FEDERAL INCOME TAX: DOCTRINE, STRUCTURE, AND POLICY
TEXT, CASES, PROBLEMS

FEDERAL INCOME TAX: DOCTRINE, STRUCTURE, AND POLICY
TEXT, CASES, PROBLEMS

FOURTH EDITION

JOSEPH M. DODGE
Stearns, Weaver, Miller, Weissler, Alhadeff, and Sitterson Professor of Law
Florida State University College of Law

J. CLIFTON FLEMING, JR.
Ernest L. Wilkinson Chair and Professor of Law
J. Reuben Clark Law School Brigham Young University

ROBERT J. PERONI
Fondren Foundation Centennial Chair for Faculty Excellence
and Professor of Law
University of Texas School of Law

Library of Congress Cataloging-in-Publication Data

Dodge, Joseph M., 1941-
    Federal income tax : doctrine, structure, and policy : text, cases, problems / Joseph M. Dodge, J. Clifton Fleming, Jr., Robert J. Peroni. -- 4th ed.
       p. cm.
    Includes index.
    ISBN 978-1-4224-9338-0 (hardbound)
  1. Income tax--Law and legislation--United States--Cases. I. Fleming, J. Clifton. II. Peroni, Robert J. III. Title.
    KF6368.D636 2011
    343.7305'2--dc23

2011032243

NOTE TO USERS

To ensure that you are using the latest materials available in this area, please be sure to periodically check the LexisNexis Law School web site for downloadable updates and supplements at www.lexisnexis.com/lawschool.

Editorial Offices
121 Chanlon Rd., New Providence, NJ 07974 (908) 464-6800
201 Mission St., San Francisco, CA 94105-1831 (415) 908-3200
www.lexisnexis.com

MATTHEW◆BENDER

(2012–Pub.3059)

PREFACE TO THE FOURTH EDITION

This fourth edition continues our practice of commingling text, primary material, commentary, and problems.

Deborah Geier did not participate in the fourth edition. Her contributions to prior editions are gratefully acknowledged.

We are pleased that Robert J. Peroni, University of Texas School of Law, has joined the fourth edition team.

The fourth edition of course incorporates developments from late 2003 to early 2011. The organization has changed somewhat from the third edition. In general, our aim has been to enable the instructor to construct a syllabus suited to his or her priorities. More subdivisions exist within chapters. Part I, providing an overview of the system, has been expanded to include material on rates, family status, computations, off-the-bottom allowances, and tax credits for the poor and middle class. Chapter 1 gives an increased emphasis on administrative law, and sets the income tax in the context of other federal taxes, state taxes, and the international tax system. Material on business and investment deductions has been moved forward. Material relating to transfer payments (gifts, damages, and assignment of income) has been brought together. The part dealing with debt now includes the material on interest and tax shelters. "Advanced" material, formerly at the end of the book, has now been integrated with foundational material. No separate part exists for the personal deductions, as each is sui generis. We hope that each chapter and each part has greater flow, logic, and progression.

Addressing the fundamental differences between income taxation and consumption taxation (or wage taxation) near the beginning of the book allows us to continue this theme throughout. However, we now note competing views of a normative income tax, the Schanz-Haig-Simons accretion version and the ability-to-pay realization income tax. Exposure to the various normative tax base constructs leads students to a more sophisticated grasp of the mongrel nature of our current system, as well as a better appreciation of the growing number of tax arbitrage opportunities that arise from inconsistent premises.

There are some changes in overall tone. We have tried to convert questions (students often didn't get the point) into text, notes, or problems. We no longer command that the students read particular Code provisions—this is best left to the instructor. We have trimmed the arithmetic in examples to render them less tedious and have attempted to achieve a balanced view of the role of time-value-of-money analysis.

We hope that this book proves to be a useful tool for exploring individual income taxation. As always, we welcome your feedback.

Joseph M. Dodge
J. Clifton Fleming, Jr.
Robert J. Peroni
2011

TABLE OF CONTENTS

TABLE OF CONTENTS

TABLE OF CONTENTS

TABLE OF CONTENTS

TABLE OF CONTENTS

TABLE OF CONTENTS

TABLE OF CONTENTS

TABLE OF CONTENTS

TABLE OF CONTENTS

TABLE OF CONTENTS

TABLE OF CONTENTS

TABLE OF CONTENTS

TABLE OF CONTENTS

TABLE OF CONTENTS

TABLE OF CONTENTS

TABLE OF CONTENTS

TABLE OF CONTENTS

TABLE OF CONTENTS

TABLE OF CONTENTS

TABLE OF CONTENTS

TABLE OF CONTENTS

TABLE OF CONTENTS

INTRODUCTION

Many tax teachers have had to deal with the dilemma posed by a student deciding whether to take the course in individual income taxation. On the one hand, the student had been told (perhaps by a first-year teacher) that all law students should take the basic tax course. On the other hand, the student had majored in liberal arts, had no meaningful exposure to tax or business matters, and wondered whether she would be seriously disadvantaged. It would be tempting to ask the student if she had the same qualms about taking courses in Constitutional Law or Criminal Procedure before signing up for those classes despite having had little previous, first-hand exposure to those areas of law. Her answer surely would be no. Perhaps the difference is that all law students are presumed equally ignorant of these nontax subjects, whereas undergraduate accounting and finance majors are presumed to have a head start in tax. Prospective tax students also are prone to think that tax is a narrow area of extremely technical application using a restricted set of skills that they do not possess or cannot acquire. We think both of these perceptions are in error, and in this Introduction we aim to allay them.

Myth Number One: Those with accounting backgrounds already know this stuff and therefore have an advantage.

Well, most accountants know how to compute depreciation, and may have learned how to fill out a tax return. But this is not a course in arithmetic or how to fill out a tax return. It certainly is not necessary to have an accounting background, or any other kind of business background, before successfully studying tax law or becoming a skilled tax attorney. Two of the three authors of this book did not have business or accounting backgrounds, and many of our best students in the past similarly have not had any prior exposure to the area (except in their capacity as taxpayers). *Here* is where you are expected to learn this material — not before.

Myth Number Two: Tax lawyers wear green eyeshades and crunch numbers for a living. Tax law is a conceptual body of law. Although the concepts sometimes cannot be explored without periodically using some simple numbers for illustrative purposes — nothing more difficult than addition, subtraction, multiplication, and division — the numbers are no more than tools. Both the numbers and the computations are comfortably within the competence of the typical junior high school student.

What, then, is the work of the tax lawyer? While some tax lawyers focus on dispute settlement (with the Internal Revenue Service (IRS) or in court), most tax lawyers are transactional lawyers — whether the transaction is a divorce, personal-injury litigation, the creation of a business entity for the entrepreneur, or a corporate merger. Consequently, the practice of tax law is typically forward-looking and can be very creative. The tax lawyer is a planner who endeavors to ensure that the best tax outcome is combined with what makes sense for other reasons, such as business needs or personal desires.

"Math anxiety" or "lack of a business background" are not excuses for low expectations or performance in the study of tax law. Students won't have trouble subtracting $40,000 from $100,000 to reach $60,000 (a typical example of the arithmetic involved in the course). Rather they have difficulty understanding that the statute directs

INTRODUCTION

them to subtract $40,000 from $100,000. That difficulty has nothing to do with math anxiety or business acumen, but rather with the lack of the legal skill to apply a statute to the facts at hand.

Myth Number Three: The main reason to take this course is because some bar exams have at least one tax question. That reason is far down on the list of good reasons to take the introductory tax course. One of the better reasons to take this course is that it will affect your practice (unless you are absolutely certain that you will spend your entire career on the criminal side of the docket — and tax issues can arise there as well!). Taxation, however, touches virtually everyone in society, from the welfare recipient, to the sole proprietor trying to start a business, to the wealthy investor, to the Fortune 500 corporation. Whether you practice real estate law, corporate law, estate and trust law, tort law, family law, international law, bankruptcy law, and on and on, and whether you practice as a sole practitioner or as a member of a large firm, issues of taxation will undoubtedly arise.[1] You need to be sensitive to them, if only to get a tax lawyer involved at the appropriate time: before the transaction occurs. As stated by Dean Erwin N. Griswold, a tax lawyer, longtime Dean of the Harvard Law School, and Solicitor General of the United States:

> It is high time that tax lawyers rise up to defend themselves against the charge that tax work is narrowing and stifling. On the contrary, it seems difficult to find a field which leads practitioners more widely through the whole fabric of the law. A tort lawyer is a tort lawyer, and a corporation lawyer is a corporation lawyer. But a tax lawyer must deal constantly not only with statutes and committee reports and regulations, but also with questions of property, contracts, agency, partnerships, corporations, equity, trusts, insurance, procedure, accounting, economics, ethics, [and] philosophy. [They] must be broad in [their] background and in [their] outlook, if [they are] to deal with the manifold problems which make up the modern field of tax law.

This may be the first substantive statutory course for many of you. Unlike the common law jurisprudence of your first-year courses, the primary source of tax law is a statute (together with interpretive pronouncements made by the administrators of the statute). Although case law is not unimportant, it is ancillary to the statutory and administrative law to which you will soon be exposed. Most law that you will practice today is found in statutes and administrative materials. Much of the common law and law of crimes has been codified. Before you leave law school, you should be able to approach the language of a statute that you have never seen before, pull apart its structure, and understand what it is telling you. There is no better course in which to practice this skill than the basic tax course.

Students anxious about taxation as a subject often use the crutch of cramming "black letter rules" set out in commercial outlines into their heads. This approach misses the point not only of tax law but graduate law study in general, which is not to learn rules of law but to apply law to facts to solve client problems. This task involves finding law, understanding it, interpreting it, and applying it to facts in a way that advances the client's objectives. This enterprise requires practice rather than memorization. Learning

---

[1] See Erwin N. Griswold, *The Need for a Court of Tax Appeals*, 57 HARV. L. REV. 1153, 1183-84 (1944); see also Erik M. Jensen, *The Heroic Nature of Tax Lawyers*, 140 U. PA. L. REV. 367 (1991) (reviewing John Grisham's THE FIRM, where the hero is a tax lawyer).

INTRODUCTION

tax is akin to learning a foreign language, where one learns vocabulary, but then must learn how to use it in reading and purposeful speaking. To this end, we strongly urge that you actually read provisions of statutes and regulations as they are cited from time to time.[2]

A distinct issue from learning how to read a statute's sometimes convoluted commands is learning how to approach ambiguity or incompleteness in those commands. Where literalism fails (or is inapposite), interpretive techniques come into play. Interpretative techniques acquired in tax are "transferable" to other courses relying on text.

A course in federal income taxation exposes you to law shaped by all three branches of government. The primary source of federal tax law is the Internal Revenue Code, enacted by Congress. But the Code is administered by the IRS within the Treasury Department, which is part of the executive branch. Because the Treasury Department promulgates Treasury regulations, and the IRS issues guidance in the form of public and private rulings, all of which have the force of law in varying degrees, the basic tax course is also a course in administrative law. Moreover, the judicial branch decides disputes arising between taxpayers and the government, including whether regulations and other guidance issued by the Treasury Department and the IRS are valid. Consequently, the basic tax course is a study of the interplay between the judiciary, executive branch administrators, and Congress.

Our approach will be to expose you to the basic technical details of the law but in a conceptually anchored way. The detail that we do cover will be used not merely to equip you with the basic mechanics of current law but to illuminate the fundamental ideas underlying the income tax. The detail will inevitably change; a major tax act was enacted nearly every year between 1981 and 1993, and starting in 1996 virtually every year has seen significant tax legislation. This legislative activity induces people to over-rate the significance of tax law changes. Although changes cannot be ignored, the income tax is grounded in underlying policies, theories, and principles, which maintain continuity and predictability. The basic tax course emphasizes what doesn't change, or what changes incrementally.

We believe that learning detail for its own sake is not important, as it may become obsolete, or even if it doesn't, you are likely to forget it after the final exam. But you will find that, in the real world, being able to cope with detail in solving a problem is an important skill. The only way to gain that skill is to practice it here. Consequently, this book will lead you through an appropriate amount and level of detail so that you can practice that important skill — knowing full well that you will forget some of that detail a

---

[2] Daniel 5:1-2, 5-7 (King James) says:

In the same hour came forth fingers of a man's hand, and wrote over against the candlestick upon the plaister of the wall of [King Balshazzar's] palace: and the king saw the part of the hand that wrote. Then the king's countenance was changed, and his thoughts troubled him, so that the joints of his loins were loosed, and his knees smote one against another. The king cried aloud to bring in the astrologers, the Chaldeans, and the soothsayers. And the king spake, and said to the wise men of Babylon, Whosoever shall read this writing, and shew me the interpretation thereof, shall be clothed in scarlet, and have a chain of gold about his neck, and shall be the third ruler of the kingdom.

Although compensation rates have gone down since Balshazzar's day, you will still be well-rewarded for learning to extract meaning from difficult language.

INTRODUCTION

year from now. But the skill you acquired in *coping with* detail will remain with you.

In summing up, we hope that four of the things you take with you from this course are an understanding of the fundamental structure of the income tax and its animating policies, the ability to spot questions and deal effectively with them under current law, the ability to deal with new statutory language you have never seen before, and the ability to work with administrative materials from a variety of sources in dealing with a transaction.

Virtually all of the chapters contain explanatory text interspersed with cases and other primary materials, as well as notes and problems. The discussion in class may well revolve around the problems, and you should try your best to answer them in advance of class. You might think of the problems as a sort of legal memorandum exercise, with the text and materials preceding the problems (and in previously covered portions of the book) as being the research base for answering the problems.

We have purposefully included far more material than can be covered in a typical one-semester course. Our reason for doing so is to provide teachers with options for structuring the course so that it addresses the issues that each of them believes are most important. Accordingly, your teacher will inevitably omit some of the material in this book, but you should not be troubled by that fact or feel short-changed.

In any discussion involving policy and theory, people will hold varying opinions. This book necessarily presents our current views. Where these views are likely to be controversial, we note the existence of alternative views.

Cases and other primary materials have been edited, sometimes heavily.

For the sake of readability, the editorial deletions (as well as very minor alterations) are sometimes not indicated, although major alterations and other editorial material are usually enclosed in brackets. Original footnote numbers are retained in brackets at the start of the footnote.

THE FUNDAMENTAL STRUCTURE OF THE FEDERAL INCOME TAX

Part One provides a contextualized overview of the federal individual income tax. Chapter 1 briefly canvasses the history of taxation in the United States and surveys the institutional apparatus for administering the tax law. Chapter 2 explores the fundamental principles that pertain to the income tax base. Chapter 3 introduces the tools of tax policy analysis. Chapter 4 brings these tools to bear on the provisions of the Code that relate to the rate structure, filing status, and allowances "off the bottom," as well as to various family-oriented tax credits. Chapter 5 covers off-the-bottom personal deductions.

Chapter 1

TAXONOMY, HISTORY, AND THE INSTITUTIONAL STRUCTURE OF TAXATION IN THE UNITED STATES

The income tax is one tool for raising revenue for the federal government. For now, you can think of an income tax as one in which the tax base (constituted annually) consists of receipts for the year that are either spent on the taxpayer's personal consumption (such as expenditures for food, clothing, and housing), or are saved or invested by the taxpayer (thus increasing the taxpayer's wealth). Other modes of taxation tend to focus *either* on personal consumption (retail sales tax, value-added tax, customs duties) *or* on wealth (property tax, wealth tax). In Part Two, an income tax will be contrasted with a tax on a taxpayer's total personal consumption for the year.

This chapter begins our journey by relating some history to locate the federal individual income tax in the constellation of tax systems that are available to governments generally and that have been used at various times by the federal government, foreign governments, and state and local governments. The historical narrative is followed by material on the institutional place of tax law in the structure of our federal government today.

A. TAXES PRIOR TO THE CONSTITUTION

Before the ratification of the Constitution, there were no national taxes, and the locus of taxation was exclusively in the colonies, and then the states under the Articles of Confederation, which imposed an assortment of taxes falling principally into the following categories:

(1) the capitation tax (sometimes referred to as a head tax or a poll tax). This is a fixed dollar tax per person (or voter). Although this kind of tax is now extinct in the United States, it remains popular with a few theoretical economists because its effects on taxpayer behavior are thought to be small.

(2) imposts (later called customs duties or tariffs). These are taxes on imports generally, or on specific categories of imports.

(3) excises. These are "internal" taxes on the manufacture or sale of goods and services. The retail sales tax, currently employed by virtually every state, is an excise tax measured by the purchase price of goods and sometimes services. The most salient federal tax of this type (that is called an "excise tax") is the tax on the manufacture of alcoholic beverages and tobacco products.

(4)   duties. In the colonial period, the term "duties" was used mainly to refer to "stamp taxes" on such items as deeds, securities transactions, and probated wills (where the duty constituted a primitive succession, or estate, tax).

(5)   property taxes. These are taxes on property ownership. An *ad valorem* property tax is levied on the value of property. Some early property taxes were calculated with reference to the property's annual use value (fair rental value), and some others were figured on a fixed-dollar-per-acre basis. All of the colonies (and states) imposed real property taxes. Some states imposed taxes on livestock and farm equipment. All states currently impose *ad valorem* real property taxes, and some states impose taxes on select categories of tangible personal property, such as business equipment, business inventory, and motor vehicles. Taxes on intangible personal property are hard to enforce, and only a tiny minority of states currently impose such taxes.

(6)   faculty taxes. These taxes (not used since the 18th century) were levied by a few states on wages and on the profits of tradesmen and merchants. However, the tax base ("faculty," which was thought to represent the payor's financial well-being and thus ability to pay taxes) was estimated, rather than determined through a systematic accounting or record-keeping of *actual* wages or profits. The faculty tax may be seen as a kind of crude forerunner of the income tax.

B.   BRIEF CONSTITUTIONAL HISTORY OF FEDERAL TAXES

Following the American Revolution, the states were loosely united under the Articles of Confederation. The Articles did not empower the U.S. federal government to lay taxes of any kind except by unanimous agreement of the states, which never occurred. The Confederation government could request contributions from the states, but the latter could (and repeatedly did) refuse such requests. Without a meaningful taxing power, the Confederation government was unable to pay Revolutionary War debts or provide for an adequate national defense and desirable internal improvements. This doomed the Confederation government and led to the crisis that was ultimately resolved by ratification of the U.S. Constitution in 1788 and establishment of a new federal government in 1789.

1.   The Framing and Ratification of the Constitution

The Constitutional Convention of 1787 was brought into existence by those who thought the Confederation government was far too weak, especially on account of the absence of a taxing power. During the Convention debates, however, divisions arose along the lines of large states vs. small states, slaveholding states vs. free states, and proponents of a strong central government vs. advocates of a weak federal government. These divisions led to a host of interlocking compromises, which can be discerned in the constitutional provisions relating to taxes. On the central issue of the taxing power, the strong-government position prevailed. Under

Article I, § 8, Clause 1, of the resulting Constitution, Congress is granted authority to "lay and collect Taxes, Duties, Imposts, and Excises." This power does not require state cooperation or involvement, and there is no limitation on the types of taxpayers that are subject to it. Thus, the Constitution authorizes the federal government to impose taxes on individuals, entities, transactions, and things, without necessarily going through the states.

The afore-mentioned Article I, § 8, Clause 1 goes on to state that "all Duties, Imposts and Excises shall be uniform throughout the United States." This Uniformity requirement was initially motivated by a federalism concern to avoid discrimination among deep water ports with respect to imposts, and has since been construed by judicial decisions to apply to "taxes" as well as duties, imposts, and excises. However, the courts regard it as preventing only patent or intentional discrimination based *expressly* on geography. Thus, an excise or tax that by its terms is imposed on only the tobacco purchases of Iowa residents would violate the Uniformity requirement, whereas a tax imposed on the production of oil throughout the United States would not violate the Uniformity requirement, even though it would disproportionately affect activity in the major oil-producing states.[1] The Uniformity requirement has not been interpreted as requiring a single (flat) rate.

A slavery issue emerged in implementing the notion that taxation and representation were to be closely linked. The Framers expected that taxes were to be mostly borne by property holders, and slaves were considered property, but slaveholding states also wanted slaves to count as persons for purposes of determining the seats in the House of Representatives to be assigned to each state. A compromise was adopted in Article I, § 2, Clause 3, under which slaves were counted as three-fifths of a person for purposes of apportioning both representatives and "direct taxes." With apparent redundancy, Article I, § 9, Clause 4, states that "direct taxes" must be apportioned among the states in proportion to the "Census or Enumeration" required to be taken within three years of the first meeting of the first Congress. (It appears that this provision was intended only to bar a direct tax during the period between ratification and the taking of the first Census, but the language is not so limiting.) Under these clauses, a direct tax could be imposed on persons and property (without involving state governments), so long as the tax yield from the various states is in proportion to their respective populations.

Regrettably, there is no definition of "direct tax" in the Constitution (except insofar as a capitation tax is stated in Article I, § 9, Clause 4, to be a direct tax). Moreover, nothing in the record of the deliberations of the Constitutional Convention suggests what the delegates meant by "direct tax."[2] Nor was there any clearly settled meaning of this term in American public discourse at the time.

---

[1] See generally *U.S. v. Ptasynski*, 462 U.S. 74 (1983).

[2] Indeed, Madison's Notes state: "Mr. King asked what was the precise meaning of *direct* taxation? No one answered." NOTES ON DEBATES IN THE FEDERAL CONSTITUTION OF 1787 REPORTED BY JAMES MADISON 494 (W.W. Norton & Co. 1987).

In the ratification debates, the question of what was a "direct tax" was obfuscated, as each side characterized the federal taxing power in a way that suited its debating strategy. The opponents of ratification (the anti-federalists) argued that the power to impose direct taxes somehow violated state rights.[3] The proponents of ratification (the federalists) argued that the federal government would mainly rely on imposts and excises, with direct taxes being imposed only in an emergency, and that the apportionment requirement actually respected state interests by viewing states as taxpaying entities or communities.[4] Hardly anybody seemed to know or care about how the apportionment requirement would operate in practice.

The concept of an income tax played no role in the creation of the Constitution, although the idea of a personal income tax on individuals was taking shape, at least vaguely, in European intellectual circles in the late 18th and early 19th centuries. An *income tax* can be crudely defined as a tax on a person's annual "net income" or "profit" calculated as a person's total *gross receipts* for the year *reduced by the total costs of producing such receipts*.[5] In the late 18th century, a personal income tax was thought impractical because (1) it would impose heavy accounting burdens on numerous taxpayers and (2) it was beyond the ability of governments to enforce.

2. From 1789 to the Sixteenth Amendment

After ratification, the nascent federal government did rely on imposts and excises (mostly on luxuries and distilleries). In addition, taxes on real estate and slaves were enacted for the periods 1798-1801 and 1813-1815 to deal with national emergencies. Operating under the assumption that these taxes were "direct," Congress apportioned them among the states in accordance with population as determined by the most recent Census. A state's quota was satisfied by sufficient collections by federal officials from individuals within the state, but under the 1813-1815 tax, the state itself had the option of satisfying the quota assigned to it.

The first major case on the meaning of "direct tax" was *Hylton v. U.S.*, 3 U.S. (3 Dall.) 171 (1796). It involved an annual tax on carriages owned for personal or commercial use. Since Congress did not apportion the carriage tax (a personal property tax) among the states in accordance with population, the tax would have been unconstitutional had it been a direct tax. In accordance with early Supreme Court practice, there was no single opinion for the Court but rather individual opinions written by the four justices who heard the oral arguments in the case, each of whom voted to uphold the tax as an "indirect" tax not subject to the apportionment requirement. The following idea, which apparently originated in Alexander Hamilton's argument for the government in *Hylton*, is set forth in the

---

[3] In the ratification period, the leading anti-federalists were state government officials. The cause of "state rights" had not yet been appropriated by slaveholding interests, which generally favored ratification as a mechanism for obtaining the return of fugitive slaves.

[4] See THE FEDERALIST No. 36 (Alexander Hamilton).

[5] In contemporary parlance, the term "gross income" is used to refer to receipts that increase the tax base (such as wages, interest, dividends, rents, royalties, and so on), and the term "deductions" is used to refer to expenses and losses that decrease the tax base. The term "credit" refers to an item — often a prepayment of tax — that reduces the bottom-line tax liability itself.

opinion of Justice Chase and is echoed in the opinions of Justices Patterson and Iredell.[6] Said Justice Chase:

> The rule of apportionment is only to be adopted in such cases where it can reasonably apply; and the subject taxed, must ever determine the application of the rule.
>
> It appears to me, that a tax on carriages cannot be laid by the rule of apportionment, without very great inequality and injustice. For example: Suppose two States, equal in census, to pay 80,000 dollars each, by a tax on carriages; and in one State there are 100 carriages, and in the other 1000. The owners of carriages in one state, would pay ten times the tax of owners in the other.
>
> It seems to me, that a tax on expence is an indirect tax; and I think, an annual tax on [ownership of] a carriage for the conveyance of persons, is of that kind; because a carriage is a consumeable commodity; and such annual tax on it, is on the expence of the owner.
>
> I am inclined to think, but of this I do not give a judicial opinion, that the direct taxes contemplated by the Constitution, are only two, to wit, a capitation, or poll tax, simply, without regard to property, profession, or any other circumstances; and a tax on LAND — I doubt whether a tax, by a general assessment of personal property, within the United States, is included within the term direct tax.

The opinion of Justice Patterson in *Hylton* noted that apportionment cannot work if no carriages are found within a state. His opinion contains the following interesting observations:

> All taxes on expences or consumption are indirect taxes. A tax on [ownership of] carriages is of this kind, and of course is not a direct tax. Indirect taxes are circuitous modes of reaching the revenue of individuals, who generally live according to their income.

On the other side of the Atlantic, England and France adopted income taxes to finance the Napoleonic Wars. Furthermore, England at this time invented the idea of imposing the income tax at the source. To illustrate, the tax on wage income would be paid by the employer out of the employee's salary, and the tax on interest income would be paid by the debtor out of the interest owed the lender.

Back in the United States, from the Jefferson administration until the Civil War, federal taxes (except for the tariff) were virtually nonexistent. A high tariff was advocated by northern states but opposed by southern states, and this issue was one of the factors that contributed to the breakup of the Union.

To help finance the Civil War, the U.S. Congress enacted an unapportioned tax on income, including income from real and personal property. The tax (which lasted from 1862 until 1872) was upheld in *Springer v. U.S.*, 102 U.S. 586 (1881), where the Court stated that direct taxes included only capitation taxes, taxes on real estate,

---

[6] The fourth judge, Justice Wilson, declined to write an opinion because he had voted to uphold the tax as a Circuit Judge in the court below.

and possibly taxes on the total wealth of an individual.

A second unapportioned personal income tax was enacted in 1894, and its constitutionality was immediately challenged. This time, the Supreme Court held (1) that a tax on rents from real estate was a tax on the real estate itself and, therefore, a direct tax (thus effectively overruling *Springer*, but not *Hylton*) and (2) that, because the tax was unapportioned, its application to real property rental income was unconstitutional. *Pollock v. Farmers' Loan & Trust Co.*, 157 U.S. 429 (1895). At pp. 580-81 and 583, the majority stated:

> [I]t is admitted that a tax on real estate is a direct tax. . . . An annual tax upon the annual value . . . of real estate appears to us the same in substance as an annual tax on the real estate, which would be paid out of the rent or income. This law taxes the income received from land and the growth or produce of the land. Mr. Justice Paterson observed in Hylton's case, "land, independently of its produce, is of no value;" and certainly had no thought that direct taxes were confined to Unproductive land.

> If it be true that by varying the form the substance may be changed, it is not easy to see that anything would remain of the limitations of the Constitution, or of the rule of taxation and representation, so carefully recognized and guarded in favor of the citizens of each state. But constitutional provisions cannot be thus evaded. It is the substance and not the form which controls, as has indeed been established by repeated decisions of this court.

> [T]he law in question, so far as it levies a tax on the rents or income of real estate, is in violation of the Constitution and is invalid.

On rehearing, 158 U.S. 601 (1895), the majority extended its holdings by finding that a tax on income from personal property, including stocks and bonds, was also unconstitutional as an unapportioned direct tax (thereby overruling *Hylton*) and that the unconstitutional portions of the statute fatally infected the entire 1894 income tax.

The second *Pollock* decision created an uproar, as it was perceived to have protected the interests of the wealthy classes from the vicissitudes of majoritarian democracy. Those who voted to adopt the 1894 income tax believed that, by reducing the government's reliance on tariffs, the new tax would materially shift the burden of taxation from consumption to capital income, thereby increasing the tax on those with greater wealth. The 1894 debates are filled with such statements.[7] Typical is the following by Representative Benton McMillan of Tennessee, chairman of the Ways and Means Subcommittee on Internal Revenue:

> I ask of any reasonable person whether it is unjust to expect that a small per cent of this enormous revenue shall be placed upon the accumulated wealth of the country instead of placing all upon the consumption of the people. . . . And yet when it is proposed to shift this burden from those who can not bear it to those who can; to divide it between consumption and

---

[7] See generally Erik M. Jensen, *The Taxing Power, the Sixteenth Amendment, and the Meaning of "Incomes,"* 33 ARIZ. ST. L.J. 1057 (2001).

wealth; to shift if from the laborer who has nothing but his power to toil and sweat, to the man who has a fortune made or inherited, we hear a hue and cry raised by some individuals that it is unjust and inquisitorial in its nature. . . .

The taxes having continually increased upon consumption, and no corresponding increase having been placed upon accumulation, we see such colossal fortunes amassed as were never accumulated in any other age or in any other country of the world.[8]

With the invalidation of the 1894 income tax in *Pollock*, both Populist and Progressive movements took up the cause of an income tax. In the meantime, the Court continued to struggle with the ambiguous distinction between "direct" and "indirect" taxes. In *Knowlton v. Moore*, 178 U.S. 41 (1899), the Supreme Court upheld the validity of the federal inheritance tax of 1898, enacted to finance the Spanish-American War, as an indirect tax on the transmission of property. And, in *Flint v. Stone Tracy Co.*, 220 U.S. 107 (1911), the Court upheld an unapportioned corporation income tax enacted in 1909 as an indirect tax that did not need to satisfy the apportionment requirement. The Court reasoned that the tax, although calculated with reference to corporate net income (including real estate rentals), was actually an excise (i.e., indirect) tax imposed on the carrying on of business through the corporate form.

3.   From the Sixteenth Amendment to the Present

Although there was sentiment in favor of enacting another income tax in order to force the Supreme Court to re-examine *Pollock*, it was eventually decided by President Taft (a Progressive Republican) and a Democrat/Republican coalition in Congress to pursue the route of a Constitutional Amendment. Ratified in 1913, the 16th Amendment provides:

The Congress shall have power to lay and collect taxes on incomes, from whatever source derived, without apportionment among the several States, and without regard to any census or enumeration.

Congress enacted the modern personal (individual) income tax in 1913. The Supreme Court upheld the tax in *Brushaber v. Union Pacific Railroad Co.*, 240 U.S. 1 (1916), stating that the purpose of the 16th Amendment was to remove the apportionment requirement from federal income taxes rather than to define the contours of a "direct tax." Although *Brushaber* is nearly 100 years old, the following passages from the opinion continue to be directly relevant to many modern-day attacks on the validity of the income tax:

The statute levies one tax called a normal tax on all incomes of individuals up to $20,000 and from that amount up by gradations, a progressively increasing tax called an additional tax is imposed. No tax, however, is levied upon incomes of unmarried individuals amounting to $3,000 or less nor upon incomes of married persons amounting to $4,000 or less. The progressive tax and the exempted amounts, it is said, are based on

---

[8] See *id.* at 1096-98 (quoting 26 Cong. Rec. app. 413, 415 (Jan. 29, 1894)).

wealth alone and the tax is therefore repugnant to the due process clause of the Fifth Amendment.

So far as these numerous and minute, not to say in many respects hypercritical, contentions are based upon an assumed violation of the uniformity clause, their want of legal merit is at once apparent, since it is settled that that clause exacts only a geographical uniformity. . . .

So far as the due process clause of the Fifth Amendment is relied upon, it suffices to say that there is no basis for such reliance since it is equally well settled that such clause is not a limitation upon the taxing power conferred upon Congress by the Constitution; in other words, that the Constitution, does not conflict with itself by conferring upon the one hand a taxing power and taking the same power away on the other by the limitations of the due process clause. . . . And no change in the situation here would arise even if it be conceded, as we think it must be, that this doctrine would have no application in a case where although there was a seeming exercise of the taxing power, the act complained of was so arbitrary as to constrain to the conclusion that it was not the exertion of taxation but a confiscation of property, that is, a taking of the same in violation of the Fifth Amendment, or, what is equivalent thereto, was so wanting in basis for classification as to produce such a gross and patent inequality as to inevitably lead to the same conclusion. We say this because none of the propositions relied upon [by the taxpayer in the present case] in the remotest degree present such questions. It is true that it is elaborately insisted that although there be no express constitutional provision prohibiting it, the progressive feature of the tax causes it to transcend the conception of all taxation and to be a mere arbitrary abuse of power which must be treated as wanting in due process. But the proposition disregards the fact that in the very early history of the Government a progressive tax was imposed by Congress and that such authority was exerted in some if not all of the various income taxes enacted prior to 1894 to which we have previously adverted.

The 1913 personal income tax initially had low rates and substantial exemptions so that it chiefly reached the income of the wealthy, but it quickly became a broad-based tax with high progressive rates in order to finance the U.S. involvement in World War I. After that war ended, rates came back down and exemptions went back up. By 1939, only about 5% of the population paid income taxes. The cataclysm of World War II, however, forever transformed the federal income tax from a "class tax" to a "mass tax." By 1960, approximately 73% of the population filed taxable returns.

In spite of the *Brushaber* decision, taxpayers have continued to assert in litigation that the income tax is unconstitutional under a multitude of theories. All of these arguments have been rejected by the courts, often with expressions of disdain and the imposition of penalties.[9]

---

[9] See, e.g., *Ficalora v. Comm'r*, 751 F.2d 85 (2d Cir. 1984).

The last significant encounter between the income tax and the Constitution arose in *Eisner v. Macomber*, 252 U.S. 189 (1920). That case focused primarily on technical aspects of how the income tax applies to distributions by corporations to shareholders. For purposes of the present discussion, *Macomber*'s significance lies in its holding that the 16th Amendment prohibits an unapportioned income tax from reaching increases in the value of a taxpayer's property before the value increases are realized through a transaction, such as a sale or exchange. The pertinent language of the opinion is (252 U.S. at 207):

> Here we have the essential matter [of what is "income" within the 16th Amendment]: *not* a gain *accruing to* capital; not a *growth* or *increment* of value *in* the investment; but a gain, a profit, something of exchangeable value, *proceeding from* the property, *severed from* the capital . . . and *coming in*, being *"derived"* — that is *received* or *drawn by* the recipient (the taxpayer), for his *separate* use, benefit and disposal — *that* is income derived from property.

Today, the idea discussed above is known as the "realization requirement." It means that increases in a taxpayer's economic well-being are not taxed until they have been "realized" through an identifiable event, such as the receipt of wages or a sale of property. As you will shortly learn, however, "realization" is not limited to "receipt of cash," because compensation received in the form of property or services and exchanges of property for other property are acknowledged to be realization events.

Although *Macomber* said that the realization requirement was a constitutional mandate, the Supreme Court has subsequently repudiated that position. In *Helvering v. Horst*, 311 U.S. 112, 116 (1940) and *Cottage Savings Ass'n v. Comm'r*, 499 U.S. 554, 559 (1991), the Court stated that the realization requirement is merely a statutory principle to which Congress can make exceptions.

Subsequent to *Macomber*, courts have taken a more nuanced approach when analyzing the constitutionality of income tax provisions. Thus, a particular provision contained in the portion of the U.S. Code that comprises the federal income tax is constitutional if it is *either* consistent with the notion of "income" under the 16th Amendment *or* entails a nondirect tax.[10]

As a result of the preceding developments, the federal income tax's major features have been accepted into the American constitutional order, and the principal disputes now revolve around (1) how the power to levy a national income tax has been exercised in fact (i.e., issues of interpretation of the Internal Revenue Code and supporting Treasury regulations) and (2) how the power to levy a national income tax should be exercised (i.e., issues of tax policy). These are the central inquiries of this book.

---

[10] *Penn Mutual Ins. Co. v. Comm'r*, 277 F.2d 16, 19-20 (3d Cir. 1960) (upholding "income tax" on gross receipts of mutual life insurance company); *Murphy v. IRS*, 493 F.3d 170 (D.C. Cir. 2007), *cert. denied*, 553 U.S. 1004 (2008) (holding that Congress could tax tort recoveries under the income tax even if they are not "income" within the 16th Amendment because such taxation is "indirect").

4. State Taxation under the Constitution

State taxing jurisdiction is limited by the Due Process Clause of the U.S. Constitution, which requires sufficient contacts between the subject of a tax and the taxing authority. Tangible property can only be taxed by the state in which the property is located, but income can be taxed by the state in which the owner resides, as well as by the state in which the income occurs.[11] The problem of multiple taxation is dealt with by the Commerce Clause of the U.S. Constitution. There is significant Supreme Court constitutional jurisprudence concerning state taxation issues. State (and local) taxation is dealt with in a separate course (or possibly in a Constitutional Law course) and is not pursued further in this book.

PROBLEMS AND NOTES

1.   (a) A friend tells you that the federal income tax is unconstitutional because it violates the apportionment requirement found in Article I, § 2, Clause 3 and Article I, § 9, Clause 4 of the Constitution. According to *Brushaber*, how should you respond?

(b) Tax protestors have attacked the validity of the 16th Amendment. These attacks have been rejected without exception by the federal courts. The following passage from *U.S. v. Stahl*, 792 F.2d 1438 (9th Cir. 1986), is typical of decisions on this point (citations and internal quotations are omitted):

> Stahl argues that the Sixteenth Amendment was never ratified by the requisite number of states because of clerical errors in the ratifying resolutions of the various state legislatures and other errors in the ratification process. He further argues that Secretary of State Knox committed fraud by certifying the adoption of the amendment despite these alleged errors.
>
> Since the Secretary of State proclaimed that the sixteenth amendment had been duly ratified, this assertion presents a political question. . . . Stahl's suggestion of fraud on the part of the Secretary does not render the [political] question justiciable, for judicial action based upon such a suggestion is forbidden by the respect due to a coordinate branch of the government. Moreover, the Court in discussing judicial review of the ratification process characterized the political question doctrine as a tool for maintenance of governmental order. Consideration of Stahl's contention, 73 years after certification of the amendment's adoption and after countless judicial applications, would promote only disorder.
>
> We conclude that the Secretary of State's certification under authority of Congress that the Sixteenth Amendment has been ratified by the requisite number of states and has become part of the Constitution is conclusive upon the courts.

Although the attacks on the 16th Amendment that were rejected by the 9th Circuit in *Stahl* have never been directly litigated before the United States

---

[11] See *New York ex rel. Cohn v. Graves*, 300 U.S. 308 (1937).

Supreme Court, the Court denied certiorari in *Stahl*, 479 U.S. 1036 (1987), and in every similar case in which certiorari has been requested. The only reasonable conclusion is that the Supreme Court agrees with the *Stahl* opinion.

(c) Your friend next tells you that because the federal income tax's progressive rates result in some individuals being taxed at higher rates than others, the federal income tax violates the Uniformity Clause of Article I, § 8, Clause 1 of the Constitution. How should you respond in light of *Brushaber*?

(d) You've read that the federal income tax has always had progressive rates — i.e., a taxpayers's income is viewed as a stack of blocks, called brackets, and the upper blocks bear higher rates of tax than the lower blocks so that high-income taxpayers pay a greater percentage of their income in tax than do low-income taxpayers. This suggests that the federal income tax violates the Constitutional requirement of equal protection of the law. But the Constitution does not expressly apply an equal protection restraint on the federal government. The only express equal protection restraint is imposed on the states by the 14th Amendment. Consequently, equal protection objections to federal legislation have to be characterized as violations of the Due Process Clause of the 5th Amendment. So it's no surprise that your friend next tells you that the federal income tax's progressive rates violate the Due Process Clause of the 5th Amendment of the Constitution. How should you respond in light of *Brushaber*?

(e) Finally, your friend tells you that the federal income tax violates the Takings Clause of the 5th Amendment to the Constitution. How should you respond in light of *Brushaber*?

2.   Would Congress have the power to:

(a) treat gifts received as gross income of the donee,

(b) tax the gross receipts of a business (i.e., not allowing costs of producing income to be subtracted),[12]

(c) tax the annual increase in value of a person's investment portfolio, or

(d) tax (annually) the value of the portfolio itself,

assuming that the tax in question is not apportioned among the states in accordance with population?[13]

3.   The *Pollock* case is now considered to be obsolete on the issue of whether (in the absence of the 16th Amendment) the income tax is a direct tax. See *Stanton v. Baltic Mining Co.*, 240 U.S. 103, 112-13 (1916) (repudiating *Pollock* on this point); *New York ex rel. Cohn v. Graves*, 300 U.S. 308, 315 (1937) (holding that a tax on rents

---

[12] *Doyle v. Mitchell Bros. Co.*, 247 U.S. 179 (1918), is often (but erroneously) cited for the proposition that "income" means sales price reduced by the cost of the sold item. However, that case arose under the corporate income tax law of 1909, not the 16th Amendment, and the actual holding was that the 1909 Act (which was expressly a tax on "net income") was not intended to reach income that accrued before 1909. Thus, the taxpayer was allowed to subtract from its sales proceeds the December 31, 1908 value of the goods that it sold, rather than the lower original cost.

[13] See generally Joseph M. Dodge, *What Federal Taxes Are Subject to the Rule of Apportionment Under the Constitution?*, 11 U. Pa. J. Const. Law 839 (2009).

was not a tax on the property itself). Nevertheless, the *Pollock* case raises an issue of substance over form (or vice versa) as applied to various modes of taxation. That is, are there meaningful distinctions among various modes of taxation? To be specific:

(a) Can a retail sales tax be distinguished from a tax on the gross receipts of a business?

(b) Can a gross receipts tax be distinguished from an income tax? If so, does the 16th Amendment authorize a tax on gross income (without deduction for the costs of producing income)? Is this last question constitutionally relevant?

(c) Can a tax on investment income be distinguished from a tax on the property itself? If not, does the 16th Amendment authorize a federal property tax?

C.   INTERNATIONAL TAXATION

The U.S. income tax operates in a global context and interacts with the tax systems of other countries.

1.   National Taxing Jurisdiction over Income

The ability of the U.S. federal government to impose income tax on international income is a matter partly of U.S. constitutional law and partly of customary international law as modified by treaties. Basically, the "international system" was devised by the major commercial nations in the 1920s and has been little influenced by Supreme Court decisions.

Regarding "jurisdiction to tax," it is necessary to determine who is subject to taxation and to what extent. Under the Internal Revenue Code, an individual is subject to federal income taxation on his or her worldwide income (i.e., the sum of U.S.-source and foreign-source income) if he or she is either a U.S. citizen *or* a U.S. noncitizen who is a "resident" as defined in § 7701(b) ("green card" holder or person with physical presence in the United States for a specified period). The U.S. approach of taxing its nonresident citizens on worldwide income is almost unique among major countries but the constitutionality of this practice was nevertheless upheld in *Cook v. Tait*, 265 U.S. 47 (1924). Corporations organized under the laws of the United States (or U.S. states or the District of Columbia) are taxable on their worldwide incomes regardless of the location of the corporation's owners or business activities.

In accordance with customary international law, the United States taxes foreign persons (nonresident alien individuals and foreign corporations) on only U.S.-connected income. This form of taxation is commonly referred to as "source taxation" and it is practiced by most countries.

2.   Mitigating Double Taxation

Since there are dual jurisdictional tax principles (nationality of the taxpayer and source), the possibility arises of international double taxation. Thus, a U.S. citizen, U.S. resident, or U.S. corporation doing business in the United Kingdom is subject to U.S. tax on U.K.-source income as well as to U.K.-source tax on the same income. A principal goal of the international system is to eliminate such double taxation because it inhibits free trade and the free movement of capital. The principal mechanisms for eliminating double taxation (under statutory tax law or treaty) is for the country of the taxpayer's nationality to cede primary jurisdiction to the source country by (a) exempting (certain) foreign-source income from nationality-country tax or (b) giving credit, against the nationality-country tax on the foreign income, for the foreign tax on that same income. (A tax "credit" is a dollar-for-dollar reduction in tax liability.) Under treaties, the source country may, in turn, agree to cede source jurisdiction to the residence country in exchange for similar treatment for its own citizens from the treaty partner.

To illustrate these mechanisms, consider the situation of Billie, a U.S. citizen, who has total (worldwide) taxable income of $1M, of which $200K comes from investments in France. For the sake of simplicity, assume that both the U.S. and French tax rates are a flat 35%. The United States can (and generally does) tax the entire $1 million (which would produce a tax of $350K), and France can (and generally does) tax Billie on the $200K of French-source income (producing a tax of $70K). With no mechanism to ameliorate double taxation of the $200K earned in France, Billie would owe $420K of worldwide tax, which is $70K more than if he earned the $1 million entirely in the United States and paid tax of only $350K. Such an outcome would effectively bar Billie (and other owners of capital) from making foreign investments, and the resulting lack of mobility for capital would reduce worldwide economic efficiency (and worldwide wealth).

The double-tax problem is completely "solved" by the United States granting a tax credit (in general, not to exceed the U.S. tax on the same income) for the $70K French income tax imposed on the $200K of French-source income. This foreign tax credit system effectively gives the source country (France in this case) jurisdictional priority. Billie would credit (subtract) the $70K French tax from the $350K U.S. tax, leaving a U.S. tax liability of only $280K. Added to his $70K French tax, Billie's worldwide tax liability would be $350K. Because Billie would owe the same worldwide $350K tax whether he earns his income in the United States or in France, Billie will base his decisions regarding where to invest on nontax reasons.

The second major technique for eliminating double taxation in the international arena is for the country of nationality to exempt foreign-source income. Here the United States would exempt the $200K French-source income from U.S. taxation. Under such a system, Billie's U.S. income would be only $800K (instead of $1M), and Billie would pay $280K of tax to the United States and $70K to France, just as under the tax credit approach.

The U.S. tax law (including treaties) relating to international transactions employs a mixture of both of these mechanisms to mitigate double taxation. The U.S. taxation of international transactions is sufficiently complicated so that it is typically a separate law school course.

PROBLEM

Richard is a U.S. citizen who personally owns and operates an unincorporated business in the United States and a separate unincorporated business in Mexico City, Mexico. Ricardo is not a U.S. citizen or a § 7701(b) resident of the United States. He personally owns and operates an unincorporated business in the United States and a separate unincorporated business in Mexico City, Mexico.

(a) What part of Richard's business profits is subject to the U.S. federal income tax?

(b) What part of Ricardo's business profits is subject to the U.S. federal income tax?

3.   Value Added Tax

Virtually every country of commercial significance has individual and corporate income taxes, and many countries also impose significant excise taxes. A common excise tax used by U.S. trading partners (but not the U.S. itself) is the "value added tax" (VAT). A VAT is essentially a sales tax collected in stages.

> *Example*: Assume the VAT rate is 10%. Adobe Industries makes adobe bricks from mud and straw obtained on its own land. It produces 1 ton of bricks that is sold to Brick Distributors for $400. The tax is $40, which is paid by Brick to Adobe, which remits the $40 to the government. Thus, Brick pays $440 for the bricks, which Brick (in turn) sells to Deuce Hardware for $700, the tax on which is $70. Again the tax is added to the price (i.e., Deuce pays a total of $770 to Brick) and remitted by Brick to the government, but at the same time Brick obtains a credit for (a refund of) the $40 tax included in the purchase price it paid to Adobe, so that the government's net tax collection from the Brick-to-Deuce sale is only $30. Finally, Deuce sells the bricks to a retail customer for $1,000, and the customer pays a tax-inclusive price of $1,100. The $100 is paid by Deuce to the government, and Deuce gets a credit (refund) of the $70 tax it paid, so that the government nets only $30 of tax on the Deuce-to-customer sale. In the end, the government has collected $100 of tax ($40 on the Adobe-to-Brick sale, $30 net on the Brick-to-Deuce sale, and $30 net on the Deuce-to-customer sale) but the $100 tax is borne entirely by the retail customer, just as would be the case under a retail sales tax (RST). The refund system has cancelled out the $40 of VAT paid by Brick to Adobe and the $70 of VAT paid by Deuce to Brick.

The advantage of the VAT over an RST is that there are no "cascading" (multiple) taxes on the same item, but at the same time no sale for consumption escapes tax. Thus, the ultimate tax is always the amount paid by the end consumer no matter how many, or few, intermediate sellers there are between the producer and the consumer. Moreover, it is not necessary for Adobe to determine (in the example above) if Brick is buying the items for resale (not taxable under an RST) or for its own use (taxable under an RST). Brick pays the $40 VAT regardless, but if Brick *does* resell the items it obtains a refund of the $40 it paid. In addition, because the VAT is collected in stages while the RST is collected at only one point (the final retail sale to the consumer), the VAT is less vulnerable to total tax avoidance by tax cheating.

The VAT is worth mentioning in this book, because it is widely used outside of the U.S., and constitutes a tempting source of potential revenue for the U.S.

4. Comparative Tax Burdens

It is often claimed that U.S. taxpayers are overburdened, but — at least in the comparative sense — this appears to be a myth, as the chart below indicates.[14] This chart shows the percentage of national income (GDP) collected through all forms of taxation by all levels of government (including state and local governments). Of all the member states of the OECD (Organization for Economic Cooperation and Development) for which data were available, which includes essentially the countries of the Western industrialized world, the U.S. had the fourth lowest aggregate tax burden in 2008. Only Mexico, Turkey, and Korea had lower burdens.

CHART 1
TOTAL TAX REVENUE AS A PERCENTAGE OF GDP IN OECD COUNTRIES, 2008

Mexico	21.1	Ireland	28.3
Turkey	23.5	Slovakia	29.3
Korea	26.6	Switzerland	29.4
United States	26.9	Greece	31.3
Canada	32.2	Austria	42.9
Spain	33.0	France	43.1
New Zealand	34.5	Italy	43.2
United Kingdom	35.7	Belgium	44.3
Iceland	36.0	Sweden	47.1
Germany	36.4	Denmark	48.3
Portugal	36.5	Australia	Not available
Czech Republic	36.6	Japan	Not available
Hungary	40.1	Netherlands	Not available
Norway	42.1	Poland	Not available
Finland	42.8		

D. OTHER FEDERAL TAXES OF NOTE

The federal taxes described herein are those that resemble or interact with the income tax or are income taxes with respect to business or investment entities.

1. The Payroll Taxes

The term "payroll taxes" refers to the Social Security tax and the Medicare tax. As the name implies, labor income (wages and self-employment income) is almost exclusively the base of the payroll taxes. Investment income — such as interest,

---

[14] Data in this chart is from OECD Factbook 2010.

dividends, rents, and royalties — generally is not covered.[15]

The Social Security tax was enacted in 1935 at a time when the wages of the lower and middle classes were not subject to income taxation because of high exemptions then in effect. Originally, the first $3,000 of wages was subject to Social Security tax at a rate of 1% to the employer and 1% to the employee (for a total of 2%). Wages above that amount were exempt. Over time, the rate and the "wage ceiling" have increased. As of 2010, the Social Security wage ceiling was $106,800, and the tax rate was 6.2% on each of the employer and employee. Self-employed persons pay tax (called "the self-employment tax") of 12.4% on their self-employment income. The first dollar of wages (or self-employment income) is taxed. That is, there is no personal exemption, as there is under the income tax.[16] Wages above the ceiling continue to be exempt from tax, however.

Employees cannot deduct their Social Security taxes from the income tax base, though the self-employed can deduct one-half of their self-employment taxes (to mimic the fact that employers can deduct their half of the Social Security tax).

The Medicare tax was enacted in 1966. Today, it is imposed on all wages and self-employment income, without a ceiling, at a rate of 1.45% on each of the employer and employee. (The self-employed pay the entire 2.9% on their self-employment income.)[17]

The combined Social Security and Medicare taxes are officially referred to as the FICA tax, and unofficially as "the payroll tax(es)."

Because money is fungible, matching particular government outlays to any particular tax stream is conceptually problematic. Nevertheless, the Social Security taxes are commonly perceived to be the source of funds for retirement benefits paid to those who have worked at least 40 quarters (three-month periods) in the paid labor force (and to their surviving spouses), while the Medicare taxes are commonly perceived to fund medical care provided to the elderly under the Medicare program. However, until recently, the taxes collected under Social Security and Medicare exceeded the amounts spent under those programs for the currently retired generation, and the excess tax collected was spent on general government operations.

---

[15] For the lone exception, see note 17, infra.

[16] However, § 36A provided for a credit against the income tax (called the "making work pay" credit) equal to 6.2% of wages, but the credit was phased out for persons whose net income exceeded $70K. This credit amounted to a rebate of the employee's share of the Social Security tax. This credit was allowed to expire at the end of 2010.

[17] Beginning in 2013, two changes affecting Medicare will become effective. First the self-employment tax and the employee portion of the Medicare tax will increase by 0.9% with regard to both annual self-employment income and annual wages in excess of $125K in the case of married individuals filing separately, $250K in the case of married individuals filing jointly and heads of household, and $200K in the case of other individuals.

Second, a new 3.8% unearned income medicare contribution tax will be imposed on the lesser of an individual's (1) net investment income or (2) the amount by which modified adjusted gross income exceeds $250K in the case of a joint return or a surviving spouse, $125K in the case of a married individual filing separately and $200K in all other cases. This new tax is a departure from the historic pattern of excluding investment income from the base of the Medicare tax.

The combination of increased "off-the-bottom" allowances under the income tax (the personal exemptions and the standard deduction) and substantial increases in the payroll tax in the last three decades have resulted in a situation in which approximately two-thirds of households now pay more in payroll taxes than income taxes. This is particularly true for the middle class.[18] Not surprisingly, the payroll taxes have constituted a growing share of federal revenue in the last several decades. Before 1963, the individual income tax produced more than twice as much revenue as the payroll taxes, whereas by 1995, the payroll taxes contributed almost as much to federal revenue as the individual income tax. This trend is shown in the following chart.[19]

CHART 2
AGGREGATE FEDERAL RECEIPTS BY SOURCE, 2005-2009
(IN MILLIONS OF DOLLARS)

	Individual Income Tax	Corporate Income Tax	Employment Taxes	Excise Taxes	Estate and Gift Taxes	Others	Total
2005	927,222	278,282	794,125	73,094	24,764	56,138	2,153,625
2006	1,043,908	353,915	837,821	73,961	27,877	69,394	2,406,876
2007	1,163,472	370,243	869,607	65,069	26,044	73,566	2,568,001
2008	1,145,747	304,346	900,155	67,334	28,844	77,573	2,523,999
2009	915,308	138,229	890,917	62,483	23,462	74,576	2,104,995

Aggregate Federal Receipts by Source as a Percentage of GDP, 2005-2009

	Individual Income Tax	Corporate Income Tax	Employment Taxes	Excise Taxes	Estate and Gift Taxes	Others	Total
2005	7.5	2.2	6.4	0.6	0.2	0.5	17.3
2006	7.9	2.7	6.3	0.6	0.2	0.5	18.2
2007	8.4	2.7	6.3	0.5	0.2	0.5	18.5
2008	7.9	2.1	6.2	0.5	0.2	0.5	17.5
2009	6.4	1.0	6.3	0.4	0.2	0.5	14.8

The payroll taxes are not considered to be "income taxes" either for constitutional purposes or for purposes of the international income tax system (although treaties expressly deal with such taxes). Because the base of the Social Security tax is simply "gross wages," there are few doctrinal issues relating to this tax, and these

---

[18] In 2010, 80.9% of all individual taxpayers were projected to bear payroll taxes in excess of their income tax liabilities. See STAFF OF JOINT COMM. ON TAX'N, PRESENT LAW AND BACKGROUND DATA RELATED TO THE INDIVIDUAL INCOME AND SOCIAL INSURANCE TAXES AS IN EFFECT FOR 2010 AND 2011, 32 (JCX-1-10 Jan. 13, 2010).

[19] This data is from STAFF OF JOINT COMM. ON TAX'N, PRESENT LAW AND BACKGROUND DATA RELATED TO THE FEDERAL TAX SYSTEM IN EFFECT FOR 2010 AND 2011, 25-26 (JCX-19-10 Mar. 22, 2010).

issues are not discussed at any length in this book. The term "wages" means "remuneration for employment" in whatever form, unless exempted under § 3121. The tax base of the self-employment tax is the net income from any business carried on by an individual (other than employment). See § 1402. Thus, self-employment income is not limited to income from personal services, but includes some of the income derived from the capital used in a person's business. It follows that income tax concepts implicitly determine the tax base of the self-employment tax, even though this tax is in addition to, and not part of, the self-employed person's income tax. Finally, the payroll tax scheme requires the distinction between an "employee" and an "independent contractor," the former being subject to the Social Security tax and the latter being subject to the self-employment tax.

2. The Federal Wealth Transfer Taxes

The term "federal wealth transfer taxes" (or just "federal transfer taxes") refers to the federal taxes on the value of gratuitous transfers (gifts, bequests, transfers by intestacy, and other transfers that occur by reason of death). These taxes are constituted by the estate tax, the gift tax, and the generation-skipping tax. *These taxes are wholly separate and apart from the income tax*, and are not discussed in this book (but are dealt with in a separate course).

The *income* taxation of gratuitous transfers is discussed in Chapter 15. Briefly, gratuitous receipts are excluded from the gross income of the recipient under § 102, and gratuitous transfers are not deductible by the transferor (i.e., do not reduce the transferor's taxable income).

3. Federal Income Taxation of Entities

This book is about the individual income tax, but it is impossible to ignore the question of federal income taxation of other legal "persons."

The existence of the federal corporate income tax is widely known. For those incorporated entities that are subject to this tax (known as "C corporations"), the tax base is taxable income, computed in pretty much the same way as it is for an individual. *However, no deduction is allowed for dividends paid to shareholders.* The C corporation's taxable income is subject to the rate schedule found in § 11. Since dividends paid by a corporation are gross income to the individual shareholder (but not deductible by the corporation), corporate profits are said to be subject to a "double tax," at least to the extent that dividends are paid out. Corporate taxation is dealt with in a separate tax course.

Entities treated as partnerships (and S corporations as defined in § 1361) are not "taxpayers," and therefore are not liable for tax on entity net profits. (Most limited liability companies are treated as partnerships for federal income tax purposes.) Instead, the net income (or loss) from these entities is attributed directly to the partners, members, or shareholders (as the case may be), whether or not the profits are actually distributed to them. (As a corollary, actual distributions of profits are *not* gross income to the partners, members, or shareholders.) The taxation of partnerships and S corporations is dealt with in separate courses.

Trusts, like corporations, can be taxable entities. Unlike corporations, distributions from a taxable trust (sometimes referred to as a "Subchapter J trust") to its beneficiaries are deductible to the trust (but cannot reduce trust net income below zero). The beneficiaries are taxed on trust distributions to the extent of the trust's deduction for distributions. This deduction/inclusion scheme avoids double taxation of trust net income. The net income (if any) of the trust (after the distribution deduction) is subject to the steeply progressive rate schedule of § 1(e). Trust income taxation is sometimes, but not typically, dealt with in a separate course, and accordingly, more material on this topic is found elsewhere in this book.

NOTE

The distinction between substance and form, alluded to in *Pollock*, is an ongoing theme in tax law. As we shall see, sometimes form matters a lot. For example, a C corporation is generally respected as a taxable entity apart from its shareholder(s) or manager(s), even where a particular shareholder or manager exercises complete control.

PROBLEMS

1. X is a legal entity under state law. It has taxable income (ignoring distributions) of $100K. During the year, it distributes $40K to those who are eligible to receive distributions. State how much is taxed to entity X and how much is taxed to the collective distributees if X is:

(a) a C corporation, and the distributions are "dividends" to shareholders?

(b) an entity treated as partnership for income tax purposes, and the distributions are made to partners in proportion to their respective interests in profit and loss?

(c) a Subchapter J trust, and the distributions are made to trust beneficiaries?

2. Same facts (and questions) as above, except that X suffers a loss of $10K during the year.

3. The material about different modes of taxation raises issues about who actually bears the economic burden ("incidence") of these taxes, as opposed (perhaps) to who nominally pays them.

(a) The estate tax is payable out of the estate (the decedent's property). Who bears the burden of this tax? Can this burden be controlled by the decedent?

(b) Can the burden of a tax lie on a thing? In other words, does the burden of a property tax fall on the property itself?

(c) Can the burden of a tax on an entity be borne by the entity itself? Where lies the burden of the income tax on a trust? Where lies the burden of the corporate income tax? Can we simply assume that it lies upon the corporation's shareholders?

(d) Is an RST borne by the buyer (consumer) or seller (merchant)? Similarly, is the property tax nominally imposed on a landlord passed on to the tenant? What does elementary economic analysis tell us about these questions?

(e) More broadly, does a tax "on" consumption (RST or VAT) necessarily *reduce* the overall consumption (as opposed to investments) of the consumer (to the extent that the consumer bears the tax in the first place)?

(f) Is it likely that a tax on a person's wages, or profits from a sole proprietorship business, is passed on to others?

E.   FEDERAL TAX LAW IN THE STRUCTURE OF GOVERNMENT

Under the Constitution, the government is divided into the legislative, the executive, and the judicial branches. This section discusses the roles of the three branches of government in making and enforcing tax law.

1.   Federal Tax Law as Statutory Law

The primary source of tax law is federal statutory law. Starting in 1913, Congress produced Revenue Acts that operated on an annual or bi-annual basis. In 1939 most of the tax law was "permanently" codified in the Internal Revenue Code of 1939. Of course, the 1939 Code was amended from time to time, but because it was permanent it did not need to be periodically reenacted in its entirety. The tax law underwent a re-codification in 1954 that entailed re-numbering the sections of the 1939 Code (plus the addition of much detail). Officially, there was another re-codification in 1986, although that re-codification did not materially change the 1954 numbering system. The current tax law is referred to as the "Internal Revenue Code of 1986, as amended," and is located in Title 26 of the U.S. Code. In addition, there exist narrow tax rules (largely transition rules, provisions affecting miniscule numbers of taxpayers, and quasi-subsidies provided through the tax system but which are part of government programs relating to such areas as agriculture and veterans and military affairs) in other parts of the U.S. Code and in the U.S. Statutes at Large.

Federal statutory law is a product of the legislative branch. Under Article I, § 7, Clause 1, of the Constitution, all revenue bills must originate in the House of Representatives. In the House, the Ways and Means Committee deals with taxation, as well as Social Security and international trade. The Chair of the Ways and Means Committee is, thus, one of the most powerful actors in the tax legislative process. Ways and Means bills are forwarded to the full House through the Rules Committee, which usually prohibits the offering of amendments from the House floor. In spite of the Constitution's grant of originating authority in the House, the Senate can always amend revenue bills passed by the House. This amendment power has been interpreted as allowing the Senate to effectively write a new bill by deleting everything in the House bill and starting over.

On the Senate side, the Finance Committee has jurisdiction over tax matters, and floor amendments are usually allowed to bills reported to the full Senate by the Finance Committee. Senate Rules allow most bills to be effectively blocked or stalled by a filibuster that can only be halted by a vote of at least 60 Senators.

If the House and Senate bills are not identical — and they virtually never are — they go to a Conference Committee composed of senior members of both the Ways and Means Committee and the Finance Committee. The Conference Committee's failure to reach agreement kills both the House and Senate bills. If the Conference Committee produces a compromise bill, it is then voted on by the House and Senate without possibility of further amendment. If approved by both Houses, the Conference agreement is then forwarded to the President as a bill for the President's action (or inaction).

Tax bills rarely make a successful passage through this process without the backing of both the congressional leadership and the Treasury Department (in the executive branch). The Ways and Means Committee and the Senate Finance Committee have professional staffs that actually draft tax legislation and scrutinize its technical aspects. The Committee members usually limit themselves to making the policy decisions eventually embodied in the statutory language. In addition, experts from the executive branch, the staff of the Joint Committee on Taxation,[20] and the drafting staffs of the House and Senate all review tax legislation.

The staffs of the House Ways and Means Committee and the Senate Finance Committee produce Committee Reports on tax bills. There is also a Report of the Conference Committee, and often (after enactment) a summary of the Act of Congress prepared by the Staff of the Joint Committee (called the "Blue Book"). These Committee Reports, along with floor debates as reported in the Congressional Record and changes in bills on the way to enactment, collectively constitute the *legislative history* of tax provisions. As will be seen, the legislative history plays an important role in the interpretation of tax statutes by the executive branch, the courts, and tax practitioners.[21]

2. Federal Tax Law as Administrative Law

Although the primary source of tax law is the Internal Revenue Code, law is also made by the executive branch. To the Framers, the role of the executive branch was to carry out and enforce statutory law. In tax law the enforcement branch, formally under the Secretary of the Treasury, is the Internal Revenue Service (the IRS, or the Service). The IRS (among other things) processes tax returns, performs civil examinations and audits, assesses underpayments of tax, and collects taxes owed through such devices as liens and levy and execution.

a. Congressional Delegation of Rulemaking

Since at least the late 19th century, Congress has delegated rule-making and dispute-resolution functions to executive branch departments and independent commissions. Administrative law, insofar as it deals with the rule-making function of an executive branch department or independent agency, addresses the legal

---

[20] The Joint Committee on Taxation and its staff are provided for by §§ 8001 through 8005 of the Code. The Committee may hold hearings and make proposals, but the chief activity of the Joint Committee is conducted through its staff.

[21] Because the Blue Book is not prepared contemporaneously with passage of the related legislation, courts have taken varying positions regarding the weight given to the Blue Book.

problem of when a court (in the context of a case or controversy) will defer to a rule or other pronouncement promulgated by a department or agency. Specifically, the core issue is whether any given administrative pronouncement will be treated by the court: (a) as having the force of (statutory) law, (b) as being entitled to some degree of respect and deference on account of the technical expertise of the agency, or (c) as having a status akin to a litigant's brief (i.e., as merely stating the agency's position on an issue). There is no simple formula that can be applied to any given administrative pronouncement to determine where it falls on this spectrum, and indeed administrative law doctrine is both murky and in flux. Nevertheless, as a general matter, the answer in any given case depends on: (1) whether the pronouncement is compatible with the relevant statutory provision; (2) whether Congress has delegated law-making authority to the agency on the issue in question; and (3) whether the pronouncement has been issued after a thorough consideration of the merits that brings the agency's expertise to bear and gives outsiders an opportunity to be heard (such as after notice to the public and consideration of comments by the public).

b. Treasury Regulations

Both the Treasury and the IRS promulgate various kinds of administrative pronouncements, such as "regulations" and published "revenue rulings." For purposes of the study of federal taxation, the most important kind of pronouncement is a Treasury regulation that deals with tax law. The purposes of tax regulations issued by the Treasury are to illustrate the operation of the statute (the Internal Revenue Code), resolve ambiguities in the statute, and fill in gaps in statutory coverage. Tax regulations often give examples of the application of tax rules to common fact situations. These examples can be very helpful for practitioners and law students.

Income tax regulations pertaining to a particular Code section are usually preceded by a "1" and a period. Thus, the regulations pertaining to § 61 of the Code can be found at Reg. § 1.61.[22]

Of all the types of administrative pronouncement issued by the Treasury or IRS, only a Treasury regulation has a realistic possibility of being considered to have the force of law under the three-pronged approach described above. Application of the "compatibility" prong, supra, depends on a comparison of the substance and language of the specific Code and regulation provisions involved in a given case. As to the "delegation" prong, the authority of the Treasury to issue pronouncements is conferred broadly by § 7805(a) of the Code, which gives the Treasury Department of the executive branch the authority to issue "all needful rules and regulations for the enforcement of" the Internal Revenue Code.[23] Additionally, assorted provisions

---

[22] Other types of regulations have different prefixes: "20." (for the estate tax), "25." (for the gift tax), "26." (for the generation-skipping tax), "301." (for procedural sections of the Code), and "601." (for IRS procedures).

[23] Curiously, there is no administrative pronouncement in the tax area that is officially called a "rule." That term should be construed to refer to any pronouncement (other than a regulation) of general applicability (i.e., that is not taxpayer-specific). Cf. Reg. § 1.6662-3(a)(2), defining the phrase "rules or regulations" (in connection with the civil penalty for disregarding rules and regulations) as encompassing

of the Code grant "specific" regulation authority to the Treasury. Accordingly, an administrative pronouncement by the Treasury (or IRS) would flunk the delegation prong only if it did not pertain to the "enforcement" of the Code or was not authorized by a specific Code provision.

Turning to the "thorough consideration of the merits" prong, supra, matters become confused insofar as the Treasury appears to have taken the position that regulations issued under § 7805 are so-called "interpretive" regulations, and therefore exempt from the notice-and-comment requirements of the Administrative Procedure Act (APA).[24] Unfortunately, that position is a two-edged sword, because interpretative regulations (a term not defined by the APA) are often said to be worthy of less deference than so called "legislative" regulations that are issued pursuant to specific grants of authority, found in provisions such as § 7872(c)(1)(E), to make rules of substantive law.[25] However, as we shall see, this facile approach is not supported by the cases.

In any event, the Treasury usually follows the spirit of the APA, even in the case of regulations issued under § 7805(a), by first issuing "proposed regulations" that constitute notice, and then inviting comment thereon.[26] The Treasury in the past has issued "temporary regulations" without soliciting comment, but now temporary regulations are simultaneously issued as proposed regulations. After considering comments, the Treasury can either withdraw or modify the proposed regulations or issue final regulations.[27] Final regulations are formally issued through publication in the Federal Register as a Treasury Decision (T.D.) over the signature of the Commissioner of the IRS and the Assistant Secretary of the Treasury for Tax

---

the Code, temporary and final regulations, and rulings (etc.) published in the Internal Revenue Bulletin, but not proposed regulations.

[24] 5 U.S.C. § 553(b)(3)(A).

[25] It has often been said that regulations issued under the authority of specific Code provisions are "legislative regulations" entitled to a high level of deference, whereas regulations issued under the general authority of § 7805 are "interpretive regulations," entitled to a lower level of deference. However, this kind of statement not only fails to jibe with the results of the cases, but it makes no analytical sense, because the promulgation of interpretive regulations under § 7805(a) has been as fully authorized by Congress as the issuance of regulations under specific statutory authority provisions, such as § 7872(c)(1)(E), and an interpretive regulation that has gone through the notice and comment procedure has been exposed to the same degree of public input and internal consideration by the Treasury as a specific statutory authority regulation.

[26] Regulations are drafted in a collaborative effort by the IRS and the office of the Tax Legislative Counsel under the Assistant Secretary of the Treasury for Tax Policy.

[27] Proposed regulations do not have the force of law because they are issued expressly as nonbinding proposals. Practitioners discount proposed regulations at their peril, however, because when they are made final, they are usually retroactive to the date on which they were first proposed, unless substantial modifications have been made to the final form. See § 7805(b) (condoning the retroactivity of regulations).

In principle, temporary regulations should receive less deference than final regulations because temporary regulations are promulgated without first giving the public an opportunity to provide comments. Nevertheless, some lower federal court decisions have held that if a temporary regulation satisfies the two prongs of the *Chevron* test (see infra text at notes 27-29), it is entitled to the same degree of deference as a final regulation. See *Alfaro v. Comm'r*, 349 F. 3d 225 (5th Cir. 2003); *Hospital Corporation of America v. Comm'r*, 348 F. 3d 136 (6th Cir. 2003). This position is supported by the Supreme Court's *Mead* and *Mayo* decisions, discussed in the text, infra.

Policy. Final regulations eventually appear in Title 26 of the Code of Federal Regulations (26 C.F.R.).

Turning to the leading cases, tax regulations issued through a meaningful notice and comment process have been given the force of law despite having been issued under § 7805(a). The "old approach" was expressed in *National Muffler Dealers Ass'n v. U.S.*, 440 U.S. 472 (1979), in which a tax regulation issued under § 7805(a) but pursuant to a notice and comment process, was given the force of law, but only after the following type of scrutiny (440 U.S. at 477):

> In determining whether a particular regulation carries out a congressional mandate in a proper manner, the court looks to see whether the regulation harmonizes with the plain language of the statute, its origin, and its purpose. A regulation may have particular force if it is a substantially contemporaneous construction of the statute by those presumed to have been aware of congressional intent. If the regulation dates from a later period, the manner in which it evolved merits inquiry. Other relevant considerations are the length of time the regulation has been in effect, the reliance placed on it, the consistency of the Commissioner of Internal Revenue's interpretation, and the degree of scrutiny Congress has devoted to the regulation during subsequent re-enactments of the statute.

Significantly, the Court in *National Muffler* did not invoke the distinction between interpretive and legislative regulations. If such a distinction was ever meaningful, it cannot be the case that a tax regulation is "interpretive" (entitled to lesser deference) just because it "interprets" a provision of the Code, because virtually all tax regulations interpret the Code. The interpretive/legislative dichotomy is misleading and should have been considered to have been obsolete after *National Muffler*,[28] although possibly a regulation authorized by a specific Code provision would have been given an even higher level of deference without the type of analysis called for by *National Muffler*.[29]

The *National Muffler* approach was apparently superseded by *Chevron U.S.A., Inc. v. Natural Resources Defense Council*, 467 U.S. 837 (1984), which stated that the first inquiry is "whether Congress has directly spoken to the precise question at issue" (i.e., does the statutory language enacted by Congress give a clear and complete meaning) because the statute is the ultimate authority.[30] If the statute is

---

[28] See *EEOC v. Arabian Am. Oil Co.*, 499 U.S. 244, 260 (1991) (Scalia, J., concurring in part and concurring in the judgment) ("the 'legislative rules vs. other action' dichotomy . . . is an anachronism").

[29] See, e.g., *Schweiker v. Gray Panthers*, 453 U.S. 34, 44 (1981):

> [The federal Medicaid regulation issued under express statutory authority to define a statutory term] is entitled to "legislative effect" because, "[in] a situation of this kind, Congress entrusts to the Secretary, rather than to the courts, the primary responsibility for interpreting the statutory term." Although we do not abdicate review in these circumstances, our task is the limited one of ensuring that the Secretary did not "[exceed] his statutory authority" and that the regulation is not arbitrary or capricious.

[30] A court confident of its interpretation of the statute can, by pronouncing the statute to clearly cover the case at hand, ignore the administrative interpretation. Therefore, *Chevron* is potentially a two-edged sword in that it strengthens the weight of administrative pronouncements dealing with ambiguous or incomplete statutory language while allowing courts to bypass such pronouncements altogether by finding that the statute is unambiguous and complete. On the other hand, in *Mayo Foundation for*

unambiguous and complete, the regulation is invalid to the extent that it fails to conform to the statute. If the statute is silent or ambiguous (and many Code provisions have gaps or involve some degree of ambiguity), the reviewing court can ask only whether "the agency's answer [to the omission or ambiguity] is based on a permissible construction of the statute." This means that if a regulation is consistent with at least one of the reasonable alternative meanings of an ambiguous or incomplete Code provision, the regulation must be upheld even if the court would prefer a different interpretation. In principle, the reviewing court is not free to impose its own view of what the *best* construction would be.

The full meaning of *Chevron* was somewhat clarified by *U.S. v. Mead Corp.*, 533 U.S. 218 (2001), where the Court considered the validity of classifications of goods for purposes of imposing tariffs on imports. The classifications were published as rulings by the Customs Service, a branch of the Treasury Department, but were not subject to notice and comment. The Court held that the rulings were not entitled to the force of law on the ground that Congress did not intend them to have the force of law. However, the Court found that the ruling was entitled to nonbinding "respect" by courts under the doctrine of *Skidmore v. Swift*, 323 U.S. 134 (1944). Accordingly, even if an agency pronouncement does not qualify for *Chevron* deference, it is entitled to a degree of respectful consideration, principally because of the agency's expertise. In *Mead*, the Court set out the following test for *Chevron* deference, i.e., for being treated as legally binding on the Court (533 U.S. at 226):

> We hold that administrative implementation of a particular statutory provision qualifies for *Chevron* deference when it appears that Congress delegated authority to the agency generally to make rules carrying the force of law, and that the agency interpretation claiming deference was promulgated in the exercise of that authority. Delegation of such authority may be shown in a variety of ways, as by an agency's power to engage in adjudication or notice-and-comment rulemaking, or by some other indication of a comparable congressional intent.

The Court went on to state that a congressional intent to delegate may be express or implied by a gap in the statute or by a statutory grant of authority to engage in notice-and-comment rulemaking, but that lack of notice-and-comment rulemaking was not *per se* fatal to *Chevron* deference.

Despite the fact that *Mead*, by framing the issue as *either Chevron* deference *or Skidmore* respect, seemed to have relegated *National Muffler* to the dustbin, some courts (especially the U.S. Tax Court) apparently didn't get the message. In *Swallows Holding v. Comm'r*, 515 F.3d 162 (3rd Cir. 2008), the Third Circuit reversed a Tax Court determination that an income tax regulation, issued with notice and comment, was a mere "interpretive regulation" (because issued under § 7805(a)) not deserving of much deference. The Third Circuit held that the regulation had the force of law under *Chevron* precisely because the regulation (which was not incompatible with the statute) had been issued after public notice and comment.

Medical Education & Research v. U.S., 131 S.Ct. 704 (2011), discussed in the text below, the Supreme Court paused only briefly at stage one by finding the statute to be ambiguous simply by failing to define the term "student," and declined to consider as dispositive dictionary definitions of "student."

Any doubts as to the application of *Chevron* to tax regulations was resolved by *Mayo Foundation for Medical Education & Research v. U.S.*, 131 S.Ct. 704 (2011), which upheld a notice-and-comment regulation issued under § 7805(a) that defined the "student" exemption for FICA withholding in a way that excluded medical residents. Applying the *Chevron* step-one analysis, the unanimous Court held that "student" was undefined in the statute, which was therefore ambiguous with respect to medical residents. The Court declined to view dictionary definitions of "student" as foreclosing a Treasury definition of that term.

Under *Chevron* step-two analysis, the Court found the regulation to be a reasonable interpretation of "student." Here the Court suggested that drawing bright lines was itself a reasonable feature of the regulation. The Court rejected the notion that tax regulations were entitled to less deference either by reason of being tax regulations or by reason of being issued under the "general" authority of § 7805(a). Additionally, the Court unequivocally stated that tax regulations issued under a notice-and-comment procedure were to be governed by *Chevron*, not *National Muffler*. By implication, *National Muffler* factors (such as longevity, contemporaneousness, and consistency) could count in favor of the validity of a regulation, but not against it (as many lower courts had done).

In sum, *Chevron* and *Mayo* establish the doctrine that a tax regulation that is authorized by the Code (including the general authorization conferred by § 7805(a)), has gone through a notice-and-comment procedure, and is not incompatible with the statute, has the force of law.[31] *This point cannot be over-emphasized.* Beginning tax students have a hard enough time grasping the primacy of the Code, and now they have to cope with the notion that executive branch regulations generally have the force of law! In short, although courts ultimately decide the status of regulations, the courts themselves are evolving a doctrine of deference to regulations, except in cases where the statutory language is clear. Older cases invalidating tax regulations have continuing vitality only if they hold that the statute is unambiguous, but not if they simply disagree with regulations on the merits.

A final regulation may itself be ambiguous. In that case, the dispute is not over the validity of the regulation but, instead, over its meaning. Government interpretations of Treasury regulations may be found in revenue rulings and other publicly disclosed IRS documents that do not have the status of law. Nevertheless, as discussed below, the courts usually defer to an agency's interpretation of its own ambiguous regulations.[32]

c.   Revenue Rulings

The IRS publishes "revenue rulings," sometimes called "published rulings," in the weekly Internal Revenue Bulletin (I.R.B.) and the semi-annual Cumulative Bulletin (C.B.). The first two (or four beginning with the year 2000) numbers of a Revenue Ruling represent the year of issuance, and the last numbers indicate the chronology. Thus, *Rev. Rul. 91-31* was the 31st revenue ruling issued in 1991. A revenue ruling sets out a hypothetical situation, states a result, and cites authority

---

[31] See *Tax Analysts v. IRS*, 350 F.3d 100, 103 (D.C. Cir. 2003).

[32] See, e.g., *Auer v. Robbins*, 519 U.S. 452, 461 (1997).

and reasons. Revenue rulings are issued without notice and comment. A most important aspect of revenue rulings is that they are internally binding on IRS personnel.[33] Thus, a *favorable* revenue ruling issued by the IRS covering your client's situation is about as good as it gets.[34]

What kind of status does a revenue ruling have in the courts? The ruling concerning tariff classifications at issue in *U.S. v. Mead*, supra , can probably be said to be less the fully-considered position of an agency than is the case with a published tax revenue ruling. In *Mead*, the Court held that, although the tariff ruling did not have the force of law, it was entitled to respect according to the standards laid down in *Skidmore v. Swift*, 323 U.S. 134, 140 (1944), which stated: "The weight of such [an administrative action] in a particular case will depend upon the thoroughness evident in its consideration, the validity of its reasoning, its consistency with earlier and later pronouncements, and all those factors which give it power to persuade. . . ." It follows that revenue rulings should be entitled to at least *Skidmore* respect by the courts, and the U.S. Circuit Courts of Appeals are generally in agreement on this point. Older cases holding that revenue rulings are no better than government litigating briefs should now be taken with a grain of salt. At the same time, there is no judicial authority that clearly explains the degree to which "*Skidmore* respect" exceeds the "deference" that would be given a brief filed by the government.

d. Private Letter Rulings

Taxpayers engaged in tax planning may submit requests for "private letter rulings," setting forth the facts of a proposed transaction, the desired tax result, and supporting reasons, if the matter is in an area in which the IRS has agreed to provide advance rulings of this nature. The IRS charges fees for a letter ruling. The Service usually confers with the taxpayer's counsel before acting on the request. If it appears that a ruling request is about to be denied, the taxpayer is permitted to (and should) withdraw the request. If your client stays the course, the ruling will be issued. Letter rulings are titled by a long number and date. The first two (or, starting in 2000, four) numbers represent the year of the ruling, the second two numbers the week of issuance, and the last three numbers the ruling's chronological number in that week. Thus, Letter Ruling 200140026 indicates that the ruling was the 26th ruling issued in the 40th week of 2001. Although not published by the Service, letter rulings are reproduced by commercial publishers and databases (such as Tax Notes and LexisNexis), after deletion of facts that would identify the taxpayer.

A letter ruling can generally be relied on by the taxpayer submitting the request — so long as the facts laid out in the request are correct — and a copy should be

---

[33] See *Rev. Proc. 78-24* , 1978-2 C.B. 502.

[34] Some courts have imposed a duty of consistency on the IRS such that the IRS cannot depart from an on-point ruling with respect to a taxpayer who relied on it, even if the ruling has been revoked. See *Silco Inc. v. U.S.*, 779 F.2d 282, 286 (5th Cir. 1986). Nevertheless, retroactive changes in regulations and rulings are an accepted feature of tax jurisprudence. See § 7805(b); *Dixon v. U. S.*, 381 U.S. 68 (1965). See generally Steve R. Johnson, *The IRS Duty of Consistency: The Failure of Common Law Making and a Proposed Legislative Solution*, 77 Tenn. L. Rev. 563 (2010).

filed with the return. The submission of ruling requests is an extremely important aspect of tax practice. Business deals are often made conditional on the parties obtaining a favorable tax ruling.

Section 6110(k)(3) provides that private rulings cannot be relied on as "precedent" by taxpayers other than one to whom the ruling was issued. In other words, private rulings do not purport to be law.[35] Nevertheless, they are extremely helpful in advising clients because they reflect the current thinking of the IRS.

e.   Other IRS Output

The following is an incomplete list of IRS "output" other than those discussed above.[36] Old forms sometimes fade and new ones emerge. All of the following (except for closing agreements) are available online.

Revenue Procedures. A "Rev. Proc." sets forth IRS procedures, such as how to apply for letter rulings, supra, and how information returns are to be formatted. They also list areas in which the IRS will decline to issue rulings (such as purely "factual" areas, including valuation). By listing requirements to be satisfied in order to obtain a favorable letter ruling in a particular area, some revenue rrocedures can indirectly express the IRS's views regarding substantive tax law. Revenue procedures are published in the Internal Revenue Bulletin and then in the Cumulative Bulletin.

Announcements and *Notices.* These items, which are published in the Internal Revenue Bulletin, are issued when guidance is needed quickly, such as just after the enactment of a new Code provision.

Technical Advice Memoranda. A "TAM" is indistinguishable in form from a private letter ruling, and it uses the same numbering system. Whereas private letter rulings are initiated by the taxpayer for planning purposes, technical advice memoranda respond to issues raised by Service personnel on audit. Although the taxpayer cannot directly initiate this procedure, she can request that the Service field personnel do so and can submit reasons supporting the desired result.

Field Service Advice. An "FSA" serves essentially the same functions as a TAM. FSAs largely superseded TAMs for awhile, but the IRS recently stopped issuing FSAs and reverted to TAMs.

General Counsel Memorandums. A "GCM" is a memorandum prepared within the office of the IRS Chief Counsel that attempts to justify a published revenue ruling or TAM. In other words, a GCM is a back-up document for a revenue ruling or a TAM. In the distant past, GCMs were published in the Cumulative Bulletin, but

---

[35] A private letter ruling might be given *Skidmore* respect by a court, despite disclaiming to be precedential authority. See *Nathel v. Comm'r*, 2010 U.S. App. LEXIS 11244 (2d Cir. 2010) (stating that an IRS General Counsel Memorandum, containing such a disclaimer, was entitled to *Skidmore* respect, while rejecting its conclusions).

[36] For a comprehensive description and discussion of the numerous forms of legal guidance issued by the IRS, see Mitchell Rogovin & Donald L. Korb, *The Four R's Revisited: Regulations, Rulings, Reliance, and Retroactivity in the 21st Century: A View From Within*, 46 DUQUESNE L. REV. 323 (2008).

the Service ceased to do so. They are best researched through an electronic database.

Internal Revenue Manual. The IRM is a set of instructions for IRS personnel, but are not "binding" as are Revenue Rulings. These instructions do, however, disclose IRS policies and procedures and are a possible source for aid in filling out tax returns, as (of course) are the IRS instructions to various Forms and Schedules.

Closing Agreements. The IRS and the taxpayer may enter into a closing agreement with respect to certain disputed issues. A closing agreement is binding unless obtained by misrepresentation of a material fact, misfeasance, or fraud. See § 7121. Additionally, it is confidential under § 6103 (i.e., not published or made available online).

PROBLEM

Consult the definition of gross income in § 61, and assume that no other Code provision (or judicial decision) applies to your client's legal tax issue, which is whether the money he received for allowing a reality TV show to film his activities around the clock for an indefinite period is includible in his gross income. Assume that the IRS is insisting that the money is includible. What are your client's chances of successfully opposing the IRS if:

(a) a Treasury Rregulation, issued under § 7805(a) through a notice-and-comment process, states that money received for abandoning a right of privacy against another is included in gross income?

(b) a published revenue ruling states the same thing but there is no regulation on point; or

(c) a private letter ruling issued to another taxpayer (and found through a computer search) states the same thing but there is no regulation or revenue ruling on point?

3.   Federal Tax Disputes in the Courts

The income tax is operated as a self-assessment system. That is to say, a taxpayer's liability is initially determined by the taxpayer on a return filed with the IRS. Payment of tax due (to the extent not already withheld or otherwise paid) is required. A small percentage of returns are selected for audit by the IRS, and the IRS may determine that the taxpayer has paid too little tax. At this point the IRS will inform the taxpayer that a tax shortfall ("deficiency") exists and must be paid. A judicial process is available if the taxpayer disagrees. Judicial process can also be invoked by a taxpayer who believes that he has overpaid his taxes and whose refund claim has been rejected or ignored by the IRS.

There are two ways in which typical tax disputes are handled. First, if the IRS proposes a deficiency, the taxpayer can file suit in the U.S. Tax Court, without paying the proposed deficiency until a judgment against the taxpayer becomes final. The government is referred to in Tax Court cases as "Commissioner" (of the IRS). Alternatively, the taxpayer can pay the proposed deficiency (or decide that too much tax was already paid) and file a "refund claim" with the IRS, and, if the

IRS does not satisfactorily respond to the claim, the taxpayer can file a "refund suit" in either the U.S. Court of Federal Claims (in Washington, D.C.) or the local U.S. District Court, the only court where a jury is available to decide fact questions. The government in Federal Claims and District Court cases is referred to as "United States."

The losing party in the Tax Court or District Court can appeal to the U.S. Court of Appeals for the circuit where the taxpayer resides. Decisions of the Court of Federal Claims can be appealed only to the U.S. Court of Appeals for the Federal Circuit (not the same as the U.S. Court of Appeals for the D.C. Circuit). The losing party in a U.S. Court of Appeals can apply for a writ of certiorari in the U.S. Supreme Court.

PROBLEMS

1.   Your client has been audited by the IRS which has asserted an income tax deficiency. Your client would like to contest the deficiency in court but cannot afford to pay it. What advice do you give?

2.   Assume that your client can afford to pay the deficiency but that the dispute turns on a fact question with respect to which the local jury will probably feel sympathy towards taxpayers. What advice do you give?

3.   Assume that your client can afford to pay the deficiency but that the dispute with the IRS involves a legal issue on which the Court of Appeals for your client's circuit of residence has previously adopted an adverse legal rule. Assume that no other Court of Appeals has yet addressed the issue. Is there any way in which your client can escape the adverse precedent?

Chapter 2

BASIC INCOME TAX PRINCIPLES

The study of numerous tax principles, doctrines, and rules is made easier by an overview of the system as a whole, which is provided in this chapter. The content of this chapter is based on the contemporary view of the basic principles comprising a personal income tax, not the views that were current in 1913.

Section A explores "income" as a conceptual matter. Section B examines how this concept is translated into a system that can measure the personal income of individuals. Section C examines the principal tax base rules under the Code. Section D describes the requisite steps for computing and paying the income tax. There is a lot packed into this chapter, and you should review it periodically when you find yourself losing sight of the big picture.

A. EVOLUTION OF "PERSONAL INCOME" AS A CONCEPT

If "income" is the "tax base" (i.e., what is to be taxed), we need to understand what is (and is not) included.

1. Personal Income vs. National Income

National income is an aggregate amount usually defined as gross domestic product (GDP), that is, the total national output of goods and services, usually measured by "final" sales proceeds (including wages, interest, and rents). A universal VAT (with no exemptions) would be a tax on GDP.

In contrast to national income, *personal* income is calculated separately for each taxpayer by referring to each taxpayer's distinct receipts and costs. The choice in favor of taxing personal income became largely settled in 1913 when the United States adopted a personal income tax. Nevertheless, the national income alternative continues to have advocates, and the debate over these two taxation approaches continues in academic and policy-making circles.

The normative issues surrounding the topics dealt with in this section, including that of the choice between a personal income tax and a national income tax, are considered in Chapter 3. This chapter is concerned with "where are we now?" and "how did we get here?"

2. Competing Notions of Personal Income

Five different concepts of personal income vied for attention in the first 50 years of the income tax. The principal points of controversy among these concepts were:

(a) Does income include nonrecurring receipts?

(b) Does income include gains and losses from property transactions? (A "gain" occurs when, for example, X purchases property for $100K and sells it for $130K.)

(c) Does income include receipts that do not result from the taxpayer's capital and labor?

The five competing approaches for resolving these and other questions all agreed on the following points: (1) a prerequisite for having income is an increase in wealth (usually from the receipt of cash or property), and (2) income is "net income," meaning that the taxpayer can reduce the tax base by the costs of earning income. In other words, under all five income concepts, net income refers to "new wealth" acquired during the income-measuring period (usually a year), thus excluding "old wealth" acquired during a prior period.

In spite of this agreement, however, there were important differences between the competing concepts as indicated by the following descriptions:

a. Trust Accounting Income

The purpose of the concept of trust accounting income is to allocate receipts and disbursements of a trust between beneficiaries entitled to receive trust income and beneficiaries who would eventually receive the trust's assets ("principal" or "corpus"), namely, beneficiaries holding remainder interests. A basic value of the law of trusts has been to "preserve corpus." Accordingly, the notion of trust income is fairly narrowly defined to exclude gratuitous receipts by the trust, as well as gains and losses accruing to property held by the trust. The effect of this approach is to minimize income and maximize corpus.

b. Business Accounting Income

Business accounting income largely evolved in the context of corporations. Corporate dividends to shareholders can only be paid out of current and accumulated net income, and (in order to prevent speculation in shares and to avoid the misleading of investors, including creditors) corporate income should not be overstated. Among other things, this meant that income could only be determined through actual transactions. Taking unrealized asset value increases into account was anathema (as it was in trust accounting income). To show nonrecurring income and gains as "income" was discouraged, as that might also fuel speculation or create confusion.

c. Income as Return on Capital or Labor

This concept of income is derived from macro-economics and is closely related to that of national income, described earlier, but modified so that investment income and net gains received by an individual are acknowledged to be included in the individual's tax base. However, receipts of pure transfers (gratuitous or otherwise) would be excluded. Accordingly, gifts, damages, insurance recoveries, and windfalls would be excluded from the tax base unless they derived from a taxpayer's "investment" of capital or labor. Thus, punitive damages and pure windfalls (such as a discovery of buried treasure) would be excluded.

The three concepts of income described above readily lent themselves to metaphors borrowed from nature. Thus, income was viewed as a "flow" or "harvest" (such as interest or rents) from either invested capital or from services. The classic metaphor is that of "fruit" and "tree," with only the fruit constituting income and the tree being viewed as the capital that produces the income. Metaphors of this type can be found in early Supreme Court decisions under the income tax.

d. Simons Income

Henry Simons was a University of Chicago public finance economist who wrote an influential book in 1938 that principally aimed to elaborate a concept of income suitable for taxation and not tainted by values derived from other disciplines. Simons strongly favored the notion of personal income against that of national income. The Simons definition of personal income for taxation purposes is:

> Personal income may be defined as the algebraic sum of (1) the market value of rights exercised in consumption and (2) the change in the value of the store of property rights between the beginning and end of the period in question.[1]

Because Robert Haig (in the early 1920s) and Georg Schanz (an earlier German writer) had also advocated essentially the same concept, this formulation is commonly called the "Haig-Simons" (H-S) or "Schanz-Haig-Simons" (S-H-S) concept of income. But since Simons is by far the most influential of the three, it is appropriate to attribute this definition to him. Much of Simons' influence on contemporary discussions of the income tax derives from the advocacy of influential Professor Stanley Surrey of Harvard Law School, who developed the concept of "tax expenditure provisions," namely, features of the tax system which did not conform to a modified version of the Simons income concept (and which therefore should be subject to the same kind of cost-benefit analysis as other government programs). Surrey used this idea as the basis of a tax policy tool, known as tax expenditure analysis, which will be discussed in Chapter 3.

In any event, the Simons definition makes a clean break with the concepts dealt with so far: under the Simons concept, all increases in an individual's material wealth, *regardless of source*, are to be included in the tax base. This would include gifts and other transfers received, non-recurring items, and pure windfalls. At the same time, the notion of "net increases in wealth" would require frequent valuation of property which would be a time-consuming and expensive matter for both government and taxpayers.

e. Ability-to-pay income

The *éminence grise* in the room is the concept of ability-to-pay income. Although the concept of ability to pay has been around at least since Adam Smith, it was appropriated by Utilitarianism, which viewed taxes in terms of subjective sacrifice. This subjective version of ability to pay, which would take into account nonmarket items such as leisure and psychic income, has since been shunned by those wary of

---

[1] HENRY C. SIMONS, PERSONAL INCOME TAXATION 50 (1938).

Utilitarianism, including Henry Simons. Nevertheless, a concept of "objective" ability to pay (looking to market outcomes rather than subjective utility) is largely (if not wholly) compatible with the Simons concept,[2] and gives it a normative underpinning. Indeed, without a normative base, the Simons construct is vulnerable to being dismissed as being purely arbitrary.

As will be explained in Chapter 3, the ability-to-pay concept can be described as a notion of substantive (as opposed to formal) *fairness* in taxation. Additionally, an objective ability-to-pay tax base describes the material resources of a taxpayer that are available for appropriation by the government, including appropriation for the possible purpose of redistribution.

The principal ways in which the ability-to-pay concept differs from the general understanding of the Simons concept are:

(1) Changes in property values do not "register" in the tax base as income, gains, and losses until they are "realized"[3] (a concept taken up shortly); and

(2) the tax base is reduced (off the bottom) by allowances that aim to immunize subsistence income from tax (such allowances are described in Chapter 4).

As an aside, it should be noted that micro-economics has its own distinctive concept of personal income, which is basically that of a "flow of satisfactions" to an individual. Since satisfactions are subjective, and include off-market conditions and occurrences (such as good health or a great climate), it is impractical to directly take them into account in computing net income for tax purposes. Nevertheless, this concept has been influential in tax policy discussions, dealt with in Chapter 3.

3. Some Highlights in the Evolution of the Income Tax

The personal income tax has evolved away from the nontax concepts of trust accounting income, business accounting income, and income as return on capital or labor and has moved towards an ability-to-pay concept (which closely resembles the Simons definition). However, a few vestiges of non-tax concepts remain. The major steps in this evolutionary process are described in the following paragraphs.

The 1913 income tax statute defined gross income as expressly including gains from employment, business, and investment, as well as "income derived from any source whatever," but the statute followed trust accounting principles by expressly excluding gratuitous receipts (gifts, bequests, and inheritances) from gross income, and this feature continues to the present day under § 102 of the Internal Revenue Code. (Recall that such transfers are subject to the federal estate and gift taxes, but the latter are separate taxes apart from the income tax, and their large exemptions and exclusions result in the nontaxation of most gratuitous transfers.)

---

[2] Thus, Simons, supra note 1, at 206, characterized his definition of income as "a measure of the individual's prosperity."

[3] Simons, supra note 1, at 100, 207-08, stated that unrealized gains and losses must be excluded from the tax base if the income tax is to be workable. Nevertheless, the Simons concept of income is commonly understood as requiring the inclusion of unrealized gains and losses. See, e.g., JOEL SLEMROD & JON BAKIJA, TAXING OURSELVES 28-29 (4th ed. 2008).

In a very early income tax case, *Gould v. Gould*, 245 U.S. 151 (1917), the Supreme Court held that a cash support payment from husband to wife was not gross income, even though the payment was not a gift. The rationale of this case is murky, but it appears to assume that intra-family transfers were not included in the statutory phrase "income derived from any source whatever" unless Congress expressly states otherwise. Apart from what is stated in the opinion of the Court, the actual holding of *Gould* is consistent with the proposition that, to be "income derived from any source whatever," a receipt must be derived from the taxpayer's capital or labor. In the 1920 case of *Eisner v. Macomber*, 252 U.S. 189, 193, the Court reinforced this idea by stating in dictum that a receipt was not income unless it was derived from the taxpayer's capital or labor.[4]

In the 1921 case of *Merchants' Loan &Trust Co. v. Smietanka*, 255 U.S. 509, the Court held that the investment gain of a taxpayer from a single, nonrecurring sale of property was includible in gross income. This case rejects the notion that only regular and recurring gains are income. More broadly, it rejects the notion that income for tax purposes is "determined" by trust and business accounting concepts of income.

The *Eisner v. Macomber* "definition" of income was followed by courts until it was buried by the Supreme Court in *Comm'r v. Glenshaw Glass Co.*, 348 U.S. 426 (1955). *Glenshaw Glass* held that a punitive damage recovery that was not produced by the taxpayer's capital or labor was included in gross income under the same statutory language that was applied in *Gould*. Under *Glenshaw Glass*, gross income means all items expressly listed as such in the Code plus all "accessions to wealth, clearly realized and over which the taxpayer has dominion and control." The receipt of a transfer payment, therefore, is income, unless excluded by statute.

Although the version of the Internal Revenue Code that was controlling in *Glenshaw Glass* employed the same statutory phrase that governed the earlier cases described above ("income derived from any source whatever"), by the time the Supreme Court decided *Glenshaw Glass*, Congress had replaced that older language with the phrase "all income from whatever source derived," which also appears in the current definition of gross income contained in § 61(a). The *Glenshaw Glass* opinion held that this new language has the same meaning as the old phrase "income derived from any source whatever."

Glenshaw Glass is the final step in liberating the concept of personal income for tax purposes from limitations imposed by other disciplines. Of course, Congress might elect to selectively embrace some of these limitations, as is the case with the § 102 exclusion that it has provided for gratuitous receipts. Also, the Code's favorable treatment for net capital gains of individuals first appeared immediately after the decision in *Merchants' Loan & Trust Co. v. Smietanka*, supra, signifying the ambivalence of Congress about the result in that case.

---

[4] This statement, which did not bear on the decision of the case, was lifted from *Stratton's Independence v. Howbert*, 231 U.S. 399 (1913), involving the 1909 income tax on corporations.

4. Ability-to-Pay Net Income as a Useful Model for Conceptualizing the Income Tax

The ability-to-pay concept of *net* income (which can also be viewed as a "modified" Simons concept) can be tentatively defined as:

Net income = Realized net increases in wealth plus consumption, both accounted for on an annual basis.

Note that this is a concept of "net income" (gross income reduced by costs of producing such income). Therefore, it does not mention allowances "off the bottom" (such as personal and dependent exemptions) that are necessary for purposes of transforming ability-to-pay net income into ability-to-pay *taxable* income, which is the amount that should ultimately be taxed. A discussion of these "off the bottom" allowances and deductions, being somewhat controversial and imprecise, is postponed to Chapters 4 and 5.

It needs to be forthrightly stated that the ability-to-pay concept of net income does not appear explicitly in the Internal Revenue Code and that several important features of the federal income tax deviate from it. Nevertheless, mastering this concept offers two potential benefits for students. First, the ability-to-pay concept of net income roughly describes the federal income tax base in general, thus enabling you to conceptualize it as a whole. Second, understanding the contours of this concept of net income is a great time saver, because it defines issues, structures the analysis of them, and provides an "initial" answer as a starting point, *even before looking up the "final" answer in the Code or regulations*. Of course, it is imperative to consult the Code and regulations, but with an understanding of ability-to-pay net income, you will often know where to start — as opposed to randomly thumbing through voluminous pages of indecipherable text or, more likely, spending excessive time with electronic databases.

5. The Income Tax Base and its Effect

The tax base of any tax on personal net income reaches both net-increases-in-wealth and personal consumption. In contrast, a sales tax and other forms of consumption taxes reach only personal consumption, and a tax on property, wealth, or the transfer of wealth reaches only wealth. Moreover, an income tax does not apply to the full value of a taxpayer's wealth. It only reaches a taxpayer's *increase* in wealth for the year, rather than the total value of the taxpayer's entire stock of net wealth. If a taxpayer's entire net wealth were taxed each year and if the tax rate were higher than the "normal" rate of return on investments, the tax would render investments pointless, because the tax would wipe out all investment earnings. By taxing only the taxpayer's net *increase* in wealth *for the year*, a personal income tax ensures that wealth is taxed just once to a particular individual (in the year it is acquired or saved), thus placing it on an equal footing with consumption.

B. MEASURING NET INCOME

It is important that a concept of income can be translated into a workable scheme that can be administered on a self-assessment basis by individual taxpayers and a relatively small bureaucracy. There are two potential "measurement" (accounting) problems that present challenges to the creation of such a scheme. One has to do with measuring "net increases in wealth" and the other with measuring "personal consumption." The material below explains how these problems are solved under the existing income tax.

1. Measuring Changes in Net Wealth: The Realization Principle

The "net increase in wealth" concept implies valuation of positive wealth (savings and investment) and negative wealth (debts and liabilities) at the beginning and end of each year. One way to reckon changes in net wealth could be to subtract the value of Net Wealth at the beginning of Year 1 from the value of Net Wealth at the beginning of Year 2. Not only is valuation difficult and contentious in itself, but it would have to be carried out annually. The task of periodically locating and valuing every item of property owned by U.S. taxpayers would overwhelm the tax system.

The principal means of avoiding annual valuation is to take a transactional approach. Instead of valuing all assets at the beginning and end of each year, changes in value can be ignored until the sale, exchange, or other disposition of the asset. At that time, the net disposition proceeds can be compared to the original net cost of the asset to determine the gain or loss for the entire holding period of the asset. Indeed, where both the purchase and sale are for cash, there is never any need to value anything because the cash price in an arms-length transaction fixes both the purchaser's cost and the seller's net sales proceeds. Even where valuation would be required (e.g., upon receiving in-kind property in an exchange), it would need to be determined only once (at the time of the exchange), rather than on an annual basis.

> ***Example***: Adam purchases shares of stock on July 17 of Year 1 for $10K. At the last nanosecond of Year 1 the stock is worth $12K. Under the Simons concept of income, Adam would have $2K of income for Year 1 because his wealth has increased by that much, but there has been no transaction to "fix" this income in Year 1, and so the system ignores such income for the time being. In Year 2 Adam sells the stock for $13K. The sales transaction fixes the income at $3K (relative to the original $10K cost) over the entire period Adam held the asset. The $3K gain is assigned entirely to Year 2. Under this transactional approach, increases and decreases in wealth are accounted for only in the year when "realized."

The principle that gains and losses are only to be reckoned when realized is justified not only by administrative convenience but also by the ability-to-pay notion. Since taxes are payable only in cash, the determination of a taxpayer's ability to pay taxes has to consider taxpayer liquidity.

If, however, conversion to cash were the sole indicator of liquidity, taxpayers could avoid accounting for gains by exchanging property for other property. Thus, the "realization" principle is not confined to the situation where the taxpayer receives cash in a sale, but includes property exchanges as well. Nevertheless, in a market economy, sales for cash, or for a promise to pay future cash, are the norm, because noncash bartering is generally inconvenient. Consequently, exchanges of one property for another would rarely occur in the absence of a special tax provision that encourages such exchanges. Accordingly, treating noncash property exchanges as events that produce taxable gain does not detract from the fact that the primary consequence of the realization principle is to give effect to the ability-to-pay concept by ensuring that taxpayers usually do not have a tax liability until they have engaged in a transaction that yields cash.

The federal income tax has, since the beginning in 1913, followed this transactional, or "realization," approach to increases and decreases in the value of property. This approach was familiar to lawmakers in 1913, because it was a central tenet of business accounting. We will see, however, that the Internal Revenue Code makes important modifications to the realization principle.

Recall that as explained above, an income concept that is based on the sum of net increases in the taxpayer's wealth plus the taxpayer's consumption must deal with the problems of measuring wealth increases and consumption amounts. The preceding discussion has dealt with the first of these measurement issues and we now turn to the second.

2. Measuring Consumption: Personal Consumption as a Deduction-Disallowance Principle

The term "consumption" refers to "personal consumption," which generally means the goods and services that an individual consumes for personal purposes, such as shelter, food, clothing, entertainment, and so on. Personal consumption, an end in itself, is distinguishable from costs of producing income, which are but a means towards an end.

It turns out that consumption can be effectively taxed under an income tax by viewing consumption as a subset of changes in wealth, and practical considerations favor taking this approach.

Treating consumption as a separate element of the tax base creates a degree of accounting complexity. For example, assume that Bob earns $100 of cash wages in Year 1. He immediately deposits the $100 in his bank account where it sits until Year 2, when he withdraws it and spends it on groceries. To keep things simple, assume (unrealistically) that these are the only financial events in Bob's life during Years 1 and 2. His income computation for Year 1 would be: net increase in wealth ($100) plus consumption (0) equals $100 income. For Year 2 it would be: net decrease in wealth (− $100) plus consumption ($100) equals zero income.

Requiring Bob in Year 2 to subtract the $100 from wealth and immediately add it to consumption increases systemic complexity and also implies that taxpayers must keep track of all consumption outlays (meals, movie tickets, dry cleaning, and on and on) *plus* free consumption benefits received in kind (such as free food at the employer's annual picnic). This would be an impossible task against which taxpayers would rebel.

As suggested above, however, these problems can be avoided simply by viewing consumption as a subset of changes in wealth. To be specific, the vast bulk of personal consumption is obtained through purchases. Amounts expended on consumption either decrease wealth in the short run or buy property (consumer assets, like a car) that will decrease in wealth over time. It would be redundant to account for such items by first decreasing wealth and then increasing the tax base by the same amount. This process can be made more manageable by simply foregoing the separate inclusion of consumption in the tax base and disallowing any deduction against the tax base for decreases in wealth that represent consumption. In effect, these items simply can be ignored in computing the tax base!

To illustrate this point, return to the example of Bob above. His tax result ($100 of Year 1 income and zero Year 2 income) can be computed in a much simpler way by ignoring the Year 2 consumption instead of subtracting $100 from wealth and adding $100 to consumption in Year 2. Under this simplified approach, Bob's accounting for Year 1 would show a net increase in wealth of ($100), resulting in $100 income. For Year 2 it would show a net increase in wealth of zero (the decrease in wealth attributable to consumption being ignored), equaling zero income. This approach avoids having to value consumption when it occurs.

Consumption received in kind (without paying for it) can also be handled under this shortcut approach by characterizing it as an increase in wealth for which there is no offsetting deduction. Thus, if one wins a free trip to Las Vegas as a prize, the *rights* to the plane trip, lodging, meals, and so on, are items of in-kind wealth possessing a market value until consumed. As such, the package of rights can be included in income without an offsetting deduction. Alternatively, the consumption obtained can be viewed as the equivalent of the receipt of cash income that is tied to a particular nondeductible expenditure. (The extent to which the income tax actually reaches to in-kind consumption is dealt with later.)

3.   The Resulting Structure of the Income Computation

The considerations outlined above result in a system in which you compute your net income *indirectly* by annually totaling your includible-in-gross-income receipts and subtracting your allowable deductions, rather than figuring (on an annual basis) the sum of (1) net realized increases in wealth and (2) aggregate consumption. This indirect system is based on the proposition that when only the costs of producing wealth are subtracted from a taxpayer's total gains for the year (wages, interest, rent, sale profits, etc.), the remainder will equal the sum of the taxpayer's consumption and net additions to wealth for the year — i.e., her ability-to-pay income.

It is worth stressing that expenditures to acquire tangible or intangible assets yielding significant future benefits do not reduce current wealth and, therefore, should not reduce current net income, even if the outlays and expenditures are not for consumption items. These outlays (called "capital expenditures") merely involve a conversion of one form of wealth (cash) into another form of wealth (an asset that provides future benefits). From an ability-to-pay perspective, a taxpayer cannot avoid tax on cash receipts by choosing to convert the cash to another asset.

The forgoing indirect system is relatively simple from the accounting angle because information about most realized wealth-increase items, namely, wages, interest, dividends, rents, and royalties, is provided by payors and transferors on information returns filed with the IRS and copied to the taxpayer. Furthermore, there is no need for the taxpayer to keep track of myriad consumption expenditures. Appreciation and loss in the value of property are accounted for only when "realized," thereby avoiding annual property valuations.

NOTES

1. The "annual accounting principle" refers to the practice of computing net income on an annual basis, even if an item (or the overall result for the year) may in some larger economic sense be viewed as tentative or provisional. The realization principle is an exception to the annual accounting principle insofar as it delays accounting for gain or loss with respect to a particular property item until its sale or other disposition. But realization of a gain or loss fixes the final tax accounting for that item. That is, unless the Code provides otherwise, the realized gain or loss is "recognized" (entered into gross income or eligible for deduction) even in the case of a property exchange or even where the proceeds of sale are used to purchase an investment of a similar type.

2. Most adherents of the Simons income tax concept oppose the realization principle. (An income tax without the realization principle is called an "accretion" income tax.) It is true that the rationales offered in defense of the realization principle are not, taken singly, overwhelmingly persuasive.

(a) Assets are not always difficult to value. Publicly traded securities and commodities are quite easy to value. On the other hand, some assets are not easy to value, and the difficulty of valuation ranges from moderate (as with real estate) to profound (closely held business interests and untested mineral rights and intellectual property). If exceptions were made to realization, an issue would be where to draw the line. Also, nonliquid assets would be tax-favored relative to liquid assets.

(b) A taxpayer's liquidity to pay taxes cannot be ascertained on an asset-by-asset basis; his or her entire panoply of resources should be taken into account. But this point perhaps cuts both ways. That is, a system that would judge a taxpayer's liquidity on the basis of his or her entire asset portfolio would find that many taxpayers have sufficient liquidity to pay tax on gain resulting from transactions in which no cash was received, but the burden of analyzing the taxpayer's entire asset portfolio would increase costs for both taxpayers and the IRS.

3. Despite the foregoing, the realization principle appears to be an immovable object not only in the United States, but also in every other country that has an income tax. This persistence might be largely based on a perception that unrealized gains and losses are "unreal," "temporary," or "ephemeral" until the taxpayer terminates her relationship to the asset. This perception is perhaps inevitable on account of volatile markets for securities and real estate. The political resistance to

abolishing the realization principle may be evidence of the public's subliminal acceptance of the ability-to-pay principle coupled with a "liberty" impulse, namely, that the tax system shouldn't "force" people to convert assets to cash by taxing gains before realization.

C.   THE TAX BASE UNDER THE CODE

Now let's turn to the language of the Internal Revenue Code and see how the indirect approach to computing ability-to-pay income is translated into positive law.

The Internal Revenue Code sections that comprise the fundamental structure of the income tax and that should be read in connection with this chapter are: §§ 61(a), 162(a), 165(a)-(c), 167(a), 262(a), 263(a), 1001(a)-(c), 1012, and 1211(b). A few additional Code sections will be noted in passing.

Start with § 1. Each subsection begins with "There is hereby imposed on the *taxable income* of . . . ." (The different sorts of filing status mentioned there will be explored in Chapter 4.) Thus, the tax base under the Code is "taxable income." Taxable income for the taxable year is subjected to the tax rate schedule specified in § 1 of the Code that corresponds to the taxpayer's filing status. The result is the tentative tax due for the taxable year before any credits (such as the Earned Income Tax Credit) are taken into account. For individuals, the taxable year is almost always the calendar year.

Section 63(a) provides that "taxable income" means "gross income minus the deductions allowed by this chapter . . . ." As one would expect, "gross income" refers to "inflows" (realized accessions to wealth) and "deductions" are derived from "outflows" (realized decreases in wealth). A "deduction" is thus a subtraction or a reduction of the tax base. *Dollars that are deducted are effectively not taxed.*

Note that only deductions "allowed by this chapter" are permitted, which means that if one wishes to deduct an item from gross income, *one must find a Code section specifically authorizing the deduction,* i.e., a section that contains the "magic words" "there shall be allowed as a deduction . . . ."

1.   Gross Income Overview

Gross Income is the starting point in the personal income tax computation. Look at § 61. (It is advisable to look at § 61 now, rather than later — say, during the exam — when it will be too late!) *In general, and presumptively, gross income includes all receipts by the taxpayer of money and property during the year, because such items represent an increase in wealth.* Most students grasp easily the notion that gross income includes such things as compensation for services rendered (§ 61(a)(1)), interest (§ 61(a)(4)), rents (§ 61(a)(5)), and dividends (§ 61(a)(7)).

Certain receipts are "excluded" from gross income, which means that they do not enter into "gross income" and thus are not taxed on receipt. They are, in other words, ignored. Virtually all exclusions are prescribed by specific Code provisions. The principal statutory exclusions are: (1) gratuitous transfers received (§§ 101(a) and 102(a)), (2) interest on certain state and local debt obligations (§ 103), (3) recoveries for physical personal injuries and sickness (§ 104), and (4) certain (but by no means all) fringe benefits of employees (numerous Code provisions). The only true non-statutory exclusion, derived from the holding of the *Gould* case supra, is that gross income does not include receipts that constitute "support" under state law.[5] The statutory exclusions of general interest are dealt with later in this book.

The part of the Code entitled "Items Specifically Included in Gross Income" (§§ 71-99) contains special rules that perform such tasks as overriding certain exclusions (in whole or in part), attributing a certain kind of income to a certain taxpayer, determining the year in which certain in-kind income is taxed, and refining the computation of certain investment income. For example, the result of the *Gould* case referred to in the preceding paragraph has been partially overturned by § 71, and § 74 removes prizes and awards from any possibility of being excluded under § 102(a).

2. Gain and Loss from Property Dispositions

One of the items specifically iterated as being included in gross income by § 61 is that of "gains derived from dealings in property." § 61(a)(3). How is "gain" defined? If John buys Blackacre (unimproved land) for $70K and eventually sells it for $120K in cash, intuition suggests that his includible "gain" is $50K. But why is the gain not $120K, or something else?

The answer is found by a careful reading of § 1001(a), (b), and (c). According to § 1001(a), "gain" is the excess of the "amount realized" over the "adjusted basis." "Loss" is the reverse: the excess of adjusted basis over amount realized. The terms "gain," "loss," "amount realized," and "adjusted basis" are precisely defined terms of art. It is important to learn the correct usage of these terms now, as they are foundational to the income tax.

Section 1001(b) states that, in John's case, the "amount realized" is the amount of money that John received for Blackacre — $120K. Note how the definition of "gain" for gross income purposes incorporates the idea of "realization." That is, gain is defined in terms of "amount realized" *on a sale or other disposition of property*. The property's appreciation or loss in value during the taxpayer's ownership years is ignored until the occurrence of a "realization event" (namely, a sale or other disposition of the property).

Any costs of disposition, such as broker's commissions incurred in selling property, reduce the amount realized. Let's assume that in John's case no such costs are present.

Section 1001 commands subtraction of the "adjusted basis" from the "amount realized" to reach "gain" (or "loss"). But what is Blackacre's "adjusted basis" in John's hands? "Adjusted basis" is defined by § 1011 as the taxpayer's initial basis,

---

[5] The fact that borrowed money is not included in gross income, despite the absence of a Code provision specifically excluding borrowed money, does not derive from a nonstatutory "exclusion" but is instead based on the notion that, because of the repayment obligation, the borrowing transaction does not increase the borrower's wealth.

adjusted thereafter in accordance with rules found in § 1016. John's initial basis will depend on how he came to own the property. Because John acquired Blackacre by purchase, § 1012 sets his initial basis at $70K — his "cost." Other initial basis rules, such as those that apply to property acquired by gift or inheritance, will be covered in due course.

"Adjusted" basis is, as one would expect, initial basis, adjusted upward or downward to reflect subsequent tax events. Shortly we shall describe two common basis adjustments under § 1016. For present purposes however, we'll stipulate that there are no such adjustments to John's initial $70K cost basis, so that his adjusted basis at the time of sale is $70K.

Thus, John has realized a "gain" equal to $50K ($120K "amount realized" *less* $70K "adjusted basis"). Under §§ 1001(c) and 61(a)(3), that gain must be "recognized," which means immediately taken into gross income, unless another Code provision steps in to defer or prohibit recognition.[6] Nonrecognition provisions of the Code exist, but none of them apply in John's case.

A "loss" occurs when the amount realized is less than adjusted basis. Note again how the "realization" principle is built into the definition of loss. In other words, under the Code a "loss" *occasioned by a sale or disposition* is synonymous with "realized loss."

A loss represents a realized decrease in wealth. Nevertheless, a loss reduces the tax base only if it can be *deducted*, and deductions can be taken only where they are authorized ("allowed") by specific Code provision. See §§ 161 and 211. The fact that § 1001(c) states that realized losses from the sale or exchange of property are "recognized" unless elsewhere provided for in the Code is not sufficient to allow losses to be *deducted*. In the case of losses, "recognition" means only that the loss now "exists" for tax purposes so as to be *potentially* deductible. Whether it is actually deductible is an issue we will return to shortly.

3. Capitalization and Basis

In the preceding section, it was explained how the Code mandates that John had gain of only $50K instead of $120K when he sells Blackacre for $120K cash. Here we explore the income tax "logic" of this result.

Two fundamental precepts in an income tax (which differentiate it from a wealth tax, for example) are:

(1) *The same dollars should not be taxed to the same taxpayer more than once*; and

---

[6] That portion of § 1001(c) that states that gains from sales or exchanges must be recognized is a redundancy because § 61(a)(3) by itself requires recognition of all realized gain "[e]xcept as otherwise provided in this subtitle." In fact, if recognition of gain depended upon § 1001(c) alone, some gain would escape tax, for § 1001(c) requires recognition of gain realized only through "sale or exchange." To illustrate, suppose a factory with a basis of $100K burns down, and the taxpayer receives $150K in insurance proceeds. Here, the realized gain of $50K would escape tax if § 1001(c) were the sole recognition mechanism because the gain was not produced by "sale or exchange." Section 61(a)(3) nevertheless captures that gain in gross income.

(2) *The same dollars should not be deducted by the same taxpayer more than once (or otherwise allowed to provide a double tax benefit).*

These precepts are inherent, by the way, in all notions of personal income, which refer to (realized) net *increases* in wealth, that is, "new" wealth of a taxpayer. Previously taxed "old" wealth (sometimes referred to as "capital") cannot be taxed again to the same taxpayer under a theoretically correct income tax. The same is true in reverse for a decrease in wealth. Such a decrease cannot reduce income more than once.

These precepts are not expressly stated as such in any single section of the Code. Rather, the Code is designed to carry out these precepts automatically. Of course, stating a principle is often easier than applying it. Thus, it is not always clear when a current transaction implicates dollars that, to the same taxpayer, have been taxed earlier or have previously reduced the tax base through a deduction. The problem of identifying "same dollars" is a pervasive one in the tax law, but it is not difficult in John's case.

How would "same dollars" be taxed twice to John if his entire $120K cash receipt were included in gross income? The answer begins with the observation that the $70K cash with which John purchased Blackacre was derived from a receipt, perhaps wages that were included in John's gross income. John took the $70K and purchased Blackacre. This cash expenditure of $70K raised a "deduction issue" at the time of purchase. Under the ability-to-pay and Simons concepts of personal income, the $70K should *not* (as a conceptual matter) have been deducted when John bought Blackacre, *because John's buying of Blackacre did not decrease John's wealth.* John merely changed the *form* of his wealth from dollar bills to land (Blackacre).

And, in fact, the $70K was *not* deductible under the Code. *A cash outlay that merely changes the form of wealth is called a "capital expenditure."* Section 263 of the Code gives examples of capital expenditures that are not deductible. This section is not really necessary, however, since there is no Code provision allowing a deduction for capital expenditures.

Generally speaking, the Code recognizes only three generic categories of the concept of "decrease in wealth" that can yield allowable deductions, namely:

(1) expenses (dealt with generically by §§ 162(a) and 212(1) and (2)),

(2) depreciation and amortization (dealt with generically by § 167(a)), and

(3) losses (dealt with generically by § 165).[7]

John's $70K expenditure to acquire Blackacre was not deductible depreciation because, as will be explained shortly, depreciation does not involve a present outlay of funds. Nor was John's expenditure a deductible loss. He obtained $70K of property in exchange for $70K of cash; no loss there. (Blackacre may decline in

---

[7] Other Code sections dealing with deductions are not "generic" (dealing with broad categories) but instead address narrow matters such as charitable contributions and residential mortgage interest, and can, therefore, be ignored in painting the big picture.

value and subsequently be sold at a loss, but that is a future possibility that has nothing to do with the tax treatment of John's $70K expenditure at the time it occurs.) Finally, John's $70K outlay did not qualify as deductible under §§ 162, 212(1) or 212(2), because these provisions only allow certain *expenses* to be deducted, and a capital expenditure is not an "expense" for this purpose. *An "expense" in tax jargon is an outlay (expenditure) for a benefit that is consumed or dissipated within a relatively short period of time.* Thus, buying paper for a business's copier constitutes the purchase of "property," but the property obtained is expected to be used up in the short term, and so its cost is a deductible expense under § 162. In contrast, a capital expenditure is an outlay that obtains value that is expected to last at least beyond the current taxable year, such as the purchase of the copier itself.

But imagine for a moment that John *had* been permitted — contrary to current law — to deduct his $70K capital expenditure when he purchased Blackacre. The $70K cash wages that he used to purchase Blackacre would, of course, have been includible in gross income, but this inclusion would have been offset (cancelled) by the $70K deduction. Thus, the $70K would not yet have been taxed in John's hands. Under those assumptions, the full $120K amount realized on the later sale of Blackacre *would* properly be included in John's gross income, since none of those dollars would have yet been taxed to John. But since the Code, in fact, *denied* John a $70K deduction when he purchased Blackacre (because the purchase did not decrease his wealth), those dollars *were* taxed to John in the year of purchase. It was the *nondeductibility* of the $70K outlay on the purchase of Blackacre, *because it was a capital expenditure*, that produces the conclusion that $70K of the $120K amount realized is a recovery of dollars that have already been taxed to John and, therefore, should be protected from taxation a second time to him. Sections 1001 and 1012 of the Code prevent the previously taxed $70K from being taxed again to John by assigning John a $70K "basis" in Blackacre and then allowing that basis to offset John's $120K amount realized in defining includible "gain." Thus, John's taxable gain is limited to the $50K that has not previously been taxed in his hands.

Up to now, we have assumed that John purchased Blackacre for cash. What is the basis for Blackacre if, instead of purchasing it for cash, John receives Blackacre as in-kind compensation for services rendered at a time when Blackacre has a fair market value of $70K? The basis question is dependent upon the resolution of the issue of whether John's receipt of land worth $70K is included in gross income. Of course it is, because § 61(a)(1) expressly identifies "compensation for services" as gross income. Income need not be paid in the form of cash in order to be cognizable for tax purposes. Otherwise, it would be terribly easy to never pay taxes; we would simply become a barter society. Thus, John must include $70K in gross income on the receipt of Blackacre. And since John pays tax on the $70K value of the land, the land represents $70K of previously-taxed dollars, and he must have a basis of $70K in the land. Reg. § 1.61-2(d)(2)(i) confirms this result.[8]

---

[8] John's $70K basis is clearly the correct result as a matter of both theory and existing law. Nevertheless, it is a result that is difficult to square with § 1012 which defines the basis of property as "cost." This matter is explored in the Notes below.

Would John still have a basis of $70K if he had obtained the cash as a cash gift that was excluded from gross income under § 102(a)? The answer is "yes" in order to prevent the "backdoor" taxation of the $70K that would occur upon the sale of Blackacre for $120K if John were assigned a zero basis. In other words, basis should still be obtained if "permanently" tax-excluded dollars are used to buy property. Otherwise, the exclusion would be lost retroactively. This result is also practical: If creating basis depended on whether the source of the funds was initially included in gross income, then all excludible amounts would have to be traced forward to the things on which they were spent. Such a system would be complex and could be a trap for those who would be unaware of the significance of the source of expenditures.

Basis is the tax term for a previously taxed amount which should not be taxed again (or an amount deliberately not taxed and which should remain untaxed). Viewed from another angle, basis can be thought of as amounts that have not yet been deducted from the tax base but that might be deducted in the future. For example, John's $70K outlay in purchasing Blackacre was prevented from being deducted in the year of purchase because it was a "capital expenditure," but the basis thereby created is effectively "deducted" (technically, "offset") against the proceeds from his later sale of Blackacre. In sum, basis becomes an accounting tool that allows us to keep track of previously taxed dollars that have not yet been deducted from the tax base.

PROBLEM

Mark uses salary income to purchase General Electric stock in Year 1 as an investment for $20K on Mar. 16. On Dec. 31, Year 1, the stock is worth $17K, and on Dec. 31, Year 2, it is worth $22K. Mark sells the stock on Sept. 1, Year 3, for $23K.

(a) What tax result to Mark in Years 1, 2, and 3 under (1) the Simons concept of income, (2) the ability-to-pay concept of income, and (3) the Code?

(b) Are the results altered if Mark receives the stock free and clear as compensation for services in Year 1 when its then fair market value was $20K?

(c) Are the results under the Code altered if the cash that Mark used to buy the stock came from a cash gift from Gramps that was excluded from Mark's income under § 102(a)?

NOTES

1. (a) An argument sometimes made by tax protestors is that wages are not "income" because there is no "gain" or "profit," measured by comparing the value of what is received (cash wages) over the *value* of what is given up (services). This kind of argument, if accepted, would eviscerate the income tax, because all market transactions entail equal exchanges of value. The whole point of markets is to fix the value at which "even" trades will occur. Essentially, this kind of argument was rejected in the early case of *Stratton's Independence v. Howbert*, 231 U.S. 399 (1918), arising under the Corporate Income Tax Act of 1909. There, the taxpayer unsuccessfully argued that it had no income from mining because the *value* of its ore at the time of sale equaled the sales proceeds. *In an income tax, the benchmark*

for figuring gain (or loss) is the basis of the thing given up, not its value.

(b) Basis is initially defined by § 1012 as "cost." So what does that term mean? As a result of what is said in (a), it cannot mean the *value* of what is given up. The usual meaning of this term is "purchase price." In the case where property is not purchased for cash but received for services rendered (and the fair market value of the property received is included in gross income), how can it be said that basis equals cost? This result is explained in terms of the *function* of basis, which is to prevent double counting of the same dollars as income to the same taxpayer. In terms of that function, "cost" (that creates basis or supports a deduction) refers exclusively to dollars *previously subject to tax*. Thus, if stock received in return for services is included in gross income, the amount included now represents previously taxed dollars, and that in turn justifies the wage earner as having a basis in the stock equal to the previously taxed dollars.

(c) Does a taxpayer obtain a basis in the case where the property received should have been included in income (i.e., was "includible") but was not in fact included because the taxpayer made an innocent mistake? This question is complicated by the federal income tax statute of limitations (which is generally three years). To simplify matters, we will assume that in the present situation, the IRS is barred by the statute of limitations from requiring the taxpayer to correct the mistake and pay the tax that was properly due. In that case, the basis should be zero.[9] Basis determinations are not subject to the tax statute of limitations.[10] (If the statute of limitations has not run, then both the income-inclusion issue and the "dependent" basis issue would still be open to correction.)

(d) The term "tax cost" is often used to describe the basis rule for in-kind property receipts. That is, writers refer to the $20K that Mark includes in gross income, on account of receiving the stock as compensation in Problem (c), supra, as his "tax cost" for the stock. That term can be misleading, however, because it could be understood to suggest that basis equals the amount of *tax paid* as a result of including the value of the property in gross income. This is clearly *not* the law. It is important to recognize that the amount included in basis is equal to the *amount included in gross income*, not the tax paid thereon. We can correctly say that this is "the cost for tax purposes under § 1012," and that the amount of income tax paid with respect to an in-kind property receipt is irrelevant.

2.   When a business sells inventory, "gain" is not computed separately for each inventory item. (Think about the practical difficulty of assigning a basis to, and figuring gain or loss on the disposition of, each can of beans on a supermarket's shelf, each screw in a hardware store's bin, etc.) Instead, both "amount realized" and "basis" are computed on a mass (aggregate) basis by means of inventory accounting conventions. Gain from inventory is not included under § 61(a)(3) ("gains derived from dealings in property") but rather under § 61(a)(2) ("gross income

---

[9] See, e.g., *Charley v. Comm'r*, 91 F.3d 72 (9th Cir. 1996); *Continental Oil Co. v. Jones*, 177 F.2d 508 (10th Cir. 1949); cf, e.g., *Hughes & Luce v. Comm'r*, 70 F.3d 16 (5th Cir. 1995) (amounts erroneously deducted, but barred by the statute of limitations, cannot be included in basis). This issue is revisited in Chapter 26.C.3.

[10] See *Dobson v. Comm'r*, 320 U.S. 489 (1943).

derived from business"). Gross income from business, insofar as it refers to net inventory gains (or losses), means aggregate Gross Receipts from the sale of inventory less aggregate Cost of Goods Sold. See Reg. § 1.61-3(a). Cost of Goods Sold is the "mass basis" for all inventory disposed of during the year. The details of inventory accounting are spelled out in Chapter 23.A.1.

4. The Character of Gain and Loss from Property: Capital vs. Ordinary

The Internal Revenue Code, except for the years 1913-1921 and 1986-1990, has provided favorable tax treatment with respect to certain "capital gains" in comparison to "ordinary" gains and income, such as wages, interest, rents, and dividends. On the flip side, "capital losses" are subject to deductibility restrictions that do not apply to other kinds of losses. It is important to grasp the basics of "character" ("capital" vs. "ordinary" gains and losses) now, because every includible gain or deductible loss poses this character issue. While a later chapter (Chapter 25) is devoted to exploring the capital gain and loss regime in some detail, we feel that it is important to introduce the concept here, because character issues pervade income tax law and its application.

Section 1222 provides that a § 1001 gain or loss is "capital" under current law only if *all three* of the following requirements are satisfied:

(a) the § 1001 gain or loss must be an *included* gain or an *allowable* (deductible) loss

(b) from the "sale or exchange" of

(c) a "capital asset."

The first requirement simply means that the status of any gain or loss as "capital" is relevant only if the gain or loss is realized and recognized so that it is actually going to show up on the tax return this year.

Regarding the second requirement, judicial decisions establish that the "sale or exchange" requirement is satisfied if all of the following are present:

(a) a complete transfer of property to another party (as distinguished from say a lease of property)

(b) in return for consideration, and

(c) the property disposed of "survives" the transaction (i.e., continues to exist in the hands of the transferee).

As to the third requirement, the term "capital asset" is defined in § 1221 to encompass *all* "property" (*including personal-use property*) that does *not* fall into the following excluded categories: (1) inventory, (2) self-created art works, copyrights, and letters held by the original creator, (3) notes and accounts receivable from the sale of inventory or services, (4) most property "used" in a trade or business, and (5) some other stuff that is not of general interest. The general idea (not to be confused with the detailed rules themselves!) is that the concept of capital gain and loss excludes gain and loss attributable to the sale of inventory and services (i.e., *ordinary business and wage income*) and excludes gains and losses attributable to the sale of property and receivables connected with the production and sale of inventory and services. It might also be helpful to keep in mind that corporate stock held by an investor (as opposed to a dealer who sells it as inventory), investment real estate, and jewelry worn for personal adornment are prototypical capital assets.

The regime described above simply distinguishes "capital" gains and losses from "ordinary" gains and losses. Nothing has been said so far about the tax treatment of capital gains and losses. Character "matters" when the taxpayer has *either* (a) a "net capital gain" *or* (b) "excess capital losses" for the *entire* taxable year. It is mathematically impossible for a taxpayer to have *both* a net capital gain *and* excess capital losses for the year.

The existence of net capital gain or excess capital losses for a taxable year is determined by working through § 1222, which specifies that:

1. Gains and losses are long-term if they result from the sale or exchange of a capital asset held for more than one year (or deemed, under § 1223, to have been held for more than one year). Where the holding period is one year or less, gains and losses are short-term.

2. Net long-term capital gain (NLTCG) means long-term capital gains (LTCG) for the year minus long-term capital losses (LTCL) for the year.

3. Net short-term capital loss (NSTCL) means short-term capital losses (STCL) for the year minus short-term capital gains (STCG) for the year.

4. Net capital gain (NCG) means the NLTCG amount for the year minus the NSTCL amount for the year.

5. The word "excess" in §§ 1222(6), 1222(7) and 1222(11) prevents any of the computations described in paragraphs 2-4 above from resulting in a negative number. For example, if the taxpayer has $75 of LTCG for the year and $100 of LTCL for the year, the NLTCG amount is zero, not minus $25. Likewise, if the NSTCL amount for the year exceeds the NLTCG amount for the year, NCG is zero.

6. NCG = (LTCG minus LTCL) minus (STCL minus STCG). A taxpayer cannot have NCG greater than zero unless the taxpayer's long-term capital gains for the year exceed the sum of the taxpayer's long-term capital losses for the year plus the taxpayer's net short-term capital losses for the year.

What is the significance of NCG? The bottom line is that, under current law, NCG is usually taxed separately under § 1(h) at rates lower than what apply to the taxpayer's ordinary income.[11] The actual rates assigned to NCG change frequently with the political winds, however. C corporations (i.e., corporations subject to the § 11 corporate income tax) are not eligible for the special tax rates on NCG.

---

[11] It can happen that a taxpayer's capital gains exceed her capital losses for the year (so that she does not have excess capital losses), and yet she may still have no "net capital gain" if (for example) all of her capital gains are "short term." Short-term capital gains are not taxed at a favorable rate.

Turning to the deductibility of capital losses, recall that a realized loss can be a "capital" loss only if it is allowable as a deduction. As will be noted shortly, a realized loss of an individual taxpayer can be deducted only if it passes muster under § 165(c). Section 165(f) says that (deductible) capital losses shall be allowed as deductions in the current year only to the extent specified in §§ 1211 and 1212. Section 1211(b) states that, for taxpayers other than C corporations, the amount of otherwise-allowable capital losses that may be allowed in any one year is limited to the amount of capital gains (long-term and short-term) included in gross income in that same year *plus*, in the case of individuals, the lesser of (a) excess capital losses or (b) $3K.[12] Any nondeductible excess can be carried forward indefinitely for use in future years.

> *Example 1*: For Year 1, Sam has salary income of $200K, LTCGs of $50K, zero LTCLs and STCGs, and STCLs of $20K. The $50K gains are included in gross income under § 61(a)(3). Assume that the $20K losses are investment losses that are deductible under § 165(c). The "net capital gain" of $30K ($50K net long-term capital gain *less* $20K net short-term capital loss) is subject to a special rate under § 1(h). Notice that the capital losses effectively offsets Sam's capital gains, not his higher-taxed ordinary salary income.

> *Example 2*: Assume that Ivan, an unmarried individual who has $30K of Year-1 salary income, realizes (and recognizes) in Year 1 only $10K of STCGs and $17K of (otherwise-allowable) LTCLs. The $10K of STCGs is included in gross income under § 61(a)(3). Only $13K of Ivan's $17K LTCLs can be deducted in Year 1. That is to say, capital losses of $10K can be deducted against the $10K of Year 1 short-term capital gains. The "excess capital loss" of $7K ($17K less $10K) can be deducted against Ivan's ordinary salary income up to a maximum limit of $3K in Year 1. (There is no "net capital gain" in Year 1, both because Ivan has no net long-term capital gain and because his capital losses exceeded his capital gains.) The remaining $4K of (disallowed) capital loss from Year 1 is carried over to Year 2. If Ivan recognizes no capital gain in Year 2, $3K can be deducted against his Year 2 salary income, and the remaining $1K would be carried forward to Year 3.

The reason for the rule generally limiting capital loss deductions to the amount of capital gain inclusions is that the taxpayer has control over the timing of realization. A taxpayer owning an investment portfolio with assets that have both increased and decreased in value would, in the absence of § 1211, sell the loss assets and deduct the losses currently against ordinary income while deferring tax on the gains by continuing to hold the gain assets and subsequently realizing the gains at the favorable rates applicable to net capital gains.[13] Congress has blocked this strategy of "selective realization" or "cherry picking" with § 1211.

---

[12] In the case of C corporations, capital losses for the year can be deducted only to the extent of capital gains for the year, § 1211(a), and excess capital losses can be carried back 3 years and forward 5 years. § 1212(a).

[13] Even if there were no favorable rate for net capital gain, this cherry picking would still be objectionable because losses would be deducted as they were incurred while gain recognition, and the tax

The significance of capital gains and losses can thus be summarized roughly as follows:

> • First, capital gains are generally fully included in gross income, just as are other recognized gains.

> • Second, if an individual's aggregate capital gains for the year equal or exceed aggregate deductible capital losses for the year, the capital losses are allowable as deductions in full *and* any "net capital gain" (excess of net long-term capital gain over net short-term capital loss) will be taxed at a preferential rate.

> • Third, if an individual's aggregate deductible capital losses for the year exceed the aggregate capital gains for the year, the capital losses are allowed only to the extent of the capital gains (long-term and short-term) plus $3K, and any remaining loss is carried forward for use in future years.

PROBLEMS

1.   Assume that Jennifer, an unmarried individual, has long-term capital gains for the year of $40K, long-term capital losses for the year of $14K, and no other capital gains or losses. What is the amount favorably treated under § 1(h)? Why isn't the full $40K favorably treated under § 1(h) and the $14K losses deducted against Jennifer's ordinary wage income?

2.   Same facts as 1., except the $40K gain is from stocks held for less than one year. What result?

3.   Same facts as 1., except that long-term capital gains are $10K. What result?

NOTE

The term "capital" appears in several terms of art. Although these terms all employ the word "capital," they have distinct meanings that differ in the following ways:

(a) In business accounting and corporate law, the term "capital" (or "capital account") refers to amounts contributed by the owners of a business (in the case of a corporation) or amounts to which the owners of a business are entitled in the event of liquidation (in the case of a partnership or limited liability company). This use of "capital" has virtually no relevance for the individual income tax.

(b) In modern income tax lingo, the word "capital," standing alone, usually means the same thing as "basis." The phrase "(tax-free) return of capital" (or "recovery of capital") refers to receipts that are not taxed because they represent basis recovery (previously taxed dollars). "Capital," like "basis," is what is *not* "income" or *not* "gain."

(c) The term "capital expenditure" refers to an outlay that is not a currently deductible expense because it produces or procures an asset or benefit with a

---

thereon, would be deferred to a future time. This creates an unwarranted tax benefit that is illustrated in Chapter 6.F.2.

useful life extending substantially beyond the end of the taxable year. As previously noted, "capital expenditure" and "expense" are mutually exclusive terms.

(d) The term "capital asset" refers to property defined in § 1221, the sale or exchange of which can produce "capital gain" or "capital loss." The concept of capital asset encompasses most property, other than property involved in the production and sale of inventory or services. *Personal-use property, as well as investment property, is encompassed by the statutory definition of capital asset.* It is a common nomenclature error to think that any asset resulting from a "capital expenditure" must be a "capital asset." A capital expenditure produces basis but does *not* determine the "character" of the asset as a "capital asset" or an "ordinary" asset. "Capital asset" is also not to be confused with "capital equipment" or "capital investment," terms used *outside* of tax to refer to purchases of property used in business (especially assets, such as equipment and buildings, involved in manufacturing, construction, and processing). Indeed, capital equipment and assets resulting from capital investment may well *not* be "capital assets" in the tax sense. See § 1221(a)(2). An amount paid for property referred to in that provision (principally business equipment and buildings) is a capital expenditure and such property will often be referred to as capital equipment or a capital investment. Nevertheless, § 1221(a)(2) provides that this property is not a capital asset for purposes of the income tax.

5. The Borrowing Exclusion

A series of future chapters will examine the tax treatment of borrowed money in detail, but the topic is so fundamental that we briefly introduce it here. Just as a capital expenditure is not a decrease in wealth (and thus generates no deduction), so the borrowing of money is not an increase in wealth that is considered to be gross income. This is because the borrower's receipt of the amount borrowed is offset by the obligation to repay that amount. (An obligation to pay out an amount in the future is "negative wealth," and in accounting is called a "liability.") Sometimes the rule that borrowed money is not income is called the "borrowing exclusion." This rule is so basically inherent in the idea of "income" that it is not stated in the Code. Several rules that *do* appear in the Code, however, presuppose the existence of the borrowing exclusion.

The repayment of loan *principal* reduces the borrower's assets but is instantly matched by a decrease in the negative wealth represented by the liability. Thus, repayment of loan principal does not reduce the taxpayer's net wealth and thus does not generate a deduction. The payment of loan *interest*, on the other hand, is treated as an "expense," an instant decrease in wealth, rather than a capital expenditure. Interest expense *may* be currently deductible; that issue is governed by § 163, discussed in Chapter 18.D.

With respect to the tax results of the lending side of the equation, the lending of money is a nondeductible capital expenditure because it creates an offsetting asset — the claim for repayment — which has a basis equal to the amount of the lent cash. The receipt of loan principal repayments is not income, because it is offset by the lender's basis. Interest received is new wealth, and is treated as income.

PROBLEM

Slade lends $10K to Darlene with 6% *per annum* market rate simple interest payable at the end of each 12-month period and with the principal repayable in full after 5 years (60 months). Darlene pays interest and principal on schedule. What tax results to Slade and Darlene in each year? See § 61(a)(4). The facts here do not give enough information to determine if the interest paid by Darlene is deductible by her, because that is a complex matter reserved for future consideration. But if she used the $10K to pay for a vacation to Tahiti, the interest is not deductible under § 163(h)(1). Why not?

NOTE

Even consumption obtained with borrowed money is taxed, eventually. Thus, Gordon borrows $10K to buy a lavish vacation package. The borrowed money is excluded, and the vacation expense is not deducted. But Gordon has to repay the loan, with money that is subject to tax (say, as includible salary), and the loan principal repayment is not deductible. Thus, in an income tax system, the consumption is taxed, belatedly, by not allowing a deduction for the money used to repay the loan (coupled with the nondeductibility of the consumption spending).

6. Deductions under the Code

This section looks at the "core" Code rules pertaining to deductions. The term "deduction" should be viewed as being distinct from "basis offset" that we encountered in connection with calculating § 1001 "gain" from the sale or other disposition of property, as well as § 61(a)(2) "gross income derived from business" with respect to inventory dispositions. In both of these cases, basis is "built into" the notion of "gross income" itself.

a. General Rules

As noted earlier, a core principle is that only deductions specifically granted by the Code are allowable. Consequently, one often reads in judicial opinions that deduction provisions in the Code "are a matter of legislative grace" and thus are to be "strictly construed" against the taxpayer. The "strictly construed" conclusion does not necessarily follow, as a matter of logic, from the fact that deductions must be authorized by language in the Code. One might reasonably draw a distinction between deductions that are fundamental to the notion of income (deductions relating to the costs of producing income) and deductions that are not fundamental (charitable contributions, etc.) and apply the strict construction rule only to the latter. But even in the latter category, Congress might have been moved by generosity rather than tight-fistedness, so that even there a lenient construction would be appropriate. Nevertheless, courts regularly recite the mantra that "deduction provisions are strictly construed."

While *gross income* consists of realized wealth *accessions*, you can think of *deductions* as being keyed to realized decreases in wealth. As noted earlier, the income tax recognizes three categories of realized wealth reduction that potentially give rise to deductions, namely:

(1) expenses (an outlay purchasing an item whose value is used up or dissipated in the short term — the opposite of a capital expenditure),

(2) losses with respect to property, and,

(3) depreciation and amortization with respect to property (not yet discussed, but *not* to be equated with "decrease in value" or "unrealized loss").

Recall from Section A that a core principle is that personal consumption is a key component of the tax base, and that the simplest way to tax most personal consumption is by disallowing a deduction for it. Under the Code, this end is accomplished by generally *disallowing deductions for personal-consumption expenses, losses, and depreciation.* See §§ 165(c), 262. Although there are exceptions to this "rule," they will be dealt with later.

Implicit in the concept of "income," however, is the notion that the costs of producing income, as opposed to the costs of enjoying consumption benefits, should be subtracted, so that only net gain or profit is taxed. This point has already been made with respect to the concept of "gain" on property dispositions, where the cost of producing the amount realized (the adjusted basis) is subtracted from the amount realized in arriving at the gain. The same analysis dictates that other *costs of producing gross income must be subtracted from that gross income so that only net profit is taxed.* It should be mentioned that there are some rules in the Code that disallow or reduce business and investment deductions that would otherwise be fully allowed under the general rule, but these will be discussed in due course.

There are different "core" Code provisions linked to each of the three categories of decrease in wealth listed above (expenses, losses, and depreciation). With respect to "expense" deductions, one looks to §§ 162 and 212, which categorically allow deductions for business and investment expense decreases in wealth, and fail to allow deductions for personal consumption decreases in wealth. Additionally, but redundantly, § 262 expressly disallows deductions for personal consumption "expenses." The exclusive gateway for the deduction of a realized "loss" by an individual taxpayer is provided by § 165(c), which categorically allow losses incurred in a business or in "transactions entered into for profit" (investments in the broad sense). Section 167(a) is to the same effect with respect to depreciation and amortization.

b. Business and Investment Expenses

The statutory authority for deducting *business* "expenses" is § 162 of the Code, allowing the deduction of all "ordinary and necessary expenses paid or incurred during the taxable year in carrying on any trade or business." Congress intended to enact an "income tax" as opposed to a "gross receipts tax." Thus, the § 162 deduction for business expenses is part of the fundamental structure of a tax on "income." Nevertheless, Congress can (and does) enact rules disallowing or diluting certain kinds of business deductions.

To illustrate the preceding points, assume that Jean earns $100K of gross receipts in practicing law. Jean would be overtaxed (in the normative sense) if she were prevented from reducing that *gross* income by the $20K salary that she must pay her secretary, the $10K in rent she must pay for her office space, and the $5K she must pay for office supplies that are rapidly used up in carrying on her business. These expenses are not additions to wealth (Jean no longer has the expended amounts), nor are they outlays to procure consumption benefits (they are incurred to produce business gross receipts rather than consumption). Thus, these expenses should not be part of the income tax base. The Code allows Jean to achieve that result by subtracting the $35K total amount of business expenses from her $100K of gross receipts so that she is ultimately taxed only on her $65K profit.

The analog to § 162 with respect to income-producing activities that do not rise to the level of a "trade or business" is § 212. For example, investment activities — such as holding stocks, bonds, and investment real estate in order to collect dividends, interest, rents, and capital gain — have been definitively held *not* to constitute a trade or business, even if the taxpayer stays very "busy" in pursuing these activities.[14] Yet, expenses incurred to produce gross investment income should nevertheless reduce that gross income so that only net profit is taxed, just as in the case of business profits, and § 212 provides the authority for those expense deductions.

Students are often thrown off track by the requirement that business and investment expenses, to be deductible, must be "ordinary" and "necessary." These terms, however, are not to be taken literally. They are basically devices to screen out personal-consumption expenses that are clothed as business expenses. Thus, "ordinary" does not mean "regular or recurring," but only "accepted in business culture," and "necessary" does not mean "required" but only "rationally related to earning income" and "appropriate in the taxpayer's judgment" as a means of earning income.

Students often, but incorrectly, infuse common morality into expense deduction issues. For example, costs of dumping industrial wastes into a pristine lake are not disallowed, and many payments of punitive damages are deductible under § 162, even though the underlying behavior is widely considered to be morally abhorrent.

c. Business and Investment Losses

Section 165 is the provision that generically allows loss deductions. The term "loss" can itself cause confusion. In the present context, the term has the meaning given by § 1001(a), that is, a realized loss with respect to a particular item of property (hence, a "transactional loss," as opposed to a net overall loss from the operation of an economic activity). A net overall loss from the operation of an activity, referred to as a "net operating loss" (or "NOL"), is a loss resulting from the excess of allowable deductions over the gross income from the activity for the year. In this chapter, the issue is when a *transactional* loss deduction with respect to an item of property is allowed in the first place.[15]

---

[14] See *Higgins v. Comm'r*, 312 U.S. 212 (1941). Section 212 was enacted in 1942 precisely to overturn the result of *Higgins*.

[15] NOLs are discussed in Chapter 26.A.3.

In the case of individuals, section 165(c) allows business and investment (transactional) losses to be deducted, as we would expect. (Section 165(c)(3) also allows deductions for losses of personal-use property arising from casualty or theft. This "personal casualty loss deduction" is discussed in Chapter 24.)

A prerequisite for the deduction of losses is that the loss must be "sustained." See § 165(a). A loss that is not sustained is a loss not "realized." A loss that is realized by reason of a sale or disposition under § 1001 automatically satisfies the sustained-loss requirement of § 165(a). The "sustained" requirement cuts two ways. It cuts against the taxpayer, because Reg. § 1.165-1(d)(2)(i) states that a loss is not sustained if "there exists a claim for reimbursement for which there is a reasonable prospect of recovery" (i.e., by making a casualty insurance claim). The sustained-loss requirement cuts in favor of taxpayers insofar as a loss may be "sustained" under § 165(a) by means other than a § 1001 sale or disposition. An example would be partial loss by fire. In general, to be "sustained" without a sale or disposition, the loss must be permanent and irrevocable. The IRS will not allow a deduction for a partial loss unless the property in question suffers a physical impairment, as opposed to, say, a loss in value due to a change in zoning regulations. See generally Reg. § 1.165-1(d) (requiring that the loss be "evidenced by closed and completed transactions and as fixed by identifiable events occurring in such taxable year").

Under § 165(b), a loss deduction cannot exceed the basis of the property. This is consistent with the larger principle that all deductions are subtractions from income (past, present, or future) and, therefore, that *all deductions (in the larger, conceptual, sense) derive from dollars subject to tax.*

d. Depreciation of Business and Investment Property

Suppose that Jean — the attorney whose office expenses were deductible from her gross income under § 162 — purchases office equipment, such as a photocopy machine, for use in her business. Should the cost of the equipment be deducted entirely in the year of purchase, as was the cost of the office supplies that she quickly used up? The answer is clearly no. With respect to the photocopier, she has merely changed the form of her wealth, i.e., she has made a capital expenditure. See Reg. § 1.263(a)-2(a). Thus, the cost of the photocopier is not an "expense," and Jean has a basis under § 1012 in the photocopier equal to its cost. Yet the cost of the photocopier is a "business cost," in the larger sense, and it should (at some point) be deducted in arriving at business net profit or loss. Will Jean have to wait until she sustains a loss under § 165(c) from selling or junking the machine before any part of the cost can be deducted?

In certain circumstances, the deduction is *not* deferred but instead takes the form of a series of deductions, which are called "depreciation deductions," over a period of years, starting with the year of acquisition. Depreciation deductions, of course, are allowed only with respect to property used in a trade or business or otherwise held for the production of income. See § 167(a). It follows that depreciation deductions are not obtainable for personal-use assets, such as homes and personal-use automobiles.

Depreciation deductions are calculated pursuant to the Code-supplied formula that is applicable to the business or investment asset in question. In other words, the depreciation deduction for a year is *not* equal to the asset's actual decline in value for the year. Nevertheless, the very existence of an allowance for depreciation might seem to contradict the realization principle. But depreciation has long been commonplace in business accounting, which also (generally) adheres to the realization principle. In business accounting, depreciation derives from the so-called matching principle, which holds that costs should be matched (allocated), as best as reasonably possible, to the income generated by the costs, according to a formula (as opposed to changes in value). The theory purporting to justify depreciation under a realization *income tax* (as opposed to financial accounting) is not so much "matching" as the idea that an asset having a limited useful life suffers a series of *partial realized* losses solely on account of the passage of time. Thus, if an asset is expected to last for five years in the taxpayer's business, at the end of 12 months the future income-producing capacity of the asset has been "permanently" (and irreversibly) reduced compared to its initial income-producing capacity. In a crude sense, one-fifth of the asset has been lost for good and if considerations of simplicity (rather than financial theory) reigned, then the cost of the asset would be pro rated over its expected period of use. Unfortunately, the depreciation methods actually deployed under the Code depart from both simplicity and financial theory. The theory and practice of depreciation deductions are explored in Chapter 28.

Section 167(a) sets forth two basic requirements for whether depreciation is allowed at all. One is the business-or-investment requirement. The other is that the property be subject to exhaustion, wear and tear, or obsolescence. This old-fashioned language is an indirect way of stating that the property must have either a finite (and ascertainable) useful life (or a "deemed" useful life) specified by the Code and that the property's utility to the taxpayer must be "used up" during that useful life. This requirement rules out depreciation of land (as distinct from mineral deposits), shares of stock, precious metals and gems, and collectibles, because none of these items "permanently" lose value in any predictable way due to the mere passage of time.

Under the Code, depreciation deductions are spread over the useful lives of assets pursuant to artificial formulas and rules contained in §§ 167, 168, and 197 of the Code. These formulas disregard actual changes of value and are independent (except by coincidence) of the depreciation formulas used for financial accounting purposes. Basically, the depreciation of *tangible* property (real and personal) is governed by § 168 and *intangible* property by §§ 167(f) and 197. Various other ad hoc depreciation rules are found in the Code. Finally, there are rules disallowing or limiting depreciation in certain cases. The complexity of depreciation rules is far too vast to delve into here, but an example dealing with some basics is worthwhile at this point.

Assume that Jean's photocopier cost $10K. Since the photocopier is depreciable tangible business property, the depreciation method is provided by § 168. Section 168 contains a lot of impenetrable verbiage that can be distilled into a series of formulas. The formulas are set out in tables found in *Rev. Proc. 87-57*, 1987-2 C.B. 687, relevant parts of which are reproduced in the West abridgement of the Code and regulations at the beginning of the Appendix and in the CCH abridgement at the beginning of the book, before § 1. Table 1 of *Rev. Proc. 87-57* provides a table for tangible *personal* property having "recovery periods" of 3, 5, 7, 10, 15, and 20 years, respectively. What recovery period does office equipment fall within? To a tax practitioner, that question is answered by consulting various published revenue procedures and the fine print in § 168. However, it turns out that most business equipment falls within the 5-year recovery-period category, and we shall simply assume that the photocopier is in that category. Note that the column under "5 year" has six entries, which happen to be percentages. The sum of the 6 percentages is 100%. These percentages are multiplied by the property's original *unadjusted* basis to reach the depreciation deduction allowable in each year.

The rest is simple. The year that the photocopier is placed in service by Jean is Year 1, followed by Year 2, and so on. For each year, the depreciation deduction is simply the unadjusted (initial) basis ($10K) times the percentage for that year. Thus, the depreciation deduction for Year 1 is $2K. (The percentage for Year 1 is based on the mandatory "half-year convention," which conclusively assumes that the asset was placed in service by Jean at the halfway point in Year 1, producing a depreciation deduction for Year 1 that is half of the amount that would be deductible under the underlying mathematical model if the asset were placed in service at the beginning of Year 1.) In Year 2, applying the percentage in the table, the depreciation deduction is $3.2K, and so on, through Year 6, assuming that the machine is used in Jean's business for all six years. Note that the percentage for Year 6 is half of that for Year 5, because the half-year convention applies at the back end as well as the front end. At that point, Jean will have depreciated 100% of her basis (cost) over five full years (four full years plus two half years) spanning six taxable years, so that no more deductions can be taken after Year 6, even if Jean continues to use the machine in her business. In other words, as with loss deductions, aggregate depreciation deductions cannot exceed basis.

Depreciation deductions are "ordinary" deductions (i.e., fully deductible against ordinary income such as wages), not "capital losses" subject to the § 1211 capital-loss-limitation rule. This is true whether or not the asset being depreciated happens to be a "capital asset."

At some point Jean will dispose of her machine, and at that point it will be necessary to determine her depreciation deduction for the year of disposition and her § 1001 gain or loss (or her § 165(c)(1) abandonment loss). It turns out that Jean's disposition of the machine (i.e., before Year 6) affects the depreciation formula for the year of disposition. Specifically, the depreciation deduction in the year of disposition is arbitrarily set at half of the formula amount, regardless of when during the year Jean disposes of the machine. This result again derives from application of the half-year convention at the back end. See § 168(d).

Allowable depreciation deductions require a reduction in basis under § 1016(a)(2) for purposes of computing gain or loss. (Adjustments to basis do not affect the depreciation computation itself.) Failure to reduce the original cost basis by amounts deducted as depreciation during the ownership period would allow the taxpayer a double deduction when the property is disposed of, thereby violating the precept that the same taxpayer should not enjoy a double tax benefit for the same dollars. Thus, if Jean used the property until year 6, taking the entire $10K cost as depreciation deductions, and then sold the machine for $1.2K, her basis for gain and loss purposes must be zero (as opposed to $10K), and she must report a $1.2K gain instead of an $8.8K loss. Otherwise, Jean would be using the same dollars twice to reduce income or gain.

Depreciation can affect the character of § 1001 gain or loss. Specifically, gain with respect to depreciable *personal* property (such as Jean's photocopy machine that she used in her business), as opposed to depreciable *real* property, is treated as "ordinary" (as opposed to "capital") gain to the extent of prior depreciation deductions. This result is provided under § 1245 (an excessively wordy provision) and is referred to as "depreciation recapture." The idea is that, just as depreciation deductions are "ordinary" deductions, so should gain "caused by" the reduction in basis on account of excessively generous depreciation be "ordinary," at least in the case of personal property.

For example, suppose Chuck purchases business equipment for $20K, takes $12K of depreciation (reducing the basis to $8K), and sells the equipment for $10K. Notice that the depreciation allowed during Chuck's ownership exceeded the economic loss in value of the property. The § 1016(a)(2) basis reduction ensures that the $2K of excess depreciation (relative to the decline of value) results in § 1001 gain. And § 1245(a) ensures that this gain is recaptured (characterized) as ordinary gain. If, instead, Chuck sold the equipment for $21K (a very unlikely occurrence), the gain would be $13K, of which $12K would be recaptured as ordinary gain under § 1245. (The character of the remaining gain is discussed in due course, as is the character of any loss realized on the disposition of depreciable property.)

PROBLEMS

1.   Sara is a dentist and spends $20K on salary for her dental assistant in Year 1. Is this amount deductible by Sara? What would have been the result if, instead, Sara had spent this $20K on groceries for herself and her family during Year 1? See §§ 162 and 262.

2.   (a) Ryan buys a car for commuting and pleasure for $20K in Year 1. (It is well-settled that commuting between home and work is a personal activity, see Reg. § 1.262-1(b)(5).) In Year 3 Ryan sells the car for $5K. What tax results to Ryan in Years 1, 2, and 3? See §§ 165(c) and 167(a).

(b) Same as (a), except that the car was a limited-production model that caught the fancy of the public, so that Ryan manages to sell it for $22K in Year 3.

3.   Same as item 2, except that the car is used exclusively in Ryan's business and has been assigned a "class life" of 5 years, and that Ryan sells the car for $11K in Year 3. What results? See §§ 167(a), 168, and 1245 and *Rev. Proc. 87-57* (and ignore §§ 168(k), 179, and 280F for now).

NOTES

1.   In the real world, many outlays smack of both personal consumption and business or investment activity. Thus, it is not surprising that the distinction between business and investment, on the one hand, and personal consumption, on the other, is problematic in its application. A common example is the cost of commuting from home to work and back. Another example is an expensive

restaurant dinner with a business client to close a deal. The meal provides nourishment (personal consumption), but the dinner is consumed in a business context and the amount paid likely exceeds what the taxpayer would otherwise have spent (business). A vast body of law (statutory and otherwise), discussed in later chapters, has developed concerning the difficult distinction between consumption and business and investment.

2.   (a) The distinction between "personal property" and "personal-use property" must be kept in mind, as both are terms of art. "Personal property" is a legal term of art in property law, meaning any property, tangible or intangible, that is not "real" property. Different depreciation and characterization rules apply to real property as opposed to personal property. For example, depreciation recapture under § 1245 applies only to (depreciable) personal property. In contrast, a "personal-use asset" is any property (almost always tangible), real or personal, devoted to personal-consumption use. Personal-use property is not depreciable, and it can generate a loss deduction only if the loss is sustained and caused by casualty or theft.

(b) The function of basis is to account for dollars previously subject to tax so that those dollars are not taxed again to the same taxpayer. Additionally, the basis system operates to prevent the same dollars from reducing the tax base more than once. Accordingly, basis is adjusted under § 1016 to reflect additions and subtractions from the store of previously taxed dollars. Basis of an existing asset is adjusted upwards for nondeductible capital expenditures (e.g., additions to the asset, such as enlarging a building) and downwards for any depreciation and loss deductions taken with respect to the asset. Capitalization and basis are the fundamental structural principles of an income tax. *An understanding of the role of capitalization and basis is crucial to an understanding of the income tax.*

3.   (a) Before any regular depreciation is taken under § 168(a), all or a portion of the property's initial cost may be treated as an "expense" (and thus immediately deductible) under some "special" Code rule, such as § 179. In such a case, the expensing rule has priority, and only the remaining basis is factored into the depreciation formula under § 168(a).

(b) Inventory (and other property held for sale to customers in the ordinary course of business) is not depreciable, because it is not considered "used" in a trade or business or "held" for the production of income.

(c) Apart from § 1245, the determination of the character of gain and loss from the disposition of property "used" in the trade or business is a complex affair. First, note that all business-use property (except for nondepreciable personal property) is excluded (removed) from the definition of "capital asset" under § 1221(a)(2). Thus, except in the case of nondepreciable business-use personal property, gain or loss on such property would be "ordinary." In theory, the gain or loss *should* be "ordinary," just as the income from the sale of the goods produced (inventory) and the services delivered with the business-use property is ordinary. However, it turns out that "long term" gain or loss on § 1221(a)(2) business-use property falls into (i.e., is picked up by) § 1231. Section 1231, enacted in 1942 as a World War II "tax relief" measure for business taxpayers, commands that all such gains and losses for the year be thrown into a "hotchpot." If the overall (net) result in the § 1231 hotchpot for the year is gain, then *all* such gains and losses emerge as "capital" gains and losses. If the net hotchpot result for the year is a loss (or zero), then *all* gains and losses in the hotchpot become "ordinary." Section 1231 is a "best of all possible worlds" haven for business taxpayers.

(d) Section 1245, enacted in 1962, takes priority over all other character rules. Thus, § 1245 gain is always ordinary gain, notwithstanding §§ 1221 and 1231.

(e) Section 1245 does not apply to depreciable real property (such as buildings), and neither does any similar "depreciation recapture" rule (with minor exceptions found in § 1250). Therefore, recognized gain on real property used in the trade or business and held for more than one year is (almost) always § 1231 gain or loss.

D.   COMPUTING AND PAYING THE INCOME TAX

In actually figuring the tax liability of individuals, matters are complicated by the fact that deductions are assigned to several categories. Additionally, one's liability under the income tax is not final, but may be increased on account of the Alternative Minimum Tax.

1.   Computing the Federal Income Tax of Individuals

It would be convenient if "taxable income" were simply "gross income" minus aggregate allowable deductions (as discussed in the previous section), but unfortunately under the Code not all deductions "count" equally. Basically, under the Code, taxable income is "adjusted gross income" ("AGI") minus the § 151 "deductions for personal and dependency exemptions" (discussed in Chapter 4) and minus the *greater* of (a) the standard deduction (also discussed in Chapter 4) *or* (b) aggregate allowable itemized deductions. See §§ 62(a) and 63(a) & (b). This resulting scheme requires that deductions be sorted into the following categories (in order of appearance):

(1) deductions (from gross income) taken in arriving at adjusted gross income,

(2) the deductions for personal and dependency exemptions,

(3) the standard deduction, and

(4) itemized deductions, broken down into:

(a) "miscellaneous itemized deductions," and

(b) all other itemized deductions

The complex structure of the individual income tax return (the Form 1040) is understandable once these categories are explained.

a.   Adjusted Gross Income

Adjusted gross income is defined in § 62(a) as gross income minus the deductions listed there. It is important that the student understand that § 62(a) does not provide the authority for *allowing* any deductions. It simply states that *certain* deductions allowed by the Code are deducted directly from gross income, i.e., they are taken "first" or, if you will, "off the top." The deductions listed in § 62(a) are colloquially called "above-the-line deductions." The "line" in question is the bottom line of page 1 of the Form 1040.

The above-the-line deductions listed in § 62(a) are generally those that Congress has thought to be the most important, or those that should be subtracted in describing a taxpayer's "economic net income." It is not surprising then that item (1) on the list is "trade or business" deductions (other than deductions connected with the taxpayer's "business" of being an employee). Here, "trade or business" is clearly meant to exclude "investment." The distinction between business and investment, which is not defined in the Code or regulations, is (to state the matter crudely) a distinction between active and passive income-producing activity. The term "business" conjures up visions of activity involving continuity and frequency, plus the taxpayer's addition of value to the final product (goods or services). Nonbusiness income-producing activity (often referred to in this book as "investment," to be understood in a broad sense) has the connotation of passively harvesting the fruit of the tree or benefitting from market fluctuations. The business vs. investment distinction is examined more closely in Chapter 8.A. Because of the fact that (nonemployee) business deductions are above the line, the instructions to the Form 1040 are able to require that these deductions be subtracted from business gross income on a separate Schedule C, so that only business net income or (operating) loss is entered on page 1 of the Form 1040. (Schedule C net income is subject to the self-employment tax described in Chapter 1.)

Although working for wage income as an employee generally constitutes carrying on a trade or business, § 62(a)(1) states that trade or business deductions attributable to being an employee are excluded from the above-the-line category. Nevertheless, § 62(a)(2) modifies § 62(a)(1) by listing certain employee business deductions as above-the-line items. The principal one of these is employee-deduction items that are reimbursed by an employer under a "reimbursement or other expense allowance arrangement." § 62(a)(2)(A). Under § 62(c), the expense-allowance arrangement must require the employee to substantiate the covered expense to the employer and remit any excess of the reimbursement over the substantiated amounts. Arrangements that satisfy these requirements are referred to in the Treasury regulations as "accountable plans." See Reg. § 1.62-2. The effect of treating reimbursed employee expenses as above-the-line deduction expenses is to make possible the accounting shortcut of (1) ignoring the deduction item and (2) ignoring the reimbursement. If the deduction were actually taken on the return, then the reimbursement would have to be reported as gross income, because the claim to the reimbursement would have a zero basis.[16] In this particular case, reimbursements are excluded by administrative grace (by ignoring them on the return) on the condition, imposed by Reg. § 1.62-2(c)(4), that the fully offsetting

---

[16] Stated differently, if the deduction were allowed to stand and the reimbursement were excluded from income, a double tax benefit would attach to the same dollars: the transaction, which leaves the taxpayer's wealth unchanged, would produce a deduction against the taxpayer's other income.

above-the-line deduction be likewise ignored.[17] This "don't show this stuff on the tax return" approach for reimbursed employee business expenses is expressly approved by the instructions to Form 1040.

The "administrative exclusion" for employer reimbursements is only available if the corresponding expense item is actually allowable as a deduction to the employee. Employee reimbursements of nondeductible items are included in gross income.

As an aside, the discussion of reimbursed employee expenses demonstrates that reimbursements are not always excludible from gross income. Reimbursements for deducted expenses are includible, as are employer reimbursements of nondeductible expenses. The topic of reimbursements (along with rebates and recoveries) is explored further in Chapter 26.

Unreimbursed employee expenses that are allowable as deductions are not "above the line" except in the case of certain deductions of government officials, teachers (K-12), and performing artists. (Trial lawyers, expert witnesses, and entertaining professors are not performing artists!)

Unfortunately, the regulations under § 62 do not define "employee" or "independent contractor." "Employees," however, are subject elsewhere in the Code to withholding of income and Social Security taxes on "wages," and for these purposes a definition of "employee" is found in Reg. § 31.3401(c)-1. In general, the regulations adopt the common-law rule that defines an "employee" as being one who is subject to the control of the employer both as to the ends to be accomplished and the means of accomplishing it. Factors taken into account under this inquiry that tend to indicate employment status are the right of the employer to discharge, the furnishing by the employer of tools, and the provision by the employer of a place to work.

The next two above-the-line deduction items in § 62 serve to reduce the significance of the distinction between business and investment. (Remember that all nonemployee business deductions are already above the line.) Section 62(a)(3) identifies all allowable loss deductions from the sale or exchange of property as being above-the-line deductions. Recall that net inventory gain or loss will have already been entered on Schedule C. Schedule D processes all capital gains and losses (which, by definition, must result from a sale or exchange), and the net capital gain, or the net capital loss (but not to exceed $3,000), is entered on page 1 of Form 1040. Form 4797 processes ordinary gains and losses from sales or exchanges, and the net result is entered separately on page 1 of the 1040. (Section 1231 gains and losses are netted first on Form 4797, and any net gain is transferred to Schedule D as net long-term capital gain.)

Section 62(a)(4) allows all deductions (not already entered on Schedules C and D) connected with the nonbusiness production of rents and royalties, such as mortgage interest, property taxes, repair expenses, and depreciation deductions in connection with a rental unit, to be taken directly from gross income. Again, the above-the-line

---

[17] The reimbursement is also exempt from withholding for other taxes, such as the Social Security tax.

status of these deductions allows them to be netted against the related gross income. Here the netting is carried out on Schedule E, and the net income or loss (i.e., after applying relevant disallowance rules) is entered on page 1 of Form 1040.

Several deductions identified by Code section are also above the line. The alimony deduction under § 215 is an above-the-line item, as is the moving expense deduction under § 217, the § 219 deduction for contributions to IRAs, and the § 220 deduction for contributions to medical savings accounts. The remaining above-the-line items are too esoteric to note at this time.

b. Deductions for Personal and Dependency Exemptions

These deductions, allowed by § 151, are unrelated to a taxpayer's loss of wealth by way of expense, loss, or depreciation. Instead, they are fixed dollar amounts (indexed for inflation) awarded on a per capita basis for the taxpayer and the taxpayer's qualifying "dependents," as defined in § 152. For example, a married couple with two qualifying dependents obtains four exemptions. If the "exemption amount" is $3,700 (the exemption amount in 2011), the total deduction is $14,800. The details are presented in Chapter 4.

c. The Standard Deduction

The "standard deduction" is a fixed dollar amount (indexed for inflation) that is awarded simply for being a taxpayer. The amount depends on filing status (married filing jointly, married filing separately, unmarried, or head of household). The amount is increased if the taxpayer has reached the age of 65 or is blind.

d. Itemized Deductions

The taxpayer deducts the greater of the standard deduction or the aggregate allowable itemized deductions. Thus, the taxpayer must "lose" one or the other of these deduction categories. Another way of looking at this rule is to note that aggregate itemized deductions have value only to the extent that they exceed the standard deduction. A taxpayer who claims itemized deductions (rather than the standard deduction) is said to be an "itemizer."

The term "itemized deductions" refers to all deductions *other than above-the-line deductions, deductions of personal and dependency exemptions, and the standard deduction.* See § 63(d). Do not be mislead by the caption "Part VI — Itemized Deductions for Individuals and Corporations" (referring to §§ 161-199) and the caption "Part VII — Additional Itemized Deductions for Individuals" (referring to §§ 211-223). Captions are not definitions. For example, business deductions allowed by §§ 161-199 are not "itemized deductions" because they are above-the-line deductions, except for unreimbursed employee business expenses.

Before one aggregates itemized deductions, it is first necessary to cull out the subcategory of "miscellaneous itemized deductions" (MIDs). Aggregate MIDs are allowable, under § 67, only to the extent they exceed a "floor" equal to 2% of the taxpayer's adjusted gross income (AGI). Stated differently, MIDs are *disallowed* in an amount up to the amount which is 2% of the taxpayer's AGI.

MIDs are itemized deductions that are *not* listed in § 67(b). The itemized deductions that *are* listed in § 67(b) and, therefore, are not subject to the 2% floor, include the popular personal deductions, such as those for mortgage interest, state and local taxes, charitable contributions, extraordinary medical expenses, and net personal casualty and theft losses (all of which are discussed later in this book). Conspicuously absent from the favored § 67(b) list are (1) unreimbursed employee business expenses and (2) investment deductions not covered by § 62(a)(3) and (4).

The rationale of § 67 is explained as follows:[18]

> The Congress concluded that the prior-law treatment of employee business expenses, investment expenses, and other miscellaneous itemized deductions fostered significant complexity, and that some of these expenses have characteristics of voluntary personal expenditures. For taxpayers who anticipated claiming such itemized deductions, prior law effectively required extensive record keeping with regard to what commonly are small expenditures. Moreover, the fact that small amounts typically were involved presented significant administrative and enforcement problems for the Internal Revenue Service. These problems were exacerbated by the fact that taxpayers frequently made errors of law regarding what types of expenditures were properly allowable.

> The use of the deduction floor takes into account that some miscellaneous expenses are sufficiently personal in nature that they would be incurred apart from any business or investment activities of the taxpayer. For example, membership dues paid to professional associations may serve both business purposes and also have voluntary and personal aspects; similarly, subscriptions to publications may help taxpayers in conducting a profession and also may convey personal and recreational benefits. Taxpayers presumably would rent safe deposit boxes to hold personal belongings such as jewelry even if the cost, to the extent related to investment assets such as stock certificates, were not deductible.

Section 68, enacted in 1990 but repealed for 2010 and thereafter, operated to cut down (but not in excess of 80%) aggregate itemized deductions (after MIDs are cut down or wiped out) other than those for medical expenses, net personal casualty and theft losses, gambling losses, and investment interest, as AGI rose above $100,000 (as indexed for inflation). This provision is mentioned because § 68 could be revived, or something similar to it could be enacted, as cutting back on itemized deductions for the well-off (without repealing the deduction provisions) could be a politically-expedient way of raising revenue.

The itemized deduction "final tally," which is figured on Schedule A of Form 1040, is (if greater than the standard deduction) entered on a single line on page 2 of Form 1040.

---

[18] STAFF OF THE JOINT COMM. ON TAX'N, GENERAL EXPLANATION OF THE TAX REFORM ACT OF 1986 78-79 (1987). As explained in Chapter 1, in the tax community, the report of the staff of the Joint Committee on Taxation describing a recently enacted piece of tax legislation is referred to as the "Blue Book" for that legislation.

The taxpayer then computes the tax under the rate schedule that keys to the taxpayer's filing status, except that net capital gains are wrung through § 1(h), which requires filling out a worksheet in the instructions to Form 1040. To the tentative tax, one adds "additions to tax" (such as self-employment tax) and subtracts available credits (including credits for prepayments of tax by way of income tax withholding and of estimated tax payments). The result is the final tax under the regular federal income tax.

2.   The Alternative Minimum Tax

For some individuals, the process described in Section B is not final. All taxpayers must pay the larger of the regular income tax or the tax due under the Alternative Minimum Tax ("AMT"), which is contained in §§ 55-59. The top tax rate for individuals under the AMT is only 28% (compared with a 35% maximum regular rate), but the tax due under the AMT can be larger than the regular tax due because "AMT taxable income" is broader than taxable income under the regular income tax by reason of eliminating certain deductions and exclusions. For example, in the case of individuals, three items mentioned so far are totally disallowed, namely, the standard deduction, the § 151 deductions for personal and dependency exemptions, and MIDs (in excess of the 2% floor). Additionally, the widely used deductions for mortgage interest, state and local taxes, and medical expenses may be reduced. Modifications of regular income tax rules under the AMT are noted as these rules are covered later in this book.

A specified amount of AMT taxable income is "exempt," i.e., subject to a zero AMT tax rate. The exemption amount is phased out as AMT taxable income rises above a certain amount. § 55(d). (The exemptions have often been raised by Congress on an ad hoc basis in order to prevent large numbers of upper-middle-class taxpayers from being subject to the AMT.) The first $175K of AMT taxable income in excess of the exemption is subject to a rate of 26%, and above that level the rate is 28%. § 55(b). The only credit allowed is a modified foreign tax credit.

Under § 55(a), the taxpayer pays the sum of (1) the regular tax liability for the year and (2) the excess of the year's AMT liability over the year's regular tax liability, which is why we stated above that the taxpayer, in essence, pays whichever is the greater of her AMT liability for the year or the regular income tax liability for the year. In subsequent taxable years, the "excess" referred to in the previous sentence can be credited against regular tax liability to the extent that the regular income tax liability for the year exceeds the putative AMT for the year. § 53. Ultimately, then, the AMT can operate chiefly as a "timing" mechanism that has the effect of requiring affected taxpayers to pre-pay their regular tax liability.

Congress obviously believes that each allowable deduction, credit, exclusion, or other income-reducing mechanism that it has created is defensible if viewed alone. At the same time, however, Congress does not want any single taxpayer to take advantage of income-reducing mechanisms in the Code to the extent that very little tax is paid on a substantial amount of economic income. In short, the AMT is designed to backstop the regular income tax by ensuring that taxpayers with substantial economic income cannot wholly avoid income tax.

3. Returns, Payments, and Tax Controversies

The individual income tax return must be filed by April 15 following the end of the taxable year (if a calendar year). See § 6072(a). A six-month filing extension (until October 15) can be had as a matter of right by filing Form 4868. Any tax due must be paid by April 15, *without regard to extensions for filing returns.* Thereafter, interest runs against the taxpayer for any amounts ultimately owed to the government.

Income taxes on wage income (as well as Social Security and Medicare taxes) are withheld by the employer. (Employers who fail to fulfill their withholding obligation incur heavy penalties.) Persons whose income does *not* consist mostly of wages subject to withholding must file quarterly declarations of estimated tax, accompanied by installment payments of the estimated amount. Estimated tax payments are a kind of quarterly "self-withholding." If estimated tax payments are inadequate, the taxpayer may be subject to an interest charge. See § 6654.

The IRS obtains tax information about a taxpayer from third parties. In addition to employers reporting wages, payors of interest, dividends, royalties, consulting fees, etc., and real estate brokers file information returns with the IRS indicating who was paid what.

Some returns are "corrected" by the IRS on account of arithmetic errors, errors in following the instructions, and information obtained by third parties. In other cases, the IRS asks for justification of the tax treatment of a particular item. In yet other cases, tax returns are selected for audit by the local office of the IRS District Director. Most audits are triggered on the basis of one or more factors entered into an IRS computer program, such as tax-shelter deductions, excessive business expenses, hobby "business" losses, unrealistically low reported income of independent contractors, and other suspected abuse areas. A low percentage (less than 2%) of individual returns are typically audited. A taxpayer who is audited is requested to explain and verify her return or a portion thereof. If a dispute arises regarding the proper treatment to be given certain items, the taxpayer is given the opportunity to appeal to the Regional Appeals Office. Most disputes are settled at Appeals. If it is not settled, the matter can be litigated in the forums described in Chapter 1. If a deficiency is not contested or if a contested deficiency is settled or finally resolved in litigation, the IRS will "assess" the deficiency, assuming the statute of limitations has not run out. Section 6851 *et seq.* provides for a "jeopardy" assessment procedure under which an assessment can be made summarily (without deficiency notice, etc.) in certain cases, such as where the taxpayer or his assets might disappear from the United States.

The collection procedure (liens, levy, and execution) can be commenced by the IRS if payment is not received in due course following assessment.

Under § 7421, a person cannot bring an injunction, declaratory judgment, or mandamus action to disrupt the normal procedures for resolving disputes. There are some insignificant statutory exceptions to this rule. The Supreme Court, in *Enochs v. Williams Packing & Navigation Co.*, 370 U.S. 1 (1962), held that this prohibition was overcome only where (1) the government, under the most liberal view, has no chance of success, and (2) the taxpayer would suffer irreparable injury.

Finally, it should be mentioned that §§ 7430-7433 provide taxpayers with various civil remedies regarding overbearing action by the IRS.

PROBLEMS

1. Larry, an associate lawyer with a small town law firm, pays $100 per year to the ABA for membership and section dues (a deductible expense under § 162). The firm does not reimburse him. Curly is an associate with a Wall Street firm and pays the same $100, but is reimbursed by the law firm. Moe, a solo practitioner, pays the same $100 out of his own pocket. To what extent are the dues deductible by each?

2. Which of the following deductions are subject to § 67 and/or § 68:

(a) Excess capital loss for the year (not to exceed $3K)?

(b) Nonbusiness bad debt deduction? (See § 166(d).)

(c) State property tax on building used in a business?

(d) State property tax on (nonbusiness) rental property?

(e) State property tax on personal residence?

3. Joseph is a professor who writes books for law student use. Are Joseph's royalties reportable on Schedule C or Schedule E? Does it make any difference? (Are royalties from leasing a mineral interest in property reportable on Schedule E?)

Chapter 3

TAX POLICY: EVALUATING TAX SYSTEMS AND PROVISIONS

Chapter 2 dealt with principles that are "internal" to an income tax in a somewhat mechanical sense. That is, they are derived from the notion of personal income, especially the notion of personal income that is founded on the ability-to-pay principle. However, taxes don't exist in a vacuum. Taxes (like any government institution) should have normative underpinnings that relate to "external" values and social practices, such as fairness, economic efficiency, and improving social welfare. But at the same time a tax system needs to be reasonably capable of administration and enforcement. In particular, the notion of ability-to-pay calls for some explanation and justification. Various norms external to a concept of personal income can be brought to bear for the purpose of evaluating specific tax provisions and even entire tax systems. The most important of these norms are outlined in this early chapter, because they can then be deployed in subsequent chapters.

The articulation of tax norms and their application is commonly referred to as "tax policy." Because these norms are imprecise, sometimes conflicting, sometimes difficult to implement in the real world, and often accepted or rejected on the basis of personal taste, political views, and/or self-interest, tax policy analysis is an inexact science leading to disagreements, which play out in the political process. The pedagogical aims of this chapter include (1) giving students the basic tools for constructing and evaluating tax policy claims and (2) helping to explain why some features of the income tax are stable and others are unstable.

The relevant norms are implied by the function of taxation, which is to raise cash revenue for the government to spend. The issues of (1) the total amount to be raised and (2) the total amount to be spent during a year by the federal government are not exactly aligned, but both are basically political issues. The lack of alignment between taxing and spending is partly due to the fact that the deliberate creation of a federal government deficit may be used as a macroeconomic tool to stimulate consumer demand and/or private investment during economic recessions. At the same time, however, the deficit, which must be made up by federal borrowing, can put upward pressure on interest rates, and rises in interest rates may dampen economic activity. Moreover, federal government borrowing shifts the burden of paying for current spending to future years (where a portion of the taxes must repay government debt and interest thereon). This can raise the issue of intergenerational equity. Although these kinds of issues are interesting and important, whether the $X to be raised by federal taxes in a given year is too high or too low (in either an absolute or relative sense) lies outside the appropriate focus of a student's first course in federal tax law.

A. FAIRNESS NORMS

In general, "fairness" has to do with the relative treatment of persons in a given (institutional) setting. In taxation, the issue of fairness pertains to the manner in which the *burden* of a particular tax (income tax, estate tax, etc.), as opposed to the *amount* of the total tax burden, is to be allocated across the population. Allocation of the tax burden in turn depends on (1) the choice of tax base (consumption, wealth, or income) and (2) the tax rate schedule.

As noted in Chapter 1, the economic burden of the tax does not necessarily fall on the nominal taxpayer. Nevertheless, in the case of any tax on the total income, consumption, or wealth *of an individual,* the likelihood that the tax will be passed on by the individual taxpayer to others is relatively low. Therefore, these kinds of "personal" taxes can reasonably be discussed in terms of fairness, because by definition they are taxes on (and are borne by) the persons who have the legal liability to pay them. In contrast, taxes on entities (e.g., the corporate income tax), transactions (sales taxes), and things (property taxes) are generally not connected to particular persons, and taxes of this sort are likely to be passed on to some degree, although it is often not clear to whom they are passed on. Therefore, it is rather meaningless to discuss taxes on entities, transactions, and things in terms of fairness unless the ultimate payers of these taxes can be identified with reasonable accuracy so that their situations can be the focus of the fairness discussion.

1. Formal Fairness: The Concept of Horizontal Equity

Perhaps the most noncontroversial concept of fairness, dating back at least to Aristotle (and intuitively understood even by small children), is that "likes should be treated alike." The tax version of this fairness maxim is *horizontal equity*, which stipulates that *like-situated taxpayers should be taxed the same.*

The issue of whether given taxpayers are "like," however, cannot be addressed in the abstract. How should "likeness" be measured? Suppose taxpayer *A* owns wealth (assets less liabilities) of $500K, earns income of $100K per year, and spends $50K each year on consumption needs, saving the remaining $50K (adding to her wealth). Suppose taxpayer *B* owns wealth (assets less liabilities) of $100K, earns income of $100K per year, and spends $100K each year on consumption needs. How should we measure their "likeness"? Do we conclude that they should pay the same amount of tax because they earn the same income? This view looks to "income" as the relevant criterion of "likeness." Should we conclude that *A* should pay 5 times the tax that *B* pays because *A* is 5 times wealthier than *B*? Or should we conclude that *A* should pay only ½ as much tax as *B*, since A spends on consumption only ½ of what *B* spends? Simply reciting the words "horizontal equity" doesn't get us far in answering these questions. Even if we decide that the tax base (the standard of comparison) should be "income," other difficulties arise. For example, should it make a difference whether income is produced by the taxpayer's labor or from an inherited stock portfolio and whether the income is spent on education or gambling? Stated more broadly, should differences in the *source* or *use* of income matter?

In short, the concept of horizontal equity depends upon a prior determination of what criteria we look at to determine sameness or difference. Until those criteria are identified, horizontal equity is only a concept of "formal" fairness that lacks necessary content.

2. Vertical Equity

The term "vertical equity" posits that differently situated taxpayers should be taxed differently. (This proposition is totally obvious — even vacuous — unless one takes the position that all individuals should pay the same dollar amount in tax.) "Differentness" would presumably be ascertained by the same criterion or index as "likeness" is determined. Whereas horizontal equity is incomplete in the sense that it doesn't specify the standard by which likeness (and difference) is ascertained, vertical equity is also incomplete because it doesn't specify *how differently* differently situated taxpayers should be taxed. This problem is essentially about tax rates. Thus, if the index is "income," and X has income of $100 (paying a tax of $10 under a 10% tax rate) and Y has income of $200, what should be the tax on Y? The answer isn't necessarily $20 (the amount obtained by applying the same 10% tax rate), unless one thinks that the arithmetic norm of proportionality is self-justifying as applied to social problems. Basically, what is needed to give content to the norm of vertical equity is a principle of distributive justice that tells us whether a high income individual should (1) pay the same dollar amount of tax as a low income individual, (2) pay a greater dollar amount but the same percentage of income as a low income individual, or (3) pay both a greater dollar amount and a higher percentage of income than a low income individual. Since agreement on a principle of distributive justice is highly unlikely, and since economics and administrative considerations also bear on tax rates, it is not surprising that the issue of tax rates is politically contentious.

3. Norms of Substantive Tax Fairness

Despite the shortcomings of both horizontal equity and vertical equity as concepts, they are widely used in tax discourse. But both presuppose a conception of the tax base — *what* should be taxed to *which* individuals. The definition and contours of the normative tax base for fairness purposes, in turn, depend upon what one considers to be *the most appropriate criteria by which to apportion the total federal tax burden (whatever that may be) among individuals*. This issue is that of "substantive" tax fairness.

Four norms of substantive tax fairness have emerged over the years, each of which derives from differing views regarding the relationship of citizens to government or society. These are: (1) the equal burden principle; (2) the principle that persons should contribute to government according to the benefits received from government; (3) the principle that persons should sacrifice to government according to what they withdraw from the store of social goods (i.e., according to what they consume); and (4) the principle that persons should sacrifice to government according to their respective abilities to pay (meaning material wealth, which, for this purpose, includes income).

a.   Equal-Burden Principle

The *equal-burden principle* would *tax people in equal dollar amounts*. A "head tax" of $20K per person would be an example of a tax premised on the equal-burden principle. The principle derives from the idea that the purpose of government is solely to guarantee equal rights and liberties to all persons ex ante. That is, the government's coercive power to tax is legitimate only to the extent that government protects life and liberty by way of defense and police and the basic economic infrastructure of a market economy. This view might be called a hard-core Libertarian view, although it is not adhered to by all that call themselves Libertarians.

Of course, no modern political entity has found it expedient to follow such a principle, because material resources are so unequally distributed in society that an equal-burden tax set at a level affordable by low-income persons could not come close to funding adequately a modern government. Even colonial-era head taxes and poll taxes exempted significant classes of people. The one thing that all people could contribute equally would be their time. A universal military draft (or national service obligation) would follow the equal-burden principle, although it would not be a "tax" in the usual sense. But universal service has never taken root in the United States, and the military draft has been riddled with exemptions.

The equal-burden principle assumes that a properly limited government will benefit all individuals equally. Thus, this principle is oblivious to the fact that even the most limited kind of government that eschews all redistributive programs does not really benefit people equally. Those with greater wealth and talent have more to lose from external aggression, civil disorder, etc., and are protected more by even a minimalist government than those with little or no wealth. For this reason, many who might be attracted to the equal-burden notion fall back on the benefit principle.

b.   Benefit Principle

The *benefit principle* asserts that *individuals should pay tax in proportion to the varying benefits they receive from government*. Originally, this view was tied to a conception of a limited government, but it was extended to encompass a government that provided "public goods." (A public good is one whose use by a particular individual or entity does not preclude its availability to others.) More recently, the benefit principle concept has been expanded by the notion that the market outcomes of individuals (income, wealth) are themselves a benefit provided by government.

There are problems with the various versions of the benefit notion. The largest of these problems is that a major form of benefits provided by a modern government is that of welfare transfers directed to certain individuals precisely because the individuals are considered too poor to pay for these benefits. Thus, it would be oxymoronic to require these persons to pay taxes as a quid pro quo for the largesse conferred on them. Stated differently, a major portion of the benefits provided by modern governments is outside the practical scope of a tax based on the benefits principle.

A second problem with the benefits principle is that other major benefits provided by a modern government such as national defense, the societal good of public education in excess of benefits enjoyed by students and their parents, environmental protection, the rule of law, etc., cannot be valued and properly apportioned among individuals with any acceptable degree of accuracy.

Moreover, the benefit principle doesn't tell us much about the tax base (i.e., whether it should be income or wealth) other than that the tax base should mimic prices one would pay in a hypothetical (but non-existent) market for government services of various types. Furthermore, the notion of a hypothetical market with government as the seller posits that the government is a principal, whereas the political theory that generated the benefit principle views government as an agent.

These difficulties cannot be avoided by announcing that the market outcomes experienced by individuals (i.e., their income or wealth) establishes the extent to which they have benefited from governmental activities, because other factors besides government activities (innate talent, luck, inheritance, physical appearance, etc.) contribute significantly to market outcomes. Finally, attempting to base the benefits principle on market outcomes could produce some odd results. For example, a sociopath who lives comfortably by thievery would pay no tax because his financial success is the result of anti-social behavior rather than participation in market activities. It is perhaps best to view the benefit principle as a justification for taxation as such rather than as a prescription for tax system design.

The benefit principle does, however, account for some taxes and user fees that operate as the quid pro quo for receiving government services. For example, an assessment imposed by a city on landowners enjoying a new sewer system installed by the city is a tax premised on the benefit principle. Similarly, gasoline taxes, bridge tolls, public college tuition, national park fees, etc., are common varieties of benefit taxes, and government insurance programs could fit into this category if they were stripped of redistributive features, but that is hardly ever the case.

c. Consumption Principle

Neither the consumption principle nor the ability-to-pay principle, infra, are derived from a limited conception of government. The *consumption principle* posits that taxation should be based on the amount of an individual's consumption. This notion traces back at least to Hobbes, who had (along with many of his contemporaries) an aversion to luxurious living, both as a matter of morality and because it was thought that it sapped the state. (To Hobbes, the rival to a tax on consumption was the property tax; the income tax had yet to be conceived of.)

Unlike the benefit principle, the consumption tax notion is capable of specifying the tax base for a personal tax, namely, a tax on the total consumption of a person for the year. Such a tax (variously called a personal consumption tax, a cash-flow consumption tax, or a consumed-income tax) has had significant academic and political backing in recent years. It is considered in some detail in Part Two.

Although the consumption principle has intuitive appeal, its pseudo-moralistic foundations (as Hobbes and later commentators conceived them)[1] do not hold water. Consumption in general does not sap the economy (take away from the store associated with social goods). The view that it does is associated with 17th century mercantilism.[2] Mercantalism in turn is based on a conception of competition among nations in a zero-sum game (mostly involving control and enjoyment of natural resources), whereas the modern free-trade ideal is based on the idea of a global economy that lifts all boats. Moreover, the modern view of economics holds that the economy is driven by demand, which, in turn, is largely a function of consumption wants. Economic assets would not be produced (or harvested) without demand. In short, consumption is the force behind the creation of wealth. The optimal balance between consuming and saving to create investment capital to expand the economy is a technical economics issue, not an ethical issue. In any event, in a global economy, capital can come from anywhere on the planet.

A personal-consumption tax is not the same as a sumptuary tax on specific luxury goods, such as expensive consumer items. A personal-consumption tax would be universal, and (if the rate is "flat") would disproportionately affect low-income persons who consume a higher percentage of their total income than high-income persons. Also, a personal consumption tax that strictly follows the Hobbesian ideal would arguably not allow for subsistence allowances off the bottom. Without such allowances, a personal consumption tax could operate in a way that is opposite to that of a luxury tax.

Finally, a tax on personal consumption (in whatever form) is still a tax payable in cash. Hence the tax (as with any tax) can reduce a person's consumption *or* wealth.

d. The Ability-to-Pay Principle

The objective *ability-to-pay principle* posits that taxes should be apportioned among the population according to the net economic resources of persons. This conception, which dates back at least to Adam Smith,[3] can be made to equate with "realized net income" as elaborated upon in Chapter 2. Under the ability-to-pay concept, income is net of decreases in wealth devoted to the production of income. That leaves two end uses for income, namely, personal consumption and retention (savings, investment, and hoarding). Since both kinds of end use are "in" the tax base, there is no need for an ability-to-pay tax regime to distinguish between them. In contrast, this distinction is critical under a consumption tax regime.

---

[1] Adam Smith, John Stuart Mill, and Victorian-era thinking in general thought that luxurious consumption weakened society.

[2] Mercantilism holds that the economic strength of a nation is measured by a state's holdings of hard currency (gold bullion), obtainable by subsidizing domestic industry and exports and keeping out imports. Adam Smith's WEALTH OF NATIONS, published in 1776, was a rebuttal of mercantilism and a paean to free trade.

[3] Writing in 1776, Adam Smith, in AN INQUIRY INTO THE NATURE AND CAUSES OF THE WEALTH OF NATIONS, stated that individuals "ought to contribute to the support of the government, as nearly as possible, according to their respective abilities; that is, in proportion to the revenue which they respectively enjoy under the protection of the state." Note the slight "benefit" flavor of the last clause of this quote, which is understandable given that the benefit theory of taxation was then dominant.

The ability-to-pay principle (like the consumption principle) is not dependent upon a particular conception of what activities are legitimate for government to undertake. Income happens to be a convenient baseline for redistribution, but it is not necessary that government in fact pursue a program of redistribution. At the same time, the ability-to- pay principle inherently recognizes two limitations of government *in exercising its taxing power.* First, the subsistence needs of individuals have priority over the needs of government. Second, because what the government requires from taxation is cash, an ability-to-pay tax should be sensitive to the liquidity (cash) position of taxpayers, and that in turn posits a principle of "realization."

B. DISTRIBUTIVE NORMS

Theories of government vary along a spectrum on the issue of whether government can legitimately redistribute (in an explicit or self-conscious way) material resources from the well-off to the less well-off. The branch of political philosophy that deals with this issue is that of distributive justice. Apart from theories concocted by thinkers, it would appear that most people simply possess charitable impulses, and, to solve the collective-action problem, such impulses are channeled (in part) through government (and in part through private charity). It is pretty obvious that one favoring redistribution through government would favor a "personal" tax having a comprehensive tax base that included an individual's wealth and consumption above the subsistence level. Redistribution has two sides, the "taking" side and the "distributing" side, and for redistribution to be meaningful the taking must be from those who have "more than enough."

The alternative to an "objective" approach to the tax base is a "welfarist" approach that plays off of the *subjective* "well-being" of individuals. A subjective concept of well-being does not fit with taxation, because government cannot directly redistribute well-being, and government activity undertaken simply to destroy well-being would have no rationale apart from envy. Government can, however, obtain cash from those who objectively have it in relative abundance and then use cash to create or foster well-being in the less-well-off members of society. Since well-being is not a proper subject of taxation, those aspects of well-being that are not represented by material wealth (such as the pleasures of nature, society, and family) have no reason to be included in the tax base. It misses the mark, therefore, to assert that a tax base comprised of material resources is a "proxy" for well-being. Well-being is not the real subject of objective ability-to-pay taxation. Besides, the empirical relation of personal income or wealth to well-being is uncertain. Assuming that the promotion of well-being is a proper "end" of government activity, the end should not be confused with the means, which (as far as taxation is concerned) is strictly about money.

Even if one were to assume arguendo that the well-being of individuals is the proper subject of tax, such a notion would translate into an expansive (rather than narrow) conception of the tax base. Since saving, investing, and gift-giving are all matters of personal choice, the choices must all be deemed to have been made to enhance the current well-being of the chooser. In short, there is no reason to think that a "well-being" conception of the tax base would be limited to personal consumption.

C. ECONOMIC NORMS

The task of taxation in relation to economics is to provide a tax system that furthers (or at least does not interfere with) economic efficiency. Although there are various concepts of economic efficiency, the core idea is to increase the material wealth of society (i.e., to increase social wealth, or the output of goods and services). Some conceptions of economic efficiency attempt to incorporate notions of distributive justice,[4] but such notions are external to economics itself, which (insofar as it claims to be a science) is inherently quantitative. In any event, the governing model of efficiency in economics is an unfettered free-market exchange (with no negative externalities, like pollution), which leaves the parties both better off and no one else worse off. Of course, matters are usually not so neat and clean, thanks to transaction costs, negative externalities, and market failures (such as those that flow from the exercise of monopoly power). Thus, in principle, government has a role not only in facilitating markets but also in correcting market imperfections.

The fundamental free market economic norm relevant to tax systems and provisions is that of *neutrality*, which posits that *the tax system should not interfere with the free market by either encouraging or discouraging particular economic activities*. People should not be affected in their economic choices by the tax laws. A common metaphor for neutrality is the "level playing field." Under the neutrality norm, tax incentives, subsidies, and penalties keyed to certain economic behaviors are anathema. The neutrality norm suggests a broad tax base with minimal exemptions and low tax rates. In theory, the Simons income concept would come closer to the neutrality ideal than would the ability-to-pay income concept, because the realization principle discriminates between investments that grow through unrealized appreciation (land, "growth" stocks, etc.) and investments that produce realized income (interest-paying corporate bonds, etc.).

The idea that the tax system can have the effect of providing an incentive or disincentive to engage in certain behaviors (contrary to what the person would do in the absence of tax) is called the *"substitution effect."* The notion is that a person would tend to substitute a low-taxed activity (or item), such as leisure, for a higher taxed one (work). The substitution effect views taxes like a selective price increase or decease. Of course, taxes are not simply "added onto" prices in the real world to the extent that the tax can be shifted to others. The same is true in reverse: a tax decrease does not necessarily translate into a price decrease.

No realistically possible tax system can be completely neutral, because some activities will always avoid being taxed and, therefore, the very existence of any form of taxation will have some effect on behavior. For example, an income tax

---

[4] For example, the notion of Pareto efficiency refers to a move that makes at least one person better off and no one worse off, which implies that making a person worse off (to make another better off) is undesirable or at least questionable. But such a notion would not seem to come from economics itself. Utilitarianism favors policies that create winners and losers, so long as there is a net social gain. Opponents of Utilitarianism object precisely to the legitimacy of social netting.

lowers the economic rewards from working and may therefore discourage work in favor of untaxed leisure. At the same time, the baseline concept of a no-tax world is also unrealistic, because government (and taxes) are necessary for the existence of basic personal security and modern-day markets.

In fact, taxes do not necessarily distort behavior in the way hypothesized by substitution-effect analysis. Take again the work-leisure distinction. Substitution-effect analysis predicts that people will react to a tax on wages by *reducing* work effort relative to leisure. But the tax might instead cause them to increase hours worked to reach the *same level of after-tax income* that they enjoyed before the tax was imposed. This incentive is called *the income effect*. The income effect is likely to be strong if the person aims for a "target level" of say, retirement savings or cash to purchase some "necessity." Moreover, it may be that neither the substitution effect nor the income effect is significant in a given context. For example, if a person likes her job and if market conditions make pay significantly unresponsive to work time or effort, taxes are unlikely to cause her to work more or less than she would in the absence of taxation. That is, a given economic choice might be swamped by factors unrelated to taxation.

Many government activities (including tax provisions) explicitly violate the neutrality norm, but usually under cover of a claimed social benefit. For example, penalty taxes might be used to combat negative externalities (i.e., social harms that are not reflected in market prices), such as those that flow from the use of alcohol, tobacco, and environmentally harmful products. Alternatively, taxes can be used for raising funds necessary to create positive externalities (social benefits not reflected in market prices), such as providing jobs for persons who would otherwise be unemployed. A question is always whether these deliberate market distortions really work. For example, a drug addict is not likely to respond to a tax on drugs by reducing consumption of drugs. Instead, the likely effect would be to induce the addict to consume cheaper (and less safe) drugs or to reduce consumption of other goods.

To generalize, the actual economic effect of almost any policy cannot be predicted in advance, but instead ultimately boils down to an empirical question.[5]

The conventional understanding of the neutrality norm, as described above, has been criticized for being too simplistic, even without taking into consideration fairness norms or distributive justice norms. The *general theory of the second best*[6] takes a more sophisticated approach to issues of economic neutrality and can be loosely stated as: a government policy that moves towards neutrality (e.g., by removing a tax preference that induced behavior that would otherwise not occur) cannot simply be assumed to improve overall economic efficiency, because the new policy might combine with other policies (either inside or outside the tax system) so

---

[5] Incidentally, there is a technical distinction to be made between a tax incentive and a tax subsidy. A tax *incentive* is designed to *modify behavior*. Thus, tax benefits obtained by persons who would have performed the desired activity without the tax incentive are "windfalls," which are economically inefficient. A tax *subsidy*, in contrast, is designed to *transfer resources to some deserving or needy group*. Of course, in practice, incentives create subsidy effects and vice versa.

[6] See R.G. Lipsey & Kelvin Lancaster, *The General Theory of Second Best*, 24 REV. ECON. STUDIES 11 (1956).

as to reduce overall economic efficiency. Similarly, a policy move that appears to violate neutrality could improve overall economic efficiency by offsetting other behavior-distorting aspects of the tax system or market imperfections. The theory of the second best requires economic models that can account for complex cause-and-effect relationships. A good lesson to be learned from the theory of the second best is that the tax system — or any individual piece of it — does not operate in a vacuum. Additionally, not every economic problem demands to be solved by a *tax* provision, as opposed to other government action. (The same lesson applies outside of the economics realm as well: not every social problem requires solution by a tax provision; the problem can be addressed by other kinds of government action.)

The theory of *optimal taxation* also modifies the neutrality norm. This theory begins by observing that tax preferences and penalties disturb the free market — i.e., are non-neutral — only to the extent that behavior is, in fact, subject to modification. Optimal taxation suggests, therefore, that taxes (whether a sales tax, income tax, or some other tax) should be heavier on "inelastic" goods, services, and behavior (in the jargon of the economist) than on "elastic" goods, services, and behavior. An inelastic item is one that does not have a readily available substitute to which individuals and businesses would be likely to turn if the item were taxed (and thereby rendered more expensive), i.e., an item that has a low "response rate" to a tax. Examples of inelastic items or behaviors might include basic subsistence food and housing, fossil fuels, antibiotics, and death. In addition, some economists believe that the decision regarding how much to work is unaffected by tax rates over a broad range, at least in the cases of single individuals and primary earners in married couples. According to this view, working is an inelastic activity for many taxpayers. Since behavior is not modified by taxes on inelastic items or activities, optimal taxation tells us that the neutrality norm is not violated by taxing them more heavily. An optimal tax system, in other words, would heavily tax some of the very items that give rise to political demands for subsidy, such as basic nutrition and health care, as well as activities favored by important social norms, such as work. But a system of this type would also heavily tax windfalls, such as prizes, lottery winnings, and perhaps inheritances, because economic behavior is not significantly modified by the tax in these cases.

The notion of economic neutrality, which implies a minimum level of government intervention, lies in tension with the notion that government should undertake programs (often of a redistributive nature) that improve social well-being. Policy makers adopting this interventionist approach are sometimes called *"welfare economists,"* because they view the improvement of social welfare as a science that can be practiced by constructing and testing social-welfare functions. (Optimal taxation theorists purport to combine classical economics with a welfarist approach.) To a welfarist, government action (including changes in the tax law) is analyzed from the vantage point of social gains and losses. A government action is said to be "Pareto efficient" if it makes at least one person better off and no person worse off than before. Although this "standard" would be unobjectionable to most,[7] it is a largely worthless policy guide, because almost all government action

---

[7] The concept of Pareto efficiency bears a striking resemblance to the Rawlsian principle that social

(including tax system design) inevitably produces losers (at least losers who perceive themselves as such). Thus, if government has set a revenue target, a tax break aimed at some segment of society would result in a tax increase for the rest. Assertions that the tax break will make everyone better off are properly met with skepticism.

The prevalent norm of welfare economics that has significance for tax policy is *Kaldor-Hicks efficiency.* (Kaldor-Hicks efficiency is related to *cost-benefit analysis,* but the latter tends to view benefits and costs in terms of dollars rather than welfare.) A government policy is Kaldor-Hicks efficient if, net of administrative costs, the *aggregate welfare gains of the winners exceed the aggregate welfare losses of the losers.* In such a case, the winners could afford to compensate the losers, and if that occurred (say, by taxation that finances redistributive transfer payments) then the scheme (as a whole) would be Pareto efficient. However, a Kaldor-Hicks efficient policy does not require that such compensation actually take place. (And many find the whole idea that government can improve society in this way to be objectionable in principle.) If a *tax law* change would produce a net social gain, a devotee of Kaldor-Hicks efficiency would support the change, whether or not it violated the neutrality principle.

Since Kaldor-Hicks efficiency is viewed in terms of welfare (subjective "utility"), as opposed to nominal dollars, redistributive schemes are virtually self-recommending, under the assumption that money has a declining marginal utility to individuals (i.e., that the last dollar of a wealthy person has less value than that same dollar would have to a person on the verge of starvation). Economists often use the term "equity" to refer to the kind of downward redistribution that seems to be prima facie mandated by Kaldor-Hicks efficiency. Such "equity" is typically contrasted with "efficiency" in the sense of wealth-maximizing market efficiency expressed in the "neutrality" concept discussed above. It is commonly thought that "equity" (having to do with the *optimal distribution* of resources) and "efficiency" (having to do with the *maximization* of aggregate resources) inherently conflict, or at least lie in tension, with each other.

D. THE "TAX EXPENDITURE" CONCEPT

Since direct spending programs to improve social welfare tend to be politically unpopular (especially if they smack of welfare for the poor or "corporate welfare"), it has been expedient for politicians to use the tax system to disguise such programs as tax benefits in the form of (1) exclusions from income, (2) deductions for phantom costs or costs of personal consumption, or (3) tax credits. It can fairly be said that any tax credit (other than one based on the payment of a tax to the U.S. Treasury or to another government) is a government spending program (subsidy).

The *tax expenditure* concept expresses an attitude of skepticism towards this use of the tax system. This skepticism is independent of the merits of any government goal. That is, the skepticism is over the means (using the tax system) rather than over the ends. In the United States, the tax expenditure concept was coined in 1967

---

arrangements (that inevitably produce inequalities) should be structured in such a way as to improve the lot of the worst-off members of society.

by Stanley Surrey, then the Assistant Secretary of the Treasury for Tax Policy, to refer to *tax preferences, incentives, and subsidies that are the functional equivalents of direct spending programs.* As Surrey conceptualized it, a tax expenditure is not a true tax provision because a tax expenditure has nothing to do with trying to arrive at the proper measure of "income."

Surrey argued that tax expenditures are usually inappropriate spending mechanisms for at least two reasons. First, they are hidden in the Internal Revenue Code. Without a line in the budget, politicians and the public can be deluded into thinking that the program is "cost free." To counter this phenomenon, both Congress and the executive branch are currently required to submit a "tax expenditure budget" along with the conventional budget. (The tax expenditure budget, however, does not enter into the calculation of the overall deficit or surplus.) Second, the tax bureaucracy, which focuses on collecting revenue, is not an efficient or appropriate mechanism to implement social policy or economic programs. Moreover, the congressional tax committees and the IRS lack programmatic expertise and political accountability in the areas that would be the province of other committees and bureaucracies in the case of a direct spending program. However, a common retort to Surrey's second point is that once a new government bureaucracy is created to administer a direct spending program, it is hard to cut back or remove.

Surrey tied the tax expenditure concept to the Simons concept of income, which, in turn, is anchored in the norm of economic neutrality. This triggered academic disputations, as it was doubted in some quarters whether such long-standing features of the income tax as the realization principle and the exclusion for gifts were really disguised spending programs.

Surrey, however, readily conceded that the realization principle should not be considered a tax expenditure, so that this point was a false issue. Other disputes about the proper content of the income tax base involved items at the periphery. Although tax expenditure analysis continues to have serious detractors, it also has energetic defenders who regard it as a sound and workable concept that has the salutary effect of revealing government spending programs disguised as tax provisions and then requiring those programs to undergo the same rigorous cost/benefit analysis that would (should?) be applied to direct spending programs. Moreover, tax expenditure analysis has in fact become an institutionalized element within the tax-law-making processes of the U.S. government, several state governments, and many foreign governments.[8]

Despite the foregoing, tax expenditures are here to stay. It is not difficult to see why tax expenditures appeal to people along the entire political spectrum: government programs can be undertaken without explicit appropriations. If some goal sounds good, just create a tax break for it! It looks like free money! The points made in this chapter are raised by features of the existing income tax that are mentioned in Chapters 4, 6, and 16.

---

[8] See J. Clifton Fleming, Jr. & Robert J. Peroni, *Reinvigorating Tax Expenditure Analysis and its International Dimensions*, 27 Va. Tax Rev. 437 (2008).

PROBLEMS

1.   Jane owns a business that pollutes the air heavily and that employs a work force receiving only subsistence, or below subsistence, wages for performing simple repetitive tasks. Jane's business produces gross income of $100K per year. Because of her low labor costs and her decision not to incur the cost of pollution control equipment, Jane's business expenses are relatively small, $10K per year, and so her net profit is $90K per year. Sue likewise owns a business that produces $100K per year of gross income. Sue has installed expensive pollution control equipment and employs a highly trained, well-paid work force that performs sophisticated tasks. Sue's business costs are much higher than Jane's because Sue pays higher wages and has incurred pollution-control costs. Consequently, Sue's net profit is only $10K per year. The jurisdiction in which Jane's and Sue's businesses are located proposes to enact a 10% tax on *gross* business income. Critique this proposal in terms of all of the policy norms covered in this chapter.

2.   Joe Bob is an associate in a law firm who earns $60K each year and who incurs no business expenses. This year, Joe Bob spends $50K on personal consumption and saves $10K. Chauncey III receives $60K each year from a trust fund created by his grandfather, and spends it all on personal consumption. What *should* be the tax bases of Joe Bob and Chauncey, respectively, applying the policy criteria discussed above?

Chapter 4

RATES AND ALLOWANCES FOR BASIC MAINTENANCE

This chapter deals with the subject of rate structures, allowances (deductions) "off the bottom" for basic maintenance of the taxpayer and his/her dependents, and tax expenditures (tax credits) aimed at the bottom of the income scale. Much of what might be loosely categorized as "the income taxation of low-income taxpayers" is found in this chapter.

A. RATE STRUCTURES

This section discusses the causes and effects of a progressive rate structure.

1. Defining Progressivity

If an income tax is "progressive," the taxpayer's "average tax rate" (defined as her/his tax payment divided by total income[1]) rises as income rises.

It is a common misunderstanding to think that an income tax with only "one" tax rate can never be "progressive." An income tax can be "progressive," even if it nominally contains only one tax rate, *so long as some income is protected from taxation*, such as occurs with the allowances off the bottom described in Section B (the standard deduction and the § 151 deductions for personal and dependency exemptions). Thus, a tax rate schedule under which the first $10K of income is not subject to tax (or, more accurately, is subject to a tax rate of 0%) and all income above that amount is subject to a flat rate, say 25%, is nevertheless progressive because the average tax rate would increase as income rises.

For example, compare Anna (with $20K of income) and Andy (with $50K of income). Anna's total tax would be $2.5K under the schedule described above (25% of the $10K earned above the tax-free $10K amount), and her average tax rate would be 12.5% ($2.5K/$20K). Andy's total tax would be $10K (25% of the $40K earned above the tax-free $10K amount), and his average tax rate would be 20% ($10K/$50K). Because Andy's average tax rate (20%) is higher than Anna's (12.5%), and Andy's total income ($50K) was higher than Anna's ($20K), this tax is progressive, even though it's a "flat" tax that nominally contains only "one" rate.

---

[1] Economists sometimes refer to the "effective tax rate" in discussions of the "incidence" of a tax, i.e., who actually bears the economic burden of a tax. In that context, "effective rate" may describe the rate of tax for a particular taxpayer after accounting for the fact that all or part of the tax was "passed on" to others.

As the Anna/Andy example illustrates, no meaningful difference with respect to progressivity exists between (1) a system with an allowance off the bottom in arriving at taxable income (as where each taxpayer obtains a "free" deduction of say $10K) and (2) a system without such an allowance, but which taxes the first $10K at a zero rate.[2] At the present time, the federal income tax uses the former approach of allowances off the bottom.

In addition to allowances off the bottom, the federal income tax augments progressivity by incorporating a "bracket" system under which incremental brackets of taxable income are subject to ever-higher tax rates. A bracket can be visualized as a tax base "tier" or "layer."[3] As of 2011, the rates under the federal income tax applicable to various income tax brackets of individuals were 10, 15, 25, 28, 33, and 35%. Thus, the 10% rate applied to the first tier of an individual taxpayer's taxable income (TI), the 15% rate to the next higher tier, and so on. The level of TI at which the tax rate for a particular bracket initially becomes effective is called the "bracket floor," and the TI level where the bracket ends and the next higher rate kicks in is called the "bracket ceiling." The highest bracket has no ceiling.

A bracket system can be conceptualized as a flat rate coupled with exemptions formulated as a decreasing percentage of the TI in each successively higher bracket. To illustrate, assume a taxpayer has $100K of taxable income, that the applicable rate schedule contains three brackets of TI (0 to $20K, above $20K to $50K, and above $50K), that the respective exemption percentages for each bracket are 100%, 80%, and 60%, and that the flat rate is 50%. Such a system translates into a progressive rate structure as follows (the "taxable percentage" being 100% minus the exemption percentage):

---

[2] More broadly, the Anna/Andy example illustrates that an income tax with an allowance off the bottom is inevitably a progressive income tax unless it employs a rate table that cancels out the progressive effect of the off-the-bottom allowance by expressly imposing tax rates that decline as income rises. Such a rate table is a political impossibility. In contrast, an allowance off the bottom that shelters a modest amount of income from taxation is a political necessity. This means that some degree of progression in the income tax is also a political necessity. From this standpoint, debates over whether the income tax should be progressive or not are irrelevant. The only meaningful controversy is with regard to how progressive the income tax should be. That, however, is a question that lacks an objective answer.

[3] An alternative way to incorporate progressivity — a "cliff" approach — is not used in the federal income tax. Under a "cliff" approach to progressivity, an increase in the tax base above a certain mark causes the *entire tax base* to be subject to a higher tax rate (not merely the amount in excess of that mark). An example would be a tax system in which the tax rate is 10%, but if TI goes above (say) $50K, the rate applicable to the *entire tax base* increases to 20%. Under this approach, a taxpayer having TI of exactly $50K would incur an additional tax of $5K on account of earning only *one additional dollar* in the tax base! Thus, a cliff system would create major disincentives for acquiring additional income and would create major incentives for cheating.

TABLE 1
FLAT RATE COMBINED WITH
DECREASING EXEMPT FRACTION

Bracket	Bracket TI	Taxable %	Taxed Amount	Rate	Tax	Bracket Rate
0-20K	20K	0%	0	50%	0	0%
20K-50K	30K	20%	6K	50%	3K	10% (3K/30K)
Above $50K	50K	40%	20K	50%	10K	20% (10K/50K)

To repeat a point made with respect to the Anna/Andy example, this table shows that an income tax can be structured as progressive over multiple brackets even if it has only a single "flat" rate.

2. Rationales for Progressivity

A progressive tax may be favored (or opposed) strictly on the basis of a taste for (or against) redistribution from the well-off to the less well-off. This taste might derive from adherence to (1) a theory of justice that favors or opposes redistribution, (2) a charitable impulse or lack thereof, or (3) political predilection. The conceptual weakness in justifying (or opposing) progressivity in taxation purely on the basis of one's view of redistribution is that the "spending" side of government is left out of the picture. Thus, a progressive tax can be combined with a regressive spending pattern that results in a "net" redistribution from the "bottom" to the "top." But views about the role and size of government generally are beyond the scope of this book. We therefore limit ourselves, in the discussion below, to two theories of progressivity that are independent of how government spends tax revenues.

a. Objective Ability to Pay

A widely held notion is that the bare subsistence existence of individuals should be "out of bounds" to income taxation. This view is supported by the "ability to pay" tax fairness norm, discussed in Chapter 3, that holds that subsistence-level income does not represent an ability to pay taxes and, therefore, should not be taxed. Bare subsistence income can be protected from tax by means of free deductions "off the bottom" that approximate a subsistence or poverty level of existence. This level can be established objectively by the use of data establishing averages for the population.

As mentioned earlier, free deductions are the functional equivalent of a simple "zero" tax rate applicable to subsistence levels of income, and a zero rate bracket combined with a flat-rate tax produces a simple progressive income tax system.

A variation of the ability-to-pay notion would replace the concept of "subsistence level" income by the more "flexible" (elusive?) concept of "nondiscretionary income."[4] That is to say, "nondiscretionary income" should be protected from

---

[4] This approach was developed in 3 REPORT OF ROYAL COMMISSION ON TAXATION 1-24 (1966) (Canada).

taxation, instead of "subsistence income," which means that the tax base should be limited to "discretionary income." This theory also postulates that nondiscretionary income increases as total income increases, because the more income one has the more income one considers to be "essential" to maintain an "appropriate" standard of living at that level (relative to other levels). At higher levels of net income, a higher standard of living becomes "required": a TV, a car (or two), a home (or two), life insurance coverage, decent health care, and so on. Nevertheless, it is taken to be the case that nondiscretionary expenditures rise at a slower rate than total net income, so that as total income increases, nondiscretionary income decreases as a percentage of total income. Thus, as one's net income rises, higher and higher percentages of net income are considered "discretionary." Under this approach, the real tax base is the discretionary amount at each income level, and this amount can be taxed at a flat rate and yet yield a progressive result. The system described in Table 1, supra, embodies precisely this approach.

b. Sacrifice Theory

A progressive rate structure has also been justified in terms of subjective "ability to sacrifice." The core intuition is that taxation involves sacrifice, and that the system should be designed so that the real burden of this sacrifice is minimized.

Sacrifice theory is based on the proposition that the "real" (subjective) value of each additional dollar (its "utility") to a person declines in absolute terms as that person's wealth or income increases. In other words, $1 means much less to Bill Gates than to the Little Match Girl. This postulate will be referred to as the *declining marginal utility* (DMU) principle as applied to a person's wealth or income. If each incremental dollar provides reduced utility per dollar, an income tax will have a less deleterious effect on individual welfare if government revenue needs are met by taxing the rich more heavily than the poor.

It turns out that the DMU concept can be applied to various conceptions of distributive justice. Thus, an adherent of the "equal burden" norm can, by applying the DMU concept, arrive at a tax that imposes equal sacrifice among members of society. Suppose, for example, that a society consists only of X and Y, that the government needs to raise $12, that X's income is $10 (with each dollar having a marginal utility of $1), and that Y's income is $100 (with each dollar having a marginal utility of 9.1 cents). If X and Y are taxed in a way that results in equal pain for each while raising the $12 needed by the government, X will be taxed $1 and Y $11.[5] Note that this approach yields a mildly progressive rate structure relative to nominal dollars because X pays a tax equal to 10% of her income while Y pays 11%.

It seems highly unlikely, however, that a person basing policy preferences on subjective utility would favor an equal burden norm for taxation. Instead, that person would be more likely to fall within the Utilitarian camp. Utilitarianism is a form of welfarism that favors the greatest subjective good for the greatest number. The logic of Utilitarianism in relation to taxes in isolation would be that taxes should impose minimum *aggregate sacrifice* on the society as a whole. Accordingly, in the

---

[5] X's "sacrifice" computation is $1 tax paid × $1 marginal utility = $1 sacrifice. Y's computation is $11 tax paid ×.091 = $1 sacrifice.

example involving X and Y, the entire tax would be imposed on Y because the total utility sacrifice would then be only $1.09 ($12 × 0.091) instead of $2 in the preceding example where X and Y bore equal sacrifices of $1 each.

One can play the "flat rate game" here as well. That is, if a "flat rate" is applied against dollars that represent declining marginal utility, one ends up with a progressive rate schedule. Thus, in Table 1, instead of a decreasing exemption percentage (translating into an increasing "discretionary income" percentage), one substitutes "decreasing utility percentage."

There are, however, several objections to Utilitarianism as a normative justification for a progressive income tax. First, Utilitarianism, which focuses on subjective sacrifices borne by individuals, requires that the sacrifice-mitigating effects of benefits provided by government spending should be taken into account. Thus, Utilitarianism cannot serve as a guide to designing an income tax that is normatively correct in isolation from other government activities.

Second, even if money has declining marginal utility, that fact is an incomplete policy guide. It is still necessary to find a prescriptive norm that explains why the fact of declining marginal utility should be used as the criterion for allocating the tax burden among individuals.

Third, the empirical basis of DMU can be challenged: the subjective value of money might decline at a faster rate for the poor (as evidenced by their failure to seek wealth) than it does for those rich who have sought mightily to obtain it. That leads to the issue of why we should care about DMU. Should a wealthy miser escape tax because she places an extremely high subjective value on money?

Fourth, since DMU is a subjective phenomenon, various individuals have differing utility curves. Therefore, subjective fairness is an impossible objective, because the utility functions of individuals cannot be reliably ascertained.

If utility functions for individuals were known, a different rate schedule would apply to different individuals, thereby negating any "objective" fairness. Fairness-type arguments are not important to Utilitarian welfarists, who are concerned with obtaining a net improvement in *aggregate* social welfare. A Utilitarian might concede that a person can have a taste for *objective* fairness, and that this taste should be incorporated into that person's utility curve. But then the task of discerning utility curves takes on added complexity. In any event, the tastes of individuals regarding desirable social arrangements can be expressed through the political process, where it appears that most people want both objective fairness and welfare improvement from government. For those who are concerned with both, the DMU idea that a dollar means more to the Little Match Girl than to Bill Gates holds a nearly irresistible intuitive allure. Most importantly, this intuitive appeal of the DMU construct allows it to provide a widely accepted normative basis for an income tax that is based on the ability-to-pay principle and that employs progressive rates. Thus, DMU plays an important role in tax policy debates regardless of its weaknesses.

3. A Brief History of Rates

Prior to World War II, the income tax was more of a "class tax" than a "mass tax." The 1913 income tax reached taxable income only above $3K (a hefty chunk of change in that era) at a rate of only 1%, with a 6% rate kicking in at $20K (the higher rate being referred to as a "surtax"). In 1914, the total number of personal tax returns amounted to 0.5% of the total population. This structure was consistent with the goal of reaching income from the wealthy, who were regressively taxed (relative to income) under the various forms of consumption taxation that were used to fund the federal government prior to the adoption of the income tax.

Revenue needs escalated drastically during World War I, when the highest marginal rate was nearly 80%. In the late 1920s and early 1930s, the exemption amount rose somewhat and the highest marginal rate did not exceed 25%. In the New Deal period, the maximum marginal rate climbed to more than 60%, but high exemptions meant that only about 5% of the population paid income taxes in 1939, though the lower classes paid Social Security tax (introduced in 1935) on their labor earnings. World War II brought a top marginal rate of 94% to finance military expenditures, and this was accompanied by low exemption amounts. In this period, the income tax became a "mass tax" for the first time. The withholding mechanism for collection on certain types of gross receipts was also introduced in this era.

Rates stayed high during the Cold War, but major tax-rate cuts occurred in 1962, 1969, and 1981, the latter lowering the maximum marginal rate from 70% to 50%. The 1986 Act drastically reduced the number of rate brackets. Since then, the highest marginal rate has not exceeded 39.6% and presently rests at 35%.

NOTES

1. It is hard to gauge the extent to which intellectual theories and norms influence tax policy. Many theories and norms (such as ability-to-pay, horizontal equity, a tolerance of moderate redistribution, and DMU) have a basis in common intuition. Theory-based proposals advanced by the Treasury Department to improve the tax system often have traction.[6] An example is the Tax Expenditure concept, which has been incorporated into the budgetary process. Theories, by helping to shape the "culture" of tax, affect legislation and perhaps explain why basic features of the tax system, such as progressive rates, personal and dependency exemptions, and the support exclusion, persist over time, although the details change from time to time.

2. There are numerous surveys that purport to measure the perceived fairness of various kinds of taxes. These surveys have to be taken with a grain of salt, because the questionnaire typically does not define fairness, and the subjects do not have to explain their responses. It would appear that people (in these surveys) tend to equate unfairness with "having to write a check," because sales taxes tend to win these popularity contests.

---

[6] In the United States, massive and comprehensive Treasury studies of the tax system occurred in 1969, 1977, and 1984, and significant tax legislation resulted, sooner or later, from these studies.

3. It is misleading to say that a retail sales tax is "regressive" relative to net income, because this statement implicitly begs two separate normative questions, namely, (1) what *should* constitute the tax base, income or consumption, and (2) what rate structures *should* apply to the various taxes that the government deploys, progressive, regressive, or proportional.

B. FILING STATUS

The rate schedule that applies to a given taxpayer depends on that taxpayer's filing status. See § 1(a)-(d). That status can be (1) married filing jointly (or "surviving spouse" as defined in § 2(a)), (2) married person filing separately, (3) unmarried individual (not head of household), or (4) unmarried individual qualifying as "head of household" under § 2(b). The significance of status classification cannot be discerned without grasping the marginal rate concept.

1. The Marginal Rate Concept

The term "marginal rate" means the rate applicable to the bracket in which a taxpayer's *last* ("marginal") dollar of income falls. In Table 1 above, the hypothetical taxpayer having TI of $100K is "in" the 20% marginal rate bracket, because her "last" dollar is taxed at a 20% rate. In contrast, the *average* tax rate for the taxpayer in Table 1 is 13% (tax of $13K divided by TI of $100K).

The marginal rate concept is crucial for tax policy analysis and tax planning because it is at the margins that decisions are made; it is at the margins that behavior may be altered because of the potential tax consequences. The marginal rate concept also allows you to analyze a potential income item or a potential deduction item from an *after-tax* perspective.

For example, suppose Employer pays Employee a year-end bonus of $100. What is the bonus worth to the Employee? From a *before-tax* perspective, a $100 bonus is obviously worth just that — $100. But in determining the *after-tax* benefit, the critical variable is the marginal rate — the rate at which that additional income is taxed. A taxpayer in the 15% tax bracket will have that additional income taxed at 15%. After taxes, $85 will be left, the after-tax benefit of the $100. A taxpayer in the 28% tax bracket will have that additional $100 taxed at 28%, so it will be worth $72 after taxes. And so on.

On the deduction side, suppose Joe gives $100 out of current income as a charitable contribution, deductible under § 170(a). How much does the contribution cost Joe? From a before-tax perspective, it cost Joe $100 out of pocket. From an after-tax perspective, however, it cost Joe only $85 if Joe is in the 15% bracket, because Joe's deduction will save $15 in taxes that would otherwise have been paid on the $100.[7] Similarly, a $100 charitable gift costs Joe only $72 if he is in the 28% bracket, and so on.

---

[7] An alternative way to reach the same conclusion is to note that if Joe had not given the $100 to charity, $15 would have gone to the government and Joe could have consumed or saved only the remaining $85. Therefore, the real cost to Joe of his $100 contribution is only the $85 consumption or saving that he sacrificed.

The relationship that is emerging here is important. *Taxpayers in higher marginal brackets benefit less from incremental income than taxpayers in lower marginal brackets, while taxpayers in higher marginal tax brackets benefit more from deductions derived from incremental costs than taxpayers in lower brackets.* These concepts can be expressed in simple mathematical formulas: the after-tax benefit from an addition to a taxpayer's income is the amount of the additional income multiplied by the expression "the number 1.0 *minus* the taxpayer's marginal rate," and the tax savings generated by an additional deduction is the deduction amount multiplied by the taxpayer's marginal rate.

Tax savings can be generated by *shifting income* from a high-bracket taxpayer to a lower-bracket taxpayer. (Of course, this only makes economic sense if the parties are related or can otherwise share the tax savings.) Thus, if mother can move $30K from her 35% marginal rate bracket to her daughter's 15% marginal rate bracket, the net tax saving is $6K (mother saves $10.5K in taxes and daughter pays additional tax of $4.5K). Techniques for accomplishing income shifting are considered in Part V, but the point about income shifting is also relevant to the discussion of filing status.

2. Tax Pros and Cons of Marriage

If a married couple files a joint return, the taxable income shown on the return is the combined (aggregate) taxable income of the couple. If the couple files separately, each spouse reports his or her own taxable income on a return.

The federal Defense of Marriage Act (1996), § 3, provides that for purposes of federal law (and notwithstanding any state law to the contrary) the term "marriage" is limited to the union of one man and one woman. This provision has been challenged on constitutional grounds. Unless this provision is held to be unconstitutional or is repealed, a same-sex married couple cannot file a federal joint return.

Marital status generally is determined as of the last day of the taxable year. § 7703(a)(1). Thus, if one marries on December 31, the couple is deemed to have been married for the entire year. This rule avoids the possibility of having a different filing status for part of the year as opposed to the rest of the year.

A married person who is "separated" under a decree of separate maintenance is deemed to be unmarried. § 7703(a)(2). A married person who files separately and meets the other head-of-household requirements of § 7703(b) is also deemed to be unmarried (and therefore eligible for "head of household" status).

The most favorable rate schedule is that for married persons filing jointly (and surviving spouses), because this schedule has the widest brackets, so that it takes a greater amount of TI (compared to the other schedules) to move into higher marginal rate brackets. The worst schedule (for individuals) is for married persons filing separately, where the brackets are precisely half as wide compared to the joint-filing schedule. This is deliberate: the tax on a married couple filing jointly is equal to twice the tax (figured as if each spouse filed separately) on half of the couple's aggregate (combined) taxable income.

A joint return effectively treats the married couple like an equal partnership. First the income and deductions of both spouses are aggregated in arriving at a "marital partnership" taxable income figure. Then the aggregate income is divided in two halves, with each spouse being assigned one-half of the aggregate. Last, a tax is calculated on each spouse's half (using the rate schedule for a married person filing separately), and the two taxes are combined. However, these steps are invisible to the taxpayer, because they are incorporated into the joint return rate schedule itself.

The implicit "income splitting" embedded in the joint return is favorable if the separate taxable incomes are unevenly split between husband and wife. For example (using the rate schedules for the year 2011), suppose W's taxable income is $68K and H's is zero. If W and H file jointly, their joint tax on the aggregate TI of $68K is $9,350. If W and H were to file separately, W's tax on $68K would be $13,125 and H's tax on nothing is zero. Filing jointly has the effect of moving $34K of W's TI from the 25% marginal rate bracket to lower marginal rate brackets. The tax for filing jointly ($9,350) is the same aggregate tax amount as if each of W and H had TI of $34K and filed separately, each paying a tax of $4,675.

The schedule for unmarried individuals is the same as for a married individual filing separately through low and moderate levels of TI. In this zone, the couple with unequal TIs can save aggregate taxes by getting married and filing a joint return, as illustrated in the previous paragraph. This phenomenon is called the "marriage bonus." However, if the couple's respective TIs are equal (and within the zone where the rate schedules for unmarried individuals and married persons filing separately are the same), their aggregate tax will be the same whether they are married or single.

At a certain point the brackets for unmarried individuals widen (relative to that of a married individual filing separately). The effect of this bracket widening at higher income levels is to create a scenario in which two unmarried persons with significant TIs will pay a somewhat lower aggregate tax relative to what they would pay if married filing jointly. (Using the 2011 rate schedules, and assuming that each of A and B has TI of $150K, their aggregate tax if unmarried is $35,617 times 2 = $71,234. In contrast, their tax if married and filing jointly is $76,454.50, a $5,220.50 increase.) Such a scenario is often described as entailing a "marriage penalty" (or "singles bonus").

As the preceding paragraphs indicate, when one spouse in a married couple earns all of the couple's taxable income, joint return filing usually provides a substantial tax benefit. But where both members of a couple are substantial income earners, there will be a tipping point at which the members save tax by being unmarried and filing separately. Figuring the tipping point between the singles bonus and the marriage bonus for higher-income couples depends on the amount of taxable income and the rate schedules in effect for the taxable year in question. The schedules have changed from year to year because the dollar figures that define the brackets are annually adjusted for inflation. The rate schedules that you see in § 1 of the Code are not the schedules applicable for the current taxable year.

The available empirical data indicates that, overall, the marriage-bonus effect outweighs the marriage-penalty effect.[8]

The schedule for Head of Household status (which requires that at least one other person is being supported in the taxpayer's home by the taxpayer) is less favorable than the joint return schedule, but not by much, and more favorable than that for unmarried persons.

3.   A Brief History of Filing Status

At the 1913 beginning of the modern income tax, and for a long time thereafter, there was only one rate schedule for individuals. There was no joint return and no aggregation of the TI of a married couple. What set the ball rolling for future statutory changes was the Supreme Court's decision in *Poe v. Seaborn*, 282 U.S. 101 (1930). The *Seaborn* couple lived in a community property state (Washington). Their income consisted of the husband's wages plus income from their property. State law deemed all property and income to be owned by the "marital community" rather than by the individuals comprising that marital community. The Court decided that, under Washington community property law, the husband earned his wages as an "agent" of the marital community. The marital community was not, however, regarded as a taxpaying entity. Instead, its income was attributed to the two spouses in proportion to their equal ownership interests in the marital community, i.e., 50/50. Thus, each spouse was properly taxed on half of the husband's labor earnings. Moreover, the Court concluded that the marital community also owned the couple's investment property. Since income from property is taxed to the owner(s) thereof, the preceding analysis that governed taxation of the husband's labor income meant that the investment income of the Seaborns also had to be attributed 50% to each spouse.

The upshot of *Seaborn* was that married couples residing in community property states were able to combine their TIs and then split the aggregate TI in half, with each spouse reporting half on his or her individual income tax return.[9] This situation of tax favoritism towards community property married couples led many states to consider adopting community property laws in order to garner their citizens the advantage of *Seaborn*.

In 1948, Congress responded by creating the joint return option for married couples. Because of the advantages of income splitting and the convenience of a single return, most one-earner couples (the predominant paradigm in 1948) filed joint returns under the new, advantageous rate schedule, even if they lived in a community property state (where there is no real advantage to filing a joint return).

---

[8] See JOEL SLEMROD & JOHN BAKIJA, TAXING OURSELVES: A CITIZEN'S GUIDE TO THE DEBATE OVER TAXES 94-95 (4th ed. 2008).

[9] Not all investment income of a couple residing in a community property state is split 50-50. These states recognize a category of "separate property" (mainly, property acquired by one spouse by gratuitous transfer from a third party). Income from separate property is taxed to the sole owner thereof.

A potential disadvantage attaches to the filing of a joint return, namely, each member of the couple is jointly and severally liable for the couple's aggregate tax liability. See § 6013(d)(3). If a married couple chooses to file separate returns under the rate schedule for married filing separately, joint and several liability is avoided. Moreover, in certain cases involving omissions of the gross income of one spouse on a joint return, the other ("innocent") spouse is relieved of any tax liability attributable to the omission if the innocent spouse did not know, or had no reason to know, of the omission. See §§ 66(b) and 6015(b). In addition, divorced or separated taxpayers can generally limit their liability to the portion of the joint return tax allocable to their own income and deductions. See §§ 66(a) and 6015(c), (d).

In 1951, unmarried persons having a dependent in the household were given some tax relief by way of a new "head of household" rate schedule. But other unmarried persons complained about suffering a singles penalty that was unrelated to the issue of income splitting. The argument was (and is) that Bob and Mary, married and with a total taxable income of $100K, enjoy a higher aggregate standard of living than Ted and Alice, each being unmarried (and presumably living apart) and each having a taxable income of $50K. The claim is that Bob and Mary's higher standard of living is attributable to (1) economies of scale and (2) the value of off-market household and child care services provided by a nonworking spouse.[10]

In response, Congress, in 1969, enacted a new rate for unmarried individuals (see § 1(c)) that was more favorable across the board than the rate schedule for married individuals filing separately, now found in § 1(d). This new rate schedule for unmarried individuals eventually spawned awareness that a marriage penalty could exist in the case of a married two-earner couple relative to an unmarried couple living together (and enjoying an enhanced standard of living). (The marriage penalty yielded to a marriage bonus for filing jointly as the income inequality of the couple increased.) The marriage penalty generated a great deal of negative publicity, with horror stories of professional couples divorcing in December (at a posh resort in the Caribbean, of course) and remarrying in January (or not remarrying at all).[11]

In 2001, Congress took the easy way out by abolishing the marriage penalty for low-to-moderate-income couples by conforming the brackets and rates of the § 1(c) schedule for unmarried individuals to the § 1(d) schedule for married persons filing separately (except at the high end). Congress has done nothing to abolish the marriage bonus.

---

[10] It is common wisdom that divorce lowers the standard of living of at least one spouse, and that reduction is probably greater than the increase (if any) in the standard of living of the other spouse. Marriage creates a similar dynamic in reverse.

[11] Recall that a person's status as married or single is generally tested on the last day of the taxable year. These stories caused the IRS to challenge the annual divorce-and-remarry cycle. See *Boyter v. Comm'r*, 74 T.C. 989 (1980) (divorce disregarded on theory that state law wouldn't recognize the divorce), *remanded*, 668 F.2d 1382 (4th Cir. 1981) (suggesting sham-transaction theory).

4.   Equity Among Individuals or Married Couples?

Couples with the same aggregate taxable incomes that file joint returns are taxed the same regardless of residence and regardless of how their aggregate TI is allocated between the spouses under state law. Thus, adoption by Congress of the new joint return rate schedule had the effect of rejecting the goal of tax equity among individuals and adopting that of tax equity among married couples.[12] It is impossible to have a progressive rate system that simultaneously achieves *both* individual equity (individuals with equal incomes are taxed equally regardless of marital status) and marriage equality (married couples with equal aggregate incomes are taxed equally regardless of which spouse earned the income or owned the property that produced the income).

Achieving individual equity is easier said than done, however. Going back to the pre-1948 system of individual returns would again give community property residents the benefit of automatic income splitting under the *Seaborn* rule. Of course, Congress could override *Seaborn* by providing that community property laws would be ignored for purposes of attributing income between husband and wife.[13] But community property states, which account for about 30% of the U.S. population, and beneficiaries of the marriage bonus for one-earner married couples, would strenuously object.

NOTES

1.   (a) A "surviving spouse," as defined in § 2(a), can file under the joint return schedule for the two taxable years following the year of the other spouse's death. In the year of death, a conventional joint return can be filed that aggregates the surviving spouse's income for the full taxable year and the deceased spouse's income for the period from the year's start to the date of death. See § 6013(a)(2).

(b) The estate of the deceased spouse is a separate taxpayer subject to the § 1(e) rate schedule for estates and trusts. The income taxation of estates is covered in Chapter 17.F. The estate of the deceased spouse cannot file a joint return with the surviving spouse. The income taxation of a decedent's estate is not to be confused with the federal estate tax, described in Chapter 1.D.2., which is an excise tax on the value of wealth passing from a decedent.

2.   (a) It would be misleading to think of a married couple filing a joint return as a "taxable unit," like a C corporation. The joint return system treats the couple like an equal partnership is treated for tax purposes: the partnership is an accounting entity but not a taxpayer, and the taxable income (computed at the partnership level) is attributed 50-50 to each partner.

(b) The notion of spousal income splitting under the joint return might appeal to one who thinks that married couples in fact split up their income. Such empirical

---

[12] A policy of equity among individuals would also be "marriage neutral" because a taxpayer's marital status would have no effect on the tax owed.

[13] Congress has in fact done this in various Code provisions of a more procedural nature. See, e.g., § 66.

research as exists suggests that this occurs mostly for couples at the bottom of the income scale. But the identity of which spouse spends the income is irrelevant to one who thinks that income should (as a policy matter) be attributed to the earner (who controls the disposition), rather than the spender. Doctrinally, income (except for married persons filing jointly) is usually attributed to the earner, as will be demonstrated in Chapter 17.A.

(c) Commentators disagree as to whether standard of living should be taken into account with respect to matters discussed in this chapter. For example, it has been disputed whether (as a policy matter) a one-earner married couple should be taxed more heavily than a two-earner married couple. Whatever one's view on this matter, it is not necessary that any such standard-of-living adjustments be the cause of creating a separate rate schedule (as occurred with the creation of separate rate schedules for head of household and unmarried individuals). Instead, downward adjustments can be made to the tax base of disfavored taxpayers. Stay tuned.

3.   The aggregation of spousal incomes in the joint return is argued to operate as an economic disincentive for the "secondary earner" to enter the workforce, since the perception would be that the "incremental" earnings of the secondary earner would be taxed at the couple's highest marginal rate. On the other hand, the secondary earner's income tax *withholding* rate is likely to be quite low, as it would be based solely on her expected earnings. Thus, her paycheck is likely going to be a higher percentage of her gross earnings than is the case of the "primary" earner, even with payroll taxes also being withheld. If (as is likely) there is under-withholding for the couple's aggregate TI, the couple will have to write one or more checks to the IRS to make up the difference.

PROBLEMS

1.   You are a lobbyist for gay and lesbian groups, but it appears that the federal Defense of Marriage Act will be around for a while. The state in which you operate already allows same-sex marriages. What kind of state legislation would enable same-sex couples to obtain the benefit of income-splitting?

2.   (a) Joseph has taxable income of $150K and Molly has taxable income of $50K. They are thinking about marriage during the winter. If tax consequences control the decision, should they marry in December of Year 1 or January of Year 2? What if Joseph earned the entire $200K and Molly had no earnings?

(b) Same as (a), except that Joseph and Molly are now married. Can you think of any situations in which they would be better off tax-wise by filing separate returns using the rates in § 1(d)? What if they live in a community property state?

C. ALLOWANCES OFF THE BOTTOM

The Code provides for various allowances (deductions) off the bottom in computing taxable income. When we say "off the bottom," we mean that the taxpayer's *first* chunk of income is protected from taxation entirely through these deductions before any tax liability attaches. The deductions dealt with in this chapter are purely a function of existence (status), as opposed to being obtained by spending money in a certain way. Deductions that derive from decisions as to how to spend money are usually viewed as being "off the top," i.e., as involving marginal dollars.

1. The Standard Deduction

The first "free" deduction is the "standard deduction," conferred by § 63(c)(2). This deduction is free simply for being a taxpayer, and is unrelated to how a person spends money. The standard deduction varies according to filing status. The numbers you see in the Code are not applicable for the current year, because the numbers in the Code are indexed for inflation. (In 2011, the standard deduction is $11,600 for a married couple filing jointly, $8,500 for a head of household, and $5,800 for unmarried individuals and married persons filing separately.)

The standard deduction is increased somewhat if the taxpayer is over the age of 65 or blind.

As noted in Chapter 2.D.1., the standard deduction effectively vanishes if the taxpayer's aggregate allowable itemized deductions exceed the standard deduction. Stated differently, a taxpayer claims whichever is the *greater* of allowable itemized deductions *or* the standard deduction. (The concept of "itemized deductions" is also discussed in Chapter 2.D.1.) Commonly claimed itemized deductions are those for home mortgage interest, state and local taxes, and charitable contributions, which (as well as others) are discussed in later chapters. Itemized deductions derive from spending money in prescribed ways.

2. Deduction for Personal Exemption

The term "exemption" has no precise meaning, but in the present context it refers to a deduction (unrelated to any specific expenditure) that shields income from tax *regardless of the type or source* of the income. (An "exclusion," such as the § 102 exclusion of gratuitous receipts, prevents economic income of a *particular type or source* from being included in gross income.)

Section 151(a) provides a deduction ("personal exemption") for the taxpayer in an amount equal to the "exemption amount," which is $2K as indexed for inflation after 1991. (By 2011, the exemption amount had grown through indexing to $3.7K.) A married couple filing jointly claims two such exemptions, as two individual taxpayers (husband and wife) are reporting their combined incomes on a single return.[14]

The personal exemption(s) and the standard deduction can both be taken by the same taxpayer(s). Together, these off-the-bottom deductions might be seen as approximating the subsistence level of an individual or household. However, this aim is achieved incompletely, as seen in Table 2 below, which compares the sum of the two tax benefits with the poverty level as determined by U.S. Department of Health and Human Services,[15] using 2010 figures.

---

[14] The unmarried person obtains one personal exemption, the married couple two, and the head of household two (really, one personal exemption and one dependency exemption).

[15] See U.S. DEP'T HEALTH AND HUMAN RESOURCES, OFFICE OF THE SEC'Y, 2010, DELAYED ANNUAL UPDATE OF

TABLE 2
COMPARISON OF OFF-THE-BOTTOM
DEDUCTIONS WITH POVERTY LEVELS (2010)

	Unmarried	Married Couple	Head Household + Dependent
Poverty Level	$10,830	$14,570	$14,570
Deductions	$9,350	$18,700	$15,700

3. Deduction for Dependency Exemptions

When a parent is required to support a dependent child, the child's subsistence needs are effectively those of the parent, not the child, who is unlikely to have income. However, the tax system is unwilling to give a deduction to the parent for actual support expenditures for four reasons: (1) support obligations are the product of personal choice and would otherwise be disallowed as personal expenses, (2) legal support requirements vary from state to state, (3) support obligations (being a function of accustomed standard of living) increase as parental income increases, and (4) accounting for actual support would be extremely burdensome for taxpayers. Accordingly, the Code adopts the crude but simpler solution of allowing a fixed dollar deduction (equal to the same "exemption amount" as exists for the personal exemption) for each dependent. The definition of "dependent" under § 152 is de-coupled from state law and is instead based on the taxpayer's action of actually treating another as a dependent (using objective criteria). Thus, dependent status is by no means limited to the taxpayer's children.

The definition of "dependent" is found in § 152, which requires that the putative dependent be *either* a "qualifying child" (as defined in § 152(c)) *or* a "qualifying relative" (as defined in § 152(d)). It would be tedious to paraphrase the Code, which here is prolix but also relatively straightforward. Nevertheless it is worth noting that a dependency exemption cannot be claimed for a person who is married *and* files a joint return. See § 152(b)(2). There is an age ceiling for "qualifying child," and an income ceiling for "qualifying relative." Amazingly, a nonrelative can be a "qualifying relative." See § 151(d)(2)(H). One's spouse is never a "dependent," although a married individual filing a separate return can claim an "additional personal exemption" for the other spouse if the latter has no gross income and is not claimed as a dependency exemption by a third party. See § 151(b).

Each of the definitions of qualifying child and qualifying relative posit a "support" test. A person who provides more than half of her support for the year cannot be a qualified child, and a person who does not receive more than half of her support from the person(s) claiming the exemption cannot be a qualifying relative. Each of these "support" tests is applied by constructing a fraction, the numerator of which is the support supplied by the dependent or the claimant(s), as the case may be, and the denominator of which is the putative dependent's total support from all sources. Scholarships for student dependents are excluded from the denominator of the fraction. See § 152(f)(5). Otherwise, the concept of support is quite broad, and is not to be equated with "support mandated by state law," "gross

---

THE HHS POVERTY GUIDELINES FOR THE REMAINDER OF 2010, 75 Fed. Reg. 45,628 (Aug. 3, 2010).

income," or "cash received." The revenue ruling below somewhat clarifies the concept of "support" for purposes of § 152.

REVENUE RULING 77-282
1977-2 C.B. 52

Advice has been requested whether expenditures for capital items are includible in support for purposes of determining whether an individual is a dependent. Reg. § 1.152-1(a)(2)(i) provides:

> The term "support" includes food, shelter, clothing, medical and dental care, education, and the like. Generally, the amount of an item of support will be the amount of expense incurred by the one furnishing such item. If the item of support furnished an individual is in the form of property or lodging, it will be necessary to measure the amount of such item of support in terms of its fair market value.

As a result of various cases dealing with support for dependents, the Service has concluded that expenditures should not be excluded from the support computation merely because the support takes the form of a capital item. See *Cramer v. Comm'r*, 55 T.C. 1125 (1971) (acq.), wherein the court included in support the cost of an electric organ purchased for the sole benefit of the dependent; and *Jones v. Comm'r*, T.C. Memo. 1969-104, wherein the court included in support the cost of a television set purchased as a gift for the dependent.

However, this conclusion does not affect the requirement of § 152 that the item must, in fact, be support. See *Flowers v. U.S.*, Civil No. 412 (W.D. Pa., Apr. 4, 1957), wherein the court determined that a lawn mower was not includible in the support of a 13-year-old child; and *Gajda v. Comm'r*, 44 T.C. 783 (1955), wherein the court determined that a typewriter and a microscope were not includible in the support of children under six years of age because of the remoteness of the benefit to the children.

In considering whether an expenditure for a capital item such as an automobile is support, it is noted that transportation costs incurred by or for a dependent are generally support within the meaning of § 152(a). *Hopkins v. Comm'r*, 55 T.C. 538 (1970).

Rev. Rul. 58-404, 1958-2 C.B. 56, holds that the year in which the support is received and not the year of payment is controlling.

Accordingly, the position of the Service with regard to various capital items is as follows:

Situation 1. A power lawn mower costing $200 was purchased by the parent for a 13-year-old child to whom the parent had assigned the duty of keeping the lawn trimmed. A mower is ordinarily an item that will benefit all members of the household. The lawn mower is such a family item and its cost is not includible in the support of the child for whose benefit it was ostensibly purchased.

Situation 2. A television set costing $150 was purchased by the parent as a Christmas gift for a 12-year-old child and was set up in the child's bedroom. The taxpayer bought the television set on credit and paid the entire amount of the charge in the following year. The television set was an item of support. This is a gift of property that is to be measured by the fair market value of the property. The fair market value of the television set was its purchase price of $150, which amount is includible in the child's support in the year of the gift. This is true even though the parent made no payment on the indebtedness for the item in the year of the gift.

Situation 3. An automobile costing $5,000 was purchased by the parent of a 17-year-old. The automobile was owned by the parent, who merely permitted the dependent to use it. Therefore, the automobile itself is not support furnished to the dependent. However, the out-of-pocket expenses of operating the automobile for the benefit of the dependent are includible in the dependent's support.

Situation 4. A youth purchased an automobile costing $4,500 using personal funds to make the purchase. The total support furnished by the parent in that year amounted to $4,000. The car's fair market value was its purchase price of $4,500, which amount is includible in the youth's support for the year of purchase. Thus, the $4,000 of support furnished by the parent for the youth's support was less than half of the total support of $8,500 in that year, and the parent cannot claim a dependency exemption. If the parent had purchased the automobile as a gift for the youth and registered title in the youth's name, the parent thereby would have provided support.

In the case of divorce, the custodial parent obtains the dependency exemption for any otherwise-eligible child, provided that more than half of the child's support comes from both parents. The custodial parent can, however, shift the dependency exemption to the non-custodial parent by signing a written declaration to that effect. See § 152(e). Thus, divorcing parents frequently bargain over this point.

The "multiple support agreement" referred to in § 152(d)(3) typically pertains to the support of aged parents by a group of children. In that situation, § 152(d)(3) describes whether and how one of the children may take the dependency exemptions for the parents.

4. The Tax Treatment of Dependents

Although persons under the age of majority and/or dependent on others for support are taxpayers in their own right, the federal income tax can be said to "absorb" a dependent into the income tax realm of the person claiming the dependency exemption (the claimant) to the extent of the support itself, due to the combination of the following income tax rules: (1) the nondeductibility (see § 262) of the actual cost of providing support, (2) the child or other dependent's "tax common law" exclusion for support received, (3) the deduction for dependency exemptions described above, and (4) the (leaky) prohibition against a dependent claiming her own standard deduction and personal exemption. In connection with this last item, § 151(d)(2) provides that a person who can be claimed as a dependency exemption by another cannot claim her own personal exemption, and § 63(c)(5) provides that a person claimed as a dependent by another can claim only a limited standard deduction. This limited standard deduction is adjusted annually for inflation, and for 2011 it is the greater of $950, or the sum of $300 and the dependent's "earned income" (basically, income from services) for the year (if any).

The overall effect of the four rules cited above is as follows. First, the dependent's personal exemption is wholly shifted from the dependent to the person claiming the dependency exemption. This result reflects the fact that the claimant is incurring additional costs off the bottom, whereas the dependent is presumably incurring no such costs. The larger rationale is that the notion of allowances off the bottom should adjust for family size. Next, as explained in the preceding paragraph, the dependent's standard deduction is substantially limited because support received (conceptualized as providing for subsistence) is non-income. The rule that support received (within a functioning household) is not income has never been officially explained,[16] but the best rationale would seem to be that the support provider (not the dependent) is in control of the spending of his own income.[17] Whatever the merits of the non-income rule, it would be error for the tax system to *both* exclude subsistence income *and also* provide a deduction for subsistence itself. Finally, it would be redundant if the person claiming the dependency exemption *also* were able to obtain a deduction for actual support outlays (which are personal outlays).

The rule that a dependent does get a limited, rather than a zero, standard deduction is rationalized by the legislative history as neutralizing any disincentive for dependent children to seek summer employment. This rationale seems weak where the lowest marginal rate is only 10%.

The dependent child is taxed on her earnings from services even if the parents have the power (under state law) to obtain the child's income. See § 73. This rule prevents full absorption of the working dependent child into the tax personality of the parents. Since parents have a duty to support children without regard to the child's own income, the child's wage income is, in the practical sense, presumably her own to spend. However, if the family is poor, the dependent may in fact be contributing the income to the common pool, in which case she is then effectively supporting herself (at least in part). Where a child (or any other putative dependent) effectively provides more than half of her own support, the parent loses the dependency exemption. In that case, the nondependent child obtains back both her personal exemption and her full standard deduction.

NOTES

1.　The tax treatment of support payments (no deduction to the provider and no inclusion by the beneficiary) is an illustration of the general doctrinal principle that income is taxed to the person who earns and spends on "personal" consumption, not the person who enjoys the spending. The income-splitting rule for joint returns, insofar as it can is rationalized on the notion of shared consumption, is contrary to this principle.

---

[16] The rule derives from the old case of *Gould v. Gould*, 245 U.S. 151 (1917), but the opinion in that case fails to adequately explain the result.

[17] There is an analogous doctrine whereby consumption-type benefits received by a person (outside of a family context) is not income where the benefits received are incidental to a noncompensatory business purpose of the provider. See Chapter 13.C.

2.　The standard deduction and § 151 deductions serve to further the cause of administrative convenience, because they relieve many taxpayers of any tax liability. Under § 6012, taxpayers with gross incomes less than the sum of the standard deduction and personal exemption(s) have no obligation to file an income tax return.

3.　(a) The § 151 deductions were subject to a phase-out rule for high-income taxpayers. The phase-out rule expired in 2010.

(b) Phasing out a tax benefit at a given income level has the same economic effect as increasing the taxpayer's marginal rate over the phase-out span. To illustrate, suppose a married couple has two personal exemptions totaling $10K, which are phased out at the rate of 10% of AGI in excess of $100K. The phase-out span is from $100K to $200K of AGI, meaning that each additional dollar of AGI in this range results in an additional tax base amount of 10 cents. Thus, the couple's marginal rate between $100K and $200K of AGI and above is really 110% of the marginal rate specified in the rate schedule. A rate schedule with such a "blip" is hard to justify on theoretical grounds, but it a politically-expedient way of raising taxes without raising rates or repealing the tax benefit.

(c) The § 151 deductions are disallowed for purposes of computing Alternative Minimum Taxable Income.

4.　In 2011, an unmarried taxpayer obtains free deductions totaling $9.5K simply by existing. This is the equivalent of having a zero rate bracket for the first $9.5K of taxable income. Assume that (using 2011 rate schedules) an unmarried person has $30K of TI, producing a tax of $4,075. Her "average tax rate" is 13.6% by using TI as the denominator ($4,075/$30K). It would perhaps be a more accurate measure of her "average tax rate" to factor in the 0% tax rate applicable to the first $9.5K that she earned. That is to say, in order to have ended up with $30K of TI (after taking account of her personal exemption and Standard Deduction), she must have had adjusted gross income (AGI) of $39.5K. This means that her "average tax rate" was, more accurately, 10.3% ($4,075/ $39,500), not 13.6%. This example demonstrates how such seemingly "objective" terms as "average tax rate" can be manipulated to serve the ends of political rhetoric. Thus, an anti-tax advocate would prefer to use a narrow tax base construct (such as actual TI) to demonstrate how burdensome existing taxes are, whereas a pro-government advocate would prefer to use a broad tax base construct (AGI) or perhaps "economic income" (AGI plus excluded income) to show that taxes are not nearly as high as they seem.

PROBLEM

Rita (whose husband died the previous year) has GI (and AGI) of $40K for the year, all of which is from wages. Rita can claim itemized deductions totaling $3K. State Rita's filing status and TI for the year, considering the following facts concerning her young relatives, Alice, Brinley, and Charles. Also, what are the TIs of Alice, Brinley, and Charles, based only on the facts given?

(a) Alice is Rita's child, age 12, who lives at home with Rita. Except for having earned $2K in a summer job, Alice has no source of support other than Rita.

(b) Brinley, a niece of Rita's, age 19, lives with Rita and attends Public University. Rita is not legally obligated to support Brinley. Brinley is a beneficiary of a trust established by her deceased mother and receives distributions from the trust of $14K, which (under the rules governing the federal income taxation of trusts and beneficiaries) is deemed to consist of $2K that is includible by Brinley as gross income and $12K that is excludible under § 102(a). Brinley socks $4K of this $14K away in a savings account and spends the remaining $10K on living expenses. Brinley receives an $8K scholarship from Public University and a $3K cash allowance (which is spent on food, travel, clothing, and recreation) from Rita. Rita gives Brinley a car worth $6K.

(c) Rita's son Charles, age 23, is a student at State University and lives with his wife, Marjorie, also a student at State University. Charles and Marjorie receive $5K and $2K as cash allowances (excludible gifts) from their respective parents. Charles and Marjorie earn wages of $10K and $15K, respectively.

D. WELFARE TAX EXPENDITURES

The income tax is a vehicle for providing welfare payments for households with children and for the working poor through the mechanism of tax credits, namely, the child tax credit (CTC), the earned income tax credit (EITC), the making-work-pay tax credit (MWPTC), and the household-and-dependent-care tax credit (HDCTC). All of these tax credits (except for the HDCTC) are wholly or partly "refundable." That is, if the credit(s) exceed the taxpayer's tax liability, the excess credit amount is refunded by the Treasury to the taxpayer, which makes these credits the functional equivalent of welfare payments. Like welfare payments, these credits impose "means eligibility" requirements in the sense that the credits are phased out (at various income levels) for higher-income taxpayers.

The description of these credits below is based on the rules in place for 2011.

1. The Child Tax Credit

The § 24 child tax credit (CTC) is equal to $1K per "qualifying child" (as defined under § 152(c)) under the age of 17 for whom the taxpayer is entitled to claim a dependency exemption. A credit of $1K is the equivalent of a deduction of $10K to a person in a 10% marginal rate bracket!

The credit is refundable (after exhausting any income tax liability) in an amount determined under the complex formula set out in § 24(d).

The CTC is "phased out" for taxpayers having AGI in excess of $110K (married filing jointly) or $75K (unmarried).

2. The Earned Income Tax Credit

The fully refundable "earned income credit" (EITC) provided by § 32 is a tax benefit targeted at the working poor. The calculation of the credit is so complex that it requires the filling out of a Schedule EIC which the IRS will do for you! Consequently, the details are not spelled out here.

The credit is, basically, an amount equal to a specified percentage of "earned income" (wages) up to certain indexed ceilings. Both the percentages and earned income ceilings are lowest for childless taxpayers and increase sharply if one or more qualifying children live with the taxpayer. A "qualifying child" (QC) under the EITC is basically the same as a "qualifying child" as defined under § 152(c), except if the child is married the taxpayer must be able to claim a dependency exemption for such child.

3. The Household and Dependent Care Credit

The express purpose of the § 21 household and dependent care tax credit (HDCTC) is to enable the taxpayer to be gainfully employed. This credit basically relates to child-care and housekeeping costs, which (of course) are not deductible (because they are personal or family expenses). This is the one credit (of the four considered here) that is not refundable.

The idea of conferring a limited tax credit for such outlays is to mitigate a tax disincentive for entering the labor force, namely, the tax on the portion of incremental wages dedicated to enabling the person to work in the first place. Other work-enabling expenses (those of commuting and work attire) are not deductible, nor do they generate a tax credit. The reason for singling out household and dependent care is probably that commuting and work-attire costs are incurred by virtually all workers, whereas the expenses that give rise to the § 21 credit are not. Also, some would argue that commuting costs are more a matter of personal choice than of quasi-necessity.

The targets of the § 21 tax credit — namely, single parents (heads of household), married parents with disabled spouses, and two-earner married couples with helpless dependents — are identified by the qualification rules found in § 21(a), (b), and (d), which limit eligible expenses to the earned income of the *lower*-earning spouse (unless the lower-earnings spouse is disabled or a student). The taxpayer must have at least one "qualifying individual," meaning (under § 21(b)(1)) a "dependent" as defined in § 152 who is under 13, or a spouse or dependent of the taxpayer who is disabled and lives with the taxpayer at least half of the year.

The credit is equal to the sum of qualified household and dependent care expenses not to exceed $6K ($3K if there is only one qualifying dependent) multiplied by 35%, if the taxpayer's AGI is no more than $15K. Above $15K, the percentage is reduced, but not below 20%. The maximum credit is therefore $2,100 ($1,050 if there is only one qualifying dependent).

4. Other Non-Business Credits

There are numerous other non-business tax credits for individuals, but only the adoption credit of § 36C is refundable. All of these credits amount to subsidies that have no inherent connection to concepts of income or of an ability-to-pay tax base. Therefore, they are not discussed here and will at best receive only cursory mention elsewhere.

PROBLEM

Return to the previous problem. What is Rita's tax liability (after the child credit) if Rita spends $3.2K on maid service and $5K on private school tuition for Alice?

NOTES

1.   (a) Welfare payments and subsidies are generally delivered by tax credits. In contrast, "tax incentives" usually take the form of deductions for outlays that a taxpayer might make at the margin. The standard deduction and § 151 deductions are not tied to outlays, and would not be tax incentives, nor are they "subsidies" because they are (in principle) used to arrive at a measurement of ability-to-pay net income.

(b) A common objection to deductions (that are not for costs of producing income) is that they are worth more to higher-bracket taxpayers than to lower-bracket taxpayers, because the tax savings attendant upon a deduction is the product of the deductible amount and the taxpayer's marginal rate. This objection seems misplaced if the deduction is designed as an incentive, because the whole point of a deduction is to lower the taxpayer's net cost for (as a percentage of) the outlay. Also, high-income taxpayers would (in most cases) be more susceptible to influence at the margin.

(c) Tax incentives can be critiqued on other grounds: (1) the goal might not be worthwhile, (2) the tax incentive may have little effect, or (3) the goal may be more easily obtained by non-tax means.

2.   (a) A tax credit tied to a particular kind of spending can be converted into a "deduction equivalent," which would be the credit amount divided by the taxpayer's marginal rate. For example, a credit of $1K to a taxpayer in the 25% marginal rate bracket is the equivalent of a deduction of $4K.[18] The HDCTC, which is of this type, is typically calculated as a percentage of a qualified expenditure. If qualified child care expenses are $3K, the taxpayer is in the 15% marginal rate bracket, and there is no phase-out, then the credit amount of $1,050 (.35 × $3K) is the equivalent of a deduction of $7K, which is more than twice the outlay! Still, the credit amount is less than the $3K cost.

(b) Phase-outs and "ceilings" are techniques of targeting tax benefits to the not-so-well-off. Phase-outs and ceilings are also characteristics of welfare programs. But ceilings and phase-outs can create "bubbles" of high marginal rates for those just above the ceiling or within the phase-out range, as was pointed out earlier. In the context of designing welfare programs (in the form of tax credits or otherwise), phase-outs and ceilings create disincentives to earn incremental income within the sensitive range. For this reason, welfare benefits are usually subject to long, drawn-out phase-outs that "start" at varying points. It is also hoped that the not-so-well-off do not comprehend the effect of phase-outs and ceilings and reduce work effort in the sensitive range in response to them.

---

[18] A credit of .25 × $4K wipes out $1K of tax liability.

3.　A "negative income tax" is a welfare system that would automatically provide a transfer payment to a person whose income was "negative" with respect to some positive dollar figure. For example, suppose every taxpayer is entitled to a nontaxable $8K check from the government (called a "demogrant"), but the tax rate (say, a flat rate of 40%) is applied to the first dollar of taxable income, and no deductions are allowed "off the bottom." If this system was adopted, the net transfer to the taxpayer (tax-free demogrant *less* tax on taxable income) would decrease until the taxpayer's income reached $20K ($8K tax), after which the taxpayer would make a net contribution to the government at an increasing rate. Perhaps the present system of multiple overlapping refundable credits could be simplified.[19]

---

[19]　See JONATHAN BARRY FORMAN, MAKING AMERICA WORK ch. 6 (2006).

Chapter 5

DEDUCTIONS FOR OFF-THE-BOTTOM PERSONAL EXPENSES

This chapter deals with those deductions for non-income-producing expenditures that might reasonably be thought of as being "off the bottom" because, although not directly related to the earning of income, they are significantly nondiscretionary and they plausibly reduce the taxpayer's objective ability-to-pay income tax base. Included here are the "personal" deductions for alimony, state and local taxes, and costs of medical care.

A. RELATION OF OFF-THE-BOTTOM PERSONAL DEDUCTIONS TO OFF-THE-BOTTOM ALLOWANCES

The term "personal deductions" refers to deductions for costs that are unrelated to business or investment activities. Under the Simons concept of income, outlays that do *not* contribute to the production of business or investment income, hereinafter referred to as "personal" outlays, should not be deductible at all. Under an ability-to-pay concept of income, however, subsistence outlays off-the-bottom should be deductible, even though they are personal outlays. Instead of attempting to identify actual subsistence outlays, an ability-to-pay income tax provides for "off-the-bottom *allowances*" of fixed dollar amounts, which (in the aggregate) adjust for family size and composition. As noted in the previous chapter, these allowances take the form of the standard deduction, the § 151 personal and dependency exemption deductions, and perhaps the rate schedules themselves.

These off-the-bottom allowances create a design problem, which is that any personal deductions for *specific kinds* of personal outlays should not duplicate allowances for the same items that are *already* built into the off-the-bottom allowances dealt with in Chapter 4. Although there is no official "breakdown" as to what is included in the off-the-bottom allowances, the concept of "subsistence" suggests that such allowances encompass basic living costs (food, housing, clothing, essential transportation, and basic health care) that are *universal* (common to everyone). It follows that personal deductions for specific kinds of outlays should be allowed for only those outlays that (1) reduce ability-to-pay *and* (2) are not universal (not already implicitly accounted for in the off-the-bottom allowances).

The deductions allowed under the Code for specific personal outlays that can be plausibly characterized as satisfying these two requirements for being off-the-bottom are those for (1) court-ordered alimony, (2) taxes paid to state and local governments, and (3) extraordinary medical expenses. These items can be said to be "compelled" by the state or by natural necessity. A fourth deduction for the costs of tax compliance might possibly be viewed as ancillary to the deduction for taxes (see

Section D, infra). A fifth deduction, for personal casualty and theft losses, might also seem to fall within this category. However, this deduction is not dealt with in this chapter because it relates to the larger problem of loss deductions relating to property, which poses a host of additional tax issues (namely, realization, basis recovery, deferred recognition of gain, and "character" of gain or loss) that deserve to be considered together. Accordingly, a discussion of that deduction is deferred to Chapter 24.

Court-ordered alimony is certainly not universal. On the other hand, taxes are universal. (Although the federal income tax is hardly universal, it is hard to escape the payroll tax and state sales taxes.) Allowing a deduction for taxes is therefore problematical, unless taxes are deemed to be omitted entirely from the existing off-the-bottom allowances (perhaps on the ground that they don't purchase subsistence existence). Costs of medical care are to some extent universal and included within the notion of subsistence. Accordingly, the deduction is allowed only for *extraordinary* medical costs for the year. Specifically, a taxpayer's qualified medical expenses are deductible only to the extent that the aggregate exceeds 10% (7.5% before 2013) of adjusted gross income (AGI). Thus, a taxpayer with AGI of $100K and qualifying medical expenses of $11.5K can deduct (after 2012) only $1.5K ($11.5K *less* $10K). (The deduction for net personal casualty and theft losses discussed in Chapter 24 is also subject to a 10%-of-AGI floor.) Amounts below the floor(s) are disallowed and cannot be carried forward for deduction in future years.

B.   DEDUCTION FOR ALIMONY

Section 215 allows an above-the-line deduction (see § 62(a)(10)) for the payment of cash alimony, as defined in § 71(b).

1.   Tax-Common-Law Background

The § 215 deduction cannot be understood without reference to the tax treatment of alimony that would exist in the absence of specific Code provisions. First, if § 215 did not allow a deduction for alimony payments, those expenditures would be nondeductible, because (1) deductions are not allowed unless authorized by a Code provision, and (2) alimony is not deductible under § 162 or § 212 because it is not an expense of producing income, and (3) alimony is made nondeductible by § 262 because it arises out of a personal relationship. (These same reasons explain the nondeductibility of child support expenditures.)

On the side of the alimony payee, the early case of *Gould v. Gould*, 245 U.S. 151 (1917), held that even cash payments received by a wife under a state court's decree of separation were not gross income under the predecessor of § 61(a). The opinion is murky (and is not reproduced here), but the holding is consistent with the dictum pronounced in the nearly contemporaneous case of *Eisner v. Macomber*, 252 U.S. 189 (1920), defining income as the "gain from labor or capital, or both combined." Alimony and child support are naked transfers and not the yield of the recipient's economic inputs (capital or labor). It should also be noted that alimony and child support are not excluded from the beneficiaries' incomes under § 102 as gifts. The fact that they are payments in satisfaction of legal obligations disqualifies them as gifts for purposes of § 102.

2.   Enactment of §§ 71 and 215

The restrictive *Eisner v. Macomber* construction of "income" described above was not overturned until the 1955 decision of the Supreme Court in *Comm'r v. Glenshaw Glass*, 348 U.S. 426, which adopted a broader concept of income as an "accession to wealth, clearly realized, and over which the [taxpayer has] complete dominion and control." In the meantime, tax rates had risen sharply to finance U.S. involvement in World War II (1941-1945). Some alimony payors found that the sum of their nondeductible alimony payments and nondeductible federal tax liabilities exceeded their gross incomes. Congress responded in 1942 by enacting the predecessors of §§ 71 and 215. These provisions "flip" the "tax common law" results in the case of "alimony or separate maintenance payments" as defined in § 71(b), but they assume the continued existence of the background rules described above. Even though *Glenshaw Glass* has sapped *Gould* of any vitality relating to a general conception of income, the history concerning the enactment and retention of §§ 71 and 215 amounts to a congressional "adoption" of the tax-common-law treatment of support payments that are not covered by §§ 71 and 215. In other words, support that is not "alimony and separate maintenance" as defined under § 71(b) continues to be governed by a rule of payor nondeductibility coupled with one of payee exclusion.

3.   Rationale

Alimony is a forced exaction over which the payor has no control, and the recipient obtains a cash increase in wealth under her full control. Alimony is not universal, nor does it purchase subsistence for the payor. Thus, there is no overlap with the standard deduction and personal exemption. Therefore, alimony should be (and is) deducted above the line, in addition to the standard deduction and other off-the-bottom allowances.

Pretty much the same things could be said about child support paid to the custodial spouse. The payee spouse doesn't have to earmark or segregate child support, and only in extreme cases of neglect would she have to account for how it is spent. The payor has no control over how it is spent. Perhaps the rationale for nondeductibility is that the payor is buying visitation rights and the pleasures of contact with the children. However, this is not necessarily the case.

The tax law would be simpler if child support was treated like alimony. Moreover, the payor is presumably in a higher marginal rate bracket than the payee. If that is the case, the tax savings to the payor of a deduction would exceed the tax cost to the payee of inclusion, and the net tax savings could be used to increase the before-tax payments. In other words, a deduction/inclusion scheme for child support (as with alimony) would be likely to enhance the welfare of the payee household. Nevertheless, child support payments continue to be nondeductible by the payor and excluded from both the payee's and the child's gross incomes.

4. Tax Alimony Defined

Under the Code, the deduction/inclusion scheme applies only to "alimony or separate maintenance payments" as defined in § 71(b), which will be referred to herein as "tax alimony." The definition of tax alimony in § 71(b) is a uniform "federal" definition that is independent of the various state law definitions of alimony. It is not even necessary that tax alimony be called "alimony" in the court papers.

All of the requirements listed in § 71(b) must be satisfied in order for an amount to qualify as tax alimony. One requirement is that the amounts be paid in cash. See § 71(a)(1) (preamble). A requirement that might raise a sticking point in the negotiations between the divorcing spouses is that the payments must stop on the death of the payee. (If the payee spouse is dead, she can no longer be supported.) See § 71(b)(1)(D).

The parties can "switch off" tax alimony characterization by expressly stating in the divorce or separation instrument that the payments *either* are not tax alimony (see § 71(b)(1)(B)) *or* are "child support." See § 71(c)(1). Additionally, payments that otherwise comply with the definition of tax alimony but which cease on the death, attainment of majority, or similar events with respect to a child will be treated as nondeductible, nonincludible child support in substance. See § 71(c)(2).

5. Front-Loaded Alimony Payments

An excessively front-loaded "tax alimony" payment stream looks like a lump-sum property settlement in disguise. A "special rule" for this situation is found in § 71(f), which contains a mechanism that focuses on the first three years in which payments are to be made. This mechanism, in essence, recharacterizes a portion of payments made in Years 1 and 2 as a property settlement, ineligible for the tax alimony inclusion/deduction scheme. Rather than requiring the taxpayers to submit amended returns for Years 1 and 2 (deleting what are considered inappropriate inclusions by the payee and inappropriate deductions by the payor), section 71(f) takes care of the problem by requiring the payor to include in Year-3 income the "excess alimony payments" made in Years 1 through 3 and provides the payee with a Year-3 deduction in the same amount.

This remedy can, however, produce unhappy results for taxpayers by creating a large Year-3 income item for the payor (pushing the payor into a higher tax bracket), as well as by creating a large Year-3 deduction item for the payee, which can exceed her Year-3 income after all other deductions are taken into account. That excess portion of the payee's § 71(f) deduction cannot be carried to other taxable years and deducted; it is lost for tax purposes if it cannot be used entirely in Year 3.

Section 71(f) can be avoided if the total alimony payments for the second year do not exceed the third year total by more than $15K *and* the total payments for the first year do not exceed the *average* of the second-year and third-year total payments by more than $15K. Thus, well-advised taxpayers always escape the consequences of § 71(f) by correctly structuring their payments. Moreover, the fact that § 71(f) cannot possibly apply unless either the first-year or second-year payments total at least $15K renders it irrelevant for many divorcing couples.

6. Alimony trusts

An ongoing support obligation might be made more secure through advance "funding," i.e., through the use of an irrevocable trust created by the payor spouse that provides for distributions to an ex-spouse and/or one or more children (minor or adult). Some early Supreme Court cases[1] held that the income from an "alimony trust" distributed to the ex-wife was taxable to the trust grantor (usually the husband) in most (if not all) cases, but the results could vary depending on state law.

Geographical uniformity was imposed in this area thanks to the enactment of § 682 in 1954, which provides that income distributed from an alimony trust is taxable to the distributee. This rule parallels §§ 71 and 215 for tax alimony payments not using a trust.

Child support trusts are subject to § 677(b), which provides that income that is actually distributed in satisfaction of an ongoing child support obligation of the trust grantor is taxed to the grantor. This rule is in alignment with the tax treatment of direct child support payments.

7. Property Transfers Incident to Divorce

Until Congress intervened in this area by enacting § 1041, the tax treatment of property settlements often depended on state law determinations of marital property rights. In many cases, property transfers and divisions pursuant to divorce were treated as taxable exchanges or sales.[2]

Section 1041 overrides prior law by treating all property transfers to a current spouse or (if incident to divorce) to an ex-spouse as nonrecognition events for both spouses and providing that the transferor's basis in the property becomes the transferee's basis.[3] A transfer to an ex-spouse is deemed to be "incident to divorce" if it (a) occurs within 1 year of the divorce or (b) is related to the termination of the marriage.

It should be re-iterated that *§ 1041 applies to all property transfers between husband and wife during marriage*, including a cash sale by one spouse to the other spouse, regardless of what the transactions are called by the parties. In other

---

[1] *Douglas v. Willcuts*, 296 U.S. 1 (1935); *Helvering v. Fuller*, 310 U.S. 69 (1940).

[2] In *U.S. v. Davis*, 370 U.S. 65 (1962), the Supreme Court held that a transfer by a divorcing husband of appreciated property to the divorcing wife was a taxable sale on the theory that the divorcing wife gave up inheritance and marital support rights of equal value to the transferred property. As a result, the excess of the transferred property's fair market value over the husband's basis was taxable gain to him. (Perhaps surprisingly, the IRS ruled that the former wife had no gain and ended up with a fair-market-value basis in the property received, presumably on the theory that the receipt was "in lieu of" excludible support payments and inheritances. See *Rev. Rul. 67-221*, 1967-2 C.B. 63.) In spite of *Davis*, property divisions could be tax-free if done properly, but, if done improperly prior to enactment of § 1041, they could end up as taxable exchanges of interests in property.

[3] This rule also applies to any property transfer to an alimony trust. (A transfer to a child support trust is not a realization event in any event.)

words, the importance of § 1041 transcends divorce taxation. Thus, if H "sells" Blackacre (having a basis to H of $100K) to W for $150K cash, the sale is not a taxable event to H, and W has a basis of $100K in Blackacre. The cash transfer is a gift having no income tax consequences for either spouse.

NOTES

1.   (a) If the *Gould* case had come out differently, the cash support payments would have been income to the wife but not deductible by the husband because there was no provision authorizing an alimony deduction at that time. (Recall that husbands and wives were viewed as separate taxpayers before 1948.) The Supreme Court could not have created a deduction for the husband (even if the husband had been a party in that litigation). Congress would have been forced to act, either by giving a deduction to payors or an exclusion to payees.

(b) Allowing husbands and wives to file joint returns implies that the married couple is an accounting entity (like a partnership) with two equal partners. This "entity" aspect of marriage lies in tension with the "aggregate" view of each spouse as an individual. Transactions within a taxable entity are invisible, both factually and as a matter of social norms. As a result, it is not necessary to decide whether the income that comes into the married couple is taxed to the earning spouse or the spending spouse — but it surely could not be taxed to both!

(c) The tax rules discussed above simply preserve the policy of "taxation once within the marital entity," even as the entity is in the process of unraveling. The rules, including those of § 1041, insure that untangling the marriage creates no new income or gain.

2.   (a) The tax alimony requirement that has prompted the most litigation is the "stop-at-death" requirement in § 71(b)(1)(D), which is often overlooked by litigants and judges in structuring divorce settlements and decrees. The stop-at-death requirement can nevertheless be satisfied if there is an applicable state law rule (statutory or judicial) that would excuse the payor spouse from making payment after the payee spouse's death. This requires federal judges, in a post-divorce tax case, to delve into the murky recesses of state law to try to divine whether the payment in question would not have to be made if the payee (who is still living) were to have died prematurely.

(b) In *Berry v. Comm'r*, T.C. Memo. 2000-373, *aff'd unpub. op.*, 2002-1 USTC (CCH) ¶50,453 (10th Cir. 2002), for example, the taxpayer was ordered to pay his spouse's legal fees incurred in their divorce proceedings and he did so. But the divorce settlement was silent regarding whether the payment obligation would survive if the ex-spouse were to die before payment (she did not). The Tenth Circuit held that the payment was not "tax alimony" because it divined that the Oklahoma Supreme Court would decide, in a case of first impression, that the husband's obligation would survive his wife's death. There are numerous cases dealing with the stop-at-death issue,[4] but in most of them there is no on-point state law precedent.

---

[4] See also *Preston v. Comm'r*, 209 F.3d 1281 (11th Cir. 2000) (court-ordered car repair expenses not "tax alimony" because payment obligation would have survived death); *Smith v. Comm'r*, T.C. Memo.

The federal judge in the tax litigation is trying to determine whether the state court *would* order the payment to be made to the payee's estate if the payee were dead (but is not in fact dead), a purely hypothetical question.

(c) The situation described above is ironic in view of the fact that one purpose for enacting the present version of § 71(b) in 1984 was to avoid having to consult state law. Congress could repeal the stop-at-death requirement, which is a trap for unsophisticated lawyers and serves no real tax value. A decision contrary to the tax expectations of the parties undermines their bargain made in the shadow of the tax rules. This type of wasteful litigation would disappear if all post-divorce cash payments were taxed the same.

PROBLEMS

1. Donald, if single, would be in the 35% marginal rate bracket, and Daisy would be in the 15% marginal rate bracket. Donald and Daisy are about to be divorced. Consider the following:

(a) Daisy demands $1K per month child support. You represent Donald, who does not object to the dollar figure. Nevertheless, what counteroffer do you recommend for Donald? (Hint: who pays tax on child support, and who pays tax on tax alimony?) How would you implement it in the divorce settlement? What if Daisy insists that nothing be called "alimony?"

(b) Instead of (a), the divorce decree requires Donald to pay Daisy $14K per year for 10 years (or until her earlier death), but when each of their two children reaches age 21 (or dies or marries prior to reaching age 21), the amount is reduced by $2K ($4K total). See § 71(c)(2)(A). The first year after the divorce, Donald pays Daisy only $5K of his total $14K obligation. See § 71(c)(3).

(c) Pursuant to the divorce decree, Donald pays Daisy's mortgage payment for the first five years (or until her earlier death) on the house she now owns as well as the life insurance premiums on a five-year term policy owned by Daisy on Donald's life. See Reg. § 1.71-1T(b), Q&A 6.

(d) Daisy demands custody of the two children, and Donald will probably agree. Can he negotiate for any consolation prize? See § 152(e).

2. John and Martha own two pieces of investment property (neither is a principal residence) as equal joint tenants. Blackacre has a $90K basis and $100K FMV, and Greenacre has a $110K basis and $100K FMV. They decide to divorce. What tax consequences result under the following scenarios?

(a) They sell the two pieces of property to third parties, split the cash equally, and divorce.

(b) Martha takes Blackacre, John takes Greenacre, they divorce, and they sell both properties to third parties.

(c) Change the facts so that John is the sole owner of both properties, and he

---

1998-166 (court-ordered attorney's fees held not to be tax alimony because payment obligation would have survived death); *Ribera v. Comm'r*, T.C. Memo. 1997-38 (same); *Zinsmeister v. Comm'r*, T.C. Memo. 2000-364 (same); *Burkes v. Comm'r*, T.C. Memo. 1998-261 (coming to the opposite result).

transfers Greenacre to Martha as part of the divorce settlement. Should John sell Greenacre instead and transfer $100K in cash to Martha (say, in five equal installments)? Would it make any difference if Greenacre's basis were $20K?

C. DEDUCTIONS RELATING TO TAXES PAID

Section 164(a) allows certain nonfederal taxes to be deducted even if not incurred in carrying on a trade, business, or other-income producing activity. This rule seems straightforward enough, but there is more here than meets the naked eye.

1. Tax Payments in the Absence of § 164

In the absence of any Code provision specifically dealing with the deductibility of taxes, they would be deductible (or not) under general tax principles. To begin with, income taxes and property taxes are considered to be "expenses" rather than capital expenditures. It is commonly thought that sales taxes (paid by a buyer of goods or services) would be expenses or capital expenditures depending on what was being purchased, but an argument can be made that sales taxes are always expenses because these taxes fund current government operations.[5] A similar ambivalence might apply to payroll taxes, which (at some point) entitle one to future social security benefits. Any tax payment that qualified as an "expense" would be deductible if it satisfied the requirements of § 162 or § 212.

Costs of tax compliance would be dealt with in a similar fashion.

2. What Does § 164 Accomplish?

The income tax does not, however, rely entirely on §§ 162 and 212 to determine the deductibility of tax obligations. The first sentence of § 164(a) lists taxes that are per se deductible (that is, even if not connected to "business" or "investment"). Stated differently, taxes of the types listed in the first sentence of § 164(a) are deductible even if they are connected with personal consumption. State and local income taxes and state, local, and foreign property taxes are the most important items on the list. Under § 164(b)(5), a taxpayer can make an election to treat state and local "general" sales taxes as being on the list in lieu of state and local income taxes.[6]

Additionally, the taxes listed in § 164(a) are always deemed to be "expenses" (and not capital expenditures), unless some other Code section mandates capitalization in the particular case. This "expense" characterization results from the phrase "for the taxable year within which paid" near the beginning of § 164(a).[7]

---

[5] However, as a matter of capitalization doctrine, to be covered in Chapter 7, transaction costs (which would include sales taxes) of acquiring property (where the cost of the property is a capital expenditure) are also capitalized and added to the basis of the acquired item.

[6] This rule is now scheduled to expire at the end of 2012, but this is the kind of "sunsetted" tax benefit that is often renewed.

[7] Sections 162 and 212 apply only to outlays that are initially characterized as "expenses" under the rules that characterize costs as either expenses or capital expenditures. In contrast, § 164(a) applies to the listed "taxes paid or accrued," with no prior determination that the taxes are "expenses." The

Taxes withheld, such as state income taxes withheld from wages, are deemed "paid" at the time of withholding, not the (later) time the return is filed or it is determined that the taxes are "owed."

An exception to the no-capitalization rule is found in § 164(c)(1) for (property) taxes assessed as a charge for local benefits (such as roads or sewers) "tending to increase the value of the property assessed."

Taxes that are not listed in the first sentence of § 164(a) are dealt with under general tax principles as described in subsection 1 above.[8]

Taxes are deductible under § 164 only if they are paid by the person who owes the taxes.[9] Thus, the payment of another person's property tax does not generate a deduction for the payor under § 164. Nevertheless, the other person may be entitled to a § 164 deduction for the payment, and the payor may (or may not) be allowed a deduction under a provision other than § 164, depending on the facts. See the discussion in Chapter 12.A of *Old Colony Trust Co. v. Comm'r*, 279 U.S. 716 (1929).

3. Property Taxes on Real Estate Sold During the Year

The rules just described are modified somewhat in the case of property taxes with respect to real property sold during the year. Real property taxes for a year are usually "imposed" on the owner of the property as of a specific assessment date, say, January 1. Typically, these taxes are payable in a lump sum. Thus, the property taxes for a year in which real estate is sold will usually be paid entirely by the buyer or entirely by the seller. Nevertheless, § 164(d)(1) treats the property tax as being "imposed" on the buyer and seller in proportion to each person's ownership period during the year of sale, regardless of state law. Thus, if the real property tax is assessed to the owner of the property on January 1, the real property tax year runs from January 1 to December 31, and the sale occurs halfway through the year, one-half of the tax is treated as being imposed on each of the buyer and the seller for purposes of § 164. But, in order to claim a deduction for taxes imposed, or deemed imposed, an individual taxpayer must also actually pay the taxes. At this point, § 164(d)(2) provides that the taxpayer is deemed to have paid the taxes "imposed" on such taxpayer under § 164(d)(1), regardless of who actually paid (or owed) them. Thus, in this example involving a sale halfway through the year, the taxes would be deducted half by the seller and half by the buyer, even though the seller actually paid all of them.

---

meaning of "accrued" is explained in later chapters, but the term only applies in the context of the "accrual method" of tax accounting, which is not a concern for individuals in their personal capacity.

[8] The second and third sentences of § 164(a) reflect general law in the case of taxes not on the § 164(a) list. They authorize the deduction of nonlisted taxes connected with the carrying on of *business and investment* activities, but require capitalization where appropriate. Thus, if the taxpayer elects to deduct state income taxes (instead of sales taxes) across the board, sales taxes (which then are not on the § 164(a) list) connected with the purchase of business, investment, or personal-use property should be capitalized.

[9] Reg. § 1.164-1(a).

But that is not the end of the story. In a real estate closing, some reimbursement may (or may not) be made by the underpayer to compensate the overpayer for the taxes allocable to the underpayer's period of ownership. Any overpayment (net of reimbursement) relative to the amount of the tax allocated to the overpayer by § 164(d)(1) is, in effect, an adjustment to the sales price under § 1001. Thus, if the seller is the overpayer, the excess tax payment by the seller is a reduction in the sales price (and not a deductible tax payment). See § 1001(b)(1). Conversely, if the purchaser ends up being the overpayer, the excess payment is treated as an addition to the sales price (and is not a deductible tax payment). See § 1001(b)(2). These adjustments to the sales price are reflected in the buyer's basis.

4. Federal Taxes

None of the major revenue-raising *federal* taxes are listed in the first sentence of § 164(a). In the absence of any other Code provision, such taxes would be deducted or capitalized to the extent permitted by general tax rules. However, section 275 steps in and prevents the deduction of federal income taxes, estate and gift taxes, and the employee portion of federal payroll taxes. However, section 275 doesn't list the employer's portion of federal payroll taxes, meaning that such taxes can be deducted as § 162 business expenses (or capitalized) in the same manner as the wages themselves are treated. Similarly, half of an individual's self-employment tax is deductible (above the line). See § 164(f).

Nondeductible federal taxes can be capitalized, where appropriate, under general capitalization principles.

The disallowance rule for federal income, estate, and gift taxes makes practical and logical sense. As Senator Henry F. Hollis said when a deduction for federal taxes was repealed in 1917, "It is a pure matter of expediency. If you so arrange the income tax this year that you allow those who pay it to take back a third of it next year, you have simply got to put on a bigger tax . . . ."[10]

In the case of the Social Security tax, matters are somewhat different, because the Social Security retirement program can be viewed as a kind of government-run pension scheme. But then the taxes would be capital expenditures. The system obviates the need for capitalization (and having to keep track of basis) by simply excluding a portion of Social Security retirement benefits under the complicated rules found in § 86. The alternative view is that Social Security taxes are not an investment in a personal retirement plan, because such taxes fund current benefit payments, and therefore are no different than other federal taxes.

5. Foreign Taxes

Foreign income taxes are eligible for the § 901 foreign tax credit (FTC), which is explained in Chapter 1.C.2.

---

[10] 65 CONG. REC. 6324 (1917).

The taxpayer can elect out of the FTC system for any year,[11] in which case the foreign income taxes for that year are on the list of deductible taxes. See § 164(a)(3). Since tax credits are usually more valuable than deductions, it is uncommon for taxpayers to claim deductions for foreign income taxes.[12]

Foreign real property taxes are also "on the list." See § 164(a)(1).

6. Status of Deduction for Taxes

A deductible tax that falls within any of the categories of § 62(a) is an above-the-line deduction. Examples are property taxes on real estate used in a trade or business (see § 62(a)(1)), property taxes on rental real estate (§ 62(a)(4)), and the deductible half of a person's self-employment tax (see §§ 62(a)(1) and 164(f)(2)).

Otherwise, deductible taxes are itemized deductions. Thanks to § 67(b)(2), they are not "miscellaneous itemized deductions" (MIDs).

7. Is the § 164 Deduction Justified?

As we have seen, certain taxes are deductible as a matter of positive law. Should they be? The answer to that question requires a consideration of the Simons income concept, the ability-to-pay concept, federalism concerns, and distortionary effects. In the following discussion of those matters, the term "§ 164 deduction" refers to the deduction for taxes that would not otherwise be deductible under § 162 or § 212 as business or investment expenses.

a. Simons Income Concept

Adherents of the Simons concept of income have argued that, in principle, an outlay (decrease in wealth) that does not represent "consumption" should be deducted and, conversely, that a consumption outlay should not be deducted. If one accepts this principle, then the issue becomes one of defining "consumption" under the Simons concept of income. Arguably, "consumption" is only a residual category that includes all costs not aimed at producing income for the taxpayer. In this sense, the taxes that generate a § 164 deduction are consumption that should be non-deductible.

Alternatively, "consumption" may be defined in terms of personal pleasure or self-interest. This is not a helpful approach, however. Obtaining personal pleasure from an outlay may (or may not) be a factor in helping distinguish true income-

---

[11] The FTC is subject to a limitation, which (to state it crudely) is the taxpayer's average U.S. federal income tax rate on worldwide TI times the taxpayer's foreign-source TI. See § 904(a). "Source" is determined under U.S. tax law. See §§ 861-865.

[12] A taxpayer would deduct foreign income taxes only if the FTC is not available or is diluted because of the FTC limitation, described in the preceding footnote. To take an extreme example, if the taxpayer's foreign income taxes are $20K but the FTC limitation is zero (because of no foreign-source income under U.S. income tax law), the FTC is zero. In this case, the taxpayer can stay in the FTC system, in which case the uncredited foreign taxes for the current year can be carried over to other taxable years for possible credit in those years. Alternatively, the taxpayer could elect out of the credit system for the current year and claim all foreign taxes for the year as deductions under § 164(a)(3).

producing outlays from non-income-production outlays at the margin,[13] but generally tax results should not hinge on a taxpayer's subjective state of mind, because that is a fact question that is costly to litigate and for which determinations are unreliable.

Perhaps a more objective notion of "self benefit" may help to identify consumption. Some government charges (such as bridge tolls, fishing license fees, gasoline taxes dedicated to highway use, and tuition at public educational institutions) appear to "purchase" direct benefits for the taxpayer. Thus, it is appropriate that these types of "benefit taxes" are not listed in § 164(a) as deductible. Of the taxes that are deductible under § 164, property taxes would appear to benefit those homeowners who have children in public schools to the extent that property taxes are used for this purpose. But this benefit approach is too broad to be useful because people benefit to some extent from the spending of most tax revenues, although they may not admit it or even realize it. Thus, the denial of a deduction for taxes on the ground of benefit to the taxpayer should probably be confined to the "benefit taxes" referred to above.

Deciding tax policy issues regarding the deductibility of taxes by engaging in arguments over the definition of "consumption" seems to us to be a fruitless approach. The category of "transfer payments" (which includes taxes) isn't really susceptible to analysis in terms of any concept of "consumption," a word that denotes "end use." The Simons concept of income requires that consumption not be deductible but that costs of producing income are to be deductible. Transfers fall into neither category.[14] The Simons concept simply fails to account for transfers made by a taxpayer.

b.   Ability-to-Pay Income

In terms of the ability-to-pay income concept, a deduction not connected with business or investment activity can be justified if (a) the item represents "subsistence" existence or (b) the item is an extraordinary nondiscretionary (forced) outlay.

Any taxes on subsistence existence (such state and local sales taxes on purchases of basic food and clothing) would be implicitly included in the taxpayer's available off-the-bottom allowances. If property taxes are viewed just as a cost of housing, there is likewise no subsistence justification for deducting them in addition to the universal off-the-bottom allowances. Income taxes cannot be viewed as a cost of subsistence, however, especially given that income taxes are not paid by a substantial portion of the population.

The § 164 deduction might be justified on the ground that the payment of taxes is involuntary or nondiscretionary and therefore reduces a person's ability to contribute to the federal government. This characterization is reasonable in the case of income taxes. In the case of sales taxes, the threshold issue is whether they

---

[13] This issue is taken up in Chapter 10.

[14] By "transfers," we mean transfers of money or property that are not economic income to the recipient. Gifts and welfare benefits are transfers; wages, interest, and rent are not.

should be treated as "taxes" or as part of the cost of whatever they purchase. Treating sales taxes as part of the purchase price avoids having to account for them separately, which would be an impossible task for most taxpayers. It would also accord with capitalization doctrine: transaction costs incurred by a buyer are treated as part of the purchase price (included in basis). Therefore, we think that sales taxes should not be viewed as "taxes."

That leaves property taxes. Property taxes are the cost of owning real estate (as opposed to being a cost of *acquiring* real estate). Property taxes on second and third homes are wholly discretionary, because owning such homes in the first place is highly discretionary. Property taxes on a principal residence are somewhat discretionary, as one has the choice of renting. As mentioned above, property taxes on a principal residence are (as part of basic housing costs) already included (in principle) in the standard deduction.

In sum, the off-the-bottom argument for deducting state and local taxes is plausible only in the case of income taxes, which are fairly independent of how one chooses to spend money. Since state, local, and foreign income taxes are avoided by many individuals (by reason of residence or relative poverty), they cannot be assumed to be included in the standard deduction. Therefore, if § 164 were amended to cover only income taxes, the deduction should be converted into a § 62 above-the-line deduction, i.e., a deduction in addition to the standard deduction. But such a deduction may be objected to on the grounds that it would tend to benefit only the well-off, an outcome that appears to sit rather uncomfortably with the notion that the deduction is an off-the-bottom allowance.

c. Federalism

Taxes paid to state and local governments supposedly serve similar or parallel functions to taxes paid to the U.S. government, namely, to promote the public good. Some political theorists consider it desirable that such parallel institutions thrive and not be "swamped" by the federal government and the federal income tax. Various reasons are cited in support of this position, such as pluralism, programmatic experimentation, and local control.

Nevertheless, the notion of "carving out" a sphere for state and local governments does not *require* a universal deduction for state and local taxes, because the federal tax take is not so high as to crowd out state and local governments. Moreover, the federal government is effectively barred by the Constitution's apportionment requirement for direct taxes from levying a real property tax, which is imposed by all the states. Finally, the concept of semi-autonomous spheres is not very helpful in the end, because it doesn't specify how much "territory" these spheres should occupy, the degree of autonomy, or the mechanism for accommodating conflicts among these spheres.

It can be argued that the federal government should not interfere in the *choice* of states as to what taxes they should impose. But this argument is basically that the federal government should allow *all* state and local taxes to be deducted or to allow *none* of them to be deducted. Allowing them all to be deducted would effectively reduce the net state and local tax burden of taxpayers in that state. Part of this tax saving would be captured by state and local governments, because they would be able to raise taxes to a greater extent than they might otherwise be able to do. Thus, a rule of nondeductibility may be more "neutral" than a rule of deductibility.

In any event, federalism arguments have no relevance to the tax treatment of foreign taxes.

d. Distortionary Effects

Allowing an unlimited § 164 deduction for *real estate* taxes creates severe economic distortions, given that other living costs are not deductible. The deduction not only distorts the choice between owning and renting, but also distorts the choice as to how much to invest in housing as opposed to other objects of spending or investing. The distortion is worst at high-income levels, where people have lots of discretionary income, and where the dollar value of the tax benefits is disproportionately high. Moreover, even if home ownership is a good thing, high-income persons don't need a tax incentive to acquire homes. As a "housing program," this deduction is inefficient, because it doesn't target first-time home buyers at the margin. Finally, the tax benefits can be captured not only by state and local governments but also by home sellers, because home prices can be raised to reflect the present value of future tax benefits. Thus, the deduction for property taxes actually operates as a barrier to first-time home buyers!

e. Conclusion

On balance, the case for deducting all state and local taxes, or just state and local income taxes, is not overwhelming.

NOTES

1.   (a) The federal government accommodates state and local governments by way of the § 164 deduction rather than a tax credit. An unlimited tax credit would allow state governments to soak up all federal tax revenue at no political cost. For example, New York could enact a law that provides that a New Yorker's state income liability is equal to the (before-credit) federal income tax liability. Thus, if the taxpayer's federal tax bill is $10K (before any credit for state taxes), the New York income tax would also be $10K. The federal income tax would be zero on account of the credit.

(b) The scenario described in (a) shows that a tax credit for another jurisdiction's taxes gives the other jurisdiction taxing priority. Foreign tax credit systems (described in Chapter 1) operate by allowing a credit against the residence country tax in an amount equal to the source country's tax (on the same income). Effectively, the source country has taxing priority.

(c) Obviously, a taxing jurisdiction (Government I) cannot allow a refundable tax credit for Government II's tax (on the same tax base) that exceeds the tax imposed by Government I. Otherwise, Government II could reach into the Treasury of Government I. For this reason, tax credit systems limit the credit for other-jurisdiction taxes.

2.   (a) A provision supposedly aimed at aiding state and local governments (but not wealthy investors) is § 103, which provides an exclusion from gross income for interest received with respect to bonds issued by state and local governments. Section 103 is aimed to operate as a subsidy to state and local governments by reducing their costs of borrowing money (their interest costs). To illustrate how this subsidy is supposed to work, assume that the prevailing interest rate on secure (taxable) federal and private bonds is 10%, and that the highest individual tax rate is 35%. The local authority wants to issue $100M of bonds. If the subsidy operates efficiently, the local authority will obligate itself to pay interest at 6.5%, instead of 10%, because an investor will obtain an after-tax rate of return of 6.5% on both taxable and nontaxable bonds. Here, the annual subsidy to the local authority would be 3.5% of the principal (10% − 6.5%).

(b) In practice, investors in the 35% rate bracket are not sufficient to absorb all the bonds that are issued by state and local governments. Thus, those governments must attract investors in lower marginal rate brackets in order to sell all of the bonds. Suppose that this requires the interest rate to be set at 7.2% (instead of 6.5%) in order to attract investors in the 28% rate bracket. The subsidy is now reduced to 2.8% of the principal. Meanwhile, the 35% bracket investors are obtaining a higher after-tax rate of return (7.2%) than the 6.5% return that would be sufficient to attract them to the state and local government bonds. In effect, part of the subsidy that was aimed at the state or local authority (equal to 0.7% of the principal annually) has been diverted as a windfall to high-bracket investors! This waste could be avoided by a direct government subsidy to the states equal to 3.5% of annual interest costs.

(c) Under § 265(a)(2), interest on debt "incurred or continued to purchase or carry" § 103 bonds is not deductible. This "nexus" language requires tracing debt to its uses. In general, debt used to purchase a personal residence or expended in business will not be linked to any § 103 bonds also owned by the debtor. If, however, debt cannot be tied to a personal residence or the taxpayer's business, an allocable portion of such indebtedness will be apportioned to the taxpayer's ownership of any § 103 bonds in his investment portfolio, and no deduction will be allowed for the related interest expense. See *Rev. Proc. 72-18*, 1972-1 C.B. 740.

3.   (a) An apartment renter cannot deduct the portion of the rent that is attributable to property taxes "passed on" to the renter by the landlord, because the landlord, not the renter, owes the tax (and also pays the tax). Additionally, as a matter of economic theory, it cannot be assumed that the tax is simply passed on to the renter. Prices (rent levels) are supposed to be set by the operation of supply and demand, and those forces may not allow property taxes to be passed on to tenants.

(b) The concept of "horizontal equity" arguably is not very helpful here. To begin with, relevant differences exist between owners and renters. (Renters don't have to pay the costs associated with ownership.) Second, even if owners and renters were thought to be in the same position, it doesn't follow that renters should be able to deduct a portion of their rent. Perhaps owners should lose the deduction for property taxes instead. Nevertheless, in the political arena, horizontal-equity notions can sometimes be effective to extend one unwarranted tax benefit to other groups of taxpayers that are superficially similar.

PROBLEMS

Analyze the tax treatment of the outlay in each of the following cases:

(a) Gail pays a property tax on a single family residence that she rents to others.

(b) Eli purchases an automobile for $20K, paying an additional $2K of state and local sales tax. The normal sales tax rate is 7.5%. The automobile will not be used in any trade or business.

(c) Willard is assessed $10K by the local water district for hooking up his home to the sewage system, plus a maintenance fee of $200 a year thereafter. See § 164(c)(1).

(d) Andrew sells his home to Barney on April 1 of Year 1 for $500K. The property taxes for the same year (imposed on a calendar-year basis) are $4K and are paid by Andrew on January 20 of Year 1. Barney does not reimburse Andrew for the Year 1 taxes allocable to Barney's ownership.

8.   Expenses Relating to the Determination of Tax Liability

Section 212(3) allows an individual a deduction for any expense paid or incurred "in connection with the determination, collection, or refund of any tax." Note that the deduction relates to compliance with *any* tax, whether the tax be local, state, federal, or foreign.

a.   Background

Section 162(a) allows a deduction for business expenses, including the costs of tax compliance (or tax planning) incurred in the operation of a trade or business. Prior to the enactment of § 212(3), controversy existed over the deductibility of tax compliance (and tax planning) costs not connected with a trade or business.

In *Higgins v. Comm'r*, 312 U.S. 212 (1941), the taxpayer attempted to deduct as business expenses the costs incurred in connection with managing his extensive portfolio of stocks and bonds. The Supreme Court, denying the deductions, agreed with the IRS that management of an investment portfolio did not rise to the level of a "trade or business" under the predecessor of current § 162. Rather than amend the statutory language to include investment activity within the scope of "business," Congress responded by enacting a new provision, now designated as § 212(1) and (2), which allows the deduction of expenses paid or incurred "for the production or collection of income" and "for the management, conservation, or maintenance of property held for the production of income." The phrase "for the production of income" encompasses "investment."

The issue of the deductibility of nonbusiness tax compliance and planning costs then shifted to § 212(1) and (2). In *Lykes v. U.S.*, 343 U.S. 118 (1952), the Supreme Court held that the expenses of contesting a possible federal gift tax liability were outside the scope of § 212(1) and (2), even though the subject of the gift was investment property, because the underlying transaction (effecting a gratuitous transfer of property) was inherently personal.

Section 212(3) was enacted in 1954 to overturn the *Lykes* result, but the scope of § 212(3) extends beyond the federal gift tax scenario, as it allows a deduction for expenses paid or incurred "in connection with the determination, collection, or refund of any tax."

b.   The Expanded Scope of § 212(3)

The language used in § 212(3) to overturn the result in the *Lykes* case — referring to expenses for "the determination, collection, or refund" of a tax — seems clearly to allow the deduction of "compliance" costs, including litigation expenses. But does that language go further?

Perhaps the leading case construing § 212(3) is *Merians v. Comm'r*, 60 T.C. 187 (1973) (reviewed) (acq.), which generated numerous concurring and dissenting opinions. That case involved a fee paid to a lawyer for estate planning services, which included the preparation of wills, the establishment of an irrevocable trust and transfers of property thereto, the dissolution of a corporation and the creation of a partnership (with the trust as a limited partner), and the creation of an irrevocable life insurance trust and the transfer of life insurance policies thereto. Various aspects of the foregoing were influenced by tax considerations, and the preparation of federal gift tax returns was required. The most significant aspect of this case is that *the IRS had conceded that tax planning expenses fell within the scope of § 212(3)*. See *Rev. Rul. 72-545*, 1972-2 C.B. 179. The majority accepted this concession but held that the taxpayer had the burden of proof in establishing what portion of the fee was allocable to the tax advice and the filing of the gift tax returns. The majority opinion stated:

> The petitioners rely on the testimony of the attorney. He testified that he did a "great deal of tax work," that the estate plan was based on his recommendations, and that such recommendations were made "for tax implications only." . . . [H]e did not testify as to the time spent evaluating such factors as each beneficiary's ability to manage funds, the state of the title to property, the amount of control that Dr. Merians desired to maintain over his property during his life, Dr. Merians' present and future financial needs, the reliability of potential trustees, or the state law difficulties which might be encountered in disposing of the property. . . . We recognize that in estate planning choices made for personal nontax reasons may have tax implications, but the consideration of such implications does not convert into tax advice the advice given concerning nontax problems.
>
> The bill for the legal services did not include an itemization of the services performed and the time spent on each activity, nor did the attorney's testimony provide such information. The attorney's testimony convinces us that a significant portion of his services consisted of tax advice. Yet, because of the vagueness of such testimony, the allocation must be weighted heavily against the petitioners. We find that 20% of the fee was for tax advice. *Cohan v. Comm'r*, 39 F.2d 540 (2d Cir. 1930). Such amount is deductible. The petitioners have not claimed that any additional amount is deductible under a section other than § 212(3).

Various concurring opinions raised the possible relevance of § 212(2) if the IRS had not conceded the broad scope of § 212(3). Another concurring opinion took the other concurring opinions to task for discussing an issue not raised by the parties. Yet another concurring opinion and the dissenting opinions argued that the IRS was wrong to extend § 212(3) to tax planning advice. Stated Judge Withey in his dissent:

> The legislative history clearly indicates the congressional intent to limit the provisions of the new paragraph (3) to actual contested tax liability, and precludes [a deduction for] expenses incident to a determination of tax liability prior to the period when it becomes due or contested. In my opinion, the words of § 212(3) "determinations, collections and refunds," connote an appraisal of tax liability on the basis of past or of settled events, not a molding of future events to reduce taxes.

Despite this rebuke, the IRS continues to allow tax planning expenses to be deductible under § 212(3), and this position seems to be confirmed by Reg. § 1.212-1(*l*) (referring to costs "for tax counsel").

c.   Possible Doctrinal Rationales for an Expanded § 212(3)

It is possible that the IRS has made its concession regarding the deductibility of *tax planning* expenses in order to avoid having to litigate this issue under § 212(2), where there are competing lines of authority that can bear on planning for the transmission of income-producing property. In *Trust of Bingham v. Comm'r*, 325 U.S. 365 (1945), costs of winding up a trust (including tax compliance costs) were allowed as deductions under the predecessor of § 212(1) and (2), on the grounds that they arose out of the activity of managing an investment portfolio, which is a core task of a trustee. Another line of authority (anticipated by *Lykes*) is represented by *U.S. v. Gilmore*, 372 U.S. 39 (1963), holding that costs of litigating a divorce were not deductible under § 212(2), because unwinding the marriage was a personal matter. It appears that these cases posit a distinction between *managing* investments and *transferring* investments to current or former family members, but applying this distinction to a given set of facts is difficult (as is evidenced by those opinions in *Merians* which ventured conflicting views on the application of § 212(2)).

A third possible view (not raised in *Merians* but possibly foreclosed by the two preceding Supreme Court cases) is that tax planning expenses should be analyzed apart from the underlying activity (of investing or effecting transfers). Under this approach, the activity of saving taxes would not support a § 212(1) or (2) deduction because saved taxes are not gross income, and the "production of income" requirement of § 212 (1) and (2) requires that the income in question be includible. See Reg. § 1.212-1(d) & (e). Section 212(3), expanded to include tax planning costs, avoids having to deal with these doctrinal intricacies.

It needs to be mentioned that § 212 only allows deductions for "expenses." Thus, tax compliance and planning costs that are capital expenditures are not currently deductible. See Reg. § 1.212-1(n).

The deduction under § 212(3) is insignificant for most persons on account of the fact that it is a "miscellaneous itemized deduction" (MID) that can be taken only "below the line." Of course, MID status is avoided (and above-the-line status attained) where the tax planning and compliance expenses are incurred in the taxpayer's business (other than the business of being an employee).

d.   Is There Any Policy Rationale for § 212(3)?

Apart from the possible practical rationale, suggested above, there appears to be no persuasive tax policy rationale for § 212(3).

Under the Simons income concept, these costs would not be deductible. They don't contribute to the production of includible income. Instead, they purchase conventional consumption, which surely includes avoiding the inconvenience attendant upon tax compliance.

Under an ability-to-pay conception of income, tax compliance and planning costs are highly discretionary. Taxpayers can read various IRS publications and do their own work. Stated differently, a broad range of tax compliance costs reduce the taxpayer's material wealth only if the taxpayer elects to incur them. Thus, they are not subsistence costs.

It might be argued that transaction costs of complying with a tax should be treated as part of the tax itself. But this rationale would only support the costs of complying with deductible taxes and would not cover tax planning.

A subsidy argument can be made along the lines that the government should bear a portion of the costs of dealing with burdens (aggravated by complexity) created by government itself. If so, the deduction should be limited to tax compliance costs (expenses of preparing tax returns and resolving disputes over tax liability). Additionally, the cost of § 213(3) is borne entirely by the U.S. Treasury, but the § 212(3) deduction pertains to compliance costs for any tax, not just federal taxes. Why should the federal government subsidize costs of dealing with foreign, state, or local governments? Moreover, it is usually desirable to deliver a subsidy by way of a tax credit rather than a deduction. In any event, the subsidy rationale is thwarted by the fact that the § 212(3) deduction is a below-the-line MID, meaning that routine tax compliance costs are hardly ever deducted in practice. The subsidy is mainly for tax litigation.

NOTES

1.   (a) It would appear that the text of § 212(3) does not support the government's position that tax planning costs are deductible under that section. In addition, the IRS concession on this point appears to ignore the mandate of § 265(a)(1) that otherwise-deductible expenses are disallowed if they are for obtaining tax-exempt income; the savings resulting from the reduction of taxes is not includible in income.

(b) Can a civic-minded taxpayer challenge an unjustified IRS concession, such as that noted in *Merrians*? Under current "standing" doctrine, a taxpayer cannot challenge the government's granting of unwarranted tax concessions in regulations and rulings.[15] The ability of an enforcement agency to use its discretion in enforcing

---

[15] See *Simon v. Eastern Kentucky Welfare Rights Org.*, 426 U.S. 26 (1976).

(rather than making) rules would be even harder to challenge.[16]

2. The stated purpose of § 67(a) — which disallows aggregate MIDs up to an amount equal to 2% of AGI — is to sweep certain borderline trivia out of the system. Examples cited in the legislative history include safe-deposit-box rental fees, membership dues payable to professional organizations, and subscriptions to periodicals.[17] Presumably, routine tax compliance costs are similar to these examples.

PROBLEM

State which of the following fees are deductible under § 212(3):

(a) A fee to an accountant to prepare one's income tax return.

(b) A fee to a lawyer to defend a tax fraud prosecution.

(c) A fee to a lawyer for estate planning advice and the drafting of a will and trust.

(d) A fee to a lawyer to submit a ruling request to the IRS relating to the acquisition of a business. See Reg. § 1.212-1(n).

D.   THE MEDICAL EXPENSE DEDUCTION

Section 213 allows a deduction for medical care costs for the year (unreimbursed by insurance or otherwise) that, in the aggregate, exceed 7.5% of AGI (10% of AGI beginning in 2013). Essentially, the deduction is for extraordinary uninsured medical care costs for the year.

1.   What Is "Medical Care"?

Section 213(d)(1)(A) provides the baseline definition of "medical care" as amounts paid "for the diagnosis, cure, mitigation, treatment, or prevention of disease, or for the purpose of affecting any structure or function of the body." This language has the effect of disqualifying the costs of maintaining or improving "general" health or fitness, such as gym membership or yoga lessons for those interested in exercising to maintain good health. In addition, other subsections in § 213(d), as well as Reg. § 1.213-1(e), contain refinements and special rules that include the following within the term "medical care":

(1) transportation primarily for (and essential to) medical care;

(2) certain lodging primarily for (and essential to) medical care;

(3) prescribed drugs (or insulin);

(4) qualified long-term care services as defined in § 7702B(c); and

---

[16] See *Allen v. Wright*, 468 U.S. 737 (1984) (holding that third parties can't challenge IRS grants of tax-exempt status to particular hospitals).

[17] STAFF OF THE JOINT COMM. ON TAX'N, GENERAL EXPLANATION OF THE TAX REFORM ACT OF 1986 78-79 (1987).

(5) healthcare insurance premiums (including Medicare Part B premiums and certain long-term-care insurance premiums).

However, cosmetic surgery is generally excluded. See § 213(d)(9).

A 10% excise tax is imposed on amounts paid for ultraviolet light tanning services.

Starting in 2014, low to moderate income taxpayers (not covered by Medicaid or Medicare) who purchase insurance through American Health Benefit Exchanges will be able to claim a refundable tax credit under § 36B with respect to such premiums.

2. Medical Care Capital Expenditures

An interesting feature of § 213 is that it is construed in a manner that overrides the capitalization principle. Although § 213(a) uses the term "expense," Reg. § 1.213-1(e)(1)(iii) provides that an outlay for medical care is deductible in full in the year actually "paid," even though it purchases an asset (e.g., eyeglasses, a wheelchair, or an artificial limb) that would normally require capitalization. Perhaps the deduction is allowed because the asset is not a business or investment item that would yield future tax benefits through depreciation and loss deductions. Thus, the tax system must either deliver the § 213 medical care subsidy by means of a deduction in the year of purchase or effectively deny the subsidy forever by requiring the purchase cost to be capitalized. In addition, allowing a deduction in the purchase year is much simpler than overcoming this dilemma by creating a special regime for the depreciation of medical capital expenditures.

There is a limit, however, to this generosity: a medical capital expenditure that improves *existing* property (e.g., an elevator or swimming pool added to a home for specific medical purposes) qualifies as a medical expense *only* to the extent that the cost of the improvement exceeds the increase in the property's value attributable to the improvement. The value-increase portion of the cost (i.e., the portion that does *not* qualify as a "medical expense") is deemed to be an "improvement" that is added to the basis of the property.

3. Who Obtains the Deduction?

The person who actually pays the expenses is the one who deducts them, provided that the person receiving the benefits is the taxpayer, the taxpayer's spouse, or any "dependents" (as defined in § 152) of the taxpayer. Under § 213(d)(5), a child of divorced parents is deemed to be a dependent of both parents for purposes of § 213.

The preceding rule allows "deduction shifting" to some extent. Thus, a married couple could file separate returns and arrange that the lower-earning spouse (having the lower AGI) would pay (and deduct) the family medical expenses.

4. Accounting for Medical Expenses

Only the *net* medical costs for the year (costs paid by the taxpayer in the year *less reimbursements during the same year*) are eligible for current deduction. Amounts paid directly to medical care providers by an insurance company, Medicare, or other third-party, aren't "paid" *by the taxpayer* during the year. The same is true for medical care provided without cost by or through the taxpayer's employer.

In the situation where a medical expense is paid by the taxpayer in Year 1 and the taxpayer receives a reimbursement or recovery in a later year, the receipt of the reimbursement or recovery raises a gross income issue that is discussed in Chapter 26.B. Nowadays this kind of delayed reimbursement or recovery is relatively uncommon.

5. Status as Itemized Deduction

The medical expense deduction as described above is classified as a garden-variety itemized deduction (not an MID).

Section 162(*l*) allows a self-employed person to deduct health insurance premiums *in full* as an above-the-line business deduction, provided that the taxpayer is not eligible to be covered by a health plan maintained by an employer of the taxpayer (apart from the self-employment) or by the employer of the self-employed person's spouse.

6. Relation to Other Deduction Provisions

Section 213 preempts other potential deduction sections in case of an overlap. For example, if an opera singer incurs expenses to cure his laryngitis, the expense is deductible (if at all) under § 213. The singer cannot claim the deduction under § 162(a) as a business expense, hoping to avoid the "floor" under the § 213 deduction. See *Rev. Rul. 57-461*, 1957-2 C.B. 116 (costs of maintaining a seeing-eye dog used by a blind taxpayer in the daily conduct of her business are deductible only as medical expenses).

Outlays that are related to health but fall outside of the § 213 definition of "medical care" may be eligible for deduction under other provisions of the Code. For example, interest paid on a home mortgage, the proceeds of which are used to finance an organ transplant, would not be a medical expense but may nonetheless be deductible as qualified home equity interest under § 163(h)(3), discussed in Chapter 18.D.5.

7. Policy Analysis

Under a Simons income rubric, personal health care costs fall into the category of consumption, because they aim to improve personal welfare. The costs of medical care represent consumer preference. Arguments to the effect that health care costs are not consumption operate by redefining "consumption" to mean something that satisfies the taxpayer's needs or wants only above some baseline.

This "baseline" argument not only smacks of dictating the conclusion by redefining the premise, but also seems to import ability-to-pay notions into the concept of consumption.

In any event, insofar as the Simons income concept is founded on the norm of economic efficiency (neutrality), no basis exists for distinguishing medical costs from other garden-variety consumption. The deduction for health care costs creates at least two economic distortions: (1) creating an incentive to prefer health care over other consumption, and (2) creating some incentive to forego health insurance. And, both of these incentives operate most strongly at high-income levels, where health insurance is affordable.

Under the rubric of ability-to-pay income, at least some medical care can be said to be "compelled" ("nondiscretionary") in the sense that a rational person would give utmost priority to at least some kinds of medical care. However, this principle is not easy to apply to medical care, because it involves "judgment" with respect to borderline issues. That is, how far does the off-the-bottom concept go in this context? We think that it does not go very far. Only objectively determined subsistence health care costs should, in principle, be subtracted from a tax base constituted according to the ability-to-pay principle. Subsistence health care would include those health care costs that prevent premature death or incapacitating illness or that keep a person in normal functioning condition relative to a person's genetic endowment and stage of life. Subsistence medical care would not encompass the costs of obtaining the following: (1) improvements in human capital, physical appearance, reproductive capacity, or physical (or sexual) performance, (2) meals and lodging in an institutional setting, (3) the attainment of heightened psychological states, (4) the avoidance of discomfort and non-debilitating pain, and (5) the maintenance or improvement of personal hygiene and general health. A tax base keyed to the ability-to-pay principle cannot be adjusted with reference to subjective states, such as pain or discomfort (and the relief thereof). In other words, the notion of subsistence would exclude treatments that are basically elective, discretionary, and lifestyle-enhancing. The definition of medical care currently found in the Code is much broader than one founded on that of ability-to-pay income.

A relatively narrow definition of subsistence health care would raise the issue of whether health insurance premiums should be nondeductible to the extent that the coverage under the policy is broader than the narrow definition of deductible medical care. Since such a discrepancy would operate as a tax incentive to acquire health insurance, it might be an acceptable tax expenditure, but a full cost/benefit analysis would be required.

The standard deduction is intended to include an implicit allowance for some "normal" amount of subsistence medical care. In principle, the floor under the § 213 medical care deduction should be synchronized with the implicit medical expense deduction that is included in the standard deduction. This is clearly not the case under current law because the 7.5% (or 10%) of AGI floor can easily be greater than the *entire* standard deduction.

Perhaps this deduction should be phased out at high income levels. The deduction is basically for uninsured health care costs, but persons of means should be able to acquire health insurance against most risks. Stated simply, extraordinary costs that can be reasonably avoided through insurance should not qualify as "subsistence." Lack of health insurance can be excused only where the taxpayer is too poor to afford it or where the treatment qualifies as subsistence health care but is not covered by policies that are readily available at higher-income levels.

8.   Overview of the Taxation of Health Care

Since national health care policy is in the limelight, it might be useful to review the various ways the tax system interacts with the health care system. In each case below, we assume (in order to isolate the effect of tax rules) that insurance reimbursements (if any) cover 100% of medical costs and occur in the same year in which medical care is paid for, and we also assume an unmarried (and dependent-free) taxpayer, Jo, with AGI of $50K (apart from health care transactions) and no allowances off the bottom, subject to a flat tax rate of 20%, and a § 213 deduction floor of 10%.

a.   Unreimbursed Health Care

Jo is an employee not covered by an employer health plan and without health insurance. She pays $10K of health care costs. Here Jo, who is "self insured," can deduct $5K [$10K *less* (.10 × $50K)] under § 213, leaving TI of $45K (and a tax of $9K). Jo has $31K left after taxes ($50K − $10K costs − $9K taxes).

b.   Health Care Covered by Self-Purchased Insurance

Here Jo pays a premium of $4K that fully covers her medical costs of $10K. Her net medical care costs for the year are $4K ($4K + $10K − $10K), which is less than the § 213 floor (and, therefore, nondeductible). The $10K insurance payment is excluded income under § 104(a)(3). Jo has $36K left after paying taxes on TI of $50K ($50K − $4K net costs − $10K taxes).

Jo is $5K better off here than in (a). It should be noted that the income tax views the insurance premium as a (nondeductible) expense (not as an investment in the insurance recovery), and the insurance recovery and the medical costs are treated as having offset each other. This is explained in Chapter 26.B.4.

c.   Employer-Provided Health Insurance

Here Jo's salary is reduced by $4K, an amount equal to the employer's cost of health insurance for Jo. Jo has no net health care costs of her own for the year (because the $10K is fully paid by the insurance company). The $4K value of the insurance coverage is excluded from income under § 106. Jo's tax (on $46K) is $9.2K. Jo ends up with $36.8K ($46K − $9.2K taxes).

Jo is better off here than in (b) to the tune of $800, because the § 106 exclusion is the equivalent of deducting the full $4K (from $50K), thereby avoiding the § 213 floor. (The $800 advantage in this scenario is the same as the tax savings from deducting $4K from income taxable at 20%.)

d. Self-Employed Health Insurance

This time around, Jo is not employed but has self-employment income of $50K, out of which she pays the $4K premium. Thanks to § 162(*l*), Jo can deduct the $4K premium in full (that is, above the line). Jo's income tax is again $9.2K, leaving $36.8K ($50K − $4K premium − $9.2K tax), the same result as in (c), where Jo was covered by employer-provided health insurance.

This scenario shows that an above-the-line deduction for dollars spent (that would otherwise be taxed) is the functional equivalent of an exclusion of the same amount.

e. Self-Purchased Insurance Through Health Savings Accounts (HSAs)

Health Savings Accounts (HSAs) are the creature of § 223. Ignoring eligibility requirements,[18] contributions to an HSA trust are deductible[19] above the line.[20] Internal earnings of the trust accumulate tax free, which is the equivalent of making additional deductible contributions. Finally, distributions from the HSA to pay for "medical care" as defined under § 213(d) are fully excludible.[21] This is the equivalent of inclusion coupled with a full offsetting deduction, not limited by any floors. As applied to Jo, these rules will leave Jo with $36.8K, the same result as in (c) and (d), and better off than in (b), the other self-purchase-insurance scenario.

NOTES

1. The tax results shown above for various health care financing options indicate that tax policy is already interacting with health care policy. However, the *tax* rules have been skewed against those who can't afford health insurance and who do not receive medical care financed by the employer (or by themselves as self-employed persons). To remedy this regressive feature of the tax system in a way that accords with the current general policy of increasing the percentage of the population covered by private health insurance, we would propose that the premiums on self-purchased insurance be fully deductible above the line, and that employer-provided health insurance would continue to be excluded. However, since co-payments and insurance deductibles can operate as an incentive not to over-use the health care system, deductibility and excludibility (as the case may be) for income tax purposes can be conditioned on the insurance being of the "moderate-deductible" type, at least for taxpayers over a certain AGI level. Conditions would also be imposed to weed out policies that cover items other than subsistence health

---

[18] An HSA participant must purchase "high deductible" insurance. Thus, HSAs are a feasible option only for the fairly well off who can afford to pay deductibles and co-pays out of their own pockets.

[19] If an employer makes a contribution to the trust, the contribution is excludible.

[20] See § 62(a)(19).

[21] Distributions for purposes other than medical care are fully taxable and may be subject to an additional 15% penalty tax. However, if a withdrawal occurs after the age at which the taxpayer is eligible for full Social Security payments there are no penalties. In that case, HSAs end up being supplementary tax-favored retirement plans.

care. (These items can be covered by separate insurance for which the premiums would not be deducted or excluded.) A refundable tax credit (in lieu of a deduction) for low-income individuals that is tied to the purchase of qualified health insurance was enacted in 2010 and is § 36B of the Code. If all of these reforms were enacted, section 213 would play a reduced role. Subsistence health care costs not covered by insurance (other than co-payments, but including deductibles) would be deductible to the extent they exceed a floor, which would be the greater of (a) a de minimis amount (say, $500) designed to sift out the chaff or (b) an amount equal to (say) 2% of AGI. The deduction should be phased out for high-income taxpayers, except (perhaps) in cases where extraordinary medical costs could not have been insured against.[22]

2.   The health reforms enacted in 2010 included other "taxes" (really, penalties) for individuals and businesses (with over 50 employees) who fail to participate in health insurance programs. Additionally, starting in 2013 the Medicare tax rate will increase to 3.8% (from 2.9%). Investment income for high-income taxpayers will be subject to a new 3.8% tax.

PROBLEMS

1.   Under the Code and Reg. § 1.213-1(e)(1) and (2), which of the following does (should) the § 213 deduction cover?

(a) The cost of a stop-smoking program or weight-loss program undertaken by an otherwise healthy individual as good preventive medicine. What if a physician ordered the programs because of the patient's prior heart attacks? See Reg. § 1.213-1(e)(1)(ii) (last sentence). Notwithstanding the implication of the language of the cited regulation, see *Rev. Rul. 99-28*, 1999-1 C.B. 1269; *Rev. Rul. 2002-19*, 2002-1 C.B. 778.

(b) The $1,000 cost of a hot tub with Jacuzzi, prescribed by a physician, to be installed in the taxpayer's home (which increases the home's value by $200) and used daily in order to relieve arthritic pain. See Reg. § 1.213-1(e)(1)(iii).

(c) An exotic dancer spends $2K on breast implants that enlarge her breasts to a size 56FF, which renders her appearance (outside of work) grotesque and subject to ridicule.

(d) A person suffering from "gender identity disorder" who undergoes sex-change surgery, hormone therapy, and breast augmentation surgery. See *O'Donnabhain v. Comm'r*, 134 T.C. 34 (2010) (reviewed).

2.   Might it be rational to forego health insurance despite the current tax benefits? Assume that Jay has AGI of $200K, and can buy private health insurance for $8K a year (assume the insurance covers all health care costs). Over a ten-year span, Jay incurs no health care costs in nine of those years and in one year suffers medical costs of $50K. How much will Jay have (after health-related costs and tax savings), assuming a 30% marginal rate and a 10% § 213 floor, if:

---

[22] The health care policy issue here is whether the government should be a partial insurer (through the tax system) of health care procedures that the private insurance market is unwilling to underwrite.

(a) Jay foregoes health insurance?

(b) Jay purchases the insurance, and the insurance premium is deductible under § 162(*l*)?

(c) Jay purchases the insurance, but the insurance premium is not deductible under § 162(*l*)?

Part Two

INCOME TAXATION vs. CONSUMPTION TAXATION

What we commonly refer to as "the income tax" is today actually a hybrid between an income tax and a consumption tax. While the fundamental structure of current law continues to revolve chiefly around income tax principles, the number and importance of consumption tax features continue to grow — so much so that we believe the growing tension between those alternative tax bases is a defining tax policy theme of recent decades.

Chapter 6 explores the structure of annual consumption taxation and compares that to the structure of an income tax. Chapter 6 reviews policy arguments for and against consumption taxation (relative to income taxation), describes major consumption tax features of the existing income tax, and notes the effects of having a hybrid tax. Chapter 7 explores the extent to which the capitalization principle is followed and implemented under current tax law.

Chapter 6

VIEWING THE INCOME TAX THROUGH A CONSUMPTION TAX LENS

As explained in Chapter 2, the major structural outlines of the federal income tax are based on the ability-to-pay concept of income, which asserts that an individual's annual income equals the total realized increase in her wealth (meaning all forms of savings and investment) minus any realized net decrease in her wealth other than consumption computed for the taxable year. However, some economists, politicians, and political action groups advocate replacing the federal income tax with a consumption tax regime that would omit all forms of savings and investment from the tax base.

There is, indeed, nothing to prevent a government from contemplating the possibility of relying on consumption taxes, and, in fact, at the time the 16th Amendment was adopted, our federal government raised most of its revenue through various forms of taxes on consumption (namely, tariffs and excises). The possibility of replacing the federal income tax with one or more consumption tax regimes is both one of the hottest public policy controversies in the United States and poses something of a back-to-the-future scenario.

In this chapter we will explore the principal consumption tax regimes and contrast them with an ability-to-pay income tax. The aim is not merely to inform you that alternative approaches to taxing the receipts of individuals exist, but also to demonstrate the structural importance of the capitalization principle under the income tax. Additionally, the distinction between income and consumption taxation allows application of the policy tools set out in Chapter 3. Finally, the consumption tax features embedded in the federal income tax produce behavioral effects and create planning opportunities.

A. DESCRIPTION OF THE MAJOR CONSUMPTION TAX REGIMES

How could a tax be structured to reach only consumption and not wealth increases? There are several approaches.

1. Retail Sales Tax and Value Added Tax

Perhaps the easiest consumption tax to understand is a retail sales tax (RST), which is commonly imposed by state and local governments. Under this method of taxation, amounts spent, usually to purchase consumption goods and (sometimes) services,[1] are typically subject to a flat-rate tax, whether the purchase is made with current income, borrowed funds, or funds previously saved by the taxpayer. For example, suppose Eli purchases an automobile for $10K to be used for personal purposes, and suppose further that the state in which Eli lives imposes an RST at the rate of 5% on retail sales of consumption goods. Whether Eli pays for the car with previously saved funds, with borrowed money, or with money received by a bequest, Eli will pay a tax of $500 on this purchase. Stated more broadly, the general exclusions from the income tax base of borrowed funds and gratuitous receipts, briefly described in Chapter 2, have no analog in an RST regime. But, on the other hand, an RST does not apply to receipts (from a salary or investments) until (and unless) the receipts are spent on consumption items. In other words, *an RST differs structurally from an ability-to-pay income tax in that (1) borrowed amounts are taxed if they are spent on consumption, and (2) amounts saved or invested are not taxed at the time they are earned nor at the time they are saved or invested.* Thus, investments can be made with *before-tax* dollars (instead of undeducted, or *after-tax*, dollars, as occurs under an income tax). This critical difference, which will be developed more fully in this chapter, is at the heart of the difference between income and consumption taxation.

Because of this exclusion for amounts saved, notice that a lower-class or middle-class household, whose earnings (and consumer borrowings) are spent entirely on "making ends meet," would see 100% (or more) of its "income" taxed under an RST when the income is earned. In contrast, a more affluent household, having income "left over" after meeting consumption needs, and thus able to save, can have *less* than 100% of its "income" taxed when earned. For this reason, an RST is typically referred to as a *"regressive tax"* relative to income because *the "average tax rate"[2] decreases as income increases.*

For example, assume that Donna and Dan both live in a state that imposes a 5% RST on all purchases of personal consumption goods and services. Assume further that Donna earns $50K per year and spends it entirely on meeting consumption needs, while Dan earns $100K and spends $75K on consumption, depositing the remaining $25K in a passbook savings account. Donna's "average tax rate" relative to income is 5% ($2,500 RST/$50K) and Dan's is 3.75% ($3,750 RST/$100K). Since the average tax rate is lower for Dan, who earned $100K, than for Donna, who earned $50K, this RST is a regressive tax *relative to income.*[3]

---

[1] In practice, sales taxes vary in the degree to which they focus exclusively on consumption. However, in theory, a sales tax on a business input, such as raw materials or equipment, is undesirable, because by the time a good is sold at retail for ultimate consumption, it will have been effectively taxed more than once, taking into account taxes imposed on materials and equipment used in the production and distribution process. (This problem is referred to as "cascading.") Even if a sales tax is properly designed to be limited to purely retail consumption purchases, it is not easy to enforce. Typically, a business buyer can obtain an exemption by presenting a "tax certificate" to the seller, stating that the purchased item will be used as a business input rather than for a consumption purpose. But the certificate is no guarantee that the purchased item will actually be used as a business input. In addition, out-of-state purchasers are usually exempt from sales tax, but that is another story (relating to the Due Process and Commerce Clauses of the U.S. Constitution) and would not inhibit the federal government in imposing a sales tax (although similar issues might arise for international sales).

[2] The average tax rate of an individual is his or her tax liability divided by total income.

[3] In the United States, state and local RSTs often attempt to avoid this regressive effect by applying

A variation of a retail sales tax used by some other countries (in addition to their national income taxes) is a "value added tax" (VAT), described briefly in Chapter 1. To review, a VAT is essentially a sales tax that is collected piecemeal at each stage of the manufacturing and distribution process, rather than all at once at the retail sale (and is also more difficult to evade than an RST). As explained in Chapter 1, however, the full amount of the VAT is ultimately paid by the consumer, and, for that reason, VATs are consumption taxes that are as regressive (relative to income) as RSTs.

2. Wage Tax

Robert E. Hall and Alvin Rabushka advocate what they call the "flat tax,"[4] which is a single-rate VAT, except that (unlike a traditional VAT) wages would be permitted to be deducted by business taxpayers and employees would be subjected to a separate *annual* tax on their aggregate wages for the year above a basic exemption amount. The wage tax rate would be set at the same percentage as the VAT rate.[5] In other words, only labor returns (wages) would be taxed under the wage tax component of the "flat tax" and they would be taxed even if saved or invested. Capital returns (interest, dividends, capital gains, etc.) would be exempted under the wage tax component. Thus, there would be no need for a capitalization principle or a basis concept. However, capital returns spent on consumption would be taxed under the VAT component at the time of consumption. Some progressivity is introduced (compared to a straight VAT) because of the personal exemption under the wage tax component. But investment returns that are reinvested would not be taxed at all, and to that extent the flat tax would be regressive relative to income.

It is possible to have an annual stand-alone personal wage tax. Such a tax would apply exclusively to aggregate labor income without regard to how funds are spent or saved. Borrowed money would not be taxed, and neither would business and investment returns. At the same time, business and investment costs would never be deducted. Basis would be irrelevant, because all business and investment returns, including gains from asset sales, would be wholly exempt.

Since the tax would be one on aggregate annual wages, the wage tax base could be subject to exemptions or progressive rates.

The current payroll taxes on wages and self-employment income (briefly described in Chapter 1.D.1) constitute stand-alone wage taxes. Recall that both the Social Security tax and Medicare tax apply only to labor income (in the case of the Social Security tax, up to a maximum ceiling) and contain no exemptions or deductions.

---

a lesser, or zero, tax rate to purchases of necessities (food, clothing, medicines, etc.). But because high-income people also purchase necessities and, therefore, benefit from the reduced or zero rates thereon, this approach has not succeeded in eliminating the regressive effect of RSTs.

[4] See ROBERT E. HALL & ALVIN RABUSHKA, THE FLAT TAX (2d ed. 1995).

[5] The uniformity in the VAT rate and the wage tax — as well as the fact that there is only a single tax rate instead of progressive tax rates imposed on higher wage amounts — creates the "flat" in "flat tax."

3.   Cash Flow Consumption Tax

Another kind of annual consumption tax is called a "cash flow consumption tax." Under a cash flow consumption tax, *all* cash flows are accounted for in the annual tax base. For example, all the following would be initially included as potential consumption: wages, borrowed money, and the entire "amount realized" on the sale of property. Any cash amount that is *not* spent on consumption, including repayments of principal and interest on loans and all business and investment outlays (including capital expenditures), would then be deducted from the tax base, leaving only amounts spent on consumption in the tax base.[6] Of course, sticky questions of categorization would remain. (Would students be taxed on the amount borrowed for college in the year of receipt, with no offsetting deduction for the tuition paid?) But the intent is, generally speaking, to tax only amounts spent on consumption and not business and investment outlays.

Since the cash flow consumption tax is an annual tax, it can be subject to exemptions and progressive rates.

The core structural difference between a cash flow consumption tax and an income tax is that *the cash flow consumption tax is unconcerned with changes in wealth*. This distinction causes a cash flow consumption tax (as well as an RST, a VAT, or a wage tax) to be lacking three essential features of an income tax, namely, (1) the capitalization principle (i.e., the rule that capital expenditures are per se nondeductible); (2) the no basis mechanism, and (3) the is no borrowing exclusion. Each of these points is now explored in greater detail.

First, the capitalization principle provides that capital expenditures under an income tax are nondeductible, because these expenditures do not result in any decrease in wealth (a decrease in wealth being a prerequisite for any deduction under an income tax). Under a cash flow consumption tax, in contrast, an outlay that would be characterized as a capital expenditure under an income tax is currently deductible *if* the acquired asset is a business or investment asset, because such an outlay represents a nonconsumption use.

Second, because of the absence of the capitalization principle, no need exists for assets to have basis representing previously taxed dollars. In an income tax, basis serves the function of a baseline for discerning between the taxpayer's old, previously taxed wealth residing in an asset and a new, untaxed increase in wealth with respect to that asset. This function is not relevant under a cash flow consumption tax, because 100% of the dollars invested in business and investment assets represent untaxed amounts (due to the deduction allowed at the time of purchase). Where basis doesn't exist, it follows that the entire amount realized on the sale of such an asset is initially included in the tax base as *potential* consumption. Indeed, *all* economic gross returns with respect to business and

---

[6] Although an annual personal consumption tax was favored in principle by such illustrious persons as John Stuart Mill, Alfred Marshall, and A.C. Pigou, the concept and details were first worked out by Irving Fisher (1867–1947), with refinements by William Vickrey (1914–1996) and Nicholas Kaldor (1908–1986). The concept achieved academic prominence in the United States as the result of William D. Andrews, *A Consumption-Type or Cash-Flow Personal Income Tax*, 87 HARV. L. REV. 1113 (1974).

investment assets (both principal and income) are includible in the cash flow consumption tax base.

Third, borrowed cash is not included in the ability-to-pay income tax base, because the borrowing does not increase net wealth (due to the offsetting liability). Under a cash flow consumption tax, in contrast, borrowed cash represents potential consumption power and is thus included in the tax base, but repayments of debt principal are deductible. It might seem odd to include borrowed amounts in the tax base under a cash flow consumption tax, but the oddity quickly dissipates if you compare the result to an RST, which the cash flow consumption tax is intended to mimic. Recall the car purchase in Section A.1, supra, for $10K, which was subject to an RST at 5%, even if the car were purchased entirely with borrowed money.

PROBLEM

If we were to eliminate the capitalization principle from the federal income tax, into what kind of tax would it be transformed?

4. Comparison of Retail Sales Tax, Wage Tax, and Cash Flow Consumption Tax

A stand-alone wage tax is actually a form of consumption taxation, even though wages used to fund investments are still subject to tax. This resemblance will be revealed by a comparison of investment results under a wage tax, an RST, and a cash flow consumption tax. Although these three kinds of taxes look superficially quite different, a wage tax (which applies only to labor returns, such as wages and salaries, and specifically exempts capital returns, such as interest, dividends, and capital gains), an RST, and a cash flow consumption tax can all reach identical investment results under certain conditions, such as identical pre-tax returns and no change in tax rates over time. The only difference is that the tax comes at the *front end* under a wage tax and at the *back end* under an RST and a cash flow consumption tax.

To illustrate, assume that Jane invests $100K from her current wages for one year at an interest rate of 10% per year, where the tax rate is 30%, and that after one year Jane liquidates the investment and consumes the total net return (income and principal after tax). Compare the results below under an RST, a cash flow consumption tax, and a wage tax.

RST

Gross Wages Invested (excluded from tax base)	$100,000
Tax on Invested Wages	$0
Net Investment After Tax	$100,000
Gross Return [$100,000 + (0.10 × $100,000)]	$110,000
Tax (30%) on Consumption of Gross Return	$33,000
Net Consumption	$77,000[7]

Cash Flow Consumption Tax

Gross Wages Invested (fully deductible)	$100,000
Tax on Invested Wages (30%)	$0
Net Investment After Tax	$100,000
Gross Return [$100,000 + (0.10 × $100,000)]	$110,000
Tax (30%) on Consumption of Gross Return	$33,000
Net Consumption	$77,000[8]

Thus, the RST and cash flow consumption tax outcomes are identical even though these taxes have very different structures as explained supra.

Wage Tax

Gross Wages Available for Investment	$100,000
Tax on Wages (30%)	$30,000
Net Investment After Tax	$70,000
Gross Return [$70,000 + (0.10 × $70,000)]	$77,000
Tax (30%) on Consumption of Gross Return	$0
Net Consumption	$77,000

In sum, Jane's outcomes under all three consumption tax regimes are the same ($77K net consumption)! Thus, although the wage tax looks like a narrow-base income tax (wage income only), its equivalence in result to the RST and the cash flow consumption tax shows that the wage tax is actually a form of consumption taxation.

And these identical $77K after-tax outcomes are notably different from the result under an income tax, where: (1) The capitalization principle makes the purchase of an investment a nondeductible capital expenditure; (2) the nondeductibility of the capital expenditure creates basis; and (3) the return on the investment, after subtracting basis, is includible in gross income. Thus, the results of Jane's

---

[7] Under a 30% RST, when Jane makes consumer purchases totaling $110K, she will pay $110K to the sellers but $33K of that amount will go to the government, and only $77K will pay for the goods and services that she actually enjoys.

[8] If Jane is informed and self-disciplined, she will understand that the inclusion of $110K in a 30% cash flow consumption tax base means that she must pay $33K of tax on the $110K. Thus, she will set aside this amount for her tax payment, and can spend only $77K on consumption items.

investment under an income tax would be:

Income Tax

Gross Wages Available for Investment	$100,000
Tax on Wages (30%)	$30,000
Net Investment After Tax	$70,000
Gross Return [$70,000 + (0.10 × $70,000)]	$77,000
Tax on $7,000 "Income" ($77,000 – $70,000 basis)	$2,100
Net Consumption ($77,000 – $2,100)	$74,900

PROBLEM

In Year 1, Clara has wage income of $60K, borrows $10K cash with which she purchases stock. She also puts $1K in a savings account. In Year 2, Clara again has wage income of $60K, sells the stock for $9K pays $400 interest on the loan, and earns $40 interest on her savings account. She withdraws the interest and spends it on groceries. What results for Clara under an income tax? The cash flow consumption tax? The wage tax? The RST? Don't forget the varying treatments of borrowing under the four taxes.

B.   AN INTRODUCTION TO THE TIME VALUE OF MONEY

An understanding of the significance of consumption taxes (relative to income taxes) requires application of time-value-of money analysis. Under time-value-of-money analysis, an amount paid or received in Year 1 is carried forward to a future date (and translated into a future value or cost) by using compound-interest analysis, and an amount to be paid or received at a future date is brought backwards to the present (and translated into a present value or cost) through present-value analysis. Present-value analysis is basic to tax policy analysis and tax planning, as well as to the valuation of assets.

1.   Compound-Interest Analysis

Compound interest means that interest is earned on principal plus prior earned interest that has not yet been paid to the investor.[9] Interest can be compounded on an annual, semi-annual, quarterly, monthly, or daily basis. To keep things manageable, our examples compute compound interest on an annual basis.

Assume that Anne loans Matthew $1K at the beginning of Year 1 for three years at a rate of 10% per annum compounded annually, with the principal and compound interest payable to Anne in a lump sum at the close of Year 3. When Year 1 ends, Anne will have earned $100 of interest ($1K × .10), *but Matthew will not pay it* to her. At the start of Year 2, the loan amount will effectively become $1,100 ($1,000 + $100 of unpaid interest), and at year end Anne will have earned $110 of interest for

---

[9] In contrast, simple interest is interest earned only on the original principal. Simple interest would be used in commerce and finance only if the interest is actually paid out on a periodic basis, as in the case of a coupon bond.

Year 2 ($1,100 × .10). Once again, the interest will not be currently paid to Anne but will, instead, be added to the loan amount at the beginning of Year 3, causing it to increase to $1,210 ($1,100 + $110). Consequently, Anne will earn $121 of interest for Year 3 ($1,210 × .10), and at the close of the year Matthew will pay her $1,331 composed of the following elements:

Original loan principal	$1,000
Year-1 interest	100
Year-2 interest	110
Year-3 interest	121
Total	$1,331

The total receipts of $1,331[10] are often called "total return(s)," "future return(s)," or "future value." Note that the interest component grows larger year by year, since the interest is computed on a "principal" amount that includes the accrued (earned) but unpaid interest of prior years. If the loan were for, say, thirty years, the $1K would grow to $17,450. The demonstrated capacity of compound interest to make an initial investment grow very large over time causes some people to get positively euphoric and refer to the "miracle of compound interest," a hyperbolic phrase that you will encounter from time to time in financial literature.

2. Present-Value Analysis

Present-value analysis is simply the reverse of compound-interest analysis. To illustrate, go back to the example of Anne and Matthew. Now, however, assume that Anne sells Blackacre to Matthew on January 1 of Year 1 in exchange for Matthew's promise to pay her a lump sum of $1,331 three years later. Intuition suggests that money not available until a future time isn't presently worth as much as money in hand. This intuition is correct, because Matthew would have to set aside cash of only $1K on January 1 of Year 1 to generate the $1,331 needed to pay Anne on

---

[10] This example grinds out a compound-interest calculation in a methodical step-by-step fashion. Fortunately, there is a formula that short-cuts the intermediate steps. In the compound-interest formula set forth immediately below, and in the present-value formula explained in Subsection 2 below, "P" stands for present value or present amount (as the case may be), "A" stands for the future amount, "n" stands for the number of interest computation periods between the present and future (days, months, years, etc.), and "i" stands for the interest rate or discount rate (as the case may be) expressed as a decimal amount per period. Thus, a 12% annual interest rate is expressed as 0.12, which is 0.01 (0.12/12) when converted to a monthly rate and 0.0003287 (0.12/365) when converted to a daily interest rate. The "n" and the "i" must be expressed in terms of the same time unit. For example, if compounding (or discounting) is to occur on a monthly basis for a 30-month period, the "n" is 30 and the "i" is a monthly rate (not an annual or daily rate). Applying the preceding terminology to a compound-interest computation, if P dollars are invested at an annually compounded interest rate "i" for say 3 years, the principal "P" will grow to "A" future value as follows:

$$A = P + Pi + i(P + Pi) + i[P + Pi + i(P + Pi)], \text{ or}$$
$$A = P(1 + i)^3$$

If "n" periods is substituted for "3," the general compound-interest formula is produced:

$$A = P(1 + i)^n$$

Table A of the Appendix to this book allows one to perform compound-interest calculations easily without a calculator or this formula.

December 31 of Year 3, if Matthew can earn 10% interest per annum compounded. Thus, if Matthew and Anne negotiate a January 1, Year 1 payment by Matthew to Anne that will discharge Matthew's Year 3 obligation, Anne cannot legitimately demand more than $1K, and Matthew cannot legitimately offer to pay less than $1K. Any amount other than $1K would alter the initial bargain, because $1K is the present value of $1,331 from Anne's point of view and the present cost of $1,331 from Matthew's perspective.[11]

C. REPLACING THE INCOME TAX WITH A CONSUMPTION TAX

An understanding of time-value-of-money analysis facilitates the task of investigating the contrasts between consumption taxation and ability-to-pay income taxation. At the present time, each of the three forms of consumption taxation has advocates who insist that Congress should enact their favored regime as a replacement for the federal income tax. To simplify the analysis of that debate, we will focus on the cash flow consumption tax, while keeping in mind that all three forms of consumption taxation effectively remove saved amounts from the tax base and that all three can be structured to produce identical results.

1. Effect on Savings

The basic argument in favor of the cash flow consumption tax is that it would produce true tax "neutrality" between consumption and savings. To illustrate this point, assume that Julie presently has $100 of wage income to consume or save for one year and that she can save at a 10% per annum interest rate. If there were a flat-rate 50% ability-to-pay income tax, Julie would actually have only $50 to save after tax because the capitalization principle would deny her a deduction for her savings. She would earn $5 ($50 × .10) over the next year, pay a $2.50 tax on that amount, and have $52.50 to consume at the end of the one-year saving period. But Table B in the Appendix shows that the present value of Julie's $52.50 at a 10% discount rate is only $47.72, whereas she could have immediately consumed $50 if she had refrained from saving. Therefore, it is argued, the income tax has made present consumption more appealing than saving for future consumption.

---

[11] As was the case with compound interest, our elegant and engaging explanation of present value and present cost has been boiled down to a dry formula, which is derived from the compound-interest formula. Whereas "A" is the "unknown" in the compound-interest formula, "P" is the "unknown" in the present-value formula. That is to say, the present value of a known or estimated future amount ("A") is, conceptually speaking, that unknown amount ("P") which, if invested at rate "i" over period "n" on a compound basis, would produce the known or estimated "A." Thus, the present-value formula is the compound interest formula "solved" for "P" (instead of "A"):

$$P = A/(1 + i)^n$$

In the present-value formula, the "i" is referred to as the "discount rate" because the formula discounts (shrinks) a future amount to a smaller present value. Generally, the discount rate used for a particular computation is the interest rate that could be obtained on investments of a comparable risk and duration to the investment being considered. The lower the risk, the lower the discount rate. The lowest-risk type of investment (U.S. government obligations), being the most certain, is often used to obtain a "default" discount rate. Table B in the Appendix facilitates present value calculations without having to use the formula.

In contrast, under a 50% flat-rate cash flow consumption tax, Julie could consume $50 today ($100 cash *less* 50% consumption tax) or save for one year and then consume $55 ([$100 deductible savings *plus* $10 investment return] *less* $55 tax). Assuming a 10% discount rate, the present value of Julie's $55 of deferred consumption is $50, which exactly equals the amount she could have consumed if she had not saved. Thus, in this example, the cash flow consumption tax is neutral with respect to Julie's decision to consume $50 now or to save and consume $55 one year from now. The argument might be that neutrality is good in itself (i.e., it is economically efficient by not distorting choices). Others may make the behavioral claim that Julie and millions of others will save more under a cash flow consumption tax regime than they would under an income tax, and follow that with the economic claim that the incremental savings will result in greater economic growth.

There are, however, reasons to be uncertain about these claims. First, savings is not solely about deferring consumption: savings may be devoted to making bequests or gaining power. Even assuming that savings equates with deferred consumption, it is not clear that an income tax significantly distorts the consumption/savings choice. Suppose Julie is choosing between a $50 restaurant dinner today and a restaurant dinner one year from now. Since most people prefer present consumption to the future consumption of the same thing to such an extent that they are willing to borrow money and pay interest to obtain it, it is implausible to assume that a consumption tax will override this preference.[12] Even if Julie has a slight preference for future consumption, it is unlikely that her choice will be driven by a financial calculation.[13] After all, she can spend slightly less on dinner next year.[14]

The claims of increased savings and an expanding economy are also somewhat elusive. A switch to a 50% cash flow consumption tax could cause the market interest rate on Julie's savings to fall from 10% (as it was under the realization income tax) to 5%, because obligors could pay less interest and still give investors the same after-tax rate of return as before. (Only $5 of before-tax interest on $100 savings would be required to produce the same $2.50 after-tax net return that Julie earned in the 50% income tax scenario). If interest rates adjust downward, the incentive for Julie to save is reduced. Nevertheless, a reduction in interest rates (etc.) would reduce costs of raising business capital, a point that will be taken up shortly, but this can also be accomplished by action of the Federal Reserve Board.

Another problem is that a tax "on" consumption does not necessarily result in a shift to savings. Because of the fact that the cash flow consumption tax base is

---

[12] Stated differently, it would seem that the discount rate would have to be vastly larger than 10% in order for the difference, under an income tax, between the value of present consumption ($50) and the present value of future consumption ($47.72) to be sufficiently large to play a significant role in Julie's thinking.

[13] However, where a taxpayer is *choosing between different financial investments* offering the same before-tax rate of return, and one alternative is taxed under income tax rules and the other is taxed under cash flow consumption tax rules, this disparate tax treatment can have a powerful effect on the taxpayer's decision to select one investment or the other, as shown infra Sections E and F.

[14] And people spend less on basic living after they retire even if income remains unchanged.

smaller than that of an ability-to-pay income tax (because savings are deducted), the cash flow consumption tax rates will surely have to be higher than the income tax rates in order to generate the same revenue for the government. The table below illustrates what might happen as a result. It assumes that, under either the income tax or the cash flow consumption tax, Julie has $100K of total income, must pay a nondeductible $30K tax to provide the necessary amount of revenue for the government, and has grown accustomed to consuming $60K per year (and will do her best to maintain that lifestyle regardless of changes in the tax regime).

	Income Tax	Cash Flow Consumption Tax
Total Income	$100,000	$100,000
Consumption	$ 60,000 (nondeductible)	$ 60,000 (nondeductible)
Savings	$ 10,000 (nondeductible)	$ 10,000 (deductible)
Tax Base	$100,000	$ 90,000
Tax	$ 30,000 (nondeductible)	$ 30,000 (nondeductible)

Thus, since Julie is "locked in" to $60K of annual consumption and $30K of tax, the cash flow consumption tax does not allow her to increase her $10K of savings because $10K is all that she has left after consuming $60K and paying $30K of tax. Stated differently, she cannot increase her savings because the switch to a consumption tax does not produce the tax reduction that is necessary to make a savings increase possible. Also note that the consumption tax rate is here 33.33 percent ($30K/$90K), whereas the income tax rate is 30 percent ($30K/$100K).

If Julie and her fellow taxpayers do respond to replacement of an income tax by a cash flow consumption tax, then the tax rate must be raised even higher, as illustrated by the following example, in which Julie, under the cash flow consumption tax, increases her savings by $10K and reduces her consumption by the same amount:

	Income Tax	Cash Flow Consumption Tax
Total Income	$100,000	$100,000
Consumption	$60,000 (nondeductible)	$50,000 (nondeductible)
Savings	$10,000 (nondeductible)	$20,000 (deductible)
Tax Base	$100,000	$80,000
Tax	$30,000 (nondeductible)	$30,000 (nondeductible)
Tax Rate	$30,000/$100,000 = 30%	$30,000/$80,000 = 37.5%

This would be a problematic scenario, because not only would higher tax rates provide a greater incentive for taxpayers to engage in economically inefficient tax avoidance, but they would also create a constituency that would politically oppose switching to a cash flow consumption tax system.

The foregoing analysis is theoretical. What about the empirical evidence? In economics jargon, the response of individual taxpayers to savings incentives is referred to as the "elasticity of savings." Empirical research on this issue is inconclusive, but in general it seems that the elasticity of savings in the United States is fairly low, meaning that individuals are largely unresponsive to tax system savings incentives. As two respected public finance economists who surveyed the literature put it: "given the state of the evidence, any claim that reducing or eliminating the tax on the return to saving would lead to large increases in saving must be regarded with skepticism."[15]

It is also claimed that if a switch to a cash flow consumption tax did produce a significant savings increase, economic growth would likewise increase because the additional savings would make more capital available to finance business expansion. Alternatively, the market would react to the increased supply of savings by reducing the before-tax rates of return that businesses must pay to attract those savings. Either way, the resulting business prosperity would, so this argument goes, ultimately result in increased wages for laborers (who would be the ones taxed).

Several reasons are usually given, however, for being uncertain about a strong economic growth effect from a changeover to a cash flow consumption tax. First, in this worldwide economy, investment dollars to expand the U.S. economy don't need to come from American savers; German, Japanese, etc., investors are perfectly acceptable. However, a decrease in before-tax rates of return resulting from increased savings by Americans could drive foreign investors away.[16] Nor is there any guarantee that if Americans increased their savings, the extra investment dollars would be invested in the United States instead of overseas, or invested at all. Second, a change to a cash flow consumption tax with its narrower base could cause the government to chill economic growth by either raising tax rates or incurring deficits and borrowing to such a degree as to dampen economic growth.

Perhaps most provocatively, there is historically a negative correlation between wealth and income inequality on the one hand and economic growth rates on the other. The "golden age" of high U.S. growth rates of 5% per year occurred between the end of World War II and roughly 1973, a time of high marginal rates on the wealthy and much less income and wealth inequality than in the period after 1973. Since replacement of the federal income tax with a cash flow consumption tax, even with graduated rates, may result in even greater wealth and income concentration at the top (as the savings of wealthy persons are freed entirely from tax), the historical trend suggests that replacement could actually correlate with *lower* economic growth rates (though, as any good statistician will tell you, correlation is *not* causation).

2. Distributional Considerations

In evaluating the wisdom of replacing the federal income tax with a consumption tax regime, it is useful to consider distributional consequences, i.e., the extent to which a revenue-neutral replacement (a switch that does not change total tax collections) would shift the burden of taxation from lower-income individuals to wealthier individuals or vice versa. Economic studies of this issue have consistently shown that the shift would be downward, with the result that the highest income

---

[15] JOEL SLEMROD & JON BAKIJA, TAXING OURSELVES: A CITIZEN'S GUIDE TO THE DEBATE OVER TAXES 130 (4th ed. 2008).

[16] Many foreign investors owe little or no tax on U.S. portfolio investments. For them, a shift to a consumption tax would not increase their likelihood of investing in the United States, and, if pre-tax returns fell, would encourage them to invest elsewhere.

taxpayers would get a tax cut, in comparison to their situation under the present federal income tax, and everyone else would experience a tax increase.[17]

To understand why this is so, recall that the effect of consumption tax regimes is to remove amounts that are saved from the tax base. In the United States, savings are heavily concentrated in the hands of wealthy individuals.[18] Thus, a switch from an ability-to-pay income tax, which taxes additions to savings, to a consumption tax regime that exempts saved amounts would inevitably favor those who save the most — generally high-income taxpayers.[19]

Are high-income individuals overtaxed under the present regime and in need of the relief that would come to them from replacing the federal income tax with a consumption tax regime? The case for a positive answer is hard to make, because the latest IRS data in the table below unequivocally shows that, since 1986, the percentage of overall adjusted gross income received by the top 10% of U.S. individual taxpayers has always been disproportionately large and has been steadily increasing in spite of prevailing income tax rates:[20]

Year	% AGI Rec'd by Top 10%
1986	35.12
1990	38.77
1994	39.19
1998	43.77
2002	41.77
2006	47.32
2008	48.05

3. Tax Justice Norms

As previously noted, the federal income tax fits comfortably under the ability-to-pay tax justice norm because receipts that are saved or invested (capital expenditures) are nondeductible and thus remain in the tax base.

The "benefit" norm might also require that if Taxpayer A is able to exploit the market to earn $500K, saving $400K, and consuming $100K she should be required to contribute more to the costs of maintaining our economic infrastructure (which

---

[17] See SLEMROD & BAKIJA, supra note 15, at 253-62; John Buckley & Diane Lim Rogers, *Is a National Retail Sales Tax in Our Future?*, 104 TAX NOTES 1277, 1280-82 (Sept. 13, 2004); Office of Tax Analysis, U.S. Treas. Dep't, *"New" Armey-Shelby Flat Tax Would Still Lose Money, Treasury Finds*, 70 TAX NOTES 451, 453-56 (Jan. 22, 1996).

[18] See Brian G. Rauh, *Personal Wealth, 2004*, IRS STATISTICS OF INCOME BULLETIN 282, 298 (Fall 2008) (in 2004, the 357,000 U.S. adult individuals with a net worth of $5M or larger owned slightly more than 50% of all assets, i.e., savings and investments, owned by the U.S. adult population).

[19] Wealthy individuals are also generally high-income taxpayers, because the types of income produced by the invested savings of individuals (rents, royalties, interest, capital gains, etc.) are concentrated among high-income taxpayers. See Justin Bryan, *Individual Income Tax Returns, 2007*, IRS STATISTICS OF INCOME BULLETIN 5, 22-29 (Fall 2009).

[20] Adrian Dungan & Kyle Mudry, *Individual Income Tax Rates and Shares, 2007*, IRS STATISTICS OF INCOME BULLETIN 18, 63 (Winter 2010).

creates the institutional conditions for lawfully acquiring income and wealth) than Taxpayer B, who earns $100K and spends it all on consumption.

If the tax base is defined under the "standard of living" (i.e., well-being or "utility") norm, the status of savings and investment is somewhat ambiguous. On the one hand, receipts that are saved or invested do not produce immediate personal consumption as such. On the other hand, the noncash wealth that results from savings and investment contributes to a taxpayer's present standard of living by providing current utility in the form of security and power over and above the anticipated future returns. As a practical matter, however, this utility cannot be readily valued. Indeed, consumption taxes do not purport to tax utility. They tax spending, not enjoyment of economic benefits.

It has been claimed since the time of Hobbes that a consumption tax accords with a general (nontax) moral norm that favors rewarding contributions to social resources (savings), but that views consumption as suspect because it allegedly reduces society's resources. This argument is pseudo-economics disguised as a moral norm.[21] Demand drives the economy as well as supply. Supply without demand is waste. As far as individual morality is concerned, savings is not motivated by impulses of generosity, but of self-aggrandizement. Finally, the moral issue of ecology (the resources of the planet) is violated only as to nonrenewable resources, a problem which far transcends the tax system.

4. Pragmatic Norms

Advocates of a cash flow consumption tax claim that these taxes better satisfy pragmatic norms than the ability-to-pay income tax. Various problems that exist in the income tax that would not exist under a cash flow consumption (or wage) tax include: (1) distinguishing between capital expenditures and expenses, (2) having to keep track of basis, and (3) having to choose correct capital recovery (depreciation) methods.

The cash flow consumption tax is not free of implementation problems, however. One is the tax treatment of personal-use assets (i.e., assets, such as a personal residence, that produce consumption benefits). If the purchase of such assets is not deductible, then a cost basis for such assets would have to be attached to these assets to avoid inclusion of the full proceeds of their sale and double taxation of the same dollars. Alternatively, their cost could be deducted as investments, but then it would seem necessary to include "imputed income" (the annual rental value of the property), as well as the sales proceeds, in the tax base. Either approach would diminish the alleged simplicity of a cash flow consumption tax.

A second issue is the tax treatment of gratuitous transfers and receipts. Contrary to the "model" advanced at the beginning of this discussion of savings being the "same" (in present-value terms) as future consumption, much wealth is not consumed (by the saver) but, rather, is the subject of gratuitous transfer.

---

[21] The argument traces back to mercantilist economics, based on a wholly nationalistic premise, that the economic welfare of the state was advanced by acquiring and hoarding "hard wealth" (gold). In the 19th century, the mercantilist pedigree was discredited (in favor of free trade) but was replaced by the Victorian notion of the inviolability of capital, which (in part) had its origins in trust law.

Should gratuitous transfers be treated as "consumption" of the transferor? Alternatively, should gratuitous receipts of cash and noninvestment property be included in the tax base of the transferee? Either solution would be a radical departure from the current income tax. But, if neither of these solutions is adopted, donees and legatees would be able to obtain savings and business expense deductions with dollars that have not been included in the tax base of *either* the transferor or the transferee. Dynastic wealth could avoid tax for perpetuity.

A third issue would be the tax treatment of debt. Under the cash flow consumption tax model, borrowing is included in the tax base (and principal and interest payments are deducted). Such a system would create bunching-of-income effects and would hit the lower and middle classes (and students) the hardest.[22] No bill providing for such treatment of debt has been seriously put forward in the U.S. Congress, and it is unlikely that one would appear in the future. But the issue would have to be dealt with, and the resolution would not be simple. Allowing *both* exclusion of borrowed funds (as under an income tax) and immediate deduction of all investments (even those made with borrowed funds) would provide dramatic tax-arbitrage effects (described in Section F, infra.)

Finally, there would be transition problems in moving from a realization income tax to a cash flow consumption tax. Under an income tax, "old capital" (basis) is recovered tax free, but under a cash flow consumption tax, investments are supposed to be deductible, and *all* returns (including a return of the original investment) are included in the tax base without a deduction for basis. Holders of old capital would surely press for a "transition rule" that would allow them to include in the new cash flow consumption tax base only the excess obtained over the old basis. But if such a transition rule were allowed, a taxpayer could sell existing assets and use old tax-free "capital recovery" dollars (the "basis" created under the income tax paradigm) to re-invest and claim deductions against the consumption tax base. The resulting double tax benefit for the same dollars would violate the internal norms of *both* an income tax and a consumption tax. Some cash flow consumption tax advocates, therefore, argue that no transition rule should be allowed. But the lack of a transition rule for "old capital" held by the propertied class would be a difficult sell politically, because the owners would lose the tax benefit from asset basis that they enjoyed under a realization income tax. However, their opposition might be mitigated by the fact that a switch from a realization income tax to a cash-flow consumption tax would presumably cause the value of their old assets to increase, because potential buyers would be allowed to deduct the purchase price and so would be willing to pay somewhat more. There is no certain answer as to how these factors would ultimately play out. For our purposes, it is sufficient to note that the transition could be complex and contentious.

PROBLEM

Explain why consumption tax devotees argue that U.S. savings would increase, to the benefit of us all, if the federal income tax were replaced with a consumption tax regime. Then evaluate this argument.

---

[22] Speaking of political liabilities, a cash flow consumption tax would also severely affect retirees who are consuming out of earlier savings.

D. FINANCIAL ANALYSIS AND THE TAXATION OF CAPITAL INCOME

Some advocates of consumption taxation argue that an ability-to-pay income tax *doubly* taxes capital returns to the same taxpayer, while a consumption tax reaches capital returns only *once*, thus putting the treatment of wealth on an equal footing with the treatment of consumption (which is also "taxed once"). This is a formal way of putting the argument that a consumption tax is more *neutral* between savings and consumption than is an ability-to-pay income tax, but there is also the rhetorical implication that double taxation of anything is bad in itself.

This argument that the income tax entails "double taxation" relies on the analytical construct borrowed from financial analysis, examined in Section B, supra. That analysis shows that one way to think about the fair market value of an asset is that it represents the *present value of all future returns* (whether called "income" or "principal"). Thus, an asset which the market values at $100 will, the market predicts, produce a stream of future payments that, when discounted to present value, is equal to $100. Now, under the capitalization principle of an ability-to-pay income tax, the purchase of a $100 investment asset represents a nondeductible capital expenditure, which means that the outlay remains in the tax base (and is thus taxed). This nondeductibility at the time of purchase effectively taxes the present value of all future returns on the investment but also creates a $100 basis. Thus, only returns *in excess* of that basis are taxed under an ability-to-pay income tax. But this represents double taxation of those excess returns *if* one accepts the proposition that the nondeductibility of the $100 purchase price *already implicitly taxed* those future returns.

It is then argued that, in contrast to an ability-to-pay income tax, all versions of a consumption tax reach the returns to investment only "once." The wage tax hits those returns *going into the investment* on a present value basis (by denying a deduction for the investment purchase but then exempting the returns when they are actually realized), while the cash flow consumption tax taxes those returns only when *coming out of the investment* (by allowing a deduction for the investment purchase but taxing *all* returns, both principal and "income," when not reinvested, i.e., available for consumption). An RST (or VAT) imposes a tax on consumption when it is purchased.

But isn't it the case that realization of future investment returns in excess of basis (as under an ability-to-pay income tax) represents *new* taxpaying *ability* that has not yet been tapped, even though the cost of the *original principal investment* was nondeductible and, therefore, taxed?[23] When viewed in this way, there is no

---

[23] One well-known early champion of a cash flow consumption tax was Nicholas Kaldor, but he disagreed with the "double taxation" proposition. He wrote that some people argued that an income tax was a double tax on the return to capital "on the ground that the market value of property is merely the discounted value of its expected future yield. . . . This may well be true from some points of view, *but from the point of view of the measurement of taxable capacity — which is the only purpose in question here — it is not correct to say that the one is just a reflection of the other.*" Nicholas Kaldor, An Expenditure Tax 31–32 (3rd ed. 1955) (emphasis added). Kaldor nevertheless supported a cash flow consumption tax over an income tax on the primary ground that it taxed consumption financed with borrowed money, which he viewed as additional taxpaying capacity.

"actual" double taxation under an ability-to-pay tax *in the flow of real time*, since the nondeductible (taxed) purchase price of an investment is exempt from tax (as basis) at the later time when investment returns are actually realized. This analytical approach seems compelling, because investment "income" exists *only as* a function of *real time*. Interest and dividend income is essentially compensation for the use of money *over real time*, and rents and royalties are compensation for the use of property *over real time*. Without such compensation (in one form or another), no investment would make sense, *since the investor would receive less (in present value terms) than what he or she parted with*.[24] Moreover, a system that raises revenue *on an annual basis* must look to a taxpayer's taxpaying capacity *in each separate year*. From that standpoint, gains on an investment are, in the years when realized, *new* taxpaying capacity that has not previously been tapped, and taxing them does not result in double taxation.

At the other extreme, ability-to-pay income tax advocates sometimes argue that a cash flow consumption tax *entirely* frees returns to capital from tax. The argument starts from the observation that the wage tax *explicitly* exempts capital returns (such as dividends, interest, and capital gains) from tax, proceeds to the further observation that a wage tax (under certain assumptions) produces the same economic result as a cash flow consumption tax, and reaches the conclusion that the latter tax must also, in economic effect, free capital returns from taxation. (See Section A.4, supra.)

But is not this "zero tax on investments" argument based on the notion of collapsed time rather than real time, as well? Under a cash flow consumption tax, if $1 is invested today and grows to $1 million after x years, the $1 is deductible in Year 1, but the $1 million is taxed in full when consumed. The argument that the cash flow consumption tax actually exempts the $1 million return relies on the proposition that allowing a deduction for the investment of $1 in Year 1 is the "same" as exempting $1 million after x years. (See Section A.4, supra.) That may (or may not) be true (viewed in the year of initial investment) in collapsed time,[25] but it is not true in real time. In terms of real time, a cash flow consumption tax does reach investment returns when spent on consumption.

It is easy to become over-infatuated with the time-value-of-money concept (which is based on collapsed time) in the context of taxes. But, unlike private individuals and entities, the government is not itself an investor (that creates future revenue for itself), and the financing of government does not operate on an "endowment" basis. That is to say, government (unlike a trust or other investment vehicle) is not financed by capital contributions that are invested and expected to generate revenue sufficient to support government for all future time. Instead, the essence of politically accountable government finance is the pay-as-you-go concept under which government relies on annual receipts. In light of this fact, it seems

---

[24] Investment return can also compensate for risk, but that also relates to time, i.e., the fact that the funds are beyond the investor's control over time.

[25] The claim that taxation in the year of investment under a wage tax really "taxes" extraordinary investment returns (as in the text example involving a return of $1 million on a $1 investment) defies common sense, but that is a separate issue from that of whether the cash flow consumption tax exempts all future returns in real time.

appropriate to evaluate the treatment of investment returns under various tax regimes in terms of annual accounting periods (real time, instead of collapsed time).

Although the rhetoric in this area often sheds more heat than light, some noncontroversial propositions remain. First, taxation of investments under an ability-to-pay income tax is less favorable to taxpayers than the tax treatment *of the same investments* under an RST, a wage tax, or a cash flow consumption tax and the reverse is true: each of those regimes taxes such investments more favorably than does an ability-to-pay income tax. This point is demonstrated by the examples in Section A.4. Second, a current deduction of a business or investment capital expenditure means that the investment is made with pre-tax dollars, and, therefore, that the investment is taxed as it would be under a cash flow consumption tax instead of under the less favorable ability-to-pay income tax rules. Thus, *the issue of whether capital expenditures should be capitalized (not deducted) or expensed (deducted) is a high-stakes matter involving more than the "mere" timing of deductions.*

E. SOME CONSUMPTION TAX FEATURES OF CURRENT LAW

Our so-called income tax is actually chock full of consumption tax features, and many commentators refer to it as a hybrid between an income and a consumption tax. Indeed, the consumption tax provisions have been expanding significantly in recent decades. Some of the more important consumption tax features of the federal income tax are described below.

1. Savings Vehicles

The differences among an ability-to-pay income tax, a cash flow consumption tax, and a wage tax can be seen in the tax treatment accorded three different kinds of savings vehicles under current law. The conventional savings account (or bank Certificate of Deposit (CD)) is governed by ability-to-pay income tax principles: (1) additions to savings (or the cost of the CD) are nondeductible capital expenditures (after-tax dollars), (2) recoveries of "principal" (basis) are free of tax, and (3) interest income is taxable.[26]

In the Individual Retirement Account (IRA) regime, additions to the account, unlike deposits in a conventional savings account or CD, are *deductible* by the investor up to a specified yearly limitation. See § 219(b). Moreover, earnings within the account are not taxed as they build up. See § 408(e)(1). Finally, distributions from the account to a taxpayer are *fully* included in gross income. See § 408(d)(1). Thus the taxation of IRAs clearly conforms to the cash flow consumption tax model. The investment is made with pre-tax dollars (instead of after-tax dollars), and no basis is created in the investment. All withdrawals are therefore taxed.

---

[26] It is worth noting here that both interest and principal receipts are in the form of cash, so that it becomes necessary to distinguish the two. As explained in Chapter 27, the labels assigned to payments by the contract do not always control for this purpose.

Health Savings Accounts (HSAs), discussed at the end of Chapter 5, follow the same approach as IRAs.[27]

There is also the Roth IRA, which is taxed according to the wage tax model: (1) additions to the account are *not* deductible, but (2) all future returns are fully exempt from tax. See § 408A(c)(1), (d)(1). To prevent investors from making all investments in Roth IRAs, the wage tax treatment is confined to additions to IRAs only up to the same annual limits that apply to conventional IRAs. See § 408A(c)(2).

2.   Qualified Retirement Vehicles

So-called qualified pension plans, profit-sharing plans, and other employer-sponsored qualified retirement vehicles (including "§ 401(k) plans") adhere to the cash flow consumption tax model. First, additions to the plan are "before tax," meaning that they are (a) excludable from the employee's income where made by the employer or (b) deductible by the employee where made by the employee. Second, inside earnings in the plan are not taxed as they build up. (Technically, the contributions are held by a "trust," and the trust is a "tax-exempt organization.") Finally, since the distributee has no basis in his or her account or interest in the plan, all distributions are includible by distributees.

To be a "qualified" plan, etc., the plan must conform to numerous restrictions relating to such matters as eligibility, funding, vesting, contribution (or distribution) amount limits, too-early distributions, too-late distributions, and other matters. Many of these restrictions derive from ERISA (the Employee Retirement Income Security Act of 1974, as amended). In the tax Code the restrictions are found in §§ 401-417. This entire area is so complex that it is typically the domain of specialists.

3.   Section 179 Deduction and Accelerated Depreciation

For many years, Congress has believed that market rates of return on investments in depreciable business equipment do not adequately reflect the resulting benefits to the U.S. economy and, therefore, that the income tax should include provisions encouraging this type of investment.[28] Two important provisions of current law that are based on this congressional belief are § 179 and § 168(k).

Subject to limitations, § 179 creates an exception to the capitalization principle by allowing taxpayers to deduct (expense) the cost of business tangible personal property and off-the-shelf business computer software placed in service during the year. For taxable years beginning in 2010 and 2011, the maximum amount that a taxpayer can expense under § 179 is $500K per year, but this figure is reduced by the amount that the cost of eligible property placed in service during the year exceeds $2M, so that the § 179 deduction is zero where investments during the year

---

[27] Unlike IRAs, payouts from HSAs are excluded, but only if they are used to pay for medical expenses that would (potentially) be deductible under § 213.

[28] The contrary argument is that § 179 is wasteful because its effects are to create a windfall for investments that would be made anyway and to subsidize other investments that are not economically competitive without a subsidy.

equal or exceed $2.5M.[29] The § 179 deduction is taken prior to depreciation deductions.

Congress did not feel that § 179 was sufficient in light of the recession that began in 2008, and so it has provided in § 168(k) that 100% of the cost of eligible property placed in service after September 8, 2010 and before 2012 can generally be expensed. There is no limitation on the amount of the deduction.[30] The complex rules defining eligible property are somewhat broader than the eligibility rules under § 179.

For present purposes, the important points regarding § 179 and § 168(k) are that (1) to the extent these provisions allow a present deduction for the acquisition costs of assets, they fully disregard the capitalization principle and achieve a cash flow consumption tax result, and (2) to the extent that § 168(k) allows excessive depreciation deductions, it partially disregards the capitalization principle and moves the federal income tax towards a cash flow consumption tax outcome. Further details regarding cost recovery are dealt with in Chapter 28.

4.   Exclusion for Interest on State and Local Bonds

Amounts invested in bonds and other debt obligations of states (and subdivisions thereof) are nondeductible (after-tax) dollars, but the interest thereon is excluded from gross income under § 103. This exclusion, sometimes called the "municipal bond exclusion," is a consumption tax feature of the income tax based on the "wage tax" paradigm, because such excluded income will never be taxed even if it is ultimately spent on consumption.

Historically, it was thought that the exclusion was mandated by the Constitution, and the notorious *Pollock* case (described in Chapter 1.B.2) so held. However, this holding of *Pollock* was subsequently overruled. See *South Carolina v. Baker*, 486 U.S. 1062 (1988). But Congress has chosen not to repeal § 103.

Gain from the sale or redemption of a § 103 obligation is not exempt under § 103. Only the interest is exempt.

5.   Gain on Personal Residence

A personal residence must be purchased with nondeductible (after-tax) dollars. Section 121, however, provides an exemption for gain on the sale or exchange of property used as the taxpayer's principal residence for 2 out of the last 5 years. This mimics the wage tax paradigm. The excluded gain under § 121 cannot exceed $250K ($500K in the case of a joint return).

A taxpayer exempting gain under § 121 generally cannot use § 121 again until two years have elapsed.

---

[29] These dollar amounts are scheduled to be reduced in taxable years beginning in 2012, and off-the-shelf business computer software is no longer eligible property for taxable years after 2012.

[30] In addition, § 168(k) specifies that for eligible property placed in service during 2012, a depreciation deduction is available for the first year of use that substantially exceeds actual depreciation during that year.

PROBLEM

(a) Explain why both the taxation of regular (not Roth) IRAs and the allowance of expensing under § 179 are applications of the cash flow consumption tax approach.

(b) Explain why the § 103 exclusion, the § 121 exclusion, and the taxation of Roth IRAs are all applications of the wage tax approach.

6. Unrealized Appreciation as Mimicking a Consumption Tax Result

As explained in Chapter 2, the realization principle, which causes unrealized gains and losses to be excluded from the tax base, is a fundamental characteristic of an ability-to-pay income tax. The realization principle is, however, also inherent in a cash-flow consumption tax, where realization is a necessary (if not sufficient) condition for taxation. That is, under a cash flow consumption tax, investment returns cannot be taxed prior to realization but even realized returns are nontaxable if fully reinvested. In an ability-to-pay income tax, however, realization is a sufficient condition of taxation, since realized returns will be taxed even if reinvested. In any event, realization has the effect of deferring income that is earned (or accrues) at an earlier date, and therefore it would be accurate to refer to realization as a "quasi-consumption-tax feature" of the current income tax, in that deferral due to nonrealization has the same effect as realization combined with reinvestment under the cash flow consumption tax. Fine points of categorization aside, the realization principle distorts investment decisions by treating investments differently.

To illustrate this point, assume that Thelma Taxpayer is a rich person who has $10M available for investment. For purposes of the following illustrations, also assume that the interest and discount rates are 10% per annum.

a. Sole Proprietorship Business Scenario

Thelma has an opportunity to use the $10M to purchase a new unincorporated business that she will own directly as a sole proprietor. Consequently, each year the profits of the new business will be taxed on her personal return. Her tax rate is 35%. The new business will earn a $1M Year 1 before-tax profit. The Year 1 after-tax profit will be invested in an expansion of the business. The business will earn a Year 2 before-tax return of 10% on invested capital. Thelma's results for Years 1 and 2 with respect to the business will be:

Year 1

$1,000,000	Profit
−350,000	Tax at 35%
$650,000	After-tax profit added to investment in Year 2
+ 10,000,000	Original investment
$10,650,000	Invested in Year 2 at 10%

Year 2

$10,650,000	Investment in Year 2
+ 1,065,000	Earnings thereon at 10%
− 372,750	35% tax on earnings
$11,342,250	Net to Thelma after taxes

b. Land Purchase Scenario

Alternatively, assume that Thelma, who is a real estate dealer, could use her $10M to purchase a piece of land on the first day of Year 1. The land will appreciate at the rate of 10% per year, compounded annually. She will hold the land as part of her dealer activities and at the end of Year 2, she will sell the land and realize her profit. Her tax rate is 35%. At the end of Year 1, she will have a 10% economic gain on her $10 million investment, but this will be an unrealized gain. Because of the realization principle, Thelma will defer all of her tax payment until the end of Year 2 when she sells. Her results are:

Year 1

$1,000,000	Unrealized profit
− 0	U.S. tax on unrealized profit
$1,000,000	Added to investment in Year 2
+ $10,000,000	Original investment
$11,000,000	Amount invested in Year 2

Year 2

$11,000,000	Investment in Year 2
+ 1,100,000	Year 2 10% appreciation
$12,100,000	Sale price at end of Year 2
− 10,000,000	Basis (original investment)
$2,100,000	Sale gain at end of Year 2
− 735,000	35% tax on sale gain
$1,365,000	After-tax gain to Thelma
+10,000,000	Original investment
$11,365,000	Net to Thelma after taxes

The following table contrasts the results between the sole proprietorship business scenario (where Thelma paid tax at the end of each year on that year's earnings) and the land purchase scenario (where Thelma deferred all tax payment until the end of Year 2):

$11,365,000	Net to Thelma in land purchase scenario
–11,342,250	Net to Thelma in business scenario
$22,750	Advantage of land purchase scenario

Because Thelma is a dealer, the foregoing ignores the favorable tax treatment accorded to the net capital gain of investors. The lower rates applied to net capital gain operate as the functional equivalent of an exclusion of a portion of net capital gains from income. A partial exclusion is a quasi-wage-tax feature of the income tax.

c. The Lesson

Thelma came out $22,750 ahead in the land purchase scenario (even without a capital gains preference) because her investment compounded tax free. In short, other things (such as before-tax return, risk level, and tax rates) being equal, an investor will do better if the return takes the form of unrealized appreciation instead of taxable periodic receipts. To repeat, the nontaxation of unrealized appreciation under the income tax is the equivalent of inclusion combined with an offsetting deduction for reinvestment, as occurs under a cash flow consumption tax.

The principal lesson to be drawn from the preceding analysis is that if a taxpayer can postpone her tax payment by making use of a consumption tax feature found in the Internal Revenue Code, she comes out ahead, provided that she doesn't incur an offsetting interest charge or penalty on the deferred tax. Thus, lawyers will always be looking for ways to help their clients with tax (or income) postponement strategies that legally employ consumption tax aspects of federal income tax law and that do not require payment to the government of interest or penalties. This will be a recurring theme throughout this book.

F. THE HYBRID TAX ANDS ITS EFFECTS

The consumption tax features of the income tax render it into a hybrid income/consumption tax, which creates tax-avoidance opportunities not available in either tax in its pure form.

1. What income tax?

Because the large majority of low- and middle-income taxpayers can save and invest through qualified pension plans, IRAs, Roth IRAs, and home ownership,[31] it is not farfetched to say that a majority of Americans *already* operate under a consumption tax or wage tax regime with regard to investments.

Higher-income taxpayers who engage in business and investment activities have easy access to outright expensing provisions, expensing-equivalent features (namely, the realization principle), partial expensing provisions (such as

---

[31] Another common middle-class investment is life insurance, which is also tax-favored, as explained in Chapters 15 and 27.

accelerated depreciation), full exclusions (such as for § 103 interest), and partial exclusions (such as the lower tax rate on net capital gain).

The more affluent, whose savings exceed the limits under many of the tax-favored savings vehicles, suffer "some" income taxation of their investments. Therefore, one way of phrasing the debate regarding whether the current Code should be replaced by some form of pure consumption taxation is whether the consumption tax treatment currently enjoyed by the poor and middle class ought to extend to the very affluent without limit.

The various consumption tax features in current law lead many to argue that our federal tax policy has adopted a hybrid income-consumption tax rather than an ability-to-pay income tax. Another way of viewing the situation, however, is to say that our federal *tax* policy generally adheres to the ability-to-pay income tax model but that Congress has chosen to implement federal *retirement* policy, federal *home ownership* policy, and other federal *nontax* policies (such as the relationship between the federal government and the states) by employing subsidy regimes in the form of consumption tax features grafted onto the ability-to-pay income tax.

2. Tax Arbitrage

Understanding how the current Code mixes income and consumption tax features allows you to appreciate the issues that can arise when the two regimes meet. Obviously, any of a wage tax, an RST, or a cash flow consumption tax regime is more favorable to savers than an income tax regime. In large part, the consumption tax features of the income tax are not accidental and are expressly intended to attract certain kinds of investments relative to others. The creation of tax-preferred investments violates the neutrality principal (discussed supra Chapter 3.C) on its face and creates complexity in the Code (an example being the "qualification" requirements relating to retirement plans). Whether tax favoritism is nevertheless warranted — either to counteract other government interventions or to achieve an increase in net social welfare — would have to be addressed on a case-by-case basis, which is beyond the scope of this book.

In one respect, however, the co-existence of income tax and consumption tax features in the same system can be said to be dysfunctional. Consider, for example, what happens when the law allows immediate deduction of business and investment capital expenditures (a cash flow consumption tax feature) while continuing to allow the exclusion of loan proceeds from the tax base (an income tax feature that would not be allowed in a cash flow consumption tax). To illustrate, suppose that Sam, in Year 1, borrows $2,000 at 4% interest to invest at a 4% rate of return. Under a pure ability-to-pay income tax, Sam would exclude the $2,000 borrowed money, get no deduction for the $2,000 investment (because it is a capital expenditure), include the $80 annual interest in income, and deduct the $80 interest expense, resulting in zero net income and no tax liability with respect to the investment. The economic wash-out would be reflected in a tax wash-out. Under a pure cash flow consumption tax, Sam would include the $2,000 borrowed money, deduct the $2,000 investment, include the $80 interest income, and deduct the $80 interest expense. Again, there would be no net income and no tax liability; the tax wash-out would accurately reflect the economic wash-out.

But what happens if the investment of the borrowed money is currently deductible? Here Sam excludes the $2K borrowed money and deducts the $2K investment. (It will be assumed either that the interest received from the investment is excluded and the interest paid is not allowed as a deduction, or that the interest received is included and the interest paid deducted.) Under current law, there is no provision or doctrine that prevents the taking of a (lawful) deduction for investments purchased with excluded borrowing (or other excluded funds). Thus, Sam ends up with *better than consumption tax treatment* by allowing him *both* to exclude the $2K borrowed money *and* to deduct the $2K investment purchased with that borrowed money, resulting in a current $2K tax loss for an economic wash-out (and a $700 tax savings if he's in the 35% tax bracket). *In short, Sam realizes a double tax benefit for the same dollars (exclusion and deduction).*

The double tax benefit for the same dollars that arises when the income tax treatment of debt is combined with the consumption tax features of current law is often referred to as "tax arbitrage."

The example above involved a cash flow consumption tax feature of the Code (the IRA deduction).

A second tax arbitrage possibility in the example above would have occurred if the $80 interest expense had been deductible "against" the $80 of currently-excluded IRA income. A second net tax loss (deductible against other income) would result, even though the interest aspect of this transaction broke even overall on a current basis. To generalize, a tax arbitrage scenario exists where *expense deductions* are allowed for costs incurred with respect to *tax-exempt (or tax-deferred) income.*

Congress has dealt with this second general problem, most notably in § 163(d), discussed in Chapter 18.D.3, which requires deferral of investment interest in excess of net investment income for the year, and § 265(a), discussed in Chapter 8.D.4, which simply disallows deductions (that would otherwise be allowed) for expenses allocable to wholly tax-exempt income. But whether §§ 163(d) and 265(a) are adequate to wholly solve this particular form of tax arbitrage remains to be seen. A more elaborate discussion of tax arbitrage is found in Chapter 21.A.

3.   Possible Distortionary Effects of a Hybrid Tax

Instead of a wholesale move from an income tax to a consumption or wage tax, the pattern has been to "load up" the income tax with consumption tax (or wage tax) features. The effect of these (and kindred) provisions is to differentiate some investments from others. Any provision of the Internal Revenue Code that adopts a consumption tax approach by allowing either a deduction for a certain category of capital expenditure or an exemption for a particular investment return has the effect of dramatically favoring that category of savings or investment over savings and investments that are subject to income tax principles. On their face, these consumption tax provisions (by being embedded in an income tax) violate neutrality and are, indeed, "tax expenditures" designed to provide incentives for various purposes such as saving for retirement, investing in equipment or machinery, conducting research and experimentation activities, promoting the extraction of oil and gas, and so on.

Although tax expenditure provisions are non-neutral on their face, whether they are non-neutral in practice is an empirical question, depending both on the "elasticity" (substitutability) of the favored activity compared to competing activities and on the existence or not of other government policies that may negate or aggravate the behavioral effects of a tax expenditure.

Nor do tax expenditure provisions *necessarily* confer higher net returns on favored investments. Since the value of an asset is the sum of the present values of all future *net* receipts, the reduction of a built-in cost (here, income taxes) with respect to a particular type of investment should result in an increased rate of return so that the investment becomes more valuable. But if this happens, more people will want the investment and its price will be driven up, which will cause its rate of return (yield/cost ratio) to drop, thereby achieving "equilibrium" among investments (whether or not tax-favored). In other words, the tax-favored investor may well end up paying a higher price for the tax-favored investment, thereby obtaining about the same *net* rate of return on tax-favored investments as on non-tax-favored investments. This point is illustrated by § 103 bonds, which offer a lower rate of return than taxable bonds. Nevertheless, equilibrium takes time, and even then it appears to be never fully achieved, partly because the future tax treatment of any given type of investment is uncertain. Even the rate of return on § 103 bonds is not as low as would be expected.[32]

Tax-favored investments are likely to provide a higher net rate of return in the *short run* (immediately after enactment of the favorable tax provision). As noted earlier, persons *already* owning the investment at the time a tax expenditure provision is enacted are likely to reap "windfall" gains, since such investments should instantly appreciate in value. Any equilibrium referred to above is established only because more investors buy the tax-favored investment than would do so if the tax advantage were not present. Thus, tax-favored investments tend to distort the allocation of investment capital (relative to the status quo), but this effect was presumably intended by the authors of the relevant tax provisions. Whether these distortions are ultimately good or bad is beyond the scope of a tax course.

PROBLEM

Why do tax advisers urge clients to borrow money to purchase regular IRAs?

---

[32] If the rate of return on comparable taxable bonds is 10%, the rate of return on § 103 bonds should be 6.5% (10% minus 3.5%), to reflect the tax that a taxpayer in the highest marginal rate bracket (35%) would have to pay on the 10% return. See Note 2 at the end of Chapter 5.C.7.

Chapter 7

THE CAPITALIZATION PRINCIPLE IN PRACTICE

As explained in Chapter 2.C.3, the capitalization principle embedded in a "theoretically pure" ability-to-pay income tax requires all outlays that transform money into other types of assets to be treated as nondeductible basis-creating capital expenditures. In the previous chapter it was explained how the capitalization principle is the defining characteristic of an "income" tax, that exceptions to the capitalization principle move the federal income tax in the direction of becoming a cash flow consumption tax, and that the income tax does not apply the capitalization principle with absolute strictness.

In this chapter, we will explore capitalization as it exists under the federal income tax. There is no general definition of capitalization in the Code, although § 263 provides some examples. Until fairly recently, there has been no comprehensive set of regulations dealing with capitalization. Apart from scattered ad hoc statutory rules applicable to specific situations, the law has largely developed through judicial decisions.

A. CREATION OF INTANGIBLE ASSETS AND BENEFITS

It has long been recognized that the costs of creating an intangible asset are capital expenditures.

1. Intangible Benefits

The following opinion is the most recent decision of the Supreme Court in the capitalization area. It deals with the creation of intangible benefits and can be thought of as establishing a baseline version of the capitalization principle. Because it represents the Supreme Court's most recent foray regarding capitalization, it should be read with care.

INDOPCO, INC. v. COMMISSIONER
United States Supreme Court
503 U.S. 79 (1992)

JUSTICE BLACKMUN delivered the opinion of the Court.

Petitioner INDOPCO, Inc., formerly named National Starch and Chemical Corp., manufactures adhesives, starches, and specialty chemical products. In October 1977, representatives of Unilever U.S., Inc. expressed interest in acquiring National Starch, which was one of its suppliers, through a friendly transaction.

National Starch at the time had outstanding over 6,563,000 common shares held by approximately 3700 shareholders.

In November 1977, National Starch's directors were formally advised of Unilever's interest. At that time, Debevoise, Plimpton, Lyons & Gates, National Starch's counsel, told the directors that under Delaware law they had a fiduciary duty to ensure that the proposed transaction would be fair to the shareholders. National Starch thereupon engaged the investment banking firm of Morgan Stanley & Co., Inc., to evaluate its shares, to render a fairness opinion, and generally to assist in the event of the emergence of a hostile tender offer.

Although Unilever originally had suggested a price between $65 and $70 per share, negotiations resulted in a final offer of $73.50 per share, a figure Morgan Stanley found to be fair. Following approval by National Starch's board and the issuance of a favorable private ruling from the IRS that the transaction would be tax-free for those National Starch shareholders who exchanged their stock for preferred stock [of a Unilever subsidiary],[1] the transaction was consummated in August 1978. [Since Unilever acquired the *stock* of National Starch, the latter continued to exist as a corporate subsidiary of Unilever.]

[Morgan Stanley and the Debevoise firm charged National Starch fees totaling about $2.7M, and other fees and charges were another $150K.]

The Court has recognized that the "decisive distinctions" between current expenses and capital expenditures "are those of degree and not of kind," *Welch v. Helvering*, 290 U.S. at 114, and that because each case "turns on its special facts," *Deputy v. Du Pont*, 308 U.S. at 496, the cases sometimes appear difficult to harmonize. National Starch contends that the decision in *Comm'r v. Lincoln Savings & Loan Assn.*, 403 U.S. 345, 354 (1971), changed these familiar backdrops and announced an exclusive test for identifying capital expenditures, a test in which "creation or enhancement of an asset" is a prerequisite to capitalization. In *Lincoln Savings*, we were asked to decide whether certain premiums, required by federal statute to be paid by a savings and loan association to the Federal Savings and Loan Insurance Corporation (FSLIC), were expenses or capital expenditures. We found that the "additional" premiums, the purpose of which was to provide FSLIC with a secondary reserve fund in which each insured institution retained a pro rata interest recoverable in certain situations, "serve to create or enhance for Lincoln what is essentially a separate and distinct additional asset." "[A]s an inevitable consequence," we concluded, "the payment is capital in nature and not an expense."

Lincoln Savings stands for the simple proposition that a taxpayer's expenditure that serves "to create or enhance a separate and distinct" asset should be capitalized. It by no means follows, however, that only expenditures that create or enhance separate and distinct assets are to be capitalized. We had no occasion in *Lincoln Savings* to consider the tax treatment of expenditures that did not create or enhance a specific asset, and thus the case cannot be read to preclude capitalization in other circumstances.

---

[1] [Editor's note: Certain corporate reorganizations involve "exchanges" that are tax-free to both the corporation and its shareholders under various provisions of the Code that are intensively studied in a course in corporate taxation.]

Nor does our statement in *Lincoln Savings* that "the presence of an ensuing benefit that may have some future aspect is not controlling" prohibit reliance on future benefit as a means of distinguishing an expense from a capital expenditure.[2] Although the mere presence of an incidental future benefit — "some future aspect" — may not warrant capitalization, a taxpayer's realization of benefits beyond the year in which the expenditure is incurred is undeniably important in determining whether the appropriate tax treatment is immediate deduction or capitalization. See *U.S. v. Mississippi Chemical Corp.*, 405 U.S. 298 (1972) (expense that "is of value in more than one taxable year" is a capital expenditure); *Central Texas Savings & Loan Assn. v. U.S.*, 731 F.2d 1181 (CA5 1984) ("While the period of the benefits may not be controlling in all cases, it nonetheless remains a prominent, if not predominant, characteristic of a capital item."). Indeed, the text of the Code's capitalization provision, § 263(a)(1), which refers to "permanent improvements or betterments," itself envisions an inquiry into the duration and extent of the benefits realized by the taxpayer.

Although petitioner attempts to dismiss the benefits that accrued to National Starch from the Unilever acquisition as "entirely speculative" or "merely incidental," the Tax Court's and the Court of Appeals' findings that the transaction produced significant benefits to National Starch that extended beyond the tax year in question are amply supported by the record. For example, National Starch's 1978 "Progress Report" observed that the company would "benefit greatly from the availability of Unilever's enormous resources, especially in the area of basic technology." Morgan Stanley's report to the National Starch board noted that National Starch management "feels that some synergy may exist with the Unilever organization given (a) the nature of the Unilever chemical, paper, plastics and packaging operations . . . and (b) the strong consumer products orientation of Unilever U.S."

In addition to these anticipated resource-related benefits, National Starch obtained benefits through its transformation from a publicly held, freestanding corporation into a wholly owned subsidiary of Unilever. The Court of Appeals noted that National Starch management viewed the transaction as "swapping approximately 3500 shareholders for one." Following Unilever's acquisition of National Starch's outstanding shares, National Starch was no longer subject to what even it terms the "substantial" shareholder-relations expenses a publicly traded corporation incurs, including reporting and disclosure obligations, proxy battles, and derivative suits.

Courts long have recognized that expenses such as these, "incurred for the purpose of changing the corporate structure for the benefit of future operations are not ordinary and necessary business expenses." *General Bancshares Corp. v. Comm'r*, 326 F.2d 712, 715 (CA8 1964).

---

[2] [6] Petitioner contends that, absent a separate-and-distinct-asset requirement for capitalization, a taxpayer will have no "principled basis" upon which to differentiate business expenses from capital expenditures. We note, however, that grounding tax status on the existence of an asset would be unlikely to produce the bright-line rule that petitioner desires, given that the notion of an "asset" is itself flexible and amorphous.

PROBLEMS

1. What test did the Supreme Court use in *INDOPCO* to distinguish capital expenditures from current expenses?

2. In Chapter 2 it was stated that a capital expenditure is an outlay that transforms one form of wealth into another form of wealth and that a capital expenditure becomes basis with respect to the new wealth. In *INDOPCO*, National Starch's cash payments of approximately $2.85M were held to be capital expenditures. Into what form of new wealth was the cash transformed? To what does the new $2.85M basis attach?

2. The Post-*INDOPCO* Intangible Asset Regulations

INDOPCO created anxiety that the IRS would use the case as a tool to require capitalization of many outlays previously treated as deductible expenses. In response, the Service issued several revenue rulings confirming prior doctrine.[3] But these rulings failed to satisfy the business tax bar, which called for clarification through Treasury regulations. In December 2003, Treasury issued final regulations dealing with costs relating to intangible assets. See Reg. § 1.263(a)-4 and -5. Rather than expressly adopting the *INDOPCO* "significant future benefit" language as a positive rule in the regulations, the Treasury drafters stated that they used this test as a "standard" in creating an exclusive list of expenditure categories that *must* be capitalized. Here are some highlights of the regulations:

• If an item is not on the "capitalization category list," the IRS will not assert *INDOPCO's* "significant future benefits" test as *sufficient* basis for capitalizing it. However, the IRS reserves the right to use the *INDOPCO* test to add items to the list through published guidance, but any such guidance will have prospective force only. See Reg. §§ 1.263(a)-4(b)(1)(iv), -4(b)(2).

• Amounts paid to create or enhance intangible benefits or rights are treated as "expenses" if they do not extend beyond the *earlier* of (i) 12 months after the first date on which the taxpayer realizes the right or benefit (including reasonably expected renewal periods) or (ii) the end of the taxable year following the payment year. This rule, sometimes known as the "12-month rule," will apply even if most of the future benefit falls into the year following the year in which the cost was incurred. See Reg. § 1.263(a)-4(f)(1)–(5).

• Employee compensation and overhead costs will not be attributed to the acquisition of intangibles, no matter how much employee time is spent on the acquisition. See Reg. §§ 1.263(a)-4(e)(4)(i), -5(d)(1).

---

[3] See, e.g., *Rev. Rul. 96-62*, 1996-2 C.B. 9 (employee training costs are generally expenses); *Rev. Rul. 94-77*, 1994-2 C.B. 19 (employment severance benefits are usually expenses); *Rev. Rul. 95-32*, 1995-1 C.B. 8 (dealing with land conservation expenditures); *Rev. Rul. 94-38*, 1994-1 C.B. 35 (costs of cleaning up hazardous waste deposited by taxpayer on its own land are business expenses); *Rev. Rul. 94-12*, 1994-1 C.B. 36 (INDOPCO does not bar the deductibility of repairs to business or investment property); *Rev. Rul. 92-80*, 1992-2 C.B. 57 (ordinary business advertising expenses remain deductible after INDOPCO even if they create goodwill).

• Certain created or enhanced intangibles without an ascertainable useful life (e.g., memberships of indefinite duration) can be amortized over 15 years. See § 1.167(a)-3(b).

• The costs incurred in directly defending against a hostile takeover (such as costs incurred to seek an injunction against the takeover or to seek a "white knight") are deductible as expenses, but costs incurred to undertake a defensive recapitalization (corporate restructuring) must be capitalized. See Reg. § 1.263(a)-5(*l*), Ex. (11).

In business accounting, prepaid expenses are treated as creating intangible assets. The most common prepayments are for insurance, rent, interest, and membership dues. Prepayments of expenses would generally be governed (one way or the other) by the 12-month rule of the post-*INDOPCO* regulations. Prepaid interest, however, is specifically governed by § 461(g), which generally requires capitalization and amortization, except for certain home mortgage "points."

PROBLEMS

1. On October 1 of Year 1, LouAnn pays $6K for a 12-month insurance policy covering business property. Coverage commences on February 1, Year 2 and ends January 31, Year 3.

(a) Can LouAnn deduct the $6K outlay on her Year 1 return? See Reg. § 1.263(a)-4(f)(1), (f)(8) Ex. (1), (2).

(b) What significant future benefit did LouAnn acquire in exchange for her $6K expenditure?

(c) It was previously stated (in Chapter 2) that the capitalized cost of a business intangible, such as LouAnn's prepaid insurance coverage, is usually deducted by straight-line amortization over the life of the intangible. How (when) would LouAnn deduct her $6K cost?

2. Assume that coverage under LouAnn's policy begins on December 1, Year 1 and ends on November 30, Year 2.

(a) Can LouAnn deduct the $6K October 1, Year 1 outlay on her Year 1 return?

(b) Is your answer consistent with *INDOPCO*?

(c) How closely does your answer match the result LouAnn would get under a cash flow consumption tax?

3. Advertising and Goodwill

Advertising outlays (apart from structures, such as billboards) have long been generally considered to be expenses, even when the advertising is intended to have long-term effects. See Reg. § 1.162-20(a)(2); *Rev. Rul. 92-80*, 1992-2 C.B. 57.

The creation of business goodwill typically occurs as an incidental byproduct of other (usually currently deductible) outlays in connection with such things as advertising, leasing a favorable business location, possessing an easily remembered business name, hiring effective sales personnel, putting forth high quality goods and services over time, etc. Thus, self-created goodwill rarely has a basis. In contrast, the cost of *purchased* goodwill (as part of the acquisition of a going business) would not qualify as an "expense" and would have to be capitalized. Because purchased goodwill typically has no ascertainable useful life, it would not be depreciable under general principles. See Reg. § 1.167(a)-3(a). Nevertheless, it often falls within the special 15-year amortization rule of § 197 (discussed in Chapter 28).

NOTES

1. *Cleveland Electric Illuminating Co. v. U. S.*, 7 Cl. Ct. 220 (1975), apparently the only case of its kind, held that advertising costs incurred to allay public opposition to the granting of a nuclear power plant construction license had to be capitalized. In *Rev. Rul. 92-80*, supra, the IRS characterized *Cleveland Electric Illuminating* as involving "the unusual circumstance where advertising is directed towards obtaining future benefits significantly beyond those traditionally associated with ordinary product advertising or with institutional or goodwill advertising."

2. Although the purchase price of an asset is the prototypical capital expenditure, it should be noted that the Treasury has created a *de minimis* expensing rule in Reg. § 1.162-6, which allows expense deductions for capital expenditures by professionals for the cost of books, furniture, equipment, and instruments, the "useful life of which is short."

PROBLEM

Hardball Mart, Inc. operates retail stores throughout the United States. It expends large sums on the following forms of advertising:

(i) Weekly advertisements in local newspapers limited to providing price information regarding sales at the respective local stores during the particular week.

(ii) Nationwide advertising to build brand recognition and goodwill by informing the public about Hardball's various charitable activities.

(iii) Nationwide advertising to resist union organization drives by telling Hardball's workers and the general public that Hardball is a great workplace without unions.

Which of these classes of advertising expense are deductible under current law? On what basis could the IRS, in *Rev. Rul. 92-80*, have excepted most advertising from the reach of *INDOPCO*?

B. COSTS OF PRODUCING TANGIBLE ASSETS (INCLUDING INVENTORY)

In the case of the creation, production, and manufacture of tangible assets, are any costs included in the basis of such assets in addition to the cost of raw materials (which are referred to as "direct" costs)?

Much of the law on this question relates to manufactured, produced, or created *inventory*, i.e., property held by sellers for sale to customers. Recall that inventory cannot be depreciated and cannot produce capital gain or loss. The ordinary gain or loss produced by the sale of inventory (called "gross income derived from business") is calculated on a mass basis by adding together Gross Receipts for the year and then subtracting Cost of Goods Sold for the year. Cost of Goods Sold, in turn, is figured by adding Purchases to Opening Inventory and subtracting Closing Inventory (determined under the FIFO or LIFO cost convention). Cost of Goods Sold is the inventory counterpart to "basis," and so it is important to be able to determine what, if anything, enters into Cost of Goods Sold, in addition to such obvious items as the cost of a merchant's purchased goods or the costs of raw materials of a manufacturer or producer.

Growing awareness of the importance of the capitalization principle stimulated the government to push for more stringent capitalization rules in this area, and this effort eventually led to the enactment of § 263A. The following opinion provided the initial impetus for this development.

COMMISSIONER v. IDAHO POWER CO.
United States Supreme Court
418 U.S. 1 (1974)

Mr. Justice Blackmun delivered the opinion of the Court.

For many years, the taxpayer has used its own equipment and employees in the construction of improvements and additions to its capital facilities [power lines and related assets]. During 1962 and 1963, taxpayer owned a wide variety of automotive transportation equipment, including cars, trucks, power-operated equipment, and trailers. The equipment was used in part for operation and maintenance and in part for the construction of capital facilities having a useful life of more than one year. For federal income tax purposes, the taxpayer claimed as a deduction all the year's depreciation on the transportation equipment, using a life of 10 years. The Commissioner disallowed the deduction for the construction-related depreciation. He added the amount of the depreciation so disallowed to the taxpayer's adjusted basis in its capital facilities.

The issue comes down to a question of timing, that is, whether the construction-related depreciation is to be amortized over the shorter life of the equipment or, instead, over the longer life of the facilities constructed. Our primary concern is with the necessity to treat construction-related depreciation in a manner that comports with accounting and taxation realities. Over a period of time a capital asset is consumed and, correspondingly over that period, its theoretical value and utility are thereby reduced. Depreciation is an accounting device which recognizes that the physical consumption of a capital asset is a true cost, since the asset is being depleted. When the asset is used to further the taxpayer's day-to-day business operations, a current depreciation deduction is an appropriate offset to gross income currently produced. It is clear, however, that different principles are implicated when the consumption of the asset takes place in the construction of other assets that, in the future, will produce income themselves. In this latter situation, the cost represented by depreciation is related to the future and is appropriately allocated as part of the cost of acquiring an income-producing asset.

Established tax principles require the capitalization of the cost of acquiring an asset. This principle has obvious application to the acquisition of an asset by purchase, but it has been applied, as well, to the costs incurred in a taxpayer's construction of capital facilities.

There can be little question that other construction related expense items, such as tools, materials, and wages paid construction workers, are to be treated as part of the cost of acquisition of a capital asset. The taxpayer does not dispute this. Of course, reasonable wages paid in the carrying on of a trade of business qualify as a deduction from gross income. § 162(a)(1). But when wages are paid in connection with the construction or acquisition of a capital asset, they must be capitalized and are then entitled to be amortized over the life of the capital asset so acquired. Construction-related depreciation is not unlike expenditures for wages for construction workers. The significant fact is that the exhaustion of construction equipment does not represent the final disposition of the taxpayer's investment in that equipment; rather, the investment in the equipment is assimilated into the cost of the asset constructed.

An additional pertinent factor is that capitalization of construction-related depreciation by the taxpayer who does its own construction work maintains tax parity with the taxpayer who has its construction work done by an independent contractor. The Court of Appeals' holding would lead to disparate treatment among taxpayers because it would allow the firm with sufficient resources to construct its own facilities and obtain a current deduction, whereas another firm without such resources would be required to capitalize its entire cost charged to it by the contractor.

Finally, the priority-ordering directive of § 161 — or, for that matter, § 261 of the Code — requires that the capitalization provision of § 263(a) take precedence over § 167(a). The clear import of § 161 is that, with stated exceptions set forth either in § 263 itself or provided for elsewhere, none of which is applicable here, an expenditure incurred in acquiring capital assets must be capitalized even when the expenditure otherwise might be deemed deductible.

[Dissenting opinion of JUSTICE DOUGLAS omitted.]

––––––––––

It should be noted that the *Idaho Power* opinion, supra, clumsily misuses the term "capital asset," a *tax* term of art defined in § 1221(a), to refer to what accountants call "capital equipment" or "capital facilities," namely, assets used in the income-producing function of the business. This use of the term "capital asset" is misleading, because assets of this type happen to be *excluded* from the tax definition of capital asset. See § 1221(a)(2). (The character of gain or loss from such assets was briefly described in Chapter 2 and is pursued in more detail in Chapter 25.) But this glitch does not detract from the force of the analysis, which is noncontroversial.

Section 263A, added to the Internal Revenue Code in 1986, codifies and elaborates on the principle set forth in *Idaho Power*. It requires the capitalization (or addition to Cost of Goods Sold) of not only the "direct" costs, but also the "indirect" costs, of (1) *producing* real property (i.e., buildings) or tangible personal property (whether inventory or otherwise) and (2) *acquiring* inventory for resale. For purposes of category (1), films, sound recordings, video tapes, books, etc., are treated as "tangible" personal property.

"Direct" costs are, as one would expect, the costs of raw materials, but direct costs also include the compensation paid to production workers. "Indirect" costs include (but are not limited to) repairs, depreciation, utilities, rent, sales taxes, property taxes, and insurance premiums, etc. — all with respect to plant and equipment — plus storage, packaging, and administrative costs allocable to production activities. Excluded from the scope of § 263A are selling expenses, state income taxes, and advertising and distribution costs. See generally Reg. § 1.263A-1T.

There are statutory exceptions to the § 263A rules of a de minimis nature for: (1) wholesalers and retailers of personal property whose average annual gross receipts do not exceed $10M (§ 263A(b)(2)(B)); (2) personal-use property created by individuals (§ 263A(c)(1)); (3) outlays that can be expensed under certain other Code provisions; and (4) certain animals and plants produced by farmers and ranchers. See § 263A(b)-(d). Presumably these situations are governed by rules found elsewhere, including case law.

Artists, writers, and photographers were initially subject to § 263A, but § 263A(h), added in 1988, now exempts self-employed professional artists, writers, and photographers from § 263A. Presumably, these activities are governed by such authorities as *Faura v. Comm'r*, 73 T.C. 849 (1980), *Snyder v. U.S.*, 674 F.2d 1359 (10th Cir. 1982), and *Rev. Rul. 63-275*, 1963-2 C.B. 85, where costs of creating books and art were allowed to be expensed on the theory that allocating costs to particular creations (completed, uncompleted, abandoned, or destroyed) would be too difficult. Nevertheless, the direct cost of prints, photographic plates, films, video and audio tapes, and similar tangible items must, under § 263A(h)(2), be capitalized.

Section 263A(f) requires the capitalization of certain construction-period interest as part of the cost of the constructed property. This rule applies where the constructed property is real property (or personal property having a long useful life for depreciation purposes) or else has an estimated production period of two years or more (one year if the property has an estimated cost exceeding $1 million). However, deductible home mortgage interest is not subject to this rule.

Under § 266, a business taxpayer can elect to capitalize interest, taxes, and other "carrying charges" with respect to the development and construction of property. Section 266 applies only to expenses that would otherwise be currently deductible and which are not subject to capitalization under § 263A.

Outside of §§ 263A and 266, interest is never capitalized, except to the extent that it is prepaid. The same can be said of taxes, except acquisition-related excise taxes, certain real property "assessments" by local governments, and certain property tax reimbursements provided for in real estate closings, all of which are discussed in

Chapter 5.C. Income taxes are never capitalized. Rent (other than prepaid rent) is not capitalized except to the extent it is considered an "indirect" production cost under § 263A. Interest, rent, property taxes, and income taxes are generally considered to be "period" costs allocable to the periods of time that property, money, or government services are "used."

PROBLEMS

1. In Year 1, the Big Hurt law firm pays $10K in salary to associates for work done during Year 1 to prepare pleadings and write a trial brief for use in Year 2 personal injury litigation which, if successful, will result in a contingency fee for Big Hurt. Can Big Hurt deduct the $10K as a Year 1 business expense, or does § 263A require that the expense be capitalized and treated as the basis of the brief and pleadings? See § 263A(a)(1), Reg. § 1.263A-2(a)(2)(ii)(B)(2) (stating: "Tangible personal property does not include de minimis property provided to a client or customer incident to the provision of services, such as wills prepared by attorneys, or blueprints prepared by architects."). Should these costs, instead, be treated as the cost of creating an *intangible* asset?

2. In Year 1, the Big Deal law firm pays $10K in salary to associates to do research used during Year 1 to create a form LLC agreement which Big Deal will use for many years whenever one of its lawyers forms an LLC for a client.

(a) Does the regulation cited in the preceding problem allow Big Deal to deduct the $10K expenditure in Year 1, or does § 263A(b)(1) require the $10K to be capitalized and treated as the basis of the form? See Reg. § 1.263A-2(a) (stating: "Section 263A applies to real property and tangible personal property produced by a taxpayer for use in its trade or business") and Reg. § 1.263A-2(a)(2)(ii) (stating that "tangible personal property includes . . . books, and other similar property embodying words, ideas, concepts.").

(b) Does Reg. § 1.162-6 (second sentence) allow Big Deal to deduct the $10K expenditure in Year 1?

C. COSTS RELATED TO ASSET ACQUISITIONS

Under the *INDOPCO* baseline, the paradigm capital expenditure is the purchase of an asset with a life that extends "substantially" beyond the current tax year. Moving beyond the purchase price itself, what about costs that are associated with (or related to) the acquisition (or disposition of an asset). This section deals with (1) transaction costs, (2) costs that are antecedent to the transaction, (3) development costs, and (4) start-up costs.

1. Transaction Costs

The transaction cost issue has long been dealt with by Reg. § 1.263(a)-2(c) and (e), as well as by cases such as the following:

WOODWARD v. COMMISSIONER

United States Supreme Court

397 U.S. 572 (1970)

Mr. Justice Marshall delivered the opinion of the Court.

Taxpayers owned or controlled a majority of the common stock of the Telegraph-Herald, an Iowa corporation. The Telegraph-Herald was incorporated in 1901, and its charter was extended for 20-year periods in 1921 and 1941. On June 9, 1960, taxpayers voted their controlling share of the stock of the corporation in favor of a perpetual extension of the charter. A minority stockholder voted against the extension. Iowa law requires "those stockholders voting for such renewal to purchase at its real value the stock voted against such renewal."

Taxpayers attempted to negotiate the purchase of the dissenting shares, but no agreement could be reached on the "real value" of those shares. Consequently, in 1962 taxpayers brought an action in state court to appraise the minority stock. In July 1965, taxpayers purchased the minority stock at the price fixed by the court. During 1963, taxpayers paid attorneys', accountants', and appraisers' fees of over $25,000 for services rendered in connection with the appraisal litigation. Taxpayers claimed deductions for these expenses, asserting that they were "ordinary and necessary expenses paid for the management, conservation, or maintenance of property held for the production of income" under § 212.

It has long been recognized, as a general matter, that costs incurred in the acquisition or disposition of an asset are to be treated as capital expenditures. The most familiar example of such treatment is the capitalization of brokerage fees for the sale or purchase of securities, as explicitly provided by a longstanding Treasury Regulation, § 1.263(a)-2(e), and as approved by this Court in *Helvering v. Winmill*, 305 U.S. 79 (1938). The Court recognized that brokers' commissions are "part of the acquisition cost of the securities," and relied on the regulation, which had been approved by statutory re-enactment, to deny deductions for such commissions even to a taxpayer for whom they were a regular and recurring expense in his business of buying and selling securities.

The regulations do not specify other sorts of acquisition costs, but rather provide generally that "the cost of acquisition of property having a useful life substantially beyond the taxable year" is a capital expenditure. Reg. § 1.263(a)-2(a). Under this general provision, the courts have held that legal, brokerage, accounting, and similar costs incurred in the acquisition or disposition of property are capital expenditures. The law could hardly be otherwise, for such ancillary expenses incurred in acquiring or disposing of an asset are as much part of the cost of that asset as is the price paid for it.

More difficult questions arise with respect to another class of capital expenditures, those incurred in "defending or perfecting title to property." Reg. § 1.263(a)-2(c). In one sense, any lawsuit brought against a taxpayer may affect his title to property. The courts, not believing that Congress meant all litigation expenses to be capitalized, have created the rule that such expenses are capital in nature only where the taxpayer's "primary purpose" in incurring them is to defend or perfect title. This test hardly draws a bright line, and has produced a melange of decisions. Such uncertainty is not called for in applying the regulation that makes the "cost of acquisition" of a capital asset a capital expense. In our view application of the latter regulation to litigation expenses involves the simpler inquiry whether the origin of the claim litigated is in the process of acquisition itself.

[T]here can be no doubt that legal, accounting, and appraisal costs incurred in negotiating a purchase of the minority stock would have been capital expenditures. Yet the appraisal process was no more than the substitute that the state law provided for the process of negotiation.

This is not a borderline case. Where property is acquired by purchase, nothing is more clearly part of the process of acquisition than the establishment of a purchase price. Thus, the [costs] incurred in that litigation were properly treated as part of the cost of the stock that the taxpayers acquired.

The post-*INDOPCO* intangibles regulations provide that transaction costs (referred to as "costs to facilitate the acquisition or creation of an intangible"), including appraisal costs, are to be capitalized.[4] However (and contrary to *Woodward!*), the same regulations provide that facilitation costs under $5K for the transaction are considered to be de minimis and need not be capitalized.[5]

With respect to Reg. §§ 1.212-1(k) and 1.263(a)-2(c), classifying the cost of defending or perfecting title to property as capital expenditures,, the idea is that defending or perfecting title is a kind of "delayed" acquisition cost made to "complete" the property-acquisition process.

Section 280B requires that the unrecovered basis of a demolished structure, plus the costs of demolition, be treated as capital expenditures with respect to the underlying land (and not as separately deductible items). In effect, these are treated as costs of acquiring the land, even if the purpose of the demolition was to make way for a replacement structure, and even if the demolition occurred well after the acquisition of the property.

Although the payment of real property taxes prevents the government from seizing the property, they are not costs of defending title to property, because they don't relate back to the acquisition of the property, but rather to its ongoing ownership.

Similarly, except as provided in §§ 263A(f) and 266 (noted in Section B, supra), interest on acquisition indebtedness is not treated as an acquisition-related cost of the property. Instead, interest is treated as a "period cost" (like rent) for the "use" of someone else's *money*. The costs of obtaining money cannot be added to the basis of the money itself, which always has a basis equal to its face amount. However, the cost of obtaining a loan is capitalized to a separate asset account and amortized over the life of the loan. See Reg. § 1.446-5. A larger point, to be developed in Chapter 20, is that loan transactions are generally (but not always) accounted for separately

---

[4] See Reg. § 1.263(a)-4(b)(1)(v).

[5] See Reg. §§ 1.263(a)-4(d)(6)(v), -4(e)(4)(iii), -5(d)(1), (3).

from property transactions, even where the loan is specifically earmarked for the purchase of the property.

The cost of acquiring a lease (not involving minerals) must be capitalized and amortized over the term of the lease under § 178.

If an incorporated business is acquired, the acquisition may take the form of either a stock purchase or a purchase of the assets. In the first case, acquisition costs are added to the basis of the stock. In the second case, aggregate acquisition costs are allocated among all of the acquired assets in proportion to their respective fair market values. See generally § 1060, discussed further at Chapter 29.A.1.

PROBLEMS

1. How does a buyer capitalize real estate closing costs? How does a seller capitalize such costs? See Reg. § 1.263(a)-2(e).

2. What is the proper income tax treatment of the dissenting shareholders' appraisal litigation expenses in *Woodward*?

3. Should legal costs incurred in obtaining a private letter ruling from the IRS in connection with the taxpayer's proposed acquisition of business or investment property be capitalized where consummation of the acquisition is contingent on a favorable ruling, the favorable ruling is obtained, and the property is actually acquired? See generally Reg. §§ 1.263(a)-5(a), 1.263(a)-5(e)(2)(ii).

4. *Lychuk v. Comm'r*, 116 T.C. 374 (2001) (reviewed), involved the acquisition of dealer installment sale contracts by a business that then collected for itself the future interest and principal payments. In acquiring the contracts, the taxpayer's employees ran credit checks, analyzed loan applications, and so on. The Tax Court held that the cost of employee salaries allocable to installment contract acquisitions were capital expenditures because this cost was incurred in the process of acquiring assets, also citing *INDOPCO*. To what extent is *Lychuk* still good law? See Reg. § 1.263(a)-4(e)(4)(i).

2. Costs Preliminary to the Transaction

Various stages might have been passed through prior to the actual acquisition or production of the asset. The earliest stage can be called the "investigation" stage. Analytically, the category of investigation costs can in turn be broken down into (1) costs of searching for properties to acquire and (2) costs of evaluating specific potential acquisitions. This area of the law is very confusing, partly because it is often not easy to separate these two steps (often the effort is not even attempted), and sometimes the distinctions don't appear to make a difference.

a. Search Costs

The taxpayer in the following ruling was not yet engaged in a trade or business, but was trying to buy a business which she would thereafter carry on. Can you spot the language in §§ 162(a) and 165(c)(1) that precluded the taxpayer from deducting (under those provisions) the costs in question?

REVENUE RULING 77-254
1977-2 C.B. 63

An individual taxpayer began to search for a business to purchase. The individual placed advertisements in several newspapers and traveled to various locations throughout the country to investigate various businesses that the individual learned were for sale. The individual commissioned audits to evaluate the potential of several of these businesses. Eventually, the individual decided to purchase a specific business and incurred expenses in an attempt to purchase this business. For example, the individual retained a law firm to draft the documents necessary for the purchase. Because of certain disagreements between the individual and the owner of the business that developed after this decision was made, the individual abandoned all attempts to acquire the business.

Rev. Rul. 57-418, 1957-2 C.B. 143, holds that losses incurred in the search for a business or investment are deductible [under § 165(c)(2)] only when the activities are more than investigatory and the taxpayer has actually entered a transaction for profit and the project is later abandoned. In *Seed v. Comm'r*, 52 T.C. 880 (1969), (acq.), the Tax Court allowed a deduction for expenses incurred by a taxpayer during an unsuccessful attempt to secure a charter to operate a savings and loan association. The court found that the taxpayer's extensive activities in the venture qualified as a transaction entered into for profit. Following the decision in *Seed* the court has continued to find that a taxpayer has entered a transaction for profit in cases in which the facts indicated that the taxpayer has gone beyond a general search and focused on the acquisition of a specific business or investment.

In view of the decision in *Seed*, *Rev. Rul. 57-418* is amplified to provide that a taxpayer will be considered to have entered a transaction for profit if, based on all the facts and circumstances, the taxpayer has gone beyond a general investigatory search for a new business or investment to focus on the acquisition of a specific business or investment.

Expenses incurred in the course of a general search for or preliminary investigation of a business or investment include those expenses related to the decisions whether to enter a transaction and which transaction to enter. Such expenses are personal and are not deductible under § 165 of the Code. Once the taxpayer has focused on the acquisition of a specific business or investment, expenses that are related to an attempt to acquire such business or investment are capital in nature and, to the extent that the expenses are allocable to an asset the cost of which is amortizable or depreciable, may be an amortizable part of the asset's cost if the attempted acquisition is successful. If the attempted acquisition fails, the amount capitalized is deductible in accordance with § 165(c)(2). The taxpayer need not actually enter the business or purchase the investment in order to obtain the deduction.

Accordingly, in the present case, the individual's expenses in retaining a law firm to draft the purchase documents and any other expenses incurred in the attempt to complete the purchase of the business are deductible [under § 165(c)(2)]. The expenses for advertisements, travel to search for a new business, and the cost of audits that were designed to help the individual decide whether to attempt an acquisition were investigatory expenses and are not deductible.

Rev. Rul. 77-254 is modeled largely on the facts of *Frank v. Comm'r*, 20 T.C. 511 (1953), which focused on whether investigation costs that the taxpayer (not then carrying on a business) incurred in a general search for a business to purchase could be deducted as an expense or loss. The Tax Court held that § 162(a) (business expenses) did not apply because the taxpayer was not currently engaged in any business. Section 212 (investment expenses) was held to apply only with respect to existing, not prospective, investments. Finally, § 165(c)(2) was held not to apply with respect to various "possibilities" that never panned out, the court stating (20 T.C. at 514-515):

> It cannot be said that the petitioners entered into a transaction every time they visited a new city and examined a new business property. Nor can we hold that petitioners entered into such transactions and then abandoned them, as they here contend. Rather, they refused to enter into such transactions after the preliminary investigation. If the general search for a suitable business property itself be considered as a transaction entered into for profit, no abandonment of such project occurred in the taxable year so as to enable deduction of these expenses as losses.

Neither *Rev. Rul. 77-254* nor *Frank* tell us how the nondeductible search costs should have been characterized. Were they disallowed expenses? Disallowed losses? Capital expenditures to be added to the basis of the property that was eventually acquired?

Presumably, if the taxpayer in *Frank* or *Rev. Rul. 77-254* was *already* in a business, the preliminary investigation costs would have been deductible either as business expenses under § 162 or business losses under § 165 (business losses not being subject to a "transaction" requirement). Nevertheless, the timing of such a deduction would depend on whether these costs were capital expenditures or expenses, and that in turn might depend on whether the aim was to acquire a new business (clearly a capital expenditure) or expand an existing business (where the answer is less clear), but this distinction is itself elusive.

In any event, *Rev. Rul. 83-105*, 1983-2 C.B. 51, suggests that preliminary search costs are inherently capital expenditures. There an oil and gas producer (a business taxpayer) undertook a reconnaissance survey (RS) that identified three geographical areas of interest (A, B, and C). The RS was followed up by a detailed survey (DS) of each of areas A and B, which resulted in the acquiring of mineral leases in area A only. The ruling held that RS costs were capital expenditures that should be allocated equally among the three areas. All the RS costs for area A were capitalized to the three leases that were ultimately acquired, even though the RS covered other lease tracts of area A that the taxpayer chose to reject. Area B was abandoned, and a business loss deduction was allowed for that area. No final decision had been made for area C, and so the capital account for that area continued forward. The ruling implicitly holds that the cost of the abandoned area B was not to be added to the basis of the area A property that was ultimately acquired, but that all of the costs allocable to area A were to be added to the basis of the acquired leases even though other potential leases in that area were rejected.

b. Evaluation Costs

Rev. Rul. 83-105, supra, holds also that evaluation (DS) costs were to be capitalized to the respective areas of interest. Therefore, the DS costs regarding area B were deductible as a business loss under § 165 when that area was abandoned.

Rev. Rul. 77-254, supra, appears to summarily hold that evaluation costs are indistinguishable from search costs, but *Rev. Rul. 83-105* holds otherwise, and also holds that both are capital expenditures. Analytically, three separate issues are presented: (1) are the costs capital expenditures, (2) to what asset(s) do they relate, and (3) whether abandonment (etc.) of an asset gives rise to a loss deduction.

Search and evaluation costs are both capital expenditures under the *INDOPCO* principle, because they both look to the (future) acquisition of property. It is a tougher call whether these capital expenditures should be allocated to both rejected and acquired properties or should (instead) all be allocated only to the cost of acquired properties, assuming that all of them are of the same type. (Costs of actually completing the transaction are garden-variety transaction costs.)

The post-*INDOPCO* regulations on intangibles are of little help. Regs. §§ 1.263(a)-4(e)(1)(i) and -5(b)(1) require capitalization of costs of "facilitating" a "transaction," and "facilitating" includes "investigating and pursuing" a transaction. However, "transaction" appears to refer only to an actual acquisition of an intangible. Effectively the regulations expand the concept of "transaction cost" backward in time, but fail to provide for the costs of nonacquired properties.

Even though preliminary investigation costs and evaluation costs are both inherently capital expenditures, they might be allocated to different assets (or allocated in different ways). The distinction would be especially difficult to manage in the area of research and experimentation, but Congress has here simplified accounting by enacting § 174, which allows expensing by a business of "research and experimentation" costs of a scientific or technical nature.

NOTES

1. The notion apparently advanced in *Rev. Rul. 77-254* that preliminary investigation costs are *never* deductible seems astonishing, but it might appear to be analogous to the doctrine, explored in Chapter 9, that the costs of putting oneself in a position to carry on a profession (e.g., education costs) are nondeductible "personal" outlays. The analogy, however, is not persuasive, because education costs are concededly the price of acquiring an asset that is personal to the taxpayer ("human capital") in the sense of being nontransferable and also in the sense of providing benefits in the personal (social, family, non-income producing) realm. The outlays described in *Rev. Rul. 77-254,* supra, in contrast, hardly appear to be personal in any sense, although they do appear to be "capital."

2. Excluded from the category of capital expenditures (as transaction costs, broadly construed) are employee compensation and overhead, as well as de minimis (under $5K) costs. See Reg. § 1.263(a)-4(e)(4).

3. *Exploration* expenses with respect to mineral interests other than oil and gas can, under § 617, be deducted currently. Any costs deducted under a § 617 election must be "recaptured" (i.e., included in gross income) if and when production commences, and the recaptured amount is to be deducted or capitalized, as appropriate, in the manner described in § 617(b)(1). If production does not occur, the earlier deduction is unaffected; in effect, the earlier deduction is an acceleration of a future loss.

3. Development Costs

Development costs are incurred *after* the acquisition of a property and are undertaken to prepare the property for production, use, or sale. Development costs resemble indirect acquisition (i.e., transaction) costs that should be capitalized. However, product development that comes within § 174 can be expensed. Additionally, § 263(c) and Reg. § 1.612-4 allow expensing of "intangible drilling and development costs" (IDCs) associated with oil and gas wells. IDCs essentially include the costs of preparing the land and drilling the wells. The cost of permanent structures, such as pumps, storage tanks, and pipelines, must still be capitalized. Section 616 provides similar rules for the development (as well as the exploration) of minerals other than oil and gas.

Sections 174, 263(c), and 616 are clearly tax expenditures by reason of treating outlays that are (wholly or partly) capital expenditures as expenses.

4. Pre-Opening Costs

Pre-opening costs can be described as costs which would be business expenses if the business were in operation, but which are not deductible because of the § 162(a) requirement that the taxpayer be presently "carrying on" a trade or business. The IRS does not consider that a business is being carried on until it begins to sell goods and services to the public.[6] This approach left open the question of what to do, if anything, with disallowed pre-opening costs. The argument for capitalization is that these "expenses" are preparatory to establishing the business as a going concern. But this approach would yield no benefit to the taxpayer by reason of the fact that the resulting "asset" (once created) is not depreciable (because it does not waste with the passage of time). Section 195 was enacted as a legislative compromise over this issue.

Section 195 is an elective provision that allows the taxpayer a deduction for the year in which a new active trade or business begins. The deduction equals the lesser of (1) the start-up expenditures for that trade or business or (2) $5K reduced (but not below zero) by start-up expenditures for that trade or business that exceed $50K. Start-up expenditures greater than the currently deductible amount are amortized (depreciated) evenly over a 180-month period starting when the active trade or business begins.

---

[6] The leading case taking this approach is *Richmond Television Corporation v. U. S.*, 345 F.2d 901 (4th Cir. 1965).

"Start-up expenditures" are defined broadly as outlays incurred in creating or investigating an active trade or business, as well as outlays incurred in anticipation of transforming a profit-seeking investment activity to an active business. But only outlays that *would have been treated as expenses if they had been incurred by an operating trade or business* are governed by § 195. See § 195(c)(1)(B). Thus, true capital expenditures (*i.e.*, the cost of business buildings and equipment and other items that would be capital expenditures even if incurred by an ongoing business) must be capitalized in the usual fashion.

In *Rev. Rul. 99-23*, 1999-1 C.B. 998, which relied on the legislative history to § 195, which in turn relied in part on *Rev. Rul. 77-254*, supra, the IRS held that preliminary search and investigation costs fell within § 195 (despite being capital expenditures), but that (transaction) costs relating to the actual acquisition of a business were capital expenditures beyond the reach of § 195.

Section 195 is discussed again in Chapter 8.B.5 in connection with the "carrying on" requirement of § 162.

Rules similar to § 195 are provided in § 248 regarding the organizational expenses of a new corporation and in § 709 with respect to the costs of organizing a new partnership.

NOTE

Rev. Rul. 99-23, supra, and the legislative history of § 195 both assume that costs of expanding an existing trade or business are deductible as expenses.[7] However, this scenario only satisfies the "carrying on" requirement of § 162. Expansion costs would still appear to be capital expenditures under *INDOPCO*, because the aim is to expand the earnings base of the business. See *FMR Corp. v. Comm'r*, 110 T.C. 402 (1998) (holding that not every business expansion cost is an expense). The post-*INDOPCO* regulations do not address this issue.

PROBLEMS

1. Mammoth Corp. negotiates an agreement to acquire all the stock of Pipsqueak, Inc., contingent on getting a favorable private letter ruling from the IRS regarding Mammoth's tax consequences from the acquisition. The IRS rules unfavorably, and the transaction is abandoned. According to *Rev. Rul. 77-254*, what is the correct income tax treatment of the legal and accounting expenses that Mammoth incurred in getting the ruling?

2. In *Rev. Rul. 77-254*, did the IRS correctly classify as "personal" the taxpayer's expenses "incurred in the course of a general search for, or preliminary investigation of, a business or investment?" In approaching this question, consider the following:

---

[7] Pre-*INDOPCO* cases had generally held that business expansion costs (not involving the acquisition of particular assets such as buildings and equipment) were expenses, see, e.g., *Briarcliff Candy Corp. v. Comm'r*, 475 F.2d 775 (2d Cir. 1973), and § 195 seems to be based on this (dubious) assumption. But see *Central Texas Savings & Loan Assoc. v. U.S.*, 731 F.2d 1181 (5th Cir. 1984).

(a) If the search had been successful, would the investigation costs be considered "indirect acquisition costs?" If so, does abandonment render them any less capital expenditures?

(b) If the costs were capital expenditures, what Code sections are ruled out as the basis for allowing a deduction? What was the asset? Was it a personal use asset?

(c) Is *Rev. Rul. 77-254* an exercise in misguided literalism? What is the probable function of the term "transaction entered into profit" in § 165(c)(2)? If the function is to weed out losses from personal-use assets, what (then) is the function of the word "transaction?" (Did Congress likely give this much thought?) Since § 165 deals with "transactional" losses with respect to specific assets (as opposed to overall "operating" losses of an activity or business), couldn't "transaction" simply be viewed as shorthand for "asset" or "account"? Under the narrow view of "transaction" adopted by *Rev. Rul. 77-254*, if the transaction (deal) isn't consummated, how can there be a "transaction" at all? Stated differently, how could "transaction" then mean "deal?"

(d) Is there abuse potential in the scenario raised by *Rev. Rul. 77-254* that commends a restrictive view of "transaction?"

3.   Does § 195 change the result in *Rev. Rul. 77-254*? *Rev. Rul. 83-103*?

D.   THE REPAIR EXPENDITURE EXCEPTION

Many (most?) repair and maintenance activities with respect to business and investment property create benefits that last substantially into future years. Accordingly, most repair and maintenance costs would be capitalized under a strict application of *INDOPCO*. Nevertheless, "expensing" of these costs with respect to business and investment property has been allowed by the regulations since the early days of the income tax, and in *Rev. Rul. 94-12*, 1994-1 C.B. 36, the IRS held that *INDOPCO* made no change on this point.

Apparently, neither the Treasury nor the IRS has ever explained the rationale for the repair and maintenance expense deduction allowance. But in the early days of the income tax when computers did not exist and tax records were kept by hand, it would surely have been an unbearable nuisance to have to increase basis and to adjust schedules of future depreciation allowances whenever property was repaired. Consequently, the repair deduction allowance may have originated as a rule of administrative expediency that is now so deeply ingrained in income tax law that the IRS felt compelled to rule that it had survived *INDOPCO*. Regardless of its origin, the repair expense exception to the general capitalization principle is now a bedrock feature of federal income tax law.

Repair and maintenance expenses are deductible only if they pertain to business or investment property. Costs of repairing damage or deterioration to a taxpayer's personal residence, for example, are nondeductible. Also, the rules outlined below for distinguishing between repair and maintenance expenses and capital expenditures are nonelective. Thus, an outlay that qualifies as a repair or maintenance expense must be treated as such even if it would be advantageous in a particular case for the taxpayer to capitalize the expenditure.

The regulations state that amounts "expended in restoring property or in making good the exhaustion thereof" are capital expenditures, not repair or maintenance expenses. The regulations also state that an outlay that "adapts property to a new or different use" is a capital expenditure, not a repair or maintenance cost. In contrast, an outlay that "neither materially add[s] to the value of the property nor appreciably prolong[s] its life, but keep[s] it in an ordinarily efficient operating condition" qualifies as a repair or maintenance expense. See Reg. §§ 1.162-4, 1.263(a)-1(a) & (b). The "materially adds to the value of the property" and "appreciably prolongs its life" tests for capitalization should not be taken too literally in this context because (as stated in *Rev. Rul. 2001-4*, 2001-1 C.B. 295):

> Any properly performed repair, no matter how routine, could be considered to prolong the useful life and increase the value of the property if it is compared to the situation existing immediately prior to that repair.

Thus, it is important to understand that the "baseline" for applying the "added value" and "prolonged life" tests is not necessarily the asset as it existed immediately before the outlay (with the asset not functioning or in disrepair) but rather (and this is somewhat hard to articulate) the asset in the normal operating condition and useful life that was projected upon *acquisition*.

These tests are admittedly vague, and it is necessary to turn to cases and rulings to flesh them out.

AMERICAN BEMBERG CORP. v. COMMISSIONER
United States Tax Court
10 T.C. 361 (1948) (reviewed),
aff'd, 177 F.2d 200 (6th Cir. 1949) (per curiam)

BLACK, JUDGE:

[In 1925–1928, petitioner built a factory. In 1940 and 1941 portions of the floor caved in. In 1941 and 1942 petitioner expended almost $1 million to fill in large cavities in the subsoil between the bedrock and the building's floor with grout (essentially low-grade cement). Petitioner claimed these amounts as business expense deductions.]

In deciding whether the expenditures may be classed as expenses of the business or whether they [were capital expenditures], we think it is appropriate to consider the purpose, the physical nature, and the effect of the work for which the expenditures were made. In connection with the purpose of the work, [the outlays were] intended [to] avert a plant-wide disaster and avoid forced abandonment of the plant. The purpose was not to improve, better, extend, or increase the original plant, nor to prolong its original useful life. Its continued operation was endangered; the purpose of the expenditures was to continue in operation not on any better scale, but on the same scale and as efficiently as it had operated before. The purpose was not to rebuild or replace the plant, but to keep it as it was and where it was.

In connection with the physical nature of the work, the drilling and grouting was not a work of construction nor the creating of anything new. While the amount of grout introduced was large, it by no means represented a large percentage of the tremendous cube of earth standing between the plant floor and the bedrock which lay at an average depth of over 50 feet below the plant floor. The work could not successfully have been of smaller scope.

In connection with the effect of the work, the accomplishment of what was done forestalled imminent disaster and gave petitioner some assurance that major cave-ins would not occur in the future. The original geological defect has not been cured; rather its immediate consequences have been dealt with.

One of the leading cases in the field of what are capital expenditures and expenses is *Illinois Merchants Trust Co. v. Comm'r*, 4 B.T.A. 103 (acq.).[8] In that case the taxpayer owned a warehouse resting on wooden piles. During the taxable year unprecedentedly low water exposed parts of the piles usually under water. Dry rot set in and the warehouse began to settle so badly as to threaten collapse. To prevent a total loss and halt this accelerated deterioration the taxpayer had all piles sawed off below the low water mark and installed concrete sections between the stumps of the piles and the bottom of the building. Much of the floor was removed in the process and one exterior wall was considerably shored up. It was held in that case that the expenditures there involved were not for permanent betterments and improvements but were repairs and deductible as ordinary and necessary business expenses.

We hold that the expenditures in question were business expenses rather than capital expenditures.

Reviewed by the Court.[9]

MURDOCK, J., dissenting: These large expenditures created a substantial underground structure, a part of the plant, which did not exist, had no previous counterparts, and was not a part of the petitioner's capital previously. Its life and benefits would last for considerably more than one year. The expenditures were capital in their nature and should be recovered ratably over its useful life.

In *United Dairy Farmers, Inc. v. U. S.*, 267 F.3d 510 (6th Cir. 2001), the taxpayer knowingly purchased two pieces of contaminated business real estate. Cleanup costs, however, proved to be more than twice the amount of the good-faith expert estimates on which the taxpayer had relied in making the purchases. Nevertheless, the court held that these costs were not deductible repair expenses but, instead, had to be capitalized. The opinion stated that "when a taxpayer improves property

---

[8] [Editor's note: The "B.T.A." cite refers to the Board of Tax Appeals, which was the predecessor of the Tax Court. The "(acq.)," standing for "acquiescence," refers to the fact that the IRS has acquiesced in the result and/or decision of the Board of Tax Appeals or the Tax Court. Acquiesences (and nonacquiescenses) are noted in the Cumulative Bulletins. A "(nonacq.)" means that the IRS will not follow the decision but will continue to litigate the issue.]

[9] [Editor's note: A "reviewed" decision of the Tax Court means that all judges participated in the final decision (an en banc decision), even though only one judge presided at the actual trial. Reviewed decisions carry more precedential weight than single-judge decisions, which are the norm.]

defects that were present when the taxpayer acquired the property, the remediation of those defects [is] capital in nature." In an earlier case, the Tax Court explained that the rule applied in *United Dairy Farmers* is based on the notion that when a taxpayer acquires property with a known defect, the acquisition is not completed until the defect is cured. See *Mt. Morris Drive-In Theatre Co. v. Comm'r*, 25 T.C. 272, 275 (1955).

Cinergy v. U.S., 55 Fed. Cl. 489 (2003), is a contrasting case. There the taxpayer had acquired a building in 1972 that contained newly installed asbestos fire-proofing material. At the time, the material did not pose either a present or anticipated health hazard. It gradually deteriorated, however, and by 1989, it had become a potential threat to workers in the building. The court allowed the taxpayer to currently deduct the costs of removing and encapsulating the asbestos materials. *United Dairy Farmers*, supra, was distinguished on the ground that the asbestos material did not constitute a defect at the time the building was acquired in 1972.

If the building in *American Bemberg* had collapsed, then the issue would have been whether costs of restoration are repairs or capital expenditures. Where a loss deduction is taken on account of the collapse, the basis would be adjusted downward for the loss, and the restoration costs would almost certainly be capital expenditures. Being able to deduct both the loss and the costs of making good the loss would somewhat have the effect of deducting the same loss twice, despite ending up with a functioning asset.

An outlay that replaces a part or component of a whole (say, a new transmission in a truck) might conceivably be viewed as a capital expenditure, even if the *effect* of the replacement of the component on the whole is to maintain the whole in normal operating condition or to prevent premature loss. But it is generally agreed that it would be too hard to account for separate components of an asset,[10] unless there is a strong justification for the separate-component approach in a particular situation. For example, a business or investment building is treated as a separate asset apart from the underlying land for a compelling reason: the building can be depreciated, whereas the land cannot. Thus, the cost of surveying land boundaries and the alteration of the land surface to effectuate drainage would all normally be treated as additions to the basis of the land, and the costs of erecting a building thereon would be included in the basis of the building. In contrast, the separate-component approach would normally not be applied with respect to personal-use property (no part of which is depreciable) or to the various components (elevators, heating and air conditioning systems, etc.) of business or investment buildings. See generally § 168(i)(6).

In *Rev. Rul. 2001-4*, 2001-1 C.B. 295, the IRS considered various kinds of maintenance outlays with respect to large airplanes. Some airplane components, such as engines, seats, and radar systems, are detachable or obtainable separately. However, the ruling eschewed treating any replacement item as a separate asset and looked to the plane as a whole. The ruling states:

---

[10] If a replacement component were a capital expenditure, then logic would dictate that the basis of the replaced component should be subtracted from the basis of the asset. It would be illogical for the basis of, say, a car to include both the cost of the replaced engine and the cost of the replacement engine. But it would be hard to determine the depreciated basis of the separate component.

[If replacement parts] are a relatively minor portion of the physical structure of the asset, or any of its major parts, such that the asset as a whole has not gained materially in value or useful life, then the costs may be deducted as repairs. If, however, a major component or a structural part of the asset is replaced and, as a result, the asset as a whole has increased in value, life expectancy, or use, then the costs must be capitalized.

Rev. Rul. 2001-4 also refers to "the plan of rehabilitation doctrine," under which "a [repair-like] expenditure made as part of a general plan of rehabilitation, modernization, and improvement must be capitalized, even though, standing alone, the item may be classified as a repair." However, the fact that an improvement is made together with repairs does not by itself indicate the existence of a general plan of rehabilitation. Unfortunately, neither the IRS nor the courts have provided any meaningful guidelines for determining the existence of a general plan of rehabilitation. Consequently, this is a highly uncertain, fact-sensitive issue.

In 2008, the Treasury promulgated Prop. Reg. § 1.263(a)-3, which provides detailed rules regarding the distinction between capital expenditures and maintenance or repair expenses with respect to tangible assets. These rules are lengthy and detailed, but they generally follow the principles explained above, although with some significant modifications. As this book goes to press, these regulations are only in proposed form, and therefore have not attained the status of law.

PROBLEMS

1.   Cliff buys a boat for $100K and then spends $50K fixing it up. Explain why Cliff would prefer to characterize this expenditure as a repair cost if the boat is used in his business but as a capital expenditure if the boat is used for his personal recreation. Can Cliff elect to treat these costs as repairs or improvements?

2.   State which of the following are repair expenses:

(a) Cost of patching a leaky roof.

(b) Cost of correcting termite damage which, if left untreated, would cause the collapse of the building, assuming that the damage was discovered after the taxpayer owned the property for a few years.

(c) Same as (b), except the taxpayer knew of the damage when the property was acquired.

(d) Cost of adding additional units to a motel.

(e) Cost of refurbishing a hotel that the taxpayer had owned for several years. The refurbishing consisted of new wallpaper, attached light fixtures, paint, carpets, furniture, and flat-screen TVs.[11]

(f) Cost of salvaging the taxpayer's barge, which had sunk as the result of a hurricane.

---

[11] See *Moss v. Comm'r*, 831 F.2d 833 (9th Cir. 1987).

Part Three

DIFFERENTIATING AMONG THE BUSINESS, INVESTMENT, AND PERSONAL SPHERES

Part One set out the basic principle that business and investment costs are deductible (sooner or later), whereas personal costs are not (with certain exceptions). Part Two explained both the importance of the capitalization principle and how the capitalization doctrine actually works. This Part deals with business and investment *expenses*, i.e., outlays that are not characterized as capital expenditures under the rules explored in Chapter 7.

Chapter 8 discusses the distinction between business and investment, and then proceeds to lay out the basic statutory requirements for deducting business and investment expenses. Chapter 9 elaborates on what is "personal" by examining the concept of human capital in general and educational costs in particular. Chapter 10 deals with situations (such as operating losses from hobby activities) where the taxpayer's activity shows, Janus-like, both a personal and an income-production "face" throughout. Chapter 11, which generally covers techniques for allocating deductions between income-production and personal activity, includes a discussion of travel and entertainment (T & E) expenses.

Chapter 8

THE BASIC FRAMEWORK GOVERNING BUSINESS AND INVESTMENT DEDUCTIONS

All respectable theories of an ability-to-pay income tax hold that decreases in a taxpayer's wealth relating to income-producing activities *should* be deductible, but those relating to personal consumption should not be deductible. At the same time, and as noted in Chapter 2, no expense, loss, or depreciation is deductible unless a Code provision specifically allows it. When these two principles collide, the first (that costs of producing income *should* be deductible) is usually the loser, meaning that the expense or loss will not be deductible in the absence of statutory authority. Hence, it is essential to grasp the statutory framework governing business and investment deductions.

A. THE DISTINCTION BETWEEN BUSINESS AND INVESTMENT

Deductions for *business* expenses, depreciation, and losses have always been allowed by the Code. The relevant provisions are §§ 162(a), 167(a)(1), and 165(c)(1). However, the realm of "income production" extends beyond "business" activity to encompass investments, wagering, and perhaps more.

1. How the Code Came to Allow Deductions for the Production of Nonbusiness Income

The Supreme Court confronted the tension between what should be deductible as a matter of theory and what was allowable as a deduction under the Code in the 1941 case of *Higgins v. Comm'r*, 312 U.S. 212 (1941). With respect to "expenses," the statute then in effect contained only the predecessor of § 162, allowing deductions for ordinary and necessary expenses of carrying on a "trade or business." The taxpayer in *Higgins* carried on extensive activities in managing his personal investment portfolio and incurred expenses for rent, salaries, etc., in connection with that activity. Although these expenses clearly related to the production of investment income and gains (and not to personal consumption), the Supreme Court held that the taxpayer's activities did not rise to the status of a "trade or business" and, therefore, that the individual's management expenses were not deductible under the statute! Thus, literal adherence to the Code resulted in a decision that clearly violated income tax theory.

Congress immediately (in 1942) overturned the result of *Higgins* by enacting the predecessor of § 212(1) and (2), allowing a deduction for nonbusiness *expenses* incurred in (1) the production or collection of income or (2) the management, conservation, or maintenance of property held for the production of income. Congress also adopted §§ 165(c)(2) and 167(a)(2) to make it clear that deductions would be allowed for nonbusiness property losses realized in a "transaction entered into for profit" and for depreciation on nonbusiness property held for the "production of income." By way of shorthand, this book sometimes uses the term "investment" to refer to the realm of nonbusiness activities and transactions that give rise to deductions under these provisions.

2. Significance of Distinction between Business and Investment

It is noteworthy that Congress did not address *Higgins* by redefining "business" to include "investment," but instead enacted a set of Code provisions that independently allow investment deductions. Thus, the *Higgins* principle that even extensive investment activity does not constitute a trade or business still stands. But if *both* business and investment expenses, depreciation, and losses are allowable under the post-*Higgins* amendments, the obvious question is whether the distinction between business and investment has any continuing significance. It turns out that there are several areas where the distinction "makes a difference."

Historically, the most important area where the distinction matters has been the distinction between "business" and "nonbusiness" bad debts under § 166 (also, by the way, enacted in 1942). Business bad debt losses are ordinary losses (and can generate a deduction to the extent of their partial worthlessness), but "nonbusiness" (i.e., investment) bad debt losses are treated as short-term capital losses under § 166(d)(1) (and the unpaid portion of the debt must be wholly worthless before any deduction is allowed).

Another area where the distinction between business and investment is important is in sorting out above-the-line deductions, regular itemized deductions, and "miscellaneous itemized deductions" (MIDs), the significance of which is explained in Chapter 2.D.1.d. Recall that nonemployee business deductions are above the line, i.e., are deductible in addition to the standard deduction. Investment deductions are above the line only in limited cases: (1) loss deductions from the sale or exchange of property, (2) deductions connected to rent and royalty income, and (3) deductions relating to tax-favored investment vehicles (such as IRAs, MSAs, and qualified retirement plans). See § 62(a)(3), (4), (6), (7), and (19). Otherwise, investment deductions of an individual are itemized deductions, and, what is worse, they are (with some exceptions) miscellaneous itemized deductions (MIDs) that are (1) deductible for regular income tax purposes only to the extent that the aggregate of them exceeds 2% of AGI and (2) disallowed in full under the Alternative Minimum Tax (AMT), described in Chapter 2.D.2.

A third area is capital gains and losses. Investment gains and losses are typically characterized as capital gains and losses because investment assets are usually "capital assets" within the meaning of § 1221(a). Property used in a trade or business is mostly taken out of "capital asset" characterization, but then it might sneak back in through § 1231. Property "held primarily for sale to customers in the ordinary course of trade or business" (often referred to as "dealer property") is neither a capital asset nor a § 1231 asset, and therefore always yields ordinary income or loss.

A fourth area in which the distinction between business and investment is important is § 163(d), which limits the deductibility of "investment interest" to the amount of "net investment income" for the year.[1] Excess investment interest for the year that is disallowed under § 163(d) can be carried forward to other taxable years until it used. Incidentally, none of the interest deductions are MIDs.[2] See § 67(b)(1).

A fifth area is net operating loss (NOL) carryovers. The net operating losses of a business can be carried over to other years, but nonbusiness losses cannot. See § 172(d)(4).

A sixth area is the U.S. taxation of foreign taxpayers. A separate tax regime exists for certain U.S. nonbusiness income of foreign taxpayers as opposed to U.S. business income.[3]

3.   Distinguishing between Business and nonbusiness Income Production

There is no definition of "business" or "investment" in the Code or regulations. Most of the law is found in court decisions.

Higgins was anticipated by *Burnet v. Clark*, 287 U.S. 410 (1932). There a principal stockholder and CEO of a corporation guaranteed the corporation's notes and later had to make good the guarantee. In denying an NOL carryover with respect to the guarantee payment, the Court stated that the taxpayer's loss was not a business loss because he had given the guarantee to protect his stock investment. The Court added that a corporation's business is not generally attributed to its shareholders.

Snyder v. Comm'r, 295 U.S. 134 (1935), arose in a context where the IRS had been treating full time stock traders as being engaged in a business. A "trader" makes a living by buying and selling stock on a short-term basis for the trader's own account. Although in this particular case the taxpayer failed to establish that he was in a trade or business by reason of trading part time, the case is cited for the proposition that stock trading on a full time basis is a business.

In *Higgins*, supra, which is still good law as to what "business" is (or is not), the Court stated (312 U.S. at 318):

> The petitioner merely kept records and collected interest and dividends from his securities, through managerial attention for his investments. No

---

[1] See *Yaeger v. Comm'r*, 889 F.2d 29 (2d Cir. 1989) (examining whether the taxpayer was an "investor" subject to § 163(d) or a "trader" who was not). The technicalities of § 163(d) are dealt with in Chapter 18.D.3.

[2] Nor is it subject to the § 68 rule (that expired at the end of 2009, but could reappear in some form) reducing aggregate allowable itemized deductions. See § 68(c)(2)).

[3] See §§ 871(a) and 881(a) (certain nonbusiness gross income taxed at 30% rate); 871(b) and 882(a) (taxable income effectively connected with a U.S. trade or business taxed under normal rate schedules).

matter how large the estate or how continuous or extended the work required may be, such facts are not sufficient as a matter of law to permit the courts to reverse the decision of the Board [of Tax Appeals that active management of a securities portfolio does not constitute carrying on a business].[4]

In *Whipple v. Comm'r*, 373 U.S. 193 (1963), the Court dealt with a claimed business bad-debt loss arising from a loan by a promoter of corporations to one of the corporations he formed (and in which he held stock). To prevail, the promoter needed to show a sufficient connection between the loan and a business carried on by him. He was not engaged in a money-lending business, and, because he received no salary or fees from the corporation for his efforts, he was not carrying on the business of being a corporate employee. Therefore, the promoter was forced to argue that being a promoter was itself a business. The Commissioner argued that the loan was made to the corporation in the taxpayer's capacity as a shareholder, which would put the loan into the "nonbusiness" category. The Court agreed with the Commissioner, stating (373 U.S. at 202):

> Devoting one's time and energies to the affairs of a corporation is not of itself, and without more, a trade or business of the person so engaged. Though such activities may produce income, profit or gain in the form of dividends or enhancement in the value of an investment, this return is distinctive to the process of investing and is generated by the successful operation of the corporation's business as distinguished from the trade or business of the taxpayer himself.

Being an "employee" constitutes a business in itself. Hence, if a person who lends to a corporation is both a shareholder (investment capacity) and employee (business capacity) and the debt becomes uncollectible, the person will usually claim that the debt should be characterized as "business" because of her employee status. However, Reg. § 1.166-5(b) provides that a debt is a "business" debt only if its relationship to the taxpayer's business is a "proximate" one. While the term "proximate" is construed broadly in the field of tort causation, in *U. S. v. Generes*, 405 U.S. 93 (1971), the Court interpreted that term much more narrowly for purposes of characterizing a debt as business or nonbusiness. In *Generes*, the Court held that a taxpayer who is both an employee and investor with respect to a corporate debtor can succeed in asserting that a debt of the corporation is a "business" debt only if protecting salary was the taxpayer's "dominant" motivation for making the loan. Mr. Generes's debt failed to qualify as a "business" bad debt because the Court was convinced that he made the loan to the corporation to protect his substantial initial investment in the corporation (approximately $200K in stock and earlier loans) rather than his salary in the corporation ($12K per year before tax). In addition to the comparatively small size of his salary, he worked only 6 to 8 hours per week for the corporation, had another full time job, and had significant

---

[4] *Higgins* was followed by *City Bank Farmers Trust Co. v. Helvering*, 313 U.S. 121 (1941), and *U.S. v. Pyne*, 313 U.S. 127 (1941), which held that the efforts of an estate or trust in asset conservation and maintenance did not constitute a trade or business. The language of § 212(2), which overturns these results, clearly references these cases.

outside earnings. Thus, his bad debt was deductible only as a nonbusiness bad debt.[5]

Comm'r v. Groetzinger, 480 U.S. 23 (1987), is the Supreme Court's most recent decision in this area. That case held that a full time gambler who made wagers solely for his own account was engaged in a business. The Court relied upon dictum in *Snyder*, stating (480 U.S at 33):

> If a taxpayer devotes his full time activity to gambling, and it is his intended livelihood source, it would seem that basic concepts of fairness (if there be much of that in the income tax law) demand that his activity be regarded as a trade or business just as any other readily accepted activity, such as being a retail store proprietor or, to come closer categorically, as being a casino operator or as being an active trader on the exchanges.

The Court rejected a test for what constitutes a business that would have required that the taxpayer sell goods or services, but added (480 U.S. at 35):

> We do not overrule or cut back on the Court's holding in *Higgins* when we conclude that if one's gambling activity is pursued full time, in good faith, and with regularity, to the production of income for a livelihood, and is not a mere hobby, it is a trade or business within the meaning of the statutes with which we are here concerned.

NOTES

1. (a) Around the time that *Higgins* was decided in 1941, the Supreme Court was giving heavy deference to the Board of Tax Appeals and its successor, the Tax Court, on both questions of fact *and* questions of law, as though the Tax Court were an administrative body with a high degree of technical expertise. Indeed, the Board of Tax Appeals was a quasi-administrative agency within the Treasury Department. This rule of deference came to be known as the "*Dobson* rule," named after *Dobson v. Comm'r*, 320 U.S. 489 (1943), set forth in another context in Chapter 26.B.6.a. Congress overturned the *Dobson* rule in 1948 by enacting what is now § 7482(a), mandating appellate court review of Tax Court decisions in the same manner as review of U.S. District Court decisions.

(b) Since the Supreme Court continues to treat the business/nonbusiness distinction as a question of fact, the appeals courts will typically defer to the trial courts. And decisions like *Higgins*, supposedly based on the facts, tend to harden into bedrock rules of tax law: managing one's own investments, even if they are very extensive and engage one full time, does not amount to carrying on a trade or business.

2. (a) Is the *Snyder/Groetzinger* duo compatible with *Higgins* and the others?

---

[5] In contrast, the taxpayer in *Haslam v. Comm'r*, T.C. Memo. 1974-97, convinced the Tax Court that his dominant motivation in making a loan to the corporation that employed him (in which he also owned stock) was to protect his full time job, at an annual salary of $15K, not his investment in shares of $20K. An important factor to the court was that Haslam's skills were idiosyncratic enough (an explosives expert) that when the employer corporation ultimately failed, he was unable to find another job at that same pay level.

Both a gambler and a successful stock trader claim skill, and both activities can produce a livelihood. Perhaps the interest, dividends, and gains of an investor constitute a kind of "passive" return, whereas a gambler has personal interaction with other gamblers and the house. That might seem to leave stock traders (who operate by making numerous purchases and sales on a short-term basis) as being closer to investors like Higgins than to gamblers like Groetzinger, but the well-settled rule that stock traders are engaged in business is ultimately based on an IRS concession of such long standing that it may now be effectively irreversible.

(b) The "livelihood" test applied to traders and gamblers initially appears to be somewhat inconsistent with the rule that a taxpayer can be in more than one business at a time. Thus, a full time employee can have a consulting business or a business as a writer or artist. Such side businesses may sometimes look like personal hobbies rather than livelihoods, which raise issues dealt with in the next chapter. Perhaps the "livelihood" test only comes into play in marginal situations where the taxpayer is not selling goods and services to others.

(c) Perhaps, as stated by Ralph Waldo Emerson, consistency is the hobgoblin of little minds.[6] Nevertheless, in this and other heavily caselaw laden areas of tax law, cases may often appear to be inconsistent. This state of affairs creates opportunities for tax attorneys to exploit.

(d) Another theme is the degree with which courts approach deduction issues by literal adherence to the Code. Under income tax *theory* (and policy), includible gross income *should* be reduced by directly related costs in order to avoid effectively doubly taxing the same dollars twice to the same taxpayer (by both including the *gross* return *and* denying deduction of — and thus indirectly taxing — the related expenses producing that return). Perhaps the most salient example of such double taxation occurred where attorney fees incurred to obtain (includible) tort and anti-discrimination-law recoveries were disallowed under the AMT, because they were MIDs.[7] Congress responded by enacting § 62(a)(20), which causes these deductions to be above-the-line, but only in certain discrimination cases.

(e) The problem of plaintiff attorney fees might be approached by viewing them as capital expenditures (either as costs of creating or developing the claim or as transaction costs) and then offsetting these costs against the recovery. If successful,

---

[6] The full quote, from Essay on Self-Reliance (1841), is,

"A foolish consistency is the hobgoblin of little minds, adored by little statesmen and philosophers and divines. With consistency a great soul has simply nothing to do. He may as well concern himself with his shadow on the wall. Speak what you think now in hard words, and to-morrow speak what to-morrow thinks in hard words again, though it contradict every thing you said to-day. — 'Ah, so you shall be sure to be misunderstood.' — Is it so bad, then, to be misunderstood? Pythagoras was misunderstood, and Socrates, and Jesus, and Luther, and Copernicus, and Galileo, and Newton, and every pure and wise spirit that ever took flesh. To be great is to be misunderstood."

[7] The deduction is initially allowed by § 212(1) as an expense for the production of (includible) income. Alternatively, the deduction could be conferred by § 162(a) in cases where the claim arose from the taxpayer's business as an employee. In either case, the deduction would be an MID. In *Comm'r v. Banks*, 543 U.S. 426 (2005), the Supreme Court rejected an attempt to bypass the deduction issue by treating the attorney fees as income received by the attorney directly from the defendant.

the costs would be "offsets," rather than "deductions,"[8] and the disadvantageous treatment of MIDs would be avoided. The litigation and business bars would strongly oppose capitalization of legal costs, however.

PROBLEM

State which of the following are "business" loans, the worthlessness of which will support an ordinary deduction under § 166(a):

(a) Accounts receivable of a department store;

(b) High-interest loans by a Mafia-connected person to various individuals with troubled credit histories;

(c) A one-time loan by a law firm's client, not in the lending business, to the law firm to allow it to pay off various firm debts; and,

(d) Same as (c), except that the lender is a leading partner in the law firm.

B. THE BASIC REQUIREMENTS OF DEDUCTIBILITY

This section explores the basic deductibility requirements under the Code, particularly under §§ 162(a) and 212(1) and (2).

1. The *Welch* Case

The famous case of *Welch v. Helvering* resists assignment to a single doctrinal pigeonhole. Instead, it interprets (perhaps obliquely) the various deductibility requirements contained in the lead-in clause of what is now § 162(a).

WELCH v. HELVERING
United States Supreme Court
290 U.S. 111 (1933)

Mr. Justice Cardozo delivered the opinion of the Court.

In 1922 petitioner was the secretary of E.L. Welch Company, a corporation engaged in the grain business. The company was adjudged an involuntary bankrupt, and had a discharge from its debts. Thereafter the petitioner made a contract with the Kellogg Company to purchase grain for it on a commission. In order to re-establish his relations with customers whom he had known when acting for the Welch Company and to solidify his credit and standing, he decided to pay the debts of the Welch business so far as he was able. In fulfillment of that resolve, he made payments of substantial amounts during five successive years. The Commissioner ruled that these payments were not deductible as ordinary and

---

[8] This approach is developed in Joseph M. Dodge, *The Netting of Costs against Income Receipts (Including Damage Recoveries) Produced by Such Costs, without Barring Congress from Disallowing Such Costs*, 27 VA. TAX REV. 297 (2007). The theory was offered in an amicus brief in *Comm'r v. Banks*, 543 U.S. 426 (2005), but the Supreme Court declined to consider it on the ground that it had not been presented to the courts below.

necessary expenses, but were rather in the nature of capital expenditures, an outlay for the development of reputation and good will.

We may assume that the payments to creditors of the Welch Company were necessary for the development of the petitioner's business, at least in the sense that they were appropriate and helpful. He certainly thought they were, and we should be slow to override his judgment. But the problem is not solved when the payments are characterized as necessary. Many necessary payments are charges upon capital [capital expenditures]. There is need to determine whether they are both necessary and ordinary. Now, what is ordinary, though there must always be a strain of constancy within it, is none the less a variable affected by time and place and circumstances. Ordinary in this context does not mean that the payments must be habitual or normal in the sense that the same taxpayer will have to make them often. A lawsuit affecting the safety of a business may happen once in a lifetime. The counsel fees may be so heavy that repetition is unlikely. None the less, the expense is an ordinary one because we know from experience that payments for such a purpose, whether the amount is large or small, are the common and accepted means of defense against attack. The situation is unique in the life of the individual affected, but not in the life of the group, the community, of which he is a part. At such times there are norms of conduct that help to stabilize our judgment, and make it certain and objective. The instance is not erratic, but is brought within a known type.

The line of demarcation is now visible. We try to classify this act as ordinary or the opposite, and the norms of conduct fail us. No longer can we have recourse to any fund of business experience, to any known business practice. Men do at times pay the debts of others without legal obligation or the lighter obligation imposed by the usages of trade or by neighborly amenities, but they do not do so ordinarily, not even though the result might be to heighten their reputation for generosity and opulence. Indeed, if language is to be read in its natural and common meaning, we should have to say that payment in such circumstances, instead of being ordinary, is in a high degree extraordinary. There is nothing ordinary in the stimulus evoking it, and none in the response. Here, indeed, as so often in other branches of the law, the decisive distinctions are those of degree and not of kind. One struggles in vain for any verbal formula that will supply a ready touchstone. The standard set up by the statute is not a rule of law; it is rather a way of life. Life in all its fullness must supply the answer to the riddle.

The Commissioner resorted to that standard, and found that the payments in controversy came closer to capital outlays than to ordinary and necessary expenses in the operation of a business. His ruling has the support of a presumption of correctness, and the petitioner has the burden of proving it to be wrong. Unless we can say from facts within our knowledge that these are ordinary and necessary expenses according to the ways of conduct and the forms of speech prevailing in the business world, the tax must be confirmed. But nothing told us by this record or within the sphere of our judicial notice permits us to give that extension to what is ordinary and necessary. Indeed, to do so would open the door to many bizarre analogies. One man has a family name that is clouded by thefts committed by an ancestor. To add to his own standing he repays the stolen money, wiping off, it may be, his income for the year. Another man conceives the notion that he will be able to practice his vocation with greater ease and profit if he has an opportunity to enrich his culture. Forthwith the price of his education becomes an expense of the business, reducing the income subject to taxation. There is little difference between these expenses and those in controversy here. Reputation and learning are akin to assets, like to the good will of an old partnership. For many, they are the only tools with which to hew a pathway to success. The money spent in acquiring them is well and wisely spent. It is not an ordinary expense of the operation of a business.

Sections 162(a) and 212(1) and (2) require that all of the following requirements be satisfied:

(1)   the outlay must be an "expense,"

(2)   that is "ordinary,"

(3)   and "necessary,"

(4)   in "carrying on" a business, producing or collecting (nonbusiness) income, or managing, conserving, or maintaining (nonbusiness) income-producing property.

That the expense must be "paid or incurred" only affects the taxable year in which the expense is deemed to occur, a question that normally depends on whether the taxpayer is on the cash method of tax accounting ("paid") or the accrual method of tax accounting ("incurred"). Tax accounting methods are dealt with in Chapter 23.A.

2.   The Outlay Must Be an "Expense"?

The distinction between "expense" and "capital expenditure" was the theme of the previous chapter. Only "expenses" can be deducted under §§ 162 and 212.

The last portion of Justice Cardozo's opinion in *Welch* seems to argue that the outlays were "capital expenditures" (instead of "expenses") to acquire an asset called "reputation," which is akin to "goodwill," a recognized business asset in the world of accounting and tax. This reference to reputation and goodwill creates confusion, because goodwill is not acquired directly (except where it is acquired as part of a pre-existing business), but is built up over time as a by-product of operating a business in a way that results in the retention of customer loyalty. What goes into developing goodwill is accounted for (and deducted) separately (e.g., as advertising expense, salary costs, rent for a prime location, and so on). Indeed, the Code and regulations dealing with capitalization do not mention "costs of creating goodwill." Thus, self-created business goodwill generally has no basis.

More importantly, the facts indicate that the reputation and goodwill referred to in *Welch* might have been those of the taxpayer personally. Attributes of a person that enhance a person's capacity to sell his or her services on the market are referred to collectively as "human capital." Human capital raises unique problems that are dealt with at the beginning of the next chapter, but here it can be confidently stated that human capital (and the "components" thereof) have no recoverable basis for income tax purposes. In any event, *Welch* is yet another authority (like *Rev. Rul. 77-254*, supra Chapter 7.C.2, dealing with the costs of searching for a business) that disallows deductions while leaving the reader (and the taxpayer) hanging as to the true tax character of the outlays in question.

3. The Expense Must Be Ordinary

In the early days of the income tax, before the enactment of § 263, the primary function of the term "ordinary" was to distinguish an "expense" from a "capital expenditure." Indeed, many cases, including *INDOPCO, Inc. v. Comm'r*, 503 U.S. 79 (1992), set forth in the previous chapter, have cited *Welch* for this very proposition. However, just as the borrowing exclusion is not in the Code (because borrowing does not result in an increase in wealth), it is equally unnecessary that the capitalization principle be found in a specific Code section like § 263, because a capital expenditure, not representing a decrease in wealth, cannot be an expense within the meaning of §§ 162 and 212. Additionally, numerous Code provisions, including § 263 (enacted in 1954), presuppose capitalization as a foundational directive under an income tax. Therefore, it is no longer necessary or desirable to peg capitalization to "ordinary" in §§ 162(a) and 212.

In *Welch*, Justice Cardozo discerned an additional role for the term "ordinary" that did somewhat match common usage, namely, the notion of the expense being accepted by the business community, even if it is not common or frequent in the experience of the particular business. Indeed, it appears that most cases (not involving capital expenditures) disallowing deductions under the "ordinary" requirement involve expenses that are voluntary, eccentric, or idiosyncratic. See, e.g., *Deputy v. Du Pont*, 308 U.S. 488 (1940) (expenses of arranging short sales that were not within the normal role of being an estate executor); *Friedman v. Delaney*, 171 F.2d 269 (1st Cir. 1948) (voluntarily assuming a client's obligation); *Heidt v. Comm'r*, 274 F.2d 25 (7th Cir. 1959) (failing to obtain reimbursement); *Trebilcock v. Comm'r*, 64 T.C. 852 (1975), *aff'd*, 557 F.2d 1226 (6th Cir. 1977) (per curiam) (fee paid to a minister for prayer sessions with taxpayer's employees).

Of course, the characteristic of eccentricity suggests "satisfying a personal need." See *Henry v. Comm'r*, 36 T.C. 879 (1961) (costs of maintaining a yacht carrying flag promoting taxpayer's business are not ordinary). Perhaps that explains why the "ordinary" requirement has never been used to disallow deductions merely because the expenses were for "cutting edge" services or technology that had not yet come into common use.

4. And Necessary

As indicated in *Welch*, the "necessary" concept in §§ 162 and 212 is rarely brought into play to disallow a deduction. Contrary to its literal meaning ("required," "forced," "because of need"), the term "necessary" is here watered down to mean "appropriate and helpful," which suggests that the taxpayer's "business (or investment) judgment" will be respected in virtually all cases. The problem with this formulation is not so much the delegation-to-the-taxpayer aspect (how could it, practically- speaking, be otherwise?), but rather the failure to complete the idea: appropriate or helpful to what? The "what" is carrying on a trade or business (or an investment activity), and the purpose of business and investment is to make a profit. Therefore, an expense should be disallowed where it cannot possibly contribute to increased profit (after the expense itself) or where the expense is predominantly personal in nature. Reg. § 1.212-1(d) somewhat captures this notion by stating that expenses not "reasonable in amount" and which do not "bear a reasonable and proximate relation to . . . the production of income" are nondeductible.

One of the very few cases where the "necessary" concept was cited as preventing a § 162 deduction is *Lucas v. Comm'r*, 79 T.C. 1 (1982), where the taxpayer was denied an employment-related deduction because he could have been reimbursed for the expense had he bothered to ask his employer. In *Henry v. Comm'r*, supra, the costs of maintaining a yacht were way out of proportion to the advertising value obtained from a business-related pennant flown from the mast. Another in this small group of cases is *Car-Ron Asphalt Paving Co. v. Comm'r*, 758 F.2d 1132 (6th Cir. 1985), which held that *legal* bribes paid to get jobs from a general contractor did not satisfy the necessary concept, because (1) the bribes reduced the taxpayer's profit, and (2) the taxpayer had been able to get most of its jobs without paying bribes. These cases might be cited for the proposition that wanton economic waste (or disguised personal consumption) does not satisfy the "necessary" test. But, otherwise, "necessary" is only rarely applied to disallow deductions, apparently because business-judgment rationalizations can be readily concocted after the fact, and courts are very reluctant to second-guess the appropriateness of "business" decisions.

5. In Carrying on a Trade, Business, or Investment Activity

Under § 162, the taxpayer must be "carrying on" an *existing* (as opposed to a planned future) trade or business. In *Welch*, it was not entirely clear if the taxpayer had already embarked upon a new trade or business, or was just preparing to do so. If the latter, the deduction could have been disallowed on the ground that the taxpayer was not carrying on a trade or business.

Prior to the enactment of § 195 (discussed in Chapter 7.C.4, supra), what to do with pre-opening business costs posed a dilemma. In theory, nonpersonal costs clearly aimed to produce income should be deductible sooner or later. But the Code seems to bar the deduction of "expenses" prior to when the business is carried on. One might strain to find that these are really capital expenditures for "establishing the business," but that would not appreciably help the taxpayer because there is no *depreciable* "asset" obtained thereby. Section 195 largely solved this problem by creating a separate amortizable account for start-up costs that would have been expenses if the business were operating. Nevertheless, it still has to be decided if expenses of this type are incurred before or after the business commences operations in order to determine if they are deductible under § 162 or by way of § 195, which often requires costs to be deducted more slowly than does § 162. Prior to the enactment of § 195, there were two lines of cases. One line (favored by the IRS) equated "carrying on" with commencing operations in the sense of producing goods or selling goods or services to the public.[9] Other cases resisted adopting a

---

[9] See, e.g., *Richmond Television Corporation v. U. S.*, 345 F.2d 901 (4th Cir. 1965); *Madison Gas &*

rule that allowed "expenses" that were clearly business-oriented to fall through the cracks just because the business hadn't yet opened its doors.[10] Since § 195 is now available, courts no longer have to play fast and loose with § 162 to allow pre-operating costs to be deductible. In any event, § 195(c)(2) specifically authorizes the Treasury to issue regulations on precisely the question of when a business commences, but so far no such regulations have appeared.

The "carrying on" phrase is not found in § 212, and § 195 only applies with reference to the beginning of an *active* trade or business (not a nonbusiness income-producing activity). Is there an implicit requirement under § 212 that the taxpayer must be "carrying on" a nonbusiness income-production activity before expense deductions may be taken? General statements can be found to the effect that § 212 must be construed *in pari materia* with § 162(a). See *U.S. v. Gilmore*, 372 U.S. 39, 45-46 (1963). On the other hand, none of the § 212 regulations purport to impose a "carrying on" requirement similar to the requirement in § 162. Additionally, Reg. § 1.212-1(b) states that an outlay to manage, conserve, or maintain income-producing property does not lose eligibility for deduction under § 212 just because it relates to future income.

In *Hoopengarner v. Comm'r*, 80 T.C. 538 (1983) (reviewed) (8 judges dissenting), *aff'd without pub. op.*, 745 F.2d 66 (9th Cir. 1984), lease payments on undeveloped property that would eventually become the site of an office building were allowed as deductions under § 212(2). The government unsuccessfully argued that allowing the deduction under § 212(2) would undermine the pre-opening doctrine, supra, in cases where the activity was headed toward business status. The Tax Court majority held that, because no carrying-on language can be found in § 212, there was no pre-opening doctrine under § 212, or at least § 212(2), in cases where the taxpayer currently owns property that can produce future income.

However, it is now agreed that *Hoopengarner* has been superseded by § 195(c)(1)(A)(iii) in cases where the activity is intended to ultimately become an active trade or business (and it does so).[11] At the same time, if a nonbusiness (but for-profit) activity has clearly commenced operations but then *unexpectedly* metamorphoses into a business, § 195 does not preclude § 212 deductions during the nonbusiness period just because the activity eventually became a business.[12]

Other than *Hoopengarner*, there appears to be no salient authority as to whether § 212 has an implicit carrying-on requirement for profit-making activity

---

Electric Company v. Comm'r, 72 T.C. 521 (1979); *Kennedy v. Comm'r*, T.C. Memo. 1973-15 (all disallowing pre-opening expenses).

[10] See, e.g., *Blitzer v. U.S.*, 684 F.2d 874 (Ct.Cl. 1982) (pre-opening expenses of low-income housing project); *U.S. v. Manor Care, Inc.*, 490 F. Supp. 355 (D. Md. 1980) (allowing deductions for pre-opening expenses of nursing homes).

[11] See, e.g., *Johnsen v. Comm'r*, 794 F.2d 1157 (6th Cir. 1986) (disapproving *Hoopengarner* on the grounds that pre-opening costs are capital expenditures and that following that case would render § 195 meaningless). Section 195(c)(1)(A)(iii), enacted after *Hoopengarner*, treats investment outlays incurred "in anticipation of [the investment] activity becoming an active trade or business" as nondeductible (but amortizable) start-up expenditures.

[12] See *Toth v. Comm'r*, 128 T.C. 1 (2007).

that never achieves business status.[13] In principle, however, because virtually all nonbusiness income-production activity involves *property* held for the production (sooner or later) of income, expenses of management, etc., should (if not capital expenditures) be allowable under § 212(2) even if income production hasn't commenced. Indeed, § 212(2) was construed broadly in *Trust of Bingham v. Comm'r*, 325 U.S. 365 (1945), where it was held that costs of terminating a trust and distributing the trust property to remainder beneficiaries fell within § 212(2), even though the trust itself would no longer be holding the trust assets for the production of income.

NOTES

1. The "ordinary and necessary" requirement cuts two ways. On the one hand, it calls attention to the fact that not all expenses occurring in the context of a business are deductible (because they might be personal expenses in disguise). On the other hand, it effectively delegates the business character of the deduction first to the taxpayer (a kind of tax business-judgment rule) and then to the business community. These delegations effectively create a strong presumption in favor of allowance.

2. There are numerous tax expenditure provisions relating to business operations and expenses.

(a) Section 199 allows a deduction equal to 9% of "qualified [domestic] production activities income," not to exceed 50% of "domestic production" W-2 wages paid for the year. The deduction is aimed to provide an incentive not to export jobs from the United States.

(b) Various business tax credits come, evolve, and go. These credits have been aimed at subsidizing such activities or items as the purchase of business equipment, the rehabilitation of old business-use buildings, the production of energy, the use of renewable energy sources, the undertaking of incremental technological research, the hiring of low-income workers, the hiring of persons in "empowerment zones," and the construction of low-income housing.

PROBLEMS

1. Ulrich is the CEO of a major corporation, and has a "retreat" on an isolated mountain lake in the Cascade Mountains in Washington. The property cost $20M, of which $4M is attributable to a 3,500 sq. ft. architecturally-significant building that is used exclusively an "office away from the office." Ulrich claims that the occasional quiet and isolation help keep his "engines" running "on all cylinders." Can Ulrich deduct depreciation on, and the costs of operating and maintaining the office building? See *Heineman v. Comm'r*, 82 T.C. 538 (1984). Ignore § 280A.

2. Mary has a JD and worked full time for a law firm from 2001-2006. From 2007 to 2010, Mary (having triplets to raise) worked sporadically as a legal

---

[13] In *Frank v. Comm'r*, 20 T.C. 511, 514 (1953), the court held that costs of searching for an investment were not deductible as expenses, but the rationale is that these were capital expenditures, and no loss deduction was allowable on the grounds that no "transaction" had been entered into.

consultant. In 2011, she performs no legal work as a consultant, but incurs various costs in preparation for resuming work. Are these costs deductible? See *Forrest v. Comm'r*, T.C. Memo. 2009-228.

C. CONNECTING EXPENSES TO AN INCOME-PRODUCING ACTIVITY

An issue (related to the carrying-on requirement) that sometimes arises is whether a given cost item *relates to* (is connected with) business or the production of income, or whether it instead relates to the personal realm. This issue is distinct from the question (dealt with in the next chapter) of whether *the activity itself* is primarily personal or primarily one of income production.

The *Gilmore* case below dealt with the deductibility of legal fees in a divorce action, and the issue was whether the legal fees were "personal" (because the unwinding of a personal relationship "caused" the litigation) or "investment" (because an unsuccessful outcome would have had the "effect" of causing the taxpayer to lose ownership of investment property). At a more mundane level, the case deals with the construction of § 212(2), which allows a deduction for expenses of maintaining or conserving income-producing property.

UNITED STATES v. GILMORE
United States Supreme Court
372 U.S. 39 (1963)

MR. JUSTICE HARLAN delivered the opinion of the Court.

In 1955 the California Supreme Court confirmed the award to the taxpayer of a decree of divorce, without alimony, against his wife Dixie Gilmore. The case before us involves the deductibility for federal income tax purposes of that part of the husband's legal expense incurred in such proceedings as is attributable to his successful resistance of his wife's claims to certain of his assets asserted by her to be community property under California law. The claim to such deduction is founded on [the 1939 Code predecessor of § 212(2)], which allows as deductions from gross income "ordinary and necessary expenses . . . incurred during the taxable year . . . for the . . . conservation . . . of property held for the production of income."

At the time of the divorce proceedings, instituted by the wife, respondent's property consisted primarily of controlling stock interests in three corporations, each of which was a franchised General Motors automobile dealer. As president and principal officer of the three corporations, he received salaries from them aggregating about $66,800 annually, and in recent years his total annual dividends had averaged about $83,000. The husband's overriding concern in the divorce litigation was to protect these assets against the claims of his wife. The respondent wished to defeat those claims for two important reasons. First, the loss of his controlling stock interests might well cost him the loss of his corporate positions, his principal means of livelihood. Second, there was also danger that if he were found guilty of his wife's sensational and reputation-damaging charges of marital infidelity, General Motors Corporation might find it expedient to exercise its right to cancel these dealer franchises.

The end result of this bitterly fought divorce case was a complete victory for the husband. The wife's community property claims were denied in their entirety, and she was held entitled to no alimony. Respondent's legal expenses in connection with this litigation amounted to $40,611 for the two taxable years in question.

Initially, it may be observed that the wording of [§ 212(2)] more readily fits the Government's view of the provision than [the taxpayer]. For in context "conservation of property" seems to refer to operations performed with respect to the property itself, such as safeguarding or upkeep, rather than to a taxpayer's retention of ownership in it.

The purpose of the 1942 amendment [that added § 212] was merely to enlarge "the category of incomes with reference to which expenses were deductible." And committee reports make clear that deductions under the new section were subject to the same limitations and restrictions that are applicable to those allowable under [§ 162]. Further, this Court has said that [§ 212] "is comparable and *in pari materia* with [§ 162]." *Trust of Bingham v. Comm'r*, 325 U.S. 365 (1945).

A basic restriction upon the availability of a [§ 162] deduction is that the expense item involved must be one that has a business origin. The pivotal issue in this case then becomes: was this part of respondent's litigation costs a "business" rather than a "personal" or "family" expense? The answer to this question has already been indicated in prior cases. In *Lykes v. U.S.*, 343 U.S. 118, the Court rejected the contention that legal expenses incurred in contesting a gift tax liability were deductible. The taxpayer argued that if he had been required to pay the original deficiency he would have been forced to liquidate his stockholdings, and that his legal expenses were therefore incurred in the "conservation" of income-producing property and hence deductible under [§ 212(2)]. The Court first noted that the "deductibility (of the expenses) turns wholly upon the nature of the activities to which they relate," and then stated:

> Legal expenses do not become deductible merely because they are paid for services which relieve a taxpayer of liability. That argument would carry us too far. It would mean that the expense of defending almost any claim would be deductible by a taxpayer on the ground that such defense was made to help him keep clear of liens whatever income-producing property he might have. For example, it suggests that the expense of defending an action based upon personal injuries caused by a taxpayer's negligence while driving an automobile for pleasure should be deductible.

In *Kornhauser v. U.S.*, 276 U.S. 145, this Court formulated the rule that "where a suit or action against a taxpayer is directly connected with, or . . . proximately resulted from, his business, the expense incurred is a business expense."

The principle we derive from these cases is that the characterization, as "business" or "personal," of the litigation costs of resisting a claim depends on whether or not the claim arises in connection with the taxpayer's profit-seeking activities. It does not depend on the consequences that might result to a taxpayer's income-producing property from a failure to defeat the claim, for, as *Lykes* teaches, that "would carry us too far" and would not be compatible with the basic lines of expense deductibility drawn by Congress.[14] Moreover, such a rule would lead to capricious results. If two taxpayers are each sued for an automobile accident while driving for pleasure, deductibility of their litigation costs would turn on the mere circumstance of the character of the assets each happened to possess, that is, whether the judgments against them stood to be satisfied out of income- or nonincome-producing property. We should be slow to attribute to Congress a purpose producing such unequal treatment among taxpayers, resting on no rational foundation.

Did the wife's claims respecting respondent's stockholdings arise in connection with his profit-seeking activities? It is enough to say that the wife's claims stemmed entirely from the marital relationship, and not, under any tenable view of things, from income-producing activity.[15] This is obviously so as regards [to claims that] depended entirely on the wife's making good her charges of marital infidelity on the part of the husband. The same conclusion is no less true respecting the claim relating to the existence of community property. For no such property could have existed but for the marriage relationship. In view of this conclusion it is unnecessary to consider the further question suggested by the Government: whether that portion of respondent's payments attributable to litigating the issue of the existence of community property was a capital expenditure.

MR. JUSTICE BLACK and MR. JUSTICE DOUGLAS believe that the Court reverses this case because of an unjustifiably narrow interpretation of the 1942 amendment of the Code and would accordingly affirm the judgment.

Although the phrase is found nowhere in the opinion, the test applied in *Gilmore* is commonly called the "origin of the claim" test.

Gilmore was anticipated by the case of *Trust of Bingham v. Comm'r*, 325 U.S. 365 (1945), where the Court held that costs of winding up a trust and distributing the trust assets to beneficiaries arose out of the activity of trust administration and were deductible under the predecessor to § 212(2). A trust exists as a medium of gratuitous transfer, but (at the same time) trust (and estate) administration is concerned with maintaining (etc.) property that is (or could be) productive of income. Following *Bingham*, Reg. § 1.212-1(i) allows such administration expenses to be deducted in full, without regard to the actual use of the property during the time it is held by the trustee or executor.

---

[14] [15] The Treasury Regulations have long provided: "An expense (not otherwise deductible) paid or incurred by an individual in determining or contesting a liability asserted against him does not become deductible by reason of the fact that property held by him for the production of income may be required to be used or sold for the purpose of satisfying such liability." Reg. § 1.212-1(m).

[15] [22] The respondent's attempted analogy of a marital "partnership" to the business partnership involved in the *Kornhauser* case, supra, is of course unavailing. The marriage relationship can hardly be deemed an income-producing activity.

NOTES

1.   (a) The origin test probably has operated to expand (rather than contract) the allowability of business and investment deductions for litigation costs, because the cost itself no longer has to be justified in terms of incremental business or investment revenue. Thus, if a person incurs legal costs as the result of a car accident while on business travel, the taxpayer might cite the origin test as a possible basis for allowing these costs to be deducted, even though the costs have no relation to the production of business revenue. See *Dancer v. Comm'r*, 73 T.C. 1103 (1980) (litigation expenses arising out of a negligent car accident on a business trip); *Clark v. Comm'r*, 30 T.C. 1330 (1958) (reviewed) (nonacq.) (defending criminal assault and rape charges arising from a business house call). Compare *Kelly v. Comm'r*, T.C. Memo. 1999-69 (denying deduction on the basis of a narrow construction of scope of taxpayer's employment); *Gilliam v. Comm'r*, T.C. Memo. 1986-81 (legal expenses incurred by a noted artist that resulted from his psychotic and bizarre behavior on a business plane trip disallowed as not being "ordinary," thereby finessing the business-connection issue).

(b) Punitive damages are usually deductible where they result from acts committed in the ordinary course of business. See *Rev. Rul. 80-211*, 1980-2 C.B. 57.

(c) The origin test poses the problem of "how far back" to go in the chain of causation. See *Boagni v. Comm'r*, 59 T.C. 708, 713 (1973) (acq.) (critiquing a mechanical application of the origin test). For example, in *Trust of Bingham*, the trust existed as a vehicle for effecting a gratuitous transfer by the person creating the trust, and the costs of distributing the assets to remainder beneficiaries were a direct costs of effecting such a transfer. Moreover, the transfer would not have occurred unless the transferor had descendents (a personal matter). However, the taxpayer in *Bingham* was not the creator of the trust, but rather the trust itself, which (in this case) was a separate taxpayer charged with managing the trust assets.

2.   (a) It would seem that the Supreme Court in *Gilmore* should have considered the "capitalization" issue before the "personal expense" issue, since capital expenditures are nondeductible without regard to whether they are also "personal" or "family." The apparent explanation is that the government, as appellant, argued the personal expense issue first and the capitalization issue second, the Supreme Court took up these issues in the order presented by the government, and, after deciding that the litigation costs were nondeductible personal outlays, had no need to address the capitalization point.

(b) On remand in *Gilmore*, it was held that the outlays were, in fact, capital expenditures. See *Gilmore v. U.S.*, 245 F. Supp. 383 (N.D. Cal. 1965), where the District Court relied on § 1.212-1(k), stating that costs of "defending or perfecting" title are to be capitalized as acquisition costs. However, the District Court erred by reading this language without reference to its function, which is to capitalize a certain type of acquisition cost. Defending a cloudy *title* is arguably different from the threat of being forced to relinquish ownership as a remote consequence of losing a lawsuit. Nevertheless, in *Spector v. Comm'r*, 71 T.C. 1017, 1027-28 (1979), *rev'd on other grounds*, 641 F.2d 376 (5th Cir. 1981), the IRS and the Tax Court took the same approach as did the District Court in the *Gilmore* remand, and there appears to be no contrary authority.

3. *Gilmore* has often been applied to disallow costs of retaining one's job (or professional license) against publicity arising from one's personal life. Mike Harden was a professional football player with the Denver Broncos. A woman with whom he was "involved" filed criminal sexual assault charges. The Broncos told Harden that if the matter were publicized, Harden's contract would not be renewed. Harden paid $25K to the woman in return for dropping the charges and keeping the matter confidential, his contract was renewed, and he sought to deduct the $25K under § 162. In *Harden v. Comm'r*, T.C. Memo. 1991-454, the deduction was denied as having an origin in a personal relationship. Here the possible effect on Harden's job was not merely speculative. Although the settlement can be said to have been a cost of carrying on Harden's personal life, it was also directly related to maintaining Harden's income stream. As shall be noted in the next chapter, job-retention costs are generally deductible as business expenses.

PROBLEMS

1. McDonald was an attorney, and Hazel was a client and friend of McDonald and a friend of his wife. Hazel executed a will (prepared by an outside attorney) and a codicil (prepared by McDonald) leaving most of her estate to McDonald. Hazel's heirs sought to invalidate the will by claiming that McDonald and his wife had used friendship to exercise undue influence over Hazel. McDonald paid a settlement in order to avoid bad publicity that would damage his professional reputation. He then attempted to deduct the payment as being connected to his law practice. What result? See *McDonald v. Comm'r*, 592 F.2d 635 (2d Cir. 1978).

2. Jack and Jill, childless, divorce. Jill incurred $5K in legal expenses for representation in the divorce. Jill obtained alimony and property. Can Jill deduct any of the $5K? See Reg. § 1.262-1(b)(7); *Wild v. Comm'r*, 42 T.C. 706 (1964) (reviewed) (acq.).

D.   LIMITATIONS ON DEDUCTIONS

The following material explores rules and doctrines that limit business and investment deductions for costs that are clearly aimed at generating income. These limitations fall into three categories: (1) bad-actor (i.e., public policy) limitations, (2) limitations related to the operation of the political system, and (3) limitations pertaining to the type of income obtained. Disallowance rules designed to weed out "personal" items are dealt with in the next two chapters.

1.   Public Policy Disallowance Rules

Starting in the 1950s, courts applied the "necessary" requirement of what are now §§ 162 and 212 to disallow deductions for expenses where "allowance of the deduction would frustrate sharply defined national or state policies proscribing particular types of conduct, evidenced by some declaration thereof." *Tank Truck Rentals, Inc. v. Comm'r*, 356 U.S. 30 (1958). After a period of uncertainty, courts limited this so-called public policy doctrine to cases where (1) the payment itself was illegal (e.g., an illegal bribe) or (2) the payment was in the nature of a fine.

In contrast, the lawful ordinary and necessary expenses of an illegal business were conceded to be allowable. See *Comm'r v. Sullivan*, 356 U.S. 27 (1958) (allowing deduction for rent and reasonable salaries paid by illegal bookmaking establishment); *Comm'r v. Tellier*, 383 U.S. 687 (1966) (allowing deduction for legal expenses of defending criminal prosecution arising out of taxpayer's securities business even though the defense was unsuccessful).

Congress has since intervened, adding several provisions pertaining to this area:

(1) Payments illegal in themselves (bribes, kickbacks, etc.) cannot be deducted *if* they are described in § 162(c), enacted in 1969. "Illegality" in the case of a payment to a foreign official or government body is defined in terms of the Foreign Corrupt Practices Act (rather than general U.S. law or the law of the foreign country). Under the Foreign Corrupt Practices Act, payments are illegal only if aimed to influence "political" or "discretionary" (as opposed to routine administrative) action.

(2) Section 162(f), enacted in 1969, provides that fines and penalties paid to governments cannot be deducted.

(3) Punitive damages paid to a nongovernmental party are not considered to be penalties and fines for purposes of § 162(f). See *Rev. Rul. 80-211*, 1980-2 C.B. 57. However, § 162(g), enacted in 1969, makes two-thirds of antitrust treble damages nondeductible if the taxpayer has been found guilty or has pleaded nolo contendere to a criminal antitrust charge.

(4) Section 280E, enacted in 1982, denies deductions and credits with respect to a trade or business activity that involves trafficking in illegal drugs (but does not deny basis offsets or inventory costs).

Under Reg. § 1.212-1(p), subsections (c), (f), and (g) of § 162 apply to investment expenses as well.

The 1969 legislative history underlying § 162(c) and (f) states that Congress intended these (then) new statutory rules to preempt the area. Thus, *expenses* not specifically barred by the above Code provisions are *no longer* to be disallowed under the common law "public policy doctrine" that was articulated in *Tank Truck Rentals*. See Reg. § 1.162-1(a). Nevertheless, the public policy doctrine continues to be applied to disallow *loss* deductions under provisions other than §§ 162 and 212. See, e.g., *Mazzei v. Comm'r*, 61 T.C. 497 (1974) (reviewed) (disallowing § 165 loss deduction by taxpayer defrauded during course of criminal conspiracy in which the taxpayer was a co-conspirator); *Rev. Rul. 81-24*, 1981-1 C.B. 79 (disallowing § 165 deduction of taxpayer's loss from his own arson).

Another set of provisions motivated by Congress's moral disapproval of certain conduct limits deductions for on executive compensation. Section 162(m) caps the compensation deduction for the 5 highest paid executives at $1M per executive. However, this provision is a toothless tiger, as it doesn't apply to performance-based compensation. Sections 280G disallows a deduction for an excess golden parachute payment (and § 4999 imposes a 20% excise tax on the same).

2. Political Expenditures

Otherwise-allowable deductions relating to the political process have been singled out for disallowance.

a. Costs of Lobbying Government

The Treasury issued regulations in 1918 denying any deduction for *business-related* political expenditures on the ground that they were not "ordinary and necessary." The Supreme Court upheld the validity of these regulations (which have since been repealed) in *Textile Mills Securities Corp. v. Comm'r*, 314 U.S. 326 (1941) (lobbying expenses) and *Cammarano v. U.S.*, 358 U.S. 498 (1959) (expenditures to mold public opinion). The rationale underlying disallowance was that the availability of a business deduction for political lobbying gave businesses an advantage not available to the rest of the citizenry, which could lobby only with after-tax dollars. In other words, the Court reasoned that the rationale that citizens should stand on an equal footing tax-wise in attempting to influence government policy was a reasonable one and thus within the Treasury's authority in interpreting § 162.

This "political neutrality" policy has been changed by legislation and withdrawal of the regulations. Current § 162(e) purports to disallow the deduction of business expenses (including research expenses) "in connection with" influencing (whether directly or by influencing the public): (a) legislation or (b) political campaigns and referenda or direct lobbying of high-level officials of the federal executive branch. This disallowance rule cannot be evaded by paying deductible dues or similar payments to tax-exempt organizations that do lobbying. Under § 6033(e), the exempt organization must report to the contributor the portion of any such contributions allocated to lobbying activities, and that portion is nondeductible. The disallowance rule does not apply to: (a) lobbying local government bodies (including Indian tribal governments), (b) certain de minimis in-house lobbying expenses, and (c) expenses incurred by taxpayers who are in the business of being lobbyists who work for others. See Reg. § 1.162-29 for illustration of how these rules are supposed to operate.

b. Campaign Costs of Political Candidates

As will be seen in the next chapter, job-seeking (and job-retention) costs can be considered to be "expenses" of a trade or business. However, deductibility is subject to the "carrying-on" rule. Presumably, being an "elected official" is a separate trade or business, so that a candidate seeking her first elective office could not deduct her campaign expenses. But perhaps each office is itself a separate trade or business, so that a current office holder seeking election to a different position also would not be entitled to deduct campaign expenses. What about a current office holder seeking re-election?

In *McDonald v. Comm'r*, 323 U.S. 57 (1944), the Supreme Court disallowed an elected official's deduction of expenses incurred in trying to obtain re-election. The result in *McDonald* is based on a public policy rationale, namely, that incumbents should not be given an income tax advantage that their challengers lack. *McDonald* is still considered good law. However, it has been held that expenses of defending against a recall during the term of office are deductible. See *Rev. Rul. 71-470*, 1971-1 C.B. 121.

Contributions to political candidates are not deductible. At the same time, contributions to a candidate's political campaign organization are not includible in the gross income of the candidate if spent on the campaign. (This result is the same as an inclusion followed by a deduction.) Campaign funds appropriated for personal use are gross income. See *Rev. Rul. 71-449*, 1971-2 C.B. 77.

To avoid circumventing the foregoing by "loaning" money to a party or candidate and then writing off the debt, § 271 disallows loss deductions for worthless debts to political parties, committees, and campaign organizations. Section 276 disallows expense deductions for attendance (or advertising) with respect to programs benefitting a political party or candidate.

3. Excessive Compensation

Section 162(a)(1) limits a deduction for compensation for services (actually rendered) to the extent that the compensation is reasonable. This limitation is almost always called into play where a closely held corporation is attempting to claim the deduction in order to reduce its corporate income tax liability. In this context, excessive salary is often a means to disguise a dividend (which is not deductible by the corporation) or perhaps a gift.[16] Nevertheless, a court will occasionally disallow a compensation deduction simply by reason of its being "excessive." There are numerous cases dealing with the issue of what is "excessive" and almost as many tests.[17]

4. Expenses Allocable to Exempt Income

Theory commands that deductions only be allowed where they produce includible income. Section 265(a)(1) disallows otherwise allowable deductions that are "allocable" to income that is "wholly exempt" from tax. Section 265(a)(2) disallows interest expense on debt "incurred or continued" to "purchase or carry" tax-exempt (§ 103) obligations. Section 264 disallows any deduction for premiums on (and interest on debt incurred to purchase or carry) a life insurance policy if paid by a beneficiary thereof who can anticipate excluding the proceeds under § 101(a).

The "wholly exempt" of § 265(a)(1) requires further elaboration. On the one hand, § 265(a)(1) has been applied to situations where income was partly includible and party excludible. In such a scenario, the expenses are allocated between the two portions on a pro rata basis. See Reg. § 1.265-1(c); *Rev. Rul. 87-102*, 1987-2 C.B. 78 (legal fees to obtain partially excluded social security benefits); *Rev. 85-98*,

---

[16] See *Smith v. Manning*, 189 F.2d 345 (3d Cir. 1951), in which the excessive salary was obviously a gift, but (since the taxpayer called it salary) was treated as (includible) salary to the proprietor's daughters receiving it. This case is an example of the principle that a taxpayer is bound by the form of the transaction.

[17] For a case fairly summarizing the trends, see *Haffner's Service Stations v. Comm'r*, 326 F.3d 1 (1st Cir. 2003), *aff'g*, T.C. Memo. 2002-38.

1985-2 C.B. 51 (legal fees to obtain partially excluded personal injury recovery under § 104). On the other hand, income that is tax-favored (like net capital gain, income that is deferred, and income from a business that can expense certain capital expenditures) is not considered to be wholly exempt from tax, so that none of the expenses allocable thereto are disallowed under § 265(a).

MANOCCHIO v. COMMISSIONER
United States Tax Court
78 T.C. 989 (1982), *aff'd*, 710 F.2d 1400 (9th Cir. 1983)

DAWSON, JUDGE:

Petitioner was employed as an airline pilot with Hughes Air West. He attended flight-training classes approved by the Veterans' Administration (VA), [which] classes maintained and improved skills required in petitioner's business. As a veteran, petitioner was eligible for an educational assistance allowance from the VA. During 1977, petitioner received $3,743 from the VA as a direct reimbursement of his flight-training expenses. On his 1977 tax return, he excluded the VA payments from income pursuant to 38 U.S.C. § 3101(a). He also claimed a deduction of $4,193 for educational expense [regarding his flight-training classes].

We agree with respondent that § 265 bars the deduction of the reimbursed expenses [but not the expenses in excess of the reimbursement]. The reimbursement clearly qualifies as a class of exempt income for purposes of § 265. Petitioner argues that the expenses are not allocable to the reimbursement, but rather to the income derived from his employment as a pilot. More specifically, his position is that § 265(1) should not be construed to apply to expenses which were merely paid out of exempt income.

Unquestionably, a principal target of [§ 265] was expenses incurred in connection with an ongoing trade or business or investment activity, the conduct of which generates exempt income. Nevertheless, we do not infer from [the examples cited in the Committee Reports] that Congress intended to limit the application of the statute to such situations. The words it selected to describe the necessary relationship between the expense and exempt income — "allocable to" — do not carry an inherently restrictive connotation. [W]e think the language employed is broad enough, particularly when construed in light of the policy behind the statute, to embrace the reimbursement situation where, but for the expense, there would simply be no exempt income. The right to reimbursement for the flight-training expenses arises only when the VA receives a certification from the flight school of the [cost of the veteran's training]. Thus, there is a fundamental nexus between the reimbursement income and the expense which, in our opinion, falls within the scope of any reasonable interpretation of the "allocable to" requirement.

[W]e do not view our decision as having any effect on the exemption provided by § 3101(a) with respect to flight-training benefits. Although it is true that petitioner is left in the identical situation from the standpoint of tax consequences as if he had received a taxable reimbursement, in which case § 265 would not bar his deduction, there will be instances where the flight training expenses will be nondeductible irrespective of § 265. In these situations, he would realize additional taxable income in the absence of the exemption provision.

Finally, we note that our result, although not our approach, is consistent with the outcome in *Wolfers v. Comm'r*, 69 T.C. 975 (1978), [which] held that a taxpayer cannot deduct an expense when it has a fixed right to reimbursement at the time the expense is incurred. While we think the result in *Wolfers* is sound, we prefer to rest on § 265 because we believe it provides a more direct and appropriate rationale for disallowing a deduction which is subject in part to tax-free reimbursement.

Reviewed by the Court.

[Concurring opinions omitted.]

NOTES

1.   (a) The public policy doctrine has not prevented the subtraction of Cost of Goods Sold in arriving at Gross Income from Business under § 61(a)(2). See *Max Sobel Wholesale Liquors v. Comm'r*, 630 F.2d 670 (9th Cir. 1980); *Rev. Rul. 82-149*, 1982-2 C.B. 56. The cost incurred by a drug dealer in purchasing illegal drugs is similarly not disallowed by § 280E. Cost of Goods Sold is not an "expense deduction," but rather a basis offset. Basis offsets are not affected by the expense disallowance rules discussed above.

(b) The public policy doctrine was unusual in holding tax law to be subordinate to nontax policy without any explicit congressional expression of which policy should prevail. The decisions that shaped the public policy doctrine were rationalized along the lines of "surely Congress wouldn't have intended allowance of a deduction here." But Congress itself rebuked this approach in enacting § 162(c), (e), (f), and (g). As noted in a dissenting opinion in *Mazzei v. Comm'r* (61 T.C. at 506):

> The Senate Finance Committee report for the 1969 Tax Reform Act states "The provision for the denial of the deduction for payments in these situations which are deemed to violate public policy is intended to be *all inclusive*. Public policy, in other circumstances, generally is not sufficiently clearly defined to justify the disallowance of deductions." (Emphasis added.) S. Rept. No. 91-552, 91st Cong., 1st Sess. (1969), 1969-3 C.B. 597. In expanding the category of nondeductible expenditures, the legislative history of the 1971 Tax Reform Act states, "The committee continues to believe that the determination of when a *deduction* should be *denied* should remain under the *control* of Congress." (Emphasis added.) S. Rept. No. 92-437, 92d Cong., 1st Sess. (1971), 1972-1 C.B. 599.

(c) The Supreme Court usually ignores the possible effect of its tax decisions on external policies (other than those relating to crimes). See, e.g., *Comm'r v. Glenshaw Glass*, 348 U.S. 426 (1955) (ignoring the effect of including punitive damages in gross income on antitrust policy).

PROBLEMS

1. Kurt, a tax professor, viciously beats up Mark, another tax professor, in Mark's office over a heated dispute about whether § 212 should be available to avoid the pre-opening doctrine. Mark sues Kurt for compensatory and punitive damages, and receives both. Kurt, uninsured, pays the damages. Deductible?

2. Recall the earlier problem where Jack and Jill divorce. Jill incurred $5K in legal expenses for representation in the divorce, whereby Jill obtained alimony and property. Now assume that Jack and Jill have children, and Jill obtains custody of the children and child support. Do these additional facts affect the tax treatment of Jill's legal fees?

3. Trey is executor of the estate of Darius Fontaine, a wealthy person who held investment securities worth about $100M, tax-exempt (§ 103) bonds worth $20M, and personal residences worth a total of $30M. Fontaine's estate is a taxable entity for federal income tax purposes, and computes its taxable income like an individual. See § 641(a)(3) and (b). The executor fee for the Fontaine estate is $10M in the year 2012. How much, if any, of this fee is deductible (assume that all the investments yield the same rate of return)? See Reg. §§ 1.212-1(i), 1.652(c)-4(c).

Chapter 9

DEFINING THE PERSONAL REALM: OF HUMAN CAPITAL

Before dealing with the question of whether an activity or item is connected to income production, thus justifying deductions for related costs, or is personal, resulting in disallowance of deductions, it is necessary to define the realm of "personal." This chapter deals with the ambivalent concept of "human capital," which allows an individual to earn wages but also has a powerful effect on the quality of one's personal life.

A. WHAT IS "HUMAN CAPITAL"?

In the last paragraph in *Welch* (in Chapter 8.B.1), Justice Cardozo stated that spending money for the acquisition of learning, culture, and personal reputation ("character") may be a wise "investment" but that such costs are not *business* expenses. This passage in *Welch* essentially sets forth the doctrine that human capital acquisition costs are not deductible. Why not? The initial response is that human capital acquisition costs are capital expenditures and not expenses, since they clearly have value that lasts beyond the current taxable year. But acquisition costs relating to *conventional* investments (such as business equipment or stocks), although likewise not currently deductible, create "basis" that is *eventually* recovered by depreciation, loss deduction, or as an offset in computing gain. Nevertheless, it is settled that there is no recovery of basis in human capital by any of these means under the income tax. Why not? The short answer is that human capital is an "inherently personal" asset that differs importantly from business assets, investment assets, and ordinary personal-use assets (such as homes and family cars).

B. DISTINGUISHING HUMAN CAPITAL FROM CONVENTIONAL CAPITAL

In its most basic form, "human capital" refers to all the physical and mental attributes of a human being necessary to earn compensation for services, such as a functioning body and a mind sufficient to follow instructions or obey orders. At higher levels, human capital includes acquired skills, training, and education, but it also includes traits such as cooperativeness, motivation, energy, sociability, willingness to assume responsibility, IQ, stamina, and physical attractiveness. Human capital incorporates good health and the ability to locate jobs, be hired (and promoted), and move to a new or better job. In short, human capital encompasses any attribute of a person (whether inherited or acquired) that has value in the market for services or talent. But, importantly, those same attributes are certain to have value in a nonmarket context as well, such as attracting potential spouses and partners, making friends, influencing people, and enjoying life generally (through recreation, culture, psychological well-being, and so on). These latter activities are clearly "personal" in the tax sense. In short, human capital yields extensive personal benefits in addition to compensation income.

Thus, to give human capital the same tax treatment as conventional assets would require that human capital first be divided into its personal component and its business and investment component, because the personal component cannot generate expense, loss, or amortization deductions. This separation would be an extremely difficult task. Moreover, the outcomes would lack precision and differ for each individual, thereby inviting endless disputes.

But even if a taxpayer's human capital could be apportioned between its personal and income-producing components (or even if it were thought that such an allocation would be unnecessary), the tax system would need to deal with the fact that much human capital is costless to the taxpayer and, therefore, does not present a case for inclusion in the various basis recovery schemes. To be specific, substantial amounts of human capital (such as genetic make-up, personality type, most general education, and general learning through social experiences) are not acquired by the taxpayer in any identifiable "cost" transaction.[1] Indeed, a great deal of very important human capital comes "for free" as a consequence of the family and economic class into which the taxpayer is born. Thus, the costless income-producing human capital (which would have no basis) would next have to be identified and removed from consideration. Then the taxpayer's human capital costs that were attributable to the remaining income-producing human capital items would have to be calculated and apportioned among those items. These would be difficult and contentious exercises.

Even if the cost of human capital relevant to wage-earning capacity could be identified, it is not a necessary requirement of an income tax that it be deducted (sooner or later). As explained above, *human capital provides personal benefits* as well as income-earning ability, and the concept of income does not necessarily dictate that the principle that income-producing costs should be deductible must trump the counter-principle that costs of obtaining personal well-being are nondeductible.

---

[1] Under an accretion income tax, the free acquisition of human capital could (in theory) be treated as a series of income-inclusion events (creating basis). But clearly such in-kind acquisitions are not "realized" under an ability-to-pay income tax, because their value is highly contingent on future events. (A Harvard degree has a substantial "free" element because tuition payments cover only part of the cost, but, nevertheless, the degree does not guarantee financial success.) Alternatively, including free acquisitions of wage-earning potential in gross income (before the wage income is realized) would create huge liquidity problems for taxpayers that would impinge on liberty values by forcing everyone to earn to their highest market potential. Taking lesser-paying, but more satisfying, jobs would be off the table, and the message would be that in our society people are nothing more than wage-earning machines. It also might be argued that much of the free acquisition of human capital would fall within the exclusions for gifts, bequests, support, and government welfare benefits. Assuming that is true, should the lucky recipient obtain a free basis (donor cost or FMV) in the capital? If so, taxpayers who receive large intra-family transfers of human capital would have a large tax advantage over less-fortunate taxpayers who must purchase the same human capital with their own after-tax dollars.

Even if the tax system overcame all of the preceding difficulties and assigned appropriate cost bases to a taxpayer's items of human capital, the bases could never be recovered as offsets against the amount realized in sale or disposition transactions or as losses realized on such transactions.[2] This is because human capital is inherent in the taxpayer, part of his or her body or being. Human capital cannot be transferred (although it can be acquired, dissipated, or allowed to lie fallow). For example, your legal education is an acquisition of human capital. But although you can choose whether or not to produce and sell the product of this capital (legal services) for income, you cannot transfer the capital to another and thus rid yourself of it. Accordingly, the only way human capital basis could have any consequence in the tax system would be through depreciation deductions (or loss deductions upon permanent disability).[3] Designing an "accurate" depreciation system for human income-producing capital would be challenging, as labor markets indicate that the value thereof *actually increases* with age, experience, and the assumption of responsibility. Any remaining human capital would disappear at death, but the tax system generally takes the position that the unused tax attributes of a person (loss carryovers and unrealized losses) are also "lost" at death, and do not carry over to the decedent's estate or successors.

In light of the foregoing, income tax systems around the world universally treat human capital as an inherently personal asset that has no recoverable basis. But despite this general principle, there are some situations (noted below) in which outlays that "relate to" human capital can generate tax benefits.

C. DISTINGUISHING HUMAN CAPITAL FROM GOODWILL

How is it that, as suggested by Justice Cardozo in *Welch*, reputation and learning are "akin" to business assets, but not themselves business assets? Specifically, how does personal reputation (at issue in *Welch*) differ from business "goodwill," a recognized business asset?

The conceptual basis for distinguishing the two is easy enough to articulate: unlike conventional business and investment assets, *human capital cannot be transferred*. But stating the distinction is much easier than applying it, even assuming awareness of the proper basis of the distinction. In *Marks v. Comm'r*, 27 T.C. 464 (1956) (acq.), an individual who was an investment banker and corporate director made payments to a corporation to head off possible liability to the corporation. The Tax Court noted that the payments, although voluntary, protected

---

[2] In the property context, a "sale" of a "temporal" portion of an income-producing asset (such as a term for years) is simply treated as an acceleration of ordinary income, with no basis offset (apart from normal depreciation, if any). See Chapter 29.B.

[3] The disability scenario would present significant practical difficulties. For example, if Sara Surgeon's surgical career is ended when an uninsured drunk driver severs her hand in an accident, would Sara (who is unable to collect any damage award from the uninsured driver) be entitled to deduct the remaining basis in her lost human capital? Even if she could continue working as a consultant to other surgeons or as a nonsurgical M.D.? Would self-inflicted losses of human capital (due, say, to poor lifestyle choices and premature retirement) be deemed to be "sustained," and (if so) how would one calculate the portion of the basis allocable to the lost portion of the human capital?

the taxpayer's existing business (as opposed to personal, nonbusiness) reputation and were, therefore, deductible.

In *Jenkins v. Comm'r*, T.C. Memo. 1983-667, the Tax Court allowed a business expense deduction to country music singer Conway Twitty for voluntarily paying off investors in Twitty Burger, Inc., which had failed, on the ground that the payments protected his existing "personal *business* reputation." The Tax Court noted that the payments would have been nondeductible if they had been made purely out of a sense of moral obligation.

Marks and *Jenkins* both seem to flirt with the notion that expenses for protecting human capital are deductible. But, if that were the case, § 213 (allowing a deduction for medical expenses) would be largely superfluous. This confusion is unfortunate, because it would have been sufficient in *Jenkins* to find that the payments protected Twitty's existing *business* (as a performer and celebrity who could license his name) without extending the court's rationale to "personal business reputation."[4] Under this "business" approach, Twitty's payments had nothing to do with his human capital. Granted, the business wouldn't have existed without Twitty's human capital. Countless businesses rely on human capital for the provision of services. Similarly, it would have been sufficient in *Marks* for the Tax Court to find that the payments protected the taxpayer's existing business as an investment banker and corporate director.

D. EDUCATION COSTS

It has not seriously been argued in court that the costs of K-12 education, or a general liberal arts college education, are deductible. These are clearly nondeductible human capital acquisition costs that do not produce a recoverable basis for the reasons discussed in Section B, supra. But some have argued for the deductibility (one way or another) of costs of obtaining *professional or vocational* degrees (such as a law or medical degree) on the theory that these relate to a *particular* trade or business.

1. Deductibility under the Regulations

Even if one gets past the *theoretical* barriers surrounding the acquisition of human capital, purely doctrinal hurdles remain. As noted in the previous chapter, § 162 requires that the taxpayer must already be "carrying on" an *existing* business in order to deduct expenses paid or incurred with respect to that business.

An issue might be whether costs of vocational or professional education fall within § 195. However, educational outlays leading to degrees fail the "expense" requirement of § 195, because the benefit created by a law school or medical school education surely has a useful life extending substantially beyond the taxable year. The outlays, therefore, look to be nondeductible "capital expenditures" instead of "expenses."

---

[4] Taking such an approach is *Lohrke v. Comm'r*, 48 T.C. 679 (1967).

But what if one is *already* in a trade or business, where the "carrying on" requirement is satisfied, and *additional* education is obtained? The Treasury has issued Reg. § 1.162-5 to deal precisely with the possibility that education costs might be deducted as "business expenses." This regulation is required reading. You should (we hope) notice that the tests set out in Reg. § 1.162-5 strongly resemble the tests differentiating between "repairs" (expenses) vs. "permanent improvements" (capital expenditures) pertaining to conventional business or investment property. To be specific, in order to be deductible under Reg. § 1.162-5, an education outlay *must* satisfy one of two requirements. It must *either*:

> (1) maintain or improve skills required by the individual in his (existing) employment or other trade or business, *or*

> (2) meet the express requirements of the individual's employer imposed as a condition to retention by the individual of existing employment, status, or compensation (this mainly applies to public school teachers, nurses, and other professions where continuing education is mandatory to retain a license).

The effect of these requirements is to deny a deduction for education expenses unless they are in the nature of maintenance or repairs. Although repair and maintenance costs usually have value beyond the current year, they have always been treated as "expenses." Even if the repair analogy is valid, a conceptual problem is that these costs appear (like medical expenses) to pertain to a person's human capital. This problem is finessed (in the above-noted regulations) by the notion (fiction?) that the taxpayer has a trade or business apart from his or her human capital. These types of costs are considered to be "direct" costs of earning income from services rather than of increasing one's *capacity* to earn income.

However, even though an educational outlay satisfies either or both of the two requirements noted above, it is nevertheless nondeductible if it *either*:

> (1) pays for education required to meet the minimum educational requirements for qualification in the taxpayer's employment or other trade or business, *or*

> (2) leads to qualifying the taxpayer for a new trade or business.

In these instances, the addition to human capital is considered to be predominant, and the costs are nondeductible capital expenditures.

SHARON v. COMMISSIONER
United States Tax Court
66 T.C. 515 (1976), *aff'd*, 591 F.2d 1273 (9th Cir. 1978) (per curiam)

SIMPSON, JUDGE:

[Taxpayer graduated from Brandeis University in 1961 and from Columbia University School of Law in 1964. He took a New York bar review course, took the bar exam, passed the bar, and worked in New York as an attorney for a law firm. In 1967 he accepted a position as an IRS attorney in California and took the same steps to enter the California bar. In 1970 he expended funds on travel and other items in connection with admission to practice before the U.S. Supreme Court.]

The petitioner contends that he is entitled to amortize the cost of obtaining his license to practice law in New York over the period from the date of his admission to the bar to the date on which he reaches age 65, when he expects to retire. In his cost basis of this "intangible asset," he included the costs of obtaining his college degree ($11,125), obtaining his law degree ($6,910), a bar review course and related materials ($175), and the New York State bar examination fee ($25). As justification, he points out that, in order to take the New York bar examination, he was required to have graduated from college and an accredited law school. The petitioner relies upon Reg. § 1.167(a)-3, which provides:

> If an intangible asset is known from experience or other factors to be of use in the business or in the production of income for only a limited period, the length of which can be estimated with reasonable accuracy, such an intangible asset may be the subject of a depreciation allowance.

There is no merit in the petitioner's claim. His college and law school expenses provided him with a general education which will be beneficial to him in a wide variety of ways. The costs and responsibility for obtaining such education are personal. In the words of § 1.162-5(b), costs of "minimum educational requirements for qualification in employment" are "personal expenditures or constitute an inseparable aggregate of personal and capital expenditures." There is no rational or workable basis for any allocation of this inseparable aggregate between the personal component and a deductible component.

Such expenses are not made any less personal by attempting to capitalize them. Since the inseparable aggregate includes personal expenditures, the preeminence of § 262 over § 167 precludes amortization. The same reasoning applies to the costs of review courses and related expenses taken to qualify for the practice of a profession.

The $25 fee paid for the license was not an educational expense but was a fee paid for the privilege of practicing law in New York, a nontransferable license which has value beyond the taxable year, and such fee is a capital expenditure. The Commissioner apparently concedes that the fee may be amortized.

The next issue is whether the petitioner may deduct or amortize the expenses he incurred in gaining admission to practice before the state and federal courts of California. It is clear that the amount paid for the bar review course was an expenditure "made by an individual for education." Although the petitioner was authorized to practice law in some jurisdictions when he took the California bar review course, such course was nevertheless educational in the same sense as the first bar review course. Nor may the petitioner treat the payment for the bar review course as a part of the costs of acquiring his license to practice in California. Educational expenses which qualify him for a new trade or business are "personal expenditures or constitute an inseparable aggregate of personal and capital expenditures." Reg. § 1.162-5(b). We find that the bar review course helped to qualify the petitioner for a new trade or business so that its costs are personal expenses.

If the education qualifies the taxpayer to perform significantly different tasks and activities than he could perform prior to the education, then the education qualifies him for a new trade or business. Thus, we have held that a professor of social work is in a different trade or business than a social caseworker. *Davis v. Comm'r*, 65 T.C. 1014 (1976). A licensed public accountant is in a different trade or business than a certified public accountant. *Glenn v. Comm'r*, 62 T.C. 270 (1974). A registered pharmacist is in a different trade or business than an intern pharmacist, even though an intern performs many of the same tasks as a registered pharmacist, but under supervision. *Antzoulatos v. Comm'r*, T.C. Memo. 1975-327.

Before taking the bar review course and passing the bar exam, the petitioner was an attorney licensed to practice law in New York. As an attorney for the Regional Counsel, he could represent the Commissioner in this Court. However, he could not appear in either the state courts of California, the federal courts located there, nor otherwise act as an attorney outside the scope of his employment with the IRS. After receiving his license to practice law in California, he became a member of the state bar with all its accompanying privileges and obligations. By comparing the tasks and activities that the petitioner was qualified to perform prior to receiving his license to practice in California with the tasks and activities he was able to perform after receiving such license, it is clear that he has qualified for a new trade or business. Consequently, the expenses of his bar review course were personal and are not includable in the cost of his license to practice law in California.

It is true that even before he became a member of the bar of California, the petitioner was engaged in the business of practicing law. However, in applying the provisions of Reg. § 1.162-5 to determine whether education expenses are personal or business in nature, it is not enough to find that the petitioner was already engaged in some business — we must ascertain the particular business in which he was previously engaged and whether the education qualified him to engage in a different business. Before taking the bar review course and becoming a member of the bar of California, the petitioner could not generally engage in the practice of law in that state, but the bar review course helped to qualify him to engage in such business.

The Commissioner does not argue that the capital expenditures incurred in obtaining his license to practice law in California may not be amortized. The courts have held that the fees paid by physicians to acquire hospital privileges are capital expenditures amortizable over the doctor's life expectancy. *Walters v. Comm'r*, 383 F.2d 922 (6th Cir. 1967). We hold that the petitioner may treat the costs of acquiring his license to practice in California in a similar manner. Such costs include [the registration fee, the general bar exam fee, the attorney's bar exam fee, the admittance fee, the U.S. District Court fee, and the U.S. Court of Appeals fee]. Although petitioner testified that he would retire at age 65 if he were financially able to do so, such testimony is not sufficient to establish the shorter useful life for which he argues.

The next issue is whether the petitioner may deduct or amortize the cost of gaining admission to practice before the U.S. Supreme Court. There is little evidence concerning the petitioner's "use" in 1970 of his license to practice before the Supreme Court. However, it is altogether appropriate for any attorney to become a member of the bar of the Supreme Court whenever it is convenient for him to do so. No one can know when the membership in such bar may be useful to him in the practice of law — it may bring tangible benefits today, tomorrow, or never. We find that the intangible asset acquired by becoming a member of such bar was used by the petitioner in 1970 and hold that he may amortize the costs of acquiring such asset over his life expectancy.

The critical factor in cases like *Sharon* is the definition of a "new" trade or business, and licensing requirements generally define a business as being new. See, e.g., *Johnson v. Comm'r*, 77 T.C. 876 (1981) (real estate broker is in a different business than real estate agent). On the other hand, teaching and business administration are viewed broadly. See Reg. § 1.162-5(b)(3)(i) (teaching); *Allemier v. Comm'r*, T.C. Memo. 2005-207 (allowing costs of an MBA where the MBA was not a required credential). The absence of a license requirement does not guarantee deductibility, however. See *Hudgens v. Comm'r*, T.C. Memo. 1997-33 (deductions for obtaining tax LL.M. were disallowed because taxpayer in fact entered new business of asset management, which was distinct from previous business of accounting although both required tax skills; hence, the expenses were not incurred in carrying on an existing business); *Blair v. Comm'r*, T.C. Memo. 1980-488 (deduction allowed only for MBA courses related to taxpayer's job).

An issue that crops in cases where the taxpayer has a J.D. degree and is trying to deduct the costs of an LL.M. degree is whether the taxpayer is carrying on the trade of being an attorney. Merely being licensed to practice law is not good enough. See *Wassenaar v. Comm'r*, 72 T.C. 1195 (1979) (no deduction allowed for costs of LL.M. in taxation where taxpayer had not practiced law before entering the degree program); cf. *Fielding v. Comm'r*, 57 T.C. 761 (1972) (deduction denied for cost of medical residency because taxpayer had not previously practiced as a physician).

2. Tax Expenditures for Education

Congress has enacted several provisions that benefit the pursuit of (nondeductible) education. The most longstanding one is § 117(a), discussed in Chapter 15, which allows qualified scholarships to be excluded from gross income. Two excluded kinds of employee fringe benefits relate to education: § 117(d) (certain free education by an employer that is itself an educational institution), and § 127 (certain education paid for by an employer). (Under current law, § 127 will expire at the end of 2012.)

Section 222 provides an above-the-line deduction, not to exceed $4K (per taxpayer per year) for "qualified tuition and related expenses" (which excludes living expenses and expenses financed by certain loans and excludible income). The deduction is for the payor, and the tuition, etc., must be that of the payor, the payor's spouse, or a person claimable as a dependency exemption under § 151. The deduction is phased out for higher-income taxpayers. Although the deduction is currently scheduled to expire at the end of 2011 it has already been extended at least twice.

The same "qualified tuition and related expenses" can qualify for the HOPE credit or the Lifetime Learning credit, both found in § 25A. In that case, the taxpayer must choose between the two. The Lifetime Learning credit is nonrefundable. The HOPE credit is partially refundable through 2012 and then becomes completely nonrefundable. The HOPE credit (not to exceed $1,800 per student per year; $2,500 for 2009-12) is only for the first two years of post-secondary education (extended to four years for 2009-12). The Lifetime Learning credit (20% of qualified tuition and related expenses, not to exceed $2K per taxpayer) covers post-secondary education, but it cannot be taken in any year in which the Hope credit is taken. Both credits are phased out for higher-income taxpayers.

Section 221 confers an above-the-line deduction (not to exceed $2,500 per taxpayer per year) for interest on a qualified education loan. This deduction is phased out for higher-income taxpayers.

Sections 529 and 530 cover "qualified tuition programs" (of states and educational institutions) and "Coverdell Education Savings Accounts," respectively. These devices are essentially special-purpose accounts that accumulate earnings tax-free. Distributions to the beneficiary for education are excluded (the equivalent of being included and then deducted).

Complex rules exist to prevent double benefits (deductions, credits, and exclusions) for the same dollars. In this connection, recall the *Manocchio* case from the previous chapter, which disallowed an educational expense deduction that was paid for with tax-exempt benefits.

E. JOB-SEEKING COSTS

Exploiting human capital often involves incurring costs to find a job. The rules for deducting job-seeking expenses derive from court decisions rather than Treasury regulations.

PRIMUTH v. COMMISSIONER
United States Tax Court
54 T.C. 374 (1970) (reviewed) (acq. in result only)

STERRETT, JUDGE:

[Primuth was a corporate executive who was dissatisfied with the future prospects of his current employment. He paid more than $3K to an employment agency to assist him in procuring a new corporate executive position while he continued to toil at his old job. The agency succeeded in arranging several interviews, one of which resulted in a new position for Primuth. Respondent Commissioner disallowed deduction of Primuth's payment to the agency on the ground that it was a personal expense.]

Over the years we have held on more than one occasion that a taxpayer may be in the trade or business of being an employee, such as a corporate executive or manager. The fact that the petitioner was employed at the time the fee was paid, which resulted in his securing new employment, is of no moment. We held in *Haft v. Comm'r*, 40 T.C. 2 (1963), that a costume jewelry salesman who had worked as an employee for some 25 years "did not cease to be in the costume jewelry business" simply because he was temporarily unemployed and had no merchandise to sell. A comparable result was reached in *Furner v. Comm'r*, 393 F.2d 292 (CA 7, 1968), reversing 47 T.C. 165 (1966), where the Seventh Circuit held that a professional teacher, who took a year off to secure a master's degree, was still carrying on a trade or business with the result that the cost of her courses taken during that year off was deductible.

The obvious principle to be evolved from the *Furner* and *Haft* cases is that it is possible for an employee to retain, at least temporarily, his status of carrying on his own trade or business independent of receiving any compensation from a particular employer. This being so, it certainly cannot be held against the petitioner that, while actively and gainfully carrying on his trade or business of being a corporate executive, he incurred an expense with a view to receiving his paychecks from a different employer than the one for whom he was working at the time of payment.

Once we have made our decision that the petitioner was carrying on a trade or business of being a corporate executive, the problem presented here virtually dissolves for it is difficult to think of a purer business expense than one incurred to permit such an individual to continue to carry on that very trade or business — albeit with a different corporate employer. There can be no question that the fee paid resulted directly in petitioner's securing new employment.

Furthermore, the expense had no personal overtones, led to no position requiring greater or different qualifications than the one given up, and did not result in the acquisition of any asset as that term has been used in our income tax laws. It was an expense which must be deemed ordinary and necessary from every realistic point of view in today's marketplace where corporate executives change employers with a noticeable degree of frequency.

It might be argued that the payment of an employment fee is capital in nature and hence not currently deductible. Presumably, under this view the fee would be deductible when the related employment is terminated. However, the difficulty with this view is to conjure up a capital asset which had been purchased. Certainly, the expense was not related to the purchase or sale of a capital asset. Further, we do not find the instant situation analogous to the capital expense incurred by an individual in the course of changing his field of endeavor.

A further objection can be made on the basis that the expenditure is basically personal in nature, analogous perhaps to general educational expenses. However, there was no element in incurring the expense of qualifying for a new trade or business or better preparing oneself to take advantage of any number of unknown opportunities or of making life more enjoyable generally. Nor is it analogous to commuting expenses which are dependent in extent upon one's own convenience in choosing a personal residence. An employment fee by its very nature bears a direct relationship to the receipt of income.

TANNENWALD, J., concurring:

To me, the drawing of distinctions based upon the difference between "seeking" and "securing" employment, upon whether the fee of the employment agency is contingent or payable in any event, or upon whether the agency's efforts are successful or unsuccessful simply adds unnecessary confusion and complexity to a tax law which already defies understanding even by sophisticated taxpayers. I would similarly reject any attempt to import a capitalization of expenditure concept into a situation such as is involved herein. That concept has generally been confined to cases of acquisition of tangible assets or intangible assets, such as a license or goodwill of a going business, or preparation for engaging in a new field of endeavor. By way of contrast, current deductibility has normally been permitted for advertising expenditures and for educational expenditures to improve one's skills utilized in existing employment, even though there were indications that some general benefit would in all probability last beyond the year of expenditure.

[Concurring opinion of SIMPSON, J., omitted.]

TIETJENS, J., dissenting:

I respectfully dissent. Of course, as the majority points out, the taxpayer was in the business of being a salaried corporate employee. But I would confine that concept much more narrowly than does the majority. I would say the taxpayer was in the business of being an employee of Foundry [Primuth's employer before he quit in order to accept the new position secured through the employment agency] when the claimed deductible expenses were incurred. The expenses, however, were not related to his employment by Foundry but were paid to obtain a new job with another employer. To me this is the same as incurring expenses in locating or finding a new business. Such expenses are not deductible as business expenses because they were not connected with the taxpayer's existing employment.

In *Cremona v. Comm'r*, 58 T.C. 219 (1972) (reviewed) (acq.), the Tax Court allowed the deduction of a fee paid by an employed administrator for job-search counseling even though the taxpayer failed to obtain any offers of employment and stayed at his old job. The IRS has generally caved in on this issue. See, e.g., *Rev. Rul. 78-93*, 1978-1 C.B. 38. However, in *Estate of Rockefeller v. Comm'r*, 762 F.2d 264 (2d Cir. 1985), expenses incurred by Nelson Rockefeller (who had been Governor of New York) in obtaining confirmation as Vice President of the United States were denied on the grounds that the Vice Presidency was sui generis and not just another position as "government executive."

F. MOVING COSTS

Section 217 has long been in the Code, and its current form allows an above-the-line deduction for certain costs of moving to a new work location. "Moving expenses" means the cost (including lodging but not meal costs) of moving oneself, members of one's household, and personal belongings to the new work location.

Section 217(c) provides mechanical thresholds pertaining to "minimum distance" and "period of work" at the new location before any moving expenses are deductible. There is no requirement that the taxpayer be employed in the "same business" at the new location. Indeed, there is no requirement that the taxpayer be already carrying on an existing trade or business. That is to say, § 217 can apply to a move required by a taxpayer's first job. Section 217 overrides any possibility of capitalization. Stated differently, moving costs that are deductible under § 217 are not subject to the capital-expenditure rule.

Moving costs are to be distinguished from business "travel" expenses, considered in the next chapter.

Section 132(g) provides for an exclusion of employer-provided moving costs to the extent that the amounts reimbursed would have been deductible under § 217 if paid for by the reimbursed employee. Of course, the taxpayer cannot both claim this exclusion *and* take the § 217 deduction for the same expenses. Thus, the exclusion is not available if the taxpayer deducts moving expenses under § 217 in Year 1 and then receives an employer reimbursement of the expenses in Year 2. Under § 82, any reimbursement for a moving expense that is not excluded under § 132 is included in gross income.

NOTES

1. (a) It is sometimes argued that identifiable costs of human capital should yield amortization deductions, as is the case with conventional capital having an ascertainable useful life. This is basically a "neutrality" argument, which cannot be answered without looking at the broader question of whether human capital is treated less (or more) favorably than investment capital overall. In thinking about this issue, consider the following scenario. George Genius wants to do complex, cutting edge work with calculus. Assume that he could work, earn $500K, and buy a supercomputer that would do the calculus for him. Alternatively, he could pursue a university education in calculus that would make him competitive with the computer (not so fast, to be sure, but competitive once we recognize that he can be more creative with his knowledge than the computer can be). Since the work George does at the university makes him the competitive equivalent of a computer that would have cost him $500K of taxable wages, his studies at the university have resulted in the acquisition of additional untaxed human capital worth $500K. This amount is far greater than his education outlays. The income tax system takes a rough justice approach to these issues by denying amortization deductions with respect to all human capital.

(b) The various tax expenditures for education, especially the § 25A tax credits, raise the problem of "capture," namely that educational institutions will just raise their tuition and fees and thereby obtain the benefits of the credits (instead of the intended beneficiaries, the students of the educational institutions).

2. (a) In *Primuth*, the Tax Court refused to capitalize the job-seeking expenses on the ground that there was no separate and distinct asset to capitalize "to." This doctrinal position was flatly rejected in *INDOPCO* in Chapter 7.A.1, supra. Yet the

IRS still follows *Primuth* and *Cremona*. Additionally, the IRS has failed to issue regulations on this issue.

(b) Note that the law regarding deductibility of job-seeking expenses exists entirely in judicial decisions, whereas the similar law governing the deductibility of education expenses is predominantly found in Reg. § 1.162-5. This can be significant because, if an aggressive taxpayer ignores a regulation, she is subject to the penalty for "negligence or disregard of rules or regulations," but apparently she may not be if she disregards a judge-created rule. See Reg. § 1.6662-3(b)(2).

(c) Isn't employment in a particular position a separate and distinct asset? It is true that such an asset has no ascertainable useful life, but depreciability is a separate issue apart from capitalization. In any event, the basis in the particular position would (if capitalized) be a business loss deduction when the taxpayer leaves that position.

(d) The rationale used by the *Primuth* court, namely, that one can be "carrying on" a business of being an "employee (of a certain category) in general" (as opposed to being an employee holding a particular position) is just a fancy way of describing human capital, is it not? Even if that is the case, it is a plausible position that obtaining a new position is not an accretion to human capital, but a manifestation of its exercise. But that still leaves open the issue of whether the outlay is an expense or a nonpersonal capital expenditure.

(e) Is it possible to draw a line cleanly between expenses relating to the carrying on of a *services* business and expenses relating to human capital? Isn't a professional license human capital, because it cannot be transferred? If so, the IRS should not concede amortization of the direct cost of professional license fees. In contrast, an employment position is not human capital, because it exists independently of the person who occupies it. A person can quit or retire from an employment position without losing any personal attributes.

(f) Regardless of the points raised above, *Cremona*, *Primuth*, and *Sharon* reflect the current state of the law.

PROBLEMS

1. (a) Can an accountant deduct the cost of going to law school? Assume the accountant intends to stay in the accounting profession and is attending law school only to improve her skills in those areas in which law and accounting overlap. See Reg. § 1.162-5(b)(3)(ii) Exs. (1) & (2); *Weiler v. Comm'r*, 54 T.C. 398 (1970).

(b) Suppose this book really turns you on to tax, and you decide to obtain an LL.M. in taxation in order to market yourself. Following the award of your J.D. degree, will you be able to deduct the costs pertaining to the LL.M. program if you begin your studies immediately? If not, can such costs be capitalized and amortized? Suppose instead that you begin as an associate in a law firm in the tax department and then earn your LL.M. in taxation either part time or, by taking a year off from work, full time. Or suppose that you begin your practice in the corporate securities area, but after a few years decide you would like to switch to tax and earn your LL.M. in taxation at that time. Is being a tax lawyer a different trade or business than being a corporate securities lawyer? Is tax law merely a specialty within the single business of "law?" How do you think the *Sharon* court would respond, in view of its decision that being a tax lawyer in New York was a different trade or business than being a tax lawyer in California? What advice would you give yourself? For guidance, consult Reg. § 1.162-5(b)(3)(i) (end) and (ii), Ex. (4); *Rev. Rul. 74-78*, 1974-1 C.B. 44; *Weyts v. Comm'r*, T.C. Memo. 2003-68; *Kohen v. Comm'r*, T.C. Memo. 1982-625; *Ruehmann v. Comm'r*, T.C. Memo. 1971-157; *Johnson v. U.S.*, 332 F. Supp. 906 (E.D. La. 1971); *Hudgens v. Comm'r*, T.C. Memo. 1997-33 (discussed earlier in this chapter); and *PLR 9112003* (Dec. 18, 1990).

(c) Ruth is a chemical engineer who works as a project manager. Then she obtains an M.B.A. and obtains a job with the same company as a marketing manager. Is the cost of the M.B.A. deductible? See *Foster v. Comm'r*, T.C. Summary Op. 2008-22.

2.   (a) Can a law student deduct the costs of obtaining her first job as an attorney under § 162(a)? Section 212? Section 195?

(b) Is § 217 available to the law student upon moving from the law school to the locale of the first job? What distance requirements must be satisfied?

3.   Daneeka, an attorney, receives an excludible gift and uses the money to pay for continuing legal education (CLE) courses. What result?

Chapter 10

DUAL-PURPOSE OUTLAYS

An activity or item may be both personal and productive of income at the same time. This chapter deals with what are basically "tie-breaker" rules for these dual-nature or dual-purpose cases. These rules operate mostly on an all-or-nothing basis. That is, they usually assign a dual-purpose activity or cost entirely to either the income-producing sphere or the personal sphere without attempting any allocation between the two.

A. PERSONAL-USE PROPERTY WITH APPRECIATION POTENTIAL

Property held for personal use may also generate future income in the form of appreciation. Can a taxpayer claim depreciation, losses, repairs, and other expenses with respect to such property (assuming that the property is not clearly put to an interim business or investment use by renting the property to others)?

The general rule is "no." The clearest case is a personal residence held for personal use (and not rented out). The property is viewed as being held for personal use even though most owners hope that the value of the residence will increase and that it can be sold at profit. Thus, depreciation, loss, repairs, etc., are not allowed at all, even if the property appreciates. (Of course, "improvements" can be added to basis.)

The courts have reached much the same result in the case of art works, collectibles, and jewelry. Although purporting to apply a "primary purpose" test to the ownership of these items, the cases tend to hold that any significant personal use indicates a primary personal use.[1] In order to claim that the property is held for investment, the property would need to be stored in a vault or put out for sale on consignment full time.

B. NOT-FOR-PROFIT ACTIVITIES

In addition to growing perceptions of the inadequacy of the ordinary-and-necessary test to weed out personal items and activities, the 1960s also witnessed a growing concern with "tax shelters." This term literally refers to an activity that generates operating losses (deductions in excess of gross income) that can "shelter"

---

[1] See *Wrightsman v. U.S.*, 428 F.2d 1316 (Ct. Cl. 1970) (expenses in connection with art collection hung in apartment used as taxpayer's residence for only one month per year were nondeductible); *Hamilton v. Comm'r*, 25 B.T.A. 1317 (1932) (no deduction for loss on sale of valuable painting displayed in taxpayer's home).

(offset) an individual's other income, such as wages. The specific concern in the 1960s was that many loss-producing ventures carried on under the rubric of "business" or "investment" were *really* disguised personal consumption activities whose deductible losses sheltered unrelated gross income from tax. Just as the basis of a personal-use asset can eliminate gain but not yield a loss deduction, so it should be the case that expenses of carrying on a personal activity should be able to offset gross income from that activity, but not to produce an operating loss that can shelter other income.

For example, suppose that Abe, a successful full-time lawyer earning $100K each year, enjoys woodworking as a hobby, and his enjoyment is increased by selling the product of his efforts at local summer craft shows. Abe generates $500 of annual gross revenue from sales, which is clearly includible in gross income. However, Abe incurs $700 in costs (for depreciation of his woodworking equipment and expenses for supplies and raw materials) in generating that gross income. This pattern is repeated (more or less) year after year. Is the $700 deductible in whole or in part? There are four possible alternative approaches:

(a) Disallow the *entire* $700 on the ground that these are costs of personal consumption.

(b) Allow the $200 operating loss to be deducted in full, thereby "sheltering" $200 of gross income from Abe's law practice.

(c) Allow $500 of deductions this year (yielding no gain and loss from the activity), and carry over the $200 loss to the next year, to be deducted to the extent of next year's net profit (if any) from the activity, and so on.

(d) Same as (c), but with no loss carryforwards.

Since Abe's activity produces income and Abe's costs directly relate to producing that income, deductions should be allowed at least to the extent of the income, thereby ruling out alternative (a). However, the fact that Abe's woodworking produced a loss and is clearly secondary to his law practice suggests that woodworking is a recreational activity and that the $200 loss is a personal cost. If so, alternative (b) must also be ruled out. Alternative (c) (the carry forward approach) effectively treats the operating loss as a capital expenditure to be matched against future income. This approach is unsatisfactory in a scenario such as this, where all indications are that these costs are not likely to generate significant future revenues. That leaves alternative (d).

Section 183, which applies to activities "not engaged in for profit," follows alternative (d), but in a roundabout way. Initially, § 183(a) provides that, if an activity is determined to be "not-for-profit" (under factors discussed shortly), then no deductions are allowable under § 162, 212, 165(c)(1) or (2), or 167 for expenses, losses, and depreciation. But then § 183(b) partially countermands this harsh result in two ways. First, § 183(b)(1) requires that the gross income from the not-for-profit activity be reduced by all deductions incurred in the activity that are allowable *without regard* to the existence of a profit motive, which would mainly be "qualified residence interest" and state and local taxes (collectively referred to as "activity-related personal deductions"). If these activity-related personal deductions exceed the not-for-profit activity gross income, then this excess is deductible against the taxpayer's gross income from other sources, but the prohibition against deductions under § 162, 212, 165(c)(1) or (2) or 167 still stands. Second, where the not-for-profit activity gross income exceeds the activity-related personal deductions, then § 183(b)(2) allows deductions for costs described in §§ 162, 212, 165(c)(1) or (2) and 167 that are attributable to the activity, but the § 183(b)(2) deduction cannot be greater than the amount by which the gross income from the activity exceeds the activity-related personal deductions. The allowance of deductions under this second prong occurs under § 183(b). *Costs in excess of these limitations are totally disallowed with no carryforward.*

The § 183(b)(2) deduction is not a "business" deduction and, therefore, is not a § 62 deduction taken in arriving at AGI. It follows that the § 183(b)(2) deduction is an itemized deduction. Worse yet, it is not on the § 67(b) list and thus is also a Miscellaneous Itemized Deduction (MID) subject to the 2%-of-AGI floor of § 67(a) (and is completely disallowed in figuring the AMT tax base). However, the activity-related personal deductions taken into account in the § 183(b)(1) computation (such as qualified residence interest) maintain the status they would have in the absence of § 183.

These rules can be illustrated by returning to Abe's woodworking activity, which generated $500 of gross income and $700 in costs, but assume now that this activity is determined to be not engaged in for profit, and that $100 of the costs were due to qualified residence interest allocated to the activity, $350 of the costs were for expenses, and $250 of the costs were for equipment depreciation. The $100 qualified residence interest is an activity-related personal deduction that is subtracted first from the $500, leaving the lesser of (a) the remaining $400 of gross income or (b) the remaining deduction items totaling $600. Therefore, only $400 would be deductible under § 183(b)(2) in the current year. This $400 is deemed to come first out of costs other than depreciation. Thus, expenses of $350 and depreciation of $50 is allowed under § 183(b)(2). The remaining $200, which is all depreciation, would be disallowed, with no carryover to other years. And, because the $400 deduction is an MID subject (along with any other of Abe's MIDs) to the 2% floor under § 67, Abe may end up deducting no part of the $400 under § 183(b)(2). The basis of the equipment is reduced by only the $50 of allowed depreciation. See Reg. § 1.183-1(b)(1).

How does one determine whether an activity is "engaged in for profit?" The *statutory* test, found in § 183(c), is remarkably unhelpful, because it merely refers to the statutory tests found in §§ 162 and 212. Reg. § 1.183-2(a) and (b), fill the void by positing a "taxpayer purpose" test that is to be applied solely on the basis of "objective standards" and by taking into account "all of the facts and circumstances," including (but not limited to) the following factors:

(1)   the profit and loss history of the activity in question;

(2)   the magnitude of activity profits (when they occur);

(3)   the taxpayer's success (or lack thereof) in similar activities in the past;

(4)   the presence or absence of appreciation in activity assets;

(5)   the presence or absence of pleasure and recreational potential;

(6)   the presence or absence of business-like "manner" (such as record-keeping, serious sales efforts, and keeping abreast of technical advances);

(7)   the presence or absence of taxpayer expertise and training;

(8)   the time and effort devoted to the activity; and

(9)   the financial status and security of the taxpayer apart from the activity.

Reg. § 1.183-2 is well worth reading (before embarking on the illustrative case below). Among other things, the regulations state that, "a reasonable expectation of profit is not required," and "it may be sufficient that there is a small chance of making a large profit." But there must be an honest "objective" of making a profit.[2]

Because the inquiry under § 183 is highly fact-intensive, much litigation has resulted. The case below is representative.

ESTATE OF POWER v. COMMISSIONER
United States Court of Appeals, First Circuit
736 F.2d 826 (1984)

Before COFFIN and BOWNES, CIRCUIT JUDGES, and PETTINE, SENIOR DISTRICT JUDGE.

BOWNES, CIRCUIT JUDGE.

Elizabeth L. Power was a taxpayer residing in Middlesex County, Massachusetts, who used a fiscal year ending June 30 for federal income tax purposes. The sole issue before the Tax Court was whether Mrs. Power's horse breeding activity was "engaged in for profit" within the meaning of I.R.C. § 183 so that losses in connection with that activity [for fiscal years 1972, 1973, 1974, and 1977] could be offset against income from other sources during the years in question. The Tax Court found that the horse breeding was not engaged in for profit, and upheld the Commissioner's determination of deficiency. T.C. Memo 1983-552. This appeal followed.

The Tax Court found the relevant facts as follows. Mrs. Power inherited a farm of some 500 acres upon her mother's death in 1941, and, with her husband, began to work much of the land as commercial fruit orchards. Although her parents had kept horses and constructed a riding ring on the property, Mrs. Power's participation in the family riding had been minimal. In the early 1950's, however, she considered the possibility of raising horses, for the farm was already equipped with the riding ring and pasture fields. After attending the National Morgan Horse Show in 1952, Mrs. Power purchased several Morgans and began to show them under the name "Waseeka Farm"; she also expanded the existing facilities and constructed new stalls on the farm. She employed a respected trainer named John Lydon beginning in the early 1960's; when Lydon left, the post was filled successively by his daughters Ginny and Priscilla until the horses were disposed of

---

[2] See *Dreicer v. Comm'r*, 665 F.2d 1292 (D.C. Cir. 1981), *on remand*, 78 T.C. 642 (1982) (finding against the taxpayer).

in 1977. In addition to the trainer, Mrs. Power employed two farmhands to care for the horses. She herself neither rode the horses nor took part in their training; she did, however, hold regular weekly meetings at which the total business of the farm was discussed. Her attorney kept meticulous records of her farming and household expenses, and her daughter helped manage the horse breeding and showing activities.

Mrs. Power attended shows in which her horses were entered, and her daughter and granddaughter rode the horses being shown. Waseeka Farm won considerable acclaim, particularly with respect to a stallion named Nocturne who was highly prized for his qualities as a show horse and sire. Nocturne's breeding career ended, though, when he unexpectedly became sterile in 1972; his projected stud fees would have amounted to $10,000 or $15,000 per year during the period in question.

For fiscal years 1958 through 1970, Mrs. Power reported an unbroken sequence of farm losses arising from the combined orchard and horse activities. After 1970, Mrs. Power gave up the orchard business, but continued to report farm losses from horse breeding alone for fiscal years 1971 through 1974. Her tax returns for the last two years were audited and her farm losses challenged on the ground that the horse breeding activity was not engaged in for profit. Mrs. Power elected under § 183(e) to postpone resolving the issue until the close of fiscal year 1977.

After the audit, Mrs. Power's daughter, Susan Annis, prepared a memorandum analyzing Waseeka Farm's income and expenses, and projected an estimated potential profit of $5,510 for the period between October 1, 1974 and September 30, 1975. This figure, however, did not take account of any legal fees, bookkeeping [fees], postage, photographs, secretarial costs, registration, or maintenance on such equipment as the tractor, horse trailer, etc. The memo also noted that it would be a "challenge" to increase income sufficiently to show even a small yearly net profit. As it turned out, Mrs. Power reported positive farm income for fiscal years 1975 through 1977 from horse breeding. The apparent showing of profit, however, reflected in reality no more than an unexplained change from accrual accounting with inventories to cash accounting without inventories; the gross income from horse sales was reported with no offsetting deduction for the cost of the horses sold. Under the prior accounting method, the Commissioner calculated that the horse operations would have yielded net losses in each year.

From 1958 through 1977, Mrs. Power's main source of income was a trust established by her parents: the trust, along with other investments, provided her with an average annual income of over $60,000. During the same period, she realized capital gains of more than $400,000, including gains in fiscal years 1973 and 1974 from the sale of land.

Appellants first contend that Mrs. Power is entitled to a presumption that her horse breeding activity was engaged in for profit under § 183(d). [The presumption applies if the activity in question shows a profit in two of the seven years ending in 1977.]

The only basis on which a finding of net profit from Waseeka Farm could arguably be shown is the sale of land in 1973 and 1974 resulting in capital gains of $67,188.30 and $ 151,695.76. If the capital gains were set off directly against the farm losses of $36,241.92 and $38,489.44 in the respective years, there would be a net profit for both years. The Tax Court, however, expressly found that "the operation of the horse farm and the holding of the land were separate activities," and accordingly refused to consider the proceeds from the land sales as gain offsetting the farm losses. The question whether several activities are to be considered separately or together for purposes of § 183 was a question of fact for resolution by the Tax Court in light of "all the facts and circumstances of the case." Treas. Reg. § 1.183-1(d)(1) [states]:

> where land is purchased or held primarily with the intent to profit from increase in its value, and the taxpayer also engages in farming on such land, the farming and the holding of the land will ordinarily be considered a single activity only if the farming activity reduces the net cost of carrying the land for its appreciation in value. Thus, the farming and holding of the land will be considered a single activity only if the income derived from farming exceeds the deductions attributable to the farming activity which are not directly attributable to the holding of the land. . . .

At no time did the farming operation produce sufficient income to reduce the net cost of holding the land. The Tax Court relied on appellants' statements that the land in question was held for appreciation and sold when it was no longer necessary for horse breeding. At trial, Susan Annis testified that during the five years before it was sold the land "wasn't really being used for much of anything" due to a reduction in the number of horses being boarded. There was also undisputed testimony that the land had been acquired for fruit orchards rather than horse breeding, and that it was later used only for the "overflow" of brood mares. The evidence was sufficient to establish that the land was not held as part of the horse breeding activity, see Treas. Reg. § 1.183-1(c)(3), and that the gain from the land sales could not be used to offset the farm losses. The Tax Court's conclusion that the § 183(d) presumption was unavailable to Mrs. Power is not clearly erroneous.

Appellants also contend that even without the benefit of the § 183(d) presumption they met their burden of proving that Mrs. Power engaged in horse breeding for profit during the years in question. The determination whether an activity is engaged in for profit is to be made by reference to objective standards, taking into account all of the facts and circumstances of each case. Although a reasonable expectation of profit is not required, the facts and circumstances must indicate that the taxpayer entered into the activity, or continued the activity, with the objective of making a profit. The Treasury Regulations set out nine relevant factors which should be taken into account in determining whether an activity is engaged in for profit. [See the text preceding this opinion.] The enumerated factors are not exclusive, nor is any single factor or combination of factors determinative.

Four considerations appear to have determined the Tax Court's conclusion that Mrs. Power did not engage in horse breeding for profit during the years in question. First, the court looked at the "unbroken string of substantial losses stretching back over decades" as strong evidence that a profit objective was lacking. This corresponds to the sixth factor in the Regulations:

> A series of losses during the initial or start-up stage of an activity may not necessarily be an indication that the activity is not engaged in for profit.

However, where losses continue to be sustained beyond the period which customarily is necessary to bring the operation to profitable status such continued losses, if not explainable, as due to customary business risks or reverses, may be indicative that the activity is not being engaged in for profit.

Treas. Reg. § 1.183-2(b)(6); see *Bessenyey v. Comm'r*, 45 T.C. 261, 274 (1965), *aff'd*, 379 F.2d 252 (2d Cir.), *cert. denied*, 389 U.S. 931 (1967) ("the goal must be to realize a profit on the entire operation, which presupposes not only future net earnings but also sufficient net earnings to recoup the losses which have meanwhile been sustained in the intervening years"). The evidence showed that a horse breeding operation might not show a profit for the first ten years. Mrs. Power's losses, however, were uninterrupted for more than twice that length of time. Although appellants stressed the unforeseeability of Nocturne's sterility and the untimely death of their last trainer as explanations for the losses, the court found that neither misfortune materially affected the lack of potential profitability of the horse breeding activity.

The second consideration mentioned by the court was the manner in which the activity was conducted, particularly with reference to Susan Annis's post-audit memorandum. Although meticulous records were kept and Mrs. Power was well advised in financial matters by her attorney and Susan Annis, the court found that the principal objective was to enable Mrs. Power to continue her horse breeding operation on a smaller scale without incurring unduly burdensome costs, not to turn the operation around and produce a profit.

The court also looked at the ninth factor in the Regulations, *viz.*, elements of personal pleasure, and found that Mrs. Power "took considerable pleasure and satisfaction in the operation of Waseeka Farm and the ownership of her prize winning Morgan horses." Not only did she attend shows, but also her daughter and granddaughter rode the horses at the shows.

Finally, the court noted that Mrs. Power's regular and substantial trust income enabled her, without lowering her standard of living, "to persist in an activity which, although enjoyable, was consistently losing money, and had no real prospects of ceasing to do so." This is clearly a valid consideration under the eighth factor in the Regulations:

> Substantial income from sources other than the activity (particularly if the losses from the activity generate substantial tax benefits) may indicate that the activity is not engaged in for profit especially if there are personal or recreational elements involved.

Treas. Reg. § 1.183-2(b)(9).

Appellants argue that the Tax Court failed to give due consideration to countervailing factors such as the potential profits from horse sales and the horse breeding expertise of Mrs. Power and her advisors. The court's conclusion concerning profit objective, however, is a finding of fact which will be reversed only if clearly erroneous. Having determined that the court properly considered the facts under the objective standards set out in [the regulations], and that its conlusions are adequately supported in the record, we decline to reweigh the evidence.

The judgment of the Tax Court is affirmed.

Cases of this type can come out the opposite of *Powers*. In *Engdahl v. Comm'r*, 72 T.C. 659 (1979) (acq.), appreciating land was considered to be part of the horse-breeding activity, and the entire operation was found to be for profit. A similar result occurred in *Fields v. Comm'r*, T.C. Memo. 1981-550, where the taxpayer, a full-time attorney carried on a cattle operation.

Because of the highly factual nature of the § 183 inquiry, the issue is much litigated. There are hundreds of reported cases, most of which are nonappealed Tax Court memorandum decisions. Reversals on appeals are uncommon. The most common types of cases involve endeavors that have the "smell" of a personal hobby, such as outdoor activities (farming, ranching, breeding, hunting, and fishing), pets, creative pursuits (art, music, and film), collecting activities, transportation (cars, planes, and boats), and the renting of vacation homes. Some cases involve syndicated tax shelters that, while lacking a hobby or pleasure aspect, are simply intended to produce operating loss deductions, typically in such areas as natural resources exploration, mining, computers, and technology.[3]

In practice, the IRS identifies activities that might not be engaged in for profit by looking for regular and recurring losses shown on Schedule C (business profit and loss) and Schedule E (profit and loss from non-business rental and royalty activities). These schedules to the Form 1040 (the individual income tax return) call for separate reporting for each activity (or property).

Activities that escape not-for-profit status may nevertheless be subject to loss limitations under other Code provisions, such as §§ 280A (rental of vacation home; business use of home) and 469 (passive activities, including rental activities), which are considered elsewhere. In these instances, net losses from an activity cannot shelter other current income of the taxpayer, but they *can* be carried forward to future years to offset (only) income from the same activity (or category of activity) in those other years.

NOTES

1.   (a) Allowing the possibility of land appreciation to count in the for-profit calculus significantly weakens § 183 in the case of the "gentleman farmer." The arguably correct approach is to *always* treat the land-appreciation aspect as a separate activity apart from the farming, etc., activity and to separately test the latter under § 183. The regulations take a different approach, however. Reg. § 1.183-1(d)(1) effectively states that the two activities will be treated as separate activities unless (1) the property is acquired or held *primarily* for appreciation (a determination that would be contentious and unpredictable) and (2) the farming

---

[3] See, e.g., *Brannen v. Comm'r*, 722 F.2d 695 (11th Cir. 1984) (movie tax shelter); *Fox v. Comm'r*, 80 T.C. 972 (1983), *aff'd by unpub. order* (2d Cir. 1984) (book publishing tax shelter).

activity reduces the net costs of carrying the land (i.e., the farming activity's receipts do not exceed its costs).[4] For this purpose, the costs of improving the soil or clearing fields should be allocated to the farming activity, not the holding activity.

(b) The regulations are overly-generous because the farming (etc.) and land-holding activities really should always be considered to be separate for several reasons. The value of rural land is usually based on its future development prospects and is rarely based on the present value of future farming and ranching profits.[5] Moreover, the value of the land cannot be assumed to appreciate by reason of the farming, etc., activity.[6] Additionally, the value of the land is not "used up" in the farming, etc., activity. Finally, the separate holding-the-land activity would often pass muster under § 212,[7] thereby avoiding § 183.

(c) In cases where the regulations allow farming and land-holding to be treated as a single activity, the result is more favorable to taxpayers than is the case with "straight" personal-use property (such as a personal residence), where the loss cannot be deducted even if there was appreciation potential when the property was purchased.

2.   (a) One reading the trial court opinions in this area would come away with the impression that there are no close cases. This is so because once the trial judge (who has no taste for being reversed) decides the yes-or-no question, all the ducks are either made to fall in line or else are ignored.

(b) A taxpayer anticipating litigation under § 183 can help her cause by (1) learning about the business, (2) obtaining the help of experts, (3) keeping records, (4) making serious efforts to sell (crops, cattle, or whatever), and (5) putting in the necessary time and effort.

(c) The taxpayer's attorney can usually manage to find at least one case where the taxpayer prevailed despite (say) keeping no records. Such a case lessens the importance of the keeping-records factor. In this way, adverse factors can be selectively downgraded.

3.   Low-income housing would often generate economic losses if it were not for the low-income housing tax credit under § 42. Reg. § 1.42-4 provides, however, that § 183(b) will not apply to the operation of a building eligible for the low-income housing tax credit of § 42. Can this unique result be inferred from congressional intent?

4.   (a) Under § 183(d), if the taxpayer shows a tax profit for three out of five consecutive years up through the current year, there is a presumption commencing in the current year, rebuttable by the IRS, that the activity is engaged in for profit.

---

[4] See *Hambleton v. Comm'r*, T.C. Memo. 1982-234 (a farming activity was held to be a not-for-profit activity, and treated as a separate activity from the § 1.212-1 land-appreciation activity; expenses relating to working the land were allocated to the farming, not the investment, activity).

[5] Section 2032A, an estate tax provision, was enacted to provide tax relief, by allowing taxpayers to value land at its present use value rather than market value. This provision makes no sense unless the use value is assumed to be the lower value in virtually all cases.

[6] See note 5, supra.

[7] See Reg. § 1.212-1(b).

(For activities involving horses, as was the case in *Power*, a profit must be shown in two out of seven years.) Failure to satisfy the terms of the presumption does not mean that the taxpayer is presumed *not* to have a profit motive; the taxpayer simply is back to having to make his or her case using the factors in Reg. § 1.183-2(b), where a string of losses is one factor indicating a not-for-profit activity.

(b) Section 183(e) supplies a mechanism so that the taxpayer commencing a *new* activity can take advantage of the § 183(d) presumption beginning in Year 1, but only if the taxpayer makes an election under § 183(e). The tradeoff for making the election is that the statute of limitations, which generally expires after three years, will be held open for two years after the five-year (or seven-year) period during which the taxpayer is attempting to satisfy the presumption.

(c) To illustrate, suppose Emma makes an election under § 183(e) in Year 1, the year the activity begins. The activity shows net tax losses during Years 1 and 2, but Years 3 and 4 yield a tax profit. The § 183(d) presumption cannot yet operate in Emma's favor, because there have not been the requisite three profit years. If Year 5 is also a profit year, the presumption in favor of the taxpayer is activated, and § 183(e) provides that it applies retroactively to Years 1 and 2. If Year 5 turns out to be a loss year, however, the pro-taxpayer presumption is not activated, and the IRS may disallow the loss in Year 1 (which, without the election, would otherwise have been a closed tax year). If Emma did not make an election under § 183(e) in Year 1, the presumption would not have operated retroactively to Year 1, but neither would the limitations period be extended.

PROBLEM

Jill, a grade-school English teacher, makes chainsaw art on weekends that she occasionally tries to sell at art and craft fairs. She uses pieces of wood that she finds in the countryside and on the beach. Jill has not obtained any art degrees nor attended any art classes. In Year 1, this activity generates $1,000 of gross income and $1,200 in total expenses that would be fully deductible under § 162 if the activity were engaged in for profit. Jill's adjusted gross income (apart from the activity in question) is $50K. Jill has other itemized deductions of $8K, none of which are MIDs. What is the effect of the foregoing on Jill's Year 1 and Year 2 taxable incomes, considering the possible application of § 183 (as well as of §§ 62 and 67)? See *Churchman v. Comm'r*, 68 T.C. 696 (1977) (struggling but dedicated artist); *Hawkins v. Comm'r*, T.C. Memo. 1979-101, *aff'd without op.*, 652 F.2d 62 (9th Cir. 1981) (secretary-poet); *Regan v. Comm'r*, T.C. Memo. 1979-340 (chemical engineer and aspiring actor).

C. GAMBLING LOSSES

Gambling is a prime example of an activity that possesses both income-producing and recreational (personal) aspects. For example, suppose Sue pursues casino gambling on her vacations solely for the entertainment value. A few of Sue's pulls of the one-arm bandits produce wins. Most, however, produce losses. (Remember, if the odds didn't favor the house, casinos would go out of business.) The cash won clearly constitutes includible gross income under § 61. Are the lost bets deductible? Even though your vacation gambling is pursued purely for personal enjoyment,

§ 165(d) allows you to deduct your losses "from wagering transactions," but only up to your gains "from such transactions" in the current year.

In *GLAM 2008-011* (Dec. 5, 2008),[8] the IRS interpreted "wagering transactions" to mean (basically) a gambling session. Under this approach, it is easy to calculate the difference between what you start with and what you end with, and it is unnecessary to keep track of the intermediate betting transactions. To illustrate, suppose that for a particular year, the taxpayer gambles with $100 for each of seven days. On each of five days, she loses the $100, and on the other two days she comes out ahead (after subtracting the $100 for each such day) by $150 each day (which amount is includible in gross income). The net gambling losses for the year ($500) exceed the net gambling gains ($300), for the year, under § 165(d), resulting in a deduction of $300, and a disallowance of $200.

Like § 183 (but unlike excess capital losses, excess investment interest, and business net operating losses), § 165(d) does *not* allow excess gambling losses for the year to be carried over and used in other years.

Deductions under § 165(d) are regular itemized deductions, but not MIDs. See § 67(b)(3).

NOTE

Section 165(d) is not limited to recreational gambling. It also applies to professional gamblers who make a business of betting on their own account. Perhaps this reflects a congressional judgment that professional gamblers cannot be readily distinguished from recreational gamblers. Or perhaps Congress regards professional gambling as a mildly reprehensible activity that should be partially disfavored by the tax law. Compare § 280E, which prohibits an illegal drug dealer from deducting any of his business expenses against drug-dealing receipts.

PROBLEM

Jack visits the casino on one occasion in Year 1. Jack's initial stake is $1K, which, by skill, soon grows to $100K, but then, thanks to luck, all of the $100K is lost. In Year 2, Jack places one bet for $1K and wins $5K. What result to Jack in Years 1 and 2?

D.   COMMUTING

Costs of commuting between home and work are classic dual-purpose items: commuting presupposes both a home (personal) and a place of work (business). (For most people, combining the living place and work place is either impossible or impractical.) The deduction provision that is most directly in point, § 162(a)(2), refers to "travelling expenses . . . while away from home in the pursuit of a trade or business" And, therefore, seems to allow a deduction for commuting costs. But that is not the case under the court decisions and regulations.

---

[8] "GLAM" stands for "generic legal advice memorandum."

COMMISSIONER v. FLOWERS
United States Supreme Court
326 U.S. 465 (1946)

MR. JUSTICE MURPHY delivered the opinion of the Court.

[The taxpayer was general counsel for a railroad having its business headquarters in Mobile, Alabama. The taxpayer lived in Jackson, Mississippi, where he had practiced law for several years prior to becoming an employee of the railroad. The taxpayer maintained an office in Jackson (mostly) at his own expense, and spent more than twice as many days in the Jackson office, performing his work for the railroad, as in the office in Mobile provided him by the railroad. There was nothing in the nature of the work that required it to be performed in Jackson; it could have been performed in Mobile. He sought to deduct the transportation expenses incurred in making trips from Jackson (where his residence was located) to Mobile as well as expenses for meals and lodgings while in Mobile.]

In this instance, the Tax Court disallowed the deductions on the ground that they represent living and personal expenses rather than traveling expenses away from home in the pursuit of business. The court below reversed on the basis that it had improperly construed the word "home" as used in [§ 162(a)(2)]. The Tax Court, it was said, erroneously construed the word to mean the post, station, or place of business where the taxpayer was employed — in this instance Mobile.

The meaning of the word "home" with reference to a taxpayer residing in one city and working in another has engendered much difficulty and litigation. The Tax Court and the administrative rulings have consistently defined it as the equivalent of the taxpayer's place of business. On the other hand, the decision below flatly rejected that view and confined the term to the taxpayer's actual residence.

We deem it unnecessary here to enter into or to decide this conflict. The Tax Court's opinion, as we read it, was grounded neither solely nor primarily upon that agency's conception of the word "home." Its discussion was directed mainly toward the relation of the expenditures to the railroad's business. The facts demonstrate clearly that the expenses were not incurred in the pursuit of the business of the taxpayer's employer. Jackson was his regular home. Had his post of duty been in that city the cost of maintaining his home there and of commuting or driving to work concededly would be nondeductible living and personal expenses lacking the necessary direct relation to the prosecution of the business. The character of such expenses is unaltered by the circumstance that the taxpayer's post of duty was in Mobile, thereby increasing the costs of transportation, food and lodging. Whether he maintained one abode or two, whether he traveled three blocks or three hundred miles to work, the nature of these expenditures remained the same.

The added costs in issue, moreover, were as unnecessary and inappropriate to the development of the railroad's business as were his personal and living costs in Jackson. They were incurred solely as the result of the taxpayer's desire to maintain a home in Jackson while working in Mobile, a factor irrelevant to the maintenance and prosecution of the railroad's legal business. The railroad simply asked him to be at his principal post in Mobile as business demanded and as his personal convenience was served, allowing him to divide his business time between Mobile and Jackson as he saw fit.

Mr. Justice Jackson took no part in the consideration or decision of this case.

[Dissenting opinion of Mr. Justice Rutledge omitted.]

The rule that commuting costs are generally not deductible is found in Reg. §§ 1.162-2(e) and 1.262-1(b)(5). There are exceptions to this rule that will be noted in due course.

E. WORK CLOTHING

Clothing would be worn for personal purposes even if the taxpayer were not working. But some jobs require the taxpayer to purchase particular items of clothing.

The IRS policy is to disallow work clothing costs unless (1) the clothing is of a type specifically required as a condition of employment, (2) it is not adaptable to general usage as ordinary clothing, and (3) it is not in fact worn outside of the work setting. See *Rev. Rul. 70-474*, 1970-2 C.B. 54. Factor (2) rules out deducting business suits and the like (even if the taxpayer swears that he would always wear jeans if it weren't for the job).

In *Pevsner v. Comm'r*, 628 F.2d 467 (5th Cir. 1980), the taxpayer, a manager of an upscale clothing boutique in Dallas, sought to deduct under § 162 the costs incurred in purchasing and maintaining ready-to-wear clothes sold by the store and designed by Yves St. Laurent. Her employer expected her to buy and wear (while on the job) clothing stocked by the store. The taxpayer did not wear these clothes away from work, because they were too expensive for her everyday lifestyle. The court, in denying the deductions, followed *Rev. Rul. 70-474* and held that whether the clothing is "adaptable to general usage" is to be determined *objectively*, not subjectively according to an individual taxpayer's self-image.

F. CHILD CARE

In *Smith v. Comm'r*, 40 B.T.A. 1038 (1939), the taxpayer, a working wife, tried to deduct the cost of child care on the ground that, "but for" the child care, she would not be able to work. The court held that the child care costs were inherently personal and nondeductible, stating (40 B.T.A. at 1039-40):

> We are not unmindful that, as petitioners suggest, certain disbursements normally personal may become deductible by reason of their intimate connection with an occupation carried on for profit. The line is not always an easy one to draw nor the test simple to apply. But we think its principle is clear. It may for practical purposes be said to constitute a distinction between those activities which, as a matter of common acceptance and

universal experience, are "ordinary" or usual as the direct accompaniment of business pursuits, on the one hand; and those which, though they may in some indirect and tenuous degree relate to the circumstances of a profitable occupation, are nevertheless personal in their nature, of a character applicable to human beings generally, and which exist on that plane regardless of the occupation, though not necessarily of the station in life, of the individuals concerned. In the latter category, we think, fall payments made to servants or others occupied in looking to the personal wants of their employers. See *Sonenblick v. Comm'r*, 4 B.T.A. 986. And we include in this group nursemaids retained to care for infant children.

A limited deduction for child care (former § 221) of two-earner married couples (not to exceed $3K) was justified as an expense to enable one to work. That deduction no longer exists, but has been effectively replaced by the § 21 household and dependent care credit, described in Chapter 4.

G. BUSINESS-SETTING MEALS NOT INCURRED IN A TRAVEL OR ENTERTAINMENT MODE

The consumption of food and beverages would seem to be the archtypical act of personal consumption. However, it turns out that special statutory rules allow meals to be deducted in certain business-travel and business-entertainment situations, to be discussed in the next chapter. In the case set forth below, however, the meal costs, incurred in a business setting, were not subject to any special statutory rules.

MOSS v. COMMISSIONER
United States Court of Appeals, Seventh Circuit
758 F.2d 211 (1985)

Before CUMMINGS, CHIEF JUDGE, and BAUER and POSNER, CIRCUIT JUDGES.

POSNER, CIRCUIT JUDGE:

Moss was a partner in a small trial firm specializing in [insurance] defense work. Each of the firm's [seven] lawyers carried a tremendous litigation caseload, averaging more than 300 cases, and spent most of every working day in courts in Chicago and its suburbs. The members of the firm met for lunch daily at the Cafe Angelo near their office. [The partnership paid for the meals, and Moss claimed his share of the meal cost as a business deduction, which was disallowed by the Tax Court.][9] At lunch the lawyers would discuss their cases with the head of the firm, whose approval was required for most settlements, and they would decide which lawyer would meet which court call. Lunchtime was chosen for the daily meeting

---

[9] [Editor's note: The posture of this case is confusing to one not versed in partnership tax. The issue here is not whether the value of the meals was gross income to Moss. Nor can the case be analogized to a reimbursed employee business expense, because Moss was acting as a partner, not as an employee. The case is best understood by thinking of Moss as a self-employed individual claiming a business expense deduction for his share of the amount paid for the meals.]

because the courts were then in recess. The alternatives were to meet at 7:00 a.m. or 6:00 p.m., and these were less convenient times. There is no suggestion that the Cafe Angelo is luxurious.

The problem is that many expenses are simultaneously business expenses in the sense that they conduce to the production of business income and personal expenses in the sense that they raise personal welfare. This is plain enough with regard to lunch; most people would eat lunch even if they didn't work.

Although an argument can be made for disallowing any deduction for business meals, on the theory that people have to eat whether they work or not, the result would be excessive taxation of people who spend more money on business meals than they would spend on their meals if they were not working. Suppose a theatrical agent takes his clients out to lunch at the expensive restaurants that the clients demand. Of course he can deduct the expense of their meals, from which he derives no pleasure or sustenance, but can he also deduct the expense of his own? He can, because he cannot munch surreptitiously on a peanut butter and jelly sandwich brought from home while his client is wolfing down *tournedos Rossini* followed by *soufflé au grand marnier*. No doubt our theatrical agent, unless concerned for his longevity, derives personal utility from his fancy meal, but probably less than the price of the meal. He would not pay for it if it were not for the business benefit; he would get more value from using the same money to buy something else; hence the meal confers on him less utility than the cash equivalent would.

The law could require him to pay tax on the fair value of the meal to him; this would be (were it not for costs of administration) the economically correct solution. But the government does not attempt this difficult measurement; it once did, but gave up the attempt as not worth the cost. The taxpayer is permitted to deduct the whole price, provided the expense is "different from or in excess of that which would have been made for the taxpayer's personal purposes." *Sutter v. Comm'r*, 21 T.C. 170 (1953) (acq.).

Because the law allows this generous deduction, which tempts people to have more (and costlier) business meals than are necessary, the Service has every right to insist that the meal be shown to be a real business necessity. This condition is most easily satisfied when a client or customer or supplier or other outsider to the business is a guest. It is undeniable that eating together fosters camaraderie and makes business dealings friendlier and easier. It thus reduces the costs of transacting business, for these costs include the frictions and the failures of communication that are produced by suspicion and mutual misunderstanding, by differences in tastes and manners, and by lack of rapport. But it is different when all the participants in the meal are coworkers, as essentially was the case here. They know each other well already; they don't need the social lubrication that a meal with an outsider provides — at least don't need it daily.

It is all a matter of degree and circumstance (the expense of a testimonial dinner, for example, would be deductible on a morale-building rationale); and particularly of frequency. Daily — for a full year — is too often, perhaps even for entertainment of clients, as implied by *Hankenson v. Comm'r*, T.C. Memo. 1984-200, where the Tax Court held nondeductible the cost of lunches consumed three or four days a week, 52 weeks a year, by a doctor who entertained other doctors who he hoped would refer patients to him, and other medical personnel.

We may assume it was necessary for Moss's firm to meet daily to coordinate the work of the firm, and also that lunch was the most convenient time. But it does not follow that the expense of the lunch was a necessary business expense. The members of the firm had to eat somewhere, and they do not claim to have incurred a greater daily lunch expense than they would have incurred if there had been no lunch meetings. Although it saved time to combine lunch with work, the meal itself was not an organic part of the meeting, as in the examples we gave earlier where the business objective, to be fully achieved, required sharing a meal. The case might be different if the location of the courts required the firm's members to eat each day either in a disagreeable restaurant, so that they derived less value from the meal than it cost them to buy it, cf. *Sibla v. Comm'r*, 611 F.2d 1260 (9th Cir. 1980); or in a restaurant too expensive for their personal tastes. But so far as appears, they picked the restaurant they liked most. Although it must be pretty monotonous to each lunch at the same place every working day of the year, not all the lawyers attended all lunch meetings and there was nothing to stop the firm from meeting occasionally at another restaurant proximate to their office in downtown Chicago; there are hundreds.

The reviewed Tax Court decision that was affirmed in *Moss* had this to say (80 T.C. 1073, 1080-81 (1983):

> The common thread which seems to bind the cases [in this area] together is the notion that some expenses are so inherently personal that they simply cannot qualify for § 162 treatment irrespective of the role played by such expenditures in the overall scheme of the taxpayers' trade or business. "A businessman's suit, a saleslady's dress, the accountant's glasses are necessary for their business but the necessity does not overcome the personal nature of these items and make them a deductible business expense. * * *" *Bakewell v. Comm'r*, 23 T.C. 803, 805 (1955). In the instant case, we are convinced that petitioner and his partners and associates discussed business at lunch, that the meeting was a part of their working day, and that this time was the most convenient time at which to meet. We are also convinced that the partnership benefited from the exchange of information and ideas that occurred. But this does not make his lunch deductible any more than riding to work together each morning to discuss partnership affairs would make his share of the commuting costs deductible. If petitioner is correct, only the unimaginative would dine at their own expense.

NOTES

1. (a) The *Moss* case raises the issue of subjective value in the following sentence: "The law could require him to pay tax on the fair value of the meal to him; this would be (were it not for costs of administration) the economically correct solution." Elsewhere Judge Posner poses hypotheticals in which business enter-

tainment meals are not "enjoyed" by the host.[10] Of what relevance is subjective value? In an ability-to-pay income tax, the cost of consumption is disallowed regardless of the level of the taxpayer's subjective enjoyment.

(b) Judge Posner's point can only have relevance on the issue of "business connection" (causation): to the extent that a cost item would be incurred *in any event* for personal purposes, it should not be deductible, since in that case the item is not incurred *because of* business or investment activity. There is no point (in terms of economic efficiency) in conferring a deduction for a cost that would be incurred anyway for purely personal reasons. A business-context meal with a cost in excess of what one would ordinarily pay might be assumed to be business motivated. On the other hand, if such business meal costs were generically deductible in full, then business people would find pretexts to have more business meals at a higher cost because of the tax benefit itself, which operates as a government subsidy for a portion of the meal cost. Additionally, how can one know what would ordinarily be paid? Why would one assume that people don't want the occasional fancy dinner?

(c) The logic of Judge Posner's analysis is that business meal costs should be deductible in part, at least, in cases where the circumstances suggest that "excess cost" exists and is attributable to a business motivation. Since the next chapter is about allocating costs between income-production and personal uses, the *Moss* case operates to set up the next chapter, where the issues considered in these notes will be revisited.

(d) In 1986, subsequent to *Moss*, Congress enacted § 274(n)(1). *The current version of § 274(n)(1) limits any otherwise allowable meal (or entertainment) expense deduction to 50% of the cost thereof.* [11] This provision would not affect the result in *Moss*, because there the costs were totally disallowed. Section 274(n)(1) does not cause any meal cost to be *allowed* in part; it merely disallows 50% of the meal (or entertainment) expense that otherwise would be deductible under § 162.

2.   In *Sibla v. Comm'r*, 611 F.2d 1260 (9th Cir. 1980), cited in *Moss*, firefighters were allowed to deduct under § 162 the meal costs they incurred in order to participate in an organized mess (group meal) while on duty during 24-hour shifts. The organized mess was made mandatory under a court order in a race discrimination case. The firefighters had to pay the costs even if they chose not to eat the meals or were unable to eat the meals on account of being present at fires. The Tax Court views *Sibla* as an aberration confined to its facts. See *Moss*, 80 T.C. at 1078-80. In *Christey v. U.S.*, 841 F.2d 809 (8th Cir. 1988), *cert. denied*, 489 U.S. 1016 (1989), members of the Minnesota Highway Patrol were permitted to deduct under § 162 the cost of restaurant meals eaten while on patrol. Applicable Highway Patrol regulations required the officers to eat their meals in public restaurants adjacent to the highways, to radio in the telephone number of the restaurant where they were

---

[10] These statements are a transparent reference to a passage in HENRY C. SIMONS, PERSONAL INCOME TAXATION 122-24 (1938), discussing whether in-kind benefits should be gross income to the employee. Simons concludes that this raises an "insuperable" problem for a personal income tax. But (in our opinion) the problem is insuperable only for an income tax based on subjective utility!

[11] Both subsections (k) and (n) of § 274 are subject to various exceptions listed in § 274(e), discussed in the next chapter in the context of entertainment expenses.

eating, and to be subject to interruption by duty calls and inquiries from the public. We think this decision is, like *Sibla*, aberrational in relation to the weight of authority, represented by *Moss*.

PROBLEMS

1. Suppose X Corporation has a weekly lunch, catered on its premises, for its 6 top executives (plus occasional additional employee attendees). Business is always the principal topic for discussion. (This hypothetical raises gross income issues for the executives that will be dealt with in the chapter on employee fringe benefits, but ignore the income issue for now, and assume that this meal is not intended to be employee compensation.) Can the corporation deduct the cost of this meal (or any portion thereof)?

2. Should meal costs be deductible if the meal was part of a "package" that included a deductible component, such as a continuing-education legal seminar that does not involve any out-of-town travel (see § 1.162-5, discussed in the previous chapter)? Should the portion of the seminar fee allocable to the meal be wholly disallowed?

Chapter 11

ALLOCATING COSTS BETWEEN THE INCOME-PRODUCTION AND PERSONAL REALMS

This chapter deals with situations where costs are allocated between income-production and personal activities, property, or acts. The chapter covers dual-use property, transportation of work tools, travel, entertainment, and business use (or rental) of homes.

A. ALLOCATION ACCORDING TO USE OF ASSETS

Costs relating to certain assets can be allocated among the business, investment, and personal categories on the basis of how these assets are used in time or space.

1. Allocations by Space

If the taxpayer owns a duplex, living in one unit and renting out the other, any deduction item pertaining to the entire structure (such as depreciation, insurance, upkeep of the grounds, and losses on sale) should be allocated between the "personal" and "income-producing" spaces on a square-footage basis. However, any item that is directly attributable to a particular unit, such as a repair to the rental-unit plumbing, should be allocated entirely to that particular unit.

2. Allocations by Time

If the taxpayer uses her car in part for business, the total depreciation, repairs, and fuel costs can be allocated to the business use in the ratio of business miles to total miles. This "time" allocation can apparently also be used if the property is sold at a loss. See generally, Reg. § 1.165-7(b)(4)(iv).

Alternatively, and for the sake of simplicity, the IRS allows taxpayers to claim a "standard mileage allowance" per business mile deduction in lieu of allocating actual expenses and depreciation.[1]

---

[1] For 2011, the mileage rate is 51 cents a mile (19 cents for the moving and medical expense deductions and 14 cents for service to charity). These rates are issued in annual IRS Notices, but can be more easily found on the IRS website: www.irs.gov. Obviously, the mileage rate cannot be taken if the motor vehicle was already expensed under § 179.

3. Converted-Use Property

Suppose that Rose purchases property used by her as a personal residence for $90K and, five years later, moves out and rents the property to Val. At the time of conversion to rental use, the building's fair market value (FMV) has fallen to $70K. Following the conversion, Rose can deduct expenses for producing rent and maintaining rental property under §§ 162 or 212 and can take depreciation on the building (but not the land) under § 167(a). But what is her basis in the building for depreciation purposes, and, if she sells the property, how is any § 1001 loss allocated between personal and profit-seeking use?

Regs. §§ 1.165-9(b)(2) and 1.167(g)-1 solve these issues by providing that the building's basis for depreciation and loss purposes is the lesser of (a) the cost of the building at the time of purchase or (b) the FMV of the building at the time of conversion to income-producing use.[2] In our hypothetical, that means that Rose's basis in the building is $70K for depreciation and loss purposes. The $20K loss in the building's value (from $90K to $70K) occurred when the building was used for personal purposes, and thus that $20K of original cost basis will not support either depreciation deductions or a loss deduction. However, for purposes of computing *gain*, the basis in the building remains at $90K in order to prevent double taxation of the same dollars. Rose's "dual" $70,000/$90,000 building basis will then be further reduced for post-conversion depreciation deductions, which cannot exceed $70K (i.e., the basis for depreciation purposes).

When is a property, in fact, converted from personal to income-producing use? Perhaps the leading case on this issue is *Newcombe v. Comm'r*, 54 T.C. 1298 (1970) (reviewed). There the taxpayer in December of Year 1 retired, moved to Florida, and put his old house up for sale at a price of $70K, which was slightly below its original cost. The former residence remained unoccupied until it was sold at a loss in Year 3, and the taxpayer never attempted to rent the house. The taxpayer argued that abandonment coupled with the offer to sell marked a conversion to income-production use for purposes of depreciation and maintenance expenses under §§ 167(a)(2) and 212, but the government contended that a conversion required rental (or at least having put the property on the rental market). The Tax Court majority rejected both categorical positions, adopting instead a facts-and-circumstances test. It ultimately decided for the government, largely because of (1) the long prior personal use by the taxpayer, (2) the fact that the property was placed on the market for immediate sale soon after the taxpayer ceased using it as a residence (instead of postponing the sale until post-abandonment appreciation had occurred), and (3) the absence of attempts to rent the property.

In dictum, the Tax Court majority intimated that a conversion to investment use was possible, even if there were no rental efforts, if the facts (such as a long delay between abandonment and putting the property on the market) indicated that the taxpayer was seeking "to realize a profit representing post-conversion appreciation

---

[2] In *Heiner v. Tindle*, 276 U.S. 582 (1928), decided before these regulations were issued, the Court held that a post-conversion sale loss on property converted to rental use in 1901 was to be computed with reference to the lesser of the FMV at the date of conversion or the FMV on March 1, 1913 (the effective date of the income tax).

in the market value of the property" (net of selling expenses).

Newcombe involved only maintenance expenses and depreciation during the period the residence was being offered for sale. In *Horrmann v. Comm'r*, 17 T.C. 903 (1951) (acq.), the Tax Court held that the test for deducting a loss on sale under § 165(c)(2) was different than that for expenses and depreciation, because the § 165(c)(2) "loss" language ("transaction entered into for profit") differed from the language found in §§ 212 and 167 ("for the production of income") pertaining to expenses and depreciation. Specifically, the Tax Court held that *actual rental* was required before a loss on a later sale could be deducted under § 165(c)(2). Merely listing for rental or sale was insufficient.

The Tax Court in *Horrmann* distinguished *Estate of Assman v. Comm'r*, 16 T.C. 632 (1951), where the taxpayer was permitted to deduct his sale loss without a prior rental. The facts said to distinguish the two cases were that the taxpayer in *Assman* abandoned the residence only a few days after it was inherited and then later demolished the residence (whereas in *Horrmann* the taxpayers had lived in the residence almost two full years after acquiring it by inheritance and before abandoning it). The *Horrmann* court said that the facts of *Assman* "indicated that from the moment the property was inherited the taxpayer did not intend to occupy it as a personal residence."

The scenario where property is converted from business or investment use, resulting in an adjusted basis of $70K to personal use is not clearly dealt with in the regulations. When the conversion occurs, the taxpayer must cease taking expense and depreciation deductions, leaving only the issue of how to account for any loss. The rule appears to be that the loss deduction is simply disallowed in full, with no attempt to allocate the loss between periods of business and personal use.[3] Thus, suppose a building is purchased for $100K and depreciation deductions totaling $30K are claimed during the building's years of business or investment use. When the FMV of the building is $75K, it is converted to personal use and later sold for $60K. The sale yields a $10K loss (adjusted basis of $70K less amount realized of $60K), which is treated as a nondeductible personal loss. Perhaps the correct theoretical result would be a $15K nondeductible personal loss ($75K − $60K) coupled with a $5K business or investment gain to reflect the excess of the $30K depreciation deductions over the $25K decline in value of the property during its period of business or investment use. However, depreciation deductions, based on statutory formulas, are never corrected to reflect actual (but unrealized) declines in market values, except in the case of "listed property" of the type mentioned in Section B.1, immediately below.[4]

If the converted property in this example were nondepreciable (say, unimproved land), the adjusted basis would remain at $100K, raising the specter of the entire loss of $40K being nondeductible, even though (by value) $25K of it was attributable to the period of business or investment use. This problem might possibly be solved by reference to Reg. § 1.165-7(b)(4)(iv), which states that a

---

[3]   See *Gevirtz v. Comm'r*, 123 F.2d 707 (2d Cir. 1941).

[4]   See § 280F(b)(2) (providing for statutory recapture of excess depreciation where "listed property" as defined in § 280F(d)(4) is converted to personal use).

casualty loss sustained with respect to an automobile used 60% for business and 40% for personal purposes is 60% allowable. This rule apparently assumes continuous business/personal mixed use during the taxpayer's ownership of the asset, but the principle could be extended to exclusive business use followed by conversion to exclusive personal use. Under this approach, the entire loss could be allocated between the personal and business (or investment) categories in the ratio of the personal holding period to the business (or investment) holding period. This approach would not achieve the "correct" result (keyed to the conversion-date FMV), except by coincidence, but perhaps that failure is a necessary corollary of the realization principle. There is, however, no extant authority applying this analysis.

PROBLEM

Don purchased personal-use property for $120K ($20K for the land and $100K for the building). At the time he converted it to rental use the land was worth $50K and the building was worth $80K. The building was "fully" depreciated over the following 40 years, after which Don sold it for $14K along with the land for $60K. What result? What if the building had been sold for $23K (and the land for $60K)?

B. STATUTORY OVERRIDES OF ALLOCATION RULES

Congress has enacted various provisions to curb taxpayer abuses involving allocations.

1. Listed Property

Because Congress perceived that taxpayers commonly overstate the business use of vehicles, boats, computers, and cell phones ("listed property"), it enacted § 280F, which provides (among other things) that listed property owned or leased by an employee and *used in the course of his employment* will not be treated as being used in the employee's business *at all* (for depreciation and lease-payment deduction purposes) unless such use is (1) for the "convenience of the employer" and (2) "required as a condition of employment."[5] See § 280F(d)(3). According to Temp. Reg. § 1.280F-6(a)(2), these terms generally have the same meaning as they do under the § 119 regulations (discussed in Chapter 12.B.1). The "condition of employment" test means that the item must be required for the employee to properly perform his duties. Other aspects of § 280F, which affect the rate of depreciation for listed property, are discussed in Chapter 28.D.1.c.

2. Home Offices

Section § 280A deals with costs related to a claimed business use of part of the taxpayer's personal residence as an office or other work area (hereinafter referred to as a "home office"). The relevant costs are the part of the taxpayer's total

---

[5] The exceptions to the term "listed property" include computers used exclusively at a regular business establishment, certain trucks and vans, and any vehicle weighing more than 6,000 pounds. Certain models of SUVs are designed to barely exceed the 6,000 pound threshold.

residential utility bills, upkeep expenses, insurance, depreciation, and so on, that are initially apportioned to the home office on a space basis, typically by comparing the square footage of the home office to the total square footage of the residence.

Prior to the enactment of § 280A in 1976, taxpayers who generally worked elsewhere but did some work at home in the evenings or on weekends would claim these apportioned home office items as deductions under §§ 162 and 167, and the lax interpretation of the "ordinary and necessary" requirement offered little resistance to such claims. In addition, there was no way that the IRS could monitor taxpayer claims as to the duration or extent of business use.

a.   When Home Office Deductions Are Allowed at All

Section 280A(a) initially disallows all deductions for an individual's costs that are proportionately allocable on a space basis to a home office or work area in a personal residence, except costs that are allowable as deductions even when not connected to income production (such as home mortgage interest and property taxes). But § 280A(c)(1) then revives the disallowed deductions, but only if the home office is:

(1) *exclusively* used in the taxpayer's business,

(2) on a regular basis, *and*

(3) if the home office is

(A) the taxpayer's principal place of business for any business of the taxpayer,

(B) used for meeting (in person) patients, clients, or customers in the ordinary course of business, *or*

(C) occupies a separate structure that is detached from the dwelling place and used in the taxpayer's business.

Nonbusiness for-profit activity does not count as "business" use, and hence cannot support any home office deduction.[6] In addition, if the taxpayer is an employee, the business use must be for the "convenience of the employer." This term was construed narrowly (in the absence of regulations on point) in *Hamacher v. Comm'r*, 94 T.C. 348 (1990), to mean "necessary for the functioning of the employer's business" or "necessary to allow the employee to perform his duties properly."

The "the principal place of business for any trade or business of the taxpayer" language in subparagraph (A) contemplates the possibility of a taxpayer having more than one business. Thus, the taxpayer with more than one trade or business can satisfy this requirement if the home office is the principal place of business for only one of her multiple businesses. An example would be an attorney who uses the home office exclusively for her "side business" as a fiction writer. However, use of the home office for more than one business of the taxpayer is problematic. See *Hamacher*, supra. For example, if the lawyer-author uses her home office occasionally to do legal research (as well as to write fiction), the possibility of home office

---

[6] See *Moller v. U.S.*, 721 F.2d 810 (Fed. Cir. 1983).

deductions would be lost under the exclusive-use requirement in § 280A(c)(1) unless the home office was also the principal place of the attorney's law business.

The meaning of "principal place of business" has generated much litigation. For example, is the "principal place of business" of a musician employed by the Metropolitan Opera in New York the place where he performs (the opera house) or the place where he practices many hours (his apartment)? See *Drucker v. Comm'r*, 715 F.2d 67 (2d Cir. 1983) (the apartment). Is the principal place of business of an anesthesiologist the hospital, where he cares for all of his patients and spends most of his working hours, or in his condominium, where he spends a substantial amount of time performing all the management tasks of his business, such as billing patients and doing professional reading? The hospital provided him with no office in which to perform such activities. In *Comm'r v. Soliman*, 506 U.S. 168 (1993), the Supreme Court decided on just these facts that the principal place of business was the hospital. The "primary considerations," according to the Court, are (1) the relative importance of activities performed at each business location (and where the services are performed or goods are delivered is of prime importance) and (2) the time spent at each location. In applying these tests, the Court focused on the fact that Dr. Soliman performed his medical services entirely at three hospitals and that he spent much more of his time performing those services than performing management tasks in his home office.

In response to *Soliman*, Congress enacted what might be called "the Doctors' Bill." It amended the flush language following § 280A(c)(1)(C) to provide that the subparagraph (A) "principal place of business" includes a home office used by the taxpayer to conduct administrative or management activities if there is no other fixed location of the trade or business where the taxpayer *actually* conducts substantial administrative or management activities. (The *Soliman* test remains relevant in cases not involving the performance of administrative or management activities.) According to the House Committee Report, the "no other fixed location" test can be satisfied even if the taxpayer has another fixed location where such activities *could* have been performed if the taxpayer had so chosen. But this flexibility is available only to self-employed persons (independent contractors). An employee who chooses to perform such activities at home even though her employer provides another fixed location at which to perform them would fail the "convenience-of-the-employer" requirement applicable to employees but not to independent contractors.[7]

b. Confinement of Home Office Deductions to the Home Office Business

Even if a taxpayer succeeds in meeting each of the tests in § 280A(c)(1) for deducting home office costs, not all such costs may be deductible in the year incurred. Congress, in enacting § 280A, was also concerned that depreciation and other deductions pertaining even to "legitimate" home offices could provide shelter from taxation to income having no connection to the home business. For example,

---

[7] See the first sentence of the flush language at the end of § 280A(c)(1); Prop. Reg. § 1.280A-2(g)(2); *Bernard v. U.S.*, 11 Cl. Ct. 437 (1986) (convenience-of-employer requirement not satisfied where noise concerns caused taxpayer to work at home instead of at the employer-provided office).

consider a full-time lawyer who earns $100K per year from law practice and who also operates an internet business, exclusively from a home office, selling tax preparation software that he developed and copyrighted. If the allowable costs allocable to the home office exceed the gross revenue generated from his software sales, the "net loss" from the internet business (the excess of aggregate deductions over gross income) could offset income from his law practice.

To prevent this result, section 280A(c)(5) provides that the deductions allocable to the home office are allowable in the current year only to the extent that the gross income from the business use of the space[8] exceeds the sum of (i) nonbusiness deductions (such as home mortgage interest and property taxes) allocable to such space and (ii) deductions incurred in the home office business but not attributable to the home office.[9] In other words, the allocable home-related deductions that don't require a business connection to be deductible (such as mortgage interest and property taxes) and the deductions that are related to the home business but have no connection to the home itself (such as advertising expense) are aggregated and taken first against gross income from the home business. The taxpayer can take the § 280A(c)(1) home office deductions only to the extent of the remaining home office business gross income.[10]

Any excess deductions are carried forward for possible use in future years against the home office business gross income.

3. Vacation Homes

Section 280A also applies to deductions attributable to a residence (usually referred to as a "vacation home") that the taxpayer both occupies for personal purposes and rents to others during the same year. Section 280A(a) initially disallows all deductions with respect to any "dwelling unit" which is "used by the taxpayer . . . as a residence," meaning (according to § 280A(d)(1)) that the taxpayer's personal use exceeds the greater of 14 days or 10% of days rented (at fair rental). This disallowance rule does not apply to personal deductions (such for mortgage interest and property taxes). See § 280A(b). Additionally § 280A(c)(3) cancels out the total-disallowance rule for (nonpersonal) deductions allocable to the rental use of the property, but in that case the anti-tax-shelter rule of § 280A(c)(5), described above, is applicable. The following discussion explores the effect of § 280A in several different scenarios.

a. No Personal Use

Section 280A is irrelevant with respect to costs incurred regarding a residence that is not used by the taxpayer to any extent for personal purposes.

---

[8] Gross income derived from other locations of the business is excluded. See Prop. Reg. § 1.280A-2(i)(2)(ii).

[9] Deductions of the business not attributable to the use of the home office would include everything *not* subject to § 280A itself, such as office supplies and labor, transportation, and advertising.

[10] Depreciation deductions (that reduce the basis of the property) are deemed to come last.

b. Minimal Personal Use Combined with Significant Rental Use

As noted above, if the taxpayer's personal use is not more than the greater of 14 days or 10% of rental days, § 280A does not apply, because the property is not considered to be "used as a residence." See § 280A(d)(1). Nevertheless, assuming the property is rented for at least 15 days, the expenses are subject to the allocation rule of § 280A(e)(1), under which the deductible expenses are the expenses multiplied by a fraction, the numerator of which is days actually rented at fair rental, and the denominator of which is total days of actual rental and personal use. This formula is favorable to taxpayers, because days of nonuse are excluded from the denominator. Deductions allowable regardless of whether connected to a business or investment activity (such as mortgage interest and property taxes) are not subject to this allocation scheme.

c. Minimal Rental Use

If the unit is "used by the taxpayer as a residence" but is rented for less than 15 days during the year, the rental income is excluded from gross income, and the deductions related to the rental (other than deductions allowable without regard to business or investment purpose, such as mortgage interest and property taxes) are disallowed. See § 280A(g); Prop. Reg. § 1.280A-1(b). This provision has been famously used by residents of U.S. Olympic host cities to create tax-free income from 14-day rentals of homes during the games.

d. Non-Minimal Rental and Personal Use

If the residential unit is "used by the taxpayer as a residence" and is rented for at least 15 days, then the deductions allocable to the rental use of the property[11] (other than deductions allowable in any event, such as mortgage interest and property taxes) are subject to the net income limitation of § 280A(c)(5) described above in connection with home offices. In applying § 280A(c)(5), it has been held that nonbusiness deductions (such as mortgage interest and property taxes) are to be allocated (in a manner different from the allocation rule found in § 280A(e)(1)) according to a fraction constituted by dividing rental days by total days in the year (as opposed to total days of use).[12]

e. Rental of Principal Residence

The taxpayer's personal use of his or her principal residence during a particular year does not count as such for purposes of the § 280A(c)(5) anti-tax-shelter rule if the use occurred either (1) before or after a 12-month period during which the residence is continuously rented at, or held for rental at, a fair market rent or (2)

---

[11] The deductions allocable to the rental use of property are determined by multiplying the repair expenses, depreciation, interest, property taxes, etc., with respect to the property for the entire year by a fraction, the numerator of which is actual rental days for the year and the denominator of which is total days of actual rental and personal use for the year; this allocation rule applies even if § 280A is otherwise avoided. See § 280A(e).

[12] See § 280A(e)(2); *Bolton v. Comm'r*, 694 F.2d 556 (9th Cir. 1982).

before a period of less than 12 consecutive months that begins during the year and ends with the sale of the residence, provided that the residence was rented at, or held for rent at, a fair market rental during the period. See § 280A(d)(4). However, the § 280A(e)(1) allocation rule would apply in either case.

NOTES

1.   Section 280A does not apply to (1) space used in a licensed day-care business, and (2) space used to store inventory where the taxpayer's home is the only fixed place of business. See § 280A(c)(2) and (4).

2.   (a) Section 183 could apply to a business operated out of a home or to the rental of a vacation home. If so, § 280A has priority over § 183. See § 280A(f)(3). Both sections prevent any net loss to be deducted against unrelated income, but § 280A allows a carryforward of the net loss and § 183 does not.

(b) If § 280A does not apply in the vacation home situation, § 183 could be a problem. Compare *Jasionowski v. Comm'r*, 66 T.C. 312 (1976) (applying § 183 to seven-year lease where rent was less than out-of-pocket costs), and *Dyer v. Comm'r*, T.C. Memo. 1983-628 (applying § 183 to rental to relative for less than fair rental value), with *Allen v. Comm'r*, 72 T.C. 28 (1979) (acq.) (rental to relative at loss not subject to § 183 where rent was prevailing rent for similar slum housing in the area).

3.   The § 121 exclusion for home sale gain does not apply to the extent of depreciation deductions taken under § 280A(c)(1). See § 121(d)(6). Thus, if Mary purchases a personal residence in 2000 for $300K, properly deducts $5K of depreciation for business use of the home under § 280A(c)(1), sells the home for $400K in 2004, and otherwise satisfies the requirements of § 121, she must include $5K of the $100K realized gain in her gross income.[13]

PROBLEMS

1.   Suppose that Candice moves to another residence, puts her house up for sale, and, finding no buyers, rents it out instead. Does § 280A apply in this situation? See § 280A(d)(4). What if she rents to a relative pending the sale of the home? See § 280A(d)(3).

2.   For the taxable year in question, assume that (1) Sheldon's nonbusiness net income from his investment portfolio is $20K, (2) business gross income attributable to his residence is $15K, (3) deductions pertaining to the same business but not derived from the residence (such as advertising expenses) are $4K, and (4) the following deduction items are attributable to his exclusive and regular business use of a portion of his residence:

(i) property taxes: $6K,

(ii) depreciation: $5K,

(iii) repairs: $1K, and

---

[13] This gain would likely be characterized as long-term capital gain (via § 1231) and constitute "unrecaptured § 1250 gain" under § 1(h), which means that it would likely be subject to a tax rate of 25%.

(iv) utilities: $3K.

Determine the tax consequences of the above facts for Sheldon in the following alternative situations:

(a) Sheldon is a psychologist, with the home office being used regularly to interview and counsel certain clients and to write up reports; Sheldon has no other place of business.

(b) Sheldon is an artist who paints in his home but produces lithographs and prints at a rented facility.

(c) Sheldon is a professor with an office at his university who uses the home office to write articles and books, some of which generate royalties.

3.   Sheldon (in his incarnation as an artist) has a small room in his home where he stores his artistic production (inventory). How, if at all, does § 280A apply to this room?

4.   Sheldon owns a computer to write books in connection with his university employment as a professor. The computer stays in his home office. Can Sheldon deduct the cost of the computer under § 179 or depreciate it?

C.   TRAVEL AND ENTERTAINMENT (T & E) EXPENSES

This section deals with business travel (and related costs) and entertainment expenses, which are traditionally lumped together.

1.   Transporting Work Tools

As noted in Chapter 10.D, daily *commuting* costs of the taxpayer are treated as nondeductible personal expenses. See Reg. § 1.262-1(b)(5). But transporting work tools and equipment, by itself, would often be a business expense. What if a person transports both herself and her tools at the same time (e.g., in the same car)? *Fausner v. Comm'r*, 413 U.S. 838 (1973) (per curiam), dealt with an airline pilot who carried work-related baggage in his car while commuting to and from the airport. The pilot would have commuted by car even if he hadn't carried baggage, and he failed to offer evidence as to the amount by which the baggage increased his commuting costs. The Supreme Court held that, in these circumstances, the pilot could not deduct any part of his commuting costs.

But what if a taxpayer can show that there were incremental commuting costs resulting from the need to carry equipment or tools? In *Rev. Rul. 75-380*, 1975-2 C.B. 59, the IRS ruled that it would allow a deduction only for that portion of the cost of transporting the work equipment that is in excess of the cost of commuting without the equipment by the mode of transportation *actually used*, even if the taxpayer would have used a less expensive mode of transportation if it were not necessary to carry the equipment. In other words, a taxpayer who would otherwise have commuted by public bus but who used her car to carry tools that were too bulky for the bus can deduct only the part of her automobile commuting costs that she can prove are greater than what the automobile (not bus) commuting costs would have been without the tools. This is usually an extremely difficult evidentiary burden for the taxpayer.

2. Business Transportation

We use the term "transportation expenses" to mean the direct cost of getting from one place to another, such as air fare or automobile expenses. Transportation expenses are a part of the more inclusive category of "travel expenses," which includes not only transportation expenses but also meals, lodging, and other costs, such as laundry, that are "incidental" to travel. See Reg. § 1.162-2(a). The category of "travel expenses" does not include "moving expenses" dealt with under § 217 (and discussed in Chapter 9.E). These two categories are quite distinct, because travel expenses are incurred "while away from home," whereas moving expenses are related to a permanent *change* of "home."

To be deductible, travel (including transportation) expenses must satisfy § 162(a)(2), which requires (1) that the expenses be "in pursuit of a trade or business" (thereby generally eliminating conventional commuting expenses), (2) that the expenses not be lavish or extravagant under the circumstances, and (3) that they be "away from home." For now we will put aside the "lavish and extravagant" rule (which requires little comment) and the "away from home" requirement, to be discussed shortly, which is highly contentious but most often comes up in the case where the taxpayer is attempting to deduct the cost of meals, lodging, and incidentals. For now, we will concentrate on the straight issue of transportation expenses unencumbered by this other baggage.

To be deductible, transportation expenses must satisfy the general rules of § 162, which include a requirement that the expense in question have a *primary business purpose*. Accordingly, a *transportation* expense (e.g., air fare) is deductible on an all-or-nothing basis. Thus, if the primary purpose of the trip is business, all of the transportation expense is deductible; if not, none of it is deductible. See Reg. § 1.162-2(b) and (d). Obviously, the relative time devoted to business and pleasure is a principal (if not exclusive) deciding factor.

In the case of travel *outside the United States*, where the primary purpose of the trip is business, § 274(c) modifies the all-or-nothing rule by providing that only the portion of the transportation expenses (e.g., air fare) that is attributable to business days (as a percentage of total travel days) is deductible (assuming that the trip first satisfies the primary purpose test). However, note that two exceptions in § 274(c)(2) and the exceptions in Reg. § 1.274-4(d)(2) often render this allocation rule inapplicable.

Section 274(h) disallows all business deductions (to the taxpayer or her employer) in the case of certain foreign business conventions and seminars. A convention or seminar on a cruise ship is considered foreign for this purpose unless the ship is registered in the United States and all ports of call are in the United States, and even if those tests are satisfied a dollar cap is imposed on the deduction. See § 274(h)(2). For conventions and seminars not on cruise ships, the disallowance rule applies if the meeting is outside of "North America," but it is waived if (1) the meeting is directly related to the active conduct of the taxpayer's trade or business and (2) it is as reasonable (considering various factors) that the meeting be held outside North America as within North America. See § 274(h)(1).

Under § 274(m)(2) travel cannot itself be viewed as a form of business-related "education." Thus, a French teacher in a U.S. high school cannot tour France and deduct the costs on the theory that that the primary purpose of the trip is to absorb the French language and culture.

Travel expenses of spouses and dependents are, with one narrow exception, not deductible. See § 274(m)(3); Reg. § 1.162-2(c).

Finally, no deduction (travel, entertainment, or otherwise) can be taken under § 212 for expenses allocable to an investment-oriented convention, seminar, or meeting. See § 274(h)(7).

3. Exceptions to the Nondeductibility of Commuting Expenses

The previous chapter set out the general rule that daily commuting expenses are nondeductible. See Reg. § 1.162-2(e). However, the following Revenue Ruling outlines exceptions to this baseline prohibition against deducting commuting expenses. (The ruling does not deal with the issue of what "home" means for purposes of the away-from-home rule for meals, lodging, and incidentals.)

REVENUE RULING 99-7
1999-1 C.B. 361

A taxpayer's costs of commuting between the taxpayer's residence and the taxpayer's place of business or employment generally are nondeductible personal expenses under Regs. §§ 1.162-2(e) and 1.262-1(b)(5). However, the transportation costs of going between one business location and another business location generally are deductible. *Rev. Rul. 55-109*, 1955-1 C.B. 261.

In general, daily transportation expenses incurred in going between a taxpayer's residence and a work location are nondeductible commuting expenses. However, such expenses are deductible under the circumstances described in paragraph (1), (2), or (3) below.

(1) A taxpayer may deduct daily transportation expenses incurred in going between the taxpayer's residence and a *temporary* work location *outside* the metropolitan area where the taxpayer lives and normally works. However, unless paragraph (2) or (3) below applies, daily transportation expenses incurred in going between the taxpayer's residence and a *temporary* work location *within* that metropolitan area are nondeductible commuting expenses.

(2) If a taxpayer has one or more regular work locations away from the taxpayer's residence, the taxpayer may deduct daily transportation expenses incurred in going between the taxpayer's residence and a *temporary* work location in the same trade or business, regardless of the distance.

(3) If a taxpayer's residence is the taxpayer's principal place of business within the meaning of § 280A(c)(1)(A), the taxpayer may deduct daily transportation

expenses incurred in going between the residence and another work location in the same trade or business, regardless of whether the other work location is *regular* or *temporary* and regardless of the distance.

The following rules apply in determining whether a work location is *temporary*. If employment at a work location is realistically expected to last (and does in fact last) for 1 year or less, the employment is *temporary* in the absence of facts and circumstances indicating otherwise. If employment at a work location is realistically expected to last for more than 1 year or there is no realistic expectation that the employment will last for 1 year or less, the employment is *not temporary*, regardless of whether it actually exceeds 1 year. If employment at a work location initially is realistically expected to last for 1 year or less, but at some later date the employment is realistically expected to exceed 1 year, that employment will be treated as temporary (in the absence of facts and circumstances indicating otherwise) until the date that the taxpayer's realistic expectation changes, and will be treated as *not temporary* after that date.

———————

Since the concept of commuting presupposes a separation between one's home and a place of work, it is not surprising that holdings (1) and (2) of *Rev. Rul. 99-7* are quite narrow. Essentially these holdings merely render it unnecessary in these two scenarios for the taxpayer to first commute to an office or work location in the metropolitan area where he lives before then proceeding on to the temporary work location (this leg of the trip would be deductible as transportation between two business locations in any event). Presumably, the rationale of these holdings (which is not stated) is that there could be no business reason for such a pointless stopover. (The significance of the "temporary" requirement will be revealed shortly.) The third holding of the ruling involves defining the situation where one's home and principal work location are deemed to be the same, in which case the notion of "commuting" is inapplicable. Prior to the ruling, it was always understood that an independent contractor (say, an electrician) operating out of her home (as her principal place of business) could deduct transportation costs for travel to job sites. In light of that rule, the third holding of the ruling, citing § 280A(c)(1)(A), hardly seems surprising, as the latter provision refers to a dwelling unit that is the "principal place of business." This third holding of the ruling is basically an acquiescence in the decision in *Curphey v. Comm'r*, 73 T.C. 776 (1980). So what's new? What is new was the addition in 1997 of the flush language at the end of § 280A(c)(1) to provide that the subparagraph (A) "principal place of business" includes a home office used by the taxpayer to conduct administrative or management activities *if* there is no other fixed location of the trade or business where the taxpayer actually conducts substantial administrative or management activities. Thus, the ruling in effect allows the Dr. Solimans of the world to deduct the cost of commuting to the hospital.

PROBLEMS

1.   Brian is a general contractor who manages his business from his home, and visits several worksites each day. Are the costs of going from home to the worksites nondeductible commuting?

2. Lorna Litigator is a solo trial lawyer whose office is in the downtown business district. Lorna needs her car almost daily to travel from the office to court appearances and to depositions. Consequently, Lorna drives her car to the office from her suburban home each day, instead of taking public transportation. Lorna spends eight to nine hours of each business day working downtown. What portion, if any, of Lorna's daily automobile expenses is deductible? Can Lorna drive directly from home to the courthouse?

3. Can the "commuting rule" be avoided by talking to clients and colleagues about business on a cellular car phone while driving (or being driven by a chauffeur) between one's home and office? Cf. *Pollei v. Comm'r*, 877 F.2d 838 (10th Cir. 1989) (allowing a deduction under § 162 by police officers for the costs of commuting from home to work in personally owned, radio-equipped cars, because regulations required them to be on duty from the time they left home and to monitor the police radio channels).

4. Larry lives in Las Vegas, Nevada, and (employed by a construction firm) works as a laborer at a large, top-secret military installation in the Nevada desert 100 miles from Las Vegas. Between Las Vegas and the work site, there's practically no reasonable place to live. Can Larry deduct his daily expenses of traveling to and from work? What if Larry's work sites are all within the Las Vegas metropolitan area?

4. Travel Meals and Lodging

Section 162(a)(2) expressly includes "meals and lodging" within the scope of deductible business "travel expenses." So-called "incidentals" (laundry, local transportation costs, and internet hook-up costs) are also included. See Reg. § 1.162-2(a). These costs again have to satisfy the basic requirements of § 162(a) (or § 212). According to Reg. § 1.162-2(a), these expenses are deductible only to the extent they are "directly attributable to" the taxpayer's trade or business. Thus, expenses incurred for meals and lodging on vacation days tacked on to the end of a business trip are entirely disallowed, even if the air fare to and from the destination is wholly deductible on account of the fact that the trip's "primary purpose" is business. Similarly, the costs (including the cab fare) of attending a play without the client and the purchase of postcards are nondeductible personal expenses.

a. Sleep-or-Rest Rule for Business Travel Meals

The case below affects only the deductibility of business travel meals.

UNITED STATES v. CORRELL
United States Supreme Court
389 U.S. 299 (1967)

Mr. Justice Stewart delivered the opinion of the Court.

[The taxpayer was a traveling salesman who customarily left his home early in the morning, ate his breakfast and lunch on the road while covering many miles, and returned home for dinner. The issue was whether the cost of his breakfasts and lunches were deductible as business travel expenses under § 162(a)(2).]

Under § 162(a)(2), taxpayers "traveling . . . away from home in the pursuit of a trade or business" may deduct the total amount "expended for meals and lodging." Because of the special demands of business travel, the [business-travel] taxpayer receives something of a windfall, for at least part of what he spends on meals represents a personal living expense that other taxpayers must bear without receiving any deduction at all. Not surprisingly, therefore, Congress did not extend the special benefits of § 162(a)(2) to every conceivable situation involving business travel. It made the total cost of meals and lodging deductible only if it occurred in the course of travel that takes the taxpayer "away from home." The problem before us involves the meaning of that limiting phrase.

In resolving that problem, the Commissioner has avoided the wasteful litigation and continuing uncertainty that would inevitably accompany any purely case-by-case approach to the questions of whether a particular taxpayer was "away from home" on a particular day. Rather than requiring "every meal-purchasing taxpayer to take pot luck in the courts," the Commissioner has consistently construed travel "away from home" to exclude all trips requiring neither sleep nor rest,[14] regardless of how many cities a given trip may have touched, how many miles it may have covered, or how many hours it may have consumed. By so interpreting the statutory phrase, the Commissioner has achieved not only ease and certainty of application, but also substantial fairness, for the sleep or rest rule places all one-day travelers on a similar tax footing, rather than discriminating against intra-city travelers and commuters, who of course cannot deduct the cost of the meals they eat on the road.

Any rule in this area must make some rather arbitrary distinctions, but at least the sleep or rest rule avoids the obvious inequity of permitting the New Yorker who makes a quick trip to Washington and back, missing neither his breakfast nor his dinner at home, to deduct the cost of his lunch merely because he covers more miles than the salesman who travels locally and must finance all his meals without the help of the Federal Treasury.

The language of the statute — "away from home" — is obviously not self-defining.[15] And to the extent that the words chosen by Congress cut in either

---

[14] [10] The Commissioner's interpretation, first expressed in *I.T. 3395*, 1940-2 C.B. 64, was originally known as the overnight rule. [Eds. note: The overnight rule was incorporated into Reg. § 1.162-17(b)(4) & (c)(2) in 1958.]

[15] [16] . . . The very concept of "traveling" obviously requires a physical separation from one's house.

direction, they tend to support rather than defeat the Commissioner's position, for the statute speaks of "meals and lodging" as a unit, suggesting — at least arguably — that Congress contemplated a deduction for the cost of meals only where the travel in question involves lodging as well. Ordinarily, at least, only the taxpayer who finds it necessary to stop for sleep or rest incurs significantly higher living expenses as a direct result of his business travel.[16] In any event, Congress certainly recognized that the Commissioner had so understood its statutory predecessor. This case thus comes within the settled principle that "Treasury regulations and interpretations long continued without substantial change, applying to unamended or substantially reenacted statutes, are deemed to have received congressional approval and have the effect of law."

Alternatives to the sleep or rest rule are of course available. Improvements might be imagined. But we do not sit as a committee of revision to perfect the administration of the tax laws. Congress has delegated to the Commissioner, not to the courts, the task of prescribing "all needful rules and regulations for the enforcement" of the Code. § 7805(a). The role of the judiciary in cases of this sort begins and ends with assuring that the Commissioner's regulations fall within his authority to implement the congressional mandate in some reasonable manner.

Dissenting opinion of MR. JUSTICE DOUGLAS, joined by MR. JUSTICE BLACK and MR. JUSTICE FORTAS.

The statutory words "while away from home," may not in my view be shrunken to "overnight" by administrative construction or regulations. "Overnight" injects a time element in testing deductibility, while the statute speaks only in terms of geography.

In *Barry v. Comm'r*, 435 F.2d 1290 (1st Cir. 1970), a consulting engineer, who frequently made automobile business trips of 16 to 19 hours duration but who was never away from home overnight, unsuccessfully sought to make his workday meals deductible under *Correll* by pulling to the side of the road and taking short naps in his car. The court stated (id. at 1294) that *Correll* "requires a stop of sufficient duration that it would normally be related to a significant increase in expenses . . . . [T]he taxpayer did not meet this requirement by catnapping in his automobile."

Section 274(k)(1) disallows any deduction for the cost of meals and beverages that is "lavish or extravagant under the circumstances."

To read the phrase "away from home" as broadly as a completely literal approach might permit would thus render the phrase completely redundant. But of course the words of the statute have never been so woodenly construed. The commuter, for example, has never been regarded as "away from home" within the meaning of § 162(a)(2). See *Comm'r v. Flowers*, 326 U.S. 465 (1946). More than a dictionary is thus required to understand the provision here involved, and no appeal to the "plain language" of the section can obviate the need for further statutory construction.

[16] [18] The taxpayer must ordinarily maintain a home for his family at his own expense even when he is absent on business, and if he is required to stop for sleep or rest, continuing costs incurred at a permanent place of abode are duplicated. . . .

Section 274(n) generally cuts down otherwise-deductible food and beverage costs to 50% thereof.

b. "Away from Home in the Pursuit of a Trade or Business"

The language in § 162(a)(2) referring to "away from home in the pursuit of a trade or business" has generated a good deal of litigation. In general, the IRS takes the position that "home" means "principal (or regular) place of business" (as opposed to principal residence). *Rev. Rul. 93-86*, 1993-2 C.B. 71. (*Rev. Rul. 99-7*, supra, which dealt with the distinction between "home" and "workplace" for purposes of the "commuting rule," does not bear on the concept of "away from home" for purposes of deducting meals, lodging, and incidentals.) The cases have taken a less rigid approach than the IRS but have not achieved consensus. The cases can perhaps be sorted out according to the situation presented.

i. Temporary vs. indefinite stay

In holdings (1) and (2) of *Rev. Rul. 99-7*, supra, the deductibility of commuting was conditioned on the work location being "temporary." The significance of "temporary" relates to the concept of "tax home," i.e., "home" for purposes of the away-from-home requirement. The definition of "home" is not a meaningful issue if the travel is away from the area where both the taxpayer's historic residence and historic workplace (or headquarters) are located, and the travel is short-term.[17] But if the travel is long-term, an issue arises as to whether the taxpayer is "away from" that home *or, instead, has established a new tax home.* If the taxpayer is deemed to have established a new tax home, then meals, lodging, and incidentals at the new job location are not deductible.

Under this dichotomy, if a move to a new job location was "temporary," the taxpayer was deemed to be in "business travel status," i.e., away from home. If the move was "indefinite," the taxpayer was deemed to have moved his tax home to the new location. The underlying rationale was that, if the new post was expected to be of a sufficiently long duration, the taxpayer would be expected to move his household to the new job location. A decision *not* to move was considered a personal choice, like that of Mr. Flowers, to simply have a long (nondeductible) commute.

Prior to 1992, this distinction between "temporary" and "indefinite" produced voluminous litigation. In that year, however, Congress amended § 162(a) by adding the middle sentence in the flush language after § 162(a)(3), which provides that "the taxpayer shall not be treated as being temporarily away from home during any period of employment if such period exceeds 1 year." Under this rule, a job that was originally expected to last eight months but does, in fact, last thirteen months can support deductions until the time that the expectation (that the job would end before one year elapsed) changed. (This point is noted in *Rev. Rul. 99-7*,

---

[17] In *Notice 2007-47*, 2007-1 C.B. 1393, the IRS relaxed the "same metropolitan area" rule with respect to lodging expense where an employer requires an employee to stay at a local lodging facility in order to participate in the employer's business meeting or function.

supra.) The IRS also maintains that a job that lasts just ten months is not "temporary" under this language if the taxpayer originally anticipated that the job would last eighteen months. See *Rev. Rul. 93-86*, 1993-2 C.B. 71.

ii.   Two business locations

Occasionally it happens that the taxpayer has two "permanent" business locations in different metropolitan areas. Here the IRS has maintained that the taxpayer's "tax home" is generally the location of the taxpayer's "principal" place of business, wherever that may be. See *Rev. Rul. 75-432*, 1975-2 C.B. 60. This issue is determined objectively by reference to a three-factor test: (1) business time spent at each location, (2) total time spent at each location, and (3) revenue generated from each location. See *Markey v. Comm'r*, 490 F.2d 1249 (6th Cir. 1974). Travel between such a "principal" place of business and a "secondary" place of business (or work site) is, thus, travel away from "home."

For example, the taxpayer in *Andrews v. Comm'r*, 931 F.2d 132 (1st Cir. 1991), was engaged in a New England swimming pool construction business for six months each year and in a Florida horse business (racing and breeding) for six months each year. Both businesses were profitable. He maintained a residence in each place and attempted to deduct the cost of transportation to, and the cost of meals and lodgings in, Florida. The Tax Court concluded that Andrews had two "tax homes," one at each of his businesses. Thus, he was not "away from home" while in Florida, and none of his travel costs were deductible. The First Circuit reversed. It reasoned that the purpose behind the travel expense deduction is to ameliorate the cost of duplicate living expenses created by business needs. Thus, on remand, the Tax Court was to apply the preceding three-factor test and decide which of the two locations was the taxpayer's "tax home" and then allow deduction of the travel expenses incurred in connection with the other business location.

iii.   Spouses having different business locations

Ethel Merman, a noted stage performer, was married to Robert Six, the CEO of Continental Airlines, which had its business headquarters in the Denver area, where the couple lived. Merman went to New York to star in the Broadway musical *Gypsy*. Six stayed behind at the marital residence in Colorado. Merman's New York engagement lasted more than two years and, towards its end, she and Six divorced. Merman incurred substantial living expenses in New York that were deductible only if Colorado continued to be her tax home. Her case was litigated in the Second Circuit, which rejects the IRS definition of tax home and holds that a taxpayer's home for purposes of § 162(a)(2) is one's "permanent abode or residence." In *U.S. v. Six*, 450 F.2d 66, 69 (2d Cir. 1971), the court stated that:

> The key inquiry is whether, under all the circumstances, Miss Merman's residence in New York during 1959 may be viewed as temporary in nature or as sufficiently indefinite to expect that a reasonable person in her position would pull up stakes and make her permanent residence in New York.

The Second Circuit remanded the case to the District Court for additional findings of fact, but cited Merman's marriage to Six as a factor on the side of deeming a permanent move to New York to be unreasonable. There is no published opinion regarding the final disposition of this case.

In *Hantzis v. Comm'r*, 638 F.2d 248 (1st Cir.), *cert. denied*, 452 U.S. 962 (1981), the taxpayer attended law school in Boston and lived there with her husband. She was unemployed during the school year, but he worked in Boston. Following her second year of law school, she worked as a paid summer law clerk in New York and then returned to Boston for her third year. She was denied a § 162(a)(2) deduction for the travel expenses related to her New York employment, the court stating (638 F.2d at 252-55):

> The meaning of the term "home" in the travel expense provision is far from clear. When Congress enacted the travel expense deduction, it apparently was unsure whether an expense must be incurred away from a person's residence or away from his principal place of business. This ambiguity persists and courts have divided over the issue.

> We think the critical step in defining "home" is to recognize that the "while away from home" requirement has to be construed in light of the further requirement that the expense be the result of business exigencies. The traveling expense deduction seeks to mitigate the burden of the taxpayer who, because of the exigencies of his trade or business, must maintain two places of abode and thereby incur additional and duplicate living expenses. Whether it is held in a particular decision that a taxpayer's home is his residence or his principal place of business, the ultimate allowance or disallowance of a deduction is a function of the court's assessment of the reason for a taxpayer's maintenance of two homes. If the reason is perceived to be personal, the taxpayer's home will generally be held to be his place of employment rather than his residence and the deduction will be denied. If the reason is felt to be business exigencies, the person's home will usually be held to be his residence and the deduction will be allowed.

> Mrs. Hantzis' trade or business did not require that she maintain a home in Boston as well as one in New York. Though she returned to Boston at various times during the period of her employment in New York, her visits were all for personal reasons. It is not contended that she had a business connection in Boston that necessitated her keeping a home there; no professional interest was served by maintenance of the Boston home as would have been the case, for example, if Mrs. Hantzis had been a lawyer based in Boston with a New York client whom she was temporarily serving.

> We are not dissuaded from this conclusion by the temporary nature of Mrs. Hantzis' employment in New York. The temporary employment doctrine does not, however, purport to eliminate any requirement that continued maintenance of a first home have a business justification. We think the rule has no application where the taxpayer has no business connection with his usual place of residence. If no business exigency dictates the location of the taxpayer's usual residence, then the mere fact of his taking temporary employment elsewhere cannot supply a compelling

business reason for continuing to maintain that residence. Only a taxpayer who lives one place, works another and has business ties to both is in the ambiguous situation that the temporary employment doctrine is designed to resolve.

Married couples pursuing careers (and having homes) at different (indefinite) locations are out of luck, because neither of them can come within the "temporary" doctrine. See *Chwalow v. Comm'r*, 470 F.2d 475, 477-78 (3d Cir. 1972):

> Where additional expenses are incurred because, for personal reasons, husband and wife maintain separate domiciles, no deduction is allowed. The fact that taxpayers have filed a joint tax return does not mean that they must have a single "tax home."

Accord *Daly v. Comm'r*, 662 F.2d 253 (4th Cir. 1981); *Foote v. Comm'r*, 67 T.C. 1 (1976).

iv.   Itinerant workers

In *Rev. Rul. 75-432*, 1975-2 C.B. 60, the IRS stated:

> In the rare case in which the employee has no identifiable principal place of business, but does maintain a regular place of abode in a real or substantial sense in a particular city from which the taxpayer is sent on temporary assignments, the tax home will be regarded as being that place of abode. This should be distinguished from the case of an itinerant worker with neither a regular place of business nor a regular place of abode. In such case, the home is considered to go along with the worker and therefore the worker does not travel away from home, and may not deduct the cost of meals or lodging.

This result (but not the reasoning) as to the itinerant worker without a regular place of abode was confirmed in *Rosenspan v. U.S.*, 438 F.2d 905 (2d Cir.), *cert. denied*, 404 U.S. 864 (1971), which disallowed meal and lodging costs for an itinerant salesman on the ground that the taxpayer had no home (in the sense of "residence").

What does *Rev. Rul. 75-432* mean by "a regular place of abode in a real or substantial sense?" The answer can be crucial to a worker with a series of temporary jobs. In *Rev. Rul. 73-529*, 1973-2 C.B. 37, the IRS stated that one factor to consider in determining whether a residence is a "regular place of abode" is the extent to which the taxpayer incurs costs to maintain the abode, which would be duplicated by the travel expense. Ethel Merman in the *Six* case probably had a regular place of abode in a real and substantial sense.

In *Henderson v. Comm'r*, 143 F.3d 497 (9th Cir. 1998), the taxpayer lived in Boise for two or three months out of the year, and spent the rest of the time on the road with a travelling ice show. The court disallowed the deduction of the taxpayer's road expenses on the ground that he had no business reason to live in Boise. Also, he had no duplicative living expenses, because he stayed rent-free at his parent's home while in Boise. *Sapson v. Comm'r*, 49 T.C. 636 (1968), came to the opposite result on somewhat similar facts, except that (1) the taxpayer paid nominal rent for a single room in his sister's home, and (2) it was found (dubiously) that the taxpayer's business headquarters were in the same city as the part-time residence.

In *Johnson v. Comm'r*, 115 T.C. 210 (2000), the taxpayer was a merchant ship captain who had a permanent residence with his family, but no business headquarters as such (apart from his ship). Here the travel deductions were allowed, despite the fact there was no business reason for the location of his home.

NOTES

1.   (a) The meals and lodging deduction is over-generous. It covers (after § 274(n), 50% of) meals even where there is "nothing special" about either the meals or the cost thereof. An example would be where a law professor visits at another law school for nine months, renting an apartment, buying the same groceries that she would have purchased at home, and cooking the same meals that she would have cooked at home. (This is a far cry from having to entertain a client or staying at an expensive hotel on a short business trip.) And it covers lodging costs that are nonduplicative. In the visiting law professor example, there is no requirement that the professor rent (or sublet) her existing home or even maintain a residence. And if she does rent her home, she may be able to claim deductions with respect thereto, subject to the rules of §§ 183 and 280A, supra. Finally, commuting (and other ordinary living) expenses at the temporary location can be deducted as being "incidental" to travel.

(b) In the visiting law professor example, however, the deductible travel expenses would be MIDs, because they would be nonreimbursed employee business deductions. Reimbursed employee business expenses are fully deductible above the line under § 62(a)(2)(A). (Actually, both the reimbursement and the expenses are ignored under Reg. § 1.62-2(c).) Most routine employee business travel is reimbursed. It is not unheard of for a visiting law professor to negotiate to convert part of her salary from the visited law school into a reimbursement for (deductible) travel expenses.

(c) Employer reimbursements also allow the employee to "get around" the 50% limitation on deductions for food or beverages (or entertainment). See § 274(n)(2)(A), which refers to § 274(e)(3). The 50% cut-down rule is then shifted to the employer, but that is of no consequence if the employer is itself a tax-exempt entity such as a university!

(d) Employer-provided meals and lodging (on the business premises of the employer) can be excluded as an employee fringe benefit if certain conditions are met under § 119. Also certain meal money provided by an employer to enable an employee to work overtime may be excludible by the employee under Reg. § 1.132-6(d)(2). (These and other employee fringe benefits are dealt with in Chapter 12.B). Tax-free employee fringe benefits finesse the issue of whether the cost, if incurred by the employee, would be deductible by the employee, because an exclusion from GI is the equivalent of inclusion (as compensation) and full offsetting deduction.

2.   (a) Although courts endlessly debate the meaning of "home," wasn't that issue actually settled by *Correll*? Did *Correll* reject a "plain meaning" reading, and

endors the "business headquarters" construction of "home" adopted by the IRS and the Tax Court?

(b) The pure itinerant, who has no home and no business headquarters apart from where she happens to be from time to time, can't be said to have a home to be away from. Should the tax result be different for one who does have a home base, but no business reason for having a home in the place chosen by the taxpayer? In this type of case, having a (permanent) home at all (incurring the duplicative expenses) would appear to be personally motivated. For example, self-employed "unique talents" (film and stage actors, fashion models, and athletes) can choose to live almost anywhere. Should it be enough that they perform *some* business functions at home (such as read scripts, phone their agents, and keep in shape)?

3.   (a) Under the first sentence in the flush paragraph at the end of § 162(a), members of the U.S. Congress are deemed to have their tax home in the district or state that they represent, but expenses of living in Washington, D.C., are deductible only up to $3K per year.

(b) Under § 162(h), added in 1981, *state* legislators living more than 50 miles from the state capitol can elect to deduct living expenses while at the capitol according to a complex formula.

(c) If federal or state officials maintain two homes and are not covered by one of the two preceding statutory rules, the "principal place of business" test applies for purposes of determining "tax home," but, of course, each trip away from such home would have to satisfy the primary purpose test (as well as other rules).

PROBLEM

Jason is a professional football player, currently employed by the Detroit Lions. Jason maintains his principal residence in Orlando, where his family lives. Jason stays in a luxurious hotel while in the Detroit area. Can Jason deduct transportation expenses between Orlando and Detroit or living expenses at either place?

5.   Business Entertainment Costs

"Entertainment expenses" are expenditures incurred for entertainment, food and beverages, recreation, or amusement to entertain *one or more other persons*, such as clients, potential customers, and business associates. Entertainment expenses include outlays for the use of boats, planes, and athletic or country clubs, for attendance at plays, musical events, or sporting events, and for hosting cocktail or dinner parties. See Reg. § 1.274-2(b)(1)(i).

In the absence of any special Code provisions, business entertainment expenses would be deductible if they met the relatively low thresholds of the "ordinary," "necessary," and "carrying-on-a-trade-or-business" requirements of § 162(a). Under these standards, the conflict between the business and personal aspects of business entertainment is normally resolved in favor of the taxpayer's deduction under § 162, unless the situation is abusive, such as when a boss and a secretary alternately take each other to lunch on a frequent basis (somewhat as in the *Moss* case, supra).

Moreover, under the *Sutter* rule discussed in *Moss*, if the expense of entertaining the guest is deductible, the taxpayer's cost of participation is also generally allowed as a deduction. Furthermore, deduction of the entertainment costs attributable to persons "closely connected" to either the taxpayer or the persons entertained, including spouses, is permitted. See Reg. § 1.274-2(d)(2) and (d)(4). (Compare § 274(m)(3), generally disallowing business *travel* costs of spouses, dependents, and companions.)

a. Section 274 Disallowance Rules

The above summary describes only the generous "threshold" rules regarding the deduction of business entertainment costs under § 162. At this point, § 274 swings into action with a bevy of disallowance rules.[18]

Section 274(a)(1)(B) disallows any deduction with respect to the cost of using, maintaining, or operating entertainment *facilities*, such as boats, planes, hunting lodges, vacation condominiums, fishing camps, swimming pools, and bowling alleys. (Additionally, section 274(g) treats any such facility as a personal-use asset for income tax purposes in general.)

Section 274(a)(3) mandates nondeductibility for club dues paid for membership in any club "organized for business, pleasure, recreation, or other social purpose."

The otherwise-deductible cost of an entertainment *activity* is disallowed by § 274(a)(1)(A) unless the cost *either*

(1) is "directly related to the active conduct of the taxpayer's trade or business" (commonly called the "directly related" test), *or*

(2) is *both* "associated with" the "active conduct of the taxpayer's trade or business" *and* directly precedes or follows a "substantial and bona fide business discussion" (commonly called the "associated with" test).

The "directly related" test is designed to weed out activities undertaken with a mere general expectation of some future business benefit, such as the creation of goodwill. See Reg. § 1.274-2(c)(3)(i) and *Rev. Rul. 63-144*, 1963-2 C.B. 124. In order to satisfy the "directly related" test, business must be conducted during the activity. A restaurant dinner during which a deal is negotiated is a prime example.

"Goodwill" entertainment costs are not, however, absolutely foreclosed from deduction by § 274(a). It is possible to deduct these outlays under the "associated with" test. But while the creation of goodwill can satisfy the "associated with" test, that test requires complying with the additional requirement that the entertainment be directly preceded or followed by a "substantial and bona fide business discussion." The "substantial and bona fide business discussion" rule has been interpreted to require discussion of actual or contemplated transactions, as opposed to mere "shop talk." See Reg. § 1.274-2(d)(3). The "directly precedes or follows" rule

---

[18] These § 274 rules do not apply to the costs of providing entertainment (etc.) to the public for profit, such as sales of meals by restaurants and sales of tickets by theaters. See § 274(e)(7) and (8); Reg. § 1.274-2(f)(2)(ix).

does not, however, mean that the discussion must be followed immediately by the entertainment or vice versa. Thus, if a taxpayer takes a client to a Broadway show in the evening following the negotiation of a business deal that afternoon, the "associated with" test would be satisfied.[19] The substantial and bona fide business discussion need not even take place on the same day as the entertainment. For example, if a client comes from out of town to the taxpayer's place of business, entertainment provided to the client on the night before the next day's substantial and bona fide business discussion would be considered "directly preceding" such discussion. See Reg. § 1.274-2(d)(3)(ii). If, on the other hand, the taxpayer takes an existing client to a Broadway show merely to maintain a good relationship with the client and without any proximate connection to a substantial and bona fide business discussion, neither the "associated with" test nor the "directly related" test would be satisfied.[20]

A perusal of Reg. § 1.274-2(c) and (d) will convey a fuller understanding of these tests.

Entertainment meals are deductible only if the taxpayer (or employee thereof) is present, and only if the cost is not lavish or extravagant under the circumstances. See § 274(k).

In the case of the rental cost of a "luxury" box (or skybox), the deduction generally is cut down to the cost of nonluxury box seats). See § 274(l)(2).

Finally, any business entertainment expenses that have overcome the various hurdles mentioned above can, of course, generally be deducted only to the extent of 50%. See § 274(n)(1).

b. Exceptions to § 274

There are several exceptions to the various hurdles and disallowance rules found in § 274(a) and other subsections of § 274. First of all, § 274 does not affect items that are deductible without regard to their connection to an income-producing activity, namely, mortgage interest, property taxes, and casualty losses. See § 274(f).

Second, employer food and beverages outlays for employees (and related facilities) furnished on the employer's business premises are excluded from all but the 50% reduction rule in § 274(n). See §§ 274(e)(1), (n)(2).

Third, employer-provided recreation (or recreational facilities) for employees who are not shareholders or highly compensated employees are exempted from the § 274 hurdles specific to entertainment (including the 50% reduction rule). See §§ 274(e)(4), (n)(2).

---

[19] Suppose that the taxpayer bought the two Broadway tickets from the doorman at his hotel for $150 each (a total of $300) when the face amount of the tickets was $100 each. The taxpayer's total deduction for the two tickets is limited to $100 (50% × $100 per ticket). See § 274(l)(1)(A), (n)(1).

[20] See, e.g., *Berkley Machine Works & Foundry Co. v. Comm'r*, 623 F.2d 898 (4th Cir.), *cert. denied*, 449 U.S. 919 (1980).

Fourth (and as noted above), paragraphs (2) and (3) of § 274(e) operate in tandem to prevent redundant application of § 274 where the employer reimburses an employee. The reimbursed employee is excepted from § 274 in order to preserve the integrity of the reimbursement "exclusion" in Reg. § 1.62-2(c)(4).[21] However, if the employer elects to treat the reimbursement as compensation, or if the employer provides an entertainment-type fringe benefit that is includible by the employees, the burden of the § 274 restrictions shifts from the employer to the employee (attempting to claim a § 162 deduction).[22]

Other items exempted from § 274(a) (and from other subsections, including the 50% reduction rule) are of an obvious or minor nature and are listed in § 274(e)(5)-(9).

6. Substantiation Requirement

In addition to the substantive rules discussed here, travel and entertainment (T & E) expenses, as well as expenses relating to "listed property" (and business gifts), are subject to the procedural requirement that they *must* be "substantiated" under § 274(d) and Reg. § 1.274-5T. *If not properly substantiated, an otherwise allowable deduction is totally disallowed!* The time, place, business purpose, and amount of the expense, as well as the taxpayer's relationship to those who were entertained, must be shown by "adequate contemporaneous records," meaning an account book or diary in which the various items are currently recorded. In addition, documentary evidence, such as receipts or bills, are needed for all lodging expenses away from home and any other expenditures of $75 or more. See Reg. § 1.274-5(c)(2)(iii)(A).

If the taxpayer is an employee who is fully reimbursed by the employer, the employee must make an "adequate accounting" to the employer of this information so that the employer can satisfy the substantiation requirements when it takes the deduction. See Reg. § 1.274-5T(f)(2).

Under revenue procedures, the IRS will allow meal expenses to be deducted at a specified *per diem* rate in lieu of detailed recordkeeping.[23]

NOTES

1. T & E expenses might be claimed under § 212 with respect to income-producing activities that do not rise to the level of a "trade or business." It appears that the language in § 162(a)(2) ("meals and lodging" . . . "away from home in

---

[21] To qualify for this exclusion (which is a shortcut for inclusion with an offsetting allowable above-the-line deduction under §§ 162 and 62(a)(2)(A)), the reimbursement must be for an expense that would be deductible if paid by the employee. See Reg. § 1.62-2(d)(1) Thus, if the employee deduction were disallowed in whole or in part by § 274, the reimbursement exclusion would not be available.

[22] Section 274(e)(2) also provides that an employer deduction (based on cost) for entertainment that is includible by an employee cannot exceed the amount includible by the employee (its FMV). The employee deduction (if any) is likely to be an MID.

[23] See, e.g., *Rev. Proc. 2002-63*, 2002-2 C.B. 691.

pursuit of . . .") is deemed to reside implicitly in § 212 as well.[24] Moreover, the restrictions of § 274 clearly apply to potential § 212 T & E deductions. See § 274(a)(2)(B).

2.   Recall that no deduction can be taken under § 212 for expenses allocable to an investment-oriented convention, seminar, or meeting. See § 274(h)(7). (This rule applies even where travel and entertainment are not involved.)

PROBLEMS

1.   (a) Ralph lives and works in Boston at his employer's headquarters, and he is sent to inspect the employer's branch operations in New York. He flies to New York on Monday morning, has a restaurant lunch alone, inspects the operations in the afternoon, dines alone at another restaurant, and flies home Monday evening. What are the tax consequences to Ralph if he is not reimbursed for these expenses?

(b) Suppose instead that Ralph decides to catch a Broadway show Sunday evening and flies down to New York Sunday afternoon, thereby adding to his trip costs (1) a night's lodging, (2) a visit to the Museum of Modern Art in the morning, and (3) cab fare from the hotel to the branch's office after lunch and back to the hotel to pick up his luggage. What tax consequences now?

(c) Are the results different in (a) or (b) above if the employer reimburses Ralph for the plane fare, meals, lodging, and local transportation, and Ralph adequately accounts to the employer for these expenses? What result to Ralph's employer?

(d) When Ralph returns to Boston, his employer requires him to take an important client to lunch at an exclusive dining club following a lengthy business meeting with the client at the employer's headquarters. The employer pays only for the client's lunch. Ralph's own lunch (which he enjoys immensely) costs him $50. (Ralph normally lunches for $2 at Burger Bash.) Who may deduct what?

2.   Schulz is a self-employed agent for film actors and actresses. His business depends heavily on his personal relationships with movie and theatrical producers and directors.

(a) Schulz and his wife often take producers and directors and their spouses out to dinner and then to shows and plays. Are Schulz's costs deductible? Those relating to his wife? Do you need any additional information?

(b) Schulz has a yacht which he uses extensively to entertain producers and directors in the company of their wives. Can any part of the mooring and maintenance expenses and depreciation of the yacht be deducted by Schulz?

(c) Schulz has a membership in the Downtown Athletic Club, where he sometimes swims and works out. He also meets clients for lunch or dinner there. Can the club membership dues and the direct food and beverage costs be deducted?

(d) About once a week Schulz has lunch with other agents, where they exchange gossip over clients and jobs and exchange information about film projects that could

---

[24] The instructions to Schedule E (on the Form 1040) relating to rental activities refer to "travel" and "meal" expenses. Reg. § 1.212-1(f) provides that commuting expenses are not deductible under § 212.

be of interest to their clients. Schulz pays for his own lunch. Deductible? What if the agents took turns paying for everybody's lunch?

3.   (a) Can an employer deduct expenses of entertaining employees to build their morale? See § 274(e)(4).

(b) Can an executive deduct costs of entertaining underlings to build their morale? See *Rev. Rul. 78-373*, 1978-2 C.B. 108.

Part Four

GROSS INCOME FROM MARKET TRANSACTIONS

No mystery exists concerning the basic categories of gross income arising from market transactions, such as compensation for services, interest and dividends, rents and royalties, and gross income from business (including gains from the sale of inventories). This part focuses on the broad reach of these conventional gross income categories but also their limits.

Gross income issues relating to transfer payments (such as gifts and damages recoveries) are dealt with in Part Five, and Part Six covers income and deduction issues arising from borrowing transactions.

Chapter 12

FORMS OF COMPENSATION INCOME

This chapter deals with § 61(a)(1): the various facets of gross income in the form of "compensation for services, including fees, commissions, fringe benefits, and similar items." Even the earliest gross income definition (the 1913 version) posited an expansive concept of compensation income: "gains, profits, and income derived from salaries, wages, *or compensation for personal service of whatever kind and in whatever form paid*, or from professions, vocations, business, [or] trade." (Emphasis added.) The current version of § 61(a)(1) is similarly expansive.

A. DISGUISED COMPENSATION

The broad language in § 61(a)(1) makes it clear that in-kind compensation is included in income (unless specifically excepted by other statutory provisions, such as those presented in Section B below). In-kind compensation can take many forms, including the receipt of tangible property for free or at a reduced price, the receipt of free or reduced-price services, or the free or reduced-price use of property. Thus, Reg. § 1.61-2(d)(1) states:

> [I]f services are paid for in property, the fair market value of the property taken in payment must be included in income as compensation. If services are paid for in exchange for other services, the fair market value of such other services taken in payment must be included in income as compensation.

For example, suppose that Eleanor is employed by a florist, and the florist sells a delivery van to Eleanor for $2K when the fair market value is $20K. The $18K "discount" is disguised compensation and would be includible by Eleanor under not only § 61(a)(1) but also § 83(a).[1] Or suppose that the florist allows Eleanor to use its van on her vacation. Eleanor would have to include the rental value of the van in gross income as additional compensation.

Now suppose that a masseuse agrees to massage a house painter if the latter paints the living room in the masseuse's personal residence. Suppose also that each

---

[1] Eleanor's purchase for less than FMV is called a "bargain purchase." Bargain purchases between strangers do not usually give rise to income to the purchaser. Instead, the purchaser takes a basis in the property equal to the bargain price and experiences the tax effect thereof, in the form of increased gain or decreased loss, when the property is transferred in a realization transaction. Bargain purchases between related parties (including parties that have an ongoing, if not personal, relationship) are treated differently, however. Section 83, which explicitly holds that a bargain purchase by a provider of services (from the person to whom the services are provided) gives rise to compensation gross income, is discussed further in Chapter 22.D and E. Although both § 61(a)(1) and § 83 require Eleanor's $18K discount in gross income, she (of course) includes it only once.

service would be sold commercially for $200 and that the masseuse and painter structure their deal so that each pays the other $200 in cash. In that case, there would be two separate transactions (massage for cash and paint job for cash), and it would be patently obvious that each taxpayer has $200 of gross compensation income, and that each has made a nondeductible $200 personal expenditure. The cash payments would, however, be meaningless from an economic standpoint because the masseuse and painter would be paying equal amounts ($200) to each other simultaneously. Accordingly, in the real world they dispense with the cash payments, and each simply provides his or her service in exchange for the other's service. In that scenario, we have in form a single transaction — a swap of services. This hypothetical was essentially the subject of *Rev. Rul. 79-24*, 1979-1 C.B. 60, in which the IRS relied on the above-quoted regulation to rule that each party realized gross income equal to the value of the services that each received ($200). This result seems unsurprising.

But suppose the swap is exactly the same except that the painter paints the masseuse's business place. In this scenario, the masseuse should have a $200 business expense deduction under § 162 (in addition to the $200 of compensation income discussed above). Each party should be treated as having paid $200 in substance, even though in form they did not, so that the masseuse has effectively made a $200 business expenditure and the painter has made a $200 personal outlay.

Rev. Rul. 79-24, however, did not speak to the deduction issue, because, under the facts of that ruling, any deemed cash payment by either party would have been a nondeductible personal expense. In reading the case set forth below, consider whether it constitutes "authority" for the proposition that a barter exchange of services is really a transaction involving the constructive receipt *and payment* of cash, which *possibly* raises a capital expenditure or deduction issue.

OLD COLONY TRUST COMPANY v. COMMISSIONER
United States Supreme Court
279 U.S. 716 (1929)

Mr. Chief Justice Taft delivered the opinion of the Court.

William M. Wood was president of the American Woolen Company during the years 1918, 1919 and 1920. The American Woolen Company had adopted the following resolution, which was in effect in 1919 and 1920:

> Voted: That this company pay any and all income taxes, State and Federal, that may hereafter become due and payable upon the salaries of all the officers of the company, including the president, William M. Wood, . . . to the end that said persons and officers shall receive their salaries or other compensation in full without deduction on account of income taxes, State or Federal, which taxes are to be paid out of the treasury of this corporation. The method of computing said taxes shall be the difference between what the total amount of his tax would be, including his income from all sources, and the amount of his tax when computed upon his income excluding such compensation or salaries paid by this company.

The decision of the Board of Tax Appeals here sought to be reviewed was that the income taxes of [about $681K and $351K] paid by the American Woolen Company for Mr. Wood were additional income to him for the years 1919 and 1920.

We think the question presented is whether a taxpayer, having induced a third person to pay his income tax or having acquiesced in such payment as made in discharge of an obligation to him, may avoid the making of a return thereof. We think he may not do so. The payment of the tax by the employer was in consideration of the services rendered by the employee and was a gain derived by the employee from his labor. The form of the payment is expressly declared [by the statute] to make no difference. It is therefore immaterial that the taxes were directly paid over to the Government. The taxes were paid upon a valuable consideration, namely, the services rendered by the employee and as part of the compensation therefor. We think therefore that the payment constituted income to the employee.

Nor can it be argued that the payment of the tax was a gift. The payment for services, even though entirely voluntary, was nevertheless compensation within the statute.

[JUSTICE McREYNOLDS's dissent on a procedural issue is omitted.]

Notice that, *in form*, Wood never received the cash that was paid directly by American Woolen to the IRS. The Court's conclusion, however, is that, *in substance*, Wood was *deemed* to have received the cash first, as though the employer paid additional cash compensation to him. Since the IRS ended up with the cash, it must have been (constructively) paid to the IRS by Wood, not American Woolen. American Woolen cannot have paid the same sum to two different parties. The deemed payment by Wood to the IRS was of Wood's federal income taxes, the payment of which happens to be a nondeductible expense. See § 275(a)(1).

The *Old Colony Trust* "substance-over-form" principle is not limited to compensation situations. For example, Reg. § 1.61-8(c) states that a lessor realizes additional gross rental income if the lessee pays, say, the lessor's casualty insurance premiums. The transaction is treated, in substance, as though the lessee paid the lessor additional cash rent, which the lessor then used to pay the insurance premiums.

In *Diedrich v. Comm'r*, 457 U.S. 191 (1982), the Supreme Court held that a "gift" of low-basis appreciated property "on condition" that the donee pay the donor's gift tax liability produced § 1001 gain to the donor equal to the excess of the gift tax paid by the donee over the donor's basis in the property. In other words, the donor was treated as having sold the property to the donee for cash equal to the gift tax liability and then as having paid the cash to the IRS.

In *Comm'r v. Indianapolis Power & Light Co.*, 493 U.S. 203 (1990), discussed more fully in Chapter 18.C.1, the taxpayer, a utility company, demanded deposits from credit-risk customers to secure the future payment of their bills. In some cases the deposits were repaid, but in other cases they were used to offset the amount billed to a customer for electricity usage. The Court ultimately held that the deposits were "loans" by customers to the utility. In those situations where the utility applied the deposit against a billed amount, the Supreme Court treated the transaction as a constructive loan repayment by the utility to the customer followed by the immediate constructive payment of that same amount by the customer back to the utility company towards the bill.

These cases, especially *Indianapolis Power & Light*, surely provide authority for our masseuse and house painter to be treated as having made deemed payments of cash to each other. And here is a lesson that extends far beyond tax law: The good lawyer recognizes how a case with facts radically different from the client's facts can nevertheless serve as legal authority bearing on the client's situation.

The "substance over form" doctrine can also be used to conflate two or more events into one. An illustrative case is *Brown v. Comm'r*, T.C. Memo. 1996-310, where a waitress collected tips (which are gross income under § 61(a)(1)), but, at the end of each day, she would distribute a portion of her tips to the busboys, the bartenders, sometimes the cooks, and (if she had been unusually busy) other waitresses from whom she had received help. She included in gross income only the portion of the tips that she retained. The government argued that she must include the *entire* amount of tips that she collected and could deduct the amounts paid to others as § 162 business expenses, but it happened that these deductions were worthless (for reasons not pertinent to the present discussion). The Tax Court held in favor of the waitress, reasoning:

> Unquestionably, where petitioner shared her tip with another waitress who helped her, the tip she shared was really intended in part for the other waitress, and the other waitress's part is not income to petitioner. Whether the person leaving a tip intended a pass-through for the busboys, bartenders, and cooks is not as clear. The testimony in this record shows that the busboys stood in full view and helped in various ways with serving and clearing the table. The bartender might not be directly in sight, but people who ordered drinks were certainly aware of the work of the bartender. Therefore, in our view, the sharing by the waitress of tips with busboys, bartenders, and cooks is merely to carry out the pass-through intent of the customer, and the gross amount of the tip is not intended to be hers to keep in its entirety.

The collapsing of two or more steps into one is often referred to as the "step-transaction doctrine."

NOTES

1.   The gross income categories of "interest," "dividends," "rents," "prizes," and so on, are also construed broadly to include in-kind receipts and payments to third parties. See *Helvering v. Midland Mutual Life Ins. Co.*, 300 U.S. 216 (1937) (interest received in the form of real property); *U.S. v. Boston & Maine Rr.*, 279 U.S. 732 (1929) (lessee payment of lessor's taxes is rent to lessor); *Dean v. Comm'r*, 187 F.2d 1019 (3d Cir.1951) (shareholder living rent-free in corporation-owned residence held to be in receipt of dividend); *Strong v. Comm'r*, 91 T.C. 627 (1988)

(rent received in form of livestock); Reg. § 1.74-1(a)(2) (prizes in form of goods or services).

2. *Old Colony Trust* does *not* stand for the proposition that "avoided expenses" are gross income. Thus, a "street person" who sleeps in a large culvert does not have income equal to the avoided rent payments. Similarly, a divorced father whose child support obligation is prematurely terminated by the accidental death of the child does not have income by being relieved of this obligation. How is *Old Colony Trust* distinguishable from the avoided-cost scenario?

3. In *Brown*, the theory adopted by the Tax Court was that the waitress was only a conduit through which payment was made by the tipper to persons other than the waitress. An alternative basis for such a result would be the existence of a pre-existing agreement among the staff to share tips in this fashion. Under that theory, the waitress would still be a conduit, but the tipper's intent would be irrelevant.

PROBLEMS

1. In many poor rural communities, social norms dictate that neighbors perform services for each other when called upon and able to do so. Also, many young parents swap babysitting services. None of these recipients of services include the value of the services received in their incomes. Are they cheating on their taxes? See § 6045(a), (c)(1)(B) (requiring "barter exchanges" to file information returns). What is the significance of Reg. § 1.6045-1(a)(4), (e)? The notion that the services that the services are excluded as "gifts" does not hold water. First, a gift for income tax purposes can only be of money or property. Second, an excludible gift for income tax purposes has to be made for a gratuitous purpose, rather than for a quid pro quo. The details of the definition of "gift" are not taken up until Chapter 15.A.3.

2. (a) Federal income tax payments are not deductible by taxpayers, even though such taxes may be attributable in whole or in large part to business or investment activity. See § 275(a). In the *Old Colony Trust* situation, how should Mr. Wood's employer have treated the tax payment for purposes of its own return?

(b) As noted in Chapter 5, an individual's real property taxes paid with respect to his home are deductible under § 164(a), even though the home is a personal-use asset. What results to the parties if an employer pays an employee's real property taxes on his personal residence? Recall that only the person who both owes and pays the real property taxes can deduct them *as real property taxes* under § 164(a). See Reg. § 1.164-1(a) (in the middle of the flush paragraph after (5).

B. EMPLOYEE FRINGE BENEFITS

The term "fringe benefits" is commonly used to refer to *consumption* items (property or services) transferred to service providers as compensation. Examples would include free or reduced-price health care, free life insurance, and discounts on the purchase of goods or services sold by the employer. Note the reference to fringe benefits in § 61(a)(1), which makes it quite clear that fringe benefits are includible in gross income unless a specific statutory exclusion applies. This section explores a few of those statutory exceptions. But it begins with an historical inquiry into a tax-common-law doctrine that developed in the early days of the income tax, long before the words "fringe benefits" were added to the definition of compensation income.

1. Tax-Common-Law Exclusions

Fringe benefit matters weren't always governed by statute. Early on, nonstatutory exclusions evolved for employer-provided tools and working conditions and meals and lodging provided by the employer for the convenience of the employer.

a. Working Conditions

The "working condition" doctrine applies where the employer provides the employee with the tools of the trade (e.g., a computer) and "working conditions" (an office, electric power, and a support staff) necessary to complete assigned tasks. It has long been recognized that the employee has no gross income from these items.

This result is now codified in § 132(a)(3) and (d), where the exclusion is conditioned on the requirement that the items provided must be such that, if purchased by the employee herself, would be deductible as a business expense or by way of depreciation deductions.

The justification for the working-conditions exclusion can be best understood by considering analogous situations. For example, instead of providing the working conditions, so that the salary is purely for services, the employer could hire an independent contractor (who provides her own tools and working conditions). The amounts paid to the independent contractor in that case are, in substance, partly for services but also partly as a kind of "rent" for the independent contractor's tools and other accoutrements of the trade. Although the independent contractor includes the entire fee in gross income, the cost of the tools, etc., is deductible, either as an expense or as depreciation. This tax treatment of the independent contractor is economically the same as a worker simply being allowed to exclude the use value of employer-provided tools, etc., but not being allowed to claim any deductions. This is the result produced by the working conditions exclusion.

A similar scenario is where the worker is an employee, but the employer agrees to reimburse the employee for tools and office equipment purchased by the employee (according to employer guidelines and/or approval). Since reimbursed employee expenses are above-the-line, see § 62(a)(2)(A), both the employee deduction and the reimbursement are ignored by the regulations. This tax result is the equivalent of a tax-free employer provision of the tools and office equipment, which is the same as the effect created by the working conditions exclusion.

b. Meals and Lodging for the Convenience of the Employer

Very early on, the IRS issued administrative pronouncements that relied on a "convenience of the employer" test in concluding that certain lodging and meals provided by an employer to a worker did not constitute compensation gross income. See, e.g., *O.D. 265*, 1 C.B. 71 (1919) (berths on merchant marine vessels for seamen). This doctrine was later adopted by the courts. See, e.g., *Benaglia v. Comm'r*, 36 B.T.A. 838 (1937) (reviewed) (acq.) (value of on-premises lodging provided to the manager of Royal Hawaiian Hotel not included in gross income, because his job required him to be "on call" at all times).

The doctrine as it existed at common law might have appeared to be somewhat confusing due to its different formulations. One main line of authority looked to whether the employer had a "compensatory intent" in providing the free meals or lodging. The other main line of authority asked whether there was a sincere "business necessity" reason for providing the meals and lodging in order for the services provider to be able to perform her duties properly. Nevertheless, application of these tests would almost always produce the same results, because providing meals and lodging to enable the employee to properly perform her duties would usually preclude the existence of a compensatory intent (of transferring wealth to the employee).

As a matter of income tax *theory*, the scenario presents a conceptual problem. Some commentators interpret the Simons definition of income as positing that in-kind consumption is per se income (even if it does not entail an increase in wealth), in which case the provider's intent would not matter. This point can be buttressed by invoking notions of horizontal equity. John is paid $100 in cash by his employer, and he purchases $25 worth of meals with a portion of that salary. The $100 is fully included as compensation, and the meal purchases constitute nondeductible personal expenses. Johanna, in contrast, is paid $75 by her employer but is also provided $25 worth of free meals on the employer's premises. *If* Johanna is permitted to ignore the value of the free meals for tax purposes, her taxable income would be only $75, and John and Johanna, who would be in the same economic position, would be taxed differently. But the construction of the example loads the dice. John and Johanna are probably not really performing equivalent jobs in the free market if Johanna is required to take her meals on the premises and John is not. If the jobs were in fact economically identical, would Johanna accept a $25 pay cut even though she loses control over this meal? On the other hand, if the jobs really are economically the same, and Johanna finds the meals to be an acceptable substitute for the loss of $25 cash, then maybe John and Johanna should both be taxed on $100. Here it can be said that Johanna in substance receives cash wages of $100 and chooses to spend $25 on on-premises meals. Such a characterization satisfies those who adopt an ability-to-pay concept of income that holds that gross income is constituted only by any (realized) net increase in wealth.

Nevertheless, the convenience-of-the-employer doctrine (which would allow Johanna to exclude the value of the meals on the right set of facts) appears to be a modest extension (or perhaps application) of the working-condition doctrine.[2] If the employee herself purchased meals and lodging, would a deduction ever be allowed (apart from the special rules applicable to away-from-home meals and lodging)? It would seem that a meal (or lodging) cost that is necessary to carry on a business would be deductible, even though meals and lodging are viewed as prototypical consumption. One example would be fancy restaurant meals consumed by a free-lance food critic, or lodging costs incurred by an author of travel guides. (Abuses are dealt with by § 183, limiting deductions from a not-for-profit activity to the gross income from the activity.)

The foregoing suggests that the convenience-of-the-employer doctrine is quite narrow. It would not extend to such fringe benefits as life insurance coverage, child care services, legal services, or even healthcare coverage, but it would apply to on-the-job training. The required analysis is wholly objective, and not dependent on any notion of "utility" or the provider's subjective intent. Henry Simons agonized over whether a military attaché had income by reason of being forced to accept such employer-provided perks as a fine uniform, lodging in the palace, fancy banquet meals, and attendance at the opera with the royal employer, in the case where none of these benefits accorded with the attaché's personal tastes. But, as Simons himself acknowledged, personal preference is an impractical basis for determining whether income has been realized, because subjectivity cannot be reliably tested on a case-by-case basis.

Nevertheless, Simons' qualms about the absence of free choice have had some impact on tax doctrine. The Supreme Court in the seminal case of *Comm'r v. Glenshaw Glass*, 348 U.S. 426 (1955), stated (albeit in dictum and without explanation) that a characteristic of gross income is "dominion and control" of new wealth by the taxpayer. However, this concept is of little help in deciding when employee fringe benefits should be included in gross income. Does the employer or the employee have dominion and control in the case of a fringe benefit? In this connection, it cannot be assumed from the mere fact that the employer provides the item in question (or that an employee accepts it subject constraints, e..g., the meal on the employer's business premises) that the employee was reluctant to receive it, particularly when the item is the sort of consumer good or service that is routinely purchased by a wide range of individuals out of their personal funds. Regardless of this theoretical controversy, however, the employee fringe benefit area is now almost entirely statutory, and it is unlikely that a court would hold that a fringe benefit (not excluded by statute) would be excluded under a lack-of-control theory.

c. Meals and Lodging under § 119

In 1954, Congress made an attempt to rescue the tax system from the vagaries of the judicial convenience-of-the-employer doctrine by enacting § 119. Today, employer-provided meals and lodgings can be excluded from gross income *only* if they satisfy the requirements of § 119. That section imposes a "business premises" requirement and a "convenience of the employer" requirement. For lodging, there

---

[2] Cf. Reg. § 1.119-1(f) Ex. (7) (meals and lodging provided at remote construction site in Alaska).

is the additional requirement that the employee be required to accept the lodging as a condition of the employment.

The regulations have adopted a relatively liberal view of "convenience of the employer" as meaning only that the employer has "a substantial noncompensatory business reason" for the arrangement. See Reg. § 1.119-1(a)(2)(i).

The "condition of employment" requirement for lodging is interpreted to mean that the employee is "required to accept the lodging in order to enable him properly to perform the duties of his employment." See Reg. § 1.119-1(b) (second sentence).

The regulations offer examples, which are well worth reading.

The case of *Comm'r v. Kowalski*, 434 U.S. 77 (1977), involved state troopers who sought to exclude a cash allowance for meals taken (at the place of their choice) while being on call in their assigned patrol areas. The troopers were not required to spend the meal allowance on meals or account for how the money was spent. The Court rejected the claim of exclusion under § 119, stating (434 U.S. at 82-84, 90, 93, 95-96):

> [T]his Court has stated that "Congress applied no limitations as to the source of taxable receipts, [but intended] to tax all gains except those specifically exempted." *Comm'r v. Glenshaw Glass Co.*, 348 U.S. 426 (1955). In the absence of a specific exemption, therefore, respondent's meal-allowance payments are income within the meaning of § 61 since the payments are "undeniable accessions to wealth, clearly realized, and over which the respondent has complete dominion."
>
> By its terms, § 119 covers meals furnished by the employer and not cash reimbursements for meals. Accordingly, respondent's meal allowance payments are not subject to exclusion under § 119.
>
> [The taxpayer then invoked the convenience-of-the-employer doctrine.] Even if we assume that respondent's meal-allowance payments could have been excluded from income pursuant to the [convenience-of-the-employer] doctrine, we must nonetheless inquire whether such an implied exclusion survives. In enacting § 119, Congress was determined to "end the confusion as to the tax status of meals and lodging furnished an employee by his employer." [A discussion of the relevant committee reports follows.] Thus, § 119 comprehensively modified the prior law, both expanding and contracting the exclusion for meals and lodging previously provided, and it must therefore be construed as its draftsmen obviously intended it to be — as a replacement for the prior law, designed to "end [its] confusion."
>
> Finally, respondent argues that it is unfair that members of the military may exclude their subsistence allowances from income while respondent cannot. While this may be so, arguments of equity have little force in construing the boundaries of exclusions and deductions from income many of which, to be administrable, must be arbitrary. In any case, Congress has already considered respondent's equity argument and has rejected it in the repeal of § 120 of the 1954 Code. That provision allowed state troopers like respondent to exclude from income up to $5 of subsistence allowance per

day. Section 120 was repealed after only four years, however, because it was inequitable [relative to the general population].

Discounted meals offered by the employer for optional purchase by the employee are not excluded (to the extent of the discount) under § 119, because the optional meals are considered as failing the convenience-of-the-employer requirement. See Reg. § 1.119-1(a)(3)(i). However, under § 132(e)(2), an employer-run eating facility on the employer's business premises does not entail additional compensation to the employee just because the employees are charged an amount that is only sufficient to cover "direct operating costs."

NOTES

1. It is not clear (as a matter of principle) why lack of dominion and control should ever wholly negate a gross income inclusion. Even if the employee's lack of choice regarding an employer-provided benefit results in a subjective utility to the employee that is below fair market value, this should not result in *zero* inclusion of a consumption-type item, especially where the benefit is of the type that virtually any non-eccentric person would want. Control is, nevertheless, a legitimate factor in deciding questions of timing or questions regarding "who is the taxpayer?" with respect to a given item of income, as will be revealed in Chapters 17 and 23.

2. *Kowalski* holds that the common-law convenience-of-the-employer doctrine cannot be invoked by a taxpayer in a case involving employer-provided meals and lodging. But it is not clear if the doctrine has been wholly removed from the U.S. tax map. Nevertheless, as a practical matter, if a fringe benefit is of the type that is dealt with by a statutory provision, a court will likely not look beyond the statutory provision.

PROBLEMS

1. The average bulldozer operator does not own a bulldozer. The bulldozer is ordinarily furnished by the operator's employer. This is an economic benefit to the operator in the sense that she cannot pursue her trade without a bulldozer, but she usually cannot afford the enormous cost of this equipment. The employer also pays the operator an hourly wage, which is included in gross income. What distinguishes the operator's free use of the bulldozer from the hourly wage so that the value of free use of the bulldozer is not included in the operator's gross income? Should the matter hinge on how much enjoyment the employee obtains from operating the bulldozer?

2. Z Corp. provides its 10 top executives with a lavish office that includes artworks, a wet bar, an exercise machine, a flat-screen TV, and an on-call masseuse. What result to the executives?

2. Other Fringe Benefits Excluded by Statute

With the passage of time, several other fringe benefit exclusions have been codified. In addition to § 119, those of broadest economic importance are § 79 (exclusion for employer-provided, group-term life insurance coverage up to $50K),

§ 105 (amounts received by employees for medical care and permanent disability under employer health and accident plans), § 106 (employee coverage under employer-provided health and accident insurance plans), § 127 (educational assistance programs), and § 129 (dependent care assistance programs).

In the 1984 Tax Act, Congress attempted to end once and for all the confusion about fringe benefits not already addressed by other Code provisions. It did so by adding the phrase "fringe benefits" to § 61(a)(1) and by enacting § 132, which excludes several fringe benefits not addressed in other Code sections. *Thus, except as otherwise provided in the Code, employee fringe benefits received as compensation by service providers are includible in gross income.* As stated in the House Report to the 1984 Act:[3]

> [An] objective of the committee's bill is to set forth clear boundaries for the provision of tax-free benefits. In addition, the committee is concerned that without any well-defined limits on the ability of employers to compensate their employees tax-free by using a medium other than cash, new practices will emerge that could shrink the income tax base significantly, and further shift a disproportionate tax burden to those individuals whose compensation is in the form of cash. And an unrestrained expansion of non-cash compensation would increase inequities among employees in different types of businesses, and among employers as well.
>
> Under the bill, most [excludible] fringe benefits may be made available tax-free to officers, owners, or highly compensated employees only if the benefits are also provided on substantially equal terms to other employees. The committee believes that it would be fundamentally unfair to provide tax-free treatment for economic benefits that are furnished only to highly paid executives. Further, where benefits are limited to the highly paid, it is more likely that the benefit is being provided so that those who control the business can receive compensation in a nontaxable form.

One of the fringe benefits codified by § 132 is the "qualified employee discount" fringe, which allows *certain* employee discounts up to a maximum per-item amount to be excluded. This rule should be understood as a (partial) exception to § 83(a), which (as noted earlier) generally provides that a "bargain purchase" of property by a service provider from the recipient of the services *does* produce gross income in an amount equal to the excess of the fair market value of the property over the price paid for it. Recall Eleanor, the employee of a florist mentioned near the beginning of this chapter, who purchased a van from her employer at a discount. This particular discount could not be excluded as a "qualified employee discount," because Eleanor's employer is not a car dealer, see § 132(e)(4)), and so the full discount would be included in Eleanor's gross income. Section 83 is an important provision relating to employee compensation, the many permutations and ramifications of which will be explored in Chapter 22.

Another fringe benefit worth commenting upon is the de minimis fringe referred to in § 132(a)(4) and (e)(1), because this category can include cash and pure

---

[3] H.R. REP. No. 98-432, 98th Cong., 1st Sess. 285-305 (1983).

consumption items, is not limited by use or function, and is not restricted to employees in the strict sense.

Excludible fringe benefits are generally available only to "employees," as opposed to those who perform services as independent contractors (self-employed individuals). In some cases, however, the term "employee" is expanded to include self-employed persons, retired employees, family members of employees, or even all recipients of the fringe benefit. See, e.g., §§ 129(e)(3) and 132(h); Reg. § 1.132-1(b).

As a matter of tax practice, the typical tax adviser would be dealing only with employers, because the obligations of employers with respect to income tax withholding and payroll taxes generally track the distinction between included and excluded compensation. See §§ 3102(a), 3202(a), and 3402(a). Indeed, employers can incur severe penalties for failure to perform their withholding and payroll tax obligations. See §§ 6651(a) and 6656.

NOTES

1.   (a) In *American Airlines, Inc. v. U.S.*, 204 F.3d 1103 (Fed. Cir. 2000), a labor dispute at a major competitor forced American's employees to handle unusually heavy passenger loads. As a "gesture of appreciation," American distributed two $50 "Be My Guest" vouchers to each employee. These vouchers were actually blank American Express charge slips imprinted with American's account number and a statement that each was good for an amount "not to exceed fifty dollars." American's purpose was to recognize the employees' efforts without holding an unwieldy company-wide appreciation dinner. Vouchers in the total face amount of $4,250,000 were issued, and over 97% were redeemed. American claimed that the vouchers were excluded from the recipients' gross income as a de minimis fringe under § 132(e) and, accordingly, did not withhold federal income tax or payroll taxes or pay the employer portion of the latter. The Court of Appeals for the Federal Circuit disagreed, rejecting the claim that it would have been administratively impracticable to account for the vouchers.

(b) An employee's personal use of frequent flyer miles earned on company-paid business trips can perhaps be viewed as a "fringe benefit" or extra compensation, because the employer could (try to) recapture the miles for itself. How would such income be measured? How could the employer fulfill its withholding and payroll tax obligations with respect to such a benefit? After many years of nonaction (political paralysis?), the IRS finally stated that it would generally not pursue this issue against employees or employers. See *Announcement 2002-18*, 2002-1 C.B. 621. However, the IRS can assert income inclusion if the employee redeems accrued benefits for cash or converts them into some other form. See *Charley v. Comm'r*, 91 F.3d 72 (9th Cir. 1996).

2.   (a) A self-employed person cannot provide excludible fringe benefits to herself, because the person is not receiving anything from another person. In addition, the person could not usually deduct the cost of purchasing the benefit for herself, because the cost would usually be considered a personal outlay. Recall, however, § 162(*l*), which allows a deduction to a self-employed person for health insurance.

(b) A person could create a controlled C corporation[4] that would be the person's employer, and the corporation could then provide tax-free (or taxable) fringe benefits to the taxpayer as its employee. (A controlled C corporation is viewed as a separate tax person apart from the individuals who control it.) The fringe benefit cost would be deductible as a business expense by the corporation. In contrast, fringe benefit exclusions are not always available for a partner/employee of a partnership, see § 707(c), or an employee who is a 2% shareholder of an S corporation, see § 1372. The availability of a particular excludible fringe benefit can be a factor in the choice of what type of business organization to use. Accordingly, this topic is often discussed in courses dealing with taxation of business organizations.

PROBLEMS

Consider whether or to what extent the fringe benefits listed below may be excluded from gross income. In answering these questions, start with the statutory language (§ 132). In addition, the regulations should be perused exhaustively because they answer many important questions left unanswered by the statute and supply some surprising answers.

1.   (a) Jerry, a flight attendant for Divided Airlines, decides to fly to Disney World for a vacation with Dorothy, his wife. Divided allows any employee and accompanying family members to take a certain number of flights each year on the employer's aircraft without charge on a space-available (standby) basis. Jerry and Dorothy take advantage of this privilege and fly to Disney World and back home for free. On the flight, they enjoy meal and beverage service.

(b) Same as (a), except that the airline allows Jerry and Dorothy to book advance tickets rather than fly on a space-available basis. (Is failing to qualify as a no-additional-cost fringe the end of the analysis?)

(c) Same as (a), except that Jerry is the CEO of Divided, and free tickets are provided on a stand-by basis only to officers of the airline; all other employees pay 50% of the normal fare.

2.   Jane is a salesperson employed in an art gallery. She purchases for her wall a small etching valued at $100, but she paid only $80 because she is allowed a 20% employee discount. The etching is by an unknown artist that Jane believes is an up-and-coming star. During the year the gallery has $1M in sales and $700K for cost of goods sold. (Does the employee need to know this?) Is all or a part of the etching gross income to Jane? A few years later, the artist is "discovered" and his art work appreciates considerably in value. Jane is thus able to sell the etching for $200. What should her basis be for purposes of calculating gain or loss under § 1001?

3.   (a) Jeff works as an attorney for a small law firm in Laramie, Wyoming. The pace of work is low-key, and Jeff usually goes home about 5:30 p.m. About once each month, however, he is required to work until 10:00 p.m., and on those nights the firm pays for the cost of his supper at a nearby restaurant with modest prices. The firm

---

[4] The distinctions among the tax treatment of a C corporation, an S corporation, and an entity (partnership or LLC) treated as a partnership for tax purposes is briefly discussed in Chapter 1.D.3.

does not pay the cost of his secretary's dinner, who also stays late on these nights. Does it make any difference whether Jeff's firm gives him cash to pay for the suppers in advance, reimburses Jeff, or has the restaurant bill the firm?

(b) Julia works for a big law firm until 10:00 p.m. at least four nights each week, and Julia's firm pays for her supper at a nearby restaurant on those nights.

4.   (a) A hospital charges employees at an employee-only cafeteria prices equal to 5% above the cost of providing the meals (which is substantially less than the value of the meals). The cafeteria is located in the hospital. See § 132(e)(2).

(b) Same as (a), except that the employees are not charged *at all* for meals. The employees consist of doctors employed by the hospital who are on call to meet emergencies and who may not leave the hospital, nurses who are given a thirty-minute meal break and who may be called back to their posts during meals, and, in comparison, relatively few clerical personnel. Consider the application of § 119, as well as § 132.

C.   POLICY CONSIDERATIONS

What would occur if *all* fringe benefits were excluded from gross income and only *cash* compensation were taxed? Employees and their employers would be under great pressure to convert at least a sizeable portion of taxable compensation into nontaxable fringe benefits, such as health insurance, free meals, free groceries, free transportation to and from work, or maybe even free campus lodging. The employees would favor this approach because they would perceive their incomes as being increased by the amount of the avoided tax (a perception that we shall challenge below). The employers would encourage this employee attitude because the employers would avoid having to pay Social Security and Medicare taxes to the extent that taxable cash wages were converted into nontaxable fringe benefits and (as noted shortly) would perhaps be able to "capture" all or a portion of the benefit of the exclusion aimed ostensibly at the employee.

On the other hand, since compensation income is the mainstay of the income tax base, as well as the sole item in the Social Security and Medicare tax bases, Congress is unwilling to tolerate a categorical exclusion for all fringe benefits. Moreover, if all fringe benefits were excludible, distributional equity concerns would be raised insofar as highly compensated individuals have more leverage to negotiate for a higher proportion of their compensation to be received in kind than do rank-and-file employees. Perhaps this latter concern explains why many (but by no means all) tax-free fringe benefits allowed under the Code are subject to nondiscrimination rules. Nondiscrimination rules, however, are not easy to draft and to implement.

A problem with any fringe benefit exclusion would be the likelihood that the tax benefit ostensibly belonging to the employee would be "captured" in whole or in part by the employer. Capture can occur, especially in the case of relatively powerless rank-and-file employees, because employers would be able to transfer less *value* to the employees to produce the same *after-tax* compensation to the employees. To illustrate, suppose that X Corp is paying $60K cash to its employee Dave, who has no deductions available, and is subject to a flat 20% tax rate. Dave's after-tax income would be $48K ($60K − $12K). Now suppose, however, that X Corp proposes that Dave be paid $40K in cash and $20K in the form of tax-free fringe benefits. Dave might like that because he would apparently save taxes of $4K ($20K excluded income × 20% marginal tax rate). Noting this fact, however, X Corp might decide to offer a compensation package of $40K taxable cash and only *$16K* of tax-free fringe benefits, arguing that this package is just as good for Dave, after tax, as $60K cash, because Dave still would end up with $48K ($40K cash + $16K excluded fringes − $8K tax). Dave might balk somewhat on the grounds that the compensation in kind limits spending choice, but Dave's resolve would greatly weaken if X Corp offered fringe benefits of the type that he would have purchased with cash in any event (e.g., medical and life insurance, use of the company's gym, meals in the company cafeteria, etc.). Or Dave might settle for $18K excluded fringes, but the employer still saves $2K ($58K compensation paid instead of $60K). The compensation is fully deducted by X Corp under all of these variations.

This example illustrates several important points. One is that tax benefits are not always fully reaped by their ostensible targets. Furthermore, many would complain that the capture of tax benefits aimed at the working class by employers is yet another way in which "the rich get richer." The Daves of the world likely think they benefit mightily from the exclusions for employer-provided health care, for example, but a good chunk of that benefit is likely to be captured by employers (not to mention health insurance companies and health care providers, who can charge higher prices than they would be able to demand if the exclusion were repealed). To generalize, almost any subsidy (tax or otherwise) to workers or consumers can be captured (in part) by employers and suppliers, especially if the subsidy is targeted to specific goods and services.

Finally, to the extent that a tax-free fringe benefit alters a person's free-spending choices, the exclusion violates the economic-efficiency tax policy norm. Recall that economic efficiency — or the increase in aggregate societal wealth that is assumed to flow when people are free to engage in economic decisionmaking without interference — suggests that the tax law should interfere as little as possible with people's behavior and economic decisions. Thus, tax commentators and public finance economists are virtually unanimous in the proposition that fringe benefits should *not* be broadly excluded.

NOTES

1.   (a) A "cafeteria plan" under § 125 is a plan that allows employees to select among various (but not all) nontaxable and taxable benefits (including cash). Exclusion of nontaxable benefits is not lost solely because the participant may choose among plan benefits, at least one of which would be taxable. In the absence of § 125, the taxpayer would be in "constructive receipt" of the taxable benefit in this situation. The § 125 election to receive any *nontaxable* benefit must be made by the first day of the plan year and prior to the time any *taxable* benefit becomes available to the participant. The election often takes the form of a salary reduction of a specified amount. See Prop. Reg. § 1.125-2(a)(2)

(b) A cafeteria plan cannot be a vehicle for deferring compensation. It follows that any nontaxable benefit elected under a cafeteria plan must be used in the current taxable year; otherwise, it is forfeited — a "use-it-or-lose-it" feature. See Prop. Reg. § 1.125-5(c). This feature virtually forces people to incur unnecessary health care expenditures at the end of the year.

2. (a) Does the concept of "no additional cost" to an employer justify an exclusion to the employee? The employee receives an economic benefit that she could have paid for, but can it be said that the transaction is equivalent to a cash payment by the employer coupled with a free spending choice? Are the wages of eligible employees likely to have been reduced? (Of course, as a general matter, in cases where an item is includible in income, the transferor's cost is usually irrelevant to tax analysis.)

(b) In any event, the providers of "no additional cost services" (usually airlines, hotels, and entertainment operations) often really do incur additional costs (such as jet fuel for the additional weight). For that reason, the phrase "(including forgone revenue)" was inserted in § 132(b)(2). But even the no-forgone-revenue notion is dubious, because the employer/service provider could auction off unused capacity at the last minute (although it might prefer not to do this).

PROBLEM

Acme, Inc., a widget manufacturing corporation, is constructing a new headquarters building, and, for the first time, employee parking spaces will be available on Acme's headquarters premises. The FMV of a parking space will be $230 per month. By coincidence, Acme is about to design a new set of compensation contracts. Acme has determined that if it charges the headquarters employees for parking, labor market conditions will force it to add a sufficient amount to the employees' annual raises to compensate them for their parking cost. Thus, Acme cannot realize any net revenue from charging the headquarters employees for parking. Assuming that all Acme headquarters employees have a 20% marginal income tax rate (and that there are no payroll taxes involved) and that Acme's marginal income tax rate is 35%, what should Acme do, given the existence of § 132(f)?

Chapter 13

CAN IN-KIND CONSUMPTION BE "RESIDUAL GROSS INCOME"?

As explained in Chapter 12, the value of consumption (or property) received in kind as *compensation* is includible gross income, unless an express Code section (such as § 119 or § 132) provides otherwise. The same is true with the other specifically identified items in § 61(a), such as interest and dividends. This chapter deals with the tax status of in-kind benefits that are not listed in § 61(a)(1) – (15) and are thus not includible in gross income unless they fall within the "residual" or "catchall" language at the beginning of § 61(a) ("gross income means all income from whatever source derived").

The Supreme Court fumbled this issue early on. Cases such as *Eisner v. Macomber*, 252 U.S. 189 (1920), appeared to restrict "income" to the return on capital and/or labor. Thus, *Gould v. Gould*, 245 U.S. 151 (1917), held that even cash alimony was not catch-all income. In *U.S. v. Supplee-Biddle Hardware Co.*, 265 U.S. 189 (1924), the Supreme Court stated that a one-time receipt should not be included as catch-all gross income unless expressly provided by Congress. These cases were influenced by nontax notions of "income" borrowed from other intellectual disciplines. It was not until *Comm'r v. Glenshaw Glass*, 348 U.S. 426 (1955), that a purely tax concept of gross income came into focus. *Glenshaw Glass* itself held that a one-time cash receipt (punitive damages) was includible as catch-all income, stating (348 U.S. at 431):

> Here we have instances of undeniable accessions to wealth, clearly realized, and over which the taxpayers have complete dominion.

This language, however, involved a cash receipt. It doesn't clearly resolve the issue of whether an in-kind consumption benefit — say, a free consumer product sample or a free meal in connection with listening to a real estate developer's pitch — falls within the catch-all concept of income. To this issue we now turn.

A. IN-KIND CONSUMPTION BENEFITS UNDER TAX THEORY

Henry Simons defined income as the algebraic sum of net wealth increases and consumption. There are two ways of "deconstructing" this language. The first one, which we can call the "consumption-oriented approach," operates in three steps. Step 1 would be to aggregate all gross increases in wealth for the year. Under step 2, all of the year's wealth decreases — *even outlays to purchase consumption* — would be subtracted. In step 3, the value of all consumption during the year (whether purchased or received in kind) would be added back in. Thus, under this interpretation of the Simons definition, all in-kind consumption would be income.

However, no income tax systematically operates in this fashion. Suppose, for example, that Elmer receives a personal use automobile worth $30K as a sales bonus. According to a literal interpretation of the Simons income concept, the taxation of the auto would entail three steps. In step 1, Elmer's income would increase by $30K on account of an accession to wealth. In step 2, Elmer's income over time would be decreased in an amount equal to the decline in value (depreciation) of the auto. In step 3, Elmer's income would be increased by the value over time of his consumption use of the auto. The amount subtracted in step 2 would not (except by chance) be the same amount added back in step 3 (which would be the rental value of the car). Of course our actual income tax system employs only step 1 in Elmer's case and ignores steps 2 and 3. Step 2 is ignored because depreciation deductions are not allowed with respect to personal-use property and because the realization principle prevents unrealized value declines from being taken into account. Step 3 is also ignored because it would be irrational to follow it if step 2 is not taken. Thus, the consumption-oriented version of the Simons definition simply does not reflect what happens under an income tax in actual practice.

Another difficulty with the consumption-oriented approach to the Simons definition is that the distinction between "wealth" and "consumption" is not as clean as might first appear. Assume that Elmer receives in Year 1 a bonus from his employer in the form of a $100 certificate entitling him to a gourmet restaurant meal within the next 12 months, and Elmer uses the certificate in Year 2. Is Year 1 the year of taxation because receipt of the certificate is a wealth increase and enjoyment of the meal in Year 2 involves (1) a wealth decrease and (2) a consumption increase that cancel each other out? Or is Year 2 the year of taxation because there is no wealth increase until a waiter puts the meal on Elmer's table?

These difficulties are avoided by an alternative interpretation of the Simons income concept that is strictly wealth-oriented. It views the taxation of consumption as a principle of nondeductibility (rather than one of additions to the tax base).

This wealth-oriented approach has only two steps. Step 1 includes all increases in wealth (including receipts of rights to consumption), but step 2 allows deductions only for wealth decreases other than decreases resulting from consumption. Thus, neither consumption expenses nor the using up of consumption rights are deductible. The receipt of a right to future consumption is taxable as an addition to wealth but the act of consumption is not taxed. No valuation is required except for the initial receipt of wealth (including consumption rights).

This alternative view of income is compatible with the ability-to-pay tax fairness norm, because cash and property (including rights to consumption) represent enforceable claims to social resources. In contrast, the pure act of consumption is nothing more than psychic pleasure (utility), which (among other salient characteristics) is not transferable, and is of no use to the government.

Most importantly, in actual practice, the federal income tax base is calculated almost wholly according to this alternative, wealth-oriented version of income. Consumption is typically taxed by disallowing any deduction for it. The act of consumption is almost never taxed unless there is good reason to tax it. Usually the "good reason" is a judgment that failure to tax the consumption benefit would open the door to undermining the tax system, or, to state the matter in a more concrete fashion, that the act of consumption is the equivalent of a receipt of cash followed by a relatively unconstrained spending choice. This kind of judgment informs the taxation of in-kind benefits received as compensation for services, discussed in the preceding chapter.

This chapter is mostly about consumption benefits received by an individual that are not considered to be gross income.

B.   NONMARKET BENEFITS

This section considers nonwealth economic benefits that are obtained "outside" of market transactions. This category can perhaps be broken down into three categories, to wit, (1) general psychic benefits, (2) imputed income from self-provided services, and (3) imputed income from the use of consumer assets. As a matter of doctrine, *none of these are considered to produce catch-all gross income for income tax purposes under current law.* This result is exactly compatible with the view that the tax base is basically "about" wealth and not utility or subjective well-being.

1.   General Psychic Benefits

"General" psychic benefits are those that are obtained from a person's external environment or the person's own internal physical and mental resources, such as sunlight, clean air and water, pleasant dreams, free TV, good health, police and fire protection, a high IQ, being well liked, being physically attractive, having a good home and/or sex life, living in a community with lots of amenities, and so on. Economists operating out of the Utilitarian tradition (sometimes called the "welfarist" tradition) have long treated these psychic benefits as "income." In welfare economics, improving the overall well-being of society is the prime directive. Because the welfarist conceives of the ideal tax base as being measured by "utility" or "well-being," the items noted above would be added to "income."

Nevertheless, even a person steeped in this tradition, for whom the exclusion of psychic benefits from the income tax base seems to be an aberration, recognizes that the exclusion is necessary due to the administrative infeasibility of attempting to take these benefits into account. The administrative problem is two-fold. First, subjective utility cannot be directly measured, and the market transactions that would supply a proxy for subjective value are lacking in the case of the free goods under consideration here. Even Henry Simons acknowledged that the tax base had to be capable of objective measurement, which meant that the system had to be keyed to *market* transactions and *market* values.[1] To Simons, objective measurability was a "principle," although based on pragmatic concerns, which often trumped strict adherence to economic concepts. The second administrative

---

[1] According to Simons, income is measured "by appeal to market prices." HENRY C. SIMONS, PERSONAL INCOME TAXATION 50 (1938).

problem with attempting to tax psychic benefits is that there is no payor who can be required to withhold tax or provide information returns, and without these the IRS has no way of learning that the benefits have been enjoyed.

But there are substantive reasons, even apart from administrative infeasibility, *not* to tax general psychic benefits. One is that the government's proper role is limited to the public use (including redistribution) of *material* resources (cash and assets). Psychic benefits are not any kind of "currency" that can be spent or redistributed. Taking away one person's happiness does not make anyone else better off (in the material sense). In contrast, material wealth can be transferred (redistributed) or redeployed for public purposes. Second, the tax base is a "difference" principle (like a grading curve). There is no point in including in the tax base nonwealth items that most people have (such as adequately clean air), could have if they so desired (like free TV or life in the country), or are distributed randomly among the population regardless of economic class (such as good looks or a good family life). Inclusions of this sort are of little help in distinguishing those who are more able to pay taxes from those who are less able. Third, psychic benefits that might be *statistically* weighted in favor of one class or another (such as, in the upper classes, a higher level of personal security and good health), might better be taken into account in adjusting the tax *rates* than in attempting to take them into account in computing the tax *bases* of individuals.

Another cluster of reasons has to do with the fact that excluding most of these psychic benefits does not raise significant economic efficiency concerns. Many of these benefits fall into the category of "public goods," defined as benefits that can be obtained without depriving another person of them. Public goods are not scarce resources that need to be efficiently allocated through the price (supply and demand) mechanism. Economic efficiency is also, by stipulation, not a concern for items that might be scarce resources in the physical sense, but which society judges should not be commodified, such as personal relationships, children, and various rights and liberties. For example, a tax on leisure or unused "earning capacity" (e.g., a tax on professionals who have the capacity to work but instead retire at age 40 and spend the rest of their lives on the beach) would impinge on liberty values. Some economists may claim that more such goods *should* be commodified and taxed in the interests of economic efficiency, but that is an eccentric view, and we shall take the existing level of noncommodification as a given.

2. Imputed Income from Self-Provided Services

A hypothetical will help to illustrate the catch-all gross income issue with respect to self-provided services. Assume that lawyer Alice, who would normally charge a client $300 to prepare a will, drafts her own will. This is the same result (and involves the same effort) as would have been obtained if Alice had first earned a $300 fee by performing services for a paying client and then had paid $300 to lawyer Bill to draft her will, in which case Alice would have $300 of cash income without any offsetting deduction for the $300 fee paid to Bill (a nondeductible personal expense). On the other hand, Alice did not actually perform any will-drafting service for a client, and did not spend any money to have a will prepared.

There were no actual *market* transactions involving other parties. Should that matter?

Economists would say that Alice has realized "imputed income" in the form of a $300 self-created economic benefit. Moreover, the economic neutrality norm suggests that this benefit should be taxed, because, if it is not taxed, Alice will have a tax incentive to perform all kinds of other services for herself — food production, home repairs, etc. — rather than entering into market transactions. Economists are of the view that economic efficiency is maximized by market transactions in which individuals sell what they do best and acquire the services at which they are less skilled by hiring others. This is known as the "principle of comparative advantage." A lawyer can draft a will for a plumber better and faster than the plumber can, and a plumber can fix Alice's clogged drain more efficiently than Alice can.

Nevertheless, the value of self-created services is not considered to be gross income under the income tax. Even if one's services create an asset for oneself, neither the value of the asset nor the excess of the product's value over the costs of materials is gross income. See *Morris v. Comm'r*, 9 B.T.A. 1273 (1928) (acq.) (excluding from gross income the value of self-grown crops consumed by a farmer). Presumably, neither the finding of wild mushrooms or strawberries in the woods and fields, nor their consumption, would be gross income. Of course, the personal effort devoted to these activities is not a "cost" that can be deducted or added to the basis of anything.

Obviously, taxing imputed income items such as these would be administratively impossible, due to the reasons for nontaxation previously mentioned in connection with general psychic benefits. In addition, providing services to oneself is just one possible way of spending leisure time, and leisure (in whatever form) is not taxed. Moreover, self-provided services usually entail the use of nondeductible tools, materials, instructions, and supplies. The tax savings "lost" by not being able to deduct these costs may be viewed as a sufficient proxy for the tax that is "lost" by failing to include in income the value obtained from self-provided services. Alternatively, if the value of self-consumed services were income, then the associated costs would have to be deducted, and this would create an accounting burden.

Moreover, taxing self-provided services would be viewed by many as an inappropriate governmental intrusion into the (personal) private sphere. In contrast, by entering into a market transaction, a person engages with society to a sufficient extent to also require engagement with the government, which secures property rights and provides economic infrastructure.

Finally, many types of self-service activities are probably engaged in disproportionately by lower-income persons, so that taxing their value would have an overall regressive effect on the distribution of the tax burden.

3. Imputed Income from Ownership of Consumer Assets

The most commonly understood meaning of "imputed income" is the fair rental value of self-owned consumer assets (homes, vehicles, and consumer durables). Economists bemoan the fact that the tax system ignores gross imputed income because it results in systematic tax favoritism for investments in consumer assets relative to conventional investments (such as stocks and bonds), the economic returns on which are taxed. Economists would say that taxing imputed income in this situation is not administratively impossible, at least with respect to homes carried on local property tax rolls. Nor would taxing this kind of imputed income violate liberty and privacy concerns to the same extent as would be the case with imputed income from self-consumed services. Finally, imputed income from homes has been taxed in other countries (and even in some of the American colonies).

To frame the matter as an economic-efficiency problem, assume that Greg and Lou each earns $50K of annual salary; and each comes into $80K of inherited cash, which each uses to purchase identical homes, but Greg rents his out for $8K per year and lives in an apartment, whereas Lou lives in her home. Greg's rent receipts are gross income, and, because his house is investment property, he is allowed to deduct annual depreciation and repairs, which total, say, $3K, producing net rental income for income tax purposes of $5K. Lou, who lives in her house, has excluded gross imputed income of $8K, but cannot deduct her $3K of depreciation and repairs. Economists would say that Greg and Lou have equal pre-tax net incomes of $5K from their houses. However, Greg is taxed on his $5K, whereas Lou is not. Awareness of the foregoing may drive Greg to live in his own home, thus violating the neutrality economic norm. Accordingly, an economist would favor taxing Lou on her $5K of net imputed income, thereby putting her and Greg on the same tax footing. Note that taxation of Lou's imputed income would accord with the view (rejected by us) that the Simons "income" concept posits consumption as an independent category of income.

Of course, Lou is not in fact required to include the $5K net rental value in income, a rule that accords with the view that consumption is not an independent category of income but just a principle of nondeductibility.

It turns out that the neutrality argument described above for taxing imputed income is not as strong as it first appears, because it was framed (as a choice between "investments") in a way that loaded the dice. An arguably more appropriate framing begins by noting that the cost of a consumer asset (a personal residence, car, etc.) represents the net present value of the future consumption benefits flowing from the use of the asset. Under the present income tax, this deferred consumption is taxed once by reason of disallowing a deduction for the asset cost. This treatment of consumer *assets* and the deferred benefits they yield accords with the taxation of present consumption *expenses* (groceries, movie tickets, etc.), which are also taxed once. Thus, the income tax is neutral as between current consumption and deferred consumption. Taxing net imputed income produced by consumer assets would effectively impose a second tax on deferred consumption and would violate the neutrality norm by discriminating against deferred consumption purchases relative to current consumption. The real complaint of the economist is that consumer assets are not taxed the same as conventional investments (which are also nondeductible but which produce a taxable net yield). That complaint was analyzed at length and questioned in Chapter 6.C.

Historically, taxes on imputed income have foundered over problems clustering around enforcement, compliance, income measurement, invasion of privacy, and taxpayer liquidity. Dealing with these problems would probably not be worth the effort, because inclusion of gross imputed income from personal-use assets would require that deductions be allowed for related depreciation, repairs, and other expenses, as well as mortgage interest and property taxes, perhaps resulting in even a net revenue loss in some cases.

Finally, economics and politics don't always mix, but politicians have the ultimate power to decide taxation issues. Can you imagine trying to explain the concept of imputed rental income to the average voter? Politicians understand this impossibility and would not alter the *status quo* by enacting a provision taxing imputed income.

NOTES

1.   (a) Imputed income from a consumer asset can be expressed as a percentage of the asset's value. From this standpoint, a tax on imputed income is a tax on the value of property and could be challenged as being a direct tax that is unconstitutional because of not being apportioned among the states in accordance with population. Although arguments can be made to the contrary, there is dictum in *Helvering v. Independent Life Insurance Co.*, 292 U.S. 371, 379 (1934), to the effect that a tax on imputed income from property would indeed be a direct tax. The actual holding of this case, however, was that Congress did have the power to enact a provision that disallowed deductions with respect to owner-occupied buildings unless the owner also included the annual fair rental value of such property in income. See § 834(d), which is applicable only to insurance companies. The Court's rationale was that this "optional" inclusion of imputed income was a legitimate, if indirect way, of disallowing deductions, which is clearly within the power of Congress. Presumably, then, Congress could (if it chose to do so) "condition" various existing homeowner deductions (mortgage interest and real property taxes) on the inclusion of imputed income.

(b) If a personal residence yields net imputed income equal to 4% of its value, then a 1% property tax (state property taxes rarely go much above 1%) is equivalent to a tax of 25% on the net imputed income from the residence. From this standpoint, state *ad valorem* property taxes on homes and consumer assets are the functional equivalent of taxes on net imputed income, but without any need to inquire about the facts of actual use.

2.   (a) If imputed income from actively used consumer assets is not income in the tax sense, then it follows that income cannot be imputed on idle cash or property (such as unimproved land allowed to lie fallow or an unexploited patent right).

(b) Some commentators favor an "accretion" income tax devoid of a realization requirement in which all changes in the FMV of assets would be taken into account each year. In this context, it is sometimes proposed that hard-to-value assets (family businesses, land, etc.) be taxed on an "imputed return" basis. If taxing imputed income from consumer assets poses a constitutional issue, imputed-return taxation would also pose a constitutional issue.

(c) Treating imputed income and imputed returns as non-income leaves us with a system that levies tax according to what was actually done (economic outcomes) as opposed to what *might* have been done.

(d) In the exclusion for imputed income from services or property simply a facet of the basic principle that self-help (or fortuitous) "avoided costs" (such as reducing consumption or avoiding legal support obligations) are not income?

3.   It has sometimes been argued that, given the exclusion for imputed income from residences, residential rental payments should be deductible (contrary to present law), in the name of horizontal equity. If this notion encompassed all rentals of personal use property, it would extend quite far. Consider leased autos, vacation rental cars, vacation home rentals, hotel stays, tool rentals, furniture rentals, DVD rentals, transportation fares, attending sporting and entertainment events, and fees for parks and recreation.

4.   (a) It might appear that the taxation of consumer assets under the income tax (by denying a deduction for the purchase cost and excluding future imputed income from consumer assets) is an example of how consumption tax features have been grafted onto the income tax. This *assumes*, however, that a theoretically pure income tax would tax gross imputed income from consumer assets. To the contrary, as explained in Section B.3, supra, single taxation of current and deferred consumption can legitimately be viewed as a core income tax principle. Accordingly, what really distinguishes an income tax from a consumption (or wage) tax is the tax treatment of investments.

(b) It is still the case that certain features of the income tax relating to consumer assets (the deductions for mortgage interest and real property taxes and the § 121 limited exclusion of gains from a sale of one's principal residences) deviate from a theoretically pure income tax and can be classified as tax expenditures.

C. PERSONAL BENEFITS PROVIDED BY ANOTHER PARTY

The material below involves consumption-type benefits that, instead of being self-provided, are provided by another party (usually a business) for its own selfish reason. But these benefits are distinguishable from conventional market exchanges in that there is no primary intent by the provider to compensate or reward the taxpayer for specific services or goods bargained-for by the provider.

1. Benefits Incidental to Business Activity

The case below deals with what amounted to an expense-paid recruiting trip. Except possibly for the portion of the trip paid for by the taxpayer's employer, the trip did not constitute "compensation," a "dividend," or any other enumerated category of income. Therefore, if the (nonemployer-provided) value of the trip is to qualify as "gross income," it must be because it falls within the "residual gross income" catchall language in § 61(a).

UNITED STATES v. GOTCHER
United States Court of Appeals, Fifth Circuit
401 F.2d 118 (1968)

Before JOHN R. BROWN, CHIEF JUDGE, and BELL and THORNBERRY, CIRCUIT JUDGES.

THORNBERRY, CIRCUIT JUDGE:

In 1960, Mr. and Mrs. Gotcher took a twelve-day expense-paid trip to Germany to tour the Volkswagen facilities there. The trip cost $1372. His employer, Economy Motors, paid $349, and Volkswagen of Germany and Volkswagen of America shared the remaining $1023. Upon returning, Mr. Gotcher bought a 25% interest in Economy Motors, the Sherman, Texas Volkswagen dealership, that had been offered to him before he left. The Commissioner determined that the taxpayers had realized income to the extent of the $1372 for the expense-paid trip. The District Court, sitting without a jury, held that the cost of the trip was not income or, in the alternative, was income and deductible as an ordinary and necessary business expense. 259 F. Supp. 340. We affirm the determination that the cost of the trip was not income to Mr. Gotcher ($686); however, Mrs. Gotcher's expenses ($686) constituted income and were not deductible.

Appellant argues that the cost of the trip should be included since it is not specifically excluded by §§ 101-123, reasoning that § 61 was drafted broadly to subject all economic gains to tax. This analysis is too restrictive since it has been generally held that exclusions from gross income are not limited to the enumerated exclusions.

In determining whether the expense-paid trip was income within § 61, we must look to the tests that have been developed under this section. The concept of economic gain to the taxpayer is the key to § 61. This concept contains two distinct requirements: There must be an economic gain, and this gain must primarily benefit the taxpayer personally.

In some cases, as in the case of an expense-paid trip, there is no direct economic gain, but there is an indirect economic gain inasmuch as a benefit has been received without a corresponding diminution in wealth. In two cases, *Rudolph v. U.S.*, 291 F.2d 841 (1961), and *Patterson v. Thomas*, 289 F.2d 108 (1961), this Court has examined expense-paid trips and held that the value of these trips constituted income. The instant case differs from *Rudolph* and *Patterson* in that there is no evidence in the record to indicate that the trip was an award for past services, since Mr. Gotcher was not an employee of VW of Germany and he did nothing to earn that part of the trip paid by Economy Motors. The trip was made in 1959 when VW was attempting to expand its local dealerships in the United States. The "buy American" campaign and the fact that the VW people felt they had a "very ugly product" prompted them to offer these tours of Germany to prospective dealers. [VW] determined that the best way to remove the apprehension about this foreign product was to take the dealer to Germany and have him see his investment first-hand. It was believed that once the dealer saw the manufacturing facilities and the stability of the "New Germany" he would be convinced that VW was for him.

A substantial amount of time was spent touring VW facilities and visiting local dealerships. Moreover, at almost all of the evening meals VW officials gave talks about the organization and passed out literature and brochures on the VW story. Some of the days were not related to touring the VW facilities, but that fact alone cannot be decisive. The dominant purpose of the trip is the critical inquiry, and some pleasurable features will not negate the finding of an overall business purpose.

The question, therefore, is what tax consequences should follow from an expense-paid trip that primarily benefits the party paying for the trip. In several analogous situations the value of items received by employees has been excluded from gross income when these items were primarily for the benefit of the employer. Thus it appears that the value of any trip that is paid by the employer or by a businessman primarily for its or his own benefit should be excluded from gross income of the payee on similar reasoning.

In analyzing the tax consequences of an expense-paid trip one important factor is whether the traveler had any choice but to go. Here, the trial judge found that the invitation did not specifically order the dealers to go, but that as a practical matter it was an order or directive that if a person was going to be a VW dealer, sound business judgment necessitated his accepting the offer of corporate hospitality. Besides having no choice but to go, he had no control over the schedule or the money spent. VW did all the planning.

The Supreme Court has defined income as accessions of wealth over which the taxpayer has complete control. *Comm'r v. Glenshaw Glass Co.* Clearly, the lack of control works in taxpayer's favor here. *McDonnell* also suggests that one does not realize taxable income when he is serving a legitimate business purpose of the party paying the expenses. The cases involving corporate officials who have traveled or entertained clients at the company's expense are apposite. Indeed, corporate executives have been furnished yachts, *Challenge Mfg. Co. v. Comm'r*, 37 T.C. 650 (1962), and taken safaris as part of an advertising scheme, *Sanitary Farms Dairy Inc. v. Comm'r*, 25 T.C. 463 (1955), but have been held accountable for expenses paid only when the court was persuaded that the expenditure was primarily for the officer's personal pleasure. On the other hand, when it has been shown that the expenses were paid to effectuate a legitimate corporate end and not to benefit the officer personally, the officer has not been taxed though he enjoyed and benefited from the activity. Thus, the rule is that the economic benefit will be taxable to the recipient only when the payment of expenses serves no legitimate corporate purpose. *See Comm'r v. Riss*, 374 F.2d 161 (8th Cir. 1967).

The decisions also indicate that the tax consequences are to be determined by looking to the primary purpose of the expenses and that the first consideration is the intention of the payor. The personal benefits and pleasure were incidental to the dominant purpose of improving VW's position on the American market and getting people to invest money.

As for Mrs. Gotcher, the trip was primarily a vacation. She did not make the tours with her husband to see the local dealers or attend discussions about the VW organization. This being so the primary benefit of the expense-paid trip for the wife went to Mr. Gotcher in that he was relieved of her expenses. He should therefore be taxed on the expenses attributable to his wife. Nor are the expenses deductible since the wife's presence served no bona fide business purpose for her husband. Only when the wife's presence is necessary to the conduct of the husband's business are her expenses deductible under § 162. Also, it must be shown that the wife made the trip only to assist her husband in his business.

[Concurring opinion of JOHN R. BROWN, CHIEF JUDGE omitted.]

In *Hornung v. Comm'r*, 47 T.C. 428 (1967), a football star's rent-free use of an auto provided by Ford Motor Co. for promotional purposes was held to be gross income on the ground that the taxpayer had unfettered personal use of the auto.

Since the doctrine in this area is related to the old "convenience of the employer" doctrine, cases involving employer-provided travel and entertainment are relevant, although in these situations the suspicion is one of disguised compensation. The *Gotcher* majority (in a passage omitted above) cited *Rudolf v. U.S.*, 370 U.S. 269 (1962) (per curiam), as authority for the proposition that the statutory gross income exclusions were not exclusive. Actually, the Supreme Court in that case did not really set any precedent at all. There the majority (of 4 justices) dismissed the writ of certiorari as having been improvidently granted and affirmed the holding below on the basis of the fact finder's conclusion that an employer-paid trip to a convention in New York, which the trial court found to be "in the nature of a bonus reward" and which was mostly devoted to entertainment, was "compensation," Even though every detail of the trip, including the entertainment, was planned in advance. (The Supreme Court generally avoids "fact" issues unless it believes that the wrong legal standards were applied by the fact finder.) Justice Harlan would have affirmed on the merits, citing the broad reach of "income" under *Glenshaw Glass*. Justices Douglas and Black dissented essentially on the ground that the paying of another's expenses is generally not income unless it is disguised compensation. This view was rejected by the other five sitting justices (two justices did not participate). The government conceded (at the court of appeals level) that the payor's intent was controlling under a "primary business purpose" test, which was essentially the same test as would apply on the deductibility side. No nonstatutory exclusions relevant to the facts were discussed in any opinion, except that of Justice Douglas, who tossed in the "convenience-of-the-employer" doctrine.[2]

In *Patterson v. Thomas*, 289 F.2d 108 (5th Cir.), *cert. denied*, 368 U.S. 837 (1961), the value of an employer-paid convention trip was included in the employee's gross income, the Fifth Circuit holding that the convenience-of-the-employer test was

---

[2] Justice Douglas was then voting for the taxpayer in virtually every tax case. See Bernard Wolfman, Jonathan L. F. Silver & Marjorie A. Silver, *The Behavior of Justice Douglas in Federal Tax Cases*, 122 U. PA. L. REV. 235 (1975).

limited to meals and lodging. The employee's attempt to take a deduction was disallowed.

But employees do not always lose cases of this type. In *McDonell v. Comm'r*, T.C. Memo. 1967-18, the taxpayer, a manager in his employer's headquarters, was sent, with his wife, to chaperone a Hawaiian vacation awarded by the employer as a sales contest prize to salesmen who sold a specified amount of the employer's products. The IRS asserted that the employer-paid trip benefits of both taxpayer and his wife were includible in gross income as either a prize within the meaning of § 74 or as compensation under § 61(a)(1). The Tax Court held for the taxpayers. The pertinent portions of its opinion are:

> At the time of initiating the contest, DECO [the employer] decided to send one [manager] and his wife for each three contest winners. This decision was based upon the company's past experience that unguided gatherings of salesmen and distributors often turned into complaint sessions and were otherwise damaging to the company's business interests. DECO assigned four managers and their wives to the trip. They were selected by placing names in a hat and drawing out four names. A manager chosen one year was eligible the next year. Those selected to go on a particular trip received no cut in pay and did not lose vacation time. Those not chosen received no substitute benefit.

> [Petitioner] was one of the four chosen. They were instructed that they should consider the trip as an assignment and not as a vacation and that their job was to stay constantly with the contest winners, to participate in all the scheduled activities, and not to go off alone. The wives were considered essential participants in the achievements of this objective. DECO felt it would be impossible for stag salesmen to host a trip for couples.

> Petitioners performed their assigned duties, which consumed substantially all of the trip time. Neither had any spare time, as they had hoped to have, to go swimming or shopping.

> The mere fact that petitioners were selected by a random drawing does not make the trip a taxable prize or award under section 74. The method of selection was founded on a sound business reason, namely, to choose those who were to serve DECO's business objectives on a basis which would obviate any feeling of discrimination.

> Unlike the contest winners, petitioners were expected to go as an essential part of petitioner's employment. More importantly, petitioners herein were expected to devote substantially all of their time on the trip to the performance of duties on behalf of DECO in order to achieve, albeit subtly, DECO's well-defined business objectives.

> Nor do we consider it material that petitioners enjoyed the trip. Pleasure and business, unlike oil and water, can sometimes be mixed. It is noteworthy that neither of petitioners went swimming or shopping during their entire stay, two activities for which Hawaii is famous.

We hold that, under all the facts and circumstances herein, the expenses of the trip are not includable in the gross income of petitioners.

NOTES

1. We can refer to the doctrine established by *Gotcher* (and not questioned in principle by the IRS) as the "incidental benefits" doctrine. The doctrine is clearly kin to the "convenience of the employer" doctrine in the employee compensation area, where (prior to 1954) there was a strict version ("necessary to perform one's job") and a loose version ("primary noncompensatory business reason of the employer"). The court in *Gotcher* adopted the loose version in a case involving a scenario where the principal mover of the trip was not the taxpayer's employer. Where the parties are basically at arm's length, the presumption (as it were) of disguised compensation is greatly reduced.

2. (a) If Mr. Gotcher had initiated the transaction and paid for the trip himself, his costs would not necessarily have been deductible. (How would they be treated, considering that Mr. Gotcher ultimately purchased an asset?) Where the costs would not be currently deductible, then a person receiving a paid-for recruiting trip likely obtains a better tax result than one who pays for it herself. Is that doctrinally relevant? Troubling?

(b) Is lack of control a sufficient ground for exclusion? One aspect of control is the decision to accept the trip offer in the first place. Was Mr. Gotcher "forced" to accept? Would Mr. Gotcher have voluntarily undertaken to take such a trip at his own expense?

(c) Another aspect of control had to do with the details of the actual trip. Should lack of control matter with respect to clear personal-use items, such as meals? How do meals differ from air fares, lodging, and sales presentations?

(d) *Gotcher* is not an avoided-expense case; the trip was purchased and used. Nor is it a "no gain" case, because (as even the *Gotcher* majority acknowledges) receiving a free benefit is the same (in the mechanical sense) as receiving cash and then paying for the benefit. There's "no gain" only if Mr. Gotcher wouldn't have undertaken the trip himself, but this observation doesn't really add anything new to the analysis.

(e) Economists regard advertising as a valuable benefit (free information) received by viewers and hearers of advertising messages. Advertising is often blended with entertainment, as in "free" TV. This benefit is rarely provided with the disinterested motive that is required to make the § 102(a) gift exclusion applicable. See Chapter 15.A.3. Nevertheless, the IRS never has, and never will, attempt to tax individuals on the "value" of "information" received by them in the form of advertising. The IRS has never explained why this is the case, but it is probably due to the fact that the benefits to recipients of advertising information are very hard to value. Also, advertising information may not actually be free; the cost of it may be built into the prices of goods and services. Regardless of what is the rationale for the exclusion of advertising messages, can the exclusion explain why the value of Mr. Gotcher's trip was excludible from his gross income?

3.   The Fifth Circuit majority included the value of Mrs. Gotcher's trip in *Mr. Gotcher's* gross income. Nowadays, recruiting often is pitched at spouses (etc.), especially if a geographical move is involved. In that case, the recruiter is providing the benefit directly to the spouse, and the spouse should receive the same tax treatment as the "principal" recruitee.

PROBLEMS

1.   Did the contest winners in *McDonell* have to treat the value of their trip as gross income? See § 74.

2.   How did (i) Mr. McDonell's trip and (ii) Mr. Gotcher's trip differ from the trip taken by the contest winners in *McDonell*?

3.   Section 132 did not exist when the McDonells took their free trip to Hawaii. If it had been applicable:

(a) Would § 132(a)(3) and (d) operate to exclude the value of Mr. McDonell's trip from his gross income?

(b) Would Reg. § 1.132-5(t)(1) operate to exclude the value of Mrs. McDonell's trip from both her income and Mr. McDonell's income?

4.   Mr. McDonell presumably received salary compensation for the time he was in Hawaii. Would he have been able to exclude that compensation or is it different from the value of his free trip?

5.   The tax year involved in *Gotcher* was 1960. At that time, it was likely the case that Mrs. Gotcher took a vacation only when Mr. Gotcher paid for it. Assuming that is so, can you use *Old Colony*, discussed in Chapter 12, to explain why the value of Mrs. Gotcher's trip was includible in Mr. Gotcher's gross income?

6.   Sally, a third-year law student, is reimbursed by the LAX law firm in Los Angeles for the expenses incurred by her and her husband while she interviews for a job. They arrive in Los Angeles Thursday night, Sally interviews with the firm on Friday, and they both attend social functions with the firm through early Saturday afternoon. They spend the rest of Saturday and all day Sunday visiting friends, returning home Monday morning. Sally is eventually hired by LAX and starts work there the following autumn. Does Sally have income with respect to this junket on account of herself or her husband? Would Sally be able to deduct the cost of the trip if she had paid for it herself?

7.   Law professors Joseph, Cliff, and Bob attend the annual convention of the Association of American Law Schools. Their respective schools reimburse their expenses of attending the convention to the extent of the required fee, transportation, hotels, and a per-diem allowance for food. They each attend three seminar-type sessions in two days. Their publisher hosts a lavish "authors party," which the three attend. The party features an open bar, and the dinner features foie gras, lobster, and a selection of premier wines. The party is interrupted by only 7 minutes of welcoming remarks, introductions, and other pleasantries. Does any of the trio have any income as a result of these activities?

2. Free Samples

The next case involved the receipt of free samples but in an unconventional context.

HAVERLY v. UNITED STATES
United States Court of Appeals, Seventh Circuit
513 F.2d 224 (1975)

Before HASTINGS, SENIOR CIRCUIT JUDGE, SWYGERT and CUMMINGS, CIRCUIT JUDGES.

HASTINGS, SENIOR CIRCUIT JUDGE:

This case presents for resolution a single question of law which is of first impression: whether the value of unsolicited sample textbooks sent by publishers to a principal of a public elementary school, which he subsequently donated to the school's library and for which he claimed a charitable deduction, constitutes gross income.

In [1967 and 1968] publishers sent to the taxpayer unsolicited sample copies of textbooks which had a total fair market value at the time of receipt of $400. The samples were given to taxpayer for his personal retention or for whatever disposition he wished to make. The samples were provided, in the hope of receiving favorable consideration, to give taxpayer an opportunity to examine the books and determine whether they were suitable for the instructional unit for which he was responsible. In 1968 taxpayer donated the books to the school library. The parties agreed that the donation entitled the taxpayer to a charitable deduction under § 170, in the amount of $400, the value of the books at the time of the contribution.[3] The parties further stipulated that the textbooks received from the publishers did not constitute gifts under § 102, since their transfer to the taxpayer did not proceed from a detached and disinterested generosity nor out of affection, respect, admiration, charity or like impulses.

The District Court held that receipt of the samples did not constitute income. 374 F. Supp. 1041 (1974). We reverse.

The taxpayer concedes that receipt of the books does not fall within any of the specific exclusions from gross income. The only question remaining is whether the value of the textbooks received is included within "all income from whatever source derived." The Supreme Court has frequently reiterated that it was the intention of Congress "to use the full measure of its taxing power" and "to tax all gains except those specifically exempted." *James v. U.S.*, 366 U.S. 213 (1961). The Supreme Court has also held that the language of § 61(a) encompasses all "accessions to wealth, clearly realized, and over which the taxpayers have complete dominion." *Comm'r v. Glenshaw Glass Co.*, 348 U.S. 426, 431 (1955).

---

[3] [2] Since the tax year at issue in this litigation is 1968, the amount of the charitable deduction that could be taken was unaffected by [present] § 170(e)(1), which was added by the Tax Reform Act of 1969. [Eds. note: That section would have limited the deduction to the taxpayer's basis in the samples.]

There are no reported cases which have applied these definitions of income to the question of the receipt of unsolicited samples. The parties have cited to the court a number of cases applying income definitions to other fact situations. We have considered these cases, but we find them of no particular assistance in resolving the question before us. In view of the comprehensive conception of income embodied in the statutory language and the Supreme Court's interpretation of that language, we conclude that when the intent to exercise complete dominion over unsolicited samples is demonstrated by donating those samples to a charitable institution and taking a tax deduction therefor, the value of the samples received constitutes gross income. The receipt of textbooks is unquestionably an "accession to wealth." Taxpayer recognized the value of the books when he donated them and took a $400 deduction therefor. Possession of the books increased the taxpayer's wealth. Taxpayer's receipt and possession of the books indicate that the income was "clearly realized." Taxpayer admitted that the books were given to him for his personal retention or whatever disposition he saw fit to make of them.

Although the receipt of unsolicited samples may sometimes raise the question of whether the taxpayer manifested an intent to accept the property or exercised "complete dominion" over it, there is no question that this element is satisfied by the unequivocal act of taking a charitable deduction for donation of the property.

[Our] conclusion is consistent with *Rev. Rul. 70-498*, 1970-2 C.B. 6, in which the IRS held that a newspaper's book reviewer must include in his gross income the value of unsolicited books received from publishers which are donated to a charitable organization and for which a charitable deduction is taken. This ruling was issued to supersede an earlier ruling, *Rev. Rul. 70-330*, 1970-1 Cum. Bull. 14, that mere retention of unsolicited books was sufficient to cause them to be gross income.[4] The Service has apparently made an administrative decision to be concerned with the taxation of unsolicited samples only when failure to tax those samples would provide taxpayers with double tax benefits. It is not for the courts to quarrel with an agency's rational allocation of its administrative resources.

———————

The holding in *Haverly* appears to be incoherent by reason of holding that in-kind receipt (in 1967) is includible by reason of its receipt (as an accession to wealth) but includible in a year other than the year of receipt (1968).[5] This scenario raises an issue of transactional accounting of the type to be examined in Chapter 26. If an in-kind receipt isn't reported as income, the item would have a zero basis, and a double tax benefit would not normally be obtainable. However, before 1969 a double tax benefit actually was attainable in the *Haverly* scenario, because the basis of donated property was then irrelevant to the determination of the charitable

———————

[4] The District Court considered *Rev. Rul. 70-498* distinguishable from the instant case on the ground that, for the book reviewer, the books were the tools of his trade. The District Court did not explain why "tools of the trade" should be a significant factor in determining what is income, but even if it were, textbooks would seem to be a tool of the trade of being a school principal. The facts indicate that it was one of taxpayer's functions as a principal to review sample textbooks to determine their suitability for his students.

[5] In *Rev. Rul. 70-498*, the books were donated in the same year that they were received.

deduction amount. The problem in *Haverly* might have been solved by the "inconsistent events" doctrine, except that this doctrine did not appear until 1983 in the case of *Bliss Dairy, Inc. v. U.S.*, 460 U.S. 370 (1983), where the taxpayer expensed the cost of some animal feed and then distributed the feed in a corporate liquidation governed by rules that gave the distributees a basis in the feed equal to its FMV. The Court in *Bliss Dairy* held that the corporate distribution of the feed to the shareholders was inconsistent with the earlier expensing of the feed as supplies for current use in business, and the remedy was to include the expensed amount in gross income in the year of the corporate distribution. Similarly, a charitable deduction is inconsistent with treating the books for tax purposes as having not been received (or as received but offset by an equal business expense deduction).

It is quite possible that free samples are now excludible under § 132(e), relating to de minimis fringe benefits. This conclusion may seem incredulous, but note that Reg. § 1.132-1(b)(4) (1989), defines "employee" for purposes of the § 132(e) de minimis fringe benefit exclusion as "meaning *any* recipient of a fringe benefit" (emphasis added). Recall also that the statutory definition of the de minimis "fringe benefit" is any property or service "the value of which is (after taking into account the frequency with which similar fringes are provided by the employer to the employer's employees) so small as to make accounting for it unreasonable or administratively impracticable." The reference to "employee" in this quotation must be read as having the meaning given to it by the aforementioned Reg. § 1.132-1(b)(4).

NOTES

1.   (a) Just what did the *Haverly* decision hold? That free samples are gross income only if they are claimed as a charitable (or perhaps a business) deduction? That free samples are income if (and when) they are consumed (which is what the provider intends)? That free samples are always income as an accession to wealth? That free samples are probably income, but that the IRS usually doesn't try to enforce inclusion?

(b) Does § 7805(a) empower the Treasury to issue a regulation excluding items from gross income simply on the basis of administrative considerations? Is this sort of thing better handled by an IRS published revenue ruling or revenue procedure? Private letter rulings? Admissions in litigation?

2.   (a) Is the typical free sample (e.g., a small box of laundry detergent) better viewed as an accession to wealth or as consumption in kind? Does this "factual" distinction make a doctrinal difference?

(b) How does the "dominion and control" notion play out in the free sample scenario? The taxpayer has the "personal" options to use it, put it on the shelf, or to throw it into the trash. Should the choice matter from a tax point of view? Note that it is a choice that the IRS would be unable to monitor.

3.   (a) Are free textbook samples received by teachers excluded under the *Gotcher* doctrine, because the point is for the publisher to obtain an adoption as a required or recommended text?

(b) Is *Haverly* a "realization" case, on account of the charitable donation? Would there be realization if the teacher doesn't adopt the book but uses it to prepare lessons or to do research?

(c) Was there anything to the taxpayer's "tools-of-the-trade" argument?

PROBLEM

PalmCoast Properties offers a free expenses-paid one-week trip to their new beachside condo development in Honduras (in an area aptly known to locals as the "Mosquito Coast"). The developers provide meals in the club house. Sales pitches are discreetly limited to relatively short periods during or around meals. Movies are shown, preceded by a promotional "short" extolling the qualities of the development. Is the value of this trip income?

Part Five

WEALTH TRANSFERS

Wealth transfers raise both income and deduction issues under an income tax. Wealth transfers received by individuals did not fit comfortably within early 20th century views of income as recurring receipts that were the product of labor or capital. Indeed, business accounting treated nonrecurring receipts as nonincome, and under trust accounting rules gratuitous receipts were "principal" (corpus) and not income. However, traditional views were given a jolt when Henry Simons claimed that all accessions to wealth, including gratuitous receipts, were income under an ideal personal income tax.

A gratuitous transfer, on the transferor's side, does not fit the traditional deductibility-issue distinction between costs of producing income and personal consumption. "Consumption" literally means the using up or destruction of material resources, which is not the case with a gratuitous transfer, whether to an individual or to a charity.

In this Part Five, Chapter 14 deals with tort recoveries (the classic nongratuitous wealth transfer) and other windfall receipts, Chapter 15 with gratuitous transfers to individuals, Chapter 16 with contributions to charities, and Chapter 17 with income-shifting arrangements effected through gratuitous transfers, trusts, and otherwise.

Chapter 14

RECOVERIES FOR PERSONAL INJURY AND OTHER WINDFALL RECEIPTS

Tort recoveries entail a transfer of wealth mandated by law on an ad hoc basis. This chapter is mainly concerned with § 104(a), which excludes from gross income various kinds of recoveries for personal injury or sickness, whether by way of damages, litigation settlements, accident or health insurance, or worker compensation. Health insurance often covers only the costs of medical care arising from personal injury or sickness. The tort system (supplemented by liability insurance) can compensate not only for medical costs but also for lost wages, lost earning capacity, pain and suffering, and emotional distress, plus punitive damages. Thus, the most wide-ranging part of § 104 is subsection (a)(2), which covers damages and damage settlements, but only for *physical* personal injury or sickness. The last section of this chapter covers windfall gains other than litigation (or insurance) recoveries.

A. HISTORY AND POSSIBLE RATIONALES OF SECTION 104

This section examines the history of § 104(a), with particular emphasis on subsection (a)(2), and its possible justifications in theory and policy.

1. Background: Recoveries in Commercial Litigation

In the very early days of the income tax there was debate over whether "income" was limited to "periodical" income and gains (such as wages, rent, ordinary business profits, interest, etc.), thereby excluding "irregular," "nonrecurring," and "extraordinary" gains. Indeed, the notion that income was limited to periodical income was then current in business accounting. However, doubts as to whether the 16th Amendment prohibited Congress from taxing nonperiodic gains were soon removed by the decision in *Merchants' Loan & Trust Co. v. Smietanka*, 255 U.S. 509 (1921), holding that an investor's capital gain from a single, isolated sale is income under the 16th Amendment.

Damage recoveries are not a specifically listed category of gross income under § 61 or any of its predecessors. Hence, the inclusion of such damages had to be dealt with under general tax principles applicable to income or gain. Damages and settlement proceeds from *commercial* litigation were treated, in the early days of the income tax, as follows:

(1) Recoveries of lost income or profits were includible ordinary income. See, e.g., *Armstrong Knitting Mills v. Comm'r*, 19 B.T.A. 318 (1930); cf. *Burnet v.*

Sanford & Brooks Co., 282 U.S. 359 (1931) (damages for misrepresentation of costs involved in carrying on contract work).

(2) Recoveries for property losses were treated as if they were an amount realized in a § 1001 sale or disposition, i.e., as gross income only to the extent the recovery exceeded the basis of the damaged or destroyed property. See *Raytheon Production Co. v. Comm'r*, 144 F.2d 110 (1st Cir.), *cert. denied*, 323 U.S. 779 (1944).

(3) Punitive damages were treated as non-income because they were not considered to be the yield of the taxpayer's capital or labor. See *Highland Farms Corp. v. Comm'r*, 42 B.T.A. 1314 (1940). (This result was not overthrown until 1955. See *Glenshaw Glass*, infra subsection 4.)

2.   Personal Injury Recoveries from Inception to *Glenshaw Glass*

In the very early years of the income tax, it was not clear whether *personal injury* recoveries were income, first, because they (for a given taxpayer) were nonrecurring, and, second, because they were not the product of capital or labor. Congress somewhat eliminated this uncertainty in 1918 by enacting a provision that excluded "amounts received . . . as compensation for personal injuries or sickness, plus the amount of any damages received whether by suit or agreement on account of personal injury."[1] (The word "physical," which is now part of § 104(a), did not appear in the 1918 version of the statute.)

Notwithstanding the 1918 enactment, the possible nonstatutory basis for exclusion continued to evolve. In *Solicitor's Opinion 132*, I-1 C.B. 92 (1922), the IRS considered three kinds of tort recoveries that it then regarded as outside the scope of "personal injury" under the 1918 statute, namely, (1) libel and slander, (2) alienation of affections, and (3) parting with custody of a minor child. It was held that none of these recoveries were income on the theory that, since none of the rights involved could have been sold in the market, damage recoveries for their loss could not yield gain or profit. Of course, this rationale is unconvincing today, because (1) damage recoveries for a lost right amount to a disposition for consideration in the form of money,[2] and (2) gain or loss is measured with reference to basis (not value). But the central role of basis was perhaps not fully appreciated in 1922, and basis is not mentioned in *Solicitor's Opinion 132*. This error was repeated in *Hawkins v. Comm'r*, 6 B.T.A. 1023 (1927), where the Board of Tax Appeals held that, although *Eisner v. Macomber* was not controlling, damages for libel and slander were not income on the ground that the very concept of compensation ("to make the plaintiff whole as before the injury") negated profit. The Board failed to note that this kind of argument was rejected by the Supreme Court as early as 1913 in *Stratton's Independence v. Howbert*, 231 U.S. 399 (1913),

---

[1] The 1918 legislative history expressed doubt as to whether tort recoveries are income within the 16th Amendment. See H.R. Rep. No. 767, 65th Cong., 2d Sess. 9-10 (1918). The enactment of the predecessor of § 104 came shortly after an opinion by the U.S. Attorney General, 31 Op. Atty. Gen. 304, 308 (1918), that an accident insurance recovery for lost human capital was not income.

[2] Cf. *Roosevelt, Jr. v. Comm'r*, 43 T.C. 77 (1964) (grant of waiver of future privacy and publicity rights for consideration gave rise to gross income without basis offset).

holding that gain was to be measured with reference to cost (basis), not the value of what was given up. In any event, the rationales of *Solicitor's Opinion 132* and *Hawkins* rendered the 1918 predecessor of § 104(a)(2) superfluous and irrelevant, except perhaps with respect to recoveries of lost wages.

3.   Dubious Internal-to-Tax Exclusionary Theories

Tort recoveries sometimes (or to some degree) are recoveries of lost *human capital* (earning capacity). As noted in Chapter 9, human capital has no measurable basis, and does not yield depreciation or loss deductions against wage income. Thus, the exercise of human capital yields gross income (such as wages) without any basis recoveries.[3] A personal injury that produces a recovery is just another way in which human capital is converted to cash, somewhat like earning wages from a miserable or degrading job.

An early doctrinal rationale for excluding recoveries of human capital was the "replacement of capital" theory. In the very early days of the income tax, it was thought that "capital" equated with "original endowment," and it was assumed that a person's human capital was a subcategory of original endowment, and that damages for lost human capital merely replaced that endowment and did not constitute gain. However, this notion was demolished (if indirectly) in *Taft v. Bowers*, 278 U.S. 470 (1929), where the donee of an in-kind gift (another type of endowment) argued that the Constitution required that he have a basis equal to the fair market value of the gift property on its receipt. The fair market value at the time of the gift would be the donee's "starting point" in figuring future economic gain or loss. The Court held that the statutory rule (carrying the donor's basis over to the donee, i.e., a carryover-basis rule) controlled and was valid under the 16th Amendment. This holding undermined the notion that a taxpayer's endowment could not be taxed, because the effect of the carryover-basis rule upheld in *Taft* was to eventually tax part of that endowment to the donee. For example, if the donor had purchased land for $24K that was worth $100K when given to the donee, and the donee later sold the land for $100K, the donee would be taxed on the $76K gain that constituted part of the donee's endowment (received from the donor). If endowment is not wholly immune from tax, then a replacement of that endowment cannot also be wholly immune from tax. Once the replacement-of-capital notion is eliminated, then "capital" always equates with basis (which is zero in the case of human capital).

Another theory hinted at in the early authorities but not clearly articulated is the "in lieu of" theory. The theory was not only delineated, but actually embraced (in 2006!), in *Murphy v. IRS*,[4] where a panel of the D.C. Circuit held that a recovery of emotional distress damages (not excluded under § 104(a)(2), which requires a physical injury) was not income under the 16th Amendment, because the damages were in lieu of a non-income good (emotional normalcy). After a good deal of hostile commentary, the panel withdrew its opinion (!) and held that, even if the damages weren't "income" under the 16th Amendment, they were taxable as

---

[3] See *Roemer v. Comm'r*, 716 F.2d 693, 696 n.2 (9th Cir. 1983).

[4] 460 F.3d 79 (D.C. Cir. 2006).

"income" under the catch-all clause of § 61(a), and that the resulting tax was valid under the "indirect tax" power granted by the 1789 Constitution.[5]

The initial *Murphy* decision was an aberration in many respects, one of which was to misapply the "in lieu of" doctrine. That doctrine was never a "theory" or "rationale" for anything, and certainly not a ground for income exclusion. It was only a "test" for determining the tax "character" of litigation settlement proceeds, as either (a) ordinary gross income, (b) excluded income under a recognized statutory exclusion,[6] or (c) an amount realized with respect to a disposition of property.[7] It had never been used to hold that cash income was really not income of any kind by reason of replacing psychic normality. Since all income can be traced to psychic phenomena,[8] the income tax would collapse under the misapplication by the first *Murphy* opinion of the "in lieu of" notion![9]

Another theoretical angle is to view a tort recovery as the fruit of an involuntary occurrence. However, the involuntariness of an accession to wealth does not ipso facto mean that it is not income. Whether involuntariness warrants "tax relief" is up to Congress. For example, Congress has chosen to make involuntariness a ground for tax relief only in the case of involuntary conversions of property covered by § 1033.[10]

4.   *Glenshaw Glass*

The early case of *Eisner v. Macomber*, 252 U.S. 189 (1920), had declared that "income may be defined as the gain derived from capital, from labor, or from both combined, provided it be understood to include profit gained through a sale or conversion of capital assets." The *Macomber* definition implied that a gain not derived from the taxpayer's capital or labor is not income. The lower courts in *Glenshaw Glass*, below, held that punitive damages received in commercial litigation were not income under the *Macomber* definition on account of not being derived from capital or labor. In the decision below, the Supreme Court not only reversed but sent the *Macomber* definition to the junkpile .

---

[5] In *Stadnyk v. Comm'r*, 2010-1 USTC (CCH) ¶50,252 (6th Cir. 2010), the Sixth Circuit rejected all of the *Murphy* reasoning and held that personal injury recoveries are income within the meaning of the 16th Amendment.

[6] See *Lyeth v. Hoey*, 305 U.S. 188 (1938) (holding that amounts received pursuant to a settlement of a bona fide will contest were an "inheritance" excluded under § 102).

[7] See *Raytheon Production Co. v. Comm'r*, 144 F.2d 110 (1st Cir.), *cert. denied*, 323 U.S. 779 (1944).

[8] For example, interest is compensation for the frustration of having to wait for the return of money, and wages are compensation for foregoing leisure.

[9] See generally, Joseph M. Dodge, Murphy *and the Sixteenth Amendment in Relation to the Taxation of Non-Excludable Personal Injury Awards*, 8 FLA. TAX REV. 369 (2007).

[10] Section 1033 is discussed in Chapter 24.D.1.

COMMISSIONER v. GLENSHAW GLASS CO.
United States Supreme Court
348 U.S. 426 (1955)

Mr. Chief Justice Warren delivered the opinion of the Court.

The question is whether money received as exemplary damages for fraud or as the punitive two-thirds portion of a treble damage antitrust recovery must be reported by a taxpayer as gross income. It is conceded by the respondents [the taxpayers] that there is no constitutional barrier to the imposition of a tax on punitive damages. Our question is one of statutory construction: are these payments comprehended by § 22(a) of the 1939 Code? The sweeping scope of the controverted statute is readily apparent:

§ 22. Gross income

(a) General definition. "Gross income" includes gains, profits, and income derived from salaries, wages, or compensation for personal service of whatever kind and in whatever form paid, or from professions, vocations, trades, businesses, commerce, or sales, or dealings in property, whether real or personal, growing out of the ownership or use of or interest in such property; also from interest, rent, dividends, securities, or the transaction of any business carried on for gain or profit, or gains or profits and income derived from any source whatever . . . .

Respondents contend that punitive damages, characterized as "windfalls" flowing from the culpable conduct of third parties, are not within the scope of the section. But Congress applied no limitations as to the source of taxable receipts, nor restrictive labels as to their nature. And the Court has given a liberal construction to this broad phraseology in recognition of the intention of Congress to tax all gains except those specifically exempted. The importance of that phrase has been too frequently recognized since its first appearance in the Revenue Act of 1913 to say now that it adds nothing to the meaning of "gross income."

Nor can we accept respondents' contention that a narrower reading is required by the Court's characterization of income in *Eisner v. Macomber*, 252 U.S. 189, as "the gain derived from capital, from labor, or from both combined." In that context — distinguishing gain from capital — the definition served a useful purpose. But it was not meant to provide a touchstone to all future gross income questions.

The question raised by the instant case is clearly distinguishable. Here we have instances of undeniable accessions to wealth, clearly realized, and over which the taxpayers have complete dominion. Respondents concede, as they must, that the recoveries are taxable to the extent that they compensate for damages actually incurred [in the form of lost profits]. It would be an anomaly that could not be justified in the absence of clear congressional intent to say that a recovery for actual damages is taxable but not the additional amount extracted as punishment for the same conduct which caused the injury.

It is urged that re-enactment of § 22(a) without change since the Board of Tax Appeals held punitive damages nontaxable in *Highland Farms Corp.*, 42 B.T.A.

1314, indicates congressional satisfaction with that holding. Re-enactment — particularly without the slightest affirmative indication that Congress ever had the *Highland Farms* decision before it — is an unreliable indicium at best. Moreover, the Commissioner promptly published his non-acquiescence in the *Highland Farms* holding and has, before and since, consistently maintained the position that these receipts are taxable. It therefore cannot be said with certitude that Congress intended to carve an exception out of § 22(a)'s pervasive coverage.

Reversed.

MR. JUSTICE DOUGLAS dissents. MR. JUSTICE HARLAN took no part in the consideration or decision of this case.

One of the reasons *Glenshaw Glass* is of interest is its approach to the issue of statutory construction. Is the term "income" in the catchall phrase of § 61(a) to be construed according to "original (1913) intent," its "plain meaning," or as a definition borrowed from another discipline? The majority opinion in *Glenshaw Glass* did not even discuss its interpretive approach, but implicitly the majority rejected both the "original intent" and "other discipline" definitions of "income. The majority's accession-to-wealth idea is clearly linked to the term "income" (literally "coming in," or, in German, "einkommen"). Thus, the *Glenshaw Glass* approach is "textually based" but "open-ended," meaning that its meaning can change over time (as, indeed, it *had* changed over time since 1913).

The obvious import of *Glenshaw Glass* is that it abolished the *Macomber* source-based definition of gross income but without also doing away with the realization principle.

5.   Evolution of § 104(a)(2) from 1955 to the Present

Solicitor's Opinion 132 implied that the three categories of "dignitary harms" discussed therein were not covered by the § 104(a)(2) exclusion (although this was irrelevant at the time because the Opinion held that recoveries for these harms were not income in the first place). This 1922 Opinion perhaps indicates that § 104(a)(2) was originally thought of primarily in terms of recoveries for *physical* (personal) injury. The overthrow of the *Eisner v. Macomber* definition of income by the 1955 *Glenshaw Glass* decision rendered *Solicitor's Opinion 132* obsolete. The IRS then seems to have taken the position that the various nonphysical injury recoveries considered in *Solicitor's Opinion 132* were now covered by the § 104(a)(2) exclusion,[11] which until *Glenshaw Glass* had been largely ignored as

---

[11]   *Rev. Rul. 74-77*, 1974-1 C.B. 33, held that amounts received as damages for alienation of affections or surrender of custody of a child were not income. No mention was made of § 104, but the ruling states that it supersedes *Solicitor's Opinion 132* "since the position stated therein is set forth under the current statute," and *Rev. Rul. 74-77* was published in the portion of the Cumulative Bulletin devoted to interpretations of § 104. *Rev. Rul. 74-77* was subsequently declared obsolete by *Rev. Rul. 98-37*, 1998-2 C.B. 182 pursuant to an IRS program of identifying rulings that "are no longer considered determinative because: (1) the applicable statutory provisions or regulations have been changed or repealed; (2) the ruling position is specifically covered by a statute, regulation or subsequent published position; or (3) the

being superfluous. The courts also got into the act by expanding the § 104(a)(2) concept of "personal injury" to encompass all damages arising from violations of "tort-type" personal rights, whether or not involving a physical injury. Thus, in *Roemer v. Comm'r*, 716 F.2d 693 (9th Cir. 1983), libel and slander damages were held to be within § 104(a)(2). The broad construction of § 104(a)(2) by the lower courts extended to employment-based claims (where much of the recovery consisted of back wages) arising under federal anti-discrimination statutes. Moreover, the issue of whether the phrase "any damages" in § 104(a)(2) covered punitive damages in personal injury litigation was regarded as an unsettled question.

The Supreme Court put the brakes on this expansion of § 104(a)(2) in three cases decided in the 1990s, all based on the notion that damages (the remedy) had to be "on account of personal injury or sickness." In *U.S. v. Burke*, 504 U.S. 229 (1992), the Court held that the back-pay remedy under a federal anti-discrimination suit was not a tort-type remedy giving rise to a recovery excludible under § 104(a)(2). *Comm'r v. Schleier*, 515 U.S. 323 (1995), held that the liquidated damages award under the federal age discrimination law was not "on account of personal injury." Basically, these cases hold that purely economic damages suffered on account of wrongful discharge do not make the § 104(a)(2) grade. In *O'Gilvie v. U.S.*, 519 U.S. 79 (1996), the Court held that punitive damages are not excludible under § 104(a)(2) because they do not compensate for personal injury.

In 1996, Congress stepped in to further curb the scope of § 104(a)(2) by (1) explicitly stating that the exclusion does not extend to punitive damages and (2) by limiting the exclusion to recoveries for *physical* personal injury or sickness. However, there is an exception to the "physical injury" requirement in the case of damages paid to compensate for the medical treatment of emotional distress. See the last two sentences in the flush paragraph of § 104(a).) In addition, § 104(c) allows "punitive" damages to be excluded in the case of wrongful death claims if governing state law labels all such recoveries as being punitive.

As to the significance of the insertion of the word "physical," the 1996 Conference Report (104th Cong., 2d Sess.141-44), states:

> The House bill provides that the exclusion from gross income only applies to damages received on account of a personal physical injury or physical sickness. If an action has its origin in a physical injury or physical sickness, then all damages (other than punitive damages) that flow therefrom are treated as payments received on account of physical injury or physical sickness whether or not the recipient of the damages is the injured party. For example, damages (other than punitive damages) received by an individual on account of a claim for loss of consortium due to the physical injury or physical sickness of such individual's spouse are excludable from gross income. In addition, damages (other than punitive damages) received on account of a claim of wrongful death continue to be excludable from taxable income as under present law.

---

facts set forth no longer exist or are not sufficiently described to permit clear application of the current statue and regulations."

The House bill also specifically provides that emotional distress is not considered a physical injury or physical sickness.[12] Thus, the exclusion from gross income does not apply to any damages received (other than for medical expenses) based on a claim of employment discrimination or injury to reputation accompanied by a claim of emotional distress. Because all damages received on account of physical injury or physical sickness are excludable from gross income, the exclusion from gross income applies to any damages received based on a claim of emotional distress that is attributable to a physical injury or physical sickness. In addition, the exclusion from gross income specifically applies to the amount of damages received that is not in excess of the amount paid for medical care attributable to emotional distress.

The "physical injury" requirement only exists under subsection (a)(2) of § 104.

To date, the most definitive IRS guidance regarding the meaning of physical injury is in *PLR 200041022* (July 17, 2000), which states that "direct unwanted or uninvited physical contacts resulting in observable bodily harms such as bruises, cuts, swelling and bleeding are personal physical injuries" and that damages for sexual harassment and touching that did not involve any of these physical manifestations were not excludible under § 104(a)(2). In *Stadnyk v. Comm'r*, 2010-1 USTC (CCH) ¶50,252 (6th Cir. 2010), the court held that damages for false imprisonment involving handcuffing and eight hours of physical confinement were not excludible under § 104(a)(2) and stated that "a false imprisonment claim may cause a physical injury, such as an injured wrist as a result of being handcuffed. But the mere fact that false imprisonment involves a physical act — restraining the victim's freedom — does not mean that the victim is necessarily physically injured."

B. TAXES AND TORT POLICY

Since it is hard to square the § 104(a)(2) exclusion with income tax norms, one might look to relevant external-to-tax policy, with specific reference to tort policy, which has a "compensation" aspect, a "deterrence" aspect, and an (economics) aspect of internalization of social costs.

The "compensation" aspect of tort policy is to make injured parties whole. Since a tort involves an injury or destruction to zero-basis human capital, all compensatory damage recoveries (including pain-and-suffering damages) are akin to wages. In the case of recoveries for lost earning capacity (a form of human capital), the recovery could be a lump-sum amount equal to the present value of the lost future wages (which is then invested in an annuity), or it could take the form of an annuity. Either way, the annuity (a series of future payments, usually of a fixed dollar amount) would mimic the future wage stream. In order to evaluate the effect of tax law on the ability of such tort recoveries to "make victims whole," we would want to know how tort recoveries are determined before the tax system comes into play.[13]

---

[12] [56] It is intended that the term emotional distress includes physical symptoms (e.g., insomnia, headaches, stomach disorders) which may result from such emotional distress.

[13] The majority state law rule is that tort damages are to be computed before tax. See RESTATEMENT

If actually earned in the labor market, wages would (of course) be gross income subject to tax. There are numerous possible combinations of (1) damages-computation rules, (2) payout schemes (lump sum vs. annuity), and (3) tax rules (applicable to both lump sum recoveries and annuities). It turns out that the § 104 exclusion is compatible with full compensation of the victim under several combinations of these factors, but the easiest combination (that is compatible with § 104) to grasp (without a lot of arithmetic) is the one where the recovery takes the form of an annuity stream, and where each annuity payment is the expected gross wage reduced by the expected *hypothetical* income tax thereon. In this case, an "implicit tax" is imposed at the stage of computing the damages recovery. The same (full compensation) result can be obtained if damages are computed before the hypothetical tax thereon, and then the damages are included in gross income. Thus, if the taxpayer would have obtained gross wages of $100K over 3 years, and the tax rate is 30%, the same compensatory result is obtained by (a) setting damages at $70K a year and excluding the same from gross income, or (b) setting the damages at $100K a year and including the same in gross income.

This equivalence of these two combinations creates bargaining opportunities that undermine both tax and tort policy. Using the preceding numbers, if the § 104(a)(2) exclusion is available, plaintiff, who suffered a loss of $100K of before-tax gross wages that would have been taxed at 30%, and defendant, who inflicted a $100K injury, might settle for less than $100K but more than $70K, say $80K, excludible under § 104(a)(2). This would overcompensate the plaintiff by $10K because she would have had only $70K after tax if the wages had been earned. And this settlement would reduce the amount of damages the defendant would have to pay from $100K of lost wages to the $80K settlement amount. On these facts, the benefit of the § 104(a)(2) exclusion would be partially captured by the defendant so that it would not have to pay the full social cost ($100K) of its anti-social behavior. Thus, the § 104(a)(2) exclusion undermines two prongs of tort policy (deterrence and internalization of social cost), while not being at all necessary to carry out the third (compensation) function.[14] And as shown above, § 104(a)(2) can even result in overcompensation.

Since both plaintiffs and defendants benefit by the § 104(a)(2) exclusion, there is no group that has a direct interest in seeing it repealed.

C.   SECTION 104 IN OPERATION

In order to discern what § 104(a)(2) actually "does," think about the possible components of a physical personal injury damage award and how they would be (properly) treated in the absence of § 104(a)(2). Suppose, for example, Sara Surgeon is run over by a drunk driver, and her hand is so badly damaged that it must be amputated, destroying her established career. She sues the driver, who was insured,

---

(SECOND) OF TORTS § 914A(2) (1977). The rule for federal torts is the opposite (recoveries are to be computed after tax). See *Norfolk & Western Ry. V. Liepelt*, 444 U.S. 490 (1980).

[14] A more elaborate analysis of the interaction of tax law and personal injury law is contained in Joseph M. Dodge, *Taxes and Torts*, 77 CORNELL L. REV. 143 (1992).

and receives as damages a lump sum of $1M. The component parts of that $1M award might include the following:

(a) a recovery for medical expenses (which would have been deductible, subject to the applicable percentage of AGI floor);

(b) a recovery for earnings lost between the time of the accident and the judgment award (which would have been taxable if actually earned and received);

(c) a recovery for future lost earning capacity (the "yield" of which would have been taxable when earned in the future);

(d) a recovery for "pain and suffering" (a taxable accession to wealth under *Glenshaw Glass*); and

(e) punitive damages (a taxable accession to wealth per *Glenshaw Glass* that punishes the tortfeasor and does not compensate for any injury).

Thus, a significant amount, perhaps all, of this award would be taxable in the absence of § 104(a)(2). Section 104(a)(2), however, provides that all of these categories are excludible, since Sara's injury was a physical one, with the exception of (1) punitive damages, and (2) recoveries of medical expenses deducted in prior years under § 213.[15]

What portion of a recovery will be allocated to the includible (or excludible) components? Any allocation of damages in a verdict will usually be honored. If there is no allocation in a verdict, or if the damages are obtained by way of settlement, the IRS takes the position that any lump-sum recovery is allocable "first" to previously deducted medical expenses before being allocated to anything else. See *Rev. Rul. 75-230*, 1975-1 C.B. 93. As to punitive damages, an allocation made in a settlement agreement may be followed, but only if it can be shown that the allocation was made at arm's length.[16] However, since both parties usually prefer not to allocate any portion of the settlement to punitive damages,[17] it may be hard to show that the allocation was truly at arm's length.[18] In that case, the IRS has announced that it will ordinarily allocate the settlement amount to punitive damages in the same ratio that the complaint requested punitive damages relative to total damages, at least in the absence of better evidence pertaining to the allocation. See *Rev. Rul. 85-98*,

---

[15] Recoveries of previously deducted medical expenses fall within the lead-in clause of § 104(a): "Except in the case of amounts attributable to (and not in excess of) deductions allowed under § 213 . . . , gross income does not include . . . ." This rule prevents a double tax benefit (exclusion and deduction) with respect to the "same" dollars. Also, any portion of the recovery constituting pre-judgment interest, which is not compensation for any injury, would be included in income. See *Brabson v. U.S.*, 73 F.3d 1040 (10th Cir. 1996); *Kovacs v. Comm'r*, 100 T.C. 124 (1993).

[16] See *Delaney v. Comm'r*, T.C. Memo. 1995-378.

[17] The victim desires to avoid characterization as punitive damages for tax reasons. The defendant is indifferent for tax reasons, since punitive damages are generally no less deductible than compensatory damages, but typically doesn't want to admit that its conduct was culpable. Also, insurance typically does not cover punitive damages.

[18] See *Bagley v. Comm'r*, 121 F.3d 393 (8th Cir. 1997) (disregarding settlement that allocated nothing to punitive damages); *Robinson v. Comm'r*, 102 T.C. 116 (1994), *aff'd on this issue*, 70 F.3d 34 (5th Cir. 1995) (Tax Court looked to underlying facts in absence of an allocation).

1985-2 C.B. 51. "Better evidence" can involve re-trying the tort case in the tax forum.

Any tax-free recovery under § 104(a)(2) maintains its wholly tax-free status, even though it is payable by the perpetrator or its insurer in installments. An installment pay-out (basically, an annuity for a term of years or until the plaintiff reaches a certain age) is called a "structured settlement," and the wholly tax-free status thereof is obtained by the § 104(a)(2) parenthetical language: "whether as lump sums or as periodic payments."

The other subsections of § 104(a) deserve brief mention. Section 104(a)(1) allows exclusion of workers' compensation payments made because of personal injury. Section 104(a)(3) allows exclusion of amounts received under a health insurance policy paid for by the taxpayer, regardless of whether the amount received exceeds actual expenditures for health care. (If, however, such amounts are received by an employee under an employer health plan, the excludible portion is limited, under § 105(b) and (c), to reimbursements or payments for actual health care costs or with respect to certain permanent disabilities.[19]) Section 104(a)(4) allows exclusion of certain disability and personal injury payments made to members of the military and certain other public employees. Finally, § 104(a)(5) allows exclusion of disability income received as a result of injuries incurred in a terrorist or military attack.

D. LEGAL FEES INCURRED TO OBTAIN DAMAGES

An individual plaintiff pursuing a personal injury claim on her own behalf will incur attorneys' fees and other costs in securing damages. Since most attorney compensation in this context is on a contingency-fee basis, the brunt of the plaintiff's costs would be paid, in effect, out of the award itself. The IRS has always treated these outlays as current "expenses" (deductible, or not, under the "expense" provisions), rather than "capital expenditures" creating basis in the award which would operate as an "offset" in arriving at a "net" award amount. (Of course, the lawyer must include the fee in gross income as compensation, whatever the treatment to the payor.) Even litigation costs paid in advance have always been treated by the IRS (without analysis) as "expenses," rather than "capital expenditures" that create basis, except in cases covered by *Woodward v. Comm'r*, supra Chapter 7.C.1.

If the claim arises out of the taxpayer's business (say, for breach of contract), legal "expenses" would be deductible under § 162(a). In a personal injury case, however, the relevant Code provision for deducting legal expenses is § 212(1), which allows deduction of "expenses . . . for the production or collection of income." However, § 265(a)(1), discussed in Chapter 8, disallows otherwise-allowable deductions that are allocable to tax-exempt income (such as the excludible portion of a physical personal injury recovery).

What does "allocable" (to tax-exempt income) mean in this context? The IRS takes the position that, if a recovery comprises both § 104(a) excluded amounts

---

[19] The employer's premium payments for employee health insurance are generally excluded from the employee's gross income under § 106(a).

(such as compensatory damages for a physical personal injury) and nonexempt amounts (such as punitive damages), any related expenses are to be apportioned between the exempt and non-exempt components of the recovery on a pro rata basis, and only the expense amount allocable to the included portion is deductible under § 212. See *Rev. Rul. 85-98*, 1985-2 C.B. 51. So, for example, if Sara Surgeon, whose hand was injured by the drunk driver, receives a jury award of $1M in compensatory damages and $500K in punitive damages, she would include in gross income only the $500K punitive damages. What if she pays her lawyer one half of her gross $1.5M award (i.e., $750K) under a contingent fee contract? Under the rules discussed thus far, since only one third of her award is includible in gross income, only one third of her lawyer's fee ($250K) is deductible under § 212(1).

But, unfortunately, the story doesn't end there. The deductible portion of attorneys' fees could be effectively disallowed as a "miscellaneous itemized deduction" (MID) by reason of being a § 212 deduction, because MIDs are added back to the AMT tax base, and may well end up generating tax under the AMT. See § 56(b)(1)(A)(1). In order to try to avoid those results, plaintiff advocates took the position that a taxable damages award simply did not include the amount that went to the plaintiff's attorneys. That is, the argument was that the attorney fee was earned directly by the attorney and is never income to the plaintiff, so that the plaintiff has no deduction issue to deal with. One theory was that attorney lien statutes in some states created a property interest for the lawyer in the portion of the claim that was assigned to the lawyer under the contingent fee contract. Another theory was that a contingent fee contract creates a partnership between the plaintiff and the attorney, so that the fee is the attorney's partnership "share" of the damage recovery. The Supreme Court rejected both of these theories in *Comm'r v. Banks*, 543 U.S. 426 (2005), holding that an attorney is inherently an agent of the client (who is the sole owner of the claim) and receives compensation from the client, who is (therefore) regarded as the recipient of the full damage recovery.

Congress responded by enacting § 62(a)(20), which provides that an "expense" deduction (whether under § 212 or 162) for attorneys' fees incurred by plaintiffs in connection with certain listed discrimination actions (such as suits under the Civil Rights Act, the Age Discrimination in Employment Act, and the Americans with Disabilities Act), certain claims against the government, and certain actions brought under the Medicare Secondary Payer statute, can now be taken "above the line," thereby avoiding MID status. However, instances will occur in which includible personal injury damages, such as common law defamation damages or punitive damages, do not arise under one of the listed federal statutes. As a result, not all plaintiffs will obtain relief under § 62(a)(20).

NOTES

1. In *Banks*, an amicus brief argued that the attorney's fee in question should properly be viewed as a capitalized offset against amount realized, like a transaction cost. The Supreme Court did not reject this argument but rather decided not to reach the merits of it because the argument was "presented for the first time to this Court." The Court continued: "We are especially reluctant to entertain novel

propositions of law with broad implications for the tax system that were not advanced in earlier stages of the litigation and not examined by the Courts of Appeals. We decline to comment on these supplemental theories." Thus, the possibility remains that this capitalized-transaction-cost argument can be developed in the lower courts in future cases not covered by § 62(a)(20).[20]

2.   Section 265 does not interfere with a successful plaintiff's use of a tax-free damages award to pay costs of her business that would otherwise be deductible under § 162. For example, suppose an individual plaintiff receives $10K in damages on account of physical personal injury and uses that cash to pay salary expenses of employees in her business. If the requirements of § 162 are met, the plaintiff would be able to deduct the full $10K of salary costs. Section 265(a)(1) disallows deductions for expenses of *producing* tax-exempt income. The deductible business salary costs did not produce the tax-exempt income. To generalize, tax-exempt income (or borrowed money) can be *expended* in a deductible fashion without running afoul of § 265(a)(1). If the rule were otherwise, expenses would have to be traced to sources. That would be practically impossible, as cash is fungible, and would operate as a trap for the unwary.

3.   Damages (and settlement) *payments* are governed by the usual deduction rules, except that § 162(g) disallows any deduction for two-thirds of treble damage payments under certain antitrust law violations. Civil punitive damages are not payable to a government and, therefore, are not nondeductible fines within the meaning of § 162(f).

4.   (a) It has been argued that a structured settlement of excludible damages (i.e., a settlement amount payable in installments) results in an unjustified receipt of tax-exempt interest by tort plaintiffs receiving excludible damages. The argument begins by positing that the "norm" of a damages recovery is a lump sum. If an excludible lump-sum recovery (equal to the present value of future wages) were invested in an annuity, the investment return on the annuity would be included in income. Therefore, since a structured settlement takes the form of an annuity, it should be considered to be (and be taxed as if it were) an investment by the plaintiff in an annuity. The opposing argument is that the norm for damages for a lost future wage stream is the wage stream itself. (The law of some states actually insists on structured settlements in certain personal injury cases.) A structured settlement, therefore, has the effect of maintaining the victim in a human-capital (wage-earning) mode. Since the investment-of-a-lump-sum model deviates from this norm, it should not be followed. The policy dispute here is whether the taxpayer should be treated as being an investor (by reason of having acquired a right to a future payment stream that can be reduced to present value) or as having received a substitute for a wage stream.

(b) A related issue is whether structured settlements would occur in the absence of favorable tax rules. The main obstacle to structured settlements in the past was the absence of security for deferred-payment promises. That problem has been

---

[20] This position is developed in Joseph M. Dodge, *The Netting of Costs Against Income Receipts (Including Damage Recoveries) Produced by Such Costs, without Barring Congress from Disallowing Such Costs*, 27 VA. TAX REV. 297 (2007).

remedied by the emergence of businesses that specialize in funding structured settlements.

PROBLEMS

1.   Isabelle is fired from her job in Year 1 and sues for race-based discrimination in violation of Title VII. She receives $500K in damages, consisting of $480K in past and future wages, $10K in reimbursement of past and future psychological counseling costs for the depression that followed her termination, and $10K for the depression itself. Is any of the award includible in Isabelle's gross income?

2.   In Year 1, Paul was seriously injured by a defective chain saw that bounced off a rock and severed Paul's right arm. Paul sued Chain Saw, Inc., for compensatory damages of $10M (including lost earning capacity, lost wages, and pain and suffering) and punitive damages of $90M. Paul paid $100K of uninsured medical expenses in Year 1, $90K of which exceeded the § 213 floor and thus were fully deductible under § 213. Chain Saw does not have liability insurance coverage.

(a) Paul proved at trial that $100K of wages were lost between the accident date and the time of trial, and that he suffered $750K in lost earning capacity. Paul also proved that he experienced pain, suffering, and depression. In Year 3, the jury awarded $2M compensatory damages and $1M punitive damages. Paul's attorney collected $1M out of the $3M total. What results to the parties?

(b) Same as above, except that the parties are ready to settle before trial. The defendant offers a present lump-sum payment of $450K. Give tax advice to Paul.

(c) If Paul's wife had recovered $5K for loss of consortium during Paul's stay in a hospital and in a rehabilitation facility, could she exclude any of this amount under § 104(a)(2)?

3.   One night Fred Fan was in a crowded sports bar with friends. He loudly stated that the reason their city's NFL team had a losing record was that the quarterback was an incompetent coward who was afraid of being hit. Fred weighs 130 pounds. The quarterback in question, who weighs 230 pounds, was sitting at the next table and heard Fred's remarks. The quarterback pulled Fred out of his chair into a standing position and began shoving him across the room while loudly calling him a "gutless wimp" and daring him to resist. Fred quickly found himself pushed into a corner. For several minutes, the quarterback loudly taunted Fred and physically restrained him from leaving the corner. Finally the quarterback spat on Fred and left the bar. Fred was never punched, he suffered no meaningful physical pain, and no detectable marks on his body resulted from this incident. Everyone in the bar laughed at Fred and he quickly left. He sued the quarterback for battery, false imprisonment, and emotional distress. The suit was settled by the quarterback paying Fred $50K and issuing a public apology. To what extent is Fred's recovery excludible from gross income?

E. OTHER WINDFALLS

The punitive damages considered in *Glenshaw Glass* were characterized as a "windfall." A "windfall gain" can be described as an increase in wealth that does not occur in a market transaction (such as finding a valuable object while stolling the beach). Since *Glenshaw Glass* held that a market transaction is not a prerequisite to inclusion in the case of § 61(a) catch-all income (which encompasses windfalls), there can be little doubt that a windfall receipt of cash is gross income, because a cash receipt is both under the taxpayer's control and is realized.

In the case of in-kind windfalls (usually in the form of tangible personal property), the issue is whether the item is included immediately at its fair market value or whether inclusion is deferred to a subsequent realization event. The law is somewhat undeveloped in this area. It is not clear whether the undeveloped state of the law results from (a) the fact that the IRS simply is not aware of most noncash windfall receipts that occur, (b) an administrative practice of the IRS (as with free samples) to generally decline to assert immediate inclusion, possibly on the ground that, if the item is worth a substantial amount, it will be sold eventually (with the entire amount realized being taxed on account of the taxpayer having a zero basis), or (c) uncertainty on the part of the IRS as to what the law actually is.

What might give pause to the IRS is the doctrine that a person engaging in the economic activity of collecting, harvesting, or obtaining the bounty of nature (by hunting, fishing, agriculture, mining, or forestry) is not treated as having realized income upon the catching, harvesting, cutting, or extraction of property. In these cases, income is not realized until the subsequent sale.[21] Although the taxpayer in these cases "invests" in the activity of obtaining property, the acquisition of the natural resources at a value in excess of (or less than) the investment is not a realization event. Similarly, an arm's length purchase of property in the market at substantially below its value (a rare occurrence) is not a realization event. These points are developed further in Chapter 22.A, D.1. However, it is possible that the IRS considers cases in which there is an investment in the activity or transaction to be distinguishable from true windfalls, where something is obtained essentially for nothing.

Instances can be noted in which realization is deemed to occur upon the acquisition of a windfall item. Reg. § 1.61-14, which specifically deals with catch-all income, requires inclusion of treasure trove when the item is "reduced to undisputed possession." By implication, finding an object whose "possession" is disputed leaves the taxpayer without dominion and control, or perhaps the income is not "realized" until possession ceases to be disputed. (Acquiring legal title is not a prerequisite to having gross income. See *James v. U.S.*, 366 U.S. 213 (1961), holding that an embezzler has income, notwithstanding lack of any legal right to the embezzled funds.)

The term "treasure trove" is not defined for tax purposes, but in the law of personal property the term usually refers to coins buried under abandoned Roman

---

[21] See Joseph M. Dodge, *Accessions to Wealth, Realization of Gross Income, and Dominion and Control: Applying the "Claim of Right Doctrine" to Found Objects, Including Record-Setting Baseballs*, 10 Fla. Tax Rev. 685 (2000).

villas in England. In Reg. § 1.61-14, the term must certainly mean currency (if not necessarily legal tender), and, by extension, gold or silver ingots or bullion. See *Cesarini v. U.S.*, 428 F.2d 812 (6th Cir. 1970) (money found in old piano is income when obtained). These items can be described as cash or the near-equivalent thereof. However, Reg. § 1.61-14 states no general rule for in-kind windfalls, and, other than treasure trove, refers only to punitive damages (*Glenshaw Glass*) and illegal gains (*James*), both entailing the receipt of cash.

Beyond the foregoing, little authority exists with respect to in-kind windfalls. In *Collins v. Comm'r*, T.C. Memo. 1992-478, the taxpayer (a racetrack employee) was held to have had income by reason of printing out pari-mutuel tickets and betting them for his own account on the same day. In *Rev. Rul. 70-498*, 1970-2 C.B. 6, the IRS held that free books received (and donated to a library in the same year) are gross income. In both of these cases the in-kind income was realized upon in the same taxable year as the year of acquisition, although in unorthodox ways.

There appears to be no case holding that the acquisition of real property by adverse possession is gross income at the time the statute of limitations bars an action for recovery by the original owner. Similarly, although there are numerous cases requiring inclusion when money is stolen, embezzled, or extorted, it appears that no case has clearly held that a thief has income upon the stealing of personal property.[22] The activities of a professional thief of valuable personal property might be analogized to a fishing business, and the thief might plausibly argue that the deferred realization rule applies. But deferred realization poses a problem for objects appropriated (lawfully or not) for personal use, where a future sale at a gain is not anticipated in the foreseeable future.

Later personal use or consumption probably does not itself count as deferred realization in this context. In *Morris v. Comm'r*, 9 B.T.A. 1273 (1928) (acq.), the value of self-grown crops was held not to be gross income, even though the crops were consumed by the taxpayer. See also Reg. § 1.61-4(a) and (c). However, *Morris* might be distinguished on the ground that it dealt with imputed income from self-provided services.

Keep in mind that this discussion relates to catch-all income. In-kind receipts that fall within iterated categories of income (compensation, prizes and awards, interest, dividends, rents, etc.) that arise from market transactions or commercial relationships are generally treated as income when acquired. Also keep in mind that a failure by the taxpayer to include windfall property in income results in the taxpayer having a zero basis in the item. (Issues raised by the forfeiture or re-transfer to the legal owner of windfall gains of items that have previously been included in income are dealt with comprehensively in Chapter 26.B.8.)

To conclude, if the law and practice with respect to in-kind windfalls lacks clarity, there is no doubt that Congress has the power to clarify matters to its liking or that

---

[22] A casual reading of *Vasta v. Comm'r*, T.C. Memo. 1989-531, might appear to be to the contrary. There a drug dealer was caught and forfeited to the government not only a large amount of cash but also some heroin and cocaine. But it is not clear from the opinion whether the value of the drugs was directly included in gross income. That would seem unlikely, as the drugs had been purchased before the forfeiture.

the Treasury could issue regulations requiring that some or all in-kind windfalls (in addition to treasure trove) be immediately included in catch-all income. Even in the absence of regulations, it is possible that an IRS examiner faced with such a case of this type might require a thief (say) to include the value of the in-kind stolen property in gross income for the taxable year of its acquisition, and a court might well agree.

PROBLEMS

1. Jolly Roger is a treasure seeker who searches for wrecked Spanish ships carrying gold bullion. Roger rents a boat, hires a crew, and soon finds what he's looking for off the coast of Honduras. The treasure consists mainly of bullion, but there are some other items (such as jewelry) that might be coveted by museums. Roger has removed the treasure to Key West, where it awaits sale, except for some jewelry, which Roger has given to his wife. Does Roger have income, and (if so) when? Does the result hinge on whether Spain, Honduras, or any other possible claimant shows up to claim all or part of the treasure?

2. Connie is an avid New York Yankees fan. At one game, it happens that star player Sol Sonnenschein strokes his 3,000th career base hit, a home run, which Connie catches. The ball has considerable value on the auction market for baseball memorabilia, but both Sol and the Baseball Hall of Fame would like to have it. State the likely tax result if:

(a) Connie keeps the ball as an "investment." Would the result be altered if the New York Yankees baseball club claims legal ownership of the ball and threatens to take Connie to court to obtain it? (Ignore other possible claimants, such as Major League Baseball.)

(b) Connie, a Sol Sonnenschein fan, realizes the importance of the ball to Sonnenschein and returns the ball to him after the game. Would the result be altered if Sonnenschein, as a conscientious employee, accepts on behalf of the New York Yankees? (Assume that no "gift" issue is raised by these facts.)

(c) Connie is contacted by other interested parties, and returns the ball to the New York Yankees, who in return awards Connie season tickets in a prime location for the next five years, along with lots of baseball paraphernalia autographed by Sonnenschein.

Chapter 15

GRATUITOUS TRANSFERS

This chapter deals with the income taxation of receipts in the form of gifts, bequests, and inheritances (§ 102), government welfare payments, life insurance proceeds (§ 101), survivor benefits outside of life insurance policies, and prizes and scholarships that were formerly dealt with under § 102. These items are collectively referred to as "gratuitous transfers" and are not (except perhaps the last item) the yield from the recipient's own labor or investment capital. There is also material on criminal tax fraud worked into the "gift" material.

Recall from Chapter 1 the existence of separate federal taxes on gifts, estate transfers, and generation-skipping transfers, collectively known as the "federal wealth transfer taxes" (or, more colloquially, as the "estate and gift tax"). These taxes are separate and apart from the income tax, and wealth transfer tax rules and results rarely have any relevance to income tax!

A. TAXING GRATUITOUS TRANSFERS UNDER THE INCOME TAX

This section deals with the structural aspects of the taxation of gratuitous transfers (gifts, bequests, and inheritances) to the transferee and the transferor.

1. The Statutory Pattern

Gratuitous receipts (gifts, bequests, and inheritances) are excluded from gross income under § 102(a), but at the same time they are not deductible by the donor or decedent.

a. Exclusion for Gratuitous Receipts

Beginning in 1913, the federal income tax has expressly provided that gross income does not include the receipt of gifts, bequests, devises, and inheritances. See § 102(a). Although there is no legislative history that expressly offers a rationale for the exclusion, enough is known to permit some informed speculation.

In the early 20th century, income tax theory was undeveloped. Consequently trust and business accounting principles filled the vacuum and heavily influenced the federal income tax. Trust law treated gifts and bequests into a trust as "trust principal" that could not be distributed to trust beneficiaries who were designated to receive "income." This arrangement fit neatly into the then "fruit and tree" metaphor used to distinguish "capital" (principal) from "income." The "tree" was the representation of the principal, which periodically produces "fruit," or income. The fruit and tree metaphor was easily extended to nontrust transactions, so that original endowments of all kinds, including nontrust gratuitous receipts, were considered "tree," not "fruit." Business accounting in the early 20th century adopted a similar approach because transfers of endowment were irregular and shed little light on the likelihood that a business would prosper as an ongoing enterprise. Accordingly, business trust accounting (like trust accounting) came to view all irregular receipts as non-income. A third strand of thinking, macro-economics, reinforced this attitude. Macro-economics views national income (GDP) as being the "product" (yield) of capital or labor. In terms of the economy as a whole, transfers[1] of all types are not viewed as adding anything to GDP, because they merely move wealth around without producing anything.

The notion that income excluded the receipt of transfers generally (not just gratuitous transfers) took hold as a doctrinal principle in the early days of the income tax, most notably as a result of the early decision in *Eisner v. Macomber*, 252 U.S. 189 (1920), which stated:

> Income may be defined as the gain derived from capital, from labor, or from both combined, provided it be understood to include profit gained through a sale or conversion of capital assets.[2]

In accord with this statement was the earlier holding of *Gould v. Gould*, 245 U.S. 151 (1917), which held that cash alimony received was not income (a result that was partially overturned by the later enactment of § 71, as described in Chapter 5.B). This way of thinking was further reinforced in the 1925 case of *Edwards v. Cuba Railroad Co.*, 268 U.S. 628 (1925), which held that a nonshareholder contribution to the capital of a railroad corporation, in the form of a subsidy by the government of Cuba to build railroad beds and track, was not gross income to the corporation. Indeed, under the *Macomber* approach, the predecessor of the § 102(a) exclusion for gifts, bequests, devises, and inheritances would have been redundant, because gratuitous receipts were not gain from the recipient's capital or labor.

The *Macomber* definition reigned supreme until the 1955 case of *Comm'r v. Glenshaw Glass Co.*, 348 U.S. 426, set forth in Chapter 14.A.4. *Glenshaw Glass* stakes out an independent concept of income for income tax purposes (as opposed to the income concepts as used in other disciplines). *Glenshaw Glass* also aligns the tax concept of income with the notion of a *personal* income tax,[3] which was advanced by Henry Simons in his 1938 book titled *The Personal Income Tax*. A personal income tax looks to the individual taxpayer's net realized increase in wealth over the taxable year (as opposed to whether the item increases the nation's economic output). After *Glenshaw Glass*, § 102(a) acquired independent significance, because in its absence gratuitous receipts fit the *Glenshaw Glass* income concept.

---

[1] By "transfer," we mean a redistribution of wealth from one party to another. This includes gratuitous transfers but also encompasses damages, insurance payouts, welfare payments and taxes other than user fees.

[2] This statement wasn't harmless dictum, because the holding of the case was that a corporation's pro rata distribution of its own stock to existing shareholders did not represent realized economic yield, but was a portion of the "tree."

[3] See supra Chapter 2.A.

The persistence of § 102(a) is probably explainable by (1) the lack of any serious move (or constituency) for repealing it, (2) political inertia (people were so used to the exclusion that it seems to be a part of the natural order of things), (3) political resistance by those who benefit by its persistence, and (4) the enactment of the federal wealth transfer taxes, which are excise taxes on wealth transfers, whether or not the wealth has been "subject to" the income tax in the hands of the transferor. However, there is no doctrinal connection between the income tax and the wealth transfer taxes, which impose a tax on the *value* of gratuitous wealth transfers (of fruit or tree). Moreover, the wealth transfer taxes have such large exemptions that they reach only a small portion of gratuitous transfers. Thus, it is not persuasive to argue that something should be excluded from gross income because it will (or may) be subject to transfer tax in the future.

b.   Nondeductibility of Gratuitous Transfers

The existence of § 102 does not mean that gratuitous transfers avoid income tax completely. Since inter vivos gratuitous transfers are personal or family expenses or losses, they are not deductible by the transferor. (In contrast, charitable gifts, considered in Chapter 16, are generally deductible.) The notion that a *decedent* could obtain an income tax deduction for transmitting her net wealth by bequest or inheritance is absurd, because an individual taxpayer ceases to exist by reason of death and cannot be said to have parted with anything during her existence. Since gratuitous transfers are not deductible, they are after-tax to the transferor. One way of looking at the matter is that a person in a 35% marginal income tax rate bracket would have to earn $154 in order to have $100 left over, after paying a tax thereon of $54 (= .35 x $154), to make the gift.

The alternative system of requiring the donee to include in income cash gifts, bequests, and inheritances *and* allowing a deduction by the donor would move the tax burden from the donor to the donee. This would allow the shifting of income from higher-tax-bracket to lower-tax-bracket family members at will. By opting instead for the exclusion/no-deduction approach illustrated above, Congress has decided to leave the tax burden on the donor. (More sophisticated devices to shift income are examined in Chapter 17.)

Another alternative approach would require the donee's inclusion of gratuitous receipts while prohibiting deduction by the donor. This regime would tax the gift twice under the income tax, but to two different people, and could be justified on ability-to-pay principles: the wealth of the transferee is increased, and the transfer is an "exercise" of the transferor's ability to pay (command over economic resources).

Despite a common intuition to the contrary, there is no "general" principle that the same dollars cannot be taxed to two different taxpayers. For example, suppose a lawyer uses $100 of wages from her job as an associate in a law firm to pay a housecleaner $100 for cleaning her home. The earnings of the lawyer are included by her under § 61(a)(1), the $100 she pays to her housecleaner from those earnings are also includible as wages by the housecleaner under § 61(a)(1), and the lawyer is prohibited from deducting the payment to the housecleaner because it is a personal consumption expense. Thus, both the lawyer and the housecleaner are taxed on the

$100. But if the lawyer, instead, gives $100 to a friend as a birthday gift, only the lawyer is taxed on that $100; no tax is paid by the recipient because of § 102(a). It would not be outrageous to align the gift scenario with the housecleaner scenario, but such a change is very unlikely to occur.

The current rules applicable to gratuitous transfers align with the rules governing the provision of support (apart from § 71 alimony). In both cases, the transfer is nondeductible and the receipt is excludible by the transferee. Thus, it is not necessary for the income tax system to police the borderline between gifts and support.[4]

2.   Transfers In-Kind

If a gift, bequest, or inheritance is in the form of property other than cash, additional considerations come into play.

a.   Income from Gratuitous Transfers

Suppose that Mother gives Daughter income-producing property — stock worth $1,000 — on which $20 in dividends is paid after the gift but before Daughter sells the stock. Can Daughter exclude the $20 in dividends received on the stock before she sells by arguing that they are included within the excludible gift? The answer is "no." Section 102(b)(1) states that the exclusion does not extend to the income earned on the property Daughter received by gratuitous transfer. The same rule applies to gain that is realized after the gratuitous transfer. If the rule were otherwise, all property could be made to generate future tax-exempt income or gain simply by being gratuitously transferred to a cooperative family member or friend!

What about a gift of an "income right" only? For example, suppose that Mother's will provides that unimproved rental property (Blackacre), worth $100K at Mother's death, is to pass to Daughter for her life, with the remainder interest passing to Granddaughter. That is, Mother makes a "split gift," in which the right to the rents passes to the Daughter for life and the right to the "principal" (the remainder interest) passes to the Granddaughter. Essentially, these were the facts in the 1925 case of *Irwin v. Gavit*, 268 U.S. 161. There, the taxpayer in the Daughter's position argued that she could exclude the trust income under the predecessor to § 102(a), but the Supreme Court held otherwise, noting that the Daughter's income was generated by a "property interest" that passed at death from the Mother, that the rents were post-death income ("fruit") from this property interest, and that the Granddaughter obtained the excludible property interest (the "tree") by reason of receiving the remainder interest. To have held in favor of the Daughter would have meant that the exclusion could be "replicated" by creating a succession of income interests. The holding of *Irwin v. Gavit* did not entail the loss of the § 102(a) exclusion, however. Instead, the case meant that there was a single exclusion and it inured entirely to the remainder recipient.

---

[4] Under the federal gift tax, however, this boundary is significant, because "support" is not a gift for gift tax purposes.

Most successive-interest gifts and bequests are in fact made to trusts, which (in a general sort of way) produce tax results similar to those reached in *Irwin v. Gavit*. That is, (1) the initial gift or estate transfer is tax-free to the trust, and (2) the post-transfer income is taxed to the trust or the trust beneficiaries. The rules for allocating post-transfer income to the various eligible taxpayers are discussed in Chapter 17.E.[5]

b.   Gratuitous Transfers Are Not Gain or Loss Recognition Events

Conceivably, the transferor (or her estate) could be held to recognize gain or loss on a gratuitous transfer of in-kind property. To illustrate, assume that Pops purchased shares of stock for $1K, which are now worth $3K, and Pops is considering giving the shares to Sonny. To the extent of Pops' $1K adjusted basis, Pops has already paid income tax on the stock, because basis is, generally speaking, a record dollars previously subject to tax. Congress could presumably require transferors of gifts, bequests, and inheritances to "realize" built-in gains (or losses) under § 1001 at the time of transfer (producing a $2K gain on the stock in Pops' case), but it has thus far declined to do so.

Conversely, in the absence of a specific Code provision on point, it certainly appears that a gift is literally a "disposition" of property and hence a realization event under § 1001, and, since the "amount realized" by the donor is zero, a realized loss would appear to be the result. Under this approach, Pops would have a $1K deductible loss in the preceding hypothetical. But the tax system cannot allow taxpayers to manufacture loss deductions for themselves simply by making gifts of high-basis property to friends and relatives. So, in fact, no loss deduction is allowed by Pops, even though there is no Code section or regulation specifically blocking it. The most probable explanation for this vacuum is that, even if the loss is realized, it is not deductible under § 165(c) because the decision to make the gift negates any business or profit motive of Pops. Thus, Pops has no allowable deduction on the gift transfer of the stock.

c.   Basis Rules

In the Pops-Sonny example, Sonny's in-kind gratuitous receipts are (of course) excluded from his gross income under § 102(a). But basis rules found in §§ 1014, 1015, and 1041 determine the extent to which this exclusion results in permanent tax forgiveness or merely tax deferral.

Section 1014 provides that the basis of the party receiving a decedent's property (the estate, heir, legatee, or other recipient of property included in the decedent's gross estate for estate tax purposes) equals the estate tax value of the property — in most cases, the fair market value at the date of decedent's death.[6] This rule has the effect of totally exempting built-in gain from income tax. Thus, if Pops dies at

---

[5] Indeed, in the early days of the income tax, the predecessor of Subchapter J (dealing with the taxation of trusts) was actually part of the predecessor of § 102.

[6] Valuation for estate tax purposes is beyond the scope of this book, but we can note that the estate tax is imposed on the fair market value of the property at the decedent's death. Although the value for

a time when the stock is worth $3K, and the shares pass to Sonny under Pop's will, Sonny takes a $3K basis (commonly referred to as a "stepped-up basis") in the shares under § 1014. If Sonny were to sell the shares immediately for $3K, he would realize no gain or loss. Thus, *the $2,000 in appreciation is never subject to income tax.*

Section 1014(b)(6) provides that the § 1014 basis rule applies to all property held as community property by husband and wife as of the decedent spouse's death, even though the surviving spouse's half interest in the community property was owned by the surviving spouse all along and is not acquired by the surviving spouse from the deceased spouse at (or by reason of) the deceased spouse's death. This rule gives a significant income tax benefit to couples (and their successors) in community property states.

The basis-equals-value-at-death rule is, however, a two-way street. If Pops' property in the Pop's-Sonny example were worth only $750 on his date of death, the $750 basis that Sonny would take in the property under § 1014 (sometimes called a "stepped down" basis) would prevent him from ever realizing and deducting the built-in loss of $250. Nevertheless, because there is much more gain property than loss property (due in part to the effects of inflation), and because informed owners of loss property may sell it before death to avoid the result described here, much more gain than loss is wiped out each year by § 1014, causing significant revenue losses for the Treasury.[7]

How did the basis-equals-value-at-death rule come about? History provides the answer. The 1913 income tax law contained only one basis rule, namely, that "basis equals cost." This rule would give Sonny a zero basis for the shares in the preceding example because he paid nothing for the property. If Sonny then sold the shares for their $3K date-of-death fair market value, he would effectively realize $3K of gain, contrary to the aim of § 102(a) to exclude the $3K from Sonny's income. Thus, application of a cost basis rule would indirectly eviscerate the § 102(a) exclusion. The Treasury, under pressure to find some way to preserve the integrity of the § 102(a) exclusion, promulgated an early regulation adopting a basis-equals-value-at-transfer rule. This rule was codified in 1918 and originally applied to all gratuitous transfers of property, including inter vivos gifts. It was immediately recognized, however, that this rule, insofar as it applied to gifts, gave living individuals the opportunity to periodically remove gain from the reach of the income tax by making inter vivos gifts to relatives and friends, perhaps with the same property passing back and forth between the same two individuals over time. To preclude this behavior, § 1015, applicable to property acquired by *inter vivos* gift, was enacted in 1921.

The first sentence of § 1015(a) (up to "except that") provides that the donee of an inter vivos gift succeeds to the donor's basis. This kind of rule in tax parlance is called a "carryover basis" rule, but is now officially referred to by the Code as a "transferred basis" rule. See § 7701(a)(43). Returning to the Pops-Sonny example,

---

estate tax purposes fixes § 1014 basis, the basis concept has no relevance whatsoever under the estate tax.

[7] Because the estate-included property is more likely to have increased in value than to have decreased in value, § 1014 is often referred to as the "stepped-up basis rule."

but now assuming that Pops transfers the appreciated shares to Sonny by inter vivos gift, Sonny takes a $1K basis under § 1015(a), instead of a $3K basis under § 1014. In effect, the $2K of built-in gain is shifted from Pops to Sonny. Thus, by reason of the basis rule in § 1015(a), section 102(a) works as a permanent exclusion for Sonny only to the extent of the $1K basis and as a deferral rule with respect to the $2K of built-in gain.

Now consider the case where the basis for inter vivos gift property exceeds the value at the date of gift (i.e., the property has a built-in loss). The "except that" clause in § 1015(a) states that, *for purposes of computing loss* (realized by the donee), the donee's basis shall be the fair market value of the property at the date of gift. Thus, if Mom has stock with a basis of $10K and makes a gift of it to DeeDee when the stock is worth $7K, and DeeDee sells the stock for $5K, then DeeDee has a loss of only $2K, because in this situation DeeDee's basis is $7K (instead of Mom's basis of $10K). This rule, which effectively wipes out Mom's $3K pre-gift loss for income tax purposes, is aimed at preventing a low-bracket donor from shifting a built-in loss to a higher-bracket donee, even though, as described above, built-in gains can be shifted from higher-bracket donors to lower-bracket donees.

But what if DeeDee sells the property for $8K? The "except that" clause of § 1015(a) provides that for purposes of calculating loss, DeeDee's basis is $7K. Since her amount realized is $8K, a $7K basis would not produce a loss, but instead would produce a gain. However, the $7K basis can't be used for calculating gain; its use is expressly confined to computing loss. To calculate gain, it would seem that DeeDee should use Mom's $10K basis per the portion of § 1015(a) preceding the "except that" clause. But no gain would result if the basis were $10K and the amount realized only $8K. Does it follow that DeeDee's sale of the stock for $8K results in both zero loss and zero gain? That is exactly the correct result. See Reg. § 1.1015-1(a)(2).

If DeeDee sells the stock for $11K, her basis is $10K, which is carried over from Mom, because the fair market value ($7K) basis is used only for calculating loss. Thus, in this fact scenario, she would have a $1K gain on the sale of the stock.

Transfers between husband and wife, by gift, sale, or otherwise during marriage or, if after marriage, incident to a divorce, are *always* governed by the pure carryover/transferred basis rule of § 1041(b), rather than § 1015. See § 1015(e). Therefore, the transferee spouse takes the transferor spouse's basis for purposes of determining *both gain and loss*.

NOTES

1.   (a) Under an ability-to-pay fairness norm, gratuitous receipts are accessions to wealth that should be included in the tax base of the recipient sooner (the fair market value on receipt) or later (by giving in-kind gratuitous receipts a zero basis). If we compare a nonworking heir receiving $100K a year to a hardworking person earning the same amount in wages, it seems unfair that the former should bear no tax burden at all. Moreover, a gratuitous transfer is a personal use of wealth that should not generate a deduction for the transferor. And a deduction would be an impossibility in the case of bequests and inheritances because a transferor-decedent

is outside the income tax system. Thus, there is a plausible case for double taxation of gratuitous transfers, although such double taxation is highly unlikely to ever be enacted by Congress.

(b) A possible rationale for the exclusion of intra-family support was that in many cases, the payor was spending money (exercising command over material resources) in a way that only benefitted the support obligee by coincidence, as in the case of expenditures to provide a residence for the obligor in which the obligee also lives. Alternatively, the identity of the obligee (as a taxpayer) is subsumed into the obligor (to the extent of the support), as evidenced by the fact that the obligor effectively obtains the obligee's personal exemption. It is hard, however, to extend these rationales to gifts of investment property, business interests, and significant amounts of cash, and the rationale is even harder to extend to bequests. It is sometimes said that the § 102 exclusion treats the donor and donee as a single taxpayer, but that is just a fancy way of describing the *effect* of § 102(a), as opposed to being a justification of it. The very act of transferring material endowment to another is a social recognition of the independent status (autonomy) of the transferee.

(c) External-to-tax arguments in favor of § 102 are similar to those made against the federal transfer taxes. For example, it is argued that taxing the transferee would (under the "substitution effect") cause the wealthy to increase consumption and decrease savings. But if savings are motivated by a "bequest target amount," then (under the "income effect") savings should increase to compensate for the added taxes. Other motivations for savings (retirement security, a Midas complex, dedication to a business, or personal austerity) would be indifferent to taxes on the recipient of gratuitous transfers.

(d) There is little political constituency for repealing § 102 (or § 1014), because the benefits of doing so (possibly lower taxes for everyone else) are (if they are understood at all) perceived as being too indirect and diffuse. That the constituency for retaining these benefits is potent is evidenced by the near permanent repeal of the estate tax in 2001 (that ultimately only took in effect only for estates of decedent's dying in 2010), and the reduced potency of the transfer taxes in 2011 and 2012 due to higher exemptions ($5 million per transferor) and lower rates (35%) than was the case previously.

(e) Under the present system, the income tax simply ignores gratuitous transfers, as well as the provision of intra-family support, except for the basis rules (and, of course, rules pertaining to the taxation of trusts, etc.).

(f) It is sometimes claimed that the existence of the federal transfer taxes justifies the present income tax exclusions resulting from §§ 102(a) and 1014. But the federal estate tax applies only to net estates (after reduction by debts and qualified marital and charitable transfers) in excess of a very high threshold ($5 million for decedents dying after 2010 and before 2013, or $10 million per married couple). Less than 1% of decedents' estates would pay any federal estate tax under such high exemption levels. Nevertheless, the § 1014 rule benefits all appreciated property acquired from a decedent, whether or not the decedent's estate pays any federal estate tax. An estate tax on a portion of the net wealth of only the very few cannot justify an income tax exemption for all.

2. (a) Under present law, capital loss (and other excess loss) carryforwards expire at a decedent's death. This approach is consistent with § 1014, because loss carryforwards represent the excess of costs over values, and therefore are analogous to the excess of basis over value, which the fair-market-value-at-date-of-death basis rule in § 1014 causes to disappear from the income tax system.

(b) Canada, in the early 1970s, replaced its wealth transfer taxes with a system under which built-in gains and losses are recognized at death (or gift). If such a system were introduced in the United States, tax favoritism (say, for transfers to spouses or of interests in family businesses) could take the form of nonrecognition of gain or loss coupled with a carryover basis. Unused loss carryovers would not be lost under such a system.

(c) Another alternative to § 1014 is an across-the-board carryover basis system. Such a system was enacted in 1976 but retroactively repealed in 1981. Obviously, a carryover basis system requires keeping basis records for long periods of time. A horrendously complex carryover basis system actually does apply to property acquired from a decedent dying only in 2010, assuming that the estate executor elects not to have the estate tax apply. See § 1022. The executor can, in the alternative, allow the estate tax to apply (even if it does not generate a tax), in which case the basis will be determined under § 1014.

3. The constitutionality of the § 1015 transferred basis rule was litigated in *Taft v. Bowers*, 278 U.S. 470 (1929). There the taxpayer argued that the 16th Amendment concept of income *required* a fair-market-value basis for property obtained by inter vivos gift. The Court instead accepted the government's argument that, since Congress could tax the donor on the built-in gain if the donor sold the property, it should not be disempowered from using the carryover basis mechanism to tax the donee on the same (built-in) gain when the donee later sells the property. *Taft* undermines the claim that a taxpayer's material endowment is not "income" within the 16th Amendment. *Taft* also stands for the proposition that Congress can decide how to attribute income between (or among) taxpayers, provided at least that income exists in the first place.

4. Section 1015(d)(6) provides that the basis of property acquired by gift is to be increased (but not in excess of the fair market value of the property at the time of gift) by the amount of any federal gift tax paid "on" any built-in gain. But large gift tax exclusions and deductions mean that the donor who actually incurs a federal gift tax is a rare bird. Consequently, the examples in the text above illustrating the operation of § 1015 omit this nuance.

PROBLEMS

1. Laura purchased stock for $10K, and it is now worth $25K. Laura has a terminal illness and asks you for tax advice. Do you advise her to:

(a) sell the stock now and make a gift or bequest of the net cash proceeds to her contemplated legatee Sam,

(b) make a gift of the stock in kind now to her contemplated legatee Sam, or

(c) hold onto the stock until death and bequeath it to Sam?

2. Same as 1, except that Laura purchased the stock for $20K, and it is now worth $15K.

3. What Is a Gift?

The Internal Revenue Code does not contain a definition of "gift," "bequest," etc. Fortunately, gratuitous transfers between family members seldom raise any problems of qualification for the § 102(a) exclusion. Transactions outside the family, or transactions inside the family that resemble commercial transactions, can cause difficulty, however.

COMMISSIONER v. DUBERSTEIN
United States Supreme Court
363 U.S. 278 (1960)

MR. JUSTICE BRENNAN delivered the opinion of the Court.

[The taxpayer, Duberstein, was president of a corporation that purchased goods from another firm, whose head was Berman. Over the course of time, Duberstein passed on to Berman information about other potential customers. Berman gave Duberstein a Cadillac automobile and deducted the cost as a business expense. Duberstein excluded the value of the Cadillac as a "gift." The Tax Court held that this transfer was not a "gift" and that the car's value had to be included in gross income. The Sixth Circuit reversed. In the companion case, *Stanton v. U.S.*, the taxpayer received $20,000 cash as a "gratuity" upon resigning as comptroller of a church, which was almost equal to his annual salary. There was testimony that Stanton had done a good job and was well liked. The district court, sitting without a jury, held the receipt to be a gift, but the Second Circuit reversed.]

We are of the opinion that the governing principles are necessarily general, and that the problem is one which, under the present statutory framework, does not lend itself to any more definitive statement that would produce a talisman for the solution of concrete cases. The statute does not use the term "gift" in the common-law sense, but in a more colloquial sense. This Court has indicated that . . . if the payment proceeds primarily from "the constraining force of any moral or legal duty," or from "the incentive of anticipated benefit" of an economic nature, *Bogardus v. Comm'r*, 302 U.S. 34 (1937), it is not a gift. And conversely, "where the payment is in return for services rendered, it is irrelevant that the donor derives no economic benefit from it." *Robertson v. U.S.*, 343 U.S. 711 (1952). A gift in the statutory sense, on the other hand, proceeds from a "detached and disinterested generosity," *Comm'r v. LoBue*, 351 U.S. 243 (1956); "out of affection, respect, admiration, charity or like impulses." *Robertson*, supra. And in this regard, the most critical consideration, as the Court was agreed in the leading case here, is the transferor's "intention."

The Government says that this "intention" of the transferor cannot mean what the cases on the common-law concept of gift call "donative intent." With that we are in agreement. The Government derives its test [that gifts should be defined as

"transfers of property made for personal as distinguished from business reasons"]
from such propositions as the following: That payments by an employer to an
employee, even though voluntary, ought, by and large, to be taxable; that the
concept of a gift is inconsistent with a payment's being a deductible business
expense; that a gift involves "personal" elements; that a business corporation
cannot properly make a gift of its assets. We think that these propositions are not
principles of law but rather maxims of experience. Some of them simply represent
truisms; it doubtless is, statistically speaking, the exceptional payment by an
employer to an employee that amounts to a gift. Others are overstatements of
possible evidentiary inferences; it is doubtless relevant to the overall inference that
the transferor treats a payment as a business deduction. The taxing statute does
not make nondeductibility by the transferor a condition on the "gift" exclusion.

Decision of the issue presented in these cases must be based ultimately on the
application of the fact-finding tribunal's experience with the mainsprings of human
conduct to the totality of the facts of each case. The nontechnical nature of the
statutory standard, the close relationship of it to the data of practical human
experience, and the multiplicity of relevant factual elements, with their various
combinations, creating the necessity of ascribing the proper force to each, confirm
us in our conclusion that primary weight in this area must be given to the
conclusions of the trier of fact. This conclusion may not satisfy an academic desire
for tidiness, symmetry and precision. But we see it as implicit in the present
statutory treatment of the gift exclusion.

One consequence is that appellate review must be quite restricted. Where a jury
has tried the matter upon correct instructions, the only inquiry is whether it cannot
be said that reasonable men could reach differing conclusions on the issue. Where
the trial has been without a jury, the judge's findings must stand unless "clearly
erroneous."

A majority of the Court is in accord with the principles just outlined. And,
applying them to the *Duberstein* case, we are in agreement that it cannot be said
that the conclusion of the Tax Court was "clearly erroneous." It seems to us plain
that, as trier of the facts, it was warranted in concluding that the transfer of the
Cadillac was at bottom a recompense for Duberstein's past services, or an
inducement for him to be of further service in the future. [The Court reversed the
Court of Appeals.] As to *Stanton*, we are in disagreement. To four of us, it is critical
here that the District Court as trier of fact made only the simple and unelaborated
finding that the transfer in question was a "gift." There must be further
proceedings in the District Court looking toward new and adequate findings of fact.

Five other Justices wrote opinions. Justices Frankfurter and Harlan concurred
in the result of *Duberstein* but would have affirmed in *Stanton* (holding the transfer
to be "not a gift"), Justice Frankfurter presciently stating: "What the Court now
does sets fact-finding bodies to sail on an illimitable ocean of individual beliefs and
experiences. This can hardly fail to invite, if indeed not encourage, too individualized
diversities in the administration of the tax law." Justice Frankfurter would have
created a rebuttable presumption that business-context transfers are not gifts.
Justice Whittaker concurred in the result in both cases. Justices Black and Douglas

would have held for the taxpayer in both cases.

The *Stanton* case on remand was again won by the taxpayer, and the Second Circuit affirmed by applying the *Duberstein* review standard (such as it is).[8]

Recall that Berman claimed a deduction for the gift of the Cadillac but that the Supreme Court held that the deduction claim did not automatically preclude Duberstein from claiming the § 102(a) exclusion. Congress in 1962 responded to this aspect of the *Duberstein* case by enacting § 274(b), which imposes a $25 cap on the donor's deduction for aggregate transfers during the year that are excludible by a given donee solely because of § 102(a). This means that § 274(b) does not limit the donor's deduction where the donee's exclusion arises under a Code provision other than § 102 (such as § 132).

The language of § 274(b) is internally incoherent. For one thing, the exceptions to the $25 limit that are listed in § 274(b)(1)(B) could not qualify as "gifts" in any event, since they are promotional materials that the transferor hopes will generate business, and thus they fail the "detached-and-disinterested-generosity" test for a gift. Moreover, it is a contradiction in terms to suggest, as § 274(b) does, that a transfer can be *both* deductible under § 162 or 212 because of the close connection of the outlay to business or investment profits *and* excludible under the *Duberstein* "detached and disinterested generosity" standard. Nevertheless, the IRS erroneously seems to interpret § 274(b) as allowing a transferor who is engaged in a business or investment activity to deduct only up to $25 per year, per transferee, for gift transfers related to the activity without regard to whether the donee is entitled to exclude the transfer only as a § 102(a) gift under *Duberstein*. See *Rev. Rul. 63-144*, Q&As 87-93, 1963-2 C.B. 142.

Additionally, any deduction for a business gift is disallowed unless it is "substantiated" by adequate records (etc.) in accordance with § 274(d).

In a delayed reaction to *Duberstein/Stanton* (and subsequent decisions), Congress in 1986 added § 102(c), categorically prohibiting exclusion under § 102(a) for transfers from an employer to an employee (and thereby negating any need to apply the *Duberstein* test to such transfers).[9] The cross references in § 102(c)(2), however, remind us that exclusion may be available under § 74(c), pertaining to certain employee achievement awards of modest-value tangible personal property, or § 132(e), pertaining to de minimis fringes. In addition, by referring specifically only to employer-employee transfers, § 102(c)(1) has no effect in cases like *Duberstein* itself (where the recipient has a business relationship with the transferor but is not an employee of the transferor).[10]

---

[8] See 186 F. Supp. 393 (E.D.N.Y. 1960), *aff'd*, 287 F.2d 876 (2d Cir. 1961).

[9] Although § 102(c)(1) on its face does not seem to contemplate any exceptions, transfers between an employer and employee who are related parties, such as father and son, may continue to be excluded under § 102(a) if "the purpose of the transfer can be substantially attributed to the familial relationship of the parties and not to the circumstances of their employment." Prop. Reg. § 1.102-1(f)(2) (proposed in 1989, but never finalized or even made a temporary regulation that would have the force and effect of law). The proposed regulation follows the legislative history. See H.R. Rep. No. 99-426, 99th Cong. 1st Sess. 106 (1985).

[10] For example, if a service provider who is an independent contractor (i.e., not an employee) receives

Following *Duberstein/Stanton*, the "gift" issue has continued to be heavily litigated. One of the more interesting cases is the Ninth Circuit's decision in *Olk v. U.S.*, 536 F.2d 876 (9th Cir.), *cert. denied*, 429 U.S. 920 (1976), involving "tokes" (similar to tips) received by a craps dealer employed by Las Vegas casinos. The district court held that the tokes were gifts, finding (1) that the dealer performed no special or unique services to customers, (2) that tokes are given to dealers as a result of impulsive generosity or superstition on the part of players, and not as a form of compensation for services, and (3) that tokes are the result of detached and disinterested generosity on the part of a small number of patrons. In reversing the district court (without remand!), the Ninth Circuit stated (536 F.2d at 878, 879):

> The conclusion that tokes "are the result of detached and disinterested generosity" on the part of those patrons who engage in the practice of toking is a conclusion of law, not a finding of fact. . . . [The finding of] "impulsive generosity or superstition on the part of the players" we accept as the dominant motive [for giving tokes]. In the context of gambling in casinos open to the public such a motive is quite understandable. However, our understanding also requires us to acknowledge that payments so motivated are not acts of "detached or disinterested generosity." Quite the opposite is true. Tribute to the gods of fortune which it is hoped will be returned bounteously soon can only be described as an "involved and intensely interested" act.

Section 6053 requires reporting of tip income, and § 3401(k) imposes a withholding requirement on employers with respect to certain tip income.

The issue of what is a tax-free "bequest" arises infrequently and mostly in the context of bequests to executors who are, as a matter of the law of estate administration, entitled to compensation for their services. The leading case on this issue before *Duberstein* was *U.S. v. Merriam*, 263 U.S. 179 (1923), where such a bequest was held to be excluded on the ground that the bequest was conditioned on the legatee merely accepting the office of executor, rather than on the actual performance of services. *Duberstein* is now the controlling authority.[11]

In *Lyeth v. Hoey*, 305 U.S. 188 (1938), a disinherited heir obtained a settlement as the result of pursuing a will contest. Under the state law applicable to the heir in this case (which was contrary to that of other states), the settlement was not considered to be an "inheritance," as such. The Supreme Court applied a uniform federal standard to characterizing such will contest settlements for § 102 purposes and held that the settlement proceeds were excludible under § 102(a) as being an inheritance in substance, regardless of the state law characterization of such a settlement.

Lyeth v. Hoey has significance beyond § 102, because it manifests the prevailing approach of courts with regard to litigation settlement awards generally. As noted in Chapter 14, courts, instead of treating damage awards (not covered by § 104) as

---

a transfer from a contracting party that the service provider argues is excludible under § 102(a), the *Duberstein* test would apply in determining whether the transfer is an excludible gift and § 102(c)(1) would have no effect on such transfer.

[11] *Wolder v. Comm'r*, 493 F.2d 608 (2d Cir.), *cert. denied*, 419 U.S. 828 (1974).

being a separate (if unenumerated) class of gross income, typically look to what the damages are "in lieu of." Damages for lost profits are ordinary income. Damages for the wrongful appropriation of property constitute an amount realized with respect to the disposition of property. An often-cited authority for this general approach is *Raytheon Production Co. v. Comm'r*, 144 F.2d 110 (1st Cir.), *cert. denied*, 323 U.S. 779 (1944).

NOTES

1. (a) There are accepted procedures for construing an ambiguous tax statute. Two of these are, first, to consult the legislative history of the provision in question and, second, to consult the regulations issued thereunder. In *Duberstein*, the Court could do neither, because there were no congressional committee reports on the 1913 Act (which included the predecessor of § 102), and there were (and are) no regulations under § 102 purporting to define "gift." The decision to adopt a common-speech meaning of gift rather than the legal definition isn't really explained, but any difference between the two definitions likely wouldn't have mattered. The Court also declined to approach the meaning of gift from a consideration of the purpose of enacting § 102 or its function (if any).

(b) An accepted definition of "gift" exists under the federal gift tax: any transfer that is not in the ordinary course of business and is not for full and adequate consideration in money or money's worth. See Reg. § 25.2512-8. In *Farid-Es-Sultaneh v. Comm'r*, 160 F.2d 812 (2d Cir. 1947), it was held that the gift tax definition did not carry over into the income tax. In *Farid*, the taxpayer entered into an arm's length, pre-nuptial agreement with her wealthy suitor, S. S. Kresge, under which she received a block of common stock in the S.S. Kresge Corporation prior to marriage in exchange for her relinquishment of valuable marital property rights that would attend divorce. The stock transfer qualified as a "gift" within the meaning of the gift tax, because what the taxpayer gave up was specified by the Code not to be consideration in money or money's worth for purposes of the federal transfer taxes. But the transfer was held not to be a "gift" for purposes of the income tax. The requisite detached and disinterested generosity was lacking because of the valuable rights that the recipient relinquished in the contract negotiations. The court went on to hold that the taxpayer "purchased" the stock in question and therefore had a cost basis equal to the stock's fair market value on receipt, as opposed to a carryover basis under § 1015.

(c) Can the Treasury now issue regulations under § 102 that could define "gift" in a way that materially differs from *Duberstein*? In *National Cable & Telecommunications Ass'n v. Brand X Internet Services*, 545 U.S. 967 (2005) (known in administrative law circles as "*Brand X*"), the Supreme Court held that a judicial interpretation of a federal statute, including a Supreme Court decision, can always be reversed by a subsequent regulation that satisfies *Chevron* unless "the prior court decision holds that its construction follows from the unambiguous terms of the statute and thus leaves no room for agency discretion." Thus, if *Duberstein* regarded the term "gift" in § 102(a) as ambiguous, Treasury can now alter the *Duberstein* definition of gift with a regulation if the regulation satisfies the two-step *Chevron* test (described in Chapter 1.E.2). In a portion of *Duberstein* that was omitted above, the Court stated, "The meaning of the term 'gift' as applied to particular transfers has always been a matter of contention," and then went on to reject inferences from other revenue provisions, such as the gift tax. It is hard to tell from passage this whether or not *Duberstein* held "gift" to be an ambiguous term. In *Intermountain Ins. Serv. of Vail, LLC v. Comm'r*, 134 T.C. 211 (2010) (reviewed), the Tax Court held that a temporary regulation (on a topic unrelated to gifts) failed the *Brand X* test on the ground that an earlier Supreme Court decision had held that the statute in question was unambiguous. But the D.C. Circuit disagreed, and validated the temporary regulation, since finalized, 2011 U.S. App. LEXIS 12476 (D.C. Cir. 2011), as did the Federal Circuit in *Grapevine Imports Ltd. v. U.S.*, 2011 U.S. App. LEXIS 4967 (Fed Cir. 2011). It would now appear that the combination of *Brand X* with *Mayo Foundation for Medical and Educational Research v. U.S.*, 131 S.Ct. 704 (2011) (applying *Chevron* to tax regulations), allows the Treasury to issue regulations that override prior court decisions unless the statute was clearly held by the prior decision to be unambiguous. Since it does not appear that the *Duberstein* decision held the term "gift" to be unambiguous, it could well be open for the Treasury to issue a regulation defining "gift" under § 102(a) in a way that deviates from the *Duberstein* interpretation.

2.   (a) A "holding" of *Duberstein* is that *the tax treatment of one party to a transaction does not determine the tax treatment of the other party* (assuming that the statute itself does not create such a linkage). In most cases, it would be hard to discover the tax treatment of the other party. If linkage were required, the administrative burdens on the tax system would increase dramatically. The IRS sometimes attempts to solve this problem by taking inconsistent positions regarding the parties to a transaction, say by treating Berman as having made a nondeductible gift while simultaneously denying Duberstein a § 102(a) exclusion for receipt of a "non-gift." If both taxpayers litigate their cases in the Tax Court, then the court has an opportunity to render consistent decisions. (The Tax Court, pursuant to its own rule, occasionally allows joinder of two or more parties to a transaction.) But there is nothing to prevent one taxpayer from litigating in the Tax Court and the other from litigating in a refund court or to prevent the taxpayers from litigating in different refund courts. In those situations, there is no method for ensuring that the outcomes are consistent. Of course, cases in the same court can be consolidated if they involve the same facts or the same issue of law.

(b) In *Duberstein*, the issue of exclusion by the transferee was not identical to the issue of business deduction to the transferor. For example, a transfer can be nondeductible as a capital expenditure, or because the transferor does not satisfy the "carrying on" requirement, but at the same time the transfer can be a non-gift because it was motivated by the transferor's self-interest. Nevertheless, the issues of exclusion and deduction are doctrinally related in that, if the transferor anticipates no economic "return" from the transfer, the transfer should (in theory, if not always in practice) be nondeductible on account of failing one or more of the requirements of § 162. However, obtaining deductions under § 162 is easier for a corporation than for an individual, which can deduct almost everything (except dividends), because a corporation cannot itself engage in personal consumption.

(c) Section 274(b) does not impose on the donor the burden of knowing the donee's actual tax treatment of an item. Instead, the test is whether the item is "excludible" (as opposed to "excluded" by the donee) only as a gift under § 102(a). Incidentally, § 274(b) is meaningless in cases where the donor is a tax-exempt organization.

3. Section 132(a)(4) and (e) provides an exclusion for the receipt of "any property or service the value of which is . . . so small as to make accounting for it unreasonable or administratively impracticable." Reg. § 1.132-1(b)(4) says that this exclusion is available to "any recipient of a fringe benefit," i.e., to the entire world! Thus, these provisions create a general exclusion for the receipt of small transfers regardless of whether the transferor's motivation is consistent with a gift under *Duberstein*.

PROBLEMS

1. Which of the following are excludible, and which are subject to the limits of § 274(b)?

(a) Receipt of pencils, pens, key chains, bottle openers, etc., with the donor's business name prominently displayed.

(b) Receipt of a gold watch by an employee on retirement.

(c) Jan, an untenured professor, gives all twelve of her seminar students a $50 restaurant gift certificate on the last day of class, just before the teacher evaluations are handed out.

(d) Tony has a torrid affair with Maria and they become engaged. However, Tony gets cold feet when he finds out that Maria's family is closely connected to the Mafia. Tony writes a "dear Maria" letter and encloses a check for $20K as a "good-bye present."

2. Suppose that a war veteran who lost his leg on the battlefield is now a professional beggar. He solicits donations on the streets and subways of a major city each day, making no fraudulent statements about his past for the purpose of his solicitations. He does not state, for example, that he cannot find employment. (He simply prefers this mode of making a living.) He lives moderately well on his "donations." Suppose the donors who transfer funds to him each day on the street have the requisite "detached and disinterested generosity." Must our professional beggar include his take in gross income, or is he sheltered by § 102(a)?

3. Attorney enters into a contract with Client to perform all legal services that Client will need over his lifetime in exchange for a $100K bequest in Client's will. Attorney performs the services without charge and collects $100,000 under Client's will. *Wolder v. Comm'r*, 493 F.2d 608 (2d Cir.), cert. denied, 419 U.S. 828 (1974), holds that, under *Duberstein*, § 102(a) does not apply in this hypothetical, so that Attorney has $100K of includible compensation income. What if there had been no contract, Client had fully compensated Attorney for her services as they were performed, and Client's will left a $100K bequest to Attorney "in recognition of her long and faithful service?" With respect to § 102(c), assume that Attorney was an independent contractor (instead of an employee) with respect to Client.

4. A Detour: The Role of Substantive Tax Doctrine in Criminal Tax Fraud Prosecutions

Tax fraud is a "specific intent" crime, meaning that the taxpayer must not only understate tax liability, make false statements, fail to file a return, etc., but also must have done so "willfully." See §§ 7201, 7203, and 7206. It is the prosecution's obligation to prove the elements of the crime, which here includes willfulness. In a sense, unlike most crimes, actual ignorance of the law precludes conviction. The defendant's willfulness (or lack therof) is a question of fact, and the fact finder (jury or judge) may or may not give credence to the defendant's claims of ignorance.

The *Harris* case below illustrates some of the difficulties of prosecuting tax fraud in the context of the "gift" issue under § 102(a).

UNITED STATES v. HARRIS
United States Court of Appeals, Seventh Circuit
942 F.2d 1125 (1991)

Before Cudahy and Flaum, Circuit Judges, and Eschbach, Senior Circuit Judge.

Eschbach, Senior Circuit Judge.

David Kritzik, now deceased, was a wealthy widower partial to the company of young women. [One] of these women was Lynnette Harris. Kritzik gave Harris more than half a million dollars over the course of several years. Harris was convicted of two counts of willfully failing to file federal income tax returns under § 7203 and two counts of willful tax evasion under § 7201.

At trial, Harris tried to introduce as evidence three letters that Kritzik wrote, but the District Court excluded the letters as hearsay. These letters were hearsay if offered for the truth of the matters asserted — that Kritzik did in fact love Harris, enjoyed giving her things, wanted to take care of her financial security, and gave her the jewelry at issue as a gift. But the letters were not hearsay for the purpose of showing what Harris believed, because her belief does not depend on the actual truth of the matters asserted in the letters. Even if Kritzik were lying, the letters could have caused Harris to believe in good faith that the things he gave her were intended as gifts. This good faith belief, in turn, would preclude any finding of willfulness. We hold that the District Court abused its discretion in excluding the letters.

Our conclusion that Harris should have been allowed to present the letters as evidence would ordinarily lead us to remand for retrial. We further conclude, however, that current law provided Harris no fair warning that her conduct was criminal. Indeed, current authorities favor Harris' position that the money received was a gift. We emphasize that we do not necessarily agree with these authorities, and that the government is free to urge departure from them in a noncriminal context. But new points of tax law may not be the basis of criminal convictions. Criminal prosecutions must rest on a violation of a clear rule of law. This rule is based on the Constitution's requirement of due process and its prohibition on ex post facto laws; the government must provide reasonable notice of what conduct is subject to criminal punishment. In tax cases, only "willful" violations are subject to criminal punishment. In the tax area, "willful" wrongdoing means the "voluntary, intentional violation of a known" — and therefore knowable — "legal duty." If the obligation to pay a tax is sufficiently in doubt, willfulness is impossible as a matter of law, and the "defendant's actual intent is irrelevant."

We do not doubt that *Duberstein*'s principles, though general, provide a clear answer to many cases involving the gift versus income distinction and can be the basis for civil as well as criminal prosecutions in such cases. We are equally certain, however, that Duberstein provides no ready answer to the taxability of transfers of money to a mistress in the context of a long-term relationship. The motivations of the parties in such cases will always be mixed. The relationship would not be long term were it not for some respect or affection. Yet, it may be equally clear that the relationship would not continue were it not for financial support or payments. [The] usual sources of authority are silent when it comes to the tax treatment of money transferred in the course of long term, personal relationships.

[The opinion then cited cases holding that payments to "mistresses" were gifts. *Reis v. Comm'r*, T.C. Memo. 1974-287; *Libby v. Comm'r*, T.C. Memo. 1969-184.] The Tax Court did find that payments were income in *Blevins v. Comm'r*, T.C. Memo. 1955-211, and in *Jones v. Comm'r*, T.C. Memo. 1977-329. But in *Blevins*, the taxpayer practiced prostitution. Similarly in *Jones* a woman had frequent hotel meetings with a married man, and on "each occasion" he gave her cash. If these cases make a rule of law, it is that a person is entitled to treat cash and property received from a lover as gifts, as long as the relationship consists of something more than specific payments for specific sessions of sex. The United States does not allege that Harris received specific payments for specific sessions of sex.

Testimony showed that Harris described her relationship with Kritzik as "a job" and "just making a living." She reportedly described how she disliked it when Kritzik fondled her naked, and made other derogatory statements about sex with Kritzik. This evidence tells us only what Harris thought of the relationship. *Duberstein* held that the donor's intent is the "critical consideration." If Kritzik viewed the money he gave *Harris* as a gift, or if the dearth of contrary evidence leaves doubt on the subject, does it matter how mercenary Harris' motives were?

For the reasons stated, we REVERSE Harris's conviction and remand with instructions to DISMISS the indictments.

FLAUM, CIRCUIT JUDGE, concurring.

I part company with the majority when it distills from our gift/income jurisprudence a rule that would tax only the most base type of cash-for-sex exchange and categorically exempt from tax liability all other transfers of money and property to so-called mistresses or companions. In *Duberstein*, the Supreme Court expressly eschewed the type of categorical, rule-bound analysis propounded by the majority. After reading *Duberstein*, a reasonable taxpayer would conclude that payments from a lover were taxable as income if they were made "in return for services rendered" rather than "out of affection, respect, admiration, charity or like impulses."

Consider the following example. A approaches B and offers to spend time with him, accompany him to social events, and provide him with sexual favors for the next year if B gives her an apartment, a car, and a stipend of $5,000 a month. B agrees to A's terms. According to the majority, because this example involves a transfer of money to a "mistress in the context of a long-term relationship," A could never be charged with criminal tax evasion if she chose not to pay taxes on B's stipend. I find this hard to accept; what A receives from B is clearly income as it is "in return for services rendered."

I am thus prompted to find Harris' conviction infirm because of the relative scantiness of the record before us, not because mistresses are categorically exempt from taxation on the largess they receive. As the majority relates, the record does contain evidence showing that Harris thought their relationship to be of the "cash-for-services" kind. Such evidence is, in my view, probative — to some degree — of Kritzik's intent. But not sufficiently so to support a criminal conviction. Absent even a scintilla of direct evidence of Kritzik's intent, I cannot conclude that the government proved the nature of Kritzik's payments to be income beyond a reasonable doubt.

NOTES

1. The legal proposition that a person cannot be convicted of tax fraud if the law (at the time of the conduct) is favorable to the taxpayer or is ambiguous, even where the defendant did not rely on such law or ambiguity, was established in the case of *James v. U.S.*, 366 U.S. 213 (1961). How ambiguous does the law have to be? In *U.S. v. Garber*, 607 F.2d 92 (5th Cir. 1979) (en banc), the defendant had been convicted of tax fraud for failing to report income from the sale of her own blood. The Fifth Circuit held that the district court should have allowed the defendant to present expert testimony to the effect that (1) there was no "on point" case authority holding "blood money" to be gross income, and (2) there were theories (of the "replacement of capital" kind) as to why such receipts might not be gross income. The dissent argued that gross receipts are gross income unless there is a basis offset and pointed out that no theory had been offered as to how a person can have a basis in her own blood. The dissent also argued that questions about the state of tax doctrine should not be submitted to juries. In our opinion, the generality of statutory language ("income from whatever source derived") does not equate with ambiguity in this context. Whether "blood money" is gross income was resolved in favor of the government in *Greene v. Comm'r*, 74 T.C. 1229 (1980).

2. The principal civil penalties relating to "substance" (as opposed to timely filing returns, making timely tax payments, and other required procedures) are found in §§ 6662 (accuracy-related penalties) and 6663 (civil tax fraud). Note particularly the penalties that relate to (1) negligence or disregard of "rules and regulations" and (2) substantial understatement of income tax liability. Reg. § 1.6662-3(b)(2) defines the phrase "rules or regulations" as encompassing the Code, temporary and final regulations, and rulings (etc.) published in the Internal Revenue Bulletin, but not proposed regulations. How does the existence of a tax

regulation affect the taxpayer's duty to file a correct return?

2.   (a) The court in *Harris* took the wrong approach, in our opinion. If the payments were compensation for services, motive is simply irrelevant. A person may retain a marginal employee out of love and affection, but wages are not thereby transformed into "gifts." The category of "compensation," therefore, in practice, trumps that of "gift." Kritzik did not "anticipate" a quid pro quo, he got it!

(b) When *Harris* is framed as a case of "compensation or not," then what Harris herself thought about the situation (that it was a job) should count.

(c) The court in *Harris* framed the issue in a way that made conviction of Harris impossible, because it required Harris to *know* that Kritzik's motive was *not* one of disinterested generosity. This made Harris the beneficiary of a higher proof threshold than applies in a civil case involving § 102, where one infers motive from circumstantial evidence.

3.   (a) The civil statute of limitations on assessment by the IRS is usually three years, or in case of major omissions of gross income, six years from the filing of the return. See § 6501(a) and (e). However, the civil statute of limitations does not run against the government at all if a fraudulent return is filed. See § 6501(c)(1). Obviously, it does not run against the government if no return is filed. See § 6501(c)(3). The criminal statute of limitations is six years in all cases. See § 6531.

(b) A person can (but is not required to) file an amended return that was erroneous when filed due to a nonfraudulent error. However, a fraudulent tax return cannot be "cured" by the later filing of a nonfraudulent amended return. See *Badaracco v. Comm'r*, 464 U.S. 386 (1984) (also holding that such an amended return did not start the civil fraud statute of limitations running against the government with respect to the original fraudulent return).

PROBLEMS

1.   Consider which of the following, if proven, would avoid a conviction for criminal tax fraud:

(a) The law was totally contrary to defendant's position, but he didn't know about it.

(b) Although it was ultimately determined that the receipts in question were income, law existed to support the defendant's position; he didn't, however, know about such law.

(c) No authority was directly in point, but settled tax principles, if applied to the new fact situation, would lead to a result contrary to the defendant's position, and the defendent knew it.

2.   Suppose a taxpayer has second thoughts about having filed a fraudulent return. What can be done to avoid a prosecution for criminal and civil tax fraud?

5. Government Welfare Benefits

Government welfare and disaster benefits are paid pursuant to government's function of improving the general welfare. The IRS has never attempted to tax need-based government benefits provided to individuals under government social welfare programs (state, federal, or foreign), whether in cash or in kind. The IRS has adopted a policy of exempting welfare benefits by issuing rulings, which are too numerous to list here, covering specific government programs. Some of the rulings deal with such "borderline" issues as welfare vs. (includible) compensation. See *Rev. Rul. 71-425*, 1971-2 C.B. 76 ("workfare" requirement does not bar exclusion of welfare payments). Another boundary is between welfare vs. (includible) "general largesse." See *Rev. Rul. 76-131*, 1976-1 C.B. 16 (Alaska Longevity Bonus Act payments to 25-year Alaska residents includible because not based on any category of need). A third boundary is between welfare vs. (includible) commercial subsidies. See *Rev. Rul. 63-269*, 1963-2 C.B. 293 (agricultural and merchant marine subsidies includible).

In addition, there are assorted statutory provisions in this area, not all of which are in the Internal Revenue Code. (Some tax provisions are sprinkled through other parts of federal statutory law.) The most important of those found in the Internal Revenue Code itself are § 85 (providing that unemployment benefits are fully includible), § 86 (providing that Social Security retirement benefits are partly includible), § 126 (excluding assorted subsidies, many related to conservation and the environment), § 131 (excluding foster care payments), and § 139 (excluding qualified disaster relief payments).

The rulings that exclude government welfare payments acknowledge that the excluded payments initially appear to be gross income under *Glenshaw Glass* but then fail to offer any rationale for the exclusion in question other than that the IRS decides by fiat not to tax the item (the IRS calls this "rule" the "administrative general welfare exclusion"). In *Rev. Rul. 2003-12*, 2003-1 C.B. 283, the IRS stated that government grants to disaster victims generally do not qualify as excludible gifts because of government's "duty" to relieve hardship. On this point, the ruling cites only an unreported U.S. District Court case from Alaska. Since no legal duty exists on this score, the duty must be a moral one. However, in *CCA 200708003* (Jan. 9, 2007) (IRS Chief Counsel Advice Memorandum), it was conceded that government benefits for a class of individuals could be excluded as gifts.

NOTES

1. The "moral duty" exception to "gift" appears in an offhand statement in *Duberstein* and originated in *Bogardus v. Comm'r*, 302 U.S. 34 (1937), where the issue was whether payments by a nongovernmental entity were includible compensation or excludible gifts. Moral obligations usually derive from having received unsolicited benefits. In *Duberstein* itself, the donor's payment may be characterized as having been made pursuant to a moral duty, because the donor had received (and hoped to continue to receive) economic benefits from the donee. Thus, there was a quid pro quo, even if it was not bargained for and even if it did not rise to the level of a legal obligation. Similarly, if a person pays a reward for finding the person's lost

dog, the reward is an informal quid pro quo and should not be excluded as a gift. In our opinion, the moral duty exception to "gift" treatment (whatever its content) was misapplied in *Rev. Rul. 2003-12* . Whether government has a moral duty to provide welfare or disaster relief is, in fact, a debatable matter that depends on one's view of the proper role of government, and a "moral duty," being self-imposed, is not an "obligation." Moreover, it is hard to attribute a clear motive of moral duty to an entity whose leadership is determined by numerous constituencies and voters. Finally, it is hard to see how the government can be under a moral duty where it received no benefits from the payee, as was the case in *Rev. Rul. 2003-12* . In sum, we think that the exclusion for government welfare payments is adequately supported by § 102(a) and that the administrative welfare exclusion is redundant and unnecessary.

2. If government welfare payments were includible in income, the income inclusion would undermine the governmental purpose and increase the reporting obligations of both taxpayers and the government itself (as payor).

3. Government reimbursements for property losses and other identified expenditures of disaster victims could be treated as insurance recoveries, in which case the taxpayer would obtain a basis offset (at least if there had been no prior deduction). (This scenario is dealt with in later chapters.) However, § 139 (added in 2001) shortcuts the analysis by simply excluding certain disaster-relief payments. Presumably, any deductions for losses or expenses that created a right to receive an excluded § 139 reimbursement would be disallowed under § 265(a)(1). Such a scenario is virtually identical to that in the *Manocchio* case, set forth in Chapter 8.D.4.

B. LIFE INSURANCE

A statutory exclusion for the proceeds of life insurance is conferred by § 101(a).

1. Income Taxation of Life Insurance Proceeds

The Revenue Act of 1918 added an income tax exclusion (now contained in § 101(a)) for the proceeds of life insurance received by a beneficiary by reason of the insured's death. Life insurance proceeds payable to a beneficiary by reason of the death of the insured may be viewed as, in effect, an indirect bequest to the beneficiary from the premium payer(s), effected through contractual arrangements with a third party, the insurance company. A separate exclusion was required, because the payment of life insurance premiums is not a gift (at least if the payor is also the owner of the policy), and the proceeds do not fit within the terms "bequest," "devise," or "inheritance," which refer only to property (or cash) owned by the decedent at death.

Life insurance can also be viewed as a wager. In its pure form ("term insurance"), the annual premium goes into an annual betting pool, and the "winners" are those who die during the insurance period. Of course, the "winner" isn't around to collect, so the winnings (the proceeds) are paid to a designated beneficiary (which could be an individual, a corporation of which the insured was an employee, a trust, or the estate of the decedent). An analogy might be provided by pure gambling, in which the winner includes the winnings in excess of her bets, as described in Chapter 10.C.

Betting on one's own life for the benefit of a possibly needy beneficiary (such as the insured's widow, minor child, or 90-year-old parent) would be considered a socially desirable form of gambling. Matters are different if a person other than the insured (or other than a person dependent on the insured) places the bet and names himself as beneficiary. Betting on another's life for one's own benefit is considered to be a socially undesirable form of wagering. In that case, there is no serious argument for making the proceeds *wholly* tax free to the bettor. Nevertheless, § 101 fails to systematically weed out the opportunistic bettor for treatment as an investor. Indeed, the only situation in which § 101 adopts the "investor" (includible gain) approach over the "indirect bequest" (excludible payoff) approach is when a policy is purchased from a previous owner (rather than from the insurance company). In that case, when the insured dies, the purchaser realizes includible income equal to the difference between the proceeds received upon the insured's death and the purchaser's cost (plus premiums paid by the purchaser). For example, assume that Mary needs money and sells to Investor for $1,000 a paid-up $5,000 life insurance policy she owns on her life. When Mary dies, Investor collects $5,000. Investor, having made no additional premium payments, can exclude only $1,000 of the proceeds under § 101(a)(2). This "investor exception" (which is functionally the same as a basis offset) does not apply where (a) the transfer of the policy was by gift (or other tax-free transfer, such as an incorporation transaction), or (b) the transferee is the insured, a partner of the insured, or a partnership or corporation in which the insured has a stake.

The failure of § 101(a) to impose "investor treatment" on a third-party purchaser of the policy from the insurance company is probably based on assumptions about the life insurance market. State law treats as void a policy procured by a person without an "insurable" interest in the insured's life. A person is deemed to have an insurable interest only where the purchaser has a reasonable expectation of profit or benefit from the *continued* life of the insured.

The exclusion under § 101(a) is only "good" for the amount of the proceeds payable in a lump sum at death. A given life insurance policy may contain one or more "settlement options" that provide for deferred payments after death. The excess of such payments over the lump-sum amount is interest, which is taxed (depending on whether the option is an interest-only option or an annuity option) under § 101(c) and (d) respectively. (These subsections are the counterparts to § 102(b) for gifts and bequests: they separate the exempt "principal" proceeds from the post-death interest income, which is includible.)

The tax treatment of life insurance as an investment prior to the insured's death, particularly with respect to the "savings element" (increase in cash surrender value), is considered in Chapter 27.D.[12]

---

[12] Briefly, when the owner of a cash-value life insurance policy surrenders it to the insurer in exchange for the cash value, the investor characterization is applied, and the excess of the amount received over the owner's basis is taxable gain. However, in this situation, the owner is not actually collecting insurance proceeds because the insured is still living. Thus, this gain falls outside the realm of "insurance" gain.

2.   What Are "Life Insurance Proceeds"?

Section 101(a) allows exclusion of "amounts received under a life insurance contract, if such amounts are paid by reason of the death of the insured." Section 101(g), added in 1996 at the height of AIDS awareness, allows certain pre-death settlements of payable-on-death proceeds to be treated as satisfying § 101(a). For example, if a "terminally ill" or "chronically ill" taxpayer needs money before death to pay for expensive medical care and sells a life insurance policy (at a discounted value) to a "viatical settlement provider," the amounts received on the sale will be deemed received under the life insurance contract by reason of the death of the insured (thus allowing exclusion of the receipt). There are a number of qualifications and limitations in § 101(g).

Not all amounts payable out of some "fund" by reason of a person's death constitute the proceeds of "life insurance." The chief characteristic of a life insurance contract is that premiums are calculated with reference to the chances of the insured's death in the current period (premium year), and there is a windfall gain to the beneficiary if the insured dies earlier than expected. As stated at the beginning of this section, life insurance is basically an annual wager, not an investment. See *Rev. Rul. 65-57*, 1965-1 C.B. 56 (relying on an estate tax case, *Helvering v. LeGierse*, 312 U.S. 531 (1941)).

C.   SURVIVOR BENEFITS UNDER ANNUITIES AND RETIREMENT PLANS

In contrast to life insurance, survivor benefits under annuities, retirement plans, employee death benefit plans, and individual retirement accounts (IRAs), are totally unrelated to anyone's predicted life span and are not life insurance (except in the case specified in § 101(h) for police officers killed in the line of duty).[13] Instead, the amount of a survivor's (death) benefit depends either on (a) the amount in the fund at the decedent's death or (b) an amount based on a formula keyed to years of employment and salary level. In short, these items are more like deferred compensation or investments than life insurance.

However, the tax treatment of these items is different from that for conventional estate transfers of investment property. First, the beneficiary's acquisition, at the decedent's death, of the right to receive payments is not included in gross income. The authority for this result, however, is not § 102(a) but rather the separate rules for taxing annuities (see § 72) and rights to "income in respect of a decedent" (IRD) (see § 691(a)), which encompasses deferred compensation rights of all kinds (including IRAs). (In general, an IRD right is a right to income earned by a decedent before death but not taxed to the decedent because not received by the decedent in cash prior to the decedent's death. See Chapter 17.F.1.)

Second, the beneficiary's rights do *not* receive a § 1014 basis. See § 1014(b)(9)(A) (excepting annuities) and (c) (excepting IRD rights). It follows that the basis of the

---

[13] Various benefits relating to service in the armed forces of the U.S. are also excluded, sometimes under the portion of the U.S. Code dealing with veterans' affairs. These benefits are not catalogued in this book.

decedent carries over to the beneficiary.

Third, when the beneficiary actually receives cash under an annuity or IRD right, the cash is gross income, subject to appropriate basis offset (under § 72).

Joint bank accounts are considered to pass to the surviving joint holder(s) by excludible bequest. The accession, by reason of the other joint tenant's death, to fee ownership of property held as a joint tenancy (or tenancy by the entirety) is not a taxable realization event under the income tax. The surviving joint tenant obtains a § 1014 basis for the portion of the property included in the decedent joint tenant's gross estate (which is often half thereof). See § 1014(b)(9).

NOTES

1.   As mentioned earlier in this chapter, in the very early days of the income tax it was debated whether "income" was limited to "periodic" income and gains (such as wages, rent, ordinary business profits, interest, etc.), thereby excluding "irregular," "nonrecurring," and "extraordinary" gains. The predecessor of § 101(a) was enacted under this influence. Soon thereafter, doubts as to whether the 16th Amendment prohibited Congress from taxing nonperiodic gains were removed. See *Merchants' Loan & Trust Co. v. Smietanka*, 255 U.S. 509 (1921) (capital gain from an investor's single, isolated sale is income under the 16th Amendment). But in *U.S. v. Supplee-Biddle Hardware Co.*, 265 U.S. 189 (1924), the Court cited the periodicity concept and stated that, although Congress could tax nonperiodic income, it had to do so explicitly.[14] However, by the time of *Comm'r v. Glenshaw Glass Co.*, 348 U.S. 426 (1955), holding that a one-time windfall gain in the form of punitive damages constituted gross income under the catch-all phrase in the predecessor of § 61, the nonperiodicity concept had become so passé that the Court didn't even bother to mention it, and it is now safe to say that it is extinct both as a constitutional principle and as a principle of statutory interpretation.

2.   The concept of "insurable interest" under state law may be weakening somewhat. Today, insurance companies are increasingly willing (with the apparent blessing of state regulators) to sell businesses life insurance for their entire pool of employees, even the lowest-level employees, and these policies pay off to the business when such an employee dies, even if the employee no longer works for the business. The term used for these policies is "janitor's insurance," to contrast them with the earlier practice of insuring the lives of only key employees, such as executives. In short, the § 101(a) exclusion has caused some corporations to conclude that purchasing life insurance with respect to employees is a more valuable way to invest profits than placing them in taxable investments, including expansion of the corporation's business.

3.   All of the various types of nonprobate transfers considered above are subject to federal gift and estate taxation. Of course, the details of federal estate tax

---

[14] This case involved corporate-owned life insurance, which was not expressly excluded at that time. The Court declined to consider the question of whether insurance proceeds were income under the 16th Amendment or under the taxing statute but noted that the statutory exclusion for individual-owned life insurance did not imply that life insurance was income. Ultimately the Court held that the proceeds were excluded, because the statute stated that corporate gross income was the same as it was for individuals.

doctrine are beyond the scope of this text.

PROBLEMS

1. (a) Mary takes out life insurance on her "partner" Susan's life in the face amount of $100K. Assume that Mary has an insurable interest in Susan's life. Susan dies. Under a settlement option in the policy, Mary can elect to take either $100K in a lump sum or 10 annual payments of $13K, and Mary elects the latter. What income tax result to Mary? See § 101(c) and (d).

(b) Same as (a), except that Mary "sells" the policy (having a then cash surrender value of $12K), to her daughter Sunny for $12K. Sunny changes the beneficiary to herself. Susan dies, and Sunny opts to take the $100K proceeds in a lump sum. See § 101(a)(2).

2. Ben is an employee covered by a "qualified" retirement plan. Recall from Chapter 6 that employer contributions to a qualified plan are not included in the employee's income as they are made, and subsequent earnings are exempt from current tax until distribution. Ben makes no out-of-pocket contributions to the plan. (What is Ben's basis in his plan rights?) The plan provides that on Ben's death his wife Brenda will receive a lump-sum retirement benefit based on a formula. Ben dies at age 72, and the formula mandates that $75K be paid to Brenda in a lump sum. Assume that this amount is included in Ben's gross estate for federal estate tax purposes. What income tax result to Brenda upon receiving the $75K?

D. SPIN-OFFS FROM SECTION 102 DEALING WITH PRIZES, AWARDS, AND SCHOLARSHIPS

In 1954, Congress added § 74, dealing with prizes and awards, and § 117, dealing with scholarships, in order to bring some semblance of control over a situation in which these items were frequently claimed to be "gifts" under § 102(a). Both sections were revised to their present form in 1986.

The simultaneous existence of §§ 74, 102, and 117 presents taxpayers with a threshold "jurisdictional fact" issue regarding whether a particular benefit is a "scholarship," a nonscholarship "prize or award," or neither of the above. If the benefit is a scholarship, the tax consequences are controlled exclusively by § 117. If the benefit is a nonscholarship "prize or award," the tax consequences are determined exclusively by § 74. If the answer is "neither of the above," then any other theory (such as "gift," "government welfare," or "support") can be attempted. But a taxpayer whose receipt is governed by either § 74 or 117 and who is unsuccessful in achieving an exclusion under those provisions cannot fall back on § 102(a) or on any other theory of exclusion. See Regs. §§ 1.74-1(a)(1) and 1.102-1(a); Prop. Reg. § 1.117-6(b)(1); *Hornung v. Comm'r*, 47 T.C. 428 (1967) (prizes).

1. Prizes and Awards

In a roundabout way, the present version of § 74 basically mandates the inclusion of nearly all prizes and awards in gross income, but the road to that result has been a long one.

Prizes are often received in kind. As a preliminary matter, it should be noted that, even before *Glenshaw Glass* (set out in Chapter 14), it was never thought that a receipt's being in kind (rather than cash) presented a serious obstacle to income inclusion. See *Peabody v. Eisner*, 247 U.S. 347 (1918) (in-kind dividend includible in shareholder's gross income). An income tax that could be avoided by the expedient of making payments and transfers in kind would be hollow, indeed. We would simply become a barter society, with all its attendant inefficiencies. Thus, "income" has never been equated with "cash income." This idea is now found in the regulations, which provide that "[g]ross income includes income realized in any form, whether in money, property, or services. Income may be realized, therefore, in the form of services, meals, accommodations, stock, or other property, as well as in cash." Reg. § 1.61-1(a). Note, however, that this regulation does not state that all in-kind receipts "are" income. Income, as stated in *Glenshaw Glass*, is not included *until* realized. Realization doctrine (dealt with in Part Seven), is too context-dependent to attempt to summarize here. Suffice it to say that § 74 *treats* prizes and awards as being realized when received, whether in cash or in kind. See *Wills v. Comm'r*, 411 F.2d 537 (9th Cir.1969) (even a trophy, with no utilitarian function, is included in gross income when received at its fair market value).

Before the 1955 *Glenshaw Glass* decision, the *Eisner v. Macomber* definition of income as the yield from capital or labor might have posed an obstacle to including some prizes in gross income. Prizes awarded on the basis of entering and winning a contest based on skill or luck could be considered a return on "labor" and, thus, would be included under the *Macomber* definition. However, certain awards that came "out of the blue" (such as the Nobel Peace Prize) might have been considered to fall outside the *Macomber* definition. But most pre-1954 cases involving prizes and awards were litigated under the gift exclusion (currently § 102(a)) rather than *Macomber*. The leading § 102 case involving prizes is *Robertson v. U.S.*, 343 U.S. 711 (1952), where the taxpayer composed a symphony in connection with his activities as a university music professor and, several years later, entered the work in a newly established contest. The score was selected the winner of a cash prize, but the taxpayer retained ownership of the composition. The Court held that the prize had been paid in discharge of an obligation created by the terms of the contest and could not be excluded as a gift, even though the donor of the prize did not obtain the rights to the composition.

Section 74, as enacted in 1954, essentially codified and extended *Robertson* by generally treating prizes and awards as gross income when received, but it contained an exception in § 74(b) for prizes and awards recognizing achievement in certain listed fields and not obtained as the result of entering a contest. Even this narrow exception was functionally eliminated in 1986 by the addition of a requirement that the § 74(b) exclusion applies only if (in addition to the prize being awarded for the listed reasons and without the recipient entering a contest) the recipient assigns the prize or award to a charity or governmental unit. In other words, a Nobel Peace Prize recipient can avoid having gross income only by giving the prize to a qualified donee, which means that the exclusion is simply the equivalent of an inclusion followed by a full offsetting charitable deduction under § 170. Therefore, the only prize winners who would care much about qualifying for the narrow § 74 exclusion today would be those whose charitable contribution deductions are reduced or disallowed by limitations in § 170 (which is the subject of the next chapter).

In short, under present law, essentially all prizes and awards are taxed to the recipient, except those modest items excluded under § 74(c) as an "employee achievement award" (defined in § 274(j)). Prizes and awards are includible even when taking the form of rights to services, such as a free vacation in Maui or free chiropractic treatments.

PROBLEMS

1.   Glenda appears on a quiz show and wins a set of living room furniture, which the show proudly announces has a "retail value" of $10K. If property is included in gross income, the measure of the inclusion is the "fair market value" of the item. Glenda doesn't care much for the style and would offer only $3K for the stuff at an auction (this is the "subjective value" to Glenda). If Glenda accepts the furniture, she could sell it (as a "new" item) for $8.6K (this is the "wholesale" value). Another possibility is that Glenda could accept the furniture, use it for a year or two, and sell it "used" for $3K.

(a) What tax result (including her basis in the furniture) if she accepts it? See Reg. § 1.61-2(d)(1); *Rooney v. Comm'r*, 88 T.C. 523 (1987); *Rev. Rul. 58-347*, 1958-2 C.B. 878.

(b) What result if Glenda refuses the furniture? Cf. *Comm'r v. Giannini*, 129 F.2d 638 (9th Cir. 1942).

(c) What result if Glenda "bargains down" to something she wants, such as $3.5K cash? A large-screen TV worth $3K? See *Turner v. Comm'r*, T.C. Memo. 1954-38.

(d) What if Glenda uses the furniture for a week and then sells it for $8K as "almost new"? See *McCoy v. Comm'r*, 38 T.C. 841 (1962) (acq.).

2. Scholarships

Scholarships are received in cash or in the form of a tuition (etc.) waiver or reduction. Most scholarships are provided by government or a tax-exempt organization, but some scholarships may be provided by nonexempt taxpayers.

In the absence of § 117, most scholarships would probably be excluded as government welfare, gifts, or as a reduction in the purchase price of education (which, as will be noted in Chapter 22, is usually considered not to give rise to realized gross income).[15] On the other hand, scholarships based on "merit" or that have strings attached might be included. *Since, however, § 117 is treated as the exclusive arbiter of whether scholarships are income, any possible ground of exclusion not found in § 117 itself must be disregarded.* Consequently, all scholarships (whatever their form) are to be treated as cash grants that are not excluded as gifts or under any provision or theory, other than § 117 itself. Even when a scholarship is paid directly by the grantor to the academic institution on behalf of the student, or is provided to the student as a tuition waiver or reduction,

---

[15] For example, an ordinary traveler does not realize gross income by obtaining a discounted air fare.

the transaction is viewed in substance as though the student received the cash and then transferred it to the academic institution.

The initial (1954) version of § 117 was quite expansive, but Treasury regulations issued in 1956 provided that the following are not excludible "scholarships": (1) transfers that are disguised compensation for services rendered to the grantor, (2) transfers to "pursue studies and research primarily for the benefit of the grantor," and (3) transfers that are payment for services "subject to the direction or supervision of the grantor." These regulations were upheld in *Bingler v. Johnson*, 394 U.S. 741 (1969), and the basic theme that compensation trumped exclusion was confirmed by the addition of present § 117(c) in 1986. However, section 117(c)(1) limits the compensation exception to payments "for teaching, research, or other services by the student required as a condition" for receiving the grant.[16]

The 1986 Act narrowed § 117 by confining the exclusion to "qualified" scholarships or fellowships as defined in § 117(b). One requirement for qualification is that the grant must assist the student to pursue a program leading to a degree. See § 117(a). Under prior law, medical interns and residents clogged up the courts with claims that their stipends primarily involved education, not services, and thus should be free from tax, an argument eviscerated by the 1986 amendment.

Additionally, qualification is limited to grants used for tuition and "required" fees, books, supplies, and so on, conspicuously omitting reference to room and board, because Congress decided that payments for ordinary consumption (living) expenses should be taxed. The literal language of § 117(b)(1) might be read as implying that if the grant recipient "used" the grant funds for room and board and paid tuition, etc., out of other funds, the grant must be included in income. However, the regulations make it clear that the student does not have to "trace" the scholarship funds to qualified uses. That is to say, the student who receives a scholarship can claim the exclusion *to the extent of* qualified expenditures regardless of the source of the funds actually used to make the qualified payments.[17] A tuition reduction or waiver is a form of scholarship that is inherently a qualified expenditure.

3. Reduced-Cost Education for Employees of Educational Institutions

Section 117(d), excluding certain "tuition reductions," appears to be largely redundant with § 117(a). However, § 117(d) is confined to tuition reductions and waivers provided to an employee of an educational institution by the institution itself as her employer. In other words, § 117(d) confers an exclusion on an employee "fringe benefit." Recall from Chapter 12 that employee fringe benefits are presumptively includible under § 61(a)(1), unless expressly excluded under the Code.

---

[16] The old rule pertaining to grants for education primarily benefitting the grantor has been slightly watered down. Now the grants are disqualified only if the grantor imposes a "requirement" that the student perform services for the grantor or that the student perform studies or research must that will primarily benefit the grantor. See Prop. Reg. § 1.117-6(d)(2).

[17] See Prop. Reg. § 1.117-6(e).

This exclusion is not available for graduate education unless the student is a teaching or research assistant. See § 117(d)(5).

Note that § 117(d) is expressly subordinate to § 117(c), which provides that a tuition reduction or waiver granted to an educational institution's employee does not qualify for exclusion to the extent that it represents payment for services required as a condition for the grant. Since a § 117(d) reduction or waiver is, by definition, conditioned on the recipient being an employee of the institution, it initially seems that all § 117(d) benefits are payments for services and that § 117(c) thus deprives § 117(d) of any effect at all! The proposed regulations, however, resolve this problem by treating § 117(d) benefits as payments for services only to the extent that the recipient's other compensation is less than a reasonable amount for the employee's actual services. See Prop. Reg. § 1.117-6(d)(3), (d)(5) Ex. (6).

The § 117(d) exclusion can apply not only to free education of the employee, but also the employee's spouse and dependents. Additionally, the education might be obtainable at another institution (perhaps one in the same athletic conference as the employee's employer). See § 117(d)(2).

On the other hand, § 117(d) is subject to a nondiscrimination requirement, meaning that the benefit cannot be offered exclusively to (say) high-ranking administrators and tenured professors. See § 117(d)(3).

Various other tax-free employee fringe benefit provisions that implicate education can be found. The most notable is § 127, which excludes (up to $5,250 per year) educational costs provided by an employer that is not itself an educational institution. Section 127 is free of § 117(c).

NOTES

1.   Many scholarships are awarded by the institution itself in the form of a reduction in the tuition "sticker price." As a result, Harvard, for example, might charge $50K for tuition to student A, $20K to student B, and nothing to student C. This phenomenon looks like routine price discrimination (like that practiced by airlines). However, there are differences between market discounts and tuition waivers and reductions: (1) for some students, the price of education may be discounted to zero (and surely the educational services obtained are worth more than that), (2) educational institutions are generally nonprofit organizations operating in a highly imperfect "market" (unlike the for-profit airlines), and (3) no differences in the quality of service is connected to the price differences (unlike the difference between first-class seats on an airplane and tourist class). Also, if scholarships awarded directly by educational institutions were considered "non-income" because of being the equivalent of price discounts, then "outsider-provided" scholarships would be taxed unfavorably relative to institution-provided scholarships. In any event, the price-discount theory is off limits, because § 117 is the sole arbiter of excludibility and it eschews the price-discount theory.

2.   The scholarship exclusion may be viewed as the equivalent of an includible receipt combined with a full offsetting deduction for a deemed payment to the educational institution. The scholarship exclusion is meaningful (beneficial) precisely because educational costs are not generally deductible (as explained in

Chapter 9.D). Thus, education financed by wages is taxable (because the wages are included and are not offset by any deduction for the tuition). On the other hand, education financed by a parental gift is not taxable (to the student, at least) because of § 102(a) or the tax-common-law support exclusion.

PROBLEMS

Which of the following involve excludible scholarships under § 117?

1. Peggy Precocious, a 12-year-old genius, applied for and received a four-year scholarship of $45K per year to pursue a bachelor's degree in physics at Hi-Tech University. Peggy spent $20K per year on tuition and fees; $10K per year for books, laboratory equipment, and a computer (all required for use in Peggy's degree program work); and $15K per year on meals and lodging in Einstein Hall.

2. Peter is a top student at the Northeast Idaho State School of Law who is elected Editor-in-Chief of the Law Review. The Editor-in-Chief of the Law Review is entitled to an annual stipend of $30K, which is awarded by the Law Review Association. Tuition is $28K. What issues are raised here? Cf. *Rev. Rul. 77-263*, 1977-2 C.B. 47 (setting forth conditions attached to exclusion of athletic scholarships).

3. Julie has a J.D. degree and is a graduate student at Columbia Law School pursuing an LL.M. degree. She also teaches the J.D. students in the research and writing program. Julie receives a salary of $30K as well as full tuition remission (worth $50K). Others who teach the J.D. students in the research and writing program who are not LL.M. candidates get paid $36K per year. In addition, Julie received $6K cash from the Rotary Club of Odessa, Texas, her home town, on the condition that Julie deliver one talk to the club upon receiving the degree. Julie did not put this amount into a segregated bank account but commingled these funds with her own personal funds.

Chapter 16

CHARITABLE CONTRIBUTIONS

This chapter examines the deduction, conferred by § 170, for gifts or contributions of money or property to certain tax-exempt organizations that are customarily referred to as "charities" (in the broad sense of "improving the public good"). The deduction, which is an "itemized deduction" (but not an MID), is considered to fall within the broader category of "personal deductions," i.e., deductions not supported by any business or investment nexus.

A. WHAT IS A GIFT OR CONTRIBUTION?

Section 170 requires that the taxpayer make a "contribution or gift," but these terms are not defined in the Code, and thus the meaning of these terms has been left to the Treasury and the courts. Basically, the concept of "contribution or gift" is similar (but not identical) to the notion of "gift" under § 102(a). The term "contribution or gift" does not include a payment to a charitable organization unless (a) the donor intends to make a gift in excess of the value of goods or services received back from the charitable donee and (2) in fact does so. See Reg. § 1.170A-1(h); *U.S. v. American Bar Endowment*, 477 U.S. 105 (1986). This test has more objectivity than the *Duberstein* "donor's motive" test, and closely resembles the test for gift under the federal gift tax. An objective test makes logical sense in the deduction context: if the "donor" receives (or thinks she has received) full value in return, the donor either hasn't incurred a decrease in wealth or has purchased personal consumption. In neither case has the donor made a contribution to a charity.

Thus, payments to a church that are required in order for the church member to send her daughter to the church's parochial school are nondeductible "tuition," not deductible "contributions."[1] And if Generous Jane purchases a ticket to a United Way dinner, only the portion of the ticket cost that exceeds the value of the dinner received in return is a "contribution or gift."

In *Hernandez v. Comm'r*, 490 U.S. 680 (1989), the Supreme Court denied deductions for payments to the Church of Scientology in exchange for services known as "auditing" and "training." The Church basically had a fee schedule that charged prices according to a session's length and level of sophistication. The

---

[1] See *Rev. Rul. 83-104*, 1983-2 C.B. 46, which also held that a payment by the parent of a student to the church that sponsors the parochial school is deductible if (1) the payment is not required as a condition of the child's admission, (2) contributions are received by the church from contributors other than parents of students, (3) aggregate contributions from parents are not significantly larger than aggregate contributions from other contributors, and (4) the school's continued operation is not dependent on parental contributions to the church.

purported justification for this arrangement was a tenet of Scientology known as the "doctrine of exchange," according to which any time a person receives something he must pay something back. Here are excerpts from the majority opinion (490 U.S. at 690-94):

> The legislative history of the "contribution or gift" limitation, though sparse, reveals that Congress intended to differentiate between unrequited payments to qualified recipients and payments made to such recipients in return for goods or services. Only the former were deemed deductible. The House and Senate Reports on the 1954 tax bill, for example, both define "gifts" as payments "made with no expectation of a financial return commensurate with the amount of the gift." S. Rep. No. 1622, 83d Cong., 2d Sess., 196 (1954); H.R. Rep. No. 1337, 83d Cong., 2d Sess., A44 (1954). In ascertaining whether a given payment was made with "the expectation of any quid pro quo," the IRS has customarily examined the external features of the transaction in question. This practice has the advantage of obviating the need for the IRS to conduct imprecise inquiries into the motivations of individual taxpayers.

> In light of this understanding of § 170, it is readily apparent that petitioners' payments to the Church do not qualify as "contribution[s] or gift[s]." As the Tax Court found, these payments were part of a quintessential quid pro quo exchange: in return for their money, petitioners received an identifiable benefit, namely, auditing and training sessions.

> Petitioners argue that a quid pro quo analysis is inappropriate under § 170 when the benefit a taxpayer receives is purely religious in nature. [But] this statutory argument finds no support in the language of § 170. Petitioners' deductibility proposal would expand the charitable contribution deduction far beyond what Congress has provided. Numerous forms of payments to eligible donees plausibly could be categorized as providing a religious benefit or as securing access to a religious service. For example, some taxpayers might regard their tuition payments to parochial schools as generating a religious benefit or as securing access to a religious service. Finally, the deduction petitioners seek might raise problems of entanglement between church and state. Petitioners' proposal would inexorably force the IRS and reviewing courts to differentiate "religious" benefits from "secular" ones.

> We turn, finally, to petitioners' assertion that disallowing their claimed deduction is at odds with the IRS' longstanding practice of permitting taxpayers to deduct payments made to other religious institutions in connection with certain religious practices. The [argument is that the] IRS has accorded payments for auditing and training disparately harsh treatment compared to payments to other churches and synagogues for their religious services: recognition of a comparable deduction for auditing and training payments is necessary to cure this administrative inconsistency.

> A 1971 ruling, still in effect, states: "Pew rents, building fund assessments, and periodic dues paid to a church . . . are all methods of making contributions to the church, and such payments are deductible as charitable

contributions within the limitations set out in § 170 of the Code." *Rev. Rul. 70-47*, 1970-1 Cum. Bull. 49. We also assume for purposes of argument that the IRS also allows taxpayers to deduct "specified payments for attendance at High Holy Day services, for tithes, for Torah readings and for memorial plaques." [The majority then stated that it could not judge from the record how these other transactions worked in practice.] We do not know, for example, whether payments for other faiths' services are truly obligatory or whether any or all of these services are generally provided whether or not the encouraged "mandatory" payment is made.

The dissenting opinion in *Hernandez* stated that it had no doubt that the majority's decision discriminated against the Church of Scientology. The dissent also thought that the benefits received were religious in nature, and that there was no comparable market for such benefits in the secular world.

Hernandez was followed in 1993 by the enactment of §§ 170(f)(8) and 6115. Section 6115 imposes an obligation on charitable organizations that provide goods or services to donors as a quid pro quo for donations to inform donors (of $75 or more) of the portion of the donation that is *not* a deductible "contribution" on account of any quid pro quo. Nevertheless, certain benefits are considered to be so de minimis that they can be ignored in valuing the amount of the net contribution. Among such benefits are those normally associated with membership, such as free or reduced admission to facilities or events, preferred parking, discounts on gift shop items, posters, decals, mugs, and keychains, provided that these items are of relatively low cost to the charity.[2]

Section 170(f)(8) states that *no deduction is allowed for a contribution of $250 or more unless the taxpayer substantiates the gift by a contemporaneous acknowledgement from the donee organization*. The acknowledgement would be the vehicle for complying with § 6115. The Instructions to Schedule A of Form 1040 state that these acknowledgements are not to be attached to the return, but instead must be in the taxpayer's possession when the return is filed. (The valuation of the gift itself is dealt with in Subsection C.2, below.)

Both §§ 170(f)(8)(B) and 6115 provide an exception to the donee's duty to report the value of any quid pro quo in the case where "such goods or services consist solely of intangible religious benefits," which is defined as "any intangible religious benefit which is provided by an organization organized exclusively for religious purposes and which generally is not sold in a commercial transaction outside the donative context." The legislative history gives as an example admission to a religious ceremony but does not explicitly refer to the *Hernandez* case, and § 170(f)(8) does not purport to be a substantive rule.

In the wake of *Hernandez*, members of the Church of Scientology initiated a lawsuit against the government to establish that its practices were not materially different from the practices of other religious organizations that had been accepted by the IRS.[3] In 1993, the IRS revoked the 1978 ruling that had initially held that

---

[2] See Regs. 1.170A-1(h)(3) & (5) Ex. (1), -13(f)(8) & (9); *Rev. Proc. 90-12*, 1990-1 C.B. 471.

[3] See, e.g., *Powell v. U.S.*, 945 F.2d 374 (11th Cir. 1991).

payments for Scientology auditing and training were not deductible.[4]

Is *Hernandez* now a dead letter? The taxpayers in *Sklar v. Comm'r*, 549 F.3d 1252 (9th Cir. 2008), sent their children to a religious school where 55% of the school day was devoted to religious education and 45% to secular education. The taxpayers argued that 55% of their tuition payments purchased intangible religious benefits and that the enactment of § 170(f)(8) and the administrative abandonment of *Hernandez* supported deduction of that amount. The court held that no part of the tuition payment was deductible, because the taxpayers had not produced evidence showing that their payments exceeded the market value of the secular education their children received.

Nevertheless, in the area of payments to religious organizations (for services that do not have a secular counterpart), it appears that the notion of "contribution or gift" is broader under § 170 than it is under § 102, because neither the IRS nor the courts desire to become entangled with religious doctrine or practices.

To be deductible, the contribution must be "to" or "for the use of" the organization. The term "for the use of" generally refers to a gift through a private trust. In that case, the disallowance rules of § 170(f)(2), noted in Subsection C.1, come into play. The term "for the use of" also refers to expenses of the taxpayer in performing services for the charity. In *Davis v. U.S.*, 495 U.S. 472 (1990), the parents of an LDS missionary paid their son's expenses while the son was proselytizing. The Court held that the payment of the expenses of another individual to perform services to the charity does not qualify, especially where the charity (the LDS church) had no control over the funds.

B. THE DONEE ORGANIZATION

No deduction is allowed at all unless it is to an *organization* described in § 170(c). Thus, a contribution or gift to a needy street person is not deductible under § 170. Moreover, the character of the organization can affect the amount of the deduction. Finally, the tax treatment of the organization itself is worthy of note in its own right.

1. Classification of Organizations

Section 501(a) exempts from income tax various corporations, trusts, and other entities that fall within one or more of the categories described in § 501(c) or (d). The list of types of *exempt organizations* is long, and includes certain pension funds, schools, charities, churches, civic leagues, chambers of commerce, labor organizations, horticultural organizations, fraternal orders, veterans groups, credit unions, and social clubs.

The most important subcategory of exempt organization for present purposes is the type of organization described in § 501(c)(3). This category includes churches, hospitals, educational and literary organizations (including symphonies and museums), and a few others.[5] Organizations in this category are commonly called

---

[4] See *Rev. Rul. 93-73*, 1993-2 C.B. 75.

[5] Bob Jones University enforced racially discriminatory admissions standards based on religious

§ 501(c)(3) organizations or simply "charities" (or "charitable organizations"), even though they don't have to be charitable in the normal sense of serving the needy or poor.

A *private foundation* is a subcategory of a § 501(c)(3) organization that is defined in § 509. Private foundations are financed primarily from endowment income or large gifts and bequests from a family or narrow group of donors. Some widely known private foundations are the Ford Foundation, the MacArthur Foundation, and the Bill and Melinda Gates Foundation. A § 501(c)(3) organization that is not a private foundation is called a *public charity* (a term not used in the Code itself) and is mainly supported by contributions from, and/or fees paid by, the public. The overwhelming majority of charities are public charities, including the American Cancer Society, the Salvation Army, churches, universities, the opera company, and so on.

An *operating foundation* is a subcategory of private foundation that essentially carries on activities directly (such as a museum), rather than making grants to other charities. See § 4942(j)(3).

2. Taxation of Exempt Organizations

Exempt organizations are, of course, generally exempt from income tax on their taxable income. Nevertheless, they are taxable on any "unrelated business [net] income," which includes "unrelated debt-financed [investment or rental net] income." See §§ 501(b), 512-514. This tax is often referred to as the "UBIT."

Private foundations are taxed at a 2% rate on their net investment income. See § 4940(a). They also are subject to indirect government regulation under §§ 4941-4948 of the Code, which impose "excise taxes" that amount to penalties on self-dealing, distributing less than 5% of the foundation assets per year, retaining control of business entities, making imprudent investments, making grants to individuals for travel or study, and attempting to influence legislation or elections.

Operating foundations are exempt from some, but not all, of the restrictions applicable to private foundations, including the tax on net investment income and the excise tax on insufficient distributions.

3. Deduction-Eligible Donees

Section 170(c) allows a deduction for a contribution or gift made "to or for the use of" certain types of tax-exempt organizations. The most important category of exempt organization to which deductible contributions can be made is the § 501(c)(3) organization. That category, as noted above, subsumes private foundations, public charities, and operating foundations. Contributions to fraternal organizations can qualify only if used for a purpose that is charitable in the broad sense. The only remaining deduction-eligible donees are (U.S., state, or local)

---

doctrine. In *Bob Jones Univ. v. U.S.*, 461 U.S. 574 (1983), the Court held that the University's tax exemption could lawfully be withheld by the IRS, because the organization did not serve a "public purpose" in the broad sense, and because the organization's practices controverted fundamental public policy. Moreover, denial of the exemption did not violate the First Amendment Free Exercise Clause.

government entities, veterans organizations, and nonprofit cemetery companies.

All of the above must be organized in the United States to be deduction-eligible.

C. MECHANICS OF THE DEDUCTION

The mechanics of the charitable contribution deduction are focused on two issues: (1) the contribution amount, and (2) the amount that may be deducted in the current year.

1. Nondeductible Gifts

Some contributions to deduction-eligible organizations are not deductible at all. Contributions of services are not deductible because they are not of money or property. As previously noted, certain out-of-pocket expense payments (but not depreciation) that are incidental to the performance of services to the charity can be deducted. See Reg. § 1.170A-1(g); *Rev. Rul. 69-645*, 1969-2 C.B. 37.

Section 170(f)(2), (3) disallows the deduction entirely in the case of contributions of certain "partial" interests in property, such as income interests, life estates, and remainder interests in trust or in nontrust property, as well as the rent-free use of property. This disallowance rule is subject to some exceptions, the most important ones not involving trusts being (1) an undivided interest in property (such as an interest of a tenant in common), (2) a remainder interest in the taxpayer's personal residence or farm, and (3) the value of a qualified conservation easement in real property. The gift of a trust *interest* to charity qualifies only if the interest is an annuity interest (fixed dollar amount paid periodically), a "unitrust" interest (fixed percentage of corpus annually), or a remainder interest following an annuity or unitrust interest. A gift to charity of a trust income interest or a remainder interest following an income interest in trust does not qualify. However, a gift of a remainder interest to a charity providing a "pooled income fund" for several donors (see § 642(c)(5)) qualifies.

A qualified conservation easement is created (donated) when a property owner gives up certain valuable property rights (such as development rights) in property in perpetuity to a qualified donee (a government or § 501(c)(3) organization) for a qualified purpose (such as outdoor recreation, the preservation of scenic values, the preservation of the environment, or historical preservation). The deduction is an amount equal to the reduction in the fair market value of the affected property caused by the granting of the easement. The giving of a qualified conservation easement can leave the donor's lifestyle unchanged. The donor (and her heirs or assignees) can continue to live in and/or enjoy the property in its "conserved" state.[6]

The rules pertaining to gifts of partial interests to charity do not prevent the contribution of money or property outright to a charity subject to the charity's contractual obligation to pay an annuity to the donor. This device, called a "direct

---

[6] See *McLennan v. U.S.*, 994 F.2d 839 (Fed. Cir. 1993) (deduction for conservation easement allowed even though it benefitted the donors' retained property).

charitable annuity," is not considered to be a gift of a partial interest in property, because the annuity obligation is not a charge on the donated money or property itself. The deduction, however, is reduced by the value of the retained annuity. See Reg. § 1.170A-1(d).

2. Valuation

If cash is contributed to a public charity (as defined in § 170(b)(1)(A)), the amount of the contribution is easy to determine: it equals the cash gift.

The general rule for gifts of property is that the deduction equals the fair market value of the property.[7] *This rule deviates from the general income tax principle that deductions with respect to property cannot exceed basis.* The donor bears the burden of proof in establishing the value of any contributed property. The donor is subject to a no-fault penalty for any significant valuation overstatement, and an additional penalty for any "gross" valuation overstatement. See § 6662(e) and (h).

Neither of §§ 170(f)(8) and 6115 (dealing with the value of consideration provided by the donee organization) require or encourage the *donee organization* to estimate the value of any property donated by the donor. *Indeed, it would be inadvisable for a charity to venture a valuation,* as there is a penalty under § 6701 for aiding and abetting an understatement, and the donor suffering a penalty for understating tax could sue the charity for negligence or misrepresentation with regard to a valuation overstatement.

Congress has taken steps to curb valuation abuses at the stage of filing the return. Section 170(f)(8) (the substantiation rule for gifts of $250 or more) has already been noted. Section 170(f)(11) imposes additional reporting requirements on the donor for items (other than those that can be readily valued, such as publicly traded stock) claimed to be worth more than $500. Additionally, if the value of a contributed item exceeds $5K, the taxpayer must obtain a qualified appraisal, and attach a signed appraisal summary to the return.[8] For gifts of a claimed value in excess of $500K, the full qualified appraisal must be attached to the donor's tax return.

Section 170(f)(12) imposes special rules on gifts of motor vehicles. Not only is an elaborate acknowledgement required from the donee (to be attached to the donor's return), but the deduction generally cannot exceed the gross proceeds of sale received by the donee.

Section 170(f)(16) (with a few exceptions) totally disallows any deduction for gifts of used clothing and household items of a utilitarian nature that are not in "good used condition."

Finally, § 170(e)(1)(B)(iii) effectively limits the deduction of intellectual property, which inherently has a speculative or contingent value, to its basis (which is usually

---

[7] See Reg. § 1.170A-1(c)(1). This rule came into being by Treasury interpretation in the early days of the income tax, presumably because the statute refers to the "amount" of the contribution.

[8] Section 6050L requires that the donee must report to the IRS if it sells the item within three years.

zero). But § 170(m) allows "second look" deductions based on the actual income yield of the intellectual property over the next 12 years.

3. Cut-Down Rules for Appreciated Property

The much-criticized rule that the deduction equals the fair market value (FMV) of the property has been diluted by § 170(e)(1), enacted in 1969, which applies (only) to certain contributions of *appreciated* property. (Thus, contributions of depreciated-value property are unaffected by § 170(e).) In most cases in which § 170(e)(1) applies, the effect is to reduce the deduction to the property's basis. To paraphrase § 170(e)(1), the FMV of the donated property is reduced by the hypothetical "tainted" gain that would occur if the property were sold for its FMV, and FMV less tainted gain equals basis.[9]

So what is tainted hypothetical gain? Under paragraph (A) of § 170(e)(1), it is any gain that would not be long-term capital gain if it were sold for its FMV. Thus, ordinary gain and short-term capital gain are tainted gain. (Section 1231 gain is treated as being long-term capital gain for this purpose.[10])

Paragraph (B) provides that even hypothetical long-term capital gain is tainted if:

(1) the property is tangible personalty *not* to be used for the charity's tax-exempt purpose or,

(2) the property (if other than marketable securities)[11] is contributed to a private foundation (other than an operating foundation or a foundation that makes substantial distributions).

Amounts lost under the cut-down rules are permanently lost (and not carried forward).

Since the § 1222(3) "sale or exchange" requirement of the long-term capital gains definition is not an issue here due to the hypothetical-sale assumption that is built into the definition of tainted gain, the result under the cut-down rule often hinges on whether the asset is a "capital asset" as defined in § 1221(a). Also relevant is the donor's holding period, after taking into account the special holding-period rules of § 1223. Provisions that often come into play in the present context are §§ 1221(a)(1), (3), and (4), and 1223(1), (2), and (9).

Another issue that is sometimes relevant is whether tangible personal property (that would produce long-term capital gain on its hypothetical sale for its FMV) is

---

[9] The language in § 170(e) seems overly convoluted. Why doesn't it simply say, in each subparagraph, that the taxpayer's deduction is limited to the property's adjusted basis? The answer is that, in rare cases, the end result will not, in fact, be equal to basis, because the "tainted" hypothetical gain (say, ordinary gain) will be less than the total hypothetical gain. For instance, in the case of depreciated personal property, the § 1245 ordinary gain may be less than the total gain.

[10] In brief, § 1231 gain is long-term gain realized on the sale or exchange of depreciable business equipment and real property used in business, other than gain "recaptured" as ordinary gain under § 1245 or some other provision. Section 1231 is explained briefly in Chapter 2.C.4 and in more detail in Chapter 25.B.2.

[11] The exception for marketable securities (which are easy to value) is found in § 170(e)(5).

to be *used* by the donee organization for its exempt purpose. A gift of a Stradivarius violin to a symphony orchestra would qualify. What would not qualify is a gift of tangible personalty where it is intended at the time of the donation that the exempt organization will sell the property. A back-up rule covers cases where the donee organization actually sells the donated tangible personal property within three-years of the donation.[12] Gifts of (long-term capital gain) real property or intangible personal property (such as shares of stock) don't have to satisfy the exempt-purpose test.

In sum, a full FMV deduction for appreciated property donations is an incredible deal that provides donors both an exclusion from income of the unrealized appreciation and a deduction of the excluded dollars. Thus, the rules of § 170(e)(1) — which can defeat this desired result — are important rules to master.

4. Deduction Ceilings

Section 170(b) caps the charitable deduction for individuals in any given year at a percentage of (slightly modified) AGI. The overall contribution limit percentage is 50% of the modified AGI amount. The limitation means all of the taxpayer's deductible § 170(c) contributions (after application of the cut-down rules) are allowable up to the ceiling. It does not mean that only a percentage of all contributions is deductible, a common mistake of students. Thus, if Mr. Goode, with an AGI of $100K, makes $60K of aggregate deductible cash contributions for the year, no more than $50K of that amount (as opposed to $30K) is currently allowable.

Lower percentage limitations apply to aggregate gifts for the year (a) to private (nonoperating) foundations and (b) of appreciated capital-gain property that escapes the cut-down rules described above.[13] Since these various limitations are very complex in the way they interact — and are almost never actually applied — the gory details will be omitted here.

Deductible (but disallowed) amounts in excess of the ceilings are (usually) subject to a five-year carryforward. The mechanics of the carryforward are too complex to pursue here, and lawyers rarely deal with this matter.

NOTES

1. As noted in the text, allowing a deduction for the value of appreciated property is highly controversial on three counts. One, the rule results in a double tax benefit for the same dollars. Two, it imposes a difficult valuation obligation on the tax system. Three, it encourages taxpayers to make gifts of hard-to-value property that can be overvalued without necessarily waving a red flag. One type of solution, represented by § 170(e), is to reduce the deductible amount to basis. An

---

[12] See § 170(e)(7); see also § 170(e)(1)(B)(i)(II) (deduction limited to basis where the tangible personal property is, in fact, sold during the year of gift).

[13] A taxpayer subject to the lower percentage limit for non-cut-down appreciated capital-gain property donated to a public charity can elect out of the lower percentage limit by limiting the deductible amount to the property's basis.

alternative remedy would be to treat such a contribution as a realization-of-gain event to the donor, and the donor would be able to deduct the full value. But under this alternative approach, a successful valuation overstatement by the taxpayer would increase both capital gain and an ordinary deduction — a taxpayer-favorable trade-off that only partially solves the first of the three problems noted above. Moreover, the second and third problems are left totally unresolved.

2. Assume property with an adjusted basis of $20 and a FMV of $100 is sold to a charity for only $20. Without any special rule, the $20 basis would fully offset the amount realized, producing no gain or loss on the "sale" portion, leaving a gift of property with an $80 value and a zero basis. Instead, § 1011(b), applicable only to sales to charities, treats the transaction as a sale of 20% of the asset to the charity, producing § 1001 gain equal to $16 ($20 less 20% of the $20 basis) and a gift of property worth $80 and having a basis of $16 (80% of the $20 basis). The $16 basis is, of course, worthless to the tax-exempt charity.

3. An organization is not officially tax-exempt (and cannot represent that contributions to it are deductible) until it receives a determination from the IRS to that effect. Therefore, the entity must apply for the exemption and (where desired) establish to the satisfaction of the IRS that the organization is not a private foundation. The IRS determinations are retroactive so long as relevant facts have not changed. Organizations that have received the requisite determination are listed in IRS Publication 78, which can be accessed at www.IRS.gov.

PROBLEMS

1. (a) You are walking through downtown when a homeless person asks you for $1. A Salvation Army colonel is standing nearby. (The Salvation Army is an organization described in § 170(c)(2).) To obtain the maximum tax benefit from your generosity, should you give the $1 directly to the homeless individual or should you give it to the colonel and suggest that he give it to the individual without imposing on the colonel any obligation to comply with your wishes? See *Kessler v. Comm'r*, 87 T.C. 1285 (1986) (justifying this structure as enabling government to ensure that charitable contributions are truly charitable by auditing the donee organizations instead of the much larger number of ultimate beneficiaries).

(b) You are a Wall Street Lawyer (charging $400 an hour), and also a big fan of Meals on Wheels, a public charity. State which of the following is the better overall option for you from a tax planning point of view:

(i) Perform volunteer services for eight hours for Meals on Wheels. (Meals on wheels would pay $25/hour for the same services.)

(ii) Work an extra hour at the law firm and donate $400 cash.

(iii) Donate shares of Intel stock worth $400 that cost you $100 ten years ago.

2. In the following, assume that each of the organizations are public charities (as opposed to being private foundations). How much is deductible by Jay in each situation? Ignore the deduction ceilings.

(a) At an auction conducted by the local PBS station during a capital fund drive, Jay purchases a signed photograph of Elvis for $3K.

(b) Jay, an alumnus of Ohio State University (OSU), contributes $1K to OSU, and the contribution entitles him to purchase (at full list price) the much-sought-after tickets to the OSU/Michigan football game. See § 170(*l*).

(c) Jay purchases two tickets for the opening night of the local nonprofit opera company, which cost $500 each. On any other night, the cost of the same tickets would be $50 each. Due to a death in the family, Jay is not able to attend, and tosses the tickets in the wastebasket.

(d) Same as (c), except that Jay turns the tickets back into the box office.

(e) Jay owns stock with a basis of $10K and a current FMV of $1K, and donates the same to OSU. (What should Jay have done instead?)

(f) At another charity auction, Jay, a decent amateur artist, donates a pastel landscape that he painted, which has a $20 basis. A local gallery that represents Jay charges $300 for similar items. See § 1221(a)(3).

(g) For that same auction (in September), Jay contributes an artwork that was inherited from his father (the artist) who died in January of the current year, at which time it was valued at $20K for estate tax purposes. At the time of contribution, the art work is appraised at $60K (death does wonders for the value of an artist's work!), but it sells for $40K at the auction. See §§ 170(e)(1); 1223(11).

(h) If, in (g), Jay had only "consigned" the work to the charity for purposes of the auction (with an agreement that the work would be returned if a minimum bid is not achieved), there has arguably been no "contribution" of the property in kind. Rather, the charity might be viewed as being Jay's agent, with the result that the gain or loss on the sale would be attributed to Jay, who would then be deemed to make a cash contribution to the charity of the sales proceeds. Can Jay argue that an irrevocable contribution of the property occurs at such earlier time (if at all) that the charity receives a minimum bid?

(i) Same as (g), except that instead of donating the work to the charity auction, Jay donates it to the local art museum, which places the work in one of its storage vaults, available for inspection by scholars and others intensely interested in Jay's father's work.

D. IS THE CHARITABLE DEDUCTION JUSTIFIED?

Obviously, the deduction for charitable contributions is not justified on the basis that the contributions represent subsistence or nondiscretionary outlays. Even if one is a member of a church that imposes "compulsory" tithes, membership in the church is voluntary.

Arguments pro and con over the charitable deduction sometimes rage over whether charitable contributions are "consumption." But one can invoke whatever definition of consumption is expedient to reach the conclusion one desires. Thus, it can be asserted that charitable donations are consumption simply because they are not income-production outlays. But it can be argued with equal fervor that they are not consumption in the literal sense because they do not use up or destroy material resources. A similar split occurs over whether the characteristic of "consumption" is personal pleasure or utility. Commentators that assume that personal utility is the touchstone of consumption have argued over the degree to which contributions to performing arts organizations, churches, and alma maters are self-benefiting.[14] However, this line of analysis leads nowhere, because it can be assumed that all charitable donations entail significant psychic benefits to the donor, or else they would not be made. Additionally, the receipt of psychic benefits does not negate the fact that a donation decreases the taxpayer's wealth in the tax sense unless there is an express or implied bargained-for quid pro quo. Taking psychic benefits into account here would be inconsistent with the objective market-based approach that permeates the income tax generally.

A mechanical view of the ability-to-pay norm would indicate that a person's charitable donations were available to finance the federal government, and therefore should not be deductible. However, the ability-to-pay norm is based on a political theory that can accommodate the charitable domain. The U.S. government and charities both serve to promote the public good, and both conform to the same triadic structure: (1) contributors, (2) a mediating institution administered by accountable agents, and (3) a class of beneficiaries (clients).[15] The "accommodating" nature of the federal government is already evident by the practice of subordinating taxation to the subsistence needs of individuals. A more controversial way in which the federal government cedes "territory" is by accommodating state and local governments, while retaining the power to override them (in most cases). Whether to cede more territory to the charitable sphere — while at the same time retaining the ultimate power to control it — is a matter of institutional judgment. The arguments for doing so include pluralism, the ability to pursue minority preferences, programmatic experimentation, the provision of positive externalities, and local control. Arguments contra include the lack of political control of charities, agency problems and an inability to effectively monitor them, the lack of transparency, domination by the very wealthy, and inefficiency. Nevertheless, the charitable domain has long been entrenched in the United States, and is expressly accommodated by the federal income tax (as well as by the federal estate and gift tax). Resources of taxpayers committed to the charitable sphere can (within limits) be viewed as being unavailable to the federal income tax system.

Under this "accommodation" approach to analyzing the proper tax treatment of charitable contributions, the preferred tax provision is a deduction. A tax credit for charitable contributions denies the semi-autonomous nature of the charitable sphere by taxing the contribution and then giving money back to the donor — but surely subsidizing donors is inappropriate in terms of a political theory based on accommodation of charitable entities. A third possible scheme would be one in which the donor received neither a deduction nor a tax credit, but the donee organization would receive a matching government cash subsidy. Such an approach would treat

---

[14] One might characterize most alumni contributions to institutions of higher education as "delayed tuition" or "degree-enhancing payments." And contributions to the regional orchestra may be viewed as "additional ticket charges" or a "fee for membership on the Board of Trustees." However, these benefits are psychic, and are not assignable in commerce.

[15] In the law of trusts, a charitable trust (which is exempt from the rule against perpetuities) cannot benefit named individuals or a definite class (such as "relatives within the 6th degree" of a certain named person).

charities as once-removed government organs.

In contrast to the political theory (institutional) approach just outlined, another possible approach is a purely instrumental one of designing the system to maximize the net welfare output of charities. Here, every design issue would ultimately be judged by empirical research. Any tax benefit to the donor would be viewed as an "incentive" to contribute, and a choice would have to be made between a deduction and a credit as the preferred incentive device. The efficiency of the deduction or credit could be tested empirically. The tax aspects of the system would be viewed as "tax expenditures." Additionally, the tax system would not be viewed as a necessary or essential component of a "program" to support charities.

The same sort of analysis, by the way, can be applied to the issue of possible tax accommodations to state and local government, dealt with in Chapter 5.C.7.

NOTES

1. The fact that the monetary value of a deduction is the amount of the deduction multiplied by the taxpayer's marginal rate is often cited in condemnation of the charitable deduction, especially given the fact that the well-off are disproportionately in a better position (with high discretionary incomes) to make deductible contributions. But this is perhaps too simplistic a view:

(a) From a political-theory view of charities as a semi-autonomous domain apart from the federal government, a deduction (subject to some kind of limit, perhaps) is as appropriate as are subsistence allowances or (perhaps) deductions for state and local taxes.

(b) From the instrumental perspective of maximizing donations, a deduction operates more efficiently than the alternatives by being conspicuously attractive to the group with the most ability to give, i.e., the wealthy.

(c) Is the charitable deduction a "subsidy," and, if so, who benefits from it? If the donor gives more to the charity because of the deduction (and resulting tax savings), the charity is reaping at least part of the subsidy. (This is a form of "capture," because the charity can point to the tax savings as a way of trying to increase the deduction.)

(d) Although a given theory may focus on only one of these "effects," in fact they all occur simultaneously. That is, the § 170 deduction embodies a particular institutional perspective, operates as an incentive, and operates as a subsidy.

2. These various angles can variously influence the *design* of the tax benefit:

(a) From an institutional perspective, because charities are much less subject to control through democratic processes than governments, it is not desirable that the federal government cede its entire territory to charities. Nor is it desirable that a wealthy taxpayer who enjoys the benefits of government in various ways be allowed to give her entire financial allegiance to a private organization and contribute nothing to government. A ceiling on the deduction is one way of preventing these scenarios from occurring. The government can also regulate to curb the excesses of the charitable sphere through the tax system. Examples are the UBIT and the various rules applicable to private foundations.

(b) It is axiomatic that a tax incentive should not be provided for an activity that would occur in the absence of the tax benefit. Perhaps contributions to churches (at least at the bottom end of the income ladder) are unresponsive to the § 170 deduction. If so, a floor under the deduction may increase efficiency. Likewise, a diluted deduction would be in order for the types of gifts that are most likely to give the donor a psychic benefit (gifts to churches, one's alma mater, and cultural organizations).

(c) A subsidy to charities could take the form of a direct government grant, instead of tax benefits. However, if the federal government were to decide what charities were deserving of subsidy (and to what degree), then the whole point of having a charitable sphere (decentralization, experimentation, etc.) would be eroded. The government could operate these activities more efficiently, because it could dispense with the high-cost fund-raising apparatus that burdens most charities. (The IRS blows away the charitable sphere in fund-raising efficiency.) But efficiency is not the point of having a charitable sphere in the first place.

Chapter 17

INCOME-SHIFTING STRATEGIES

This chapter deals first with income-attribution (and deduction-attribution) rules and then with devices to shift income from high-bracket to lower-bracket taxpayers. Gifts (in trust or otherwise) are the usual (but not exclusive) means of achieving income shifting.

A. INCOME ATTRIBUTION

The term "income attribution" refers to rules that deal with the problem of what income "belongs to" which taxpayer(s). Deductions present a similar attribution problem. Recall from Chapter 4 that each individual is a separate taxpayer. This is true even for infants and other dependents. Spouses are separate taxpayers as well. However, shifting income from one spouse to another is inconsequential if the spouses file a joint return. Indeed, filing a joint return automatically achieves income-splitting between spouses. Tax alimony, discussed in Chapter 5.B, is another "legal" income-shifting device. As noted in Chapter 4.C.4, the support of dependents has the ultimate effect of shifting the dependent's personal exemption to the person claiming the dependency exemption.

The core income attribution principles were developed relatively early by the Supreme Court. Recall that husband and wife were separate taxpayers unable to file a joint return prior to 1948.

1. Income from Property

By way of review of material covered in Chapter 4, it has always been understood that income from property is taxed to the owner of property. If there is more than one owner (as is the case with community property), the income from the property is attributed among the owners in proportion to their respective ownership interests.

2. Income from Services

The case set forth below, one of the most cited cases in federal taxation, deals with the taxation of income from services.

LUCAS v. EARL
United States Supreme Court
281 U.S. 111 (1930)

MR. JUSTICE HOLMES delivered the opinion of the Court.

This case presents the question whether the respondent, Earl, could be taxed for the whole of the salary and attorney's fees earned by him in the years 1920 and 1921, or should be taxed for only a half of them in view of a contract with his wife. By the contract, made in 1901, Earl and his wife agreed "that any property either of us now has or may hereafter acquire in any way, either by earnings (including salaries, fees, etc.) or otherwise, during the existence of our marriage, or which we or either or us may receive by gift, bequest, or inheritance, and all the proceeds, issues, and profits of any and all such property, shall be treated and hereby is declared to be received, held, and owned by us as joint tenants, and not otherwise, with the right of survivorship."

The validity of the contract is not questioned. The Revenue Act of 1918 imposes a tax upon the net income of every individual. A very forcible argument is presented to the effect that the statute seeks to tax only income beneficially received, and that taking the question more technically the salary and fees became the joint property of Earl and his wife on the very first instant they were received. We well might hesitate upon the latter proposition because however the matter might stand between husband and wife he was the only party to the contracts by which the salary and fees were earned, and it is somewhat hard to say that the last step in the performance of those contracts could be taken by anyone but himself alone. But this case is not to be decided by attenuated subtleties. It turns on the import and reasonable construction of the taxing act. There is no doubt that the statute could tax salaries to those who earned them and provide that the tax could not be escaped by anticipatory arrangements and contracts however skillfully devised to prevent the salary when paid from vesting even for a second in the man who earned it. That seems to us the import of the statute before us and we think that no distinction can be taken according to the motives leading to the arrangement by which the fruits are attributed to a different tree from that on which they grew.

Earl stands for several propositions. First, and most obviously, *income from services is taxed to the earner thereof*, notwithstanding any advance arrangement to the contrary (referred to as an attempted "anticipatory assignment of income"). The rationale is opaque. It appears to go something like this: (1) the statute is not clear; (2) the statute should be construed to reach a reasonable result (not one dictated by attenuated subtleties of contract law); (3) allowing such assignments would undermine the progressive rate structure; and (4) the result (attribution to the earner) is not only sound policy but is doctrinally reasonable by analogy to the attribution rule for property income (the property here being human capital).

Earl also stands for the proposition that *the presence or absence of tax-avoidance motive generally is irrelevant in connection with assignment-of-income questions.*

In *Earl*, there could have been no income-tax-avoidance motive when the contract was entered into (in 1901) because the federal income tax didn't then exist and the previous one had been held to be unconstitutional.

Third, *Earl rejects the argument that income is taxed to the person who beneficially enjoys it*. If this argument were accepted, then the fact-finder would have to decide how beneficial enjoyment was allocated, an impossible task in the case of a married couple. Moreover, the logical implication of such a rule would be to tax children (and others) on support and gifts received.

3. Who Is the Real Earner?

A few months following *Earl* — in the very same term — the Supreme Court decided *Poe v. Seaborn*, 282 U.S. 101 (1930). This case, described in Chapter 4.B.3, held that personal services income earned by the husband in a community property jurisdiction ended up being taxed half to the husband and half to the wife. This result on the surface appears to fly in the face of *Earl*. In *Seaborn*, the Court finessed this difficulty by holding that (under state law) the husband earned his wages as an "agent" of the marital community. The marital community was not itself a separate taxable entity under the income tax, and so the community income was allocated 50% to each member of the community, according to their interests under state law. Similarly, although the husband (then) had the sole power to manage the property owned by the marital community, he did so as agent.

Since business and investment entities can act only through the activities and decisions of agents, income earned for the entity by the services of the agents are attributed to the entity. If the entity is treated as a partnership for income tax purposes, or is a Subchapter S corporation, the entity income is then re-attributed to the equityholders (partners, shareholders, or whatever). See *U.S. v. Bayse*, 411 U.S. 940 (1973) (income earned by partnership but paid to a trust is includible by the partners in proportion to their partnership interests).

4. Who Is the Real Owner of Income-Producing Property?

The *Blair* and *Clifford* cases, infra, cannot be grasped without a minimal understanding of how trust income is normally taxed. This topic was briefly touched upon in Chapter 1.D.3, and is discussed in more detail at the end of this chapter. The Code has long provided that a (noncharitable) trust is a taxpayer subject to income tax. The taxable income of a trust is generally computed like that for an individual. The receipt by a trust of its "funding" gift, bequest, or life insurance proceeds payment is excluded from the trust's gross income. The core distinguishing principle of trust income taxation is that distributions to beneficiaries are gross income to the beneficiaries to the extent of the trust's net income for the year. At the same time, distributions are deductible by the trust to the extent they are includible by the beneficiaries. Thus, the trust is taxed only on the excess (if any) of its net income over deductible distributions. (These rules, operating in tandem, assure that trust income is not taxed both to the trust and to the beneficiaries.) Distributions to beneficiaries in excess of the trust net income for the year are treated as "corpus" (principal), and are excludible to the beneficiaries.

> *Example*: The trust has net income (gross income less ordinary deductions) for the year of $10K. On January 10th of that year, the trust distributes $13K to Deanna, the trust's sole beneficiary. No other distributions are made during the year. Deanna has gross income of $10K (lesser of distribution or trust net income). The remaining $3K is tax-free to Deanna. The trust's taxable income is zero (net income of $10K less distribution deduction of $10K).

In *Blair v. Comm'r*, 300 U.S. 5 (1937), grandfather William Blair created a trust that provided that the trust income was payable to his son Edward for life. Edward made a gift of fractional shares of his income interest to his children, so that they would actually receive what was considered "income" under the law of trusts (which at that time meant mainly interest and dividends) during Edward's lifetime. If Edward's gift were respected for income tax purposes, the distributions would, under the income tax, be includible by the distributees (to the extent of trust net income as computed for income tax purposes) and deductible by the trust. However, the government argued that this assignment was ineffective to shift trust income from Edward to Edward's children, its theory being that Edward assigned only the future income itself, as opposed to a property interest. In rejecting the government's position, the Supreme Court stated (300 U.S. at 333-34):

> The will creating the trust entitled the petitioner during his life to the net income of the property held in trust. He thus became the owner of an equitable interest in the property. By virtue of that interest he was entitled to enforce the trust, to have a breach of trust enjoined, and to obtain redress in case of breach. The interest was alienable like any other in the absence of a valid restraint upon alienation. We conclude that the assignments were valid, that the assignees thereby became the owners of the specified beneficial interests in the income, and that as to these interests they and not the petitioner were taxable for the tax years in question.

This quote from the *Blair* case suggests that its rationale is strictly that the donor transferred a true property interest. Nevertheless, it is significant that Edward's gifts were of fractional shares in Edward's income interest for life and that Edward retained no interest in these gifts, because Edward only had an income right in the first place. Hence, *Blair*, is distinguishable from later cases in which the owner of a fee interest in property made a gift of an income right (the fruit) while retaining a reversion in the underlying property (the "tree").

The issue in the next case, *Clifford*, was whether the grantor of (i.e., the donor of property to) an inter vivos trust (who made himself the trustee) was entitled as a matter of law to shift the trust income to the trust and/or its beneficiaries. When this case arose (and subsequently through 1986), the § 1(e) rate schedule applicable to trust taxable income was essentially the same as the § 1(d) schedule, meaning that income taxed to the trust or its beneficiaries would obtain the benefit of marginal income tax rate brackets that were likely to be lower than those of the grantor.

HELVERING v. CLIFFORD
United States Supreme Court
309 U.S. 331 (1940)

Mr. Justice Douglas delivered the opinion of the Court.

In 1934 respondent declared himself trustee of certain securities which he owned. During the continuance of the trust respondent was to pay over to his wife the whole or such part of the net income as he in his "absolute discretion" might determine. The trust was for a term of five years. On termination of the trust the entire corpus was to go to respondent, while all [accumulated] income was to be treated as property owned absolutely by the wife. [Respondent as trustee also had various administrative powers, such as the right to vote stock, to sell or borrow on the credit of trust assets and reinvest the proceeds, and to invest trust assets in virtually anything.] An exculpatory clause purported to protect him from all losses except those occasioned by his "own willful and deliberate" breach of duties as trustee.

It was stipulated that while the "tax effects" of this trust were considered by respondent they were not the "sole consideration" involved in his decision to set it up, as by this and other gifts he intended to give "security and economic independence" to his wife.

During 1934 all income from the trust was distributed to the wife. The Commissioner determined that income from the trust was taxable to him. The broad sweep of [the predecessor of § 61] indicates the purpose of Congress to use the full measure of its taxing power within [the enumerated] categories. Technical considerations, niceties of the law of trusts or conveyances, or the legal paraphernalia which inventive genius may construct as a refuge from taxes should not obscure the basic issue. That issue is whether the grantor after the trust has been established may still be treated, under this statutory scheme, as the owner of the corpus. In absence of more precise guides supplied by statute or regulations, the answer to that question must depend on an analysis of the terms of the trust and all the circumstances attendant on its creation and operation. And where the grantor is the trustee and the beneficiaries are members of his family group, special scrutiny of the arrangement is necessary lest what is in reality but one economic unit be multiplied into two or more by devices which, though valid under state law, are not conclusive [for income tax purposes].

In this case we cannot conclude as a matter of law that respondent ceased to be the owner of the corpus after the trust was created. Rather, the short duration of the trust, the fact that the wife was the beneficiary, and the retention of control over the corpus by respondent all lead irresistibly to the conclusion that respondent continued to be the owner for [income tax] purposes.

So far as his dominion and control were concerned, it seems clear that the trust did not effect any substantial change. In substance his control over the corpus was in all essential respects the same after the trust was created as before. The wide powers which he retained included for all practical purposes most of the control which he as an individual would have. There were, we may assume, exceptions, such as his disability to make a gift of the corpus to others during the term of the trust and to make loans to himself. But this dilution in his control would seem to be insignificant and immaterial, since control over investment remained. If it be said that such control is the type of dominion exercised by any trustee, the answer is simple. We have at best a temporary reallocation of income within an intimate family group.

Since the income remains in the family and since the husband retains control over the investment, he has rather complete assurance that the trust will not effect any substantial change in his economic position. It is hard to imagine that respondent felt himself the poorer after this trust had been executed, for as a result of the terms of the trust and the intimacy of the familial relationship respondent retained the substance of full enjoyment of all the rights which previously he had in the property. For where the head of the household has income in excess of normal needs, it may well make but little difference to him (except income-tax-wise) where portions of that income are routed, so long as it stays in the family group.

Our point here is that no one fact is normally decisive but that all considerations and circumstances of the kind we have mentioned are relevant to the question of ownership. We cannot say that the triers of fact committed reversible error when they found that the husband was the owner of the corpus.

[JUSTICE ROBERTS, joined by JUSTICE MCREYNOLDS, dissented on the ground that it was up to Congress to draw the lines as to what constituted retained ownership.]

Although *Clifford* has been superseded by statute in the area of attribution of trust income to an inter vivos trust grantor, *Clifford* still retains vitality on the issue of "tax ownership" of nontrust property.

Clifford also contains two often-cited maxims of tax law. One is that transactions between related parties will be closely scrutinized to ascertain their substance.

The other is the maxim of statutory construction that "Congress has fully exercised its taxing power." Obviously, this cannot be taken literally, because it would mean that all statutory exclusions are redundant (because required by the Constitution). Also, Congress can, under its power to lay indirect taxes without apportionment, tax subjects, under the income tax, that are not "income." The purpose this maxim was intended to serve was only that the *enumerated* categories of gross income in § 61(a) (compensation, interest, dividends, etc.) were to be construed broadly to include in-kind receipts and to foreclose subterfuges based on (nontax) legal technicalities. Because this maxim has sown confusion, its use in Supreme Court opinions has dropped off since the 1960s.

B.   OTHER JUDICIAL DOCTRINES PREVENTING INCOME ASSIGNMENTS

This section deals with additional judicially developed doctrines relating to attempted assignments of income in a nontrust context.

1.   Nontrust Retained-Reversion Transfers

A case decided very shortly after *Clifford* is *Helvering v. Horst*, 311 U.S. 112 (1940). There, a father who owned a "coupon bond" retained the ownership of the bond but transferred the interest coupons to his son for collection shortly before the coupons became due. The taxpayer-father argued that the coupons, which represented a right to interest income, were "property" under *Blair*, that the donee's receipt of the coupons was itself a completed tax-free gift under § 102, and that the bond interest should be taxed to the donee-son when received as "income from" a gift of property. But the Supreme Court majority held that the father was taxable on the interest collected by the son. (The son's actual receipt of the cash would be excludible from his income under § 102(a) as a gift from his father.)

The majority opinion in *Horst* is murky. It fails to cite the fruit-and-tree metaphor, perhaps because bond coupons have an independent legal existence apart from the bond, just as an income beneficiary of a trust has an interest that derives from but is distinct from interests in the trust principal. The basis of *Horst* appears to be a reinterpretation of *Earl* as filtered through *Clifford*. The pertinent part of the rambling opinion states (311 U.S. at 118):

> The power to dispose of income is the equivalent of ownership of it. The exercise of that power to procure the payment of income to another is the enjoyment and hence the realization of the income by him who exercises it. We have had no difficulty in applying that proposition where the assignment preceded the rendition of the services, *Lucas v. Earl*, for it was recognized that the rendition of the service by the assignor was the means by which the income was controlled by the donor and of making his assignment effective.

But why didn't the Court cite *Clifford* (decided earlier in the same term) if the rationale was retained *control*? To confuse matters further, the facts in *Horst* and *Clifford* have a major point in common, namely, the *retention of a reversion* following the assigned income right: in *Horst*, the reversion consisted of the bond itself (representing the right to the bond principal at maturity) and the interest coupons that were to come due after the gifted interest coupons were redeemed for cash.

One year after *Horst*, the Court decided *Harrison v. Schaffner*, 312 U.S. 579 (1941). There, a trust's income beneficiary assigned by gift only a fixed sum of money payable out of next year's trust income. These facts are distinguishable from those in *Horst*, because here the donor retained no reversion in the corpus itself. Nevertheless, the Court stated that this arrangement was closer to *Earl* than to *Blair*. The donor in *Schaffner* continued to own the ongoing income interest out of which the future sum was "carved out." The Court taxed the income to the donor, stating (312 U.S. at 583) that the donor had "parted with no substantial interest in property other than the specified payments of income."

Thus, it appears that any assignment by gift of a *temporal* interest carved out of a greater interest held by the donor is not effective to assign income.[1] In *Galt v. Comm'r*, 216 F.2d 41 (7th Cir. 1954), *cert. denied*, 348 U.S. 951 (1955), the court, in holding a property owner's assignment by gift of 20 years' rent to be ineffective for income tax purposes, stated that "it is immaterial whether the assignment . . . is for a short or long term."

These cases don't really explain *why* a carve-out gift of a temporal interest with a retained reversion is ineffective, but there are parallels with other areas of tax law, particularly that regarding leases. The lessor of property is treated as the full owner for income tax purposes. The entering into of a lease is not treated as a sale of an interest in the property for a term for years. Rent is treated as pure fruit. The retention of a reversion by the lessor is indicative of full ownership of the property (the tree).

Treating the holder of a reversion as the (full) owner of the property simplifies matters tax-wise. But this "single owner" approach is not the only possible way of treating temporal-carve-out transactions. An alternative approach is exemplified by § 1286, which governs cases in which bond coupons are stripped from the bond, and the owner of the coupons is a different person than the owner of the bond. Basically, the "coupon (income) interest" is treated as a separate "wasting" (depreciable) asset that is separate from the "bond" asset, which appreciates with the passage of time. Both of these interests are treated as "trees" with basis that can yield net income.[2] But this approach involves a lot of arithmetic, and the calculations depend on knowing the amount and timing of all future payments.[3] Thus, this approach is practical only for fixed-term debt obligations.

2. Nontrust Gifts of Accrued but Unpaid Income Rights

In the companion case to *Horst, Helvering v. Eubank*, 311 U.S. 122 (1940), the taxpayer assigned by gift his right to renewal commissions that he was entitled to receive if and when customers renewed insurance policies that he had earlier sold them. The taxpayer had fully earned the right to the commissions prior to the assignment. The taxpayer (predictably) argued that the right to commissions already earned was an interest in "property," so that the amounts received by the donee by reason of owning such right would be taxable to the donee (so long as the rights were fully transferred). Not surprisingly, the Supreme Court majority held for the government. In its brief opinion, the majority (confusingly) cited *Horst*, dealing with the assignment of future income to be earned on retained property,

---

[1] In a case with similar facts but involving a different issue, the Court held that a purported sale of a carved-out income right was not a sale of a portion of the underlying property, so that no basis offset was allowed and capital gain treatment was denied. See *Comm'r v. P.G. Lake, Inc.*, 356 U.S. 260 (1958) (where the Court cited *Clifford, Horst*, and *Schaffner*).

[2] It appears that § 1286 supersedes *Horst* on its specific facts. If § 1286 applies to gifts of bond coupons, then a portion of the coupon amounts will be taxed to the donee.

[3] The financial analysis involved in figuring out what the net income would be from each property interest is explained in Chapter 27.B.

rather than *Earl*, dealing with the assignment of services income (although *Horst* itself mainly relied upon *Earl*).

Although *Eubank* might be seen as merely foreclosing a possible way of avoiding *Earl* (by making gifts of services income *after* the services have been performed), it is best viewed as standing for a separate rule in the income-assignment pantheon, namely, that a gift of earned but unpaid income ("ripened fruit") — whether services income or property income — is ineffective to shift the taxation of the income *even if the tree is also transferred along with the fruit*. See, e.g., *Salvatore v. Comm'r*, 434 F.2d 600 (2d Cir. 1970) (gain on sale of property given to children, where donor had already negotiated the sale, was taxed to the donor); *Austin v. Comm'r*, 161 F.2d 666 (6th Cir. 1947) (gift of accrued but unpaid interest was ineffective to shift the interest income to the donee); *Smith v. Comm'r*, 292 F.2d 478 (3d Cir. 1961) (dividend on stock gifted one day before payment of previously declared dividend was taxed to the donor).

As with carve-out gift transactions, a doctrine that is kin to that exemplified by *Eubank* comes into play where rights to accrued income are sold (instead of being transferred by gift): § 1001 gain on the disposition of a right attributable to accrued but unpaid ordinary income is ordinary gain (not capital gain).[4]

C. ATTRIBUTION OF DEDUCTIONS

What about the attribution of deductions? It is clear that deductions derived from *property* itself (depreciation and losses) are claimable only by the owner(s) of the property. One should be reminded that § 1015 operates to prevent the assignment by gift of a built-in loss. (At the same time, § 1015 facilitates the assignment of a built-in gain.)

Expense deductions are generally taken by the taxpayer who incurred (owes) the item in question, provided that such taxpayer also pays (or is deemed to have paid) the item. Thus, if X pays Y's deductible mortgage interest, the deduction (as an *interest* deduction under § 163) can be claimed only by Y (who, under the *Old Colony Trust* rule, supra Chapter 12.A) is deemed to have received the cash from X and then paid the same cash to the mortgage lender. By making the payment to Y, X may or may not have a deduction or a capital expenditure under applicable tax rules, but whatever the tax treatment of X may be, X is not paying "interest." Recall also that if a person (engaged in a business) pays another party's debts, the payor risks disallowance of an expense deduction under the "ordinary and necessary" test as applied in *Welch v. Helvering*, Chapter 8.B.1.

Nevertheless, some situations exist where a person can claim a deduction on the basis of payment alone. For example, current § 213 allows the payor of medical expenses to obtain the deduction even when the expenses were incurred by the taxpayer's spouse and dependents. See § 213(a). And, because charitable donations

---

 [4] See § 1221(a)(4) (denying capital asset status to receivables resulting from the taxpayer's performance of services or sale of inventory); *U.S. v. Midland-Ross Corp.*, 381 U.S. 54 (1965) (sale of a bond with accrued interest); *Ayrton Metal Co. v. Comm'r*, 299 F.2d 741 (2d Cir. 1962) (sale of earned but undistributed profits from joint venture); *Lasky v. Comm'r*, 22 T.C. 13 (1954), *other issues appealed*, 235 F.2d 97 (9th Cir. 1956), aff'd *per curiam*, 352 U.S. 1027 (1957) (accrued but unpaid royalties).

are gratuitous, the payor obtains the deduction. Deductions for certain state and local taxes and mortgage interest can be obtained by the payor in the case of joint and several liability, which is common.

Community property law operates on the deduction side as well as the gross income side. Deductions relating to community property investments (repairs, depreciation, and losses) are attributed 50-50 to each spouse. Other expenses paid out of community funds are also split 50-50. However, as noted earlier, the split attribution of deductions has no significance if the couple files a joint return.

NOTES

1.   (a) *Horst, Eubank,* and *Schaffner* are sometimes said to stand for the proposition that the assignment of a pure income right is ineffective. However, these cases can be explained on other grounds (retained reversion, gift of ripened fruit), and the proposition is contradicted by *Blair.*

(b) In *Comm'r v. First Security Bank of Utah,* 405 U.S. 394 (1972), fees for services rendered by the taxpayer were successfully shifted to another party, the Court holding that *Earl* does not apply where the taxpayer is prohibited *by law* from initially receiving the fees.

(c) In *Rev. Rul. 73-390,* 1973-2 C.B. 12, the IRS ruled that an agreement, valid under state law, to convert income from rendering services from community property income into the separate income of the spouse who earned it was valid for tax purposes (i.e., the income was taxable entirely to the earner spouse unless a joint return was filed). The ruling relied on 1934 and 1940 court of appeals decisions that in turn relied on *Seaborn,* but ignored a later Supreme Court case, *Comm'r v. Harmon,* 323 U.S. 44 (1944), which invalidated (for tax purposes) an election under then-Oklahoma law to opt into a community property regime (rather than Oklahoma's "standard" non-community property regime). The ruling, therefore, is questionable, but apparently little used, and (being pro-taxpayer) is unlikely to be challenged.

2.   (a) It is not always easy to tell when income is from property or services in situations where a creative talent creates intellectual property (such as a copyrighted manuscript), assigns her rights to a publisher, producer, or manufacturer in return for future royalties (that are contingent on sales to the public), and then assigns the royalty right to a related party. The royalty right is viewed as a separate property right apart from the underlying intellectual property right, and the gift of it is usually successful to assign the income. See, e.g., *Heim v. Fitzpatrick,* 262 F.2d 887 (2d Cir. 1959).

(b) In contrast, an assignment of sales proceeds is ineffective to shift income. See *Court Holding Co. v. Comm'r,* 324 U.S. 331 (1945); *Malkan v. Comm'r,* 54 T.C. 1305 (1970) (acq.). The distinction between assigning sales proceeds and the author-royalty scenario is probably that an assignment of sales proceeds is an assignment of earned income (ripened fruit, as in *Eubank*), whereas the royalties are to be earned in the future. However, the author-royalty scenario is hard to distinguish from *Eubank,* where the future commissions depended on events beyond the donor's control, as is also the case in the author-royalty situation. Perhaps a right to renewal commissions (a right to compensation for past services) is what distinguishes *Eubank* from the creator of intellectual property, even though the intellectual property was created by the creator's labors.

3.   (a) Entities are not considered to be operating as an "agent" of the entity's equityholders (owners) simply because of their equity ownership and ultimate control of the entity's operations. See e.g., *Moline Properties v. Comm'r*, 319 U.S. 436 (1943); *Nat'l Carbide Corp. v. Comm'r*, 336 U.S. 422 (1949). Instead, an actual agency arrangement must exist apart from ownership control. See *Comm'r v. Bollinger*, 485 U.S. 340 (1988). The strong presumption against the agency status of business entities operates to maintain the integrity of the tax systems dealing with entities and their owners. Thus, if K owns all of the stock of KMAX Corp., the income and deductions of KMAX will not be attributed to K individually unless an actual agency relationship exists. In the absence of such a relationship, the income and deductions from KMAX's activities will be attributed to KMAX Corp.

(b) Agent-principal issues are sometimes hard to sort out. In *Rev. Rul. 74-581*, 1974-2 C.B. 25, a law school operated an in-house legal clinic as part of its teaching program. In connection with their teaching duties, full-time salaried clinical faculty members were appointed to represent indigent defendants, and they supervised students in preparing the cases. Afterwards, the faculty members received fees under the Criminal Justice Act for their services and turned this compensation over to the law school as required by their law school employment contracts. On these facts, the IRS ruled that "the attorney-faculty members involved are working solely as agents of the law school . . . and realize no personal gain from payments [under the Criminal Justice Act] for their services in representing the indigent defendants." Thus, the clinical faculty members were not taxed on the fees turned over to the law school.

(c) In contrast, the following members of religious orders were each held to have received their compensation in their individual capacities and not as agents of their religious orders, even though each was obligated by a vow of poverty to transfer all compensation to his or her order (and each did so): (1) a Franciscan priest who received wages from a federal hospital for serving as its chaplain, see *Kircher v. U.S.*, 872 F.2d 1014 (Fed. Cir. 1989); (2) a Jesuit priest who received wages from a state university for teaching Catholic theology and history, see *Fogarty v. U.S.*, 780 F.2d 1005 (Fed. Cir. 1986); and (3) a Roman Catholic nun who was paid by the federal government for serving as a nurse-midwife at a public health clinic, see *Schuster v. Comm'r*, 800 F.2d 672 (7th Cir. 1986). Is it significant that the decision to hire these particular individuals was made by the employers, that all day-to-day supervision and control of their services was done in the workplace by their employers, and that there were no contracts between the religious orders and the employers regarding the individuals' services?

PROBLEMS

1.   (a) Dr. Smith is a garden-variety internist. He is president, chairman of the board, and sole stockholder of Smith P.C., a professional corporation that is also a C corporation (a taxable entity). Pursuant to an employment contract that gives the corporation an employer's normal authority to direct and control Dr. Smith's work,

Dr. Smith performs all services for patients except for those rendered by an employee medical technician. There are other employees of the corporation who act as receptionists, clerks, and accountants. The patients are billed by the "Smith P.C." and make out their checks to it. Can the IRS tax Dr. Smith directly on the corporation's profits under *Earl* or *Clifford*? If Dr. Smith finds it advantageous to do so, can he argue that *Earl* or *Clifford requires* that the corporation's profits be included in his gross income (rather than the corporation's income)?

(b) Same facts as (a), except that it is the Jones Corp., the sole shareholder of which is pro basketball superstar Djibouti Jones, which enters into a contract with a professional basketball club to provide Jones' services as a basketball player. Compare *Leavell v. Comm'r*, 104 T.C. 140 (1995) (income attributed to player), with *Sargent v. Comm'r*, 929 F.2d 1252 (8th Cir. 1991) (income attributed to corporation).

2. Consider the assignment of income by gifts of stock and dividend rights in each of the following situations. Who is taxed on the income (and when) in each case?

(a) Clive owns a 10-year U.S. Series E Savings Bond, the interest on which is not taxed (nor paid) until the bond is redeemed at its maturity. (See § 454.) Clive gives the bond to Doug after nine years, at which time the accumulated but unpaid and untaxed interest is $3,456. Doug redeems the bond at the end of Year 10, at which time the total accrued interest is $4,000. See *Rev. Rul. 55-278*, 1955-1 C.B. 471; *Rev. Rul. 69-102*, 1969-1 C.B. 32.

(b) Clio, who owns shares of Intel Corp., puts the stock in her friend Carlotta's name on Intel's books but retains the stock certificates and has Carlotta endorse all of the dividend checks (received by Carlotta) over to Clio. Clio also instructs Carlotta on how to vote the Intel stock.

(c) Serge, a high-stakes speculator, makes an arm's length purchase of a 40% right to a possible contingent fee in pending litigation from the law firm trying the case. Serge then gives half of his 40% interest to his son Ivan.

(d) Gramps owns stock of ConEd (a utility company) that pays regular dividends. He gives Junior the right to receive the ConEd dividends for the next two years.

(e) Randy, who owns shares of stock in AT&T, gives his friend Charles the right to all dividends from the stock for 30 years and validly agrees in writing not to sell the stock in the meantime. The stock remains registered on AT&T's books in Randy's name. AT&T will send an information return to the IRS reporting Randy as the recipient of the dividends.

D. NONTRUST STRATEGIES FOR SHIFTING INCOME

Previous sections of this chapter were somewhat doctrinal in orientation. This section takes an instrumental approach to common techniques (successful or unsuccessful) of shifting income that do not involve the use of trusts.

1. Gifts of Income-Producing Property to Minors: The Kiddie Tax

Cash gifts, to minors or otherwise, fail to immediately shift income, because gifts are excluded by the donee and are not deductible by the donor. Of course, the donee can invest the cash in income-producing property. Alternatively, the donor can make a gift of income-producing property, so long as the donor does not retain ownership "in substance" or a reversionary interest.

Individuals who, due to their age of minority, tend to have little or no income of their own, are a tempting category of donee. Outright gifts to minors would normally be subject to court-supervised guardianship, but guardianship can be avoided by using a trust (in which one or more minors are beneficiaries) or a "custodial" gift under the Uniform Gift to Minors Act, which has been enacted by all of the states. A custodial gift vests immediate title in the minor, subject to management powers held by an adult custodian. (The custodian is often a parent of the minor or perhaps the donor.) Thus, income from custodial property is taxed to the minor (whereas in a trust the income could be taxed to the trust, if not distributed).

Custodial gifts to minors became so popular that Congress responded in 1986 by enacting § 1(g), known as the "Kiddie Tax." Under § 1(g), the net unearned income of a (non-orphaned) child who has not attained the age of 18 by the close of the taxable year[5] is taxed at the higher of the child's rate or, more likely, the rate at which such income would have been taxed if the income were attributed to the parent(s) and treated as the "last" dollars in the tax base of the parent(s). If the parents are unmarried, the relevant parent is the custodial parent. If the parents are married but file separately, the higher-income parent is the relevant parent. See § 1(g)(5).

The term "unearned income" essentially means investment income, because "earned income" means wages and income from a services business. If the minor owns a business in which capital is a material income-producing factor, at least 70% of the net income will be treated as unearned income.[6]

The "net" unearned income is the excess of unearned gross income less any above-the-line deductions allocable to such income. This amount is then reduced by the greater of (a) two times the standard deduction amount available to a person being claimed as a dependent or (b) the sum of (i) one such standard deduction amount and (ii) the itemized deductions directly connected to the production of the unearned income.

Section 1(g) applies even if the source of the unearned income is property transferred by a person other than the child's parent. A grandparent is a common example. Indeed, § 1(g) applies even to investment income derived from the child's own savings out of earned income.

---

[5] Section 1(g) also may apply to a child who is a full-time student under the age of 24 and whose earned income constitutes 50 percent or less of that child's amount of support for the taxable year. See § 1(g)(2)(A)(ii). But it does not apply if the child files a joint return. See § 1(g)(2)(C).

[6] See § 911(d)(2), which provides the relevant definition of "earned income."

Section 1(g) affects only the *rate* at which a child's unearned income is taxed. The income is still taxed to the child. Thus, the child is not generally relieved of having to file a return and pay the tax. Nevertheless, if the gross income of the child consists only of interest and dividends not exceeding an amount equal to 10 times the standard deduction amount available to a person being claimed as a dependent, the parent can elect to have the child's net unearned income attributed to the parent (and thus included on the parent's return) to avoid the hassle of filing a return for the child. See § 1(g)(7).

2. Below-Market Gift Loans

Gifts of money or property are subject to the federal gift tax, and gifts of property run up against the potential problem of retained ownership in substance. Both problems are avoided by a loan, which is neither a gift to, nor the income of, the borrower. The money that the high-bracket lender could have invested is now in the hands of the low-bracket borrower, who can then invest the money on her own account. Since an obligation of the borrower to pay interest would reduce (or eliminate) the borrower's investment income and increase the lender's investment income, it is necessary (to achieve income shifting) that the lender simply forgoes the charging of interest. Of course, the principal has to be repaid, or else the transaction might be viewed as a disguised gift for gift tax purposes.

Congress eventually reacted to this and other transactions involving below-market loans by enacting § 7872, which is examined in some detail in Chapter 18.B. Section 7872 applies slightly differently to gift loans than it does to compensation (or dividend) loans. To illustrate the operation of § 7872 to gift loans, assume that Dad lends $100K to adult daughter Sammy, without interest, for a 10-year term. Section 7872(b)(1), made applicable by § 7872(d)(2), treats Dad as having made a gift of the excess of the amount lent ($100K) over the present value of Sammy's non-interest-bearing repayment obligation as calculated according to the discounting rules of § 7872. Assuming that the present value of Sammy's repayment obligation is $62K, it follows that Dad is deemed to have presently transferred $38K of value to Sammy, and this is treated as a "gift" for both gift and income tax purposes.

In addition, § 7872(a) treats Sammy as making annual payments of the foregone interest to Dad. The foregone interest amount is keyed to the "applicable federal rate" (AFR) for each year the loan is outstanding.[7] The foregone interest amount is includible by Dad as interest income, and is treated as an interest expense by Sammy. Whether it is deductible by Sammy depends on what she did with the $100K. (The deductibility of interest is considered in Chapter 18.D.) Since the topic here is "assignment of income," assume that Sammy invested the $100K in taxable bonds. In that case, the foregone interest amount would be investment interest that is deductible by Sammy under § 163(a), subject to the limitation (of net investment income) imposed by § 163(d). In that case, the effect of the deemed payment of foregone interest would be to shift the investment income earned on

---

[7] This rule differs from that applicable to other below-market term loans subject to § 7872, where the imputed interest is calculated as if the repayment obligation were an original-issue-discount (OID) obligation taxed according to § 1272. OID is explained in Chapter 27.B.1.

the $100K from Sammy back to Dad *but only at the applicable federal interest rate.*

Section 7872 contains some rules that apply only to "gift loans." First, the entire section is waived if the aggregate of below-market gift loans by the individual taxpayer to another individual is less than $10K (unless the loan is connected to purchasing or carrying investments by the donee). Second, if such loan amount does not exceed $100K, the imputed interest amount deemed paid from the borrower to the lender shall not exceed the borrower's net investment income for the year. If the borrower's net investment income for the year is less than $1K, it shall be treated as zero for purposes of the preceding sentence. (The rationale of this exception is that, if the borrower isn't investing, no income shifting is being attempted.) Note that this second special rule does *not* change the amount of the deemed gift (for both gift and income tax purposes) from the lender to the borrower.

PROBLEMS

1.   Daughter, age 25, needs $10K per year to finance her law school education. Mother is in the 35% tax bracket and daughter is in the 15% bracket. Assume that the applicable federal rate (AFR) at all times is 10%. Mother makes an interest-free loan of $117,650 to Daughter, repayable on Mother's demand. A demand loan cannot be reduced to present value, because the future date for repayment is not known. Daughter buys a $117,650 certificate of deposit (CD) from a bank, which pays Daughter 10% interest ($11,765) per year, yielding $10K after taxes. After three years, Daughter cashes in the CD and repays Mother the $117,650 principal amount. How does § 7872 affect this transaction?

2.   Same as problem 1, except that the loan is a three-year term loan. Assume that the present value of the repayment obligation of $117,650, determined under the § 7872 rules (using an AFR of 10%), is $88,350.

3.   Paying Salary to the Natural Object of One's Bounty

Can income be shifted by a high-bracket person paying wages to a lower-bracket person within the "family?" The hope is that the wage payment would be deductible by the payor under § 162(a) as an ordinary and necessary business expense and includible by the payee under § 61(a)(1). Additionally, wages are normally "earned income" exempt from the Kiddie Tax (and able to increase the standard deduction of a "dependent").

This idea is a non-starter if the services are of a domestic, personal, or household nature, because, in that case, the wages, although includible by the payee, would be considered to be nondeductible personal and household expenses of the payor. See § 262. This plan would be a disaster because it would actually *increase* the aggregate taxable income of the pair without increasing their aggregate economic income.

The current deductibility of wages presupposes (1) that the wages are not capital expenditures and (2) that such expenses are incurred in a business (or income-production) activity being carried on by the payor. In addition to the usual requirements of § 162(a) or 212 (as the case may be) described in Chapter 8,

§ 162(a)(1) adds a proviso stating that expenses in the nature of compensation for services are deductible only to the extent they are "reasonable" and "for personal services actually rendered." As noted in connection with the *Clifford* case, transactions between related parties are scrutinized as to their substance. Thus, to be deductible, the wages paid to a related person in a business context must be for real work and must not exceed what would be paid in an arm's length transaction. Additionally, income from services is subject to the payroll tax or self-employment tax.

The case below ties together several strands set out in this section, while adding a new Code provision to your repertoire, § 73.

FRITSCHLE v. COMMISSIONER
United States Tax Court
79 T.C. 152 (1982)

FAY, JUDGE:

[Petitioners Robert and Helen Fritschle, residents of Missouri, had eleven children, the eight youngest of which lived at home. Since 1956 Robert had been employed as general manager by American Gold Label Co. (AGL), which was in the printing business. Starting in 1970, AGL undertook printing on cloth ribbons and rosettes of the type awarded at horse shows, county fairs, etc. AGL needed outside help to assemble the ribbons and rosettes and contracted this job out to Helen, who was to be paid on a piecework basis. Materials were provided by AGL. From 1970 to 1976, Helen, with the help of her children, did the work at home.] The children performed approximately 70% of the work. The children were not employees of either Helen or AGL, nor was there any other arrangement for them to share directly in the compensation paid to Helen by AGL.

Since a portion of the compensation was attributable to work performed by their children, petitioners argue that a proportionate amount of the payments should be included in the income of the children. It is axiomatic that income must be taxed to him who earns it. *Lucas v. Earl*. Moreover, it is the command of the taxpayer over the income which is the concern of the tax laws. Recognizing that the true earner cannot always be identified simply by pointing "to the one actually turning the spade or dribbling the ball," this Court has applied a more refined test — that of who controls the earning of the income. *Johnson v. Comm'r*, 78 T.C. 882 (1982)[, aff'd, 698 F.2d 372 (9th Cir. 1983)].

Applying this test, it is clear that, for purposes of taxation, Helen, and not the children, was the true earner of the income. Helen was solely responsible for the performance of all services, AGL contracted only with Helen, and no contract or agreement existed between AGL and any of the children. All checks were made payable to Helen and the children received no direct compensation for their work. Clearly, the compensation was made purely for the services of Helen. Although AGL knew the children were performing part of the work, that does not change the fact that AGL looked exclusively to Helen for performance of the services. In short, Helen managed, supervised, and otherwise exercised total control over the entire operation. It was she who controlled the capacity to earn the income, and it was she who in fact received the income. It does not necessarily follow that income is taxable to the one whose personal efforts produced it.[8]

Nevertheless, petitioners argue § 73 mandates a result in their favor. Section 73(a) provides: "Amounts received in respect of the services of a child shall be included in his gross income and not as the gross income of the parent, even though such amounts are not received by the child."

Petitioners argue the language and meaning of § 73 are clear. However, § 73(a) was enacted in response to a different situation and, under these facts, does not purport to tax the children on a portion of the income at issue herein. Prior to 1944, a parent was required to include in income all earnings of a minor child if, under the laws of the state where they resided, the parent had a right to those earnings. Since parents in all states were not entitled to the earnings of their minor children, different tax results obtained depending on state law. To eliminate this discrepancy, Congress enacted § 73 to provide a uniform rule that all amounts received "in respect of the services of a child" shall be included in the income of that child regardless of the fact that, under state law, the parent may be entitled to those amounts. Thus, § 73 taxes a minor child on income he is deemed, in the tax sense, to have earned. It does not purport to alter the broad principle of taxation that income is taxed to the earner. Helen is the true earner of the income herein. If, on the other hand, we made a finding that it was the services of the children that were being contracted for and that the children were the true earners of the income, then § 73 would tax the children on that income. This is so despite state law.

PROBLEMS

1. Wanda earns $100K in annual salary. Do any of the following effectively shift income to her son Shawn, age 25, for federal income tax purposes?

(a) Wanda makes a cash gift of $20K to Shawn.

(b) Wanda enters into an enforceable contract with Shawn, under which Shawn is deemed to "own," at the moment of earning, 20% of Wanda's wages. (Assume that the contract is legally valid and enforceable.)

(c) Wanda pays Shawn a salary of $20K for doing household chores.

(d) Wanda pays Shawn a salary of $20K for running occasional errands and doing odd jobs in Wanda's business.

2. What if, in *Fritschle*, the mother actually paid reasonable wages to the children by depositing money in custodial bank accounts in their names, designating herself as custodian? Assume that, under applicable state law, the parents are not

---

[8] [7] . . . Petitioners make no claim for a deduction with respect to the services rendered by the children. Indeed, no such deduction would be allowable since no payments to the children were made or set aside. See *Romine v. Comm'r*, 25 T.C. 859 (1956), wherein a father's expenditures on his son's behalf for college were held not to be payments for services actually rendered. Compare *Hundley v. Comm'r*, 48 T.C. 339 (1967), wherein a professional baseball player, Randy Hundley, was allowed a business expense deduction for paying over to his father 50% of the bonus he received for signing with the San Francisco Giants.

entitled to the income of their minor children. A custodian of a custodial account has the power to apply funds for the benefit of the minor children. Assume that the mother in fact uses all of the custodial funds to pay for the children's support. Since the parents have a duty to support the children without regard to the children's other resources, it is likely that the mother, by using the funds in this fashion, is unlawfully appropriating the children's property.

4. Gifts of Interests in Entities Carrying on a Services Business

Gifts of property (without strings attached) are usually effective to shift future income to the donee. Can an entity be used to transform services income into income from property for the donee of an equity interest in the entity? This issue is examined here in the context of entities taxed as partnerships, S corporations, and C corporations. In all cases, the attempt to shift income depends on an arrangement whereby the entity does *not* pay adequate "salary" to the provider of services because salary payments would be income to the service provider and would reduce or eliminate the entity-level profit. It is the entity-level profit that can (through gifts of equity interests in the entity) be more easily shifted to other family members.

a. Family Partnerships

Why not take a cue from *Seaborn* (which treated married couples in community property states as, in effect, equal partners in a partnership), and create a partnership in which Pat, successful lawyer, forms a partnership with daughter Celia (the PC law partnership) in which Pat and Celia have 80% and 20% interests in partnership profits and losses respectively? (An LLC can be used instead of a partnership, since LLCs are usually treated as partnerships for tax purposes.) Assume that this arrangement (which entails a gift of a 20% partnership interest from Pat to Celia) is valid under state law in all respects.

Recall (from Chapter 1.D.3) that an entity treated as a partnership for federal income tax purposes (a "tax partnership") is not a taxpayer and owes no tax itself. See § 701. Instead, the net income of the tax partnership is generally attributed to the owners (here, the partners) as it is earned (whether or not distributed) essentially in proportion to their ownership interests. See § 704(a) and (b). Moreover, the character of the income at the partnership level (as earned income) passes through to the partners.[9] Thus, all the pieces appear to be in place for a successful assignment to Celia of 20% of Pat's income from the PC partnership (but which is essentially Pat's law practice), which is income from services, so long as the PC partnership does not pay salary to Pat equal to the net income the PC partnership (really Pat) earns by performing services. For example, if the PC partnership earns net income of $500K (all attributable to Pat's services) and pays no salary to Pat, the net income of $500K would, according to the partnership tax rules described so far, be allocated $400K to Pat and $100K to Celia.

---

[9] See § 702(b); *Rev. Rul. 67-158*; 1967-1 C.B. 188.

Two barriers exist, however, to achieving income splitting through a partnership formed to receive and divvy-up a given income stream among members of a related group, such as family members. The PC partnership scheme for shifting income won't work unless clients are willing to hire the partnership rather than Pat individually. Recall the *Fritschle* case, supra, where the payor hired Mrs. Fritschle to provide the goods. Only PC partnership income can possibly be allocated 20% to Celia.

Second, even if the PC partnership manages to contract to perform services for clients, the principle of *Lucas v. Earl* was applied in early Supreme Court cases[10] to attribute the ostensible partnership income that was attributable to the performing of services to the partner who *actually* performed the services in cases where the other "partners" are family members who obtained their interests by gift from the services. But the doctrine that emerged from these cases was imprecise, causing Congress to enact § 704(e). To the extent § 704(e) applies, it supersedes prior case law.

The language of § 704(e) is unusually opaque, even to a person savvy in income tax doctrine, but the general idea is (1) that services income must first be allocated to a partner who made gifts of partnership interests and also performs services for the partnership to the extent that such partner is undercompensated, and (2) that, as to the remaining partnership net income, the donee of a partnership interest will be recognized as a partner only if (a) the donee has a capital interest (liquidation right) in a partnership in which capital (investment) is a material income-producing factor *and* (b) the donor does not retain control over the donee's partnership interest. These tests are fairly objective. Test (1) codifies the *Lucas v. Earl* principle, and the two-pronged test (2) codifies the principle that a true owner of income-producing property is taxed on the income therefrom. Although a partnership interest won't be disregarded for income tax purposes just because it was acquired by gift, the gift, under prong (2)(a), has to transfer "real" ownership of a true "property" interest to the donee. The Treasury has dealt with the ownership-in-substance principle of prong (2)(b) in Reg. § 1.704-1(e)(2). One rule found therein is that a gift of a partnership interest to a minor child in trust virtually requires an independent trustee for the assignment to have any chance of being recognized for income tax purposes.

Section § 704(e) comes into play only if capital is a material income-producing factor in the partnership. Thus, a pure services partnership (like the PC partnership) lies outside of § 704(e), and is exposed to being totally disregarded for income tax purposes under the case law.[11]

---

[10] See *Burnet v. Leininger*, 285 U.S. 136 (1932) (holding that an attempted assignment by a husband of half of his partnership interest was not a true gift of an interest in the partnership); *Comm'r v. Tower*, 327 U.S. 280 (1946) (family partnership not recognized, despite wife's ownership of a capital interest, where husband performed all the services and totally controlled the partnership business); *Comm'r v. Culbertson*, 337 U.S. 733 (1949) (partnership interest acquired by gift can be valid even if the donee partner contributes neither services nor original capital).

[11] See *Payton v. U.S.*, 425 F.2d 1324 (5th Cir.), *cert. denied*, 400 U.S. 957 (1970) (ordering district court to enter judgment n.o.v. for the government); *Ketter v. Comm'r*, 70 T.C. 637 (1978), *aff'd sub nom. Frank v. Comm'r*, 605 F.2d 1209 (8th Cir. 1979) (partnership interests disregarded).

b. Family Subchapter S Corporations

A Subchapter S corporation is a corporation whose shareholders unanimously elect to be taxed (under Subchapter S of the Code) in a way that resembles the tax scheme applicable to partners and partnerships. Thus, corporate profit and loss is passed through, along with the character thereof. The Subchapter S counterpart to § 704(e) is § 1366(e), which allows the IRS to impute salary (or investment return) to a contributor of services (or capital) to an S corporation having shareholders who are family members (spouse, ancestors, descendants, and trusts for any such person).

Even if a family member is not involved, the IRS has weapons other than § 1366(e) at its disposal. If the S corporation actually makes payments to the service provider that are called "dividends," the payments run the risk of being re-characterized as "salary" (which also renders them subject to payroll tax).[12]

Additionally, § 482 allows the IRS to re-allocate income between two businesses controlled by the same taxpayer in order to clearly reflect the income of each. In this case, the two businesses would be a family S corporation and the shareholder's business of being an employee. Section 482 would operate in this context by re-attributing the corporation's services income to the employee. See *Rev. Rul. 88-38*, 1988-1 C.B. 246. However, section 482 appears to be seldom used in this context.

c. Family C Corporations

Since a C corporation (briefly described in Chapter 1.D.3) is a taxable entity, and since the dividends paid by it are income to the shareholder (without a deduction by the corporation), the formation of a C corporation expected to earn net profits followed by gifts of dividend-paying stock would have little tax-planning appeal, because the dividends would be a second tax on corporate profits. Moreover, dividends are inherently "unearned" income.[13] In a C corporation context, the tax incentive is to pay *too much* salary to the services provider (which can hopefully be deducted by the corporation and, thus, is subject to tax only at the service provider level). Excessive salary payments may be disallowed as deductions, as explained in Chapter 8.D.3. But that is another story, the point here being that one would not form a C corporation just to make gifts of dividend-paying stock. But if one were already "stuck" with being a shareholder in a closely-held C corporation, gifts of stock would generally be effective to shift dividend income.

Nevertheless, a controlled corporation might be used in other income-assignment schemes. In *Comm'r v. Sunnen*, 333 U.S. 591 (1948), the taxpayer, an inventor, entered into nonexclusive licensing arrangements with a family corporation controlled by him in return for the corporation's agreement to pay royalties based on the corporation's income derived from the inventions. He then assigned

---

[12] See *Dunn & Clark, P.A. v. Comm'r*, 57 F.3d 1076 (9th Cir. 1995); *Spicer Accounting, Inc. v. U.S.*, 918 F.2d 90 (9th Cir. 1990).

[13] Gifts of corporate stock are sometimes made for estate planning purposes, but typically the stock is not expected to pay dividends, but instead is anticipated to be held by the donees for long-term appreciation.

the royalty agreements to his wife (who in those days was a separate taxpayer). The Supreme Court held that the taxpayer was taxed on the royalties because (1) the taxpayer controlled the corporation and (2) the taxpayer had not granted an exclusive license to the corporation (in effect, he retained the right to license the inventions to others). *Sunnen* appears to be a "substantial ownership" case, and it is not often invoked by the IRS. *Sunnen* is not considered to be an obstacle to forming a corporation with garden-variety investments (or a viable business) and then making gifts of stock to family members. The gifts of stock are not disregarded for income tax purposes just because the donor continues to control the management of the corporation. Control of the corporation is distinguishable from not really parting with ownership of the gifted stock.

PROBLEM

1.   Kent and Mabel (who are married) operate a dairy farm. Kent, Mabel, and their six children (ranging in age from 12 to 28) all do farm work (although the younger ones also attend school), as well as household chores. The farm is a labor-intensive operation, but it has also been highly profitable. Up to now, the children have never been paid wages as such. What tax advice would you give Kent and Mabel?

2.   Same facts as 1, but instead of operating a dairy farm Kent and Mabel both perform accounting services from their home, and the children have no particular knowledge of accounting.

E.   INCOME SHIFTING THROUGH TRUSTS

This section deals mainly with the income taxation of trusts insofar as it relates to income shifting. (Technical details of trust taxation that are only marginally germane to income shifting are omitted.) Trusts are funded by gratuitous transfers (i.e., bequests, gifts, life insurance, and beneficiary designations under retirement plans, IRAs, and the like). Trusts created by gift obviously have income-shifting potential, but even trusts funded with bequests (etc.) can serve an "income-dispersal" function.

1.   The Trust as an Accounting Entity

The trust receiving one or more gratuitous transfers is a tax *accounting* entity, meaning that income, gains, deductions, losses, and so on, are initially "reckoned" at the trust level before being attributed to one or more taxpayers. This means that the usual rules (including basis rules) governing gratuitous transfers, namely, §§ 101(a), 102, 691, 1014, and 1015, apply to transfers that fund trusts. Assets *purchased* by the trust take a § 1012 cost basis, and property dispositions by the trust (whether of assets acquired by gratuitous transfer or by purchase) are dealt with at the trust level according to the usual rules concerning sales, exchanges, basis, and so on.

Since a trustee is under a duty to invest (prudently), the typical trust is invested in stocks, mutual funds, bonds, and other interest-bearing obligations. Less commonly, a trust might receive annuities, rents, and royalties, and on occasion may operate a business (or own an interest in a business).

Since trusts are usually invested exclusively in passive investments, the expenses of a trust are usually those of managing the investments. The manager in charge is the trustee, who may delegate some investment functions to investment advisors. Trustees are paid commissions (fees). In short, most deductions of a trust are expenses that are deductible under § 212(1) and (2). In *Trust of Bingham v. Comm'r*, 325 U.S. 365 (1945), § 212(2) was construed broadly to cover expenses of winding up and distributing trust assets (some of which did not produce income), which are neither expenses of producing income or of managing income-producing property, but were held to have arisen out of the function of a trustee to manage a portfolio of assets. If a trust invests in § 103 bonds, § 265(a)(1) comes into play to disallow a portion of the expenses that would otherwise be deductible under § 212.[14]

Since a trust has no standard deduction, the category of "itemized deduction" is not directly relevant, but it is indirectly relevant because an itemized deduction (such as would usually be the case with a § 212 deduction) might be an MID subject to the 2%-of-AGI floor. Section 67(e) provides that the following deductions of trusts are "above-the-line" (thereby avoiding MID treatment): (1) the § 642(b) personal-exemption-equivalent deduction, supra, (2) the "distribution deduction," described shortly, and (3) "the deductions for costs which are paid or incurred in connection with the administration of the . . . trust and which would not have been incurred if the property were not held in such trust." This last clause was construed in *Knight v. Comm'r*, 552 U.S. 181 (2008), which held that investment advisory fees paid by a trust were subject to the 2% floor, on the ground that such fees are commonly incurred by individuals holding an investment portfolio. Presumably trustee commissions and trust legal fees would usually avoid the 2% floor.

Once having determined the net income of a trust as an accounting entity, the basic issue under the income tax is whether (and to what extent) the resulting trust net income is taxed to the trust itself (as a separate taxable entity), the trust's grantor (if living), or one or more beneficiaries. This issue in turn is governed by three sets of income tax rules: (1) the "Subchapter J" rules, (2) the "grantor trust" rules, and (3) the "beneficiary-owned trust" rules, which will be considered in turn.[15]

2. Subchapter J Trusts

Although all tax rules dealing with trust income taxation are found in Subchapter J (§§ 641-691), the term "Subchapter J trust" is used here to refer to a trust that is neither a "grantor trust" in the income tax sense (defined and discussed in Subsection 3 below) nor a "beneficiary-owned trust" in the income tax sense (defined and discussed in Subsection 4 below). The crucial difference between

---

[14] See Regs. §§ 1.265-1(c), 1.642(c)-4(c).

[15] Alimony and child support trusts have already been briefly discussed in Chapter 5.B. The discussion of trusts in this chapter does not include the U.S. taxation of foreign trusts or of U.S. trusts with foreign beneficiaries.

a Subchapter J trust and the other two types of trust is that only a Subchapter J trust is *a separate taxable entity* capable of having taxable income subject to the trust rate schedule found in § 1(e).

A trust is an investment vehicle often characterized by split-interest beneficial ownership. That is to say, there are one or more beneficiaries who will or might, from time to time, receive current distributions of "trust income" and/or "trust corpus" (i.e., principal, as determined under trust accounting rules), and then there are (usually different) beneficiaries (holders of "remainder interests") who obtain the trust property upon termination of the trust. An example of a prototypical trust would be one where "income" (under the law of trusts, not in the income tax sense) is to be distributed to Barbara for life; on the death of Barbara, the trust terminates and its assets are distributed outright to the remainder beneficiary, Charles. Until termination, the trustee is the legal owner of the trust assets, but the beneficiaries (Barbara and Charles) are the equitable (beneficial) owners, who have the right to enforce the trust against the trustee.

It should be noted that the law of trusts and the income tax each impose separate sets of rules to identify "income" and "principal." The trust law rules (which are not discussed here) determine what is currently distributable to "income" beneficiaries.[16] The tax rules independently determine what amounts are taxed (or not taxed) to whom and when.

An initial tax issue is whether the trustee, as the legal owner of the property, is *personally* taxed on the income of the trust. The answer is "no," because the trustee does not beneficially own the trust property. In terms of income-attribution doctrine, the trustee (in its fiduciary capacity as trustee) is an agent for the trust, not a principal.

There are various possible theoretical models for taxing successive-interest arrangements, such as trusts, but the model chosen by the Code in Subchapter J is the relatively straightforward one wherein the trust is viewed as the "tree" which generates an annual crop of "fruit" that may (or may not) fall into the hands of the beneficiaries. Fruit that is harvested by beneficiaries during the year is taxed to them, and not to the trust. Fruit that is not harvested by beneficiaries during the current year is treated as absorbed by (and hence taxed to) the trust as a taxpayer in its own right. Accrual notions are banished from the system: (1) there is no amortization of wasting trust interests (like a right to income for life), (2) there is no accrual of gain as vested remainders move closer to possession, and (3) there are no "realizations" (taxable events) by reason of the expiration, vesting, divestment, or coming-into-possession of interests that beneficiaries have in trusts.

In the case of a Subchapter J trust, the trust net income (discussed above) is the starting point for computing the trust's taxable income. See § 641(b), which states that the trust's taxable income is to be (initially) computed in the same manner as for an individual. In addition to the normal income tax deductions (such as trustee fees), *a trust obtains a deduction for distributions to beneficiaries (the "distribution deduction"), and an amount equal to the distribution deduction is*

---

[16] See § 643(b) (stating that the use in Subchapter J of the word "income," when standing alone, means trust accounting income).

gross income to the distributees. This deduction/inclusion scheme has the effect of "shifting" income from the trust's tax base (and the trust's marginal tax rate) to the tax bases of one or more beneficiaries (and their marginal tax rates).

Turning to specifics, the distribution deduction (as well as the resulting aggregate beneficiary income inclusion) is an amount equal to the *lesser* of (a) "Distributions" *or* (b) the trust's "distributable net income" (DNI). Both Distributions and DNI are technical terms of art,[17] but the following discussion assumes (in the interest of simplicity) that Distributions means actual distributions to beneficiaries during the year (whether paid "out of" trust income or trust principal) and that "DNI" is equal to pre-distribution trust net income *less* net capital gains.

When the smoke clears, the *current* net income of the trust is taxed either to the trust or to the beneficiaries, or partly to the trust and partly to the beneficiaries (as a group). This trust/beneficiary allocation scheme neither adds income to the tax system nor removes income from the tax system, because the trust-level distribution deduction gives rise to a corresponding beneficiary-level gross income inclusion. Current-year Distributions in excess of the current-year DNI are not deducted by the trust, nor are they gross income to the beneficiaries (even if attributed to trust net income of prior years). The noninclusion to the beneficiaries derives from the fact that any Distribution in excess of DNI can only be "from" amounts that were (1) taxed to the trust in prior years or (2) received by the trust tax-free under §§ 101(a) and 102(a).

The trust obtains a $100 or $300 "personal exemption" deduction under § 642(b) in cases where its net income exceeds the distribution deduction.

> ***Example***: G dies in 2010, and creates a $1M trust under her will. The trustee has discretion to pay income and/or corpus to B or to accumulate trust income. On B's death, the trust will terminate and the assets will be paid over to C. In 2011, the trust obtains the initial $1M funding as a gratuitous transfer, which is wholly excludible from the trust's 2011 gross income under § 102(a). Assume that, in 2011, the trust has net ordinary income (after deductions) of $40K (and no net capital gains), and, thus, has DNI of $40K, and the trustee distributes $27K to B. The trust obtains a distribution deduction of $27K and a personal exemption of $100, resulting in a 2011 taxable income amount of $12.9K, which is subject to the § 1(e) rate schedule. B has gross income of $27K in 2011. C has no 2011 gross income with respect to the trust.
>
> In 2012 the trust has net ordinary income (and DNI) of $50K, and the trustee distributes $62K to B. The trust's distribution deduction is limited to the trust's current DNI of $50K. The trust, therefore, has zero taxable income and owes no tax. B has gross income of $50K in 2012, and the other $12K that she received is tax-free to her (as it is deemed to come from the original bequest that created the trust and/or income previously taxed to the trust).

---

[17] Certain rules in § 663 bear on the concept of Distributions, and DNI is defined in § 643.

If Distributions are made to more than one beneficiary during a year (and the aggregate of such Distributions exceeds DNI), the includible amount (the DNI amount) is allocated among the distributees in proportion to the distribution amounts received by each. However, where amounts (such as "income") are *required* to be distributed to one or more beneficiaries *and* other amounts are distributed to beneficiaries under a discretionary power in the same year, the DNI for the year is allocated first to the required distributions. See § 662(a).

A few technical observations are in order at this point, two of which relate to the definition of DNI (found in § 643(a)) as (essentially) being trust net *ordinary* income. Recall that DNI limits the amount deductible by the trust and includible by beneficiaries in the aggregate.

First, the fact that DNI is *net* of allowable ordinary deductions assures that such ordinary deductions are not lost. Assume that the trust has gross ordinary income of $12K and $2K of allowable § 212 deductions (after deduction-disallowance rules and deduction floors), and that the trust distributes $12K to B during the year. The DNI is $10K, the distribution deduction is $10K (which, combined with the § 212 deduction of $2K, reduces the trust's taxable income (TI) to zero), and B includes $10K. If (instead) the DNI were $12K, the trust's TI would still be zero (the distribution deduction cannot create a net loss for tax purposes), and B would include $12K, resulting in a waste of the § 212 deduction.

Second, the fact that DNI usually excludes net capital gains means that net capital gains are usually taxed to the trust. (Nevertheless, net capital gains *are* included in DNI in the year the trust terminates, and in a few other situations.[18]) Assume that the facts are the same as in the previous example, except that the trust has additional net capital gains of $5K, and the distribution to B is $18K. The DNI is still $10K ($12K ordinary income less $2K allowable deductions), the distribution deduction is $10K, B includes $10K, and the trust is taxed on net capital gains of $5K.

The third technical point is that the character of distributed income passes through to the beneficiary. In the previous example, the $10K included by *B* is all ordinary income, because all of the capital gains are taxed to the trust. Similarly, if the distributed income includes tax-exempt interest (under § 103), the exemption passes through to the beneficiary, and the distribution deduction is reduced by the same amount.[19]

In sum, under the system described above, the trust taxable income is taxed either to the trust or to the distributees in accordance with distributions actually made, as described above. If the distributees and/or the trust are in lower marginal income tax rate brackets than the grantor of the trust, an income tax savings can be obtained.

However, at this point, two factors intervene to reduce or eliminate the possible tax savings obtainable by dispersing income to a trust and/or its beneficiaries. One is the Kiddie Tax already mentioned. For a minor beneficiary, gross income

---

[18] See Reg. § 1.643(a)-3(b), (e).

[19] See §§ 643(a)(5), 661(b) & (c), 662(b).

resulting from a trust distribution is unearned income likely to be taxed at the parent's highest marginal rate. The second factor is the § 1(e) rate schedule applicable to trust taxable income, which has very narrow brackets, causing trust ordinary taxable income to be taxed in the highest bracket having a very low threshold.

3. Grantor Trusts

Although *Clifford* and other cases of similar ilk are still viable authority on the issue of property ownership for tax purposes *outside* of the trust area, Congress felt that this body of case law was too uncertain to be able to predict outcomes in cases involving inter vivos gifts to trusts, and, accordingly, enacted §§ 671-677. The last sentence of § 671 makes it clear that the rules of §§ 671-677 are to wholly supersede and pre-empt *Clifford* (and related case law) with respect to the issue of whether a *trust grantor* is deemed to be the owner of the inter vivos trust's assets, which results in attribution of the trust's net income to the grantor for so long as the grantor is alive. Sections 671-677 are known as the "grantor trust rules" (or "*Clifford* trust rules"), and an inter vivos trust is called a "grantor trust" (or a "*Clifford* trust") to the extent that §§ 671-677 cause the grantor to be taxed on trust income not actually received by the grantor.

Section 671 states that that the effect of a grantor being treated as the owner of a trust (or a portion thereof) is that the grantor is taxed on the income from the trust (or relevant portion thereof). The "ownership-in-substance" rules are found in §§ 673-677, as supplemented by definitions and operating rules found in § 672. Income attributed to the grantor under § 671 is not taxed again to the trust or the beneficiary actually receiving it. The actual receipt by a taxpayer (other than the grantor) is treated as an excludible § 102(a) gift from the grantor.

Section 676, which actually predated the *Clifford* case,[20] states that a grantor is deemed to be the owner of any trust that she (or, under § 672(e), her spouse) can revoke. (The trust in *Clifford* was irrevocable, and thus avoided this particular rule.)

Section 673(a) provides (with a minor exception) that a trust grantor is deemed to be the owner of a trust in which the grantor (or the grantor's spouse) has a reversionary interest worth, at the creation of the trust, more than 5% of the value of the trust property. (Valuation of reversionary interests requires actuarial tables.) Recall that the grantor in *Clifford* had a reversion after five years, which would have easily exceeded the 5% ceiling of current law.

Under § 677(a), the grantor is the owner of the trust, or any portion thereof, if the income will *or might* be paid to the grantor (or to the grantor's spouse), unless an "adverse party" can block such payment.

Section 677(b) states that the grantor shall be taxed on income that is *actually* paid to a person whom the grantor is obligated to support (in full or partial

---

[20] The predecessor of § 676 was upheld in *Corliss v. Bowers*, 281 U.S. 376 (1930), where the Court stated: "The income that is subject to a man's unfettered command and that he is free to enjoy at his own option may be taxed to him as his income, whether he sees fit to enjoy it or not."

satisfaction of a support obligation), but the grantor won't be taxed on income just because it *might* be used for this purpose.

Sections 674 and 675 treat the grantor as the owner of the trust on account of certain dispositive and administrative powers held by the grantor, the grantor's spouse, a related party, or even a "nonadverse party" acting as trustee. These sections are too complex or esoteric for summarization, especially if the reader lacks familiarity with the intricacies of trust law (or estate and gift tax doctrine that plays off trust law).

If all of the §§ 673-677 triggering conditions are avoided, then the grantor is *not* treated as the owner of the trust, and the income is taxed to the trust and/or distributees, as explained earlier, unless the trust is a beneficiary-owned trust (described immediately below). Obviously, the grantor can be taxed on trust income only so long as he or she is alive.

4. Beneficiary-Owned Trusts

Under § 678, a beneficiary who can demand, withdraw, or appropriate trust *income or capital gains* is taxed on the income or capital gains, whether or not any demand is actually made. A power to demand (etc.) only trust *corpus* causes the person holding the power to be the tax owner of the property itself.[21] For § 678 to apply, the beneficiary's power must be exercisable solely by the beneficiary, and must not be limited by ascertainable standards governing distributions, such as "support." Accordingly, § 678 can be easily avoided, if that is desired.

5. Use of Trusts in Family Income Tax Planning

It is generally advisable to avoid the compressed § 1(e) rate schedule for Subchapter J trusts. Since the § 1(e) tax applies only where trust net ordinary income exceeds distributions for the year, an obvious technique is to avoid accumulations by making sufficient discretionary distributions (where the trust does not mandate distributions of all the income or an amount equal to or in excess of trust income). However, in some situations, it may be advisable (usually for nontax reasons) to avoid distributions. (Trust accumulations of net capital gains are relatively harmless because net capital gains, wherever "located," are subject to maximum marginal rates under § 1(h) well below that for ordinary income.)

An alternate means to avoid the high rate brackets of § 1(e) is for a grantor to deliberately create a trust that will be treated under §§ 671-678 as a grantor trust or a beneficiary-owned trust. A grantor trust that is intentionally created to avoid § 1(e) is often called a "defective grantor trust." (A power that violates one on the provisions of § 675 is usually used, because such a power would not cause inclusion of the trust in the grantor's gross estate.) This technique is useful if one desires to set up a trust that will accumulate income for nontax reasons. Because the income is taxed to the grantor, the high rates of § 1(e) won't apply to the trust

---

[21] Section 678 is a codification of *Mallinckrodt v. Nunan*, 146 F.2d 1 (8th Cir. 1945). Trusts of this type are occasionally referred to as "*Mallinckrodt* trusts."

accumulations (unless the grantor happens to be in the highest marginal rate bracket).

Grantor trusts raise transactional issues as well. The IRS takes the position that a sale by a grantor to a grantor trust (or vice versa) should not be given any tax effect, on the theory that one cannot make a sale to oneself. See *Rev. Rul. 85-13*, 1985-1 C.B. 184.[22] Additionally, Reg. § 1.1001-2(c), Ex. (5), states that the cessation of grantor trust status during the grantor's lifetime constitutes a "disposition" of the property from the grantor to the trust at such time.[23]

PROBLEMS

1. Heather creates an inter vivos trust, naming herself as trustee, to support her elderly mother. The property transferred to the trust will produce $10K of net ordinary income per year, which will be distributed entirely to Heather's mother. State whether Heather is taxed on the trust income under the grantor trust rules of §§ 671-677 under the following variations:

(a) The trust is revocable.

(b) The trust is irrevocable, and the trust provides that the trust will terminate, and the property will revert to Heather's ownership, on the earlier of 11 years from the date the trust is created or the mother's death. Heather's mother has a five-year life expectancy.

(c) Same as (b), except that upon termination, the trust property will be distributed to Heather's husband. See § 672(e).

(d) The trust is irrevocable, the trustee is National Bank, and the trustee can pay corpus to Heather in the trustee's discretion. Does it matter whether corpus is actually distributed to Heather?

2. Grandmother creates an irrevocable trust with $1M of securities, income and/or corpus to be paid to her granddaughter Janis (or income accumulated), until Janis reaches age 30 (or dies before reaching 30), at which time the trust assets shall be distributed outright (and free of the trust) to Janis, if living, or (if Janis is not then living) to Grandmother's then living issue per stirpes. In trust Year 1, the trust has taxable ordinary income of $60K, and distributes $50K to Janis. In trust Year 2, the trust has taxable ordinary income of $70K and distributes $100K to Janis.

(a) What income tax results to the trust and Janis, assuming Janis is age 7 when the trust is created? Do you need to know more facts?

(b) Same as (a), except assume that Janis is age 20 when the trust is created.

---

[22] Although the opposite result was reached by the Second Circuit in *Rothstein v. U.S.*, 735 F.2d (2d Cir. 1984), only one of the three judges on the panel took the position that an installment sale from the trust to the grantor should be treated as a realization event. One judge concurred in the result on the ground that the trust was not a grantor trust. *Rothstein* was viewed with veiled disapproval in *Madorin v. Comm'r*, 84 T.C. 667 (1985).

[23] The disposition could be a realization event in certain cases, such as where a trust asset is (1) a partnership interest, (2) any asset encumbered by liabilities, or (3) an installment obligation.

(c) Same as (b), except assume that the trust also has $10K of net capital gains for trust Years 1 and 2 and that such net capital gains are not included in trust DNI.

F. INCOME TAXATION OF ESTATES AND SURVIVORSHIP RIGHTS

An individual taxpayer's existence ends on the date of death. Death is final in the sense that all carryovers (of NOLs, capital losses, and so on) simply expire. Immediately following death, a new income-tax taxpayer, the decedent's "estate," springs into being and continues as a taxpayer for (roughly) as long as there is an estate administration with respect to the decedent under state law. The representative of the estate is required to file the estate's income tax return (Form 1041). (The estate as an income tax taxpayer is distinct from the federal estate tax and the legal responsibility of paying the estate tax.)

1. Transfers at Death of Accrued but Unpaid Income Rights

Recall from Section B.2, supra, that *gifts* of accrued (i.e., earned) income rights are generally ineffective to shift the accrued income to the donee. What about rights to income accrued or earned by a taxpayer but unpaid at her death? Such rights, if they pass to a legatee, heir, or under a beneficiary designation in a contract, are referred to as rights to "income in respect of a decedent" (IRD rights). In dollar terms, the largest category of IRD rights is deferred wages, including retirement plan rights and IRAs, but also included are more mundane items, such as the unpaid final salary check, accrued but unpaid interest, rentals, royalty incomes, and so on. Annuities are treated the same as IRD rights as far as post-death payouts are concerned. Rights to succession and survivorship benefits are discussed in connection with §§ 101(a), 102(a), and 1014 in Chapter 15.C, but further elaboration is in order here.

The problem posed by IRD rights is that the decedent taxpayer used the cash method of accounting but her existence terminated at death *prior* to the reduction of the IRD rights to cash or its equivalent. Who (if anybody) should be taxed on such items? There are three possibilities: (1) allow these items to disappear from the tax system (in the same way that unrealized appreciation and depreciation disappear from the tax system pursuant to the § 1014 basis rule), (2) include these items on the taxpayer's final income tax return, or (3) tax such items to the taxpayer's successor in interest (estate, legatee, trust, or designated individual beneficiary). The decision was made that these items should not avoid tax just because the earner died. In contrast to *gifts* of accrued but unpaid income rights, the at-death transfer of such rights is not considered abusive or motivated by tax-savings considerations. And inclusion of these items on the decedent's final income tax return would possibly raise liquidity (i.e., accelerated realization) problems in the case of retirement plan rights, annuities, and IRAs. For these (and other) reasons, Congress decided that IRD rights are to be taxed *entirely* to the decedent's successors in interest.

In order to carry out this decision, § 1014(c) provides that *IRD rights are excluded from the § 1014 fair-market-value-at-date-of-death basis rule*. Thus, the successor acquires the same basis (if any) in the right that the decedent had (which is typically zero). Section 691(a) states that the successor is taxed on the IRD right as and when the IRD is reduced to cash. In the case of retirement plan rights and annuities, any basis that the decedent had (and which carries over to the successor) is recovered under the § 72 rules (described in Chapter 27.C).

The flip side of the coin is a "deduction in respect of a decedent" (DIRD), which is an expense incurred but unpaid by the decedent that § 691(b) allows to be deducted by the successor who pays it (usually the decedent's estate). The DIRD concept is a much narrower concept than IRD, as it is limited to incurred but unpaid *expense* items that would be deducted under any of §§ 162, 163, 164, and 212, plus depletion under § 611, as well as the foreign tax credit under § 901. Non-DIRD items are not deducted by anybody for income tax purposes, but they are usually deducted for estate tax purposes, as they reduce the decedent's net estate.

If (contrary to fact), a decedent's "net IRD" (IRD less DIRD) were accruable on the decedent's final income tax return, any income tax paid or owed thereon would necessarily have reduced the decedent's net estate subject to estate tax. Since such is *not* the case, however, Congress has given the successor (the person including the IRD in income) an *income tax* deduction equal to the estate tax (if any) attributable to the inclusion of the IRD right in the estate tax base of the decedent. See § 691(c). This obscure deduction is an itemized deduction but not an MID.

2. Income Taxation of Estates

The income tax rules applicable to an estate and its beneficiaries, i.e., legatees and heirs, are generally the same as those that apply to a Subchapter J trust, described above. Like a Subchapter J trust, the estate is subject to the highly compressed § 1(e) rate schedule. As with any trust, the initial "funding" of the estate with the decedent's property is excluded from the gross income of the estate by reason of § 102(a). The subsequent income received by the estate during its period of administration (including IRD income received) is gross income of the estate, and the estate takes deductions for such "estate administration" items as executor's commissions, estate attorney fees, and appraisal fees, *so long as such items are not also deducted for federal estate tax purposes*. See § 642(g). The estate can also deduct DIRD items paid by it.

As with Subchapter J trusts, estates obtain a distribution deduction equal to the lesser of Distributions (to legatees and heirs) or the estate's DNI, and the distributees (as a group) include in gross income an amount equal to the estate's distribution deduction.

One major difference exists between trust and estate taxation: Distributions from the estate in satisfaction of specific property bequests ("I leave Blackacre to B") and fixed monetary bequests ("I leave $10,000 to C") are *not* treated as deductible Distributions for purposes of the deduction/inclusion scheme. See § 663(a)(1). This means that only distributions in satisfaction of "residuary bequests" ("I leave [all, the rest of] my property to D") and of inheritances are deductible Distributions in the Subchapter J tax sense. This rule increases the possibility that estate net income will exceed deductible Distributions and thus increases the possibility that the estate will have income subjected to the steep § 1(e) rate schedule. This fact, in turn, has implications for the way wills are drafted, as well as for discretionary decisions of the estate fiduciary.

NOTES

1.   The income taxation of trusts and estates is a sufficiently broad topic that it typically constitutes a separate course in tax LL.M. programs and even some J.D. programs, but the core concepts aren't difficult, and every professional person dealing with tax, estate, and trust issues should be acquainted with these concepts.

2.   (a) When a Subchapter J trust or an estate distributes property in kind, the default rules are: (1) the "amount" of the Distribution is the lesser of the property's basis or its fair market value (FMV) at the time of the distribution, (2) the trust or estate does not recognize gain or loss on the distribution, and (3) the basis to the trust or estate carries over to the distributee. (But remember that an estate itself takes a FMV basis when it acquires the property by reason of death under § 1014, so its basis may be very close to FMV at the time of later distribution to the ultimate legatee.)

(b) The fiduciary can elect into a deemed-realization treatment for property distributions, in which case the Distribution for Subchapter J purposes is deemed to be equal to the FMV of the property, the estate or trust recognizes gain or loss, and the distributee takes the property with a FMV basis. See § 643(e)(3).

(c) When an estate distributes in-kind property in satisfaction of a *fixed-dollar bequest*, the estate realizes (and recognizes) gain or loss equal to the difference between the property's FMV and its basis, and the legatee takes a FMV basis.[24] (Recall that such a distribution in satisfaction of a fixed-dollar bequest is not a deductible Distribution for Subchapter J purposes because of § 663(a)(1).)[25]

(d) Any losses realized on a *sale* between (a) a grantor and a trust created by that grantor, (2) a trustee and a beneficiary of the trust (or another trust created by the same grantor), or (3) an estate and a beneficiary of an estate, fall within the loss-disallowance rule of § 267(a)(1). There is an exception for transactions described in (c), supra. See § 267(b)(4)-(7), (13).

PROBLEM

What are the income tax pros and cons of the alternative will formats set out below? What additional facts would you like to know? (Disregard the federal estate tax considerations.)

(a) "I bequeath my entire property and estate to my wife Gladys."

---

[24] This is called the *Kenan* rule, after *Kenan v. Comm'r*, 114 F.2d 217 (2d Cir. 1940). The theory (explained in Chapter 19.A.1) is that the fixed-dollar legacy is a "debt" of the estate that is satisfied with the property distribution.

[25] In the case of certain farm real estate which is valued for estate tax purposes at a discount below FMV, the gain is computed as if the § 1014 basis were the actual FMV at death. See § 1040 (post-2010 version).

(b) "I leave my property and estate as follows:

    1. all my tangible personal property to my wife Gladys;

    2. my interest in any real property to my wife Gladys; and

    3. all the rest and residue of my estate to my wife Gladys."

Part Six

BORROWING, LENDING, AND INTEREST

Debt is a paramount characteristic of the U.S. economy. Indeed, it is a persistent thread that runs through many prominent aspects of investments, business activities, and everyday life. Consequently, important statutory and judicial rules have been developed to define the tax consequences of debt transactions. The materials in this part are structured to guide you through the relevant law. Chapter 18 considers how borrowing and quasi-borrowing transactions can be (and are) treated. Chapter 19 explains how borrowing can produce "income from the discharge of indebtedness" under § 61(a)(12) of the Code (variously called "debt-discharge income," "discharge-of-indebtedness income," "cancellation-of-debt income," or even "COD income"), which can then possibly be deferred under § 108. Chapter 20 deals with the effect of mortgages on the purchase and sale of property. Chapter 21 examines the role of debt (especially nonrecourse debt) in tax shelters.

Chapter 18

BORROWING, LENDING, AND INTEREST

This chapter covers the tax treatment of basic borrowing and lending transactions, the effect of interest (or the lack thereof) on the tax treatment of loans, the tax treatment of receipt/repayment scenarios that are not really loans, and the deduction of interest expense.

A. "STRAIGHT" BORROWING AND LOAN REPAYMENT TRANSACTIONS

Recall from Chapter 2 that the ability-to-pay formulation of "income" calls for adding increases in realized "net wealth" and deducting decreases in realized "net wealth" (except those net wealth decreases spent on consumption). The role of the realization principle in the income tax treatment of borrowing is perhaps under-appreciated, because at least three different ways exist (in theory) for treating borrowing (and lending) transactions for income tax purposes, and the differences among these approaches all pertain to "timing." To illustrate these differences, assume that Steve borrows $5K in Year 1 from National Bank at a market rate of interest and repays the $5K in Year 2, along with the interest.

The first approach, the "accrual-at-face approach," is the paradigm primarily adopted in the income tax. Consider first the lender. Because National Bank has merely changed the form of its wealth from cash to Steve's note, the bank's $5K cash outlay is viewed as a nondeductible "capital expenditure." Moreover, since Steve's note is treated as wealth to the extent of its full face (i.e., stated principal) amount of $5K, no change in National Bank's wealth results from its lending of the $5K. At this point, National Bank has a $5K basis in Steve's note, and Steve's $5K repayment of loan principal in Year 2 will be treated by National Bank as a tax-free recovery of basis.[1] Interest received by National Bank, however, is "new" wealth and, thus, is includible in gross income. If Steve does not repay the loan, National Bank will incur a sustained loss that will be deductible as a business bad (i.e., worthless) debt loss under § 166 to the extent of National Bank's remaining basis in the note. (Bad debt losses are discussed further in Chapter 23.A.4.)

Now consider the borrower, Steve. Under the accrual-at-face approach, his receipt of the $5K cash is not considered "gross income" because his $5K face amount offsetting liability (negative wealth) prevents the borrowing transaction as a whole from increasing his net wealth.[2] Putting it in the language of *Glenshaw*

---

[1] Tax-free cash treated as a "return of capital" with respect to an underlying investment uses up (and reduces) the basis of that underlying investment, dollar for dollar.

[2] If a business accounting balance sheet were to be set up for Steve, with "assets" listed on the left

Glass, Steve has not realized an "accession to wealth." Some refer to this rule as the "borrowing exclusion." Subsequently, when Steve repays the loan principal, he realizes no net wealth reduction because the $5K decrease in his cash assets is matched by an identical decrease in the face amount of his liabilities, thus negating any realized reduction in his net wealth. Consequently, Steve is precluded from deducting any of his principal repayment. Because the cash used to repay principal is not deductible, it will be effectively taxed (by remaining in Steve's tax base) in the repayment year. Thus, rather than being taxed when the loan is received, Steve is effectively taxed on the borrowed amounts at the time of repayment, which means that he pays back the principal with dollars that have been previously subject to tax. (Steve's payment of interest is, however, an "expense," a current wealth decrease, which he may or may not be able to deduct. The deduction for interest expense is examined in Section D, infra.)

The second possible approach to borrowing, which is polar opposite of the accrual-at-face approach, is the "annual-accounting approach," under which the receipt of borrowed money and its repayment would be viewed as independent transactions. Under this approach, borrowed amounts would be included in the tax base when the loan proceeds are received. When repayment is made, deductions would be allowed to the borrower for both principal and interest payments, since they would be neither consumption outlays nor additions to savings.

A third possible approach to borrowing transactions lies between the accrual-at-face and annual-accounting approaches. It would allow Steve to offset against his $5K Year-1 receipt only the fair market value of his repayment obligation. A variation would allow Steve to offset against the $5K loan proceeds only the discounted present value of his repayment obligation. We can call either variation the "accrual-at-value approach." (Indeed, if the discount rate for ascertaining present value properly accounts for the risk of nonpayment, there would be no meaningful distinction between fair market value and present value.[3]) Under the accrual-at-value approach, Steve would have a realized wealth increase or decrease in Year 1 equal to the difference (if any) between his $5K receipt of borrowed funds and the fair market value (or the present value) of his $5K repayment obligation.

One appealing feature of the accrual-at-face approach (the primary paradigm used in the income tax) is that it entails virtually no accounting. Under it, the "plain vanilla" borrowing and lending of principal is simply ignored for tax purposes, as are loan principal repayments, whereas they would create reportable events under the other approaches. Also, the annual-accounting approach would result in the "bunching" of large amounts of income when mortgage loans are taken out and (perhaps less commonly) the bunching of deductions when large amounts of loan principal are repaid. Consequently, the temptation would exist to evade taxes by not reporting borrowing income, while claiming principal repayment deductions. The accrual-at-value approach would impose the burden of an initial valuation of the

---

and "liabilities" listed on the right, his assets on the left would increase by $5K on receipt of the cash, but his liabilities on the right would increase by an identical amount, leaving his "net worth" (assets less liabilities) unchanged.

[3] In practice, there is usually a difference between fair market value and present value, because interest rates are rarely "customized" to individual borrowers to reflect their creditworthiness..

repayment obligation, and would require an accounting for the difference (if any) between such value and the amount ultimately collected in the way of principal payments.[4] These burdens would appear to be mostly unnecessary because, if the loan is obtained in an arm's length transaction, it can be assumed that the lender values the borrower's note in an amount equal to its face amount, and, if that is good enough for the lender, it ought to be good enough for the tax system. Nevertheless, the accrual-at-value approach may be appropriate in non-arm's length borrowing transactions and, as we shall see, is actually used in certain of those cases. Nevertheless, it can be said that the accrual-at-face approach is the "general rule" under the federal income tax.

Recall from Chapter 6 that borrowing produces a very different set of results under a cash flow consumption tax, which adopts a version of the annual-accounting approach. On the lender's side, the transfer of principal to the borrower is a deductible investment, and all receipts of cash (both principal and interest payments) are includible in the lender's tax base. On the borrower's side, the borrowed cash is includible as potential consumption,[5] and payments of both principal and interest would be deductible as nonconsumption expenditures.[6] Under a wage tax, the lender cannot deduct the amount lent, but both interest and principal payments are excludible from the lender's income.[7] The borrower includes no income on account of the borrowed cash (only wages are includible), but neither principal nor interest payments are deductible by the borrower.

B. BELOW-MARKET LOANS

As noted above, the accrual-at-face approach has prevailed in the federal income tax, probably out of considerations of convenience. Tax advisors, however, began to figure out that the accrual-at-face approach could be used to effect a disguised "transfer" (gift, compensation, dividend, etc.) by making a loan that bore either no interest or interest below the prevailing market rate for similar loans. Such loans are called "below-market loans." Below-market *gift* loans were briefly discussed in Chapter 17.D.2.

---

[4] For example, if Steve's $5,000 cash borrowing were offset in Year 1 by only $4,800 (the value of Steve's note), causing Steve to include $200 in Year-1 income, and if Steve in fact repaid the entire $5,000 principal, Steve would be entitled to a $200 deduction at some point.

[5] If the borrower uses the borrowed principal to purchase an investment rather than to purchase consumption, the inclusion of the borrowed funds would be effectively offset by a deduction for the new investment.

[6] Under a cash flow consumption tax, it is axiomatic that there must not be double taxation of the same dollars *in present-value terms*. Since, in an arm's length borrowing transaction, the borrowed amount should equal the present value of future principal and interest payments, the inclusion of the borrowed amount in the borrower's tax base in the year of the loan commands deduction by the borrower of both principal and interest payments in order to prevent the double taxation of any of the same dollars *in present-value terms*.

[7] These results flow from the fact that a wage tax reckons only wage income and allows no deductions, but the effect of these rules on borrowing results in the same no-double-taxation-in-present-value-terms result as operates under the cash flow consumption tax, discussed in the preceding footnote.

To illustrate the economics of a below-market nongift loan, suppose an employer lends $100K to a key employee for 10 years at a zero interest rate. (Such a loan is called a "term loan" because it has a fixed repayment period.) Assuming that the prevailing interest (discount) rate is 5% compounded annually, then the present value of the employee's repayment obligation is $61.4K.[8] Thus, the lender has parted with $100K but has "gotten back" an asset (the employee's repayment obligation) worth only $61.4K. The true loan principal amount is, therefore, $61.4K, because only the $61.4K is a true capital expenditure. It follows that the lender/employer has made a present wealth transfer of $38.6K — the excess of the employer's $100K cash "loan" over the $61.4K present value of the repayment obligation. Similarly, the employee/borrower has received $100K cash while giving back an obligation with a present value of only $61.4K, meaning that the employee has received a current accession to wealth equal to $38.6K.

Under the accrual-at-face approach, however, these economic realities would be ignored: the lender would be deemed to have transferred nothing, and the borrower would be deemed to have no accession to wealth. When challenged by the IRS, the lower federal courts doggedly followed the accrual-at-face approach, declining to use present-value analysis with respect to below-market repayment obligations.[9] However, in *Dickman v. Comm'r*, 465 U.S. 330 (1984), the Supreme Court held that an interest-free loan from one family member to another involved "transfers" for federal gift tax purposes from the lender to the borrower. In 1984, in the shadow of the *Dickman* litigation, Congress enacted § 7872, the odd numbering of which reflects the fact that it applies for both income and gift tax purposes.

Section 7872 provides that certain below-market loans are to be treated in accordance with the economic model laid out in the preceding paragraph, that is, as involving a wealth transfer from the lender to the borrower in an amount equal to the excess of the amount lent over the present value of the repayment obligation. See § 7872(b)(1). The treatment of this wealth transfer is governed by the substantive Code rules that "fit" the relationship between the borrower and the lender. For example, in the *Dickman* family-transfer situation, the transfer was in the nature of a "gift" made by the lender, excludible by the borrower under § 102 for income tax purposes, but taxed to the lender-donor under the gift tax. In the hypothetical posed at the beginning of this section, involving the below-market loan from a corporation to its employee, the transfer would be in the nature of "compensation," includible by the employee under § 61(a)(1), and possibly deductible by the employer as a wage cost.[10] If a corporation makes a below-market loan to a shareholder, the forgone interest would be in the nature of a "dividend," includible under §§ 61(a)(7) and 301 by the borrower and nondeductible to the corporation.

---

[8] For ease of comprehension, the numbers in this example are rounded.

[9] In *Dean v. Comm'r*, 35 T.C. 1083 (1961) (reviewed), for example, the Tax Court held that an interest-free loan from a corporation to a shareholder did not result in a constructive dividend to the shareholder in an amount equal to the forgone interest.

[10] The wage cost could be a deductible business expense under § 162 or possibly a capital expenditure or inventory cost under § 263A.

The application of § 7872 is limited to below-market loans that are gift loans, compensation-related loans, corporation-shareholder loans, continuing-care-facility loans, "tax avoidance loans,"[11] and below-market loans (to be specified in regulations) that "have a significant effect on any Federal tax liability of the lender or the borrower."

Section 7872 clearly applies to our initial hypothetical, resulting in a payment of compensation in the amount of $38.6K (ordinary income to the employee/borrower and potentially deductible by the employer/lender) and an "investment" (i.e., the loan principal amount) by the employer of the remaining $61.4K in the employee's $100K repayment obligation. This investment is, of course, a capital expenditure, producing a basis in the repayment obligation of $61.4K for the employer/lender. Because our employee will pay $100K in Year 10 to the employer/lender, the lender will have investment income (interest) of $38.6K, since the lender's basis is only $61.4K. Similarly, because the borrower will use $100K cash to repay loan principal of $61.4K (which is not deductible), the remaining $38.6K will be in the nature of interest expense, which is potentially deductible under § 163, examined in Section D, infra.[12]

The *Dickman* case itself involved a "demand" loan under which the lender could "call" the principal back at any time. Discounting to present value is impossible where it is not known when the loan will be repaid. In the case of demand loans, § 7872(e)(2) deems there to be an annual (gift, compensation, etc.) transfer equal to the "forgone interest," which is calculated with reference to the interest rate paid by the federal government on certain of its debt.[13] This rate is referred to as the "applicable federal rate" (AFR). (Since the AFR changes from time to time, it cannot be inserted into the statutory language but is instead gleaned from revenue procedures published bi-monthly.) The same foregone interest amount is deemed to be repaid annually from the borrower to the lender as "interest." (The deemed equal-amount cross payments reflect the fact that no money actually changes hands except at the inception and repayment of the loan.)

Crucial terms (like "below-market loan") and rules for calculating the present value of repayment obligations under term loans are spelled out in § 7872(e) and (f).

PROBLEMS

1. Z Corp. lends its chief executive officer (CEO) $1M for 10 years at zero interest. Assume that the present value of $1M after 10 years, using the current AFR and discounting on a semi-annual basis, is $700K and that the loan is not described in § 7872(f)(3). What tax results to the parties?

---

[11] An example of a "tax avoidance loan" might be a below-market loan from a tax-exempt person (to whom a deduction would be meaningless) to a taxable person in an effort to disguise an income item (other than compensation or dividend income).

[12] It happens that the $38.6K of forgone interest deemed paid from the borrower to the lender is allocated over the 10-year period as it is earned. See § 7872(b)(2). The actual mechanics of the allocation are explained under the rubric of "original issue discount," discussed in Chapter 27.B.1.

[13] With respect to gift loans, see the special limitations in § 7872(d)(1).

2.   Same as 1, except the borrower is the sole shareholder of Z Corp., instead of its CEO.

C. WHAT COUNTS AS A BORROWING

The existence of the rule that borrowing is not an income realization event has necessitated the development of doctrine that defines what is a true borrowing under the income tax.

1. Contingent Repayment Obligations

A true loan, for tax purposes, is an amount that is subject to an *absolute and unconditional* obligation to repay. It is only because of the offsetting absolute obligation to repay that the borrower is not considered to have realized a "net wealth accession" in the year of receipt. This section deals with the situation where the taxpayer receives cash subject to a *contingent* obligation to repay the cash in the future. Sometimes the taxpayer knows of the contingency in advance, but in many cases, he or she is taken by surprise. Regardless of the taxpayer's foreknowledge, however, the tax law generally follows the "annual-accounting approach" (see Section A, supra) in these situations by requiring inclusion in the year of receipt and allowing a deduction if and when the contingency ripens and repayment occurs. The following case illustrates this general pattern.

NORTH AMERICAN OIL CONSOLIDATED v. BURNET
United States Supreme Court
286 U.S. 417 (1932)

Mr. Justice Brandeis delivered the opinion of the Court.

The question for decision is whether money received by North American Oil Consolidated in 1917 was taxable to it as income of that year. Among many properties operated by it in 1916 was a section of oil land, the title to which stood in the name of the United States. The Government had instituted a suit to oust the company from possession, and on February 2, 1916, it secured the appointment of a receiver to operate the property and to hold the net income thereof. The money paid to the company in 1917 represented the net profits from that property in 1916 during the receivership. After entry by the District Court in 1917 of the final decree dismissing the suit, the money was paid by the receiver to the company. The Government took an appeal to the Court of Appeals. In 1920, that Court affirmed the decree. In 1922, a further appeal to this Court was dismissed by stipulation.

The net profits were not taxable to the company in 1916. The company was not required in 1916 to report as income an amount which it might never receive. Throughout 1916 it was uncertain who would be declared entitled to the profits. It was not until 1917, when the District Court entered a final decree dismissing the suit, that the company became entitled to receive the money. The net profits earned by the property in 1916 were not income of 1922, the year in which the litigation was finally determined. They became income of the company in 1917, when it first became entitled to them and when it actually received them.

If a taxpayer receives earnings under a claim of right and without restriction as to its disposition, he has received income which he is required to [include on his tax] return, even though it may still be claimed that he is not entitled to retain the money, and even though he may still be adjudged liable to restore its equivalent. If in 1922 the Government had prevailed, and the company had been obliged to refund the profits received in 1917, it would have been entitled to a deduction from the profits of 1922, not from those of any earlier year.

Not every situation that looks like a receipt accompanied by a contingent repayment obligation is treated as such for purposes of applying *North American Oil*. An example of an arrangement that appears to result in immediate income recognition under *North American Oil*, but does not, is a "security deposit," the most common form of which is cash received in advance by a landlord to cover the possibility of damages to the premises or nonpayment of rent. In form, it seems that the landlord's repayment obligation is contingent because repayment of the deposit will occur only if the lessee leaves the premises intact and with no rent arrears. If the premises are damaged, or if the lessee owes rent to the landlord (common occurrences in the landlord-tenant world), the landlord will keep all or a portion of the deposit.

The Supreme Court considered a deposit scenario in *Comm'r v. Indianapolis Power & Light Co.*, 493 U.S. 203 (1990). There an electric utility required deposits from certain customers to secure the payment of utility bills. These deposits appeared to be accompanied by a mere contingent liability, because the repayment of each deposit hinged on the customer satisfying his or her contractual obligations. Under this interpretation, *North American Oil* would treat the deposits as gross income to the utility at the time they were received (and the utility would deduct any actual repayment of the deposits to customers). The Supreme Court, however, characterized the transaction as follows (493 U.S. at 209–13):

> These deposits were acquired [by the utility] subject to an express "obligation to repay," either at the time service was terminated or at the time a customer established good credit. So long as the customer fulfills his legal obligation to make timely payments, his deposit ultimately is to be refunded, and both the timing and method of that refund are largely within the control of the customer.
>
> The Commissioner emphasizes that these deposits frequently will be used to pay for electricity, either because the customer defaults on his obligation or because the customer, having established credit, chooses to apply the deposit to future bills rather than to accept a refund. The problem with petitioner's argument perhaps can best be understood if we imagine a loan between parties involved in an ongoing commercial relationship. At the time the loan falls due, the lender may decide to apply the money owed him to the purchase of goods or services [from the borrower] rather than to accept repayment in cash. But this decision does not mean that the loan, when made, was an advance payment after all. The lender in effect has

taken repayment of his money (as was his contractual right) and has chosen to use the proceeds for the purchase of goods or services from the borrower. Although, for the sake of convenience, the parties may combine the two steps, that decision does not blind us to the fact that in substance two transactions are involved.

Our decision is also consistent with the Tax Court's long-standing treatment of lease deposits. The Tax Court traditionally has distinguished between a sum designated as a prepayment of rent — which is taxable upon receipt — and a sum deposited to secure the tenant's performance of a lease agreement.

In other words, while the "form" of the transaction appeared to indicate that the utility had only a "contingent" obligation to repay, the Court concluded that in "substance" the utility had an absolute obligation to repay every deposit. In those instances where the utility appeared to "keep" the deposit for nonpayment of an electric bill, the Court reasoned that there was actually a deemed repayment of the deposit by the utility to the customer, followed by a deemed payment immediately back to the utility as an "electricity payment." Thus, at the time the deposits were received, the utility was entitled to exclude them as "true loans." If and when a deposit was applied to a bill in default, the amount so applied would constitute gross income at that later time.

The opinion in *Indianapolis Power & Light* warrants critique for an inappropriate use of the concept of "dominion and control" by stating that a borrower lacks dominion and control over borrowed money. But that was not the case with the utility deposits in *Indianapolis Power & Light*, where the deposits could have been spent in any fashion the utility desired. Properly understood, the borrowing exclusion is premised on the "accession-to-wealth" notion (i.e., that the borrower does not have income on account of receipt of the loan proceeds because of the borrower's absolute obligation to repay).

The case of *U.S. v. Lewis*, 340 U.S. 590 (1951), is similar to *North American Oil*, except that when the *Lewis* taxpayer received the cash he was not aware of any contingency that might cause him to disgorge the payment later on. In 1944, Lewis received a $22K bonus from his employer and included it in gross income. Subsequent litigation, however, determined that there had been a mistake in the bonus computation, and Lewis was required to return $11K to the employer in 1946. Since the reimbursement was an expense incurred in his trade or business of being an employee, Lewis was clearly entitled to a 1946 deduction for the $11K repayment. Lewis did not wish to deduct the amount in that year, however, because his 1946 marginal rate was lower than his 1944 marginal rate, which meant that the tax savings from the 1946 deduction would be less than the 1944 tax paid on the $11K amount. (Tax rates went down at the end of World War II.) Instead, Lewis sought to file an amended 1944 return (since the statute of limitations had not yet run) and re-compute his 1944 tax by excluding from gross income the $11K item that he repaid in 1946. In other words, Lewis would have treated the $11K as borrowed money (rather than compensation) in 1944. The Court, following *North American Oil*, held that the taxpayer's only remedy was a 1946 deduction. That is to say, since inclusion of the full bonus in 1944 was "correct" under the facts then known to Lewis, an amended return for 1944 was inappropriate.

The issues of amended returns, the deductibility of repayments, and the application of § 1341 (enacted in response to *Lewis*) are dealt with in Chapter 26 (especially Section B.8 thereof).

The "annual-accounting" approach for receipts subject to a contingent obligation to repay is preferable to that of including the original receipt reduced by the value of the repayment obligation for various reasons. First, in many of these cases the taxpayer is unaware of any possibility of disgorgement. Second, there is no way to accurately value such contingencies as losing a case on appeal or (in the case of ill-gotten gains) being caught and held to account.[14] Finally, the disgorgement either will or will not occur, meaning that the initial valuation will always prove to be inaccurate, and that in turn would seem to call for some "adjustment" to compensate for the initial valuation error.

The annual-accounting approach is theoretically correct, because a deduction for the disgorgement of previously included income replicates the tax treatment of an interest-free loan for the same period under § 7872. To illustrate this point, suppose Jolene in Year 1 wins $100K in a contest but exactly one year later is forced to refund the $100K (without interest) when it is discovered that she was not eligible to compete. The contest sponsor has, in effect, made an interest-free loan to Jolene. Jolene's situation does not actually fit within any of the § 7872(c) categories, but if § 7872 were to apply, Jolene would have an offset (against the initial receipt) equal to the present value of the (then unknown) repayment obligation. Instead of an offset equal to the present value of $100K, Jolene deducts $100K one year after she includes the $100K, which is functionally the same result as occurs under § 7872.

This exercise undertaken in the preceding paragraph also demonstrates that the later deduction should be automatic, and not dependent on whether the transaction had a business or investment flavor.[15]

PROBLEM

Becky, a landlord, collects a security deposit equal to one-month's rent from the tenant. If the premises are in good condition at the end of the rental term and no back rent is then due, Becky will return the deposit to the tenant. If the tenant damages the rental unit and does not pay for its repair, or if the tenant owes rent, Becky will retain all or some of the deposit to cover the rent or repair the damage. The deposit is not deposited in escrow and does not bear interest.

(a) What result if the deposit is repaid? Does § 7872 apply?

---

[14] The § 7872 approach, by using the AFR as the discount rate, ignores the various elements that constitute risk, such as the lack or inadequacy of security, the borrower's creditworthiness, or the possibility that a creditworthy borrower may become insolvent in the future. Risks of this sort are conventionally "compensated for" by the charging of a higher interest (discount) rate. But the AFR (the § 7872 discount rate) is based on the rate for U.S. federal government obligations, traditionally considered to be virtually risk-free.

[15] The deduction can best be characterized as a loss (of $100K cash) in a transaction entered into (initially) for profit.

(b) What tax consequences result if the tenant, who had kept the property in good condition, fails to pay the last month's rent, and thus Becky keeps the deposit?

(c) What tax result occurs if the tenant paid all rent due but trashed the premises, so that Becky keeps the deposit?

2.   Phantom Repayment Obligations

In *James v. U.S.*, set forth below, the Court held that an embezzler must include stolen amounts in gross income in the embezzlement year, even though the embezzler might have been eventually caught and forced to refund the money to the victim. Thus, *James* can be viewed as a special kind of "contingent liability" case. However, it can also be viewed as one where the alleged repayment obligation (which was created by state law) was so unlikely to be satisfied that it "didn't count" in determining whether the embezzled amount was subject to an absolute obligation to repay for purposes of deciding whether it was an excludible "loan" for tax purposes).

JAMES v. UNITED STATES
United States Supreme Court
366 U.S. 213 (1961)

Mr. Chief Justice Warren announced the Judgment of the Court and an opinion in which Mr. Justice Brennan and Mr. Justice Stewart concur:

The petitioner is a union official who embezzled in excess of $738,000 during the years 1951 through 1954. Petitioner failed to report these amounts in his income and was convicted for willfully attempting to evade the federal income tax in violation of § 7201 of the Code.

Because of a conflict with the Court's decision in *Comm'r v. Wilcox*, 327 U.S. 404 (1946), a case whose relevant facts are the same as those in the case now before us, we granted certiorari. In *Wilcox*, the Court held that embezzled money does not constitute income to the embezzler in the year of the embezzlement. Six years later, this Court held, in *Rutkin v. U.S.*, 343 U.S. 130 (1952), that extorted money does constitute income to the extortionist in the year that the money is received. In *Rutkin*, the Court did not overrule *Wilcox*. However, examination of the reasoning used in *Rutkin* leads us inescapably to the conclusion that *Wilcox* was thoroughly devitalized. The basis for the *Wilcox* decision was "that a taxable gain is conditioned upon the absence of a definite, unconditional obligation to repay or return that which would otherwise constitute a gain." Since Wilcox embezzled the money, and therefore "was at all times under an unqualified duty and obligation to repay the money to his employer," the Court found that money embezzled was not includible within "gross income." But, Rutkin's legal claim was no greater than that of Wilcox. Both Wilcox and Rutkin obtained the money by means of a criminal act. Nor was Rutkin's obligation to repay the extorted money to the victim any less than that of Wilcox. The victim of an extortion, like the victim of an embezzlement, has a right to restitution. Furthermore, it is inconsequential that an embezzler may lack title to the sums he appropriates while an extortionist may gain a voidable title. Questions of federal income taxation are not determined by such "attenuated subtleties." What is important is that the right to recoupment exists.

It has been a well-established principle, long before either *Rutkin* or *Wilcox*, that unlawful, as well as lawful, gains are comprehended with the term "gross income." The Income Tax Act of 1913 provided that "the net income of a taxable person shall include gains, profits and income . . . from . . . the transaction of any lawful business carried on for gain or profit, or gains or profits and income derived from any source whatever. . . ." When the statute was amended in 1916, the one word "lawful" was omitted. This revealed, we think, the obvious intent of Congress to tax income derived from both legal and illegal sources, to remove the incongruity of having the gains of the honest laborer taxed and the gains of the dishonest immune. The language of § 61(a) has been held to encompass all "accessions to wealth, clearly realized, and over which the taxpayers have complete dominion." *Comm'r v. Glenshaw Glass Co.*, 348 U.S. 426 (1955). A gain "constitutes taxable income when its recipient has such control over it that, as a practical matter, he derives readily realizable economic value from it." *Rutkin*, supra.

When a taxpayer acquires earnings, lawfully or unlawfully, without the consensual recognition, express or implied, of an obligation to repay and without restriction as to their disposition, "he has received income which he is required to [report on his] return, even though it may still be claimed that he is not entitled to retain the money, and even though he may still be adjudged liable to restore its equivalent." *North American Oil v. Burnet*. In such case, the taxpayer has "actual command over the property taxed — the actual benefit for which the tax is paid." This standard brings wrongful appropriations within the broad sweep of "gross income"; it excludes loans. When a law-abiding taxpayer mistakenly receives income in one year, which receipt is found to be invalid in a subsequent year, the taxpayer must nonetheless report the amount as "gross income" in the year received. *U.S. v. Lewis*. We do not believe that Congress intended to treat a law-breaking taxpayer differently. Just as the honest taxpayer may deduct any amount repaid in the year in which the repayment is made, the Government points out that, "If, when, and to the extent that the victim recovers back the misappropriated funds, there is of course a reduction in the embezzler's income."

[The portion of the opinion dismissing the criminal tax fraud indictment is omitted, but this aspect of the case is discussed in Chapter 15.A.4, supra.]

There are numerous cases dealing with the issue of whether a purported loan is "real." The issue in many of these cases is whether the obligor can claim deductions for interest payments, as the idea of "interest" presupposes a valid debt obligation.[16] Another group of cases involves the issue of whether the lender can claim a

---

[16] See, e.g., *Knetsch v. U.S.*, 364 U.S. (1960) (Chapter 21.B.1, infra, holding that a purported loan was a "sham"); *John Kelley Co. v. Comm'r*, 326 U.S. 521 (1946) (dealing with possible treatment of corporate debt as equity); *Gilbert v. Comm'r*, 248 F.2d 399 (2d Cir. 1957) (in dealing with the debt vs. equity distinction in the corporation context, the test is one of "reasonable expectation of repayment"); *Estate of Franklin v. Comm'r*, 544 F.2d 1045 (9th Cir. 1976) (a tax shelter case, disallowing interest deductions

§ 166 bad debt deduction, which also requires a valid debt obligation.[17] A third group of cases deals with the issue of whether a "loan" is really a disguised gift or other transfer that lacks a bona fide repayment obligation.[18]

It is hard to generalize with any precision from this mass of case law, but, roughly speaking, a valid debt for tax purposes requires a reasonable expectation of repayment and an intent on the part of the lender to enforce the debt. In determining whether these requirements are satisfied, courts consider such factors as whether (1) there is a repayment schedule, (2) interest payments are provided for, (3) the borrower has a sufficient cash flow (present and future) to repay, (4) the borrower's net worth can realistically support repayment, (5) the loan is secured by meaningful collateral, and (6) the loan is not subordinate to other debt. In short, this issue is highly fact-dependent.

PROBLEMS

1. Jim borrows $10K from his sister, Lori, evidenced by a 5-year note with a market rate of 5% interest. State whether the "normal" tax results for Jim are altered if:

(a) Jim intends to repay the debt but is insolvent, without a job, and suffering from assorted problems that will likely prevent him from obtaining and holding a job, and Lori makes the loan in ignorance of these facts. Does it matter if the reason for Lori's ignorance is that she didn't inquire or that Jim concealed his financial information?

(b) Jim has financial resources but subjectively intends not to repay the loan, and Lori is unaware of this intent. Does it matter if Jim signs a note or verbally acknowledges that it is a loan?

(c) Jim has financial resources, but Lori has no intention of enforcing the loan. Does it matter if Jim is aware of this intent?

2. In Year 1, Fred embezzles $10K from his employer. In Year 2 he is caught. The employer agrees not to press criminal charges after Fred agrees to repay the embezzled amount plus $3K. What are Fred's tax consequences? Is Fred likely to report income in Year 1? When apprehended in Year 2, can (and should) Fred file an amended return for Year 1?

D. INTEREST EXPENSE

The receipt of interest clearly produces an accession to wealth and, therefore, it is not surprising that § 61(a)(4) expressly identifies interest as a gross income item. The income tax treatment of the payment of interest is somewhat more complex, however. (The distinction between interest and principal is explored in Chapter 27.A, infra)

---

and also involving the issue of whether purchase-money debt could be included in basis).

[17] See, e.g., *Eckert v. Burnet*, 283 U.S. 140 (1931); *Brenhouse v. Comm'r*, 37 T.C. 326 (1961) (acq.).

[18] See, e.g., *Andrew v. Comm'r*, 54 T.C. 239 (1970) (acq.) (income tax); *Estate of Mitchell v. Comm'r*, T.C. Memo. 1982-185 (estate tax); *Rev. Rul. 77-299*, 1977-2 C.B. 14 (gift tax).

1. Interest as an Expense

Interest costs are generally treated as expenses, even if the underlying debt is connected to the acquisition of property. Interest is viewed as a cost of using (renting) another person's *money*. In finance circles, interest is treated as a "period cost" that becomes owed with the passage of time.

Section 163, which governs virtually all tax issues concerning interest costs, treats interest as an expense by stating that interest is deducted (if at all) when paid (by a cash-method taxpayer) or accrued (that is, owed) by an accrual-method taxpayer. (The doctrinal significance of the cash method and the accrual method is explained in Chapter 23.A.3, infra)

The exceptions to the expensing of interest are relatively insignificant: (1) capitalization of interest that is prepaid (§ 461(g)), (2) capitalization of certain construction-period interest (§ 263A(f)), and (3), at the taxpayer's election, carrying charges (§ 266). These exceptions are not discussed further in this chapter.

2. Incurred to Produce Income

When interest is paid for a loan of money used to facilitate a business or investment activity, the interest deduction should not be (and is not) disallowed just because of the fact that the borrowed money was excluded from the debtor's gross income by the borrowing exclusion. The following example illustrates why this is so. Individual B borrows $10K on January 1, Year 1. The loan principal and 10% interest are due on January 1, Year 2. B uses the borrowed money to make a January 1, Year 1 purchase of a bond that will pay $10K of principal and 10% ($1K) interest on January 1, Year 2. The $10K of loan proceeds are excluded from B's gross income and she takes a $10K basis in the bond. On January 1, Year 2, B collects $10K of bond principal that is offset by her $10K basis, and she makes a nondeductible $10K principal payment to the lender. On January 1, Year 2, B also collects $1K of bond interest, but there is no economic profit because B must pay $1K of interest expense on January 1, Year 2. The entire borrowing/investment scheme produces an economic wash, and the only way to make the tax system reflect this fact is to allow B a $1K January 1, Year 2 interest deduction. Denial of the deduction for interest expense would leave B with $1K of net income from a scheme that yielded no overall economic gain. Thus, income tax logic requires B to be allowed a deduction for her January 1, Year 2 interest outlay regardless of the January 1, Year 1 exclusion of the loan proceeds for her gross income.

The example above assumed that B's interest income is includible. If the income is excluded, the interest should not be deducted. Otherwise, the same economic wash as occurred in the example would generate a tax loss. Accordingly, § 265(a) disallows any deduction for interest on debt used to purchase or carry tax-exempt (§ 103) bonds or which is allocable to tax-exempt income.

Not surprisingly, business interest is allowed as a deduction, except where the interest is allocable to a business of being an employee (in which case the interest is treated as nondeductible personal interest under § 163(h)(1)). See § 163(h)(2)(A). The deduction for allowable business interest is above-the-line under § 62(a)(1).

3.   Excess Investment Interest

Assume that Investor borrows $100K at 10% ($10K) interest payable annually for 10 years to buy Blackacre, which appreciates at a rate of $10K per year. After 10 years, Investor sells Blackacre for $200K, realizing a gain of $100K. Assume that the interest is deducted annually (against other income) in the years paid and that the tax rate is always 30%. The tax savings from the interest deduction is $3K per year, which (if invested at a 10% gross return that is taxed annually at 30%) will grow to about $45K after 10 years, which is about $15K more than is needed to pay the $30K tax on the investment profit of $100K. The important points here are (1) this borrowing/investment transaction yields an economic profit of about $15K out of an economic wash, and (2) the profit is due solely to the fact that the interest deductions are taken annually, whereas the appreciation is not taxed until the end of the 10-year period.

The theoretically appropriate correction is to defer the interest deductions to match the deferred gain after 10 years.[19] A deferral of deductions is the functional equivalent of capitalizing the interest deductions and adding them to basis. The solution fashioned by Congress for this problem is, under § 163(d), to defer interest deductions but without capitalizing the deferred interest deductions to particular assets. Specifically, § 163(d) prevents taxpayers (other than corporations) from deducting each year's aggregate "investment interest" to the extent that it exceeds the year's aggregate "net investment income," which is investment income minus allowable investment expenses (after applying the § 67 two-percent floor under MIDs) other than investment interest expense itself. Investment interest in excess of net investment income can be carried forward indefinitely in a deferred-interest account and deducted in a future year or years in which the taxpayer has net investment income in excess of that year's investment interest.

Thus, in the preceding example, if Investor has no other investment interest, income, or expenses over the 10-year period in question, all of Investor's interest deductions (totaling $100K) would be deferred and deducted in the year that the taxpayer has $100K (or more) of gain on the sale of Blackacre (assuming that such gain is treated as "investment income").

If, however, Investor had realized (in each of the 10 years) at least $10K of net investment income, Investor would have been able, under § 163(d), to deduct currently the entire $10K of investment interest expense on her returns for each of the 10 years.

Section 163(d) creates a problem by not capitalizing the interest to a specific asset. Investment interest (deferred or not deferred) is a deduction against ordinary income rather than capital gain. In the example, Investor's gain on the sale of Blackacre is capital gain. Under a strict capitalization approach, the capital

---

[19] If the investment appreciated at a rate of 10% compounded annually (instead of $10K per year), the Year 10 value would be $259K (due to the compound interest effect). To obtain a tax wash from deferral in this scenario, it would have to be assumed (contrary to fact) that the interest paid increased each year at a compound interest rate of 10%. Additionally, the deferred deductions would also have to be compounded forward on a before-tax basis. But the tax system does not compound deduction, basis, or inclusion amounts forward, and doing so here would add unnecessary complexity to the system.

gain would be zero (because Investor's basis would be $200K, the initial $100K cost plus 10 years of deferred interest of $10K per year). To control this character-mismatching problem, the Code provides that net capital gain (and qualified dividend income taxed at capital gains rates) is treated as investment income only to the extent that the taxpayer elects to forego the preferential § 1(h) rates with respect to these items. See §§ 1(h)(3) & (h)(11)(D), 163(d)(4)(B). Thus, in the Investor example, the deferred interest of $100K would be deducted in the year that Blackacre is sold for a $100K capital gain only if Investor declined to take advantage of the lower § 1(h) rates on such gain.

The distinction between "business" and investment is obviously crucial to the application of § 163(d). This distinction was discussed in Chapter 8.A, supra. "Investment interest" includes all interest on debt incurred to purchase or carry investment property. It does not, however, encompass qualified residence interest (Subsection 5, infra) or "passive activity" interest taken into account under § 469 (discussed in Chapter 21.D, infra). Allowable investment interest with respect to a property that produces rents and royalties is an above-the-line deduction under § 62(a)(4). Otherwise, it is an itemized deduction, but not an MID. See § 67(b)(1).

4. Consumer Interest Generally

Consider the example of individual A who borrows $10K at 10% per annum interest. Assume that she uses the $10K to finance a consumption purchase, say a personal-use automobile. If imputed income from the automobile (i.e., the annual rental value of the automobile) were treated as gross income for federal income tax purposes, she would be allowed to annually deduct the related interest expense (as well as repairs and appropriate depreciation). The income tax does not, however, tax imputed income. Accordingly, interest, repairs, and depreciation should be (and are) disallowed. In the case of interest expense, the deduction is initially allowed by § 163(a) but is then cancelled out by § 163(h)(1), which disallows (with exceptions to be shortly noted) any deduction for personal interest.

A horizontal equity argument can, nevertheless, be made that consumer interest should be deductible by comparing A (the debt-financed purchaser of an automobile) with B, who purchases the automobile with $10K of cash salary. The argument (which ultimately fails) is that A and B will be equally taxed on the identical $10K of automobile cost only if A is allowed to deduct interest. But this argument does not prove the case for B's interest deduction. Initially, B uses $10K of after-tax dollars to buy the car, whereas A uses $10K of excluded borrowed cash to buy the car. At the same time, the present value of the total future, but nondeductible, principal and interest payments that A is obligated to make on her $10K debt, (assuming a market rate of interest) is $10K. In other words, disallowing deductions for all principal and interest payments that A will ultimately make on the debt that she incurred to buy her automobile is the equivalent, in present value terms, of disallowing the deduction for B's $10K cash outlay. This analysis demonstrates that awarding an interest deduction to A would actually violate horizontal equity by putting A in a better tax position than B. This analysis of consumer debt is consistent with the analysis of the income taxation of consumer assets (and imputed income) outlined in Chapter 13.B.3, where it was demonstrated that the income tax reaches only the present value of future consumption by disallowing any deduction for the costs of such assets.

In sum, allowing taxpayers to deduct consumer interest expense against salary income would effectively amount to a government subsidy for debt-financed consumer purchases.

5. Consumer Interest on Debt Secured by a Personal Residence

Under § 163(h)(2), personal consumption interest is disallowed unless it is either (1) "qualified residence interest," discussed immediately below, or (2) education interest to the extent allowed under § 221 (an above-the-line deduction mentioned in Chapter 9.D.2).

"Qualified Residence Interest" is defined in § 163(h)(3) as interest paid with respect to either "Acquisition Indebtedness" or "Home Equity Indebtedness." A prerequisite for falling within either category is that the debt be secured by a "qualified residence," which is one's principal residence and one other "residence" (which could be a mobile home or even a boat).

Acquisition Indebtedness is debt that is used for certain purposes (purchasing, constructing, or substantially improving a qualified residence that secures the debt) and that, along with all other Acquisition Indebtedness, does not exceed $1M.

Home Equity Indebtedness is qualified-residence-secured debt (other than Acquisition Indebtedness) that does not, along with all other Home Equity Indebtedness, exceed the lesser of $100K or the "equity" of the securing residence (meaning the FMV of the residence less any outstanding Acquisition Indebtedness secured by that residence). Unlike Acquisition Indebtedness, no provision constrains the use to which Home Equity Indebtedness can be put. Thus, the proceeds of a "home equity loan" can be spent on a college education, a fancy car, a private plane, or a lavish vacation, without jeopardizing the deductibility of the interest!

Note that the $1 million and $100K "ceilings," which are not indexed for inflation, apply to debt principal, not the interest itself.

In *Rev. Rul. 2010-25*, 2010-2 C.B. 571, the IRS ruled that the first $100K of Acquisition Indebtedness in excess of $1M could qualify as Home Equity Indebtedness. The ruling rejects a contrary holding in *Pau v. Comm'r*, T.C. Memo. 1997-43.

Qualified Residence Interest is an Itemized Deduction, but not an MID. See § 67b)(1).

PROBLEMS

1. Ten years ago, Evelyn purchased a home for $750K, taking out a mortgage (secured by the residence) of $600K with 12% interest from National Bank. She has used this residence continuously as her principal residence. How much interest can Evelyn deduct in the current year with respect to this debt?

2. (a) Jack purchased a home for $200K in Year 1, taking out a mortgage (secured by the residence) of $160K with 12% interest from National Bank. He has used this home continuously as his principal residence. The residence was still worth $200K in Year 3 when Jack borrowed $75K to finance a kidney transplant for his dying child. (For the sake of simplicity, assume that the first mortgage was an interest-only "balloon mortgage" and that no principal payments had yet been made on it.) To what extent is the interest on the two loans deductible?

(b) How would the answer change if Jack spent the proceeds of the second loan on adding a sauna or a racquetball court to his residence?

6. Sorting Interest into Categories

The rules disallowing the deduction of both consumer interest that does not qualify under §§ 163(h)(3) or 122 and excess investment interest generally require that the debt from which the interest arises be characterized according to the use or uses made of the debt proceeds. This, in turn, requires that the debt proceeds must be traced to specific expenditures. See Reg. § 1.163-8T(a)(1), (3).

This tracing approach creates at least two problems. First, where the debtor has multiple debts or makes multiple uses of debt proceeds, the tracing exercise can be quite complex and can require maintenance of extensive, detailed records. Second (and perhaps more important), the tracing approach creates disparate treatment among taxpayers. To be specific, taxpayers who have sufficient cash can avoid the restrictions on the deduction of interest expense by (1) using their cash to pay costs that would (if the costs were debt-financed) give rise to deduction-restricted interest and (2) using their borrowing capacity to pay costs that do not trigger restrictions on interest deductions. In contrast, cash-poor taxpayers who must borrow for everything, do not have this manipulation opportunity. This inequity could be mitigated by characterizing debt according to its collateral, if any, rather than the use of the borrowed funds. But this approach would also favor the wealthy, who could mortgage business and investment assets (which they own disproportionately to the rest of the population) to finance personal consumption. Yet another possibility (known as "stacking") would be to allocate debt first to assets of a certain character (to the extent of their value), next to assets of another character (to the extent of their value), and so on. The rationale would be that debt is fungible and supports, at least indirectly, ownership of all of the debtor's assets even if the debt proceeds are spent on current consumption. The stacking approach, unfortunately, would require a burdensome annual inventory and valuation of all taxpayer-owned assets. Moreover, if the stacking rule were to allocate debt first to business or investment assets, the wealthy would again be favored. A final alternative would allocate interest *proportionately* to all property owned by the taxpayer, but this too would require annual valuations of assets. In short, none of these alternative approaches are particularly appealing or workable.

The only other path out of this conundrum is to allow unlimited deductions for investment and consumer interest expense and to tolerate the resulting anomalies described in the examples above. In 1986, Congress concluded that the tracing approach of current law was the lesser evil in spite of its imperfections.

Chapter 19

CANCELLATION-OF-DEBT INCOME

This chapter deals with the tax consequences to those who avoid having to pay their debts. In this chapter, "debts" refers not only to obligations to repay loans but also obligations to pay liabilities not arising from loans.

Section 61(a)(12) lists as a gross income item the "income from discharge of indebtedness." Two other widely-used terms that are used synonymously are "debt-discharge income" (DDI) and "cancellation-of-debt income" (COD income). The concept of "debt discharge" actually encompasses three situations, namely:

(1) the debtor's satisfying the debt (Section A of this chapter);

(2) the satisfaction of the debt by a third party (the *Old Colony* doctrine, discussed in Chapter 12.A); and,

(3) the cancellation of the debt by the creditor or by operation of law (true debt-discharge or cancellation-of-debt income under § 61(a)(12)) (Section B of this chapter).

Section C of this chapter deals with § 108, which mitigates the effect of certain debt-discharge income.

Section 61(a)(12), enacted in 1954, doesn't define debt-discharge income. It simply confirms established judicial doctrine to the effect that such a category of income exists, and that such category is distinct from such other categories as "gains from dealings in property" (§ 61(a)(3)) and "catch-all income." Thus, § 61(a)(12) income cannot be capital gain, and it is the only category of income that is subject to § 108. The definition of debt-discharge income is found in the caselaw, which continues to evolve.[1]

A. SATISFACTION OF LIABILITIES

A debt can be satisfied (paid off) by the debtor or by a third party. This scenario does not give rise to debt-discharge income as such.

1. Satisfaction by the Debtor

That § 61(a)(12) cannot mean that *every* discharge of debt produces debt-discharge income is evident from the most common scenario of all, namely, that of the debtor paying off the debt or liability in cash. Recall the example in the last

---

[1] The legislative history indicates that the enactment of § 61(a)(12) was not intended to arrest judicial development. See H.R. Conf. Rep. No. 2543, 83d. Cong., 2d Sess. 23 (1954).

chapter of Steve, who borrowed $5K from National Bank. Assuming that this loan is not a below-market loan governed by § 7872, Steve has no income at the time of the borrowing, because the receipt of the $5K is offset by the face amount of the $5K repayment obligation. And when Steve repays the $5K principal amount of the loan in full, his positive wealth (assets on hand) and negative wealth (his liabilities) will both be reduced by $5K, resulting in no change in Steve's net wealth (or "net worth"). Because Steve's repayment of the loan principal does not reduce his net wealth, he cannot deduct the repayment. Clearly there is no new gross income on account of the repayment. Nevertheless, it can be said that Steve is effectively "taxed" on the borrowed money at the time of *repayment*, because Steve is using previously taxed dollars for this purpose.

If P performs services to discharge a debt owed by P to C, P has compensation income equal to the amount of the discharged debt (not debt-discharge income). See Reg. § 1.61-12(a).

Gain or loss can arise if the debtor uses property as a medium of debt satisfaction. Suppose, for example, that Virginia owes $10K to Jefferson, but instead of paying Jefferson in cash, Virginia transfers property with a $3K basis and a $10K value to Jefferson in satisfaction of the debt. Numerous cases have held this transaction to be a "realization event" under § 1001. The transaction is deemed to be the equivalent of (1) a sale by Virginia of the property for $10K cash to Jefferson, followed by (2) Virginia using the cash to satisfy the liability. While there are no tax consequences to the second step, the first step produces a $7K realized gain within the meaning of § 1001(a), which Virginia must include in her gross income under § 61(a)(3) (as opposed to § 61(a)(12)) and a $10K basis in the property to Jefferson.

Several well-known cases in the literature, as well as one of the examples cited in Reg. § 1.61-12, apply this principle:

1. *U.S. v. Davis*, 370 U.S. 65 (1962), held that a husband's transfer of appreciated property in satisfaction, in a divorce settlement (having a value deemed to be equal to the value of the transferred property) produced gain (or loss). This result in the marital transfer context has since been superseded by § 1041, treating husband-wife transfers (in marriage or divorce) as nonrecognition events with carryover basis. However, *Davis* remains good authority on the issue of whether the transfer of property in satisfaction of an obligation is a realization event for federal income tax purposes.

2. *International Freighting Corp. v. Comm'r*, 135 F.2d 310 (2d Cir. 1943), held that an employer's payment of employee compensation by a transfer of appreciated property resulted in gain recognition, which in turn allowed the full value of the property to be deducted as a business deduction; this result is now "codified" in Reg. § 1.83-6(b).

3. *Kenan v. Comm'r*, 114 F.2d 217 (2d Cir. 1940), held an estate executor's satisfaction of a fixed-dollar legacy under the decedent's will (considered to be a "debt" of the estate) with appreciated property produced gain to the estate (an income tax entity).

The gain or loss in this type of situation may qualify as capital (or § 1231) gain or loss, because a transfer of property in satisfaction of a debt or liability is considered to be a "sale." Whether the realized loss is *deductible* would be governed by § 165, with possible disallowance under § 267(a)(1) if the "buyer" is a related party.

2. Third-Party Satisfaction of Debt

Although virtually all debt-discharge situations involve only the debtor and the creditor, situations arise where a *third party* satisfies a debtor's obligation to a creditor. An example already encountered in Chapter 12.A is offered by *Old Colony Trust Co. v. Comm'r*, 279 U.S. 716 (1929). In this type of case, the third-party payor is deemed to transfer cash to the obligor (the first party) who in turn is deemed to pay over the cash to the obligee (the second party). The tax nature of the first deemed payment depends on the context (perhaps the relationship between the first and third parties). In *Old Colony*, the first deemed payment was characterized as compensation for services. The tax nature of the second deemed payment from the obligor to the obligee depends on the nature of the obligation. In *Old Colony*, it was characterized as a payment of a nondeductible federal income tax.

Another Supreme Court case of this ilk is *Diedrich v. Comm'r*, 457 U.S. 191 (1982), which held that a gift of property conditioned on the donee paying the donor's gift tax liability was to be characterized as a sale by the donor to the donee for an amount equal to the gift tax amount, followed by a nondeductible gift tax payment by the donor to the IRS.[2] (However, a realized loss in such a scenario would not be allowed as a deduction, because a gift is a "personal" loss.)

In *Ashby v. Comm'r*, 50 T.C. 409 (1968), a corporation's payment of a major shareholder's debt was held to be a "dividend" paid by the corporation to the shareholder followed by a nondeductible debt repayment by the shareholder to the lender.

None of these cases involved § 61(a)(12) debt-discharge income.

PROBLEMS

1. (a) Charlotte owes Calvin $5K. They are unrelated and deal with each other at arm's length. Instead of repaying with dollars, Charlotte transfers stock with a fair market value of $5K to Calvin in full satisfaction of the debt. Charlotte bought the stock three years ago for $3.5K. What results for both parties assuming that Calvin's basis in Charlotte's debt is $5K?

(b) Same as (a), except that Charlotte's basis in the property is $8K, and Calvin and Charlotte are siblings. What if Calvin subsequently sells the stock for $10K? See § 267(a)(1), (b)(1), (c)(4), (d).

2. In *Friedland v. Comm'r*, T.C. Memo. 2001-236, a father transferred property with a built-in gain to a creditor of his son's corporation, in which the father owned

---

[2] The Court in *Diedrich* seemed confused concerning how to categorize the facts, but *Old Colony* is clearly on point.

no stock. The Tax Court held that because the transfer did not satisfy a liability of the father, the father did not engage in a constructive sale.

(a) Was the Tax Court correct?

(b) What should be the son's tax treatment?

B. COD INCOME

Income can arise for the obligor where the creditor itself cancels or waives all or part of the debt or liability or allows it to become unenforceable (say, by allowing the statute of limitations to run). This debt-discharge scenario is commonly referred to as cancellation-of-debt income, or "COD income" for short, and it is this scenario that is referred to by § 61(a)(12). Most debt cancellations arise where the debtor is in financial difficulty and persuades (or threatens) one or more of its creditors that everybody would be better off if the debt were cancelled or reduced.

1. A Doctrine in Search of a Theory

The principal doctrinal issue is whether all debt and liability cancellations give rise to income, and the answer depends on which of two competing theories is sound. One is the balance-sheet (reduction-in-liability) theory, and the other is the inconsistent-events theory (namely, that the cancellation of the debt is inconsistent with the tax treatment of the event that gave rise to the obligation).

a. The Balance-Sheet Approach

In *U. S. v. Kirby Lumber*, 284 U.S. 1 (1931), the taxpayer corporation issued bonds to investors and received an amount equal to the stated principal (i.e., face) amount. By so doing, the corporation borrowed the bond proceeds, which it was obligated to repay at a fixed date. Market-rate interest was payable periodically. Subsequent to the original issue, the market value of the bonds decreased, probably due to an increase in market interest rates. The corporation repurchased some of these bonds in the market for a price that was about $138K less than the face amount. Since a debtor cannot owe money to itself, the liability represented by the face amount of the repurchased bonds disappeared. The Supreme Court held that the $138K excess of the face (principal amount) of the repurchased bonds over the purchase price was gross income to the corporation, stating in a typically short opinion by Justice Holmes:

> By the Revenue Act of 1921, gross income includes "gains or profits and income derived from any source whatever," and by the Treasury Regulations, that have been in force through repeated re-enactments, "If the corporation purchases and retires any of such bonds at a price less than the issuing price or face value, the excess of the issuing price or face value over the purchase price is gain or income for the taxable year." We see no reason why the Regulations should not be accepted as a correct statement of the law.

> In *Bowers v. Kerbaugh-Empire Co.*, 271 U.S. 170, the [taxpayer] owned the stock of another company that had borrowed money repayable in

[German] marks for an enterprise that failed. At the time of payment the marks had fallen in value [relative to the U.S. dollar], which so far as it went was a gain for the [taxpayer], and it was contended by the [government] that the gain was taxable income. But the transaction as a whole was a loss, and the contention was denied. Here there was no shrinkage of assets and the taxpayer made a clear gain. As a result of its dealings it made available $138,000 of assets previously offset by the obligation of bonds now extinct. We see nothing to be gained by the discussion of judicial definitions. The defendant in error has realized within the year an accession to income, if we take words in their plain popular meaning, as they should be taken here.

In *Kirby Lumber*, Justice Holmes appeared to rely on financial accounting analysis in concluding that the taxpayer realized gross income when it extinguished debt that had a face amount that exceeded by $138K the price paid to extinguish such debt. The key language indicating this reliance was: "As a result of its dealings it made available [$138K of] assets *previously offset* by the obligation of bonds now extinct." (Emphasis added.) To appreciate the implications of this language we need to briefly explore the financial accounting concept of a "balance sheet," which shows the "net worth" (assets minus liabilities) of a business as of the balance sheet's date. Under financial accounting rules, a borrowing transaction produces a simultaneous *increase* in both the borrower's cash (a balance sheet "asset") and the borrower's "loan payable" account (a balance sheet "liability," which is the opposite of an asset). Because these items offset each other, the borrowing does not change the borrower's balance sheet "net worth." Changes in the fair market value (FMV) of an asset or liability do not affect the balance sheet. When the borrowed principal is repaid, the repayments would simultaneously *reduce* both the borrower's cash account (an asset) and the loan payable account (a liability) by equal amounts. Because these reductions would offset each other, there would be no change in the borrower's net worth. But the *Kirby Lumber* facts deviated from the ordinary pattern. Its cash payment eliminated debt that was $138K greater than the reduction in its cash account. Thus, Kirby Lumber's accounting "net worth" was increased by $138K. Because Justice Holmes saw Kirby Lumber as having "freed" $138K of its assets from the previously offsetting liability, his analysis has often been referred to as the "freeing-of-assets" approach to the debt-discharge issue.

Justice Holmes's discussion of *Bowers v. Kerbaugh-Empire Co.*, 271 U.S. 170 (1926), was regrettably mischievous, because it suggested that, at least in some cases, the liability reduction arising from the debt discharge (an economic gain) might be offset by a loss of the borrowed cash (or assets purchased with the cash). In *Kerbaugh-Empire*, a U.S. corporation borrowed German Marks and was obligated to repay an equal amount of Marks. Although it squandered these funds in a losing venture, the loan transaction on its own happened to produce a gain because the U.S. dollar rose in value against the German Mark, and the taxpayer was able to repay the German Marks that it originally borrowed using fewer U.S. dollars than would have been required if the dollar's value had remained unchanged. Nevertheless, the Supreme Court held that since the loss suffered when the borrowed funds were squandered exceeded the gain arising on the foreign currency borrowing transaction, the taxpayer had no overall gain from the transaction.

Leaving aside the question whether *Kerbaugh Empire* was really a debt-cancellation case,[3] a more fundamental reason exists to discredit it. In terms of tax principles, we have seen that a borrower is allowed to exclude borrowed amounts from gross income because the borrower has an offsetting obligation to make nondeductible repayment of the principal. To the extent that the borrower escapes the offsetting repayment obligation, he realizes a gain *with respect to the borrowing transaction itself.* Accordingly, *the use to which the borrower puts the borrowed amount* is irrelevant to the borrowing transaction. What happens to the borrowed cash can (and is) accounted for separately. If this were not so, both timing and character rules would be undermined. Every debt-financed transaction would have to be held open until the final results on both sides could be tallied. Similarly, the scheme of capital gains taxation would be violated if a capital loss on the asset side were able to be offset by an ordinary gain on the debt side. Finally, rules would have to be developed to decide when the two sides would be integrated (that is, when loan proceeds would have to be traced to their uses). Tracing itself would be messy.

Although *Kerbaugh-Empire* has never been expressly overruled by the Supreme Court, its incompatibility with other income tax principles has been acknowledged to the point where it is now considered to be a dead letter.[4] Unfortunately, the "freeing-of-assets" rationale advanced in *Kirby Lumber* planted the seeds of dubious doctrine. Take the case of the insolvent debtor who has a negative net worth both before and after the debt discharge. For example, assume that Dugald's only liability is for $20K that he had previously borrowed and that he has assets worth only $8K. Because his total liabilities exceed his assets by $12K, he has a negative net worth of $12K, i.e., he is "insolvent." Assume further that his creditor is willing to reduce the debt by $5K in order to rehabilitate Dugald, a good customer. Dugald will then have $8K of assets and $15K in liabilities but still no positive net worth. There has been no "freeing up" of any of his assets, as his total debt obligations still exceed all of his assets.

Based on the freeing-of-assets rationale implied in *Kirby Lumber*, early decisions concluded that insolvent debtors did not realize gross income when the debt discharge failed to make them solvent. That is to say, the courts created a judicial "insolvency exception" to the general rule that debt-discharge income must be included in gross income. However, if a debt discharge resulted in a previously insolvent debtor achieving a positive net worth, the debtor *did* realize gross income, but the amount was limited to the positive net worth.[5] For example, if Dugald's creditor had discharged $14K of the $20K of total debt, Dugald would have gross income $2K (the excess of his $8K of assets over his $6K remaining liability). To that extent, he was rendered solvent by the debt cancellation. (This result, as well as other "derivations" of the balance-sheet approach, are codified in § 108, which is discussed in Section C.)

---

[3] In *Kerbaugh-Empire*, no debt was cancelled, the borrowed German Marks having been fully repaid. Rather, *Kerbaugh-Empire* involved the taxation of foreign currency transactions, a subject that is now governed by §§ 985–989 of the Code, which are sometimes covered in a course in international taxation.

[4] See, e.g., *Vukasovitch v. Comm'r*, 790 F.2d 1409 (9th Cir. 1986); *Rev. Rul. 92-99*, 1992-2 C.B. 35.

[5] See, e.g., *Lakeland Grocery Co. v. Comm'r*, 36 B.T.A. 289 (1937).

Really, the balance-sheet sheet approach applied in *Kirby Lumber* does not require consideration of asset values. In principle, a liability is considered in financial accounting to be a "negative asset," and a reduction in a liability, from whatever cause, increases balance sheet wealth (net worth) by decreasing negative wealth. Accordingly, Dugald should (in theory) be required to include the entire debt-reduction amount (in both scenarios) as COD income.

NOTES

1.   In the *Kirby Lumber* case, the issue (sales) price of the bonds equaled their face amount. In actual practice, however, the issue price of a bond can be greater or lesser than its face amount, and this discrepancy implicates the distinction between "interest" and "principal," which is dealt with in Chapter 27. In this chapter, *it should generally be assumed that the amount borrowed and the amount of principal to which the lender is entitled at maturity are the same.* This assumption will indeed hold true with respect to bank loans, private loans, consumer debt, and other nonpublicly traded debt.

2.   A 1943 Supreme Court case[6] held that a debt cancellation not made for consideration is a "gift" (and was thus excluded from the debtor's gross income under the predecessor to § 102). However, in *Comm'r v. Jacobson*, 336 U.S. 28 (1949), the Court backtracked, holding that the gift exclusion does not apply where the creditors appear to be acting out of their own self-interest, which is usually the case. In other words, the gift exclusion *can* apply to a debt-cancellation scenario only under the demanding *Duberstein* test, discussed in Chapter 15.A.3.

PROBLEM

Mary, who was not in the lending business, loaned her son Bob $10K to help him start a business. The business struggled and, to provide further help, Mary forgave the debt even though Bob was not insolvent. She did so because of her affection for her son. Does Bob have gross income?

b. The Inconsistent-Events Theory

In the typical COD income scenario the borrower received cold, hard cash in the prior year that would have been a wealth accession at that time under § 61 if it were not for the offsetting obligation to repay, but now that obligation is gone. While the exclusion was proper in the year of the borrowing (because repayment was expected) the borrowing exclusion should not continue to hold sway with respect to the cash that we now expect will *never* be repaid. The reason justifying exclusion in the borrowing year has disappeared. Insolvency is irrelevant. The notion of debt-cancellation income is simply a *delayed realization* approach that causes borrowed amounts to be included in income when, and to the extent that, the repayment obligation ceases to exist (apart from its satisfaction).

---

[6] *Helvering v. American Dental Co.*, 318 U.S. 322 (1943).

The foregoing is a description of the inconsistent-events theory of COD income as applied to cash borrowings.[7] Under this theory, the insolvency exception is unsound as tax doctrine, because the debtor's asset holdings are irrelevant. The flip sits theory is that no COD income should be held to arise in cases involving the reduction or elimination of tax liabilities, support obligations, fines, penalties, or obligations arising under tort law, *because in these cases the taxpayer never received cash (or other property) that was excluded from income on account of an obligation to repay.*[8]

c. Evaluation of the Theories

The balance-sheet approach is (we think) incorrect, because it is based on two false premises. The first is that COD income cannot exist except to the extent that it increases the positive net worth of the debtor. The second false premise is that all liabilities, even those not incurred in connection with the receipt of money or property, are "negative wealth" in the tax sense (so that the cancellation thereof must increase the debtor's net wealth). Both premises are based on a business accounting convention that is at odds with general income tax principles. Business accounting is based on a universal concept of "accrual," in which income items are taken into account when the right to future cash is acquired (as opposed to when the cash itself is received) and expenses are taken into account when the liability to make future payments is fixed (rather than when cash is actually paid). Under the income tax, most corporations and many businesses follow the accrual method, but virtually all individuals are on the cash method, meaning (in part) that expense deductions are taken only when paid in cash. (Tax accounting methods are explained in Chapter 23.) For cash-method taxpayers, application of accrual concepts is severely limited. For present purposes, it suffices to say that the accrual concept is relevant to a cash-method taxpayer only to the extent of the offsetting obligation to repay borrowed money and debt incurred to purchase items that are deductible or which acquire basis. (Such purchase-money debt is discussed in the next chapter.)

Accordingly, "liabilities" of a cash-method taxpayer not arising from the receipt of money or property *do not represent negative wealth in the income tax sense.* These obligations merely express an expectation that the taxpayer will pay cash in the future. If this expectation is negated, the taxpayer is in the position of having neither received nor parted with material wealth. Therefore, the cancellation of these liabilities should not result in gross income (unless the liability resulted in a prior tax benefit, such as basis or an expense deduction).

---

[7] Another scenario, discussed in Chapter 23, is where an accrual-method taxpayer properly takes a current expense deduction for a future liability, but the future liability disappears or turns out to be less than the amount deducted. In such a case the proper tax treatment is an "adjustment," taking the form of an income inclusion in the current year (not the earlier year in which the expense was accrued). See Reg. § 1.461-1(a)(3). This adjustment is not COD income.

[8] This statement assumes that the taxpayer did not previously deduct the item (or include it in basis). See footnote 7.

d. Where Is the Law Headed?

Although the theory is clear (in our opinion), the positive tax law, unfortunately, is unsettled. The IRS (since the mid-1990s) appears to be asserting the existence of COD income in what we consider to be inappropriate situations. Thus, under the inconsistent-events theory, the cancellation of an obligation to pay accrued (owed) interest should arguably not give rise to COD income, because the obligation to pay interest was not matched with the receipt of cash or property. However, in *Payne v. Comm'r*, T.C. Memo 2008-66, *aff'd per curiam*, 2010-1 USTC (CCH) ¶50,132 (8th Cir. 2009), *cert. denied*, 131 S. Ct. 151 (2010), the courts found COD income to exist in such a situation. The taxpayer owed approximately $21K on a credit card. Although taxpayer was neither insolvent nor in bankruptcy proceedings, the creditor bank agreed to accept approximately $5K in full settlement of the account balance. The taxpayer asserted, and the Tax Court did not disagree, that this payment was equal to 100 percent of the principal amount of the credit card debt, so that the $16K discharged amount was entirely unpaid interest. The taxpayers in *Payne* represented themselves, and relied on a statutory exception that had no relevance, failing to argue that no COD income arose in the first place.

In *Hahn v. Comm'r*, T.C. Memo 2007-75 (appeal not taken), the taxpayer in a similar case was represented by counsel, who argued that there was no COD income on the basis that no cash or property was received. The Tax Court again found that there was COD income, citing the freeing-of-assets theory, and stating that the taxpayer received the economic benefit of the use of money. (This raises the issue of whether the receipt of services without payment therefore is gross income, an issue raised in Chapter 13 and again in Subsection 2 below.)

Both of these cases ignored, and reached results contrary to, *Rev. Rul. 76-316*, 1976-2 C.B. 22, which held that COD income arose with regard to unpaid interest only to the extent that the debtor, an accrual-method taxpayer, had previously deducted the accrued but unpaid interest.

The cases noted above appear to be oblivious to the current (if somewhat ambiguous) attitude of the Supreme Court. In a case involving purchase-money debt incurred to acquire depreciable property, the Supreme Court, in *Comm'r v. Tufts*, 461 U.S. 300 (1983), set out in the next chapter, embraced the inconsistent-events theory:

> The rationale for [current inclusion] is that the original [borrowing exclusion] rested on the assumption that the mortgagor incurred an obligation to repay. Moreover, this treatment balances the fact that the mortgagor originally received the proceeds of the nonrecourse loan tax-free on the same assumption. Unless the outstanding amount of the mortgage is deemed to be realized, the mortgagor effectively will have received untaxed income at the time the loan was extended.

However, since the debt in *Tufts* was incurred to purchase property, the inconsistent-events theory did really affect the result in *Tufts*.

More to the point is *U.S. v. Centennial Savings*, 499 U.S. 573 (1991), which held that a reduction of interest owed to depositors did not give rise to COD income. (The depositors had purchased bank CDs on which interest accrued at a certain rate, but (under the terms of the CDs) the interest owed was reduced in the case of premature withdrawal by the depositors.) Here the Court stated (499 U.S. at 482):

> Borrowed funds are excluded in the first instance because the taxpayer's obligation to repay the funds offsets any increase in the taxpayer's assets; if the taxpayer is thereafter released from his obligation to repay, the taxpayer enjoys a net increase in assets equal to the forgiven portion of the debt, and the basis for the original exclusion thus evaporates.

However, the decision rested on the narrower ground that the reduction in owed interest did not produce COD income for the bank because the reduction in its interest obligation was already built into the agreement.[9]

In sum, the state of the law is uncertain, because, although the Supreme Court appears to have embraced the inconsistent-events theory, it hasn't clearly rejected the freeing-of-assets theory or decided whether the inconsistent-events theory produces COD income only in cases where the taxpayer obtained cash or property (or obtained an earlier tax benefit from the borrowing).

NOTES

1.   (a) *Payne* and *Hahn* might have reached the right result if the receipt of a service (the use of money) without paying for it is gross income. In Chapter 13, we express skepticism that unpaid-for services obtained in an arm's length transaction are gross income, except where the transaction amounts to the receipt of cash followed by its expenditure. This issue is raised again in the *Zarin* case, below.

(b) Where the liability in question is not incurred in connection with the receipt of cash, property, or services (as in the case, e.g., of tax a liability or a fine), it is hard to discern any increase in wealth or income in the tax sense. Some older cases support this view. In *Comm'r v. Rail Joint Co.*, 61 F.2d 751 (2d Cir. 1932), it was held that no COD income arose where a corporation purchased, at less than face amount, its own bonds that had been distributed to its shareholders without receipt of consideration, i.e., as a dividend). *Bradford v. Comm'r*, 233 F.2d 935 (6th Cir. 1956), held that a bank's cancellation of a taxpayer's note did not produce COD income where the taxpayer had given the note to the bank for no consideration other than the bank's cancellation of debt owed by the taxpayer's husband. The taxpayer had given the note to financially strengthen her husband's separate business. The court said that the taxpayer "received nothing of value."

2.   If the payment (satisfaction) of the (cancelled) liability would have given rise to a deduction to the obligor, inclusion of the cancelled debt in the obligor's income produces the wrong end result because the deduction for the payment (which is lost because no payment occurs) would have offset the income used to make the payment. Section 108(e)(2) recognizes this point, and "excludes" such COD income from gross income. However, we think that cancellations of obligations not incurred for cash or property (or which did not previously produce a tax benefit) are not

---

[9] Apparently it was conceded (on what basis we don't know) that the early-withdrawal penalties were income to the bank of some type, but the case was fought over whether § 108 applied, because § 108 only comes into play for COD income.

income in the first place, regardless of whether payment would be deductible.

2. The Disputed-Debt Doctrine

Further light on the tension (or conflict) between the balance-sheet approach and the inconsistent-events approach is provided by an examination of the disputed-debt doctrine. The chosen vehicle for this examination is the *Zarin* case, below, involving a settlement of gambling debts. The reader should especially ponder the question: "What did Mr. Zarin receive in the year in which he became indebted to Resorts?" Another potential angle on this case is the rule that "bargain purchases" (purchases of goods and services) involving strangers at arm's length do not give rise to income. (This doctrine is explored in Chapter 22.D.) More broadly, as discussed in Chapter 13.C, it appears that, generally, "consumption" is measured by what you pay for it (the cost being nondeductible), not its value. Additionally, recall from Chapter 10.C that § 165(d) disallows the deduction of aggregate gambling losses for the year in excess of aggregate gambling gains for the year, even if the taxpayer is a professional gambler. This disallowance is permanent, there being no "carryover" of excess gambling losses to other taxable years.

ZARIN v. COMMISSIONER
United States Tax Court
92 T.C. 1084 (1989)

COHEN, JUDGE:

The sole issue for decision is whether petitioners had income from discharge of gambling indebtedness during 1981. David Zarin (petitioner) was a professional engineer. Petitioner occasionally stayed at Resorts Int'l Hotel, Inc., in Atlantic City. Petitioner had gambled on credit both in Las Vegas, Nevada, and in the Bahamas. In June 1978, petitioner applied to Resorts for a $10,000 line of credit to be used for gambling. After a credit check, the requested line of credit was granted, despite derogatory information received from Credit Central. The game most often played by petitioner, craps, creates the potential of losses or gains from wagering on rolls of dice. Petitioner usually bet the table limit. Resorts quickly became familiar with petitioner. At petitioner's request, Resorts would raise the limit at the table to the house maximum. When petitioner gambled at Resorts, crowds would be attracted to his table by the large amounts he would wager. Gamblers would wager more than they might otherwise because of the excitement caused by the crowds and the amounts that petitioner was wagering. Petitioner was referred to as a "valued gaming patron." By November 1979, petitioner's permanent line of credit had been increased to $200,000. Despite this increase, at no time after the initial credit check did Resorts perform any further analysis of petitioner's creditworthiness. Beginning in the late summer of 1978, petitioner was extended the complimentary use of a luxury suite at Resorts. Resorts progressively increased the complimentary services to include free meals, entertainment, and 24-hour access to a limousine. By late 1979, Resorts was extending such comps to petitioner's guests as well. By this practice, Resorts sought to preserve not only petitioner's patronage but also the attractive power his gambling had on others.

Once the line of credit was established, petitioner was able to receive chips at the gambling table. Patrons of New Jersey casinos may not gamble with currency, but must use chips. Chips may not be used outside the casino for any purpose. Petitioner received chips [on 90-day credit]. At all times pertinent hereto, petitioner intended to repay any credit amount properly extended to him by Resorts. Between June 1978 and December 1979, petitioner incurred gambling debts of approximately $2.5 million. Petitioner paid these debts in full. [In 1980,] petitioner was gambling 12–16 hours per day, 7 days per week in the casino, and he was betting up to $15,000 on each roll of the dice. Petitioner was not aware of the amount of his gambling debts.

During April 1980, petitioner delivered personal checks in the total amount of $3,435,000 that were returned to Resorts as having been drawn against insufficient funds. On April 29, 1980, Resorts cut off petitioner's credit. On November 18, 1980, Resorts filed a complaint in New Jersey state court seeking collection of $3,435,000 from petitioner based on the unpaid personal checks and markers. On March 4, 1981, petitioner filed an answer, denying the allegations and asserting a variety of affirmative defenses. On September 28, 1981, petitioner settled the Resorts suit by paying $500,000. The difference between petitioner's gambling obligations of $3,435,000 and the settlement payments of $500,000 is the amount that respondent alleges to be income from forgiveness of indebtedness.

In general, gross income includes all income from whatever source derived, including income from the discharge of indebtedness. § 61(a)(12). The gain to the debtor from such discharge is the resultant freeing up of his assets that he would otherwise have been required to use to pay the debt. See *U.S. v. Kirby Lumber Co.*, 284 U.S. 1 (1931).

Petitioner argues that the debt instruments were not enforceable under New Jersey law. In *Comm'r v. Tufts*, 461 U.S. 300 (1983), the Supreme Court examined the economic realities associated with the cancellation of an obligation. Indicating a concern with symmetry, the Supreme Court observed in *Tufts*:

> The . . . [taxpayer] originally received the proceeds on the . . . loan tax-free [on the assumption that the mortgagor incurred an obligation to repay]. Unless the outstanding [liability that the taxpayer is relieved of] is deemed to be realized, the [taxpayer] effectively will have received untaxed income at the time the loan was extended. . . .

In the instant case, symmetry from year to year is not accomplished unless we treat petitioner's receipt of the loan from Resorts (converted to chips) and the subsequent discharge of his obligation to repay that loan in a consistent manner. Petitioner received credit of $3,435,000 from Resorts. He treated these amounts as a loan, not reporting any income on his 1980 tax return. The parties have stipulated that he intended to repay the amounts received. Certainly if he had won, the amounts borrowed would have been repaid.

We conclude here that the taxpayer did receive value at the time he incurred the debt and that only his promise to repay the value received prevented taxation of the value received at the time of the credit transaction. When, in the subsequent year, a portion of the obligation to repay was forgiven, the general rule that income results from forgiveness of indebtedness, § 61(a)(12), should apply.

[Petitioner argued that his debt was unenforceable and, therefore, that there was no debt to be discharged.] Legal enforceability of an obligation to repay is not generally determinative of whether the receipt of money or property is taxable. *James v. U.S.* [For accrual-method tax accounting purposes], legal liability is not required. *Burlington Northern R.R. v. Comm'r*, 82 T.C. 143 (1984); *Flamingo Resort, Inc. v. U.S.*, 664 F.2d 1387 (9th Cir. 1982).

Petitioner also relies on the principle that settlement of disputed debts does not give rise to income. Prior to the settlement, the amount of petitioner's gambling debt to Resorts was a liquidated amount. There is no dispute about the amount petitioner received. The parties dispute only its enforceability. A genuine dispute does not exist [for purposes of the disputed-debt doctrine] merely because petitioner required Resorts to sue him before making payment of any amount on the debt.

Petitioner incurred gambling losses in 1980, but his gain from the discharge of his gambling debts occurred in 1981. That gain is separate and apart from the losses he incurred from his actual wagering transactions. If we were to effectively allow petitioner to deduct [his 1980 gambling losses] from the [1981] discharged debt, we would ignore annual accounting and undermine § 165(d) by in effect allowing gambling losses in excess of gambling winnings.

Reviewed by the Court.

NIMS, PARKER, KORNER, SHIELDS, HAMBLEN, CLAPP, GERBER, WRIGHT, PARR, and COLVIN, JJ., agree with the majority opinion.

TANNENWALD, J., dissenting:

The foundation of the majority's reasoning is that Mr. Zarin realized income in an amount equal to the amount of the credit extended to him because he was afforded the "opportunity to gamble." I think it highly significant that in all the decided cases involving the cancellation of indebtedness, the taxpayer had, in a prior year when the indebtedness was created, received a nontaxable benefit clearly measurable in monetary terms which would remain untaxed if the subsequent cancellation of the indebtedness were held to be tax free. Such is simply not the case herein. The concept that petitioner received his money's worth from the enjoyment of using the chips (thus equating the pleasure of gambling with increase in wealth) produces the incongruous result that the more a gambler loses, the greater his pleasure and the larger the increase in his wealth.

Under the circumstances, I think the issue of enforceability becomes critical. I think it significant that because the debts involved herein were unenforceable *from the moment they were created*, there was no . . . increase in petitioner's wealth that could constitute income. This is particularly true in light of the fact that the chips were given to Mr. Zarin with the expectation that he would continue to gamble and, therefore, did not constitute an increase in his wealth when he received them in the same sense that the proceeds of a non-gambling loan would. Cf. *Rail Joint Co. v. Comm'r*, 61 F.2d 751 (2d Cir. 1932), where it was held that there was no income from the discharge on indebtedness when the amount [of] the discharge was in excess of the value of what had been received by the debtor at the time the indebtedness was created.

I find further support for my conclusion from the application of the principle that if there is a genuine dispute as to liability on the underlying obligation, settlement of that obligation will not give rise to income from discharge of indebtedness. *N. Sobel, Inc. v. Comm'r*, 40 B.T.A. 1263 (1939). Respondent simply has not met his burden of showing that the dispute between Resorts and Mr. Zarin was not a genuine dispute as to Mr. Zarin's liability for the underlying obligations.

WELLS, J., agrees with this dissent.

JACOBS, J., dissenting:

In my opinion, petitioner's obligation to Resorts was void *ab initio*, and therefore, I would first hold that petitioner realized income (herein referred to as chip income) in 1980 (a year at issue) to the extent of the value of the chips received. In my opinion, for purposes of § 165(d), the chip income constitutes gain from a wagering transaction, because no such income would have been realized but for the wagering transactions in which petitioner's losses occurred.

[The dissenting opinion of JUDGE RUWE, arguing that § 108(e)(5) negated income inclusion because gambling chips were "property," is omitted, as are portions of the other opinions that deal with this issue. Judges Chabot, Swift, Williams, and Whalen, agreed with that dissent. Section 108(e)(5) is discussed in the next chapter.]

ZARIN v. COMMISSIONER
United States Court of Appeals, Third Circuit
916 F.2d 110 (1990)

Before STAPLETON, COWEN and WEIS, CIRCUIT JUDGES.

COWEN, CIRCUIT JUDGE:

The Tax Court held that gambling chips were "a medium of exchange within the Resorts casino" and a "substitute for cash." Alternatively, the Tax Court viewed the chips as nothing more than "the opportunity to gamble and incidental services." We agree with the gist of these characterizations, and hold that gambling chips are merely an accounting mechanism to evidence debt. Nor did the chips have any independent economic value beyond the casino.

Instead of analyzing the transaction at issue as cancelled debt, we believe the proper approach is to view it as disputed debt or contested liability. Under the contested liability doctrine, if a taxpayer, in good faith, disputed the amount of a debt, a subsequent settlement of the dispute would be treated as the amount of debt cognizable for tax purposes. Thus, if a taxpayer took out a loan for $10,000, refused in good faith to pay the full $10,000 back, and then reached an agreement with the lender that he would pay back only $7000 in full satisfaction of the debt, the transaction would be treated as if the initial loan was $7000. When the taxpayer tenders the $7000 payment, he will have been deemed to have paid the full amount of the initially disputed debt.

[Here,] Zarin incurred a $3,435,000 debt while gambling at Resorts, but in court, disputed liability on the basis of unenforceability. A settlement of $500,000 was eventually agreed upon. It follows that the settlement served only to fix the amount of debt. When Zarin paid the $500,000, any tax consequence dissolved.[10]

The Commissioner argues that the contested liability doctrine only applies when there is an unliquidated debt: that is, a debt for which the amount cannot be determined. When a debt is unenforceable, it follows that the amount of the debt, and not just the liability thereon, is in dispute. Although a debt may be unenforceable, there still could be some value attached to its worth. This is especially so with regards to gambling debts; they are often collected, at least in part. Resorts is not a charity; it would not have extended illegal credit to Zarin and others if it did not have some hope of collecting debts. Although casinos attach a dollar value to each chip, that value is not beyond dispute, particularly given the illegality of gambling debts in the first place. This proposition is supported by the facts of the present case. Such a debt cannot be called liquidated, since its exact amount was not fixed until settlement.

STAPLETON, CIRCUIT JUDGE, dissenting.

Resorts sells for cash the exhilaration and the potential for profit inherent in games of chance. Zarin, like thousands of others, wished to purchase what Resorts was offering in the marketplace. He chose to make this purchase on credit and executed notes evidencing his obligation to repay the funds that were advanced to him by Resorts. As in most purchase money transactions, Resorts skipped the step of giving Zarin cash that he would only return to it in order to pay for the opportunity to gamble. Resorts provided him instead with chips that entitled him to participate in Resorts' games of chance on the same basis as others who had paid cash for that privilege.[11] Whether viewed as a one or two-step transaction, however, Zarin received either $3.4 million in cash or an entitlement for which others would have had to pay $3.4 million. Despite the fact that Zarin received in 1980 cash or an entitlement worth $3.4 million, he correctly reported in that year no income from his dealings with Resorts. He did so solely because he recognized

---

[10] [10] Had Zarin not paid the $500,000 settlement, it would be likely that he would have had income from cancellation of indebtedness. The debt at that point would have been fixed, and Zarin would have been legally obligated to pay it.

[11] [1] I view as irrelevant the facts that Resorts advanced credit to Zarin solely to enable him to patronize its casino and that the chips could not be used elsewhere or for other purposes. When one buys a sofa from the furniture store on credit, the fact that the proprietor would not have advanced the credit for a different purpose does not entitle one to a tax-free gain in the event the debt to the store is extinguished for some reason.

an offsetting obligation to repay Resorts $3.4 million in cash. In 1981, Resorts surrendered its claim to repayment of the remaining $2.9 million of the money Zarin had borrowed. As of that time, Zarin's assets were freed of his potential liability for that amount and he recognized gross income in that amount.[12] In 1980, neither party was maintaining that the debt was unenforceable.

I regard it as far preferable to have the tax consequences turn on the manner in which the debt is treated by the parties. For present purposes, it will suffice to say that where something that would otherwise be includible in gross income is received on credit in a purchase money transaction, there should be no recognition of income so long as the debtor continues to recognize an obligation to repay the debt. On the other hand, income, if not earlier recognized, should be recognized when the debtor no longer recognizes an obligation to repay and the creditor has released the debt or acknowledged its unenforceability. In this view, it makes no difference whether the extinguishment of the creditor's claim comes as a part of a compromise. Resorts settled for 14 cents on the dollar presumably because it viewed such a settlement as reflective of the odds that the debt would be held to be enforceable.[13]

I would affirm the judgment of the Tax Court.

In *Rood v. Comm'r*, T.C. Memo. 1996-248, *aff'd*, 97-2 USTC ¶50,619 (11th Cir. 1997) (unpublished per curiam opinion), the Tax Court stuck by its guns and held that a casino's discharge of gambling debts resulted in debt-discharge income to the patron. The taxpayer tried to fit within the Third Circuit *Zarin* opinion by arguing that he disputed the debt with the casino, but the Tax Court in its fact findings found that there was no bona fide dispute regarding either the amount or the enforceability of the debt. The 11th Circuit affirmed based on the fact findings.

The Third Circuit majority's view of the disputed-debt doctrine in *Zarin* to encompass any settlement of a debt "in good faith" (whatever that means) is much broader than that advanced in any prior case. The leading case involving the disputed-debt doctrine is *N. Sobel, Inc. v. Comm'r*, 40 B.T.A. 1263 (1939), cited in Judge Tannenwald's Tax Court dissent. *Sobel* involved the purchase of shares of stock on credit. The taxpayer disputed both the *enforceability and amount* of the debt on the basis of the seller's misrepresentation of the stock's value, and settled the matter by paying half the face amount. The Board held that there was no debt-discharge income.

---

[12] [2] This is not a case in which parties agree subsequent to a purchase money transaction [that what was] purchased has a value less than thought at the time of the transaction. In such cases, the purchase price adjustment rule is applied. Nor is this a case in which the taxpayer is entitled to rescind an entire purchase money transaction, thereby to restore itself to the position it occupied before receiving anything of commercial value.

[13] [5] A different situation exists where there is a bona fide dispute over the amount of a debt and the dispute is compromised. Rather than require tax litigation to determine the amount of income received, the Commissioner treats the compromise figure as representing the amount of the obligation. I find this sensible and consistent with the pragmatic approach I would take.

The Third Circuit's expansive view of the disputed-debt doctrine in *Zarin* was criticized at length in *Preslar v. Comm'r*, 167 F.3d 1323 (10th Cir. 1999), which agreed with the Tax Court that only the enforceability, not the amount, of the discharged debt was contested in *Zarin* and that the disputed-debt doctrine does not apply in that circumstance. According to *Preslar*, the disputed-debt doctrine is based on the proposition that, if there is a good faith dispute over the *amount* of the debt, then the sum ultimately fixed by settlement or final judgment is "the debt," and if the taxpayer pays that sum in full, there is no debt-discharge income.

NOTES

1.   As a postscript, Mr. Zarin sued his attorneys on the theory that their failure to assert that he was covered by the § 108(a)(1)(B) insolvency exception constituted malpractice. His complaint was dismissed on multiple grounds. See *Zarin v. Reid & Priest*, 585 N.Y.S.2d 379 (App. Div. 1992).

2.   In *Libutti v. Comm'r*, T.C. Memo. 1996-108, Taxpayer gambled at the Atlantic City Trump Casino and lost approximately $4.1M in 1987, $3.1M in 1988, and $1.2M in 1989. (Either he was improving as a gambler or running out of money.) Because Taxpayer was such a profitable patron, the casino rewarded him with so-called "comps" consisting of cars, jewelry, all-expense-paid vacations, alcohol, and entertainment tickets with total values of $443K for 1987, $975K for 1988, and $1.13M for 1989. Taxpayer argued that the comps were gains from wagering transactions and, therefore, that § 165(d) allowed each year's total casino gambling loss to be deducted against the value of that year's comps so that the comps were wiped out by the deductions. The Tax Court agreed because: "The relationship between petitioner's comps and his wagering is close, direct, evident, and strong." Do you think this result is correct? Compare *Boyd v. U.S.*, 762 F.2d 1369 (9th Cir. 1985).

PROBLEMS

1.   (a) In *Zarin*, did the taxpayer receive money, property, or consumption on credit? In which of these categories does "the opportunity to gamble" (cited in Judge Tannenwald's dissent) fall into? Is the opportunity to gamble the same as the pleasure of gambing? How do these possible characterizations make a difference in the result? (*Zarin* highlights the importance in tax litigation of being able to present the facts in a way that fits into one's best legal arguments.)

(b) Is the Tannenwald dissent based on the theory that there is no COD income unless the transaction as a whole entails an increase in material wealth? Under that theory, the avoidance of paying a debt or liability is not per se COD income. But did Judge Tannenwald unwittingly invoke the *Kerbaugh-Empire* fallacy? In any event, the inconsistent-events theory of COD income raises the problem of how do treat the transactions described in (c) and (d), which follow.

(c) Does a seller of services usually extend credit as such? (Why not?) In any event, if a seller of goods or services does expressly extend credit, is the transaction essentially equivalent to a loan of cash, which if not repaid, results in COD income? Was this the case in *Zarin*?

(d) Is the scenario where consumption is simply not paid for distinguishable from a sale on credit? How would you resolve the case where Dave, a writer, rents a place in Greenwich Village under a one-year lease for $1K a month (payable monthly in advance), but after going six months without actually paying the rent, settles the landlord's $6K claim for $2K? What if Dave can't pay anything, and he and the landlord settle on zero rent but with Dave having to vacate the premises immediately? If the scenario just described is not COD income, is it "catch-all" income (discussed in Chapter 13)?

2. (a) The disputed-debt doctrine as articulated in *Sobel* is consistent with the inconsistent-events theory of COD income, because the settlement fixes both the value of what was received and its cost to the taxpayer. Statements to the effect that the settlement fixes the amount of the "debt" are factually inaccurate, because the usual applications of the disputed-debt doctrine, involving breach of warranty and fraud in credit sales, are grounds for complete rescission.

(b) Since rescission of a credit sale transaction would not give rise to COD income (why not?), can the supposed distinction between disputes over the amount of the debt and disputes over its existence or validity be relevant?

(c) If *Zarin* was indeed a purchase-money debt case, which view of value is relevant between the value of the chips to Zarin or the value to Resorts of the claim against Zarin?

(d) Should the disputed-debt doctrine be extended to non-purchase-money debt cases? Suppose Brent borrows money from a loan shark, refuses repayment, and could (at least in court) resist repayment on the basis of a legal defense? Should Dave in problem 1(d), who didn't pay the rent, be able to invoke the disputed-debt doctrine if, say, his Village pad was infested with roaches and the lead paint on the walls was disintegrating?

3. (a) Normally, taxation of wealth increments and consumption under an income tax are measured with reference to the taxpayer's cost, which fixes basis, the amount deductible as an expense, or the amount not deducted (and thereby taxed) as personal consumption. (Exceptions exist to account for disguised wealth transfers.) Treating the cancellation or reduction of debt with respect to credit sales of goods or services as gross income cuts against the grain of this general principle. Can this aberration be justified?

(b) Cancellation of bank-issued credit card debt, which is owed to a bank (not individual vendors), raises a doctrinal problem, because it is hard (perhaps impossible) to trace such debts to specific transactions, some of which may have been for cash advances, deductible expenses, or assets with a basis. The IRS has responded in a way that renders tracing unnecessary by treating bank-issued credit card transactions as involving a cash loan by the bank to the credit card holder, who then is deemed to pay cash to merchants accepting the card as payment for goods and services. See *Rev. Rul. 78-38*, 1978-1 C.B. 68. Is it feasible to treat debt on bank issued credit cards as anything other than expenditures of borrowed money? How about debt on merchant-issued credit cards?

C. SECTION 108

Section 108, originally enacted in 1939 but modified many times since, accommodates both tax policy (the delayed-realization approach) and the bankruptcy policy of debtor rehabilitation by providing rules that generally *defer* recognition (inclusion) of COD income in certain defined situations, rather than completely *forgiving* it.[14]

Although § 108 purports to apply to all "income from discharge of indebtedness," it actually only applies to § 61(a)(12) COD income. Thus, gain on the in-kind satisfaction of an obligation would be "sale" gain, and income in an *Old Colony* situation would be compensation income, dividend income, or whatever, and thus § 108 would not apply in these scenarios.

First consider § 108(a)(1)(B), (a)(3), and (d)(3). These provisions continue, but supersede, the common law insolvency doctrine illustrated in Section B.1 by the hypothetical involving Dugald, whose total liabilities are $20K and who has only $8K of assets. If Dugald negotiates a complete discharge of the $20K debt, $12K (the amount of his insolvency before the debt discharge) of his $20K debt-discharge income would be excluded under the authority of § 108(a)(1)(B), but $8K would be included in his gross income. Unlike the common law rule result, the $12K of debt-discharge income that Dugald is entitled to exclude under § 108(a)(1)(B) is not completely forgiven. Rather, it is only *deferred* through the mechanism found in § 108(b). Section 108(b) achieves deferral by mandating that a sum equal to the amount excluded under § 108(a)(1) must reduce certain favorable tax attributes that Dugald may possess. These attributes, listed in § 108(b)(2), include certain deduction carryovers, certain tax credit carryovers, and the basis of property owned by Dugald, all of which would ordinarily reduce Dugald's tax liability in future years. The effect, then, of § 108(b) is to *increase* Dugald's *future* tax liability. For example, in our case where Dugald excluded $12K of his $20K debt discharge, and assuming that Dugald has no deduction and credit carryovers, he will suffer a $12K reduction in the basis of property he owns, thereby depriving him of $12K of future depreciation deductions or basis offsets, which in turn will have the effect of increasing his future taxable income by $12K. Of course, tax deferral will turn into complete tax forgiveness if Dugald has none of the tax attributes listed in § 108(b). Since the tax on income deferred under § 108(b) does not bear any interest, however, Dugald (whose understanding of the time value of money is keen) is grateful for § 108(b), even where it turns out to be merely a deferral of income and not complete tax forgiveness.

Perhaps the most important § 108 exception is found in § 108(a)(1)(A), which excludes *all* debt-discharge income (even if the taxpayer is thereby made solvent) realized in connection with federal bankruptcy proceedings pursuant to Title 11 of

---

[14] The "delayed realization" approach to debt-discharge income that results from § 108(b) means that Congress has recognized that taxation of debt-discharge income is logically necessary to prevent the taxpayer from receiving permanently tax-free dollars even if the debtor is insolvent. But discharged debtors are often financially strapped and have a substantially diminished current ability to pay taxes as well as other debts. Section 108's deferral of income recognition is driven by this reality and is thus based on solicitude for the financially unfortunate rather than any internal tax logic. See S. Rep. No. 1035, 96th Cong. 2nd Sess. 9-11 (1980).

the U.S. Code.[15] As with the insolvency exception, however, any tax attributes listed in § 108(b) that Dugald possesses would be reduced by the amount excluded under § 108(a)(1)(A), so that the bankruptcy exception usually accomplishes tax deferral rather than tax forgiveness (unless Dugald possesses none of the tax attributes listed in § 108(b)).

Other § 108 exclusions not detailed here relate to "qualified farm indebtedness," "qualified real property business indebtedness," and "qualified principal residence indebtedness." See § 108(a)(1)(C), (D) & (E), (c), (f), and (g). Property-acquisition debt is dealt with in the next chapter.

Section 108(f) excludes COD income arising from a cancellation, under the terms of the loan agreement, of certain student loans contemplating certain kinds of post-education (low-wage) employment. *Rev. Rul. 2008-34*, 2008-2 C.B. 76, deals with a student's loan under the Loan Repayment Assistance Program. Pursuant to the program, the student agreed to work "in a law-related public service position for, or under the direction of, a tax-exempt charitable organization or a government unit, including a position in (1) a public interest or community service organization, (2) a legal aid office or clinic, (3) a prosecutor's office, (4) a public defender's office, or (5) a state, local, or federal government office," and the law school forgave the loan after the graduate worked for a specified period of time in a qualifying position. The ruling concluded that the terms of the program satisfy the requirements of § 108(f).

PROBLEMS

1.   Suppose that Hallie owed $20K to the local grocer by reason of buying subsistence food items on credit and she had no assets. She had been taught that she was morally obligated to pay her debts. Consequently, she worked the graveyard shift at a deep coal mine, where the prevailing temperature was 115° F, until she had earned $20K and paid her liabilities in full. She was insolvent throughout this period of time. Are any of her coal mining earnings excludible? Should Hallie have sought tax advice?

2.   (a) X Corp borrows $100K from Donna at 6% interest per year over 10 years with repayment of the principal in Year 10. The debt is evidenced by a bond in registered form having a face amount of $100K, and the interest is payable annually. The interest is paid according to schedule for a few years. Interest rates go up and the bond is worth only $78K. (Why does this occur?) At this point X Corp, which is solvent, "calls" (redeems) the bond for that amount pursuant to a call privilege contained in the terms of the bond. What result for X Corp?

(b) Same as (a), except that after a few years X Corp enters Title 11 bankruptcy, and the entire $100K principal amount of the debt obligation is extinguished. X Corp continues in business.

3.   What are the tax results if Jacob owns assets worth $100K and has liabilities

---

[15] Title 11 of the U.S. Code contains the entire law pertaining to federal bankruptcies, including Chapter 11 (pertaining to certain business reorganizations), Chapter 7 (pertaining to liquidations), and Chapter 13 (pertaining to consumer reorganizations).

of $150K when a creditor, acting to promote the creditor's own business interests and not to provide Jacob with a gift, cancels a $60K debt that Jacob owed him? What if the cancellation occurs in bankruptcy court? Outside bankruptcy? See § 108(a)(3), (d)(3).

Chapter 20

DEBT AND PROPERTY

This chapter considers how the tax principles relating to borrowing and the discharge of debts (set forth in the preceding two chapters) operate in the context of acquisitions, sales, and dispositions of property.

Some transactional jargon requires elucidation. A "nonrecourse debt" is a debt obligation secured by the property but for which the debtor is not personally liable. The nonrecourse lender's only remedy on default of a nonrecourse debt is foreclosure on the property securing the debt. A "recourse" debt, in contrast, is one for which the debtor is personally liable; whether or not the debt is secured by property, the lender can proceed against the debtor and garnish his wages, impose liens on his other property, etc., if the recourse debt is not repaid. The term "equity" refers to the excess (if any) of the fair market value (FMV) of the property (at any given time) over the outstanding amount of principal debt secured by the property (similar to the concept of "net worth" but as applied to a single asset).

A. THE EFFECT OF DEBT ON BASIS

If Rachel buys Whiteacre from Farmer White for $10K of her own cash, Rachel has a cost "basis" in Whiteacre of $10K under § 1012. If Whiteacre is not depreciable and Rachel sells it for $10K in cash, she will realize no gain or loss under § 1001, because her $10K amount realized (AR) equals her $10K adjusted basis.

But what if in Year 1 Rachel borrowed $9K cash from National Bank, deposited it in a checking account, and in Year 2 used this $9K, along with $1K of her current wages, to purchase Whiteacre? Adjusted basis (AB) is generally a running record of previously taxed dollars, and borrowed money is "before tax" by reason of being excluded from gross income. So would Rachel's initial basis in Whiteacre be limited to $1K or would it be $10K? That is, if Rachel immediately sold Whiteacre for $10K, would her gain be $9K or zero?

Rachel's initial basis should be (and is) $10K. Cash (being wholly fungible) *must* have a basis equal to its face amount. It is inconceivable that a $20 bill could have a basis of, say, $3. For this reason alone, Rachel's initial basis in Whiteacre should be (and is) $10K, because the purchase price is all in cash. Such a result is not a tax loophole for Rachel, because the debt transaction is accounted for separately. In effect, Rachel is taxed on the $9K of borrowed money when she repays it with after-tax dollars. If Rachel's initial basis were limited to $1K, she would end up paying tax twice on the same $9K, once by reason of having gain of $9K on a cash sale of Whiteacre for $10K, and again by repaying the loan with after-tax dollars. Moreover, a basis of $10K results in no gain or loss on the Whiteacre transaction, which is appropriate, given that what Rachel takes out of Whiteacre ($10K) is exactly the same as what she put in ($10K). Whiteacre hasn't changed in value. Likewise (but in reverse), what Rachel took out in the loan transaction ($9K) is identical to what she puts back in by repaying the $9K principal.

Now suppose that Rachel's borrowing is an integral part of the property purchase. The conventional way in which this happens is that Rachel, desiring to purchase Whiteacre from Farmer White for $10K but having only $1K of cash, goes to National Bank, which lends her $9K secured by a mortgage on Whiteacre. At a real estate closing, Rachel obtains the deed to Whiteacre from Farmer White, and Farmer White receives $10K in cash, $1K of which comes from Rachel's personal funds and the other $9K of which comes from National Bank. Rachel never personally touches the borrowed cash. We refer to this scenario as "third-party financed sale" involving a "third-party mortgage." Here Rachel again should have (and does) have an initial basis in Whiteacre of $10K. The debt transaction can (and is) accounted for separately from the property transaction.

A third transactional possibility is that Rachel buys the property from Farmer White for $1K cash and takes over a $9K mortgage-secured debt that Farmer White had incurred in acquiring Whiteacre from the prior owner. If Farmer White was personally liable on the debt (i.e., the debt was recourse), Rachel could "assume" it, which means that Rachel becomes personally liable for repaying it. Or Rachel might only take the property "subject to" the debt, in which case the property remains as security for the debt but she is not personally liable for repaying it. (This might occur either if the debt was already nonrecourse to Farmer White or if the debt was recourse but Rachel succeeded in avoiding personal liability on the debt.) Whether or not Rachel assumes or takes subject to the debt, the mortgage lender can foreclose on the property for nonpayment. Thus, if Rachel fails to pay the debt as and when it is due, Rachel can lose the property and her "equity" in it. Rachel's basis in this scenario should be (and is) $10K for the reasons already stated.

Finally, suppose that Rachel did not even go to a bank. Instead, she agrees with Farmer White to give him $1K in cash and her own note for $9K (the note representing her promise to pay $9K in the future, plus interest). We call this a "two-party purchase-money debt" situation. In commercial jargon, this type of transaction is also called a "seller-financed sale" or an "installment sale." Here it might be tempting to suppose that Rachel's AB begins at only $1K (the cash that she parted with), and will increase as and when she makes principal payments, since those nondeductible principal payments would then represent "after-tax" dollars. But the temptation should be (and is) resisted, because, if Rachel were to sell the property before making any principal payments, she would be taxed twice on the borrowed $9K under the reasonable assumption that she pays this off. (Moreover, if Rachel sold the property for an amount in excess of $1K but not more than $10K, she would have a tax gain without economic gain.) Thus, Rachel's initial basis is $10K in this fourth scenario as well.

In summary, these property-acquisition scenarios involving debt financing show that the buyer's initial basis includes acquisition (purchase-money) debt. Although these results are dictated by logic, the tax literature typically attributes this doctrine to the Supreme Court's decision in *Crane v. Comm'r*, 331 U.S. 1 (1947), which actually involved a fifth scenario.[1] Thus, the doctrine that requires inclusion of acquisition debt in basis is commonly, if somewhat misleadingly, called the "*Crane* doctrine." In any event, Rachel's initial basis in Whiteacre is $10K, regardless of whether the debt is recourse or nonrecourse, regardless of the source of the credit, and regardless of whether the debt she incurs in connection with the purchase is new or pre-exists the purchase.

In addition to the reasons already given, the inclusion of acquisition debt in basis is supported by considerations relating to depreciation. As the Supreme Court stated in *Crane* (331 U.S. at 9–11):

> If the mortgagor's [i.e., the taxpayer's] equity were the basis, it would also be the original basis from which depreciation allowances are deducted. If it is, and if the amount of the annual allowances were to be computed on that value, as would then seem to be required, they will represent only a fraction of the cost of the corresponding physical exhaustion, and any recoupment by the mortgagor of the remainder of that cost can be effected only by the reduction of his taxable gain in the year of sale. If, however, the amount of the annual allowances were to be computed on the value of the property, and then deducted from an equity basis, we would in some instances have to accept deductions from a minus basis or deny deductions altogether. The Commissioner also argues that taking the mortgagor's equity as the basis would require the basis to be changed with each payment on the mortgage, and that the attendant problem of repeatedly recomputing basis and annual allowances would be a tremendous accounting burden on both the Commissioner and the taxpayer. Moreover, the mortgagor would acquire control over the timing of his depreciation allowances.

A corollary of the so-called *Crane* basis rule is that if the purchase-money (or acquisition) debt is included in the basis of property, the repayment of the debt principal does not increase the taxpayer's basis. If it did, the taxpayer would be double counting the debt principal in basis.

Rachel's acquisition-debt scenario must be distinguished from that of Jon, who borrows against property that he *already owns* in circumstances that show that the debt is unrelated to the debtor's earlier acquisition of the property. The basis of property used to secure *post-acquisition debt* (*sometimes called "after-acquired debt"*), i.e., debt unrelated to the acquisition of the property securing the new debt, does *not* include the new debt. For example, assume that Jon purchases Blackacre (vacant land) for $100K in cash, establishing a cost basis of $100K. A few years later, after Blackacre appreciates in value to $500K, Jon borrows $200K, using the property as security. Whether the debt is recourse or nonrecourse, it is *not* included

---

[1] *Crane* involved previously-mortgaged property acquired by bequest. (This scenario is not commonplace, because mortgage balances are often paid off by the decedent's estate, but that was not the case in *Crane*.) The governing statutory basis rule in such cases is § 1014, stating that the basis of property acquired from a decedent equals its FMV at the decedent's death. The taxpayer argued that the "property" referred to by § 1014 was only the equity, but the Court held that it was the unencumbered FMV of the property, including the mortgage, even though the mortgage was nonrecourse.

in the basis of Blackacre because it was not used to acquire (or improve) Blackacre.

The bottom line: *Debt used to acquire property — whether recourse or nonrecourse and regardless of its origin — is included in the basis of the acquired property.*[2] *Post-acquisition debt that happens to be secured by a piece of property does not increase the basis of that property, except to the extent that the debt proceeds are used to permanently improve the property, which would cause a basis increase under § 1016(a)(1).*

PROBLEM

Return to the example of Rachel, who purchased Whiteacre for $1K in cash and $9K in debt. If Whiteacre were depreciable property, would the depreciation deductions to which Rachel would be entitled if she held the property for its full life add up to $1K or $10K? See § 167(a) & (c).

B.   REDUCTION IN ACQUISITION DEBT

If acquisition or purchase-money debt is included in basis, could it be the case that *relief* from such indebtedness (other than by payment), in whole or in part, operates as a *reduction* in basis, *where the taxpayer continues to own the property*?[3] Alternatively, might not such debt relief be § 61(a)(12) cancellation-of-debt (COD) income, possibly deferrable under § 108 if the taxpayer is insolvent or the debt reduction occurs in a bankruptcy proceeding?[4] The answer depends principally on whether the debt is owed to the seller ("two-party purchase-money debt") or to a third party (such as a bank).

1.   Third-Party Debt

What happens if *third-party* purchase debt is reduced, *but the taxpayer-debtor continues to own the property*? Perhaps *nonrecourse* debt may be seen as so closely tied to the ownership of the property securing it that relief from it ought to be accounted for entirely under the property rules (by way of reduction in basis) rather than the debt rules (COD income). In contrast, recourse debt, even when secured by property, is not as closely identified with the property, since the owner is independently liable on the debt. The ruling below considered precisely this issue.

---

[2] In some scenarios, such as where mortgaged property is acquired in a transaction in which the transferor does not recognize gain or loss, some special basis rule might apply that produces a basis to the transferee that is less than the mortgage. An example of such a basis rule is § 1041, involving transfers between husband and wife, explained at Chapter 5.B.7.

[3] As noted above, the repayment of loan principal by the taxpayer herself has no effect on basis because the debt transaction is accounted for separately from the property transaction.

[4] Since there is no disposition of the property, no § 1001 gain or loss can exist, as in the case where property is transferred in satisfaction of an existing liability (as noted in Chapter 19.A.1).

REVENUE RULING 91-31
1991-1 C.B. 19

If the principal amount of an undersecured nonrecourse debt is reduced by the holder of the debt who was not the seller of the property securing the debt, does this debt reduction result in the realization of discharge of indebtedness income or in the reduction of the basis in the property securing the debt?

In 1988, individual A borrowed $1M from C and signed a note payable to C for $1M that bore interest at a fixed market rate payable annually. A had no personal liability with respect to the note, which was secured by an office building valued at $1M that A acquired from B with the proceeds of the nonrecourse financing. In 1989, when the value of the office building was $800K and the outstanding principal on the note was $1M, C agreed to modify the terms of the note by reducing the note's principal amount to $800K.

The facts here do not [come within any of] the specific exclusions provided by § 108(a).

In *Rev. Rul. 82-202,*, 1982-2 C.B. 35, a taxpayer prepaid the mortgage held by a third party lender on the taxpayer's residence for less than the principal balance of the mortgage. At the time of the prepayment, the fair market value of the residence was greater than the principal balance of the mortgage. The revenue ruling holds that the taxpayer realizes discharge of indebtedness income, whether the mortgage is recourse or nonrecourse and whether it is partially or fully prepaid. *Rev. Rul. 82-202* relies on *U.S. v. Kirby Lumber Co.*, 284 U.S. 1 (1931), in which the United States Supreme Court held that a taxpayer realized ordinary income upon the purchase of its own bonds in an arm's length transaction at less than their face amount.

In *Comm'r v. Tufts*, 461 U.S. 300 (1983), the Supreme Court held that because a nonrecourse note is treated as a true debt upon inception (so that the loan proceeds are not taken into income at that time), a taxpayer is bound to treat the nonrecourse note as a true debt when the taxpayer is discharged from the liability upon disposition of the collateral, notwithstanding the lesser fair market value of the collateral.

In *Gershkowitz v. Comm'r*, 88 T.C. 984 (1987), the Tax Court, in a reviewed opinion, concluded, in part, that the settlement of a nonrecourse debt of $250,000 for a $40,000 cash payment (rather than surrender of the collateral) resulted in $210,000 of discharge of indebtedness income.

The Service will follow the holding in *Gershkowitz* where a taxpayer is discharged from all or a portion of a nonrecourse liability when there is no disposition of the collateral. Thus, in the present case, A realizes $200,000 of discharge of indebtedness income in 1989 as a result of the modification of A's note payable to C.

In an earlier Board of Tax Appeals decision, *Fulton Gold Corp. v. Comm'r*, 31 B.T.A. 519 (1934), a taxpayer purchased property [taking subject to] an outstanding mortgage [without being personally liable on it] and subsequently satisfied the mortgage for less than its face amount. The Board of Tax Appeals, for purposes of determining the taxpayer's gain or loss upon the sale of the property in a later year, held that the taxpayer's basis in the property should have been reduced by the amount of the mortgage debt forgiven in the earlier year.

The *Tufts* and *Gershkowitz* decisions implicitly reject any interpretation of *Fulton Gold* that a reduction in the amount of a nonrecourse liability by the holder of the debt who was not the seller of the property securing the liability results in reduction of the basis in that property, rather than discharge of indebtedness income for the year of the reduction. Therefore, that interpretation is rejected and will not be followed.

The 1993 Tax Act modified the result of *Rev. Rul. 91-31* by adding § 108(a)(1)(D). A discharge of "qualified [depreciable] real property business indebtedness," as defined in § 108(c)(3) is, at the taxpayer's election, excluded from gross income, but only to the extent (if any) that the pre-reduction debt principal amount exceeds the then FMV of the depreciable real property (this excess being the "negative equity" amount). The amount excluded reduces the basis of the depreciable real property. Other tax attributes of the taxpayer are unaffected.

The Mortgage Forgiveness Debt Relief Act of 2007 created a new category of excluded COD income by adding § 108(a)(1)(E) and (h), which applies to "qualified principal residence indebtedness." To illustrate these provisions, assume that there is a $1M recourse mortgage debt with respect to individual A's principal residence, that she is not insolvent or in bankruptcy, and that her basis in the residence is $1M but that the FMV has fallen to $750K. The lender reduces the debt principal to $750K and allows A to retain ownership and make payments on the diminished debt principal. Here, A clearly realizes $250K of ordinary COD income, but it is excluded from gross income if discharged before 2013. This exclusion is only good for "qualified principal residence indebtedness," defined as "acquisition indebtedness" within the meaning of § 163(h)(3)(B), except that the $1M and $500K ceilings are doubled. "Principal residence" has the same meaning as in § 121. Contrary to the usual rules in § 108(b), the amount excluded reduces only the basis (but not below zero) of the principal residence. Other tax attributes are unaffected. This effectively means that the taxpayer will realize either a smaller nondeductible loss or increased gain on a simultaneous or later sale of the residence, but (of course) all or a portion of any such gain may be excludible under § 121. Thus, the exclusion in § 108(a)(1)(E) may turn out to be permanent.

If only a portion of the discharged debt is "qualified principal residence indebtedness," an ordering rule provides that the § 108(a)(1)(E) exclusion is applied last. IRS Publication 4681 provides the following example. Ken incurred a recourse debt of $800K when he purchased his principal residence for $880K. When the FMV of the property went up, Ken refinanced the then principal debt of $740K by raising the principal amount to $850K. Ken used the $110K "new" (but non-acquisition) funds to pay off his credit cards. Later, Ken's residence declined in value to somewhere in the $700K–$750K range. The lender agreed to allow a sale of the property for $735K and to cancel the remaining $115K of the $850K. Ken can exclude only $5K of the cancelled debt ($115K canceled debt minus the $110K amount of the debt that was not qualified principal residence indebtedness), and must include the remaining $110K in income, unless another exclusion applies.

2.   Two-Party Debt

The two-party acquisition-debt situation is governed by § 108(e)(5), a crucially-important provision. In this scenario, the seller wears two hats: lender as well as property seller. For example, suppose Boris purchases a personal residence from Sylvia for $20K cash at closing plus Boris's promise to pay $80K in a single balloon payment 5 years from now, with payments of market-rate interest in the meantime. As noted in the discussion of acquisition debt, Boris has effectively borrowed $80K from Sylvia which is used to purchase the property, resulting in Boris having an initial basis of $100K. Subsequently, the FMV of the property is discovered have been worth only about $75K, perhaps because of a latent defect in the property. Boris threatens a lawsuit, which is settled by an agreement between Boris and Sylvia to reduce the principal debt amount from $80K to $55K.

Prior to the enactment of § 108(e)(5), the disputed-debt doctrine, discussed in Chapter 19.B.3, prevented transactions of this sort from giving rise to COD income, but only if there was a dispute over the value of the property received by the purchase-money debtor, in which case the reduction in the debt was viewed as a reduction in the price (and a reduction in Boris's basis). The reach of the disputed-debt doctrine was (and continues to be) uncertain (as is evidenced by the *Zarin* case). In addition, there was doubt as to whether the basis-reduction result of *Fulton Gold*, discussed in *Rev. Rul. 91-31*, extended to cases not involving a disputed debt.[5]

Section 108(e)(5) resolves these uncertainties by providing that *any* reduction in two-party acquisition (purchase-money) debt is treated as a "purchase price reduction" rather than as producing COD income. This rule applies regardless of the reason for the reduction of the principal debt or whether the debt is recourse or nonrecourse.

NOTES

1.   In *Zarin*, one of the arguments made by the taxpayer was that § 108(e)(5) applied to exclude the COD income because the debt was incurred in order to purchase "property" — gambling chips — from Resorts (the seller/lender). The Tax Court majority rejected the argument, stating (92 T.C. at 1097–1100):

> It seems to us that the value received by petitioner does not constitute the type of property to which § 108(e)(5) was intended to be applied. The "property" argument overemphasizes the significance of the chips. As a matter of substance, chips in isolation are not what petitioner purchased. Obviously the chips in this case were a medium of exchange within the Resorts casino, and in that sense they were a substitute for cash, just as Federal Reserve Notes, checks, or other convenient means of representing

---

[5] In *Fulton Gold*, there appeared to be a defect (unspecified) in the mortgage itself and not in the property, and so the disputed-debt doctrine (as it existed before the Third Circuit's decision in *Zarin*) would not have applied.

credit balances constitute or substitute for cash.

Judge Ruwe dissented on this point, but both the Third Circuit majority and dissent agreed with the Tax Court majority, noting that § 108(e)(5) presupposes that the taxpayer continues to own the property subject to the reduced purchase-money debt.

2.   (a) Section 108(e)(5) applies only to reductions of purchase-money debt owed to sellers of *property*. It does not apply where the debt is owed to a *services* provider. In the latter situation, the disputed-debt doctrine is still available.

(b) Should § 108(e)(5) be extended to the purchase of services on credit? Recall § 108(e)(2). What if the cost of the services had previously been deducted (by an accrual-method taxpayer)?

3.   A basis-reduction rule has the effect of blending debt doctrine and property-transaction doctrine. A basis reduction can reduce depreciation deductions (or future losses) or increase future (capital) gain. The realization of the COD income (or gain) is effectively deferred to the disposition of the property by way of sale, depreciation, or other disposition.

PROBLEM

Dmitri Debtor purchased business equipment for $10K from Sam Seller. He paid $1K in cash and gave Sam a $9K note on which he was not personally liable but which was secured by a mortgage on the equipment. Dmitri holds the property for some months, pays interest but no principal on the debt, and properly deducts $3K of depreciation.

(a) When the property declines in value to $6.8K, Dmitri persuades Sam to reduce the nonrecourse principal on the debt from $9K to $6K. What are the tax results?

(b) Does it affect the results if Dmitri claims that the property was only worth $7.5K when acquired due to a defective part, and now worth only $7K?

(c) Would the results of (a) and (b) be different if Dmitri had borrowed the $9K from a bank, and the bank agreed to the debt reduction? Would it make a difference if the property were real estate used in Dmitri's business, instead of business equipment?

C. THE DISPOSITION OF DEBT-ENCUMBERED PROPERTY

Annoyingly, the tax rules dealing with dispositions of mortgaged property vary according to whether (at the time of disposition) the party disposing of the property has positive or negative equity in the property. (Recall that "equity" is the excess of the value of the property over the unpaid principal amount of the mortgage debt.)

1. Positive-Equity Property

Suppose an owner of positive-equity mortgaged property sells it, and the buyer either assumes personal liability under a recourse mortgage or takes the property subject to a mortgage (recourse or nonrecourse). Take Rachel, who purchased Whiteacre with $1K of her own cash and a $9K loan. Her initial basis is $10K. Let's assume that Rachel has not repaid any of the $9K debt and that Rachel is now ready to sell, with the property now being worth $12K. How would a buyer pay for it? A buyer could come up with $12K cash (without incurring any debt) in order to pay Rachel, in which case Rachel would undoubtedly be required to pay off the $9K debt. But if the buyer has only $3K cash and has trouble getting a loan from either a bank (or from Rachel herself), an alternative is for the buyer to pay Rachel the $3K cash and to assume (or take subject to) the outstanding $9K debt. The tax issue presented by this alternative is to determine Rachel's "amount realized" in computing § 1001 gain or loss. (The buyer's initial basis, as explained in Section A, includes the purchase money mortgage debt and is $12K.)

A problem in resolving this issue is posed by the language in § 1001(b), which states that the "amount realized" consists of money (cash) and/or the fair market value of property received in connection with the sale or other disposition of the property. It says nothing about "debt relief." Nevertheless, the amount of relief from *recourse* debt (by the buyer's assumption of the debt) has always been considered to be included in the amount realized. In effect, the single sale for $3K in cash and a $9K assumption of Rachel's recourse mortgage is reconceptualized as two transactions: (1) a sale for $12K in cash followed by (2) Rachel then using $9K to "satisfy" her liability on the $9K debt. Because Rachel was personally liable on the loan, the "economic benefit" that she enjoys on account of the buyer assuming the recourse debt is relief from the full amount of the debt, even though the debt continues to exist with a new debtor (the buyer). Since the economic benefit occurs on account of the disposition of the property, the debt relief is treated as "amount realized" from the property sale rather than separate COD income. By reason of having a deemed "cash" amount realized of $12K, Rachel has a gain of $2K after subtracting her $10K basis. The gain is realized by Rachel entirely at the time of sale. None of the realization is deferred until the buyer actually pays off the assumed debt.

Until *Crane* was decided, there was considerable uncertainty regarding whether relief from *nonrecourse* debt in the situation described above should also be included in amount realized. After all, does Rachel really enjoy an "economic benefit" from being relieved of debt for which she is not personally liable? *Crane* resolved this issue by holding that *nonrecourse debt relief is included in the amount realized on the transfer under § 1001*. The Court explained its holding as follows (331 U.S. at 13–14):

> Petitioner concedes that if she had been personally liable on the mortgage and the purchaser had either paid or assumed it, the amount so paid or assumed would be considered a part of the "amount realized." The cases so deciding have already repudiated the notion that there must be an actual receipt by the seller himself of "money" or "property," in their narrowest senses. It was thought to be decisive that the taxpayer was the

"beneficiary" of the payment in "as real and substantial [a sense] as if the money had been paid it and then paid over by it to its creditors."

It is immaterial as to our problem whether the [seller] is also to receive money from the purchaser to discharge the mortgage prior to sale, or whether he is merely to transfer subject to the mortgage — it may make a difference to the purchaser and to the mortgagee, but not to the [seller]. We are rather concerned with the reality that an owner of property, mortgaged [on a nonrecourse basis] at a figure less than that at which the property will sell, must and will treat the conditions of the mortgage exactly as if they were his personal obligations. If he transfers subject to the mortgage, the benefit to him is as real and substantial as if the mortgage were discharged, or as if a personal debt in an equal amount had been assumed by another.

The *Crane* "debt-relief-as-amount-realized" rule can produce § 1001 gain or loss in the case of dispositions "for nothing." Thus, a foreclosure or an abandonment of property can result in § 1001 gain or loss equal to the difference between the outstanding principal amount of the mortgage debt amount and the property's adjusted basis, even though the taxpayer loses the property and receives nothing other than relief from mortgage debt. See *Parker v. Delaney*, 186 F.2d 455 (1st Cir. 1950). Even a gift to an individual or to a charity can produce gain for the donor to the extent the donated property is encumbered by debt in excess of the property's basis.[6] See, e.g., *Johnson v. Comm'r*, 495 F.2d 1079 (6th Cir.), *cert. denied*, 419 U.S. 1040 (1974); *Guest v. Comm'r*, 77 T.C. 9 (1981).[7]

Returning to Rachel, if her amount realized (in both the recourse and nonrecourse situations) were not to include the debt relief, her amount realized would be only the $3K cash she received, producing the absurd result of a $7K capital loss ($3K amount realized *less* $10K basis) on property that actually increased in value from $10K to $12K after she acquired it. But that result could be "compensated for" by requiring Rachel to simultaneously realize $9K of COD ordinary income along with a capital loss of $7K.[8] (Keep in mind that COD income is subject to the various rules found in § 108.) After all, Rachel is escaping $9K of debt. However, the tax law has always treated consideration (in money or money's worth) for the transfer of property as "amount realized" in computing gain or loss. This result achieves "symmetry" in the sense that the acquisition debt that is included in basis is (except to the extent paid off in the interim) also included in amount realized. However, achieving symmetry is not itself the rationale of this result. The rationale (as

---

[6] The excess (if any) of the property's value over the debt is the gift portion of the transaction. See Reg. § 1.1015-4 (describing some of the tax consequences of part gift/part sale transactions). A bequest of encumbered property does not give rise to gain or loss, at least where the FMV of the property exceeds the debt, because § 1014 creates a new basis equal to such value, as was confirmed by *Crane*.

[7] No loss, however, is allowed to the donor of a gift when the debt relief is less than basis. This is usually a result of the § 165(c) disallowance rule and sometimes the rule of § 267(a)(1) that losses on sales to related parties are disallowed.

[8] Whether COD income would exist might depend on whether Rachel continues to be secondarily liable on the mortgage or whether Rachel wholly shucks it off. This would require a determination of state law and perhaps the actions of the lender. The rule that treats the taking over of the debt as "amount realized" in all recourse-debt cases eliminates having to make these inquiries.

explained in *Crane*) is that debt relief is, to the seller, the equivalent of cash sales proceeds, just as acquisition debt is treated by the buyer as the borrowing of cash to purchase the property.

Symmetry is actually absent in the case of after-acquired debt secured by the property but not included in the property's basis. Relief from such debt upon sale or disposition is included in amount realized, because relief from such debt is (again) viewed as the equivalent of receiving cash proceeds from the sale or disposition.

Another lack-of-symmetry feature is that the basis (created by the debt) can generate ordinary depreciation deductions, whereas the inclusion of the same debt in amount realized can produce capital gain. This problem can be cured separately, as occurs under § 1245 for depreciable personal property, by recapturing gain attributable to depreciation as ordinary gain. But recapture does not (ordinarily) occur in the case of depreciable real property.

PROBLEMS

1. Doris Debtor purchased business equipment for $10K from Sergio Seller. She paid $1K in cash and gave Sergio a $9K note on which she was not personally liable but which was secured by a mortgage on the equipment. Doris properly deducted $3K of depreciation with respect to the equipment, paid interest, and did not make any principal payments. What is the tax result to Doris if she sells the equipment to a third party, Bob Buyer, for $1K in cash, subject to the $9K nonrecourse debt?

2. Same as problem 1, except that Doris made $1K in principal payments before selling the property to Bob for $1K in cash, subject to the remaining $8K of nonrecourse debt, at a time when the property was worth $9K.

3. (a) Rita bought Redacre for $30K in cash. When the property appreciated to $80K, she mortgaged it on nonrecourse terms for $40K, which she used to pay off personal credit card debt. The property has further appreciated to $100K when she sells it to Paul, who pays $60K cash and takes the property subject to the $40K mortgage. What are the tax consequences to Rita and Paul?

(b) Would the answer to (a) change if Rita spent $10K of the $40K loan proceeds on having a surveyor establish the building lot boundaries necessary to subdivide Redacre?

4. Marge owns Greenacre having a FMV of $100K and a basis of $20K, but subject to a nonrecourse debt of $30K, which she gives to her nephew Ron. What are the tax consequences to the parties?

2. Negative-Equity Property

The discussion of amount realized has so far assumed that the fair market value of the property is greater than the outstanding principal debt. But what if the value of the property falls below the outstanding debt principal amount, and the taxpayer transfers or abandons it? The answer here depends on whether the debt is recourse or nonrecourse.

a. Nonrecourse Debt

Suppose, for example, that Rachel, who purchased Whiteacre with $1K cash and $9K of *nonrecourse* debt, discovers (at a time when the unpaid principal remains $9K) that the property's FMV has fallen to $7K. Would Rachel make payments on the debt when she no longer has any equity to protect? Would Rachel pay an additional $9K to keep property that is now worth only $7K?

The answer is "no" *if* we assume that Rachel is acting rationally (with no moral qualms) and suffers no negative collateral consequences. It is often suggested that Rachel should undertake to pay the $9K because the property *might* regain its value. To do so, however, would be economically irrational. The fact that Whiteacre was *once* worth $10K is no indication that it will increase in value at a more rapid rate than any other investment that Rachel can make with $7K. Additionally, because the $9K debt is nonrecourse, Rachel can walk away from it without giving anything to the lender other than the property with a $7K FMV. By doing so, Rachel can shift $2K of the $3K economic loss from herself to the lender. The lender in effect is acquiring a property worth $7K with $9K of loan proceeds, and Rachel is losing her $1K down payment.

Assuming that Rachel makes no mortgage principal payments, and that the lender forecloses on the property and takes title, should the *entire* $9K debt relief be included in Rachel's § 1001 "amount realized" under *Crane*? If it were, Rachel would realize a $1K loss ($9K debt relief amount realized *less* $10 basis), which would equal her $1K economic loss of the down payment. Another theoretical possibility might be to say that Rachel has realized a capital loss on the property of $3K ($7K FMV *less* $10K basis) combined with COD income of $2K (since Rachel is giving up only $7K of FMV to get rid of a $9K liability). (This is the same result as a cash sale for Whiteacre's $7K FMV followed by paying the $7K cash to get rid of the $9K liability.) Any COD income would be "ordinary" but also eligible for deferral under § 108 on the right facts.

A third possibility was raised by footnote 37 in *Crane*, which stated:

> Obviously, if the value of the property is less than the amount of the mortgage, a mortgagor who is not personally liable cannot realize a benefit equal to the [full amount of the outstanding] mortgage. Consequently, a different problem might be encountered where [such] a mortgagor abandoned the property or transferred it subject to the mortgage. That is not this case.

Presumably, the idea informing the quoted passage is that if the value of the security for a nonrecourse debt falls below the principal amount, and the taxpayer surrenders the property to the lender, relief from the excess principal portion of the debt (over the FMV of the property) is not meaningful to the taxpayer (being only the problem of the lender) and should not be included in amount realized. If this is correct, then Rachel would only realize a $3K capital loss, and no COD income would exist.

In *Tufts*, which follows, the taxpayer in a negative-equity situation involving nonrecourse debt sold the property to a third party, who took subject to the debt. The Fifth Circuit, 651 F.2d 1058 (5th Cir. 1981), adopted the approach hinted at by the *Crane* footnote. The Supreme Court reversal is set forth below. In reading the opinion, be aware that Justice Blackmun used some eccentric and confusing vocabulary. To be specific, he suggested that the taxpayer/seller's obligation was "cancelled." Actually, the debt remained outstanding but it would never be paid by the taxpayer/seller because it was shifted (if it was shifted at all) to the buyer of the property. Justice Blackman also suggested that the buyer "assumed" debt, but in fact one cannot "assume" a nonrecourse debt. But these errors had no effect on the outcome.

COMMISSIONER v. TUFTS
United States Supreme Court
461 U.S. 300 (1983)

JUSTICE BLACKMUN delivered the opinion of the Court.

[Tufts transferred property with a fair market value of $1.4M to a buyer, Bayles, who agreed to reimburse sale expenses and to take the property subject to an outstanding nonrecourse mortgage. Tufts had financed the property's construction entirely with a $1.85M nonrecourse mortgage, and thus the property's initial basis was $1.85M under the *Crane* rule. Because of $400K of depreciation deductions, the adjusted basis of the property was $1.45M at the time of the sale. Tufts had not made any principal payments on the $1.85M loan before selling the property. Tufts claimed a $50K loss on the sale, arguing that the "amount realized" was limited to the $1.4M FMV of the property transferred, citing footnote 37 in *Crane*.]

Over 35 years ago, in *Crane v. Comm'r*, 331 U.S. 1 (1947), this Court ruled that a taxpayer, who sold property encumbered by a nonrecourse mortgage (the amount of the mortgage being less than the property's value), must include the unpaid balance of the mortgage in the computation of the amount the taxpayer realized on the sale. The case now before us presents the question whether the same rule applies when the unpaid amount of the nonrecourse mortgage exceeds the fair market value of the property sold.

In *Crane*, this Court took the first and controlling step toward resolution of this issue. . . . The Court concluded that Crane obtained an economic benefit from the purchaser's assumption of the mortgage identical to the benefit conferred by the cancellation of personal debt. Because the value of the property in that case exceeded the amount of the mortgage, it was in Crane's economic interest to treat the mortgage as a personal obligation; only by so doing could she realize upon sale the appreciation in her equity.

This case presents [the issue raised by footnote 37 of *Crane*]. We are disinclined to overrule *Crane*, and we conclude that the same rule applies when the unpaid amount of the nonrecourse mortgage exceeds the value of the property transferred. *Crane* ultimately does not rest on its limited theory of economic benefit; instead, we read *Crane* to have approved the Commissioner's decision to treat a nonrecourse mortgage in this context as a true loan. This approval underlies *Crane*'s holdings that the amount of the nonrecourse liability is to be included in calculating both the basis and the amount realized on disposition. That the amount of the loan exceeds the fair market value of the property thus becomes irrelevant.

When a taxpayer receives a loan, he incurs an obligation to repay that loan at some future date. Because of this obligation, the loan proceeds do not qualify as income to the taxpayer. When he fulfills the obligation, the repayment of the loan likewise has no effect on his tax liability.

Another consequence to the taxpayer from this obligation occurs when the taxpayer applies the loan proceeds to the purchase price of property used to secure the loan. Because of the obligation to repay, the taxpayer is entitled to include the amount of the loan in computing his basis in the property; the loan, under § 1012, is part of the taxpayer's cost of the property. Although a different approach might have been taken with respect to a nonrecourse mortgage loan,[9] the Commissioner has chosen to accord it the same treatment he gives to a recourse mortgage loan. The Court approved that choice in *Crane*, and the respondents do not challenge it here. The choice and its resultant benefits to the taxpayer are predicated on the assumption that the mortgage will be repaid in full.

When encumbered property is sold or otherwise disposed of and the purchaser assumes the mortgage, the associated extinguishment of the mortgagor's obligation to repay is accounted for in the computation of the amount realized. Because no difference between recourse and nonrecourse obligations is recognized in calculating basis, *Crane* teaches that the Commissioner may ignore the nonrecourse nature of the obligation in determining the amount realized upon disposition of the encumbered property. He thus may include in the amount realized the amount of the nonrecourse mortgage assumed by the purchaser. The rationale for this treatment is that the original inclusion of the amount of the mortgage in basis rested on the assumption that the mortgagor incurred an obligation to repay. Moreover, this treatment balances the fact that the mortgagor originally received the proceeds of the nonrecourse loan tax-free on the same assumption. Unless the outstanding amount of the mortgage is deemed to be realized, the mortgagor effectively will have received untaxed income at the time the loan was extended and will have received an unwarranted increase in the basis of his property.[10] The Commissioner's interpretation of § 1001(b) in this fashion cannot be said to be unreasonable.

The Commissioner in fact has applied this rule even when the fair market value of the property falls below the amount of the nonrecourse obligation. Reg. § 1.1001-2(b); *Rev. Rul. 76-111*, 1976-1 C. B. 214. Because the theory on which the rule is based applies equally in this situation, we have no reason, after *Crane*, to question this treatment.[11] Respondents received a mortgage loan with the concomitant

---

[9] [5] The Commissioner might have adopted the theory, implicit in *Crane*'s contentions, that a nonrecourse mortgage is not true debt, but, instead, is a form of joint investment by the mortgagor and the mortgagee. On this approach, nonrecourse debt would be considered a contingent liability, under which the mortgagor's payments on the debt gradually increase his interest in the property while decreasing that of the mortgagee.

[10] [8] . . . Our analysis applies even in the situation in which no deductions are taken. It focuses on the obligation to repay and its subsequent extinguishment, not on the taking and recovery of deductions.

[11] [11] . . . The Commissioner has chosen not to characterize the transaction as cancellation of indebtedness. We are not presented with and do not decide the contours of the cancellation-of-

obligation to repay by the year 2012. The only difference between that mortgage and one on which the borrower is personally liable is that the mortgagee's remedy is limited to foreclosing on the securing property. This difference does not alter the nature of the obligation; its only effect is to shift from the borrower to the lender any potential loss caused by devaluation of the property. This, however, does not erase the fact that the mortgagor received the loan proceeds tax-free and included them in his basis on the understanding that he had an obligation to repay the full amount. When the obligation is canceled, the mortgagor is relieved of his responsibility to repay the sum he originally received and thus realizes value to that extent within the meaning of § 1001(b).

JUSTICE O'CONNOR, concurring:

I concur in the opinion of the Court, accepting the view of the Commissioner. I do not, however, endorse the Commissioner's view. Indeed, were we writing on a slate clean except for the decision in *Crane*, I would take quite a different approach — that urged upon us by Professor Barnett as amicus.

Crane established that a taxpayer could treat property as entirely his own, in spite of the "coinvestment" provided by his mortgagee in the form of a nonrecourse loan. That is, the full basis of the property, with all its tax consequences, belongs to the mortgagor. That rule alone, though, does not in any way tie nonrecourse debt to the cost of property or to the proceeds upon disposition.

The logical way to treat this case is to separate the two aspects of these events and to consider, first, the ownership and sale of the property, and, second, the arrangement and retirement of the loan. The fair market value of the property on the date of acquisition — the purchase price — represents the taxpayer's basis in the property, and the fair market value on the date of disposition represents the proceeds on sale. The benefit received by the taxpayer in return for the property is the cancellation of a mortgage that is worth no more than the fair market value of the property, for that is all the mortgagee can expect to collect on the mortgage. Thus, the taxation of the transaction *in property* reflects the economic fate of the *property*.

In the separate borrowing transaction, the taxpayer acquires cash from the mortgagee. He need not recognize income at that time, of course, because he also incurs an obligation to repay the money. Later, though, when he is able to satisfy the debt by surrendering property that is worth less than the face amount of the debt, we have a classic situation of cancellation of indebtedness, requiring the taxpayer to recognize income in the amount of the difference between the proceeds of the loan and the amount for which he is able to satisfy his creditor. The taxation of the financing transaction then reflects the economic fate of the loan.

The reason that separation of the two aspects of the events is important is, of course, that the Code treats different sorts of income differently. A gain on the sale of the property may qualify for capital gains treatment, while the cancellation of

---

indebtedness doctrine. We note only that our approach does not fall within certain prior interpretations of that doctrine. Although the economic benefit prong of *Crane* relies on a freeing-of-assets theory, that theory is irrelevant to our broader approach.

indebtedness is ordinary income, but income that the taxpayer may be able to defer. § 108.

Persuaded though I am by the logical coherence and internal consistency of this approach, I agree with the Court's decision not to adopt it judicially. We do not write on a slate marked only by *Crane*. The Commissioner's longstanding position, *Rev. Rul. 76-111*, 1976-1 C.B. 214, is now reflected in [Reg. § 1.1001-2(b)]. In the light of the numerous cases in the lower courts including the amount of the unrepaid proceeds of the mortgage in the proceeds on sale or disposition, it is difficult to conclude that the Commissioner's interpretation of the statute exceeds the bounds of his discretion. One can reasonably read § 1001(b)'s reference to "the amount realized *from* the sale or other disposition of property" (emphasis added) to permit the Commissioner to collapse the two aspects of the transaction. As long as his view is a reasonable reading of § 1001(b), we should defer to the regulations promulgated by the agency charged with interpretation of the statute.

––––––––

The *Tufts* holding is that *relief from nonrecourse debt resulting from the transfer of the property securing the debt is included in amount realized — regardless of the FMV of the property at the time of the transfer. Tufts* upholds Reg. § 1.1001-2(a)(1) and (b), promulgated during the *Tufts* litigation.[12] Since this result is also (apparently) codified in § 7701(g), added in 1984 (the year after the *Tufts* decision), the Treasury is seemingly barred from changing the regulations on this point.

Under the majority's approach and the regulations cited above, Rachel (in the earlier example) realizes a § 1001 (capital) loss of $1K ($9K debt relief amount realized *less* $10K basis), with no COD income being present. In contrast, under the approach taken in Justice O'Connor's concurrence, Rachel would be considered to have sold her property for cash equal to its $7K FMV, producing a $3K loss, and to have shucked off her $9K liability by paying $7K (in FMV terms) to the creditor, producing COD income of $2K (possibly subject to § 108). The loss could be a nondeductible personal loss or a capital loss (subject to deduction restrictions). The O'Connor approach would have cleared away for good the residue of the old *Kerbaugh-Empire* case which "mixed" the tax treatment of debt with the tax treatment of the property acquired with the borrowed money. Rachel's $2K wealth accession in this scenario is *not* the result of appreciation (in fact, the value of the property *decreased* by $3K). The $2K wealth accession is the result of Rachel's avoiding repayment of borrowed funds that were excluded from her gross income on the premise that they would be repaid (the rationale underlying COD income).

Compare *Rev. Rul. 91-31*, supra Section B, where the creditor agreed to reduce a nonrecourse debt without foreclosing on the property. Since the property was not disposed of by the debtor, there was no realization event, so there was no possibility of immediate § 1001 "gain" or "loss." Significantly, the IRS ruled there that the reduction in debt produced COD income rather than a reduction in basis. Thus, in

––––––––

[12] [12] When that regulation uses the phrase "liabilities from which the transferor is discharged as a result of the sale or disposition," it is using the word "discharge" in the sense of "effectively gotten rid of," which occurs upon a disposition of property subject to a nonrecourse debt. See Reg. § 1.1001-2(a)(4)(i).

that scenario the debt transaction was kept separate from the property transaction. However, in the two-party debt situation, governed by § 108(e)(5), the opposite approach is taken: the reduction in debt reduces the basis and does not produce COD income. And third-party debt falling under § 108(a)(1)(D) and (E) is similarly treated — a reduction of the basis of the (depreciable or residential) mortgaged property instead of COD income.

b. Recourse Debt

Now reconsider the Rachel hypothetical, except that Rachel's debt is *recourse* instead of nonrecourse. As the following ruling indicates, current law adopts Justice O'Connor's two-step approach in this situation!

REVENUE RULING 90-16

1990-1 C.B. 12

X was the owner and developer of a residential subdivision. To finance the development of the subdivision, X obtained a loan from an unrelated bank. X was unconditionally liable for repayment of the debt. The debt was secured by a mortgage on the subdivision. X became insolvent (within the meaning of § 108(d)(3) of the Code) and defaulted on the debt. X negotiated an agreement with the bank whereby the subdivision was transferred to the bank and the bank released X from all liability for the amounts due on the debt. When the subdivision was transferred pursuant to the agreement, its fair market value was 10,000x dollars, X's adjusted basis in the subdivision was 8,000x dollars, and the amount due on the debt was 12,000x dollars, which did not represent any accrued but unpaid interest. After the transaction X was still insolvent.

Section 1.1001-2(a)(2) [of the regulations] provides that the amount realized on a sale or other disposition of property that secures a recourse liability does not include amounts that are (or would be if realized and recognized) income from the discharge of indebtedness under section 61(a)(12). Section 1.1001-2(c) illustrates these rules as follows: *Example (8)*. In 1980, F transfers to a creditor an asset with a fair market value of $6,000 and the creditor discharges $7,500 of indebtedness for which F is personally liable. The amount realized on the disposition of the asset is its fair market value ($6,000). In addition, F has income from the discharge of indebtedness of $1,500 ($7,500–$6,000).

In the present situation, X transferred the subdivision to the bank in satisfaction of the 12,000x dollar debt. To the extent of the fair market value of the property transferred to the creditor, the transfer of the subdivision is treated as a sale or disposition upon which gain is recognized. To the extent the fair market value of the subdivision, 10,000x dollars, exceeds its adjusted basis, 8,000x dollars, X realizes and recognizes gain on the transfer. X thus recognizes 2,000x dollars of gain.

To the extent the amount of debt, 12,000x dollars, exceeds the fair market value of the subdivision, 10,000x dollars, X realizes income from the discharge of indebtedness. However, under section 108(a)(1)(B) of the Code, the full amount of X's discharge of indebtedness income is excluded from gross income because that amount does not exceed the amount by which X was insolvent.

If the subdivision had been transferred to the bank as a result of a foreclosure proceeding in which the outstanding balance of the debt was discharged (rather than having been transferred pursuant to the settlement agreement), the result would be the same. A mortgage foreclosure, like a voluntary sale, is a "disposition" within the scope of the gain or loss provisions of section 1001 of the Code. See *Helvering v. Hammel*, 311 U.S. 504 (1941); *Electro-Chemical Engraving Co. v. Comm'r*, 311 U.S. 513 (1941); and *Danenberg v. Comm'r*, 73 T.C. 370 (1979)(acq.).

Relief from *recourse* debt in excess of the FMV of the securing property produces an amount realized on the transfer equal to the property's FMV and COD income in the amount of the excess of the outstanding principal amount of the debt over the FMV of the property. Accord *Gehl v. Comm'r*, 102 T.C. 784 (1994), *aff'd without op.*, 95-1 USTC (CCH) ¶50,191 (8th Cir. 1995).

If property is sold in foreclosure for less than the full amount of an outstanding recourse liability and (unlike the creditors in *Rev. Rul. 90-16*) the creditor does *not* abandon its rights to collect the deficiency, the debtor's amount realized for purposes of calculating gain or loss under § 1001 upon transfer of the property equals the proceeds generated by the sale. If the creditor eventually abandons its claims regarding the deficiency (or the statute of limitations runs), the debtor will be charged with COD income at that later time. If the debtor pays the deficiency in full, COD income is avoided. See *Aizawa v. Comm'r*, 99 T.C. 197 (1992).

3. Unpaid Interest

In the real world, borrowers who lose property through foreclosure due to nonpayment of principal may owe unpaid interest as well. What is the impact of unpaid interest on the borrower's amount realized? The answer is not clear, with authority being sparse.

In *Allan v. Comm'r*, 86 T.C. 655 (1986), *aff'd*, 856 F.2d 1169 (8th Cir. 1988), it was held that, because the unpaid interest had been added to principal pursuant to the loan agreement, the unpaid interest was properly included in amount realized under *Tufts*. (Adding the unpaid interest to principal was viewed as the equivalent of an additional cash loan because it increased the interest that would accrue.) Hence, this holding would appear not to cover the case of garden-variety unpaid interest. Nevertheless, adding interest to principal is just an accounting move, and does not reflect any advance of additional cash.

In *Catalano v. Comm'r*, T.C. Memo 2000-82, *rev'd on other grounds*, 279 F.3d 682 (9th Cir. 2002), the Tax Court held that past due interest on a nonrecourse mortgage (not added to principal) was both included in the amount realized on the foreclosure and deducted. *Catalano* was reversed by the Ninth Circuit on the ground that no property disposition had occurred, with no discussion of the unpaid interest issue, which then became moot.

Both cases involved nonrecourse debt. In a case where recourse debt is involved, and the value of the property is less than the loan principal, a COD issue would be raised, and the unpaid interest would not be included in amount realized.

NOTE

The Tax Court holding in *Catalano* that the inclusion of unpaid interest in amount realized entitles the taxpayer to deduct the same interest (at least where the interest, if paid, would have been deductible) produces an outcome analogous to that obtaining under § 108(e)(2), which excludes COD income in cases where the liability, if paid, would be deductible. But an equally symmetrical result would be no inclusion in amount realized and no deduction. It is not clear that *Catalano* (a Tax Court memorandum decision) will hold up or create a general rule for all unpaid interest dispositions. The theory of the Tax Court opinion was that the debtor actually paid the interest, citing the principle (see Chapter 19.A.1) that a transfer of property in satisfaction of a debt is a sale generating a cash amount realized equal to the debt followed by a satisfaction of the debt with cash. The in-kind-satisfaction theory does not fit the scenario of a foreclosure on a nonrecourse debt, because a sale for cash is not an option (unless the bank agrees), and any sale would be at FMV (which, in *Catalano*, was lower than the outstanding principal debt). At this point the Tax Court relied on *Tufts* for the proposition that FMV is irrelevant. That may be so as to amount realized, but not as to the issue of the deemed payment of interest. Moreover, as to the amount realized issue, *Tufts* dealt with relief from acquisition debt, and rested on the theory that the seller had earlier received tax-free cash. The *Catalano* decision (as well as *Allan*, supra) fails to explain how unpaid interest represents a prior receipt of material wealth within the rationale of *Tufts*. (In cases where unpaid interest had been *previously* deducted because the debtor was on the accrual method, then the relief from the interest obligation would clearly give rise to a later income inclusion. See *Rev. Rul. 76-316*, 1976-2 C.B. 22.) The relief-from-unpaid-interest issue is also discussed at Chapter 19.B.1.b in the context of COD income.

PROBLEMS

1. Dennis Debtor purchases business equipment for $10K (its FMV) from Sophie Seller. Dennis pays $1K in cash and gives Sophie a $9K note on which he was not personally liable but which was secured by a mortgage on the equipment. Dennis properly deducts $3K of depreciation over time, makes interest payments, but does not make principal payments. The property falls in value to $8.5K.

(a) Dennis transfers the property to Bennie Buyer for no cash (because the property is worth only $8.5K), subject to the $9K nonrecourse debt. (Why would Bennie buy it?) What result to Dennis (and Bennie)?

(b) Same as (a), except that, instead of selling the property, Dennis fails to make principal payments on the debt when required, and Sophie forecloses on the property.

(c) Same as (a), except that the $9K debt is recourse, Sophie forecloses when the property is worth $8.5K, and agrees not to pursue a deficiency judgment.

(d) Same as (c), except that Sophie obtains a $500 deficiency judgment against Dennis.

2. Simon owns property that was purchased with $200K of third-party nonrecourse debt secured by the property. It has been depreciated, so that its basis is now $50K, but its value has plummeted to $10K. Assume that Simon has not paid any debt principal. The mortgagee is demanding payment and threatening foreclosure. Simon is insolvent. What tax advantage would accrue if Simon (instead of suffering foreclosure) pays the bank $15K to fully settle its debt, while keeping the property? Might the bank agree to this?

Chapter 21

TAX SHELTERS

The topic of tax shelters can be described as a set of solutions to a problem that is hard to pin down. Section A considers some possible definitions of tax shelters. Section B involves judicial doctrine that re-characterizes the facts of abusive transactions. Section C explores the role of nonrecourse debt in tax shelters. Section D considers the passive activity rules.

A. WHAT'S A "TAX SHELTER"?

The search for an accepted definition of "tax shelter" is elusive. One commentator has defined a "tax shelter" as "an investment that is worth more after tax than before tax."[1] Taken at face value, this definition reaches every investment resulting in a net loss that can be deducted against (and which "shelters") other income,[2] because the tax saving from the sheltering deduction for the net loss leaves the taxpayer better off than she was before the tax consequences were taken into account. However, this definition is overinclusive, because nonconsumption losses that accurately reflect economic decreases (such as a loss on a sale of investment real estate) are legitimate. At the same time, this definition is underinclusive, because an investment producing a tax profit is worth more *before* tax than after tax and is, therefore, not a tax shelter under the preceding definition, even if the deductions are illegitimate (i.e., the deductions are costs that should be treated as nondeductible capital expenditures or they exceed actual economic costs).

Perhaps, then, a "tax shelter" is any investment that produces a lower tax liability than would be the case if the investment's *tax* result conformed to the "correct" result as measured by "correct" tax principles. But this definition of tax shelter would encompass numerous transactions involving tax provisions that deviate from the normative concept of income in a taxpayer-favorable way, such as the § 121 exclusion for gain on the sale of a principal residence and the retirement savings provisions (IRAs, etc.) discussed in Chapter 6.E.2. That makes this alternative definition problematic if the term "tax shelter" is intended to have an aura of opprobrium, because Congress clearly wants taxpayers to benefit from these provisions or to use these provisions to achieve certain social and economic goals without any stigma being attached. These provisions may be bad policy on

---

[1] See David Cay Johnston, *A Shelter Can Be Simple, or Ornate*, N.Y TIMES, July 13, 2003, at § 3, p. 11 (quoting Professor Calvin Johnson).

[2] If the asset produces a profit that is taxed, the investment is worth less after tax than before tax. If the asset produces a profit that is not taxed, produces neither profit nor loss, or produces a loss that cannot reduce other income, the asset has the same value before tax as it has after tax.

their own merits, but they should not be considered "illegitimate" solely because they deviate from income tax norms.

Thus, one avenue to explore in our search for a tax shelter definition would be to try to determine which transactions that produce tax benefits that deviate from ability-to-pay principles were "intended" by Congress (and thus legitimate), such as investments in principal residences and contributions to retirement plans, and which transactions that produce tax benefits that deviate from ability-to-pay principles were *not* "intended" by Congress. But how can we discern this intent? Although legislative history often gives examples of anticipated applications of a legislative enactment, such a list of examples would rarely be exhaustive, and legislative history rarely identifies results that are not intended. In short, attempting to define "tax shelter" by relying on expressions of congressional purpose is unlikely to produce a definitive list of tax shelters.

Perhaps a distinction can be made between subsidization of favored economic activities, on the one hand, and *being able to profit solely from the tax system,* on the other. To illustrate this distinction, suppose that Sam, in Year 1, earns a $50K salary and spends it entirely on personal consumption. However, Sam could reduce his tax base by investing $2K in an IRA, because the $2K would be deductible from Sam's income under § 219. The income earned by the IRA (say, at 5% or $100 over the first 12 months) would be exempt from tax as it is being earned, but if Sam withdrew the full $2.1K after 12 months, the $2.1K would be taxed. At a 30% rate, the tax would be $630, leaving Sam with $1,470 after taxes. If there were no § 219 deduction, Sam would end up with $1,449 [($2K − $600) + ($70 return − $21 tax)]. The IRA scheme (which reflects cash flow consumption tax principles) increases the already-positive return on the investment compared to the conventional income tax treatment. This favorable treatment creates the desired incentive to save for retirement in this fashion.

In the alternative, suppose Sam borrows the $2K at 5% per annum to invest in the IRA. Under conventional income tax principles, Sam would include in gross income his $50K compensation, exclude the $2K borrowed money, and be prohibited from deducting the $2K IRA investment (because it's a capital expenditure), and his bottom-line Year 1 taxable income would be $50K. In Year 2, the $100 interest received and included in income would be offset by the $100 interest on the loan. Alternatively, if Sam were taxed under cash flow consumption tax principles, he would include the $50K and the $2K borrowed money, and deduct his $2K IRA investment, again leaving a taxable consumption income of $50K. In Year 2, the $2.1K proceeds of cashing out the investment would be offset by $2.1K of deductions for interest and principal repayments. In either case, he would be prohibited from obtaining a tax profit from an economic wash.[3]

However, under current law Sam both *excludes* the $2K borrowed money and *deducts* the $2K IRA investment in the investment year. His bottom-line Year 1 taxable income is only $48K. Sam pockets $600 ($2K x .30) from the tax saving. In

---

[3] Under any of the income tax, cash flow consumption tax, and wage tax models, the tax treatment of positive investing and negative investing (borrowing) is internally consistent, i.e., the tax treatment of the one is the "mirror image" of the tax treatment of the other.

Year 2, Sam has an included $2.1K cash return from the IRA and a $100 interest deduction, resulting in a tax of $600. So, if the Year 2 tax "offsets" the Year 1 tax, what's the problem? The problem is an unwarranted time-value-of-money advantage. The $600 obtained in Year 1 could have been invested at 3.5% (5% minus 30% tax), resulting in a $21 after-tax profit on an economic wash (zero net investment and zero net return).

There is no Code provision that would defeat Sam's tax benefits. The only Code section that might disallow his § 219 deduction for investing in the IRA, § 265(a)(1), does not reach this scenario, because § 265(a)(1) disallows deductions only to the extent that they are allocable to "wholly exempt" income. The only receipt to which Sam's § 219 deduction is allocable is the borrowed money, which is non-income (and therefore cannot be "wholly exempt income"). Section 265(a)(2) disallows the interest deduction relating to wholly tax-exempt income, but the earnings inside the IRA are eventually taxed to Sam (see § 408(d)).[4] (In the present case, the IRA yield is actually taxed in Year 2.) So here we have the confluence of the income tax treatment of borrowed money combined with the cash flow consumption tax treatment of the IRA investment. The term that we introduced in Chapter 6.F.2 for this confluence is "tax arbitrage."

Is this tax arbitrage a "tax shelter" because Congress could not rationally desire a tax savings for a net investment of zero, or is it a not a tax shelter because Congress has failed to take steps to correct the problem? How *could* Congress correct this problem?[5] A permanent disallowance of the $100 interest deduction would result in overkill (a tax penalty of $30). A rule, such as § 163(d), that defers the investment interest deduction until investment income is realized does not fix the problem raised by the Sam hypothetical (where the interest deduction in fact matched the interest inclusion). A rule that *generally* defers the § 219 deduction (until the IRA is cashed in) amounts to a repeal of § 219. A rule that deferred the § 219 deduction only where it was obtained with borrowed money would require tracing, and would be hard to enforce. Presumably, it would defer the § 219 deduction to match principal payments on the loan, raising an additional complication. Congress might rationally decide that fixing this particular problem isn't worth the effort. In that case, what could a court possibly do to fix the Sam problem? Courts are supposed to follow the mandate of the Code.

In the meantime, the notion of a tax shelter is beginning to take shape in the haze. A tax shelter appears to result from a *combination* of tax rules applied to a transaction or activity that are out of sync with each other, and produce a result that goes beyond a reasonable congressional purpose of simply incentivizing (politically determined) socially desirable investments. A near-constant ingredient in the stew is the income tax treatment of debt (and interest) combined with a consumption (or wage) tax treatment of investments. But this combination does not appear to "cinch" a determination of illegitimacy. What more might be need?

---

[4] For § 265(a)(1) to apply, the otherwise-deductible expense must actually give rise to the excludible dollars (as where an otherwise-deductible expense confers on the taxpayer a right to receive an excluded reimbursement). See Chapter 8.D.4.

[5] Another example of a "permissible" tax shelter in this sense would be borrowing money to invest in assets that are "expensed" under § 179 or depreciated rapidly under § 168. See Chapter 6.E.3.

B. ROLE OF COURTS IN ATTACKING "ILLEGITIMATE" ARRANGEMENTS

Courts have developed doctrines to defeat certain kinds of tax shelters.

1. Sham Transactions

The classic case below involves a more elaborate and "packaged" version of the Sam scenario discussed immediately above, and raises the issue of when courts can legitimately intervene in defeating tax-motivated transactions.

KNETSCH v. UNITED STATES
United States Supreme Court
364 U.S. 361 (1960)

MR. JUSTICE BRENNAN delivered the opinion of the Court.

[Eds. note: The facts are quite complex, and to aid in comprehension some of the numbers have been rounded off.]

[The Sam Houston Life Insurance Company placed ads in the *Wall Street Journal* and other places promising income tax savings on the purchase of annuity contracts with borrowed money. Responding to the ad, Karl Knetsch, age 60, purchased a 30-year-deferred-maturity annuity on December 11, 1953, in the face amount of $4M for $4,004,000. Of the $4K amount in excess of the annuity's face amount, $3K was, in essence, a fee to buy the tax product and $1K was Knetsch's net investment. Knetsch paid this $4K excess in cash and borrowed the remaining $4M from Sam Houston at 3½% interest, which was $140K per year. The loan (used to purchase the annuity) was nonrecourse, secured only by the annuity. Knetsch's $4M annuity "investment" was to earn interest at 2½%, which was $100K per year, though annuity payments would not begin until Knetsch reached age 90. In the meantime, the $100K interest Knetsch earned each year was to be held by the insurance company and was not currently taxed to Knetsch. Nevertheless, each year Knetsch "borrowed" the $100K and used that, plus $40K of his own cash, to pay that year's $140K interest obligation. Knetsch's net equity in the annuity was maintained at only $1K, which means that, if he lived to age 90, Knetsch's annuity would begin to pay him $43 per month for the remainder of his life.[6] In sum, Knetsch incurred an economic, out-of-pocket loss for each year by entering into this investment, figured *before* tax. He paid an up-front fee of $3K in Year 1 for one "circle" of cash ($4M borrowed from Sam Houston and paid immediately back to purchase the annuity contract). And in Year 2 and in each year thereafter, he paid $40K for additional "circles" of cash ($100K borrowed from Sam Houston against the $100K interest earned (but retained by the company) and paid immediately back as part of his annual $140K "interest" payment on the original $4M loan). Under the tax rules then in effect, all of the tax results appeared to be proper. The

---

[6] [Eds. note: If Knetsch had died before reaching age 90, his beneficiaries would have received the existing net equity. Knetsch would have had to live to an age over twice that of Methuselah (2,100 years, to be exact) to break even economically (disregarding taxes).]

bottom line was Knetsch's taking a $140K "interest" deduction each year against his then very high marginal rate, yielding an annual tax savings of $112K, at an out-of-pocket annual cost of $40K, which yielded a net after-tax profit of $72K per year.]

The [District Court] made findings that "there was no commercial economic substance to the . . . transaction," that the parties did not intend that Knetsch "become indebted to Sam Houston," that "no indebtedness of [Knetsch] was created by any of the . . . transactions," and that "no economic gain could be achieved from the purchase of these bonds without regard to the tax consequences." His conclusion of law was that "while in form the payments to Sam Houston were compensation for the use or forbearance of money, they were not in substance. As a payment of interest, the transaction was a sham."

We first examine the transaction between Knetsch and the insurance company to determine whether it created an "indebtedness" within the meaning of [the predecessor to § 163(a)], or whether, as the trial court found, it was a sham. We put aside a finding by the District Court that Knetsch's "only motive was to attempt to secure an interest deduction." As was said in *Gregory v. Helvering*, 293 U.S. 465, 469: "The legal right of a taxpayer to decrease the amount of what otherwise would be his taxes, or altogether avoid them, by means which the law permits, cannot be doubted. But the question for determination is whether what was done, apart from the tax motive, was the thing which the statute intended." When we examine "what was done" here, we see that Knetsch paid the insurance company [$284K] during the two taxable years involved[7] and received [$200K] back in the form of "loans." What did Knetsch get for the out-of-pocket difference of [$84K]? In form he had an annuity contract with a so-called guaranteed cash value at maturity of $8,388,000, which would produce monthly annuity payments of $90,171, or substantial life insurance proceeds in the event of his death before maturity. This was a fiction, because each year Knetsch's annual borrowings kept the net cash value, on which any annuity or insurance payments would depend, at the relative pittance of $1K. Plainly, therefore, Knetsch's transaction with the insurance company did not appreciably affect his beneficial interest except to reduce his tax. For it is patent that there was nothing of substance to be realized by Knetsch from this transaction beyond a tax deduction. What he was ostensibly [borrowing] back was in reality only the rebate of a substantial part of the so-called "interest" payments. The [$84K] difference retained by the company was its fee for providing the facade of "loans" whereby the petitioners sought to reduce their 1953 and 1954 taxes in the total sum of [($140,000 + $140,000) × .80)].

Mr. Justice Douglas, with whom Mr. Justice Whittaker and Mr. Justice Stewart concur, dissenting:

It is true that in this transaction the taxpayer was bound to lose if the annuity contract is taken by itself. At least the taxpayer showed by his conduct that he never intended to come out ahead on that investment apart from this income tax deduction. Yet the same may be true where a taxpayer borrows money at 5% or 6%

---

[7] [Eds. note: $4,000 "up front" plus $140,000 of Year-1 "interest" and $140,000 of Year-2 "interest."]

interest to purchase securities that pay only nominal interest; or where, with money in the bank earning 3%, he borrows from the selfsame bank at a higher rate. His aim there, as here, may only be to get a tax deduction for interest paid. Yet as long as the transaction itself is not hocus-pocus, the interest charges incident to completing it would seem to be deductible under the Internal Revenue Code. While the taxpayer was obligated to pay interest at the rate of 3½% per annum, the annuity bonds increased in cash value at the rate of only 2½% per annum. The insurance company's profit was in that 1-point spread.

Tax avoidance is a dominating motive behind scores of transactions. It is plainly present here. Will the Service that calls this transaction a "sham" today not press for collection of taxes arising out of the surrender of the annuity contract? I think it should, for I do not believe any part of the transaction was a "sham." To disallow the "interest" deduction because the annuity device was devoid of commercial substance is to draw a line which will affect a host of situations not now before us and which, with all deference, I do not think we can maintain when other cases reach here. The remedy is legislative. Evils or abuses can be particularized by Congress. We deal only with "interest" as commonly understood and as used across the board in myriad transactions. Since these transactions were real and legitimate in the insurance world and were consummated within the limits allowed by insurance policies, I would recognize them tax-wise.

Congress does frequently respond to perceived tax abuses by enacting anti-abuse rules. Two such rules impact a *Knetsch*-type transaction. In 1954, before the Supreme Court decision in *Knetsch*, Congress enacted § 264(a)(2),[8] which now explicitly prohibits the deduction of interest paid on indebtedness incurred to purchase single-premium annuity contracts. (Sections 264(a)(3) and (4) extend this rule to non-single-premium policies, with certain exceptions.) Congress has also amended the rules involving the taxation of annuities so that borrowings against such policies are deemed to be includible "distributions" to the extent of the untaxed inside build-up.

2. Business Purpose

Turning to the question of the ability of *courts* to attack tax-motivated transactions, in *Gregory v. Helvering*, 293 U.S. 465 (1935), one of the most cited tax cases of all time (and quoted by the *Knetsch* majority), the Supreme Court stated that taxpayers are free to enter into tax-motivated transactions to obtain favorable tax treatment. Indeed, Judge Learned Hand, at the Second Circuit level, memorably stated (69 F.2d 809, 810 (2d Cir. 1934)):

A transaction, otherwise within an exception of the tax law, does not lose its immunity because it is actuated by a desire to avoid or, if one choose, to

---

[8] The new law was made prospective only, however, and one argument made by *Knetsch* was that Congress, by making the new law prospective only, intended to allow deduction of interest with respect to pre-1954 contracts like his. The Court rejected this argument by noting that the new law prohibited interest deductions even with respect to bona fide indebtedness and thus had no bearing on the issue of whether purported indebtedness is actually a "sham."

evade, taxation. Anyone may so arrange his affairs that his taxes shall be as low as possible; he is not bound to choose that pattern which will best pay the Treasury; there is not even a patriotic duty to increase one's taxes.

But the taxpayer nevertheless *lost* the Gregory case both in the Second Circuit and in the Supreme Court, the latter quoting Judge Hand's follow-up: "[b]ut the question for determination is whether what was done, apart from the tax motive, was the thing which the statute intended." Thus, tax-avoidance motive is not *itself* a basis for deciding against a taxpayer who literally complies with the statute, but perhaps one can consider taxpayer motive when attempting to ascertain congressional intent as to the intended *reach* of the statute. The facts in *Gregory* involved a complex transaction that was structured to garner "capital gains" treatment for the receipt of a plain vanilla dividend, which at that time, and for most of the history of the income tax has been treated as ordinary income taxed at a significantly higher rates than capital gains. There was no business (i.e., nontax) purpose for structuring the transaction in that way except to transform (high-taxed) ordinary income into (low-taxed) capital gain. It was this lack of "business purpose" for structuring the transaction in a more complex way than necessary to achieve a distribution of the dividend that caused the Court to agree with the IRS that the receipt should be treated as a plain ordinary-income dividend.

Gregory is usually cited for the proposition that a taxpayer must have a "business purpose" (i.e., a nontax purpose) for structuring a business transaction in a chosen way to garner the tax benefits of that selected form. If a taxpayer lacks a sufficient business purpose for structuring the transaction in that particular way, the government may succeed in arguing that the transaction should be taxed as though it were structured in a less tax-favorable form *that better reflects the "substance" of the transaction. Gregory* has left a huge wake, in which the roles of congressional intent, "business purpose," "substance-over-form," "sham transaction," and "economic substance" have played out in a not wholly comprehensible fashion.

Knetsch does not suggest that Congress, in enacting § 163, *specifically* included an implied economic-purpose requirement in the § 163 language. Therefore, if the absence of economic (nontax) purpose was relevant in *Knetsch*, it must have been because such an "economic profit" requirement is a pervasive limitation to be read by the courts into *all* taxpayer-friendly tax provisions (unless Congress clearly intends otherwise).[9] It is not surprising, then, that subsequent cases have carried the message of *Knetsch* beyond "sham debt" cases to situations involving bona fide debt (or transactions not involving debt at all).

3.   Economic Substance

In *Goldstein v. Comm'r*, 364 F.2d 734 (2d Cir. 1966), Tillie Goldstein was a retiree living on a pension of approximately $1K per year when she won $140K in the Irish Sweepstakes in 1958. Later that year, her son, a CPA, set up a tax

---

[9] Prior to the 1969 enactment of § 183, discussed at Chapter 10.B, courts disallowed *all* deductions whose allowability was contingent on a business or investment nexus unless the "primary purpose" of the activity or the cost was to seek a profit. The interest deduction (in the days of *Knetsch*) was not so contingent.

reduction plan for her. The plan was complex, but, in simplified form, two banks loaned Tillie nearly $1M at 4% interest for relatively short terms, the longest being for less than three years. Tillie immediately used the borrowed funds to purchase U.S. Treasury notes paying 1½% interest. Although she was personally liable on the bank loans, her assets were grossly insufficient to pay it off. The Treasury notes, however, were safe securities that could likely be sold for more than enough to repay the loans, and under the plan the banks immediately took the notes as collateral. In short, the banks were looking to the Treasury notes for repayment of the loan principal, and Tillie had only a theoretical personal exposure. Contemporaneously with these transactions, and as part of the plan, Tillie transferred about $80K to the banks as a prepayment of the entire interest due for the term of the loans. In structuring the plan, her son estimated that she would receive sufficient yield on the Treasury notes to offset about $61.5K of her interest prepayment so that her before-tax economic loss from the plan would be about $18.5K. But because Tillie's 1958 Irish Sweepstakes winnings pushed her into a high tax bracket for that year, her $80K deduction for the interest prepayment would save about $55K in federal income tax in 1958. Thus the *after-tax* result of the plan would be a $36.5K after-tax profit ($55K tax saving *less* $18.5K before-tax economic loss).[10]

The Second Circuit concluded that, unlike the debt in *Knetsch*, the bank debt incurred by Tillie Goldstein was not a "sham" but rather was "bona fide debt" because, among other reasons: (1) the bank loans (unlike the *Knetsch* loans) were third-party debts owed to independent lenders other than the seller of the investment (the U.S. government); (2) the two loan transactions "did not within a few days return all the parties to the position from which they had started," since Ms. Goldstein retained legal ownership of the Treasury notes until she sold them and repaid the loan principal; and (3) the loans were recourse. The court nevertheless ruled in favor of the government. First, the Second Circuit found that "the Tax Court was justified in concluding that petitioner entered into [the plan] without any realistic expectation of economic profit and 'solely' in order to secure a large interest deduction in 1958." The court then ruled that "Section 163(a) does not 'intend' that taxpayers should be permitted deductions for interest paid on debts that were entered into solely in order to obtain a deduction."

In short, *Goldstein* took *Knetsch* a step further by holding that, even though the debt was not a sham, Tillie's failure to satisfy the before-tax-profit-expectation test per se resulted in disallowance of the interest deduction.

The "before-tax-economic-profit" requirement elucidated in *Goldstein*, decided in 1966, was incorporated into § 183(a), enacted in 1969, which permanently disallows net losses with respect to "activities not engaged in for profit." Section 183, discussed in Chapter 10.B, is commonly applied to "hobby" activities having an element of personal pleasure, but it has also been applied to tax-shelter activities (that don't resemble a hobby).[11]

---

[10] Today, this result is foreclosed by § 461(g), added in 1976, requiring that prepaid interest be capitalized and amortized over the term of the loan (except for certain "points" paid on home mortgage loans).

[11] See, e.g., *Hildebrand v. Comm'r*, 28 F.3d 1024 (10th Cir. 1994); *Rose v. Comm'r*, 88 T.C. 386 (1987),

4.   Codification of the Economic Substance Doctrine

Section 183 disallows operating losses from an "activity," but discrete investment transactions involving financial constructs (as in *Knetsch* and *Goldstein*) are arguably not "activities." Attacks under § 183 sometimes are unsuccessful, because the nine-factor test under § 183 can be manipulated to the taxpayer's advantage.[12] Also, § 183 does not apply to C corporations (i.e., corporations taxed under Subchapter C of the Code). Accordingly, the judicial doctrines referred to above have continued to play a role, although with mixed results.[13] Many of the litigated corporate tax shelters have relied on complex combinations of rules found in Subchapter C (pertaining to corporations), Subchapter K (pertaining to partnerships and limited liability companies), and Code provisions dealing with international transactions, which are beyond the scope of this book. Common ingredients are the creation of tax losses or credits (that do not represent economic losses) and the shifting of income or gain to a nontaxed entity (such as a charity, governmental unit, or foreign corporation). These deals are often marketed to potential clients under agreements that they keep the details of the transaction confidential (so that the tax shelter can be sold to multiple clients).

The judicial doctrines described above have become collectively known as the economic substance doctrine.[14] This doctrine "[i]n general . . . denies tax benefits arising from transactions that do not result in a meaningful change to the taxpayer's economic position other than a purported reduction in Federal income tax."[15] Unfortunately, the judicial decisions that created and elaborated this general rule were vague and inconsistent regarding critical details. Congress responded by enacting § 7701(o) and a companion penalty provision, both with an effective date of March 30, 2010. Regrettably, § 7701(o) does little on its face to clarify the details of the economic substance doctrine. New § 7701(o) states that:

> In the case of any transaction to which the economic substance doctrine is relevant, such transaction shall be treated as having economic substance only if—
>
> (a) the transaction changes in a meaningful way (apart from Federal income tax effects) the taxpayer's economic position, and
>
> (b) the taxpayer has a substantial purpose (apart from Federal income tax effects) for entering into such transaction.[16]

---

aff'd, 868 F.2d 851 (6th Cir. 1989); *Ronnen v. Comm'r*, 90 T.C. 74 (1988).

[12]   See, e.g., *Gefen v. Comm'r*, 87 T.C. 1471 (1986); *Zegeer v. Comm'r*, T.C. Memo. 1989-590.

[13]   Compare *ACM Partnership v. Comm'r*, 157 F.3d 231 (3d Cir. 1998) (government win), with *Compaq Computer v. Comm'r*, 277 F.3d 778 (5th Cir. 2001) (government loss).

[14]   *See* Martin J. McMahon, Jr., *Living with the Codified Economic Substance Doctrine*, 128 TAX NOTES 731, 732-36 (Aug. 16, 2010).

[15]   STAFF OF JOINT COMM. ON TAX'N, TECHNICAL EXPLANATION OF THE REVENUE PROVISIONS OF THE "RECONCILIATION ACT OF 2010," AS AMENDED, IN COMBINATION WITH THE "PATIENT PROTECTION AND AFFORDABLE CARE ACT," 142 (JCX-18-10 2010).

[16]   § 7701(o)(1).

The critical terms "meaningful" and "substantial" are undefined, and the terms "economic position," "transaction," and "business purpose" are only partially defined. The full impact of this new provision will not be known until regulations are issued and perhaps not until sufficient time passes to allow the development of a line of interpretive cases.

Of more immediate importance is the new penalty provision that is coupled with § 7701(o). Sections 6662(a) and (b)(6) impose a penalty equal to 20% of any underpayment of tax resulting from claimed tax benefits being disallowed by § 7701(o). Where the taxpayer does not make an adequate tax return disclosure of the facts relevant to the disallowed tax benefits, the penalty rate doubles to 40%. See § 6662(i). Both the 20% and 40% versions of this penalty are "no fault" in the sense that they cannot be deflected by the § 6664 "reasonable cause/good faith" defense. See § 6664(c)(2), (d)(2).

PROBLEM

Sam borrows $2K from a bank on a recourse basis at 5% interest, and contributes the $2K to an IRA, the 5% earnings on which are not taxed until withdrawn in retirement.

(a) In the absence of § 163(d), can Sam deduct, under the Code, his current interest payment against his current salary income? Are any of the judicial doctrines applicable? § 7701(o)? What if the interest owed is at a 4% rate?

(b) Does § 163(d) apply? Is that an adequate remedy for the government? What if Sam borrowed the $2K as § 163(h)(3)(C) home equity indebtedness? See § 163(d)(3)(B).

C. NONRECOURSE DEBT IN TAX SHELTERS

Nonrecourse debt played a critical role in early tax shelters, begetting anti-abuse rules in its wake.

1. Inflated Two-Party Nonrecourse Debt

Recall that the buyer in the *Tufts* case in the previous chapter willingly acquired property that was encumbered with nonrecourse debt in excess of its fair market value. Good reasons once existed for making this move, which appears to make no sense on its face. First, the nonrecourse debt produces *Crane* basis that can generate depreciation deductions in excess of economic loss. In addition, the debt generates interest deductions, another common ingredient in tax-shelter losses. And what did these anticipated tax benefits cost the buyer? At some future point the buyer would suffer foreclosure, but the gain in the case of business real estate would ultimately be taxed at low capital gains rates (by way of § 1231). Moreover, the ordinary deductions were annual, but the capital gain was deferred. Section 163(d) was avoided by C corporations and generally avoided if the property was used in a trade or business.

Consider the case of Sara Surgeon, a doctor whose marginal tax rate is 35%. Sara purchases an apartment building worth $100K at the beginning of Year 1 and finances the purchase by paying $5K in cash and borrowing the remainder from National Bank on a nonrecourse basis. The loan provides for annual payments of market-rate interest but requires no principal payments until the beginning of Year 6. Assume that the building will retain its FMV, and Sara will sell it at the beginning of Year 6 for $5K cash, subject to the $95K nonrecourse debt. If the rent paid by the tenants exactly equals Sara's tax-deductible cash expenses for mortgage interest, real property taxes, and building maintenance during her five years of ownership, Sara has neither a net tax liability with respect to the includible rental income nor any "carrying costs" to fund out of pocket. During that five-year period, however, Sara is also entitled to take depreciation deductions on her $100K basis, which would come to about $3.6K per year, resulting in a net ordinary loss for tax purposes. In the absence of any statutory rule to the contrary, Sara's net loss of $3.6K would shelter gross income from other sources, such as salary income. The annual tax saving is $1,260 ($3,600 × .35) per year. The present value in Year 1 of this five-year stream of tax savings is about $5,248, using a 7% discount rate. When Sara sells the investment in Year 6, she will have an amount realized of $100K ($5K cash + $95K debt relief) and an adjusted basis of $82K [$100K − (5 × $3.6K)], resulting in $18K of "unrecaptured § 1250 gain" taxed at a 25% rate.[17] Her tax due will be $4.5K ($18K × .25). But the tax payment is six years in the future, so the present cost is only about $3K using a 7% discount rate.

When this $3K Year 1 present cost is matched against her $5,248 Year 1 present-value tax savings, Sara has made a $2,248 Year 1 profit (in present value terms) on a $5K cash investment — a 45% return — *even assuming an economic wash.*

The larger the debt that Sara incurs, the larger the tax benefits that she enjoys! A rational third-party lender, however, would not be willing to lend Sara any more than the $100K FMV of the apartment building when she buys it in Year 1. But if Sara finances the purchase from the *seller* of the building, rather than a third-party bank, *both* parties may be willing to inflate the debt to amounts far in excess of the property's FMV.

To illustrate this point, assume that Cliff has owned an office building for several years as an investment. The building, with a current FMV of $100K, was purchased for $100K, and $90K of depreciation was deducted to produce a current basis of $10K. Cliff sells the building to Reese for $105K cash *plus* Reese's nonrecourse note requiring Reese to pay $1.9M in a lump sum 40 years from the sale date, in addition to annual payments of market-rate interest. The nonrecourse note is secured by a mortgage on the property. As in Sara's case, the building is rented to long-term tenants who will pay at least enough rent to cover the note interest, the building property taxes, and the building maintenance and management costs — all of which are deductible expenses (which means that the includible rental income will produce no net tax liability for Reese).

Reese has just purchased a $100K building for a total price of $2,005,000! Moreover, Reese has even paid $5K more cash on the front end than the building is worth! Is Reese crazy to do this deal? Perhaps not. Under the principles covered in Chapter 20.A, Reese can include the $1.9M debt in his basis to produce a total

---

[17] See Chapter 25.

basis of $2,005,000. If he depreciates the building using the straight-line method over 40 years, this basis will generate depreciation deductions of $50,125 each year. If Reese is in the 35% tax bracket, his depreciation deductions will save him approximately $17,544 in tax each year for 40 years ($50,125 × .35). The present value of this stream of savings is about $233,891, assuming a 7% discount rate. At the end of 40 years, Reese will walk away from the building and from the $1.9M debt, and Cliff will take the building back. Because Reese will have fully depreciated the building, his basis will be zero. His amount realized under *Tufts* will be $1.9M, producing a $1.9M § 1231 gain on which he will pay a tax of $475,000 using the 25% rate for "unrecaptured § 1250 gain." Because this tax will not arise until 40 years in the future, however, the present cost of the tax is only $31,721, assuming a 7% interest rate. Thus, Reese's net tax saving from the transaction is $202,170 ($233,891 present-value tax saving *less* $31,721 present cost). Since Reese paid only $105K out of pocket, he has a net profit of $97,170 (a 92.5% return on his cash investment) purely from gaming the tax system — even though he appears, to the uninitiated, to be a fool who laid out $105K for property worth only $100K! Reese will be quite happy with his deal.[18]

So will Cliff. If, contrary to the deal described above, Cliff had sold the building to Reese for a cash payment equal to the building's $100K FMV, Cliff would have had a $90K gain, yielding a tax (at a 25% rate) of $22.5K, leaving $77.5K in cash for Cliff. But Cliff sold the building for $105K in cash plus a $1.9M note, a total price of $2,005,000, yielding a total gain of $1,995,000. Cliff reports his sale gain under the § 453 "installment method" (Chapter 23.D.2, infra), which allows him to recognize the gain in proportion to the cash received relative to the sale price. Because Cliff received only .052369 of the sale price in cash at the time of sale ($105,000/$2,005,000), he would report only $104,476 of gain at that time ($1,995,000 × .052369). Since he never collects any more cash, he never reports additional sale gain.[19] Most of this gain is taxed (in 2011) at a 15% rate,[20] resulting in a tax of approximately $16,194, leaving Cliff with $88,806 of cash ($105,000 *less* $16,194). *Thus, Cliff is $11,306 better off than if he had simply sold the building for $100K cash* ($88,806 *less* $77,500)! Furthermore, if the building is still commercially viable at the end of the 40-year period, Cliff could do this deal all over again with a new buyer.

But because of the artificial depreciation, interest, and other deductions that can arise from inflated two-party debt, courts have struck down such debts as "shams." The leading case of this type is *Estate of Franklin v. Comm'r*, 544 F.2d 1045 (9th Cir. 1976). There the taxpayers purchased a motel worth no more than $700K for approximately $1.2 million, paying $75K as "prepaid interest" (but nothing as a

---

[18] For that reason, Cliff is likely to insist that Reese pay cash in excess of the $100K FMV of the building. We arbitrarily set the cash payment at $105K to reflect this fact.

[19] Section 1038 applies to Cliff on the repossession of the property, but § 1038(b)(1) causes Cliff to recognize only $524 gain on the repossession. See Chapter 22.A.6. The tax on this amount would be miniscule and, to simplify matters, we have omitted it from the example.

[20] Of the entire $1,995,000 realized gain, $1,905,000 (95% of the total) is attributable to "appreciation" that is subject to a 15% rate, with the remaining $90K (5% of the total) being attributable to depreciation that is taxed (as "unrecaptured § 1250 gain") at a 25% rate. This results in a 15.5% average tax rate on Cliff's recognized gain of $104,476.

down payment) and giving a nonrecourse note to the seller for the entire purchase price. The note provided for monthly payments in an amount only slightly greater than the interest, with a large balloon payment due in 10 years. The taxpayers leased the property back to the sellers; the monthly "rent" due from the sellers equaled the monthly "interest" payments due from the buyers on the note. The deed wasn't recorded. Thus, neither cash nor possession of the property actually changed hands, except for the $75K "prepaid interest." The Ninth Circuit, in *Estate of Franklin*, disallowed the taxpayer's interest deductions and also held that the nonrecourse liability did not create any depreciable basis on the theory that, from the inception, the loan was not "real" because, being so inflated, there was no realistic expectation that it would ever be paid.

Returning to the example of Cliff and Reese, the holding of *Estate of Franklin* would today limit Reese's basis for computing depreciating deductions to the $105,000[21] that he actually invested out-of-pocket, thus reducing his depreciation deductions over the assumed 40-year period to $2,625 per year. In addition, Reese would not get a deduction for interest payments.

2. Limited Partnerships

The three common business entities are "C corporations" taxed under Subchapter C of the Code, "S corporations" taxed under Subchapter S, and "tax partnerships" (including most LLCs) taxed under Subchapter K.[22] The common tax-shelter investments in the 1970s and 1980s marketed to individuals used "tax partnerships" to house the tax shelter. There are good reasons why corporations — particularly the C corporation — made poor tax shelter vehicles for individuals. Most important, a C corporation is a separate taxable entity. Thus, corporate-level deductions — including tax shelter net losses — can be used only by the corporation to offset entity-level gross income and cannot be "passed through" and used by the shareholders on their individual tax returns to offset salary and other investment income. Both S corporations and tax partnerships are better on this count, as these entities generally are *not* treated as taxpayers separate from their owners. Hence, the gross income and deductions of the entity (and thus the net loss arising from a tax shelter) *are* passed through to the entity owners and deducted on their individual tax returns. See §§ 702(a), 704(a) & (b), and 1366(a). For this reason, S corporations and tax partnerships are commonly called "pass-through entities."

It happens that the "outside basis" rules, described below, rule out the S corporation as a viable entity for tax shelters using debt, leaving the "tax partnership" as the vehicle of choice for multiple-owner tax shelters. A shareholder's basis in S corporation stock and a tax partner's equity basis in his or her tax partnership interest is typically referred to in tax jargon as "outside basis."

---

[21] *See Lebowitz v. Comm'r*, 917 F.2d 1314 (2d Cir. 1990); *Odend'hal v. Comm'r*, 748 F.2d 908 (4th Cir. 1984).

[22] Partnerships, general and limited, and limited liability companies (LLCs) are usually treated for federal income tax purposes as partnerships, unless they elect to be treated as corporations under Reg. § 301.7701-3. Thus, we use the term "tax partnership" to refer to any kind of entity that is taxed under the partnership rules.

(The entity's basis in its assets is called "inside basis.") The entity owner's initial outside basis is usually equal to the initial cash purchase price paid by the owner for her interest in the entity. Outside basis is thereafter *increased* by the owner's subsequent contributions to capital *as well as the owner's share of net profits that are passed through to the owner and included on his or her individual tax return.* Similarly, if the business is operating at a loss, outside basis is *decreased by the owner's share of net losses that are passed through to the owner and deducted on his or her individual tax return.* Outside basis is also decreased by any distributions made to the owner by the entity.[23] In short, outside basis is used as a tax accounting tool to keep track of the investor's "after tax" investment in the entity.

The outside basis rules described above serve to protect the tax principle that *deductions must generally be supported by basis (previously taxed dollars)* in order to avoid a double tax benefit for the same dollars. Specifically (and of immense importance), the owner of an interest in a pass-through entity can currently deduct his or her share of entity-level net losses *only* to the extent of outside basis. It follows that, *when outside basis has reached zero, the passed-through losses can no longer be deducted.* See §§ 704(d) and 1366(d)(1).[24] Instead, such losses are held "in suspense," i.e., carried forward, to be used in future taxable years (if any) when and to the extent that the owner's outside basis increases above zero (by reason of a contribution by the owner or the pass through of net profit).

To the rescue of tax partners comes § 752(a), providing that entity-level liabilities are treated as additional cash contributions by the tax partners, which in turn (under § 722) increases their outside bases in the tax partnership interests pro tanto, resulting in an increase in the amount of entity-level losses that can be passed through and deducted by them! This rule is essentially an extension of the *Crane* doctrine to tax partners, who are treated as though they had individually borrowed the money (or incurred the liability) and contributed the cash proceeds (or property) to the tax partnership. Thus, basis in tax partnership interests can be created and increased through the use of borrowed funds without an inclusion in income. Because no such rule exists for S corporations, tax partnerships are the preferred investment vehicle for tax shelters.

To illustrate, assume that Sara and Sam create an equal partnership to purchase an apartment building worth $100K at the beginning of Year 1, with each contributing $2.5K to the partnership in exchange for their 50% partnership interests. The *partnership* borrows the remaining $95K needed to purchase the apartment building from National Bank. Sara and Sam each take an initial outside basis in their partnership interests of $2.5K. But under § 752, the $95K debt incurred by the partnership is treated as though cash were borrowed by the partners and then contributed to the partnership, which increases their outside bases by $47.5K each (to $50K each). Recall that the building produces a net loss of

---

[23] See §§ 705, 722, 733, 1367(a), and 1368(b). Cash distributions must necessarily take a basis equal to the face amount of the cash, necessitating a pro tanto reduction in the investor's remaining outside basis.

[24] Since the loss in excess of outside basis is not deducted currently, the outside basis cannot fall below zero.

$3.6K per year. In Year 1, the partnership's $3.6K net loss is passed through, $1.8K to each partner (and deducted on their individual tax returns), and the outside bases are reduced by $1.8K to $48.2K. The same occurs in Year 2, reducing the outside bases to $46.4K, and so on in succeeding taxable years.

If Sam and Sara had formed an S corporation instead of a tax partnership, Sam and Sara would each take an initial outside basis of $2.5K in his or her S stock, but the outside basis of each would not be increased to reflect the $95K debt incurred by the S corporation. In Year 1, the S corporation's $3.6K net loss is passed through $1.8K to each (and deducted on their individual tax returns), and the outside bases of each is reduced by $1.8K to $700. In Year 2, however, Sam and Sara can deduct only $700 of the $1.8K net loss passed through to each of them, and the outside basis of each shareholder is reduced to zero. The remaining $1.1K loss for each is carried forward by each of them for possible deduction in such future years as their outside bases increase above zero. In Year 3, Sam and Sara can deduct none of the S corporation's net loss; it must be carried forward by them entirely. In sum, the inability to include entity-level debt in the owners' outside bases causes S corporations to be poor tax-shelter vehicles.

3. At-Risk Rules

By the early 1980s, partnership tax shelters were publicly marketed to thousands of individuals. One response enacted by Congress in 1987 was to treat certain publicly traded partnerships as C corporations, which deprived the owners of the ability to deduct the entity's tax-shelter losses on their individual tax returns. See § 7704.

A second response was the enactment in 1976 of § 465, which was strengthened in 1978 and 1986, in an attempt to curb most tax-shelter losses financed by nonrecourse debt. Nonrecourse debt was the lynchpin of these syndicated tax shelters, because it increased the outside basis of limited partners in limited partnerships. Limited partnership interests were readily marketable, because a limited partner is not personally liable for partnership debts. The at-risk rules of § 465 operate to limit the deductibility of net losses attributable to a particular activity (the excess of deductions over income from the activity) to the amount that the taxpayer (i.e., limited partner) has "at risk" in the activity as of the end of that particular year, with any disallowed net loss being carried forward to be set off against future profits and/or future increases in the taxpayer's at-risk amount. In the case of a partner in a tax partnership, the partner's at-risk amount is an account that is separate and independent from the partner's outside basis account.

The mechanics of § 465 are fairly complex, but the general idea is similar to the pass-through-entity rule in that it limits the deductibility of current losses to the at-risk amount (if less than the outside basis amount). The taxpayer's at-risk amount is calculated in a manner similar to the way outside basis is figured in a tax partnership, but (unlike a tax partnership) the at-risk amount generally excludes nonrecourse debt. However, under § 465(b)(6) certain nonrecourse debt representing loans *by third-party commercial lenders* in connection with *real estate activities* (excluding mineral activities) is treated as recourse debt (and therefore increases the at-risk amount).

The existence of § 465 renders it impossible to market nonrecourse debt-financed tax shelters through limited partnerships, except in the case of real estate activities where the nonrecourse debt financing is provided by a third-party commercial lender. In cases not involving nonrecourse debt (as defined for purposes of § 465), the results under § 465 will essentially be identical to (or no worse than) the results obtainable under the tax partnership rules. For the forgoing reasons we think that examining the § 465 rules in detail is not worthwhile in a basic income tax course.

D. SECTION 469 AND PASSIVE LOSSES

The *coup de grâce* to common abusive tax shelters marketed to individuals was administered by the 1986 enactment of the § 469 "passive activity" rules (one of the worst oxymorons to be found in the Code). The general structure of § 469 is similar to that of §§ 465 and 163(d): net losses arising from certain activities are not allowed to shelter income from other sources, such as salary. While § 465 is aimed at taxpayers who do not have a sufficient amount *at risk* in the activity, § 469 is aimed at taxpayers who do not *materially participate* in the activity, i.e., who are passive investors.

A road map through the alleyways of § 469 is helpful. Section 469(a)(1) disallows deduction of the taxpayer's "passive activity loss,"[25] which is defined by § 469(d)(1) as the excess of the taxpayer's aggregate losses from "passive activities" over the taxpayer's aggregate income from such activities for the year. Since "passive activity loss" is an aggregate concept for a given year, it follows that net losses from some passive activities can offset net profits from other passive activities. (In contrast, § 465 operates strictly on a per-activity basis.)

A "passive activity" is defined in § 469(c) and (h) as any business or investment activity in which the taxpayer does not "materially participate." Under § 469(h)(1), participation must be "regular, continuous, and substantial" to be considered "material." In the case of a real estate professional holding rental property, there is a special material-participation exception in § 469(c)(7). *All rental activities not engaged in by real estate professionals* are per se passive activities, while certain working interests in oil and gas properties are per se not passive activities, in both cases without regard to the presence or absence of material participation. See § 469(c). Thus, third-party nonrecourse-debt rental real estate activities that escape the jaws of § 465 end up in the maw of § 469, unless the taxpayer is a "real estate professional." Except for narrow exceptions in the regulations, no limited partner interest in a limited partnership can qualify under the "material participation" test. See § 469(h)(2).

Section 469(e)(1) provides that "portfolio investments" (i.e., investments that yield interest, dividends, annuities, or certain royalties) are *not* treated as passive activities, even though owning stocks and bonds seems to be an essentially "passive" activity in the colloquial sense. The purpose of this rule is to prevent the affluent

---

[25] Section 469(a)(1) also disallows "passive activity credits" for the year.

from using their tax-shelter net losses to offset net income from their portfolio investments.

An exception to the disallowance rule is provided by § 469(i), which allows deduction of up to $25K of otherwise-disallowed net losses from passive rental real estate activities, if the taxpayer "actively participated" in the activity (an easier standard to meet than the "materially participated" standard). The $25K allowance is phased out as the taxpayer's AGI rises from $100K to $150K. This provision is aimed at the small investor who owns a rental unit or two.

Disallowed passive activity net losses for the year are carried forward to the next year under § 469(b), to be deducted against net passive activity profit for the year (if any), and so on, indefinitely.

When a passive activity is disposed of, the cumulative undeducted net passive activity loss *of that particular activity* is allowed by § 469(g) to be deducted (without limitation) in the year the activity is completely disposed of.[26]

Loss-deduction limitations imposed by the partnership tax rules (limiting such deductions to the taxpayer's "outside basis") and by the at-risk rules (limiting such deductions to the taxpayer's "amount at risk") apply *before* § 469. That is, losses disallowed (and suspended) elsewhere do not enter into the § 469 computations.[27]

It is time for another example. Assume that Dr. Krank earns $300K from his medical practice in the current year, $10K in taxable interest, and $20K in dividends. Krank purchases a limited partnership interest in a partnership that produces exercise videos, but he has no other § 469 passive investments. Krank's share of the net loss from the partnership for the current year is $40K (*after* possible application of partnership tax rules and § 465). Under § 469, *none* of that net loss is deductible in the current year against either his medical practice income or his portfolio interest and dividend income. Krank can carry the loss forward to future years in which the partnership becomes profitable, he earns a net profit from another passive activity to absorb it, or he disposes of his limited partnership interest.

In sum, § 469, like §§ 465 and 163(d), is a *timing* rule; it is not intended to disallow business and investment losses entirely. Many tax shelters, though they produce early net losses because of front-loaded depreciation and interest deductions, would produce positive economic and tax income if held throughout their lifetimes. For example, most shelters (including Sara and Sam's apartment building) would produce *Tufts* gain on disposition or abandonment of the activity. By delaying deductions of net losses from passive activities until sufficient passive income is earned or until the activity is disposed of, § 469 chiefly prevents the deduction of losses that do not represent *current economic* losses. Only upon

---

[26] This rule necessitates keeping track of disallowed passive activity losses on a per-activity basis, which in turn would require a rule for allocating passive activity net profits (both overall and from a particular activity) among "loss" activities. This problem (which probably does not arise often) is supposed to be dealt with by regulations issued under § 469(j)(4), which suggests that such profits are to be allocated among loss activities in proportion to the amount of passive activity losses in such activities.

[27] See Reg. § 1.469-2T(d)(6).

disposition, when built-in gain or loss is realized, can such a *final* economic reckoning be made.

NOTES

1.   (a) Losses disallowed under §§ 163(d) (discussed in Chapter 18.D.3), 465, and 469, as well as capital losses deferred under § 1211, are separately carried forward. "Investment interest" subject to § 163(d) is defined so as to be exclusive of "passive activity interest" subject to § 469.

(b) Loss carryovers generally expire at the taxpayer's death, and do not pass to the taxpayer's estate or other successors in interest. However, unused passive activity losses are (apparently) allowed on the decedent's final income tax return to the extent they exceed the § 1014 basis step-up with respect to the activity.

2.   Other Code provisions single out "tax shelters" (as variously defined) for special treatment:

(a) A "tax shelter" cannot use the cash method of accounting. See § 448(a)(3), (d)(3).

(b) "Farming syndicates" cannot deduct the cost of certain items prior to actual use thereof, see § 464, and must match net losses with gross income (resulting in deferral of the net losses) for Alternative Minimum Tax (AMT) purposes. See § 58(a).

(c) All tax shelters (as defined under intricate regulations) must be registered with the IRS, and any "potentially abusive tax shelter" must keep lists of investors. See §§ 6111, 6112. Penalties are imposed for failure to comply. See §§ 6707, 6708.

(d) The IRS also attempts to combat tax shelters by publicly announcing that certain tax shelters that have come to its attention do not "work" as hoped and that the agency will contest them. See, e.g., *Rev. Rul. 2002-69*, 2002-2 C.B. 260 (dealing with lease-in, lease-out — or LILO — transactions); *Notice 2000-44*, 2000-2 C.B. 20 (dealing with so-called Son of BOSS shelters); *Notice 2002-70*, 2002-2 C.B. 765 (dealing with so-called PORCs); 2003-2 C.B. 1181, Notice 2003-76 (containing "listed transactions" that must be disclosed under § 6011).

PROBLEM

Gilligan, a trial attorney, is involved with each of the following investments during the years in question. Assume that Gilligan's AGI (disregarding the following) is $120K, that the activities described below survive a § 183 inquiry, and that neither Gilligan nor his spouse is a real estate professional as defined in § 469(c)(7)(B). What are the tax consequences in each of the following situations?

(a) Last year (Year 1), Gilligan purchased a rental duplex for $200K, using $20K of his own money and $180K borrowed on a nonrecourse basis from a commercial bank, with 10% interest payable annually. In Year 1, Gilligan paid interest expense of $10K and made a principal payment of $2.5K on the debt. He received net rents of $5K. Depreciation for tax purposes was $7K.

(b) In the current year (Year 2), Gilligan pays interest expense of $18K and makes a principal payment of $3K. He receives net rents of $6K. Depreciation for tax purposes is $6K.

REALIZATION AND RECOGNITION

This Part Seven deals with timing issues under the income tax, most of which can be subsumed under the rubric of "realization," which has to do with *when* gross income, expense deductions, gains, and losses are deemed to exist under the income tax. The related concept of "recognition" deals with the issue of when a realized item is actually taken into account under the income tax system.

Chapter 22 deals with the realization and recognition of gross income, gains, and losses, and it does so mostly in connection with the receipt of, or exchanges of, in-kind property. A principal focus is on in-kind compensation devices involving stock and options to buy stock. Chapter 23 deals with what are traditionally referred to as the "tax accounting" rules (cash method and accrual method) relating to credit sales (and purchases) of services and inventory, as well as the accounting rules for deferred payment sales of property (including the installment method). This chapter includes material on the cash-method doctrines of cash equivalency, constructive receipt, and the economic-benefit doctrine. Chapter 24 deals with gains and losses arising from casualties and other involuntary conversions. Chapter 25 discusses "character" aspects of recognized gains and losses.

Chapter 22

REALIZATION OF GROSS INCOME

Chapter 2 introduced the "realization" principle as applied to a property owner's gains and losses. Under that principle, value changes are ignored and gain or loss with respect to property is not "realized" until there is a sale, exchange, or other disposition. Thus, in the gain and loss context, the realization principle operates as a timing rule, deferring the taxation of gain or loss on property until a realization event occurs. This chapter moves beyond the basic idea of realization as it applies to sales of property to issues involving the receipt of in-kind property as gross income or as "amount realized" in an exchange.

A. NONMARKET TRANSACTIONS

Although a *complete* disposition of property is clearly a realization event, other generalizations about "realization" are hazardous. Nevertheless, the following proposition can be advanced as a hypothesis: nonmarket transactions *generally* do not give rise to income, gain, or loss.

1. Obtaining the Bounty of Nature

This topic was already alluded to in Chapter 14.E, but the realization "angle" is worth going over again at this point. Recall that obtaining the bounty of nature (through agriculture, husbandry, mining, fishing, etc.) is not gross income, despite being an increase in the taxpayer's wealth, because of nonrealization. A possible explanation for nonrealization is that these increases in wealth were not obtained in a market transaction, and therefore are beyond the capacity of the tax system to monitor. Also, to the extent that these activities are profit-seeking, income, gain, or loss will eventually be realized. To the extent that these activities are not profit-seeking, they occur in the private sphere that is perhaps off-limits to government.

A scenario that is somewhat similar to the foregoing is that of free samples received anonymously. The *Haverly* case on free samples, Chapter 13.C.2, may be "read" as a realization case holding that free samples are not income until converted to cash or claimed as a deduction. Similar considerations apply to the finding of objects (other than cash or its near equivalent) abandoned by other humans, but here deferral until subsequent realization is a more controversial proposition. In any event, free samples and found objects are distinguishable from activities involving obtaining the bounty of nature, because the latter activities involve some kind of investment on the part of the taxpayer, so that the "harvesting gain" (the excess, if any, of the value of what is harvested over the cost of obtaining the harvest) can be analogized to unrealized appreciation with respect to a particular item of investment property.

2.   Changes in Value Brought about by External Events

An identifiable increase or decrease in the value of an asset brought about by an external event is not considered to be a realization event. Examples of such events include the government building a major highway next to the property, or the taxpayer herself making improvements. The same principle works for losses.[1] These situations simply involve conspicuous and sudden unrealized appreciation or depreciation.

To be distinguished from the foregoing are cases involving deductions for a "partial" loss, in which it can be said that there has been a disposition of a physical portion of the property itself.[2]

3.   Subdividing Property

A property owner does not recognize gain or loss when she subdivides her existing property into smaller units or parcels, even if this action is a matter of public record, and even if the act of subdividing is itself expected to enhance the aggregate value of the property. Here there is no sale or exchange, both of which presuppose another party to the transaction, nor is there a "disposition."

The sale of lots resulting from a subdivision posits the issue of ascertaining the basis of the lots that are sold. The basis for each lot is its appropriate portion of the *original* cost basis for the entire original tract (its initial purchase price), plus the cost of any capital expenditures made with respect to that particular lot. The lot's allocation of the original cost basis for the entire tract would be figured by looking to that lot's FMV back *at the time of the original tract purchase*. This approach might be difficult to apply, however, because the purchase price for the undivided tract would not, at the time of purchase, have typically been broken down into components corresponding to the future subdivided lots. In other words, the allocable cost of a given lot has to be determined retroactively. If, at the time the lots are disposed of, their values at the time of acquisition cannot reasonably be determined, but the lots are relatively fungible, the basis of each lot may reasonably be said to equal a pro rata portion (by relative acreage) of the basis in the whole.

4.   The Ripening of Existing Rights and Interests

Suppose Granny creates a trust in Year 1, with the income to be distributed to Beth for life, and on Beth's death the trust is to terminate and its assets are to be paid over to Chuck if Chuck is living at Beth's death, but if Chuck is not then living, the assets are to be paid over to Dick. In this case, Chuck and Dick initially acquire alternate contingent remainder interests. Chuck's remainder interest is contingent

---

[1] See, e.g., *Pulvers v. Comm'r*, 407 F.2d 838 (9th Cir. 1969) (landslide on adjacent land is not realized loss on taxpayer's land, which declined in value); Henley v. U.S., 396 F.2d 956 (Ct. Cl. 1968) (same).

[2] In *Selig v. Comm'r*, T.C. Memo. 1967-253, no loss was allowed when development plans for agricultural land were abandoned due to a change in the law. In *Cox v. U.S.*, 537 F.2d 1066 (9th Cir. 1976), a partial loss deduction was allowed for the physical destruction (by a salt water intrusion) of an oil deposit under land that was still good for other uses.

on Chuck outliving Beth, and Dick's remainder interest is contingent on Chuck predeceasing Beth. In Year 12, Chuck dies while Beth is still alive, causing Dick's interest to "vest," i.e., to become noncontingent. Vesting causes the value of Dick's interest to suddenly increase in value by a significant amount.

In Year 20, Beth dies and Dick acquires all of the then trust assets (both in-kind and in cash). In the jargon of trust law, Dick's vested remainder interest is said to "come into possession."

The issue on the table is whether Dick is deemed to realize income, gain, or loss either upon the vesting of the interest (at Chuck's death) or at the time the interest comes into possession (at Beth's death). The IRS has never asserted that either occurrence is a realization event. There is no sale, exchange, or disposition at either time.[3] Instead, the existing interest of Dick merely changes form ("ripens") according to its inherent nature. The same results occur if Dick has a nontrust remainder interest in specific property.

Although the complete failure, lapse, or termination of an interest in trust or property would appear to entail a realized loss, a loss deduction is only possible in the rare case where the interest was purchased. Virtually all such interests are acquired by gratuitous transfer, and Congress has made the policy decision that interests acquired by gratuitous transfer should be dealt with rules that (mostly) render the concept of basis irrelevant in this scenario. At the level of intuition, it would be hard to justify an income tax deduction for failing to obtain gratuitous receipts. A technical explanation for the irrelevancy of basis in this context is found in Chapter 29.B.

5.   The Exercise of Options and Conversion Privileges

If a person paid $1K in an arm's length transaction for a call option (i.e., option to purchase) that is subsequently exercised to purchase property currently worth $13K at a price of $10K, it is plausible (if somewhat of a stretch) to view the exercise as an "exchange" of the option (plus $10K cash) for the property. Viewing the exercise of the option in this fashion would produce gain of $2K for the purchaser ($13K FMV of property received *less* cash paid of $10K *less* $1K basis in the option). However, the tax law has generally not treated the exercise of an option as entailing an "exchange" of the option for the property purchased on exercise. Instead, option exercises are generally treated as nonrealization events. Thus, the taxpayer described above would not realize any gain on the option exercise and would take a basis of $11K in the property obtained on the exercise ($1K original option price *plus* $10K exercise price). As with obtaining the bounty of nature (having a value greater than the cost of obtaining it), the obtaining (by the exercise of an option) of property having a value in excess of the investment

---

[3] In Dick's case, the termination of the trust on Beth's death entails a "distribution" of all of the trust assets to Dick. This distribution is taxable to Dick only to the extent of the trust's distributable net income (DNI) for the taxable year of the terminating trust. Thus, this distribution will be mostly tax-free to Dick. (To treat the distribution as an "amount realized" in a sale or exchange by Dick of his remainder interest would also happen to undermine the § 102(a) exclusion for gratuitous receipts.) The bases of the trust assets to the trust generally carry over to Dick. See § 643(e). See Chapter 17.E for a discussion of the income taxation of trusts.

therein is not a realization event, because the "instant gain" is viewed as a form of unrealized appreciation. (However, if an option is used as a device to disguise an intended wealth transfer, as occurs with "compensation" stock options, explored in Section D, different rules come into play.)

The option-exercise scenario is different than the "vesting" or "coming into possession" scenarios, supra, only in that the exercise of an option involves some action on the part of the taxpayer, whereas the taxpayer is passive in the gratuitous receipt scenarios. Nevertheless, in all these situations, the property ultimately acquired was inherent (or latent) in the remainder interest or option that the taxpayer initially acquired.

A somewhat more plausible case for "exchange" treatment can be illustrated by the situation where Brock purchases "convertible debentures" issued by X Corp. for $10K. The conversion feature allows Brock to convert the debentures into 100 shares of X Corp. preferred stock. Assume that Brock exercises this conversion right when the preferred stock has a value of $120 per share, so that the 100 shares received have a total value of $12K. Does Brock realize gain here of $2K pursuant to an "exchange?" The IRS has ruled that there is no "realization" in this scenario, although no rationale was given.[4] Perhaps a "conversion right" into other property is not materially different from an option. Both scenarios can be said to involve unrealized appreciation with respect to the property (or right) obtained by the taxpayer's initial investment.

In both the option and conversion-right scenario, another party is involved in the transaction, but the other party is passive and has no power to prevent, modify, or renegotiate the transaction.

The option and conversion-right rules are fairly narrow, and cover only property-to-property transactions. If a shareholder of a corporation has the right to "put" her stock to the corporation for a price, or the corporation has the right to "call" the shareholder's stock for a price, the exercise of such rights is a realization event, even if the corporation distributes property (rather than cash) to the shareholder in exchange for the latter's stock. These types of transactions in interests in entities are studied in courses in corporate and partnership tax.

6. Repossessing Sold Property

Suppose Saul sells Blackacre worth $1M (in which Saul's basis is $200K) to Betty, who pays $100K down and promises to pay $900K in the future (with market-rate interest). Saul "has" $800K gain on the sale. Under rules discussed in Chapter 23.D, Saul might have been taxed on all or a part of this gain in the year of sale (Year 1). If Betty fails to pay the remaining $900K on time, Saul may legally repossess the property. One might call this a "ripening" of a pre-existing security interest retained by Saul, the seller. Or maybe this right can be analogized to an option or conversion right. However, a security interest is not viewed as a "reversionary interest" in property (such as is held by a lessor of property). In any

---

[4] See *Rev. Rul. 72-265*, 1972-1 C.B. 222. The ruling essentially held that a regulation so holding issued under the 1918 Revenue Act continued to be in effect, even though that regulation was never re-issued under the 1921 Act and subsequent revenue acts and codifications.

event, Saul began with Blackacre, sold that in return for cash and an asset (Betty's deferred-payment obligation), and ends up back with Blackacre instead of the deferred-payment obligation.[5]

The deferred-payment obligation (the note) should have a basis equal to Saul's after-tax investment in the note. That amount, in turn, depends upon how much gain Saul has already been taxed on. If the sale of Blackacre produced gain of $800K under § 1001 that was fully taxed, then Saul would have a basis of $900K in Betty's note ($200K cost basis in Blackacre *plus* $900K gain recognized *minus* $100K cash received). (Thus, the collection of the $900K on the note from Betty would produce no further gain or loss.) But let's assume that Saul properly was taxed on gain of only $80K in Year 1, according to the installment method provided by § 453(c). (The $80K is 10% of the total $800K gain, based on the fact that Saul received 10% of the consideration in cash in the year of sale.) In that case Saul's basis in Betty's note would be $180K ($200K cost basis in Blackacre + $80K taxed gain − $100K cash received). This result is logical, because Saul used up $20K of his $200K basis in Blackacre as an offset against the $100K cash received in the year of sale in order to produce the $80K of taxable gain.

Two possible ways exist to conceptualize the repossession. One is to treat Blackacre as being received by Saul in an "exchange" for giving up Betty's note, because the repossession involves two persons and two distinct items of property. Here, the gain or loss would depend upon the fair market value (FMV) of Blackacre at the time of repossession. If the property continues to be worth $1M,[6] the realized gain on the exchange would be $820K ($1M FMV of property received *less* Saul's $180K basis in the obligation). Although Saul will have had aggregate gain of $900K ($820K + $80K) over the life of this investment (instead of $800K gain realized on the initial sale of Blackacre), keep in mind that Saul has received a total of $1.1M ($100K cash + $1M Blackacre FMV).

The second way is to view the transaction as a "ripening" of Saul's security interest, analogous to a coming into possession of a reversionary interest, or (in contract-law terms) as analogous to a rescission. Either way, the repossession would not be a realization event. Nevertheless, Saul would have to take into account the fact that he has $100K cash "in pocket" (that he can keep), the receipt of which caused Saul to be taxed on only $80K of gain.[7] The conventional way of wholly implementing a reversion (or rescission) approach would be to treat Saul as having no further gain or loss upon the repossession, but having a basis in Blackacre of $180K (the same basis as Saul would have had in Betty's note). This approach would treat the $20K nontaxed cash received ($100K cash - $80K gain taxed by reason of receiving the cash) as a basis reduction.

---

[5] If the debt is nonrecourse, the foreclosure essentially satisfies the obligation in full. If the obligation is recourse the value (or proceeds from the sale of) the collateral will be applied towards satisfaction of the debt. Even if the debt is not satisfied in full, the sale or exchange issue would still exist to the extent of the discharged portion of the obligation.

[6] If it were worth more than $1M, state mortgage law might require Saul to return the excess value to Betty.

[7] In *Rev. Rul. 80-58*, 1980-1 C.B. 11, the IRS ruled that the prior recognized gain could not be "erased" unless the rescission occurred in the same year as the sale.

Prior law had followed the exchange approach but it was replaced by the 1964 enactment of § 1038, which adopts a variation of the reversion approach, the only difference being that the excess cash of $20K (so far not taxed) is treated as (additional) taxable gain upon the repossession, instead of as a basis reduction.[8] Thus, the basis of Saul in Blackacre should (and does) end up at $200K (rather than $180K). Saul's $200K basis in Blackacre consists of the $180K original basis in Blackacre that has so far not been used up, plus the $20K gain recognized under § 1038.

Section 1038(a) accomplishes these results by first setting forth a general rule that no gain or loss is realized to the seller on a repossession, but § 1038(b) goes on to provide that gain shall be recognized in an amount equal to the *lesser* of (a) the gain on the original sale not yet recognized (less any costs of repossession, which we deem to be zero in order to simplify matters) *or* (b) the excess (if any) of money (and other property) already received (other than amounts received as interest and the buyer's obligation itself) over the gain previously reported. The amount described in (a) has the effect of limiting the repossession gain to the amount of unrecognized gain on the original sale. The amount described in (b) is none other than the untaxed consideration already received. Plugging Saul's numbers into the formula, his yet-to-be recognized gain is $720K ($800K sale gain *less* $80K gain already recognized), and the excess of (cash) payments received ($100K) over reported gain ($80K) is $20K. The lesser amount ($20K) prevails.

Section 1038(c) provides that Saul's new basis in Blackacre is equal to his basis in the unpaid installment obligation increased by any gain recognized under § 1038 (and any costs of repossession). Accordingly, Saul's basis is $200K ($180K basis in the installment obligation *plus* $20K of § 1038 gain). This is the sum of the previously taxed dollars still "in" Blackacre ($200K original basis *plus* $80K of included sale gain *plus* $20K of included § 1038 gain *less* $100K cash).

Section 1038 applies only to repossessions of real property. Repossessions of personal property (for failure to pay an installment obligation) are governed by § 453B(a), which treats the transaction as a taxable disposition of the installment obligation in exchange for the property at its FMV.[9]

NOTES

1. A conversion of bonds to stock of the *same* corporation pursuant to a conversion privilege (which requires action on the taxpayer's part) is not quite the same as the ripening (vesting, coming into possession) of a future interest, which occurs passively. A conversion also involves the (passive) involvement of another party. Thus, conversions are a kind of "exchange" transaction, but not one that takes

---

[8] See S. Rep. No. 1361, 88th Cong., 2d Sess. 11-14 (1964), 1964-2 C.B. 828, 835.

[9] The repossession of personal property will satisfy all or a portion of the liability. See U.C.C. §§ 9-504 and 9-505. In most cases, the creditor will either have purchased the obligation for its value from the seller (and have a cost basis) or itself be the seller of the goods (say, a car dealer) on the accrual method of accounting (and have a basis equal to the face amount of the installment obligation), in both cases reduced by principal payments received. In such a case, the repossession will result in a relatively small (ordinary) gain or loss.

place in the market. Nevertheless, the IRS treats conversions of bonds to stock of the same corporation (entailing a move from greater to lesser liquidity with respect to corporate assets) as nonexchanges, precluding realization of gain or loss. (A conversion from stock to bonds in the same corporation is a move in the other direction, because a bond is a right to cash, and therefore such a conversion amounts to a sale.)

2.   In *Rev. Rul. 69-135*, 1969-1 C.B. 198, the IRS ruled that the conversion of a bond into stock of a *different* corporation, pursuant to the exercise of a conversion right, was a taxable exchange.

PROBLEMS

1.   Assume that Erin owns Blackacre, a 100-acre tract of undeveloped land that she bought for $10K more than 20 years ago. The land is now worth $100K and she holds it primarily for sale to customers in the ordinary course of her real estate development business. Blackacre has a beautiful running creek flowing through one corner of the property, but the opposite corner is treeless and close to a noisy rock quarry. Erin subdivides Blackacre into 20 residential building lots and records a plat reflecting this action. The act of subdivision causes the lots in the aggregate to be worth $180K.

(a) Is Erin's act of subdividing the real property a realization event? Should the result hinge on whether the subdivision itself enhances the value of the total property?

(b) How does Erin determine the basis of the lots to be sold?

2.   Suppose that Daisy creates a trust in Year 1 with $100K, income to Abner for 25 years, remainder to Sylvia if Sylvia is living at the end of 25 years, but if Sylvia is not then living, reversion to Daisy.

(a) In Year 11, Sylvia dies, meaning that the property will definitely revert to Daisy (or her successors in interest). Does Daisy realize any gross income at this point?

(b) In Year 17, Daisy's partner Flora contributes $40K to this trust. Does Daisy realize gross income as a result of this transfer either in Year 17 or in Year 25, when the trust terminates and its assets are distributed to Daisy?

3.   Suppose Saul sells Blackacre worth $1M (in which Saul's basis is $200K) to Betty, who pays $100K down and promises to pay $900K in the future (with market-rate interest). Assume that Saul properly reports $800K gain on the sale under § 1001 in the year of sale. Subsequently, Betty defaults, and the property is then worth $1.3M. What are the tax results of the repossession to Saul? (And, by way of review, what are the tax results to Betty?)

B.   WHEN DOES A TAXABLE EXCHANGE OCCUR?

This section is a virtual continuation of the previous section. The basic doctrinal point continues to be that a transaction that merely changes (from within) the form of a taxpayer's existing asset is *generally* not considered a realization event, even if the transaction involves another party. As was the case with repossessions, supra, transactions of this sort can sometimes come close to being "exchanges" of one asset for another, which *are* acknowledged realization events under § 1001.

1. Stock Dividends and Stock Splits

Eisner v. Macomber, 252 U.S. 189 (1920), which has been mentioned before, is perhaps the first major realization-of-income case. In *Macomber*, a corporation distributed additional shares of its own common stock, pro rata, to its existing common shareholders.[10] Thus, the dividend did not change the proportions in which the corporation's common stock was owned. For example, a common shareholder who owned 5% of the corporation's common stock before the stock dividend continued to own 5% after the dividend, even though the number of her shares increased in "absolute" terms. Accordingly, the receipt of the pro-rata stock dividend in *Macomber* was analogous to merely subdividing the shareholders' existing proportionate stock interests into smaller, more numerous pieces (on the initiative of the corporation) without changing the proportionate size of each shareholder's aggregate interest. Ms. Macomber, in other words, merely had more pieces of paper representing her same slice of the corporate pie. The Court stated (252 U.S. at 194-96):

> The essential and controlling fact is that the stockholder has received nothing out of the company's assets for his separate use and benefit; on the contrary, every dollar of his original investment, together with whatever accretions and accumulations have resulted from employment of his money and that of the other stockholders in the business of the company, still remains the property of the company, and subject to business risks which may result in wiping out the entire investment. Having regard to the very truth of the matter, to substance and not to form, he has received nothing that answers the definition of income.

> It is said that a stockholder may sell the new shares acquired in the stock dividend and so he may, if he can find a buyer. It is equally true that if he does sell, and in doing so realizes a profit, such profit, like any other, is income. The same would be true were he to sell some of his original shares at a profit. But if a shareholder sells dividend stock he necessarily disposes of a part of his capital interest, just as if he should sell a part of his old stock, either before or after the dividend. What he retains no longer entitles him to the same proportion of future dividends as before the sale.

> It is said there is no difference in principle between a simple stock dividend and a case where stockholders use money received as cash dividends to purchase additional stock contemporaneously issued by the corporation. But an actual cash dividend, with a real option to the stockholder either to keep the money for his own or to reinvest it in new

---

[10] The media often uses the term "stock dividend" to refer to a cash dividend. This usage is incorrect because *all* dividends pertain to corporate stock. Correctly used, the term "stock dividend" means a dividend in the form of the corporation's own stock, as opposed to a cash dividend or an in-kind dividend other than in the form of the corporation's own stock.

shares, would be as far removed as possible from a true stock dividend, such as the one we have under consideration, where nothing of value is taken from the company's assets and transferred to the individual owner-ship of the several stockholders and thereby subjected to their disposal.

In *Macomber*, Congress had actually enacted a statutory provision expressly taxing stock dividends. The Supreme Court in *Macomber* held that such enactment was unconstitutional because pro-rata stock dividends were not "income" under the 16th Amendment. This specific holding of *Macomber* is obsolete for three reasons. First, an "income tax" provision can be constitutionally valid as a nonapportioned "indirect tax," even if the item taxed is not "income." (But arguably the tax in *Macomber* was a tax on a percentage of the value of Ms. Macomber's stock, and, therefore, a property, i.e., "direct," tax.) Second, the 1940 case of *Helvering v. Bruun*, set forth in the next section, substantially broadened the notion of realized income to include accretions to the "tree" under some circumstances. Third, the "realization" principle probably no longer has any *constitutional* status.[11]

Nevertheless, Congress has repealed the statutory provision involved in *Macomber*, and the current rules, found in § 305 (examined in a corporate tax course), follow *Macomber* in providing that pro-rata stock dividends are not gross income but that non-pro-rata stock dividends are. Moreover, *Macomber* follows the "subdivision" rule of nonrealization, and *Glenshaw Glass* (supra Chapter 14) acknowledged that "realization" continues to be a prerequisite for catch-all gross income.

A "stock split" is very close to a stock dividend, but it actually takes the form of an "exchange." A typical stock split involves the issuance of (say) two "new" shares for each "old" share, the old shares being returned to the corporation and cancelled. Section 1001 expressly treats exchanges of property as realization events. However, section 1036 states that a shareholder does not "recognize" gain or loss in a stock-split type of exchange, provided that the stock received (of the same corporation) is of the same general type (common or preferred) as the stock given up. The theory of § 1036 is that this type of transaction, although an exchange in form, in substance is a mere subdivision of existing property.

If a stock dividend or a stock split does not give rise to realized or recognized income, gain, or loss, the taxpayer's basis in her aggregate investment remains the same. The taxpayer's old basis is reallocated among the increased number of shares now evidencing her investment.[12]

---

[11] See *Cottage Savings Ass'n v. Comm'r*, excerpted in Subsection 3 below.

[12] For example, in the case of certain pro-rata stock dividends, the old basis is allocated between the old shares and the new dividend shares based on the relative FMV of each block. See § 307. To illustrate, suppose that Sue's block of common stock has a basis of $60 and a FMV of $100 when she receives an excludible stock dividend of common shares with an aggregate value of $25 (thus reducing the value of her old common to $75). Since the new shares are worth 1/4 of the total value of what Sue now owns, she assigns 1/4 of her old basis ($15) to them, and the remaining 3/4 of her old basis ($45) is assigned to the old shares.

2. Modification of Debt Instruments

Suppose a party lends cash in return for the borrower's debt instrument (a promissory note or a debenture if the borrower is a corporation). Later, the loan is renegotiated and this lender receives from the borrower a new debt instrument, with significantly different terms, in exchange for the original instrument. Such a transaction would clearly constitute an "exchange" that produces realized gain or loss to the lender to the extent of the difference between the fair market value of the *new* instrument and the lender's basis in the *old* instrument. See *Rev. Rul. 77-415*, 1977-2 C.B. 311.

But suppose that, instead of receiving a new instrument in exchange for the old one, the lender and borrower merely negotiate *modifications* to the terms of the old instrument, so that the old instrument is transformed into a substantially different obligation. Is this situation a *constructive* exchange of the original debt instrument for a new one, despite the absence of an exchange in form? That is the issue dealt with by Reg. § 1.1001-3, promulgated in 1996. That regulation treats any "significant modification" of an outstanding debt instrument, with or without an actual substitution of a new instrument for the original one, as a constructive "disposition" of the old instrument "in exchange" for a new one containing the modified terms.

An alteration of the terms of a debt instrument is generally not considered a "modification" if it occurs (1) by the operation of an automatically triggered mechanism contained in the instrument's original terms (such as the periodic resetting of the interest rate based on changes in the prime rate) or (2) pursuant to the unilateral exercise of a right conferred by the instrument's original terms (such as the debtor's exercise of a right to convert the instrument from a variable interest rate to a fixed rate). These exceptions echo the nonrealization rules for future interests and conversion rights, respectively. Nor does a modification occur simply because the debtor temporarily fails to perform. An example would be the making of a late payment. In all other cases, however, any change in the terms of a debt instrument is a "modification."

But a modification does not result in an *exchange* under the regulations unless it is economically "significant." The regulations provide numerous rules and examples that deal with particular situations. A substitution of collateral securing a recourse note or the assumption of a debt by a purchaser of property would not be deemed "significant." Other modifications, including significant changes in the interest rate, significant extensions of the maturity date, reductions in stated principal, changes in the identity of the obligor of a recourse note, and any other change that has the effect of materially altering the annual yield, are treated as "significant" modifications.[13]

The amount realized on an exchange is normally the FMV of the property received (here, the modified debt instrument), but the actual FMV would be hard to determine unless the modified debt instrument were offered for sale. A special

---

[13] Reg. § 1.1001-4, issued in 1998, adopts a "no exchange" posture for certain modifications relating to "notional principal contracts," such as commodity or interest rate swaps, which are not generally addressed in this book.

rule exists in this case under Reg. § 1.1001-1(g), also issued in 1996: the amount realized is the FMV of the obligation only if the obligation is publicly traded; otherwise the FMV is deemed to be equal to the discounted present value of the obligation.[14]

3.   Exchanges of Virtually Identical Properties

If a change or ripening of an item of property into a different form is not a realization event (i.e., not an "exchange"), then perhaps a "nominal" exchange of properties that are identical or virtually identical is not an exchange *in substance*. Although § 1001(a) literally states that a "sale or other disposition of property" causes gain or loss to be regarded as realized, Reg. § 1.1001-1(a) elaborates on § 1001(a) by stating:

> [e]xcept as otherwise provided . . . , the gain or loss realized from . . . the exchange of property for other property *differing materially either in kind or in extent*, is treated as income or as loss sustained "[i.e., realized]." (Emphasis added.)

This language seems to leave open the possibility that an exchange of identical (or nearly identical) properties is *not* a "disposition" that would constitute a realization event.

The government raised this very issue in *Cottage Savings Ass'n v. Comm'r*, 499 U.S. 554 (1991). In that case, the taxpayer, a savings and loan association, exchanged its interests in one group of residential mortgage loans that had lost significant value for another lender's interests in a different group of residential mortgage loans that also had depreciated in value. The taxpayer sought to deduct the loss that it contended was realized on the exchange of the mortgage portfolios. All of the loans were secured by single-family homes, most of which were in the same geographical area. Under financial accounting rules adopted by the relevant federal regulatory body, the interests received by the taxpayer were deemed "substantially identical" to the interests transferred, and, thus, the exchange did not produce a loss for financial accounting purposes. The government argued that, because the exchanged interests were "essentially economic substitutes," they were not "materially different" within the meaning of Reg. § 1.1001-1, quoted above, so that the exchanges were not realization events. The Supreme Court disagreed, stating:

> Precisely what constitutes a "material difference" for purposes of § 1001(a) is a complicated question. The Commissioner argues that properties are "materially different" only if they differ in economic substance. To determine whether the participation interests exchanged in this case were "materially different" in this sense, the Commissioner argues, we should look to the attitudes of the parties, the evaluation of the interests by the secondary mortgage market, and the views of the Federal Home Loan Bank Board. We conclude that § 1001(a) embodies a much less demanding and less complex test. Unlike the question whether § 1001(a) contains a

---

[14] The present value is determined pursuant to § 483.

material difference requirement, the question of what constitutes a material difference is not one on which we can defer to the Commissioner. For the Commissioner has not issued an authoritative, prelitigation interpretation of what property exchanges satisfy this requirement. Thus, to give meaning to the material difference test, we must look to the case law from which the test derives and which we believe Congress intended to codify in enacting and reenacting the language that now comprises § 1001(a).

[The relevant cases[15]] stand for the principle that properties are "different" in the sense that is "material" so long as their respective possessors enjoy legal entitlements that are different in kind or extent. Thus, separate groups of stock are not materially different if they confer "the same proportional interest of the same character in the same corporation." However, they are materially different if they are issued by different corporations, or if they confer "different rights and powers" in the same corporation.

We find no support for the Commissioner's "economic substitute" conception of material difference. The Commissioner's test is incompatible with the structure of the Code. Section 1001(c) provides that a gain or loss realized under § 1001(a) "shall be recognized" unless one of the Code's nonrecognition provisions applies. One such nonrecognition provision [§ 1031, discussed immediately below], withholds recognition of a gain or loss realized "on the exchange of property . . . for property of like kind." If Congress had expected that exchanges of similar properties would not count as realization events under § 1001(a), it would have had no reason to bar recognition of a gain or loss realized from these transactions.

As the result of *Cottage Savings*, it is virtually impossible to maintain that an exchange in form is not a realization event in substance. However, "realization" is not the last step in the analysis, because it is possible that some Code provision (such as § 1031, infra, or § 1036, supra) will cause the realized gain or loss to go unrecognized in whole or in part. If a gain or loss is not "recognized," it is not currently included in gross income nor eligible to be currently deducted.

NOTES

1.   (a) *Macomber* rejected the notion that a transaction should be taxed as if the taxpayers chose the most tax-disadvantaged way of reaching the same end result. It follows that taxpayers can opt to take transactional paths so as to take advantage of favorable tax rules, so long as such transactional paths are not shams and have economic substance, etc. as explained in Chapter 21.B..

(b) In addition to the "subdivision" rationale for not taxing pro rata stock dividends, an additional rationale is that it could be thought to be "unfair" to tax the stock dividend, while at the same time treating the partial loss on the old shares as not being realized. As noted above, the IRS and the cases practically never treat

---

[15] The Court cited *U.S. v. Phellis*, 257 U.S. 156 (1921), *Weiss v. Stearn*, 265 U.S. 242 (1924), and *Marr v. U.S.*, 268 U.S. 536 (1925), all involving transactions in corporate stock and securities.

partial losses as being realized in the absence of a physical "disposition" of a portion of an asset. In the case of a pro rata stock dividend, the FMV of the shareholder's *total* stockholding is unlikely to significantly change as the result of the pro rata stock dividend. In other words, the FMV of the new (dividend) stock is correlated with (indeed, causes) the partial loss in the FMV of the old stock, and both the gain and the loss pertain to the same stockholdings of the *same taxpayer* in the form of the new stock.

(c) A *cash* dividend (which also reduces the value of existing stock), is clearly income, because the cash has been extracted from the underlying investment. Cf. *Lynch v. Hornby*, 247 U.S. 339 (1918) (dividend declared after the 1913 effective date of the income tax is entirely taxable even though traceable to pre-1913 corporate earnings and profits).

2.   (a) The losses in *Cottage Savings* were ordinary losses, not capital losses, because they were a kind of "bank inventory" and (hence) not "capital assets" as defined in § 1221(a).

(b) *Cottage Savings* was a product of the savings-and-loan crisis of the 1980s. This e swap transactions were effectively encouraged by the federal Home Loan Bank Board, which allowed savings and loan associations to avoid showing financial accounting losses on swaps of troubled mortgage portfolios while the same losses were allowed as income tax deductions, thereby allowing the financially-shaky institutions to have the best of both the accounting and tax worlds.

3.   (a) In *Shoenberg v. Comm'r*, 77 F.2d 446 (8th Cir. 1935), the court disallowed a loss deduction in a case where the taxpayer purchased the same type of stock from the same publicly-held corporation very shortly thereafter. The court stated that the loss was not sustained, because the taxpayer had not changed his economic position. Section 1091 can be avoided by delaying the purchase beyond 30 days of the sale.

(b) The type of transaction dealt with in *Shoenberg* is called a "wash sale." Wash sales of stock and securities are now governed by § 1091, which (basically) disallows the loss if substantially identical stock or securities are acquired within 30 days before or after the sale date. The basis of the old investment carries over, increased (or decreased) by any excess (shortfall) of the purchase price over the sale price.

4.   (a) A "straddle" is a pair of offsetting investments in the same economic risk (such as a commodity futures contract), so that if one investment leg goes up, the other leg will go down. The classic tax strategy with a straddle is to realize the loss leg and postpone realizing on the gain leg, but without change in one's overall wealth position. Section 1092 curbs this strategy by essentially treating the straddle as a unitary investment. Thus, a realized loss can be deducted only to the extent that it exceeds unrealized gain on the same straddle.

(b) Section 1092 is subordinate to § 1256, which deems certain option and future contracts to be sold for their FMV at the end of the year. A tax rule of this type (which treats unrealized gains and losses as having been realized annually) is called a "mark-to-market" rule.

5. Section 267(a)(1) provides that losses on sales between (specified) related parties are disallowed. The rationale of this provision is close to the traditional rationale of nonrealization cases, namely, that nothing has really changed. See *McWilliams v. Comm'r*, 331 U.S. 694 (1947) (holding that a loss sale on a stock exchange by one spouse and the near-simultaneous purchase of identical stock on the same exchange by the other spouse fell within the loss-disallowance rule of § 267(a)(1)). In a § 267(a)(1) scenario, the disallowed loss is held "in solution" pending a subsequent sale to a nonrelated party. That is, any gain realized by the related-party buyer on the disposition of the property is reduced by the disallowed loss. See § 267(d). Thus, if X sells $10K basis property to daughter Y for its FMV of $7K (resulting in disallowance to X of the $3K loss), and Y (having a $7K basis) sells the property to an unrelated party for $11K, Y's $4K gain is reduced (by the previously disallowed loss of $3K) to $1K.

6. Where a debtor issues new debt in satisfaction of old debt, the debtor, in principle, has debt-discharge income in an amount equal to the reduction (if any) in the principal owed. Section § 108(e)(10) defines the new principal as the FMV of the new debt obligations where they are publicly traded, or the discounted present value of the obligations in other cases. That is, the stated principal amount might well be disregarded. This is basically the same valuation rule as exists on the lender side for modifications of debt interests.

7. Many Code provisions (§ 1031 et seq.) exist that cause a realized gain or loss to go unrecognized (in whole or in part). Already noted are §§ 1036, 1038, 1091, and 1092. Others will be noted in due course. Far less common are provisions that treat unrealized gains and losses as being realized (and recognized). Apart from § 1256, supra, the other conspicuous provision of this type is § 475, which provides for mark-to-market accounting for the "inventory" of securities dealers.

PROBLEM

Assume that (1) Erik loaned $100 to individual X for five years under terms requiring annual interest payments, (2) interest rates have fallen and X's note is presently worth $120, (3) the note will mature and require the $100 of principal to be repaid one year from now, and (4) X anticipates being unable to make full payment at that time because of a cash flow problem. Therefore, Erik and X agree to extend the loan for five years past the maturity date on the same terms as the original loan. They do so by making a handwritten change to the maturity date provision of the original note. The note as modified now has a discounted present value of $128, but has a FMV of $123. What is the tax result to Erik? See Reg. § 1.1001-1(g) and -3(e).

4. Like-Kind Exchanges

The most important exchange nonrecognition provision covered in a course on the individual income tax is § 1031, which (subject to various exceptions) provides that no gain or loss shall be recognized by a transferor in an "exchange" of "like-kind" property.

a. Eligibility for § 1031

The properties exchanged must be of a "like kind" to each other. With respect to real estate, the term "like kind" is broadly construed to encompass virtually all types of interests therein. See Reg. § 1.1031(a)-1(b) and (c). Essentially, "anything goes" with respect to real property, except that U.S. real estate is never of like kind with respect to foreign real estate. See § 1031(h)(1). Even unimproved farm land is of a like kind with respect to a city lot with an office building on it.

The standard of "likeness" is much stricter in the case of personal property. See generally Reg. § 1.1031(a)-2. An exchange of an automobile for a truck would probably not be a like-kind exchange.[16] *Rev. Rul. 79-143*, 1979-1 C.B. 264, held that numismatic coins, which are valued on the basis of various factors, such as rarity, condition, and aesthetics, are *not* of like kind with bullion-type coins, which are valued on the basis of their metal content alone.

Many types of common investments, such as stocks, bonds, other debt instruments, certificates of trust, and partnership interests, as well as choses in action, are simply ineligible for § 1031. See § 1031(a)(2)(B)-(F). Moreover, stock in trade or other property held primarily for sale (i.e., "dealer property) is ineligible for § 1031. See § 1031(a)(2)(A).

Not surprisingly, then, real property exchanges account for the vast bulk of like-kind transactions obtaining § 1031 treatment.

Both the property exchanged (given up) and the property received in exchange must be business or investment property in the transferor's hands. Thus, if the transferor used either the property given up or the property received in the exchange for personal purposes, such as a personal residence, § 1031 would not apply, even if the properties are "like-kind." This rule sometimes operates to disqualify one party to the exchange from § 1031 treatment but not the other party.

Finally, the properties must be "exchanged." Section 1031(a)(3) allows, within specified time limits, for the exchange not to be simultaneous.[17] But a sale immediately followed by a reinvestment of the sales proceeds into like-kind property — even within the time limits specified by § 1031(a)(3) — simply doesn't qualify as an exchange.[18]

It is often not easy for one seeking a § 1031 exchange to find an owner of desired property of a near equal value who also wants to engage in an exchange. A common technique is for the first party (A) to find a buyer (B), who wants A's property, and then to locate a willing seller (C) of a desired property. Then, it is arranged for B to buy the desired property from C, which B then exchanges with A for A's property. See *Coupe v. Comm'r*, 52 T.C. 394 (1969) (reviewed) (acq.).

---

[16] See Reg. § 1.1031(a)-1(c)(1).

[17] In *Starker v. Comm'r*, 602 F.2d 1341 (9th Cir. 1979), the taxpayer transferred property in Year 1 and did not receive like-kind property in exchange until Year 5, but the court held that the Year-1 transfer came within § 1031. In 1984, Congress gave limited sanction to this result by enacting § 1031(a)(3), which is now the exclusive rule for achieving § 1031 qualification for a delayed exchange.

[18] See *Carlton v. U.S.*, 385 F.2d 238 (5th Cir. 1967).

However, it may be undesirable to incur transaction costs (including real estate transfer taxes) twice on the property owned by C. Or perhaps B is reluctant to take title to C's property even momentarily for fear (say) of someday becoming liable for environmental hazards. In *Rev. Rul. 90-34*, 1990-1 C.B. 154, A transferred investment real estate to B. B, in turn, purchased like-kind investment property owned by C, but arranged for the title to be transferred directly from C to A. The IRS ruled that A had engaged in a § 1031 exchange, even though A's transferee, B, never owned the like-kind property.

An example of a transaction that failed to qualify under § 1031 was presented by *Klein v. Comm'r*, T.C. Memo. 1993-491, where the taxpayer attempted to use an escrow arrangement whereby B would pay cash for A's property, but the cash would go into escrow and ultimately pay for C's property. Here, § 1031 treatment was denied because the taxpayer could have (but didn't) withdraw funds from the escrow. The court stated that the transferor must not have actual or constructive receipt of cash.[19] The courts don't allow taxpayers here to apply an "end result," step-transaction test.[20]

Regulations added in 1991, now provide "safe harbors" regarding the use of "qualified intermediaries," such as escrow agents.[21] A properly structured escrow allows title to *C*'s property to go directly to *A*, bypassing *B*, and for *B*'s cash to go directly to *C*. Businesses have come into existence just to handle multi-party § 1031 transactions.

b.　Mechanics of § 1031

The materials below take you through the mechanics of § 1031(a). In each hypothetical, Barbara owns Blackacre, a parcel of real estate held for investment with an adjusted basis of $4K and FMV of $10K. If Barbara sells it to Wally for $10K in cash, Barbara realizes, and must recognize (include in gross income), gain of $6K. (The issue of "character" will generally be ignored in this discussion.)

Now suppose instead that Barbara transfers Blackacre to Wally in exchange for $10K worth of IBM stock. This transaction flunks § 1031 (the properties are not "like kind" *and* stock is not an eligible type of property). Barbara will have the same $6K realized gain as in the initial example, because "amount realized" is defined by § 1001(b) to mean cash and/or the FMV of any property received. The gain is recognized, because there is no Code provision stating that it is not. See § 1001(c). Barbara's cost basis under § 1012 in the IBM stock is $10K, the amount taxed to Barbara by being included in the amount realized (sometimes called "tax cost basis").

Now suppose that, instead of receiving IBM stock from Wally, Barbara receives Greenacre, a parcel of investment real estate with a FMV of $10K, in exchange for Blackacre. Barbara once again has a $6K *realized* gain under § 1001, but this

---

[19] Compare *Biggs v. Comm'r*, 632 F.2d 1171 (5th Cir. 1980) (three-party transaction through escrow held to qualify under § 1031 because taxpayer never actually or constructively received cash).

[20] See *Bell Lines, Inc. v. U.S.*, 480 F.2d 710, 714 (4th Cir. 1973) (taxpayer cannot advance a substance-over-form theory in this context).

[21] Regs. §§ 1.1031(b)-2, 1.1031(k)-1(g).

exchange qualifies under § 1031, if Barbara holds or uses Greenacre for business or investment purposes.

Under § 1031(a), Barbara's $6K realized gain will go unrecognized. *But Barbara's unrecognized gain is not permanently forgiven. Rather, it is "preserved" (and thereby deferred). The mechanism for preserving this gain for future reckoning is the basis rule found in § 1031(d), which requires* Barbara to take a basis in Greenacre equal to her old basis in Blackacre, which is $4K. Thus, if Barbara sold Greenacre for $10K, she would recognize the $6K of gain that § 1031(a) allowed to go unrecognized on the exchange.[22]

Next assume that, at the time of the exchange, Greenacre is worth only $8K, so that Wally must add $2K cash consideration "to boot" in order to equalize the exchange. (Additional consideration in the form of cash, or non-like-kind property, is referred to in tax jargon as "boot"). Barbara could be (but is not) viewed as having "sold" 1/5 of the value of Blackacre for $2K cash, which would be offset by 1/5 of Barbara's basis in Blackacre ($800), resulting in "sale gain" of $1.2K. Simultaneously, there would be an "exchange" of $8K worth of Blackacre for $8K worth of Greenacre under § 1031. But that is *not* how § 1031 operates. Under § 1031(b), Barbara must recognize her *realized* gain ($6K) *to the extent of* the boot received ($2K). Stated differently, § 1031(b) requires Barbara to recognize *gain* in an amount equal to the *lesser* of her entire realized gain *or* the boot received. (The gain recognized is "capital gain" if Blackacre is a capital asset in her hands.) The $4K remainder of her $6K realized gain is not recognized.

The receipt of boot can only cause gain to be recognized. It cannot cause any loss to be recognized.

Conceptually, Barbara's basis in Greenacre should be an amount equal to her after tax dollars "in" her investment in Greenacre. Her original basis in Blackacre was $4K, and her gain recognized was $2K. But Barbara not only received Greenacre, but also cash, and cash must have a basis equal to its face amount. Thus Barbara's basis in Greenacre should be (and is) $4K ($4K starting basis + $2K recognized gain − $2K cash boot).

Another way of conceptualizing the basis issue is to work backwards from the desired end result of "preserving" the unrecognized gain of $4K for future inclusion. This result can be accomplished by reducing Greenacre's $8K acquisition-date value by the unrecognized gain amount of $4K (realized gain of $6K reduced by recognized gain of $2K).

In this case, the Code in § 1031(d) follows the first approach. Thus, Barbara's basis in Greenacre equals her basis in Blackacre ($4K), plus any cash paid (or the basis of any boot given up) (0), increased by any gain recognized ($2K), and decreased by any boot received ($2K), which comes out to $4K.[23] If Barbara then

---

[22] If Barbara were later o sell Greenacre for $9K, she would realize (and recognize) gain of only $5K. In other words, the $1K decline in Greenacre's value following the exchange would effectively eliminate $1K of the $6K of unrecognized gain that was preserved for future reckoning by § 1031(d).

[23] Section 1031(d) says that basis is reduced by any loss recognized, but loss can only be recognized with respect to depreciated-value (i.e., FMV-less-than-basis) in-kind boot given up in the exchange.

immediately turned around and sold Greenacre for its $8K value, she would realize and recognize $4K of gain, which is precisely the amount that went unrecognized on her exchange with Wally under § 1031.

Assume the same facts as the last hypothetical, except that Greenacre is only worth $3K and the cash boot is $7K. Again Barbara realizes $6K of gain, but this time she recognizes all of it. (She cannot recognize more gain than she has realized.)

Barbara's basis in Greenacre under § 1031(d) would be $3K ($4K Blackacre basis *plus* $6K gain recognized *less* $7K money received), which happens to be its FMV at the time of the exchange. Consequently, if Barbara immediately sold Greenacre for its $3K FMV, she would recognize no gain, which is the right answer, because (1) she has already recognized her entire Blackacre gain, and (2) Greenacre has not appreciated in value subsequent to her acquisition of it.

What is the effect on the party *giving* boot in an exchange qualifying for § 1031? Assume that the FMV of Greenacre is $15K, the FMV of Blackacre remains $10K, and Barbara throws in $5K of cash boot to even the deal. Barbara has essentially purchased $5K worth of Greenacre for cash and has exchanged Blackacre, worth $10K, for $10K worth of Greenacre. Thus, Barbara's amount realized "for" exchanging Blackacre is $10K, none of which is recognized (because she *received* no boot). Her basis in Greenacre would be $9K (her $4K Blackacre basis *plus* her $5K basis in the cash she transferred). If she then immediately sold Greenacre for its $15K value, she would realize and recognize the $6K of gain that was deferred under § 1031(a).

How does § 1031 operate if the properties involved are subject to mortgages? The following rules come into play, all of which are illustrated in Reg. § 1.1031(d)-2:

 • Net liability relief (the excess of any liability of which the transferor is relieved over any liability assumed by the transferor in the exchange is treated as "boot" received for purposes of gain recognition under § 1031(b). (Any cash given up by the transferor would reduce this boot amount.)

 • A net liability *increase* does not offset the amount of any boot received.

 • Gross liability relief is treated as "money received" for purposes of calculating basis under § 1031(d).

 • Any (gross) liability taken on is added to basis under the so-called *Crane* basis rule for acquisition debt.

These rules can be illustrated in the situation where Blackacre, worth $10K and subject to a $2K mortgage, is exchanged for Wally's Greenacre, worth $9.4K and subject to a mortgage of $1K. Since Barbara's net equity of $8K ($10K FMV *less* $2K mortgage) is less than Wally's net equity of $8.4K ($9.4K - $1K), Barbara throws in another $400 of cash to equalize the exchange. Barbara's *net* liability relief of $1K ($2K - $1K), reduced by the $400 cash she transfers, is treated as "boot" for purposes of § 1031(b). Thus, Barbara must recognize $600 ($1K - $400) of her $6K realized gain. Her basis in Greenacre is $4K ($4K Blackacre basis *plus* $400 cash *less* $2K "money received" in the form of liability relief *plus* $600 gain recognized *plus* $1K acquisition debt). If Barbara were to immediately sell Greenacre for $9.4K cash, she would realize the $5.4K of gain that went unrecognized on the exchange.

The holding period of property acquired in a § 1031 exchange relates back to the acquisition date of the exchanged property if the property exchanged is a capital asset or § 1231 property in the transferor's hands (which it normally would be, given the requirements for § 1031 to apply). See § 1223(1).

NOTES

1. *Philadelphia Park Amusement Co. v. U.S.*, 126 F. Supp. 184 (Ct. Cl. 1954), stands for the following propositions regarding *taxable* property-for-property exchanges:

(a) The basis of the acquired property under § 1012 is its FMV on receipt, which also is the measure of the amount realized in the taxable exchange, even though such a result (which conforms to tax logic) might be hard to square with a literal reading of the term "cost" in § 1012. (This result is often referred to as a "tax cost basis.") Basis is one's previously taxed dollars in the property received in the taxable exchange.

(b) If the value of the property received can't be determined, such value is deemed to be equal to the value of the property given up (under what is sometimes called the "barter equation" method of valuation).

(c) If *neither* value can be determined with a reasonable degree of accuracy (a rare and extraordinary occurrence), there is a "tax common law" tax-free exchange, with the basis of the property given up becoming the basis of the property acquired. This rule is the "exchange" analogue to the *M.E. Blatt Co.* case, in Section C below, essentially deferring the in-kind gain (instead of deferring rental gross income as in *Blatt*). See *Helvering v. Tex-Pen Oil Co.*, 300 U.S. 481, 499 (1937); cf. *Burnet v. Logan*, 283 U.S. 404 (1931) (sale of speculative-value property for contingent-payment consideration).

2. Although in-kind boot is unlikely in a § 1031 nonrecognition exchange, here are the rules:

(a) The recipient of in-kind boot treats its FMV as the amount of the boot, and the basis of the boot received equals its FMV on receipt (under § 1012 "tax cost" principles).

(b) The transferor of in-kind boot recognizes gain or loss on the difference between its FMV and the transferor's basis in the in-kind boot property. This result derives from the fact that the in-kind boot is being exchanged for the portion of the acquired property having a FMV equal to the in-kind boot, but that this portion of the exchange is taxable to both the transferor and the recipient of the in-kind boot. Any loss is subject to loss allowance (and disallowance) rules. Any gain recognized or loss allowed to the transferor is factored into the basis of the like-kind property received.

3. Personal residences are not eligible for § 1031 exchanges. Under § 121(d)(10), if business or investment property is obtained in a § 1031 exchange, converted to use as the principal residence of the taxpayer, and sold within five years of the exchange, the sale is disqualified from the § 121 exclusion.

4. (a) Section 1031 is commonly defended with three arguments: (1) continuity of investment, (2) difficulty of valuation, and (3) lack of liquidity to pay the tax. The argument against favorable tax treatment for like-kind property exchanges (especially of real estate) is that such exchanges would be fairly uncommon in the absence of § 1031. Sales for cash are the norm, and avoid all three of the problems said to justify § 1031 in the first place. Even with genuine exchanges, the existence of these problems is a question of fact.

(b) An alternative viewpoint might be that § 1031 isn't broad enough, and that the proceeds of any sale of any investment should be allowed to be reinvested (rolled over) into any other investment tax-free. (This approach is a principal feature of a cash flow consumption tax.) How would the basis of the new investments be determined?

(c) A few discrete tax roll-over rules exist in the Code. One is § 1033, covered in Chapter 24.D, dealing with gains (but not losses) in involuntary conversions. Others deal with withdrawals from tax-favored retirement plan accounts.

5. (a) Tax-free exchanges (conversions) of certain life insurance policies are allowed under § 1035. The operative rules of § 1035 (as well as of § 1036) basically track those for § 1031.

(b) Nonrecognition rules abound in Subchapters C and K, dealing with corporations and partnerships, especially with respect to exchanges involving equity interests resulting from formations, mergers, and (for partnerships) liquidations. Understanding § 1031 is great preparation for understanding the mechanics of numerous corporate and partnership tax rules.

PROBLEM

Daisy owns Cowacre worth $200K, adjusted basis (AB) $100K, which she transfers to Misty in exchange for Horseacre worth $170K, AB $90K, and $30K cash.

(a) What are the results to *both* Daisy and Misty, including basis in the property received, assuming that the exchange fails to qualify under § 1031?

(b) Same as (a), except that the exchange qualifies under § 1031 for both of them?

(c) Same as (b), except that Cowacre is subject to a mortgage of $70K, Horseacre is subject to a mortgage of $60K, and the cash boot is $20K?

C. LESSEE IMPROVEMENTS

A reversionary interest in a trust is essentially a remainder interest retained by the creator of the trust. In Chapter 17.B.1 it was shown that the retention of a reversion in gratuitously-transferred property generally prevented the tax ownership of the property (and the income therefrom) from being shifted to the donee of the income interest for income-attribution purposes. And in Section A.4 of this chapter it was shown that the coming into possession of a reversion (or remainder) was not a realization event. But by far the most common form of a reversion occurs in commerce (rather than in the context of gratuitous transfers): where a property owner enters into a lease (with the tenant in possession expected to pay rent), the owner thereby creates a reversion in herself to take effect upon the expiration of the lease. Not surprisingly, the coming into possession of the reversion upon the expiration or termination of the lease is not generally a realization event. The owner is just regaining possession of property of which ownership was maintained all along.

Two cases were decided by the Supreme Court where a commercial lessee made *improvements* on the lessor's property that would pass to the lessor upon the termination of the lease. Lessee improvements made for the benefit of the grantor can constitute "rent" and thus be includible in the lessor's gross income as ordinary income under § 61(a)(5). But even if lessee improvements are required by the lease terms, they will constitute "rent" (currently includible by the lessor) under Reg. § 1.61-8(c) only when they are designated as such by the parties.[24] Such in-kind rent is deductible by the lessor (as opposed to being a capital expenditure).

However, the vast majority of lessee improvements are made to benefit the lessee, and only incidentally benefit the lessor if the improvements happen to possess economic value to the lessor at the termination of the lease. In the two cases below, the improvements in question did not constitute "rent" (because not designated as rent by the lease), but lessee improvements are new wealth obtained by the lessor, and would appear to be catch-all income at some point. The issue before the Court in each case was *when* the improvements are income within the meaning of the catchall phrase in § 61(a). The three "timing" possibilities are (1) the year the improvements are constructed by the lessee, (2) the later year in which the lease terminates (and the lessor's reversion comes into possession), or (3) the even later year in which the property (with the improvements) is sold by the lessor. If (as is usually the case) the improvements decrease in value over time, then the later that the realization event occurs, the lesser is the amount included by the lessor in gross income.

In the first such case, decided in 1938, the government argued that the improvements produced catch-all gross income to the lessor *in the year the improvements were made.*

M. E. BLATT CO. v. UNITED STATES
United States Supreme Court
305 U.S. 267 (1938)

MR. JUSTICE BUTLER delivered the opinion of the Court.

Lessor purchased the real estate in 1927, and September 13, 1930, leased it for use as a moving picture theater for a term of ten years, beginning upon completion of improvements to be made. At its own cost and expense, lessor agreed to make alterations in accordance with plans prepared by an architect selected by the parties. Lessee agreed to install the latest type of moving picture and talking

---

[24] See *Comm'r v. Cunningham*, 258 F.2d 231 (9th Cir. 1958).

apparatus, theater seats and all other fixtures, furniture and equipment necessary for the successful operation of a modern theater, to become the property of lessor at the expiration or sooner termination of the lease. The total cost of all improvements [made by lessee was about $40,000].

[The Commissioner took the *cost* of various items constituting the lessee's improvements and reduced these amounts by 10 years of future depreciation charges under various business accounting conventions, omitting some items which would then have no value, and proposed including the resulting amounts in the lessor's gross income in the taxable year when the improvements were completed.]

[The Court first held that, although the lessee-made improvements had been required by the lease terms, they were not "rent" income to the lessor because there was no "plainly disclosed" intention of the parties to regard the improvements as "rent."]

It remains to be considered whether the amount in question represented taxable income, other than rent, in the first year of the term. The findings fail to disclose any basis of value on which to lay an income tax or the time of realization of taxable gain, if any there was. The findings do not show whether [the Commissioner's figures] are intended to represent value of improvements if removed or the amount attributable to them as a part of the building.

It does not appear that, if detached from the building, the [various items] would then have any value, even as junk, over the necessary cost of removal. It is clear that, if any value as of that time may be attributed to them, it is included in and not separable from that of the leased premises.

[Assuming] that the improvements increased the value of the building, [such enhancement] is not distinguishable from excess, if any there may be, of value over cost of improvements made by lessor. Each was an addition to capital; not income within the meaning of the statute.

[Even] assuming that at some time the value of the improvements would be the income of lessor, it cannot be reasonably assigned to the year in which they were installed. The Commissioner found that at the end of the term some would be worthless and excluded them. He also excluded depreciation of other items. These exclusions imply that elements which will not outlast lessee's right to use are not at any time income of lessor. The inclusion of the remaining value is to hold that petitioner's right to have them as a part of the building at expiration of the lease constitutes income in the first year of the term in an amount equal to their estimated value at the end of the term without any deduction to obtain present worth as of the date of installation. It may be assumed that, subject to the lease, the lessor became the owner of the improvements at the time they were made. But it had no right to use or dispose of them during the term. Mere acquisition of that sort did not amount to contemporaneous realization of gain within the meaning of the statute.

MR. JUSTICE STONE: I acquiesce in that part of the Court's opinion which construes the findings below as failing to establish that the lessee's improvements resulted in an increase in market value of the lessor's land in the taxable year. As it is unnecessary to decide whether such increase, if established, would constitute taxable income of the lessor, I do not join in so much of the opinion as, upon an assumption contrary to the findings, undertakes to discuss that question.

In the following case, decided only two years later, the Supreme Court considered the issue of whether a lessor realizes catch-all gross income *in the year the lease terminates* with respect to an entire building erected by the lessee. In this case, the lease terminated prematurely because of the economic collapse of the Great Depression, so that the acquisition of the building by the lessor was akin to an in-kind windfall of the type discussed in Chapter 14.E.

HELVERING v. BRUUN
United States Supreme Court
309 U.S. 461 (1940)

MR. JUSTICE ROBERTS delivered the opinion of the Court.

In 1929 the tenant demolished and removed the existing building and constructed a new one. On July 1, 1933, the lease was cancelled for default in payment of rent and taxes and the [taxpayer] regained possession. The parties stipulated "that as of said date, July 1, 1933, the building had a [net] fair market value of $51,434.25.

The [taxpayer] insists that the realty — [an asset of the lessor] at the date of the execution of the lease — remained such throughout the term and after its expiration; that improvements affixed to the soil became part of the realty indistinguishably blended in the capital asset; that such improvements cannot be separately valued; that they are, therefore, in the same category as improvements added by [taxpayer] to his land, or accruals of value due to extraneous and adventitious circumstances. Such added value, it is argued, can be considered capital gain only upon the owner's disposition of the asset. The position is that the economic gain consequent upon the enhanced value of the recaptured asset is not realized within the meaning of the Sixteenth Amendment and may not, therefore, be taxed without apportionment.

We hold that the petitioner was right in assessing the gain as realized in 1933.

We might rest our decision upon the narrow issue presented by the terms of the stipulation. It does not appear whether the building was readily removable from the land. It is not stated whether the [stipulated value of the building] accurately reflects an increase in the value of land and building considered as a single estate in land. [Even if that were the case,] we think that gain in the amount named was realized by the respondent in the year of repossession.

Essentially the [taxpayer] relies upon expressions found in [*Eisner v. Macomber*] to the effect that gain derived from capital must be something of exchangeable value proceeding from property, severed from the capital, and received by the recipient for his separate use, benefit, and disposal. These expressions, however, were used to clarify the distinction between an ordinary dividend and a stock dividend. We think they are not controlling here.

While it is true that economic gain is not always taxable as income, it is settled that the realization of gain need not be in cash derived from the sale of an asset. Gain may occur as a result of exchange of property, relief from a liability, or other profit realized from the completion of a transaction. The fact that the gain is a portion of the value of property received by the taxpayer in the transaction does not negative its realization.

Here, as a result of a business transaction, the respondent received back his land with a new building on it, which added an ascertainable amount to its value. It is not necessary to recognition of taxable gain that he should be able to sever the improvement begetting the gain from his original capital. If that were necessary, no income could arise from the exchange of property; whereas such gain has always been recognized as realized taxable gain.

The CHIEF JUSTICE concurs in the result in view of the terms of the stipulation of facts.

MR. JUSTICE McREYNOLDS took no part in the decision of this case.

After *Bruun*, Congress enacted § 109, which provides that a lessor generally does not realize gross income with respect to lessee improvements upon the termination of the lease. Since, if § 109 applies, the improvements are not included in the lessor's income at the time of termination of the lease, the lessor has no basis with respect to the improvements. See § 1019. Thus, the lessor is taxed (if at all) only when the improved property is sold or otherwise disposed of, at which time the value of the improvements (if any) augments the amount realized (if any) under § 1001. Moreover, the resulting gain or loss may well be treated as capital gain or loss or § 1231 gain or loss (if it was realized on the "sale or exchange" of a "capital asset" or § 1231 property) instead of ordinary income, as in *Bruun*.

The effect in § 109 of the parenthetical phrases "other than rent" is to cause the rare improvements that do constitute rent to be *currently* includible in the gross income of the lessor under Reg. § 1.61-8(c). The deferred-realization holding of the *Blatt* case only applies to improvements that are *not* current rent. These results illustrate the point that deferred realization is highly unlikely in the case of the iterated categories of gross income, but possible in the case of catch-all income, assuming that there is a strong case for deferred realization. Since §§ 109 and 1019 only pick up where *Blatt* and *Bruun* leave off, it appears that there is no scenario in which lessee improvements are income to the lessor at the termination of the lease.

NOTES

1. (a) The government in *Blatt* advanced a theory that was twice flawed: (1) starting with the future depreciated cost (rather than the future value) of the improvements, and (2) failing to discount the future value to the present. But it is likely that the government would have lost *Blatt* anyway.

(b) *Blatt* might be read as standing for any of the following propositions:

(i) In-kind catch-all income is never realized on receipt. But even if *Blatt* can be read for this holding, it didn't survive *Bruun*, at least as a general rule.

(ii) A nonassignable (but vested) right to future income is not currently realized income. The material in Section E, which follows shortly, contradicts this possible reading.

(iii) A nonassignable but vested right to future income is not realized if the value of the right to future income is uncertain due to future contingencies. This position is the one that is most harmonious with current doctrine. Stay tuned.

2.   (a) The taxpayer in *Bruun* didn't help its cause by stipulating as to the value of the improvements at the termination of the lease. The Court in *Bruun* suggested that it didn't care whether the stipulated amount referred to (a) the FMV of the building as a separate asset or (b) the enhancement of the FMV of the lessor's property attributable to the building.

(b) The taxpayer in *Bruun* argued that the improvement was an addition to the taxpayer's "capital," citing *Macomber*. *Bruun* establishes that "capital" in the tax sense refers to "taxpayer's investment" (basis). The lessee improvements were "new wealth" to the taxpayer transferred to the taxpayer by another party. The tax concept of "capital" does not refer to economic, accounting, physical, or metaphysical reality.

3.   (a) The lessee would rarely undertake an improvement (unless treated by the lease as a substitute for rent) where it did not expect to recoup its investment, but expectations can be thwarted, as happened in *Bruun*. Yet a loss to the lessee is not necessarily a gain to the lessor. Suppose a strip-mall space is rented to a group that operates a Chinese restaurant, and the group installs the usual Chinese restaurant furnishings and kitchen equipment. The lease ends, and now the landlord is stuck with stuff that may actually render the space more difficult to rent or that is expensive to remove. Even if the improvements benefit the lessor, the enhancement in value might be hard to ascertain. Considerations such as these (as well as possible nonliquidity, if the improvements did have significant value) presumably contributed to the enactment of § 109.

(b) Nevertheless, where the lessee improvements do increase the income-producing capacity of the property, § 109 is another Code section that you can add to your list of cash flow consumption tax features embedded in current law, because it results in part of the lessor's investment being "before tax." However, it is unlikely that § 109 will distort transactions, because a lessee would have no economic motivation to accommodate a lessor's desire to take advantage of § 109.

(c) A lessee may be required, under a "net lease" arrangement, to pay certain expenses of the lessor (real property taxes, repairs, and possibly mortgage payments). Here such payments are generally considered to be additional current rental income. See Reg. § 1.61-8(c), which is an application of the *Old Colony Trust* doctrine (supra Chapter 12.A).

4.   Relief granted by Congress in a particular fact situation is not the same as "reversing" a principle established by a Supreme Court decision. Thus, the

enactment of § 109 did not "overrule" *Bruun* with respect to its realization holding. It just changes the result with respect to lease terminations. The value of lessee-constructed improvements (that are not rent) is still *realized* income at the termination of the lease. It just happens to be income that is excluded by statute (really, deferred income, given the zero-basis rule in § 1019). On the other hand, *Bruun* modifies *Macomber*, not only as to what is "capital" (vs. income) but to the effect that "severability" is not a necessary attribute of "income" in either the statutory or constitutional sense.

D. BARGAIN PURCHASES OF PROPERTY

Here we consider the bargain-purchase scenario, which has been already been anticipated by certain scenarios considered earlier in which an initial investment results in the obtaining (immediately, or as the result of subsequent transformations) of property with a greater (or lesser) FMV than the investment amount. The "bargain purchase" type of transaction discussed herein is a purchase of property from a second party for an amount less than the FMV of the property. A bargain purchase can occur at arm's length in commerce by reason of a seller's mistake or may be a non-arm's-length transaction in which the "seller" intends to effectuate a disguised transfer of value to the buyer. The tax issue posed by the bargain-purchase scenario is whether the buyer "realizes" income or gain *at the time of purchase*, when his or her wealth increases, or instead can defer realization until the property purchased at a bargain is ultimately sold.

1. Commercial Bargain Purchases

Cliff enters a car dealership, sees a car he likes, pays the full sticker price of $20K, and uses the car for personal purposes. Pat goes to the same dealership, sees the same model of car and, after bargaining for two hours, purchases it for $17K. She also uses it for personal purposes. Neither party is in any way related to the car dealership or its owners. In other words, the transaction is at arm's length.

No Code provision specifically addresses the general category of "bargain purchase." The issue is whether the excess of the $20K sticker price over Pat's cost is income on account of being an immediate in-kind accession to wealth ($3K worth of "free" car) or whether the $3K "bargain" element avoids immediate tax on the ground that it is not realized. If the $3K is included in Pat's gross income, Pat would have a § 1012 basis of $20K (purchase price of $17K *plus* included income of $3K). If the $3K is not included, Pat's basis would be $17K.

Because a bargain purchase is a one-time, identifiable event, forcing Pat to include in gross income the $3K bargain would not present the same degree of administrative difficulty as would be encountered in treating *all* property appreciation as includible gross income as it accrues annually. Additionally, the $3K should be included in income immediately if the substance of this transaction is (1) a transfer of $3K of cash to Pat from the dealership coupled with (2) the free and willing purchase of the car by Pat for $20K.

But in general — and as illustrated by *Eisner v. Macomber* — taxpayers are judged by what actually occurred, not by the highest-tax way in which a given economic result *might* have been obtained. Since Pat and the dealership are unrelated and at arm's length, no reason exists to think that the transaction involves a disguised cash payment to Pat.

Transactions of Pat's type have aroused no interest on the part of the IRS. It is considered to be a "rule" that a bargain purchase — *if negotiated at arm's length by unrelated parties* — does not result in gross income to the buyer.[25] This is sometimes called the "commercial bargain purchase" (or "good deal") exception or rule. This is a deferred realization rule because Pat's adjusted basis in the property purchased will be the $17K paid for the car, so that, if Pat were able to resell the car for $20K, he would have $3K of gain on sale.

Another reason for not treating Pat's situation as giving rise to $3K of current gross income begins by noting that because retail car prices (and the prices for homes, land, and many other items) are individually negotiated, the $20K sticker price in Cliff's and Pat's hypothetical was simply the car dealer's opening offer and not a true benchmark for measuring any realized wealth increase of a purchaser. Thus, Cliff's $20K purchase merely shows that he is a poor negotiator. It does not establish that Pat had a $3K gain any more than it establishes that Cliff had a $3K loss. Moreover, price discrimination among customers is a fact of economic life. It can be said for both Cliff and Pat that the value of what they purchased was exactly equal to what they paid for it. That is to say, as a matter of "fact," there was no "bargain" purchase by Pat at all! Certainly, it would be virtually impossible to administer the tax laws if every commercial transaction were subject to scrutiny to determine the existence of a discount (bargain-purchase) component (or its opposite, a purchase in excess of value).

But sometimes the value of a purchased item is *greatly* in excess of (or below) its true value. Nevertheless, these transactions are not considered to be realization events. This approach is related to that applicable to the person seeking to reap the bounty of nature. Suppose Mary purchases land (together with mineral rights) in a remote section of the Sierra Nevada for $5K on a hunch that "ther's gold in them thar hills." After the purchase, Mary pokes around and discovers the legendary Lost Chance Mine, rich with veins of precious minerals. The property is now worth millions, but the exact value depends upon further exploration, development, and production activity. In the objective sense, the high value was "there" all along. Nevertheless, Mary realizes no gross income until the minerals, the mineral rights, or the property is sold. In short, the bargain-purchase amount is treated as unrealized appreciation.

NOTES

1.   (a) A rule of deferred "realization" results in ultimate exclusion where the item in question loses its value over time (and is not converted to cash) or is consumed. Examples are self-grown crops consumed by the grower and free samples of consumable goods.

---

[25] See *Palmer v. Comm'r*, 302 U.S. 63 (1937) (dictum); *Pellar v. Comm'r*, 25 T.C. 299 (1955) (acq.); *Rev. Rul. 91-36*, 1991-2 C.B. 17.

(b) Presumably, a bargain purchase of services is possible. Since services received are instantly consumed, no future realization of income or gain is possible. Recall the *Zarin* case, about the compulsive gambler, in Chapter 19.B.2. Mr. Zarin ended up paying $500K for gambling opportunities having a "list price" of $3.4M. To repeat a question raised there, is avoiding having to pay for items purchased on credit a common type of commercial bargain purchase, or should Mr. Zarin have been deemed to have received cash that he then lost at the gambling table?

2.   (a) The reverse of a bargain purchase is where the price exceeds the FMV of the property or service. We can call this a commercial *premium* purchase, which often involves the seller concealing or misrepresenting the nature or quality of the property or service. Not surprisingly, the taxpayer is not deemed to have a realized loss in this case. Because premium purchases are likely as common as bargain purchases, the IRS would have little to gain by scrutinizing both, because it can be assumed that premium-purchases would be more frequently reported than bargain purchases if consumers could claim loss deductions in such cases.

(b) If a commercial premium purchase is made on credit and the parties subsequently agree to retroactively reduce the amount owed, the disputed-debt doctrine (or § 108(e)(5)) discussed in Chapters 19.B.2 and 20.B.2 may come into play.

2.   Non-Arm's-Length Bargain Purchases

In a commercial arm's length context, sellers have an overpowering economic incentive not to simply give value away to customers. But the reasons for ignoring commercial bargain purchases made at arm's length do not apply to situations where bargain purchases might be used as a subterfuge to cause economic income to be invisible to the income tax system. This possibility exists where the parties have a pre-existing relationship that involves the systematic transfer of wealth from one party to the other, as occurs with employers and employees, corporations and shareholders.

Consider a price discount extended from a corporation to its shareholders or from an employer to its employees. Under case law, it is settled that a bargain sale by a corporation to a shareholder produces gross income for the shareholder equal to the amount of the discount. The "discount" is nothing more than a disguised dividend, and § 61(a)(7) specifically lists dividends as includible in gross income. Similarly, it has long been understood that a bargain purchase by an employee from an employer is compensation income to the employee. This rule appears in Reg. § 1.61-2(d)(2), stating:

> Except as otherwise provided . . . , if property is transferred by an employer to an employee or if property is transferred to an independent contractor, as compensation for services, for an amount less than its fair market value, then regardless of whether the transfer is in the form of a sale or exchange, the difference between the amount paid for the property and the amount of its fair market value at the time of the transfer is compensation and shall be included in the gross income of the employee or independent contractor.

This result is now codified in § 83(a), enacted in 1969, which provides some additional clarifications to address situations where the property obtained is subject to a "substantial risk of forfeiture," a wrinkle that is addressed shortly. Also, statutory exceptions exist to § 83(a) for certain fringe benefits that take the form of discounts. Examples are §§ 117(d) (tuition reductions for employees of educational institutions) and 132(a)(2) (qualified employee discounts).

For example, if Priscilla is a valued paralegal employee of a law firm, and the firm sells her a car for $5K when the car's FMV is $20K, the $15K "discount" represents disguised compensation for services rendered. Thus, Priscilla would include $15K in gross income under §§ 83(a) and 61(a)(1). The $15K is ordinary compensation income.

Unlike true arm's length bargain purchases, where the discount is "latent" (not known to the seller) because of the seller's ignorance or lack of sophistication, in the disguised-compensation or disguised-dividend situations the assets are typically standard consumer and investment items (such as autos or shares of stock) that have a known current value. Moreover, the "seller" is *intending* to transfer value to the "buyer." Without an inclusionary rule to govern these situations, shareholders and employees could collude en masse with corporations and employers to avoid the compensation and dividend gross income inclusions under §§ 61(a)(1) and (7) through price discounts. In these cases, the exclusion of bargain purchase income would defeat Congress's intent to treat compensation and dividends as major components of the income tax base. Moreover, if tax results differed dramatically according to the mechanism of payment (cash vs. bargain purchase), the norm of economic efficiency would be violated, as the tax law would provide a strong inducement for taxpayers to engage in behavior that they would not otherwise practice.

A below-market loan transaction really entails a "bargain purchase" of *money* by the borrower, because the consideration given by the borrower is worth less (in present-value terms) than the amount of cash received. However, deferral of income in this situation is impossible, because the borrowed cash cannot have a basis that is lower than the amount of the cash itself. Below-market loans are unlikely in arm's length transactions because lenders will demand market-rate interest. But below-market loans are likely in the same situations in which bargain purchases are likely (employer-employee, corporation-shareholder, etc.). Not surprisingly, in these situations, § 7872 (discussed at Chapter 17.D.2 and Chapter 18.B) treats certain below-market loans as resulting in current transfers (of wages, dividends, etc.).

PROBLEMS

1.   Pilar, an art history professor, is browsing around an art gallery in Year 1 and notices a small Holy Family painting attributed to the minor Renaissance artist Guido da Bologna with a price tag of $2K. Pilar recognizes this as a long-lost work (last seen in 1895 in the private collection of the Earl of Tweed) painted by the major Florentine master Andrea del Sarto, who was the subject of Pilar's doctoral dissertation. Pilar, who is familiar with the trade in paintings of this period, thinks the work is worth at least $500K, and so she gladly forks over the $2K purchase price, barely concealing her glee. In Year 3, a panel of experts confirm that the

painting purchased by Pilar is the long-lost del Sarto work, and in Year 4 Pilar sells the work to a museum for $800K. What tax results to Pilar?

2.   Same facts as above, except that, instead of selling the work to a museum for $800K in Year 4, Pilar sells the work to her daughter Francesca in Year 5 for a $100K note, payable in full at the end of Year 10 (with market-rate interest). In Year 9 Francesca sells the work for $1M and pays off the debt (with interest) owed to her Mother. What tax results to Pilar and Francesca? See Reg. § 1.1015-4 (and ignore § 453).

3.   Employee Stock Options

Employee stock options are "call" options "granted" (or "issued"), usually without explicit charge, by corporate employers to their employees. The option gives the employee a right to purchase the *employer's* stock at a fixed (or perhaps formula) price during a specified future period. It is expected (as with any call option) that the employee will exercise the option if the stock FMV rises above the option price, because only then will the employee be in a position to make a bargain purchase of the stock. If the stock value never rises above the option price, it is expected that the option will be allowed to lapse.

In the absence of any "special rules," one would analyze employee stock options along the lines suggested by material discussed previously. That is, first, does the grant of the option (which is "property") give rise to current compensation income equal to the value of the option, or are there features of an option that would cause realization of such income to be deferred until the exercise of the option, which would appear to fall squarely under § 83(a) as an employee bargain purchase? But on the other side is the "rule" noted in Subsection A.5 that the exercise of an option is not a realization event. If there is no realization event until the stock (obtained by exercising the option) is sold, is the resulting gain capital gain or compensation (ordinary) gross income? Finally, can more than one of these events (grant of option, exercise of option, and sale of stock) give rise to "compensation" (ordinary) income? Although the tax treatment of stock options is now governed by explicit statutory rules, discussed shortly, this was not always the case. But it happens that the current treatment of stock options is mostly modeled on cases decided prior to the 1969 enactment of § 83.

COMMISSIONER v. SMITH
United States Supreme Court
324 U.S. 177 (1945)

MR. CHIEF JUSTICE STONE delivered the opinion of the Court.

Respondent's employer [Western Cooperage Co.] gave to him, as compensation for his services, an option to purchase from the employer certain shares of stock of another corporation at a price not less than the then value of the stock. In two later tax years, when the market value of the stock was greater than the option price, respondent exercised the option, purchasing large amounts of the stock in each year. The question for decision is whether the difference between the market value and the option price of the stock was compensation for personal services of the employee, taxable as income in the years when he received the stock, under [the predecessor of § 61].

The Tax Court sustained the Commissioner. The Court of Appeals for the Ninth Circuit reversed, 142 F.2d 818, holding that the exercise of the option was a mere purchase of a capital investment which could result in taxable income only upon sale of the stock.

Respondent has never contended that the option itself had value when given, and there was no finding by the Tax Court that it then had value. The Tax Court quoted from *Estate of Connolly v. Comm'r*, 45 B.T.A. 374, as follows: "If the options had never been exercised, the optionees would never have received any additional compensation."

[The predecessor of current § 61(a)] is broad enough to include in taxable income any economic or financial benefit conferred on the employee as compensation, whatever the form or mode by which it is effected. [The regulations] specifically include in income property "transferred . . . by an employer to an employee, for an amount substantially less than its fair market value," even though the transfer takes the form of a sale or exchange, to the extent that the employee receives compensation.

When the option price is less than the market price of the property for the purchase of which the option is given, [the option] may have present value and may be found to be itself compensation for services rendered. But as the option here was not found to have any market value when given, it could not itself operate to compensate respondent. It could do so only as it might be the means of securing the transfer of the shares of stock from the employer to the employee at a price less than their market value, or possibly, which we do not decide, as the option might be sold when that disparity in value existed.

We find no basis for disturbing [the Tax Court's] findings, and we conclude it correctly applied the law to the facts found. Its decision is affirmed, and the judgment of the Court of Appeals below is reversed.

Mr. Justice Roberts is of opinion that the judgment should be affirmed for the reasons stated by the Court of Appeals.

In *Smith*, the Tax Court found that the option itself had no ascertainable value when it was granted. This holding echoes that in the *M. E. Blatt Co.* case, supra Section C, in that the ultimate value of the option depends upon contingent future facts. Moreover, since the exercise date cannot be known, it is impossible to discount a known future amount back to the present.

Modern financial theory holds that this type of option must indeed have a positive value, because a call option is a right to share in future stock value appreciation without any obligation to share in future value depreciation. Suppose the current value of Dell Corporation stock is $30, and the value of such stock might go up or down in the future. It cannot be seriously maintained that a right to buy Dell stock for $30 at any time during the next five years has absolutely "no" value. It may be that the measure of value is not obvious, but it is (now) theoretically possible to come up with a value, if necessary. The policy question is whether the valuation exercise would be worth the effort, given that the value would only be a statistical guess.

An option is said to be "in the money" if the value of the underlying property (the stock) is greater than the option price at the date of grant. Thus, if the option were to buy Dell stock at a price of $28 commencing immediately (when the current FMV of Dell stock is $30), then the option would have a "minimum" value of $2 per share, but its actual value would be more than that.

In any event, the *Smith* opinion implied that, if the option itself *did* have an ascertainable value when granted, the "compensation" attributable to the option would be considered received (and includible) then. Moreover, *Smith* strongly implied that the later exercise would be a nonrealization event. In *Comm'r v. LoBue*, 351 U.S. 243 (1956), the options were in the money when the options were granted, and the taxpayer argued that the *exercise* of the options didn't give rise to compensation income because the options *did* have an ascertainable fair market value when granted. The Supreme Court rejected the taxpayer's argument (351 U.S. at 249):

> It is of course possible for the recipient of a stock option to realize an immediate taxable gain. The option might have a readily ascertainable market value and the recipient might be free to sell his option. But this is not such a case. These three options were not transferable, and LoBue's right to buy stock under them was contingent upon his remaining an employee of the company until they were exercised. The taxable gain to LoBue should be measured as of the time the options were exercised and not the time they were granted.

The dissenting opinion of Justice Harlan stated (351 U.S. at 250-51):

> When the respondent received an unconditional option to buy stock at less than the market price, he received an asset of substantial and immediately realizable value, at least equal to the then existing spread between the option price and the market price. At the exercise of the option, the corporation "gave" the respondent nothing; it simply satisfied a previously-created legal obligation. The option should be taxable as income when given, and any subsequent gain through appreciation of the stock, whether realized by sale of the option or by sale of the stock acquired by its exercise, is attributable to the sale of a capital asset. Any other result makes the division of the total gains between ordinary income and capital gain dependent solely upon the fortuitous circumstance of when the employee exercises his option. [Justice Harlan went on to say that the options that could be exercised only at a future date if the taxpayer was still employed by the company should not be taxed until that future date.]

The results of *Smith* and *LoBue*, which were decided under the general language of the predecessor of § 61(a)(1), have been codified by § 83(a) and (e)(3) and (4). Under § 83(a), the employee realizes ordinary compensation income on the grant date of the option *if* the option has a readily ascertainable value at that time. In such a case, the ordinary income amount is the option's FMV on the grant date, the employee takes a FMV "cost" basis in the option, and, under § 83(e)(4), no further income is realized when the option is exercised. The employee's § 1012 basis in the stock obtained through exercise of the option is the sum of her basis in the option (equal to the amount included in gross income on receipt of the option) plus the price paid under the option to obtain the stock. On a subsequent sale or exchange of the stock, the excess of the amount realized over the stock's basis (even if attributable solely to a low option price) would be capital gain. But *granted options are hardly ever taxed at the date of grant*, because Reg. § 1.83-7(b) provides that a stock option can have a "readily ascertainable fair market value" *only* if it meets stringent conditions, including immediate transferability, that are usually not satisfied by options granted by employers to employees.

An employee receiving an option *without* a "readily ascertainable fair market value" (as defined by the regulations) realizes no income on receipt, see § 83(e)(3), but has *ordinary income under § 83(a) when the option is exercised.* The income amount is, of course, the bargain-purchase amount, i.e., the difference between the price paid for the stock and its FMV at the time of exercise. The employee's § 1012 basis in the stock is the sum of the purchase price plus the amount of income arising from exercise of the option, i.e., the total basis will equal the stock's FMV at the time the option is exercised. Any appreciation in the stock after its purchase can be realized by sale or exchange as capital gain.

Stock options that are "in the money" when granted are subject to § 409A, enacted in 2004, with the likely result of immediate inclusion in income, plus a 20% penalty.[26] It is not clear that inclusion under § 409A precludes inclusion under § 83 when an option is exercised. In any event, it appears that § 409A has effectively killed in-the-money options.

Notwithstanding the foregoing, there is a category of employee stock options called *incentive stock options* (ISOs) — or sometimes "qualified options" — that must "qualify" under numerous requirements set forth in § 422. One of these requirements is that the options must be nontransferable, and another is that the options must not be in the money when granted.

Both the grant *and* the exercise of ISOs are deemed to be nonrealization events. See § 421(a)(1). (However, the "spread" on the exercise date, i.e., the bargain-purchase amount, is gross income to the employee for purposes of the Alternative Minimum Tax (AMT) under § 56(b)(3).) Any gain or loss realized on the ultimate sale of the stock is "capital" gain or loss. The "price" to be paid for the employee exemption, however, is loss of the employer's § 162 deduction. See § 421(a)(2). However, ISOs are immune from the rules of § 409A.

---

[26] This result would be triggered by flunking the fixed-payout rules of § 409A(a)(2). See Reg. § 409A-1(b)(5)(i).

E. NONVESTED PROPERTY TRANSFERS UNDER SECTION 83

The majority opinion in *LoBue* suggests that a *transferable* option might be income at the date of grant. The reverse implication is that nontransferability must result in deferred realization. It is true that, under Reg. § 1.83-7(b), the nontransferability of a (non-ISO) employee stock option results in nonrealization of income on the date the option is granted. But it does not follow that the nontransferability of other in-kind property received as compensation always defeats immediate inclusion. Indeed, in *U.S. v. Drescher*, 179 F.2d 863 (2d Cir. 1950), the court decided that transferability was *not* a prerequisite to realization, at least of compensation income *other* than stock options. In *Drescher*, the employer purchased property (an annuity contract) for the taxpayer-employee from an insurance company. The contract obligated the insurance company to make future payments to the employee commencing when the employee reached age 65. The employee's rights under the contract were not only "funded" but "vested" (i.e., were nonforfeitable), although he could not sell or otherwise transfer the contract to another. The employee argued that he realized no compensation until annuity payments were received in the future. A previous case, *Ward v. Comm'r*, 159 F.2d 502 (2d Cir. 1947), had held that the receipt by an employee of an *assignable* annuity contract was gross income because the property could be reduced to cash by being sold for its present value. The *Drescher* court held that the fact that property could not be assigned did not change the basic rule of inclusion under *Ward*, even though nonassignability meant that the contract in *Drescher* could generate only future cash receipts. The court nevertheless remanded for an assessment of the effect of nonassignability on the present *value* of the annuity, because the employee's income inclusion would be limited to that value.

Another factor bearing on realization has been the significance of "vesting" (acquiring a nonforfeitable right to the property). Justice Harlan's dissent in *LoBue* argued that the options should have been included when granted (despite nontransferability) but not prior to their being vested. In contrast, case law doctrine holds that the receipt of *cash* is current gross income notwithstanding the possibility that the cash will have to be repaid or refunded (forfeited) in the future. See Chapter 18.C. The repayment would raise a deduction (or perhaps a § 1341 credit), issued in the later year in which the cash were paid back. However, in the case of *property* subject to a risk of forfeiture, it would seem that the forfeiture risk would depress the value of the property itself.[27] But valuing a forfeiture risk is virtually impossible, especially if the forfeiture condition depends on the "will" of the employee or employer.

These issues were eventually sorted out with the enactment of § 83 in 1969, which comprehensively deals with in-kind compensation received by an employee or other provider of services. Section 83 treats a transfer of "property" to a services provider as gross income in an amount equal to the excess of the FMV of the property over any consideration paid by the services provider *in the first year the property is*

---

[27] Since U.S. cash must have a basis equal to its face amount, the amount includible on the receipt of cash cannot be discounted on account of the risk of forfeiture. Hence, a contingent liability to repay cash is something separate and apart from the cash itself.

"transferable or [is] not subject to a substantial risk of forfeiture." As noted momentarily, the "transferability" concept is subordinate to the "risk of forfeiture" idea. Section 83, by delaying realization until the risk of forfeiture lapses (when the right to the property "vests"), avoids the problem of having to take the risk of forfeiture into account in valuing the property received.[28] Restricted property transfers are not subject to § 409A.[29]

Section 83(c)(2) states that the property in the hands of the services provider is "transferable" *only* if any transferee of the property would not be subject to a substantial risk of forfeiture. Thus, "transferability" has no significance apart from the concept of "substantial risk of forfeiture." Whether or not a transferee is bound by forfeiture conditions is determined by applicable property and commercial law. In the case of stock, forfeiture conditions and other restrictions endorsed on the stock certificate are binding on any transferee.

To illustrate the operation of § 83 regarding transfers of property (other than stock options), assume that in Year 1 an employer transfers stock with a FMV of $100 to an employee at no charge and without restriction. Since the stock is fully vested in the employee, the employee must include $100 of ordinary income and take a $100 cost basis in the stock (under § 1012 "tax cost" principles).

Now assume the same facts as before except that the terms of the transfer stipulate that if the employee quits her job or is fired without cause before three years have elapsed, she must return the stock to the employer. Assume further that the employee's failure to satisfy the three-year requirement will cause any transferee to forfeit the stock. (Such stock is colloquially referred to as "restricted stock.") Because quitting one's job and being fired without cause are considered substantial risks of forfeiture under Reg. § 1.83-3(c), the employee need not include anything in Year 1 gross income. When the restrictions lapse in Year 3, however, she would include in gross income the FMV of the stock *at that time.* If, for example, the stock were then valued at $150, she would include $150 of ordinary income (rather than the $100 value at the time of the original transfer) and take a $150 cost basis in the stock under § 1012. Any appreciation thereafter would result in capital gain when the stock was sold by her.

In the case of property subject to a substantial risk of forfeiture transferred to a services provider, the latter may make the election described in § 83(b). If our taxpayer in the preceding example made the § 83(b) election, she would accelerate her ordinary income inclusion to Year 1 (usually a bad result in light of the time value of money). The amount included would not be discounted on account of the risk of forfeiture. Any further appreciation in value would then be capital gain (a

---

[28] Property received as compensation is often subject to transfer restrictions (permanent or temporary), restrictions on voting (where the property is voting stock), and restrictions on the use of the property as security for debt. The only restrictions that are taken into account in *valuing* the property for purposes of § 83 are restrictions in the nature of permanent limitations on the property's transfer that require the taxpayer to sell, or offer to sell, the property for a formula price at some future time and that will also be enforced against a transferee. See Regs. §§ 1.83-1(a)(1)(i), -3(h), -3(i). Thus, there is no valuation discount in the case of § 83 in-kind compensation on account of the forfeiture conditions themselves.

[29] See Reg. § 1.409A-1(b)(6).

good result). Thus, our hypothetical employee would include $100 in Year 1 gross income as ordinary compensation income and would take a cost basis of $100 under § 1012; if she later sold the stock for $175 after it vested in Year 3, she would realize $75 of capital gain. However (and at odds with the alternative model, as well as tax logic), if she forfeits the stock, she obtains no loss deduction. That is to say, she loses her basis (created by the $100 income inclusion). See § 83(b)(1) (last clause). Thus, in determining whether to make the § 83(b) election, one important factor is the services provider's best estimate as to whether she will be able to satisfy the restriction. Any basis attributable to actually paying for the stock would not be lost.

NOTES

1.   (a) A vested right to a future amount is a present increase in wealth capable of present valuation. In the area of employee compensation, such rights are typically nonassignable in order to tie the employee's future performance to the future success of the company.

(b) The employee can bargain for tax deferral by paying the "price" of reduced security (by accepting forfeiture conditions). Employers view forfeiture conditions as an effective mechanism for tying the employee to the employer.

(c) Section 83 deals with the issue of when does an employee "convert" from being treated as a wage earner (taxed only as wages are received) to being treated as an investor (whose investments are supposed to be with previously taxed dollars). The tax treatment of ISOs follows that of a cash flow consumption tax approach, rather than an income tax approach.

2.   (a) As a general matter, when a taxpayer transfers property (other than its own stock) to another as compensation, the transferor realizes (and recognizes) gain or loss equal to the difference between the FMV of the property transferred and the transferor's basis in the property. See Reg. § 1.83-6(b), which incorporates the holding of *International Freighting Corp. v. Comm'r*, 135 F.2d 310 (2d Cir. 1943). This rule, in effect, treats the transferor as having transferred cash compensation to the services provider, followed by a purchase (with the same cash) by the latter of the transferor's property. The possible alternative approach of treating the transfer as a nonrealization event is not followed, because the transferor is treated as having an amount realized equal to the FMV of the property, and the norm of a market exchange is one of an exchange of equal values.

(b) In the same scenario as (a), the employer obtains a deduction (assuming the compensation is an "expense" rather than a capital expenditure) equal to the amount included by the services provider in income under § 83(a) (which is the full value of the property if the services provider pays no consideration for it), but only in the same year that the amount is includible by the employee. See § 83(h); Reg. § 1.83-6(a).

3.   (a) Where a corporation transfers its *own stock* to an *investor* in return for cash, the corporation has no income or gain by reason of § 1032. This rule also applies where a corporation issues its own stock to a services provider.

(b) Nevertheless, the corporation issuing its own stock for services still obtains a deduction equal to the amount included in gross income by the services provider, provided that the requirements for taking an expense deduction as compensation under § 162 are satisfied. Since a corporation is not required to pay dividends on stock, it is hard to see what present or future cost is being incurred by the corporation, other than the foregone but tax-free cash proceeds that could be obtained by issuing the stock in the market. The issue of whether employee stock options are real "costs" of a corporation has been hotly debated in financial accounting circles.

PROBLEMS

1.   In Year 1, X Corp. issues to its employee, Betty, nontransferable options to purchase up to 1,000 shares of X Corp. stock at $10 per share beginning January 1 of Year 2. On the issue date, X Corp. stock was worth $10 per share and, on January 1 of Year 2, $13 per share. Betty exercises the options for 600 shares, paying $6K, in Year 4, at which time X Corp. stock is selling for $17 per share (so that the value of the acquired stock is $10.2K). Betty sells the 600 shares in Year 7 for $30 a share ($18K total).

(a) What results to Betty and to X Corp as a result of the foregoing, assuming (in the alternative) that these are (or are not) ISOs?

(b) Betty's options for the other 400 shares expire on December 31 of Year 6 without having been exercised. What result to Betty? What if she paid $1 per option in Year 1? See § 1234.

2.   Y Corp. sells shares of its own stock (worth $100K, determined without regard to any restriction on the stock) to its officer, Wilma, for $20K, on condition that Wilma repay the stock to Y Corp. should Wilma be terminated without cause or quit her job during the next 10 years. This restriction is endorsed on the stock certificates issued to Wilma.

(a) What are the tax consequences to Wilma and Y Corp. if, at the expiration of 10 years, Wilma is still employed by Y Corp. and the stock is then worth $135K?

(b) What are the tax consequences to Wilma and Y Corp. if, instead, Wilma quits her job after seven years, at which time the stock is worth $107K?

(c) Same as (a) and (b) but assume that Wilma makes a § 83(b) election. Why would an employee make such an election?

(d) What is the tax treatment of the dividends payable on the Y Corp. stock to the parties under the above variations? See Reg. § 1.83-1(a)(1); *Rev. Rul. 83-22*, 1983-1 C.B. 17.

Chapter 23

TAX ACCOUNTING METHODS

Tax accounting methods pertain to the timing of gross income items and expense deduction items. Because tax accounting rules are timing rules, they belong within the larger rubric of "realization" doctrine. The principal "tax accounting methods" are (1) the "cash receipts and disbursements" method of tax accounting (the "cash method"), (2) the accrual method of tax accounting, and (3) the installment method of accounting for certain noninventory property sales. See §§ 446(c), 453.

Most (if not all) of the transactions dealt with in this chapter involve the purchase and sale of goods, services, and property on credit. The term "on credit" means that the buyer is obligated to pay all or part of the price in cash in the future, whether or not that promise is evidenced by a promissory note.

A. ROLE OF CASH AND ACCRUAL ACCOUNTING METHODS

This section deals with (1) the substantive issues addressed by the cash and accrual methods of tax accounting, and (2) how one determines which method to use. (The installment method is dealt with in Section D.2.)

1. Inventory Accounting

The cash and accrual methods of accounting deal generally with the *timing* of (1) *gross income inclusions* and (2) *expense deductions*. These methods also control the timing with respect to inventory accounting. When a business sells inventory, "gain" is not computed separately for each inventory item. Instead, both "amount realized" and "basis" are computed on a mass (aggregate) basis by means of inventory accounting conventions. Gain from inventory is excluded from § 61(a)(3) ("gains derived from dealings in property") but instead is included within § 61(a)(2) ("gross income derived from business"). Gross income derived from business, insofar as it refers to inventory gains or losses, means aggregate gross receipts from the sale of inventory less aggregate "cost of goods sold" (CGS). See Reg. § 1.61-3(a).

The CGS amount is the "mass basis" for all inventory disposed of. CGS is computed as follows: (1) cost of Opening Inventory *plus* (2) cost of Purchased Inventory during the taxable year *minus* (3) cost of Closing Inventory (which is also cost of Opening Inventory for the following taxable year). The sum of Opening Inventory and Purchases represents the aggregate cost of the total inventory available for sale during the taxable year. The subtraction of Closing Inventory (i.e., the cost of what's left at the end of the taxable year) yields the cost of inventory disposed of during the taxable year, whether by sale, "loss," theft, or abandonment.

The cost of Closing Inventory is figured by taking a physical inventory and then applying either the FIFO (first-in, first-out) or LIFO (last-in, first-out) cost convention. To illustrate, suppose that in Year 1 the taxpayer purchases 100 widgets, none of which are sold in Year 1, for $10 each (a total of $1K), and in Year 2 the taxpayer purchases another 100 widgets for $13 each (a total of $1,300). The sum of Opening Inventory and Purchases (200 units) is $2,300. At the end of Year 2, Closing Inventory consists of 80 widgets, meaning that 120 units have been disposed of during the year. Under FIFO, the cost of Closing Inventory is $1,040 (80 × $13) because "what's left" is deemed to be the most recently acquired widgets. Using FIFO produces a CGS figure of $1,060 ($800 + $1,300 - $1,040). Under LIFO, the cost of Closing Inventory is $800 (80 × $10) because "what's left" is deemed to be the earliest inventory acquired. LIFO produces a higher CGS figure of $1,300 ($800 + $1,300 - $800) due to the lower amount subtracted. The higher the CGS figure, the lower the income from inventory sales.

2. What Issues Are Affected by Tax Accounting Methods?

To simplify things for the reader, in this subsection the term "gross income" refers to *both* gross receipts in the case of inventory sales *and* items of gross income (such as services income), and the term "expense" refers to *both* inventory costs *and* deductible expense items generally.

Tax accounting methods determine *when* gross income (and gross receipts) items are includible and *when* expenses (and inventory costs) are deductible. They have nothing to do with the more fundamental questions of *whether* or not an item constitutes "gross income" or is (or is not) deductible as an "expense." *Nor do tax accounting methods alter the rules pertaining to capitalization (and noninventory basis), borrowing, and basis recovery*, even though the latter topics also deal with "timing" issues.

The "gross income" timing issue for the seller with respect to credit sales of services or inventory is whether the seller's claim against the buyer, arising from the buyer's promise to pay cash in the *future*, is to be treated as "property" received by the seller. If the claim is *not* treated as property, the seller would realize gross income only as the buyer makes cash payments in satisfaction of the claim. If, on the other hand, the seller's receipt of the claim against the buyer *is* treated as property, then it would be included in gross income or gross receipts. In cases where rights or claims to future cash are to be considered property upon receipt by the seller, a second issue arises, which is: "At what amount should such property be taken into account?" Its face amount? The "discounted present value" of the face amount? Its fair market value (FMV), which would take into account not only the time delay in payment but also the risk of nonpayment (i.e., the creditworthiness of the buyer)? Recall that inclusion at FMV is the norm for includible in-kind property income in contexts *not* involving credit sales. For example, if you receive an automobile as a prize, the amount includible is its (retail) FMV.

In the case of credit sales, if the discount rate itself were to take creditworthiness into account (as would happen in commerce), there would be little difference between FMV and "present discounted value" (PV). Also, if the seller charges market-rate interest, the PV of a deferred-payment obligation (and maybe its FMV if the obligor has an impeccable credit rating) will be equal (or nearly equal) to its face amount. However, the three possible measures of the includible amount can diverge. If no interest (or a below-market rate of interest) is charged, the face amount will diverge from both the PV and FMV. Additionally, PV *for tax purposes* can diverge from FMV because the Code imposes a "standard" discount rate keyed to U.S. government obligations, called the "applicable federal rate" (AFR), which is basically a risk-free discount rate.

Whichever of face amount, PV, or FMV is the rule for credit sales, the seller would take a basis in the claim to future cash equal to the amount included. However, if either the PV or the FMV of the purchaser's obligation when acquired is the amount included in gross income or gross receipts then, when the seller actually receives the principal cash owed under the claim in the future, there would be a second realization event giving rise to gain or loss, because the claim is "disposed of" (extinguished) at the moment it is satisfied. The buyer's satisfaction of the claim in full by the payment of cash would result in no further gain or loss to the seller *only if* the amount actually received by the seller precisely equals the amount previously included, but this will systematically be the case only if the amount included in gross income or gross receipts – which amount, recall, fixes the basis in the claim – is the face amount of the obligation (the stated principal amount).

Thus, assume that Christa, a tax expert, prepares Rudi's tax return and bills Rudi in the amount of $1K in November of Year 1, payable in 90 days, but with no interest charge on late payments. Rudi pays $1K to Christa in January of Year 2. The fact that the transaction occurs in Year 1 and the payment occurs in Year 2 *requires* a system of tax accounting to sort out the issue of what year(s) the transaction is reportable. (If this transaction were an isolated transaction and the payment were received in the same year as that in which the services were performed, then tax accounting rules would not be necessary.)

Figuring the PV in Year 1 of Christa's claim against Rudi is impossible, because it is basically an open account debt that can be paid at any time. And, short of offering the claim for sale in the marketplace and seeing what offers come along, it would be even harder to figure its FMV, but we shall stipulate that the FMV is $900 because Rudi has a poor credit record. If the claim were treated as "property" (and included) in Year 1, Christa would (under general tax principles) include $900 in Year 1, creating a basis in the claim of $900 and resulting in $100 of additional "satisfaction gain" (or collection gain) in Year 2 when Rudi *actually* pays the full $1K of cash.

Both the PV and FMV methods would pose administrative problems, namely, figuring out the amount to be included (which also fixes the seller's basis in the claim), (2) keeping track of the basis, and (3) figuring the gain or loss on collection or disposition of the claim. Additionally, is the collection gain "ordinary" income or "capital" gain? Each item, by itself, may involve relatively trivial amounts, and yet the taxpayer (if a business taxpayer) may have to account for thousands or millions of such items in a taxable year.

3.   The Cash and Accrual Approaches in a Nutshell

Only two simplifying approaches are possible. One is to treat the claim as "not property" and simply await the receipt of cash. The *cash method of accounting* adopts this approach. If Christa (in the above example) uses the cash method, she realizes no gross income in Year 1. Rather, she realizes gross income only when the claim is paid in Year 2. If Rudi never pays, Christa never realizes gross income from this transaction. Accordingly, Christa never acquires a tax basis in the claim against Rudi, and can have no deductible loss if her claim against Rudi becomes worthless.

The second simplifying approach is to treat the claim as "property" but to measure it at its *face amount* (instead of at its PV or FMV). The *accrual method of accounting* adopts this approach. Thus, if Christa uses the accrual method, she realizes Year 1 gross income of $1K (the face amount of the claim against Rudi), which creates a $1K basis for Christa in the claim against Rudi. If Rudi pays the face amount of $1K in Year 2, Christa realizes no further gain or loss because the $1K received is precisely offset by Christa's $1K basis created in the prior year. Since the collection gain or loss is zero, the issue of its "character" dissolves. If Christa's claim against Rudi becomes worthless at some point, she has a basis of $1K in her claim that will support a business (bad debt) loss deduction.

In short, both the cash and accrual methods avoid having to value claims (rights) to future cash.

Since Rudi's cost of having his tax return prepared is an "expense" that happens to be deductible under § 212(3) (or possibly under §§ 162(a) and 212(2)), Rudi faces the same tax accounting options as Christa, only in reverse: (1) deduction of $1K *when paid in Year 2* (the cash method) or (2) deduction of $1K *face amount in Year 1* (the accrual method).

The *concept* of "accrual" means that rights and obligations involving future payments are taken into account at the time (prior to receipt or payment of cash) when the right or obligation is fixed (established), assuming that the amount of the future receipt or payment is known with reasonable accuracy. The idea is that one's wealth is increased or decreased at that time. The concept of accrual permeates business/financial accounting where a right to receive future payment (a "receivable") is an "asset," and an obligation to make future payment (a "payable") is a "liability."

The accrual concept has been encountered previously, most notably in the case of the "borrowing exclusion," where the "offsetting liability" (obligation to repay principal) is viewed as an immediate decrease in wealth taken into account at its face amount as an offset against the borrowed cash amount. A related example is the so-called *Crane* basis rule, discussed in Chapter 20.A. Thus, if Don purchases noninventory property on credit for $1M, his basis would be $1M immediately upon purchase. Here, the obligation to pay in the future is treated as a current payment of the purchase price at its face amount. However, it bears emphasis that the accrual concepts embodied in the treatment of borrowing and the *Crane* basis rule are mandatory, and are not dependent upon a taxpayer's tax accounting method! The same is true of capitalization. These rules trump cash-method and accrual-method rules.

The differences between the cash and accrual methods only come into play when the issue is the timing of gross income inclusions and item deductions where cash payment is to be made in the future. Accounting methods have no bearing on the inclusion of in-kind income apart from future-payment obligations. Thus, if an employer transfers an automobile to its employee, the automobile is gross income to the employee when received (under §§ 61(a)(1) and 83), and the amount included is its FMV. The fact that the employee is on the cash method does not allow the employee to avoid or defer immediate inclusion in income of the value of the automobile. In cases where in-kind income is subject to a deferred-realization rule (such as those encountered in the previous chapter), the deferred-realization rule is independent of cash-method accounting rules, and is applicable to cash-method and accrual-method taxpayers alike. As will be explained in Section D, cash-method and accrual-method rules are not applicable to sales of noninventory property.

It should also be pointed out that interest is accounted for separately from the "principal" component of deferred-payment transactions. Thus, if the Christa/Rudi example involved a one-year term note bearing market-rate interest, the interest payments would be accounted for separately from the $1K principal obligation itself. The issue of the distinction between principal (face amount) and interest is dealt with in Chapter 27.

4.   Accounting Methods and Bad Debt Losses

Recall that borrowed money is excludible from the borrower's gross income only because the offsetting repayment obligation prevents a wealth accession. Thus, a borrower who escapes the repayment obligation generally realizes § 61(a)(12) debt-discharge income (possibly deferrable under § 108). We have not, until now, however, considered the tax consequences to the *creditor* when a debt is not repaid. Bad debt losses are considered here because of their close relationship to tax accounting methods.

When a debt or claim becomes worthless, the creditor has sustained a loss in the *economic* sense. Whether a loss exists in the *tax* sense depends on the extent, if any, of the creditor's "basis" in the debt or claim. Recall that under § 165(b) *any* loss deduction is limited to the taxpayer's basis. For example, if uninsured investment property Blackacre, with a basis of $100 and FMV of $500, burns to the ground, the taxpayer's *economic* loss is $500, but his *tax* loss is limited to only $100. Since the $400 of unrealized appreciation in Blackacre's value was never included in the taxpayer's gross income, that $400 of appreciation cannot be deducted as a loss, or else the taxpayer will enjoy *both* an exclusion *and* a deduction of the same $400 (a prohibited double tax benefit for the same dollars to the same taxpayer).

It happens that bad debts are governed by a specific Code provision, § 166, rather than the § 165 general loss-deduction provision. Predictably, however, § 166(b) provides that the amount deductible in the year of a debt's worthlessness is limited to the creditor's basis in the debt. When a lender transfers cash to a borrower, the lender has made a nondeductible capital expenditure, which creates basis. That basis prevents any loan principal repayments from constituting "gross income" to the lender. Rather, any such principal repayment is a tax-free "return of capital," which reduces the lender's basis in the amount loaned. When the cash loan becomes "worthless," § 166 allows the lender to deduct as a bad-debt loss any remaining basis in the loan.

The ruling below deals with the issue of whether the taxpayer actually made a "loan" of cash to the borrower that would support a bad-debt deduction.

REVENUE RULING 93-27
1993-1 C.B. 32

The taxpayer, *A*, was divorced in 1989 from *B* and was granted custody of their two minor children. Pursuant to a property settlement and support agreement that was incorporated into the divorce decree, *B* agreed to pay to *A* $500 per month for child support. During 1991, *B* failed to pay $5,000 of this obligation. Because of *B*'s arrearage, *A* had to spend $5,000 of *A*'s own funds in support of *A*'s children.

In *Swenson v. Comm'r*, 43 T.C. 897 (1965), the taxpayer claimed a bad debt deduction for an uncollectible arrearage in child support payments from a former spouse. The Tax Court denied the deduction on the ground that the taxpayer had no basis in the debt created by the child support obligation. The taxpayer had argued that her basis consisted of the expenditures for child support she was forced to make from her own funds as a result of the father's failure to make his required payments. The court pointed out, however, that the father's obligation to make the payments had been imposed by the divorce court and was not contingent on the taxpayer's support expenditures.

In the present case, *A*'s own child support expenditures did not create or affect *B*'s obligation to *A* under the divorce decree. Accordingly, *A* did not have any basis in *B*'s obligation to pay child support, and *A* may not claim a bad debt deduction under § 166.

As noted above, a cash lender, having made a capital expenditure by advancing money, possesses a basis that can support a bad debt deduction. In contrast, a seller of goods and services on credit does not have a basis in the buyer's debt obligation unless that obligation has a basis to the seller by reason of an earlier income inclusion. Such an inclusion would have been caused by the credit seller being on the accrual method of tax accounting for the sale. To illustrate, suppose that Mary buys dancing lessons on credit from John in Year 1 and in Year 2 is fully discharged from this debt in a bankruptcy proceeding. John acquires an "account receivable," which is an asset of sorts, in Year 1. Can John deduct this $100 debt in Year 2 when it becomes wholly worthless? The answer depends simply on whether John uses the cash or accrual method of accounting. If John uses the cash method, he would have included nothing in Year 1 in his gross income. Having not included any gross income in Year 1, John has no basis to deduct in Year 2 when the debt becomes worthless. If, in contrast, John uses the accrual method, he would have accrued the

$100 account receivable in gross income in Year 1 at its face amount. Therefore, when the account receivable becomes worthless in Year 2, John has a $100 basis in it (i.e., the amount that he included in gross income in Year 1) to deduct under § 166.

In short, an "account receivable" has a basis only if and to the extent that it has been included in gross income, and that depends on the workings of cash-method and accrual-method doctrines.

Other aspects of § 166 are worth noting. Notice how § 166 treats "nonbusiness" bad debts unfavorably compared to "business" bad debts. "Business" bad debt losses are fully deductible as ordinary losses instead of capital losses, because a loss due to worthlessness does not involve a "sale or exchange." In contrast, nonbusiness bad debts are conclusively treated as short-term capital losses. See § 166(d)(1)(B).

Moreover, a business debt can generate deductions even if only a *portion* of it becomes worthless, provided that the worthless amount is charged off on the taxpayer's books. See Reg. § 1.166-3(a)(2). The ability to deduct a partially worthless business bad debt is an exception to the principle that partial losses are not realized (in the absence of a physical disposition of a part of the asset). Deductions for partially worthless bad debts appear to be quite rare. Possible scenarios include a bankruptcy proceeding that reduces amounts available to creditors or a permanent impairment of collateral.

Nonbusiness debts must be *fully* worthless in order to be deductible. This rule is satisfied where a nonbusiness debt has partially been paid off (this is sometimes referred to as a debt that is "wholly worthless in part"). For example, if $100 was originally lent, $40 was repaid, and the entire remaining $60 principal debt then became wholly worthless, the deduction of $60K is allowed.[1]

The distinction between business and nonbusiness (investment) bad debts was discussed in Chapter 8.A. Note that § 166 acknowledges no such thing as a nondeductible "personal" debt. There are only two categories of worthless debts (business and nonbusiness), and both are deductible, although their treatment differs. Thus, a bona fide cash loan to a family member that later becomes worthless is deductible as a nonbusiness bad debt loss. However, a creditor cannot create a bad debt deduction by gratuitously cancelling a family member's debt (that was bona fide when made), because gifts (however disguised) are not deductible. If the loan to the family member was not bona fide (because it was a disguised gift at the time made), the lent cash is a nondeductible gift "expense," and does not create a basis in the debt that can later be deducted. See Chapter 18.C.2.

The issue of worthlessness is a factual one that has given rise to much litigation. In general, a debt is worthless only when there is discharge in bankruptcy, the statute of limitations has run, or there is no practical hope of repayment after considering bona fide efforts by the lender to obtain repayment. See Reg. § 1.166-2.

The worthlessness of certain "securities," which includes debt instruments issued by corporations or governmental units that are either in registered form or have

---

[1] See *Alexander v. Comm'r*, 26 T.C. 856 (1956) (acq.).

interest coupons attached,[2] is governed by § 165(g) instead of § 166. If such a security is a capital asset, § 165(g) treats its worthlessness as a "sale or exchange" on the last day of the taxable year. This rule usually results in a long-term capital loss.

Worthlessness of a debt is to be distinguished from the situation where a debt is satisfied for its full face amount, but such face amount differs from the taxpayer's basis therein. This can happen where, say, a $1K face amount bond was purchased on the market for $1.1K, and the corporation redeems the bond for $1K. Section 1271(a)(1) provides that amounts received on the retirement of a debt obligation are deemed to be received "in exchange" for the obligation. In *McClain v. Comm'r*, 311 U.S. 527 (1941), the word "retirement" was construed to mean any kind of satisfaction of the debt, whether at or before maturity. The effect of § 1271(a)(1) is usually to produce a capital gain or loss to the obligation holder.

5.   Which Method of Accounting Does a Taxpayer Use?

Certain taxpayers ("tax shelters," as defined in the Code, many corporations, and certain partnerships with a corporate partner) *must* use the accrual method by statutory fiat under § 448. Also, inventory sales (gross receipts) and Purchases (entering into CGS) must generally be accounted for using the accrual method, even if the taxpayer otherwise uses the cash method.[3]

Otherwise, taxpayers may choose their "overall" method of tax accounting, and § 446(a) states that a taxpayer chooses a method of tax accounting by the way the taxpayer keeps its "books." Most individual wage earners do not keep systematic books as such. The closest thing to books would be checkbook registers, credit card statements, and perhaps individual cash expenditure receipts. Nevertheless, these count as books for income tax purposes,[4] and they generally record receipts and payments as actually received and paid (and, as noted below, checks and credit card payments are treated as "cash equivalents"). Thus, virtually all individuals use the cash method (except insofar as they are a direct owner of an accrual-method business).

If the taxpayer keeps its books according to recognized business accounting principles, sometimes referred to as "generally accepted accounting principles" (GAAP), the taxpayer is usually required to use the accrual method, because the accrual method of tax accounting and GAAP are both based on accrual *concepts*.

----

[2] The term "securities" in § 165(g) also includes shares of stock. However, in the case of small business stock as specified in § 1244, worthlessness gives rise to an ordinary loss of up to $50K (or $100K in the case of a married couple filing a joint return).

[3] See Reg. § 1.446-1(c)(2). The main exceptions lie for certain farmers, but that is a subject unto itself. Under *Rev. Proc. 2002-28*, 2002-1 C.B. 815, however, a taxpayer who would otherwise be required to use the accrual method and inventory accounting can use the cash method (and forgo inventory accounting) if (1) the taxpayer's average annual gross receipts do not exceed $10 million, (2) the taxpayer is not a "tax shelter" as defined in the Code, and (3) the taxpayer's principal business activity is not mining, manufacturing, wholesale trade, retail trade, or the information industry (other than furnishing information services).

[4] See Reg. § 1.441-1(b)(7).

Essentially, then, the cash method is a kind of default system that controls a taxpayer's tax accounting issues, unless the taxpayer keeps systematic books following GAAP principles or is otherwise required to use the accrual method. For purposes of this book (and the Problems), *it should generally be assumed that individual taxpayers use the cash method, unless stated otherwise.*

A taxpayer might use the cash method for certain activities and the accrual method for others. For example, a sole proprietor may use the accrual method with respect to her retail business and the cash method for other receipts (such as investment income) and personal expenditures.[5] And (as already noted) inventories must usually be accounted for using the accrual method. As a general rule, a taxpayer cannot simply elect to treat certain items under the cash method and other items under the accrual method within a single activity. Whichever method the taxpayer uses for that activity usually controls all of the taxpayer's transactions in that activity. Taxpayers are also held to a standard of consistency from year to year.[6] Any change in accounting method requires the advance permission of the IRS. See § 446(d).

Overriding everything, however, is § 446(b), which grants the Commissioner a broad power to compel the taxpayer to change a method of accounting that the Commissioner (i.e., the IRS) finds "does not clearly reflect income." The IRS can use its § 446(b) power to shift a taxpayer to, or away from, the accrual method (or the cash method), either with respect to the taxpayer's entire return or with respect to only certain activities or items.

NOTES

1.   Recall that inventory is not a capital asset under § 1221(a)(1), and compensation for services is ordinary income. These rules are backed up by § 1221(a)(4), which provides that receivables resulting from the sale of inventory or services are not capital assets. See § 1221(4). Thus, the sale (or satisfaction) of receivables for inventory or services produces ordinary gain or income.

2.   (a) *Rev. Rul. 93-27*, set out above, held that A's cash support outlays were not loans (capital expenditures creating basis). B's unpaid support obligations arose from the divorce decree, not the expenditure of A's funds to provide the support that B was supposed to have provided. A's support outlays were just nondeductible family expenses, not loans to B.

(b) If the child support system under state law provides that support outlays by the custodial parent give rise to a claim for reimbursement from the noncustodial parent up to the amount stipulated by the custodial agreement, the nondeductible child support "expenses" of the custodial parent would become capital expenditures, by reason of creating an asset (the right to reimbursement). See Chapter 26.B.

3.   (a) To support a bad debt deduction, the debt must be *bona fide*.[7] If a

---

[5]   See Reg. § 1.446-1(c)(1)(iv).

[6]   See Reg. § 1.446-1(c)(2)(ii).

[7]   See Reg. § 1.166-1(c).

purported loan is a gift, the loan is not even a capital expenditure, but only a nondeductible expense. A gift would be indicated if the borrower is a related person and the lender didn't intend to enforce the note or the borrower had no expectation of repayment due (say) to the fact that the borrower was disabled and/or chronically unemployed.[8]

(b) If a buyer fails to pay the purchase price to the seller of real property, and the seller repossesses the property, section 1038(a) (discussed in Chapter 22.A.6) bars the seller from claiming a bad debt deduction. The effect of § 1038 is to "call off" the earlier sale (and its attendant purchase money debt). Section 453B, discussed in Section D, infra, governs repossessions of personal property that had been sold on credit. Here the most likely result is (ordinary) gain or loss equal to the difference between the FMV of the repossessed collateral and the creditor's basis in the obligation.

4. Apart from the cash method of accounting, the accrual method of accounting, and the installment method, other "permitted" accounting methods exist, but are more specialized. Accounting for long term contracts is discussed in Chapter 26.A.4. Other accounting rules for certain narrow situations are allowed under various Code provisions, regulations, and revenue procedures.

PROBLEMS

1. In Year 1, the taxpayer purchases 100 widgets, none of which are sold in Year 1, for $10 each (a total of $1K). In Year 2, the taxpayer purchases another 100 widgets on credit for $13 each (a total of $1,300), and sells 120 widgets for $15 (20 for cash and the other 100 on credit). None of the credit transactions involve an interest charge. What would be the Year-2 "gross income derived from business" under § 61(a)(2) using FIFO? Using LIFO? Note that, under § 472(c), if LIFO is used for tax purposes it must also be used for financial reporting purposes. Why would Congress attach such a condition to LIFO, but not FIFO, inventory calculations?

2. Mike performs legal services for Becky in Year 1 and shortly thereafter sends her a bill for $3K, which is not disputed. The bill requests payment in 30 days but makes no mention of interest charges for late payments. In Year 3, Becky pays the $3K in full.

(a) What tax results to both parties if they are both on the *accrual* method?

(b) What tax results to both parties if they are both on the cash method?

(c) What tax results to both parties if Becky never pays the bill? (Assume, in the alternative, that they both are on the accrual method or both on the cash method.)

(d) Suppose the provider of legal services is a corporation? *Can* it be on the cash method? Should it *want* to be on the cash method?

3. Lori, who uses the cash method, lends $10K cash to her beloved brother Jim in Year 1, evidenced by a 5-year note with a market rate of interest. What tax result

---

[8] See *Eckert v. Burnet*, 283 U.S. 140 (1931); *Van Anda v. Comm'r*, 12 T.C. 1158 (1949), *aff'd per curiam*, 192 F.2d 391 (2d Cir. 1951); *Hunt v. Comm'r*, T.C. Memo. 1989-335.

to Lori if:

(a) Lori *never* intended to (and does not) enforce the loan terms?

(b) Lori's intent was equivocal, but in Year 5, Lori (in a fit of generosity) declares that she has ripped up the note and that Jim doesn't have to pay her anything (even though he could have)?

(c) Lori intended to seek repayment, but Jim in fact never pays it back, although Lori strenuously demands payment in Year 5 and thereafter, and Jim (having moved to the Bahamas) has no assets subject to attachment or garnishment. The statute of limitations runs against Lori's claim in Year 8.

B. CASH-METHOD DOCTRINE

The core principle of cash-method doctrine is that the inclusion of gross income or the deduction of expense items occurs only as the item is received or paid (as the case may be) in cash.[9]

Use of the term "cash method" can, however, mislead some students into thinking that *only* the receipt of *cash* triggers a gross income inclusion (or expense deduction) for a taxpayer using this method of accounting. *Nothing can be further from the truth!* Being on the cash method does not avoid immediate inclusion of realized in-kind income. Thus, it does not prevent immediate inclusion of an automobile received by an employee as compensation. It only operates to defer income that takes the form of rights to future cash payments, such as receivables and (perhaps, as we shall see) notes and contract rights to future cash. Use of the cash method does not permit a current deduction for "capital expenditures" that happen to be paid in cash, nor does it allow borrowed cash to be included in current income.

The cash method of accounting has spawned three common law tax doctrines of far-reaching significance that are dealt with below: (1) the cash-equivalency doctrine, (2) the constructive-receipt doctrine, and (3) the economic-benefit doctrine.

1. The Cash-Equivalency Doctrine

The receipt of an item that is a "cash equivalent" is immediate gross income (or a gross receipt) to a cash-method taxpayer.

a. Checks

On both the income and the deduction side, *checks are generally considered to be the equivalent of cash.* Thus, income inclusions occur when checks are received by a cash-method taxpayer and allowable expense deductions are taken by a cash-method taxpayer when checks are delivered.[10] The date when the check is cashed,

---

[9] See Reg. § 1.446-1(c)(1)(i).

[10] Mailing by the payor apparently constitutes delivery for deduction purposes but not receipt for gross income inclusion purposes. Compare Reg. § 1.170A-1(b) with *Rev. Rul. 76-3*, 1976-1 C.B. 114.

deposited, or paid by the drawee bank is irrelevant for these purposes.[11] The amount included or deducted (as the case may be) is the *face amount* of the check, as opposed to its FMV (which might conceivably be discounted in commerce because of a risk of nonpayment). If the check is returned unpaid, however, there is no current income or deduction, at least until the check is paid.[12]

b. Contractual Promises to Make Future Payments

At the other end of the spectrum, "[a] mere promise to pay, not represented by notes or secured in any way, is not regarded as the receipt of income within the intendment of the cash receipts and disbursements method." See *Rev. Rul. 60-31*, 1960-1 C.B. 174, 177. Similarly, the making of such a promise is not considered "payment" and will not result in an immediate deduction. A contractual promise to pay is distinguishable not only from notes but also such financial instruments sold in commerce as bonds, debentures, annuities, corporate stock, and other interests in entities, which are considered "property" and are outside of the scope of cash-method doctrine. Receipts of property are generally included in gross income, unless a nonrealization rule provides otherwise.

c. Promissory Notes

Promissory *notes* are a problem area because a note (to the recipient) occupies the no-man's land among the territories staked out by checks (cash equivalents), mere promises to pay (not currently includible), and the financial-instrument kind of property, such as a bond, which is normally included in income when received. A *negotiable* note is a very liquid form of property. Here, the tax treatment differs according to whether the question is broached from the income side or the deduction side.

On the income side, the leading case is *Cowden v. Comm'r*, 289 F.2d 20 (5th Cir. 1961), which stated:

> If a promise to pay of a solvent obligor is unconditional and assignable, not subject to set-offs, and is of a kind that is frequently transferred to lenders or investors at a discount not substantially greater than the generally prevailing premium for the use of money, such promise is the equivalent of cash.

Under this approach, transferability (or assignability) without an excess discount is critical in determining whether a note is a cash equivalent. (Note that a note can be assignable without being "negotiable.") The *Cowden* "rule" would result in immediate inclusion of a negotiable note (which is ipso facto assignable) unless its FMV is significantly below its present discounted value (i.e., its FMV reflects a discount greater than the discount that occurs merely to compensate for the

---

[11] A dramatic illustration of this principle occurred in *Walter v. U.S.*, 148 F.3d 1027 (8th Cir. 1998), where a taxpayer had to include the face amount of a check in the year the check was received even though the taxpayer lost the check before cashing or depositing it and did not obtain a replacement check until two years later.

[12] See *Kahler v. Comm'r*, 18 T.C. 31 (1952).

delayed payment).[13] Thus, the fact that the note is already heavily iscounted by reason of not bearing interest would not preclude cash equivalency.[14]

A *third-party* obligation (such as a note, bond, or debenture issued by someone other than the buyer of goods or services) is generally treated as "property," which is generally includible at its FMV. Thus, for example, assume that Sally, a cash-method taxpayer, is employed by sole proprietor John, who pays Sally her $100 salary by transferring to her a nonassignable note, having a FMV of $100, given to John by Clare, one of John's customers. Sally must include the $100 FMV of the third-party debt instrument in her gross income under § 61(a)(1) in the year received, even though the note doesn't satisfy the *Cowden* test. Sally cannot defer inclusion of the amount until she sells it for cash or is otherwise paid cash by Clare at the note's maturity. A note made out from the buyer of goods and services to the seller (a two-party note) that flunks the *Cowden* test is treated as a mere contractual promise to pay, rather than as a cash equivalent or as property. Hence, it is not currently includible.

It is perhaps confusing to say that (under *Cowden*) a second-party assignable note that lacks an excess discount is really a "cash equivalent," because true cash equivalents (checks, supra, and credit card transactions, infra) are taken into account at their face amount.[15] A *Cowden* note is really a kind of "property," includible at its FMV (not its face amount),[16] just as is any third-party note (assignable or not). Despite the foregoing, *Cowden* notes are spoken of as being cash equivalents to the extent of their FMV.

On the deduction side, *the giving of one's own promissory note is not the equivalent of paying cash and thus cannot currently trigger an expense deduction,* even if the note satisfies the *Cowden* test or is payable on demand. The taxpayer/ payor is viewed as not having parted with anything, except a piece of paper, until actual payment of the note. See *Don E. Williams Co. v. Comm'r,* 429 U.S. 569 (1977).[17] Of course, the giving *of a third-party note* (instead of one's own note) would give rise to a current deduction. For example, if cash-method Joe transferred to Jane a $100 note originally issued to Joe by Conglomerate Corporation, Joe could deduct the value of the Conglomerate note (assuming, of course, that the payment to Jane is a deductible expense), regardless of whether the note meets the *Cowden* test.[18]

---

[13] See *Williams v. Comm'r,* 28 T.C. 1000 (1957) (acq.) (insolvent payor).

[14] In *Cowden* itself, the promise to make future payment did not bear interest, and the IRS valued the obligation simply by discounting it to present value.

[15] In *Cowden,* the Tax Court had included the note at face, but the Fifth Circuit remanded on this point.

[16] *See Cowden v. Comm'r,* 289 F.2d 20, 23 (5th Cir. 1961); *Board v. Comm'r,* 18 B.T.A. 650 (acq.).

[17] A post-dated check is treated as a promissory note. See *Griffin v. Comm'r,* 49 T.C. 253, 261-62 (1967).

[18] As already noted in Chapter 22.E, where a transfer of property represents payment for services, the amount deductible is the FMV of the property under § 162, and the difference between the property's basis and FMV is deemed to be a § 1001 realized gain or loss to the payor. See Reg. § 1.83-6(a)(1) and (b).

d.   Credit Card Transactions

The proper analysis of credit card transactions is initially somewhat nonobvious, and perhaps would depend on whether one is considering the income side or the deduction side. On the income side, the signing by the customer of the credit card slip is very much like the giving of a check, because the merchant has a "demand right" against the bank that issues the credit card. On the deduction side, however, the issue is whether signing the slip is more like giving a check or like giving *one's own* note.

The ruling below also focuses on whether the credit card used is a third-party credit card, rather than a two-party credit card (i.e., where the issuer of the card is also the payee of the deductible expense item). In the third-party credit card situation, the cardholder use of the credit card is treated as if she had used borrowed funds to pay the expense item (which is treated as a cash payment for cash-method purposes). In contrast, in the two-party credit card situation (which is basically a charge-account arrangement), a cash-method cardholder's use of the credit card is treated as equivalent to the cardholder's promising to pay for the item in the future, and is not treated as a cash payment for cash-method purposes.

REVENUE RULING 78-38
1978-1 C.B. 68

Treas. Reg. § 1.170A-1(a)(1) provides that a deduction is allowable to an individual under § 170 only for charitable contributions "actually paid" during the taxable year, regardless of when pledged and regardless of the method of accounting employed by the taxpayer in keeping books and records. In *Rev. Rul. 71-216*, 1971-1 C.B. 96, the assumption was made that a charitable contribution made by a taxpayer by use of a credit card was tantamount to one made by the issuance and delivery of a promissory note by the obligor.

It has been concluded that there are major distinctions between contributions made by the use of credit cards and contributions made by promissory notes. In *Rev. Rul. 68-174*, 1968-1 C.B. 81, the charitable organization that received the promissory note from the obligor received no more than a mere promise to pay. Conversely, the credit card holder in *Rev. Rul. 71-216*, by using the credit card to make the contribution, became immediately indebted to a third party (the bank) in such a way that the cardholder could not thereafter prevent the charitable organization from receiving payment.[19] The credit card draft received by the charitable organization from the credit card holder was immediately creditable by the bank to the organization's account as if it were a check.

Since the cardholder's use of the card creates the cardholder's own debt to a third party, the use of a bank credit card to make a charitable contribution is equivalent to the use of borrowed funds to make a contribution. The general rule is that when a deductible payment is made with borrowed money, the deduction is not

---

[19] [Eds. note: Actually, a credit card holder can "stop payment" by notifying the bank (before or after the bank pays the merchant) that she won't pay that particular charge, but checking accounts also work somewhat in this fashion, and the risk of stopping payment is considered to be so de minimis that it can be disregarded for doctrinal purposes.]

postponed until the year in which the borrowed money is repaid.

Accordingly, the taxpayer who made a contribution to a qualified charity by a charge to the taxpayer's bank credit card is entitled to a deduction in the year the charge was made. *Rev. Rul. 68-174* is distinguished.

It is safe to say that the holding of *Rev. Rul. 78-38*, supra, is not limited to situations involving the § 170 charitable contribution deduction.

e. Effect of § 83

As noted in the previous chapter, § 83 governs the tax treatment of "property" received by a services provider as payment for services. If a deferred-payment obligation is "property" within the meaning of § 83, then it would result in immediate inclusion (assuming that the property is not subject to a substantial risk of forfeiture). But Reg. § 1.83-3(e) defines (currently includible) "property" for purposes of § 83 as "property *other than either money or an unfunded and unsecured promise to pay money or property in the future*." Since notes are inherently unfunded,[20] and (where received for services) unlikely to be secured by property, the FMV of an unsecured note received as compensation by a services provider is *not* included in the services provider's gross income *under § 83* when received.

Since § 83 does not apply, we are presumably back to cash-method doctrine. Therefore, to avoid immediate inclusion, any deferred-compensation promise must avoid the various cash-method doctrines discussed herein. See *Rev. Rul. 60-31*, 1960-1 C.B. 174 (applying pre-§ 83 cash-method doctrine to unfunded deferred compensation arrangements); *Evans v. Comm'r*, T.C. Memo. 1988-288 (promissory notes included as compensation income under *Cowden* test but not § 83).

2. The Constructive-Receipt Doctrine

A cash-method taxpayer is not allowed to avoid current income inclusion by voluntarily postponing receipt until some future time. In the absence of this prohibition, cash-method taxpayers could easily defer their tax liabilities with respect to earned and available income merely by delaying their collection of the income. Thus, *the constructive-receipt doctrine provides that the taxpayer must include an item in gross income at the time the taxpayer has both the right to the item (whether it is cash or property) and the power to obtain possession of it.*

On the other hand, a meaningful restriction on the taxpayer's current right or power will preclude constructive receipt. What's a "meaningful restriction"? In *Roberts v. Comm'r*, T.C. Memo. 2002-281, a cashier's check was delivered to the taxpayer's residence in 1997 while he was incarcerated. He did, however, have access to a telephone and could have arranged for assistance in immediately cashing the check. Nevertheless, the taxpayer did not cash the check until after his

---

[20] The concept of "funding" implies a segregated fund that is set aside to ensure payment. Trusts and escrows are examples of funded arrangements.

release in 1998. The Tax Court held that the amount of the check was gross income constructively received in 1997.

The doctrine is spelled out in some detail in Reg. § 1.451-2, which is recommended reading.

There is no "constructive-payment doctrine" on the deduction side. Just as in the case of transferring one's own note, a cash-method taxpayer must *actually* part with cash or its equivalent in order to take an expense deduction.

The case below deals with the possible application of the constructive-receipt doctrine at the stage of constructing the transaction itself.

REED v. COMMISSIONER
United States Court of Appeals, First Circuit
723 F.2d 138 (1983)

Before CAMPBELL, CHIEF JUDGE, GIBSON and TIMBERS, SENIOR CIRCUIT JUDGES.

FLOYD R. GIBSON, SENIOR CIRCUIT JUDGE:

Reed acquired stock in Reed Electromech Corporation in 1963. In 1967, Reed and several of his fellow shareholders entered into an agreement with Joseph Cvengros, also an Electromech shareholder, granting Cvengros an option to purchase the stock. The agreement set a $3,300 per share price and provided that, if Cvengros purchased the stock, the closing would be on December 27, 1973. In November of 1973, Cvengros exercised his option to purchase the stock. Shortly thereafter, Reed and his fellow selling shareholders became concerned about the federal income tax implications of a sale in 1973. Reed, in particular, wanted to defer closing until 1974 so that he would have time to make an orderly sale of certain securities, the capital loss from which he desired to write-off against the capital gain on the Electromech sale. Reed was understandably reluctant to sell the loss securities prior to the December 27 closing, fearing that Cvengros' outside financing might fall through, thus preventing the Electromech stock sale. On the other hand, Reed believed that after the December 27 closing there would not be enough time remaining in 1973 to properly identify and sell these loss securities in that year.

In early December 1973, Reed and Cvengros, desiring to accommodate all involved, orally agreed to modify the agreement to provide that Reed and the other selling shareholders would not be entitled to receive payment until January 3, 1974. Both Reed and Cvengros considered the deferred payment provision to be part of the purchase/sale agreement and legally binding. Reed indicated that he would not have gone through with the transaction if Cvengros had not agreed to the deferred payment provision. Under the terms of the escrow agreement, the stock sales proceeds were to be paid by Cvengros to the escrowee bank at the December 27, 1973 closing and the escrowee was then to make disbursements of the sales proceeds to a number of selling shareholders, including Reed, on January 3, 1974. The selling shareholders were not entitled to receive interest, investment income or any other incidental benefits on the sales proceeds while they were in escrow. [The closing and escrow were carried out according to the agreement.]

The Commissioner contends Reed constructively received the stock sales proceeds when they were deposited in the escrow account on December 27, 1973. A cash basis taxpayer such as Reed is required to recognize income from the sale of property in the taxable year in which he actually or constructively receives payment for the property. Reg. § 1.451-2(a) explains the constructive receipt doctrine as follows:

> Income although not actually reduced to a taxpayer's possession is constructively received by him in the taxable year during which it is credited to his account, set apart for him, or otherwise made available so that he may draw upon it at any time. However, income is not constructively received if the taxpayer's control of its receipt is subject to substantial limitations or restrictions.

Thus, a taxpayer recognizes income when he has an unqualified right to receive immediate payment. However, a seller has the right to enter into an agreement with the buyer that he, the seller, will not be paid until the following year. As long as the deferred payment agreement is binding between the parties and is made prior to the time when the seller has acquired an absolute and unconditional right to receive payment, then the cash basis seller is not required to report the sales proceeds as income until he actually receives them.

Applying the language of Reg. § 1.451-2(a) quoted above, if the deferred payment agreement provides that the seller has no right to payment until the taxable year following the sale, then the income received from the sale is not "set apart for him, or otherwise made available so that he may draw upon it" in the year of the sale. Alternatively stated, such a deferred payment agreement restricts the time of payment and therefore serves as a "substantial limitation" on the taxpayer control of the proceeds in the year of the sale.

Courts have generally recognized that a cash basis seller may effectively postpone income recognition through the use of a *bona fide* arms-length agreement calling for deferred payment of the sales proceeds. [Citations omitted.] Similarly, an existing agreement which has been amended or modified to provide for deferred payment of an amount not yet due serves to postpone income recognition. This is true even though: 1) the purchaser was initially willing to contract for immediate payment; and 2) the taxpayer's primary objective in entering into the deferred payment agreement was to minimize taxes. A deferred payment agreement is considered *bona fide* if the parties intended to be bound by the agreement and were, in fact, legally bound.

The Commissioner claims the escrow modification providing for disbursement of the sales proceeds to Reed in 1974 was not a *bona fide* arms-length agreement between Cvengros and Reed and, hence, did not "substantially limit" Reed's access to the sales proceeds deposited in escrow. Instead, the purported escrow modification was nothing more than Reed's self-imposed limitation, designed to defer income recognition on proceeds he already had an unqualified, vested right to receive on December 27, 1973. The Commissioner claims the record reveals that

Reed could have taken the sales proceeds immediately after the December 27, 1973 closing, had he so requested. However, in this case the escrow arrangement was the product of an arms-length, bona fide modification to the agreement between Reed and Cvengros. The modification became effective prior to the time when Reed had an unqualified right to demand immediate payment under the then-existing purchase agreement. The record reveals that the provision was the product of some arms-length negotiations between Cvengros and Reed. Cvengros, at his financial backer's insistence, was initially unwilling to make the deferred payment but agreed to the escrow device after Reed promised to remain on the Electromech Board of Directors to insure a smooth ownership transition.

The instant case is close to *Busby v. U.S.*, 679 F.2d 48 (5th Cir. 1982), involving a cotton farmer's use of an escrow device to defer income from the sale of a cotton crop until the year after it was harvested and delivered to the buyer. In *Busby*, the farmer emphasized the importance of a deferred payment and conditioned the sale upon it. Accordingly, the buyer's purchasing agent agreed to establish an irrevocable escrow account in a bank. Under the terms of the purchase agreement, the buyer was to deposit the proceeds of the sale into the escrow account following the delivery of the cotton in 1973. The escrowee was to then pay the purchase price to the farmer in 1974. The 5th Circuit concluded that there was an arms-length agreement to defer payment which was effective to shift the farmer's tax on the proceeds until the year following the sale.

The Commissioner's next argument is that the bank served as Reed's agent in holding the sales proceeds in 1973. The escrow agreement provided that the bank was acting on the behalf of both Reed and Cvengros. Courts have generally recognized that an escrowee does not serve as a taxpayer's agent for income recognition purposes where, as in this case, the escrowee represents both the buyer and seller. [Citations omitted.] To establish an agency relationship between the escrowee and the taxpayer, the Commissioner must show that the escrow was set up unilaterally by the taxpayer or that the escrowee was functioning under the exclusive authority of the taxpayer.

On the constructive receipt issue, *Reed* is consistent with other "contract for the sale of goods" cases, many of them involving farmers.[21] Regarding contracts involving the performance of services, the IRS has long conceded that unfunded and unsecured agreements to defer compensation not yet earned generally do not trigger the constructive receipt doctrine. See *Rev. Rul. 60-31*, 1960-1 C.B. 174. More controversially, court decisions often declined to impose constructive receipt in situations where compensation earned but not yet due was deferred by an arm's length agreement.[22] However, § 409A(a)(4) now disregards such attempts at deferral unless the election to defer compensation is made in the year before the

---

[21] See, e.g., *Amend v. Comm'r*, 13 T.C. 178 (1949) (acq.).

[22] See *Comm'r v. Oates*, 207 F.2d 711 (7th Cir. 1953); *Veit v. Comm'r*, 8 T.C. 809 (1947). The IRS took a stricter position, see *Rev. Proc. 71-19*, 1971-1 C.B. 698, *amplified, Rev. Proc. 92-65*, 1992-1 C.B. 428, that is now (along with other rules that trigger immediate inclusion of rights to deferred compensation) embodied in § 409A.

compensated services are performed. Section 409A, enacted in 2004, and which supersedes the constructive receipt doctrine in the arena of deferred employee compensation in many other respects, is discussed more fully in Subsection 5, infra.

3. The Economic-Benefit Doctrine

Under the "tax-common-law" version of the oddly named "economic-benefit doctrine," a cash-method taxpayer must include in gross income the value of cash or other property transferred to a trust or escrow *if* the taxpayer has an indefeasibly vested right to receipt of the cash or property in the future. The idea is that such a "funded" arrangement gives the taxpayer significantly more than a mere unfunded and unsecured promise of the obligor to pay money in the future.

An example of a routine application of the economic-benefit doctrine is found in *Sproull v. Comm'r*, 16 T.C. 244 (1951), *aff'd per curiam*, 194 F.2d 541 (6th Cir. 1952), where a corporate employer unilaterally awarded a 1945 bonus of $10,500 to its cash-method chief executive officer (CEO) but actually paid the bonus to a trustee on December 31, 1945. The agreement between the employer and the trustee specified that the latter would hold and invest the bonus amount and pay half the bonus to the CEO at the end of 1946 and the other half, plus all investment earnings, to the CEO at the end of 1947. The CEO's right to these amounts was nonforfeitable, and if he died prior to receipt of all the money, the unpaid amounts would go to his estate. Since the investment return on the $10,500 deposited with the trustee was presumably going to be earned at a market rate and would ultimately go to the CEO, the December 31, 1945, FMV of the CEO's right to future receipt of the trust fund would have been $10,500.[23] The CEO contended that he should not report income until he actually received cash in 1946 and 1947. The Tax Court held that the trust fund's FMV ($10,500) was includible in the CEO's 1945 income. The pertinent portion of the opinion states (16 T.C. at 247-48):

> Here, we think it must be held that the expenditure of the $10,500 in setting up the trust conferred an economic or financial benefit on petitioner properly taxable to him in 1945. The fund was ascertained and paid over by petitioner's employer for his benefit in that year. Petitioner had to do nothing further to earn it or establish his rights therein. The only duties of the trustee were to hold, invest, accumulate, and very shortly pay over the fund and its increase to petitioner or his estate in the event of his prior death. No one else had any interest in or control over the monies. The trust agreement contained no restriction whatever on petitioner's right to assign or otherwise dispose of the interest thus created in him. On the facts here there is no doubt that such an interest had a value equivalent to the amount paid over for his benefit.

In *Pulsifer v. Comm'r*, 64 T.C. 245 (1975), Irish Sweepstakes winnings were sequestered in a bank account until the winners (who were minors) attained the age of majority. The court applied the economic-benefit doctrine to include the winnings

---

[23] Actually, $10.5K would have been the present value (PV) of the right to the future distribution, but since the employee's right was funded and secure, there would have been no meaningful difference between PV and FMV in this and similar cases.

in income in the earlier year the sweepstakes ticket was declared a winner, stating that the result did not hinge on whether the ticket was assignable.

4. Funded Deferred Compensation under the Code

In the area of employee compensation, the economic-benefit doctrine is now embedded in the Code. To be specific, § 402(b)(1) states that employer contributions to a *non*qualified trust for the benefit of an employee are treated as a "transfer of property" to the employee under § 83(a).[24] Thus, if the employee's right to this property interest is not subject to a substantial risk of forfeiture, section 83(a) requires the employee to immediately include the employer contribution in gross income, even if the employee's interest in the trust is nonassignable.[25] The amount includible is normally the contribution amount (not the FMV of the employee's incremental interest in the trust).[26] The idea is that the trust must invest prudently, so that it can be assumed to earn a market rate of return, in which event the PV of the future receipts attributable to the employer's contribution would equal the contribution amount. Also, since the vested interest in the trust is "secure," the FMV would be very close to the PV.

Contributions to an "exempt trust" (under a "qualified" plan or IRA) are *not* taxable when made. See § 402(a).

A "rabbi trust"[27] is a type of funded nonexempt (i.e., nonqualified) employer trust arrangement with terms that make the trust assets effectively the property of the employer and potentially subject to the claims of the employer's general creditors in bankruptcy. Therefore, rabbi trusts are not, from the employee's point of view, "secured" (truly "funded") for purposes of §§ 83 and 402(b). That is to say, if the employer went bankrupt, the employee would have no greater right to the trust assets than the employer's general creditors. Because the rabbi trust is treated as being unfunded and unsecured, the employee's rights are not "property" rights under Reg. § 1.83-3(e), meaning that general cash-method principles control, resulting in the deferral of taxation until the employee's receipt of cash control. See *Rev. Proc. 92-64*, 1992-2 C.B. 422 (containing a rabbi trust model trust agreement that ensures deferral).

5. Section 409A

Congress responded to certain perceived abuses of nonqualified deferred compensation by enacting § 409A in 2004. Section 409A is not only complex in itself but has spawned 70 pages of regulations. It applies to any vested nonqualified arrangement whereby payment is deferred more than two and one-half months

---

[24] The tax treatment of "qualified" employee trusts was briefly discussed in Chapter 6.E.2.

[25] Recall from Chapter 22.E that § 83(a) requires inclusion when transferred property is *either* not subject to a substantial risk of forfeiture *or* is "transferable" (i.e., free of the forfeiture restriction).

[26] See Reg. § 1.402(b)-1(a)(1).

[27] These funded nonqualified arrangements have come to be called "rabbi" trusts in tax jargon because the first letter ruling sanctioning them was obtained by a congregation for its rabbi. A funded nonqualified trust that is not a rabbi trust and is deigned to be subject to §§ 83 and 402(b) is called a "secular trust."

beyond the year the taxpayer has acquired the right to the compensation, or, if later, the year in which a forfeiture condition lapses.[28] Thus, section 409A impacts both funded and unfunded nonqualified deferred compensation arrangements, and supersedes any tax-common-law doctrine to the contrary.

Section 409A generally causes current inclusion of compensation in gross income unless the deferral arrangement:

> (1) provides that future payments and distributions will be made only on separation from service, disability, unforeseeable emergency, death, etc.,

> (2) generally prohibits the acceleration of deferred payments and distributions,

> (3) does not allow for elective deferrals in (or after) the year the services are performed,

> (4) if a funded plan is not funded by a foreign trust or by foreign assets, and

> (5) if a funded plan does not provide for the funding of assets to be restricted as to the provision of benefits if the employer's financial health decreases.

In addition to immediate inclusion, a 20% penalty tax is imposed.

NOTES

1. (a) A disclaimer of gross income (refusing to accept it now or in the future) avoids inclusion, and is distinguishable from the constructive-receipt doctrine. See *Comm'r v. Giannini*, 129 F.2d 638 (9th Cir. 1942); *Rev. Rul. 66-167*, 1966-1 C.B. 20. A disclaimer negates the income itself, whereas constructive receipt deals with its timing.

(b) The rule that a significant restriction on withdrawal (etc.) negates application of the constructive-receipt doctrine operates as a recipe for avoiding constructive receipt. Banks commonly impose penalties for withdrawals from various kinds of accounts and CDs. However, that is not necessarily the end of the story, because earned interest might be taxable under the OID rules, discussed in Chapter 27.B.1.

2. (a) In *Reed v. Comm'r*, supra, the panel of the First Circuit rejected application of the economic-benefit doctrine to the escrow arrangement on the grounds that (1) the escrow didn't bear interest and (2) to have held otherwise would have had the result of putting a cash-method taxpayer on the accrual method. Although most funded arrangements bear interest, none of the cases prior to *Reed* considered that factor to be significant, much less decisive. The absence of interest only reduces the value of the future right, but a cash-method taxpayer includes the FMV of in-kind income, not its face amount, as occurs with accrual-method taxpayers. The FMV is considered to be equal to the face amount if the escrow or

---

[28] See Reg. § 1.409A-1(b)(1).

fund earns market-rate interest. Thus, *Reed* is an aberration as far as the economic-benefit doctrine is concerned.

(b) If the economic benefit doctrine stands (as it should) for the proposition that a vested right to a fund is "property," then *Pulsifer* was correct in holding that nonassignability is not a bar to current inclusion. Cf. *U.S. v. Drescher*, 179 F.2d 863 (2d Cir. 1950) (receipt by employee of nonassignable annuity contract was included in current income).

3.   (a) To prevent the double taxation of the same dollars to the same person, any amounts included by the taxpayer under § 83 (or otherwise) become basis in the right to future payments (sometimes called § 1012 "tax cost" basis). The taxation of distributions from employee trusts (qualified and nonqualified) are discussed in Chapter 27.C.

(b) An employer, even if it uses the accrual method, cannot deduct contributions to nonqualified funded trusts until, and to the extent that, the employee includes the same in income. See §§ 83(h); 404(a)(5). Contributions to qualified plans are deductible immediately, although certain limitations may apply.

(c) The income earned by a qualified trust or IRA is exempt from tax under § 501(a). For that reason, investments by such a trust should seek the best before-tax rate of return. Tax benefits like the § 103 exclusion or percentage depletion are useless to a tax exempt entity.

(d) Section 402(b)(3) provides that an employee will not be taxed on the income of a nonexempt trust. Presumably, the income is taxed to the trust (or perhaps the employer under the grantor trust rules).

PROBLEMS

1.   Isaac Investor has an ordinary passbook savings account that earns interest at 4% compounded daily. Isaac can withdraw from the account at any time but in fact makes no withdrawals during the year. Does Isaac's tax treatment with respect to this account depend upon whether he uses the cash or accrual method?

2.   Jim, who uses the cash method, is a domestic employee of Harry. When, and how much, does Jim include in gross income in the following situations?

(a) Jim receives a salary check for $500 on Dec. 31, Year 1, at 10 p.m. (after banking hours) and deposits it on Jan. 3, Year 2.

(b) What if Harry has such a bad reputation for writing bad checks that any local bank would refuse to cash the check, and any local check-cashing business would cash it for only $430? See *Goodman v. Comm'r*, 5 T.C.M. (CCH) 1126, 1198 (1946) (check not treated as cash equivalent where recipient knew that issuer's bank account lacked funds to cover the check).

(c) What if the check in (a) ultimately bounces? See *Premji v. Comm'r*, T.C. Memo. 1996-304, *aff'd without opinion*, 139 F.3d 912 (10th Cir. 1998).

3.   Agnes, who uses the cash method, pays a doctor's bill with a Visa card on Dec. 27 of Year 1. The bank sends Agnes a statement on Feb. 4 of Year 2. Agnes, being in financial difficulty, does not pay the statement in full until Year 3. When is Agnes

deemed to have paid this medical bill for purposes of the § 213 medical expense deduction?

4.   Adam, who uses the cash method, is an employee of Enchanted Eve Inc. According to the employment agreement, Adam is to be paid monthly. The comptroller of Enchanted Eve refuses to disburse the December check because she heard Adam was having an affair with Enchanted Eve's CEO. Adam sued Enchanted Eve in Year 2 and won a judgment in small claims court in Year 3. The right of Enchanted Eve to appeal expired in Year 5, but it still did not pay. In Year 6 Adam brought an action to collect on the judgment, and in Year 7 he finally obtained the funds. In what year is the amount includible in income?

5.   Regina (a cash-method grower) sells oranges to Sunny Fruit Company near the end of Year 1 and renders a bill in early Year 2 in the amount of $10K. The bill requests payment in 30 days but makes no mention of interest charges for late payments. Sunny Fruit pays nothing in Years 1 and 2, and in Year 3 it gives Regina an unsecured negotiable note for $10K, bearing 4% simple interest, payable in full after 4 years. The discounted PV of the note is $9.6K and its FMV is $9K. The note is paid off in Year 7.

(a) What tax results to the parties, both of whom use the cash method?

(b) Same as (a), except the note is nonnegotiable under the UCC but assignable?

6.   Lori is a cash-method farmer who sells her wheat crop to Grain Elevators, Inc. (an accrual-method taxpayer) on September 1 of Year 1 for $50K, payment to be made in January of Year 2. Lori delivered the wheat in October of Year 1, and Grain Elevators was able and willing to pay Lori the $50K at that time, but Lori insisted on payment in January of Year 2. Grain Elevator's payment obligation is unsecured and not represented by any note. When must Lori include the $50K in income?

7.   Ryan is a professional hockey player who uses the cash method of accounting. He agrees with his employer that he will play for 3 years for $1.2M total consideration, such consideration to be paid at the rate of $120K for each of the 10 years beginning in the contract year. The employer's contractual obligation is unsecured and is not represented by a note. The discounted PV of Ryan's compensation package (assuming that it will be earned and paid on time) is $700K. What tax results for Ryan?

8.   Lindsey is an employee of Y Corp, which pays a one-time $100K bonus into a nonqualified pension trust exclusively for Lindsey's benefit. After 20 years, the trust will terminate and pay out everything to Lindsey, if living, or, if Lindsey is deceased, to Lindsey's estate. Lindsey's rights in this trust are fully vested.

(a) When is Lindsey taxed and in what amount?

(b) Same as (a), but Lindsey is Executive Vice President, and can withdraw from the account to pay his children's college bills?

(c) Same as (a), except the trust (located in the Cayman Islands) can be reached by the creditors of Y Corp.

9. Same as 8, except that the trust is "qualified" under § 401. (Two of the numerous requirements for "qualification" are funding and early vesting.)

C. THE ACCRUAL METHOD

Under the accrual concept, gross income items would be included *at face* when the right to future payment is fixed, and allowable expense items would be deducted *at face* when the obligation to pay them is fixed. The actual accrual-method tax rules have deviated somewhat from the accrual concept (which was borrowed from business accounting), especially on the deduction side.

1. The All-Events Test

The accrual concept was adapted to the income tax through the "all-events test." A gross income item involving a right or claim to future cash, property, or services is includible only when (1) "all the events have occurred that fix the right to receive the income" *and* (2) "the amount of the income can be determined with reasonable accuracy." Reg. § 1.446-1(c)(1)(ii)(A). On the deduction side, the all-events test is: (1) "all the events have occurred that establish the fact of the liability" and (2) "the amount of the liability can be determined with reasonable accuracy." Reg. § 1.446-1(c)(1)(ii)(A). However, on the deduction side the all-events test is now a mere "necessary" condition for accrual, because § 461(h) provides that a deduction that satisfies the all-events test cannot occur prior to "economic performance."

a. Routine Applications

When exactly a "right" to receive gross income (or a liability) is "fixed" varies according to context. In the case of the sale of inventory or other goods, where the price is agreed to, the taxpayer is supposed to follow a consistent policy that is also used for bookkeeping purposes, such as the date of shipping, the date title passes, the date of delivery, or the date of acceptance.[29]

In the case of income from the provision of services, the all-events test is satisfied at the earlier to occur of when the services are performed or when payment is due.[30] Although a case involving a public utility allowed accrual of income at the later of these two times,[31] that result was overturned by the 1986 enactment of § 451(f), providing that accrual of income can occur no later than when utility services are performed. The IRS clearly maintains that the "earlier of" rule controls across the board.[32]

Income (or expenses) that are the function of the passage of time (interest and rent) accrue as time passes, even though the rent or interest rate is fixed in advance.

---

[29] See Reg. § 1.446-1(c)(1)(ii)(C); *Pacific Grape Products v. Comm'r*, 219 F.2d 862 (9th Cir. 1955); *Hallmark Cards, Inc. v. Comm'r*, 90 T.C. 26 (1988).

[30] See *Charles Schwab Corp. v. Comm'r*, 107 T.C. 282 (1996), *aff'd by order*, 161 F.3d 1231 (9th Cir. 1998) (income of broker accrued on trade date, not settlement date); *Decision, Inc. v. Comm'r*, 47 T.C. 58 (1966) (acq.) (billing occurred before the services were fully performed).

[31] See *Public Service Co. v. Comm'r*, 78 T.C. 445 (1982) (nonacq.).

[32] See *Rev. Rul. 79-195*, 1979-1 C.B. 177.

See Reg. §§ 1.461-4(d)(7) Ex. (8) (rent), (e) (interest).

Regardless of the context, a right to gross income need not be legally enforceable for accrual to occur.[33] On the other hand, a *disputed* right or liability is not fixed, even if one party is clearly in the right.[34] If part of an item is undisputed and part is subject to dispute, the undisputed part is accruable.[35]

The second prong of the all-events test — that the amount of gross income (or allowable expense) can be determined with "reasonable accuracy" — means just what it says; "exactitude" or "certainty" is not demanded for accrual to occur. An amount that can be figured according to a rate, formula, or set procedure usually passes muster.

If the amount accrued turns out to be incorrect, an adjustment is made in the year in which the correct amount is determined.[36] Thus, if $1K of gross income is accrued (included) in Year 1 because that amount is "reasonably" anticipated, and the precise amount turns out to be $1,100 in Year 2, an additional $100 is included in Year-2 income. Or, if the correct amount turns out to be $960 in Year 2, $40 is deducted in Year 2. Notice that the tax return for Year 1 is not amended, since the amount accrued in Year 1 was "correct" under the facts that were known in Year 1.

The fact that amounts are accrued at "face amount" necessarily implies that no account is to be given to such factors as the absence of an interest charge, the other party's unwillingness to adhere to the contract, or the risk of nonpayment (which exists with any credit transaction).[37] In other words, the mere possibility that payment may not be made in the future does not prevent accrual.

On the other hand, an item is not accruable if it is subject to a condition precedent that has not yet occurred. A fortiori, an item is not accruable just because of what might happen in the future, or even because of what statistically is probable to happen. Accordingly, if a contract is entered into for the sale of property, the gain or loss cannot accrue before the closing, where possible obstacles to the consummation of the sale are removed.[38]

b. Some Leading Accrual Cases

The Supreme Court first enunciated the all-events test in *U.S. v. Anderson*, 269 U.S. 422 (1926). There a munitions manufacturer using the accrual method of accounting was required to pay a special federal tax on its 1916 munitions sale profits. For financial accounting purposes, the taxpayer deducted the tax in 1916 but, for *income tax* purposes, deferred the deduction until 1917, the year in which

---

[33] See *Flamingo Resorts, Inc. v. U.S.*, 664 F.2d 1387 (9th Cir. 1982) (gambling casino must accrue gross income even if claims are not enforceable).

[34] See *Dixie Pine Prod. Co. v. Comm'r*, 320 U.S. 516 (1944); *Security Flour Mill Co. v. Comm'r*, 321 U.S. 281 (1944).

[35] See Reg. § 1.461-1(a)(2)(ii).

[36] See Regs. §§ 1.451-1(a), 1.461-1(a)(3).

[37] See, e.g., *U.S. v. Hughes Properties, Inc.*, 476 U.S. 593 (1986) (risk of insolvency or bankruptcy); *Georgia School-Book Depository, Inc. v. Comm'r*, 1 T.C. 463 (1943) (certainty of delayed payment).

[38] See *Lucas v. North Texas Lumber Co.*, 281 U.S. 11 (1930).

the munitions tax return was filed and the tax was actually assessed and paid. In requiring the taxpayer to deduct the munitions tax in 1916,[39] the Court stated (269 U.S. at 441):

> In a technical legal sense it may be argued that a tax does not accrue until it has been assessed and becomes due; but it is also true that in advance of the assessment of a tax, all the events may occur which fix the amount of the tax and determine the liability of the taxpayer to pay it.

The application of the all-events test often varies according to the type of transaction. For example, *Anderson* allowed accrual of the munitions tax liability prior to the year of formal assessment, because the facts necessary to calculate the amount of the 1916 tax existed at the close of 1916. The taxpayer's 1917 acts — making out (and filing) the return and assessment of the 1916 tax — were mere formalities. The same approach applies to deductible state and foreign income taxes. In accord is § 461(c), which allows an election to ratably accrue real property taxes over any definite time period to which the tax relates (as opposed to accrual on the assessment or lien date).

In *Anderson*, it seems reasonably clear that the Court was not intentionally creating a divergence between financial and tax accounting. Indeed, the *Anderson* decision required the taxpayer to claim its income tax deduction in the same year it was taken on its financial books in conformity with business accounting rules. But in the years after *Anderson*, the all-events test took on an independent doctrinal life of its own in the tax arena, mostly as the result of a long line of post-*Anderson* Supreme Court cases.

A case involving a deduction for future "contingent" liabilities, *Lucas v. American Code Co.*, 280 U.S. 445 (1930), was the first in which the Supreme Court used the all-events test to *delay* deductions for tax purposes that were currently allowed for financial accounting purposes. (Business accounting favors showing the "bad news" as early as possible.)

Closely related to the contingent-liability situation is that involving "reserve" accounting. In business accounting practice, a "reserve" account represents *future* liabilities or losses, including contingent items, which can be estimated with reasonable statistical accuracy. The most common type of reserve in financial accounting is the bad debt reserve. If a party sells goods or services on credit, financial accounting dictates that the face amount of the right to receive the future cash payment is to be added to financial accounting income. To account for the risk of uncollectibility, a loss is *currently* taken (with a corresponding addition to the bad debt reserve) to reflect the estimate of the amount of the receivables that will never be collected. This accounting move is a backhanded way of showing a reduced value for the current year's receivables as a group. (To complete the financial accounting picture, collection on the receivables reduces the receivables account on the party's books, and worthless receivables are charged against the bad debt reserve account on the party's books, with neither charge affecting net income for financial reporting purposes.) If reserve accounting were adopted for tax purposes, annual additions to

---

[39] In *Anderson*, the taxpayer wanted to *delay* the deduction until the later year, because tax rates went up significantly in 1917 because of World War I.

the reserve would be taken as current expense or loss deductions, and the subsequent actual worthlessness of receivables would be ignored. In short, reserve accounting under the income tax would accelerate the realization of expenses and losses.

Has reserve accounting been allowed to accrual-method taxpayers? It was held in *Spring City Foundry Co. v. Comm'r*, 292 U.S. 182 (1934), that receivables must be accrued in gross income for tax purposes at their full face amount, even though a predictable percentage of them would turn out to be uncollectible, because (as noted above) the mere possibility of nonpayment does not preclude income accrual under the all-events concept of fixing the right (and amount) of the future receipt. Shortly after the *Spring City Foundry* decision, Congress expressly allowed accrual-method taxpayers to deduct additions to reserves for bad debts (but not additions to other kinds of reserves). Such express statutory authorization was required, because the Supreme Court has consistently rejected reserve accounting in the tax context, despite its acceptance in financial accounting. The most recent example is *U.S. v. General Dynamics Corp.*, 481 U.S. 239 (1987), where the issue was whether an accrual-basis taxpayer providing medical benefits to its employees (by paying their medical bills out of its own funds) could deduct a reasonable estimate of its obligation to pay for medical care obtained by employees (or their dependents) for claims that had not yet been processed by the employer. The taxpayer argued that the all-events test was satisfied when the employees incurred the medical expenses, but the Court disagreed, noting that claims for reimbursement had to be submitted and then passed upon by an internal review process. The Court concluded with (481 U.S. at 246): "A reserve based on the proposition that a particular set of events is likely to occur in the future may be an appropriate conservative accounting measure, but does not warrant a tax deduction."

The dissent in *General Dynamics* argued that the facts there were hard to distinguish from those in *U.S. v. Hughes Properties*, 476 U.S. 593 (1986), which allowed a casino to accrue future liabilities arising from gamblers' use of progressive slot machines owned by the taxpayer. A progressive slot machine's jackpot gets progressively larger on each pull of the handle until it pays a winner, which the case recited took between 1.9 months and 35 months. The amount of the built-up jackpot at the end of each year can be ascertained by simply reading the machine, but payment does not occur until a winning pull. Over the objections of the IRS, the Court held that deductions could be accrued for the annual increases in as-yet-unpaid jackpots, although the identity of the winners and the time of future payment could not be known.

In 1986, Congress repealed the deduction pertaining to bad debt reserves for taxpayers other than financial institutions. In the same legislation, Congress enacted § 448(d)(5), which allows certain accrual-method taxpayers to *exclude* from gross income the appropriate percentage of currently-earned receivables that are statistically estimated to be uncollectible. This rule applies, however, only where (1) the receivables are for certain *services* rendered by the taxpayer *and* (2) the receivables do *not* bear interest or a penalty for late payment. The services rendered by the taxpayer must be in the field of health, law, engineering, architecture, accounting, actuarial science, performing arts, or consulting, unless the taxpayer's average annual gross receipts do not exceed $5 million. Taxpayers in these areas are unlikely to be on the accrual method in the first place. See § 448(b)(2).

Not mentioned so far is § 446(b), which grants the Commissioner the broad power to compel an accounting method change if the Commissioner finds that the taxpayer's existing method "does not clearly reflect income."[40] Taxpayer consistency, both between income and deduction items and from year to year, is one prerequisite to satisfying the requirement that the accounting method clearly reflects income.[41] The IRS can use its § 446(b) power to shift a taxpayer to, or away from, the accrual method, either with respect to the taxpayer's entire return or with respect to only certain activities or items.[42]

In *Ford Motor Co. v. Comm'r*, 71 F.3d 209 (6th Cir. 1995), the court held that the IRS power under § 446(b) could be invoked to override a taxpayer's accounting treatment that satisfied the all-events test. The exercise of the power was justified where application of the all-events tests resulted in economic distortion due to the long time lag between the accrual year and the payment year.[43]

NOTES

1. Although bad debt reserves might be said to be a way of indirectly approximating the FMV of receivables, the accrual method by its nature deems FMV to be irrelevant (as does business accounting generally). Additionally, a seller of inventory or services can charge an interest rate that takes the risk of uncollectibility into account (as is the case with credit card issuers). Perhaps services providers are reluctant to behave like a bank towards its customers, which would explain the limited scope of § 448(d)(5).

2. The "reasonable accuracy" prong of the all-events test does not often bar accruals, because it is only necessary that the amount be ascertainable, i.e., *capable* of being ascertained by one having access to the facts and applicable rules and standards as they exist at year end. Thus, an amount is ascertainable even though the amount is not actually calculated until a succeeding year, as in *Anderson*, with the 1917 filing of a tax return using facts that existed at the end of 1916, or as in *Continental Tie & Lumber Co. v. U.S.*, 286 U.S. 290 (1932), where the amount was determined in a future administrative proceeding, so long as these future determinations are of a "ministerial" (as opposed to "discretionary" or "contingent") character.

3. Section 461(f) was enacted to overturn the result of *U.S. v. Consolidated*

---

[40] The accrual cases are sometimes unclear as to whether the basis for decision is § 446(b) or the all-events test. The courts appear to be reluctant to allow the IRS to overturn accounting practices consistent with industry standards unless such practices are clearly unreflective of income. See, e.g., *Public Service Co. v. Comm'r*, 78 T.C. 445 (1982) (nonacq.).

[41] See Reg. § 1.446-1(c)(2)(ii).

[42] Moreover, a taxpayer can change its method of accounting only with the consent of the IRS. See § 446(e). Before giving such consent, the IRS may require certain adjustments to income to avoid the effect of a double deduction or inclusion due to the accounting change. See § 481.

[43] A well-known precursor to the *Ford Motor Co.* case is *Mooney Aircraft, Inc. v. U.S.*, 420 F.2d 400 (5th Cir. 1969), which disallowed a deduction for liabilities to be paid 15 to 30 years in the future.

Edison, 366 U.S. 380 (1961), which disallowed deduction of a contested liability even though it had actually been paid by the taxpayer (although the taxpayer continued to contest the liability, thereby barring accrual under the "disputed item" rule).

PROBLEM

Describe the tax consequences to Acme Cleaning Co. of the following, assuming that it uses the accrual method:

(a) Acme performs cleaning services for Zeta Data Services late in Year 1 and renders a bill therefore in early Year 2 in the amount of $10K, which is not disputed. Interest is charged (starting 60 days from the billing date). The fee (along with accrued interest) is paid in Year 3.

(b) What if, instead, Zeta never pays either the interest or the fee?

(c) Same as (a), except that in Year 3, Zeta objects to the fee on the grounds that it is excessive and that some of the work was shoddy. The parties agree in Year 4 to settle at $7K, which Zeta pays in Year 5.

(d) Same as (a), except that Acme is a real estate broker who negotiated a property sale for Zeta, with the fee to be a fixed percentage of the sales price of Zeta's property. The contract for sale is entered into in Year 2, and the sale closes in Year 3.

(e) Acme enters into a 24-month lease of a portion of its building, starting on October 1, Year 1, for $1K a month, with no cancellation options for either party.

2. Economic-Performance Test

The economic-performance test was added on the deduction side by the enactment of § 461(h) because accrual of a liability "at face" does not clearly reflect income unless market-rate interest is charged by the credit seller. For example, in *Hughes Properties* (the slot machine case), there was no interest charge. Interest really can't be charged until the seller performs services or delivers goods to the obligor, nor can it be charged if there is no obligor at all. Nevertheless, under prior law accrual was often allowed simply by reason of entering into a contract or performing an act that triggered a future liability, even where the liability was not "realized" in any normal sense (i.e., no cost had been suffered).[44]

One approach to the deduction-overstatement problem would have been to reduce future liabilities to present value, but that approach would entail a lot of arithmetic, and assumes that the time of future payment is fixed. Congress in 1984 decided instead on the economic-performance rule of § 461(h). Under § 461(h), obligations are accrued *at their face amount* at the *later* to occur of (a) satisfying the all-events test or (b) the time of economic performance. As stated in § 461(h)(1), "the all events test shall not be treated as met any earlier than when economic

---

[44] A conditional liability was allowed to be accrued in *Lukens Steel Co. v. Comm'r*, 442 F.2d 1131 (3d Cir. 1971), nonacq., *Rev. Rul. 72-34*, 1972-1 C.B. 132. In *Harrold v. Comm'r*, 192 F.2d 1002 (4th Cir. 1951), accrual of future reclamation costs was allowed in the year of the strip-mining activity, despite the absence of anybody that could be called a creditor.

performance with respect to such item occurs."

What constitutes "economic performance" depends on the type of transaction. Where the taxpayer's obligation arises because another party provides goods, facilities, or services to the taxpayer, economic performance occurs when the item is provided to the taxpayer (that being the earliest time that the provider could charge interest on deferred payments). In cases where the taxpayer incurs an obligation to provide goods or services to another (such as under a warranty obligation), economic performance occurs when the taxpayer incurs the costs of performance,[45] that being the earliest time that the taxpayer suffers any economic deprivation. In other cases — such as tort liabilities, workers' compensation liabilities, rebates, refunds, jackpots, taxes (other than real property taxes), and items not otherwise covered by a specific rule — economic performance occurs with the actual payment of cash. See § 461(h)(2).

Section 461(h)(3)(C) provides a de minimis rule that allows deduction prior to economic performance (so long as the all-events test is satisfied) for certain recurring, comparatively small items if economic performance occurs within eight and one-half months of the close of the taxpayer's taxable year. See Reg. § 1.461-4(g).

Detailed regulations flesh out the statutory generalities in critically important ways. See Regs. §§ 1.461-4, -5, and -6, which are well worth perusing.

Section 461(h) is subordinate to other Code provisions providing for specific rules, such as those relating to deductible compensation (§§ 83(h), 404(a)(5)) and real property taxes (§§ 164(d), 461(c)).

NOTE

Is it unfair to curb deduction accruals but not income accruals? The most common type of accrued income is represented by the trade receivable. Trade receivables are often liquid (i.e., can be readily sold or "factored" in commerce), but, if not, can be made to bear interest if the taxpayer desires. Also, professional service providers, who often must suffer nonpayment (or delayed payment) of receivables, can usually avoid being on the accrual method altogether. See § 448(d)(5).

PROBLEM

When would the following deductible items accrue under present law?

(a) rent (see also § 467),

(b) state income taxes,

(c) real property taxes (see § 461(c)),

(d) progressive slot machine jackpot, and

(e) medical care reimbursements of an employer to its employees.

---

[45] See Reg. § 1.461-4(d)(4)(i).

3. Tax Accounting Versus Financial Accounting

"Prepaid income" has been a contentious issue that exposes differences between business and tax accounting. Prepaid income refers to the receipt of cash by the taxpayer in advance of the taxpayer's performance of services (or provision of goods).

In business accounting, the cash received is not credited to the Income account but is instead credited to a Prepaid Income *liability* account that signals the fact that the cash hasn't yet been earned. When the income is subsequently earned, the Prepaid Income account is reduced and a corresponding amount is credited to Income. This treatment follows the "matching" principle of business accounting. In this case, the idea is that the income should be matched (taken in the same year as) the subsequently-incurred costs of producing such income. Prepaid income may or may not be returnable to the payor of the cash if the services are not performed. Although the recipient has full use of the money, any later refund is only of the amount received, with no interest charge.

If the recipient is on the cash method, the cash would clearly be includible in income, because of the absence of any absolute obligation to repay, and any later refund of the cash advance will raise a deduction issue. Although prepaid income can be distinguished from garden-variety contingent-repayment cases (discussed in Chapter 18.C.1), in that the taxpayer receiving the prepaid income is typically under an absolute obligation to perform services or deliver goods in the future (either as demanded or according to a schedule), the "absolute obligation" is to provide services or goods, and not repay money. . Hence, the "borrowing exclusion" does not apply,[46] and the annual accounting principle holds sway. (The annual accounting principle, discussed in Chapter 26, treats each taxable year as a discrete receptacle of gross income and deduction items realized in that year.)

Accrual-method taxpayers have attempted to avoid the no-loan character of prepaid income by invoking business accounting principles. The Commissioner's weapon is its power under § 446(b) to require deviations from financial accounting rules when necessary to "clearly reflect income."

---

[46] In *North Am. Oil Consol. v. Burnet*, 286 U.S. 417 (1932), supra Chapter 18.C.1, the Court noted (in a passage not reproduced) that its holding (that the borrowing exclusion didn't apply because the repayment obligation was contingent) would be the same regardless of whether the taxpayer was on the cash method or the accrual method.

RCA CORPORATION v. UNITED STATES
United States Court of Appeals, Second Circuit
664 F.2d 881 (1981)

Before FEINBERG, CHIEF JUDGE, and MANSFIELD and KEARSE, CIRCUIT JUDGES.

KEARSE, CIRCUIT JUDGE:

This appeal requires us to determine whether the Commissioner properly exercised his discretion when he rejected as "not clearly reflect(ing) income" within the meaning of § 446(b) the accrual method of accounting used in 1958 and 1959 by plaintiff RCA Corp. to account for revenues received from the prepayment of fees associated with certain service contracts entered into with purchasers of its products. The District Court held that the Commissioner had abused his discretion. We reverse.

Since 1946 RCA has carried on a business of servicing television sets and other products it sold. In the typical service arrangement, the purchaser of an RCA product would contract, at the time of purchase, to receive service and repair of the product for a stated period in exchange for prepayment of a single lump sum. Under these agreements, service was available to the purchaser on demand at any time during the contract term, which might range from three to twenty-four months.

For 1958 and 1959, the IRS required RCA to report its service contract revenues upon receipt, rather than deferring recognition of any portion of them. At trial, RCA contended that its accrual accounting for prepaid service contract revenues "clearly reflect(ed) income" within § 446(b), and that the Commissioner had therefore abused his discretion. For its part, the government argued that under a trio of Supreme Court Cases, *Automobile Club of Michigan v. Comm'r*, 353 U.S. 180 (1957); *American Automobile Ass'n v. U.S.*, 367 U.S. 687 (1961) ("AAA"), and *Schlude v. Comm'r*, 372 U.S. 128 (1963), methods of accrual accounting based on projections of customers' demands for services do not clearly reflect income.

The [District] Court read *Michigan*, *AAA*, and *Schlude*, *supra*, to proscribe, as "not clearly reflect(ing) income," only those methods of deferring recognition of income that are not based on demonstrably accurate projections of future expenses required to earn the income. In addition, the court expressed its belief in the continued vitality of our decision in *Bressner Radio, Inc. v. Comm'r*, 267 F.2d 520 (2d Cir. 1959), *nonacquiescence*, *Rev. Rul. 60-85*, 1960-1 C.B. 181, decided after *Michigan* but before *AAA* and *Schlude*, in which we held that deferral methods of accounting based upon reasonably accurate estimates of future costs were permissible under § 446. Finding that RCA's accrual method matched service contract revenues and related expenses "with reasonable precision" and therefore "clearly reflect(ed) income," the court held that the Commissioner had abused his discretion.

This case well illustrates the fundamental tension between the purposes of financial accounting and those of tax accounting. As the Supreme Court has recognized, these two systems of accounting have "vastly different objectives":

> The primary goal of financial accounting is to provide useful information to management, shareholders, creditors, and others properly interested; the major responsibility of the accountant is to protect these parties from being misled. The primary goal of the income tax system, in contrast, is the equitable collection of revenue; the major responsibility of the IRS is to protect the public fisc. Consistently with its goals and responsibilities, financial accounting has as its foundation the principle of conservatism, with its corollary that "possible errors in measurement should be in the direction of understatement rather than overstatement of net income and net assets." In view of the Treasury's markedly different goals and responsibilities, understatement of income is not destined to be its guiding light.

Thor Power Tool Co. v. Comm'r, 439 U.S. 522 (1979). The case also highlights the fundamentally different perspective that courts must adopt when reviewing the propriety of an exercise of administrative discretion rather than deciding a naked question of substantive law. We conclude that the District Court gave too little weight to the objectives of tax accounting and to the Commissioner's wide discretion in implementing those objectives.

Since the Commissioner has "much latitude for discretion," his interpretation of the statute's clear-reflection standard "should not be interfered with unless clearly unlawful." *Lucas v. American Code Co.*, 280 U.S. 445 (1930). The task of a reviewing court, therefore, is not to determine whether in its own opinion RCA's method of accounting for prepaid service contract income "clearly reflect(ed) income," but to determine whether there is an adequate basis in law for the Commissioner's conclusion that it did not. Our review of the relevant decisions persuades us that the law adequately supports the Commissioner's action.

In *Michigan, supra*, the taxpayer received income in the form of prepaid membership dues and promised, in exchange, to perform various services for its members upon demand at any time during the twelve-month term of the membership agreement. In order to match prepaid dues revenues with related expenses, the taxpayer assumed that members would demand services at a constant rate during the contract term and credited prepaid membership dues to current income on a monthly pro rata basis to match the hypothetical rate of demand for services. The Supreme Court upheld the Commissioner's rejection of this method, reasoning that it was "purely artificial and (bore) no relation to the services which (the taxpayer) may in fact be called upon to render." Not long after *Michigan* was decided, however, this Court, in *Bressner Radio, supra*, upheld a method of deferral accounting for prepaid service contract income that resembled the method rejected in *Michigan*. The taxpayer in *Bressner Radio* contracted to service television sets on demand for a period of one year in exchange for prepayment of a stated fee; the taxpayer recognized 25% of the prepayment as income upon receipt and the remainder over the twelve-month contract term. This Court distinguished *Michigan* on the ground that the taxpayer had shown that it experienced "a reasonably uniform demand for services."

Subsequently, in *AAA, supra*, a case that involved a method of deferring recognition of prepaid membership dues income substantially identical to that employed by the taxpayer in *Michigan*, the taxpayer argued that the Commissioner had abused his discretion in rejecting its deferral method of accounting because it had shown at trial that its method accorded with generally accepted accounting principles and was justified by its past experience in providing services. Despite this showing, the Court upheld the Commissioner's rejection of the method. The Court stated as follows:

> Findings merely reflecting statistical computations of average monthly cost per member on a group or pool basis are without determinate significance to our decision that the federal revenue cannot, without legislative consent and over objection of the Commissioner, be made to depend upon average experience in rendering performance and turning a profit.

Finally, in *Schlude, supra*, the taxpayers, operators of a dance studio, contracted with some of their students to provide a specified number of dancing lessons in exchange for a prepaid fee; the lessons were to be given from time to time, as the student specified, during the contract term. The taxpayers credited contract prepayments to a deferred income account, and then at the end of each fiscal period credited to current income for that period the fraction of the contract price that represented the fraction of the total number of hours of instruction available under the contract that the student had actually used during the period. In addition, if for more than a year a student failed to request any lessons, the taxpayer treated the contract as canceled and recognized gain to the extent of the amount of the student's prepayment. Despite the fact that the taxpayer's method of accounting was based largely on its actual performance of services during the taxable year, the court upheld the Commissioner's rejection of the method, viewing the case as "squarely controlled" by *AAA*, because the taxpayer was required to perform services under its contracts only at the student's demand.

The policy considerations that underlie *Michigan, AAA,* and *Schlude* are quite clear. When a taxpayer receives income in the form of prepayments in respect of services to be performed in the future upon demand, it is impossible for the taxpayer to know, at the outset of the contract term, the amount of service that his customer will ultimately require, and, consequently, it is impossible for the taxpayer to predict with certainty the amount of net income that he will ultimately earn from the contract. For purposes of financial accounting, this uncertainty is tolerable; the financial accountant merely estimates future demands for performance and defers recognition of income accordingly. Tax accounting, however, "can give no quarter to uncertainty." *Thor Power Tool, supra*, 439 U.S. at 543. The entire process of government depends on the expeditious collection of tax revenues. Tax accounting therefore tends to compute taxable income on the basis of the taxpayer's present ability to pay the tax, as manifested by his current cash flow, without regard to deductions that may later accrue. By the same token, tax accounting is necessarily hostile to accounting practices that defer recognition of income, and thus payment of the tax on it, on the basis of estimates and projections that may ultimately prove unsound.

In view of the relevant Supreme Court decisions and the policies they reflect, we cannot say that the Commissioner abused his discretion in rejecting RCA's method of accounting for service contract income. Like the service agreements at issue in *Michigan*, *AAA*, and *Schlude*, RCA's service contracts obligated it to perform services only upon the customer's demand. Thus, at the beginning of the contract term, RCA could not know the extent of the performance that the customer might ultimately require, and it could not be certain of the amount of income that it would ultimately earn from the contract. The Commissioner was not required to subject the federal revenues to the vicissitudes of RCA customers' future demands for services.

We think that the Supreme Court's post-*Bressner* decisions in *AAA* and *Schlude* have deprived *Bressner* of controlling force. It is not simply the "artificiality" of a taxpayer's method of deferring recognition of income from services performable on demand that offends the clear reflection principle of § 446(b), but rather the uncertainty inherent in any method that relies on prognostications and assumptions about the future demand for services. Although RCA's predictions may have been more accurate than those of the taxpayers in *AAA* and *Schlude*, they were predictions nonetheless, and the Commissioner was not required to accept them as determinants of the federal revenue.

In addition, although the District Court found that RCA's accounting practices did "clearly reflect income," we are not bound by that finding under the "clearly erroneous" standard of Fed. R. Civ. P. 52. The issue before the District Court was not whether RCA's accounting method adequately reflected income, but whether the Commissioner abused his discretion in determining that it did not. The latter question is one of law.

———————

In the Supreme Court "trilogy" of cases described in *RCA*, the Court did not explicitly or categorically deny the relevance of the matching rationale in tax accounting, but rather held that the taxpayer's *evidence* of the extent to which future costs would be incurred was infirm. The Court essentially concluded that, since both the *time* and *extent* of future expenses were unknown (because the contracts in each case were performed only on customer demand), the argument that the prepaid income should be deferred to better "match" those unknown future expenses was unpersuasive on the particular facts before it.

Thus, the cases noted so far imply that deferral of prepaid income might be allowed in cases in which both the time and extent of future services with respect to a particular contract *can* be predicted with *certainty*. Just such a situation was presented in *Artnell Co. v. Comm'r*, 400 F.2d 981 (7th Cir. 1968). The taxpayer, the successor to the Chicago White Sox, Inc., did not include the prepaid income that White Sox, Inc., had received for season tickets, parking permits, and broadcasting rights, all relating to baseball games scheduled for the following year's season. The Seventh Circuit allowed the income to be deferred to the following taxable year when the games were actually played, because each game date was known with certainty.[47]

The IRS has issued *Rev. Proc. 2004-34*, 2004-1 C.B. 991, which allows one-year deferral for prepaid income for services (and for other items described in the revenue procedure), regardless of whether they would pass muster under *Artnell*. Limited deferral of prepayments for goods can be obtained under Reg. § 1.451-5.

There are two statutory provisions that allow some deferral of prepaid income: (1) § 456, dealing with prepaid dues of certain (nonprofit) membership organizations (such as AAA), and (2) § 458, dealing with returnable magazines, paperbacks, and sound recordings.

NOTES

1.　The Supreme Court has never actually held that certainty as to future services justifies deferral of prepaid income. Rather, it merely held that *failure* to establish certainty is enough to defeat deferral. Does distinguishing the Supreme Court trilogy lead to the opposite tax result where the date and amount of future services is known with certainty? What tax doctrine justifies a distinction between certainty and statistical probability? It appears that matching has never been invoked by the IRS in an effort to accelerate income.

2.　(a) Can prepaid income be properly viewed as "borrowed money" and thus deferrable (until earned) under the borrowing exclusion? This theory hasn't been discussed in any of the cases, but some commentators have suggested that the cash received *must* equal the present value of the future services to be performed. Is this is a plausible assumption? In any event, the relative comparison is not to the future value of the services but to the future costs thereof. The present value of the future obligation can't be calculated without knowing the date and amount of the future costs. But future business costs are not fixed in either amount or date. Instead, they are determined by future decisions as to what costs to incur and by future supply and demand. Even in a case like *Artnell*, the future costs could not have been known with certainty.

(b) If the prepayment is refunded, the transaction amounts to an interest-free loan. It turns out that inclusion of the prepaid cash on receipt coupled with the deduction upon repayment gives the same result, in present value terms, as would occur under § 7872, assuming a constant tax rate.[48]

3.　(a) Section 446(b) does not override core legally-established tax principles, such as those for capitalization, borrowing, and depreciation. However, as noted earlier, it can override the all-events rule (and other tax accounting rules).

(b) The *RCA* case quoted an important passage from the case of *Thor Power Tool*

---

[47] Accord *Tampa Bay Devil Rays v. Comm'r*, T.C. Memo. 2002-248, which held that a baseball team could defer inclusion of advance payments received in 1995 and 1996 for ticket sales and private suite reservations until the related games were actually played in 1998.

[48] Assume a 10% discount rate, a tax rate of 20%, and a receipt of $10K by X that is (to be) refunded 12 months later. Under § 7872, X has Year 1-income of about $909, resulting in a tax of about $182. In the absence of § 7872, X has a Year-1 tax of $2K, and a Year 2-tax savings of $2K, the present value of which is $1,820, for a net present value loss of $182.

v. Comm'r, 439 U.S. 522 (1979), noting the different objectives of financial and tax accounting. In *Thor Power Tool*, the taxpayer attempted to "write down" (deduct) excess inventory under the "lower of cost or market" method allowed by Reg. § 1.471-2(c). The taxpayer argued that it was sufficient that the write-down conform to "best accounting practice," but the Supreme Court rejected the notion that conformity to financial accounting rules creates a presumption of correctness in the taxpayer's favor. The Court held further that the Commissioner's disallowance of the write-down was not an abuse of discretion under the "clearly reflect income" standard set forth not only in § 446(b) but also in Reg. § 1.471-2(a)(2). Specifically, the taxpayer's write-down did not clearly reflect income, because it failed to comply with burden-of-proof requirements established by the applicable Treasury Regulations. Thus, a specific holding of *Thor Power Tool* is that the Treasury can issue regulations setting forth "clear reflection of income" *rules*, as distinguished from using § 446(b) on only an *ad hoc* basis. See Reg. § 1.446-2, promulgated in 1994, dealing with accounting for interest accruals.

4.   "Prepaid income" for the recipient is "prepaid expense" for the payor. Assuming that the payment occurs in a business context, what is the tax treatment thereof to an accrual-method payor? A cash-method payor?

PROBLEM

X Corp sells large front-projection screens at retail for $4K each. As part of the purchase price, X Corp obligates its technicians to perform a maintenance call at the purchaser's home once each year (on the anniversary of the purchase date) for five years, whether or not the customer requests the call. Can X Corp defer inclusion of the portion of the purchase price attributable to the maintenance agreement until the services are performed?

D.   ACCOUNTING FOR DEFERRED-PAYMENT PROPERTY SALES

A sale of property (not subject to inventory accounting) involving future payments of principal cash from the buyer to the seller is variously called an "installment sale," a "deferred-payment sale," or a "seller-financed sale." This type of transaction involves only two parties, possibly because a bank is unwilling to lend cash to the buyer (for example, because the purchased property, the security, is nonliquid or would require extensive management if taken over by the bank). In a two-party, deferred-payment sale, it can be assumed that the buyer's obligation is secured by the property.

Various issues that arise in this type of transaction have already been discussed, namely, the buyer's basis (under the so-called *Crane* doctrine), the tax treatment of the seller who repossesses the property if the buyer defaults, and the tax results (possibly involving § 108(e)(5)) if the loan principal is reduced. Additionally, a bad debt deduction could be available if the buyer's obligation becomes worthless (unless § 1038 applies by reason of a repossession).

What hasn't been discussed so far is the tax treatment of the seller by reason of the sale itself. As will be explained below, the sale is accounted for under one of: (a)

§ 1001, (b) the § 453 installment method (where available), or (c) the open-transaction method (where available). The open-transaction method is available only for contingent-payment sales, and that method will be discussed last.

1. Gains and Losses under § 1001

Suppose that cash-method Sinead sells unimproved investment real estate (adjusted basis $30K and unencumbered by any mortgage) to Basil in Year 1 for $100K. Basil is to make a cash down payment (at the time of closing in Year 1) of $20K and promises to pay four annual installments of $20K each, starting on the first anniversary of the closing, plus market-rate interest. Assume there are no transaction costs. The property's title and possession are to pass to Basil at the closing. Basil's deferred-payment interest-bearing obligation of $80K may or may not be evidenced by a note, but in all probability the note or other promise will be secured by a mortgage running to Sinead. Assume that the discounted PV of Basil's obligation[49] is $78K, and its FMV is $75K.[50] Basil's basis is the full $100K, starting at the closing, under the rule commonly referred to as the *Crane* doctrine.

Interest is a separate income/expense item, meaning that interest it is not included in Basil's basis, nor is it included in Sinead's § 1001 "amount realized" on the sale. Interest is compensation to Sinead for Basil's use of the money, not part of the payment for the property itself.

Section 1001(b) states that the "amount realized" equals the "sum of any money received plus the fair market value of the property (other than money) received."[51] Applying this language to Sinead's situation appears to be straightforward, because Basils's deferred-payment obligation is "property" (a *right* to future money), rather than itself being money. Although the amount realized "from" the sale *could* have been construed to include future money, the text of § 1001(b) refers to money and property *received* (from the sale), not money "to be received," "money receivable," or any other expression looking to the future receipt of cash. Thus, § 1001 has long been understood as requiring that the realized gain or loss be computed in the year of sale, with no deferral of gain or loss on account of the right to receive future cash. By treating the right to future cash as "property" under § 1001, then it follows that Sinead would have, in the year of sale, gain realized of $65K, obtained by subtracting her basis of $30K from her amount realized of $95K ($20K cash plus $75K FMV of the property received). Additionally, Sinead would have further collection gain as the result of receiving $80K principal cash in satisfaction of her deferred-payment obligation, which has a basis of $75K (under § 1012, i.e., the amount included in amount realized on account of receipt of the obligation). The interest is additional gross income to Sinead, and lies outside of § 1001.

---

[49] The PV of the obligation as a whole is the *sum* of the present values of *all* future principal *and interest* payments.

[50] The FMV is likely to be lower than the discounted PV due to credit and security risks, transaction costs involved in enforcing an obligation, and the inability to convert the security to cash (nonliquidity).

[51] Where the consideration consists wholly or mostly of "property," the transaction is really an "exchange" rather than a sale. Nevertheless, transactions of the type discussed here (where the "property" is the buyer's own promise or note) are called (deferred-payment) "sales."

However, as with credit sales of inventory or services, referring to the FMV of a deferred-payment obligation is awkward, because the valuation of such an obligation (especially if given by a non-repeat player in a casual sale) can be difficult. Perhaps here resort can be had to the seller's tax accounting method, in which case an accrual-method taxpayer would treat the deferred-payment obligation as having a value equal to the face (principal) amount of the obligation. As to cash-method taxpayers, however, avoiding valuation would appear not to be an option. In *Warren Jones Co. v. Comm'r*, 524 F.2d 788 (9th Cir. 1975), the cash-method taxpayer argued that the FMV of a deferred-payment contract was not includible at all in the amount realized from the sale in question on the ground that it was not the equivalent of cash under the *Cowden* rule (Subsection B.1.c, supra), and the Tax Court agreed. But, after reviewing the legislative history of § 1001, the Ninth Circuit reversed, and held that the amount realized by a cash-method taxpayer always includes the FMV of a deferred-payment obligation, regardless of the cash-equivalency doctrine as filtered through the *Cowden* rule. This decision had the effect of requiring valuation of the deferred-payment obligation in all cases involving a cash-method seller.

In 1996, the Treasury issued Reg. § 1.1001-1(g), which *effectively abolishes reliance on either the seller's accounting method or the FMV of the obligation.*[52] This regulation is difficult to comprehend because it is littered with cross-references to unfamiliar provisions. Basically, the regulation treats the amount realized attributable to the debt instrument as being equal to its stated principal (i.e., face) amount. However, if the interest is at a below-market rate of interest, then the amount realized attributable to the debt instrument is determined under § 1274 (discussed below, but usually the discounted PV of the obligation, i.e., the sum of the present values of all principal and interest payments under the contract, and if § 1274 does not apply, the value of the instrument is its discounted PV as determined under § 483.

Thus, if the 4% interest rate charged by Sinead in the example set forth above is not below market, Sinead has gain in the year of sale equal to $70K [($20K cash + $80K stated principal) − $30K adjusted basis], and no subsequent collection gain (because the $80K basis in the obligation under § 1012 will be fully offset against the $80K of principal payments). The tax results are the same whether Sinead uses

---

[52] There is an exception in the rare case where the obligation is a publicly traded instrument (such as a corporate bond). See Reg. § 1.1001-1(g)(1), referring to Reg. § 1273-2(b) which refers to publicly traded debt issued for property. Reg. § 1.1001-1(g)(3) states that the rules of Reg. § 1.1001-1(g) supersede those of Temp. Reg. § 15A.453-1(d)(2)(ii), issued in 1981, subsequent to *Warren Jones*. Subparagraph (ii) of that superseded temporary regulation states that the value of the deferred payment obligation (to a cash-method seller) shall be its FMV, but then states that such FMV shall not be less than the FMV of the property sold less other consideration received on the sale (such as the down payment). If the stated selling price is accepted as the FMV of the property, then the FMV of the note will usually turn out to be its stated principal amount. In the Sinead example, if the property sold is accepted as being worth $100K, then the FMV of the note under the superseded temporary regulation is $80K ($100K property FMV less $20K cash down payment), resulting in gain of $70 K ($20K cash + $80K obligation FMV − $30K basis). The principal difference between the approach of Reg. § 1.1001-1(g)(1) and the approach of the superseded temporary regulation is that it is now not necessary (in the first instance) to determine the FMV of the property sold (or the FMV of the deferred-payment obligation, unless the latter is publicly traded).

the cash method or the accrual method. (Another account of Reg. § 1.1001-1(g) is found in Chapter 27.B.1.) This method of computing gain or loss on a deferred-payment sale entirely in the year of sale is referred to as the "closed-transaction method."

2. The Installment Method

The installment method, located in § 453, was enacted to provide relief from having to recognize all or most of the gain in the year of sale under § 1001(b). The installment method, spelled out in § 453(c), operates by prorating the gain "to" the payments of principal cash as and when received, in proportion to such payments. Thus, in the Sinead-Basil example, Sinead would have $14K of (capital) gain in each of Years 1 through 5 inclusive (since 70% of each $20K payment received represents gain) and no collection gain or loss.

a. Scope of Installment Method

It is helpful to start with a broad overview of the reach of § 453. An "installment sale" is defined as any disposition of property where at least one (cash) payment is to be received after the close of the taxable year in which the disposition occurs. See § 453(b)(1).

Section 453(a) only applies where the deferred-payment sale produces gain, not where it produces loss. Losses on sales are computed under the § 1001 closed-transaction method.

The installment method is *not* available for: (1) sales of inventory, (2) certain dealer dispositions,[53] (3) most gain from depreciable personal property,[54] (4) most sales to related parties, (5) sales of personal property under revolving credit plans, (6) sales of stock or securities (and certain other property) traded on an established market, and (7) sales where the debt obligation received is readily tradable or payable on demand. See § 453(b)(2), (f)(4), (g), (i), and (j). These exceptions are mostly based on the ready marketability of the property being sold and/or the obligations obtained, and in some cases on the lack of any compelling nontax reason for structuring the sale as an installment sale.

Once transactions that fall within the exceptions are eliminated, it turns out that the great bulk of transactions that are eligible for the installment method are "casual" (nondealer) gain sales of real property, especially unimproved land, farms, and ranches (for which a bank might be unwilling to lend money). Installment sales may also occur with respect to closely held businesses (and interests therein), but

---

[53] See § 453(*l*) for the definition of a "dealer disposition." In general, the term "dealer" is tax jargon for a taxpayer who sells, in the ordinary course of its business, property described in § 1221(a)(1) (inventory, etc.), which are not "capital assets."

[54] Technically, gain equal to depreciation recapture under § 1245 (mentioned briefly in Chapter 2) cannot be reported under the installment method. See § 453(i). However, in the overwhelming majority of cases involving the sale of depreciable personal property, the entire gain will be § 1245 gain. See also § 453(g) (generally disallowing the installment method for the sale of any depreciable property, real or personal, to a controlled entity).

installment sales appear to be uncommon for art works and collectibles (where cash is obtainable through auction).

If a sale is eligible for the installment method, the seller can elect to use the installment method or elect to report the gain according to the § 1001 closed-transaction method. The election is made simply by how the taxpayer reports the gain on the tax return.[55]

b. Installment Method Mechanics

Examine § 453(c). Under the installment method, eligible sale gain is recognized according to application of the following formula to the facts of each year that a payment (other than interest) is received:

$$\frac{\text{Gross Profit}}{\text{Contract Price}} \times \begin{array}{c}\text{Current Payments}\\\text{(other than interest)}\end{array} = \begin{array}{c}\text{Included Installment}\\\text{Gain}\end{array}$$

The relevant terms are defined in Temp. Reg. § 15A.453-1(b). "Gross Profit" is the Selling Price less basis. "Selling Price" means the gross selling price (other than interest), *at its face amount* (not PV or FMV), unreduced by mortgages and encumbrances. Commissions and other selling expenses augment (i.e., are added to) basis (rather than being subtracted from Selling Price). Really, Gross Profit is going to be the same as § 1001 gain in virtually all cases.[56]

Contract Price means "Selling Price,"[57] supra, *reduced by* mortgages assumed by (or taken subject to by) the buyer, *except that* the excess (if any) of mortgages over augmented basis is *not* subtracted. Stated differently, Contract Price is Selling Price reduced by so much of the mortgage balance as does *not* exceed augmented basis.

"Payments" means *cash payments received in the current year. Interest is excluded*. The down payment (if any) is a Payment, as are any cash "principal" amounts received. "Payments" also includes certain highly liquid obligations of the borrower, namely, those that are payable on demand or (if the buyer is a corporation or government) that are publicly traded. See § 453(f)(3), (4), and (5). Payments are not reduced by commissions and other transaction costs (since they are accounted for in the augmented basis). As with Contract Price, debt (mortgage) relief (in the year of sale) is not a Payment except for any excess of debt relief over augmented

---

[55] Under the statute, the installment method has priority and the taxpayer has to "elect out" of the installment method in order to use the closed-transaction method. See § 453(a) and (d). However, in practice, the election is made by how the gain is reported on the return. Form 6252 is used for installment-method reporting.

[56] An exception would lie for the rare gain in excess of § 1245 recapture gain on the sale of depreciable personal property. Section 1001 gain might be keyed to PV (rather than face amount) in the case of obligations that bear a below-market interest rate but which are not subject to §§ 483 and 1274, discussed in the text later in this chapter, which can operate to reduce the § 1001 gain and Gross Profit (§ 453 gain) to an equal extent.

[57] However, Contract Price and Payments are not reduced by any § 1245 (or § 1250) depreciation recapture.

basis. *The Payments amount is the only item in the formula that can vary from year to year.*

The formula would apply to Sinead's aggregate Payments (including the down payment) received from Basil during the year (for any year in which any Payment, including the down payment, is received), as follows:

$$\frac{\$70K}{\$100K} \quad \times \quad \$20K \quad = \quad \$14K \text{ gain (included each year)}$$

The remaining $6K of each payment would constitute a tax-free recovery of Sinead's basis in the sold property, and the aggregate tax-free basis recovery over 5 years would equal her $30K basis (5 x $6K). If the payment schedule were not uniform, the amount of Sinead's includible gain (and basis recovery) would vary from year to year because the Payments amount would vary from year to year (with the other numbers remaining constant).

To demonstrate the effect of mortgages, assume the same facts as before in the Sinead/Basil transaction (basis of $30K and selling price of $100K), except that the property is subject to a $50K mortgage, and the seller-paid transaction costs are $6K. Hence, the Gross Profit is now $64K. Again Basil pays $20K down, but he takes subject to the mortgage, and therefore he owes Sinead only $30K more, which he agrees to pay in full in Year 5. This time, the numbers plug into the formula as follows for Year 1:

$$\frac{\$64K}{\$64K} \quad \times \quad \$34K \quad = \quad \$34K \text{ Year 1 Gain}$$

The Contract Price is $100K reduced by the portion of the $50K not in excess of (i.e., up to) the augmented basis of $36K. That is, $100K *less* $36K equals $64K. Payments in Year 1 are the sum of the cash ($20K) and the excess of the mortgage over the augmented basis ($14K, i.e., $50K - $36K). These add up to $34K.

In Year 5, the formula looks like this:

$$\frac{\$64K}{\$64K} \quad \times \quad \$30K \quad = \quad \$30K \text{ Year 5 Gain}$$

Total gain is $64K ($34K in Year 1 plus $30K in Year 5).

The installment method does not affect the character of the seller's gain, which is determined at the time of sale. Thus, if the asset sold is a capital asset held for more than one year, the gain reported under the installment method will be long-term capital gain, regardless of whether that gain is reported in the year of sale or in the later years when the various installment payments are received. You will note that there is no "collection" gain or loss when the installment method is used.

c. Section 453A

Section 453 installment reporting creates a deferral opportunity relative to the closed transaction method of § 1001. Section 453 can be viewed either as a rule of deferral of *realization* or as a rule of *deferral of tax* on a realization that occurred entirely at the time of sale. Under an ability-to-pay concept of income, one can say that deferred realization is appropriate for situations in which nonliquid property is "exchanged" for a nonliquid installment obligation (secured by a mortgage on the sold property).[58] (Whether § 453 adequately identifies "deserving" transactions is, of course, a pertinent question.) In contrast, an adherent of the Simons income concept would hold that the seller acquires wealth with an ascertainable FMV (or PV) in the year of sale, and that the realized gain should be fully taxed then. It follows that § 453 should be reconceptualized as a tax-deferral mechanism, and that interest should be charged on such tax deferral.

Being somewhat ambivalent on this issue, Congress enacted § 453A, which is really two separate provisions rolled into one. First, Congress fine-tuned the concept of a nonliquid installment obligation by providing that any borrowing by the property seller in which the deferred-payment obligation is pledged as security is treated as an accelerated payment on the obligation. See § 453A(d). This rule comes into play only where the sales price exceeds $150K, and the property is not farm property or personal-use property (such as a residence). Thus, if Basil's deferred-payment obligation was $1M, and Sinead pledged this obligation as collateral to borrow $1M from a bank in Year 2, Sinead would be treated as receiving a $1 million Year 2 Payment.

Second, § 453A treats certain installment sales as "tax deferral" scenarios. If the aggregate face amount of § 453A obligations obtained in the year (and outstanding at the end of that year) exceeds $5M, the seller must pay interest to the government on the deferred tax attributable to such excess aggregate face amount. See § 453A(b)(2) and (c).

d. Disguised Interest

Installment sales are "seller-financed" sales. The seller wears two hats: seller of property and lender of money with which the buyer purchases the property. Like all debt obligations, installment obligations usually bear interest. Interest on the installment obligations does not enter into the § 453 formula (nor the computation of gain or loss under the § 1001 closed-transaction method) and is accounted for separately, according to the taxpayer's normal accounting method. The interest is includible by the seller, and is deductible by the buyer (if the requirements of § 163 are satisfied).

It did not require a great deal of sophistication to realize that installment sales can readily be structured to convert ordinary (interest) income into preferentially-taxed capital gain by the simple expedient of increasing the stated sales price (and capital gain) and reducing (or eliminating) the stated interest component of

---

[58] Installment obligations on rural property (nonliquid collateral) are heavily discounted (in FMV terms) below PV.

installment obligations by a corresponding amount, leaving the total value of the consideration unchanged. The buyer, it is true, might (if sophisticated) object to reducing or eliminating the stated interest (if the interest is deductible), but on the other hand the interest might not be deductible, and the buyer might benefit from a higher stated principal that may be depreciated or expensed. The buyer might even be able to negotiate some price reduction in return for the tax favor conferred on the seller.

To appreciate these points, suppose Sally sells Blackacre, which has a basis of $80K and a FMV of $100K, to Barry for a balloon payment due at the end of 3 years. Assuming that market-rate interest is 8%, the balloon payment would be $126K (with a little rounding off), consisting of $100K of principal and $26K of compound interest. Suppose, however, that the sale terms are changed to require Barry to pay $126K of "principal," and no "interest," in a lump sum at the end of 3 years. If the $126K were accepted by the tax law as the purchase price for Blackacre, Sally will have converted $26K of ordinary interest income into an increased amount realized (and capital gain), and Barry will have a $126K basis in Blackacre. In addition, the transaction may qualify for § 453 installment reporting, in which case Sally's $46K of capital gain would be deferred to Year 3.

Congress has responded by enacting §§ 483 and 1274, both of which recalculate *the "real principal" as being the present value (PV) of the buyer's obligation* (the sum of the present values of all principal *and* interest payments under the contract), computed in essentially the same manner as if § 7872 applied. In other words, the calculation uses the "applicable federal rate" (AFR), which is published periodically by the IRS, as the discount rate, and the discounting is done on a semi-annual basis. See §§ 483(a), 1274(b)(1) and (2). In the Sally/Barry example, the stated principal amount of Barry's obligation is $126K, but the operation of these provisions would, if the AFR were 8%, yield a present value of $100K. An alternative measure of the real principal, to be used in potentially abusive situations (such as where the debt obligation is nonrecourse), is the FMV of the property sold ($100K in this case), reduced by other consideration (none in this case). See § 1274(b)(3); Regs. §§ 1.483-2(a)(ii), 1.1274-2(b)(3), -5. (This back-up resort to the FMV of the property sold is the only way in which FMV can enter into the computation of gain or loss on a property sale, but note that the reference is to the FMV of the sold property, not the FMV of the deferred-payment obligation.)

So, if the real principal is $100K, then the (capital) gain, whether figured under § 453 or § 1001, is $20K, and the remaining $26K is really interest. In the § 453 formula, the Gross Profit would be reduced to $20K, the Contract Price would be reduced to $100K (as would the Year 3 "Payment"), yielding a Year 3 capital gain of $20K.

Sections 483 and 1274 differ with respect to how the imputed interest of $26K in the aggregate is to be accounted for. If § 1274 controls, the taxpayers (even those using the cash method) are required to take account of the imputed interest as earned, i.e., as it accrues. The method of calculation is explained in Chapter 27.B.1, but, briefly, interest compounding at 8% annually would be $8K for the first 12 months, $8,640 for the next 12 months, and $9,360 for the third 12 months, adding up to $26K. In contrast, § 483 requires that the imputed interest be taken into account according to the taxpayer's normal accounting method. For cash-method sellers and buyers, this means deferral of the entire interest until received (or paid).

Sections 483 and 1274 potentially apply in any case where the AFR is greater (or lesser) than the stated interest rate. (There is a maximum AFR in certain cases, however.[59]) Section 1274 takes priority over § 483, but § 1274 does not apply to sales of: (1) principal residences, (2) farms for less than $1M, (3) other property where total payments are $250K or less, and (4) sales of patents on a contingent-payment (royalty) basis. See § 1274(c)(3). In addition, cash-method sellers (who aren't dealers) can elect out of § 1274 under § 1274A(c) if the principal amount does not exceed $2M. (This election binds the borrower/purchaser as well.) Sales (in excess of $3K) that fall within these exceptions (other than exception (4)) or the § 1274A(c) "election out" are subject to § 483.

e. Disposition of Installment Obligations

If, subsequent to an installment sale, the seller disposes of the installment obligation, gain or loss is realized (and recognized) under § 453B in an amount equal to the difference between the seller's basis in the obligation and (1) the amount realized (in case of a sale or exchange of the obligation) or (2) the FMV of the obligation (in the case of any other kind of disposition). The "basis" of an installment obligation is its (remaining unsatisfied) face amount *less* the amount of gain that has *not yet* been recognized. (Conceptually, the basis in the obligation is the taxpayer's basis in the sold property reduced by the basis therein that has already been recovered under § 453 by reason of having received prior Payments.)[60]

For example, suppose Serge sells Blackacre, with a basis of $60K, to Brenda for $100K, consisting of a $20K down payment in Year 1 and a promise to make a balloon payment of $80K in Year 5, plus market-rate interest. The total gain is $40K, of which 20% ($8K) is recognized in Year 1 under § 453. In Year 4, Serge sells the $80K obligation to Dolly for $79K. Serge's basis in the obligation is $48K ($80K face amount reduced by the $32K of as-yet-to-be recognized gain). As indicated above, the $48K figure can also be obtained by starting with Serge's Blackacre basis of $60K and subtracting the $12K basis of Blackacre already "used up" under § 453 against the Year-1 down payment of $20K to produce the Year 1 gain of $8K. The Year-4 gain is $31K ($79K sales price *less* $48K basis).[61] This gain has the same character as that of the underlying sale.

If the obligation, on account of not being paid, is disposed of (satisfied) in a transaction involving the repossession of personal property that had previously

---

[59] The discount rate for purposes of both §§ 483 and 1274 is not to exceed 9% in the case of sales of (most kinds of) property where the stated principal amount does not exceed $2.8M. See § 1274A(a) and (b). For purposes of § 483, the discount rate interest is not to exceed 6% on certain sales of land for $500K or less between related parties. See § 483(e). These ceilings on discount rates have the effect of increasing the present value of the buyer's obligation (in relation to the real present value) during periods when the AFR is high (as it was when § 1274 was enacted).

[60] The basis of deferred-payment obligations was touched upon in connection with repossessions of sold property, discussed in Chapter 22.A.6.

[61] The figure of $31K represents the deferred § 453 gain ($32K) *less* the $1K reduction in sales price of the obligation relative to its face amount.

been sold to the obligor, the installment obligation is treated as being exchanged for the repossessed collateral at the latter's then FMV. The taxpayer in these cases is usually a merchant or finance company, in which case the original credit sale of the personal property would not have been reportable under § 453. (Recall that repossessions of real property are governed by § 1038, discussed in Chapter 22.A.6.)

If the obligation is cancelled or becomes unenforceable, the nonsale disposition rule applies, but the FMV is presumably zero, and the disposition is not treated as a sale or exchange. There, the seller would have a loss that is ordinary in character. If the obligor and obligee are related parties in this situation, however, the amount realized is deemed to be not less than the face amount of the obligation. In neither case can the transferor claim a bad debt deduction.

These rules assure that installment gain is accelerated to the seller on *any* disposition of the installment obligation. However, if an installment obligation is disposed of by reason of an individual's death, § 453B does not apply, and the decedent's successor essentially stands in the decedent's shoes (that is, takes the decedent's basis in the obligation).[62]

Finally, § 453(e) requires an acceleration of installment gain in certain cases in which the installment sale was to a related party, and the related-party buyer disposes of the property within 2 years of the installment sale.

3. Open-Transaction Method for Contingent Payment Sales

Both § 453 and § 1001 presuppose that the selling price (or amount realized) can be ascertained at the time of sale. Thus, neither the installment method nor the § 1001 closed-transaction method can function if the future payments are contingent on speculative events.

Most contingent payment rights in commerce are referred to as "royalty" rights. A royalty is a stream of payments made by a transferee of a property right to the transferor that is contingent on (1) the transferee's production from the transferred property (such as a mineral interest) or (2) the transferee's sales receipts (either gross or net) derived from use of the property (as in the case of a transferee's use of a patent right, copyright, or trade name to produce and sell products). The payments are structured to be contingent because neither party, at the time the arrangement is entered into, knows the true value of the underlying property, and, therefore, a price cannot be fixed. A royalty arrangement is a way in which the transferor and transferee "share" in the uncertain future success or failure of the property (but without entering into a "partnership" or "joint venture"). Royalty arrangements are common in the natural resources, high-tech, franchising, and entertainment industries.

If the transferor retains residual ownership of the property and the transferee only has the right to use the property, royalties are in the nature of contingent rent, and are treated for tax purposes as if they were rent. (Such a transaction, where it involves intangible property, is commonly referred to as a "license.") If, however, all substantial rights in the property are transferred to the transferee,

---

[62] See §§ 453B(c), 691(a)(4), 1014(c); Reg. § 1.691(a)-5(a). The successor does not obtain a § 1014 basis.

then the disposition is a sale (or possibly an exchange), and the royalty right is the consideration. Where some, or all, of the consideration for the purchase of property will be paid pursuant to a royalty arrangement, the transaction is a "contingent-payment sale." The distinction between a license (or lease) and a sale is an important tax issue that is taken up in Chapters 28.C.3 (intangibles) and 29.A.2.c (mineral interests). Here it is assumed that the transaction is indeed a sale, and the issue on the table is: "How are contingent-payment sales taxed?"

The answer, in brief, is the "open-transaction method." This method originated in the 1931 case of *Burnet v. Logan*, 283 U.S. 404, where the cash-method taxpayer in 1916 sold stock in a company for $137,500 cash plus a right to 60 cents per ton of ore obtained by the buyer from a mine to which the company had a long-term mineral lease. The government argued that the closed-transaction method should be applied and that the present value of the future payment right was $121,383, based on tonnage estimated to be mined over a projected 45-year period. The total cash received by the taxpayer from 1916 through 1920 was less than taxpayer's basis in the stock that was sold, and the taxpayer reported no income or gain for those years. Under the open-transaction approach advocated by the taxpayer, she would have been entitled to exclude the payments from income until she had recovered an amount equal to her stock basis. All receipts above that amount would be included as capital gain from the 1916 sale of her stock. The Supreme Court agreed with the taxpayer, stating:

> As annual payments on account of extracted ore come in, they can be readily apportioned first as return of capital and later as profit. The liability for income tax ultimately can be fairly determined without resort to mere estimates, assumptions, and speculation. When the profit, if any, is actually realized, the taxpayer will be required to respond. The consideration for the sale was the promise of future money payments wholly contingent upon facts and circumstances not possible to foretell with anything like fair certainty. The promise . . . had no ascertainable fair market value. The transaction was not a closed one. Respondent might never recoup her capital investment from payments only conditionally promised. She properly demanded the return of her capital investment before assessment of any taxable profit based on conjecture.

A contingent-payment sale fits the definition of "installment sale" in § 453(b)(1) because at least one payment will occur in a future year. However, since the Selling Price and Contract Price cannot be determined in such a case, the normal § 453 formula stated in § 453(c) cannot be used. Instead, the following alternative § 453 approaches are prescribed by Temp. Reg. § 15A.453-1(c). First, if the contingent-payment sale provides for a *maximum possible selling price*, the *maximum* price is treated as the "Selling Price" under the conventional installment-method formula, and the formula is then applied. If there is no maximum selling price but there is a *maximum period over which payments are to be received*, each year's receipts (treated as "amount realized" for the year) are offset by a portion of the basis prorated evenly over the maximum period. If (as is likely) there is *neither* a maximum selling price *nor* a maximum payment period, the basis of the property sold is prorated equally over a 15-year period against the amount realized in each year.

The seller in a contingent-payment sale situation can elect to forego the methods described in the preceding paragraph and instead use the open-transaction method approved by the *Logan* case.[63] *In order to use the open-transaction method, both the buyer's payment obligation and the value of the sold property must not be readily ascertainable.*[64] See Temp. Reg. § 15A.453-1(d)(2)(iii). In the usual contingent-payment sale, this test is readily satisfied. Despite protestations in the regulations about use of the open-transaction method being "rare and extraordinary," that would hardly appear to be the case given the prominence of the industries where transactions of this type are common.

It would be unusual for a contingent-payment sale to provide for interest, because interest usually presupposes an ascertainable "principal," and a stated principal is inherently lacking where the sale price is uncertain. Sections 483 and 1274 except certain contingent-payment sales of *patents* from their interest-imputation rules. Otherwise, interest is imputed in a contingent-payment sale *on a retroactive basis*. Thus, if the AFR for the time of sale in Year 1 was 5%, and the contingent payment received in Year 5 turns out to be $100K, the discounted present value (as of Year 1) would be about $78K (treated as the principal payment), and the remaining $22K would be deemed to be "interest," includible by the recipient and deductible by the payee (if a deduction is allowed under § 163) in Year 5.[65]

Another problem with contingent-payment sales is the buyer's basis. With no stated or ascertainable "real" principal, the so-called *Crane* basis rule cannot be applied as of the year of sale. And with no ascertainable basis (and perhaps no ascertainable useful life), how would depreciation (if any) be calculated? *These problems are finessed by allowing the buyer to deduct the full amount of each payment.*[66] This method can be viewed as the equivalent of capitalizing the payment and deeming the depreciation (and interest) for the year to be exactly equal to such payment.

4. Deferred Sales Pursuant to Put and Call Options

Whereas a deferred-payment sale involves the receipt of consideration *after* a sale has occurred, the purchase of an option to buy or sell property in the future involves the payment of cash *in advance of*, but in connection with, a *possible* future property sale. An option to buy is known as a "call option" and an option to

---

[63] The transaction must be a "sale" and not an "exchange" (e.g., a patent right for shares of stock in the buyer).

[64] Temp. Reg. § 15A.453-1(d)(2)(iii) provides: "The fair market value of a contingent payment obligation may be ascertained from, and in no event shall be considered to be less than, the fair market value of the property sold (less the amount of any other consideration received in the sale)." This statement follows the holding of *U.S. v. Davis*, 370 U.S. 65 (1962), where the consideration received by a husband in exchange for his securities (the value of the wife's support rights surrendered) was highly speculative and presumed by the Court to be equal to the securities given in exchanged. . This approach is referred to as the barter-equation method of valuation.

[65] See Reg. § 1.1275-4(c)(4)(i), (ii).

[66] See *Newton Insert Co. v. Comm'r*, 61 T.C. 570 (1974), *aff'd*, 545 F.2d 1259 (9th Cir. 1976) (government concession).

sell is a "put option." A call or put option may lapse without being exercised. The tax issue here is the relation, if any, that the option transaction bears to the later property transaction.

To illustrate the "call option" scenario, suppose Gordon for several years has owned unimproved land (Blackacre), purchased for $10K and having a current FMV of $30K. Jane, an investor, is not interested in an immediate purchase of Blackacre, but she believes that it might appreciate. Accordingly, Jane in Year 1 offers Gordon a nonrefundable $1K payment (premium) for the right (option) to purchase the property from Gordon before the end of Year 5 for $35K (the "option price"). Gordon doubts that Blackacre's value will rise above the option price ($35K) before the end of Year 5, and so he accepts Jane's offer, seeing it as an opportunity to pick up a quick $1K while retaining the property. Gordon is called the "writer" or "grantor" of the option (or the "optionor"), and Jane is called the "grantee" (or "optionee").

This transaction is not an "installment sale" (potentially eligible for § 453), because an installment sale involves one or more payments received *after* the year of sale. Instead, the issue posed by a call option is whether the call option premium is separate ordinary income (with no basis offset) to Gordon because Gordon has not yet disposed of the property (or any aspect thereof) or whether the option transaction should be held open for possible integration with the future sale.

In *Rev. Rul. 58-234*, 1958-1 C.B. 279, the IRS has adopted the open-transaction approach, stating in part (and in a somewhat conclusory manner):

> An optionor, by the mere granting of an option, may not have parted with any physical or tangible assets; but, just as the optionee thereby acquires a right to buy certain property at a fixed price on or before a specified future date, so does the optionor become obligated to deliver, such property at that price, if the option is exercised. Since the optionor assumes such obligation, which may be burdensome and is continuing until the option is terminated, there is no closed transaction nor ascertainable income or gain realized by an optionor upon mere receipt of a premium for granting such an option. It is manifest . . . that there is no Federal income tax incidence on account of either the receipt or the payment of such option premiums, unless and until the options have been terminated, by failure to exercise, or [by exercise], with resultant gain or loss.

Applying the ruling to the Gordon/Jane hypothetical, if the sale does *not* take place and the option lapses after 5 years, the option premium would be ordinary income to the property owner (Gordon) only *at the time the option lapses*. If the option is exercised, the option premium is treated as additional amount realized to Gordon, increasing his capital gain. On Jane's side, the option premium is a capital expenditure. If the option lapses, she would have a loss deduction in Year 5, assuming that the transaction was entered into for profit (as is the case here). If the option is exercised, the option premium would be added to Jane's basis in Blackacre.

The Gordon/Jane hypothetical can also be used to illustrate the "put option" scenario. Gordon wants to continue holding Blackacre because he believes that its value will continue to increase, but just in case the value actually falls, he wants to "lock in" his unrealized gain of $20K. Accordingly, Gordon offers Jane a nonrefundable $1K payment for Jane's commitment to buy Blackacre from Gordon at any time Gordon chooses to "put" the property to Jane, up to the end of Year 5, at the $30K option price. Jane, thinking that the property's value will not fall below $30K, accepts Gordon's offer.

The same tax-treatment design options exist here as for call options, and again *Rev. Rul. 58-234* treats the put option transaction as being an open transaction. Accordingly, if the value of Blackacre falls and the option is exercised, the $1K constitutes a reduction in Jane's basis in Blackacre (sort of like a price rebate received in advance of a purchase) and a reduction in Gordon's amount realized on the sale of Blackacre. If the option lapses in Year 5, Jane has ordinary income of $1K *in Year 5* and Gordon has a deductible loss of $1K in Year 5.

The "character" of any loss attributable to the lapse of an option is governed by § 1234(a)(1) and (2), which would operate in most cases to produce a capital loss. (If the underlying property is stock, securities, and commodities, § 1234(b)(1) treats any deferred income resulting from the lapse of an option as a short-term capital gain.)

NOTES

1. (a) The deferral of the seller's gain under § 453 can combine with the *Crane* basis rule on the buyer's side to create a tax arbitrage possibility in cases where the buyer's basis can be written off at a faster rate than the seller's inclusion. There is no across-the-board tax rule or principle to deal with timing mismatch situations, because generally the tax treatment of one party to a transaction does not dictate that of another party.

(b) There are ad hoc rules in the Code that deal with some situations of this type. For example, §§ 83(h) and 404(a)(5) delay an employer's deduction for certain compensation to the year of the employee's includibility. Another provision of this type is § 267(a)(2), which provides that any expense deduction by an accrual-method taxpayer to a cash-method related-party payee is to be deferred until the year of payee inclusion. Section 1239 deals with a "character mismatch" arbitrage opportunity by converting capital (or § 1231) gain into ordinary gain when a sale of depreciable property is made to (or by) a controlled entity, but not in other related-party situations.

2. The transaction in *Burnet v. Logan* today looks more like an "exchange" than a "sale," because the seller received a right to royalties based on the production of a mine. If the transaction had been treated as an exchange, it might well have been a tax-common-law nontaxable exchange (because both properties involved were not susceptible to reasonable valuation), but the royalties would have been ordinary income from mining subject to depletion.

3. The open-transaction rule for put and call options is illogical as to the person receiving payment. Normally, a payment for a person's doing something (or not doing something) is compensation for services. Compensation is included when received, not as it is earned never time. In no sense is the option payment a loan or an addition to (or subtraction from) the sales price.

PROBLEMS

1. Lance sells a large tract of unimproved land, with a basis of $700K to Kevin. The sale contract calls for Kevin to pay Lance $200K as a cash down payment in the year of sale (Year 1) and $1M at the end of 60 months (for a total consideration of $1.2M) plus 5% market interest ($50K) each year on the unpaid balance of $1M. The FMV of Kevin's deferred payment obligation is $600K, despite the market-interest rate and the fact that the obligation is secured by a mortgage on the property, because of (1) the risk of Kevin's nonpayment, (2) the high volatility of land prices in the area, and (3) the high transaction costs of enforcing a mortgage. Title and possession pass at closing.

(a) What is Kevin's basis in the property? Does it matter if Kevin uses the cash or accrual method? Does it depend on the method Lance uses to report the sale?

(b) What result to Lance under the § 1001 closed-transaction method? Does the answer depend on whether he uses the cash or accrual method?

(c) Can Lance report this transaction under the open-transaction method, assuming he otherwise uses the cash method?

(d) Assuming Lance is not a dealer in this kind of real estate, can he use the installment method? What tax results in each year under the installment method?

(e) What result in (d) if the property were subject to a nonrecourse mortgage of $300K, which Kevin takes the property subject to? In this case, the Year 5 payment would be $700K instead of $1M, the interest on which would be $35K per year.

(f) Now assume the original facts, except that the AFR at the time of sale is 8%. Assuming that discounting is done on an annual basis, the present value of the deferred-payment obligation is $880,228, derived as follows:

Time (months)	Payment Due	Present Value
12	$50K	$46,296
24	$50K	42,877
36	$50K	39,691
48	$50K	36,752
60	$1,050K	714,612
		Total $880,228

Assume that the FMV of the deferred-payment obligation is $500K. What tax results under §§ 453 and 1001, assuming that § 1274 applies? Assuming that § 483 applies? Do either of these sections in fact apply?

2. (a) Vincent, an actor, agrees to be the leading man in the film to be called The Terminated Ten, but the Executive Producer balks at paying Vincent's demanded fee of $10M. Instead, Vincent agrees to be paid an amount equal to $100K upon signing the contract plus 2% of the gross ticket sales. (Vincent's contract right is unfunded and unsecured.) The previous nine films in the "Terminated" series did fairly well, and it would be reasonable to expect that Vincent would rake in an additional one to six million dollars on this deal. What tax result to Vincent, assuming the following receipts: Year 1 (signing the deal), $100K; Years 2 and 3 (film

in production), zero; Year 4, $600K; Year 5, $300K; Year 6 $100K; Years 7 through 12, zero; and, Year 13 (from release of future rights), $50K?

(b) Same as (a), except that Vincent is not an actor but the owner of the movie rights to the Terminated Ten screenplay, which is based on characters created by Vincent and featured in the previous 9 Terminated films. Vincent didn't actually write the screenplay himself. Instead, Vincent (who owns the copyright to the Terminated concept and characters) paid a stable of scriptwriters, editors, and consultants a total of $450K to produce the screenplay. What are the possible tax results to Vincent? Among other things, is Vincent eligible for the § 453 installment method, and, if so, how would that operate in this case?

Chapter 24

REALIZATION OF LOSS ON THE DESTRUCTION OR THEFT OF PROPERTY

This chapter deals with the loss of property by reason of its destruction, theft, seizure, or other involuntary cause. This type of loss can often be recovered by insurance or a tort recovery, or through an eminent domain proceeding, and the recovery could result in a gain for tax purposes. This topic deserves a separate chapter on account of the fact that numerous special rules cluster around it. These rules include timing rules, deduction rules, nonrecognition rules, and characterization rules.

A. THE DEDUCTION FOR PERSONAL CASUALTY AND THEFT LOSSES

It is axiomatic that losses on personal-use assets are not deductible. Nevertheless, § 165(c)(3) allows a deduction for casualty and theft losses of personal-use property, although the deduction is subject to limits in § 165(h) that severely restrict its scope and thereby make it unavailable to many taxpayers. The § 165(c)(3) deduction is a regular itemized deduction (not an MID).

Sustained casualty and theft losses on business or investment property are deductible in full under § 165(c)(1) or (c)(2). Since their deductibility is not dependent on § 165(c)(3), they are *not* subject to the § 165(h) reductions.

1. What Is a Casualty or Theft?

Only sustained losses of an individual's personal-use property caused by casualty or theft are deductible under § 165(c)(3). A casualty refers to a sudden or unexpected *cause* (as opposed to effect) that results in physical damage to the property (or its uselessness).[1] The concept of "casualty" has bred countless disputes with the IRS. For example, the IRS, after considering scientific evidence that termite infestation requires three to eight years before it results in significant damage, ruled that termite damage to personal-use property was not deductible as a "casualty" because the damage was "the result of gradual deterioration through a steadily operating cause and [was] not the result of an identifiable event of a sudden, unusual or unexpected nature."[2] In contrast, the IRS ruled that a sudden infestation of southern pine bark beetles that killed ornamental trees in five to ten

---

[1] See *Citizens Bank v. Comm'r*, 28 T.C. 717, aff'd, 252 F.2d 425 (1st Cir. 1957); *Chamales v. Comm'r*, T.C. Memo. 2000-33.

[2] *Rev. Rul. 63-232*, 1963-2 C.B. 97; see *Newton v. Comm'r*, 57 T.C. 245 (1971) (acq.); *Rev. Rul. 66-303*, 1966-2 C.B. 55.

days constituted a "casualty."[3] The general idea is that § 165(c)(3) is not intended to allow backdoor depreciation deductions for the gradual loss in value of personal-use property.

The concept of "casualty" possesses some relevance for business and investment property (as well as for personal-use property) insofar as a casualty loss (for which there is no reasonable prospect of recovery) is treated as being "sustained," even where the property is not completely disposed of or destroyed, where a permanent physical impairment occurs.[4]

A person cannot create a casualty by an intentionally destructive act, such as arson.[5] On the other hand, an accident resulting from the taxpayer's own negligence can qualify as a casualty if it is "sudden, unexpected, and unusual,"[6] and not "gross" or "willful."[7]

Losses resulting from the theft of personal-use property are also allowable under § 165(c)(3). "Theft" includes any felonious taking, including embezzlement, fraud, extortion, or blackmail.[8] Since certain special rules (to be noted in due course) apply only to theft losses, the taxpayer bears the burden of proof in establishing that a theft occurred.[9] A frequent difficulty here is differentiating a theft from the simple loss of an item — jewelry falling off the wearer while walking, for example.[10]

2.   Is the § 165(c)(3) Deduction Justified?

The conventional justification for the § 165(c)(3) deduction is that the casualty or theft produces a sudden and unexpected loss in value that is not attributable to the personal consumption use of the assets by the taxpayer. This explanation is simple and appealing.

It might also accord with an interpretation of the Simons income concept that views "consumption" as an independent component of income. But that leads to a dead end, because the Simons income concept posits no clear principle for the tax treatment of economic waste. If consumption in the Simons income concept (or under the ability-to-pay concept) refers instead to a principle of the nondeductibility of consumption costs, then the consumption occurred with the original purchase of the consumer item, and subsequent events are irrelevant. Indeed, the § 165(c)(3) deduction is inconsistent with other income tax rules pertaining to personal-use assets, such as the nontaxation of gross imputed income.

---

[3] See *Rev. Rul. 79-174*, 1979-1 C.B. 99.

[4] See Regs. §§ 1.165-1(d)(2), -7(b)(3) Ex. (1).

[5] See *Rev. Rul. 81-24*, 1981-1 C.B. 79.

[6] See *Rev. Rul. 72-592*, 1972-2 C.B. 101.

[7] See *Blackman v. Comm'r*, 88 T.C. 677 (1987), *aff'd by order*, 867 F.2d 605 (1st Cir. 1988).

[8] See Reg. § 1.165-8(d); *Citron v. Comm'r*, 97 T.C. 200 (1991) (holding that the taking must be a criminal act); *Rev. Rul. 2009-9*, 2009-1 C.B. 735 (investment losses attributable to the Bernard Madoff Ponzi scheme).

[9] *Rev. Rul. 72-112*, 1972-1 C.B. 60.

[10] See, e.g., *Smith v. Comm'r*, 10 T.C. 701 (1948) (lost dog).

The net consumption value (reduced to present value) of any personal-use asset is taxed ex ante by disallowing any deduction for the purchase price (by capitalizing it). No deductions are allowed in other cases involving lack of enjoyment of a personal-use asset, such as where the personal-use asset had worn out significantly faster than anticipated, had been a lemon, or simply fell into disuse. Conversely, a purchaser of a consumer item has no income or gain on account of over-use or over-enjoyment.

The § 165(c)(3) deduction is also inconsistent with the tax treatment of personal casualty insurance, because the costs (premiums) of obtaining such insurance are considered to be nondeductible personal outlays, whereas the loss insured against is potentially deductible under § 165(c)(3). This argument posits that there is no meaningful difference between buying, say, 12 Baccarat crystal wine glasses in the expectation that 10 of them will survive breakage and buying 10 wine glasses plus paying insurance premiums to cover their possible loss. In both cases, the cost, which should be about the same in each case, results in obtaining 10 intact wine glasses.[11] In order to achieve parity of tax result in the two cases, the sudden loss of the two wine glasses should not be deductible. However the insurance may be managed, the true nondeductible cost of the personal consumption is the total amount paid to secure the 10 glasses. Stated differently, to the extent that personal casualty losses are deductible under § 165(c)(3), the self-insured (the buyer of the 12 glasses) is tax-favored over the taxpayer who pays nondeductible premiums to acquire insurance against personal casualty loss.

However, an ability-to-pay approach might allow a deduction for *some* casualty and theft losses, namely, those that result in *extraordinary, duplicative, off-the-bottom living expenses*. This rationale is in fact embodied in § 123 of the Code, which excludes insurance proceeds arising from a casualty to one's personal residence to the extent of duplicative living expenses. Under this duplicative-expense approach, the deduction would presumably be available only for losses with respect to "essential" consumer durables (homes, major appliances, and cars), and then only when the taxpayer, following the loss, *actually replaced* the lost item with a functionally equivalent one. For example, if a taxpayer's car that cost $30K, having a current FMV of $17K, is "totaled" as the result of the occurrence of an uninsured risk, perhaps deduction of the lesser of $17K or the cost of a replacement car would be justified under this analysis.

From an external policy perspective, the § 165(c)(3) deduction is flawed. In principle, the Code should not allow deductions for losses resulting from risks that can be readily insured against. The deduction operates to make the federal government (i.e., other taxpayers) the partial insurer of uninsured losses due to casualty and theft. It is unfair that conscientious property owners should insure both against their own risks and (involuntarily) against risks incurred by others. Free "insurance" coverage increases moral hazard (unnecessary risk-taking).

---

[11] To spell this point out more fully, X spends $1.2K for 12 wine glasses without insurance, and Y pays $1.2K for 10 wine glasses and insurance coverage. Y loses two glasses to casualty, and the insurance replaces them in a transaction that produces no gain or loss (because the basis equals the insurance recovery), so that Y ends up with 10 glasses. X loses 2 glasses to casualty, and ends up with 10 glasses. If X deducts the loss, X is better off than Y tax-wise.

Moreover, this subsidy favors high-rate-bracket taxpayers (who obtain greater tax savings per deduction dollar than lower-bracket taxpayers), but high-bracket taxpayers are the very group most able to obtain casualty insurance.

3. Limitations on the § 165(c)(3) Deduction

In order to maintain our focus on the § 165(c)(3) deduction, it will be *assumed* herein that the taxpayer in question has a "sustained" casualty or theft loss of a stipulated amount, referred to herein as the "loss amount," which is the lesser of the property's basis or the economic loss resulting from the casualty or theft, reduced by any insurance (or other) recovery. The concept of the loss amount, explored more fully in Section C.1 and 2, infra, is relevant for all transactional losses. The discussion here will instead focus on rules unique to the § 165(c)(3) deduction. Nevertheless, two points relating to losses generally are worth noting here. First, no loss deduction can exceed the property's basis. See § 165(b). Second, an apparent loss can end up being a *gain* by reason of an insurance recovery or other recovery. In the casualty and theft loss context, a gain is most likely to occur where a casualty insurance recovery exceeds the basis of the property lost by casualty or theft. We mention these points here because they come into play in the computation of the § 165(c)(3) deduction.

The rules unique to the § 165(c)(3) deduction are located (mostly) in § 165(h). First, section 165(h)(1) provides that the sustained loss amount from any casualty or theft event with respect to personal-use property has to be reduced by $100. This reduction is per event, not per item. The purpose is to prevent de minimis casualty losses from even appearing on the tax radar screen. Thus, if Paula accidentally steps on her drugstore reading glasses that cost her $20, Paula can forget not only the glasses but also any hope of a tax deduction. If Paula's ring is stolen and the theft loss amount is initially $3K, the loss is reduced to $2.9K by the $100-per-casualty-or-theft floor.

Section 165(h)(2)(A) provides that aggregate net personal casualty and theft losses for the year can be deducted in an amount not to exceed the aggregate *recognized* personal casualty and theft gains for the year. Thus, if Paula has $5K of recognized casualty gains in the same year as her $2.9K loss in the previous paragraph, the full $2.9K loss is allowed (and, of course, the $5K gains are included in gross income). Moreover, under § 165(h)(5)(A), this $2.9K loss becomes an above-the-line deduction! In this scenario (where the personal casualty and theft gains exceed the losses), both the gains and the losses are treated as being "capital" in character by reason of § 165(h)(2)(B) (which treats the gains and losses in such situation as if they arose from sales or exchanges of capital assets).

In the more common scenario where the personal casualty and theft losses exceed the gains, § 165(h)(2)(A) provides that the *excess* of such theft losses for the year *over* such (recognized) gains for the year is allowable only to the extent (if any) *that such excess loss* exceeds 10% of the taxpayer's AGI for the year. Thus, if Paula has zero recognized personal casualty and theft gains for the year, and Paula's AGI is $100K, the $2.9K loss is wholly disallowed, since $2.9K is less than $10K (i.e., 10% of $100K). No carryover of disallowed § 165(c)(3) losses is permitted. If Paula's AGI were, instead, $20K, then she would be allowed to deduct

$900 ($2.9K − $2K), the $2K figure being 10% of $20K. Where (as here) the personal casualty and theft losses for the year exceed such gains, both the gains and the losses are naturally "ordinary," because a casualty or theft is not a "sale or exchange," and there is no statutory rule providing a different result in this case. Finally, the personal casualty and theft loss deduction for the year (in excess of such gains for the year) is a regular itemized deduction (not an MID). See § 67(b)(3). (If there are such gains for the year, the losses are above-the-line deductions to the extent of such gains under § 165(h)(5)(A).)

NOTES

1.   The 10% floor under the § 165(c)(3) deduction suggests that routine casualty and theft losses are included in the off-the-bottom allowances. However, such losses are neither routine nor inherently off-the-bottom (i.e., relating to subsistence existence). A more likely explanation is that the floor eliminates having to account for trivia, or even that Congress is ambivalent about the justification for the deduction but is unwilling to take the heat for wholly repealing it.

2.   *Personal* casualty and theft losses raise some ancillary points.

(a) Section 165(h)(5)(E) conditions a deduction on filing an insurance claim, if the casualty or theft loss is covered by insurance. Here Congress is reluctant to subsidize a loss that was avoidable simply by filing a claim.[12] This rule is only applicable to § 165(c)(3) losses.[13]

(b) Under § 165(*l*), an uninsured loss on a bank deposit due to bank failure can be treated as either a § 165(c)(3) deduction or (up to $20K) as an ordinary investment loss, and not as a nonbusiness bad debt loss under § 166(d).

(c) Because of the floor under the § 165(c)(3) deduction, it could (in some situations) be advantageous for a married couple to file separate returns. Of course, the loss deduction is attributable to the owner(s) of the property.

3.   A loss of cash due to casualty, theft, or forfeiture is treated as a "loss" rather than as an "expense."[14] This characterization helps taxpayers come under § 165(c)(3) where the loss is not a business or investment loss but is caused by casualty or theft. It hurts taxpayers in cases where the loss would be deductible as a business or investment loss but the deduction is disallowed under the judicial public policy doctrine (which applies to losses but not expenses).[15]

---

[12] This provision was enacted to overturn the result of *Miller v. Comm'r*, 733 F.2d 399 (6th Cir. 1984).

[13] Thus, the *Miller* case cited in the preceding footnote appears to be good law for business and investment losses caused by casualty or theft.

[14] See *Kreiner v. Comm'r*, T.C. Memo. 1990-587; *Rev. Rul. 72-112*, 1972-1 C.B. 60.

[15] See, e.g., *Wood v. U.S.*, 863 F.2d 417 (5th Cir. 1989) (forfeiture by drug dealer). In contrast, current *expenses* relating to criminal activities that are otherwise deductible under § 162 or 212 could be disallowed only under a statutory disallowance rule provided by §§ 162(c), 162(f), 162(g), or 280E, but not under the judicial public policy doctrine. See Chapter 8.D.1.

B. WHEN IS A LOSS SUSTAINED?

Loss deductions *in general* are deductible only when the loss is "sustained." See § 165(a). Reg. § 1.165-1(d) states:

> [A] loss shall be treated as sustained during the taxable year in which the loss occurs as evidenced by closed and completed transactions and as fixed by identifiable events occurring in such taxable year . . . . If a casualty or other event occurs which may result in a loss and, in the year of such casualty or event, there exists a claim for reimbursement with respect to which there is *a reasonable prospect of recovery*, no portion of the loss with respect to which reimbursement may be received is sustained . . . , until it can be ascertained with reasonable certainty whether or not such reimbursement will be received.

Basically, the foregoing posits two requirements: (1) that the loss be "fixed" and "final," and (2) that there is not "a reasonable prospect of recovery" by way of insurance coverage or otherwise (government compensation or tort recovery). At the same time, the quoted passage from the regulations *allows for the possibility of a deduction for a partial loss in cases where there has been no complete "disposition" of the property.*

Note that the foregoing rules apply to losses generally. They are not limited to § 165(c)(3) situations involving the casualty or theft losses with respect to personal-use property.

What is the result if there is no reasonable prospect for recovering all of a loss, but a reasonable chance exists of recovering a portion of it? For example, perhaps Harry's homeowner's insurance excludes the first $10K of hurricane loss (i.e., contains a $10K "deductible") but covers the rest of the loss. Deduction of a partial loss is allowable under § 165 (subject to the § 165(h) limitation), so long as the deduction portion is identified by a closed and completed transaction. Thus, if Harry's total loss is $34K, a loss of $10K (the uncovered amount) is clearly sustained in the year the loss occurs. The remaining $24K loss would be "sustained" only if and when it is finally determined that Harry's insurance policy does not really cover it.

Theft losses (otherwise sustained) are deemed to be sustained no earlier than when the loss is discovered. See § 165(e).

Under § 165(i), a taxpayer may elect to treat a loss attributable to a federally-proclaimed disaster as having been sustained in the year preceding the disaster. This allows for the immediate filing of an amended return for the preceding year, which would constitute an immediate claim for a refund based on the additional deduction.

C. DETERMINING THE AMOUNT OF THE LOSS (OR GAIN)

The net gain or loss is, conceptually, the difference between the insurance (or litigation) recovery and the basis attributable to the loss resulting from the casualty or other event. Since there may be no recovery at all, one starts with a determination of the basis attributable to the loss resulting from the casualty or other event (herein referred to as the "loss amount").

1. The Loss Amount

In a *complete disposition of business or investment property* (by way of casualty, theft, abandonment, or otherwise), the loss amount is the taxpayer's (then) basis in the asset, reduced by any insurance (or litigation) recovery (which is an amount realized). Here the amount of economic loss (loss in value) is not relevant, because the investment is wholly disposed of.[16]

In all other cases, *the loss amount is the lesser of the economic loss or basis.* This rule, now found at Reg. § 1.165-7(b)(1), is designed to crudely identify the portion of the asset's basis that is attributable to the loss. The rule was upheld in *Helvering v. Owens*, 305 U.S. 468 (1939). There the taxpayer purchased an automobile for $1,825 and was using it for personal purposes when it was damaged in a collision. The fair market value (FMV) of the car was $225 prior to the collision and $190 after the collision. The taxpayer argued that he was entitled to deduct $1,635 under a literal reading of what is now § 165(b): his entire cost basis of $1,825 less the $190 value of the car after the accident. The IRS limited the casualty loss to $35, the reduction in value arising from the accident.

Although the decline in value resulting from the "casualty or other event" is the true measure of economic loss resulting from the casualty, repair expenses can be used as a proxy for such loss. See Reg. § 1.165-7(a)(2)(ii). Measuring the loss in value of damaged goods would be difficult.

A salutary effect of the lesser-of-basis-or-economic-loss rule is that it prevents a deduction of personal consumption in a § 165(c)(3) context by deeming the pre-casualty (or theft) decline in value of the property to be a proxy for the personal consumption benefit obtained from the property. To illustrate this point, suppose an automobile is purchased for $30K and declines in value to $20K, at which point it is "totaled." Here, the loss amount is $20K, meaning that the $10K value used up in personal consumption is not deductible. On the other hand, the "lesser of" rule operates in a way that treats any economic loss attributable to the casualty as coming "first" out of basis. To illustrate this point, suppose an antique table is purchased for $10K and appreciates in value to $16K. The uninsured table is damaged by floodwater, necessitating repairs of $8K, which is deemed to be the measure of the economic loss. The entire $8K loss is deductible (because less than the basis of $10K), even though some of the loss must have been "out of" the unrealized appreciation. In principle, a loss of untaxed appreciation should not be deductible, or else the taxpayer would enjoy a double tax benefit for the same

---

[16] See Reg. § 1.165-7(b)(1) (flush language after (ii)).

dollars (exclusion of the unrealized appreciation and deduction of that same appreciation as a loss when the property is damaged).

One might argue that (in the table example) the $8K economic loss should be deemed to have come first out of the $6K unrealized appreciation (resulting in a lost basis amount of only $2K).[17] Alternatively, it could be argued that 8/16 of the basis (i.e., 8/16 × $10K = $5K) should be deductible. But, if this latter approach were applied to *depreciated*-value property, the deductible amount would exceed the economic loss. Thus, if the table was only worth $6K when damaged and the repairs were $3K, the loss amount would be 3/6 of $10K, or $5K, a dubious result. In any event, the lesser-of-basis-or-economic-loss rule is well established.

If no recovery is obtained, and if:

(a) the deduction is allowed under § 165(c)(1) or (c)(2) as a business or investment loss, the loss amount is simply deducted, or

(b) the deduction is allowed only under § 165(c)(3), one then applies the rules of § 165(h), described above, to the loss amount.

2. Effect of Recovery

Since a casualty or theft loss is not "sustained" if there is a reasonable prospect of recovery, the transaction in such cases is held open until the recovery is received (or is denied) to determine the amount of the sustained loss or realized gain. Any recovery reduces the "loss" otherwise figured under the lesser-of-basis-or-economic-loss rule, and it might produce gain. The net gain or loss is realized in the year the recovery occurs.

For example, assume that Peter owns a painting, which hangs on his wall for enjoyment, and that it is totally destroyed by fire in Year 1. His basis in the painting was $8K, the FMV of the painting at the time of the destruction was $10K, and Peter receives an insurance recovery of $7K in Year 2. The $7K recovery reduces the $8K loss amount (i.e., the lesser of $10K economic loss or $8K basis), and so the net loss amount for tax purposes in Year 2 is only $1K, which is then subject to § 165(h).

Assume the same facts, except that the pre-casualty FMV was only $6K. Here the recovery of $7K is *greater* than the loss amount of $6K, resulting in no net *casualty* loss that can be deducted. But there is no tax gain under § 1001 either, since the amount realized of $7K is less than the total property basis of $8K. The result here is a nondeductible, *noncasualty* loss of $1K.[18] Because Peter's property is used for personal purposes, this *noncasualty* loss cannot be deducted under § 165(c)(3).

---

[17] The IRS made such an argument in *Cox v. U.S.*, 537 F.2d 1066 (9th Cir. 1976), where the loss was to an oil deposit that was not known to exist when the property was acquired, but it was rejected by the court.

[18] Another way of conceptualizing this scenario is to think of the $6K portion of the $8K basis as being used up against $6K (of the $7K) insurance recovery, producing a net casualty loss of zero and leaving the remaining $2K of basis being disposed of for an amount realized of $1K in a nondeductible loss transaction.

Finally, assume the same facts as initially stated, except that the insurance recovery is $10K. Here Peter realizes a personal casualty *gain* of $2K, since the entire basis in the destroyed painting is $8K. This $2K gain may or may not be recognized, as will be seen shortly.

Where a loss is correctly deducted in Year 1 (due to the lack of a reasonable prospect of recovery) and a recovery is obtained in a later year (perhaps as the result of a successful tort claim), the later recovery is includible at least to the extent of the deduction actually taken in Year 1. (The mechanics of this inclusionary rule are discussed in Chapter 26.B.6.)

3.   Tax Treatment of Casualty Insurance Premiums

Since the *full* insurance recovery is matched against all or a portion of the taxpayer's basis in the property lost (in whole or in part) by casualty or other event, it must be the case that the insurance recovery is not (also) offset by property insurance premiums. That is correct. In other words, the purchase of property insurance is not an investment, and the premiums are not capital expenditures creating basis that will be offset against any insurance recovery. Instead, the premiums are viewed as *expenses* to obtain a service (insurance coverage), which the taxpayer typically hopes never to have to use. As no Code provision deals specifically with such premium expenses, deductibility hinges on general rules pertaining to the deductibility of expenses.[19] Thus, premiums paid with respect to business or investment property are deductible under §§ 162 or 212, while premiums paid with respect to personal-use property are nondeductible. Accordingly, the premiums paid with respect to conventional homeowner's insurance are nondeductible personal expenses.

NOTES

1.   Insured property losses are treated as open transactions to the extent that there is a reasonable prospect of recovery (by insurance). In contrast, medical expenses and (insurance) reimbursements are accounted for on a year-to-year (closed-transaction) basis. A medical expense paid by the taxpayer that is not in fact reimbursed *in the same year* is an expense for that year. A medical insurance reimbursement in a later year is treated as raising a separate gross income issue. (The reimbursement is income to the extent actually deducted in the prior year under a doctrine known as the "tax benefit rule." See Chapter 26.B.6.) The taxpayer cannot simply "elect" to forgo deduction of an allowable and proper medical expense (or casualty loss) simply in order to create basis to use as an offset for a future reimbursement or recovery.

2.   The term "reasonable prospect of recovery" is pretty much limited to insurance coverage and perhaps rights to recovery under government disaster-

---

[19] As noted in Chapter 7.A.1, prepaid insurance (where the premium purchases more than 12 months of coverage) can be a capital expenditure.

relief programs.[20] The mere possibility of a tort recovery is usually considered to be too contingent, unless a suit is initiated promptly.[21]

3. If the asset is not disposed of, the taxpayer's basis is clearly reduced by the amount of the loss allowed after applying the § 165(h) floors. Should the basis also be reduced by any *disallowed* loss amount? Or what if the taxpayer did not itemize (i.e., was unable to get any tax benefit from the deduction because her total itemized deductions did not exceed the standard deduction)? In *Dobson v. Comm'r*, 320 U.S. 489 (1943), the Supreme Court held that an allowable loss deduction that could not reduce taxable income (which was already below zero) in the year sustained did not reduce the basis of the asset. *A fortiori*, casualty loss deductions disallowed by § 165(h) would not reduce basis.

4. Are repairs to fix a casualty loss treated as expenses or capital expenditures? (Repairs on personal-use property are, of course, not deductible.) Prop. Reg. § 1.263(a)-3(g)(1)(iii) (2008), states that a taxpayer must capitalize amounts "for the repair of damage to a unit of property for which the taxpayer has properly taken a basis adjustment [with respect to a casualty loss]."

PROBLEM

In the following, assume that Steve and Janice, who are married, have AGI of $60K for each year in question, disregarding the transactions described below. Analyze the following transactions *in the aggregate*, but ignore § 1033, infra.

(a) Steve and Janice had earlier purchased a car for $20K. In Year 1, when the car is worth $16K, Steve negligently runs it into a telephone pole, reducing the value to $4K. Steve has the car repaired for $11K. The loss is covered by collision insurance, except that the policy carries a $2K "deductible." Steve and Janice pay annual insurance premiums of $1K for this policy, which entitles them to recover $9K ($11K insured loss less $2K deductible), but the insurance company does not approve the claim until Year 2 and does not pay it until Year 3.

(b) Janice owns an art work inherited from her mother. Her basis in the art work (under § 1014) is $16K (the FMV of the art work at the date of her mother's death), and it is worth about $25K in Year 1, when it is stolen. The theft is discovered in Year 2. The insurance covers replacement cost, which in this case means its current FMV, minus a $5K "deductible." The insurance company agrees to pay $20K in Year 2 and does so in Year 2.

---

[20] See *Callahan v. Comm'r*, T.C. Memo. 1996-65, *aff'd by order*, 111 F.3d 892 (5th Cir. 1997) (payment by FEMA to hurricane victims).

[21] In *Johnson v. U.S.*, 74 Fed. Cl. 360 (2006), the court held that a theft loss resulting from a fraud scam could not be taken where the taxpayer was actively pursuing a lawsuit in the same year that the theft was discovered. In a later hearing of the same case, 80 Fed. Cl. 96 (2008), *appeal dismissed* (Fed. Cir. 2010), the taxpayer was allowed to deduct losses on claims that had been abandoned or settled, against the government's objection that the entire bundle of claims had to be resolved.

D. GAINS FROM INVOLUNTARY CONVERSIONS

As noted above, the receipt of a recovery or reimbursement relating to property can produce realized gain to the recipient. Here, we consider the relief that is provided to such recipients by § 1033, which deals with realized gains from "involuntary conversions." In addition to casualty and theft, the term "involuntary conversion" encompasses other involuntary realization events, such as expropriation, seizure, condemnation, requisition, or similar action.

1. Operation of § 1033

Section 1033 allows the taxpayer to take steps that will result in the deferred recognition of gains that are realized from involuntary conversions. Section 1033 differs from § 1031 (discussed in Chapter 22) in (1) being elective, (2) being inapplicable to involuntary-conversion *losses*, and (3) being available for involuntary conversions of all kinds of property (including personal-use property).

To illustrate the mechanics of § 1033, suppose that Claire owns a vacation home (which she occasionally rents to tenants), with a $100K FMV, which burns to the ground in Year 1. Her adjusted basis in the home was then $50K, and she receives (under her insurance policy) $80K in Year 2. (The land is a separate asset which is not destroyed.) Claire realizes (pursuant to an involuntary conversion) a $30K gain on the home under § 1001 when she receives the insurance proceeds in Year 2 ($80K AR *less* $50K AB). Absent an election under § 1033, that realized gain must be recognized in Year 2.

Under § 1033(a)(2), realized gain (but not loss) goes unrecognized *at the taxpayer's election* if (1) the transaction giving rise to the gain was an "involuntary conversion," (2) before the close of the second taxable year following the year in which the gain was realized (which would be Year 4 in Claire's case) the taxpayer acquires property that is "similar or related in service or use" to the converted property, and (3) such replacement property is at least equal in cost to the amount realized for the converted property. The concept of "similar or related in service or use" is applied quite narrowly.[22]

Thus, if Claire, prior to the end of Year 4, builds a new vacation home on the same land for $90K and makes the election provided in § 1033, her $30K realized gain goes unrecognized in Year 2, since she is treated as having "rolled over" the entire amount realized ($80K), plus $10K additional cash, into similar-use property.[23]

However, § 1033 is only a *deferral* provision, not a *forgiveness* provision. Claire's $30K of realized but unrecognized gain will be preserved for future reckoning

---

[22] See Reg. § 1.1033(a)-2(c)(9).

[23] If Claire wants to avoid including her realized gain in Year 2, she must file a form with her tax return informing the IRS that she is planning to purchase replacement property and to elect the benefits of § 1033. Another form will need to be filed for the year when she actually acquires the replacement property. If Claire *fails* to purchase the replacement property in a timely manner, she will have to file an amended return for Year 2, and pay additional tax (because of the recognized gain), plus interest to compensate the government for the time value of the late tax payment.

through the basis mechanism found in § 1033(b)(2). If § 1033 were intended to forever exempt the involuntary conversion gain from tax, Claire's basis in her new vacation home would be its $90K cost under § 1012. But § 1033(b)(2) requires a reduction in the basis of the replacement property by the amount of gain that went unrecognized under § 1033(a). Thus, Claire's basis in the new vacation home would be only $60K (the $90K cost of the new vacation home *less* the $30K of unrecognized gain on the involuntary conversion of her old home). Thus, if she immediately sold her new home for its $90K value, she would realize and recognize the $30K of gain that went unrecognized in the year the involuntary-conversion gain was realized.

Conceptually, $60K is the correct basis amount, because her after-tax investment in the new home is $60K ($50K unrecovered basis in the destroyed home plus additional investment of $10K).

But what if Claire, who received $80K from the insurance company, uses only $70K of it to purchase a replacement vacation home and uses the remaining $10K for some other purpose? In that case, Claire is required to *recognize* her realized gain to the extent that the proceeds are *not* rolled over into qualifying replacement property. That is to say, Claire must recognize $10K of her $30K realized gain. The nonreinvested cash is the § 1033 version of "boot" (which was discussed in the § 1031 context in Chapter 22.B.4). Section 1033(b)(2) provides that Claire's basis in the new home, which she purchased for $70K, would be $50K (the $70K cost of the new home *less* the $20K of unrecognized gain). Claire's $50K basis in the new home correctly memorializes her after-tax investment in it ($50K unrecovered basis in destroyed home, *less* $10K pocketed cash, *plus* $10K gain recognized). If Claire turned around and sold the new home for $70K, before its fair market value changed, she would realize and recognize the $20K of gain that went unrecognized on the involuntary conversion.

If Claire had a basis in the destroyed property of $75K, and received $80K in insurance proceeds, she would realize a gain of only $5K. *The gain recognized under § 1033 cannot exceed the gain realized.* Thus, if Claire spent only $70K of the $80K insurance proceeds on the replacement unit, she would have to recognize her entire $5K realized gain (not $10K), and her basis in the replacement property would therefore be its $70K cost, since the reduction to basis under § 1033(b)(2) for the amount of gain that went unrecognized would be zero. Her after-tax investment in the new vacation home is indeed $70K ($75K initial cost basis *less* $10K pocketed cash *plus* $5K gain recognized).

2. Interaction of § 1033 with § 121

Section 1033 can apply to the same transaction as does § 121, which you first encountered in Chapter 6.E.5. Recall that § 121 excludes up to $250K of gain ($500K if the taxpayers are married and file a joint return) from the sale of the taxpayer's principal residence. Section 121, unlike § 1033, is a *permanent* exclusion. Thus, § 121 is to be applied "before" § 1033 (if the § 121 exclusion is not alone sufficient, to allow the entire gain to go forever untaxed).

Thus, suppose Felix (who is unmarried) owns a principal residence with a basis of $300K that appreciates in value to $500K, at which time it is destroyed by fire, and Felix receives insurance proceeds of $500K. The involuntary conversion gain of $200K is fully excluded under § 121, and Felix's basis in his new residence (*if* he purchases one, which § 121 does not require) is exactly what he pays for it.

Now suppose instead that the value of the principal residence is $700K, so that Felix has a realized involuntary conversion gain of $400K upon receiving insurance proceeds of $700K. Felix buys a new home for $600K in the following year, meaning that he has nonreinvested cash boot of $100K. Under § 121, the first $250K of realized gain goes permanently unrecognized. Section 121(d)(5) provides that Felix's AR *for purposes of § 1033* is deemed to be only $450K (the actual AR of $700K *less* the § 121 exempt gain of $250K). Since $450K is less than the reinvested amount of $600K, Felix is *deemed* not to have received any boot (even though he really did) for purposes of § 1033. So long as Felix makes the § 1033 election, the § 1033 unrecognized gain is $150K (deemed AR of $450K less basis of $300K). Felix's basis in his new home (which he purchased for $600K) is $450K ($600K cost *less* $150K of § 1033 unrecognized gain). This basis result of $450K "checks out" in terms of Felix's after-tax investment ($300K original basis *plus* $250K of permanently exempt gain *minus* $100K pocketed cash).

3.   Character of Recognized Involuntary Conversion Gains and Losses

The character (as capital or ordinary) of *personal* casualty and theft recognized gains and allowable losses are subject to the character rules found in § 165(h), discussed above. Section 1231 is not relevant to such gains and losses.

Section 1231 is, however, potentially applicable to involuntary conversion gains or losses that are long-term and that derive from property used in the trade or business or from capital assets held in business or for investment.

First, if *casualty and theft* gains from such (business and investment) property exceed *casualty and theft losses* from such property, all such gains and losses become "involuntary conversion gains and losses" from such property. If the casualty and theft losses exceed the gains, then all such gains and losses are removed from § 1231 and are governed by other character rules.

Next, and subject to the foregoing, recognized or allowable involuntary-conversion gains and losses from long-term property used in the trade or business or long-term capital assets held in business or for investment are "§ 1231 gains" and "§ 1231 losses." The other principal category of § 1231 gain or loss is that of long-term gains or losses on the *sale or exchange* of property used in the trade or business (other than nondepreciable, nonamortizable personal property, such as goodwill, which is a capital asset).

Section 1231 is a taxpayer-friendly provision whose complex mechanics are explained in the next chapter. Here it will be noted that if the aggregate § 1231 gains exceed the aggregate § 1231 losses for the year, *all* such gains and losses are treated as capital gains and losses. If the § 1231 losses exceed (or are equal to) the § 1231 gains for the year, *all* such gains and losses are deemed to be "ordinary."

The holding period of replacement property acquired in a § 1033 rollover transaction relates back to the acquisition of the involuntarily-converted property if such property was a capital asset or § 1231 property in the taxpayer's hands. See § 1223(1).

NOTE

In tax jargon, nonrecognition of gain conditioned on a "reinvestment" of the proceeds into other eligible property is called a "tax-free rollover." A tax-free rollover (as well as a tax-free exchange) is a cash flow consumption tax feature of the income tax. Indeed, a cash flow consumption tax is one, big, tax-free rollover system! So long as sales proceeds are reinvested in business or investment property, they produce no tax under such a system. To illustrate this point, in a cash flow consumption tax system, assume that the taxpayer's investment property is sold for $100K, and the proceeds are entirely used to buy investment or business property (and not spent on personal consumption). The $100K of sales proceeds is added to the tax base but is then offset by the $100K deduction for the purchase of the new investment, and no tax is owed. Section 1033, which has been around for a long time, represents a policy of limited solicitude for victims of involuntary conversions rather than a calculated move in the direction of a cash flow consumption tax system.

PROBLEMS

1. Luke owns a house, with a basis of $200K, which he purchased on January 1 of Year 1 and has used continuously as his principal residence. He sells it for $350K on March 16 of Year 4. What tax consequences result? Does it matter whether Luke uses all or some the proceeds to buy another residence? (Does it have to be a "principal" residence?) If he does buy another residence for $400K, what is his basis in it?

2. Same as problem 1, except that Luke's house is destroyed by fire on May 15, Year 7, when the value of the home is $300K. The "relacement cost" of the new home, to which Luke is entitled under his insurance policy, is $350K, which is paid to him on June 14 of Year 8. The reconstruction of the house is completed in November of Year 9, at an actual cost of only $325K. What tax results for Luke?

3. Same as problem 2, except that the building that burned down (and is reconstructed) is Luke's restaurant rather than his home. What result? Does it matter if the reconstruction cost of $325K is financed with borrowed money, secured by a mortgage on the reconstructed restaurant?

Chapter 25

CAPITAL GAINS AND LOSSES

This chapter provides more detailed coverage of capital gains and losses than was offered in Chapter 2.

Recall that "net capital gain" enjoys favorable tax treatment for individuals through lower tax rates under § 1(h) than the rates applicable to ordinary gains and income. In contrast, capital losses of individuals are unfavorably treated under § 1211, which limits capital losses deductions for the year to the amount of the capital gains amount for the year plus $3K, with any excess being carried forward indefinitely. (In the case of a corporation, net capital gains are generally not subject to a preferential tax rate; net capital losses of corporations are carried back three years and then forward for five years, after which they expire.)

This chapter first examines, in Section A, the definitional nuances of "sale or exchange" and "capital asset," plus some "glosses" on the concept of capital gains and loss. Section B describes the special rules applicable to property that has been depreciated or otherwise used in a trade or business. Section C explores the policy implications of the system. Section D reviews the consequences of capital gain and loss treatment with a view to planning opportunities.

A. DEFINING CAPITAL GAINS AND LOSSES

Recall that § 1222 provides that *otherwise includible or deductible* gains and losses are "capital" gains or "capital" losses *only* if two requirements are satisfied: (1) the gain or loss results from the "sale or exchange" (or deemed sale or exchange) of (2) a "capital asset" within the meaning of § 1221(a). All other includible or deductible gains and losses are commonly referred to as "ordinary." Section 1222 adds that a capital gain or loss will be "long-term" if realized with respect to an asset held more than one year. All other capital gains and losses are "short-term." Section 1223 provides special holding period rules, many of which have been mentioned already.

1. The "Sale-or-Exchange" Requirement

The term "sale or exchange" is not defined in the Code or regulations. Thus, the courts were initially left with the task of giving content to this term. The relevant judicial decisions have established the following requirements, *all of which must be satisfied*:

(1) A completed transfer of property must occur. The transfer can be voluntary or involuntary. However, a transfer subject to a significant retained interest or power (other than a security interest) is inconsistent

with a sale or exchange. ("Incomplete" transfers are dealt with in Chapter 29.B.)

(2) The transfer must be from the taxpayer to another party. Thus, worthlessness and abandonment do not entail sales or exchanges.

(3) Closely related to (2), the property must survive the transaction. Thus, the satisfaction of a claim or debt obligation is not a sale or exchange of the claim or obligation by the creditor because the claim (although disposed of by being satisfied) no longer exists after it has been satisfied of the claim (which is satisfied) or the property (which no longer exists and which does not transfer to the insurance company).[1] Similarly, the collection of insurance proceeds for property destroyed by fire is not a sale or exchange.[2]

(4) Finally, the transferee must supply consideration in the form of cash (a sale) or property or services (an exchange), or some combination of both.[3] As noted in Chapter 13, relief of a transferor's debt is considered the equivalent of receiving cash.

Thus, the following property dispositions clearly qualify as sales or exchanges: a transfer from a mortgagor to a mortgagee through a mortgage foreclosure or in lieu of foreclosure,[4] a transfer of property in payment of a debt,[5] a taking of property by exercise of a government's condemnation power, and a gift of property subject to a liability in excess of the donor's basis.[6]

The rule that obtaining satisfaction of a claim (at or before its maturity) is not a sale or exchange of the claim was rationalized by the Fifth Circuit, in *Pounds v. U.S.*, 372 F.2d 342 (5th Cir. l967), as follows:

> If the interest [of the taxpayer owning the claim] had been sold to a third party shortly before [the claim matured], the income realized from the sale should be taxable at capital gains rates. If such a sale should give rise to capital treatment, the result we reach in this case may seem formalistic. One of the reasons for according special tax treatment to capital [gains] is to facilitate the disposal of appreciated property. In light of this consideration, our distinction becomes meaningful. Until [the claim matured, the taxpayer] had complete control over the timing of the realization of income from his interest. But once [the claim matured], special tax treatment was

---

[1] See *Fairbanks v. U.S.*, 306 U.S. 436 (1939) (redemption of debt); *Pounds v. U.S.*, 372 F.2d 342 (5th Cir. 1967) (satisfaction of contract right); *Fahey v. Comm'r*, 16 T.C. 105 (1951) (satisfaction of right to contingent fee). Satisfying a claim by transferring property with a built-in gain or loss *is* a sale or exchange by the transferor but not the transferee, as explained in Chapter 19.A.1.

[2] See *Helvering v. William Flaccus Oak Leather Co.*, 313 U.S. 247 (1941).

[3] This requirement has been interpreted liberally. See *U.S. v. Davis*, 370 U.S. 65 (1962) (release, upon divorce, of transferee's marital rights); *International Freighting Corp. v. Comm'r*, 135 F.2d 310 (2d Cir. 1943) (receipt of services; result ratified by Reg. § 1.83-6(b)).

[4] See *Hale v. Comm'r*, 32 B.T.A. 356 (1935), *aff'd*, 85 F.2d 819 (D.C. Cir. 1936).

[5] See *Kenan v. Comm'r*, 114 F.2d 217 (2d Cir. 1940).

[6] See *Johnson v. Comm'r*, 495 F.2d 1079 (6th Cir.), *cert. denied*, 419 U.S. 1040 (1974).

no longer necessary or even relevant. [The taxpayer] had lost control over the timing of his income realization.

A transaction that appears to involve the extinguishment, cancellation, or termination of a contract right for consideration might be held to be a sale if the right is immediately re-granted to a third party and the third party provides consideration that ends up in the hands of the terminated grantee. For example, if X leases property to Y, whose lease is terminated in a transaction in which Z, the new lessee of X, pays money to X who in turn pays Y to give up the lease, then Y may be viewed as having sold the lease to Z. (If the transaction were viewed as one where X paid Y to terminate the lease, Y would be treated as not having disposed of the lease in a sale or exchange.) See *Bisbee-Baldwin Corp. v. Tomlinson*, 320 F.2d 929 (5th Cir. 1963).[7]

Notwithstanding the tax common law rules relating to the sale-or-exchange requirement described above, Congress has enacted numerous Code provisions that *deem* various transactions to result in "sales" or "exchanges. Most of these have already been mentioned. A few provisions cut the other way by deeming certain dispositions not to be sales or exchanges. In the aggregate, these provisions greatly dilute the importance of the tax-common-law doctrine pertaining to what is a "sale or exchange."

1. § *165(g)*. The loss occasioned by a "security" (which is a capital asset) becoming worthless is treated as a loss from the sale or exchange of a capital asset at the end of the year it becomes worthless. The term "security" includes not only stock and stock rights but also corporate or government debt instruments in registered form or with coupons. (Note, however, that, notwithstanding § 165(g), an individual taxpayer may be able to claim an ordinary loss (subject to a limit) on worthlessness of "small business stock" described in § 1244.)

2. § *165(h)(2)(B)*. Where personal casualty and theft gains in a year exceed personal casualty and theft losses, all the gains and losses are treated as capital gains and losses, subject to holding period rules.

3. § *166(d)(1)(B)*. A worthless nonbusiness bad debt (other than a security) is treated as a short-term capital loss, regardless of the taxpayer's actual holding period for the debt.

4. § *1231*. This section was touched upon in the discussion of involuntary conversion gains and losses in Chapter 24.D. Section 1231 is discussed further in Section B, infra.

5. § *1234*. The lapse of an option to buy or sell property is deemed a sale or exchange by § 1234(a). The option is also deemed a capital or § 1231 asset if the option property is such.[8]

---

[7] Accord *Comm'r v. Ferrer*, 304 F.2d 125 (2d Cir.1962) (release of movie rights to copyright owner who re-granted movie rights to third party). Compare Comm'r v. Pittston Co., 252 F.2d 344 (2d Cir. 1958) (no sale where rights were terminated without reassignment; this result is overturned by § 1234A).

[8] Section 1234(b) treats the gain or loss to the grantor of a put or call option relating to stock, securities, or commodities as short-term capital gain or loss.

6.   § *1234A*. The termination of a "right or obligation" with respect to property that would be a capital (or § 1231) asset in the hands of the taxpayer is treated as gain or loss from the sale or exchange of a capital (or § 1231) asset.

7.   § *1234B*. Gain or loss from the sale, exchange, or termination of a securities futures contract is treated by § 1234B as gain or loss from the sale or exchange of property that has the same character as the property to which the contract relates has in the taxpayer's hands (or would have in the taxpayer's hands if the taxpayer acquired it).

8.   § *1235*. A transfer for consideration of property consisting of all substantial rights to a patent by a "holder"[9] is treated by § 1235 as the sale or exchange of a capital asset held for more than one year, regardless of whether the payments received by the transferor-holder in such transfer are payable over the period coterminous with the transferee's use of the patent or are contingent on productivity, use, or disposition of the patent transferred. Section 1235 is discussed further in Chapter 28.C.3.

9.   § *1241*. Amounts received in cancellation of a lease or distributorship agreement are deemed to be received in an exchange by the lessee or distributor.

10.   § *1253*. The transfer of a franchise, trademark, or trade name is *not* a sale or exchange of a capital asset if the transferor retains any significant power, right, or continuing interest in the subject matter of the transfer. Section 1253 is discussed further in Chapter 28.C.3.

11.   § *1271(a)(1)*. The receipt of consideration for the retirement or redemption (i.e., satisfaction) of a debt obligation is generally deemed to be a sale or exchange of the obligation by the creditor. Section 1271 is discussed further at Chapter 27.B.1.

12.   § *1287*. The gain realized on the sale of a debt obligation that is not in registered form is ordinary gain if the debt is required under § 163(f) to be in registered form.

Sections 165(g), 1234A, and 1271(a)(1)) were enacted to provide "equal treatment" between a person selling a financial asset just prior to a "terminal" realization event (lapse, worthlessness, redemption, or satisfaction) and a person holding onto the asset until such terminal realization event occurs.

Similar deemed-sale-or-exchange provisions exist in Subchapters C and K, dealing with corporate and partnership tax.

---

[9] A "holder" is (i) an individual who created the patent or (ii) any other individual who acquired her interest in the patent in exchange for money or money's worth paid to the creator of the patent before actual reduction to practice of the invention covered by the patent, provided that such individual is not the creator's employer or a "related person" of the creator.

2. "Capital Asset"

Section 1221 provides that *all* items of property — whether business, investment, or personal-consumption — are capital assets *except* for property listed in § 1221(a)(1) through (8).

a. Overview of the Statutory Exceptions

The common theme underlying the statutory exceptions of § 1221(a) is that compensation income and income from the sale of inventory (and property used to produce the inventory) should not generally qualify as "capital gain." Thus, exception (1) denies capital asset status to "stock in trade," "inventory," and "property held . . . primarily for sale to customers in the ordinary course of . . . business." Exception (3) denies capital asset status to copyrights, letters, and literary, musical, or artistic compositions (but, notably, not patents) *in the hands of their creators (or transferees who take a carryover basis in the property from its creator)* because this property reflects the creators' personal labor. (In the hands of buyers who take a cost basis, however, these works can become capital assets, if not held as inventory.) And exception (4) provides that accounts receivable for services rendered or for inventory sales are not capital assets, since such accounts receivables, though "property," merely memorialize a right to collect ordinary income. Additionally, the tax common law has effectively expanded these statutory exceptions.

Section 1221(b)(3) provides that a taxpayer can elect to treat "self-created" musical compositions or copyrights in musical works as capital assets, notwithstanding the exceptions in § 1221(a)(1) and (3).

Exception (2) — depreciable personal property *used* in the taxpayer's trade or business (or realty, whether or not depreciable, *used* in such trade or business) — is not a capital asset. (Amortizable personal property used in a trade or business also is excluded from the capital asset definition under this exception because amortization is simply a particular type of depreciation.) Such property, if held for more than one year, is dealt with by § 1231, discussed in Section B. The only used-in-business property that is a capital asset is nondepreciable, nonamortizable, personal property used in the trade or business (perhaps self-created business goodwill), but this exception is relatively unimportant. Exception (8) concerns "supplies of a type generally used or consumed by the taxpayer in the ordinary course of a trade or business." Thus, if a widget manufacturer sells some of its excess office supplies instead of using them in the business, the realized gain or loss would be ordinary. (Supplies deducted as "expenses" under § 162 would have a zero basis.)

The subsections below explore the "inventory" exception, the *Corn Products* doctrine and its progeny (which led to exception (7) in § 1221(a)), the *Arrowsmith* doctrine, and cases involving sales of rights to obtain ordinary income.

b. The "Dealer Property" Exception

The case below involves the often-litigated phrase in § 1221(a)(1): "property held by the taxpayer primarily for sale to customers in the ordinary course of his trade or business." Many of the litigated cases pertain to real estate originally acquired as an investment (which would be a capital asset) but which is later sold in a context that raises the issue of whether the property has crossed the line, over time, from investment property to property held "primarily for sale to customers . . . ." But the issue is not limited to real estate. It arises whenever an owner of property that was once held for personal use or investment begins to sell the property on a regular basis.

BYRAM v. UNITED STATES
United States Court of Appeals, Fifth Circuit
705 F.2d 1418 (1983)

Before WISDOM, GEE and REAVLEY, CIRCUIT JUDGES.

GEE, CIRCUIT JUDGE:

"If a client asks you in any but an extreme case whether, in your opinion, his sale will result in capital gain, your answer should probably be, 'I don't know, and no one else in town can tell you.' "[10] Sadly, the above wry comment on federal taxation of real estate transfers has, in the twenty-five years or so since it was penned, passed from the status of half-serious aside to that of hackneyed truism. Hackneyed or not, it is the primary attribute of truisms to be true, and this one is: in that field of the law — real property — where the stability of rule and precedent has been exalted above all others, it seems ironic that one of its attributes, the tax incident upon disposition of such property, should be one of the most uncertain in the entire field of litigation. But so it is, and we are called on again today to decide a close case in which almost a million dollars in claimed refunds are at stake.

During 1973, John D. Byram, the taxpayer, sold seven pieces of real property. Mr. Byram was not a licensed real estate broker, was not associated with a real estate company which advertised itself, and did not maintain a separate real estate office. He advertised none of the seven properties for sale, nor did he list any of them with real estate brokers. To the contrary, all of the transactions were initiated either by the purchaser or by someone acting in the purchaser's behalf. None of the properties sold was platted or subdivided. Byram devoted minimal time and effort to the sales in question, occupying himself chiefly with his rental properties.

From 1971 through 1973, Byram sold 22 parcels of real property for a total gross return of over $9 million.

The term "capital asset" is defined in relevant part as "property held by the taxpayer," not including property held "primarily for sale to customers in the ordinary course of [the taxpayer's] trade or business." § 1221(a)(1). The district

---

[10] [1] Comment, *Capital Gains: Dealer and Investor Problems*, 35 Taxes 804, 806 (1957).

court found that Byram "was not engaged in the real estate business" during the relevant years and that each of the seven properties in issue was held "for investment purposes and not primarily for sale to customers in the ordinary course of [Byram's] trade or business." Our first task is to decide the correct standard by which to review the district court's principal finding[11] that Byram's holding purpose was for investment rather than for sale. The choice of a standard will determine the outcome of many cases; if the issue is treated as factual, the district court's decision is final unless clearly erroneous, F.R.C.P. 52(a), but if a question of law is presented, we may decide it *de novo*.

The question whether the characterization of property as "primarily held for sale to customers in the ordinary course of [a taxpayer's] trade or business" is an issue of fact or one of law has engendered tremendous controversy and conflict both in this and other circuits. [Citations omitted.] Fortunately, it is unnecessary once again to traverse the conceptual thicket. The Supreme Court has levelled it. *Pullman-Standard v. Swint*, 456 U.S. 273 (1982). In *Swint*, the Court reviewed a decision of this court holding that by setting up and perpetuating a particular seniority system, an employer and two unions had discriminated against black employees in violation of Title VII of the Civil Rights Act. In order to establish discrimination in the operation of a seniority system, it is necessary to prove discriminatory intent. The district court found that the seniority system did not result from an intention to discriminate. This court independently reviewed the record and made its own finding of discrimination. Reversing that decision, the Supreme Court held that our accepted rule allowing *de novo* review is incompatible with the dictates of Rule 52, Federal Rules of Civil Procedure, [which] "broadly requires" that findings of fact be accepted unless clearly erroneous.

The purpose for holding property is a question of intent and motive.[12] As such it is a question of pure fact. The record and the district court's findings of fact indicate that in determining Byram's holding purpose, the court considered all the factors this court has called "the seven pillars of capital gains treatment":

> (1) the nature and purpose of the acquisition of the property and the duration of the ownership; (2) the extent and nature of the taxpayer's efforts to sell the property; (3) the number, extent, continuity and substantiality of the sales; (4) the extent of subdividing, developing, and advertising to increase sales; (5) the use of a business office for the sale of the property; (6) the character and degree of supervision or control exercised by the taxpayer over any representative selling the property; and (7) the time and

---

[11] [3] In *Suburban Realty Co. v. U.S.*, 615 F.2d 171 (5th Cir.), *cert. denied*, 449 U.S. 920 (1980), we recognized that the Code definition of "capital asset" gives rise to at least three inquiries:

(1) was taxpayer engaged in a trade or business, and, if so, what business?

(2) was taxpayer holding the property primarily for sale in that business?

(3) were the sales contemplated by taxpayer "ordinary" in the course of that business? In many situations, these questions are analytically independent.

[12] [9] We have uniformly held that the statutory exception for property "held" for sale to customers requires an inquiry into the taxpayer's intent. See, e.g., *Suburban Realty*, 615 F.2d at 182-85. Moreover, the fact that the taxpayer's subjective state of mind is not controlling and an objective inquiry must be made by the court does not render the issue any less one of intent or any less factual. See *Comm'r v. Duberstein*, 363 U.S. 278 (1960).

effort the taxpayer habitually devoted to the sales.

U.S. v. Winthrop, 417 F.2d 905, 910 (5th Cir. 1969). Recent cases have placed particular emphasis on four of these factors, noting that frequency and substantiality of sales is the most important factor, and that improvements to the property, solicitation and advertising efforts, and brokerage activities are also especially relevant considerations. *Biedenharn Realty*, 526 F.2d 409, 415-16 (5th Cir. 1976) (en banc), *cert. denied*, 429 U.S. 819. At the same time, it has been repeatedly emphasized that these factors should not be treated as talismans. Rather, each case must be decided on its own peculiar facts.

The district court found most of the *Winthrop* factors absent in Byram's case. The district court did not clearly err in determining that 22 such sales in three years were not sufficiently frequent or continuous to compel an inference of intent to hold the property for sale rather than investment. Compare *Suburban Realty* (244 sales over 32-year period). Mr. Byram has presented us with a close case. Had we been called upon to try or retry the facts, perhaps we would have drawn different inferences than did the district court. However, [the standard of review] has relieved us of that duty. Our review of the evidence convinces us that the district court was not clearly erroneous.

The portion of the *Byram* decision that relies on *Pullman-Standard v. Swint* appears to have been ignored by other appeals courts dealing with the standard of review. See *Sanders v. U.S.*, 740 F.2d 886 (11th Cir. 1984) (declining to follow *Byram* on this point, and relying on older authority). In fact, no other federal court of appeals has followed, or even cited, *Byram* on this issue, perhaps because "intent" for purposes of discrimination law is not the same as "holding purpose" in the present context. And it is not clear that the standard of review really affects the outcome in this type of case.

Byram notwithstanding, numerous cases have held that the "liquidation" of a large tract of unimproved land by way of subdivision, improvements, selling efforts, and/or frequent (if passive) sales eventually serves to convert what was originally investment property into dealer (i.e., ordinary gain) property. See, e.g., *Biedenharn Realty Co. v. U.S.*, 526 F.2d 409 (5th Cir.) (en banc), *cert. denied*, 429 U.S. 819 (1976). The cases are highly factual and the outcomes not always predictable.

The only Supreme Court foray into the § 1221(a)(1) area was *Malat v. Riddell*, 383 U.S. 569 (1966) (per curiam), a case where the taxpayer held houses for *either* rental *or* sale, whichever option turned out to be more feasible. The Court held only that "primarily" meant "principally" or "of first importance" and remanded the case to the trial court.

Congress inserted the words "to customers" in § 1221(a)(1) so that "traders" on stock and commodity markets — who sell anonymously over the exchange rather than to specific "customers" — would not fall within the dealer exception. Their gains and losses thus remain capital, even though "traders" are in a "trade or business" (e.g., for § 162 purposes).

"Dealers" in securities sell to identifiable customers and, therefore, would normally have ordinary gains and losses under § 1221(a)(1). Section 1236, however, allows dealers to obtain "capital" treatment for securities that are separately identified *on the date of purchase* as being held for investment. Thus, if the stock is later sold at a loss, the stock is subject to the capital loss limitation rules in § 1211; the taxpayer is foreclosed from opportunistically arguing that the stock was held as inventory property.[13]

Similarly, the sale or exchange of "commodities derivative financial instruments" held by a "commodities derivatives dealer" would normally produce ordinary gains and losses under § 1221(a)(1). Section 1221(a)(6), however, allows such dealers in commodities derivative financial instruments to obtain "capital" treatment for instruments that are separately identified on the date of purchase as being held for investment.

Section 1237 provides that certain development activities with respect to a given tract of land (such as subdividing, installing access roads and utilities, clearing, and selling) will not automatically result in "dealer property" status for that land if the property was held for five years. But § 1237 imposes the following "costs": (1) gains are treated as ordinary in an amount not to exceed 5% of the selling price in years in or after the sale of the sixth lot or parcel from the same tract of property, (2) selling expenses may be disallowed, and (3) certain capital expenditures cannot be added to basis. Section 1237 is not available if the taxpayer is a C corporation (or a "dealer" regarding other parcels) or if the taxpayer makes "substantial improvements" (as defined in the regulations) to the land.

A taxpayer desiring neither to use § 1237 nor to take a chance on losing in court might try to lock in capital gains by forming a corporation, selling undeveloped property to the corporation at its FMV (as undeveloped property) under the installment method, and then having the corporation develop the property and sell the lots. This approach runs risks of its own under the corporate income tax, which are beyond the scope of this text.

c. Hedging Transactions

In *Corn Products Refining Co. v. Comm'r*, 350 U.S. 46 (1955), the taxpayer manufactured products (such as corn syrup) from corn. Due to limited corn storage facilities (creating a need for a steady supply of corn in the future) and the desire to avoid wide fluctuations in the future price of corn, the taxpayer bought "futures contracts" at harvest time when it thought that prices were most favorable. These contracts entitled it to future deliveries of corn under the futures contract, thereby locking in a steady supply of corn at the cost of the futures contract and thereby "hedging" against future corn price increases. If the price of corn in the market were to go up, Corn Products would take delivery under the futures contracts or sell the contracts at a profit. If the price went down, Corn Products could sell the

---

[13] Section 475, added in 1993, generally imposes a mark-to-market regime (i.e., deemed realization at the end of each year) for securities dealers (broadly defined) and provides that gains or losses deemed realized are ordinary. Section 475 does not apply to securities identified as being for investment, which means that § 1236 controls.

futures contracts and take delivery at current lower prices.

Commodities futures contracts are clearly capital assets in the hands of the typical investor who buys them as part of his investment portfolio. But the Supreme Court nevertheless agreed with the IRS in *Corn Products* that the corn futures contracts were *not* capital assets in the hands of the taxpayer, because the contract purchases and sales were "an integral part of its manufacturing business."

For the subsequent 33 years, courts treated assets "integrally related to the taxpayer's business" as not being capital assets. In practice, taxpayers often quietly treated *gains* from such assets as "capital" but then waived the *Corn Products* flag if the assets were sold at a loss (in order to avoid the § 1211 loss-limitation rule).

Finally, in *Arkansas Best Corp. v. Comm'r*, 485 U.S. 212 (1988), the Supreme Court accepted the government's invitation to "clarify" *Corn Products*, and the Court confirmed that *Corn Products* did *not* create a nonstatutory exception to the definition of "capital asset" for "integrally related" assets. Rather, the Court now said, *Corn Products* had merely interpreted the § 1221(a)(1) "inventory" exception broadly. Since corn was a necessary raw material for the taxpayer's manufactured products in that case, gains and losses realized on sales of the corn futures contracts were tantamount to "inventory" gains and losses and thus were "noncapital" for that reason. See *Buena Vista Farms v. Comm'r*, 68 T.C. 405 (1977) (sale of contract right to obtain water produced ordinary gain because the sale of the water itself would have produced ordinary income under § 1221(a)(1)).

The re-interpretation of the meaning of *Corn Products* in *Arkansas Best* threw into doubt the treatment of common hedging transactions, and taxpayers engaging in these transactions sought guidance. The Treasury responded by issuing Reg. § 1.1221-2, which provides that sales or exchanges in "hedging transactions" produce ordinary income and loss, but *only* if the hedge is identified as such by the taxpayer on the date acquired. This approach was confirmed by the 1999 enactment of § 1221(a)(7).

d. The Arrowsmith Doctrine

The case below established the *Arrowsmith* doctrine, which holds that prior inclusion events can affect the "character" (as capital or ordinary) of a current deduction if the inclusion and deduction are transactionally related.

ARROWSMITH v. COMMISSIONER
United States Supreme Court
344 U.S. 6 (1952)

Mr. Justice Black delivered the opinion of the Court.

In 1937 petitioners decided to liquidate a corporation in which they had equal stock ownership. Petitioners reported the profits as capital gains [under the predecessor of § 331].[14] About the propriety of these returns, there is no dispute.

---

[14] [Eds. note: The shareholder's gain or loss in a corporate liquidation would equal the excess of the

But in 1944, a judgment was rendered against the old corporation. The two taxpayers were required to and did pay the judgment for the corporation, of whose assets they were transferees. Classifying the loss as an ordinary business one, each took a 100% deduction for the amount paid. The Commissioner viewed the 1944 payment as part of the original liquidation transaction requiring classification as a capital loss, just as the taxpayers had treated the original liquidating distributions as capital gains.

[Section § 1222] treats losses from "sales or exchanges of capital assets" as "capital losses" and [§ 331] requires that liquidation distributions be treated as "exchanges." The losses here fall squarely within the definition of "capital losses" contained in these sections. Taxpayers were required to pay the judgment because of liability imposed on them as transferees of liquidation distribution assets. And it is plain that their liability was not based on any transactions of theirs apart from the liquidation. It is not denied that had this judgment been paid after liquidation, but [in the same year], the losses would have been properly treated as capital ones. For payment during 1940 would simply have reduced the amount of capital gains taxpayers received during that year.

It is contended, however, that this payment which would have been a capital transaction in 1940 was transformed into an ordinary business transaction in 1944 because of the well-established principle that each taxable year is a separate unit for tax accounting purposes. But this principle is not breached by considering all the liquidation transaction events in order properly to classify the nature of the 1944 loss for tax purposes. Such an examination is not an attempt to reopen and readjust the earlier tax returns, an action that would be inconsistent with the annual tax accounting principle.

MR. JUSTICE JACKSON, whom MR. JUSTICE FRANKFURTER joins, dissenting:

Solicitude for the revenues is a plausible but treacherous basis upon which to decide a particular tax case. A victory may have implications which in future cases will cost the Treasury more than a defeat.

MR. JUSTICE DOUGLAS, dissenting:

There were no capital transactions in the year in which the losses were suffered. Those transactions occurred and were accounted for in earlier years in accord with the established principle that each year is a separate unit for tax accounting purposes.

The *Arrowsmith* case plays off the "annual accounting principle," which is a major theme of the next chapter. Basically, that principle is one that requires that

---

cash and the value of the property received in the liquidation over the shareholder's basis in the stock, which is disposed of (canceled) as a result of the liquidation, since the corporation ceases to exist. A liquidation would not ordinarily be a "sale or exchange" necessary to generate a capital gain for the shareholders, because the stock disposed of does not survive the liquidation, but § 331 deems a sale or exchange to exist.]

income and expense items be accounted for in the year they are received or paid (or accrued). Transactions and activities are generally not held open awaiting a "final outcome." The annual accounting principle isn't universal, of course, because there are exceptions for true borrowings, capital expenditures, installment sales, contingent-payment sales, in-kind compensation subject to forfeiture conditions, put and call options, and other deferred-realization rules. Nevertheless, in *Arrowsmith* the corporate liquidation was not an installment sale or a contingent-payment sale when it occurred, and accordingly it was then properly treated as a closed-transaction sale. The tax law does not require perfect prescience. It turned out that the transaction was not final due to a later unforeseen event. Nevertheless, it would not have been proper to amend the tax return for the year of liquidation, because that return was correct under the facts that then existed. (Besides, an amended return could have been barred by the running of the statute of limitations.).

In *Arrowsmith*, the payment can be characterized as being an integral part of an earlier transaction.[15] The concept of "same transaction" has since been stretched somewhat. In *U.S. v. Skelly Oil Co.*, 394 U.S. 678 (1979), the taxpayer, a natural gas producer, made refunds to its customers on account of overcharges. The earlier gross receipts had been partially offset by percentage depletion deductions. (Percentage depletion deductions are not calculated with respect to cost basis, but rather as a percentage of gross income from the natural resource property; hence, the effect is one of a partial exclusion from gross income.) The Court required that the deductions for the refunds be reduced to compensate for the earlier deductions. *Arrowsmith* has also been applied to a disgorgement of "insider profits" on stock sales, even though the payee (the corporation) was unrelated to the purchaser of the stock.[16]

e. Rights to Ordinary Income

At times, as in the *Corn Products* case,[17] the courts have stated that the definition of capital asset is to be narrowly construed. In *Comm'r v. Gillette Motor Transport Co.*, 364 U.S. 130, 134 (1960), the Court stated:

> While a capital asset is defined as "property held by the taxpayer," it is evident that not everything which can be called property in the ordinary sense and which is outside the statutory exclusions qualifies as a capital asset. This Court has long held that the term "capital asset" is to be construed narrowly in accordance with the purpose of Congress to afford capital-gains treatment only in situations typically involving the realization of appreciation in value accrued over a substantial period of time, and thus to ameliorate the hardship of taxation of the entire gain in one year.

Statements such as these have generated a body of case law that has perhaps produced more heat than light by excluding certain rights to receive ordinary

---

[15] Authorities fitting this pattern include *Estate of Shannonhouse v. Comm'r*, 21 T.C. 422 (1953); *Rev. Rul. 67-331*, 1967-2 C.B. 290.

[16] See, e.g., *Brown v. Comm'r* 529 F.2d 609 (10th Cir. 1976); *Mitchell v. Comm'r*, 428 F.2d 259 (6th Cir. 1970).

[17] See 350 U.S. 46, 52.

income from capital asset status. A casual reading of cases in this area might lead one to conclude that there is a "substitute for ordinary income" doctrine providing that any sale of a right to ordinary income produces ordinary gain, but that cannot be a correct statement of doctrine, as virtually any investment represents rights to future ordinary income.[18]

The cases that legitimately hold against capital gain treatment appear to fall into certain categories, at least three of which find echoes in assignment-of-income doctrine (discussed in Chapter 17). One such category involves "carve-out sales," with the seller retaining a reversion in the sold property.[19] See *Comm'r v. Hort*, 313 U.S. 28 (1941) (payments from lessee to property owner to cancel outstanding lease); *Comm'r v. P.G. Lake, Inc.*, 356 U.S. 260 (1958) (assignment of right to royalties from mineral interest up to fixed dollar amount); *Gillette Motor Transport*, supra (payments for term interest in taxpayer's property). These cases, which hold that the transactions in question do not involve a disposition of a "part" of the property, are discussed in Chapter 29.B, because an important aspect of these cases is the denial of any basis offset.

The second category involves a sale of rights to income already earned.[20] In *U.S. v. Midland-Ross Corp.*, 381 U.S. 54 (1965), the taxpayer purchased short-term noninterest-bearing notes from an issuer as an investment at a discount below their face (i.e., stated principal) amount, and later sold them at a gain, which was essentially the amount of accrued but disguised interest of the type encountered in connection with deferred-payment sales (where the disguised interest is now identified under §§ 483 and 1274, see Chapter 23.D.2.d).[21] The Court held the gain to be ordinary gain, stating (381 U.S. at 57):

> This Court has consistently construed "capital asset" to exclude property representing income items or accretions to the value of capital assets themselves properly attributable to income. Thus the Court has held that "capital asset" does not include compensation awarded a taxpayer representing the fair rental value of its facilities during their period of operation, *Comm'r v. Gillette Mo.tor Transport Co.*, 364 U.S. 130, 134 (1960), [and] the proceeds of the sale of an orange grove attributable to the value of an unmatured annual crop, *Watson v. Comm'r*, 345 U.S. 544 (1953). Unlike the typical case of capital appreciation, the earning of [interest] is predictable and measurable. The $6 earned on a one-year note for $106 issued for $100 is precisely like the $6 earned on a one year loan of $100 at 6% stated interest.

In the same vein, numerous recent cases have held that a sale of an existing right to be paid lottery winnings in the future gives rise to ordinary income. See, e.g.,

---

[18] This point is emphasized in *Lattera v. Comm'r*, 437 F.3d 399, 404 (3d Cir. 2006).

[19] The assignment-of-income analogue is found in the following cases: *Helvering v. Clifford*, 309 U.S. 331 (1940); *Helvering v. Horst*, 311 U.S. 112 (1940); and *Harrison v. Schaffner*, 312 U.S. 579 (1941).

[20] The assignment-of-income analogue is *Helvering v. Eubank*, 311 U.S. 122 (1940).

[21] The accrued implicit interest is known as original issue discount (OID). Such implicit interest is now taxed as it accrues (even to a cash-method taxpayer) under § 1272, discussed (along with the OID concept itself) Chapter 27.B.1.

Lattera v. Comm'r, 437 F.3d 399 (3d Cir. 2006), *cert. denied*, 549 U.S. 1212 (2007).[22]

The third category involves rights to income from services. A case that straddles this category and the second (earned income) category is *Bisbee-Baldwin Corp. v. Tomlinson*, 320 F.2d 929 (5th Cir. 1963), where it was held that ordinary income resulted from a sale of mortgage servicing contracts under which the seller received compensation for servicing mortgages held by third party investors (i.e., for receiving payments, pursuing delinquent debtors, etc., on behalf of the investors) with the compensation being calculated as a fixed percentage of payments on the mortgages.[23] Of similar cast are *Holt v. Comm'r*, 303 F.2d 687 (9th Cir. 1962) (consideration received for releasing right to movie royalties held to be ordinary income where the right had been received as compensation for services rendered in producing the movie), and *Bellamy v. Comm'r*, 43 T.C. 487 (1965) (sale of actor's contractual right to prevent TV re-runs of shows he had appeared in resulted in ordinary gain). Pure category-3 cases are those that involve the sale of a right to earn future *services* income[24] (such as termination payments to employees). These also tend to result in ordinary income or gain. See, e.g., *Elliott v. U.S.*, 431 F.2d 1149 (10th Cir. 1970) (termination of agency contract); *Foote v. Comm'r*, 81 T.C. 930 (1983), *aff'd unpub. op.*, 751 F.2d 1257 (5th Cir. 1985) (release by academic of tenure rights for lump-sum consideration held to result in ordinary income).

A fourth category involves the sale of a right to earn ordinary income that is not purely services-derived. Here, the critical factor appears to be who owns the underlying property right that generates the income. If the right is owned by a third party, then ordinary income is likely to result. See *Coleman v. U.S.*, 388 F.2d 337 (Ct. Cl. 1967) (sale of right to share in sales proceeds derived from another's property); *Martin v. Comm'r*, 50 T.C. 341 (1968) (acq.) (sale of right to receive royalties with respect to movie right owned by another). Compare *McAllister v. Comm'r*, 157 F.2d 235 (2d Cir. 1946), where the sale of an income interest in a trust produced capital gains even though the right to income was purely passive. Whether the income is passive or active appears to be irrelevant in this context. An income interest in a trust is an interest that entails equitable rights in the underlying trust corpus. The income-assignment analogue to *McAllister* is *Blair v. Comm'r*, 300 U.S. 5 (1937), discussed in Chapter 17.A.4, which allowed a gift of an income interest to shift income to the donee. Similar to *McAllister* is *Comm'r v. Ferrer*, 304 F.2d 125 (2d Cir. 1962), where the actor Jose Ferrer had obtained play-production rights from the author of the novel "Moulin Rouge" (based on the life of the artist Henri de Toulouse-Lautrec). Ultimately, Ferrer reconveyed to the author his right to produce the play. The Second Circuit held that the gain on the sale of the play-production rights back to the author was "capital," since such rights gave Ferrer an interest in the underlying property (the copyright to the play). Ferrer had also obtained a right to 40% of any royalties to be received by the author (who

---

[22] See also *U.S. v. Maginnis*, 356 F.3d 1179 (9th Cir. 2004); *Prebola v. Comm'r*, 482 F.3d 610 (2d Cir. 2007); *Watkins v. Comm'r*, 447 F.3d 1269 (10th Cir. 2006); *Womack v. Comm'r*, 510 F.3d 1295 (11th Cir. 2007); *Davis v. Comm'r*, 119 T.C. 1 (2002).

[23] The facts of *Bisbee-Baldwin* are somewhat similar to those of *Eubank*, supra note 20, an assignment-of-income case which involved renewal commissions on existing insurance policies.

[24] The assignment-of-income analogue is, of course, *Lucas v. Earl*, 281 U.S. 111 (1930).

had retained the movie rights), which he "sold" to the director John Huston (who hired Ferrer to play the lead role in the movie). But the sale of the right to a share in the movie royalties was held to produce ordinary income, because Ferrer never owned the underlying movie rights. It can be noted that this second *Ferrer* holding, as well as those in *Martin* and perhaps *Coleman*, supra, appear to be inconsistent with analagous assignment-of-income authorities, such as *Heim v. Fitzpatrick*, 262 F.2d 887 (2d Cir. 1959), which allowed a gift of a royalty interest in a patent owned by another to be effective to shift income, on the theory that the royalty right was a separate property right apart from the patent. Accord *PLR 8337055* (similar situation involving right copyright royalties).

In *Ferrer*, the right to share in the movie royalties had initially been granted to the taxpayer as an inducement to produce the play, which would generate consumer interest in the subsequent movie, i.e., would enhance the marketability of the underlying property. If, in contrast, Mr. Ferrer had *separately acquired* such a pure (but derivative) income right (the right to share in the movie royalties) as an investment and then sold that right, the right would likely have been held to rise to the level of "property" within the meaning of § 1221(a).[25]

The observation that an investment in a legal right can result in that right being treated as property raises the question of whether an "investment" (or basis) is a general prerequisite to obtaining capital asset status.[26] If so, then a fifth tax-common-law category of noncapital-asset property might exist. There are indeed some statements in the cases to the effect that investment or basis is required in order to obtain capital gain treatment.[27] But the absence of basis characterizes cases involving rights to services income (which always produce ordinary income), and it is (therefore) not yet clear that the absence of investment or basis has been definitively established as a separate ground of denying capital-asset status.

NOTES

1.   (a) It's hard to see how, as is claimed in *Byram*, that the § 1221(a)(1) dealer exception turns on "purpose" or "motive." The dominant purpose is always to make a profit, regardless of dealer or investor status. Anything will be sold if the price is right. It can be noted that § 1221(1) itself does not refer to purpose or motive, but only "held . . . primarily for . . . ." The requirements of "to customers," "in the

---

[25] See *Ayrton Metal Co. v. Comm'r*, 299 F.2d 741 (2d Cir. 1962) (right to future profits from a mine); *Pacific Finance Corp. of Cal. v. Comm'r*, T.C. Memo. 1953-129 (sale of purchased right to movie profits).

[26] Some cases have found capital gains despite no basis, although there had been an investment. E.g., *Metropolitan Bldg. Co. v. Comm'r*, 282 F.2d 592 (9th Cir. 1960) (surrender of lessee's leasehold interest); *Ofria v. Comm'r*, 77 T.C. 524 (1981) (sale of self-developed know-how). Basis might be relevant where it derives from the investment of another, as with property acquired by gift.

[27] See *U.S. v. Maginnis*, 356 F.3d 1179, 1183-84 (9th Cir. 2004) (lottery winnings not the result of investment); *Holt v. Comm'r*, 303 F.2d 687, 691 (9th Cir. 1962) (termination payment for gross receipts interest in motion pictures received by the producer of the motion pictures held to be ordinary income); *Bellamy v. Comm'r*, 43 T.C. 487, 498 (1965) (taxpayer, the actor Ralph Bellamy, sold rights relating to a movie in which he starred; the sale proceeds held to be ordinary income on ground that taxpayer had no investment in such rights). But see *Ayrton Metal Co. v. Comm'r*, supra note 25, which treated a sale of a profits interest in which the taxpayer had no basis as resulting in capital gain, but the no-basis issue appears not to have been raised.

ordinary course of," and "his trade or business," refer only to objective facts, and "primarily" can be determined objectively. The phrase "held by the taxpayer" is a nonissue.

(b) Is it necessary to have multiple factors? *Original* intent hardly seems to be relevant (even assuming "intent to hold" is relevant). The crucial issue is "in the ordinary course of his trade or business," where the principal indicators are really two: (1) "busyness" (the continuity and frequency of sales activity) and (2) value added by taxpayer activity (by subdivision, improvements, and/or marketing).

(c) Does (should) involuntariness cut one way on the capital gain side and another on the capital loss side? See *Helvering v. Hammell*, 311 U.S. 504 (1941) (holding that the capital loss limitation cannot be avoided on the ground that the sale was involuntary); *Biedenharn Realty Co. v. U.S.*, 526 F.2d 409 (5th Cir.) (en banc), *cert. denied*, 429 U.S. 819 (1976) (stating that "unanticipated, externally induced factors which make impossible the continued pre-existing use of the realty," if not coupled with activities indicative of a "full blown real estate business," can allow original investment intent to control notwithstanding dealer-like sales activities). Don't these cases have it exactly backward, considering the purposes of the capital gains preference and the limitation on capital losses?

2. Section 121, which wholly excludes gains from the sale of a principal residence, up to $250K ($500K for a joint return), has already been mentioned. Any gain on the sale of a principal residence that does not qualify for exclusion under § 121 is generally treated as capital gain (since a principal residence satisfies the definition of "capital asset" in § 1221(a)).

3. Section 1202 provides an exclusion for a substantial fraction of the gain on certain "qualified small business stock" held more than five years. (Note that the definition of "qualified small business stock" in § 1202 is not the same as the definition of "small business stock" in § 1244.)

PROBLEMS

1. Lou, a lawyer, inherited the family farm of 200 acres in 1965, when it was worth $200K. The farmhouse has lain vacant and is in dilapidated condition. The land is not seriously devoted to any farming business. The suburbs of the nearest city are reaching outwards to the general area where the farm is located, and Lou, without advertising, has been approached by several interested parties regarding whether the land is for sale. Lou has leased the land under a grazing lease for $3K a year. Preliminary investigation by Lou indicates that the land might be worth around $4K per acre for the whole tract (a total FMV of $800K) or $8K per acre if subdivided into one-acre lots with paved access roads and utilities (a total FMV of $1.6M). Lou wants to maximize his profit and also desires that as much of the profit as possible be capital gain. Advise Lou regarding his options.

2. Bubba is in the business of oil and gas discovery and development. Because the demand for drilling services is volatile, Bubba buys the stock of a company that actually does the drilling, so that Bubba can obtain drilling services on demand. After a prolonged slump in the oil exploration business, Bubba sells this stock at a loss. What result under current law? Cf. *Rev. Rul. 58-40*, 1958-1 C.B. 275.

3. In Year 1, Boris sells investment real estate, basis $900K, to Natasha, who pays $1M, $800K of which is financed by a mortgage from the X Bank. In Year 5 Natasha discovers an environmental hazard and sues Boris for breach of warranty. In settlement of the suit, Boris pays $160K in cash to Natasha. What is the tax treatment of the $160K payment to both parties?

4. Feared slugger Boniface Scyszynski sets a record by blasting five home runs in one game.

(a) Boniface's fame grows, and he becomes an "Oatsies champion," under which he obtains an annual fee from Grain Mills in return for having his likeness plastered on Oatsies boxes and otherwise for endorsing the product. About a year later, news leaks out that Boniface raises roosters for cockfighting, and Grain Mills wants to cancel the contract, but finds that it failed to insert a contract clause that clearly covers this kind of nefarious activity. Eventually, Grain Mills pays Boniface $500K and Boniface releases his rights under the contract. What tax result to Boniface?

(b) Jason, an avid Cubs fan, attends as many games as he can. As luck would have it, he caught the record-setting fifth home-run ball. This ball is much in demand by collectors (including the Baseball Hall of Fame). Will Jason obtain capital gains treatment if he sells the spheroid? (Assume that he has the right to do that.) Can he do anything to improve his chances?

B. DEPRECIATION RECAPTURE AND SECTION 1231

Property that has been depreciated, nondepreciable real property used in a trade or business, and business or investment property that is "involuntarily converted" are subject to special characterization regimes under §§ 1245, 1250, and 1231, described below.

1. Depreciation Recapture

Section 1016(a) requires that all write-offs (deductions) with respect to an asset (depreciation, amortization, and losses) reduce the asset's basis. Write-offs under provisions (such as § 179) that allow for the expensing of capital-expenditure costs either don't appear in basis in the first place or else reduce the basis (if the basis initially included such cost). In the case of personal property used in a trade business or held for the production of income, these write-offs typically result in basis falling below the FMV of the asset (perhaps even to zero), thereby resulting in gain upon the asset's sale. These write-offs are taken against ordinary business and investment income, i.e., they are not capital losses, even though the theory of these deductions (that are not blatant subsidies) is (as explained supra in Chapter 28.A.1) one of "sustained partial loss." To illustrate the problem, assume that a depreciable asset is purchased for $100K and that $60K of depreciation deductions are properly taken against ordinary income subject to a 35% rate (reducing the basis of the property to $40K) before it is sold for $70K. Obviously, $30K of the depreciation (producing a tax savings of $10.5K) was "excessive" in terms of the decline in FMV, but the reduced basis under § 1016(a)(2) will produce a gain of $30K which, if treated as long-term capital gain subject to (say) a 15% tax rate, would result in a tax of $4.5K, resulting in a net tax savings of $6K. Under tax theory, these results yield an illegitimate (in theory) excessive (i.e., 20%, the excess of the 35% marginal deduction rate over the 15% inclusion rate) tax benefit for the same ($30K) dollars. However, the courts have never applied *Arrowsmith*-type principles in this area to correct the problem, leaving the matter to Congress.[28] (The problem would not exist if the amount of depreciation allowed to be deducted tracked the annual decreases in FMV.)

In 1962, Congress reacted to this problem by enacting § 1245, *which essentially requires that the gain amount that is equal to the amount of prior write-offs of the cost of the property (other than loss deductions) be treated as "ordinary" gain.* In many instances the only write-off was depreciation or amortization, but many expensing provisions (such as § 179, but not § 174, relating to research and experimentation expenditures) are treated as depreciation for this purpose). To illustrate the operation of § 1245, if the property described above were depreciable personal property, the entire $30K gain would be treated as ordinary gain. The ordinary gain produced by § 1245 is referred to as "depreciation recapture." If depreciated property is disposed of at a loss, no gain exists to be recaptured, and § 1245 does not apply.

If the depreciable personal property in the example were sold for $110K instead of $60K, the taxpayer would realize a $70K gain, of which $60K (an amount equal to the prior depreciation deductions) would be recaptured as ordinary income under § 1245, and the remaining $10K would retain its character as capital gain or § 1231 gain (explored below), as the case may be.

In the case of depreciable *real* property, § 1250 recaptures as ordinary gain an amount equal to only the excess of accelerated depreciation over straight-line depreciation. Since real property placed in service since 1986 has been limited to straight-line depreciation, § 1250 rarely applies.

Nevertheless, § 1250 is indirectly of current relevance in that "unrecaptured § 1250 gain" is a subcategory of capital (or § 1231) gain that is taxed at a higher rate than "regular" net capital gain (in 2011, the maximum rate for unrecaptured § 1250 gain is 25% (rather than 15%). The term "unrecaptured § 1250 gain" means what it says: the portion of the gain from real property that is attributable to all depreciation (and a few other obscure) deductions taken but which (as is likely) are not recaptured under § 1250 itself. See § 1(h)(6). However, unlike § 1245 ordinary income recapture, unrecaptured § 1250 gain retains its character as capital gain or § 1231 gain, as the case may be, for all purposes in the Code (including the capital-loss limitation in § 1211).

To illustrate, suppose that the property in the example was real property that was purchased for $100K in 1990 and sold for $110K in 2011 and that (because of being used in the taxpayer's business) was subject to $60K of straight-line depreciation. The gain of $70K ($110 AR less $40 AB) is all § 1231 gain. None of this gain is actually recaptured under § 1250, because the depreciation was all taken under the straight-line method, but if this § 1231 gain ends up being long-term capital gain, $60K of it will be culled out of the "net capital gain" amount as

---

[28] See *Fribourg Navagation Co. v. Comm'r*, 383 U.S. 272 (1966) (allowing depreciation deduction in year of sale even though adjusted basis was already below selling price).

unrecaptured § 1250 gain and will instead be taxed (in 2011) at a 25% rate. The remaining $10K of gain is § 1231 gain.

A couple of technical points: first, unrecaptured § 1250 gain is computed without any offset by allowable (capital or § 1231) losses on (depreciable) real property; second, the amount of § 1231 gain that can be treated as unrecaptured § 1250 gain cannot exceed the amount (if any) of the overall "net § 1231 gain." The general significance (and operation) of § 1231 is revealed in the material immediately following.

2. Section 1231

Property *used in a trade or business* (other than the relatively insignificant category of nondepreciable personal property) is excluded from the definition of capital asset by § 1221(a)(2). Stated differently, § 1221(a)(2) excludes from the definition of capital asset any depreciable or amortizable personal property used in a trade or business and any real property (whether depreciable or not) used in a trade or business. However, gains and losses from the sale or exchange of business-use property (other than nondepreciable personal property) *held for more than one year* goes into the hopper of § 1231.[29] Other items, to be mentioned below, also go into this hopper. The significance of § 1231 is that if aggregate § 1231 gains exceed aggregate § 1231 losses for the year, *all* such gains and losses *are "treated" as long-term capital gains and losses.* If, on the other hand, aggregate § 1231 losses do not exceed aggregate § 1231 gains for the year, *all* such gains and losses *retain their status as ordinary gains and losses.* See § 1231(a)(1), (2). These rules effectively mean that any "net § 1231 gain" is treated as long-term capital gain (which may help to create "net capital gain" under § 1222(11) subject to favorable rates for noncorporate taxpayers), while any "net § 1231 loss" is free of the § 1211 deduction-restriction rules pertaining to capital losses. In other words, the taxpayer gets the best of both worlds! (For this reason, assets falling within § 1231 are sometimes referred to as "quasi-capital assets.").

Also going into the § 1231 hopper are (recognized) gains and (allowable) losses from the *involuntary conversion* (whether or not resulting in a sale or exchange) of any long-term business-use asset or long-term capital asset held for business or investment (whether depreciable or not). However, business and investment *casualty and theft* gains and losses are treated as from an involuntary conversion only if such gains exceed such losses. See § 1231(a)(4)(C).

The hopper also includes certain favored products of mining and agriculture. See § 1231(b)(2)-(4).

Section 1231 is not available for assets described in § 1221(a)(1), (3), and (5). See § 1231(b)(1).

Section 1231(c) contains a five-year, look-back rule, which somewhat dilutes § 1231's "best of both worlds" approach. To be specific, a net § 1231 gain will *not* be

---

[29] Note that property falling within § 1221(a)(2) that has been held for one year or less at the time of disposition is neither a capital asset nor § 1231 property. Accordingly, gains and losses from the disposition of such property are ordinary.

treated as long-term capital gain (i.e., will be net ordinary gain) to the extent a taxpayer has deducted net § 1231 losses as ordinary losses in the prior five years.

Section 1245 has largely displaced § 1231 with respect to gains from depreciable *personal* property used in a trade or business, which rarely appreciates over its original cost (except for amortizable intangible assets, which often do appreciate over their original cost). Section 1231 is most relevant, therefore, in connection with business *real* property, such as the factory where the widgets are produced or raw farm land, and amortizable intangible personal property used in a trade or business, such as a customer list or a purchased patent, copyright, trademark, or goodwill. The impact of § 1231 is further curtailed by reason of the fact that there is generally no capital gains preference for corporations under current law, although corporations still care about the character of gains and losses because of the capital-loss limitation in § 1211.

NOTES

1.   Section 1245 does not recapture the time-value-of-money advantage of excess depreciation.

2.   The *Byram* problem potentially exists under § 1231, which (like § 1221) has an exception for dealer property. See § 1231(b)(1)(A) and (B). With respect to real estate, the analysis is pretty much the same under § 1231 as it is under § 1221. But where the business assets consist of tangible, depreciable personal property (e.g., equipment) instead of real property, the law has developed somewhat differently. Here the courts have generally held that a "business-like" liquidation of business equipment *at the end of the equipment's normal business cycle* does not convert the equipment to dealer property and eliminate "§ 1231 asset" status. See, e.g., *Philber Equip. Corp. v. Comm'r*, 237 F.2d 129 (3d Cir. 1956). Compare *International Shoe Machine Corp. v. U.S.*, 491 F.2d 157 (1st Cir.), *cert. denied*, 419 U.S. 834 (1974), which held that business equipment held by a taxpayer principally as § 1231 property for lease to customers became dealer property when sold where such sales were a small, but accepted and predictable, part of the taxpayer's business, and the equipment had a significant useful life remaining at the time of sale. This issue is largely moot nowadays due to the effect of § 1245 depreciation recapture on the disposition of depreciable personal property.

3.   Besides unrecaptured § 1250 gain, the other category of capital gain subject to a special rate (28%) is officially referred to as "28-percent rate gain" and unofficially as "net collectibles gain." This category is defined in § 1(h)(4) as collectibles gain (plus § 1202 gain) minus the sum of collectibles losses, the net short-term capital loss, and long-term capital loss carried to the year. The term "collectibles" includes art, antiques, gems, precious metals, stamps, coins, wines, and liquors. Only collectibles that are capital assets go into this category.

PROBLEM

Assume that Patrick, an unmarried individual who has salary income of $100K, incurs the following items for the taxable year in question. These items and his salary are his only income and deductions. Characterize the following items of gain and loss. Are his capital losses, if any, fully deductible? Does he have any "net capital gain"?

(a) Sale of office equipment held for two years in his business: sales price $25K, original cost $30K, depreciation taken $8K.

(b) Sale of rental real property held for three years and actively managed by Patrick: sales price $110K, original cost $100K, straight-line depreciation taken $9K.

(c) Investment bad debt loss: $7K. See § 166.

(d) Loss on the sale of unimproved land used in his business and held for five years: $5K.

(e) Gain on the sale of stock held for four months: $3K.

(f) Recognized gain (due to an insurance recovery) stemming from the theft of bearer bonds: $2K.

C. POLICY CONSIDERATIONS

The preferential treatment of long-term capital gain has fluctuated widely over the life of the modern income tax. In some periods (such as 1986-1990), there was no preference. As of 2011, however, the top individual rate for ordinary income is 35%, while the most common rate applied to net capital gain is 15%, a significant difference. Is this benefit accorded to "net capital gain" warranted?

If one takes the Simons income tax view that gains (and losses) should be reckoned from year to year under a mark-to-market system, then the realization principle already benefits the taxpayer by deferring gains and losses past the date when they should be reckoned. From this vantage point, it is hard to see why one tax benefit should be compounded by another.

The opposite point of view would start from the premise that gains and losses are not really income (or loss) but merely changes in principal (capital). From this vantage point, capital gains tax preferences are seen as a concession in a compromise over a basic principle. (This argument overlooks that fact that realized capital gains are available for consumption.) Historically, capital gains preferences came into the Code shortly after it was established that the capital gains of investors would be taxed.

Over time, other notions have been introduced — as ex post rationales — to support the capital gains rate preference.

Pro: Reduced rates are justified because of the "bunching problem." Full taxation of capital gains realized in one year under a progressive rate schedule is unfair, because the realized gain bunched into one year is attributable to accretion over several years, and, if the accretion had been taxed as it occurred, it might have been taxed entirely in the lowest bracket, whereas part of that gain might now be taxed in a higher bracket.

Con: First, one can assert that bunching is a "problem" only if one concedes that an annual mark-to-market system, where bunching would not exist, is normatively correct. If one instead takes realization as the norm, the realized gains (and losses) are the ones that should count, especially considering that the vast bulk of them are incurred in voluntary transactions. The bunching argument may be counterfactual: it cannot be simply assumed that the value of the asset rose in even increments over a long period of time. Also, a bunching rationale would posit a holding-period requirement of no less than two years. Third, an alternate solution exists, called "income averaging," under which the excess, if any, of current taxable income over the "average" taxable income for some base period (e.g., the previous three years) is hypothetically spread back over the base period for purposes of computing the "proper" tax rate on the excess in the year of realization. No bunching problem can exist if the taxpayer was already in the highest marginal rate bracket during the period when the gains accrued (and empirical evidence shows that a high percentage of includible capital gains are accrued by high-bracket taxpayers).[30]

Pro: Reduced rates are justified because all or part of the gain is illusory due to the effects of inflation.

Con: Inflation affects not only "capital gain" but *all* gains and losses, as well as other carried-over tax attributes (such as NOLs and depreciation). Moreover, a fixed-lower-rate tax benefit for long-term capital gain is an extremely crude inflation adjustor, since it operates the same whether an asset is held for 366 days or 50 years — not to mention the fact that the rate of inflation varies from time to time. In any event, there is a "correct" technical solution to the inflation problem, which is to index the basis of all assets according to a formula:

new basis = previous basis $\times$ $\dfrac{\text{price index at end of year}}{\text{price index at beginning of year}}$

Although indexing the basis of property has support in some circles, there are practical and political obstacles. One is that it is complex; not only assets but also depreciation deductions, NOL carryovers, capital loss carryovers, etc. — anything that affects how the tax base is measured over time — would have to be indexed for this to work correctly. Another is that, if the basis of assets were indexed for inflation, then the basis (principal) of debt instruments would also have to be indexed, since they are assets owned by lenders. Borrowers enjoy a benefit in times of inflation by reason of repaying debt with deflated dollars. When debt basis is increased according to an inflation index, a portion of what is nominally called "interest" on the debt really becomes a return of "principal." Thus, indexing debt for inflation would confer a tax advantage on banks (which would be entitled to "exclude," as return of principal, part of what is called "interest" in the loan documents), whereas debtors, including homeowners paying mortgage interest, would be denied a deduction for a portion of the nominal interest that is really repayment of principal. Because the losers under comprehensive indexing would far outnumber the winners, it would be a hard political sell.

---

[30] The "flatter" the rate structure is, the less significant is the bunching problem. It was no surprise that the Code's income-averaging provision was repealed in 1986 when rates were flattened, and it has not been revived with the move to a slightly more progressive rate structure since then.

Pro: A tax benefit for capital gain lowers the tax barrier to realizations (known as the "lock-in effect"), and mitigating the lock-in effect would enhance the mobility of capital to its best economic use, consistent with the neutrality norm.

Con: The main problem with the capital-mobility argument as it applies to a capital gains preference is that it suggests that any tax benefit on liquidating investments should be conditioned on reinvesting the proceeds from the sale of the investment (as occurs under a cash flow consumption tax). The capital-mobility rationale is entirely lost with respect to capital gain realized in order to finance consumption.

On a technical economics level, the capital-mobility argument would be persuasive only to the extent that it could be shown that particular property could be put to more productive use if owned by a taxpayer different from the current owner, and the current owner does not sell to the more efficient user solely because of the tax that would be due on sale. For passive investments, like stocks, it doesn't matter who owns them. Productive assets can be disposed of in tax-free exchanges attendant upon mergers and acquisitions.[31] Thus, the problem is overstated.

A more pressing lock-in influence is exerted by § 1014, which permanently exempts unrealized gains on property owned at death and thereby encourages taxpayers to hold appreciated property until their demise in order to transfer it to their heirs with the gain laundered out of the income tax system. Of course, that particular lock-in effect can be eliminated by repealing § 1014 and substituting a realization-at-death or carryover basis regime; a capital gains preference is not essential to mitigating that lock-in effect.

The best income tax solution to any lock-in problem (as with bunching) would be a change to an annual mark-to-market system. However, no income tax has gone to a mark-to-market system. The reasons are more psychological than policy-based, but they appear to be deep-rooted, nevertheless. Unrealized gains and losses are not separated from the investment, and therefore they can't be devoted to any kind of consumption end use (unless a taxpayer borrows against unrealized gains to finance consumption). Another issue is that of volatility, which is related to the popular intuition that unrealized gains and losses are "temporary" (not final). The annual appreciation or depreciation in a volatile investment may overstate the average, and thereby be unrepresentative. Also, this year's appreciation (or its opposite) may be wiped out sooner or later. Finally, the realization-based income tax system is largely designed to avoid or at least reduce valuation issues, which would be a significant strain on the system. Valuation is often difficult and/or inaccurate.

A possible solution would be to adopt an annual mark-to-market system only for highly liquid assets, such as publicly traded securities, for which market quotes are available. But taxing unrealized gains (and losses) with respect to only *certain* assets would create tax disparities among investments and might encourage a move to nonliquid investments, contrary to the conventional preference for liquid investments. Moreover, only the fairly wealthy can tolerate nonliquidity sufficiently

---

[31] See, e.g., §§ 351, 354.

to make the move to nonliquidity.[32] Thus, adopting a mark-to-market system only for liquid investments would benefit the wealthy relative to everyone else. Of course, any system of taxing investments involves the drawing of lines. The realization requirement already favors appreciating investments over those that pay out income regularly.

Pro: Lowering the tax burden on capital gain would actually increase tax revenues by increasing the frequency of realizations sufficiently to outweigh the reduction in the tax burden per realization.

Con: This raises an empirical question on which economists are divided.

Pro: A capital-gain preference will increase new investment in the economy and thus fuel economic growth.

Con: This is an argument for lower taxes on investments generally relative to consumption, an argument that was dealt with in Chapter 6 in connection with the consumption tax as an alternative to the income tax.

One final point worth noting that relates to the whole idea of a capital-gains preference is that taxable capital gains are concentrated at higher income levels, as shown by a 2003 IRS study of the top 400 taxpayers in Adjusted Gross Income (AGI) from 1992 to 2000. The percentages of AGI consisting of wages and net capital gain, respectively, as well as their "average tax rate" (total tax paid divided by AGI) were as follows for 1992, 1996, and 2000:[33]

	Salaries and Wages Percent of AGI	Net Capital Gain Percent of AGI	Average Tax Rate
1992	26.22	36.08	26.38
1996	11.14	63.40	27.81
2000	16.70	71.83	22.29

These statistics pre-date the 2003 Act's reduction in capital gains rates.

The stocks owned by most middle-class Americans are held in tax-favored pension plans (qualified plans, IRAs, etc.), where the capital gains tax preference is useless. That is, because all net income and net gains are exempt from tax as earned in such accounts, but all distributions (in excess of the employee's basis, if any) are treated as ordinary income.

D. EXCESS CAPITAL LOSSES AND NET CAPITAL GAIN

Excess capital losses are treated unfavorably, whereas "net capital gains" are subject to reduced tax rates. This section focuses on the mechanics that produce these outcomes and their implications for planning.

---

[32] This phenomenon is visible in estate planning, where the very wealthy routinely move liquid investments into nonliquid closely-held entities for the purpose of depressing the value of assets that are subject to estate and gift taxation.

[33] IRS, 22 STATISTICS OF INCOME BULLETIN 7 (Spr. 2003).

1. Excess Capital Losses

This subsection describes the rules that apply when a taxpayer (whether an individual or an entity, such as a corporation) has allowable capital losses in excess of the includible capital gains for the year. In this case, the taxpayer will have no "net capital gain" subject to reduced tax rates.

The aggregate of a corporate or individual taxpayer's capital losses (whether short-term or long-term) can be deducted only to the extent of that year's aggregate capital gains (whether short-term or long-term). In addition, noncorporate taxpayers may deduct any *excess* of capital losses over capital gains against ordinary income for the year, but only to the extent of $3,000 ($1,500 for a married person filing separately). See § 1211(b). Deductible capital losses of individuals are taken above the line (i.e., are not itemized deductions). See § 62(a)(3).

Excess capital losses of a corporation that are not allowed in the current year are carried back three years and forward for only five years. Excess capital losses of individuals are carried forward indefinitely, but disappear at death.

The rules stated so far are indifferent to whether gains and losses are long-term or short-term, but holding period is an issue for losses carried over to a year that could generate net capital gain. Initially, long-term losses are netted against long-term gains, and short-term losses are netted against short-term gains. For carryover purposes, if the taxpayer has *both* excess short-term losses *and* excess long-term losses in the current year, the convoluted language in § 1212(b) ensures that she would be deemed to have deducted her excess net short-term losses *first* within the $3K limitation.

The purpose of the disadvantageous treatment of capital losses is to prevent a taxpayer with a portfolio of both *unrealized* gains and losses from selectively realizing (sometimes called "cherry picking") the capital losses while leaving the capital gains unrealized. Stated differently, § 1211 blocks a taxpayer from deducting losses that do not reflect *real* net wealth decreases when unrealized gains are considered. Section 1211 is a blunt instrument, and (in theory) would not serve any purpose in cases where the taxpayer has no unrealized gains. However, a more finely-tuned anti-cherry-picking rule would require valuation of assets and would be too difficult to administer for both taxpayers and the IRS.

PROBLEM

Assume that Louise, an unmarried individual, has salary income of $100K each year and that all capital gains and losses are recognized or allowable except as provided otherwise in § 1211. Describe the effects of the following on Louise's taxable income (and assume that Louise has no other capital gains and losses):

	Capital Gains		Capital Losses	
Year	long-term	short-term	long-term	short-term
1	$6,000	$2,000	$9,000	$0
2	6,000	2,000	4,000	8,000
3	6,000	2,000	11,000	3,000

2. Net Capital Gain

A taxpayer whose total capital gains exceed total capital losses can fully deduct the losses against the gains. Moreover, taxpayers in this position are the only ones who can possibly have "net capital gain," a favored class of income that is subject to various special low tax rates under § 1(h) in the case of noncorporate taxpayers.[34] (Corporations are not entitled to the capital gains rate reductions; the corporate capital gains rate reduction was eliminated in 1986.)

"Net capital gain" (NCG) is defined in § 1222(11) as the excess of "net long-term capital gain" (NLTCG) over "net short-term capital loss" (NSTCL). Thus, long-term capital gain (LTCG) must be netted against long-term capital loss (LTCL) to arrive at NLTCG, and short-term capital loss (STCL) must be netted against short-term capital gain (STCG) to arrive at NSTCL. Negative numbers within each category are treated as zero. (For example, if STCGs are $6K and STCLs are $5K, the NSTCL is zero.) The definition of NCG precludes its augmentation by STCG (thus, STCGs are essentially taxed at ordinary income tax rates). The essential ingredient for NCG is LTCG (in excess of LTCL). But NSTCL reduces NCG, so an individual taxpayer favors STCGs over ordinary income because STCGs offset STCLs (i.e., reduce NSTCL) and thereby mitigate or eliminate the impact of STCLs in reducing NCG, the portion of taxable income that is taxed at the preferential rates in § 1(h).

The various netting operations *prevent the creation of a tax profit from a net economic wash during a year*. Take the case where a 35%-bracket taxpayer has only a $10K LTCG and a $10K STCL for the year. The realized gain and loss have obviously produced a zero-sum *economic* result, i.e., neither a net gain nor a net loss. Without the netting rules (and § 1211), however, the LTCG would be taxed at a reduced rate, usually 15%, while the STCL would be worth 35 cents on the dollar (by being deducted against ordinary income that would otherwise be taxed at 35%). This outcome would effectively create a $2K tax profit where there is no economic net gain or loss (i.e., $3.5K of tax saved by deducting the loss against ordinary income minus $1.5K of tax owed on the LTCG).

NOTES

1. In the case of individual taxpayers, § 163(d), discussed in Chapter 18.D.3, limits the deduction of investment interest to the extent of a taxpayer's net investment income. This limitation was mainly designed to prevent a capital gains tax shelter, where, say, $100K is borrowed at 4% and used to purchase an asset that appreciates at a rate of 4%. In the absence of § 163(d), the interest would be deducted against ordinary income, and the economically offsetting gain would be deferred and taxed at preferential rates. Under §§ 1(h)(2) and 163(d)(4)(B), the taxpayer can elect to count all or a portion of the NCG as "net investment income," in which event it will not qualify for the capital-gains rate preferences in § 1(h),

---

[34] The language of § 1(h) is horribly complex, and is not recommended reading.

thereby trading the rate advantage for the ability to currently deduct the interest.

2.   While it is more important to appreciate that NCG is taxed at reduced rates than to understand precisely *which* lower rate will apply, it is worth mentioning the highlights of § 1(h). In practice, Schedule D of Form 1040 leads the taxpayer through the § 1(h) thicket.

(a) Except as specified below, the rate that applies to most NCG is 15% (at least for taxable years beginning before 2013).

(b) NCG from "collectibles" is taxed at the lower of 28% or the taxpayer's regular (ordinary) tax rate.

(c) As mentioned in Section B.1, capital gain attributable to depreciable real property that *would* have been recaptured as ordinary income if § 1245 (instead of § 1250) had applied ("unrecaptured § 1250 gain") is taxed at the lower of 25% or the taxpayer's regular tax rate.

(d) NCG (other than collectibles NCG or unrecaptured § 1250 gain) that would otherwise fall in the 10% or 15% *ordinary* income tax brackets is taxed at 5% (0% for taxable years beginning after 2007 and before 2013), though, empirically, there are a relatively small number of taxpayers in these brackets that have NCG.

(e) For taxable years beginning after 2002 and before 2013, "qualified dividend income" is taxed at the most favorable capital gains tax rates described in (a) and (d) above. See § 1(h)(11). "Qualified dividend income," however, is still ordinary income for all other purposes in the Code, including the capital loss limitation in § 1211.

3.   Planning Considerations

Taxpayers with timing flexibility can sometimes minimize the disadvantage of capital losses as well as maximize the advantages attaching to NCG.

For example, a taxpayer who realizes large capital losses gets little help from the de minimis rule that allows capital losses to offset up to $3,000 of ordinary income each year. Such a taxpayer will seek to sell assets that generate capital gain to immediately absorb as much of the large capital losses as possible, thus avoiding long deferral of the loss deductions, which would reduce their value to the taxpayer. Suppose, however, that the taxpayer is a small-time investor with only moderate capital gains and losses within the portfolio. In this case, the best course might be to realize long-term capital gains and capital losses in alternate years, to take advantage of the $3K limit on excess losses.

Short-term capital gains are good to pair with capital losses, because here the losses (1) offset gains that would be taxed at ordinary income rates (standing alone) and (2) don't reduce any rate benefit.

If the taxpayer already has net long-term capital gains, realization of short-term capital losses would reduce NCG qualifying for the preferential tax rates in § 1(h). If the short-term capital losses can't be avoided, the best move is to realize an equal amount of short-term capital gains.

PROBLEM

Benjamin's stock portfolio shows (1) LTCGs of $15K, (2) STCGs of $5K, and (3) STCLs of $20K. It is late December.

(a) What is Benjamin's optimum realization strategy for the current year (and anticipating the future), assuming that all realizations are discretionary?

(b) Same as (a), but assume (in the alternative) that Benjamin has *already* realized: (a) the LTCGs of $15K, (b) the STCGs of $5K, or (c) the STCLs of $20K.

Part Eight

CAPITAL RECOVERY APART FROM SALES AND DISPOSITIONS

This final part contains four chapters that explore basis (capital) recovery. Chapter 26 examines the interplay between the annual accounting principle and basis recovery. The remaining chapters are clustered around the theme that basis should be recovered only as the investment is disposed of in whole or in part. Chapter 27 deals with cost recovery in the case of financial instruments (mainly, debt obligations). Chapter 28 deals with depreciation (and who is entitled to take it). Chapter 29 covers partial dispositions of both vertical (spatial) and horizontal (temporal) interests, apart from depreciation.

Chapter 26

RECOVERIES OF EXPENSE ITEMS: THE EFFECT OF ANNUAL ACCOUNTING ON BASIS AND BASIS RECOVERY

Methods of tax accounting, discussed in Chapter 23, determine the assignment of gross income and expense deductions to particular taxable years. These rules operate in the absence of absolute certainty. Thus, in Chapter 18 it was seen that receipts are included in current income despite the fact that the income might have to be refunded in the future. The same can occur, in reverse, with expense deduction items that are paid or accrued: such items might be recovered in the future. The recovery raises a gross income issue. There is certainly no general principle or rule that recoveries (including reimbursements) are excludible per se. On the contrary, *a cash receipt (other than a borrowing) is treated as gross income unless it is excluded by statute or offset (in whole or in part) by basis recovery.* (The minor exceptions to this statement do not involve recoveries of expense items.[1])

A recovered or reimbursed expense item may have been deducted (or not deducted), and the prior deduction (or nondeduction) may have been correct or erroneous in the prior year. An issue implicitly raised by a recovery of a prior *incorrectly* treated expense is that of the correction of possible errors on prior returns. When is it appropriate to file an amended return? When, if ever, can the statute of limitations (barring the reopening of prior-year tax returns) be overcome or finessed?

A. THE ANNUAL ACCOUNTING PRINCIPLE

The annual accounting principle holds generally that income and deduction items are to be reckoned (i.e., reported, returned) on the tax return for the taxable year received or paid, or the taxable year accrued, according to the taxpayer's method of accounting and other basic tax rules (relating to capitalization, borrowing, and dispositions) notwithstanding the possibility that the transaction might be reversed in the future or that the activity to which the item pertains has not been completed.

1. The Taxable Year

The period for calculating taxable income is the "taxable year," § 441(a), which generally is the 12-month annual accounting period regularly used by the taxpayer in computing book income. See § 441(b) and (c). The two types of taxable years are

---

[1] The nonstatutory exclusions for cash received are for borrowings, premiums received under put and call options, and certain "prepaid income" of accrual-method taxpayers. The second and third of these are covered in Chapter 23, and neither are justified (in our opinion).

the *calendar year* (January 1 through December 31) and the *fiscal year*, the latter being defined in § 441(e) to generally mean a period of 12 months ending on the last day of any month other than December. For almost all individual taxpayers, the annual accounting period is the calendar year. Corporations, partnerships, and estates (as well as some individuals), but not trusts, may have fiscal years that deviate from the calendar year in order, for example, to conform to their seasonal business or marketing cycles.

A short taxable year (*i.e.*, less than 12 months) will likely occur on the death (or birth) of an individual taxpayer or the inception or termination of a trust, estate, or C corporation.[2] In that case, taxable income is computed for the short taxable year under normal rules.

2. Unfinished Business

The notion of the annual accounting system boils down to the proposition that (with a few exceptions, such as borrowing and installment sales) income-seeking activities, ventures, and transactions are not "held open" beyond the current taxable year to await the "final results." In general, income items are includible in the taxable year when received or accrued even though there is a possibility that (a), in the case of a cash-method taxpayer, the taxpayer will have to repay or refund the included income item in the future, or (b), in the case of an accrual-method taxpayer, the taxpayer will not collect the included item. Similarly, expense items are generally deducted in the taxable year when paid or accrued, even though there is a possibility that (a) the taxpayer (on the cash method) will receive a reimbursement, refund, or recovery of the deducted item, or (b) that the taxpayer (on the accrual method) will not end up paying the deducted item. In short, each taxable year is taken as it comes (and goes). The foregoing carries out what is sometimes referred to as the "integrity of the taxable year" concept.

The classic expression of the annual accounting principle is found in the following case.

BURNET v. SANFORD & BROOKS CO.
United States Supreme Court
282 U.S. 359 (1931)

Mr. Justice Stone delivered the opinion of the Court.

From 1913 to 1915, inclusive, respondent corporation was carrying out a contract for dredging, entered into with the United States. In making its returns for 1913 to 1916, respondent added to gross income the payments received and deducted its expenses paid. Over the four-year period expenses exceeded payments by $176,272. The returns for 1913, 1915, and 1916 showed net losses. That for 1914 showed net income.

In 1915 work was abandoned, and in 1916 suit was brought [against the United

---

[2] A short taxable year can also occur where the taxpayer changes accounting periods, which is allowable only with the permission of the IRS. See §§ 442, 443(b), and (d).

States] to recover for breach of warranty of the character of the material to be dredged. Judgment for the claimant was affirmed by this Court in 1920. The recovery was "compensatory of the cost of the work." In 1920, petitioner received $192,578, the sum of the $176,272 by which its expenses under the contract had exceeded receipts from it and accrued interest of $16,306.

That the recovery made by respondent in 1920 was gross income for that year cannot be doubted. [While] the money received equaled, and in a loose sense was return of, expenditures made in performing the contract, still the expenditures were expenses incurred in the prosecution of the work under the contract, for the purpose of earning profits. They were not capital investments, the cost of which, if converted, must first be restored from the proceeds before there is a gain taxable as income.

Respondent insists that the sum recovered is not income [for purposes of the 16th amendment], since the particular transaction from which it was derived did not result in any net gain. But a taxpayer may be in receipt of net income in one year and not in another. The net result of the two years, if combined in a single taxable period, might still be a loss; but it has never been supposed that this fact would relieve him from a tax on the first, or that it affords any reason for postponing the assessment of the tax until the end of a lifetime, or for some other indefinite period, to ascertain more precisely whether the final outcome of the period, or of a given transaction, will be a gain or a loss.

It is the essence of any system of taxation that it should produce revenue ascertainable, and payable, at regular intervals. Only by such a system is it practical to produce a regular flow of income and apply methods of accounting, assessment, and collection capable of practical operation. While, conceivably, a different system might be devised by which a tax could be assessed, wholly or in part, on the basis of the finally ascertained results of particular transactions, Congress is not required by the [16th] amendment to adopt such a system, even if it were practicable.

The assessments [for the tax due] were properly made under the statutes. Relief from the alleged burdensome operation which may not be secured under these provisions can be afforded only by legislation, not by the courts.

The taxpayer's unsuccessful argument in *Sanford & Brooks* was that unused *operating* losses from an activity created a basis that had to be offset against an economic recovery which was essentially "for" such losses. An "operating loss" (as opposed to a "transactional loss") is the excess of deductions for the year over gross income for the year. An implied holding of *Sanford & Brooks* is that an operating loss is not converted into a transactional loss (i.e., into basis) at the close of the loss year

3. Net Operating Loss Carryovers

Congress did respond to *Sanford & Brooks* by enacting the predecessor to § 172. In essence, this provision allows certain deductions that are unusable in the current year (because of a lack of sufficient gross income) to be carried backward and forward for use in other taxable years to the extent of sufficient gross income in those years.

Section 172(c) defines a "net operating loss" (NOL) as the excess of allowable deductions over gross income for the year. In the case of individuals, § 172(d) effectively provides that nonbusiness deductions in excess of nonbusiness gross income cannot be taken into account. (Since nonbusiness activities include investment activities, the distinction between business and investment is critical in computing NOLs of individuals.) Thus, for individuals, the application of § 172 is (with a few modifications) essentially limited to unused net losses (i.e., deductions in excess of gross income) arising from business.

Sections 172(a) and (b) allow the current-year NOL to be first carried back to the second preceding taxable year and deducted on an amended return for that year to the extent of that year's taxable income, thus generating a refund (generally without interest[3]). If any of the NOL remains, it is carried back to the taxable year immediately preceding the NOL year. If any of the NOL remains unused, it is carried forward, for up to 20 years, to be used in the first year, or years, possible.[4] Any unused NOL carryforwards of an individual expire at the end of the 20 years or, if earlier, the taxpayer's death.

If § 172 had been on the books, Sanford & Brooks Co. would effectively have obtained the end result it desired, though not by way of a basis offset against a recovery in 1920 of prior losses. Rather the NOLs created in the years 1913, 1915, and 1916 would have been carried forward and deducted in appropriate years (1914, 1917, and so on) that showed a net operating profit.

4. Accounting for Long-Term Contracts

Shortly after *Sanford & Brooks* was decided, the Treasury issued regulations pertaining to tax accounting for long-term contracts. The taxpayer (contractor) was allowed to use either the "completed-contract" method or the "percentage-of-completion" method. Under the completed-contract method, the taxpayer could defer recognition of profit or loss on the contract until its completion; thus, all income and deduction items with respect to the performance of the contract would be reckoned in the final year. In other words, project-based reporting was allowed with respect to long-term contracts. In 1986, Congress, which was concerned by the revenue loss inherent in the deferral of net income under the completed-contract method, essentially abolished it by enacting § 460. Nevertheless, § 460(e) allows the completed-contract method to be used for any home construction contract or any contract by a taxpayer whose gross receipts do not exceed $10M if

---

[3] See §§ 6611(e), (f).

[4] A taxpayer can elect to waive the carryback period and carry NOLs only to future years. See § 172(b)(3).

the construction is expected to be completed within two years.

Under the "percentage-of-completion" method, the contractor must include in income in each year the same percentage of the total contract price (whether or not received) as the expenses paid or accrued during the year bear to total expected expenses in performing the contract. This approach results in inclusion at earlier times than would normally be the case under even the cash or accrual methods, not to mention the completed-contract method.

NOTES

1.   In a business context, aren't unused net operating losses the functional equivalent of capital expenditures? They derive from costs in the same way that the basis of an asset derives from costs. The difference is that basis adheres to a particular asset and can be eventually *matched* to the income (or amount realized) generated by that asset. Operating losses, on the other hand, are not easily matched against particular income. Nor is it self-evident that such matching would be consistent with either the Simons or ability-to-pay income concepts, which both look to increases and (non-consumption) decreases in wealth during the taxable year. Indeed, the annual accounting principle of the income tax negates the idea of a matching principle, apart from transactional accounting, such as that discussed in Section B, infra. (Business accounting holds matching to be a central principle).

2.   Another carryover system is that for excess capital losses. Capital losses for a year (including capital loss carryovers "to" the year) are netted against capital gains for the year. Excess capital losses of a year are carried over to other years to offset capital gains in those years. This system suggests a "portfolio" (grouping of similar investments) approach to such gains and losses.

3.   The foregoing raises the issue as to whether losses from a given activity should be confined to (a) that particular activity, (b) a group of related activities, or (c) all of the taxpayer's business and income-seeking activities. This larger issue is dealt with by various means, depending on the context. NOLs (including carryovers) can offset taxable income of any composition. Capital-loss carryovers can only offset net capital gains, except that $3K of excess capital losses of individuals can offset any kind of taxable income. Losses from passive activities can offset only net income from other passive activities, but not "portfolio income" (mostly, interest and dividends), and any carried-over loss is allocated to the "source" passive activity. (But when a passive activity is fully disposed of in a taxable transaction, any remaining net loss from that activity is deductible against other income. See § 469(g).) Any loss carryover from the business or rental use of a residence is confined to that residence. See § 280A(c)(5).

B.   TRANSACTIONAL ACCOUNTING FOR RECOVERIES

Below are addressed the income tax consequences of reimbursements and recoveries for *identifiable* expenses or losses, in both the commercial and personal contexts, where the reimbursements are obtained through contractual arrangements (including insurance) and through the recovery of damages. These situations (unlike those for net operating losses and net portfolio losses) are "transactional" in the sense that the recovery can clearly be matched to a (prior) cost.

A "reimbursement" or "recovery" is, by definition, always connected with a specific prior loss or expense. An "expense" is deducted (if at all) only in the year paid (or accrued). A "loss" (if deductible at all) is deducted only in the year realized (or sustained) and only to the extent of tax basis. These are rules of tax law. Under the "annual accounting principle," a taxpayer cannot "elect" to forgo an allowable deduction for an expense or loss and instead capitalize the outlay (creating basis for use in future years) or otherwise "voluntarily" defer the deduction to a later year. The rules described below, in other words, are "mandatory."

1. Second-Party Refund of Expenses

The paradigm scenario is as follows: in Year 1, Millicent (a government employee) has $32K of federal income taxes withheld from her wages. Federal income tax payments are nondeductible expenses under § 275(a)(1). On April 13 of Year 2, Millicent files her federal income tax return for Year 1, showing that the federal income tax owed for Year 1 is only $29K. Therefore, her return for Year 1 constitutes a claim for a refund of $3K. On May 23, Year 2, Millicent duly receives a check for $3K from the U.S. Treasury. Is this $3K gross income to Millicent in Year 2? No, because her overpayment of $3K in Year 1 (ascertained after the fact) was really a loan to the U.S. Treasury, which wasn't entitled to keep the $3K. In other words, although Millicent apparently incurred an "expense" (for federal income taxes paid) of $32K in Year 1, it turns out that $3K (of the $32K) was actually a capital expenditure (creating a claim for refund of exactly the same amount, $3K). Millicent therefore has a basis of $3K in her asset (the claim for refund). When that claim is paid off by the refund check of $3K in Year 2, the $3K amount realized is exactly offset by Millicent's $3K basis in the claim, resulting in no income, gain or loss.

Now assume the same facts, except that in Year 1 Millicent also had $10K of Virginia income taxes withheld, and that these taxes were fully deducted in Year 1 under § 164(a). Assume further that Millicent's other itemized deductions (apart from the deduction for Virginia income tax) exceeded her standard deduction. In Year 2, Millicent fills out her Virginia state income tax return, discovers she only really owed $9K, and obtains a $1K refund from the Virginia state treasury. The first issue is whether Millicent should file an amended return for Year 1 on the grounds that her $10K deduction was "improper" in hindsight. The answer is an emphatic "no!" The $10K was the proper deduction for Year 1, because it was paid in Year 1, and Millicent could not have known of its ultimate incorrectness until Year 2, the year she is required to file her Virginia income tax return for Year 1. The deduction for Year 1 stands!

Since amending the Year 1 federal income tax return is improper in this case, the refund of $1K received in Year 2 must raise a gross income issue for Year 2. Is it excluded in Year 2, on the same ground that the federal income tax refund is excluded (i.e., by reason of a basis offset)? No, under current law, Millicent's Year 1 itemized deductions are considered to have been fully deductible "above" the standard deduction. Therefore, the $1K refund is deemed to come out of this previously deducted (and zero-basis) amount and must be included in Year 2 gross income. There is, however, no adjustment to Millicent's Year 1 taxable income and no interest is charged on any Year 2 tax that results from the Year 2 inclusion.

The effect (on later recovery receipts) of *improper* tax treatments in earlier years will be discussed in due course.

The foregoing is a classic illustration of how the annual-accounting/integrity-of-the-taxable-year principle operates in a "transactional" setting. The basic idea is that amended returns are not filed to correct "errors" that appear only by reason of hindsight. Instead, the error is corrected (if at all) by the tax treatment of the refund in the later year that the refund is received.

Another two-party refund scenario is that involving employer reimbursements of deductible employee business expenses. The employer reimbursement plan will establish a reimbursement policy for its employee business expenses. If the employee expense is deductible as a business expense by the employee and is reimbursed according to the reimbursement plan, the employee expense is an above-the-line deduction under § 62(a)(2)(A). If the employee actually took an above-the-line deduction in Year 1 and received the reimbursement in Year 2, the reimbursement would be includible, because the claim for reimbursement would have a zero basis (on account of having been properly deducted). However, under Reg. § 1.62-2(c)(4), if a reimbursement of the type described above is made under an "accountable plan,"[5] the reimbursement is not gross income, provided that the employee doesn't claim the deduction. In effect, the employee, by foregoing an above-the-line deduction for the "expense," creates a basis to be offset against the reimbursement. As a result, neither the expense nor the reimbursement is reported.

2. Third-Party Customer Rebates

In the typical customer rebate scenario, a dealer sells a car or other consumer item to an individual who is entitled to a cash rebate from a third party (usually the manufacturer). This is a kind of reimbursement, but the reimbursement is typically much less than the purchase price. An example would be where Patsy pays $20K for a personal-use car but subsequently receives a $3K "rebate" from the manufacturer under a publicized program. She has no offsetting deduction (on the initial purchase) because the purchase of a consumer item is either a nondeductible capital expenditure (as in Patsy's case) or a nondeductible expense. Is the rebate gross income?

---

[5] An "accountable plan" is one that (1) covers reimbursement only of expenses that would be deductible by the employee (if paid by the employee directly), and (2) requires the employee to properly account to the employer (including the return of any reimbursement amount in excess of the business expense).

REVENUE RULING 76-96
1976-1 C.B. 23

M, a manufacturer of automobiles, instituted a program whereby it pays 40 x dollar rebates to all qualifying retail customers who purchase or lease a new automobile. For purposes of the rebate program, a qualifying retail customer is one who independently negotiates, at arm's length, with one of M's dealers to arrive at a purchase or lease price for an automobile. The automobile must be a type specified by M and the purchase or lease must be made within a prescribed period. The rebates are made subsequent to the delivery of the automobile.

Section 1012 of the Code provides that the basis of property shall be the cost of such property with exceptions not pertinent here. Section 1016 of the Code provides, in pertinent part, that proper adjustment in respect of the property shall in all cases be made for expenditures, receipts, losses, or other items, properly chargeable to capital account.

In the case of a purchase, at the time qualifying retail customers conclude negotiations with M's dealer, section 1012 of the Code establishes a basis for the automobiles. Assuming there are no trade-in automobiles involved, the actual purchase price of the new automobiles will be their basis. The rebate represents a reduction in the purchase price of the automobile. Thus, when the qualifying retail customers each receive the $40x$ dollar rebate, section 1016 requires a downward adjustment to the basis of the automobiles. In the case of a lease, the rebate represents a reduction in the rental fee. Accordingly, the $40x$ dollar rebates paid by M to qualifying retail customers who purchase or lease a new automobile are not includible in the qualifying retail customers' gross incomes.

The result of *Rev. Rul. 76-96*, supra, is correct, but its rationale requires further discussion. One approach would be to collapse the initial purchase and the subsequent rebate into a single purchase event (which, in Patsy's case, would be a purchase of the car for $17K). The difference between the retail price of $20K and Patsy's ultimate purchase price of $17K would fall within the "exclusion" for commercial bargain purchases discussed at Chapter 22.D.1. Under the "step-transaction doctrine," interdependent steps of a transaction can be collapsed into a single transaction.

However, the ruling above seems to take a different approach. It appears to treat the rebate as a separate event, with Patsy first taking a $20K basis in the car and then obtaining the rebate as a subsequent, tax-free receipt that requires a corresponding basis reduction to be made under § 1016, which cryptically refers to a "proper adjustment [to basis] . . . for . . . receipts . . . properly chargeable to capital account." But the reference to § 1016 is question-begging, because how does one know that a rebate is an excludible receipt "chargeable to capital account"? An answer is that the $20K outlay purchased two items, a car for $17K and a right to a $3K rebate for $3K. (Since the $3K is a fixed dollar amount obtainable on demand, it can be safely assumed that it "cost" Patsy $3K.[6]) The collection of the $3K rebate

---

[6] Alternatively, the $3K cash would be excluded if Patsy had disposed of 3/20 of the car (and of its

is then offset by the $3K basis therein.

3.   Third-Party Expense Reimbursements

The case below involved a third-party reimbursement of the taxpayer's excessive nondeductible federal income tax payment.

CLARK v. COMMISSIONER
United States Board of Tax Appeals
40 B.T.A. 333 (1939)

LEECH:

The question presented is whether petitioner derived income by the payment to him of an amount of $19,941 by his tax counsel, to compensate him for a loss suffered on account of erroneous advice given him by the latter. [The tax counsel had advised filing joint income tax returns in 1932, but the filing of a separate return by each spouse would have saved petitioner $19,941 in tax. An IRS ruling prevented taxpayers who filed a joint return (or separate returns) from later changing their minds and filing amended returns using the alternative filing status, even if the statute of limitations had not yet run. The validity of this IRS ruling was upheld in *Buttolph v. Comm'r*, 29 F.2d 695 (7th Cir. 1928). Thus, the petitioner was barred from changing his filing status and claiming a refund from the IRS. The tax paid by petitioners was "properly computed" for a joint return.]

The theory on which the respondent included the above sum of $19,941 in petitioner's gross income for 1934 is that this amount constituted taxes paid for petitioner by a third party and that, consequently, petitioner was in receipt of income to that extent. *Old Colony Trust Co. v. Comm'r*, 279 U.S. 716, [Chapter 12.A, supra] is cited as authority. Petitioner, on the contrary, contends that this payment constituted compensation for damages or loss caused by the error of tax counsel.

We agree with petitioner. Petitioner's taxes were not paid for him by any person — as rental, compensation for services rendered, or otherwise. He paid his own taxes. When the joint return was filed, petitioner became obligated to and did pay the taxes computed on that basis. In paying that obligation, he sustained a loss which was caused by the negligence of his tax counsel. The $19,941 was paid to petitioner, not qua taxes, but as compensation to petitioner for his loss. The measure of that loss, and the compensation therefor, was the sum of money which petitioner became legally obligated to and did pay because of that negligence. The fact that such obligation was for taxes is of no moment here.

Moreover, so long as petitioner neither could nor did take a deduction in a prior year of this loss in such a way as to offset income for the prior year, the amount received by him in the taxable year, by way of recompense, is not then includible in his gross income.

---

basis of $20K) right after purchase. But that clearly is not what happens in the rebate scenario.

Decision will be entered for the petitioner.

The IRS has acquiesced in *Clark*. See *Rev. Rul. 57-47*, 1957-1 C.B. 23.

The import of *Clark* is to treat a third-party reimbursement of an expense in the same way as a second-party reimbursement. In *Clark*, the taxpayer had a basis in the recovery for professional malpractice because the reimbursement was "for" a nondeductible expense. If the expense had been fully deducted, the recovery would have been includible, because the "right to the recovery" would have had a zero basis.

4. Medical Insurance Reimbursements

The common type of third-party reimbursement of expenses occur with respect to health insurance. The initial issue with respect to medical insurance (as with any insurance) is whether or not the insurance premiums are "speculative investments" (capital expenditures) that create basis that is offset against any "winnings" that occur by reason of insurance company payments to medical care providers. Instead of being treated as capital expenditures or wagers, insurance premiums are generally treated as "expenses" that purchase "protection" (coverage against loss).[7] The premiums would usually be deductible expenses only if allowed under an expense-deduction provision such as §§ 162 or 212. It happens, however, that health insurance premiums are treated as deductible medical expenses under § 213, subject to the floor under that deduction. See § 213(d)(1)(D). The protection obtained by paying a premium under medical insurance (or any other type of insurance) typically lasts for 12 months or less, after which it has to be renewed.

Medical insurance recoveries are matched not against the premiums but against the costs of medical care that are insured against. Initially, all actual medical payments by an individual, whether or not they create a right of reimbursement, are treated as "medical expenses" under § 213.[8] Treating all medical costs as "expenses" is administratively convenient in that the issue of insurance coverage (whether certain, nonexistent, or "iffy") can be ignored for tax purposes. That is, medical costs are treated as expenses even if they create a certain right to an insurance reimbursement. (In theory, an outlay that creates a right to a future receipt is a capital expenditure.)

The operative rule under § 213(a) is that medical expenses paid by the taxpayer are eligible for deduction under § 213 to the extent that they are not in fact reimbursed by insurance in the same year that they are paid.[9] If the unreimbursed medical expenses for the year are deducted in full in the year paid, the taxpayer has a zero basis in the right of recovery. In that case, an insurance recovery in a

---

[7] Liability insurance is discussed immediately below. Life insurance, which has an investment aspect, is discussed in Chapter 15.B. Property (casualty and theft) insurance is discussed in Chapter 24.C.

[8] Section 213 is explored in more detail in Chapter 5.D.

[9] Section 213(a) allows the deduction of certain medical expenses "not compensated for by insurance or otherwise." "Otherwise" refers to payments received under government programs (such as Medicaid and Medicare) or damages received in personal injury litigation.

later year would be included in income. (This result is obtained under the lead-in clause of § 104(a), which removes the possibility of exclusion if the medical expenses were fully deductible in a prior year). If the unreimbursed medical expenses for the year are not deducted at all (say, due to the floor under the § 213 medical expense deduction), then the undeducted medical costs create a basis that will offset the recovery, as will be explained shortly. If the insurance (etc.) reimbursement occurs in the same year as the medical expense, not only is the expense nondeductible but the reimbursement is excluded under §§ 104(a)(3) or 105(b). Here a same-year economic wash produces a tax wash. The explanation for this result is that the outlay for medical care is here viewed as a capital expenditure creating an absolute right to the reimbursement (as evidenced by the fact that the reimbursement in fact occurred in the same year as the outlay).

Nowadays, insurance reimbursements to individual taxpayers are uncommon. Covered medical costs are usually billed by the provider of medical services directly to the insurance company. Covered amounts are never paid by the taxpayer, and hence are not deductible medical expenses. They are normally not reimbursed to the taxpayer either, and hence do not create a gross income issue. Generally, the insured only pays "co-pay amounts," "deductible amounts" (amounts payable by the insured before the insurance coverage kicks in), and noncovered amounts. When these are paid by the taxpayer, they are expenses usually eligible for deduction under § 213, but they do not (likely) create any right of reimbursement.

In sum, a medical cost that was nondeductible in Year 1 can create a basis in a later insurance (or other) recovery thereof, protecting it from inclusion, *even though the cost was not self-consciously viewed as a "capital expenditure" but rather an "expense" in the year paid.* However, this scenario would be fairly uncommon these days. It could arise, for example, if the taxpayer paid medical bills because the insurance company denied coverage, but later the insurance company has a change of heart and sends a reimbursement check to the taxpayer.

5. Liability Insurance

There are no Code provisions or regulations specifically dealing with the tax treatment of a person whose tort liabilities are absolved by liability insurance. Indeed, and oddly, no cases or rulings appear to be directly on point. Moreover, there are no reports of the IRS asserting a deficiency on account of liability coverage. Why not?

In principle, the liability insurance company reimburses the defendant/taxpayer for tort damages paid by the taxpayer to the plaintiff. In practice, the liability insurance company pays the plaintiff directly, and for good reasons.[10] But the form of the transaction doesn't matter. As *Old Colony Trust* (Chapter 12.A.) teaches us,

---

[10] The insurance company pays the claimant directly (rather than the insured), because (1) the insured often doesn't have the cash to pay the injured party, (2) the insurance company doesn't want to have to monitor the payment by the insured to the injured party, and (3) the insurance company needs to avoid having to pay both the defendant and the plaintiff (who might claim to be a third-party beneficiary).

the insurance company payment to the plaintiff must be reconstructed into two components: (1) a payment (reimbursement) from the insurance company to the defendant (the insured), and (2) a payment from the defendant to the plaintiff (by way of damages or settlement). Since there is no statutory exclusion for liability insurance reimbursements, the includibility of the reimbursement depends on whether the taxpayer has a basis in the reimbursement. In the medical expense area, we saw that the taxpayer's payment for medical care is treated as an expense *if not reimbursed in the same year*. In that case, the taxpayer has a basis in the medical insurance reimbursement only if the expense (in the prior year) was not deducted (perhaps because of floor under the deduction). It was also seen that a *reimbursement in the same year* is not treated as an expense but as a capital expenditure because in fact the medical-expense payment produced a reimbursement in the same year. So it is with liability insurance, except that here the damages payment by the taxpayer and the reimbursement from the insurance company are simultaneous. Indeed, the two are one and the same. Accordingly, the reimbursement is offset by a basis amount (equal to the reimbursement), because the taxpayer's payment to the defendant is a capital expenditure creating an absolute right to the reimbursement. This analysis renders the annual accounting principle irrelevant for this scenario, and also finesses the issue of whether the payment to the plaintiff would (viewed as an expense) be a deductible expense.

But wouldn't this kind of characterization have equally applied in *Old Colony Trust* itself, where the payment of the nondeductible federal income tax by the employee directly triggered the reimbursement by his employer? In *Old Colony Trust*, the employee's tax payment, although nondeductible, was *not* treated as a capital expenditure (creating basis that would shield from taxation the reimbursement). The tribunal that decided *Clark* believed that *Clark* and *Old Colony Trust* were distinguishable cases that required different outcomes because *any* employer reimbursement of a *non*deductible employee expense is viewed as disguised compensation gross income. In *Old Colony Trust*, the right to reimbursement arose from the employee's performance of services. In the liability insurance scenario, in contrast, the insurance coverage is purchased in an arm's length market transaction by the payment of cash premiums. The issue of the taxability of the defendant is no longer located in the taxability of the reimbursement but in the deductibility of the premium payments, which are expenses.

The tax treatment of liability insurance is perhaps bolstered by considerations of public policy. Imagine the outcry if the IRS were to hold that liability insurance reimbursements were gross income, especially in cases where the insured-against outlay (the payment to the claimant) is not otherwise deductible. Vehicle owners would have to insure not only against the possibility of the large tort award but also against the resulting tax liability! Premiums (often nondeductible) would significantly increase, and in the end the insured's reimbursed tax liability would be shifted to the mass of premium payers.

NOTES

1.   (a) In *Clark*, the taxpayer's payment of his federal tax was a nondeductible expense because of § 275(a). Does treating the nondeductible tax "expense" as creating basis in the reimbursement provide an end run around the deduction-disallowance rule? Was the recovery in *Clark* "new wealth," or was it recycled old wealth?

(b) It is too glib to explain the tax results of insurance transactions in terms of "avoiding loss" or "eliminated (or reduced) cost." Loss under the income tax is purely a function of basis. If an art work that cost $17K but is now worth $100K is stolen, and the economic loss of $100K is fully covered by casualty and theft insurance, the insured now has a realized *gain* of $83K. (In this case, all or part of the gain might be deferrable under § 1033.) In all of the situations described above, the tax result is explained by basis. If one suffers a loss of reputation due to slander, any tort recovery for the loss is fully included in income, because the taxpayer has no basis in her reputation. (In some tort scenarios, the recovery is excluded under § 104(a), an explicit statutory exclusion.)

2.   (a) Some homeowner insurance will reimburse an insured for living expenses incurred while a damaged or destroyed personal residence is rendered unusable. The cases had held that this type of insurance reimbursement was included in gross income. See *McCabe v. Comm'r*, 54 T.C. 1745 (1970) (stating, rather summarily, that the taxpayer had no cost basis in the insurance recovery). Section 123, added in 1969, modifies this result, holding that reimbursements of certain "excess" living expenses (relative to normal living expenses) are excluded from gross income. It seems to us that the result of the cases are wrong, because the insurance coverage was paid for in a market transaction, the insurance premium was a nondeductible personal expense, and the nondeductible living expenses created a basis in the right to be reimbursed by the insurance company.

(b) The previous item raises the issue of the taxation of consumption that occurs by reason of membership in a "consumer club," which can be defined as any arrangement by which the taxpayer pays an up-front fixed-dollar-amount premium that entitles the taxpayer to various on-demand or as-needed consumption benefits. Examples are legion: health clubs and spas, roadside assistance services (such as AAA), dance studios, prepaid legal services, and prepaid health care. In all of these examples, the participant is taxed by disallowing the deduction for the premium, membership fee, or whatever the payment might be called. Taxing the value of the benefits in addition to taxing the *payment* for the benefits would be unwarranted double taxation of the same thing to the same taxpayer. Ergo, the *McCabe* case was wrongly decided solely on the ground that the taxpayer (by paying the nondeductible insurance premium) had already paid for the benefits in question. The larger point is that that personal consumption is measured by what you pay for it. No gain or loss arises under the income tax just because the FMV of the consumption received is greater or less than the amount paid to purchase it at arm's length in the market. The even larger point is that consumption under the income tax is generally a principle of nondeductibility rather than of income inclusion.

PROBLEMS

1. Suppose Vijay purchased a car from a dealership for $20K and just happened to be the ten-thousandth customer of the dealership, which resulted in him winning a $3K cash door prize. What tax result to Vijay? Which authority controls, § 74 or *Rev. Rul. 76-96*, supra?

2. While driving to the theater one evening in Year 1, Dr. Dave hits Phyllis, a pedestrian. Phyllis, who was injured, sues Dr. Dave in Year 2 for damages resulting from negligence. Dr. Dave's insurance carrier, Gekko, negotiates a settlement with Phyllis in Year 3, which it pays directly to Phyllis in Year 4. What tax results to Dr. Dave in Years 1-4?

3. What if a tax shelter promoter sells a tax shelter to you and guarantees that he will pay any additional tax properly owed if the tax shelter doesn't "work" as planned? When you are held to owe additional taxes, and the shelter promoter pays them under his contract with you, do you realize gross income?

6. Figuring the Taxpayer's Basis in a Recovery

Figuring the taxpayer's basis in a recovery is easier said that done. The material presented so far has only stated that basis cannot be created by a properly taken deduction of the expense or loss in the prior year. This statement will suffice as a crude generalization, because both deducting and excluding (by way of basis offset) the same dollars effectively provides an impermissible double tax benefit. However, the generalization requires further refinement, as will be explained below.

a. The Tax Benefit Rule

In the *Dobson* case below, the deduction in the earlier year was for an investment loss allowable under the predecessor of § 165(c)(2) that was useless because the taxpayer "already" had negative taxable income for the year in which the loss was realized.

DOBSON v. COMMISSIONER
United States Supreme Court
320 U.S. 489 (1943)

MR. JUSTICE JACKSON delivered the opinion of the Court.

The taxpayer, Collins, in 1929 purchased 300 shares of stock from the National City Company. In 1930 Collins sold 100 shares, sustaining a deductible loss of $41,600.80, which was claimed on his return for that year and allowed. In 1931 he sold another 100 shares, sustaining a deductible loss of $28,163.78, which was claimed in his return and allowed. The remaining 100 shares he retained. He regarded the purchases and sales as closed and completed transactions. [The 1930 and 1931 losses, even though "allowed," did not actually reduce Collins' tax liability in those years because his taxable income was negative before considering these losses.] In 1936 Collins learned that the stock had not been registered in compliance with the Minnesota Blue Sky Laws and learned of facts indicating that he had been induced to purchase by fraudulent representations. He filed suit against the seller alleging fraud and failure to register. In 1939 the suit was settled, on a basis which gave him a net recovery of $45,150, of which $23,296 was allocable to the stock sold in 1930 and $6,454 allocable to that sold in 1931. In his return for 1939 he did not report as income any part of the recovery. Adjustment of his 1930 and 1931 tax liability was barred by the statute of limitations.

The Commissioner added to Collins' 1939 gross income the recovery attributable to the shares sold. The recovery upon the shares sold was not, however, sufficient to make good the taxpayer's original investment in them.

Collins sought a redetermination by the Board of Tax Appeals, now the Tax Court. He contended that the recovery of 1939 was in the nature of a return of capital from which he realized no gain and no income, and that he had received no tax benefit from the loss deductions. The Tax Court sustained the taxpayer's contention that he had realized no taxable gain from the recovery. The Court of Appeals concluded that the Tax Court's decision "evaded or ignored" the statute of limitation [and] the provision of the Regulations that "expenses, liabilities, or deficit of one year cannot be used to reduce the income of a subsequent year."

We do not agree. The Tax Court has not attempted to revise liability for earlier years closed by the statute of limitation, nor used any expense, liability, or deficit of a prior year to reduce the income of a subsequent year. It went to prior years only to determine the nature of the recovery, whether return of capital or income. Nor has the Tax Court reopened any closed transaction; it was compelled to determine the very question whether such a recognition of loss had in fact taken place in the prior year as would necessitate calling the recovery in the taxable year income rather than return of capital.

The Government urges that although the recovery is capital return it is taxable in its entirety because taxpayer's basis for the property in question is zero. The argument relies upon [the predecessor of § 1016(a)(1)], which provides for adjusting the basis of property for "expenditures, receipts, losses, or other items, properly chargeable to capital account." Consequently, by deducting in 1930 and 1931 the entire difference between the cost of his stock and the proceeds of the sales, taxpayer reduced his basis to zero.

But the statute does not specify the circumstances or manner in which adjustments of the basis are to be made, but merely provides that "[p]roper adjustment . . . shall in all cases be made" for the items named if "properly chargeable to capital account." What, in the circumstances of this case, was a proper adjustment of the basis was thus purely an accounting problem and therefore a question of fact for the Tax Court to determine. Evidently the Tax Court thought that the previous deductions were not altogether "properly chargeable to capital account" and that to treat them as an entire recoupment of the value of taxpayer's stock would not have been a "proper adjustment." We think there was substantial evidence to support such a conclusion.

The Government relies upon *Burnet v. Sanford & Brooks Co.* for the proposition that losses of one year may not offset receipts of another year. But the case suggested its own distinction: "While (the money received) equalled, and in a loose sense was a return of, expenditures made in performing the contract, still, as the Board of Tax Appeals found, the expenditures were expenses . . . . They were not capital investments . . . ."

We are not adopting any rule of tax benefits. We only hold that no principle of law compels the Tax Court to find taxable income in a transaction where as matter of fact it found no economic gain and no use of the transaction to gain tax benefit.

The Court, in a portion of the opinion that is omitted, held that Tax Court decisions as to matters of "accounting" should be given deference. This holding is now obsolete, as § 7482(a) now provides that Tax Court decisions are reviewable in the same way as are U.S. District Court decisions tried without a jury.

Despite the Supreme Court's denial that it was adopting a rule of law, *Dobson*'s effect was to accomplish precisely that by establishing an exclusionary rule now known as "the tax benefit rule," which might perhaps be better labeled as the "*no*-tax-benefit rule."

The holding of *Dobson* is that a properly deducted loss does not reduce the basis in a taxpayer's right of recovery unless the loss actually reduces tax liability. (The basis in the stock became the basis in the recovery for stock fraud.)

The attempt in *Dobson* to distinguish *Sanford & Brooks* is not wholly convincing, because a taxpayer's inability to use expenses in the year paid or incurred itself creates a basis in any recovery of those expenses, and basis was the rationale for deciding *Dobson*. If basis can be created by disallowed expenses (as in federal tax refunds, uncompensated medical costs, and *Clark*), then basis can be created by allowed but unusable expense deductions.

Indeed, one might argue that *Dobson* implicitly overruled *Sanford & Brooks*, because the issue in the latter case was whether a recovery (for prior operating losses that couldn't be carried over to other years) was subject to a basis offset equal to the prior unusable losses. That was *precisely* the issue litigated in *Dobson* as well, and the Supreme Court allowed the basis offset in that case. The only difference is that the *Dobson* scenario was wholly "transactional" in the sense that one started with basis in assets (stock) that became the basis in a recovery, but in *Sanford & Brooks* the scenario, which initially involved operating (as opposed to transactional) losses, arguably became a scenario that involved a "transactional" issue by reason of the taxpayer's lawsuit to recover such losses from the government. The transaction was one in which a lump-sum cash recovery raised the issue of basis offset. Viewing *Dobson* as overruling *Sanford & Brooks* does not undermine the annual accounting principle. Net operating losses continue to require statutory authorization to be carried over to other years as deductions. Treating net operating losses (unused expense deductions) as creating basis in a later recovery precisely follows the annual accounting principle, because each event that is relevant to the income tax is registered in the taxable year in which it occurs. Capitalization (a principle of nondeductibility) is not entered on the tax return, nor do tax returns keep running accounts of the basis of assets. Looked at from a distance, capitalization and basis recovery under the income tax operate as a parallel system to the reckoning of expense deductions and gross income items in the years paid or accrued.

b. The Basis-Ordering Rules of § 111

Despite the Supreme Court's attempt to distinguish *Sanford & Brooks* as a case involving "expenses" (rather than proper adjustments to basis), it is clear that the principle of *Dobson* applies to recoveries of properly deducted expenses that, for one reason or another, did not produce a tax benefit in the year paid or accrued, and this principle has been codified in what is now § 111.

The no-tax-benefit rule is all about basis in a right of recovery. Thus, if Walter correctly deducts a state income tax expense against taxable income in Year 1, and obtains a refund of a portion of the taxes paid in Year 2, the refund would normally be included in his gross income. Allowing Walter to exclude the Year 2 recovery of the Year 1 deduction amount would create a double tax benefit for the same dollars. But what if Walter did not actually reduce his tax base in the earlier year? For example, what if Walter did not itemize? Since the deduction for state income taxes of an individual is an itemized deduction, the failure to itemize (due to the sum of allowable itemized deductions being less than the standard deduction) means that Walter obtained no tax benefit from the deduction. The exclusionary aspect of the tax benefit rule, now found in § 111, provides that such a recovery is *not* gross income, because the failure to reduce the tax base with the outlay in the prior year effectively creates a basis in any right to recovery. Reasons for not obtaining a tax benefit from an allowable deduction include: (a) failure to itemize, (b) the taxpayer's taxable income being already at zero or a negative number, (c) the deductible amount being "under" a deduction floor (such as the floor in § 213 or the 2% floor for Miscellaneous Itemized Deductions in § 67), or (d) the deductible amount being "over" a deduction ceiling (as with the § 170(b) limitations on charitable contributions).

A problem with *Dobson* itself was the unexplained finding that the taxpayer's taxable income was "already" at zero in the years of the stock losses. Why didn't the stock losses themselves reduce the taxable income towards zero, with the result that *other* deductions were the ones that were "under water"? After all, taxable income is computed at the end of the year, not on a daily basis. In other words, there is an accounting issue of deciding which deduction dollars were under water (and did not produce a tax benefit). The second (and ultimately more important) accounting issue is that of whether recovery dollars are matched against dollars that did (or did not) produce a tax benefit.

These accounting issues were formerly resolved by the regulations under § 111, which are quite complex but do not reflect statutory changes made in 1984 and, therefore, probably no longer are completely valid on determining the amount of the recovery that can be excluded under § 111. The regulations state that a recovery is excludible to the extent of the "recovery exclusion," a special basis account, for the prior year of deduction. The recovery exclusion for a prior year is equal to the deductible "§ 111 items" bad debts and state and local taxes, but also including other recoverable items. These § 111 deduction items, in the aggregate, constitute the potential recovery exclusion (basis) amount for the prior year. This amount is then reduced (generally) by the decrease in taxable income (if any) caused (using a before-and-after computation of taxable income) by the deduction of these items in the prior year, which amount reduces this special basis account. (An item that, although not deducted in the prior year or any other year, produced an as-yet-unexpired loss carryover is deemed to have produced a deduction in the prior year. See § 111(c).)

The bottom line is that, under these regulations, recoveries were treated as coming first out of basis (the recovery exclusion amount), before any recoveries were included in gross income. This and other aspects of the regulations were favorable to taxpayers. Additionally, the regulations subtly altered the outcome of *Dobson* itself because an unused stock loss deduction of the *Dobson* type, instead of becoming the basis for the specific right of recovery for stock fraud, became part of the basis for the general recovery-exclusion account for the year of the unused loss, and this account could be offset against other recoveries of § 111 deduction items for that year.

However, in 1984, Congress amended the language of § 111(a) to provide that a recovery attributable to an amount deducted in a prior year can be excluded under this provision only "to the extent such amount did not reduce the amount of tax imposed by this chapter." Although the IRS did not amend or revoke the § 111 regulations, the IRS apparently no longer completely follows them regarding the accounting rules described above. Most importantly, the IRS interprets the 1984 statutory change to mean that recoveries are now treated as coming first out of the amount of the prior deduction that reduced taxable income and produced a tax benefit in the earlier year. This approach in turn increases the chances that the taxpayer will have gross income on account of the recovery (the reverse of the approach taken in the § 111 regulations written before the 1984 statutory change). The recovery will be excludible under § 111 only to the extent it exceeds the portion of the earlier deduction that reduced taxable income. Stated differently, a recovery of a previously deducted item is includible in gross income in the year of receipt to the extent of the difference between the taxpayer's taxable income in the earlier year with the refunded item taken as a deduction and the taxpayer's taxable income without deduction of the refunded item. See *Rev. Rul. 93-75*, 1993-2 C.B. 63. These revised accounting rules are unfavorable to taxpayers.

For example, suppose a taxpayer has $7K of state and local taxes in Year 1 that are deductible under § 164. Suppose further that the taxpayer's total itemized deductions for Year 1 (including the state and local tax deduction) are $13K, and the taxpayer's standard deduction for Year 1 is $11K, so, of course, the taxpayer elects to take itemized deductions in Year 1. Since her itemized deductions exceeded the standard deduction by only $2K, that is the total amount of tax benefit provided by those deductions (including the state and local tax deduction) in Year 1. In Year 2, the taxpayer files her state and local income tax return for Year 1, determines that she overpaid those taxes by $3K, and receives a refund from the state in that amount. Under current law, $2K of the refund is treated as gross income under the inclusionary component of the tax benefit rule, because the refund is treated as first coming out of the $2K of Year 1 itemized deductions that produced a tax benefit. The taxpayer may exclude the remaining $1K of the refund under § 111 and the exclusionary (i.e., basis) component of the tax benefit rule. (By contrast, under the pre-1984 Act § 111 regulations described above, the taxpayer would have been able to exclude the entire $3K refund from gross income under § 111.)

Section 111 does not alter the result of *Sanford & Brooks*, because of the § 111(c) rule (mentioned above) that provides that a prior allowable § 111 deduction that resulted in an increase in an unexpired deduction carryover (such as a § 172 NOL carryover or a capital loss carryover under § 1212) is treated as though it had already provided a tax benefit, even if it ultimately fails to do so.

Section 111(b) provides that, if a prior-year credit turns out to have been excessive (due to, say, a subsequent downward price adjustment), the current-year tax shall be increased by the amount of such excess (by-way-of-hindsight) credit.

7. The "Inconsistent Events" Rule

In the companion cases of *Hillsboro Nat'l Bank v. Comm'r* and *Bliss Dairy, Inc. v. U.S.*, 460 U.S. 370 (1983) (hereinafter referred to as *Hillsboro/Bliss*), the Supreme Court held that a taxpayer could have gross income in the current year because of an "event" in the current year that is "fundamentally inconsistent" with the tax treatment (e.g., deduction) in a prior year, *regardless of whether the prior year is closed under the statute of limitations.*

Although *Hillsboro/Bliss* was seen at the time as a new doctrine (or as an extension of the tax benefit rule), it had existed all along in the area of accrual taxation. Recall (from Chapter 23.A.3) that an accrual-method taxpayer includes an income or deduction item at its face amount, and a condition of accrual is that the amount be calculated with reasonable accuracy (but not that the amount be exactly determined). The regulations have long provided that the later receipt or payment of an amount greater or less than the amount previously accrued requires that an appropriate adjustment be made in the later year of actual receipt or payment. See Reg. §§ 1.451-1(a), 1.461-1(a)(3). Amending the return for the earlier year of accrual is incorrect, because the deduction in the earlier year was a proper application of the law based on the facts known to the taxpayer at the time of the accrual.

Another precedent for the inconsistent-events rule is that of COD income, discussed in Chapter 19: the receipt of borrowed money in Year 1 is tax-free on the assumption that the principal will be repaid with after-tax (i.e., nondeductible) dollars; the cancellation of the repayment obligation in Year 2 is an event inconsistent with the earlier exclusion of the borrowed money and gives rise to current debt-discharge income (or amount realized) for the borrower in Year 2. The case of *Comm'r v. Tufts*, supra Chapter 20.C.2, is based on an inconsistent-events rationale for debt-discharge income. (In Chapter 19.B.1.b, we argue that the inconsistent-events concept is the only correct rationale for the debt-discharge income concept.)

An illustration of the inconsistent-events doctrine divorced from its antecedents would be where a taxpayer properly deducts the cost of office supplies purchased in Year 1 for use in her business. The supplies sit on the shelf until Year 5, when the taxpayer takes them home and uses them as personal items. The Year 5 conversion from business to personal use is an event "fundamentally inconsistent" with the premise of the Year 1 deduction (that the supplies would be consumed in the taxpayer's business). Thus, the taxpayer would be required to include in her Year 5 gross income an amount equal to the Year 1 deduction. Even if Year 1 were open under the statute of limitations (which is not the case here), amending the return for Year 1 would not be the proper solution, because the Year 1 deduction has been stipulated to have then been proper under the facts and law existing in Year 1. That is to say, when Year 1 ended, the pencils were expected to be used in the taxpayer's business, and thus Amanda properly deducted their cost as a business expense in that year.

Although the inconsistent-events rule evolved independently of the tax-benefit rule, § , 1992-2 C.B. 49, supra, cited the inconsistent-events rule in support of its conclusion that a reimbursement of an overcharge of deductible interest is deemed to come first out of the previously deducted (zero-basis) amount under § 111. That is, the refund is inconsistent with the excessive deduction in the prior year (to the extent the excessive deduction caused a reduction in the prior year's tax).

NOTES

1. Section 111 (the codification of the no-tax-benefit rule) does not take account of changes in the taxpayer's tax bracket between the year of the deduction and the year of recovery. For example, suppose Joseph (a cash-method taxpayer) correctly deducts $100 in state taxes in Year 1 when he is in the 15% tax bracket, generating a tax savings of $15. Suppose in Year 2 that the $100 is refunded when Joseph earns enough money to be in the 25% tax bracket. *Must* the refund be reported in Year 2 (which would generate a $25 tax), or can Joseph amend his Year 1 return (which is still open under the three-year statute of limitations), so as to show no state tax deduction? Although Joseph would prefer amending the Year 1 return to including the refund in his gross income for Year 2, he cannot do so, because the deduction shown on the Year 1 return was correct. (Joseph's deduction under § 164 is for taxes paid, not taxes ultimately owed.) Moreover, Joseph correctly realized the income in Year 2, because Joseph had no basis in the refund. See *Alice Phelan Sullivan Corp. v. U.S.*, 381 F.2d 399 (Ct. Cl. 1967) (rejecting the notion that the tax rate applicable to the recovery should be the same tax rate that applied to the deduction).

2. Section 111(a) states that the recovery is excluded to the extent that the recovery (etc.) is "attributable" to the amount that did not reduce tax in the prior year. In applying this provision, one could follow any of three "allocation options" or "stacking rules," under which a recovery would be allocable: (a) first to basis (the recovery exclusion), (b) first to the expense or loss amount that did reduce tax, or (c) to basis (the recovery exclusion) in the same percentage as the recovery bears to the original expense or loss. The pre-1984-Act § 111 regulations, as noted earlier, allocated the recovery first to the recovery exclusion (stacking rule (a)). Under current law, the IRS allocates the recovery first to the expense or loss amount that did reduce tax (stacking rule (b) above). Stacking rule (a) is clearly incorrect, because it allows full basis recovery before the possibility of refund is fully exhausted. Stacking rule (c) is more complicated to apply than either (a) or (b). As noted above, in *Rev. Rul. 92-91*, 1992-2 C.B. 49, the IRS justified adoption of stacking rule (b) by reference to the inconsistent-events rule. That is, the refund

shows that the prior deduction (to the extent producing a tax benefit) was excessive (in hindsight). The proper remedy in such a scenario is an income inclusion in the later year.

3. The tax benefit rule, § 111, and *Arrowsmith* do not apply to depreciation, which is subject to its own rules, to be discussed in Chapter 28. Thus, recapture of capital gain (caused by depreciation deductions that reduce basis below value) as ordinary gain can only be done by statute. See § 1245.

PROBLEMS

1. (a) What result if a taxpayer overpays *federal* income taxes in Year 1, files a return in Year 2 for Year 1 claiming an overpayment of such taxes, and receives in Year 3 a refund of part of the Year 1 taxes? Is the refund includible in gross income in Year 3?

(b) Same as (a), except the overpayment is of state income taxes. Assume further that the standard deduction in Year 1 is $11K, the state income tax deduction was $5K, other itemized deductions were $7K, and the Year 2 refund amount is $3K. (Assume that no NOL was produced in year 1 and that no other § 111 deduction items, such as bad debt losses, were taken in Year 1.)

2. If the facts in *Dobson* arose today, could the taxpayer exclude his recovery (as he was permitted to do in the case), assuming that his stock sales produced capital losses that were disallowed under § 1211? See §§ 111(c), 1212(b); Reg. § 1.111-1(b)(2)(i) (last sentence).

8. Refunds of Prior Receipts

The "mirror" scenario to a recovery of a previous expense or loss item is that where the taxpayer repays or refunds to another party an item that was previously received.

a. The Misnamed "Claim-of-Right" Doctrine

The annual accounting principle reigns as well where the refund is *by* the taxpayer. Thus, in the early case of *North American Oil Consolidated v. Burnet*, 286 U.S. 417 (1932) (set out in Chapter 18.C.1), the holding was that a damages recovery received after the trial court decision in the taxpayer's favor had to be included in income even though the defendant was pursuing an appeal that, if successful, would result in a future refund of the damages recovery by the taxpayer. The Court stated that any future refund would raise a deduction issue in the refund year.

The opinion in *North American Oil* noted that the taxpayer obtained the damages under a "claim of right." Later cases assumed, on the basis of this off-hand remark, that illegal gains were not included in gross income. This notion was put to rest in *James v. U.S.*, 366 U.S. 213 (1961) (set out in Chapter 18.C.2). Nevertheless, the rule whereby a receipt is included in current income notwithstanding a possible contingency of refund or repayment is still sometimes referred to, misleadingly, as the claim-of-right doctrine.

That doctrine is a rule of income inclusion. The focus here is on the tax treatment of any repayment that occurs. Logically, if the item were fully included, the refund should be fully deductible as a matter of right, and not be dependent on a Code provision allowing the deduction. Alternatively, the deduction should be allowed under § 212(1) as a cost of obtaining includible income (in a prior year) or under § 165(c)(2) as a loss in a transaction entered into for profit. See *Rev. Rul. 82-74*, 1982-1 C.B. 110 (stating that a refund of fraudulently obtained insurance proceeds by an arsonist gave rise to a loss deduction, citing an earlier ruling coming to the same result for a refund of embezzled cash).

Logic would also dictate that a refund of an excludible item should be nondeductible. Cf. § 265(a)(1). Such was the holding of *U.S. v. Skelly Oil Co.*, 394 U.S. 678 (1969), where the Court allowed a deduction of only 72.5% of customer refunds of gross receipts that had (in the earlier years received) been offset by a 27.5% percentage depletion deduction. And, in *Arrowsmith v. Comm'r*, 344 U.S. 6 (1952), a refund of proceeds obtained in a sale that produced a capital gain was held to be a capital loss (rather than an ordinary expense). Both of these cases, discussed in the previous chapter, stand for what might be called a "no-tax-detriment rule," meaning that a refund of an item that did not increase taxable income (and the taxpayer's tax liability) should not be deducted.

Despite the foregoing, it has been held that a refund of a fully-included item is subject to deduction-disallowance rules. In *Wood v. U.S.*, 863 F.2d 417 (5th Cir. 1989), a forfeiture of cash to the government, which the taxpayer (a drug dealer) included in income, and which normally would have been deductible under § 165(c)(2), was disallowed under the public policy doctrine. In order to invoke the public policy doctrine, it was first necessary to hold that the forfeiture of cash was a "loss" initially deductible under § 165 (subject to the public policy doctrine) rather than an "expense" deductible under either § 162 or 212. (Expense deductions under §§ 162 and 212 are subject to statutory disallowance rules, but not the public policy doctrine).[11] The Fifth Circuit in *Wood* then said that allowing the deduction would undermine the penalty for forfeiture. But the deduction of an item that was included in gross income (in an earlier year) provides no economic gain to the taxpayer whatsoever. Instead, the holding of the Fifth Circuit has the effect of imposing a tax penalty on the taxpayer on top of the forfeiture itself.

b. Section 1341

The principles of *Skelley Oil* and *Arrowsmith* continue to be part of the common law of the income tax, but they have not been incorporated into the Code. Instead, Congress has seen fit to enact § 1341, which allows the taxpayer to elect between a deduction in the refund year or a tax credit in the refund year equal to the incremental tax suffered by reason of the earlier inclusion.[12] Section 1341 has bred

---

[11] The public policy doctrine and related material are discussed in Chapter 8.D.1. None of the statutory disallowance rules would have applied in *Wood* if the forfeiture had been deemed to have been an expense. Section 280E would now provide a statutory basis for disallowing the deduction of a forfeiture by a drug dealer.

[12] Section 1341 was enacted in response to *U.S. v. Lewis*, 340 U.S. 590 (1951), involving a bonus received (and taxed) in 1944 (subject to very high war-time tax rates) and a refund of a portion of the

an inordinate amount of litigation due to the statutory conditions imposed by it. These are:

(1) an item (other than from the sale of inventory) must have been included in gross income for a prior year because "it appeared that the taxpayer had an unrestricted right to such item," and

(2) a deduction (in excess of $3K) must be allowable for the taxable year of refund "because it was established after the close of such prior taxable year that the taxpayer did not have an unrestricted right to such item."

Courts have read "unrestricted right" to mean "legal" right, thereby denying § 1341 to refunds and forfeitures of ill-gotten gains. See *Culley v. U.S.*, 222 F.3d 1331 (Fed. Cir. 2000); *Wood v. U.S.*, supra. Literally, the phrase "unrestricted right" could have been construed to mean something milder, like "not then in dispute" or "not restricted as to disposition" (by being in a trust or escrow).

The IRS construes the term "appeared" in § 1341 to mean that some doubt must have existed in Year 1 as to the taxpayer's right to the income. See *Rev. Rul. 68-153*, 1968-1 C.B. 371. But the courts have generally disagreed, holding that § 1341 covers the situation where facts occurring in a later year (without warning or notice) negated the taxpayer's right to the income. See, e.g., *Van Cleave v. U.S.*, 718 F.2d 193 (6th Cir. 1983).

If the requirements of § 1341 are satisfied, the taxpayer can elect to have her tax liability for the year to be determined by taking either the deduction or the credit. Yet numerous cases appear to assume that the deduction is conferred by § 1341 itself. This assumption is plainly incorrect. Nowhere in § 1341 does it say that § 1341 itself authorizes the deduction, and § 1341 is located in Subchapter Q of the Code, dealing with readjustments of tax liability, rather than in Subchapter B, dealing with the computation of taxable income. The deduction-authorization provision in these cases is normally § 165, and § 165(a) and (c)(2), in particular.

Curiously, § 67(b)(9) states that the "deduction under section 1341" is not a miscellaneous itemized deduction (MID). It is not clear whether this means only a deduction of the type referred to in § 1341 (deriving from a refund of a previously included amount) regardless of whether the § 1341 requirements are met or a deduction that actually satisfies all the tests of § 1341 such that the taxpayer could have elected to take a tax credit in lieu of the deduction.

Another mystery is why the deduction (if any) is allowed as a "loss" under § 165(c)(2) and not under § 162(a), 212(1), or 165(a). An explanation (of sorts) of this rule appears in *Yerkie v. Comm'r*, 67 T.C. 388 (1976), which held than an employee who embezzled from his employer was not in the business of being an embezzler, nor did the embezzlement occur in his capacity of being in the business of being an employee, and therefore could not parlay the restitution of embezzled funds into a NOL carryover. (This analysis arguably ignores the "origin" test set out in *U.S. v. Gilmore*, 372 U.S. 39 (1963), not discussed in *Yerkie*, but the Tax Court perhaps indirectly dealt with this point by stating that the embezzlement was not within the scope of the taxpayer's employment.) The *Yerkie* decision fails to explain why the

---

bonus made in 1946 (when marginal rates had decreased).

repayment of the embezzled funds was not an expense deductible under § 212(1). The IRS allows the theft (or embezzlement) of cash to be deducted as a personal theft loss under § 165(c)(3). See Reg. § 1.165-8(d). But treating a cash refund as a loss (instead of an expense) undermines the distinction between the two and creates uncertainty as to what set of statutory rules apply. In any event, it may be that § 165(c)(2) only comes into play in situations involving ill-gotten gains, into which category virtually all of the cases in this area happen to fall. See, e.g., *Rev. Rul. 65-254*, 1965-2 C.B. 50.

NOTES

1. If the receipt of an income item and its repayment occur in the same taxable year, the transaction may be treated as a loan, with no tax consequences. See *Mais v. Comm'r*, 51 T.C. 494 (1968). However, this rule has been ignored in forfeiture cases. See *Vasta v. Comm'r*, T.C. Memo. 1989-531. Alternatively, the giving of a consensual agreement of repayment within the same year that an income item is received at least raises the possibility that the receipt will be treated as a borrowing. See *Collins v. Comm'r*, 3 F.3d 625 (2d Cir. 1993); *Buff v. Comm'r*, 58 T.C. 224, 232 (1972), *rev'd*, 496 F.2d 847 (2d Cir. 1974).

2. The "characterization" principle illustrated in *Arrowsmith* has been applied to *recoveries* of previously deducted items. In *Merchants Nat'l Bank v. Comm'r*, 199 F.2d 657 (5th Cir. 1952), the taxpayer properly claimed approximately $50K of ordinary business bad debt deductions in Year 1. By Year 4, however, the debtor had unexpectedly revived, and the taxpayer sold the previously written-off notes, and (while conceding a zero basis in the notes) claimed that the gain was capital gain. The court, however, held that the sales proceeds were ordinary income in Year 4, because they amounted to the recovery of ordinary deductions. Accord *Bresler v. Comm'r*, 65 T.C. 182 (1975) (later damages recovery relating to earlier ordinary loss treated as ordinary gain).

PROBLEMS

1. Boris sells investment real estate, basis $900K, to Natasha, who pays $1M, $800K of which is financed by a mortgage from the X Bank. Any gain or loss realized by Boris under § 1001 is "capital gain." In Year 5, Natasha discovers a latent defect and sues Boris for breach of warranty. In settlement of the suit, Boris pays $160K in cash to Natasha. What is the tax result to each party?

2. Suppose that in Year 1, Barney, a landowner, receives mineral royalties of $10K from the Ajax Mining Company. Ajax properly claims a business deduction for the royalties, and Barney includes the same in gross income, while properly claiming a 20% percentage depletion allowance (i.e., 20% of the $10K is deducted from gross income). In Year 2, it turns out that the royalty calculation was in error, and Barney is required to return $4K to Ajax. Also in Year 2, the tax law was changed so that the depletion percentage is reduced to 15% (effective as of the beginning of Year 2). What tax results to Ajax and Barney?

C.   TRANSACTIONAL ERRORS AND THE STATUTE OF LIMITATIONS

The material above assumes that the initial tax treatment was correct. This section explores scenarios where the earlier tax treatment was *incorrect*. In the typical case, the error (if not involving fraud) would pass into oblivion by reason of being barred by the running of the statute of limitations against the government (or the taxpayer). However, there are circumstances in which errors (barred by the statute of limitations) can be corrected either retroactively or by appropriate "adjustment" in the current year.

1.   Basic Procedures Involving Tax Returns

The tax statutes of limitations relate to the taxpayer's duty to file an income tax return.

a.   The Filing of the Return

The individual income tax return is the Form 1040 (sometimes referred to as "the long form"). Alternatively, eligible taxpayers can file shorter Forms 1040A or 1040EZ, which are aimed at taxpayers with relatively simple tax lives. For example, a taxpayer can file form 1040EZ only if (among other requirements) the taxpayer has no dependents, has less than $50K of TI that consists mostly of wages and includes no capital gains, and takes the standard deduction. Taxpayers who realize capital gains or who deduct student loan interest can file Form 1040A if (among other requirements) they earn less than $50K in wages and take the standard deduction.

An individual's income tax return must be filed by April 15 following the close of the calendar taxable year or by 3 months and 15 days following the close of the fiscal taxable year. See § 6072(a). A six-month filing extension (until October 15 for calendar-year taxpayers) can be obtained as a matter of right by filing Form 4868. A further two-month extension can be obtained with the IRS's permission (routinely granted) under § 6081. A return filed after the due date (as extended) is subject to the penalty prescribed by § 6651(a)(1).

Any tax due must be paid by April 15 (or the analogous due date for the fiscal-year taxpayer) *without regard to extensions for filing returns*. Thus, a taxpayer filing Form 4868 must do a quick "estimated" tax calculation and send the IRS a check for any estimated tax due. Otherwise, any net tax ultimately owed will be burdened with an interest charge. Taxpayers can request the IRS for an extension of time (up to six months) to pay the tax, but the granting of this permission does not suspend the accrual of interest. See §§ 6161 and 6601(b)(1). In addition to interest, a penalty will be imposed for late payment, unless the taxpayer can show reasonable cause and lack of willful neglect. See § 6651(a)(2).

A taxpayer whose income does *not* consist mostly of wages subject to withholding by an employer must file quarterly declarations of estimated tax, accompanied by installment payments of the estimated tax amount. See § 6654. Estimated tax payments are a kind of quarterly "self-withholding." If estimated tax payments are inadequate, the taxpayer may be subject to an interest penalty.

Any installment payments of estimated tax, along with any "informal" estimated tax payments mailed in with Form 4868, will be credited (along with any taxes withheld) against the ultimate tax due. If all such tax payments exceed the tax due, the taxpayer is entitled to a refund of the excess. Interest runs in favor of the taxpayer if the IRS is tardy in sending the refund check. See § 6611. Accordingly, the IRS will routinely pay the claimed refund, and, if it sees any problems with the return, will raise them later.

b. Amended Returns

In general, the tax return for the year is completed on the basis of the taxpayer's understanding of the law and on the basis of facts known or reasonably accessible to the taxpayer, in both cases as of the time the return is filed. If additional or contrary facts that existed in the earlier year are later discovered, or the taxpayer's understanding of the law applicable to the earlier year has been upgraded, the taxpayer *may* (but is not required to) file an amended return on Form 1040X.[13] As a matter of legal rule, an amended return is *not* to be filed on account of facts occurring in a later year or a change in the law occurring in a later year. In other words, recoveries and refunds in a later year than the year of the deduction or inclusion cannot be a pretext for filing an amended return for the earlier year.

An amended return would also be filed on account of an NOL (or other) carryback to a prior year or in the case of a "federally declared disaster loss" attributed to a prior year under § 165(i) and (k).

The taxpayer has an economic incentive to file an amended return where it will save taxes. In that case, the amended return constitutes a "claim for refund," which triggers the procedure relating to refund claims and refund suits. If, instead, the taxpayer will have to pay additional tax by filing an amended return, the economic incentive is reversed. Here the taxpayer is not under any legal obligation to file an amended return, and prudential considerations cut in opposite directions. If the initial return was fraudulent, filing an amended return neither cures the fraud nor starts the statute of limitations to run against the government. See *Badaracco v. Comm'r*, 464 U.S. 386 (1984). If the original return is erroneous but not fraudulent, filing an amended return (accompanied by the payment of additional tax) would stop the accrual of interest and perhaps civil penalties. On the other hand, some taxpayers choose (whether rightly or wrongly) to sit tight and play the "audit lottery."

---

[13]   Reg. § 1.451-1(a) states:

> If a taxpayer ascertains that an item should have been included in gross income in a prior taxable year, he should, if within the period of limitation, file an amended return and pay any additional tax due. Similarly, if a taxpayer ascertains that an item was improperly included in gross income in a prior taxable year, he should, if within the period of limitation, file a claim for credit or refund of any overpayment of tax arising therefrom.

c. Audit and its Aftermath

Obvious errors on the return (such as math errors, entering items on the wrong schedule, the underreporting of income known to the IRS due to third-party information returns, or the failure to provide any required substantiation) are usually settled expeditiously without audit. Tax returns are selected for audit by the local office of the IRS District Director. Most audits are undertaken on the basis of one or more triggering factors entered on an IRS computer program, such as losses from tax shelters, excessive business expenses, hobby losses, unrealistically low reported income of independent contractors, and other suspected abuse areas. An audit may be partial or comprehensive. The audit rate has recently been quite low, mostly due to inadequate IRS resources.

A taxpayer who is audited is requested to explain and verify those items of her return that are questioned. If a dispute arises regarding the proper treatment given to certain items, the taxpayer has the opportunity to appeal to the Regional Appeals Office. Most disputes are settled at Appeals or earlier. If the matter is not settled, it can be taken to court.

The litigation forums available to tax disputes were explained in Chapter 1.E.3. Formally, the litigation process is usually set in motion when the IRS proposes a *deficiency* (tax due) in what is commonly called a "90-day letter." The 90-day letter gives the taxpayer 90 days to petition the Tax Court, without paying the deficiency. See §§ 6211(a) and 6213(a). If the taxpayer does not petition the Tax Court within the 90-day period, or if the proposed deficiency is conceded, settled, or resolved in the Tax Court litigation process (including appeals), the IRS can (and usually will) *assess* the deficiency, which is the equivalent of a formal invoice and demand.[14] The *collection* procedure (liens, levy, and execution) can be commenced if payment is not received in due course following assessment. See § 6301 et seq.

If the taxpayer chooses not to litigate the matter in the Tax Court or, by paying the deficiency prior to filing such a petition, deprives the Tax Court of jurisdiction, the taxpayer can thereafter file a claim for refund with the IRS. If the claim is rejected (or not acted upon), the taxpayer can file a refund suit in the U.S. district court for the district in which the taxpayer resides or in the Court of Federal Claims.

2. Tax Statutes of Limitations

Both the IRS and the taxpayer are constrained in the processes described above by the applicable statutes of limitations.

Under § 6501(a), the IRS is barred from *assessing* a tax or deficiency after three years has run from the *later* to occur of the due date for filing the return (in most cases, April 15 of the year following the calendar taxable year) or the date the return is actually filed. However, this three-year period is extended to six years if

---

[14] The taxpayer, after filing the petition, can sign a Waiver of various rights and rules, including the normal rule barring assessment by the IRS while the Tax Court litigation is pending. In this instance the deficiency may be assessed and paid (which stops the accrual of interest in favor of the government), yet the Tax Court is not deprived of jurisdiction. See *Rev. Proc. 84-58*, 1984-2 C.B. 501.

there was unreported gross income in an amount greater than 25% of reported gross income. As previously noted, the statute of limitations does not commence to run against the government if the return is fraudulent, there was an attempt to evade tax, or (of course) no return is filed.[15]

The statute of limitations relating to assessment is suspended for a period that begins on the date on which the 90-day letter was sent and ends 60 days after either (1) the last date of the 90-day period or (2), if the taxpayer files a Tax Court petition, the date on which the Tax Court decision becomes final (upon settlement or the exhaustion of all appeals). See § 6503(a). The statute of limitations may be further extended if the taxpayer signs a Waiver of the limitations period for assessment.

The taxpayer can file a *claim for refund* (or an amended return showing an overpayment) no later than the *later* of three years after filing the return[16] or two years after paying the tax in question. See § 6511. If (as is often the case) the claim is not acted upon, the taxpayer *may* file a refund suit no earlier than six months after the claim was filed. If the claim is officially denied, the refund suit must be filed within two years of such denial. See § 6532(a).

The running of the relevant statutes of limitations renders the tax return itself as the final arbiter of all (nonfraudulent) tax matters raised by the return, except as noted in the remainder of this chapter.

NOTES

1. Sections 6851 et seq. provide for a "jeopardy" assessment procedure under which an assessment can be made summarily (without deficiency notice, for example) in certain cases, such as where the taxpayer or his assets might disappear from the United States. See § 7429 (detailing the taxpayer's rights in reviewing such actions).

2. Under § 7421, a person cannot bring an injunction, declaratory judgment, or mandamus action to head off potential tax liability. The Supreme Court, in *Enochs v. Williams Packing & Navigation Co.*, 370 U.S. 1 (1962), held that this prohibition was overcome only where (1) the government, under the most liberal view, has no chance of success, and (2) the taxpayer would suffer irreparable injury.

3. Under §§ 7430-7433, taxpayers have various civil remedies regarding overbearing action by the IRS.

3. Transactional Error-Correcting Adjustments

In the transactional accounting scenarios considered in Section B of this chapter (recoveries, refunds, and inconsistent-event scenarios), it was assumed that the earlier tax treatment of the expense, loss, or receipt was "correct." In the material

---

[15] The statute of limitations for *criminal* prosecution of most tax crimes is generally six years from the date of the offense. See § 6531.

[16] If the overpayment relates to a deduction for bad debts or worthless securities, the period is seven years. See § 6511(d)(1).

below, we consider the issue of whether these doctrines are altered in the situation *where the earlier tax treatment was erroneous and correction of the error is barred by the statute of limitations.* It should be mentioned that, where the initial treatment was erroneous, the taxpayer can always correct the error by filing an amended return if the correction of the error is not barred by the statute of limitations. See *Rev. Rul. 54-10*, 1954-1 C.B. 24.

a. Recovery of Erroneously Deducted Amounts

The case below involved a tax-benefit-rule scenario where the earlier deduction was erroneous.

HUGHES & LUCE v. COMMISSIONER
United States Court of Appeals, Fifth Circuit
70 F.3d 16 (1995)

Before REAVLEY, JOLLY, and WIENER, CIRCUIT JUDGES.

WIENER, CIRCUIT JUDGE.

[Hughes & Luce, a law firm using the cash method of accounting, deducted expenses ("Service Costs") it incurred on behalf of its contingent-fee litigation clients — such as court costs, filing fees, expert witness fees, travel and meals, telephone charges, and delivery services — in the year expended as ordinary and necessary business expenses under § 162. The firm then included in income client reimbursements when received. The taxpayer was audited for 1989, and the taxpayer and the IRS agreed that Hughes & Luce *should* have been treating the payment of client expenses as loans to the clients, resulting in no deductions when the expenses are paid and no inclusions for reimbursements received. Thus, the IRS and Hughes & Luce agreed that the firm was not permitted to deduct expenses paid in 1989 on behalf of their litigation clients. Hughes & Luce then argued that, on this theory, client reimbursements received in 1989 for amounts deducted in years prior to 1989 — which were closed by the statute of limitations — were excludible returns of loan proceeds.]

The federal income tax is based on an annual accounting system, which is "a practical necessity if [it] is to produce revenue ascertainable and payable at regular intervals" [quoting *Hillsboro Nat'l Bank v. Comm'r*, 460 U.S. 370 (1983)]. Strict adherence to the annual accounting period, however, may create transactional inequities. The tax benefit rule was adopted in an equitable effort to mitigate some of the inflexibilities of the annual accounting system by approximating the results that would be produced in a system based on transactional rather than annual accounting.

The tax benefit rule includes an amount in income in the current year to the extent that: (1) the amount was deducted in a year prior to the current year, (2) the deduction resulted in a tax benefit, [and] (3) an event occurs in the current year that is fundamentally inconsistent with the premises on which the deduction was originally based. An event is fundamentally inconsistent with the premises on which the deduction was originally based if that event would have foreclosed the deduction had it occurred in the year of the deduction.

The Tax Court held that the application of the tax benefit rule was improper in this case because of the "erroneous deduction exception." That exception provides that the tax benefit rule applies only when the original deduction was proper. In its opinion, the Tax Court noted candidly that the erroneous-deduction exception has been criticized or rejected by many Courts of Appeals.[17] The Tax Court nevertheless applied this exception in the instant case because we had not squarely addressed this issue. We do so now and join the other circuits in rejecting the erroneous-deduction exception.

The rationale underlying the erroneous deduction exception was explained by the Tax Court in *Canelo v. Comm'r*, 53 T.C. 217, 226-27 (1969), as follows:

> We realize that [the taxpayers] herein have received a windfall through the improper deductions. But the statute of limitations requires eventual repose. The "tax benefit" rule disturbs that repose only if [the IRS] had no cause to question the initial deduction, that is, if the deduction was proper at the time it was taken. Here the deduction was improper, and [the IRS] should have challenged it before the years prior to 1960 were closed by the statute of limitations.

Like the other Courts of Appeals before us, we are not persuaded by this reasoning. As other courts have observed, the inclusion of the reimbursements in income does not reopen the tax liability for the prior years — albeit the result is much the same — and does not implicate the statute of limitations. The only taxable year affected by the tax benefit rule is the year in which the reimbursements are received, which year must be open for the rule to apply at all. That these reimbursements are property treated as loan repayments does not prevent their taxation when, as here, the loan disbursements were erroneously deducted in a prior year as an expense. The tax benefit rule requires taxation because of a previously created tax benefit, regardless of an item's inherent characteristics (*i.e.*, whether repayment of a loan or recovery of a deductible expense) and regardless of whether the original deduction was proper or improper. We also agree with the court in *Unvert v. Comm'r*, 656 F.2d 483 (9th Cir. 1981), that the erroneous deduction exception is poor public policy in that it rewards the taking of improper tax deductions. We therefore reject the erroneous-deduction exception and conclude that the tax benefit rule applies regardless of the propriety of the original deduction.

The Tax Court stubbornly refuses to give in on this issue, despite lack of support from any court of appeals. See *Davoli v. Comm'r*, T.C. Memo. 1994-326.

---

[17] See *Unvert v. Comm'r*, 656 F.2d 483 (9th Cir. 1981); *Union Trust Co. v. Comm'r*, 111 F.2d 60 (7th Cir. (1940); *Kahn v. Comm'r*, 108 F.2d 748 (2d Cir. 1940); *Comm'r v. Liberty Bank & Trust Co.*, 59 F.2d 320 (6th Cir. 1932).

b. Repayment of Erroneously Excluded Amounts

The "mirror" of the erroneous-deduction scenario is the erroneous-exclusion scenario. *Skelly Oil*, supra, provided that *correctly* excluded income (because of the effect of the depletion deduction) does not support a deduction when that income is later refunded. What about *incorrectly* excluded income? It is often stated that a prior inclusion is a prerequisite to a deduction. See *Culley v. U.S.*, 222 F.3d 1331 (Fed. Cir. 2000); *McKinney v. U.S.*, 574 F.2d 1240 (5th Cir. 1978) (rejecting taxpayer's claim that "reportability" supports a deduction, but then sidestepping the issue by noting that embezzled funds were not reportable as income for the prior year); *Rev. Rul. 82-74*, 1982-1 C.B. 110 (stating that inclusion is a prerequisite for a later deduction).

c. Does a Basis Exist in Erroneously Excluded In-Kind Income?

Does erroneously excluded in-kind property nevertheless take, as a matter of law, a fair market value basis that can offset later sales proceeds?

The logic of *Hughes & Luce*, and indeed the holding of *Dobson* itself, dictates that basis determinations are not hostage to the statute of limitations. In other words, an erroneous exclusion should preclude, as a matter of law, the existence of basis, where the statute of limitations has run on the erroneous exclusion. Surprisingly, however, such a doctrine has not clearly become the norm, although there are authorities that support it. See *Timken v. Comm'r*, 141 F.2d 625 (6th Cir. 1944) (no basis for unreported in-kind dividend); *Charley v. Comm'r*, 91 F.3d 72 (9th Cir. 1996) (conversion of employer-paid frequent flyer credits to cash were fully includible in gross income, since the credits were not included when earned). The reason for this doctrinal sluggishness is that the erroneous-exclusion issue, as well as similar issues involving inconsistent tax positions of a party, has long been mired in equitable doctrines, which are discussed immediately below. These doctrines transcend the narrow issue of the basis of erroneously excluded property.

d. Duty of Consistency

Basis has been denied in erroneous-exclusion cases under the equitable doctrine of "duty of consistency," sometimes known as "quasi-estoppel" (to distinguish it from regular estoppel, immediately infra). The main difference between "duty of consistency" and a straightforward zero-basis rule of law is that the duty-of-consistency doctrine requires that the IRS must not have been on notice (within the period of limitations) that the tax position of the taxpayer was erroneous. (The idea is that the IRS should not benefit from its own laxity.) The IRS will generally be considered to have satisfied the lack-of-notice requirement in the erroneous-exclusion scenario if the item was wholly omitted or the value was understated as a factual matter (and the IRS had no obvious reason to challenge the valuation). See *Continental Oil Co. v. Jones*, 177 F.2d 508 (10th Cir. 1949); *Estate of Letts v. Comm'r*, 109 T.C. 290 (1997). However, if the error was one of law, the chances that the IRS was deemed to have been put on notice are relatively high. See *Comm'r v. Mellon*, 184 F.2d 157 (3d Cir. 1950) (refusing to apply the doctrine because the IRS itself made the error of law); *Ross v. Comm'r*, 169 F.2d 483 (1st Cir. 1948). However, an error of law by the taxpayer should not automatically render the doctrine inapplicable,[18] and the doctrine is clearly available where the issue was one of mixed law and fact. See *LeFever v. Comm'r*, 100 F.3d 778 (10th Cir. 1996).

The duty-of-consistency doctrine is often invoked in situations involving inconsistent tax results under the estate, gift, and/or income taxes derived from the same transaction.

e. Estoppel

Apparently not all courts have accepted the duty-of-consistency doctrine, and instead insist that the requirements of the traditional doctrine of equitable estoppel must be satisfied, even in an erroneous-exclusion case.[19] The main difference between equitable estoppel and the duty-of-consistency doctrine is that estoppel requires a *willful* misrepresentation of law or fact by the taxpayer, a requirement that is almost impossible to satisfy.

The argument made for rejecting a duty-of-consistency approach in favor of an equitable-estoppel approach is to preserve the policy of the statute of limitations. The argument in favor of the duty-of-consistency approach is that a taxpayer should not be able to compound error upon error, and that requiring willful misrepresentation is unrealistic, because a tax return with an erroneous tax treatment is itself not only a misrepresentation, but a misrepresentation of facts (and perhaps of legal issues) initially known only to the taxpayer. In short, the IRS cannot contest every possible issue that might be implicated by a tax return, and certainly not issues (like omissions of income) not revealed on the return. See *Estate of Ashman v. Comm'r*, 231 F.3d 541 (9th Cir. 2000); *Mayfair Minerals, Inc. v. Comm'r*, 56 T.C. 82 (1971), *aff'd per curiam*, 456 F.2d 622 (5th Cir. 1972). The trend is clearly in favor of a duty-of-consistency approach.

f. Equitable Recoupment

This doctrine allows the government in defending a refund claim to offset the tax refund owed by it by the amount of tax on a related transaction that would be owed to the government except for the fact that it is barred by the statute of limitations. In reverse, it allows the taxpayer, in resisting a deficiency claim, to offset the deficiency owed by the amount of a refund of an overpaid tax on a related transaction that would otherwise be barred by the statute of limitations.[20] The idea behind the doctrine is that, once a transaction is before a court, the court may examine all aspects of the transaction in order to avoid inconsistent results on

---

[18] See *Interlochen Co. v. Comm'r*, 232 F.2d 873 (4th Cir. 1956).

[19] See *Alsop v. Comm'r*, 290 F.2d 726 (2d Cir. 1961), construing its earlier decision in *Bennet v. Helvering*, 137 F.2d 537 (2d Cir. 1943), to have held that a taxpayer innocently excluding in-kind income has a basis therefor equal to its value upon receipt.

[20] See *Bull v. U.S.*, 295 U.S. 247 (1935) (the taxpayer was allowed a refund of a barred overpayment of estate tax against an income tax deficiency arising out of the same item). It had long been assumed that the Tax Court lacks jurisdiction to apply the equitable-recoupment doctrine, but that assumption has been recently challenged. See *Branson v. Comm'r*, 264 F.3d 904 (9th Cir. 2001).

different issues arising from the same transaction.[21] The doctrine does not require any misrepresentation, intentional or otherwise, by the other party, but it requires clean hands on the part of the party invoking the doctrine.

The scope of equitable recoupment was limited by the decision in *U.S. v. Dalm*, 494 U.S. 596 (1990), which held that a taxpayer could not invoke the doctrine as an independent jurisdictional basis for a suit for refund where a claim for refund had not been timely filed by the taxpayer.

4.   The Mitigation Provisions

In 1938, prior to *Dobson* and the other cases involving transactional accounting discussed above, Congress enacted what now appear as §§ 1311-1314 of the Code. These "mitigation provisions" (as they are called) are extremely complex. Where applicable, they (unlike transactional accounting rules) *actually permit the reopening of an item otherwise barred by the statute of limitations, and its correction, including interest*, but only if:

(1)   there is a "determination" (court decision, closing agreement, acceptance, or rejection of a claim for refund, or a formal agreement with the IRS memorialized on Form 2259) in the current year that is inconsistent with the tax treatment of the barred item,

(2)   a party has maintained inconsistent positions in both the barred year and the current year,

(3)   the treatment of the barred item was erroneous, and

(4)   the relationship between the barred item and the current item is one of those enumerated in § 1312.

It would be tedious to describe all of the relationships described in § 1312, especially as the mitigation provisions are not often invoked.

With respect to the issue of whether erroneously excluded in-kind income acquires a basis, § 1312(7) is potentially applicable, but it initially requires a "determination" of basis for the current year favorable to the taxpayer. In other words, if there is a determination that basis equals the FMV of in-kind property on receipt, the barred erroneous exclusion might be able to be reopened, notwithstanding the running of the statute of limitations. But the IRS would be expected to resist on principle a finding that such FMV basis existed, and the IRS may succeed (or obtain satisfaction under one of the equitable doctrines). Therefore, it is unlikely that a determination that a FMV basis exists will be made in such a case. Even if there is such a determination, a court might conceivably hold (as a matter of law) that the failure to report the receipt of the property as income (although erroneous) was not "inconsistent" with having a basis equal to FMV on receipt.[22]

---

[21] See *Rothensies v. Electric Storage Battery Co.*, 329 U.S. 296 (1946) (equitable recoupment not available for the re-examination of barred transactions from taxable years other than the year involved in the deficiency suit).

[22] The legal theory for such a rule of law would be that basis is acquired if the in-kind receipt is

A more likely mitigation scenario is where a taxpayer erroneously claims a bad debt deduction in Year 1, and then in Year 5 obtains a determination that the deduction is properly taken in Year 4.[23]

The mitigation provisions, where available, are alternatives to the transactional accounting rules and equitable doctrines described above. At the same time, since the mitigation rules are patterned on the general theory of equitable recoupment, it is possible that an available statutory mitigation remedy in a particular case would bar that particular judicial remedy.[24]

5. Effect of Judgments in Tax Litigation

The annual accounting principle implicates the doctrines of res judicata and collateral estoppel. A federal tax decision only resolves the issues litigated for the taxable year(s) in question. Thus, res judicata only applies to prevent relitigation of the same issues *in the same taxable year* involving the same taxpayer.

The doctrine of collateral estoppel would come into play if the same issue as was dealt with in previous litigation arose in successive taxable years with regard to the same taxpayer. In *Comm'r v. Sunnen*, 333 U.S. 591 (1948), the Supreme Court held that courts should not apply this doctrine so woodenly as to prevent relitigation of the identical tax issue where either the facts have been modified or the law has evolved to make the earlier determination erroneous.[25]

Since there are, effectively, no mandatory joinder procedures in tax litigation,[26] a decision as to one party to a transaction has no effect on other parties to the same transaction. See *Divine v. Comm'r*, 500 F.2d 1041 (2d Cir. 1974).

"includible" (as opposed to "included") in income. (This legal theory, in our view, has no basis in norms or logic.)

[23] As mentioned earlier, § 6511(d) imposes a 7-year statute of limitations for the filing of claims for refund for bad debts. There is no such special rule for deficiencies.

[24] See *Berenson v. U.S.*, 385 F.2d 26 (2d Cir. 1967).

[25] It is claimed that *Sunnen* was modified by *Montana v. U.S.*, 440 U.S. 147 (1979), a case involving the constitutionality of a state tax, but *Montana* does not appear to break new ground except insofar as it held that the United States was in substance a party to earlier litigation that it controlled. There is a statement in *Montana* that collateral estoppel only requires "substantial" identity of issues, but it also recognized the possibility of "special circumstances" cutting against the application of collateral estoppel (mainly, in the area of constitutional law, to prevent the perpetration of a judgment that was erroneous on the law).

[26] The Tax Court is an Article I Court not governed by the Federal Rules of Civil Procedure, but it has its own rules of practice and procedure. In *O'Connor v. Comm'r*, 78 T.C. 1 (1982), set out at Chapter 29.A.2.c, cases involving the two parties to a mineral lease were consolidated in the Tax Court. Tax Court Rule 34 allows a Tax Court petition by more than one party. This could occur if virtually the same notice of deficiency were sent to multiple taxpayers, such as limited partners in a tax shelter. But there is no joinder in the Tax Court as a matter of right, and the Commissioner has no role in any joinder procedure. It appears to be very rare that parties on the opposite side of the transaction are joined. However, the consolidation of cases presenting the same issue is not uncommon on appeal.

PROBLEMS

1.   In Year 1, Rachel made a contribution of $3K to the Save the World Fund and claimed a charitable deduction. In Year 1, Rachel's other itemized deductions exceeded the standard deduction. Rachel filed her return for Year 1 on March 1 of Year 2. On April 1 of Year 5, Rachel discovered that the Fund was actually *not* an organization described in § 170(c) to which a deductible contribution could be made (because it was organized under the laws of Iran, and, besides, supported terrorism).

(a) Can and should Rachel file an amended return for Year 1? Would there be any point in doing so for her or the IRS?

(b) Rachel does not file an amended return for Year 1, but on June 4 of Year 5, Rachel wrote a nasty letter to the Fund demanding her money back. However, the Fund returned only $1K along with a release form against future claims, which Rachel signed. What are the tax consequences for Rachel?

(c) Same questions as (a) and (b), except that Rachel knew, when she made the contribution, that the Fund was not an organization qualified to receive deductible contributions.

2.   EZ Loan Corp. lends $50K to Victoria in Year 1. Victoria disappears. In Year 4, EZ Loan claims a bad debt deduction on its corporate tax return, which is not contested. In Year 6, EZ Loan claims another bad debt deduction for the same debt. In Year 8, it does the same, but this time the IRS notices the deduction.

(a) Suppose that the IRS in Year 8 decides that Year 8 is actually the correct year for deducting the bad debt because that is the year in which the debt becomes worthless. Can the IRS assert a zero deduction on the ground that the taxpayer has no basis in the worthless debt?

(b) Has the statute of limitations run against the government for Years 4 and 6? Cf. § 6511(d).

(c) Can the government concede the deduction in Year 8 and reopen years 4 and 6 under § 1311 (or otherwise)?

3.   In Year 1, Karen exchanges Blackacre, with a basis of $100K, for Whiteacre, worth $350K, and treats the exchange as a nonrecogition exchange under § 1031. In Year 10, Karen sells Whiteacre for $500K, and claims that her basis should really be $350K (instead of $100K) on the ground that the Year 1 exchange did not qualify under § 1031. Assuming that the exchange really did not qualify for § 1031 treatment, can the IRS assert that Karen's basis is $100K or, in the alternative, concede a $350K basis but invoke § 1311 with respect to Karen's treatment of the exchange on her Year 1 return?

Chapter 27

THE TAXATION OF FINANCIAL INVESTMENTS

Financial instruments — such as debt obligations, annuities, and unmatured life insurance policies — are investment contracts that provide the owner with a fixed future return. The investor's tax consequences revolve around distinguishing "capital" (principal), which can be recovered by the owner as a basis offset against receipts of cash (or accruals of income) from includible "interest." The issuer of the financial instrument, such as the borrower or financial institution, also needs to be able to distinguish "interest" from principal, because interest expense is potentially deductible under § 163, whereas principal payments are not interest expense and not deductible.

The key to understanding basis recovery in the case of financial instruments is that of *realization of loss*. It is axiomatic that basis can be deducted, or used as an offset against a receipt, only when there is a *sustained loss* of the property (asset) to which the basis attaches. The paradigm example is the sale or exchange of property in its entirety: since the "whole" is disposed of, the entire adjusted basis (AB) is offset against the amount realized (AR) to produce realized gain or loss under § 1001.

Many kinds of financial instruments entail sustained *partial* losses. Partial losses (with partial basis recoveries) are familiar from the context where a taxpayer disposes of a *physical* "part" of the "whole." Thus, if one owns Blackacre and subdivides it into 100 lots, the basis of Blackacre is allocated among the 100 lots, and, as each lot is sold, the portion of Blackacre's basis that was allocated to that lot is disposed of with that lot and offsets the sales price received for that lot.

A financial instrument cannot be broken down into physical components. However, if the instrument *provides for a fixed number of fixed-dollar payments at specified future dates*, the instrument can (with the tools of present-value analysis) be viewed as a bundle of claims to the various future cash receipts, and this approach allows basis (representing principal) to be *matched* against the receipts themselves as and when they occur. The notion that a *receipt* constitutes a "disposition" of a part of the whole instrument is perhaps counter-intuitive. However, just as a sale of one subdivided lot is a disposition of a part of the whole (of, say, 120 lots), so does a receipt of one cash payment (out of an array of, say, 120 payments provided for in the instrument) mark the disposition of part of the whole, because the satisfaction of the claim to that particular payment results in its extinguishment.

A. CONVENTIONAL DEBT OBLIGATIONS

The taxation of debt obligations is a function of financial analysis and tax accounting methods.

1. Identifying Principal and Interest

The task of distinguishing principal from interest in a financial obligation implicates the distinction between substance and form. The notion of "substance" in turn requires a theory for ascertaining the substance. In this context, the theory is provided by a financial (present-value) analysis of typical financial-instrument categories. The theory sometimes identifies the substance of what is principal and what is interest in a way that differs from the form, i.e., the principal and interest designations supplied by the parties in their contract. The tax law sometimes follows the substance (as identified by the theory) and sometimes follows the contract designations.

a. Interest-Only Obligations

Assume first that Larry and Barry both use the cash method of accounting and that Larry lends $10K to Barry in Year 1, repayable in full at the end of 36 months (a "balloon payment"), with $800 interest payable at the end of 12 months, 24 months, and 36 months respectively. This kind of loan is called an "interest-only term loan." Since $800 is 8% of $10K, the *stated* (contractual) interest rate is 8%.

It is obvious that Larry is investing $10K and, since he will eventually receive $12.4K back, that $2.4K (out of the $12.4K) will be interest income. But is each $800 payment really interest (entailing no basis offset for Larry), and is the $10K payment really principal (entitling Larry to a $10K basis offset)? Financial analysis confirms that the contractual designations of interest here are correct as a matter of substance, if we assume that the current discount rate (prevailing market interest rate) for obligations of a similar term and risk is also 8%. In that case, the present values (at the beginning of Year 1) of each future payment of what the parties have labeled interest and principal are as indicated below[1] in Table 1.

TABLE 1
PRESENT VALUE OF OBLIGATION WHERE
INTEREST AND DISCOUNT RATES ARE THE SAME

Due at End of Month	Amount	Present Value
12	$ 800	$ 741
24	800	686
36	800	635
36	10,000	7,938
		Total: $10,000

Here the financial (i.e., present) value of the obligation, which is the sum of the present values of *all* future payments (both principal and interest) that Barry will make to Larry, turns out to be $10K, precisely equal to the face amount of the

---

[1] To review calculation of present values, revisit Chapter 6.B, and Table B in the Appendix.

obligation. In general, *whenever an obligation's stated interest rate is the same as the discount rate, the obligation's present value and face principal amount will be the same*. To generalize further, a lender and borrower dealing at arm's length can be presumed to set interest at the discount rate appropriate for the specific transaction. Thus, in an arm's length transaction there is generally no reason to doubt the initial assumption of the parity of the discount and stated interest rates. Where this assumption is correct (as in our Larry/Barry example), the substance and the form are the same.

The "proof" that the first $800K is entirely interest entails valuation of Larry's investment immediately after its receipt at the end of 12 months. *If we continue to use an 8% discount rate*, Larry (as shown in Table 2 below) has sustained no loss with respect to the underlying debt instrument in present-value terms, because the aggregate of the present values of Barry's remaining payments continues (at all times) to be $10K.

TABLE 2
PRESENT VALUE OF 3-YEAR OBLIGATION AT END OF YEAR 1

Due at End of Month	Amount	Present Value
24 (12 from now)	$ 800	$741
36 (24 from now)	800	686
36 (24 from now)	10,000	8,573
		Total: $10,000

The present value of the interest payment due at the end of Month 24 has increased from $686 (Table 1) to $741, because the Month 24 payment is now only 12 months off. The same analysis explains why the Month 36 interest and principal payments have increased in present value from $635 to $686 and $7,938 to $8,573 respectively. Because the present value of Barry's debt to Larry continues to equal Larry's original investment (the $10K loaned to Barry), Larry (after receiving the first $800 payment) has not disposed of any portion of his investment. The same analysis shows that there is no realized partial loss caused by the receipt of the Month 24 payment of $800. At the end of Month 36, when $10,800 is received, Larry's asset ceases to exist, which means he has a sustained loss of the asset's entire $10K basis, none of which had been previously used. Thus, the entire $10K basis will offset the $10,800 receipt, resulting in $800 of includible "interest" gross income to Larry (and interest expense to Barry).

b.   The Theory: Realized Changes in Value Due Solely to the Passage of Time

The foregoing analysis raises questions about the methodology. First, why wasn't the basis for the each receipt *fixed* at its *initial* present value ($741 for the first $800 receipt, and so on)? If that had occurred, only a small portion of each $800 receipt would have been interest income. But we did not isolate each future-receipt claim. Instead, we bundled them together and, using present-value analysis, showed that there was no loss (in present-value terms) of the investment (viewed as a bundle) by reason of each $800 receipt.

Why, then, was the package bundled? The answer is that the package was a unitary investment from the beginning. Larry did not make four separate investments of $741 (with $800 being due after 12 months), $686 (with $800 due after 24 months), $635 (with $800 due after 36 months), and $7,938 (with $10K also due after 36 months), coming to a total investment of $10K). Interestingly, if Larry had made four separate investments, the aggregate accrued (i.e., earned) interest would still be $800 at the end of 12 months, and so on. In that case, cash-method taxpayers would be treated differently from accrual-method taxpayers. That is, if Larry were on the cash method he would realize income of only $59 ($800 - $741) after 12 months, but if he were on the accrual method he would realize an aggregate of $800 after 12 months. Therefore, if the tax system were to allow Larry to follow cash-method accounting for the four separate investments, he could obtain a more favorable tax result than would be the case with the unitary (bundled) investment by reason of being able to shift most of the $2.4K interest income to the end of the 36-month period. Whether a cash-method taxpayer should be (or is) allowed to manipulate the results in this fashion is explored in Section B.

The second question is why are we using present-value analysis? The answer is that the realization principle does not allow us to refer to changes in fair market value (FMV).

Next, does the realization principle even allow us to use present-value analysis? And, while we are at it, why (in determining present value) was the initial 8% discount rate always used to determine the present value of the future payments (thereby ignoring any changes in the actual discount rate subsequent to the creation of the repayment obligation)? The answer to both questions derives from a view of the realization principle in which "finality" (as opposed to liquidity) is the touchstone for realization. With finality being the touchstone for realization, merely temporary (transient) changes in FMV cannot be taken into account. The factors that affect an asset's FMV include: (1) the amount of future yields, (2) the date of future yields, (3) the discount rate, and (4) the number of future yields. In the case of fixed-yield financial instruments, factors (1) and (2) are fixed by contract (and anything that might alter them, like the obligor's becoming insolvent, would be subject to fluctuation), and factor (3) (discount rates) is inherently subject to fluctuation. The only factor that is immutable in the case of a financial instrument providing for a determinable number of fixed payments is the passage of time, which is marked by the receipt of payments out of a bundle of a determinable number of total payments. Thus, it can be said that changes in value (both positive and negative) due solely to the passage of time are truly realized in the sense of being final and irreversible, and can be taken into account without violating this version of the realization principle.

It should be mentioned that this "finality" view of realization is not the only possible view of realization, because it omits any requirement of liquidity. But liquidity is not a problem in the Larry/Barry scenario, because (assuming Larry is on the cash-method of accounting) Larry has income only on account of (and in an amount less than) the cash received at each 12-month interval.

c. Level-Payment Obligations

So far, we only addressed an interest-only loan, where *no partial losses were realized during the instrument's term*, and thus the instrument's basis could be used only at the end of the instrument's life to offset a portion of the final payment under the contract. Let's turn now to an example illustrating the phenomenon of *realized partial losses* during the term of the financial instrument. Consider a $300K loan from Linda to Barb at 10% interest per annum, under which it is agreed that Barb will make *three* equal payments, at 12-month intervals, set at an amount that will return Linda's $300K principal in installments over the 36-month loan period and also give her a 10% per annum rate of interest on unpaid principal. Since neither party desires to be shortchanged, the amount of each payment must be calculated so that both the present cost (Barb's vantage point) and the present value (Linda's vantage point) of the repayment obligation equal $300K. Using a discount rate of 10% (compounded annually), Table 3 shows that each annual payment must be $120,634.

TABLE 3
PRESENT VALUE OF 3-YEAR LEVEL-PAYMENT OBLIGATION
AT 10% DISCOUNT AND INTEREST RATE

Due at End of Month	Amount	Present Value at Inception
12	$120,634	$109,668
24	120,634	99,698
36	120,634	90,634
	Total: $361,902	Total: $300,000

Because Barb's three annual payments will reduce the principal amount of her obligation to zero after 36 months while giving Linda 10% interest, it is obvious that each $120,634 payment is partly (tax-free) return of principal (basis) to Linda and partly interest income includible by her. But how much of each payment is principal and how much is interest? One might jump to the conclusion that $100K of each of the three payments is principal, because that sum is one-third of the principal amount owed by Barb to Linda, and that the $20,634 remainder of each payment is interest. However, such a conclusion turns out to be incorrect if one uses the same methodology that was applied in the Larry/Barry example.

Table 4, below, shows the amount of Linda's realized loss in the *present value* of Barb's obligation resulting from each receipt.

TABLE 4
LOSS IN PRESENT VALUE OF 3-YEAR LEVEL-PAYMENT
OBLIGATION OVER TIME (10% CONSTANT DISCOUNT RATE)

	(1) PV of Obligation	(2) Loss in PV
Begin Investment	$300,000	—
After 12 months	209,366	$90,634
After 24 months	109,668	99,698
After 36 months	0	109,668

Table 4 shows that immediately after the Month 12 payment (the realization event for a cash-method taxpayer), the present value of Barb's debt is the present value of the payments for Months 24 and 36, now due in 12 months ($109,668) and 24 months ($99,968) respectively (a total of $209,366). The decrease in the present value of the investment package from $300K to $209,366 after the first 12 months is, therefore, $90,634. Likewise, at the end of Month 24, the present value of the investment package is only the present value of the Month 36 payment, due in 12 months, which is now $109,668. The column (2) "Loss in PV" amounts seen in Table 4 represent real economic shrinkage in Linda's $300K investment (basis) *solely due to the passage of time*. These realized partial losses should be treated as excludible basis recoveries by Linda and as nondeductible principal repayments by Barb. Subtracting the "losses" (basis recoveries) shown in column (2) from each year's receipt of $120,634 yields the annual interest amounts (includible by Linda) and possibly deductible by Barb) as indicated in Table 5.

TABLE 5
INTEREST PORTION OF EACH PAYMENT

	Payment		Principal		Interest
Year 1:	$120,634	-	$90,634	=	$30,000
Year 2:	120,634	-	99,698	=	$20,936
Year 3:	120,634	-	109,668	=	$10,966
					Total: $61,902

Total gross receipts of $361,902 (3 × $120,634) minus aggregate interest income of $61,902 leaves Linda with an aggregate basis recovery (sustained loss) of $300K, which, as expected, equals the amount she lent to Barb.

Notice from Tables 4 and 5 how the interest component diminishes over time while the principal component increases over time. This characteristic of a "loan amortization schedule" is familiar to anybody who has made level-payment home-mortgage (or car-loan) payments. Over time, more of each payment consists of principal, and less consists of interest.

Most important, it would be incorrect (in terms of the realization theory underlying this analysis) to simply take the $300K of principal and the total interest of $61,902 and prorate them equally among the three years ($300K/3 = $100K of principal per 12-month period and $61,902/3 = $20,634 interest per period). Such an approach, by overstating the principal component (basis recovery amount) for the first two payments would have the effect of deferring interest earned in the first twenty-four months to the third payment. Deducting Linda's basis before it is really used up amounts to partial cash flow consumption tax treatment (instead of income tax treatment).

The results in Tables 4 and 5 can be replicated by an easier calculation. Note from Table 5 that the "interest" for the first 12-month period is $30K, which is 10% (the contractual rate of interest) of the initial principal balance of $300K. Since the rest of the $120,634 Month-12 receipt consists of $90,634 "principal" repayment, the remaining principal (the "principal balance") at the beginning of second 12-month period *must* be $209,366 ($300K *less* the $90,634 of principal recovered), the interest on which is $20,936 (10% of $209,366) for the second 12-month period. The same process produces interest of $10,966 in the third 12-month period. The computational method that follows this approach is called the "declining-balance method," and is illustrated by Table 6.

TABLE 6
DECLINING-BALANCE METHOD OF AMORTIZING A LOAN

	Payment	Interest Portion at 10%	Principal Portion	Principal Balance
Beginning				$300,000
End 12 months	$120,634	$30,000	$90,634	209,366
End 24 months	120,634	20,936	99,698	109,668
End 36 months	120,634	10,966	109,668	0

To repeat, the "interest portion at 10%" is simply 10% of the "principal balance" shown at the end of the *previous row* (e.g., 10% of $300K is $30K for Year 1).

The declining-balance method provides that *each payment consists "first" of the interest earned (accrued) up to the payment date on the outstanding principal balance, with the remainder of the payment being a repayment of principal.* The declining-balance method is the method that truly reflects the portion of each cash payment that represents earned interest and the portion that represents the principal repayment (basis recovery) amount. Conversion of a principal portion of an investment to cash entails an equal dollar withdrawal from (loss to) the investment, because cash always has a basis equal to the amount thereof. This loss is permanent; hence, it is realized. (The interest income portion of a payment is new wealth to the investor, and not a conversion of old wealth, i.e., basis, into cash.)

2.   Timing of Interest Inclusions and Deductions

The foregoing explains how the interest and principal components of cash payments are calculated. For income tax purposes, however, the timing of interest inclusions and deductions with respect to financial instruments is a function of the taxpayer's accounting method. Under the cash method of accounting, the realization event is the receipt or payment of cash. Tables 1-6 above were all based on the assumption that the parties were on the cash method.

Under the accrual method of accounting, interest is earned or owed solely with the passage of time, without regard to the timing of actual receipts or payments. For any taxable year, the interest included or deducted is the amount of interest accrued during the taxable year. To illustrate how the accrual method would work, assume that the loan described in Table 6 was made after 1/3 of Year 1 had expired, and that interest is compounded (discounted) on an annual basis. The interest accrued (and included or deducted) in Year 1 would be 2/3 of $30K ($20K), and the inclusion or deduction in Year 2 would be the remaining $10K (1/3 of the interest accrued over the first twelve months) plus $13,957 (2/3 of the $20,936 that accrues over the following twelve months).

The inclusion of interest by an accrual-method lender prior to the actual receipt of cash creates an "interest receivable" with a basis equal to the amount included. Thus, when the actual receipt of the interest in cash occurs, the basis in the interest receivable exactly offsets the receipt, and the lender has no additional includible income.[2] The same principle operates in reverse to prevent double deductions by borrowers. That is to say, the accrual-method borrower claims deductible interest in the year accrued and does not get a second deduction in a later year when the interest is actually paid.

In the past, accrual-method taxpayers often disregarded the declining-balance method, described in Table 6, for computing earned interest, in favor of the "Rule of 78s." This rule need not be explained here other than to say that the total interest payable on an obligation was allocated among the time periods of a loan according to a mechanical formula that did not reflect when the interest was actually earned. The Rule of 78s is widely used by finance companies and for consumer credit, but it overstates interest in the early years of a loan relative to the declining-balance method. We mention this in order to make a point about the law of tax accounting. In *Rev. Rul. 83-84*, 1983-1 C.B. 97, the IRS ruled that interest deduction accruals of an accrual-method taxpayer could not exceed the interest as figured under the declining-balance method, which the IRS calls the "economic-accrual" method. The IRS's position, based on its authority under § 446(b) to change a taxpayer's accounting method that "does not clearly reflect income," was upheld in *Prabel v. Comm'r*, 91 T.C. 1101 (1988) (reviewed), *aff'd*, 882 F.2d 820 (3d Cir. 1989), and is essentially codified in Reg. § 1.461-4(e).

NOTE

In a conventional savings account, the depositor earns interest at a rate that may well involve daily compounding. The bank is probably on the accrual method, and calculates its interest deduction for its taxable year accordingly. The depositor, although probably on the cash method, has the right and the power to withdraw the earned (accrued) interest at any time. Therefore, the depositor is in constructive receipt of interest accrued on the deposit during the taxable year (whether or not anything is actually withdrawn). In effect, the depositor is deemed to have received all interest accrued during the year. (It follows that actual withdrawals do not have to be allocated between principal and interest.) The bank is obligated to send the depositor (and the IRS) a Form 1099 describing the amount of such accrued interest for the year.

PROBLEMS

1. On March 31 of Year 1, the EZ Bank (an accrual-method taxpayer) lends $100K to Cliff (a cash-method taxpayer) at 8.5% market-rate non-compounded interest per year. The loan (with interest) is to be repaid in full by 15 annual payments of $12K each, payable on April 1 of Years 2 through 16 inclusive. What tax results to the taxpayers for Years 1 and 2?

2. Why (in terms of financial theory) are shares of dividend-paying stock not eligible for basis recovery (until disposition)?

---

[2] If interest is never received, the accrual-method taxpayer that included interest in income as it accrued can eventually claim a § 166 bad debt deduction.

B. DISCOUNT AND PREMIUM

Although corporate bonds and debentures represent loan transactions, the true loan amount is the original purchase price of the obligation as the result of market forces at the time the corporation issues the obligation. Thus, Grant Corp. issues bonds, and the bonds state that the "principal amount" is $10K payable after 10 years, and that the annual interest rate is (say) 4%. However, if the discount rate is greater than 4% and/or Grant Corp. is considered to be a credit risk, the bonds will likely sell (on original issue) for less than $10K (say, $9.8K). Whoever purchases the bonds (say, Amy) will (if she holds onto the bonds) receive the stated interest and the stated principal per the bond contract. However, because the $10K stated principal ("the stated redemption price at maturity") exceeds Amy's purchase price by $200, Amy will (in the absence of tax rules to the contrary) realize $200 gain for tax purposes when the bond principal is paid off. This excess of the stated redemption price at maturity over the issue price is known as "original issue discount" (OID). In the reverse situation where the issue price is greater than the stated redemption price at maturity, the difference is known as "(bond) premium." This section deals with the tax treatment of OID and bond premium.

1. Original Issue Discount

In the hypothetical above, the OID is only $200 per $10K face amount bond, which hardly seems to raise a serious tax problem. But suppose the X Bank comes up with the bright idea of issuing a 3-year certificate of deposit (CD) for $10K that can be redeemed for $12,597 after 36 months, with no stated interest, to individuals (all on the cash method). The bank has figured out that a discount rate of 8% compounded annually for 36 months will reduce $12,597 to a present value of $10K. Accordingly, the bank (which is on the accrual method) claims an interest deduction of $800 for the first 12 months. Since the interest is not paid, the accrued (and deducted) interest for the second 12-month period is $864 [.08 × ($10K + $800)]. Again the interest is not paid, so the interest accrued (and deducted) for the third 12-month period is $933 [.08 × ($10K + $800 + $864)]. This adds up to $12,597 ($10K + $800 + $864 + $933), which is duly paid to the depositor after 36 months. In the meantime, the cash-method taxpayer (having received no cash) reports nothing, except gain of $2,597 after 36 months (amount realized of $12,597 less basis of $10K). Moreover, the taxpayer claims that the gain of $2,597 is capital gain, because § 1271(a)(1) treats the retirement of a debt obligation as a "sale or exchange." The bank imposed a penalty for an early cashing-in of the CD, which prevents the owner of the CD from being in constructive receipt of the accruing interest.

Transactions such as the one just described were common in the late 1960s and early 1970s. However, the Supreme Court, in *U.S. v. Midland-Ross Corp.*, 381 U.S. 54 (1965), had recently held that an actual sale of an OID bond on the market (prior to its maturity) produced ordinary gain on the ground that earned OID was essentially interest (and not "market" appreciation). There the Court stated:

> This Court has consistently construed "capital asset" to exclude property representing income items or accretions to the value of capital assets themselves properly attributable to income. Earned original issue discount

serves the same function as stated interest, concededly ordinary income and not a capital asset; it is simply "compensation for the use or forbearance of money." Unlike the typical case of capital appreciation, the earning of discount to maturity is predictable and measurable . . . . The $6 earned on a one-year note for $106 issued for $100 is precisely like the $6 earned on a one year loan of $100 at 6% stated interest.

The holding of *Midland-Ross* would appear to have extended to the redemption of an OID bond at maturity from a holder who had acquired it on original issue.

Congress was not satisfied with *Midland-Ross*, because the investors could still defer the gain, whereas the issuers were accruing the deduction currently. Also, subsequent purchasers of OID obligations were cured of the OID taint, because any discount they enjoyed was not "original issue" discount but, instead, "market discount." Eventually, in 1984, Congress enacted a comprehensive set of special rules for certain debt obligations, now found in §§ 1271-1288.

As far as OID itself is concerned, a cash-method investor, under § 1272, is put on the accrual method for including OID in gross income as it accrues. This is illustrated by Table 7, which follows the CD example above. Section 163(e) requires issuers to follow the same accrual approach as investors. These accrual rules are mandatory, not elective. OID is now defined by statute (§ 1273(a)) as the excess of the stated redemption price at maturity (basically, the stated principal amount) over the issue price. There is a de minimis exception to the definition of OID, under § 1273(a)(3), for instances where the discount from the stated principal is less than 1/4 of 1% times the number of years to maturity. Exceptions to the OID accrual rule, listed in § 1273(a)(2), exist for tax-exempt bonds, U.S. savings bonds, bonds with a term of 1 year or less, and certain small nonbusiness loans made by an individual.

In an OID scenario, the implicit interest rate is not stated, but it can be figured out with a financial calculator. The implicit interest rate (for tax purposes) is that discount rate (compounded semi-annually) which reduces the stated redemption price at maturity to the issue price. The implicit interest rate (called the "yield to maturity") is then applied against the issue price (and compounded semi-annually). The accrued interest is figured for each six-month accrual period and, if an accrual period straddles two taxable years, the accrued interest for the accrual period is prorated between the taxable years on a daily basis. In practice, the computations will be performed by the issuer and reported to the holder (and the IRS) on a Form 1099-OID. In Table 7, we show how OID accrual works, but (for the sake of simplicity) all computations are made on the basis of annual compounding. It has already been determined for purposes of this exercise that the implicit interest rate (yield to maturity) is 8% compounded annually. The "principal" of an OID obligation is the issue price (the amount invested), not the stated principal (the stated redemption price at maturity).

TABLE 7
RETURN ON OID OBLIGATION WITH NO INTEREST PAYMENTS

When	Interest Accrued @ 8%	Accumulated Principal and Interest
Beginning	—	$10,000
After 12 months	$800	10,800
After 24 months	864	11,664
After 36 months	933	12,597

The last column of Table 7 shows that an OID obligation increases in value with the passage of time as the discount (earned but unpaid OID) accumulates.

Suppose the obligation was issued on March 31 of Year 1. Thus, the investor holds it for about 3/4 of Year 1, and would prorate the $800 of accrued interest for the first (12 month) accrual period on a daily basis between Years 1 and 2, resulting in the inclusion of $600 of interest (3/4 × $800) in Year 1 and $200 in year 2. The investor would report an additional $648 in Year 2 (3/4 × $864), for a total Year 2 inclusion of $848 ($200 + $648). Following this procedure, the amounts reported in Year 3 would be $916, and the amounts reported in Year 4 would be $233. The amounts reported in Years 1 through 4 add up to $2,597. The issuer deducts interest in the same fashion under § 163(e). (Keep in mind that Table 7 is not based on semi-annual compounding, as actually occurs under § 1272.)

Sections §§ 1272 and 163(e) might be justified on the grounds that gains that occur with the passage of time are realized. Of course, the OID gains are realized in the sense of being final and irretrievable. But in this case finality is obtained without regard to liquidity (the receipt of cash by a cash-method taxpayer). Nevertheless, the possible nonliquidity of the investor is treated as of no concern in this case because no investor is required to invest in an OID obligation, and any investor that does is on notice of being subject to accrual taxation. It is worth noting that the tax system generally ignores (i.e., does not require inclusion of) other passage-of-time gains, such as occur with respect to the inside build-up in annuity and life-insurance contracts (discussed in Sections C and D, infra) and vested remainder interests (discussed in Chapter 29.B).

An OID obligation can exist where an interest rate is stated but it is lower than the applicable federal rate. In that case, the accrued OID amount for a period is the interest accrued for the period less the interest paid, as is illustrated by Table 7A, in the footnote below.[3]

---

[3] Assume, for example, that Y Corp. issues a three-year $10K face amount bond providing for three annual *stated* interest payments of $800. But, unlike Table 1, the discount rate is 10% instead of 8%. Y Corp. (the borrower-issuer of the obligation) is in no position to demand $10K in return for an 8% stated-interest obligation, since investors will simply go elsewhere to obtain a return of 10%. By paying only $9,502 for the Y Corp. bond, an investor can indirectly obtain a "real" 10% *total* rate of return to maturity (despite the *stated* rate of return of 8%), which ensures economic parity with comparable investments yielding 10%. The $498 of OID ($10K - $9,502) accrues as illustrated in Table 7A, where we assume (for the sake of simplicity) that the annual accruals coincide with the taxable year.

The OID rules affect some transactions considered in previous chapters. First, consider below-market term loans governed by § 7872. In the case of "term loans" that aren't gift loans, § 7872 incorporates the OID rules in calculating the amount and accrual rate of deemed interest, which is really OID. Suppose, for example, that in Year 1 Z Corp. lends its CEO Nancy $100K for five years at zero stated interest, and the applicable federal rate (AFR) is 6%. The present value of Nancy's repayment obligation (discounted on a semi-annual basis) is $74,409, which (in effect) *is the real principal*, and the remaining $25,591 received from Z Corp. by Nancy is a Year-1 compensation cost of Z Corp. and Year-1 compensation gross income to Nancy. But, at the end of five years, Nancy must pay $100K to Z Corp. This means that Z Corp. has lent $74,409 and obtained a five-year, zero-stated-interest obligation with a stated principal of $100K. Thus, Nancy's debt is an OID obligation under which Nancy is deemed to pay $25,591 total interest to Z Corp. as it accrues under the § 1272 rules illustrated in Table 7. See § 7872(b)(2).[4]

A second important application of the OID rules is to certain below-market-interest installment sales, where a debt (installment) obligation is issued (given) for property rather than (or in addition to) cash. Here the transferor (seller) of the property is engaged in a deferred-payment sale, raising issues as to the amount realized under the closed-transaction § 1001 method or the selling price (as well as contract price and payments) for purposes of the § 453 installment method, issues that were dealt with in Chapter 23.D. The OID rules and the amount realized (or selling price) rules are meshed together, as will now be explained.

First, how do the OID rules work here? If the debt that is given for the property (or the property itself) is publicly traded, the issue price (for determining the existence of OID) is equal to the FMV value of the property. See § 1273(b)(3). This scenario would be uncommon in the case of individual taxpayers, however, and the default OID rule for debt issued for property is that the issue price equals the stated redemption price at maturity, *resulting in no OID*, unless § 1274 applies. See § 1274(b)(4). Recall from Chapter 23.D.2.d that § 1274(b)(1) treats certain below-market obligations given for property as having an "imputed principal amount" (i.e., real principal amount) equal to the PV of the obligation as determined by discounting (on a semi-annual basis) all stated principal and interest payments back to the present. Since the imputed principal amount is the "issue price" for OID

TABLE 7A
RETURN ON OID OBLIGATION WITH STATED INTEREST

When	Interest Earned @ 10%	Subtract Interest Paid	Unpaid Interest (OID)	Accumulated P & I
Beginning	—	—	—	$9,502
End 12 months	$950	$800	$150	9,652
End 24 months	965	800	165	9,817
End 36 months	983	800	183	10,000
Totals	$2,898	$2,400	$498	

[4] This OID treatment doesn't apply to demand loans or gift loans. In those cases, the borrower is deemed to pay "foregone interest" to the lender calculated by multiplying the AFR by the amount of stated principal. See § 7872(a)(1). Demand loans could not be discounted to present value because their terms are unknown in advance.

purposes, see § 1274(a), the effect is to create what we can call "§ 1274 OID" that is reportable by a cash-method seller as it accrues under § 1272. Any of the exceptions to § 1274 would eliminate the existence of § 1274 accruable OID. To recapitulate, the seller of property has § 1272 OID if publicly traded property is involved, § 1274 OID for certain other debt (bearing below-market interest) given for property, and no accruable OID in all other cases.

The seller's amount realized under the § 1001 closed-transaction method is determined under Reg. § 1.1001-1(g), which incorporates the OID rules just described by cross-referencing them. Thus, the amount realized under § 1001(b) is computed with reference to (a) the FMV value of the sold property in the uncommon publicly-traded scenario, (b) the PV of the obligation (the imputed principal amount) in the § 1274 scenario, or (c) the stated principal, but reduced by implicit interest (if any) as determined under § 483, in all other cases. Recall from Chapter 23.D.2.d that § 483 is a back-up to § 1274 for below-market debt issued for property (that escapes § 1274), except that *§ 483 does not require OID accruals by a cash-method seller.* (Section 1274A(c) provides an election out of § 1274 OID-accrual treatment for certain installment obligations that don't exceed $2M.) Hence, where § 483 (or § 1274A(c)) applies, the amount realized is less than the stated selling price, but no OID accruals are required.

Turning to the installment method, that method is not available where publicly traded property is sold, and publicly traded debt received is treated as cash received. If §§ 483 or 1274 applies, the selling price (and reportable gross profit) are reduced, and contract price and (principal) payments are also reduced. See Temp. Reg. § 15A.453-1(b)(2)(ii). If §§ 483 and 1274 don't come into play, the stated principal controls. Section 1274 creates accruable OID and §§ 483 and 1274A(c) create implicit interest (includible by a cash-method taxpayer only when received).

2. Market Discount

A debt obligation may have an original issue price equal to its face amount (and, thus, have no OID), but subsequently its value may fall as the yield on comparable investments rises. For example, assume that Maria pays $10K on original issue for a $10K face amount corporate bond maturing in three years, with 8% market-rate interest payable in Years 1 through 3. One year later, after the first interest payment, market interest rates on comparable bonds rise to 10%, and Maria sells the bond to Daphne, who, being a savvy investor, is not willing to pay the full $10K face amount, and earn only an 8% return, when she could get a 10% return by buying a comparable $10K bond with 10% interest. Thus, Daphne pays only $9,648[5] in order to equate the total return with a bond paying 10%. The $352 excess of the $10K face amount over the $9,648 purchase price is referred to as "market discount."

---

[5] Using a 10% discount rate, the present value of the Year 2 $800 interest payment is $727; the present value of the Year 3 interest payment is $661; and the present value of the Year 3 principal payment of $10K is $8,260. Thus, the present value of the obligation (the sum of the present values of the payments) is $9,648.

Market discount is economically identical to OID as far as Daphne is concerned. However, the issuer cannot know the price at which Daphne purchased Maria's bond. For this reason, the issuer is in no position to provide the IRS with information on market discount accruals for the purchasers of its bonds after original issue, and the calculation of market discount accruals by most investors would be resisted as too burdensome (not to mention incomprehensible). Not surprisingly, therefore, the tax rules pertaining to market discount are much "softer" than for OID. Under § 1276, there are no required accruals of market discount.[6] Instead, any gain realized on a sale or redemption of a market discount obligation is treated as interest (ordinary income) to the extent of the taxpayer's pro rata share of the market discount. That amount is determined by multiplying the total market discount (the excess of the stated principal amount over the purchase price) by a fraction, the numerator of which is the number of days the obligation was held by the taxpayer and the denominator of which is the total number of days between the purchase date and the maturity date. This rule essentially extends the *Midland-Ross* "character" result to market discount instruments.

3. Bond Premium

Debt-obligation (bond) "premium" is the reverse of OID, and it arises when a debt obligation bears a stated interest rate in *excess* of the market (discount) rate. Because of the higher stated interest rate, investors (lenders) will pay more for the debt than its face amount. For example, assume that a three-year, $10K face amount debt obligation paying interest at 12% per annum until maturity is issued when the discount rate is 10%. The amount that would actually be paid by a rational investor is $10,497, which is the aggregate present value (using a 10% discount rate) of the $1.2K interest payments at the end of Years 1 through 3, and of the $10K payment due at the end of Year 3. This $497 excess over the face amount is referred to as "premium."

Since the bond purchaser has lent the issuer $10,497 when the discount rate is 10%, the interest accrued after 12 months would be $1,049.70. But the first stated interest payment will be $1.2K. The excess payment of $150.30 is really a partial repayment of the $497 additional principal lent by the buyer.[7] Sections 171 and 1016(a)(5) account for these results on the purchaser's side by "amortizing" (deducting) the premium over time.[8] On the issuer's side, § 171(e) treats the amortizable bond premium as a reduction of the interest payment, so that the issuer's Year 1 interest outlay is treated as being only $1,049.70. Table 8 shows how these principles apply over the bond's three-year life (with the numbers being rounded off to the nearest dollar).

---

[6] Taxpayers can elect accrual treatment under § 1276(b)(2), but (given the time value of money) it is hard to imagine any individual investor making such an election, except where she has a § 172 NOL carryover about to expire.

[7] None of the stated $10K principal will be paid until the end of Year 3. Thus, the $150.30 excess is, by process of elimination, a partial recovery of the bond premium.

[8] Use of the word "amortize" here misleadingly implies straight line (i.e., equal or ratable) deductions or offsets, but in this context financial calculations are used.

TABLE 8
PREMIUM OBLIGATION

When	Yield @ 10%	Stated Interest	Amortized Premium	Principal Balance
Begin Year 1	—	—	—	$10,497
End Year 1	$1,050	$1,200	$150	10,347
End Year 2	1,035	1,200	165	10,182
End Year 3	1,018	1,200	182	10,000

PROBLEM

X Corp. (an accrual-method taxpayer) issues a 10-year $100K face amount bond to Investor (a cash-method taxpayer) in registered form, yielding payments of 10% stated interest per year, with the principal to be repaid in full at maturity. The bond is issued on June 30 of Year 1. Assume that §§ 171, 1272, and 1276 apply to the bond. Describe how both Investor and X Corp. will report this transaction in the first year (assuming, for the sake of simplicity, that all discounting, etc., is done on an annual basis), where:

(a) Investor purchases the bond for $100K.

(b) Investor purchases the bond for $88.7K, because the current discount rate is 12%. (This purchase price brings the yield to maturity to 12% on an annual-compounding basis.)

(c) Investor purchases the bond for $121K, because the current discount rate is 7%. (This purchase price reduces the yield to maturity to 7% on an annual-compounding basis.)

(d) Investor purchases the bond for $90K exactly one year after original issue and holds it until maturity.

C. ANNUITIES

A conventional annuity is an investment that promises a series of level payments to a payee (the annuitant) for a specified time period, such as the annuitant's life, a term of years, the life of the annuitant plus the life of one or more designated surviving beneficiaries, or the life of the annuitant plus a term of years.[9] When the annuity period expires, the stream of payments ends. Annuities can be purchased for a lump-sum consideration or by making a series of premium payments. The cost is, of course, a nondeductible capital expenditure that creates basis.

Annuities resemble level-payment mortgages: the annuity purchaser is the "lender" who lends money to the borrower (the seller of the annuity) and who is repaid the principal amount plus interest. That is, the purchaser of the annuity is in the position of the bank in the residential-mortgage situation. One difference

---

[9] A "variable" annuity also provides for payments over a specified time period, but the future payments can fluctuate to reflect the then-current investment yields. The tax treatment of variable annuities is too complex to describe here. See Reg. §§ 1.72-2(b)(3), -4(d)(3).

between a mortgage and an annuity is that annuity payments usually do not commence immediately upon the purchase of the annuity but at some future date (in tax jargon, the "annuity starting date"), such as age 65 or upon retirement. The typical annuity is a substitute for a pension.

Another difference between annuities and mortgages is that annuities that are keyed to the lives of one or more persons (the most common type) contain an element of actuarial risk as well as the conventional element of investment risk: the longer the person or persons live, the greater the investment return; the shorter they live, the worse the return. In some cases, the risk of premature death is cushioned by a "refund feature," under which all or a portion of the annuitant's unrecovered investment is paid to the annuitant's estate. An annuity for one or more lives entails a stream of payments that, although not "fixed" in terms of their number, is "determinable" in number through the use of actuarial tables.

A third way in which annuities differ from conventional home mortgages is that the rate of basis recovery (described below) is faster under § 72 than under the declining-balance method applicable to conventional debt, described in Section A.

Section 72 provides that the "inside build-up" in annuities (i.e., increase in cash surrender value due to earnings on the investment) is treated as if it were unrealized appreciation, and thus it is not taxed as it accrues. Taxation occurs only when cash payments are actually received. See § 72(a) (stating that an annuitant has income only on the receipt of a payment). Annuities are not subject to the constructive-receipt doctrine, even where the investor has the power to draw down on his or her investment, including any growth therein, at any time prior to the annuity starting date.

With respect to payments received under the annuity contract, a crucial distinction is made between payments received *before* the annuity starting date and those received *after* the annuity starting date (called "payments received as an annuity").

Withdrawals prior to the starting date are deemed to come first out of earned (but undistributed) income and, only when such income is exhausted, out of principal. See § 72(e)(2)(B). (Loans made under the contract and the proceeds of pledges or assignments are treated as withdrawals.[10]) The undistributed "income" at the time of a withdrawal is the excess of the cash surrender value of the contract (i.e., premium payments plus earnings thereon) over the investor's basis (called the "investment in the contract").[11] This treatment parallels that for conventional debt instruments held by a cash-method taxpayer.

An additional 10% penalty tax is generally imposed on withdrawals from income prior to the age of 59½. See § 72(q). Gifts of annuity contracts (except to one's spouse) are "deemed realization" events. See § 72(e)(4)(C).

Payments "received as an annuity" are governed by § 72(b)(1), which provides that each annuity payment (that would otherwise be fully included under § 72(a)) is

---

[10] See § 72(e)(4)(A).

[11] See § 72(e)(3). The investor's basis in the annuity contract equals the premiums paid except in the unusual case where the investor purchased the contract from a prior investor.

included in gross income *except for* that fraction of the payment that is obtained by dividing the "investment in the contract" (the basis) by the "expected return" under the contract (total anticipated annuity payments)[12] as of the annuity starting date. Thus:

$$\text{Excluded Amount} = \text{payment} \quad \times \quad \frac{\text{Investment in the Contract}}{\text{Expected Return}}$$

Once constituted, the fraction never changes. That is, the investment-in-the-contract amount is not reduced (adjusted downwards) to reflect prior-year basis recoveries, and the expected-return amount is not reduced to reflect payments already received. Also, the expected-return amount is the gross expected return (the aggregate of expected payments) and is not reduced to present value. In other words, § 72(b)(1) tells us to calculate the ratio of initial basis to total expected gross return and then to apply that same ratio against each payment received to determine the basis offset against that payment. (In form, the annuity formula closely resembles the § 453 installment-method formula.)

A glance at Table 6, supra, reveals that the "straight-line" (prorated) basis recovery approach of § 72 differs from the declining-balance method of capital recovery for mortgages.

Basis can be recovered under § 72(b) only until it is exhausted. Thereafter, annuity payments are entirely included in gross income. See § 72(b)(2). If the annuity expires before the basis has been fully recovered, the unrecovered basis is deductible on the tax return for the annuitant's final taxable year. See § 72(b)(3). If annuity payments continue to a survivor, the survivor simply steps into the primary annuitant's shoes and continues to recover basis under the same formula that the primary annuitant used. See §§ 691(d) and 1014(b)(9)(A) (no stepped-up basis).

D.   TAXATION OF LIFE INSURANCE CONTRACTS BEFORE THE INSURED'S DEATH

For federal income tax purposes, there are three categories of life insurance contracts:

(1) a contract that fails to qualify as life insurance for tax purposes under § 7702, because of a close resemblance to a conventional investment (an example being a "variable premium" contract), (2) a "true" life insurance contract (i.e., one having a meaningful actuarial risk component), and (3) a "modified endowment contract" as defined in § 7702A (i.e., a life insurance contract that avoids category (1) but under which the cash surrender value would equal the face amount before the insured reaches the age of 99). The discussion below deals only with the taxation of life insurance contracts *prior to* the death of the insured. (Chapter 15.B covers the tax treatment of payments made by reason of the insured's death.)

---

[12] Where the expected return is dependent on the life span of one or more individuals, the regulations provide actuarial tables for making the calculation.

Life insurance premiums are not deductible — not even if incurred by a business to protect itself against the death of a key employee. See § 264(a)(1). The entire premium amounts are capitalized and become the basis in the insurance contract, § 72(e)(6)(A), even though, in the conceptual sense, all or part of each year's premium is an "expense" of providing current insurance protection that is consumed as the premium year progresses.

Insurance contracts that fail to qualify as life insurance under § 7702 are taxed like savings accounts (rather than under § 72): each year the policyholder includes in gross income an amount equal to the increase in cash surrender value for the year, *plus* the cost of the current year's life insurance protection, *less* the net premium. See § 7702(g)(1). The policyholder's basis in the contract increases as amounts are included in gross income and as premiums are paid. Because such policies are unfavorably taxed, they are unlikely to be widely sold to the public.

Modified endowment contracts under § 7702A are subject to § 72(e) (i.e., are taxed like annuities before the annuity starting date): the investment return accruing prior to distribution under the contract (the "inside build-up") is not included by the policyholder in gross income as it accrues, but any distributions (including loans) are deemed to come first out of "income" and second out of "principal." See § 72(e)(10).

True life insurance contracts are strongly tax-favored prior to the death of the insured:

(1) Inside build-up is not taxed to the policy owner.

(2) *Withdrawals are treated as coming first out of principal* (and thus are excluded to the extent thereof).

(3) Policy loans are not treated as withdrawals. See § 72(e)(5)(A) and (C).

(4) Policy "dividends" that are retained by the insurance company and applied to reduce future premiums are generally not treated as withdrawals but as premium reductions. See § 72(e)(4)(B).

NOTES

1.   The variations in the tax treatment of the financial instruments dealt with in this chapter is problematic from a policy point of view. Many commentators take the view that the owner of an annuity or insurance policy should be taxed on the inside build-up, on the ground that these vehicles are essentially savings accounts with a power of withdrawal.

2.   Life insurance policies somewhat resemble OID obligations, because the investment is less than the future lump-sum payout. However, in a life insurance contract the date of the future payout is not fixed in advance, and the taxpayer's basis constantly increases with premium payments. Thus, an OID (accrual-at-fixed-rate) approach is not feasible.

3.   An investment that is tax-favored is not necessarily a better investment overall compared to investments that are not tax-favored. Take a conventional annuity, for example, where the inside build-up is not subject to tax as it is earned.

The annuity payments will be set by contract at a sufficiently low level so that the issuing company can expect to make a profit on the difference between its investment return and the investment return built into the contract. Moreover, the rate of return will be further reduced on account of the fact that actuarial data show that persons who buy annuities tend to outlive their life expectancies. Life insurance policies typically impose a "load," which is basically a charge to cover the company's selling expenses. Finally, the issuing company can be expected to capture part of its customers' tax benefits for itself by offering a lower rate of inside build-up (thereby increasing its profit).

PROBLEMS

1.   On his 65th birthday, George purchased a single-premium annuity contract for $100K. The contract provides for 15 annual payments of $12K to George, commencing on the first anniversary of the purchase. What tax result to George in each year of the contract? What result if George dies the day before his 75th birthday?

2.   The Rock Insurance Corp. issues a policy to Olga. As of the beginning of the current taxable year, Olga has paid net premiums totaling $50K, and the cash surrender value of the policy is $60K.

(a) During the year, the premium payment is $2K, the cash surrender value increases by $5K, the cost of life insurance protection is $1K, and Olga makes no withdrawals. State the tax result to Olga if (in the alternative):

(1) the policy is *not* a "life insurance contract" as defined in § 7702,

(2) the policy is a "modified endowment contract" as defined in § 7702A,

(3) the policy is a "life insurance contract" as defined in § 7702.

(b) Same facts and questions as (a), except that Olga withdraws $16K on December 31 of the current year.

Chapter 28

DEPRECIATION

This chapter deals with assets, such as equipment, buildings, and intangibles that that are dedicated to income production but do not produce predetermined cash returns. Suppose, for example, Cliff pays $10K for a widget-making machine. Whether widget sales revenues will restore his $10K investment to Cliff will be dictated by the dynamics of the widget market, not by any internal attribute of the machine. In more abstract terms, the widget machine does not have an "internal" capital-recovery scheme, as do those financial instruments whose contractual terms impose a definite payment schedule. In the case of assets like the widget machine, the tax system provides an external capital-recovery system in the form of depreciation for business and investment assets that are used up in helping to produce income.

A. NORMATIVE DEPRECIATION UNDER AN INCOME TAX

A mark-to-market system in which depreciation equals the annual decline in the fair market value (FMV) of an asset conflicts with the realization principle, and is unadministrable. Accordingly, this section assumes the task of attempting to accommodate the idea of tax depreciation to the realization principle (under an ability-to-pay income tax). The allowance of depreciation deductions under the income tax does initially appear to conflict with the realization principle, because a series of deductions is allowed prior to a sale, disposition, or other event fixing a loss with finality. However, depreciation deductions under a realization income tax do not purport to be based on the annual decline in value of an asset. Instead, the purported justification for depreciation is based on the view that realization only requires irreversibility or "finality."

1. Depreciation under the "Finality" View of Realization

The simplest way of grasping the "realized depreciation" idea is to view Cliff's machine as being constituted by the number of temporal segments equal to its anticipated useful life (which will be stipulated to be equal to 60 months). Accordingly, each month of use can be viewed as a using up of 1/60th of the asset. It follows that an appropriate portion of the basis should be deducted to reflect the month's realized partial loss. (The number of segments can be keyed to any time period, such as years, months, or days, but we will use months, because that time unit best accords with current rules.)

What is the "appropriate amount" of (monthly) depreciation is another issue. One could simply view each passing month as marking a loss of 1/60th of the basis of the machine. Or, one could impose a financial model that views a machine as producing a fixed yield. If the yield is assumed to be steady over 60 months (with no realizable salvage value at the end),[1] the depreciation schedule would resemble that suggested by Tables 4-6 in the preceding chapter (the declining balance method).[2] The analysis would be modified if one made different assumptions about future yields, such as (a) an obtainable salvage value at the end of 60 months or (b) a decreasing *net* yield (perhaps attributable to increasing repairs). A "correct" system for determining depreciation deductions under this approach would require accurate estimates of the useful lives and rates of return for millions of assets. Since that would be immensely burdensome, Congress has instead created a handful of standard-assumption scenarios that are subject to mechanical depreciation formulaes.

In any event, depreciation, under a tax system with a "finality" realization principle, is the method by which partial losses are deemed sustained (realized) *solely due to the passage of time*. Thus, depreciation is necessarily a function of useful life, and the other factors that affect an asset's FMV from time to time (such variable discount rates and estimates of future net yield) are ignored. It follows that assets *without* a finite useful life should not be depreciable at all, because no irretrievable losses can occur through use of the asset. At the same time, it is possible (under the finality theory of realized partial loss) for the FMV of property to actually *appreciate* at the same time that the property *depreciates for tax purposes*.

2. Depreciation under the "Liquidity" View of Realization

Depreciation under the income tax has been around for so long that it is considered sacrosanct, but the concept of depreciation under a realization income tax can be criticized along the lines sketched below.

Depreciation has long been a feature of trust accounting, where it prevents premature dissipation of trust principal,[3] and of business accounting, where it shows the age of income-producing assets (and the need to replace them), but neither of these rationales are relevant to a realization income tax. Another business-accounting rationale, namely, to match costs against the income they produce, is also not relevant for a tax system based on the annual accounting

---

[1] Salvage value is the estimated realizable value at the end of the useful life. Conceptually, this amount is not lost by reason of use, and should not be depreciated. It is possible for an asset to have a salvage value of zero, or even a negative number (representing the estimated cost of disposing of the asset).

[2] To illustrate, assume that Calvin pays $300K in Year 1 for a widget-making machine, having an expected useful life of three years (after which it will have no "salvage value") and generating a net return (after depreciation) of 10% (which comes to $120,634 annually). The proper depreciation for Years 1-3 would be: Year 1, $90,634; Year 2, $99,698; and Year 3, $ 109,668. A quick look at Tables 4-6 in Chapter 27 shows that Calvin's depreciation deductions would be identical, in timing and amount, to Barb's recovery of loan principal. This declining balance method of depreciation is sometimes referred to as Samuelson depreciation. Samuelson depreciation is said to be neutral (not causing economic distortions).

[3] Assume a trust, income to B for life, remainder to C, which is funded entirely by commercial real estate. The effect of depreciation in trust accounting is to decrease the net income payable to B, and to create a cash reserve that can be used to replace the building, thereby maintaining the value of C's remainder interest.

principle, which requires gross income and deduction items to be reckoned in the year realized without regard to possible linkages between or among them. The only plausible tax justification for depreciation is that of "realized loss." The gist of our internal-to-tax critique of tax depreciation is that the realization principle under an ability-to-pay income tax is keyed to transactions, and that the "finality" notion of realization is a "foreign" accrual concept "pulled out of the hat" to justify depreciation, the allowance of which tilts the tax system in favor of understating net income.

As a doctrinal matter, the "finality" notion might be said to derive from the § 165(a) requirement that a loss be "sustained." Depreciation is said to be a series of partial sustained losses, but partial losses are not allowed under § 165(a) in the absence of a physical destruction, loss, or disposition.[4] Thus, a partial loss is not allowed on account of re-zoning or a change in law that makes property permanently less valuable.[5] In short, "finality" is only a necessary (as opposed to sufficient) condition to realization. It cannot seriously be maintained that depreciation would be allowed under § 165 standing alone. A separate statutory provision (§ 167) is required.

Conceptually, there is no justification, under a realization income tax, for isolating losses due solely to the passage of time from other causes of changes in the FMV of an asset. Stated differently, realization under an ability-to-pay income tax doesn't allow any recognition of mere changes in FMV, regardless of "cause," including the passage of time. Moreover, useful life itself can change over time. For example, an asset's useful life might be extended indefinitely by repairs and modifications. Also, the concept of a fixed useful life, on which the concept of "finality depreciation" depends, is viewed ex ante (as are accrual concepts generally), whereas the concept of realization is always ex post.

The whole concept of discounting to present value presupposes reasonable certainty of fixed dollar amounts payable at fixed future dates (an "internal" rate of return). No internal rate of return exists for a business asset such as a machine. It is just one factor of production contributing to the production of revenue, and that revenue stream for the activity as a whole is unpredictable and potentially of infinite (or at least indefinite) duration. Depreciation, on the other hand, is allowed for any wasting asset, even though the asset does not itself yield future cash receipts, and even though nothing that might determine the FMV of the asset is fixed. No "segments" of the asset are being disposed of (as cash is collected) as is the case with a debt obligation or annuity.

That there is no general income tax principle of realization of passage-of-time changes in value is evidenced by the fact that depreciation is virtually unique. The tax system fails to tax *gains* attributable to the passage of time, except in the case of original issue discount (OID), which also follows accrual concepts and is mandated by statute. Even in the case of OID, current (i.e., accrual) taxation thereof is limited to certain cases involving fixed future payments at specified

---

[4] See *Pulvers v. Comm'r*, 48 T.C. 245 (1967), *aff'd*, 407 F.2d 838 (9th Cir. 1969); *Citizens Bank v. Comm'r*, 252 F.2d 425 (1st Cir. 1957).

[5] See *Lakewood Associates v. Comm'r*, 109 T.C. 450 (1997).

future dates. Internal consistency would require extension of OID income accruals to all rights to future cash, such as (for example) the inside build-up of life insurance and annuity contracts.

"Finality" is the same concept that accrual taxation is based on. Accrual taxation causes a present tax reckoning of a future event on account of the fixing of a right or obligation to receive or pay a determinable future amount. Depreciation doesn't even require an obligation, but only a prediction, namely, that the asset will be worthless after a period that can be reasonably estimated. These predictions are invariably based on statistics. As indicated in Chapter 23.C, predictions (based on statistics) are not a sufficient basis for realization even under tax accrual doctrine. In the operational sense, there are no realized losses until the asset is disposed of. Until then, the asset continues to be fully usable.

The foregoing critique of tax depreciation is essentially made from an internal-to-tax perspective. External-to-tax norms derived from economics would take a different view, although consistent application of economic norms would require changes of tax rules on the income side as well. For example, instead of imputing an internal rate of return to a discrete assets (such as business machines), it would make more economic sense to impute an economic return to a business activity or a business firm as a whole. Such a tax would bear little resemblance to an "income tax" as that term in generally understood.

3. Cost Recovery under the Code as a Tax Expenditure

Of course, depreciation is entrenched in the tax system, and there is no chance that it will be abolished in the context of an income tax system. If anything, the system is moving in the opposite direction towards that of a consumption tax, where all business and investment purchases are expensed. Actually, under current law, investors can obtain *even better* tax treatment for investments in depreciable property than would occur under a cash flow consumption tax in the case where expensed investments are made with borrowed money (a common practice). To take an extreme example, if Cliff were to borrow $10K to buy a business asset for $10K that is expensed, Cliff would show a tax loss of $10K despite a current economic wash.

Specifically, the cost recovery system for nonfinancial assets provided by Congress allows larger depreciation deductions in earlier years than would be obtained under any plausible formula based on "sustained" losses due to the passage of time. This "larger and sooner" approach (called "accelerated" depreciation) is accomplished through all or some of the following: (1) allowing some capital expenditures (in the case of certain business tangible personal property) to be "expensed" (deducted entirely in the year of purchase),[6] (2) disregarding "salvage value" (thereby increasing the depreciable amount),[7] (3)

---

[6] The following expensing provisions have been mentioned in previous chapters: § 174 (scientific or technical research and experimentation costs), § 179 (costs of business tangible personal property), and § 263(c) (intangible drilling and development costs).

[7] Depreciation for business accounting is based on cost less estimated realizable salvage value, which is an end-of-the-line cash receipt, and is not "lost" with the passage of time.

positing useful lives shorter than actual average useful lives (especially in the case of tangible personal property), and (4) creating depreciation formulas that provide a down-sloping or level basis recovery. The effect of accelerated basis recovery is a tax subsidy for the purchase of depreciable assets (especially business equipment), which constitutes a tax expenditure.

B.   WHAT IS DEPRECIABLE?

This section considers the threshold doctrinal issue of which assets are eligible for depreciation under current law. Such justification as exists for depreciation in the first place requires that the asset in question have a finite useful life. Thus, land, stock in a corporation (as well as analogous ownership interests in partnerships and LLCs), and any other asset with an indefinite (or at least unknowable) useful life at the time of acquisition should not be depreciable. What does positive law say about this issue?

Although the mechanics of computing depreciation and amortization are found mostly in §§ 168 and 197, § 167(a) is the provision that actually authorizes depreciation deductions (i.e., which contains the words "there shall be allowed as a depreciation deduction"). To be depreciable under § 167(a), *two* requirements must be satisfied: (1) the property must be used in a trade or business or held for the production of income, *and* (2) the property must be subject to "exhaustion, wear and tear (including . . . obsolescence)." What does the "wear-and-tear" requirement mean? Prior to the case decided below, that venerable language had always been interpreted to mean that only "wasting" assets, i.e., assets with an ascertainable useful life at the time of acquisition, could be depreciated. See Reg. § 1.167(a)-1(a) and (b). Even though that language has not been amended since its 1954 enactment, the Tax Court majority below held that the language took on a new meaning in 1981.

SIMON v. COMMISSIONER
United States Tax Court
103 T.C. 247 (1994) (reviewed)
aff'd, 68 F.3d 41 (2d Cir. 1995)

Laro, Judge:

[Petitioners, Richard and Fiona Simon, are professional violinists who play in the first violin section of the New York Philharmonic Orchestra. Both of them maintained two careers, one as a full-time player with the Philharmonic and a second as a soloist, chamber music player, and teacher.] The two violin bows in issue were made in the 19th century by Francois Xavier Tourte (1747-1835). Francois Tourte is considered the premier violin bow maker. On November 13, 1985, petitioners purchased Bow 1 for $30,000. On December 3, 1985, petitioners purchased Bow 2 for $21,500. On their 1989 Form 1041, petitioners claimed depreciation deductions in accordance with the appropriate statutory provisions that applied to 5-year property. Respondent disallowed petitioners' depreciation deduction in full.

Playing with a bow adversely affects the bow's condition. In addition, perspiration from a player's hands enters the wood of a bow and ultimately destroys the bow's utility for playing. Frequent use of a violin bow will cause it to be "played out," meaning that the wood loses its ability to vibrate and produce quality sound from the instrument. The Tourte bows were purchased by petitioners, and were playable by them during the year in issue, only because the Tourte bows were relatively unused prior to petitioners' purchase of them; the Tourte bows had been preserved in pristine condition in collections. At the time of trial, the condition of the Tourte bows had deteriorated since their purchase.

As the [Supreme] Court observed in 1927: "The theory underlying this allowance for depreciation is that by using up the plant, a gradual sale is made of it." *U.S. v. Ludey*, 274 U.S. 295, 301 (1927). Prior to the Economic Recovery Tax Act of 1981 (ERTA), personal property was depreciated pursuant to § 167. The regulations expanded on the text of § 167 by providing that personal property was only depreciable if the taxpayer established the useful life of the property. See § 1.167(a)-1(a) and (b). With respect to the pre-ERTA requirement of useful life, the Commissioner [took] the position that a taxpayer generally could not deduct depreciation on expensive works of art and curios that he purchased as office furniture. *Rev. Rul. 68-232*, 1968-1 C.B. 79.

In enacting ERTA, the Congress believed that the determination of useful lives was "complex" and "inherently uncertain," and "frequently [resulted] in unproductive disagreements between taxpayers and the IRS." S. Rept. 97-144, at 47 (1981), 1981-2 C.B. 412, 425. Accordingly, the Congress decided that a new capital cost recovery system would have to be structured which, among other things, lessened the importance of the concept of useful life for depreciation purposes. This new system [ACRS] was prescribed in § 168, [which] minimized the importance of useful life by: (1) reducing the number of periods of years over which a taxpayer could depreciate property from the multitudinous far-reaching periods of time listed for the [pre-1981] system to the four short periods of time listed in ERTA and (2) basing depreciation on an arbitrary statutory period of years that was unrelated to, and shorter than, an asset's estimated useful life.

We agree with petitioners that they may depreciate the Tourte bows under ACRS. Inasmuch as § 168(a) allows a taxpayer to deduct depreciation with respect to "recovery property," petitioners may deduct depreciation on the Tourte bows if the bows fall within the meaning of that term. The term "recovery property" is defined broadly under ERTA to mean tangible property of a character subject to the allowance for depreciation and placed in service after 1980. § 168(c)(1). The term "of a character subject to the allowance for depreciation" is undefined. We believe that Congress used the term "depreciation" in § 168(c)(1) to refer to the "exhaustion, wear and tear . . ." that is contained in § 167(a).

We are convinced that petitioners' frequent use of the Tourte bows subjected them to substantial wear and tear during the year in issue. Petitioners actively played their violins using the Tourte bows, and this active use resulted in substantial wear and tear to the bows.[8]

---

[8] [11] In this regard, we do not believe that the Tourte bows are so-called [nondepreciable] works of art. We define a "work of art" as a passive object, such as a painting, sculpture, or carving, that is

Section 168 does not support the proposition that a taxpayer may not depreciate a business asset due to its age, or due to the fact that the asset may have appreciated in value over time. *Noyce v. Comm'r*, 97 T.C. 670 (1991) (taxpayer allowed to deduct depreciation under § 168 on an airplane that had appreciated in economic value). Respondent incorrectly mixes two well-established, independent concepts of tax accounting, namely, accounting for the physical depreciation of an asset and accounting for changes in the asset's value on account of price fluctuations in the market.

We also reject respondent's contention that the Tourte bows are nondepreciable because they have value as collectibles independent of their use in playing musical instruments, and that this value prolongs the Tourte bows' useful life forever. [But] the same argument concerning a separate, nonbusiness value can be made of many other assets. Such types of assets could include, for example, automobiles, patented property, highly sophisticated machinery, and real property. For the Court to delve into the determination of whether a particular asset has a separate, nonbusiness value would make the concept of depreciation a subjective issue and would be contrary to the Congress's intent to simplify the concept and computation of depreciation.

Reviewed by the Court. PARKER, SWIFT, WRIGHT, PARR, WELLS, RUWE, and COLVIN, JJ., agree with this majority opinion.

RUWE, J. concurring:

Everyone seems to favor tax simplification until the simplified law is actually applied to a real set of facts and produces a less-than-perfect result. I can understand the dissenters' concern that § 168 might allow an asset to be written off over a period much shorter than its actual useful life and that the entire cost might be deducted despite the fact that there might be no actual economic decrease in value. However, that is the price of the tax simplification implicit in § 168.

PARKER, COHEN, SWIFT, WRIGHT, PARR, WELLS, and BEGHE, JJ., agree with this concurring opinion.

[Concurring opinion of BEGHE, J., omitted.]

HAMBLEN, C.J., dissenting:

The antique violin bows are treasured "works of art" that for 71 years the Internal Revenue Service has treated, with congressional acquiescence, as nondepreciable property because as instruments and collectibles they have an indeterminable useful life. The majority opinion concludes, as a matter of law, that if a taxpayer uses in his trade or business tangible personal property which suffers

---

displayed for admiration of its aesthetic qualities. The Tourte bows, by contrast, functioned actively, regularly, and routinely to produce income in petitioners' trade or business.

some wear and tear, irrespective of whether the wear and tear can be restored by ordinary maintenance, irrespective of whether it has a determinable useful life, and irrespective of whether it declines in value, the taxpayer is entitled to depreciate the property under ACRS (§ 168) by treating it as falling within one of the five broad classes of "recovery property." I cannot agree. That conclusion contradicts the basic underpinnings of the depreciation allowance and the holdings of this Court and other courts.

It is true that § 168 represents a restructuring of the concept of depreciation deductions and that Congress has deemphasized the concept of useful life and abandoned the concept of salvage value. But Congress did not release the concept of depreciation from the moorings of useful life. The question of whether a tangible asset used in a trade or business is subject to wear and tear is of course a starting point for determining whether an asset is depreciable. But it is not the final determinant. The premise underlying the depreciation allowance is that wear and tear or obsolescence causes a corresponding reduction in the value of an asset and diminishes its useful life.

The Blue Book states that ACRS "does not change the determination under prior law as to whether property is depreciable or nondepreciable." Staff of Joint Comm. on Taxation, General Explanation of the Economic Recovery Tax Act of 1981, at 77 (1981). The majority opinion essentially ignores these statements. Depreciation is defined as a loss in the value of property over the time the property is being used. In 1985, Bow 1 was purchased for $30,000 and appraised at $35,000; Bow 2 was purchased for $21,500 and appraised at $25,000. Petitioners' costs were simply not used up over the claimed 5-year period. Indeed, Richard Simon could not say how long the bows would be usable. Even if used in a trade or business, a "work of art" retains its character as a work of art because it does not have a determinable useful life and generally does not decline in value over a predictable period. In cases of this kind it seems that our role should begin and end with assuring that the Commissioner's authority to implement the congressional mandate has been exercised in a reasonable manner.

The concept of matching income and expenses would indicate that when the income-producing asset retains its value, the taxpayer has not expended the purchase price, but rather has merely converted it from cash to an asset of equal value. Depreciation, in a sense, departs from realization principles, allowing a taxpayer to recognize a loss in the value of an asset without the requirement of disposition. But depreciation assumes that the asset will be consumed and decline in value over a predictable period of time. When an asset increases in value, as here, there is no loss or waste to match against income, a circumstance which, to say the least, stands the concept of matching revenue and cost on its head.

There are some intermediate and ultimate findings of fact and conclusions that concern me because they appear to be incorrect or unsupported by the record. The "wear and tear" concept relates to the physical life of tangible property. The physical life must be lessened by wear and tear that cannot be corrected by regular maintenance. See *Lindheimer v. Illinois Bell Tel. Co.*, 292 U.S. 151, 167 (1934) (depreciation represents "the loss, not restored by current maintenance, which is due to all the factors causing the ultimate retirement of the property. These factors embrace wear and tear, decay, inadequacy, and obsolescence.") The majority opinion finds that the "petitioners' frequent use of the Tourte bows subjected them to substantial wear and tear during the year in issue." While there is obviously some degree of wear and tear to any wood instrument or bow, I doubt whether these particular bows suffered "substantial" wear and tear. Richard Simon, whose testimony was somewhat inconsistent, said the bows were kept in "perfect condition," and that the bows showed "a very minuscule amount of wear." Obviously the bows were in excellent condition at the time of trial when Judge Laro permitted both petitioners to play their violins with the two Tourte bows in a courtroom demonstration. That occurred 8 years after they were first used by petitioners. Even assuming the bows may eventually wear out, the unanswered question is how long this would take. They have lasted 175 years so far and may be good for another 175 years, if properly maintained. If ever they do cease to be usable, they may well continue to have independent value as collectibles.

CHABOT, JACOBS, WHALEN, AND HALPERN, JJ., agree with this dissent.

[Dissenting opinions of GERBER AND HALPERN, JJ, omitted.]

In accord with *Simon* is *Liddle v. Comm'r*, 103 T.C. 285 (1994), *aff'd*, 65 F.3d 329 (3d Cir. 1995). The IRS has indicated that it does not acquiesce in *Simon* and *Liddle* and will continue to litigate the issue. See 1996-2 C.B. 2.

C.   WHO TAKES DEPRECIATION?

The short answer is that the owner of the depreciable property is the person who can take depreciation deductions on his, her, or its investment. However, the issue of tax ownership (or investment) in a commercial setting[9] is often unclear where X transfers the use and/or possession of property to Y in return *for a stream of periodic payments*. Without more information, this type of transaction might be classifiable as either (1) a deferred-payment "sale" or (2) a lease (or license). Nevertheless, the transaction *must* be categorized as either a sale or lease (or license) not only because of the issue of tax ownership but also because the tax treatment of (installment) sales differs from that for leases and licenses in important respects. Recall from Chapter 23, that a deferred-payment sale is treated for income tax purposes as occurring in the year of sale, but gain from such a sale may be reportable under the § 453 installment method or possibly (if the sale involves contingent payments) under the open-transaction method. The "buyer," as the new tax owner, immediately acquires a *Crane* basis (or, in a contingent-payment situation, the ability to deduct each payment). The installment obligation is a debt obligation, involving principal and (stated or imputed) interest. On the other hand, in a lease or license scenario, the lessor or licensor of the property must include "rents" or "royalties" as ordinary gross income, but at the same time can (as owner of the property and its gross income) take appropriate depreciation or amortization

---

[9] Tax ownership in a family setting is dealt with in Chapter 17.

deductions. Moreover, a business or investment lessee or licensee can deduct the entire amount of rental and royalty payments and can amortize the cost of any investments made in acquiring the lease or license itself plus improvements made to the property. See §§ 168(i)(8), 178.

One should not be surprised by now to learn that whether a transaction is categorized as a "sale," on the one hand, or a "lease" (or license), on the other, is not dictated by the labels affixed by the parties to the transaction. For purposes of the income tax, the *substance* of a transaction must be examined to determine whether it is *really* a sale or a lease (or license). It happens that the tax rules may vary according to the transactional context.

1. Seller-Financed Sale vs. Lease of Tangible Personal Property

What distinguishes most tangible personal property from real property is the finite and relatively short useful life of the former. In this context, a "lease" in form can be an "installment sale" in substance where the lease term is roughly the same as (or greater than) the useful life of the property, because in that case the "lessor" gets nothing of significant value back at the end of the lease. Similarly, an "installment sale" in form can be a "lease" in substance if it is probable that the "seller" will end up with the property after the term of the "installment payments" (assuming the payments are actually made). The tax system, however, cannot wait to see who actually ends up with the property after the series of payments, or after the transferor re-takes the property if the transferee defaults.[10] Since the tax system needs to know who is the property's "tax owner" during the payment period, the issue of sale vs. lease must be resolved "up front," i.e., at the time the transaction is initially executed. Moreover, the issue of tax ownership is an all-or-nothing one.

In the area of tangible personal property (usually equipment) leases, the courts are quite willing to apply substance-over-form principles in characterizing a transfer of tangible personal property as a deferred-payment sale or as a lease. In this context, deferred-payment-sale characterization is not necessarily advantageous, because sales of inventory produce ordinary gain and are not eligible for the § 453 installment method.

For example, in *Starr's Estate v. Comm'r*, 274 F.2d 294 (9th Cir. 1959), the taxpayer had a fire sprinkling system installed in his manufacturing plant pursuant to an agreement captioned "Lease Form of Contract." Under the agreement, the sprinkler system was leased to the taxpayer for a five-year period with aggregate rentals that exceeded the system's fair market value. The taxpayer-lessee had the option to renew the lease for an additional five years at a $32-per-year rental, which was actually an inspection fee. If the taxpayer did not renew, the lease permitted the lessor to remove the system from the taxpayer's building, but the salvage value of the system's components would be insignificant, and the lessor had

---

[10] The sale/lease issue is of such importance with respect to tangible personal property that Article 2A of the Uniform Commercial Code is devoted to it. However, the issue is unlikely to arise in commercial law unless a party breaches the contract.

waived this right in similar situations. The lease was silent regarding the rights of the parties at the end of the renewal period. The court held that the lease was actually a sale by the purported lessor to the purported lessee, and that the excess of the purported rental payments over the system's fair market value was probably a finance charge. The opinion stated:

> [W]here the foreordained practical effect of the rent is to produce title eventually, the rental agreement can be treated as a sale. In this case, we do have the troublesome circumstance that the contract does not by its terms ever pass title to the system to the "lessee." Most sprinkler systems have to be tailor-made for a specific piece of property and, if removal is required, the salvageable value is negligible. Also, it stretches credulity to believe that the "lessor" ever intended to or would "come after" the system. And the "lessee" would be an exceedingly careless businessman who would enter into such contract with the practical possibility that the "lessor" would reclaim the installation. He could have believed only that he was getting the system for the rental money.

The meaningful-reversion approach is followed by the IRS and the courts. See generally *Rev. Proc. 2001-28*, 2001-1 C.B. 1156 (IRS guidelines requiring as a condition for obtaining a ruling, inter alia, that the value at the end of lease to be equal to at least 20% of cost). See, e.g., *In re Comdisco, Inc.*, 434 F.3d 963 (7th Cir. 2006); *Sun Oil Co. v. Comm'r*, 562 F.2d 258 (3d Cir. 1977).

2. Seller-Financed Sale vs. Lease of Real Property

In the typical seller-financed (deferred-payment) sale of real property, the buyer undertakes to pay interest and principal according to a fixed-payment schedule. Of course, if the buyer defaults, the seller can foreclose and re-acquire the property, which is typically used as security for the unpaid principal and interest. Moreover, if the buyer's obligation is recourse, the seller has the right to pursue the buyer for any deficiency. Here "sale" treatment is often desired by the seller, who will likely end up with capital (or § 1231) gain and possible use of the installment method.

Two Supreme Court decisions are worth mentioning in this area. In *Comm'r v. Brown*, 380 U.S. 563 (1965) (which is known as the *Clay Brown* case to tax aficionados), the issue was whether the purported bootstrap sale involved a true and complete sale. A bootstrap sale is one in which a definite purchase price is fixed in amount but the purchase price is to be paid out of future income earned by the sold property (instead of under a fixed payment schedule).

Clay Brown and other individuals owned a business. In 1952, they agreed to sell the business to a charity (the Institute) for $1.3M, payable $5K down from the assets of the business and the balance within 10 years from 72% of the net earnings of the assets, with no stated interest. The Institute had no obligation to pay this debt except from the net earnings of the sold assets, and the debt was secured by mortgages of the assets. The business was initially managed for the Institute by a corporation run by Clay Brown and his associates, but the business floundered due to a rapidly declining lumber market, and the Brown group had left by the end of 1954. In 1957, the business failed, and the sellers, instead of repossessing the properties under the mortgages, arranged for the Institute to sell the properties, keep 10% of the sale proceeds, and pay the remaining 90% to Brown and his associates. The government viewed the transaction as an attempt to convert ordinary business income into capital gain. In holding that a sale had taken place, the majority opinion of Justice White stated:

> The transaction was a sale under local law. The Institute acquired title to the [assets of the business] in return for its promise to pay over money from the operating profits of the company. If the stipulated price was paid, the Brown family would forever lose all rights to the income and properties of the company. Prior to the transfer, respondents had access to all of the income of the company; after the transfer, 28% of the income remained with the Institute. Respondents had no interest in the Institute. Any rights to control the management were limited to the management contract between Clay Brown and [the Institute], which was relinquished in 1954.

> The Commissioner claims that the transaction did not have the substance of a sale. His argument is that since the Institute invested nothing, assumed no independent liability for the purchase price, and promised only to pay over a percentage of the earnings of the company, the entire risk of the transaction remained on the sellers. [The Commissioner's argument is essentially] that because business earnings are usually taxable as ordinary income, they are subject to the same tax when paid over as the purchase price of property. This argument has rationality, but it places an unwarranted construction on the term "sale," is contrary to the policy of the capital gains provisions of the Code, and has no support in the cases. We reject it.

> A "sale" is a common event in the non-tax world; and since it is used in the Code without limiting definition and without legislative history indicating a contrary result, its common and ordinary meaning should at least be persuasive of its meaning as used in the Code.

> To require a sale for tax purposes to be to a financially responsible buyer who undertakes to pay the purchase price from sources other than the earnings of the assets sold or to make a substantial down payment seems to us at odds with commercial practice and common understanding of what constitutes a sale. A wide variety of tax results hinge on the occurrence of a "sale." To accept the Commissioner's definition of sale would have ramifications which we are not prepared to visit upon taxpayers, absent congressional guidance in this direction.

The dissenting opinion of Justice Goldberg stated:

> In numerous cases this Court has refused to transfer the incidents of taxation along with a transfer of legal title when the transferor retains considerable control over the income-producing asset transferred. See, e.g., *Helvering v. Clifford*, 309 U.S. 331 (1940). Control of the business did not, in fact, shift here.

> I do not believe that Congress intended this recurrent receipt of business income to be taxed at capital gains rates merely because the

business was to be transferred to a tax-exempt entity at some future date. [The holding of the majority will sanction] a tax-avoidance scheme under which the holder of any income-producing asset "sells" his asset for a promise to pay him the income for a period of years. The buyer would do nothing whatsoever; the seller would be delighted to lose his asset after 30 years in return in return for capital gains treatment of all income earned during that period.

The Court justifies its result in the name of conceptual purity. Though turning consequences on form alone might produce greater certainty of the tax results of any transaction, this stability exacts as its price the certainty that tax evasion will be produced.

In the second Supreme Court case of note, *Frank Lyon Co. v. U.S.*, 435 U.S. 561 (1978), Worthen Bank wanted to build an office building for its own use in Little Rock, Arkansas,, but applicable bank regulations prohibited direct ownership. Accordingly, Worthen Bank arranged for Frank Lyon Co., a home furnishings dealer, to build and own the building on ground rented from Worthen Bank, with funds borrowed by Frank Lyon Co. from an outside lender, and to lease the building to Worthen Bank for a long term, with Worthen Bank's "rental" obligation exactly covering Frank Lyon Co.'s mortgage payments. Worthen Bank had options to purchase the property at various times during the first 25 years of the building lease at a very low fixed price relative to even the estimated salvage value of the building. At the end of Worthen Bank's building lease, Frank Lyon Co. was free to rent it to the highest bidder for 10 years while paying nominal ground rent to Worthen Bank. When this 10-year rental period ended, the ground lease would terminate, and ownership of the building would pass to Worthen Bank, at which time the building would be approximately 74 years old.

The government argued that Frank Lyon Co. was not the true owner-lessor and hence could not take depreciation deductions on the building, but the Supreme Court held otherwise. While the Court stated so many factors in support of its decision that Frank Lyon Co. was the tax owner of the building that it is difficult, if not impossible, to discern a clear rationale or test from the opinion, it seems that two of the more important factors to the Court were that (1) the transaction had a business purpose (apart from saving taxes) and (2) an independent third party (the outside lender) was involved.

Both *Brown* and *Frank Lyon* lack any conceptual framework whatsoever. Such a framework might have been provided by heeding the authorities involving equipment leases, discussed above. Following those authorities, the principal issue in distinguishing a lease from a sale in *Frank Lyon* should have been whether Frank Lyon Co. possessed the possible risks and benefits associated with owning real property subject to a long-term lease. Such risks and benefits would not accrue to Frank Lyon Co. unless it had a meaningful reversion in the building following the building's lease term. This reversion would subject Frank Lyon Co. to the risk that the building would be worth less than anticipated or, alternatively, would give Frank Lyon Co. the benefit of any possible appreciation in value (or a slower decline in value than anticipated). However, it appears from the facts that Frank Lyon Co. possessed no meaningful reversion (did not bear the benefits and risks of equity ownership), and should not have been viewed as having "real" ownership for tax purposes. As it turned out, Worthen Bank exercised its earliest option to acquire the building from Frank Lyon Co. in 1981, only three years after the Supreme Court decision and 11 years after the building was occupied by it.

Brown, in contrast, dealt with what was essentially a security interest (a right of repossession on default), which is distinguishable from a reversion following a term interest. Nevertheless, the government's theory was basically that the transaction was a sham, but in this respect the Tax Court found as a fact that it was not, 37 T.C. 461 (1961) (reviewed), and this finding was accepted on appeal. The government might have profited if it had (on appeal) advanced a theory of what it thought the transaction really was (assuming the transaction not to be a sham). To us, the transactions might have been viewed as a lease to the charity, with the charity having a call option to buy the property. . This approach would leave the Clay Brown group as owners who received ordinary rent income.

An owner of *land* subject to even a very long-term lease will possess a meaningful reversion, because land has an infinite life,[11] but the shorter the useful life of the asset, the more problematic is the determination of whether a meaningful reversion exists. A building often has a very long physical life, but physical life is not by itself controlling. In *Frank Lyon*, Worthen Bank had options to purchase the property at various times during the first 25 years of the building lease at a very low fixed price relative to even the estimated salvage value of the building, making exercise of the option a virtual certainty (though the trial court had disagreed with this prediction). Those options should have negated Frank Lyon Co.'s reversion at the end of the building's lease, thus causing Worthen Bank to be treated as a purchaser (instead of as Frank Lyon Co.'s lessee) and causing Frank Lyon Co. to be treated as an installment seller or as a lender financing a purchase. Either characterization would have resulted in Worthen Bank (rather than Frank Lyon Co.) being entitled to depreciate the building. As noted above, Worthen Bank exercised its purchase option at the earliest time permitted by the agreement.

NOTES

1. (a) The Supreme Court appears to be desirous of elevating form over substance in cases involving real property, perhaps thinking that certainty is important with regard to real estate. But certainty over title is not the same as certainty over tax consequences.

(b) The *Frank Lyon* case, decided in 1978, has had little effect on the doctrine pertaining to two-party sales and leases of equipment. Thus, in *Swift Dodge Co. v. Comm'r*, 76 T.C. 547 (1981), the Tax Court relied on *Frank Lyon Co.* to uphold a lease, but was reversed on appeal on the ground that the purported lessor, in substance, had no more than a security interest, 692 F.2d 651 (9th Cir. 1982).

2. (a) Before the sale in *Brown*, the sellers (the Brown group) effectively owned 100% of the business's net profits in perpetuity. But they sold the business for an

---

[11] See *Estate of Simmers v. Comm'r*, 231 F.2d 909 (4th Cir. 1956) (lump-sum payment for 99-year Maryland ground lease held to be rent). The results of this case are overturned by §§ 163(c) and 1055.

amount equal to 72% of the net profits to be received by the Institute, subject to a $1.3M cap, over the next 10 years. This appears foolish at the outset, but the buyer was a tax-exempt entity that would avoid being taxed on the profits of the business, and it is likely that the $1.3 million was somewhat more than the business was really worth. Thus, the combination of (1) such inflated selling price, (2) treating the transaction as a sale entitled to capital gains treatment, and (3) avoiding tax at the ordinary income rate on future net profits would be expected to more than make up for the reduced future net cash flow. Subsequent to *Brown*, Congress enacted § 514, which subjects a charity to tax on unrelated debt-financed income.

(b) Chapter 21.C.1 considers the possibility that a purported deferred-payment sale is a "sham" where the installment obligation is nonrecourse and its face amount so exceeds the value of the property at the time of sale that foreclosure is inevitable from the very beginning. In *Brown*, the government argued that the parties expected default, but the Tax Court held otherwise, and the economics of the deal didn't indicate that default was inevitable.

(c) In *Brown* the buyer's note didn't bear interest, meaning that the sales price (and capital gain amount) was (simply as a matter of arithmetic) overstated. A similar transaction would now be re-cast so as to convert a portion of the selling price into ordinary income interest under §§ 1274 or 483.

3.   Section 1239 converts any capital gain from the sale of depreciable property to certain related persons as ordinary gain. The term "related person" is limited to persons and entities controlled by such persons, and excludes related individuals.

PROBLEMS

1.   Lora Landlord constructs a new rental office building that includes a fire sprinkler system furnished by Vern Vendor. The transaction's terms require Lora to pay the full price of the system in three equal annual installments and give her the option to acquire legal title by paying $1.00 at the end of the three years. Because the sprinkler system is an integral part of the building, § 168 requires it to be depreciated over 39 years. Would it be to Lora's advantage to have the transaction characterized as a lease for tax purposes?

2.   Quality Cars is an accrual-method car dealership that sells the Humm-Bee, a tiny hybrid, which retails for $20K and is often sold on a five-year installment basis. Advise Quality on whether it should inaugurate a Humm-Bee lease program for its customers and on what terms. Assume that a Humm-Bee is 5-year property to business owner-lessors for purposes of § 168. Also, under what circumstances might a lease be especially attractive to a customer?

3.   Sale vs. License of Intangibles

Certain intangibles (such as patents, copyrights, trade secrets, film rights, etc.) are commonly transferred on a contingent-payment basis, because the true value of the property is untested and speculative. Regardless of whether the transaction is a sale or a lease (which in this context is called a "license"), the payments made by the transferee would be periodic and (probably) contingent. Thus, the sale/license distinction cannot be made on the basis of the form of the consideration. The periodic and contingent payments are commonly referred to in the trade as "royalties," although it is probably correct to use this term only when referring to payments under a license.

In a true license, the royalty payments are treated by both parties as rent for income tax purposes. Thus, the licensor has ordinary income on receipt of the royalty payments under the license. If the licensor has a basis in the licensed property, the basis is potentially amortizable by the licensor according to the amortization rules for intangibles (many of which are located in § 197).

A contingent-payment sale can be reported under the open-transaction method, which allows basis recovery against receipts until basis is exhausted. Any subsequent gain is capital (or § 1231) gain if the asset sold was a capital (or § 1231) asset. Since the consideration is contingent, the buyer can have no Crane basis equal to the total debt principal amount, because the total principal amount cannot be known in advance. Instead, each payment is treated by the purchaser as an expense (rather than as a capital expenditure or loan principal repayment), as if the purchaser were a licensee paying royalties.

Early cases involving dispositions of intangibles on a contingent-consideration basis held that the transaction would be treated as a "sale" (as opposed to a license) if the transferor gave up all significant rights in the property (and its use) and did not retain significant powers with respect to the property. But, as with tangible property sales, a retained "security interest" or its equivalent would not negate the existence of a sale. Thus, at a minimum, the transferor desiring "sale" treatment would have to surrender its rights (other than any bona fide security interest) *for the full legal duration of the intangible.* Moreover, the transferee would have to acquire the *exclusive* right to the intangible.

More problematic was the situation where the intangible was carved up in a territorial (as opposed to temporal) manner. For example, the owner of a book copyright might transfer the exclusive right to use it (i.e., sell the book) in Europe but retain the right to use the copyright in the United States. The courts eventually came to treat these transactions as sales, but litigation was extensive.

Congress has codified (and modified) the above common law approach in two important areas. Section 1235 deals with transfers of patents and related rights, and § 1253 pertains to transfers of trademarks, trade names, and franchises. These provisions also affect the issue of the "character" (as capital or ordinary) of any gain or loss upon a "sale." The case below discusses the history and application of § 1235.

FAWICK v. COMMISSIONER
United States Court of Appeals, Sixth Circuit
436 F.2d 655 (1971)

Before PHILLIPS, CHIEF JUDGE, and WEICK and McCREE, CIRCUIT JUDGES.

PHILLIPS, CHIEF JUDGE.

Mr. Fawick has been an inventor since sometime before 1926 and has been issued some 200 patents during his lifetime. His normal practice has been to exploit his inventions on his own rather than to license others to develop and market them. Prior to 1928 the taxpayer was engaged in the business of manufacturing clutches. [Later] he began to conceive the idea of a flexible brake, coupling and clutch with certain of the moving parts made of rubber. Patent applications were filed on this invention and on February 23, 1937, the taxpayer entered into a license agreement with the Falk Corporation. The agreement granted to Falk:

(1) An exclusive license for the flexible couplings,

(2) An exclusive license for driving clutches but limited to marine service only, and

(3) A non-exclusive license for the complete geared-power transmission units.

In 1938 the taxpayer organized Fawick Corporation to engage in the manufacture and sale of these clutches for other than marine use. He assigned to Fawick Corporation his rights in the patents, excluding the rights previously assigned to Falk Corporation in the above-quoted agreement and also excluding certain rights which he reserved to himself.

The determinative issue on this appeal is whether a patent license containing a field-of-use restriction is a transfer of "property consisting of all substantial rights to a patent" within the meaning of § 1235. A resolution of the issue requires a consideration of the state of the law as it existed prior to the enactment of [§ 1235 in] 1954. Prior to 1954 the only way an inventor could get capital gain treatment for income received from exploitation of a patent was by qualifying under the sections corresponding to the present §§ 1221 and 1222. To qualify, the inventor must have been an "amateur" rather than a "professional." Otherwise, the sale would have been of property held primarily for sale in the ordinary course of his business. As a further qualification, it was the Commissioner's position [accepted by some, but not all, courts] that the capital gain provisions of the Code were designed to lessen the tax burden [only] on persons selling property for a gain produced over a period of years but realized in a single tax year, [but] not over a period of several years as in the usual patent royalty situation.

The report of the Senate Finance Committee contained the following:

To obviate the uncertainty caused by [the Service's position] and to provide an incentive to inventors to contribute to the welfare of the Nation, your committee intends to give statutory assurance to certain patent holders that the sale of a patent (whether as an "assignment" or "exclusive license") shall not be deemed not to constitute a "sale or exchange" for tax purposes solely on account of the mode of payment.

The emphasis of the section, as we read it, is on the tax consequence of the "sale of a patent" where the consideration is in the form of contingent royalty payments. The "incentive to inventors to contribute to the welfare of the Nation" resulted when capital gain treatment was provided under § 1235 for professional as well as amateur inventors otherwise qualifying under the statute. Thus, the two-fold purpose of the section does not point to the interpretation urged by the taxpayer, *viz.*: that the section was designed to permit capital gain treatment of income from transfers having a field-of-use restriction.

The reason for § 1235 is that even when patents are sold, the normal transaction involves periodic payments of the sale price "contingent on the productivity, use or disposition of the property transferred." This form of payment is so much like rental payments in the commonplace transactions involving other capital assets that Congress found it necessary to declare specifically that such transfers are entitled to capital gain treatment irrespective of the mode of payment.

Apparently Congress, in drafting § 1235, chose the phrase "transfer . . . of . . . all substantial rights to a patent" rather than "sale of a patent," since, due to the special character of a patent, the transferor must maintain some control over the property in order to get his maximum sale price from the transferee. Hence, Congress required only that the holder transfer "all substantial rights" to a patent rather than make a complete divestiture of title to the property. The report of the Senate Finance Committee makes it clear, however, that the preferred treatment should be limited to transfers in the nature of a sale, in the sense that the transferor must release to the transferee all substantial rights evidenced by the patent, and that interpretation should prevail regardless of whether the transaction is termed an "assignment" or an "exclusive license":

> The word "title" is not employed because the retention of bare legal title in a transaction involving an exclusive license may not represent the retention of a substantial right in the patent property by the transferor. Furthermore, retention by the transferor of rights in the property which are not of the nature of rights evidenced by the patent and which are not inconsistent with the passage of ownership, such as a security interest (*e.g.*, a vendor's lien) or a reservation in the nature of a condition subsequent (*e.g.*, a forfeiture on account of nonperformance) are not to be considered as such a retention as will defeat the applicability of this section. On the other hand, a transfer terminable at will by the transferor would not qualify.

It is our opinion that the phrase "all substantial rights to a patent" is a reference to the monopoly right for which the patent stands. The monopoly right granted by the patent is the right to exclude others from making, using, or selling the invention. This necessarily encompasses the right to exclude others from any particular industrial field in which those others might choose to use the invention. This is the right that must be sold to the transferee, and the transfer must cover all practical fields-of-use for the invention.

A field-of-use restriction in a license may not prevent the transfer from being one of property consisting of all substantial rights to a patent, where the field-of-use to which the licensee is restricted is the only field in which the invention has value.

Our approach does not affect the right of the holder to retain legal title to the patent or the right to veto sublicenses, since these powers are designed to protect the transferor's interest in the continuance of the purchase payments and do not interfere with the full use by the transferee of the monopoly right in the patent.

Applying the approach that we outline to the present controversy, we find that the record establishes that the Fawick patents had known value outside the marine service industry at the time of the license, as demonstrated by the licensing arrangement with Fawick Corporation described above. The transaction therefore fails to qualify under § 1235 for capital gain treatment.

Reversed and remanded.

In *Estate of Klein v. Comm'r*, 507 F.2d 617 (7th Cir. 1974), the Seventh Circuit upheld the position of Reg. § 1.1235-2(b)(1)(i) that an exclusive license to exploit a U.S. patent within only a *portion* of the U.S. fails the all-substantial-rights test of § 1235.

Section 1253, dealing with transfers of rights in franchises, trademarks, and trade names, appears on the surface to parallel the § 1235 approach by denying "sale" treatment "if the transferor retains any significant power, right, or continuing interest with respect to the subject matter of the franchise, trademark or trade name." The phrase "significant power, right, or continuing interest" is broadly defined in § 1253(b)(2), however, to include a right to receive payments contingent on productivity, use, or disposition if the payments are a "substantial element" of the transaction. If so, the payments are treated by § 1235(c) as being received upon the sale of a non-capital asset. A right of quality control, a right to require exclusive dealing arrangements, and certain other rights also constitute significant retained rights that result in ordinary income characterization. Thus, § 1253 generally produces the opposite result to § 1235.

PROBLEMS

1.   Georgia Genius spent $60K of her own funds developing a U.S. patent right (see § 174), which she sells to Eddie Entrepreneur for $100K cash. Eddie then grants an exclusive license to IBM Corporation to exploit the patent throughout the United States for its entire term in return for IBM's promise to pay a royalty equal to 5% of the sales price of each unit produced and sold under the patent right. The patent right will revert to Eddie if IBM fails in good faith to exploit the patent or becomes insolvent or bankrupt.

(a) How should the parties report these transactions?

(b) Would the results in (a) be different if:

(i) the license was nonexclusive?

(ii) the license covered only the Eastern United States?

(c) What results to the parties if, instead of a patent, the item was a copyright covering a novel? See § 1221(a)(3).

(d) What results to the parties if, instead of a patent or copyright, the item was the BigBurger trademark which Eddie was franchising to various franchisees?

2. In a contingent-payment sale, is any portion of each payment imputed "interest"? See §§ 483(d)(4), 1274(c)(3)(E); Reg. § 1.483-4.

D. CALCULATING DEPRECIATION UNDER THE CODE

The Internal Revenue Code prescribes the depreciation rules that are employed for tax purposes. These rules apply without regard to: (1) whether the taxpayer uses cash or accrual accounting, (2) the way in which the taxpayer computes depreciation for financial accounting purposes, (3) the actual or expected revenue to be derived from the asset in question, and (4) changes in the FMV of the property. Depreciation deductions calculated in compliance with Code rules are safe from being overturned under the Commissioner's § 446(b) power to insist on the "clear reflection of income."

Depreciation deductions are deductions of the basis created when the asset was originally acquired (or improved) and the purchase outlay (or improvement) was categorized as a nondeductible capital expenditure. Thus, depreciation deductions cannot exceed the taxpayer's basis in the asset (or improvement).

Depreciation (and other cost recovery deductions) are allowed (begin) in the year that the asset is placed in service or use, which may be later than the year of purchase.

Since it is not an aim of this book to train accountants, the descriptions below will be light on details and arithmetic.

1. Depreciation of Tangible Personal Property

Depreciable tangible personal property may generate cost recovery deductions that are taken "before" actual depreciation deductions are taken.

a. Pre-Depreciation Cost Recovery

As previously mentioned in Chapter 6.E.3, § 179 allows expensing of active-business tangible personal property (including computer software) up to a maximum annual dollar amount (but not to exceed business net income). The deduction is phased out for large business. The deduction can be allocated among the taxpayer's eligible assets as the taxpayer desires (but not to exceed $25K per sport utility vehicle).

If § 179 property is converted to personal or investment use in a later taxable year, all or part of the § 179 deduction may be "recaptured" (as gross income) in that year. See § 179(d)(10).

Section 179 deductions are treated as expenses, and therefore are never capitalized. Depreciation deductions proper are derived from basis resulting from capital expenditures. Section 168(k), also mentioned in Chapter 6.E.3, allows 50% of the cost of "qualified property" purchased (and placed into service) during the period 2010-2013 to be deducted as additional first-year depreciation. (The percentage is 100% during a window running from September 8, 2010 to the end of 2011!) Unlike § 179, there is no phase-out of this provision for large businesses, or even any requirement that the property be used in the active conduct of the taxpayer's business. "Qualified property" generally means § 168 property with a recovery period of 20 years or less, as well as certain computer software and leasehold improvements. Any amount deducted under § 168(k) reduces the taxpayer's cost basis in the particular asset for purposes of computing "regular" depreciation under § 168(a).

b. Depreciation Proper

Any cost of depreciable tangible property that is left standing after §§ 179 and 168(k) have been applied is depreciated under the so-called MACRS (modified accelerated cost recovery system) set forth in § 168(a)-(e). The verbiage in § 168(a)-(e) has mostly been reduced to a table that specifies depreciation schedules for 3-year property, 5-year property, 7-year property, 10-year property, 15-year property, and 20-year property. The schedules are published in *Rev. Proc. 87-57*, 1987-2 C.B. 687, and found in the Appendix to *Selected Federal Taxation Statutes and Regulations* (West edition) and immediately before the "Table of Contents" of *Federal Income Tax Code and Regulations Selected Sections* (CCH edition). In § 168(e)(3), Congress has prescribed the classifications for certain kinds of tangible personal property but has otherwise left classification up to the IRS, which has obliged by issuing revenue procedures.[12] Most tangible personal property happens to fall within the category of "5-year property."

The depreciation schedule for most of categories is derived by application of the 200% (i.e., double) declining-balance method,[13] switching to straight-line depreciation in the year when doing so produces a larger deduction. A declining-balance method of depreciation entails the application of a constant percentage against the property's adjusted basis *as reduced for prior depreciation*. In the case of 5-year property, the "single" declining-balance percentage is 20% (100%/5); hence, the double declining-balance rate is 40%.[14] Since declining-balance depreciation continues to infinity,[15] it is necessary to switch in mid-stream to a method that depreciates a fraction of the *unreduced* basis per year in order to fully depreciate the asset within the applicable period. (For example, a straight-line rate of 20% rate applied against the unreduced basis results in depreciating 100% of the basis in 5 years.)

---

[12] See *Rev. Proc. 87-56*, 1987-2 C.B. 674.

[13] Fifteen-year and 20-year property is subject to the 150% declining balance method.

[14] A 100% (or single) declining-balance method of depreciation would employ a constant percentage obtained by dividing one by the depreciation period. In the case of 5-year property, this rate would be 20% (1/5) per year. Twice that rate is 40%.

[15] Whacking off a percentage of something always leaves something left standing.

A "half-year convention" is imposed by § 168(d)(1), which means that all assets placed in service during the year are deemed to be placed in service halfway through the year. In the case of 5-year property to be depreciated over 60 months, that means the depreciation extends into the first 6 months of Year 6 (6 + 12 + 12 + 12 + 12 +6), assuming that the item is in service until Year 6.

All of the arithmetic involved in combining (1) the initial double-declining balance method, (2) the later switching to the straight-line depreciation, and (3) the half-year convention, are done for the taxpayer in the schedules contained in *Rev. Proc. 87-57.*

For the curious, here is how the percentages are obtained for the schedule for 5-year property. The rate for Year 1 is the double declining-balance rate of 40% cut in half by reason of the half-year convention. The rate for Year 2 is 32% [.4(100% - 20%)]. For Year 3, the rate is 19.2% [.4(100% - 20% - 32%)]. At this point, the remaining basis is 28.8% of the whole [(100% - (20% + 32% + 19.2%)], and it is time to switch to the straight-line method. Since there are 30 months to go (2.5 years), the rate for Years 4 and 5 is 11.52% (12/30ths of 28.8%), and the rate for Year 6 (where the half-year convention applies) is 5.76% (half of 11.52%). All of the percentages add up to 100%.

The taxpayer is spared having to work out the applicable percentages. *All the taxpayer has to do is to apply the percentage found in the applicable schedule for the applicable year of service to the (unadjusted) depreciable basis that was left standing after applying §§ 179 and 168(k).* The half-year convention also applies if the property is disposed of prior to the last year. Thus, if five-year property is disposed of in Year 4, the taxpayer is entitled to half of the deduction allowed by the table for Year 4 (which would be 5.76%). Obviously, no depreciation would be allowed for Years 5 and 6.

MACRS as applied to tangible personal property results in greater deductions in the earlier years compared to the later years, which is why it is referred to as "accelerated depreciation."

Section 168(b)(5) allows a taxpayer to make an election to use the straight-line method of depreciation in lieu of MACRS. A taxpayer with a small amount of taxable income in the year that the property is placed in service but who expects much larger amounts of taxable income in the later years in which the property will be in service might make this election.

MACRS does not apply to property used outside of the United States, plus other items listed in § 168(g)(1), which are depreciated under the "alternative depreciation system." This alternative depreciation system uses the straight-line method over (usually) longer recovery periods. (The alternative depreciation system *must* be used for tangible property under the Alternative Minimum Tax (AMT). See § 56(a)(1).) In addition, a taxpayer can sometimes elect to use the unit-of-production method (or some variation thereof).[16] The income-forecast method is used for films,

---

[16] See § 168(f)(1). Here the basis is multiplied by a fraction, the numerator of which is units of use (say, miles) during the current year and the denominator of which is total predicted units of remaining use calculated as of the beginning of the year.

videos, and sound recordings (which are really intangibles with a tangible embodiment).[17]

c.   Section 280F Limitations

Section 280F(a) defers and limits § 179 deductions and § 168 depreciation with respect to automobiles and certain other tangible personal property used in business.

First, subsection (a) reduces the §§ 179 and 168 deductions that would otherwise be allowable (assuming 100% business use) with respect to *business automobiles*. The per-year limitations specified in § 280F(a)(1)(A) have been indexed for inflation since 1988. The reduced deduction is further reduced by multiplying the deduction by the ratio of business use to total use. Depreciation deductions disallowed on account of personal use cannot support subsequent depreciation deductions.[18]

Second, in cases where the taxpayer's business use of automobiles and other "listed property" fails to exceed 50% for the year, the § 179 deduction is eliminated, and the taxpayer is required to use the "alternative depreciation system" found in § 168(g). See § 280F(b)(1). "Listed property" includes not only automobiles and other transportation vehicles, but also entertainment property, computers (and peripheral equipment), and cellular telephones. Computers (and peripheral equipment) are deemed not to be "listed property" if used exclusively at a regular business establishment (which may include a § 280A(c)(1) home office). See § 280F(d)(4)(B).

Third, § 280F(d)(3) states that any *employee-owned* listed property is deemed to be held wholly for personal use (for this and other purposes) — effectively disallowing any write-offs of such property — unless such use is "for the convenience of the employer and required as a condition of employment." This phrase refers to the regulations under § 119 (pertaining to employer-provided meals and lodging for an employee), and generally refers to a scenario in which the job requires the equipment but the employer fails to provide it.

2.   Depreciation of Real Property

Recall that land is not depreciable. Thus, basis has to be allocated between the nondepreciable land and any depreciable buildings or other structures.

Depreciable real property is not eligible for the deductions conferred by §§ 168(k) and 179. Thus, only § 168(a) "regular" depreciation is at issue.

Depreciable real property is classified by § 168(e)(2) as either "residential rental property" or "nonresidential real property." Section 168(c) then assigns recovery periods of 27.5 years and 39 years to residential rental property and nonresidential

---

[17] See §§ 167(g), 168(f)(3) & (4). Here the basis is multiplied by a fraction, the numerator of which is current receipts and the denominator of which is total predicted receipts calculated as of the beginning of the year. Section 167(g) limits the "total income" in the denominator to income expected to be earned by the end of the tenth year after the year the property is placed in service.

[18] See § 280F(d)(2).

real property, respectively. Section 168(b)(3) mandates use of the straight-line method of depreciation for both classes of real property. Under § 168(d)(2), a mid-month convention is mandated for both classes of real property, which means that the property is deemed to be placed in service (and withdrawn from service if the asset is disposed of prior to being completely depreciated) in precisely the middle of the month when it was actually placed in service (or taken out of service).

Again, all of the above is built into IRS Table 6 in *Rev. Proc. 87-57* (for residential rental property) and Table A-7a in IRS Publication 946 (for nonresidential real property). The applicable table lists a percentage (listed under the month in which the property was placed in service) that is multiplied by the property's *unadjusted* basis each year.

3. Amortization of Intangibles

The cost recovery allowance employed with respect to intangible assets is usually referred to as "amortization" instead of depreciation. Nevertheless, amortization is effectively a form of straight-line depreciation under which the cost of an intangible is evenly prorated over an appropriate period.

Amortizable intangible assets (patents, copyrights, contract rights, etc.) tend to be somewhat unique to the taxpayer and are not covered by the class-life system found in § 168. The default rule for intangible assets (not covered by a specific Code section) is that of amortization over their actual estimated useful lives using the straight-line method. See § 167(a); Reg. §§ 1.167(a)-3, 1.167(b)-1. However, intangible assets of speculative value, such as copyrights to unproven literary works and patents may be required to be amortized under the income-forecast method.[19]

Prior to the enactment of § 197 in 1993, a common threshold issue arising under § 167(a) was whether a given intangible asset had an ascertainable useful life. If an intangible (such as a franchise or license) could be renewed indefinitely by the taxpayer, it was deemed not to possess an ascertainable useful life and thus could not be amortized. Moreover, distinguishing certain separate intangible assets that had an ascertainable useful life from "goodwill" (which generally has no ascertainable useful life) was sometimes difficult. Both issues were posed in the case of *Newark Morning Ledger Co. v. U.S.*, 507 U.S. 546 (1993). There the purchaser of a newspaper business allocated a portion of the purchase price to an intangible asset denominated "paid subscribers" (who were largely expected to continue to subscribe after the newspaper's change in ownership). The taxpayer came up with an estimated useful life of this "paid subscribers" intangible asset based on statistical and actuarial forecasts of how long the average subscriber would continue to subscribe. Instead of challenging the quality of the evidence ostensibly establishing useful life, the IRS disallowed these deductions on the ground that the concept of "paid subscribers" was indistinguishable from goodwill and, therefore, was per se nondepreciable.

---

[19] See note 17.

In rejecting the government's position, the Supreme Court majority held (over four dissents) that the no-amortization-of-goodwill rule does not prevent amortization of a claimed intangible asset where the taxpayer proves that the intangible asset (1) has an ascertainable value separate and distinct from goodwill, and (2) has a limited useful life, the duration of which can be ascertained with reasonable accuracy. But because these issues were primarily factual and often involved expensive experts and voluminous statistical and documentary evidence, taxpayers as well as the government incurred large costs in litigating this issue. Moreover, only taxpayers that could afford the litigation route were likely to prevail. These interrelated problems of fairness and cost were publicized by the *Newark Morning Ledger* case and prompted Congress to intervene with the 1993 enactment of § 197, which provides that any "amortizable § 197 intangible" is to be amortized over 15 years beginning with the month the intangible is acquired.

The term "amortizable § 197 intangible" is very broadly defined to include purchased or acquired goodwill, going concern value, other ongoing-business intangibles, know how, franchise rights, trademarks, trade names, government permits and licenses, and covenants not to compete. A few of these items are included *only* if obtained in connection with the acquisition of a going business. The term does *not* include: (i) most intangibles created by the taxpayer (but see the next sentence), (ii) interests in entities and certain other financial assets (including debt and leases), (iii) interests in land, (iv) nonexclusive computer software, (v) professional sports franchises, and (vi) transaction costs connected with tax-free mergers, acquisitions, and other structural changes. However, the term *does include* the following intangibles created by the taxpayer: (i) any license, permit, or other right granted by a governmental unit, or agency, (ii) any covenant not to compete entered into as part of the acquisition of a trade or business, and (iii) any franchise, trademark or trade name.

The 15-year amortization rule under § 197 supersedes all competing capital-recovery rules. However, under § 167(f), certain intangible property is amortizable only as follows: (1) non-exclusive computer software over 36 months, (2) mortgage servicing rights over 108 months, and (3) certain created or enhanced intangibles without an ascertainable useful life (*e.g.*, memberships of indefinite duration) not acquired in connection with the acquisition of a business over 15 years. Lease acquisition costs are governed by § 178.

Intangibles not governed by § 197 or any other special Code provision are amortizable, if at all, under the rules in § 167, which means that the intangible must have an ascertainable useful life. Thus, for example, goodwill created by the taxpayer is not eligible for § 197 amortization, as mentioned above, and is not amortizable under § 167 because goodwill has no ascertainable useful life. A customer list created by the taxpayer is not eligible for amortization under § 197 but is eligible for amortization under § 167 if the taxpayer can establish the useful life of such list. However, a taxpayer may often have a low basis in such self-created (as opposed to acquired) customer lists, so little amortization may result in any event.

Intangibles that are "expensed" under the Code and regulations (such as research costs under § 174 and advertising costs that create goodwill) have no basis that can be amortized.

4. Effect of Depreciation on Basis

Although the rule that depreciation reduces basis under § 1016(a)(2) is fundamental, what about depreciation deductions that are claimed but disallowed? In general, depreciation that is disallowed because the asset (or part thereof) is held for personal use (or is so used part of the time) does not reduce basis for purposes of determining gain or loss, since such depreciation is not "allowed or allowable." Depreciation that is deferred under § 280F(a) does not reduce basis unless and until it is actually deducted.

In *Virginian Hotel Corp. v. Helvering*, 319 U.S. 523 (1943), the taxpayer erroneously claimed excessive depreciation deductions for years on which the statute of limitations had run so that the IRS could no longer challenge the incorrect deductions. Nevertheless, on a later sale of the property, the taxpayer claimed that its basis should *not* have been reduced by the "excess" (thus producing less gain). This claim was made on the ground that the excess depreciation produced no reduction in tax liability, because the taxpayer had net losses (aggregate deductions exceeded gross income) in those years apart from the excess depreciation. The Court rejected this argument under the predecessor of § 1016(a)(2), which stated that the basis should be adjusted for depreciation "to the extent allowed (but not less than the amount allowable)." The Court noted:

> The purpose . . . was to make sure that taxpayers who had made excessive deductions in one year could not reduce the depreciation basis by [only] the lesser amount of depreciation which was "allowable."

The Court held that "allowed" depreciation included excess depreciation that was inappropriately deducted by the taxpayer. Both the fact that the statute of limitations had run on the year of the excess deductions and the fact that the excess deductions produced no tax benefit were held to be irrelevant under the quoted language.

Section 1016(a)(2)(B) was subsequently amended to partially overturn the result of *Virginian Hotel*. Today, depreciation allowed (in excess of depreciation "allowable") reduces basis *only* if such depreciation actually reduced taxes in some year.

PROBLEMS

1. State the depreciation or amortization allowable in Years 1 and 2 with respect to each asset below. Separately state whether the asset could be written off under § 179 and/or § 168(k). Assume all assets are placed in service by the same taxpayer, who is a business executive, on April 15 of the current year. The assets are not acquired in connection with the purchase of a going business.

(a) Personal residence: cost $500K.

(b) Art work ("old master" painting) held for investment: cost $50K.

(c) Industrial machine (with a 5-year "class life") for use in a woodworking side business: cost $150K.

(d) Apartment building (on leased land): cost $1M.

(e) Nonrenewable 20-year government license to operate a cable TV system: cost $400K.

(f) Passenger car purchased that is used 75% for business and the rest for pleasure: cost $40K.

(g) Laptop computer, with software package, purchased to write the taxpayer's memoirs, which she hopes to have published: cost $3K.

2.   On January 1 of Year 1, Seller sells her business to Buyer. Such sale includes the following two assets. What is the amount of amortization allowable in Years 1 and 2 with respect to each asset?

(a) Four-year covenant not to compete entered into by Seller with Buyer in connection with Buyer's acquisition of Seller's business: payments of $7,500 per year from Buyer to Seller for the 4-year period.

(b) Goodwill in Seller's business acquired by Buyer as part of the acquisition of Seller's business: cost $60K.

3.   On January 1 of Year 1, Taxpayer, an inventor, receives a U.S. patent on an invention that he created that has a capitalized cost of $30K. Taxpayer will use the patent in his patent licensing business. The patent has a legal life under U.S. patent law of 20 years. What is the amount of amortization allowable in Years 1 and 2 with respect to this patent?

Chapter 29

THE DISPOSITION OF A PART OF THE WHOLE

What tax consequences arise when a taxpayer actually purports to dispose of part of a larger property interest? How should we determine the fraction of the taxpayer's entire basis that can be used to offset the amount realized (if any)? In this chapter, the parts are not deemed to be used up simply due to the passage of time, but rather are actually separated from the whole. The two broad categories of parts are "spatial" (physical) parts and "temporal" parts (such as a term for years or a remainder interest).

A. DISPOSITION OF PHYSICAL COMPONENTS

Here we consider dispositions of asset aggregations, the depletion of mineral deposits, and the loss of unidentified physical portions of a larger whole. We have already dealt with two analogous situations, namely, inventories (Chapter 23.A.1) and subdivisions of real property (Chapter 22.A.3).

1. Disposition of an Aggregate of Assets

A sale of real property may actually be a sale of an aggregation of separate assets rather than the sale of a single item of property. These assets are (1) the land, (2) whatever buildings and other improvements come with the land, and (3) any mineral rights going with the land. These rights may be sold separately, but if they are sold as a package the consideration for the sale must be allocated among the various assets in proportion to their respective fair market values (FMVs) at the time of sale. The seller computes § 1001 gain or loss, and determines its character, with respect to each asset. The buyer takes a separate cost basis in each asset, which can be recovered (if at all) according to the proper basis recovery mechanism for that type of asset.

> *Example*: Terry purchased (nondepreciable) land for $100K and subsequently spent $400K to construct a rental office building. She deducted $150K of depreciation on the building during her ownership period, resulting in an adjusted basis for the building of $250K, before selling the property (land and building) to Danny for $500K. At the time of sale, the FMV of the land is $300K, and the FMV of the building is $200K. Terry realizes a $200K gain with respect to the land ($300K amount realized *less* $100K adjusted basis) and a $50K loss with respect to the building ($200K amount realized *less* $250K adjusted basis) under § 1001, and the character of each gain and loss (as ordinary, capital, or § 1231) must be determined separately. Danny's nondepreciable cost basis in the land is $300K, and his depreciable cost basis in the building is $200K.

In the case of personal-use (i.e., residential or recreational) property, this allocation can be waived, and the aggregate basis can be offset against the total amount realized. This short cut is allowed because no component is depreciable and the character of the gain or loss realized on each component would be the same. See generally Reg. § 1.165-7(b)(2)(ii).

The sale of the assets of a going business involves the same sort of analysis. In computing both the seller's gain or loss and the purchaser's basis, the purchase price for the entire business is allocated among the component assets of the business according to their respective FMVs at the time of sale. For both buyer and seller, any excess of the total purchase price over the aggregate value of identifiable assets (whether tangible or intangible) must be allocated to an asset called "goodwill."[1] This allocation approach will give the buyer of a going business a basis in the purchased goodwill. See § 1060(a). The seller, in contrast, will rarely have a basis in self-created goodwill, because the seller will have capitalized the costs of creating it into other assets (e.g., trademarks) or will have currently deducted these costs under § 162 (e.g., as advertising and employee training expenses).

The buyer of a going business often insists that the seller contractually agree not to compete with the buyer in the same geographic area for a number of years. The consideration allocated to such a "covenant not to compete" is ordinary income for the seller (compensation for services *not* rendered), with no basis offset. Sellers always prefer to allocate consideration in sales contracts to goodwill rather than to a noncompetition covenant because goodwill is a capital asset.[2] Buyers are indifferent to the allocation, because purchased goodwill and noncompetition covenants are both amortizable over 15 years.[3] Because the buyer has no interest in opposing the seller's allocation, an underallocation to the noncompetition covenant can result.

To deal with these situations, the second sentence of § 1060(a) was added in 1990. It provides that a written agreement regarding the allocation of consideration to, or the FMV of, any of the assets in an applicable asset acquisition is to be binding on both parties for tax purposes, unless the IRS determines that the allocation is not appropriate. Nevertheless, the parties are able to refute the allocation or valuation under the strict standards set forth in *Comm'r v. Danielson*, 378 F.2d 771, 775 (3d Cir.), *cert. denied*, 389 U.S. 858 (1967). *Danielson* held that a party can "challenge the tax consequences of his agreement as construed by the Commissioner only by adducing proof which in an action between the parties to the agreement would be admissible to alter that construction or to show its unenforceability because of mistake, undue influence, fraud, duress, etc."[4]

A sale of a business, or an aggregation of business assets, is to be distinguished from a sale of stock in a corporation, which is considered to be a sale of a single

---

[1] Goodwill might be further broken down into goodwill and going-concern value, but this distinction is not important for tax purposes.

[2] Since self-created goodwill is nonamortizable (nondepreciable) personal property used in a trade or business, it is (unlike most business-use assets) a capital asset. See § 1221(a)(2).

[3] See § 197(a), (b), (d)(1)(E).

[4] See Reg. § 1.1060-1(c)(4).

asset, not a sale of proportionate interests in the corporation's underlying assets. This is consistent with the view that a corporation is an entity that is separate from its owners. Stock is a capital asset (except when held as inventory by a stock dealer). The sale of a partnership interest, in contrast, is treated quite differently.[5]

PROBLEM

John sells a business to Jane for cash. The business has two assets: (1) a fully depreciated widget-making machine and (2) zero-basis self-created goodwill. These assets have each been held for 10 years. In connection with the sale, John agrees not to compete with Jane for two years. How would John and Jane prefer to allocate the purchase consideration among the assets? Would Reg. § 1.1060-1 interfere with these allocations?

2.   Depletion of Natural Deposits

Assume that Owner buys land, improved or unimproved, containing mineral deposits. The first task is to allocate the total purchase price among the raw land, the mineral deposits, and any buildings or structures, in proportion to their respective FMVs. Suppose that $100K of the purchase consideration is allocated to the deposits. Owner begins extraction of the minerals. How much of his $100K cost basis in the deposit should be allocated to the minerals extracted and sold each year (and thus used as an offset against the sales proceeds)?

a.   Cost Depletion

Basis recovery with respect to natural deposits, including oil, gas, minerals, and timber, is called "cost depletion." Under § 611, a given natural deposit is simply assumed to be of a uniform grade or quality. Therefore, the taxpayer's basis in the deposit is recoverable, through "cost depletion," in proportion to the amount extracted or harvested each year as follows:

$$\text{cost depletion for year} = \frac{\text{quantity extracted in current year}}{\text{quantity in deposit at beginning of year}} \times \text{adjusted basis in deposit (reduced for prior depletion)}$$

See Reg. § 1.611-2(a). Once the entire cost of the deposit has been deducted (i.e., once the deposit's adjusted basis becomes zero), cost depletion ceases.

Thus, in our hypothetical, Owner would deduct $10K in Year 1 if 1/10 of the minerals were extracted, and his adjusted basis in the deposit at the beginning of Year 2 would be $90K. If he extracted 1/5 of the *remaining* deposit in Year 2, his cost depletion would be $18K (1/5 × $90K), and his adjusted basis in the deposit would be $72K. And so on.

---

[5] A sale of a partnership interest (or an interest in an LLC that is taxed as a partnership) is viewed in part as the sale of the partner's share in certain ordinary income assets of the partnership (generating ordinary income) and in part as a sale of the interest itself (a capital asset). See §§ 741 and 751(a), dealt with in a course in partnership taxation.

Cost depletion is very much like unit-of-production depreciation, mentioned in the previous chapter, except that cost depletion describes the actual physical disposition of portions of the mineral deposit, somewhat like the sale of subdivided (fungible) lots.

b. Percentage Depletion

In many instances, the owner can take "percentage depletion" under § 613 or § 613A in lieu of cost depletion. Specifically, the percentage depletion deduction is an amount, not to exceed a specified percentage (50%, or 100%) of current taxable income from the property (disregarding any depletion), equal to the applicable percentage (under § 613 or § 613A) of the "net" gross income from the deposit (gross income less rents or royalties paid). Percentage depletion is not available for oil and (certain) gas, except to small royalty owners and independent producers under § 613A. It is also not available for timber, water, and minerals from inexhaustible resources (such as sea water).

Percentage depletion deductions are equivalent to an exclusion from gross income of a percentage of net income earned on the deposit. Because percentage depletion is not keyed to basis, it is not a true basis recovery system. Although percentage depletion (like cost depletion) reduces basis down to zero as it is deducted, it (unlike cost depletion) can be taken *even after* basis reaches zero. Such "excess" depletion, however, is subject to the Alternative Minimum Tax (AMT) by reason of § 57(a)(1).

c. Who Is Entitled to Depletion?

In the case of mineral interests, depletion doesn't necessarily follow property law. Nevertheless, it is worthwhile to know how typical deals are structured. As a matter of property law, the right to minerals in place may either be an incident of owning the land or it may be a separate property interest ("mineral rights") capable of being owned by person(s) other than the landowner(s). Mineral rights (with or without the underlying land) may be sold or leased. Since the quantity and quality of the minerals in place are often not known with any certainty, it is common (in *either* a sale or a lease) that the consideration take the form of periodic payments that are contingent on the production (extraction) to be done by the transferee. Thus, if a contingent-payment transaction involving minerals is held to be a "sale" for tax purposes, the seller can use the open-transaction method of reporting gain. If the transaction is a lease, the royalties received would be gross income subject to depletion. Often the lessee is said to have a "working interest," because the lessee is the one to exploit the mineral deposit by drilling, mining, quarrying, or whatever (or paying others to perform needed services).

The case below explores (1) the issue of whether the transaction at issue constitutes, for tax purposes, a sale of minerals or a lease and (2) the quality of the "ownership interest" necessary to support the right of a taxpayer to take depletion deductions. The case is somewhat unusual in that both parties to the transaction were joined in the Tax Court litigation.

O'CONNOR v. COMMISSIONER
United States Tax Court
78 T.C. 1 (1982)

GOFFE, JUDGE:

[W.G. Bush & Co. was a brick manufacturer. The O'Connors, husband and wife, owned land near Nashville, Tennessee, that contained extensive clay deposits. In 1966, the O'Connors leased to Bush, for the purpose of mining clay, part of the property for seven years with an option to renew for three years. Bush was to pay the O'Connors 25 cents per cubic yard mined, with $67,000 — the payment for the first 268,000 cubic yards — payable in advance and nonrefundable. Bush agreed to undertake reasonable efforts to mine the clay and to bear the cost of improvements to the land necessary for mining, while the O'Connors remained liable for property taxes. The O'Connors had the option of cancelling the lease if Bush violated the agreement or became insolvent.]

Petitioners maintain that the agreement constituted a sale of minerals in place, so that the payments they received were for a sale of a capital asset. Respondent argues that the O'Connors retained an economic interest in the clay in place so that the payments received were [lease] royalties which, when reduced by the appropriate depletion allowance, are ordinary income.

The income tax act of October 3, 1913, recognized that, in order to arrive at a true reflection of a taxpayer's income, the law needed to provide for the recovery of capital. In the context of mining, this meant that a reasonable allowance for the exhaustion of wasting resources [i.e., cost depletion] must be allowed. The Revenue Act of 1918 created "discovery depletion," which meant that the amount the investor could deduct for depletion might be based not on cost, but rather on the [higher] fair market value of the minerals at the time of [subsequent] discovery, in effect providing for a step-up in basis on the date of discovery. The purpose of discovery depletion was "to encourage the wildcatter or pioneer," that is, to encourage those willing to bear the risks necessary to discover and develop natural resources.

Percentage depletion was created by Congress in the Revenue Act of 1926. The Conference Report explains that:

> The administration of the discovery provision has been very difficult because of the discovery valuation that had to be made in the case of each discovered well. In the interest of simplicity and certainty, the Senate amendment provides that the allowance for depletion shall be [27.5%] of the gross income from the property.

Percentage depletion was gradually extended to more and more minerals, with brick and tile clay allowed percentage depletion in the Revenue Act of 1951.

Both lessors and lessees may be entitled to depletion. This does not mean that the same income is used to compute two depletion deductions. Each is entitled to depletion only as to his economic interest therein. Accordingly, if a lessor leases mineral rights while retaining an interest therein, the depletion is allowable on the royalty income he receives from the lessee, and the lessee is entitled to depletion on the net of the gross receipts from production less the royalties he has paid to the lessor.

The concept of economic interest was defined by the Supreme Court in *Palmer v. Bender*, 287 U.S. 551 (1933), when the Court was asked to decide who was entitled to the allowance for discovery depletion after a sublease. In that case the taxpayer acquired oil and gas leases on unproven land and subsequently drilled for and discovered oil. [He] then transferred a portion of [his] lease to a third party, receiving in exchange bonus payments and retaining a one-eighth royalty. The Commissioner disallowed the [depletion], arguing that the leases were sold, based on a [Texas] law characterization that they were assigned. In allowing the depletion, the Court observed that:

> The language of the statute is broad enough to provide, at least, for every case in which the taxpayer has acquired, by investment, any interest in the oil in place, and secures, by any form of legal relationship, income derived from the extraction of the oil, to which he must look for a return of his capital. [The taxpayer's] right to a depletion allowance does not depend upon his retention of ownership or any other particular form of legal interest in the mineral content of the land. It is enough if, by virtue of the leasing transaction, he has retained a right to share in the oil produced. If so, he has an economic interest in the oil, in place, which is depleted by production.

The Court went on to explain that the investment of the taxpayer was at risk. "The loss or destruction of the oil at any time would have resulted in loss [to the taxpayer]." The Commissioner has adopted this definition of economic interest in Reg. § 1.611-1(b)(1).

The O'Connors maintain that the agreement [here] contemplated that a definite amount of clay would be mined, this expectation was met, and, thus, the minerals were sold for a fixed total consideration. The O'Connors suggest that this issue should be decided by a line of cases in which taxpayers were found to have sold their interest in quantities of minerals. In *Rhodes v. U.S.*, 464 F.2d 1307 (1972), the Fifth Circuit found that a sale was made when the contract purported to "sell, assign, and set over unto grantee, in fee simple, all of the merchantable brick clay deposits" underlying a specifically designated and described one acre parcel, the purchase price being $7,500. The Fifth Circuit again found a sale in *Whitehead v. U.S.*, 555 F.2d 1290 (1977), where the taxpayer transferred a fixed quantity of sand and gravel in place, namely 1,333,333 cubic yards, for a total fixed price of $200,000.

The foregoing indicates that it is certainly possible for a taxpayer to transfer his entire interest in all of, or a portion of, minerals in which he possesses an economic interest. The question before us is whether the O'Connors have done so. The key to the O'Connor position is their premise that the agreement unconditionally required Bush to extract and remove a certain quantity of clay. The agreement provides as follows:

> Until the deposits of commercially usable clay on the premises which can be feasibly mined have been exhausted, Bush agrees to make every

reasonable effort, consistent with its business operations, to mine same during the original term or any renewal hereof. In this connection, Bush further agrees that so long as commercially usable clay for the manufacturing of brick which can be feasibly mined is available from deposits located on the premises, at least 80% of the clay utilized in the production of clay bricks at its plants located in Davidson County during the term hereof shall be from that supply mined from the premises.

We do not view this provision as an unconditional requirement on Bush to extract and remove any certain amount of clay or all the clay. Bush's obligation is conditioned on (1) the clay's meeting Bush's specifications, (2) the "feasibility" of mining the clay, which might include any number of economic and regulatory exigencies, and (3) the requirements of Bush's plants, which might vary greatly as Bush is dependent on the vagaries of the construction industry for which it provides building materials. We also observe that the presence of an advance royalty, a royalty paid up front but recoupable out of production, is designed to protect the O'Connors in case Bush does not remove significant amounts of clay.

We find that [this] clause does not cause the agreement to effect a sale. Why then would a lease agreement include such a clause? Under a lease, the lessor grants the lessee the exclusive right to mine certain natural resources. Although there might be some cash consideration for this privilege, the "true consideration for the transaction was the expectation of development of the premises and the payment of royalties to be derived" therefrom. 5 E. Kuntz, Oil and Gas 47 (1978). Accordingly, many jurisdictions, including Tennessee, have developed an implied duty on the part of the lessee to mine the premises for minerals. The general remedy for failure to fulfill this duty is cancellation of the lease. This permits the lessor to find someone else willing to develop his minerals. The implied duty to reasonably develop may not exist in Tennessee, however, where significant consideration for the lease agreement is otherwise present, such as when the lease agreement provides for minimum payments in lieu of production. It is quite understandable, then, that Tennessee lessors would want an express duty of reasonable development included in the lease. The assurance which this duty creates does not, however, require the lessee to mine any certain quantity of minerals.

We hold that the O'Connors did retain an economic interest in minerals in place. They continued to share in the risks of production and thus were required to look solely to production to recover their capital.

The issue [in *W.G. Bush & Co. v. Comm'r*, a case consolidated with the *O'Connor* case] concerns whether Bush is entitled to depletion on clay mined from the property. The issue is whether petitioner "acquired by investment an interest in minerals in place," thereby satisfying the first prong of *Palmer v. Bender*. It might well be contended that petitioner literally made no direct "investment" at the time he initially acquired his rights as lessee. He agreed to pay [the lessor] only if, as, and when he did extract minerals. [Nevertheless], the case law convinces us that the acquisition by a mine operator of a substantial bona fide ownership or leasehold interest in the minerals in place, or the economic equivalent thereof, will satisfy the first prong test, whether or not an "investment" is made to acquire such interest, at least so long as a significant related investment is made in development of the property to facilitate exploitation of such ownership or leasehold rights.

We find that Bush has made a significant development investment. Bush built an access road across the property, cleared the overburden, installed the necessary culverts, and accomplished all other work necessary to prepare the property for mining, including acquiring the necessary mining permits.

A "lease bonus" is cash paid by the lessee to the lessor for entering into the lease. A bonus is gross income to the lessor that is subject to cost or percentage depletion and is a capitalized lease acquisition cost to the lessee. See *Rev. Rul. 80-49*, 1980-1 C.B. 127. After 1986, a lease bonus relating to an oil or gas property does not qualify for percentage depletion. § 613A(d)(5).

An "advance royalty" is a lump-sum prepaid royalty that is recoupable (i.e., earned) out of subsequent production. (The $67K advance payment in the *O'Connor* case was an advance royalty.) An advance royalty is gross income to the lessor subject to depletion (and is not a loan). The lessee's deduction for advance royalties is delayed until the later of when the mineral is produced or sold by the lessee. Reg. § 1.612-3(b)(3). Since 1986, an advance royalty relating to an oil or gas property does not qualify for percentage depletion. § 613A(d)(5).

A "production payment" (consideration for what is called an oil-payment right) refers to a transaction in which a lump-sum consideration is received by a mineral owner for an assignment of the right to exploit minerals for so long as it takes for the assignee to earn an amount equal to the lump-sum consideration (plus an additional return to the owner, similar to interest), at which point the assignee's exploitation rights terminate and revert to the assignor. In the case of *Comm'r v. P.G. Lake, Inc.*, 356 U.S. 260 (1958), the mineral owner argued that the assignment was a "sale" of an interest in the minerals (that produced capital gain), but the government prevailed on the theory that the assignment was a "carve-out sale," which, as will be seen in Section B, results in the gross proceeds being treated as (accelerated) ordinary income with no basis offset. This result, though not what the taxpayer in *P.G. Lake* wanted, was favorable to most assignors receiving production payments, because the gross ordinary income also increased the available percentage depletion deductions that are a function of the "net gross income" from the minerals. Moreover, under the holding of the *Lake* case, the assignee would also be able to claim percentage depletion deductions on *its* investment.

Section 636(a), enacted in 1969, alters the *P.G. Lake* results by treating the "sale" of the carved-out interest as a borrowing transaction, with the production payment received by the owner being treated as loan principal to be repaid (with interest) out of production. Hence, the "seller" (really the borrower) continues to be the sole "owner" of the entire property for depletion purposes, and the "buyer" (the lender) does not acquire any interest in the minerals for tax purposes, regardless of state law, and therefore has no depletable interest. Moreover, the lump-sum production payment itself (treated as the proceeds of a loan) is not gross income subject to percentage depletion. The owner-borrower therefore cannot use this type of transaction to accelerate gross income and attendant percentage depletion deductions.

On the flip side, the sale of mineral property subject to a *retained* production payment is treated, under § 636(b), as a seller-financed sale with the fixed-amount sale price (plus interest) to be paid out of production. Such a transaction is essentially a bootstrap sale in which a fixed portion of the selling price is payable from future production. The seller only has a creditor interest and not a depletable interest in the sold property.

NOTES

1.   (a) Transactions involving minerals are similar to those involving intellectual-property intangibles, discussed in the preceding chapter, but the tax doctrine is different (except perhaps for franchises, etc., governed by § 1253). The economic-interest doctrine treats both the mineral lessor and the lessee as "owners." This is not wholly irrational, as contingent-payment transactions entail the sharing of rewards, as well as the risk of nonprofitability. An alternative way of sharing risks and rewards is to form a partnership or other business entity. But this is unlikely to happen where the lessor has nothing to offer other than location. Lessors are often passive investors or speculators, leaving exploration and development to the lessee.

(b) The sale by a landowner or casual investor of mineral rights would give rise to capital gain, unless the seller is a "dealer" in such rights. See *Rev. Rul. 73-428*, 1973-2 C.B. 303.

(c) The sale of extracted minerals by the owner of the working interest (often the lessee in a mineral lease) would normally produce ordinary income subject to depletion, except for coal and iron ore (as well as timber, certain livestock, and unharvested crops sold with the land), which are treated as § 1231 assets. See §§ 631 and 1231(b)(2)-(4).

(d) If the working interest itself is sold, it would produce § 1231 gain, because the interest is treated in such owner's hands as real property used in a trade or business, unless the seller has become a dealer with respect to such interests. See *Rev. Rul. 68-226*, 1968-1 C.B. 362.

(e) Notwithstanding the above, section 1254 provides for the characterization of any gain on the sale or disposition of mineral property, or interests therein (including working interests), as ordinary gain to the extent of the lesser of (1) the gain realized (or deemed realized) or (2) the aggregate of (i) depletion deductions (that reduced basis) and (ii) deductions for intangible drilling and development costs (IDCs).

2.   Percentage depletion is the ultimate tax expenditure, bearing no relation to any kind of tax theory. In addition to percentage depletion, recall from Chapter 7.C.3 that IDCs can be expensed (rather than capitalized) under § 263(c).

PROBLEM

Vincent, an individual investor, purchases land (including the mineral rights) in an oil-producing area for $100K, but it is not known whether oil can successfully be recovered from this property. The same kind of land would be worth $60K if it were not in an oil-producing area. After a few years, Vincent conveys the mineral rights to Excel, an oil company, on the terms that Excel will recover as much oil as feasible and will pay Vincent a royalty equal to $1 for each barrel of oil produced. In Year 1, Excel produces 100K barrels, which are sold for $50 per barrel; Excel's deductions (other than royalties paid to Vincent) are $2M.

On January 5 of Year 2, Excel assigns a production right to Cashco for $4.2M, which gives Cashco the right to the oil in-kind if, as, and when produced until the $4.2M, plus interest at 10%, is recouped by Cashco. The right is expected to pay off in about two years, at which time the right to production will revert to Excel.

Excel doesn't own or operate any other oil and gas properties; it neither refines any petroleum product nor sells at retail. What are the results to Vincent, Excel, and Cashco? See also §§ 263(c), 611, 612, 613(a) & (d), 613A(a)-(c)(1), (d) & (e); Reg. § 1.612-4.

3.   Recoveries for Unidentifiable Portions of the Whole

It occasionally happens that a private party or government takes, destroys, damages, or impinges on the property rights of a taxpayer. If the loss is uncompensated, the taxpayer may have a loss deduction under § 165. If the loss is compensated by insurance, damages, or "just compensation" in an eminent domain proceeding, the amount of the recovery would be treated as an "amount realized" under § 1001 on the "disposition" of the property right, although all or a portion of the gain may go unrecognized under § 1033 (discussed in Chapter 24.D). In either case, the taxpayer must ascertain the basis of the item lost, destroyed, or appropriated. This task may be difficult, however, if it is impossible to determine the percentage of the whole that is destroyed.

Consider the following passage from the case of *Raytheon Production Corp. v. Comm'r*, 144 F.2d 110 (1st Cir.), *cert. denied*, 323 U.S. 779 (1944):

> Where the cost basis that may be assigned to property has been wholly speculative, the gain has been held to be entirely conjectural and nontaxable. In *Strother v. Comm'r*, 55 F.2d 626 (4th Cir. 1932), *aff'd on other grounds*, 287 U.S. 314 (1932), a trespasser had taken coal [from taxpayer's deposit] and then destroyed the entries so that the amount of coal taken could not be determined. Since there was no way of knowing whether the recovery was greater than the basis for the coal taken, the gain was purely conjectural and not taxed. Magill, Taxable Income, pp. 339-340, explains the result as follows: "as the amount of coal removed could not be determined until a final disposition of the property, the computation of gain or loss on the damages must await that disposition."

The no-income result in *Strother* was presumably achieved by offsetting against the dollar amount of damage recovery a precisely equal dollar amount of the taxpayer's basis in the whole. As a necessary corollary, the taxpayer's basis in the whole must have been reduced by an amount equal to the recovery. (The Supreme Court affirmance of *Strother* was only of its holding that mineral royalties received from 1920 to 1926 on leases executed before 1913 were subject to income tax.)

A similar result to *Strother* was reached in *Inaja Land Co. v. Comm'r*, 9 T.C. 727 (1947) (acq.), which involved consideration paid for an easement in land that allowed the grantee to periodically flood a portion of the taxpayer's property by discharging water.[6] But the water flow was unpredictable, and the easement did not identify any specific portion of the property as being covered by the easement. The taxpayer's basis in the entire property exceeded the amount paid for the easement. The consideration received was wholly excluded (and the basis in the property reduced by an equal amount).

One could reasonably argue that these cases, more than 50 years old, should be considered obsolete, being based on dictum in early Supreme Court cases stating that basis had to be recovered "first" before any gain could be realized.[7] None of those cases involved a disposition of a part of the whole. Moreover, the approach of *Strother* and *Inaja Land* would produce the absurd result of a total basis recovery (and zero remaining basis), if the recovery in such a case were to exceed the taxpayer's basis in the whole, even though the taxpayer still owns valuable property.

In principle, these situations should be treated in the same general manner as cost depletion, that is, the basis of the whole should be multiplied by an appropriate fraction, and only the resulting fractional part of basis should be used as an offset against the consideration received. Unlike cost depletion, however, the fraction cannot be expressed in physical units. Nevertheless, the recovery itself is a measure of the lost value. Therefore, an appropriate fraction would be the amount of the recovery divided by the estimated value of the property just prior to the loss. In *Fasken v. Comm'r*, 71 T.C. 650 (1979) (acq.), also dealing with the sale of an easement, the court stated that the taxpayer had the burden of showing that a rational allocation of basis was not possible if he wanted to obtain the favorable result in *Strother* and *Inaja Land*. The taxpayer failed, and the court upheld the government's allocation.

PROBLEMS

1. Owner owns a coal deposit with a $100 FMV and a $50 basis. Trespasser takes an undetermined amount of coal, and Owner recovers $10 in cash damages from Trespasser. What is the result for Owner? The next year, Owner mines the rest of the coal and discovers that $70 worth of coal was taken by Trespasser so that only $30 worth remained. What is the result for Owner now?

2. Suppose that a landowner loses a suit brought by a utility company in which the utility successfully claims (to the surprise of everyone else) that it has a pre-existing easement to build transmission lines over the taxpayer's property and, therefore, that it can do so without paying compensation. Can the landowner take

---

[6] The transaction was part of the scheme whereby the City of Los Angeles obtained water from the eastern side of the Sierra Nevadas. This scheme was the basis of the plot for the movie "Chinatown."

[7] The source of this notion was a passage in *Doyle* v. *Mitchell Bros. Co.*, 247 U.S. 179, 184, 185 (1918), but that case only held that basis could be no lower than the FMV of the property on the effective date of the 1909 corporate income tax. The only Supreme Court case to actually hold that basis had to be recovered "first" was *Burnet v. Logan*, 283 U.S. 404, 413 (1931), but that case (involving a contingent-payment sale) simply followed the then-existing rule for annuities, as noted by the Second Circuit in the same case, *Logan v. Comm'r*, 42 F.2d 193, 197 (1930).

a partial loss deduction in this case? See Reg. § 1.165-1(d)(1) ("closed and completed transaction" language). Although § 166 acknowledges the possibility of deducting partial business bad debt losses, that provision is rarely applied outside of bankruptcy (where the principal may be reduced, but not wiped out). As to partial losses generally, in *Parmelee Transp. Co. v. U.S.*, 351 F.2d 619 (Ct. Cl. 1965), the taxpayer obtained a proxy for a partial loss deduction to the value of its business by identifying a "sub-asset" (goodwill) that had wholly been destroyed. In *Lakewood Associates v. Comm'r*, 109 T.C. 450 (1997), a partial loss was disallowed when government wetland restrictions were imposed on taxpayer's property, because the loss in value was not fixed by a closed and completed transaction, meaning some kind of disposition.

B.   TRANSACTIONS INVOLVING TEMPORAL INTERESTS

A person might carve up an outright (fee simple) ownership of property into various "temporal" segments in property, such as a current-enjoyment interest (e.g., a leasehold, a life estate, or a term for years) and a future interest (e.g., a remainder or reversion). This section sorts out the tax consequences of the acquisition, holding, and disposition of such interests.

1.   Carve-Out Sales

In a "carve-out" transaction, the taxpayer (owning an outright or fee simple interest in property) "carves out" (and sells) a temporal portion of it — such as a term of years or a remainder interest — *with retention by the taxpayer of whatever is left*. Two major Supreme Court cases involve the tax treatment of payments received with respect to certain carved-out interests. The first, set forth below, dealt with payments received by a lessor from a lessee desiring to get out of an unfavorable lease.

HORT v. COMMISSIONER
United States Supreme Court
313 U.S. 28 (1941)

MR. JUSTICE MURPHY delivered the opinion of the Court.

Petitioner acquired a lot and ten-story office building by devise from his father in 1928. Petitioner's father had executed a contract in which the Irving Trust Co. agreed to lease the main floor and basement for a term of fifteen years at an annual rental of $25,000. In 1933, the Irving Trust Co. found it unprofitable to maintain a branch in petitioner's building. After some negotiations, petitioner and the Trust Co. agreed to cancel the lease in consideration of a payment to petitioner of $140,000. Petitioner reported a loss of $21,495 on the theory that the amount he received as consideration for the cancellation was $21,495 less than the difference between the present value of the unmatured rental payments and the [lower] fair rental value of the [premises] for the unexpired term of the lease.

The amount received by petitioner for cancellation of the lease must be included in his gross income in its entirety. Plainly the definition [of gross income] reached the rent paid prior to cancellation just as it would have embraced subsequent payments if the lease had never been cancelled. It would have included a prepayment of the discounted value of unmatured rental payments. Similarly, it would have extended to the proceeds of a suit to recover damages had the Irving Trust Co. breached the lease. That the amount petitioner received resulted from negotiations ending in cancellation of the lease rather than from a suit to enforce it cannot alter the fact that basically the payment was merely a substitute for the rent reserved in the lease. It is immaterial that petitioner chose to accept an amount less than the strict present value of the unmatured rental payments rather than to engage in litigation, possibly uncertain and expensive.

The consideration received for cancellation of the lease was not a return of capital. We assume that the lease was "property," whatever that signifies abstractly. Simply because the lease was "property," the amount received for its cancellation was not a return of capital. Where, as in this case, the disputed amount was essentially a substitute for rental payments, it must be regarded as ordinary income, and it is immaterial that for some purposes the contract creating the right to such payments may be treated as "property" or "capital."

For the same reasons, that amount was not a return of capital because petitioner acquired the lease as an incident of the realty devised to him by his father. Theoretically, it might have been possible in such a case to value realty and lease separately and to label each a capital asset. But that would not have converted into capital the amount petitioner received from the Trust Co., since [the tax law] does not distinguish rental payments and a payment which is clearly a substitute for rental payments.

Undoubtedly the lease cancellation diminished the amount of gross income petitioner expected to realize, but to that extent he was relieved of the duty to pay income tax. Nothing in [the predecessor of § 165 pertaining to deductibility of losses] indicates that Congress intended to allow petitioner to reduce ordinary income actually received and reported by the amount of income he failed to realize. We may assume that petitioner was injured insofar as the cancellation of the lease affected the value of the realty. But that would become a deductible loss only when its extent had been fixed by a closed transaction.

As *Hort* noted, it is settled that "advance rents" (rents paid in advance of when they are due) are treated as ordinary gross income to the lessor with no basis offset or recovery apart from the current annual depreciation deduction for the building. See Reg. § 1.61-8(b) (which also confirms the *Hort* result). This result holds even if the lessor uses the accrual method of accounting and the rent is received in advance of when it was earned. For a lessee, prepaid rent and lease acquisition costs are costs of acquiring a term interest and are amortizable by a nonresidential lessee over the term of the lease, as determined with the aid of § 178.

Hort also confirms the rule that a taxpayer does not have a tax loss by reason of failing to receive income, because there is no basis in the lost future income. But the taxpayer in *Hort* attempted to avoid this problem by claiming that part of the underlying property (and its basis) was allocable to the cancelled lease. The Court rejected this not-implausible argument without explanation, and did the same in the second carve-out case, *Comm'r v. Gillette Motor Transport*, 364 U.S. 130 (1960). There, the taxpayer was a trucking company whose employees went on strike during World War II. Because of the need to transport war material, the government took control of the facilities, but title was left in the taxpayer. The government operated the facilities for over a year and paid the taxpayer a "just compensation" award representing the FMV of its facilities for the requisition period, plus interest. The taxpayer argued that the award, less an appropriate basis offset, was capital gain. The Court rejected both the basis-offset and capital-gain arguments, and held that the award was ordinary income in full. The opinion of the Court stated (364 U.S. at 135):

> To be sure, respondent's facilities were themselves property. But here the Government took only the right to determine the use to which those facilities were to be put. That right is not something in which respondent had any investment, separate and apart from its investment in the physical assets themselves. Respondent suggests no method by which a cost basis could be assigned to the right. The right to use is not a capital asset, but is simply an incident of the underlying physical property, the recompense for which is commonly regarded as rent.

But Chapter 27 indicates ways in which a basis in property *could be* (as a matter of arithmetic) assigned to a future temporal segment. That such an allocation is possible is illustrated by § 1286, which deals with the tax treatment of "stripped bonds." Assume that Seller, who owns a bond with interest coupons, sells the interest coupons to Purchaser, retaining the bond proper. The Seller's original basis in the entire instrument[8] could be allocated between the retained bond and the stripped coupons according to their respective present values (PVs) at the time of purchase, but § 1286 instead makes the allocation in proportion to their respective FMVs at the time of the sale.[9] An allocation is also required if, instead, the Seller sells the bond and retains the coupons.[10]

Why is an allocation of basis to disposed-of temporal segments generally barred (apart from § 1286)? The answer is that such an allocation would greatly complicate tax accounting. Taken to its logical conclusion, any lease would have to be treated as a disposition of a term of years. The basis in the property would have to be allocated between the lease (and then to rents), on the one hand, and the lessor's reversionary interest, on the other. The allocation would be difficult on account of the possibility of (perhaps indefinite) lease renewals. Writing off the basis attrib-

---

[8] Section 1286 first requires the Seller to include in income any accrued interest and market discount that had not been included in income prior to the sale. These included amounts are added to basis before the allocation.

[9] While not central to the present discussion, it can be noted that the Purchaser of the interest coupons is then treated as having bought a series of future payment rights for less than their face amount and must accrue what is OID into income. (OID income is explained in Chapter 27.B.1.) The Seller *also* has an OID obligation, because her basis in the stripped bond is now less than the principal face amount.

[10] Again both the buyer of the stripped bond and the taxpayer holding the retained coupons hold OID obligations.

utable to the lease would seem to call for (in the interests of symmetry) treating the reversion as an original-issue-discount (OID) obligation yielding annual interest accruals includible in income by even a cash-method taxpayer (as explained in Chapter 27.B.1).[11] Without OID accruals, it would be possible to effectively convert land into a depreciable asset by leasing it, and to achieve accelerated write-offs of all leased assets (because, if present values are the key to allocating basis, the present value of nearer years is greater than that for more distant years). To avoid all of these complications, the Supreme Court in *Hort* and *Gillette Motor* considered the temporal segments (the leaseholds) to be indivisible from the whole (the underlying physical asset). Also, a simpler cost recovery system already exists, namely, depreciation (at least of assets with a finite life) with respect to the underlying asset.

At an intuitive level, no disposition of anything occurred in *Hort* and *Gillette Motor.* In *Hort,* the taxpayer could lease the property to another tenant. In *Gillette Motor,* the taxpayer actually received the equivalent of one year's rent. If nothing was disposed of that couldn't be accounted for by ordinary depreciation, the Court was justified in not allowing a basis offset (or capital gains treatment).

Because the seller obtains no basis offset for the transferred current-enjoyment interest (life estate or term of years) in a carve-out sale, it follows that the seller's entire adjusted basis in the property remains lodged in the retained reversionary interest and ultimately (when the reversion comes into possession) in the fee interest. (Recall from Chapter 22.A.4 that the coming into possession of a reversion is not a realization event.)

Now consider an arm's-length sale of a carved-out *remainder interest* in (say) unimproved land, with Seller retaining a life estate or term for years. In that scenario, does Seller have a basis offset against the sales proceeds? Here the answer is "yes." Just as the income tax basically views the owner of the reversion as the owner of the underlying property, a sale of a remainder interest is viewed as a true disposition of an interest in property. The basis allocable to the sold remainder interest is Seller's basis in the entire property multiplied by the "actuarial factor" for a remainder interest after the retained interest. The actuarial factor is a percentage figure (expressed as a decimal) representing the present value, as of the date of sale, of $1 to be hypothetically received at the expected expiration of the retained interest. The actuarial tables are issued by the Treasury under § 7520. Various tables are set out that are based on various discount rates, and the table that is to be used depends on the "applicable federal rate" (AFR) prevailing in the month in which the transaction occurs.[12] The resulting gain or loss from the sale of a carved-out remainder interest is capital gain or loss if the underlying asset is a capital asset.

Despite sparse authority, it appears that the seller of a remainder interest cannot amortize a retained term (or life) interest, but can deduct the basis allocated to such interest when it expires if the interest is used in business or held for investment.[13]

---

[11] The reversion would have a basis below the expected FMV of the property at end of the lease.

[12] The actuarial tables are found in *Notice 89-60,* 1989-1 C.B. 700.

[13] See *Lomas Santa Fe, Inc. v. Comm'r,* 74 T.C. 662 (1980), *aff'd,* 693 F.2d 71 (9th Cir. 1982), *cert.*

NOTES

1. *Hort* implicitly holds that an acceleration of rents (by paying rents in advance) does not justify accelerating future depreciation deductions to "match" the accelerated rents. The more general point is that nonfinancial (physical) assets do not suffer "losses" (either economically or in the tax sense) on account of the owner obtaining cash receipts, as do financial assets (such as annuities and bonds), which are nothing more than a right to cash receipts.

2. Cases denying capital gain treatment often have their assignment-of-income counterparts (discussed in Chapter 17). *Hort* is similar to its near-namesake *Helvering v. Horst*, 311 U.S. 112 (1940), because in both cases the taxpayer kept a reversion in the underlying property. *Gillette Motor* (and *Comm'r v. P.G. Lake, Inc.*, 356 U.S. 260 (1958), discussed in Section A.2) are both similar to *Harrison v. Schaffner*, 312 U.S. 579 (1941), in that both involved short-term assignments of the possession of, or the income from, property. *U.S. v. Midland-Ross Corp.*, 381 U.S. 54 (1965), holding that gain, from the sale of a bond, representing accrued OID, was, in substance, accrued interest taxable as ordinary income, is similar to *Helvering v. Eubank*, 311 U.S. 122 (1940), involving a gratuitous assignment of accrued commissions.

3. (a) A "premium lease" refers to a lease that calls for rents in excess of the current rental value of the property. The 1993 Tax Act settled a prior split of authority[14] by precluding any separate allocation of cost basis to a premium lease acquired together with the underlying property. See § 167(c)(2). (In *Hort*, the lease was probably not a premium lease when the taxpayer acquired the property in 1928.)

(b) In *Metropolitan Bldg. Co. v. Comm'r*, 282 F.2d 592 (9th Cir. 1960), the taxpayer was a lessee who had subleased the premises to a third party. The sublessee wished to eliminate the lessee and lease the premises directly from the lessor, and the lessor was agreeable. The sublessee therefore paid the lessee a sum of money in return for the lessee surrendering its lease with the lessor. The Ninth Circuit concluded that the amount received by the lessee was capital gain, because the lessee sold its entire interest in the underlying property (without retaining a reversion). An assignment-of-income counterpart to *Metropolitan Bldg. Co.* is *Blair v. Comm'r*, 300 U.S. 5 (1937), discussed in Chapter 17.A.4.

4. A casual reading of *Hort* suggests that amounts that are a "substitute for ordinary income" are ordinary income with no basis offset. But that cannot be correct, because virtually all sales proceeds represent the present value of future receipts. In *Hort* and *Gillette Motor* the payments *were* rent in substance (although called something else).

---

denied, 460 U.S. 1083 (1983); *U.S. v. Georgia Railroad & Banking Co.*, 348 F.2d 278 (5th Cir. 1965). Conceivably, these cases could be distinguished on the grounds (1) that the remainder interest was held by a related party and (2) the device was seen as one that illegitimately converted a nondepreciable asset into a depreciable asset.

[14] Compare *Midler Court Realty, Inc. v. Comm'r*, 61 T.C. 590 (1974), aff'd, 521 F.2d 767 (3d Cir. 1975), with *World Pub'g Co. v. Comm'r*, 299 F.2d 614 (8th Cir. 1962).

2. Investing in Temporal Interests

If the temporal interest is *purchased*, the basis thereof is initially its cost. If a purchased *life estate or term of years* is currently producing income, the purchaser can amortize the cost of the interest over its expected life (the term of years or the period determined under actuarial tables with respect to the measuring life),[15] because the interest is a wasting investment asset.[16]

A purchased *remainder* interest is not a wasting asset prior to the time it vests or comes into possession. In fact, a remainder interest *increases* in value with the passage of time, as the date it will be expected to come into possession draws ever nearer. This passage-of-time gain is not, however, included in gross income under the OID rules, since a remainder interest does not involve a sum certain payable at a fixed future date. Additionally, the eventual coming into possession (or vesting) of a remainder interest is not a realization event.[17] Assuming the remainder interest is not in trust, it follows that the cost basis of the remainder interest continues "in" the property, now owned in fee simple.[18]

If a purchased *contingent* remainder fails or is extinguished (before the taxpayer's death) by reason of not satisfying the requisite conditions, the taxpayer's unamortized basis can be taken as a loss deduction under § 165(c)(2), assuming that the transaction was entered into for profit.

It should be mentioned that there is virtually no commerce in present and future interests, except among family members incident to estate planning, where transactions of this sort will be scrutinized for, among other things, the existence of disguised gifts.

Additionally, § 167(e) provides that a current interest cannot be amortized if the terminal interest (remainder or reversion) is held (directly or indirectly) by a related person, as defined in § 267(b) or (e). This situation could arise not only in a carve-out sale to a related party but also where the related parties separately but simultaneously purchase the current and terminal interests from a third party. The main purpose of § 167(e) is to block the stratagem through which an owner of nondepreciable property, such as land or securities, could partially convert the nondepreciable property into an amortizable current interest by selling a remainder interest following a retained life or term interest to a related party. In other respects, the rules under § 167(e) closely parallel the rules for interests received by gratuitous transfer, immediately following.[19]

---

[15] Amortizable temporal interests, not being within § 197, are amortized over the actual term (or life expectancy).

[16] See, e.g., *Estate of Christ v. Comm'r*, 54 T.C. 493 (1970), *aff'd*, 480 F.2d 171 (9th Cir. 1973). If an interest lapses on the purchaser's own death, the remaining basis cannot be taken as a loss.

[17] See Chapter 22.A.4.

[18] As noted in Subsection 1, supra, the basis of the income interest stays with the seller, who probably cannot amortize it.

[19] For example, assume that Father and Son together purchase Blackacre (undeveloped land) from a third party. Father purchases a life estate for $370K, and Son purchases the remainder interest for $130K. Section 167(e) would prohibit Father from amortizing the $370K cost of the life estate, but Father's basis in his life estate would be reduced over time as though such deductions were taken, and

3. Interests Obtained by Gratuitous Transfer

Temporal interests are commonly created by gifts and bequests, often in trust, in family estate planning. The receipt of any interest by gratuitous transfer is excluded from gross income by reason of § 102, but post-transfer income is taxed.

The rules governing trusts and beneficiaries are described in Chapter 17.E. Assuming that the underlying trust property is not deemed to be owned by an individual under the grantor-trust or beneficiary-owned trust rules, it is deemed to be owned by the trust as a separate taxpayer. The trust's "inside" basis in the property it acquires by gratuitous transfer is determined by § 1014 or 1015. Recall that current net trust income and net gain (computed as for an individual) is taxed to the trust, except insofar as it is distributed to beneficiaries. Recall also that there was no mention of basis recovery by beneficiaries in the earlier discussion.

Indeed, calculating the basis of *life or term* interests acquired by *gratuitous transfer* is pointless, because the holder cannot obtain any tax benefit from such basis. To be specific, § 273 provides that such basis is not amortizable (unlike the amortizable cost basis of a *purchased* term or life interest), and § 1001(e) provides that such basis cannot offset the amount realized in the case of a sale or disposition of the interest. Thus, if the donee of an income interest in trust for life sells her life interest for $370K to Investor, she will realize and recognize the full $370K as § 1001 gain.

Turning to the situation where a *remainder* interest is acquired by gratuitous transfer, recall that remainder interests are not treated as OID obligations, nor is the vesting or coming into possession of a remainder interest considered to be a realization event. The extinguishment or lapse of a contingent remainder interest acquired by gratuitous transfer does not generate a loss deduction (because the transaction was not entered into for profit), and a gift of such a remainder interest is a nonevent for income tax purposes. In these cases, the ownership of the remainder interest merely shifts to another party. Thus, the basis of a *gratuitously acquired* remainder interest is relevant only if the interest is sold. Such a sale is uncommon, but, where one occurs, the seller's basis would be the initial basis in the property as determined under §§ 1014, 1015, or 1041, as the case may be, multiplied by the actuarial factor for a remainder interest determined as of the time of sale (as opposed to the date the remainder interest was acquired).

For example, suppose that Will was age 48 when Father died and bequeathed a stock portfolio with a FMV of $1M in trust, income to Will for life, remainder to Cassie. Assume that the appropriate "life estate factor" for a 48-year-old person is 0.77488 and the "remainder factor" is 0.22512. However, it is not necessary to determine the bases of Will's and Cassie's interests in the trust, because such basis is irrelevant to the rules governing the income taxation of trusts and beneficiaries. Because of § 1014, the trust, as a separate taxpayer, starts out with a $1M basis in all of its assets. When Will is 60 years of age, Cassie sells her remainder interest to

---

Son's basis in his remainder interest would increase by the same amount (though Son would not be required to report these increases as income under the OID rules). This shifting-basis rule parallels that for remainder interests acquired by gratuitous transfer that are later sold, as is illustrated by the Will/Cassie hypothetical in the text below.

Dickie, who will pay an amount based on the then value of the trust assets and his best estimate of how long he expects Will to live. Say that this amount is $750K. At the time of sale, Cassie's remainder factor has increased to .36774, meaning that Cassie's basis is her remainder interest is $367,740 (.36774 × the *original* $1M § 1014 basis), resulting in a $382,260 gain ($750K *less* $367,740). Dickie now has a $750K cost basis in the remainder interest, and, since he purchased it, he is not governed by the rules that applied to Cassie. Dickie's basis in the remainder is fixed and does not increase with the passage of time. His basis is of no consequence, however, unless he, in turn, sells the interest. Since Dickie is now a trust beneficiary, he is governed by the tax rules governing trusts and beneficiaries. Dickie's acquisition of the direct ownership of the trust assets upon Will's death is not a realization event, and (unlike the case of a nontrust remainder interest), his basis in the acquired trust assets will be the *trust's* basis in these assets. Dickie's basis in his remainder interest will simply disappear.[20]

In short, the rules pertaining to trust taxation generally avoid treating trust interests as being separate investments acquired by gratuitous transfer. Instead, the trust is viewed as a unitary investment vehicle which is a separate taxable entity, except for distributions to beneficiaries.[21] The scheme of taxing trusts and beneficiaries avoids the nonsymmetry that would occur if current beneficiaries could claim amortization deductions while remainder beneficiaries excluded passage-of-time gains with respect to remainder interests. In short, the policies at work here are the same that underlie the *Hort* decision!

The same principles, with some modifications, apply to nontrust split-interest transfers. Suppose, for example, that Jenny makes an *inter vivos* gift of Blackacre to Karl for life, remainder to Laura. Karl, the holder of the life estate, is treated as the owner of all of the income from Blackacre and can claim whatever depreciation, expense, and loss deductions as may be available with respect to Blackacre. See § 167(d). (By virtue of § 1015, these deductions will be calculated with reference to Jenny's basis in Blackacre at the time of gift.) Under § 273, however, Karl cannot amortize his "life estate" basis in Blackacre. Laura realizes no passage-of-time gain as her ownership interest ripens, nor does she realize gain or loss on acquiring Blackacre in fee upon Karl's death. Laura's basis in her fee interest in Blackacre is equal to the full original § 1015 basis, adjusted, of course, for any depreciation or depletion taken by Karl.[22]

Stated crudely, in the case of both trust and nontrust successive interests acquired by gratuitous transfer, the holders of the current interest are taxed on the net income (the "fruit"), and the holder of the remainder interest ends up with the basis (the "tree"). This approach is much simpler and more reflective of

---

[20] See § 643(e). Although the trust also started out with a basis in the trust assets determined by § 1014 or 1015, any assets purchased by the trust would have a cost basis under § 1012.

[21] Regs. §§ 1.1014-4 and 1.1015-1(b) refer to the basis of a trust in its inception assets, as well as the basis of beneficiaries in their interests, as the "uniform basis."

[22] Laura does not acquire a § 1014 basis, because the value of Blackacre is not included in Karl's gross estate. If the trust were a generation-skipping trust and if Karl's death is a "taxable termination" under the federal generation-skipping tax, Laura's basis might be adjusted (in whole or in part) in a manner similar to § 1014. See § 2654(a)(2).

liquidity than a fractionalized-interest approach that would allow amortization deductions to current beneficiaries and that might (or might not) require holders of remainders (including contingent remainders) to include passage-of-time gains in income.

PROBLEMS

1. (a) Sylvia, owning unimproved land in fee with a basis of $40K and FMV of $100K, sells a life estate to Tom for its then actuarial value of $75K while retaining the remainder (worth $25K) for himself. What are the results to Sylvia and Tom?

(b) Same as (a), except that Sylvia sells the remainder for its actuarial value of $30K to Tom and retains the life estate (worth $70K), instead. What are the results to Sylvia and Tom?

(c) Same as (a), except that Sylvia simultaneously sells a 30-year term interest to Dmitri for $95K and the remainder interest to Eudora for $5K. What are the results to Dmitri and Eudora?

2. Allan bequeaths a mineral interest (that generates royalties), worth $100K, to Lucy (age 25) for her life, remainder to Matthew.

(a) How is depletion allocated? What basis does Matthew take on Lucy's death? (Ignore § 2654(a)(2).)

(b) Ten years after Allan's gift, the property is worth $200K, and Lucy sells her life estate to Lucas for its then value of $130K. What result to Lucy?

3. Joseph dies, leaving his investment portfolio of stocks worth $1M in trust, income to Wendy for her life, remainder to Bridget, who immediately sells her remainder interest in the trust to Jonathan for $100K, its then actuarial value. Of what relevance is the $1M basis under § 1014 to the various parties (including the trust) in this scenario?

APPENDIX

TABLE A: COMPOUND INTEREST

Amount to Which $1 Now Will Grow by End of Specified Year at Compounded Interest*

Year	3%	4%	5%	6%	7%	8%	10%	12%	15%
1	1.03	1.04	1.05	1.06	1.07	1.08	1.10	1.12	1.15
2	1.06	1.08	1.10	1.12	1.14	1.17	1.21	1.25	1.32
3	1.09	1.12	1.26	1.19	1.23	1.26	1.33	1.40	1.52
4	1.13	1.17	1.22	1.26	1.31	1.36	1.46	1.57	1.74
5	1.16	1.22	1.28	1.34	1.40	1.47	1.61	1.76	2.01
6	1.19	1.27	1.34	1.41	1.50	1.59	1.77	1.97	2.31
7	1.23	1.32	1.41	1.50	1.61	1.71	1.94	2.21	2.66
8	1.27	1.37	1.48	1.59	1.72	1.85	2.14	2.48	3.05
9	1.30	1.42	1.55	1.68	1.84	2.00	2.35	2.77	3.52
10	1.34	1.48	1.63	1.79	1.97	2.16	2.59	3.11	4.05
11	1.38	1.54	1.71	1.89	2.10	2.33	2.85	3.48	4.66
12	1.43	1.60	1.80	2.01	2.25	2.52	3.13	3.90	5.30
13	1.47	1.67	1.89	2.13	2.41	2.72	3.45	4.36	6.10
14	1.51	1.73	1.98	2.26	2.58	2.94	3.79	4.89	7.00
15	1.56	1.80	2.08	2.39	2.76	3.17	4.17	5.47	8.13
16	1.60	1.87	2.18	2.54	2.95	3.43	4.59	6.13	9.40
17	1.65	1.95	2.29	2.69	3.16	3.70	5.05	6.87	10.60
18	1.70	2.03	2.41	2.85	3.38	4.00	5.55	7.70	12.50
19	1.75	2.11	2.53	3.02	3.62	4.32	6.11	8.61	14.00
20	1.81	2.19	2.65	3.20	3.87	4.66	6.72	9.65	16.10
25	2.09	2.67	3.39	4.29	5.43	6.85	10.80	17.00	32.90
30	2.43	3.24	4.32	5.74	7.61	10.00	17.40	30.00	66.20
40	3.26	4.80	7.04	10.30	15.00	21.70	45.30	93.10	267.00
50	4.38	7.11	11.50	18.40	29.50	46.90	117.00	289.00	1080.00

* To find what $1 invested today at a particular rate of compounded interest will be worth at the end of a specified number of years, find the year in the column at left and then find the appropriate interest rate along the top. Your answer is the number found at the intersection of the year line and interest-rate column. For example, $1 invested today at 8% compound interest will grow to $1.47 at the end of five years, $2.16 at the end of ten years, and $4.66 at the end of twenty years.

TABLE B: PRESENT VALUE

What $1 at End of Specified Future Year Is Worth Today*

Year	3%	4%	5%	6%	7%	8%	10%	12%	15%
1	.971	.962	.952	.943	.935	.926	.909	.893	.870
2	.943	.925	.907	.890	.873	.857	.826	.797	.756
3	.915	.890	.864	.839	.816	.794	.751	.711	.658
4	.889	.855	.823	.792	.763	.735	.683	.636	.572
5	.863	.823	.784	.747	.713	.681	.620	.567	.497
6	.838	.790	.746	.705	.666	.630	.564	.507	.432
7	.813	.760	.711	.665	.623	.583	.513	.452	.376
8	.789	.731	.677	.627	.582	.540	.466	.404	.326
9	.766	.703	.645	.591	.544	.500	.424	.360	.284
10	.744	.676	.614	.558	.508	.463	.385	.322	.247
11	.722	.650	.585	.526	.475	.429	.350	.287	.215
12	.701	.625	.557	.497	.444	.397	.318	.257	.187
13	.681	.601	.530	.468	.415	.368	.289	.229	.162
14	.661	.577	.505	.422	.388	.340	.263	.204	.141
15	.642	.555	.481	.417	.362	.315	.239	.183	.122
16	.623	.534	.458	.393	.339	.292	.217	.163	.107
17	.605	.513	.436	.371	.317	.270	.197	.146	.093
18	.587	.494	.416	.350	.296	.250	.179	.130	.0808
19	.570	.475	.396	.330	.277	.232	.163	.116	.0703
20	.554	.456	.377	.311	.258	.215	.148	.104	.0611
25	.478	.375	.295	.232	.184	.146	.0923	.0588	.0304
30	.412	.308	.231	.174	.131	.0994	.0573	.0334	.01551
40	.307	.208	.142	.0972	.067	.0460	.0221	.0107	.00373
50	.228	.141	.087	.0543	.034	.0213	.00852	.00346	.000922

* To find the present value of $1 that will be received in a future year under a particular rate of compound interest, find the year in which the $1 will be received in the column at the left and then find the appropriate interest rate along the top. Your answer is the number found at the intersection of the year line and interest-rate column. For example, the present value of $1 invested at 8% compound interest that will be received five years from now is just over 68 cents. The present value of that same dollar is just over 46 cents if it will be received after ten years and is 21 1/2 cents if it will be received after twenty years.

TABLE OF CASES

[References are to pages.]

[References are to pages.]

[References are to pages.]

[References are to pages.]